FURTHER MATHEMATICS FOR
ECONOMIC
ANALYSIS

PEARSON
Education

We work with leading authors to develop the
strongest educational materials in economics,
bringing cutting-edge thinking and best learning
practice to a global market.

Under a range of well-known imprints, including
Financial Times/Prentice Hall, we craft high quality print
and electronic publications which help readers to
understand and apply their content,
whether studying or at work.

To find out more about the complete range of our
publishing, please visit us on the World Wide Web at:
www.pearsoned.co.uk

FURTHER MATHEMATICS FOR
ECONOMIC ANALYSIS

KNUT SYDSÆTER
PETER HAMMOND
ATLE SEIERSTAD
ARNE STRØM

 Prentice Hall

FINANCIAL TIMES

An imprint of **Pearson Education**

Harlow, England • London • New York • Boston • San Francisco • Toronto • Sydney • Singapore • Hong Kong
Tokyo • Seoul • Taipei • New Delhi • Cape Town • Madrid • Mexico City • Amsterdam • Munich • Paris • Milan

Pearson Education Limited
Edinburgh Gate
Harlow
Essex CM20 2JE
England

and Associated Companies throughout the world

Visit us on the World Wide Web at:
www.pearsoned.co.uk

First published 2005

ISBN 0 273 65576 0

British Library Cataloguing-in-Publication Data
A catalogue record for this book is available from the British Library

10 9 8 7 6 5 4 3 2 1
09 08 07 06 05

Typeset in TEX by the authors.
Printed and bound by Ashford Colour Press Ltd., Gosport.

The publisher's policy is to use paper manufactured from sustainable forests.

CONTENTS

Supporting resource

Visit www.pearsoned.co.uk/sydsaeter to find a valuable online resource

For instructors
• Complete, downloadable Instructor's Manual with exam problems

For more information please contact your local Pearson Education sales representative or visit
www.pearsoned.co.uk/sydsaeter

PREFACE

The economic world is a misty region.
The first explorers used unaided vision.
Mathematics is the lantern by which what was before
dimly visible now looms up in firm, bold outlines.
The old phantasmagoria[1] disappear.
We see better. We also see further.
—Irving Fisher (1892)

This book is intended for advanced undergraduate and graduate students of economics whose mathematical requirements go beyond the material usually taught in undergraduate courses. In particular, it presents most of the mathematical tools required for typical graduate courses in economic theory—both micro and macro. The volume has many references to Sydsæter and Hammond's *Essential Mathematics for Economic Analysis* (Pearson Education, 2002) [generally referred to as EMEA throughout this successor volume], but that book is by no means a prerequisite. Indeed, this volume is designed to be accessible to anybody who has had a basic training in mathematical analysis and linear algebra at the level often encountered in courses taught to economics undergraduates. Like EMEA, the treatment here is deliberately quite rigorous, but rigour is not emphasized for its own sake.

An important aspect of the book is its systematic treatment of the calculus of variations, optimal control theory, and dynamic programming. Recent years may have seen control theory lose some of its prominence in economics, but it is still useful in several areas, notably resource economics and industrial organization. Furthermore, in our view the existing economics literature has paid too little attention to some of the subtler issues that frequently arise, especially when the time horizon is infinite.

Some early chapters review and extend elementary matrix algebra, multivariable calculus, and static optimization. Other chapters present multiple integration, as well as ordinary difference and differential equations, including systems of equations. There is a chapter on elementary topology in $\mathbb{R}^n$ and separation theorems. In the final chapter we discuss setvalued functions ("correspondences") and the fixed point theorems that economists most often use.

As the title suggests, this is a mathematics book with the material arranged to allow pro-

---

[1]"Phantasmagoria" is a term invented in 1802 to describe an exhibition of optical illusions produced by means of a magic lantern.

gressive learning of mathematical topics. If the student acquires some economic insight and intuition at the same time, so much the better. At times, we do emphasize economics not only to motivate a mathematical topic, but also to help acquire mathematical intuition. Obviously, our economic discussions will be more easily understood by students who already have a certain rudimentary understanding of economics, especially of what economics should be about.

In particular, this is not a book about economics or even about mathematical economics. As one reviewer of EMEA put it: "Mathematics is the star of the show". We expect students to learn economic theory systematically in other courses, based on other books or articles. We will have succeeded if they can concentrate on the economics in these courses, having mastered beforehand the relevant mathematical tools we present.

Almost every section includes worked examples and problems for students to solve as exercises. Many of the problems are quite easy in order to build the students' confidence in absorbing the material, but there are also a number of more challenging problems. Concise solutions to odd-numbered problems are suggested. Solutions to even-numbered problems will be available to instructors in a manual that can be downloaded from a restricted access part of an associated website. That website will also include other supplementary material, including exam type problems that instructors might find useful for assignments or even exams.

The book is not intended to be studied in a steady progression from beginning to end. Some of the more challenging chapters start with a simple treatment where some technical aspects are played down, while the more complete theory is discussed later. Some of the material, including more challenging proofs, is in small print. Quite often those proofs rely on technical ideas that are only expounded in the last two chapters.

The author team consists of the two co-authors of EMEA, together with two other mathematicians in the Department of Economics at the University of Oslo.

Knut Sydsæter, Peter Hammond, Atle Seierstad, and Arne Strøm

Oslo and Stanford, December 2004

1

TOPICS IN LINEAR ALGEBRA

I came to the position that mathematical analysis is not one of
many ways of doing economic theory: It is the only way. Economic
theory is mathematical analysis. Everything else is just
pictures and talk.
—R. E. Lucas, Jr. (2001)

This chapter covers a few topics in linear algebra that are not always treated in standard mathematics courses for economics students. We assume that the reader has previously studied some basic concepts and results, which are briefly reviewed in Section 1.1. A fuller treatment including many practice problems, can be found in EMEA, or in many alternative textbooks.

Next we consider partitioned matrices. These are useful for computations involving large matrices, especially when they have a special structure.

In an economic model described by a linear system of equations, it is important to know when that system has a solution, and when the solution is unique. General conditions for existence and uniqueness are most easily stated using the concept of linear independence, along with the related concept of the rank of a matrix. These topics are treated in Sections 1.3 and 1.4.

The implications of these ideas for solving linear systems is the topic of Section 1.5.

This chapter also discusses eigenvalues, which are indispensable in several areas of mathematics of interest to economists—in particular, stability theory for difference and differential equations. Eigenvalues and the associated eigenvectors are also important in determining when a matrix can be "diagonalized", which greatly simplifies some calculations involving the matrix. The chapter concludes by looking at quadratic forms— first without linear constraints, then with them. Such quadratic forms are especially useful in deriving and checking second-order conditions for multivariable optimization.

1.1   Review of Basic Linear Algebra

An $m \times n$ matrix is a rectangular array with m rows and n columns:

$$\mathbf{A} = (a_{ij})_{m \times n} = \begin{pmatrix} a_{11} & a_{12} & \cdots & a_{1n} \\ a_{21} & a_{22} & \cdots & a_{2n} \\ \vdots & \vdots & & \vdots \\ a_{m1} & a_{m2} & \cdots & a_{mn} \end{pmatrix} \tag{1}$$

Here a_{ij} denotes the element in the ith row and the jth column.

If $\mathbf{A} = (a_{ij})_{m \times n}$, $\mathbf{B} = (b_{ij})_{m \times n}$, and α is a scalar, we define

$$\mathbf{A} + \mathbf{B} = (a_{ij} + b_{ij})_{m \times n}, \quad \alpha \mathbf{A} = (\alpha a_{ij})_{m \times n}, \quad \mathbf{A} - \mathbf{B} = \mathbf{A} + (-1)\mathbf{B} = (a_{ij} - b_{ij})_{m \times n} \tag{2}$$

Suppose that $\mathbf{A} = (a_{ij})_{m \times n}$ and that $\mathbf{B} = (b_{ij})_{n \times p}$. Then the product $\mathbf{C} = \mathbf{AB}$ is the $m \times p$ matrix $\mathbf{C} = (c_{ij})_{m \times p}$, whose element in the ith row and the jth column is the inner product (or dot product) of the ith row of $\mathbf{A}$ and the jth column of $\mathbf{B}$. That is,

$$c_{ij} = \sum_{r=1}^{n} a_{ir} b_{rj} = a_{i1} b_{1j} + a_{i2} b_{2j} + \cdots + a_{ik} b_{kj} + \cdots + a_{in} b_{nj} \tag{3}$$

It is important to note that the product $\mathbf{AB}$ is defined only if the number of columns in $\mathbf{A}$ is equal to the number of rows in $\mathbf{B}$.

If $\mathbf{A}$, $\mathbf{B}$, and $\mathbf{C}$ are matrices whose dimensions are such that the given operations are defined, then the basic properties of matrix multiplication are:

$$(\mathbf{AB})\mathbf{C} = \mathbf{A}(\mathbf{BC}) \qquad \textbf{(associative law)} \tag{4}$$

$$\mathbf{A}(\mathbf{B} + \mathbf{C}) = \mathbf{AB} + \mathbf{AC} \qquad \textbf{(left distributive law)} \tag{5}$$

$$(\mathbf{A} + \mathbf{B})\mathbf{C} = \mathbf{AC} + \mathbf{BC} \qquad \textbf{(right distributive law)} \tag{6}$$

If $\mathbf{A}$ and $\mathbf{B}$ are matrices, it is possible for $\mathbf{AB}$ to be defined even if $\mathbf{BA}$ is not. Moreover, even if $\mathbf{AB}$ and $\mathbf{BA}$ are both defined, $\mathbf{AB}$ is not necessarily equal to $\mathbf{BA}$. Matrix multiplication is *not* commutative. In fact,

$$\mathbf{AB} \neq \mathbf{BA}, \quad \text{except in special cases} \tag{7}$$

$$\mathbf{AB} = \mathbf{0} \text{ does not imply that } \mathbf{A} \text{ or } \mathbf{B} \text{ is } \mathbf{0} \tag{8}$$

$$\mathbf{AB} = \mathbf{AC} \text{ and } \mathbf{A} \neq \mathbf{0} \text{ do not imply that } \mathbf{B} = \mathbf{C} \tag{9}$$

By using matrix multiplication, one can write a general system of linear equations in a very concise way. Specifically, the system

$$\begin{aligned} a_{11}x_1 + a_{12}x_2 + \cdots + a_{1n}x_n &= b_1 \\ a_{21}x_1 + a_{22}x_2 + \cdots + a_{2n}x_n &= b_2 \\ \cdots\cdots\cdots\cdots\cdots\cdots\cdots\cdots&\cdots \\ a_{m1}x_1 + a_{m2}x_2 + \cdots + a_{mn}x_n &= b_m \end{aligned}$$

can be written as $\qquad \mathbf{Ax} = \mathbf{b}$

if we define $\mathbf{A} = \begin{pmatrix} a_{11} & a_{12} & \cdots & a_{1n} \\ a_{21} & a_{22} & \cdots & a_{2n} \\ \vdots & \vdots & & \vdots \\ a_{m1} & a_{m2} & \cdots & a_{mn} \end{pmatrix}, \quad \mathbf{x} = \begin{pmatrix} x_1 \\ x_2 \\ \vdots \\ x_n \end{pmatrix}, \quad \mathbf{b} = \begin{pmatrix} b_1 \\ b_2 \\ \vdots \\ b_m \end{pmatrix}.$

A matrix is **square** if it has an equal number of rows and columns. If $\mathbf{A}$ is a square matrix and n is a positive integer, we define the nth power of $\mathbf{A}$ in the obvious way:

$$\mathbf{A}^n = \underbrace{\mathbf{A}\mathbf{A}\cdots\mathbf{A}}_{n \text{ factors}} \tag{10}$$

For **diagonal matrices** it is particularly easy to compute powers:

$$\mathbf{D} = \begin{pmatrix} d_1 & 0 & \cdots & 0 \\ 0 & d_2 & \cdots & 0 \\ \vdots & \vdots & \ddots & \vdots \\ 0 & 0 & \cdots & d_n \end{pmatrix} \implies \mathbf{D}^n = \begin{pmatrix} d_1^n & 0 & \cdots & 0 \\ 0 & d_2^n & \cdots & 0 \\ \vdots & \vdots & \ddots & \vdots \\ 0 & 0 & \cdots & d_n^n \end{pmatrix} \tag{11}$$

The **identity matrix** of order n, denoted by $\mathbf{I}_n$ (or often just by $\mathbf{I}$), is the $n \times n$ matrix having ones along the main diagonal and zeros elsewhere:

$$\mathbf{I}_n = \begin{pmatrix} 1 & 0 & \cdots & 0 \\ 0 & 1 & \cdots & 0 \\ \vdots & \vdots & \ddots & \vdots \\ 0 & 0 & \cdots & 1 \end{pmatrix}_{n \times n} \qquad \textbf{(identity matrix)} \tag{12}$$

If $\mathbf{A}$ is any $m \times n$ matrix, then $\mathbf{AI}_n = \mathbf{A} = \mathbf{I}_m\mathbf{A}$. In particular,

$$\mathbf{AI}_n = \mathbf{I}_n\mathbf{A} = \mathbf{A} \quad \text{for every } n \times n \text{ matrix } \mathbf{A} \tag{13}$$

If $\mathbf{A} = (a_{ij})_{m \times n}$ is any matrix, the **transpose** of $\mathbf{A}$ is defined as $\mathbf{A}' = (a_{ji})_{n \times m}$. The subscripts i and j are interchanged because every row of $\mathbf{A}$ becomes a column of $\mathbf{A}'$, and every column of $\mathbf{A}$ becomes a row of $\mathbf{A}'$.

The following rules apply to matrix transposition:

(i) $(\mathbf{A}')' = \mathbf{A}$ (ii) $(\mathbf{A} + \mathbf{B})' = \mathbf{A}' + \mathbf{B}'$ (iii) $(\alpha\mathbf{A})' = \alpha\mathbf{A}'$ (iv) $(\mathbf{AB})' = \mathbf{B}'\mathbf{A}'$ (14)

A square matrix is called **symmetric** if $\mathbf{A} = \mathbf{A}'$.

Determinants and Matrix Inverses

Recall that the determinants $|\mathbf{A}|$ of 2×2 and 3×3 matrices are defined by

$$|\mathbf{A}| = \begin{vmatrix} a_{11} & a_{12} \\ a_{21} & a_{22} \end{vmatrix} = a_{11}a_{22} - a_{21}a_{12}$$

$$|\mathbf{A}| = \begin{vmatrix} a_{11} & a_{12} & a_{13} \\ a_{21} & a_{22} & a_{23} \\ a_{31} & a_{32} & a_{33} \end{vmatrix} = \begin{cases} a_{11}a_{22}a_{33} - a_{11}a_{23}a_{32} + a_{12}a_{23}a_{31} \\ \quad - a_{12}a_{21}a_{33} + a_{13}a_{21}a_{32} - a_{13}a_{22}a_{31} \end{cases}$$

Determinants of order 2 and 3 have a geometric interpretation which is shown and explained in Fig. 1 for the case $n = 3$.

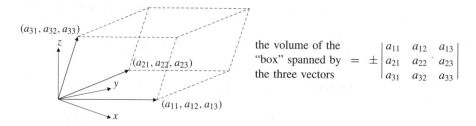

Figure 1

For a general $n \times n$ matrix $\mathbf{A} = \{a_{ij}\}$, the determinant $|\mathbf{A}|$ can be defined recursively. In fact,

$$|\mathbf{A}| = a_{i1}A_{i1} + a_{i2}A_{i2} + \cdots + a_{ij}A_{ij} + \cdots + a_{in}A_{in} \qquad (15)$$

where the *cofactors* A_{ij} are determinants of $(n-1) \times (n-1)$ matrices given by

$$A_{ij} = (-1)^{i+j} \begin{vmatrix} a_{11} & \cdots & a_{1,j-1} & a_{1j} & a_{1,j+1} & \cdots & a_{1n} \\ a_{21} & \cdots & a_{2,j-1} & a_{2j} & a_{2,j+1} & \cdots & a_{2n} \\ \vdots & & \vdots & & \vdots & & \vdots \\ a_{i1} & \cdots & a_{i,j-1} & \boxed{a_{ij}} & a_{i,j+1} & \cdots & a_{in} \\ \vdots & & \vdots & & \vdots & & \vdots \\ a_{n1} & \cdots & a_{n,j-1} & a_{nj} & a_{n,j+1} & \cdots & a_{nn} \end{vmatrix} \qquad (16)$$

Here lines have been drawn through row i and column j, which are to be deleted from the matrix $\mathbf{A}$ to produce A_{ij}. Formula (15) gives the *cofactor expansion of* $|\mathbf{A}|$ *along the ith row.*

In general,

$$\begin{aligned} a_{i1}A_{i1} + a_{i2}A_{i2} + \cdots + a_{in}A_{in} &= |\mathbf{A}| \\ a_{i1}A_{k1} + a_{i2}A_{k2} + \cdots + a_{in}A_{kn} &= 0 \qquad (k \neq i) \end{aligned} \qquad (17)$$

$$\begin{aligned} a_{1j}A_{1j} + a_{2j}A_{2j} + \cdots + a_{nj}A_{nj} &= |\mathbf{A}| \\ a_{1j}A_{1k} + a_{2j}A_{2k} + \cdots + a_{nj}A_{nk} &= 0 \qquad (k \neq j) \end{aligned} \qquad (18)$$

This result says that an expansion of a determinant along row i in terms of the cofactors of row k vanishes when $k \neq i$, and is equal to $|\mathbf{A}|$ if $k = i$. Likewise, an expansion along column j in terms of the cofactors of column k vanishes when $k \neq j$, and is equal to $|\mathbf{A}|$ if $k = j$.

The following rules for manipulating determinants are often useful:

If two rows (or two columns) of $\mathbf{A}$ are interchanged, the determinant changes sign but its absolute value remains unchanged. $\qquad (19)$

If all the elements in a single row (or column) of $\mathbf{A}$ are multiplied by a number c, the determinant is multiplied by c. $\qquad (20)$

If two of the rows (or columns) of $\mathbf{A}$ are proportional, then $|\mathbf{A}| = 0$. $\qquad (21)$

The value of $|\mathbf{A}|$ remains unchanged if a multiple of one row (or one column) is added to another row (or column). $\qquad (22)$

Furthermore,

$$|\mathbf{A}'| = |\mathbf{A}|, \quad \text{where } \mathbf{A}' \text{ is the transpose of } \mathbf{A} \tag{23}$$

$$|\mathbf{AB}| = |\mathbf{A}| \cdot |\mathbf{B}| \tag{24}$$

$$|\mathbf{A} + \mathbf{B}| \neq |\mathbf{A}| + |\mathbf{B}| \quad \text{(usually)} \tag{25}$$

The *inverse* $\mathbf{A}^{-1}$ of an $n \times n$ matrix $\mathbf{A}$ has the following properties:

$$\mathbf{B} = \mathbf{A}^{-1} \iff \mathbf{AB} = \mathbf{I}_n \iff \mathbf{BA} = \mathbf{I}_n \tag{26}$$

$$\mathbf{A}^{-1} \text{ exists} \iff |\mathbf{A}| \neq 0 \tag{27}$$

If $\mathbf{A} = (a_{ij})_{n \times n}$ and $|\mathbf{A}| \neq 0$, the unique inverse of $\mathbf{A}$ is given by

$$\mathbf{A}^{-1} = \frac{1}{|\mathbf{A}|} \operatorname{adj}(\mathbf{A}), \quad \text{where} \quad \operatorname{adj}(\mathbf{A}) = \begin{pmatrix} A_{11} & A_{21} & \cdots & A_{n1} \\ A_{12} & A_{22} & \cdots & A_{n2} \\ \vdots & \vdots & \ddots & \vdots \\ A_{1n} & A_{2n} & \cdots & A_{nn} \end{pmatrix} \tag{28}$$

with A_{ij}, the *cofactor* of the element a_{ij}, given by (16). Note carefully the order of the indices in the *adjoint matrix*, $\operatorname{adj}(\mathbf{A})$ with the column number preceding the row number. The matrix $(A_{ij})_{n \times n}$ is called the *cofactor matrix*, whose transpose is the adjoint matrix.

In particular, for 2×2 matrices,

$$\begin{pmatrix} a & b \\ c & d \end{pmatrix}^{-1} = \frac{1}{ad - bc} \begin{pmatrix} d & -b \\ -c & a \end{pmatrix} \quad \text{if} \quad \begin{vmatrix} a & b \\ c & d \end{vmatrix} = ad - bc \neq 0 \tag{29}$$

The following are important rules for inverses (when the relevant inverses exist):

$$(\mathbf{A}^{-1})^{-1} = \mathbf{A}, \quad (\mathbf{AB})^{-1} = \mathbf{B}^{-1}\mathbf{A}^{-1}, \quad (\mathbf{A}')^{-1} = (\mathbf{A}^{-1})', \quad (c\mathbf{A})^{-1} = c^{-1}\mathbf{A}^{-1} \tag{30}$$

Cramer's Rule

A linear system of n equations and n unknowns,

$$\begin{aligned} a_{11}x_1 + a_{12}x_2 + \cdots + a_{1n}x_n &= b_1 \\ a_{21}x_1 + a_{22}x_2 + \cdots + a_{2n}x_n &= b_2 \\ \cdots\cdots\cdots\cdots\cdots\cdots\cdots\cdots\cdots\cdots\cdots\cdots \\ a_{n1}x_1 + a_{n2}x_2 + \cdots + a_{nn}x_n &= b_n \end{aligned} \tag{31}$$

has a unique solution if and only if $|\mathbf{A}| = |(a_{ij})_{n \times n}| \neq 0$. The solution is then

$$x_j = \frac{|\mathbf{A}_j|}{|\mathbf{A}|}, \quad j = 1, 2, \dots, n \tag{32}$$

where the determinant

$$|\mathbf{A}_j| = \begin{vmatrix} a_{11} & \cdots & a_{1,j-1} & b_1 & a_{1,j+1} & \cdots & a_{1n} \\ a_{21} & \cdots & a_{2,j-1} & b_2 & a_{2,j+1} & \cdots & a_{2n} \\ \vdots & & \vdots & \vdots & \vdots & & \vdots \\ a_{n1} & \cdots & a_{n,j-1} & b_n & a_{n,j+1} & \cdots & a_{nn} \end{vmatrix} \tag{33}$$

is obtained by replacing the jth column of $|\mathbf{A}|$ by the column whose components are $b_1, b_2,$ $\ldots, b_n$.

If the right-hand side of the equation system (31) consists only of zeros, so that it can be written in matrix form as $\mathbf{Ax} = \mathbf{0}$, the system is called **homogeneous**. A homogeneous system will always have the **trivial solution** $x_1 = x_2 = \cdots = x_n = 0$. The following result is useful.

$$\mathbf{Ax} = \mathbf{0} \quad \text{has nontrivial solutions} \quad \Longleftrightarrow \quad |\mathbf{A}| = 0 \tag{34}$$

Vectors

Recall that an **n-vector** is an ordered n-tuple of numbers. It is often convenient to regard the rows and columns of a matrix as vectors, and an **n-vector** can be understood either as a $1 \times n$ matrix $\mathbf{a} = (a_1, a_2, \ldots, a_n)$ (a *row vector*) or as an $n \times 1$ matrix $\mathbf{a}' = (a_1, a_2, \ldots, a_n)'$ (a *column vector*). The operations of addition, subtraction and multiplication by scalars of vectors are defined in the obvious way. The **dot product** (or **inner product**) of the n-vectors $\mathbf{a} = (a_1, a_2, \ldots, a_n)$ and $\mathbf{b} = (b_1, b_2, \ldots, b_n)$ is defined as

$$\mathbf{a} \cdot \mathbf{b} = a_1 b_1 + a_2 b_2 + \cdots + a_n b_n = \sum_{i=1}^{n} a_i b_i \tag{35}$$

If $\mathbf{a} = (a_1, \ldots, a_n)'$ and $\mathbf{b} = (b_1, \ldots, b_n)'$ both happen to be $n \times 1$ matrices, $\mathbf{a} \cdot \mathbf{b}$ is again given by (35). Then the transpose $\mathbf{a}'$ of $\mathbf{a}$ is a $1 \times n$ matrix, and the matrix product $\mathbf{a}'\mathbf{b}$ is a 1×1 matrix. In fact, $\mathbf{a}'\mathbf{b} = a_1 b_1 + a_2 b_2 + \cdots + a_n b_n = \mathbf{a} \cdot \mathbf{b}$.

Important properties of the dot product include these: If $\mathbf{a}$, $\mathbf{b}$, and $\mathbf{c}$ are n-vectors and α is a scalar, then

$$\text{(i) } \mathbf{a} \cdot \mathbf{b} = \mathbf{b} \cdot \mathbf{a}, \quad \text{(ii) } \mathbf{a} \cdot (\mathbf{b}+\mathbf{c}) = \mathbf{a} \cdot \mathbf{b}+\mathbf{a} \cdot \mathbf{c}, \quad \text{(iii) } (\alpha\mathbf{a}) \cdot \mathbf{b} = \mathbf{a} \cdot (\alpha\mathbf{b}) = \alpha(\mathbf{a} \cdot \mathbf{b}) \tag{36}$$

The **Euclidean norm** or **length** of the vector $\mathbf{a} = (a_1, a_2, \ldots, a_n)$ is

$$\|\mathbf{a}\| = \sqrt{\mathbf{a} \cdot \mathbf{a}} = \sqrt{a_1^2 + a_2^2 + \cdots + a_n^2} \tag{37}$$

Note that $\|\alpha\mathbf{a}\| = |\alpha|\|\mathbf{a}\|$ for all scalars and vectors.

The following useful inequalities hold:

$$|\mathbf{a} \cdot \mathbf{b}| \leq \|\mathbf{a}\| \cdot \|\mathbf{b}\| \quad \textbf{(Cauchy–Schwarz inequality)} \tag{38}$$

$$\|\mathbf{a} + \mathbf{b}\| \leq \|\mathbf{a}\| + \|\mathbf{b}\| \quad \textbf{(triangle inequality for norms)} \tag{39}$$

The **angle** θ between nonzero vectors $\mathbf{a}$ and $\mathbf{b}$ in $\mathbb{R}^n$ is defined by

$$\cos\theta = \frac{\mathbf{a} \cdot \mathbf{b}}{\|\mathbf{a}\| \cdot \|\mathbf{b}\|} \quad (\theta \in [0, \pi]) \tag{40}$$

This definition makes sense because the Cauchy–Schwarz inequality implies that the right-hand side has absolute value ≤ 1. According to (40), $\cos\theta = 0$ iff $\mathbf{a} \cdot \mathbf{b} = 0$. Then $\theta = \pi/2 = 90°$.

By definition, **a** and **b** in $\mathbb{R}^n$ are **orthogonal** if their dot product is 0. In symbols:

$$\mathbf{a} \perp \mathbf{b} \quad \Longleftrightarrow \quad \mathbf{a} \cdot \mathbf{b} = 0 \tag{41}$$

The **straight line** through two distinct points $\mathbf{a} = (a_1, \ldots, a_n)$ and $\mathbf{b} = (b_1, \ldots, b_n)$ in $\mathbb{R}^n$ is the set of all $\mathbf{x} = (x_1, \ldots, x_n)$ in $\mathbb{R}^n$ such that

$$\mathbf{x} = t\mathbf{a} + (1 - t)\mathbf{b} \tag{42}$$

for some real number t.

The **hyperplane** in $\mathbb{R}^n$ that passes through the point $\mathbf{a} = (a_1, \ldots, a_n)$ and is orthogonal to the nonzero vector $\mathbf{p} = (p_1, \ldots, p_n)$, is the set of all points $\mathbf{x} = (x_1, \ldots, x_n)$ such that

$$\mathbf{p} \cdot (\mathbf{x} - \mathbf{a}) = 0 \tag{43}$$

1.2 Partitioned Matrices and Their Inverses

Many applications of linear algebra deal with matrices of high order. To see the structure of such matrices and to ease the computational burden in dealing with them, it is often helpful to partition the matrices into suitably chosen submatrices. The operation of subdividing a matrix into submatrices is called **partitioning**.

EXAMPLE 1   Consider the 3×5 matrix $\mathbf{A} = \begin{pmatrix} 2 & 0 & 1 & 0 & 4 \\ 1 & 2 & 1 & 3 & 4 \\ 0 & 0 & 2 & 1 & 4 \end{pmatrix}$. The matrix $\mathbf{A}$ can be partitioned in a number of ways. For example,

$$\mathbf{A} = \left(\begin{array}{cc|ccc} 2 & 0 & 1 & 0 & 4 \\ 1 & 2 & 1 & 3 & 4 \\ \hline 0 & 0 & 2 & 1 & 4 \end{array} \right) = \begin{pmatrix} \mathbf{A}_{11} & \mathbf{A}_{12} \\ \mathbf{A}_{21} & \mathbf{A}_{22} \end{pmatrix} \tag{$*$}$$

where $\mathbf{A}_{11}, \mathbf{A}_{12}, \mathbf{A}_{21},$ and $\mathbf{A}_{22}$ are submatrices of dimensions $2 \times 2, 2 \times 3, 1 \times 2,$ and 1×3, respectively. This is useful because A_{21} is a zero matrix. Other less useful partitionings of **A** include the one where **A** is partitioned into three row vectors, and the one where **A** is partitioned into five column vectors.

Though Example 1 raises the possibility of partitioning a matrix into arbitrarily many submatrices, the rest of this section considers only partitionings into 2×2 arrays of submatrices as in $(*)$.

Operations on Partitioned Matrices

One can perform standard matrix operations on partitioned matrices, treating the submatrices as if they were ordinary matrix elements. This requires obeying the rules for sums, differences, and products.

Adding or subtracting partitioned matrices is simple. For example,

$$\begin{pmatrix} \mathbf{A}_{11} & \mathbf{A}_{12} \\ \mathbf{A}_{21} & \mathbf{A}_{22} \end{pmatrix} + \begin{pmatrix} \mathbf{B}_{11} & \mathbf{B}_{12} \\ \mathbf{B}_{21} & \mathbf{B}_{22} \end{pmatrix} = \begin{pmatrix} \mathbf{A}_{11} + \mathbf{B}_{11} & \mathbf{A}_{12} + \mathbf{B}_{12} \\ \mathbf{A}_{21} + \mathbf{B}_{21} & \mathbf{A}_{22} + \mathbf{B}_{22} \end{pmatrix} \tag{1}$$

as long as the dimensions of $\mathbf{A}_{11}$ are those of $\mathbf{B}_{11}$, the dimensions of $\mathbf{A}_{12}$ are those of $\mathbf{B}_{12}$, and so on. The result follows directly from the definition of matrix addition. The rule for subtracting partitioned matrices is similar.

The rule for multiplying a partitioned matrix by a number is obvious. For example,

$$\alpha \begin{pmatrix} \mathbf{A}_{11} & \mathbf{A}_{12} \\ \mathbf{A}_{21} & \mathbf{A}_{22} \end{pmatrix} = \begin{pmatrix} \alpha \mathbf{A}_{11} & \alpha \mathbf{A}_{12} \\ \alpha \mathbf{A}_{21} & \alpha \mathbf{A}_{22} \end{pmatrix} \tag{2}$$

The following example shows how to multiply partitioned matrices.

EXAMPLE 2   Let $\mathbf{A}$ be the 3×5 matrix $(*)$ in Example 1, and let $\mathbf{B}$ be the 5×4 matrix

$$\mathbf{B} = \begin{pmatrix} 1 & 0 & \vdots & 2 & 1 \\ 0 & 1 & \vdots & 0 & 5 \\ \cdots & \cdots & & \cdots & \cdots \\ 0 & 0 & \vdots & 1 & 0 \\ 0 & 0 & \vdots & 1 & 0 \\ 0 & 0 & \vdots & 0 & 1 \end{pmatrix} = \begin{pmatrix} \mathbf{B}_{11} & \mathbf{B}_{12} \\ \mathbf{B}_{21} & \mathbf{B}_{22} \end{pmatrix}$$

with the indicated partitioning. The product $\mathbf{AB}$ is defined, and the ordinary rules of matrix multiplication applied to the entire matrices yield

$$\mathbf{AB} = \begin{pmatrix} 2 & 0 & 5 & 6 \\ 1 & 2 & 6 & 15 \\ 0 & 0 & 3 & 4 \end{pmatrix}$$

Consider next how to take advantage of the partitioning of the two matrices to compute the product $\mathbf{AB}$. Simply multiply the partitioned matrices as if the submatrices were ordinary matrix elements to obtain

$$\mathbf{AB} = \begin{pmatrix} \mathbf{A}_{11}\mathbf{B}_{11} + \mathbf{A}_{12}\mathbf{B}_{21} & \mathbf{A}_{11}\mathbf{B}_{12} + \mathbf{A}_{12}\mathbf{B}_{22} \\ \mathbf{A}_{21}\mathbf{B}_{11} + \mathbf{A}_{22}\mathbf{B}_{21} & \mathbf{A}_{21}\mathbf{B}_{12} + \mathbf{A}_{22}\mathbf{B}_{22} \end{pmatrix}$$

$$= \begin{pmatrix} \begin{pmatrix} 2 & 0 \\ 1 & 2 \end{pmatrix} + \begin{pmatrix} 0 & 0 \\ 0 & 0 \end{pmatrix} & \begin{pmatrix} 4 & 2 \\ 2 & 11 \end{pmatrix} + \begin{pmatrix} 1 & 4 \\ 4 & 4 \end{pmatrix} \\ (0 \quad 0) + (0 \quad 0) & (0 \quad 0) + (3 \quad 4) \end{pmatrix} = \begin{pmatrix} 2 & 0 & 5 & 6 \\ 1 & 2 & 6 & 15 \\ 0 & 0 & 3 & 4 \end{pmatrix}$$

Note that the two matrices $\mathbf{A}$ and $\mathbf{B}$ were partitioned with dimensions chosen so that all the needed products of submatrices are well defined.

The method suggested by Example 2 is valid in general. It is not difficult to formulate and prove the general result, though the notation becomes cumbersome. If you work through Problem 1 in detail, the general idea should become clear enough.

Multiplying matrices using partitioning is particularly convenient if the matrices have a special structure and involve simple submatrices (like identity or zero matrices).

EXAMPLE 3   Consider the problem of computing powers of the following matrix with the indicated partitioning:

$$\mathbf{M} = \begin{pmatrix} 1/3 & 1/2 & \vdots & 1/6 & 0 \\ 1/2 & 1/3 & \vdots & 0 & 1/6 \\ \cdots & \cdots & \vdots & \cdots & \cdots \\ 0 & 0 & \vdots & 1 & 0 \\ 0 & 0 & \vdots & 0 & 1 \end{pmatrix} = \begin{pmatrix} \mathbf{P} & \mathbf{Q} \\ \mathbf{0} & \mathbf{I} \end{pmatrix}$$

Then

$$\mathbf{M}^2 = \begin{pmatrix} \mathbf{P} & \mathbf{Q} \\ \mathbf{0} & \mathbf{I} \end{pmatrix}\begin{pmatrix} \mathbf{P} & \mathbf{Q} \\ \mathbf{0} & \mathbf{I} \end{pmatrix} = \begin{pmatrix} \mathbf{P}^2 & (\mathbf{P}+\mathbf{I})\mathbf{Q} \\ \mathbf{0} & \mathbf{I} \end{pmatrix} \quad \text{and} \quad \mathbf{M}^3 = \begin{pmatrix} \mathbf{P}^3 & (\mathbf{P}^2+\mathbf{P}+\mathbf{I})\mathbf{Q} \\ \mathbf{0} & \mathbf{I} \end{pmatrix}$$

In general, for all natural numbers n, it can be shown by induction that

$$\mathbf{M}^n = \begin{pmatrix} \mathbf{P}^n & (\mathbf{P}^{n-1} + \cdots + \mathbf{P}^2 + \mathbf{P} + \mathbf{I})\mathbf{Q} \\ \mathbf{0} & \mathbf{I} \end{pmatrix}$$

Inverses by Partitioning

Inverting large square matrices is often made much easier using partitioning. Consider an $n \times n$ matrix $\mathbf{A}$ which has an inverse. Assume that $\mathbf{A}$ is partitioned as follows:

$$\mathbf{A} = \begin{pmatrix} \mathbf{A}_{11} & \mathbf{A}_{12} \\ \mathbf{A}_{21} & \mathbf{A}_{22} \end{pmatrix}, \qquad \text{where } \mathbf{A}_{11} \text{ is a } k \times k \text{ matrix with an inverse} \qquad (3)$$

Hence $\mathbf{A}_{12}$ is a $k \times (n-k)$ matrix, $\mathbf{A}_{21}$ is $(n-k) \times k$, while $\mathbf{A}_{22}$ is an $(n-k) \times (n-k)$ matrix. Since $\mathbf{A}$ has an inverse, there exists an $n \times n$ matrix $\mathbf{B}$ such that $\mathbf{AB} = \mathbf{I}_n$. Partitioning $\mathbf{B}$ in the same way as $\mathbf{A}$ yields

$$\mathbf{B} = \begin{pmatrix} \mathbf{B}_{11} & \mathbf{B}_{12} \\ \mathbf{B}_{21} & \mathbf{B}_{22} \end{pmatrix}$$

The equality $\mathbf{AB} = \mathbf{I}_n$ implies the following four matrix equations for determining $\mathbf{B}_{11}$, $\mathbf{B}_{12}$, $\mathbf{B}_{21}$, and $\mathbf{B}_{22}$:

(i) $\mathbf{A}_{11}\mathbf{B}_{11} + \mathbf{A}_{12}\mathbf{B}_{21} = \mathbf{I}_k$ (ii) $\mathbf{A}_{11}\mathbf{B}_{12} + \mathbf{A}_{12}\mathbf{B}_{22} = \mathbf{0}_{k \times (n-k)}$

(iii) $\mathbf{A}_{21}\mathbf{B}_{11} + \mathbf{A}_{22}\mathbf{B}_{21} = \mathbf{0}_{(n-k) \times k}$ (iv) $\mathbf{A}_{21}\mathbf{B}_{12} + \mathbf{A}_{22}\mathbf{B}_{22} = \mathbf{I}_{n-k}$

where the subscripts attached to $\mathbf{I}$ and $\mathbf{0}$ indicate the dimensions of these matrices. Because $\mathbf{A}_{11}$ has an inverse, (ii) gives $\mathbf{B}_{12} = -\mathbf{A}_{11}^{-1}\mathbf{A}_{12}\mathbf{B}_{22}$. Inserting this into (iv) gives $(-\mathbf{A}_{21}\mathbf{A}_{11}^{-1}\mathbf{A}_{12} + \mathbf{A}_{22})\mathbf{B}_{22} = \mathbf{I}_{n-k}$, and so $\mathbf{B}_{22} = (\mathbf{A}_{22} - \mathbf{A}_{21}\mathbf{A}_{11}^{-1}\mathbf{A}_{12})^{-1}$. Next, solve

(i) for $\mathbf{B}_{11}$ to obtain $\mathbf{B}_{11} = \mathbf{A}_{11}^{-1} - \mathbf{A}_{11}^{-1}\mathbf{A}_{12}\mathbf{B}_{21}$. Inserting this into (iii) and rearranging yields $(\mathbf{A}_{22} - \mathbf{A}_{21}\mathbf{A}_{11}^{-1}\mathbf{A}_{12})\mathbf{B}_{21} = -\mathbf{A}_{21}\mathbf{A}_{11}^{-1}$. Using the expression found for $\mathbf{B}_{22}$, we have $\mathbf{B}_{21} = -\mathbf{B}_{22}\mathbf{A}_{21}\mathbf{A}_{11}^{-1}$. It follows that $\mathbf{B}_{11} = \mathbf{A}_{11}^{-1} + \mathbf{A}_{11}^{-1}\mathbf{A}_{12}\mathbf{B}_{22}\mathbf{A}_{21}\mathbf{A}_{11}^{-1}$. The conclusion is:

$$\begin{pmatrix} \mathbf{A}_{11} & \mathbf{A}_{12} \\ \mathbf{A}_{21} & \mathbf{A}_{22} \end{pmatrix}^{-1} = \begin{pmatrix} \mathbf{A}_{11}^{-1} + \mathbf{A}_{11}^{-1}\mathbf{A}_{12}\mathbf{\Delta}^{-1}\mathbf{A}_{21}\mathbf{A}_{11}^{-1} & -\mathbf{A}_{11}^{-1}\mathbf{A}_{12}\mathbf{\Delta}^{-1} \\ -\mathbf{\Delta}^{-1}\mathbf{A}_{21}\mathbf{A}_{11}^{-1} & \mathbf{\Delta}^{-1} \end{pmatrix} \tag{4}$$

where $\mathbf{\Delta} = \mathbf{A}_{22} - \mathbf{A}_{21}\mathbf{A}_{11}^{-1}\mathbf{A}_{12}$.

Formula (4) is valid provided both $\mathbf{A}^{-1}$ and $\mathbf{A}_{11}^{-1}$ exist. Similarly, if both $\mathbf{A}^{-1}$ and $\mathbf{A}_{22}^{-1}$ exist, then

$$\begin{pmatrix} \mathbf{A}_{11} & \mathbf{A}_{12} \\ \mathbf{A}_{21} & \mathbf{A}_{22} \end{pmatrix}^{-1} = \begin{pmatrix} \tilde{\mathbf{\Delta}}^{-1} & -\tilde{\mathbf{\Delta}}^{-1}\mathbf{A}_{12}\mathbf{A}_{22}^{-1} \\ -\mathbf{A}_{22}^{-1}\mathbf{A}_{21}\tilde{\mathbf{\Delta}}^{-1} & \mathbf{A}_{22}^{-1} + \mathbf{A}_{22}^{-1}\mathbf{A}_{21}\tilde{\mathbf{\Delta}}^{-1}\mathbf{A}_{12}\mathbf{A}_{22}^{-1} \end{pmatrix} \tag{5}$$

where $\tilde{\mathbf{\Delta}} = \mathbf{A}_{11} - \mathbf{A}_{12}\mathbf{A}_{22}^{-1}\mathbf{A}_{21}$.

EXAMPLE 4   Compute $\mathbf{A}^{-1}$ when $\mathbf{A} = \left(\begin{array}{cc:ccc} 2 & -3 & 0 & 0 & 0 \\ 3 & -4 & 0 & 0 & 0 \\ \hdashline 1 & -1 & 1 & 0 & 0 \\ 1 & -1 & 0 & 1 & 0 \\ -5 & 7 & 0 & 0 & 1 \end{array}\right) = \begin{pmatrix} \mathbf{A}_{11} & \mathbf{A}_{12} \\ \mathbf{A}_{21} & \mathbf{A}_{22} \end{pmatrix}$.

Solution: Because $\mathbf{A}_{22} = \mathbf{I}$, it is easier to use formula (5) than (4). Note that $\tilde{\mathbf{\Delta}} = \mathbf{A}_{11}$, so by formula (1.1.29), $\tilde{\mathbf{\Delta}}^{-1} = \begin{pmatrix} -4 & 3 \\ -3 & 2 \end{pmatrix}$. Then

$$-\mathbf{A}_{22}^{-1}\mathbf{A}_{21}\tilde{\mathbf{\Delta}}^{-1} = -\mathbf{I}_3 \begin{pmatrix} 1 & -1 \\ 1 & -1 \\ -5 & 7 \end{pmatrix} \begin{pmatrix} -4 & 3 \\ -3 & 2 \end{pmatrix} = -\begin{pmatrix} -1 & 1 \\ -1 & 1 \\ -1 & -1 \end{pmatrix}$$

and so

$$\mathbf{A}^{-1} = \begin{pmatrix} \begin{pmatrix} -4 & 3 \\ -3 & 2 \end{pmatrix} & \begin{pmatrix} 0 & 0 & 0 \\ 0 & 0 & 0 \end{pmatrix} \\ \begin{pmatrix} 1 & -1 \\ 1 & -1 \\ 1 & 1 \end{pmatrix} & \begin{pmatrix} 1 & 0 & 0 \\ 0 & 1 & 0 \\ 0 & 0 & 1 \end{pmatrix} \end{pmatrix} = \left(\begin{array}{cc:ccc} -4 & 3 & 0 & 0 & 0 \\ -3 & 2 & 0 & 0 & 0 \\ \hdashline 1 & -1 & 1 & 0 & 0 \\ 1 & -1 & 0 & 1 & 0 \\ 1 & 1 & 0 & 0 & 1 \end{array}\right)$$

(Check the result by computing $\mathbf{A}\mathbf{A}^{-1}$ using partitioning.)

We conclude this section by giving two useful formulas for the determinant of an $n \times n$ matrix $\mathbf{A}$ partitioned as in (3). (See Problem 5.)

$$\text{If } \mathbf{A}_{11}^{-1} \text{ exists, then } \begin{vmatrix} \mathbf{A}_{11} & \mathbf{A}_{12} \\ \mathbf{A}_{21} & \mathbf{A}_{22} \end{vmatrix} = |\mathbf{A}_{11}| \cdot |\mathbf{A}_{22} - \mathbf{A}_{21}\mathbf{A}_{11}^{-1}\mathbf{A}_{12}| \tag{6}$$

$$\text{If } \mathbf{A}_{22}^{-1} \text{ exists, then } \begin{vmatrix} \mathbf{A}_{11} & \mathbf{A}_{12} \\ \mathbf{A}_{21} & \mathbf{A}_{22} \end{vmatrix} = |\mathbf{A}_{22}| \cdot |\mathbf{A}_{11} - \mathbf{A}_{12}\mathbf{A}_{22}^{-1}\mathbf{A}_{21}| \tag{7}$$

PROBLEMS FOR SECTION 1.2

1. Compute the following matrix product using: (i) ordinary matrix multiplication; (ii) the suggested partitioning.

$$\begin{pmatrix} a_{11} & a_{12} & a_{13} \\ a_{21} & a_{22} & a_{23} \\ \hline a_{31} & a_{32} & a_{33} \end{pmatrix} \begin{pmatrix} b_{11} & b_{12} \\ b_{21} & b_{22} \\ \hline b_{31} & b_{32} \end{pmatrix} = \begin{pmatrix} \mathbf{A}_{11} & \mathbf{A}_{12} \\ \mathbf{A}_{21} & \mathbf{A}_{22} \end{pmatrix} \begin{pmatrix} \mathbf{B}_{11} \\ \mathbf{B}_{21} \end{pmatrix}$$

2. Compute the following matrix product using the suggested partitioning. Check the result by ordinary matrix multiplication.

$$\begin{pmatrix} 1 & 1 & 1 \\ -1 & 0 & -1 \end{pmatrix} \begin{pmatrix} 2 & -1 \\ 0 & 1 \\ \hline 1 & 1 \end{pmatrix}$$

3. Use partitioning to compute the inverses of the following matrices:

(a) $\begin{pmatrix} 1 & 0 & 0 & 0 & 1 \\ 0 & 1 & 0 & 0 & 1 \\ 0 & 0 & 1 & 0 & 1 \\ 0 & 0 & 0 & 1 & 0 \\ 1 & 1 & 1 & 0 & 1 \end{pmatrix}$ (b) $\begin{pmatrix} 2 & 3 & 0 & 0 \\ 5 & 2 & 0 & 0 \\ 0 & 0 & 4 & 3 \\ 0 & 0 & 3 & 2 \end{pmatrix}$ (c) $\begin{pmatrix} 2 & 0 & 0 & 0 \\ 0 & 0 & 0 & 1 \\ 0 & 0 & 1 & 0 \\ 0 & 1 & 0 & 0 \end{pmatrix}$

4. Let $\mathbf{A} = \begin{pmatrix} a_{11} & \cdots & a_{1n} \\ \vdots & \ddots & \vdots \\ a_{n1} & \cdots & a_{nn} \end{pmatrix}$ and $\mathbf{X} = \begin{pmatrix} x_1 \\ \vdots \\ x_n \end{pmatrix}$, where $|\mathbf{A}| \neq 0$. Show that

$$|\mathbf{A} + \mathbf{X}\mathbf{X}'| = \begin{vmatrix} 1 & -x_1 & \cdots & -x_n \\ x_1 & a_{11} & \cdots & a_{1n} \\ \vdots & \vdots & \ddots & \vdots \\ x_n & a_{n1} & \cdots & a_{nn} \end{vmatrix} = |\mathbf{A}| \cdot (1 + \mathbf{X}'\mathbf{A}^{-1}\mathbf{X}) \tag{*}$$

(This formula is useful in econometrics.)

5. If $\mathbf{P}$ and $\mathbf{Q}$ are invertible square matrices, prove that

$$\begin{pmatrix} \mathbf{P} & \mathbf{R} \\ \mathbf{0} & \mathbf{Q} \end{pmatrix}^{-1} = \begin{pmatrix} \mathbf{P}^{-1} & -\mathbf{P}^{-1}\mathbf{R}\mathbf{Q}^{-1} \\ \mathbf{0} & \mathbf{Q}^{-1} \end{pmatrix}$$

HARDER PROBLEMS

6. (a) Show that if $\mathbf{A}_{12}$ or $\mathbf{A}_{21}$ in (3) is the zero matrix, then $|\mathbf{A}| = |\mathbf{A}_{11}| \cdot |\mathbf{A}_{22}|$. (*Hint:* Use the definition of a determinant. See e.g. EMEA, Chapter 16.)

   (b) Show that $\begin{pmatrix} \mathbf{I}_k & -\mathbf{A}_{12}\mathbf{A}_{22}^{-1} \\ \mathbf{0} & \mathbf{I}_{n-k} \end{pmatrix}\begin{pmatrix} \mathbf{A}_{11} & \mathbf{A}_{12} \\ \mathbf{A}_{21} & \mathbf{A}_{22} \end{pmatrix} = \begin{pmatrix} \mathbf{A}_{11} - \mathbf{A}_{12}\mathbf{A}_{22}^{-1}\mathbf{A}_{21} & \mathbf{0} \\ \mathbf{A}_{21} & \mathbf{A}_{22} \end{pmatrix}$,

   and use this result to prove (7).

7. (a) Suppose $\mathbf{A}$ is $n \times m$ and $\mathbf{B}$ is $m \times n$. Prove that $|\mathbf{I}_n + \mathbf{AB}| = |\mathbf{I}_m + \mathbf{BA}|$. (*Hint:* Define $\mathbf{D} = \begin{pmatrix} \mathbf{I}_n & \mathbf{A} \\ \mathbf{0} & \mathbf{I}_m \end{pmatrix}$, $\mathbf{E} = \begin{pmatrix} \mathbf{I}_n & -\mathbf{A} \\ \mathbf{B} & \mathbf{I}_m \end{pmatrix}$. Then $|\mathbf{I}_n + \mathbf{AB}| = |\mathbf{DE}| = |\mathbf{D}|\,|\mathbf{E}| = |\mathbf{E}|\,|\mathbf{D}| = |\mathbf{ED}| = |\mathbf{I}_m + \mathbf{BA}|$.)

   (b) Use the result in (a) to prove that if $a_1, \ldots, a_n$ are all different from 1, then

$$\begin{vmatrix} a_1 & 1 & 1 & \cdots & 1 \\ 1 & a_2 & 1 & \cdots & 1 \\ 1 & 1 & a_3 & \cdots & 1 \\ \vdots & \vdots & \vdots & \ddots & \vdots \\ 1 & 1 & 1 & \cdots & a_n \end{vmatrix} = (a_1 - 1)(a_2 - 1)\cdots(a_n - 1)\left[1 + \sum_{i=1}^{n} \frac{1}{a_i - 1}\right]$$

   (*Hint:* Let $\mathbf{F} = \mathbf{I}_n + \mathbf{A}_{n\times 1}\mathbf{B}_{1\times n}$ where $\mathbf{A}_{n\times 1} = \left(\frac{1}{a_1 - 1}, \frac{1}{a_2 - 1}, \ldots, \frac{1}{a_n - 1}\right)'$ and $\mathbf{B}_{1\times n} = (1, 1, \ldots, 1)$.)

1.3 Linear Independence

Any system of linear equations can be written as a vector equation. For instance, the system

$$\begin{aligned} 2x_1 + 2x_2 - x_3 &= -3 \\ 4x_1 \qquad + 2x_3 &= 8 \\ 6x_2 - 3x_3 &= -12 \end{aligned}$$

can be written as the vector equation

$$x_1\mathbf{a}_1 + x_2\mathbf{a}_2 + x_3\mathbf{a}_3 = \mathbf{b} \tag{$*$}$$

where

$$\mathbf{a}_1 = \begin{pmatrix} 2 \\ 4 \\ 0 \end{pmatrix}, \quad \mathbf{a}_2 = \begin{pmatrix} 2 \\ 0 \\ 6 \end{pmatrix}, \quad \mathbf{a}_3 = \begin{pmatrix} -1 \\ 2 \\ -3 \end{pmatrix}, \quad \mathbf{b} = \begin{pmatrix} -3 \\ 8 \\ -12 \end{pmatrix}$$

In ($*$) we say that **b** is expressed as a **linear combination** of the column vectors of the coefficient matrix **A**. Solving system ($*$) we get $x_1 = 1/2$, $x_2 = -1/2$, and $x_3 = 3$. Thus $\mathbf{b} = (1/2)\mathbf{a}_1 + (-1/2)\mathbf{a}_2 + 3\mathbf{a}_3$. In this case, we say that **b** is *linearly dependent* on the vectors $\mathbf{a}_1$, $\mathbf{a}_2$, and $\mathbf{a}_3$.

More generally, if one particular member of a set of vectors in $\mathbb{R}^m$ can be expressed as a linear combination of the other vectors in the set, that vector is said to be *linearly dependent* on the others, and the whole set of vectors is said to be *linearly dependent*. But if no vector in the set can be expressed as a linear combination of the others, then the set of vectors is *linearly independent*.

It is convenient to have an equivalent but more symmetric definition of linearly dependent and independent vectors.

DEFINITION

The n vectors $\mathbf{a}_1, \mathbf{a}_2, \ldots, \mathbf{a}_n$ in $\mathbb{R}^m$ are **linearly dependent** if there exist numbers $c_1, c_2, \ldots, c_n$, not all zero, such that

$$c_1\mathbf{a}_1 + c_2\mathbf{a}_2 + \cdots + c_n\mathbf{a}_n = \mathbf{0} \tag{1}$$

If this equation holds only when $c_1 = c_2 = \cdots = c_n = 0$, then the vectors are **linearly independent**.

So a linear combination of linearly independent vectors can be the **0** vector only if all the coefficients in the linear combination are zero.

EXAMPLE 1

(a) Prove that $\mathbf{a}_1 = \begin{pmatrix} 3 \\ 1 \end{pmatrix}$ and $\mathbf{a}_2 = \begin{pmatrix} 6 \\ 2 \end{pmatrix}$ are linearly dependent. Illustrate.

(b) Prove that $\mathbf{a}_1 = \begin{pmatrix} 3 \\ 1 \end{pmatrix}$ and $\mathbf{a}_2 = \begin{pmatrix} 1 \\ 2 \end{pmatrix}$ are linearly independent. Illustrate.

Solution:

(a) Here $\mathbf{a}_2 = 2\mathbf{a}_1$, so $2\mathbf{a}_1 - \mathbf{a}_2 = \mathbf{0}$. Choosing $c_1 = 2$ and $c_2 = -1$ yields $c_1\mathbf{a}_1 + c_2\mathbf{a}_2 = \mathbf{0}$, so according to definition (1), $\mathbf{a}_1$ and $\mathbf{a}_2$ are linearly dependent. The vector $\mathbf{a}_2$ points in the same direction as $\mathbf{a}_1$, and is twice as long. See Fig. 1.

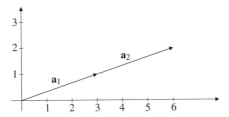

Figure 1 $\mathbf{a}_1$ and $\mathbf{a}_2$ are linearly dependent.

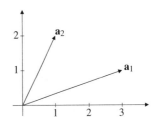

Figure 2 $\mathbf{a}_1$ and $\mathbf{a}_2$ are linearly independent.

(b) In this case the equation $c_1\mathbf{a}_1 + c_2\mathbf{a}_2 = \mathbf{0}$ reduces to

$$3c_1 + c_2 = 0$$
$$c_1 + 2c_2 = 0$$

The only solution is $c_1 = c_2 = 0$, so $\mathbf{a}_1$ and $\mathbf{a}_2$ are linearly independent. See Fig. 2.

The formal definitions of linear dependence and independence given above may seem rather odd. However, we can easily prove the following result:

A set of n vectors $\mathbf{a}_1, \mathbf{a}_2, \ldots, \mathbf{a}_n$ in $\mathbb{R}^m$ is linearly dependent iff at least one of them can be written as a linear combination of the others.

Or equivalently: A set of vectors $\mathbf{a}_1, \mathbf{a}_2, \ldots, \mathbf{a}_n$ in $\mathbb{R}^m$ is linearly independent iff none of them can be written as a linear combination of the others.

(2)

Proof: First, suppose that $\mathbf{a}_1, \mathbf{a}_2, \ldots, \mathbf{a}_n$ are linearly dependent. Then the equation $c_1\mathbf{a}_1 + c_2\mathbf{a}_2 + \cdots + c_n\mathbf{a}_n = \mathbf{0}$ holds with at least *one* of the coefficients c_i different from 0. After reordering the vectors $\mathbf{a}_i$ and the corresponding scalars c_i, if necessary, we can assume that $c_1 \neq 0$. Solving the equation for $\mathbf{a}_1$ yields $\mathbf{a}_1 = -(c_2/c_1)\mathbf{a}_2 - \cdots - (c_n/c_1)\mathbf{a}_n$. Thus, $\mathbf{a}_1$ is a linear combination of the other vectors.

Suppose on the other hand that $\mathbf{a}_1$, say, can be written as a linear combination of the others, with $\mathbf{a}_1 = d_2\mathbf{a}_2 + d_3\mathbf{a}_3 + \cdots + d_n\mathbf{a}_n$. Then $(-1)\mathbf{a}_1 + d_2\mathbf{a}_2 + d_3\mathbf{a}_3 + \cdots + d_n\mathbf{a}_n = \mathbf{0}$. The first coefficient in this equation is $\neq 0$, so the set $\mathbf{a}_1, \mathbf{a}_2, \ldots, \mathbf{a}_n$ is linearly dependent. ∎

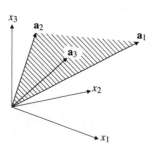

Figure 3 Vectors $\mathbf{a}_1$, $\mathbf{a}_2$, and $\mathbf{a}_3$ are linearly dependent.

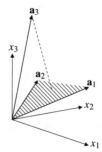

Figure 4 Vectors $\mathbf{a}_1$, $\mathbf{a}_2$, and $\mathbf{a}_3$ are linearly independent.

It is very helpful to have a geometric feeling for the meaning of linear dependence and independence. For the case of $\mathbb{R}^2$, Example 1 illustrated the possibilities. In $\mathbb{R}^3$, let $\mathbf{a}_1$ and $\mathbf{a}_2$ be two non-parallel 3-vectors starting at the origin. If t_1 and t_2 are real numbers, then the vector $\mathbf{x} = t_1\mathbf{a}_1 + t_2\mathbf{a}_2$ is a linear combination of $\mathbf{a}_1$ and $\mathbf{a}_2$. Geometrically, the set of all linear combinations of $\mathbf{a}_1$ and $\mathbf{a}_2$ is called the plane **spanned** by $\mathbf{a}_1$ and $\mathbf{a}_2$. Any vector in the plane spanned by $\mathbf{a}_1$ and $\mathbf{a}_2$ is linearly dependent on $\mathbf{a}_1$ and $\mathbf{a}_2$.

Suppose we take another 3-vector $\mathbf{a}_3$ that is *not* in the plane spanned by $\mathbf{a}_1$ and $\mathbf{a}_2$. Then the three vectors $\mathbf{a}_1$, $\mathbf{a}_2$, and $\mathbf{a}_3$ are linearly independent, because no vector in the set can be written as a linear combination of the others. In general, three vectors in $\mathbb{R}^3$ are linearly dependent iff they all lie in the same plane. Three vectors in $\mathbb{R}^3$ are linearly independent iff there is no plane that contains all three vectors. Figures 3 and 4 give geometric illustrations of these statements.

In $\mathbb{R}^m$, the two m-vectors $\mathbf{a}_1$ and $\mathbf{a}_2$ are linearly dependent iff one of the vectors, say, $\mathbf{a}_1$, is proportional to the other, so that $\mathbf{a}_1 = c\mathbf{a}_2$. If $c \neq 0$, the two vectors are called **parallel**.

Linear Dependence and Systems of Linear Equations

Consider the general system of m equations in n unknowns, written both in its usual form and also as a vector equation:

$$
\begin{aligned}
a_{11}x_1 + \cdots + a_{1n}x_n &= b_1 \\
&\cdots\cdots\cdots\cdots\cdots\cdots\cdots
\end{aligned}
\qquad \Longleftrightarrow \qquad x_1\mathbf{a}_1 + \cdots + x_n\mathbf{a}_n = \mathbf{b} \qquad (3)
$$
$$
a_{m1}x_1 + \cdots + a_{mn}x_n = b_m
$$

Here $\mathbf{a}_1, \ldots, \mathbf{a}_n$ are the column vectors of coefficients, and $\mathbf{b}$ is the column vector with components $b_1, \ldots, b_m$.

Suppose that (3) has two solutions $(u_1, \ldots, u_n)$ and $(v_1, \ldots, v_n)$. Then

$$
u_1\mathbf{a}_1 + \cdots + u_n\mathbf{a}_n = \mathbf{b} \qquad \text{and} \qquad v_1\mathbf{a}_1 + \cdots + v_n\mathbf{a}_n = \mathbf{b}
$$

Subtracting the second equation from the first yields

$$
(u_1 - v_1)\mathbf{a}_1 + \cdots + (u_n - v_n)\mathbf{a}_n = \mathbf{0} \qquad (*)
$$

Let $c_1 = u_1 - v_1, \ldots, c_n = u_n - v_n$. The two solutions are different if and only if $c_1, \ldots, c_n$ are not all equal to 0. We conclude that if system (3) has more than one solution, then the column vectors $\mathbf{a}_1, \ldots, \mathbf{a}_n$ are linearly dependent. Equivalently: *If the column vectors $\mathbf{a}_1, \ldots, \mathbf{a}_n$ are linearly independent, then system (3) has at most one solution.* Without saying more about the right-hand side vector $\mathbf{b}$, however, we cannot know if there are any solutions at all, in general.

THEOREM 1.3.1

The n column vectors $\mathbf{a}_1, \mathbf{a}_2, \ldots, \mathbf{a}_n$ of the $n \times n$ matrix

$$
\mathbf{A} = \begin{pmatrix} a_{11} & a_{12} & \cdots & a_{1n} \\ a_{21} & a_{22} & \cdots & a_{2n} \\ \vdots & \vdots & \ddots & \vdots \\ a_{n1} & a_{n2} & \cdots & a_{nn} \end{pmatrix}, \quad \text{where} \quad \mathbf{a}_j = \begin{pmatrix} a_{1j} \\ a_{2j} \\ \vdots \\ a_{nj} \end{pmatrix} \qquad (4)
$$

are linearly independent iff $|\mathbf{A}| \neq 0$.

Proof: The vectors $a_1, a_2, \ldots, a_n$ are linearly independent iff the vector equation $x_1 a_1 + x_2 a_2 + \cdots + x_n a_n = 0$ has only the trivial solution $x_1 = x_2 = \cdots = x_n = 0$. This vector equation is equivalent to a homogeneous system of equations, and according to (1.1.34), it has only the trivial solution iff $|A| \neq 0$.   ∎

According to this theorem, three vectors a_1, a_2, and a_3 in $\mathbb{R}^3$ are linearly dependent iff the determinant $|a_1\, a_2\, a_3|$ of the matrix with columns a_1, a_2, and a_3 is zero, which is true iff the volume shown in Fig. 1.1.1 (page 4) collapses to zero.

EXAMPLE 2   Suppose a, b, and c are three linearly independent vectors in $\mathbb{R}^n$. Are $a - b$, $b - c$, and $a - c$ linearly independent?

Solution: Suppose $c_1(a - b) + c_2(b - c) + c_3(a - c) = 0$. Rearranging, we get $(c_1 + c_3)a + (-c_1 + c_2)b + (-c_2 - c_3)c = 0$. Since a, b, and c are linearly independent, $c_1 + c_3 = 0$, $-c_1 + c_2 = 0$, and $-c_2 - c_3 = 0$. These equations are satisfied (for example) when $c_1 = c_2 = 1$, and $c_3 = -1$, so $a - b$, $b - c$, and $a - c$ are linearly dependent.

PROBLEMS FOR SECTION 1.3

1. Express $\begin{pmatrix} 8 \\ 9 \end{pmatrix}$ as a linear combination of $\begin{pmatrix} 2 \\ 5 \end{pmatrix}$ and $\begin{pmatrix} -1 \\ 3 \end{pmatrix}$.

2. Determine which of the following pairs of vectors are linearly independent:

   (a) $\begin{pmatrix} -1 \\ 2 \end{pmatrix}, \begin{pmatrix} 3 \\ -6 \end{pmatrix}$ (b) $\begin{pmatrix} 2 \\ -1 \end{pmatrix}, \begin{pmatrix} 3 \\ 4 \end{pmatrix}$ (c) $\begin{pmatrix} -1 \\ 1 \end{pmatrix}, \begin{pmatrix} 1 \\ -1 \end{pmatrix}$

3. Prove that $\begin{pmatrix} 1 \\ 0 \\ 1 \end{pmatrix}, \begin{pmatrix} 2 \\ 1 \\ 0 \end{pmatrix}$, and $\begin{pmatrix} 0 \\ 1 \\ 1 \end{pmatrix}$ are linearly independent. (Use Theorem 1.3.1.)

4. Prove that $(1, 1, 1)$, $(2, 1, 0)$, $(3, 1, 4)$, and $(1, 2, -2)$ are linearly dependent.

5. If a, b, and c are linearly independent vectors in $\mathbb{R}^m$, prove that $a + b$, $b + c$, and $a + c$ are also linearly independent. Is the same true of $a - b$, $b + c$, and $a + c$?

6. (a) Suppose that $a, b, c \in \mathbb{R}^3$ are all different from 0, and that $a \perp b$, $b \perp c$, and $a \perp c$. Prove that a, b, and c are linearly independent.

   (b) Suppose that $a_1, \ldots, a_n$ are vectors in $\mathbb{R}^m$, all different from 0. Suppose that $a_i \perp a_j$ for all $i \neq j$. Prove that $a_1, \ldots, a_n$ are linearly independent.

7. Prove the following results:

   (a) If a set of vectors is linearly dependent, then any *larger* set (that is, any set containing the original set) is also linearly dependent.

   (b) If a set of vectors is linearly independent, then any subset (that is, any set contained in the original set) is linearly independent.

1.4 The Rank of a Matrix

Associated with any matrix is an important natural number called its *rank*. An $m \times n$ matrix A has n column vectors, each with m components. The largest number of column vectors in A that form a linearly independent set is called the **rank** of A, denoted by $r(A)$.

DEFINITION

The **rank** of a matrix A, written $r(A)$, is the maximum number of linearly independent column vectors in A. If A is the 0 matrix, we put $r(A) = 0$. $\qquad(1)$

The rank of a matrix gives very useful information. In particular, it is of central importance in stating the main results in the next section concerning the existence and multiplicity of solutions to linear systems of equations.

EXAMPLE 1   Let A be a square matrix of order n. Because the matrix has only n columns, its rank cannot exceed n. In fact, according to Example 1.3.2, the n column vectors of A are linearly independent iff $|A| \neq 0$. We conclude that a square matrix A of order n has rank n iff $|A| \neq 0$.

The rank of a matrix can be characterized in terms of its nonvanishing minors. In general, a **minor** of order k in A is obtained by deleting all but k rows and k columns, and then taking the determinant of the resulting $k \times k$ matrix.

EXAMPLE 2   Describe all the minors of the matrix $A = \begin{pmatrix} 1 & 0 & 2 & 1 \\ 0 & 2 & 4 & 2 \\ 0 & 2 & 2 & 1 \end{pmatrix}$.

Solution: Because there are only 3 rows, there are minors of order 1, 2, and 3. There are:

(a) *4 minors of order 3.* These are obtained by deleting any one of the 4 columns:

$$\begin{vmatrix} 1 & 0 & 2 \\ 0 & 2 & 4 \\ 0 & 2 & 2 \end{vmatrix}, \quad \begin{vmatrix} 1 & 0 & 1 \\ 0 & 2 & 2 \\ 0 & 2 & 1 \end{vmatrix}, \quad \begin{vmatrix} 1 & 2 & 1 \\ 0 & 4 & 2 \\ 0 & 2 & 1 \end{vmatrix}, \quad \begin{vmatrix} 0 & 2 & 1 \\ 2 & 4 & 2 \\ 2 & 2 & 1 \end{vmatrix}$$

(b) *18 minors of order 2.* These are obtained by deleting one row and two columns, in all possible ways. Two of them are:

$$\begin{vmatrix} 1 & 0 \\ 0 & 2 \end{vmatrix}$$ (deleting the third row and the third and fourth column)

$$\begin{vmatrix} 0 & 1 \\ 2 & 1 \end{vmatrix}$$ (deleting the second row and the first and third column)

(c) *12 minors of order 1.* These are all the 12 individual elements of **A**.

NOTE 1 An $m \times n$ matrix has $\binom{m}{k}\binom{n}{k}$ minors of order k. For instance, in Example 2 the 3×4 matrix **A** has $\binom{3}{2}\binom{4}{2} = \frac{3 \cdot 2}{1 \cdot 2} \cdot \frac{4 \cdot 3}{1 \cdot 2} = 3 \cdot 6 = 18$ minors of order 2. (For the definition of the binomial coefficient $\binom{m}{k}$, see e.g. EMEA.)

The relation between the rank and the minors is expressed in the following theorem:[1]

THEOREM 1.4.1

The rank $r(\mathbf{A})$ of a matrix **A** is equal to the order of the largest minor of **A** that is different from 0.

If **A** is a square matrix of order n, then the largest minor of **A** is $|\mathbf{A}|$ itself. So $r(\mathbf{A}) = n$ iff $|\mathbf{A}| \neq 0$. This agrees with Example 1.3.2.

EXAMPLE 3   Find the ranks of the following matrices:

$$(a) \begin{pmatrix} 1 & 0 & 2 & 1 \\ 0 & 2 & 4 & 2 \\ 0 & 2 & 2 & 1 \end{pmatrix} \qquad (b) \begin{pmatrix} -1 & 0 & 2 & 1 \\ -2 & 2 & 4 & 2 \\ -3 & 1 & 6 & 3 \end{pmatrix} \qquad (c) \begin{pmatrix} -1 & 0 & 2 & 1 \\ -2 & 0 & 4 & 2 \\ -3 & 0 & 6 & 3 \end{pmatrix}$$

Solution:

(a) The rank is 3 because $\begin{vmatrix} 1 & 0 & 2 \\ 0 & 2 & 4 \\ 0 & 2 & 2 \end{vmatrix} = -4$ is a non-zero minor of order 3.

(b) Because columns 1, 3, and 4 are proportional, all four minors of order 3 are 0, whereas $\begin{vmatrix} -1 & 0 \\ -2 & 2 \end{vmatrix}$, say, equals -2, so the rank is 2.

(c) All minors of order 3 and 2 are 0. Because not all the elements are 0, the rank is 1.

EXAMPLE 4   Determine the rank of $\mathbf{A} = \begin{pmatrix} 5 - x & 2 & 1 \\ 2 & 1 - x & 0 \\ 1 & 0 & 1 - x \end{pmatrix}$ for all values of x.

---

[1] For a proof of this theorem, see e.g. Fraleigh and Beauregard (1995).

Solution: Expanding $|\mathbf{A}|$ by the third column, we see that

$$|\mathbf{A}| = -(1-x) + (1-x)[(5-x)(1-x)-4] = x(1-x)(x-6)$$

If $x \neq 0$, $x \neq 1$, and $x \neq 6$, then the rank is 3. Because the minor $\begin{vmatrix} 5-x & 2 \\ 1 & 0 \end{vmatrix} = -2 \neq 0$, whatever the value of x, we see that the rank of the matrix is 2 when x is 0, 1, or 6.

Recall that the determinant of a matrix is equal to the determinant of its transpose. The following result is therefore not surprising.

THEOREM 1.4.2

The rank of a matrix $\mathbf{A}$ is equal to the rank of its transpose: $r(\mathbf{A}) = r(\mathbf{A}')$.

Proof: Suppose $|\mathbf{D}|$ is a minor of $\mathbf{A}$. Then $|\mathbf{D}'|$ is a minor of $\mathbf{A}'$, and vice versa. Because $|\mathbf{D}'| = |\mathbf{D}|$, the result follows from Theorem 1.4.1. ∎

It follows from (1) and Theorem 1.4.2 that the rank of a matrix can also be characterized as the maximal number of linearly independent rows of $\mathbf{A}$. So we have three ways of showing that $r(\mathbf{A}) = k$:

(a) Find one set of k columns that is linearly independent, and then show that no set of *more* than k columns is linearly independent.

(b) Find one set of k rows that is linearly independent, and then show that no set of *more* than k rows is linearly independent.

(c) Find one minor of order k that is not 0, and then show that *all* minors of order higher than k are 0.

An Efficient Way to Find the Rank of a Matrix

None of the methods (a), (b), and (c) for finding the rank of a matrix is very efficient. A better approach uses the fact that *the rank of a matrix is not affected by elementary operations.*[2] In the following, if a matrix $\mathbf{A}$ can be transformed into a matrix $\mathbf{B}$ by means of elementary operations, then we write $\mathbf{A} \sim \mathbf{B}$.

EXAMPLE 5   Find the rank of $\begin{pmatrix} 1 & 2 & 3 & 2 \\ 2 & 3 & 5 & 1 \\ 1 & 3 & 4 & 5 \end{pmatrix}$.

---

[2] Elementary row (column) operations are: (a) interchanging two rows (columns); (b) multiplying each element of a row (column) by any scalar $\alpha \neq 0$; (c) if $i \neq j$, adding to each element of the ith row (column) α times the corresponding element of the jth row (column). See e.g. EMEA.

Solution: We use the elementary operations indicated. That is, we multiply the first row by -2 and add it to the second row, and also multiply the first row by -1 and add it to the third row, etc.

$$\begin{pmatrix} 1 & 2 & 3 & 2 \\ 2 & 3 & 5 & 1 \\ 1 & 3 & 4 & 5 \end{pmatrix} \begin{matrix} -2 & -1 \\ \\ \end{matrix} \sim \begin{pmatrix} 1 & 2 & 3 & 2 \\ 0 & -1 & -1 & -3 \\ 0 & 1 & 1 & 3 \end{pmatrix} \begin{matrix} \\ \\ 1 \end{matrix} \sim \begin{pmatrix} 1 & 2 & 3 & 2 \\ 0 & -1 & -1 & -3 \\ 0 & 0 & 0 & 0 \end{pmatrix}$$

The rank of the last matrix is obviously 2, because there are precisely two linearly independent rows. So the original matrix has rank 2.

PROBLEMS FOR SECTION 1.4

1. Determine the ranks of the following matrices:

(a) $\begin{pmatrix} 1 & 2 \\ 8 & 16 \end{pmatrix}$
(b) $\begin{pmatrix} 1 & 3 & 4 \\ 2 & 0 & 1 \end{pmatrix}$
(c) $\begin{pmatrix} 1 & 2 & -1 & 3 \\ 2 & 4 & -4 & 7 \\ -1 & -2 & -1 & -2 \end{pmatrix}$

(d) $\begin{pmatrix} 1 & 3 & 0 & 0 \\ 2 & 4 & 0 & -1 \\ 1 & -1 & 2 & 2 \end{pmatrix}$
(e) $\begin{pmatrix} 2 & 1 & 3 & 7 \\ -1 & 4 & 3 & 1 \\ 3 & 2 & 5 & 11 \end{pmatrix}$
(f) $\begin{pmatrix} 1 & -2 & -1 & 1 \\ 2 & 1 & 1 & 2 \\ -1 & 1 & -1 & -3 \\ -2 & -5 & -2 & 0 \end{pmatrix}$

2. Determine the ranks of the following matrices for all values of the parameters:

(a) $\begin{pmatrix} x & 0 & x^2 - 2 \\ 0 & 1 & 1 \\ -1 & x & x - 1 \end{pmatrix}$
(b) $\begin{pmatrix} t + 3 & 5 & 6 \\ -1 & t - 3 & -6 \\ 1 & 1 & t + 4 \end{pmatrix}$
(c) $\begin{pmatrix} 1 & x & y & 0 \\ 0 & z & w & 1 \\ 1 & x & y & 0 \\ 0 & z & w & 1 \end{pmatrix}$

3. Give an example where $r(\mathbf{AB}) \neq r(\mathbf{BA})$. (*Hint:* Try some 2×2 matrices.)

1.5 Main Results on Linear Systems

Consider the general linear system of m simultaneous equations in n unknowns:

$$a_{11}x_1 + a_{12}x_2 + \cdots + a_{1n}x_n = b_1$$

$$a_{21}x_1 + a_{22}x_2 + \cdots + a_{2n}x_n = b_2$$

$$\text{or} \quad \mathbf{Ax} = \mathbf{b} \qquad (1)$$

$$\cdots\cdots\cdots\cdots\cdots\cdots\cdots\cdots\cdots\cdots$$

$$a_{m1}x_1 + a_{m2}x_2 + \cdots + a_{mn}x_n = b_m$$

where $\mathbf{A}$ is the $m \times n$ coefficient matrix.

Define a new $m \times (n + 1)$ matrix $\mathbf{A_b}$ that contains $\mathbf{A}$ in the first n columns and $\mathbf{b}$ in column $n + 1$:

$$\mathbf{A} = \begin{pmatrix} a_{11} & a_{12} & \cdots & a_{1n} \\ a_{21} & a_{22} & \cdots & a_{2n} \\ \vdots & \vdots & & \vdots \\ a_{m1} & a_{m2} & \cdots & a_{mn} \end{pmatrix} \quad \text{and} \quad \mathbf{A_b} = \begin{pmatrix} a_{11} & a_{12} & \cdots & a_{1n} & b_1 \\ a_{21} & a_{22} & \cdots & a_{2n} & b_2 \\ \vdots & \vdots & & \vdots & \vdots \\ a_{m1} & a_{m2} & \cdots & a_{mn} & b_m \end{pmatrix}$$

$\mathbf{A_b}$ is called the **augmented** matrix of the system (1). It turns out that the relationship between the ranks of $\mathbf{A}$ and $\mathbf{A_b}$ is crucial in determining whether system (1) has a solution. Because all the columns in $\mathbf{A}$ occur in $\mathbf{A_b}$, the rank of $\mathbf{A_b}$ is certainly greater than or equal to the rank of $\mathbf{A}$. Moreover, because $\mathbf{A_b}$ contains only one more column than $\mathbf{A}$, the number $r(\mathbf{A_b})$ cannot be greater than $r(\mathbf{A}) + 1$.

THEOREM 1.5.1

A necessary and sufficient condition for a linear system of equations to be consistent (that is, to have at least one solution) is that the rank of the coefficient matrix is equal to the rank of the augmented matrix. Briefly:

$$\mathbf{Ax} = \mathbf{b} \quad \text{has a solution} \quad \Longleftrightarrow \quad r(\mathbf{A}) = r(\mathbf{A_b})$$

Proof: Let the column vectors in $\mathbf{A_b}$ be $\mathbf{a}_1, \mathbf{a}_2, \ldots, \mathbf{a}_n, \mathbf{b}$, and suppose that (1) has a solution $(x_1, \ldots, x_n)$, so that $x_1 \mathbf{a}_1 + \cdots + x_n \mathbf{a}_n = \mathbf{b}$. Multiply the first n columns in $\mathbf{A_b}$ by $-x_1, \ldots, -x_n$, respectively, and add each of the resulting column vectors to the last column in $\mathbf{A_b}$. These elementary column operations make the last column $\mathbf{0}$. It follows that $\mathbf{A_b} \sim [\mathbf{a}_1, \ldots, \mathbf{a}_n, \mathbf{0}]$. Evidently, this matrix has the same rank as $\mathbf{A}$, so $r(\mathbf{A_b}) = r(\mathbf{A})$, because elementary column operations preserve the rank.

Suppose on the other hand that $r(\mathbf{A}) = r(\mathbf{A_b}) = k$. Then k of the columns of $\mathbf{A}$ are linearly independent. To simplify notation, suppose that the first k columns, $\mathbf{a}_1, \ldots, \mathbf{a}_k$, are linearly independent. Because $r(\mathbf{A_b}) = k$, the vectors $\mathbf{a}_1, \ldots, \mathbf{a}_k, \mathbf{b}$ are linearly dependent. Hence there exist numbers $c_1, \ldots, c_k$ and β, not all equal to 0, such that $c_1 \mathbf{a}_1 + \cdots + c_k \mathbf{a}_k + \beta \mathbf{b} = \mathbf{0}$. If $\beta = 0$, then $\mathbf{a}_1, \ldots, \mathbf{a}_k$ would not be linearly independent. Hence $\beta \neq 0$. Then $\mathbf{b} = x_1^0 \mathbf{a}_1 + \cdots + x_k^0 \mathbf{a}_k$ where $x_1^0 = -c_1/\beta$, $\ldots, x_k^0 = -c_k/\beta$. It follows that $(x_1^0, \ldots, x_k^0, 0, \ldots, 0)$ is a solution of $\mathbf{Ax} = \mathbf{b}$.   ∎

Theorem 1.5.1 yields a simple test for deciding whether or not a linear system of equations has solutions. The system has at least one solution iff $r(\mathbf{A}) = r(\mathbf{A_b})$.

EXAMPLE 1   Apply Theorem 1.5.1 to the system $\begin{array}{l} 2x_1 - x_2 = 3 \\ 4x_1 - 2x_2 = 5 \end{array}$.

Solution: Here $\mathbf{A} = \begin{pmatrix} 2 & -1 \\ 4 & -2 \end{pmatrix}$ and $\mathbf{A_b} = \begin{pmatrix} 2 & -1 & 3 \\ 4 & -2 & 5 \end{pmatrix}$. We see that $|\mathbf{A}| = 0$, so $r(\mathbf{A}) < 2$. Because not all the elements in $\mathbf{A}$ are 0, it follows that $r(\mathbf{A}) = 1$. But $r(\mathbf{A_b}) = 2$, because the minor obtained by deleting the first column is equal to 1. Thus, $r(\mathbf{A}) \neq r(\mathbf{A_b})$, so the system has no solutions. To confirm this, multiply the first equation by 2 to obtain $4x_1 - 2x_2 = 6$. This is obviously inconsistent with the second equation.

Superfluous Equations

Consider the case where $r(\mathbf{A}) = r(\mathbf{A_b}) = k$ with $k < m$, so that the common rank of $\mathbf{A}$ and $\mathbf{A_b}$ is less than the number of equations. The maximum number of linearly independent row vectors in $\mathbf{A_b}$ is k, so there exist k row vectors in $\mathbf{A_b}$ that are linearly independent, and any other row vector in $\mathbf{A_b}$ is a linear combination of those k vectors. We will now prove that, if the vector $(x_1^0, x_2^0, \ldots, x_n^0)$ satisfies the k equations corresponding to k linearly independent row vectors in $\mathbf{A_b}$, then it also satisfies all the equations corresponding to the remaining rows in $\mathbf{A_b}$. These remaining equations are "superfluous".

To simplify notation, reorder the equations so that the first k row vectors in $\mathbf{A_b}$ are linearly independent. The other rows are dependent on these first k rows, so for $s = k + 1, \ldots, m$, we have

$$(a_{s1}, a_{s2}, \ldots, a_{sn}, b_s) = \sum_{l=1}^{k} \lambda_{sl}(a_{l1}, a_{l2}, \ldots, a_{ln}, b_l) \tag{$*$}$$

for suitable constants $\lambda_{s1}, \lambda_{s2}, \ldots, \lambda_{sk}$. From $(*)$, we see in particular that $a_{sj} = \sum_{l=1}^{k} \lambda_{sl} a_{lj}$ and $b_s = \sum_{l=1}^{k} \lambda_{sl} b_l$. Suppose that $\sum_{j=1}^{n} a_{lj} x_j^0 = b_l$ for $l = 1, \ldots, k$, so that $(x_1^0, \ldots, x_n^0)$ satisfies the k first equations in (1). For $s = k + 1, \ldots, m$, we then obtain

$$\sum_{j=1}^{n} a_{sj} x_j^0 = \sum_{j=1}^{n} \left(\sum_{l=1}^{k} \lambda_{sl} a_{lj} \right) x_j^0 = \sum_{l=1}^{k} \lambda_{sl} \left(\sum_{j=1}^{n} a_{lj} x_j^0 \right) = \sum_{l=1}^{k} \lambda_{sl} b_l = b_s$$

This confirms that if the vector $(x_1^0, \ldots, x_n^0)$ satisfies the first k equations in (1), then it automatically satisfies the last $m - k$ equations in (1).

THEOREM 1.5.2

Suppose that system (1) has solutions and that $r(\mathbf{A}) = r(\mathbf{A_b}) = k < m$. Choose any collection of k equations corresponding to k linearly independent rows. Then any solution of these equations also satisfies the remaining $m - k$ equations.

Degrees of Freedom

Consider the case where $r(\mathbf{A}) = r(\mathbf{A_b}) = k$, with k less than n, the number of variables in the system. Because $r(\mathbf{A}) = k$, we know that $\mathbf{A}$ has at least one non-zero minor of order k (Theorem 1.4.1). After rearranging the equations and the variables (if necessary), we can assume that the $k \times k$ matrix

$$\mathbf{C} = \begin{pmatrix} a_{11} & a_{12} & \cdots & a_{1k} \\ a_{21} & a_{22} & \cdots & a_{2k} \\ \vdots & \vdots & \ddots & \vdots \\ a_{k1} & a_{k2} & \cdots & a_{kk} \end{pmatrix}$$

in the upper left-hand corner of $\mathbf{A}$ has a nonzero determinant. If $k < m$, then the last $m - k$ equations in (1) are superfluous and the whole system (1) has exactly the same solutions as the first k equations on their own:

$$a_{11}x_1 + \cdots + a_{1k}x_k + a_{1,k+1}x_{k+1} + \cdots + a_{1n}x_n = b_1$$
$$a_{21}x_1 + \cdots + a_{2k}x_k + a_{2,k+1}x_{k+1} + \cdots + a_{2n}x_n = b_2$$
$$\cdots\cdots\cdots\cdots\cdots\cdots\cdots\cdots\cdots\cdots\cdots\cdots\cdots$$
$$a_{k1}x_1 + \cdots + a_{kk}x_k + a_{k,k+1}x_{k+1} + \cdots + a_{kn}x_n = b_k$$

$(*)$

Suppose we move all terms involving $x_{k+1}, x_{k+2}, \ldots, x_n$ to the right-hand side:

$$a_{11}x_1 + \cdots + a_{1k}x_k = b_1 - a_{1,k+1}x_{k+1} - \cdots - a_{1n}x_n$$
$$a_{21}x_1 + \cdots + a_{2k}x_k = b_2 - a_{2,k+1}x_{k+1} - \cdots - a_{2n}x_n$$
$$\cdots\cdots\cdots\cdots\cdots\cdots\cdots\cdots\cdots\cdots\cdots\cdots\cdots$$
$$a_{k1}x_1 + \cdots + a_{kk}x_k = b_k - a_{k,k+1}x_{k+1} - \cdots - a_{kn}x_n$$

$(**)$

According to Cramer's rule, system $(**)$ has a unique solution for $x_1, x_2, \ldots, x_k$ for each choice of $x_{k+1}, x_{k+2}, \ldots, x_n$. Thus we have the following theorem:

THEOREM 1.5.3

Suppose that system (1) has solutions with $r(\mathbf{A}) = r(\mathbf{A_b}) = k < n$. Then there exist $n - k$ of the variables that can be chosen freely, whereas the remaining k variables are uniquely determined by the choice of these $n - k$ free variables. We say that the system has $n - k$ **degrees of freedom**.

EXAMPLE 2   Determine whether the following system of equations has any solutions, and if it has, find the number of degrees of freedom.

$$x_1 + x_2 - 2x_3 + x_4 + 3x_5 = 1$$
$$2x_1 - x_2 + 2x_3 + 2x_4 + 6x_5 = 2$$
$$3x_1 + 5x_2 - 10x_3 - 3x_4 - 9x_5 = 3$$
$$3x_1 + 2x_2 - 4x_3 - 3x_4 - 9x_5 = 3$$

Solution: **Here**

$$\mathbf{A} = \begin{pmatrix} 1 & 1 & -2 & 1 & 3 \\ 2 & -1 & 2 & 2 & 6 \\ 3 & 5 & -10 & -3 & -9 \\ 3 & 2 & -4 & -3 & -9 \end{pmatrix} \quad \text{and} \quad \mathbf{A_b} = \begin{pmatrix} 1 & 1 & -2 & 1 & 3 & 1 \\ 2 & -1 & 2 & 2 & 6 & 2 \\ 3 & 5 & -10 & -3 & -9 & 3 \\ 3 & 2 & -4 & -3 & -9 & 3 \end{pmatrix}$$

We know that $r(\mathbf{A_b}) \geq r(\mathbf{A})$. All minors of order 4 in $\mathbf{A_b}$ are equal to 0 (note that several pairs of columns are proportional), so that $r(\mathbf{A_b}) \leq 3$. Now, there are minors of order 3 in

A that are different from 0. For example, the minor formed by the first, third, and fourth columns, and by the first, second, and fourth rows, is different from 0 because

$$\begin{vmatrix} 1 & -2 & 1 \\ 2 & 2 & 2 \\ 3 & -4 & -3 \end{vmatrix} = -36 \tag{$*$}$$

Hence, $r(\mathbf{A}) = 3$. Because $3 \geq r(\mathbf{A_b}) \geq r(\mathbf{A})$, we have $r(\mathbf{A}) = r(\mathbf{A_b}) = 3$, so the system has solutions. There is one superfluous equation. Because the first, second, and fourth rows in $\mathbf{A_b}$ are linearly independent, the third equation can be dropped. The number of variables is 5, and because $r(\mathbf{A}) = r(\mathbf{A_b}) = 3$, there are 2 *degrees of freedom*.

Next we find all the solutions to the system of equations. The determinant in $(*)$ is different from 0, so we rewrite the subsystem of 3 independent equations in the form

$$\begin{aligned} x_1 - 2x_3 + x_4 + x_2 + 3x_5 &= 1 \\ 2x_1 + 2x_3 + 2x_4 - x_2 + 6x_5 &= 2 \\ 3x_1 - 4x_3 - 3x_4 + 2x_2 - 9x_5 &= 3 \end{aligned} \tag{$**$}$$

or, in matrix form, as

$$\begin{pmatrix} 1 & -2 & 1 \\ 2 & 2 & 2 \\ 3 & -4 & -3 \end{pmatrix} \begin{pmatrix} x_1 \\ x_3 \\ x_4 \end{pmatrix} + \begin{pmatrix} 1 & 3 \\ -1 & 6 \\ 2 & -9 \end{pmatrix} \begin{pmatrix} x_2 \\ x_5 \end{pmatrix} = \begin{pmatrix} 1 \\ 2 \\ 3 \end{pmatrix}$$

The 3×3 coefficient matrix corresponding to x_1, x_3, and x_4 in $(**)$ has a determinant different from 0, so it has an inverse. Therefore,

$$\begin{pmatrix} x_1 \\ x_3 \\ x_4 \end{pmatrix} = \begin{pmatrix} 1 & -2 & 1 \\ 2 & 2 & 2 \\ 3 & -4 & -3 \end{pmatrix}^{-1} \begin{pmatrix} 1 \\ 2 \\ 3 \end{pmatrix} - \begin{pmatrix} 1 & -2 & 1 \\ 2 & 2 & 2 \\ 3 & -4 & -3 \end{pmatrix}^{-1} \begin{pmatrix} 1 & 3 \\ -1 & 6 \\ 2 & -9 \end{pmatrix} \begin{pmatrix} x_2 \\ x_5 \end{pmatrix}$$

It is easy to verify that

$$\begin{pmatrix} 1 & -2 & 1 \\ 2 & 2 & 2 \\ 3 & -4 & -3 \end{pmatrix}^{-1} = \frac{1}{18} \begin{pmatrix} -1 & 5 & 3 \\ -6 & 3 & 0 \\ 7 & 1 & -3 \end{pmatrix}$$

Then, after some routine algebra, we have

$$\begin{pmatrix} x_1 \\ x_3 \\ x_4 \end{pmatrix} = \begin{pmatrix} 1 \\ 0 \\ 0 \end{pmatrix} - \begin{pmatrix} 0 \\ -\frac{1}{2}x_2 \\ 3x_5 \end{pmatrix} = \begin{pmatrix} 1 \\ \frac{1}{2}x_2 \\ -3x_5 \end{pmatrix}$$

So, if $x_2 = a$ and $x_5 = b$ are arbitrary real numbers, then there is a solution

$$x_1 = 1, \quad x_2 = a, \quad x_3 = \tfrac{1}{2}a, \quad x_4 = -3b, \quad x_5 = b$$

This confirms that there are 2 degrees of freedom. (You should verify that the values found for $x_1, \ldots, x_5$ do satisfy the original system of equations for all values of a and b.)

The concept of degrees of freedom introduced in Theorem 1.5.3 is very important. Note that if a linear system of equations has k degrees of freedom, then there *exist* k variables that can be chosen freely. It may not be the first k variables that can be chosen freely. For instance, in Example 2 there are 2 degrees of freedom, but x_1 cannot be chosen freely because $x_1 = 1$.

PROBLEMS FOR SECTION 1.5

1. Use Theorems 1.5.1 to 1.5.3 to examine whether the following systems of equations have solutions. If they do, determine the number of degrees of freedom. Find all the solutions. Check the results.

   (a) $-2x_1 - 3x_2 + x_3 = 3$
   $4x_1 + 6x_2 - 2x_3 = 1$

   (b) $x_1 + x_2 - x_3 + x_4 = 2$
   $2x_1 - x_2 + x_3 - 3x_4 = 1$

   (c) $x_1 - x_2 + 2x_3 + x_4 = 1$
   $2x_1 + x_2 - x_3 + 3x_4 = 3$
   $x_1 + 5x_2 - 8x_3 + x_4 = 1$
   $4x_1 + 5x_2 - 7x_3 + 7x_4 = 7$

   (d) $x_1 + x_2 + 2x_3 + x_4 = 5$
   $2x_1 + 3x_2 - x_3 - 2x_4 = 2$
   $4x_1 + 5x_2 + 3x_3 = 7$

2. Solve the following systems and determine the number of degrees of freedom:

   (a) $x_1 - x_2 + x_3 = 0$
   $x_1 + 2x_2 - x_3 = 0$
   $2x_1 + x_2 + 3x_3 = 0$

   (b) $x_1 + x_2 + x_3 + x_4 = 0$
   $x_1 + 3x_2 + 2x_3 + 4x_4 = 0$
   $2x_1 + x_2 - x_4 = 0$

3. Discuss the solutions of the following system for all values of a and b.

$$x + 2y + 3z = 1$$
$$-x + ay - 21z = 2$$
$$3x + 7y + az = b$$

4. Let $\mathbf{Ax} = \mathbf{b}$ be a linear system of equations in matrix form. Prove that if $\mathbf{x}_1$ and $\mathbf{x}_2$ are both solutions of the system, then so is $\lambda \mathbf{x}_1 + (1 - \lambda)\mathbf{x}_2$ for every real number λ. Use this fact to prove that a linear system of equations that is consistent has either one solution or infinitely many solutions. (For instance, it cannot have exactly 3 solutions.)

5. (a) For what values of the constants p and q does the following system have a unique solution, several solutions, or no solution?

$$x_1 + x_2 + x_3 = 2q$$
$$2x_1 - 3x_2 + 2x_3 = 4q$$
$$3x_1 - 2x_2 + px_3 = q$$

   (b) Determine for each value of p the set of all vectors $\mathbf{z}$ that are orthogonal to the three vectors $(1, 1, 1)$, $(2, -3, 2)$, $(3, -2, p)$.

6. Let $\mathbf{a}_1, \ldots, \mathbf{a}_n$ be n linearly independent vectors in $\mathbb{R}^n$. Prove that if a vector $\mathbf{b}$ in $\mathbb{R}^n$ is orthogonal to all the vectors $\mathbf{a}_1, \ldots, \mathbf{a}_n$, then $\mathbf{b} = \mathbf{0}$.

7. Let the matrix $\mathbf{A}_t$ be defined for all real numbers t by $\mathbf{A}_t = \begin{pmatrix} 1 & 3 & 2 \\ 2 & 5 & t \\ 4 & 7-t & -6 \end{pmatrix}$.

   (a) Find the rank of $\mathbf{A}_t$ for each value of t.

   (b) When $t = -3$, find all vectors $\mathbf{x}$ that satisfy the vector equation $\mathbf{A}_{-3}\mathbf{x} = \begin{pmatrix} 11 \\ 3 \\ 6 \end{pmatrix}$.

   (c) When $t = 2$, determine a vector $\mathbf{z} \neq \mathbf{0}$ that is orthogonal to each vector of the form $\mathbf{A}_2\mathbf{x}$, where $\mathbf{x}$ is an arbitrary vector in $\mathbb{R}^3$.

1.6 Eigenvalues

Many applied problems, especially in dynamic economics, involve the powers $\mathbf{A}^n$, $n = 1, 2, \ldots$, of a square matrix $\mathbf{A}$. If the dimensions of $\mathbf{A}$ are very large and $\mathbf{x}$ is a given nonzero vector, then computing $\mathbf{A}^5\mathbf{x}$, or even worse, $\mathbf{A}^{100}\mathbf{x}$, is usually a major problem. But suppose there happens to be a scalar λ with the special property that

$$\mathbf{A}\mathbf{x} = \lambda\mathbf{x} \qquad (*)$$

In this case, we would have $\mathbf{A}^2\mathbf{x} = \mathbf{A}(\mathbf{A}\mathbf{x}) = \mathbf{A}(\lambda\mathbf{x}) = \lambda\mathbf{A}\mathbf{x} = \lambda\lambda\mathbf{x} = \lambda^2\mathbf{x}$, and in general, $\mathbf{A}^n\mathbf{x} = \lambda^n\mathbf{x}$. Many of the properties of $\mathbf{A}$ and $\mathbf{A}^n$ can be deduced by finding the pairs $(\lambda, \mathbf{x})$, $\mathbf{x} \neq \mathbf{0}$, that satisfy $(*)$.

A nonzero vector $\mathbf{x}$ that solves $(*)$ is called an **eigenvector**, and the associated λ is called an **eigenvalue**. Zero solutions are not very interesting, of course, because $\mathbf{A}\mathbf{0} = \lambda\mathbf{0}$ for every scalar λ.

In optimization theory, in the theory of difference and differential equations, in statistics, in population dynamics, and in many other applications of mathematics, there are important arguments and results based on eigenvalues. Here is a formal definition:

EIGENVALUES AND EIGENVECTORS

If $\mathbf{A}$ is an $n \times n$ matrix, then a scalar λ is an **eigenvalue** of $\mathbf{A}$ if there is a nonzero vector $\mathbf{x}$ in $\mathbb{R}^n$ such that

$$\mathbf{A}\mathbf{x} = \lambda\mathbf{x} \qquad (1)$$

Then $\mathbf{x}$ is an **eigenvector** of $\mathbf{A}$ (associated with λ).

It should be noted that if $\mathbf{x}$ is an eigenvector associated with the eigenvalue λ, then $\alpha\mathbf{x}$ is another eigenvector for every scalar $\alpha \neq 0$. Eigenvalues and eigenvectors are also called **characteristic roots (values)** and **characteristic vectors**, respectively.

How to Find Eigenvalues

The eigenvalue equation (1) can be written as

$$(\mathbf{A} - \lambda\mathbf{I})\mathbf{x} = \mathbf{0} \tag{2}$$

where $\mathbf{I}$ denotes the identity matrix of order n. According to (1.1.34), this homogeneous linear system of equations has a solution $\mathbf{x} \neq \mathbf{0}$ iff the coefficient matrix has determinant *equal to* 0—that is, iff $|\mathbf{A} - \lambda\mathbf{I}| = 0$. Letting $p(\lambda) = |\mathbf{A} - \lambda\mathbf{I}|$, where $\mathbf{A} = (a_{ij})_{n \times n}$, we have the equation

$$p(\lambda) = |\mathbf{A} - \lambda\mathbf{I}| = \begin{vmatrix} a_{11} - \lambda & a_{12} & \cdots & a_{1n} \\ a_{21} & a_{22} - \lambda & \cdots & a_{2n} \\ \vdots & \vdots & \ddots & \vdots \\ a_{n1} & a_{n2} & \cdots & a_{nn} - \lambda \end{vmatrix} = 0 \tag{3}$$

This is called the **characteristic equation** (or **eigenvalue equation**) of $\mathbf{A}$. From the definition of a determinant, it follows that $p(\lambda)$ in (3) is a polynomial of degree n in λ. According to the fundamental theorem of algebra, equation (3) has exactly n roots (real or complex), provided that any multiple roots are counted appropriately.

If the components of the vector $\mathbf{x}$ are $x_1, \ldots, x_n$, then (2) can be written as

$$\begin{aligned} (a_{11} - \lambda)x_1 + & \quad a_{12}x_2 + \cdots + & a_{1n}x_n = 0 \\ a_{21}x_1 + (a_{22} - \lambda)x_2 + & \cdots + & a_{2n}x_n = 0 \\ & \cdots\cdots\cdots\cdots\cdots\cdots\cdots & \\ a_{n1}x_1 + & \quad a_{n2}x_2 + \cdots + (a_{nn} - \lambda)x_n = 0 \end{aligned} \tag{4}$$

An eigenvector associated with λ is a nontrivial solution $(x_1, \ldots, x_n)$ of (4).

EXAMPLE 1   Find the eigenvalues and the associated eigenvectors of the matrices

$$\text{(a)} \quad \mathbf{A} = \begin{pmatrix} 1 & 2 \\ 3 & 0 \end{pmatrix} \qquad\qquad \text{(b)} \quad \mathbf{B} = \begin{pmatrix} 0 & 1 \\ -1 & 0 \end{pmatrix}$$

Solution: (a) The characteristic equation is $|\mathbf{A} - \lambda\mathbf{I}| = \begin{vmatrix} 1 - \lambda & 2 \\ 3 & -\lambda \end{vmatrix} = \lambda^2 - \lambda - 6 = 0.$
This has solutions $\lambda_1 = -2$ and $\lambda_2 = 3$, which are the eigenvalues of $\mathbf{A}$.

For $\lambda = \lambda_1 = -2$, the two equations of system (4) both reduce to $3x_1 + 2x_2 = 0$. Choosing $x_2 = t$, we have $x_1 = -\frac{2}{3}t$. The eigenvectors associated with $\lambda_1 = -2$ are, therefore, $\mathbf{x} = t\begin{pmatrix} -2/3 \\ 1 \end{pmatrix}$, $t \neq 0$. If we put $t = -3s$, we can equivalently represent the eigenvectors as $\mathbf{x} = s\begin{pmatrix} 2 \\ -3 \end{pmatrix}$, $s \neq 0$. For $\lambda = 3$, system (4) implies that $x_1 = x_2$, so the eigenvectors are $\mathbf{x} = s\begin{pmatrix} 1 \\ 1 \end{pmatrix}$, $s \neq 0$.

(b) The characteristic equation is $|\mathbf{B} - \lambda\mathbf{I}| = \begin{vmatrix} -\lambda & 1 \\ -1 & -\lambda \end{vmatrix} = \lambda^2 + 1 = 0$, which has the

complex roots $\lambda = \pm i$. The eigenvectors turn out to be $s\begin{pmatrix} 1 \\ i \end{pmatrix}$ and $t\begin{pmatrix} 1 \\ -i \end{pmatrix}$, with $s \neq 0$ and $t \neq 0$.[3]

EXAMPLE 2   Find all the eigenvalues and those eigenvectors that are associated with the real eigenvalues of the matrices

(a) $\quad \mathbf{A} = \begin{pmatrix} 0 & 0 & 6 \\ 1/2 & 0 & 0 \\ 0 & 1/3 & 0 \end{pmatrix}$ (b) $\quad \mathbf{B} = \begin{pmatrix} 5 & -6 & -6 \\ -1 & 4 & 2 \\ 3 & -6 & -4 \end{pmatrix}$

Solution: (a) The characteristic equation is

$$|\mathbf{A} - \lambda\mathbf{I}| = \begin{vmatrix} -\lambda & 0 & 6 \\ 1/2 & -\lambda & 0 \\ 0 & 1/3 & -\lambda \end{vmatrix} = -\lambda^3 + 1 = 0$$

which has $\lambda = 1$ as its only real root. (Because $-\lambda^3 + 1 = (1 - \lambda)(\lambda^2 + \lambda + 1)$, there are two complex eigenvalues, $\lambda = -\frac{1}{2} \pm \frac{1}{2}\sqrt{3}\,i$.) The eigenvectors associated with $\lambda = 1$ satisfy (4), which becomes

$$\begin{aligned} -x_1 &&+ 6x_3 &= 0 \\ \tfrac{1}{2}x_1 - &x_2 && = 0 \\ &\tfrac{1}{3}x_2 - &x_3 &= 0 \end{aligned}$$

This gives the eigenvectors $\mathbf{x} = t(6, 3, 1)'$, with $t \neq 0$.

(b) The characteristic equation is

$$|\mathbf{B} - \lambda\mathbf{I}| = \begin{vmatrix} 5-\lambda & -6 & -6 \\ -1 & 4-\lambda & 2 \\ 3 & -6 & -4-\lambda \end{vmatrix} = -(\lambda-2)^2(\lambda-1) = 0$$

Thus, $\lambda_1 = 1$ and $\lambda_2 = 2$ are the eigenvalues. For $\lambda_1 = 1$, the eigenvectors are $\mathbf{x} = t\begin{pmatrix} 3 \\ -1 \\ 3 \end{pmatrix}$ with $t \neq 0$. For $\lambda_2 = 2$, the eigenvectors are all the vectors of the form

$\mathbf{x} = \begin{pmatrix} 2s+2t \\ s \\ t \end{pmatrix} = \begin{pmatrix} 2 \\ 1 \\ 0 \end{pmatrix} s + \begin{pmatrix} 2 \\ 0 \\ 1 \end{pmatrix} t$, with s and t in $\mathbb{R}$, not both s and t equal to 0.

EXAMPLE 3   Let $\mathbf{D} = \mathrm{diag}(a_1, \ldots, a_n)$ be an $n \times n$ diagonal matrix with diagonal elements $a_1, \ldots, a_n$. The characteristic polynomial is $|\mathbf{D} - \lambda\mathbf{I}| = (a_1 - \lambda)(a_2 - \lambda)\cdots(a_n - \lambda)$. Hence, the eigenvalues of $\mathbf{D}$ are the diagonal elements. Let $\mathbf{e}_j$ denote the jth unit vector in $\mathbb{R}^n$, having all components 0, except for the jth component which is 1. Because $\mathbf{D}\mathbf{e}_j = a_j\mathbf{e}_j$, it follows that any nonzero multiple of $\mathbf{e}_j$ is an eigenvector associated with the eigenvalue a_j of $\mathbf{D}$.

---

[3] One can do matrix algebra with complex numbers in exactly the same way as with real matrices.

Matrices of Order 2

When $n = 2$, then $\mathbf{A} = \begin{pmatrix} a_{11} & a_{12} \\ a_{21} & a_{22} \end{pmatrix}$ and its eigenvalues are given by the quadratic equation

$$|\mathbf{A} - \lambda\mathbf{I}| = \begin{vmatrix} a_{11} - \lambda & a_{12} \\ a_{21} & a_{22} - \lambda \end{vmatrix} = \lambda^2 - (a_{11} + a_{22})\lambda + (a_{11}a_{22} - a_{12}a_{21}) = 0 \quad (5)$$

If the eigenvalues are λ_1 and λ_2, then

$$\begin{aligned} \lambda^2 - (a_{11} + a_{22})\lambda + (a_{11}a_{22} - a_{12}a_{21}) &= (\lambda - \lambda_1)(\lambda - \lambda_2) \\ &= \lambda^2 - (\lambda_1 + \lambda_2)\lambda + \lambda_1\lambda_2 \end{aligned} \quad (6)$$

Comparing (5) and (6), we see that the sum $\lambda_1 + \lambda_2$ of the eigenvalues is equal to $a_{11} + a_{22}$, the sum of the diagonal elements (also called the **trace** of the matrix and denoted by $\mathrm{tr}(\mathbf{A})$). The product $\lambda_1\lambda_2$ of the eigenvalues is equal to $a_{11}a_{22} - a_{12}a_{21} = |\mathbf{A}|$. In symbols: $\lambda_1 + \lambda_2 = \mathrm{tr}(\mathbf{A})$ and $\lambda_1\lambda_2 = |\mathbf{A}|$.

Many dynamic economic models involve square matrices whose eigenvalues determine their stability properties. In the 2×2 case, important questions are when the two eigenvalues are real and what are their signs. The roots of the quadratic equation (5) are

$$\lambda = \tfrac{1}{2}(a_{11} + a_{22}) \pm \sqrt{\tfrac{1}{4}(a_{11} + a_{22})^2 - (a_{11}a_{22} - a_{12}a_{21})} \quad (7)$$

These roots are real if and only if $(a_{11} + a_{22})^2 \geq 4(a_{11}a_{22} - a_{12}a_{21})$, which is equivalent to $(a_{11} - a_{22})^2 + 4a_{12}a_{21} \geq 0$. In particular, both eigenvalues are real if the matrix is symmetric, because then $a_{12} = a_{21}$ and so we have a sum of squares. (But a matrix may well have real eigenvalues even if it is not symmetric, as in Example 1 (a).)

It follows that for a 2×2 matrix $\mathbf{A}$ with real eigenvalues,

(A) both eigenvalues are positive $\iff$ $|\mathbf{A}| > 0$ and $\mathrm{tr}(\mathbf{A}) = a_{11} + a_{22} > 0$

(B) both eigenvalues are negative $\iff$ $|\mathbf{A}| > 0$ and $\mathrm{tr}(\mathbf{A}) = a_{11} + a_{22} < 0$

(C) the two eigenvalues have opposite signs $\iff$ $|\mathbf{A}| < 0$

Moreover, 0 is an eigenvalue iff $|\mathbf{A}| = 0$. The other eigenvalue is then equal to $a_{11} + a_{22}$.

The General Case

From the definition of a determinant, it follows that $p(\lambda) = |\mathbf{A} - \lambda\mathbf{I}|$ in (3) is a polynomial of degree n in λ. In fact, it is convenient to write it as a polynomial in $-\lambda$:

$$p(\lambda) = (-\lambda)^n + b_{n-1}(-\lambda)^{n-1} + \cdots + b_1(-\lambda) + b_0 \quad (8)$$

The zeros of this **characteristic polynomial** are precisely the eigenvalues of $\mathbf{A}$. Denoting the eigenvalues by $\lambda_1, \lambda_2, \ldots, \lambda_n$, we have

$$p(\lambda) = (-1)^n(\lambda - \lambda_1)(\lambda - \lambda_2) \ldots (\lambda - \lambda_n) \quad (9)$$

Consider the coefficients in the characteristic polynomial (8). Putting $\lambda = 0$ in (3) and in (8), we see that $p(0) = b_0 = |\mathbf{A}|$. But $\lambda = 0$ in (9) gives $p(0) = (-1)^n(-1)^n\lambda_1\lambda_2\cdots\lambda_n$. Since $(-1)^n(-1)^n = 1$, we have $b_0 = |\mathbf{A}| = \lambda_1\lambda_2\cdots\lambda_n$.

Let us also determine the coefficient b_{n-1} in (8). The product of the elements on the main diagonal of (3) is $(a_{11} - \lambda)(a_{22} - \lambda)\cdots(a_{nn} - \lambda)$. If we choose a_{jj} from one of these parentheses and $-\lambda$ from the remaining $n - 1$, then add over $j = 1, 2, \ldots, n$, we obtain the term

$$(a_{11} + a_{22} + \cdots + a_{nn})(-\lambda)^{n-1} \qquad (*)$$

Since each term in the expansion of the determinant in (3), except the product of all the elements on the main diagonal, contains at most $n - 2$ of the elements on the main diagonal (check the case $n = 3$), we cannot get other terms with $(-\lambda)^{n-1}$ except those in $(*)$. Hence, $b_{n-1} = a_{11} + a_{22} + \cdots + a_{nn}$, the **trace** of $\mathbf{A}$. By expanding (9) we see that the coefficient of $(-\lambda)^{n-1}$ in (8) is $b_{n-1} = \lambda_1 + \lambda_2 + \cdots + \lambda_n$.

THEOREM 1.6.1

If $\mathbf{A}$ is an $n \times n$ matrix with eigenvalues $\lambda_1, \lambda_2, \ldots, \lambda_n$, then

(a) $|\mathbf{A}| = \lambda_1\lambda_2\ldots\lambda_n$

(b) $\text{tr}(\mathbf{A}) = a_{11} + a_{22} + \cdots + a_{nn} = \lambda_1 + \lambda_2 + \cdots + \lambda_n$

In words: If $\mathbf{A}$ is an $n \times n$ matrix, the product of all the eigenvalues is equal to the determinant of $\mathbf{A}$, while the sum of all the eigenvalues is equal to the trace of $\mathbf{A}$. This confirms the results we found for $n = 2$.

NOTE 1   From Theorem 1.6.1 we know that in the characteristic polynomial (8), b_0 is the determinant of $\mathbf{A}$ and b_{n-1} is the trace of $\mathbf{A}$. One can prove in general that the coefficients $b_{n-1}, \ldots, b_1, b_0$ in (8) can be characterized as follows:

$$b_k = \text{the sum of all principal minors of } \mathbf{A} \text{ of order } n - k \qquad (10)$$

Thus b_0 equals the determinant of $\mathbf{A}$, since it is the only principal minor of order n, and b_{n-1} is the sum of all the principal minors of order 1, i.e. the sum $a_{11} + a_{22} + \cdots + a_{nn}$, the trace of $\mathbf{A}$.

PROBLEMS FOR SECTION 1.6

1. For the following matrices, find the eigenvalues and also those eigenvectors which correspond to the real eigenvalues:

(a) $\begin{pmatrix} 2 & -7 \\ 3 & -8 \end{pmatrix}$ 　　　(b) $\begin{pmatrix} 2 & 4 \\ -2 & 6 \end{pmatrix}$ 　　　(c) $\begin{pmatrix} 1 & 4 \\ 6 & -1 \end{pmatrix}$

(d) $\begin{pmatrix} 2 & 0 & 0 \\ 0 & 3 & 0 \\ 0 & 0 & 4 \end{pmatrix}$ 　　　(e) $\begin{pmatrix} 2 & 1 & -1 \\ 0 & 1 & 1 \\ 2 & 0 & -2 \end{pmatrix}$ 　　　(f) $\begin{pmatrix} 1 & -1 & 0 \\ -1 & 2 & -1 \\ 0 & -1 & 1 \end{pmatrix}$

2. Prove that λ is an eigenvalue of the matrix A iff λ is an eigenvalue of A'.

3. Suppose A is a square matrix and let λ be an eigenvalue of A. Prove that if $|A| \neq 0$, then $\lambda \neq 0$. In this case show that $1/\lambda$ is an eigenvalue of the inverse A^{-1}.

4. (a) Compute $X'AX$, A^2, and A^3 when $A = \begin{pmatrix} a & a & 0 \\ a & a & 0 \\ 0 & 0 & b \end{pmatrix}$ and $X = \begin{pmatrix} x \\ y \\ z \end{pmatrix}$.

   (b) Find all the eigenvalues of A.

   (c) The characteristic polynomial $p(\lambda)$ of A is a cubic function of λ. Show that if we replace λ by A, then $p(A)$ is the zero matrix. (This is a special case of the Cayley–Hamilton theorem. See (1.7.6).)

5. $A = \begin{pmatrix} a & b & c \\ b & d & e \\ c & e & f \end{pmatrix}$ has the eigenvectors $v_1 = \begin{pmatrix} 1 \\ 0 \\ -1 \end{pmatrix}$, $v_2 = \begin{pmatrix} 1 \\ 2 \\ 1 \end{pmatrix}$, $v_3 = \begin{pmatrix} 1 \\ -1 \\ 1 \end{pmatrix}$, with associated eigenvalues $\lambda_1 = 3$, $\lambda_2 = 1$, and $\lambda_3 = 4$. Determine the matrix A.

6. (a) Find the eigenvalues of $A = \begin{pmatrix} 4 & 1 & 1 & 1 \\ 1 & 4 & 1 & 1 \\ 1 & 1 & 4 & 1 \\ 1 & 1 & 1 & 4 \end{pmatrix}$. (*Hint*: Problem 1.2.7 (b).)

   (b) One of the eigenvalues has multiplicity 3. Find three linearly independent eigenvectors associated with this eigenvalue.

7. Find the real eigenvalues and associated eigenvectors of $A = \begin{pmatrix} 1 & 0 & 0 & 0 \\ 1 & 0 & 0 & 0 \\ 0 & 0 & 0 & -1 \\ 0 & 0 & 1 & 0 \end{pmatrix}$.

8. Let $A = \begin{pmatrix} -2 & -1 & 4 \\ 2 & 1 & -2 \\ -1 & -1 & 3 \end{pmatrix}$, $x_1 = \begin{pmatrix} 1 \\ 0 \\ 1 \end{pmatrix}$, $x_2 = \begin{pmatrix} 1 \\ -1 \\ 0 \end{pmatrix}$, $x_3 = \begin{pmatrix} 1 \\ 1 \\ 1 \end{pmatrix}$.

   (a) Verify that x_1, x_2, and x_3 are eigenvectors of A, and find the associated eigenvalues.

   (b) Let $B = AA$. Show that $Bx_2 = x_2$ and $Bx_3 = x_3$. Is $Bx_1 = x_1$?

   (c) Let C be an arbitrary $n \times n$ matrix such that $C^3 = C^2 + C$. Prove that if λ is an eigenvalue for C, then $\lambda^3 = \lambda^2 + \lambda$. Show that $C + I_n$ has an inverse.

HARDER PROBLEMS

9. Let $A = (a_{ij})_{n \times n}$ be a matrix where all column sums are 1—that is, $\sum_{i=1}^{n} a_{ij} = 1$ for $j = 1, 2, \ldots, n$. Prove that $\lambda = 1$ is an eigenvalue of A.

1.7   Diagonalization

We begin by noting a simple and useful result. Let $\mathbf{A}$ and $\mathbf{P}$ be $n \times n$ matrices with $\mathbf{P}$ invertible. Then

$$\mathbf{A} \text{ and } \mathbf{P}^{-1}\mathbf{AP} \text{ have the same eigenvalues} \tag{1}$$

This is true because the two matrices have the same characteristic polynomial:

$$|\mathbf{P}^{-1}\mathbf{AP} - \lambda\mathbf{I}| = |\mathbf{P}^{-1}\mathbf{AP} - \mathbf{P}^{-1}\lambda\mathbf{IP}| = |\mathbf{P}^{-1}(\mathbf{A} - \lambda\mathbf{I})\mathbf{P}|$$
$$= |\mathbf{P}^{-1}||\mathbf{A} - \lambda\mathbf{I}||\mathbf{P}| = |\mathbf{A} - \lambda\mathbf{I}|$$

where we made use of rule (1.1.24) for determinants, and the fact that $|\mathbf{P}^{-1}| = 1/|\mathbf{P}|$.

An $n \times n$ matrix $\mathbf{A}$ is **diagonalizable** if there exists an invertible $n \times n$ matrix $\mathbf{P}$ and a diagonal matrix $\mathbf{D}$ such that

$$\mathbf{P}^{-1}\mathbf{AP} = \mathbf{D} \tag{2}$$

By Example 1.6.3, the eigenvalues of a diagonal matrix are the diagonal elements. Hence, if $\mathbf{A}$ is diagonalizable, so that (2) holds, then $\mathbf{P}^{-1}\mathbf{AP} = \text{diag}(\lambda_1, \ldots, \lambda_n)$, where $\lambda_1, \ldots, \lambda_n$ are the eigenvalues of $\mathbf{A}$. Two questions arise:

(A) Which square matrices are diagonalizable?

(B) If $\mathbf{A}$ is diagonalizable, how do we find the matrix $\mathbf{P}$ in (2)?

The answers to both of these questions are given in the next theorem.

THEOREM 1.7.1 (DIAGONALIZABLE MATRICES)

An $n \times n$ matrix $\mathbf{A}$ is diagonalizable iff it has a set of n linearly independent eigenvectors $\mathbf{x}_1, \ldots, \mathbf{x}_n$. In that case,

$$\mathbf{P}^{-1}\mathbf{AP} = \text{diag}(\lambda_1, \ldots, \lambda_n) \tag{3}$$

where $\mathbf{P}$ is the matrix with $\mathbf{x}_1, \ldots, \mathbf{x}_n$ as its columns, and $\lambda_1, \ldots, \lambda_n$ are the corresponding eigenvalues.

Proof: Suppose $\mathbf{A}$ has n linearly independent eigenvectors $\mathbf{x}_1, \ldots, \mathbf{x}_n$, with corresponding eigenvalues $\lambda_1, \ldots, \lambda_n$. Let $\mathbf{P}$ denote the matrix whose columns are $\mathbf{x}_1, \ldots, \mathbf{x}_n$. Then $\mathbf{AP} = \mathbf{PD}$, where $\mathbf{D} = \text{diag}(\lambda_1, \ldots, \lambda_n)$. Because the eigenvectors are linearly independent, $\mathbf{P}$ is invertible, so $\mathbf{P}^{-1}\mathbf{AP} = \mathbf{D}$.

Conversely, if $\mathbf{A}$ is diagonalizable, (2) must hold. Then $\mathbf{AP} = \mathbf{PD}$. The columns of $\mathbf{P}$ must be eigenvectors of $\mathbf{A}$, and the diagonal elements of $\mathbf{D}$ the corresponding eigenvalues. ∎

EXAMPLE 1   Verify Theorem 1.7.1 for $\mathbf{A} = \begin{pmatrix} 1 & 2 \\ 3 & 0 \end{pmatrix}$. (See Example 1.6.1(a).)

Solution: From Example 1.6.1(a), the eigenvalues are $\lambda_1 = -2$ and $\lambda_2 = 3$. For the matrix $\mathbf{P}$ we can choose $\mathbf{P} = \begin{pmatrix} 2 & 1 \\ -3 & 1 \end{pmatrix}$, whose inverse is $\mathbf{P}^{-1} = \begin{pmatrix} 1/5 & -1/5 \\ 3/5 & 2/5 \end{pmatrix}$. Now direct multiplication shows that $\mathbf{P}^{-1}\mathbf{AP} = \text{diag}(-2, 3)$. Theorem 1.7.1 is confirmed.

NOTE 1 A matrix $\mathbf{P}$ is called **orthogonal** if $\mathbf{P}' = \mathbf{P}^{-1}$, i.e. $\mathbf{P}'\mathbf{P} = \mathbf{I}$. If $\mathbf{x}_1, \ldots, \mathbf{x}_n$ are the n column vectors of $\mathbf{P}$, then $\mathbf{x}'_1, \ldots, \mathbf{x}'_n$ are the row vectors of the transposed matrix, $\mathbf{P}'$. The condition $\mathbf{P}'\mathbf{P} = \mathbf{I}$ then reduces to the n^2 equations $\mathbf{x}'_i\mathbf{x}_j = 1$ if $i = j$ and $\mathbf{x}'_i\mathbf{x}_j = 0$ if $i \neq j$. We conclude that $\mathbf{P}$ is orthogonal iff $\mathbf{x}_1, \ldots, \mathbf{x}_n$ all have length 1 and are mutually orthogonal.

Many of the matrices encountered in economics are symmetric. For symmetric matrices we have the following important result.

THEOREM 1.7.2 (THE SPECTRAL THEOREM FOR SYMMETRIC MATRICES)

If the matrix $\mathbf{A} = (a_{ij})_{n\times n}$ is symmetric, then:

(a) All the n eigenvalues $\lambda_1, \ldots, \lambda_n$ are real.

(b) Eigenvectors that correspond to different eigenvalues are orthogonal.

(c) There exists an *orthogonal* matrix $\mathbf{P}$ (i.e. with $\mathbf{P}' = \mathbf{P}^{-1}$) such that

$$\mathbf{P}^{-1}\mathbf{AP} = \begin{pmatrix} \lambda_1 & 0 & \cdots & 0 \\ 0 & \lambda_2 & \cdots & 0 \\ \vdots & \vdots & \ddots & \vdots \\ 0 & 0 & \cdots & \lambda_n \end{pmatrix} \tag{4}$$

The columns $\mathbf{v}_1, \mathbf{v}_2, \ldots, \mathbf{v}_n$ of the matrix $\mathbf{P}$ are eigenvectors of unit length corresponding to the eigenvalues $\lambda_1, \lambda_2, \ldots, \lambda_n$.

Proof: (a) This was proved in the previous section for $n = 2$. For the general case, see e.g. Fraleigh and Beauregard (1995).

(b) Suppose $\mathbf{Ax}_i = \lambda_i\mathbf{x}_i$ and $\mathbf{Ax}_j = \lambda_j\mathbf{x}_j$ by $\lambda_i \neq \lambda_j$. Multiplying these equalities from the left by $\mathbf{x}'_j$ and $\mathbf{x}'_i$, respectively, we get $\mathbf{x}'_j\mathbf{Ax}_i = \lambda_i\mathbf{x}'_j\mathbf{x}_i$ and $\mathbf{x}'_i\mathbf{Ax}_j = \lambda_j\mathbf{x}'_i\mathbf{x}_j$. Since $\mathbf{A}$ is symmetric, transposing the first equality yields $\mathbf{x}'_i\mathbf{Ax}_j = \lambda_i\mathbf{x}'_i\mathbf{x}_j$. But then $\lambda_i\mathbf{x}'_i\mathbf{x}_j = \lambda_j\mathbf{x}'_i\mathbf{x}_j$, or $(\lambda_i - \lambda_j)\mathbf{x}'_i\mathbf{x}_j = 0$. Since $\lambda_i \neq \lambda_j$, it follows that $\mathbf{x}'_i\mathbf{x}_j = 0$, and thus $\mathbf{x}_i$ and $\mathbf{x}_j$ are orthogonal.

(c) Suppose all the (real) eigenvalues are different. Then according to (b), the eigenvectors are mutually orthogonal. Problem 1.3.6(b) then tells us that the eigenvectors are linearly independent. By Theorem 1.7.1, $\mathbf{A}$ is diagonalizable and (4) is valid with $\mathbf{P}$ as the matrix with the eigenvectors $\mathbf{x}_1, \ldots, \mathbf{x}_n$ as its columns. We can choose the eigenvectors so that they all have length 1, by replacing each $\mathbf{x}_j$ with $\mathbf{x}_j/\|\mathbf{x}_j\|$. According to Note 1, the matrix $\mathbf{P}$ is then orthogonal. For a proof of the general case where some of the eigenvalues are equal, see e.g. Fraleigh and Beauregard (1995). ∎

EXAMPLE 2 It follows from (4) that $\mathbf{A} = \mathbf{P}\,\text{diag}(\lambda_1, \ldots, \lambda_n)\,\mathbf{P}^{-1}$. If m is a natural number, then

$$\mathbf{A}^m = \mathbf{P}\,\text{diag}(\lambda_1^m, \ldots, \lambda_n^m)\,\mathbf{P}^{-1} \tag{5}$$

This provides a simple formula for computing $\mathbf{A}^m$ when $\mathbf{A}$ is diagonalizable.

NOTE 2 A famous and striking result is Cayley–Hamilton's theorem which says that any square matrix satisfies its own characteristic equation. Thus, with reference to the characteristic polynomial (1.6.8),

$$(-\mathbf{A})^n + b_{n-1}(-\mathbf{A})^{n-1} + \cdots + b_1(-\mathbf{A}) + b_0\mathbf{I} = \mathbf{0} \qquad \textbf{(Cayley–Hamilton)} \qquad (6)$$

For a proof, see Faddeeva (1959) or Lewis (1991).

PROBLEMS FOR SECTION 1.7

1. Verify (4) for the following matrices by finding the matrix **P** explicitly:

   (a) $\begin{pmatrix} 2 & 1 \\ 1 & 2 \end{pmatrix}$
   (b) $\begin{pmatrix} 1 & 1 & 0 \\ 1 & 1 & 0 \\ 0 & 0 & 2 \end{pmatrix}$
   (c) $\begin{pmatrix} 1 & 3 & 4 \\ 3 & 1 & 0 \\ 4 & 0 & 1 \end{pmatrix}$

2. (a) Prove that if $\mathbf{A} = \mathbf{PDP}^{-1}$, with **P** and **D** as $n \times n$ matrices, then $\mathbf{A}^2 = \mathbf{PD}^2\mathbf{P}^{-1}$.

   (b) Show by induction that $\mathbf{A}^m = \mathbf{PD}^m\mathbf{P}^{-1}$ for any positive integer m.

3. Use (1) to prove that if **A** and **B** are both invertible $n \times n$ matrices, then **AB** and **BA** have the same eigenvalues.

4. Cayley–Hamilton's theorem can be used to compute powers of matrices. In particular, if $\mathbf{A} = (a_{ij})$ is 2×2, then
$$\mathbf{A}^2 = \mathrm{tr}(\mathbf{A})\mathbf{A} - |\mathbf{A}|\,\mathbf{I} \qquad (*)$$

   Multiplying this equation by **A** and using (*) again yields $\mathbf{A}^3$ expressed in terms of **A** and **I**, etc. Use this method to find $\mathbf{A}^4$ when $\mathbf{A} = \begin{pmatrix} 2 & 1 \\ 1 & 3 \end{pmatrix}$. (See e.g. Goldberg (1958), Section 4.5.)

1.8 Quadratic Forms

Many applications of mathematics make use of the following special kind of double sum. A **quadratic form** in n variables is a function Q of the form

$$Q(x_1, \ldots, x_n) = \sum_{i=1}^{n} \sum_{j=1}^{n} a_{ij} x_i x_j = a_{11}x_1^2 + a_{12}x_1 x_2 + \cdots + a_{ij}x_i x_j + \cdots + a_{nn}x_n^2 \quad (1)$$

where the a_{ij} are constants. Suppose we put $\mathbf{x} = (x_1, x_2, \ldots, x_n)'$ and $\mathbf{A} = (a_{ij})$. Then it follows from the definition of matrix multiplication that

$$Q(x_1, \ldots, x_n) = Q(\mathbf{x}) = \mathbf{x}'\mathbf{Ax} \qquad (2)$$

Of course, $x_i x_j = x_j x_i$, so we can write $a_{ij}x_i x_j + a_{ji}x_j x_i = (a_{ij} + a_{ji})x_i x_j$. If we replace a_{ij} and a_{ji} by $\frac{1}{2}(a_{ij}+a_{ji})$, then the new numbers a_{ij} and a_{ji} become equal without changing $Q(x_1, \ldots, x_n)$. Thus, we can assume in (1) that $a_{ij} = a_{ji}$ for all i and j, which means that the matrix $\mathbf{A}$ is symmetric. Then $\mathbf{A}$ is called the *symmetric matrix associated with* Q, and Q is called a **symmetric quadratic form**.

EXAMPLE 1   Write $Q(x_1, x_2, x_3) = 3x_1^2 + 6x_1 x_3 + x_2^2 - 4x_2 x_3 + 8x_3^2$ in matrix form with $\mathbf{A}$ symmetric.

Solution: We first write Q as follows:

$$Q = 3x_1^2 + 0 \cdot x_1 x_2 + 3x_1 x_3 + 0 \cdot x_2 x_1 + x_2^2 - 2x_2 x_3 + 3x_3 x_1 - 2x_3 x_2 + 8x_3^2$$

Then $Q = \mathbf{x}'\mathbf{A}\mathbf{x}$, where $\mathbf{A} = \begin{pmatrix} 3 & 0 & 3 \\ 0 & 1 & -2 \\ 3 & -2 & 8 \end{pmatrix}$ and $\mathbf{x} = \begin{pmatrix} x_1 \\ x_2 \\ x_3 \end{pmatrix}$.

We are often interested in conditions that ensure that $Q(\mathbf{x})$ has the same sign for all $\mathbf{x}$.

DEFINITENESS OF A QUADRATIC FORM

A quadratic form $Q(\mathbf{x}) = \mathbf{x}'\mathbf{A}\mathbf{x}$, as well as its associated symmetric matrix $\mathbf{A}$, are said to be **positive definite**, **positive semidefinite**, **negative definite**, or **negative semidefinite** according as

$$Q(\mathbf{x}) > 0, \quad Q(\mathbf{x}) \geq 0, \quad Q(\mathbf{x}) < 0, \quad Q(\mathbf{x}) \leq 0 \tag{3}$$

for all $\mathbf{x} \neq \mathbf{0}$. The quadratic form $Q(\mathbf{x})$ is **indefinite** if there exist vectors $\mathbf{x}^*$ and $\mathbf{y}^*$ such that $Q(\mathbf{x}^*) < 0$ and $Q(\mathbf{y}^*) > 0$. Thus an indefinite quadratic form assumes both negative and positive values.

In order to prove that a quadratic form is positive semidefinite, we have to prove that $Q(\mathbf{x}) \geq 0$ for *all* choices of $\mathbf{x}$. How can this be done? Consider first the case $n = 2$. Then the quadratic form is

$$Q(x_1, x_2) = a_{11}x_1^2 + 2a_{12}x_1 x_2 + a_{22}x_2^2$$

We claim that:

$Q(x_1, x_2)$ is positive semidefinite

$$\Longleftrightarrow a_{11} \geq 0, \ a_{22} \geq 0, \ \text{and} \ \begin{vmatrix} a_{11} & a_{12} \\ a_{12} & a_{22} \end{vmatrix} = a_{11}a_{22} - a_{12}^2 \geq 0 \tag{4}$$

Proof: Suppose $a_{11} \geq 0$, $a_{22} \geq 0$, and $a_{11}a_{22} - a_{12}^2 \geq 0$. If $a_{11} = 0$, then $a_{11}a_{22} - a_{12}^2 \geq 0$ implies $a_{12} = 0$, and so $Q(x_1, x_2) = a_{22}x_2^2 \geq 0$ for all (x_1, x_2). If $a_{11} > 0$, then by completing the square, we can write

$$Q(x_1, x_2) = a_{11}\left(x_1 + \frac{a_{12}}{a_{11}}x_2\right)^2 + \left(a_{22} - \frac{a_{12}^2}{a_{11}}\right)x_2^2 \tag{*}$$

Because $a_{11} > 0$ and $a_{22} - (a_{12})^2/a_{11} \geq 0$, we see that $Q(x_1, x_2) \geq 0$ for all (x_1, x_2).

To prove the reverse implication, suppose $Q(x_1, x_2)$ is positive semidefinite. Then, in particular, $Q(1, 0) = a_{11} \geq 0$ and $Q(0, 1) = a_{22} \geq 0$. If $a_{11} = 0$, then $Q(x_1, 1) = 2a_{12}x_1 + a_{22}$, which is ≥ 0 for all x_1 if and only if $a_{12} = 0$. (If $a_{12} > 0$, then choosing x_1 as a large negative number makes $Q(x_1, 1)$ negative. If $a_{12} < 0$, then choosing x_1 as a large positive number makes $Q(x_1, 1)$ negative.) Thus, $a_{11}a_{22} - a_{12}^2 = 0$. If $a_{11} > 0$, then $(*)$ is valid and $Q(-a_{12}/a_{11}, 1) = a_{22} - a_{12}^2/a_{11} \geq 0$. ∎

The positive definite case is also easy and the proof is left to the reader:

$$Q(x_1, x_2) \text{ is positive definite} \iff a_{11} > 0 \text{ and } \begin{vmatrix} a_{11} & a_{12} \\ a_{12} & a_{22} \end{vmatrix} = a_{11}a_{22} - a_{12}^2 > 0 \quad (5)$$

NOTE 1   In (5) we say nothing about the sign of a_{22}. But if $a_{11}a_{22} - a_{12}^2 > 0$, then $a_{11}a_{22} > a_{12}^2 \geq 0$, and so $a_{11}a_{22} > 0$. It follows that since a_{11} is positive, so is a_{22}. Thus we could have added the condition $a_{22} > 0$ on the right-hand side in (5), but it is superfluous.

The negative (semi)definite versions of (4) and (5) are easy to formulate and prove because $Q(\mathbf{x})$ is negative (semi)definite iff $-Q(\mathbf{x})$ is positive (semi)definite. Be careful with the signs, though—for example, note that $\begin{vmatrix} -a_{11} & -a_{12} \\ -a_{12} & -a_{22} \end{vmatrix} \geq 0 \iff a_{11}a_{22} - a_{12}^2 \geq 0$.

The results above for quadratic forms in two variables can be generalized. In order to do so we need a few new concepts. Recall that in Section 1.4 we defined the minors of a matrix. To study the sign of quadratic forms we need some special types of minor.

Let $\mathbf{A} = (a_{ij})$ be any $n \times n$ matrix. An arbitrary **principal minor** of **order** r is the determinant of the matrix obtained by deleting all but r rows and r columns in $\mathbf{A}$ with the same numbers. In particular, a principal minor of order r always includes exactly r elements of the main (principal) diagonal. We call the determinant $|\mathbf{A}|$ itself a principal minor. (No rows or columns are deleted.) A principal minor is called a **leading principal minor** of order r ($1 \leq r \leq n$), if it consists of the first ("leading") r rows and columns of $|\mathbf{A}|$.

EXAMPLE 2   Write down the principal and the leading principal minors of

$$\mathbf{A} = \begin{pmatrix} a_{11} & a_{12} \\ a_{21} & a_{22} \end{pmatrix} \quad \text{and} \quad \mathbf{B} = \begin{pmatrix} b_{11} & b_{12} & b_{13} \\ b_{21} & b_{22} & b_{23} \\ b_{31} & b_{32} & b_{33} \end{pmatrix}$$

Solution: By deleting row 2 and column 2 in $\mathbf{A}$ we get (a_{11}), which has determinant a_{11}. (Remember that the determinant of a 1×1 matrix (a) is the number a itself.) Deleting row 1 and column 1 in $\mathbf{A}$ we get (a_{22}), which has determinant a_{22}. The principal minors of $\mathbf{A}$ are therefore a_{11}, a_{22}, and $|\mathbf{A}|$. The *leading* principal minors are a_{11} and $|\mathbf{A}|$.

The principal minors of $\mathbf{B}$ are $|\mathbf{B}|$ itself, and

$$b_{11}, \quad b_{22}, \quad b_{33}, \quad \begin{vmatrix} b_{11} & b_{12} \\ b_{21} & b_{22} \end{vmatrix}, \quad \begin{vmatrix} b_{11} & b_{13} \\ b_{31} & b_{33} \end{vmatrix}, \quad \text{and} \quad \begin{vmatrix} b_{22} & b_{23} \\ b_{32} & b_{33} \end{vmatrix}$$

while the leading principal minors are $|\mathbf{B}|$ itself, b_{11}, and $\begin{vmatrix} b_{11} & b_{12} \\ b_{21} & b_{22} \end{vmatrix}$.

Suppose **A** is an arbitrary $n \times n$ matrix. The leading principal minors of **A** are

$$D_k = \begin{vmatrix} a_{11} & a_{12} & \cdots & a_{1k} \\ a_{21} & a_{22} & \cdots & a_{2k} \\ \vdots & \vdots & \ddots & \vdots \\ a_{k1} & a_{k2} & \cdots & a_{kk} \end{vmatrix}, \quad k = 1, 2, \ldots, n \tag{6}$$

These determinants are obtained from the elements in $|\mathbf{A}|$ according to the pattern suggested by the following arrangement:

$$\begin{vmatrix} a_{11} & a_{12} & a_{13} & \cdots & a_{1n} \\ a_{21} & a_{22} & a_{23} & \cdots & a_{2n} \\ a_{31} & a_{32} & a_{33} & \cdots & a_{3n} \\ \vdots & \vdots & \vdots & \ddots & \vdots \\ a_{n1} & a_{n2} & a_{n3} & \cdots & a_{nn} \end{vmatrix} \tag{7}$$

Note that there are many more principal minors than there are leading principal minors.[4] It is notationally cumbersome to represent a specific principal minor, but we use Δ_k to denote a generic principal minor of order k.

The above concepts make it possible to formulate the following theorem:

THEOREM 1.8.1

Consider the quadratic form

$$Q(\mathbf{x}) = \sum_{i=1}^{n} \sum_{j=1}^{n} a_{ij} x_i x_j \quad (a_{ij} = a_{ji})$$

with the associated symmetric matrix $\mathbf{A} = (a_{ij})_{n \times n}$. Let D_k be defined by (6) and let Δ_k denote a arbitrary principal minor of order k. Then we have:

(a) Q is positive definite $\iff$ $D_k > 0$ for $k = 1, \ldots, n$

(b) Q is positive semidefinite $\iff$ $\begin{cases} \Delta_k \geq 0 \text{ for all principal minors} \\ \text{of order } k = 1, \ldots, n \end{cases}$

(c) Q is negative definite $\iff$ $(-1)^k D_k > 0$ for $k = 1, \ldots, n$

(d) Q is negative semidefinite $\iff$ $\begin{cases} (-1)^k \Delta_k \geq 0 \text{ for all principal} \\ \text{minors of order } k = 1, \ldots, n \end{cases}$

If we change the sign of each element in a $k \times k$ matrix, then the determinant of the new matrix is $(-1)^k$ times the determinant of the original matrix. Since $Q = \sum \sum a_{ij} x_i x_j$ is

---

[4] More precisely, there are $\binom{n}{k}$ principal minors of order k, but only one leading principal minor of order k.

negative (semi)definite iff $-Q = \sum\sum(-a_{ij})x_i x_j$ is positive (semi)definite, we see that (c) and (d) in the theorem follow from (a) and (b). For $n = 2$ we proved (a) and (b) in (5) and (4) above. For a general proof, we refer to e.g. Fraleigh and Beauregard (1995).

NOTE 2   It is a rather common misconception that if we replace each inequality $D_k > 0$ in (a) with $D_k \geq 0$, we get a necessary and sufficient condition for A to be positive semidefinite. But $Q(x_1, x_2) = 0 \cdot x_1^2 - x_2^2$ has $D_1 = 0$ and $D_2 = 0$, yet $Q(0, 1) = -1 < 0$, so Q is *not* positive semidefinite. (Theorem 1.8.1 (b) reveals that Q is not positive semidefinite, since there exists a principal minor of order 1 that is equal to -1.)

EXAMPLE 3   Use Theorem 1.8.1 to determine the definiteness of

$$\text{(a) } Q = 3x_1^2 + 6x_1x_3 + x_2^2 - 4x_2x_3 + 8x_3^2 \qquad \text{(b) } Q = -x_1^2 + 6x_1x_2 - 9x_2^2 - 2x_3^2$$

Solution: It makes sense to check the leading principal minors first, in case the matrix turns to be definite rather than merely semidefinite.

(a) The associated symmetric matrix A is given in Example 1, and its leading principal minors are

$$D_1 = 3, \quad D_2 = \begin{vmatrix} 3 & 0 \\ 0 & 1 \end{vmatrix} = 3, \quad \text{and} \quad D_3 = \begin{vmatrix} 3 & 0 & 3 \\ 0 & 1 & -2 \\ 3 & -2 & 8 \end{vmatrix} = 3$$

We conclude that Q is positive definite.

(b) The associated symmetric matrix is $A = \begin{pmatrix} -1 & 3 & 0 \\ 3 & -9 & 0 \\ 0 & 0 & -2 \end{pmatrix}$. Here the leading principal minors are $D_1 = -1$, $D_2 = 0$, $D_3 = 0$. It follows that the conditions in part (a) of Theorem 1.8.1 are not satisfied, nor are those in (b) or (c). In order to check the conditions in (d), we must examine all the principal minors of A. As described in Example 2, the 3×3 matrix A has three principal minors of order 1, whose values $\Delta_1^{(1)}$, $\Delta_1^{(2)}$, and $\Delta_1^{(3)}$ are the diagonal elements. These satisfy

$$(-1)^1\Delta_1^{(1)} = (-1)(-1) = 1, \quad (-1)^1\Delta_1^{(2)} = (-1)(-9) = 9, \quad (-1)^1\Delta_1^{(3)} = (-1)(-2) = 2$$

There are also three second-order principal minors which satisfy

$$\Delta_2^{(1)} = \begin{vmatrix} -1 & 3 \\ 3 & -9 \end{vmatrix} = 0, \quad \Delta_2^{(2)} = \begin{vmatrix} -1 & 0 \\ 0 & -2 \end{vmatrix} = 2, \quad \Delta_2^{(3)} = \begin{vmatrix} -9 & 0 \\ 0 & -2 \end{vmatrix} = 18$$

Hence $(-1)^2\Delta_2^{(1)} = 0$, $(-1)^2\Delta_2^{(2)} = 2$, and $(-1)^2\Delta_2^{(3)} = 18$. Finally, $(-1)^3\Delta_3 = (-1)^3 D_3 = 0$. Thus $(-1)^k\Delta_k \geq 0$. for all principal minors Δ_k ($k = 1, 2, 3$) in the matrix A associated with the quadratic form Q. It follows from (d) that Q is negative semidefinite.

The definiteness of a quadratic form can often be determined more easily from the signs of the eigenvalues of the associated matrix. (By Theorem 1.7.2 these eigenvalues are all real.)

THEOREM 1.8.2

Let $Q = \mathbf{x'Ax}$ be a quadratic form, where the matrix $\mathbf{A}$ is symmetric, and let $\lambda_1, \ldots, \lambda_n$ be the (real) eigenvalues of $\mathbf{A}$. Then:

(a) Q is positive definite $\iff$ $\lambda_1 > 0, \ldots, \lambda_n > 0$

(b) Q is positive semidefinite $\iff$ $\lambda_1 \geq 0, \ldots, \lambda_n \geq 0$

(c) Q is negative definite $\iff$ $\lambda_1 < 0, \ldots, \lambda_n < 0$

(d) Q is negative semidefinite $\iff$ $\lambda_1 \leq 0, \ldots, \lambda_n \leq 0$

(e) Q is indefinite $\iff$ $\mathbf{A}$ has eigenvalues with opposite signs

Proof: According to Theorem 1.7.2, there exists an orthogonal matrix $\mathbf{P}$ such that $\mathbf{P'AP} = \text{diag}(\lambda_1, \ldots, \lambda_n)$. Let $\mathbf{y} = (y_1, \ldots, y_n)'$ be the $n \times 1$ matrix defined by $\mathbf{y} = \mathbf{P'x}$. Then $\mathbf{x} = \mathbf{Py}$, so that

$$\mathbf{x'Ax} = \mathbf{y'P'APy} = \mathbf{y'}\,\text{diag}(\lambda_1, \lambda_2, \ldots, \lambda_n)\,\mathbf{y} = \lambda_1 y_1^2 + \lambda_2 y_2^2 + \cdots + \lambda_n y_n^2 \qquad (8)$$

Also, $\mathbf{x} = \mathbf{0}$ iff $\mathbf{y} = \mathbf{0}$. The conclusion follows immediately. ∎

EXAMPLE 4   Use Theorem 1.8.2 to determine the definiteness of the quadratic form in Example 3(b).

Solution: The associated symmetric matrix is $\begin{pmatrix} -1 & 3 & 0 \\ 3 & -9 & 0 \\ 0 & 0 & -2 \end{pmatrix}$. The characteristic equation simplifies to $-\lambda(\lambda + 2)(\lambda + 10) = 0$, so the eigenvalues are $0, -2,$ and -10. Theorem 1.8.2 tells us the quadratic form is negative semidefinite.

PROBLEMS FOR SECTION 1.8

1. Write down the double sum in (1) when $n = 3$ and $a_{ij} = a_{ji}$ for $i, j = 1, 2, 3$.

2. Write the following quadratic forms as $\mathbf{x'Ax}$, with $\mathbf{A}$ symmetric:

   (a) $x^2 + 2xy + y^2$ (b) $ax^2 + bxy + cy^2$ (c) $3x_1^2 - 2x_1x_2 + 3x_1x_3 + x_2^2 + 3x_3^2$

3. Using Theorem 1.8.1 or Theorem 1.8.2, or otherwise, determine the definiteness of

   (a) $Q = x_1^2 + 8x_2^2$ (b) $Q = 5x_1^2 + 2x_1x_3 + 2x_2^2 + 2x_2x_3 + 4x_3^2$

   (c) $Q = -(x_1 - x_2)^2$ (d) $Q = -3x_1^2 + 2x_1x_2 - x_2^2 + 4x_2x_3 - 8x_3^2$

4. If $x_1, \ldots, x_n$ are n independent observations $(n > 1)$ of a stochastic variable X, and $m_x = \left(\sum_{j=1}^{n} x_j\right)/n$ is the mean of $x_1, \ldots, x_n$, an estimator for the variance of X is

   $$\frac{1}{n-1} \sum_{i=1}^{n} (x_i - m_x)^2$$

   Is this a quadratic form? If yes, is it positive definite?

5. Show that if $Q = \mathbf{x}'\mathbf{A}\mathbf{x}$ in (2) is positive definite, then

    (a) $a_{ii} > 0, \quad i = 1, \ldots, n$ (b) $\begin{vmatrix} a_{ii} & a_{ij} \\ a_{ji} & a_{jj} \end{vmatrix} > 0, \quad i, j = 1, \ldots, n$

6. Let $\mathbf{A} = (a_{ij})_{n \times n}$ be symmetric and positive semidefinite. Prove that

$$\mathbf{A} \text{ is positive definite} \iff |\mathbf{A}| \neq 0$$

7. Let $\mathbf{A}$ be a symmetric matrix. Write its eigenvalue polynomial as

$$\varphi(\lambda) = \lambda^n + a_{n-1}\lambda^{n-1} + \cdots + a_1\lambda + a_0$$

Prove that $\mathbf{A}$ is positive definite iff $a_i > 0$ for $i = 0, 1, \ldots, n - 1$.

1.9 Quadratic Forms with Linear Constraints

In constrained optimization theory we need to study the signs of quadratic forms subject to homogeneous linear constraints.

Consider first the quadratic form $Q = ax^2 + 2bxy + cy^2$ and assume that the variables are subject to the homogeneous linear constraint $px + qy = 0$, where $q \neq 0$. Solving the constraint for y, we have $y = -px/q$. Substituting this value for y into the expression for Q yields

$$Q = ax^2 + 2bx\left(-\frac{px}{q}\right) + c\left(-\frac{px}{q}\right)^2 = \frac{1}{q^2}(aq^2 - 2bpq + cp^2)x^2 \qquad (*)$$

We say that $Q(x, y)$ is **positive (negative) definite subject to the constraint** $px + qy = 0$ if Q is positive (negative) for all $(x, y) \neq (0, 0)$ satisfying $px + qy = 0$. By expanding the determinant, it is easy to verify that

$$aq^2 - 2bpq + cp^2 = -\begin{vmatrix} 0 & p & q \\ p & a & b \\ q & b & c \end{vmatrix} \qquad (1)$$

Combining this with $(*)$ gives the following equivalence:

$$\left.\begin{array}{l} Q = ax^2 + 2bxy + cy^2 \text{ is positive definite} \\ \text{subject to the constraint } px + qy = 0 \end{array}\right\} \iff \begin{vmatrix} 0 & p & q \\ p & a & b \\ q & b & c \end{vmatrix} < 0 \qquad (2)$$

This is also valid when $q = 0$ but $p \neq 0$. The condition for negative definiteness is that the determinant on the right-hand side is > 0.

Consider next the general quadratic form

$$Q(\mathbf{x}) = \sum_{i=1}^{n}\sum_{j=1}^{n} a_{ij}x_i x_j \qquad (a_{ij} = a_{ji}) \qquad (3)$$

subject to m linear, homogeneous constraints

$$b_{11}x_1 + \cdots + b_{1n}x_n = 0$$
$$\dotfill$$
$$b_{m1}x_1 + \cdots + b_{mn}x_n = 0$$

(4)

or $\mathbf{Bx} = \mathbf{0}$, where $\mathbf{B} = (b_{ij})$ is an $m \times n$ matrix.

We say that Q is **positive (negative) definite subject to the linear constraints** (4) if $Q(\mathbf{x}) > 0$ (< 0) for all $\mathbf{x} = (x_1, \ldots, x_n) \neq (0, \ldots, 0)$ that satisfy (4).

Define the symmetric determinants

$$B_r = \begin{vmatrix} 0 & \cdots & 0 & b_{11} & \cdots & b_{1r} \\ \vdots & \ddots & \vdots & \vdots & & \vdots \\ 0 & \cdots & 0 & b_{m1} & \cdots & b_{mr} \\ b_{11} & \cdots & b_{m1} & a_{11} & \cdots & a_{1r} \\ \vdots & & \vdots & \vdots & \ddots & \vdots \\ b_{1r} & \cdots & b_{mr} & a_{r1} & \cdots & a_{rr} \end{vmatrix}, \quad r = 1, \ldots, n$$

Notice that the determinant B_r is the $(m + r)$th leading principal minor of the $(m + n) \times (m + n)$ bordered matrix $\begin{pmatrix} \mathbf{0}_{m \times m} & \mathbf{B} \\ \mathbf{B}' & \mathbf{A} \end{pmatrix}$. Then we have the following result. (For a proof see Farebrother (1977).)

THEOREM 1.9.1

A necessary and sufficient condition for the quadratic form

$$Q = \sum_{i=1}^{n} \sum_{j=1}^{n} a_{ij} x_i x_j$$

to be positive definite subject to the linear constraints (4), where we assume that the first m columns in the matrix $(b_{ij})_{m \times n}$ are linearly independent, is that

$$(-1)^m B_r > 0, \quad r = m + 1, \ldots, n$$

(5)

The corresponding necessary and sufficient condition for negative definiteness subject to the constraints (4) is

$$(-1)^r B_r > 0, \quad r = m + 1, \ldots, n$$

(6)

Note that the number of determinants to check is $n - m$. The more degrees of freedom (i.e. the smaller m is), the more determinants must be checked. If there is only one variable more than there are constraints, we need only examine B_n. If $n = 2$ and $m = 1$, then (6) reduces to $(-1)B_r > 0$ for $r = 2$, that is, $B_2 < 0$. (This confirms the result in (2).)

EXAMPLE 1   Examine the definiteness of $Q = 3x_1^2 - x_2^2 + 4x_3^2$ subject to $x_1 + x_2 + x_3 = 0$.

Solution: Here $n = 3$, $m = 1$. According to (5) and (6), we must examine the determinant B_r for $r = 2$ and 3. We find that

$$B_2 = \begin{vmatrix} 0 & 1 & 1 \\ 1 & 3 & 0 \\ 1 & 0 & -1 \end{vmatrix} = -2, \quad B_3 = \begin{vmatrix} 0 & 1 & 1 & 1 \\ 1 & 3 & 0 & 0 \\ 1 & 0 & -1 & 0 \\ 1 & 0 & 0 & 4 \end{vmatrix} = -5$$

Hence $(-1)^1 B_2 = 2$ and $(-1)^1 B_3 = 5$, so (6) shows that Q is positive definite subject to the given condition. (This is easy to check directly by substituting $-x_1 - x_2$ for x_3 in Q.)

PROBLEMS FOR SECTION 1.9

1. Determine the definiteness of $x^2 - 2xy + y^2$ subject to $x + y = 0$ both directly and using Theorem 1.9.1.

2. Examine the definiteness of the following quadratic forms subject to the given linear constraint using Theorem 1.9.1:

   (a) $2x^2 - 4xy + y^2$ subject to $3x + 4y = 0$

   (b) $-x^2 + xy - y^2$ subject to $5x - 2y = 0$

3. Examine the definiteness of $-5x^2 + 2xy + 4xz - y^2 - 2z^2$ s.t. $\begin{cases} x + y + z = 0 \\ 4x - 2y + z = 0 \end{cases}$

4. Examine the definiteness of $x^2 + 2xy + y^2 + z^2$ subject to $\begin{cases} x + 2y + z = 0 \\ 2x - y - 3z = 0 \end{cases}$ using Theorem 1.9.1.

MULTIVARIABLE CALCULUS

Wisdom and maturity are the last settlers in pioneering communities.
—P. A. Samuelson (1985)

In this chapter we discuss a number of topics in multivariable calculus. We begin by studying gradients and directional derivatives, which are useful tools in optimization theory. We go on to consider convex sets. Next, concave and quasiconcave functions are studied in some detail. The general Taylor's formula is briefly presented. Differentiable transformations, inverse and implicit function theorems are then studied along with functional dependence—a tricky concept which is discussed in somewhat more detail than in similar books. A discussion of existence and uniqueness results for systems of nonlinear equations concludes the chapter.

2.1 Gradients and Directional Derivatives

If $z = F(x, y)$ and C is any number, we call the graph of the equation $F(x, y) = C$ a **level curve** for F. Recall that the slope of the level curve $F(x, y) = C$ at a point (x, y) is given by the formula

$$F(x, y) = C \implies y' = -\frac{F_1'(x, y)}{F_2'(x, y)} \tag{1}$$

According to (1), if (x_0, y_0) is a particular point on the level curve $F(x, y) = C$, the slope at (x_0, y_0) is $-F_1'(x_0, y_0)/F_2'(x_0, y_0)$. The equation for the tangent line T shown in Fig. 1 is $y - y_0 = -[F_1'(x_0, y_0)/F_2'(x_0, y_0)](x - x_0)$, or rearranging,

$$F_1'(x_0, y_0)(x - x_0) + F_2'(x_0, y_0)(y - y_0) = 0 \tag{2}$$

Recalling the dot product from linear algebra (see (1.1.35)), equation (2) can be written as

$$(F_1'(x_0, y_0), F_2'(x_0, y_0)) \cdot (x - x_0, y - y_0) = 0 \tag{3}$$

The vector $\left(F_1'(x_0, y_0), F_2'(x_0, y_0)\right)$ is called the **gradient** of F at (x_0, y_0), and is often denoted by $\nabla F(x_0, y_0)$. The vector $(x - x_0, y - y_0)$ is a vector on the tangent T in Fig. 1, and (3) means that $\nabla F(x_0, y_0)$ is **orthogonal** to the tangent line T at (x_0, y_0).

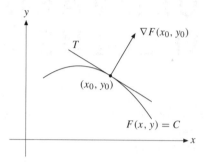

Figure 1 $\nabla F(x_0, y_0)$ is **orthogonal** to the tangent line T at (x_0, y_0).

EXAMPLE 1   Compute $\nabla F(\frac{1}{2}, 2)$ for $F(x, y) = xy$, and find the equation for the tangent to the curve $xy = 1$ at $(\frac{1}{2}, 2)$.

Solution: $F_1'(x, y) = y$ and $F_2'(x, y) = x$, so $\nabla F(\frac{1}{2}, 2) = (2, \frac{1}{2})$. Hence by (3), the equation of the tangent is

$$(2, \tfrac{1}{2}) \cdot (x - \tfrac{1}{2}, y - 2) = 0, \quad \text{i.e.} \quad 2x - 1 + \tfrac{1}{2}y - 1 = 0, \quad \text{or} \quad y = -4x + 4$$

Suppose more generally that $F(\mathbf{x}) = F(x_1, \ldots, x_n)$ is a function of n variables defined on an open set A in $\mathbb{R}^n$, and let $\mathbf{x}^0 = (x_1^0, \ldots, x_n^0)$ be a point in A. The **gradient** of F at $\mathbf{x}^0$ is the vector

$$\nabla F(\mathbf{x}^0) = \left(\frac{\partial F(\mathbf{x}^0)}{\partial x_1}, \ldots, \frac{\partial F(\mathbf{x}^0)}{\partial x_n} \right)$$

of first-order partial derivatives. Alternative notations for $\nabla F(\mathbf{x}^0)$ are $F'(\mathbf{x}^0)$ and $DF(\mathbf{x}^0)$.

Consider the level surface of $F(x_1, \ldots, x_n)$ corresponding to the level C, i.e. the set of points that satisfy

$$F(x_1, \ldots, x_n) = C$$

If $\mathbf{x}^0 = (x_1^0, \ldots, x_n^0)$ lies on this level surface, i.e. if $F(\mathbf{x}^0) = C$, then the **tangent hyperplane** to the level surface at $\mathbf{x}^0$ is the set of all $\mathbf{x} = (x_1, \ldots, x_n)$ such that

$$F_1'(\mathbf{x}^0)(x_1 - x_1^0) + \cdots + F_n'(\mathbf{x}^0)(x_n - x_n^0) = 0$$

Using the dot product we can write this as

$$\nabla F(\mathbf{x}^0) \cdot (\mathbf{x} - \mathbf{x}^0) = 0 \tag{4}$$

Since any point $\mathbf{x}$ in the tangent hyperplane satisfies (4), the gradient $\nabla F(\mathbf{x}^0)$ is orthogonal to the tangent hyperplane at $\mathbf{x}^0$. (See (1.1.43).) An illustration is given in Fig. 2 for $n = 3$. (We assume that $\nabla F(\mathbf{x}^0) \neq \mathbf{0}$.)

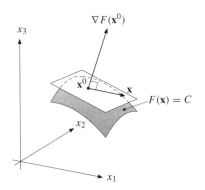
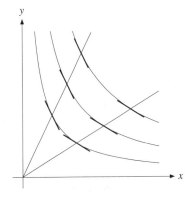

Figure 2 The gradient $\nabla F(\mathbf{x}^0)$ is orthogonal to the tangent plane of $F(\mathbf{x}) = C$ at $\mathbf{x}^0$.

Figure 3 f is homogeneous of degree k. The level curves are parallel along each ray from the origin.

NOTE 1 If the graph in Fig. 2 is defined by $z = f(x_1, x_2)$, then the tangent plane to this graph at the point (x_1^0, x_2^0, z^0) is (see e.g. EMEA),

$$f_1'(x_1^0, x_2^0)(x_1 - x_1^0) + f_2'(x_1^0, x_2^0)(x_2 - x_2^0) - 1 \cdot (z - z^0) = 0$$

Thus the vector $(f_1'(x_1^0, x_2^0), f_2'(x_1^0, x_2^0), -1)$ is orthogonal to the tangent plane of $z = f(x_1, x_2)$ at (x_1^0, x_2^0, z^0). This tangent plane is precisely the plane obtained from (4) by putting $F(x_1, x_2, z) = f(x_1, x_2) - z$.

EXAMPLE 2   Suppose that $f(x_1, \ldots, x_n) = f(\mathbf{x})$ is homogeneous of degree k. Then $f_i'(\mathbf{x})$ is homogeneous of degree $k - 1$ for $i = 1, \ldots, n$ (see e.g. EMEA). Hence, for $\lambda > 0$ we have $\nabla f(\lambda \mathbf{x}) = (f_1'(\lambda \mathbf{x}), \ldots, f_n'(\lambda \mathbf{x})) = (\lambda^{k-1} f_1'(\mathbf{x}), \ldots, \lambda^{k-1} f_n'(\mathbf{x})) = \lambda^{k-1} \nabla f(\mathbf{x})$. So, at each point on a given ray through the origin the gradients are proportional, which implies that the level surfaces are parallel. See Fig. 3. To summarize:

$$f(\mathbf{x}) \text{ homogeneous of degree } k \implies \left\{ \begin{array}{l} \text{The level surfaces are parallel} \\ \text{along each ray from the origin.} \end{array} \right. \tag{5}$$

The Directional Derivative

Let $z = f(\mathbf{x})$ be a function of n variables. The partial derivative $\partial f / \partial x_i$ measures the rate of change of $f(\mathbf{x})$ in the direction parallel to the ith coordinate axis. Each partial derivative says nothing about the behaviour of f in other directions. We introduce the concept of *directional derivative* in order to measure the rate of change of f in an arbitrary direction.

Consider the vector $\mathbf{x} = (x_1, \ldots, x_n)$ and let $\mathbf{a} = (a_1, \ldots, a_n) \neq \mathbf{0}$ be a given vector. If we move a distance $h \|\mathbf{a}\| > 0$ from $\mathbf{x}$ in the direction given by $\mathbf{a}$, we arrive at $\mathbf{x} + h\mathbf{a}$. The average rate of change of f from $\mathbf{x}$ to $\mathbf{x} + h\mathbf{a}$ is then $\big(f(\mathbf{x} + h\mathbf{a}) - f(\mathbf{x})\big)/h$. We define the *derivative of f along the vector* $\mathbf{a}$, denoted $f_\mathbf{a}'(\mathbf{x})$, by

$$f_\mathbf{a}'(\mathbf{x}) = \lim_{h \to 0} \frac{f(\mathbf{x} + h\mathbf{a}) - f(\mathbf{x})}{h} \tag{6}$$

or, with components,

$$f_\mathbf{a}'(x_1, \ldots, x_n) = \lim_{h \to 0} \frac{f(x_1 + ha_1, \ldots, x_n + ha_n) - f(x_1, \ldots, x_n)}{h}$$

(We assume that $\mathbf{x} + h\mathbf{a}$ lies in the domain of f for all sufficiently small h.) In particular, with $a_i = 1$ and $a_j = 0$ for $j \neq i$, the derivative in (6) is the partial derivative of f w.r.t. x_i.

Suppose f is C^1 in a set A, and let $\mathbf{x}$ be an interior point in A.[1] For an arbitrary vector $\mathbf{a}$, define the function g by $g(h) = f(\mathbf{x} + h\mathbf{a}) = f(x_1 + ha_1, \ldots, x_n + ha_n)$. Then $(g(h) - g(0))/h = (f(\mathbf{x} + h\mathbf{a}) - f(\mathbf{x}))/h$. Letting h tend to 0, equation (6) implies that $g'(0) = f_\mathbf{a}'(\mathbf{x})$. But according to the definition of $g(h)$ and the rule for differentiating composite functions, $g'(h) = \sum_{i=1}^n f_i'(\mathbf{x} + h\mathbf{a}) a_i$, so that $g'(0) = \sum_{i=1}^n f_i'(\mathbf{x}) a_i$. Hence we have shown that:

$$f_\mathbf{a}'(\mathbf{x}) = \sum_{i=1}^n f_i'(\mathbf{x}) a_i = \nabla f(\mathbf{x}) \cdot \mathbf{a} \tag{7}$$

Formula (7) shows that *the derivative of f along the vector $\mathbf{a}$ is equal to the dot product of the gradient of f and $\mathbf{a}$.*

If $\|\mathbf{a}\| = 1$, the number $f_\mathbf{a}'(\mathbf{x})$ is called the **directional derivative** of f at $\mathbf{x}$, in the direction $\mathbf{a}$. It is precisely when $\mathbf{a}$ is a vector with length 1 that we have the following nice interpretation of $f_\mathbf{a}'(\mathbf{x})$: Moving a distance h in the direction given by $\mathbf{a}$ changes the value of f by approximately $f_\mathbf{a}'(\mathbf{x})h$, provided h is small.

EXAMPLE 3   Find the directional derivative of $f(x, y) = x^2 + 2xy + y^3$ at the point $(x, y) = (1, 1)$ in the direction given by the vector $\mathbf{a} = \mathbf{b}/\|\mathbf{b}\|$, where $\mathbf{b} = (1, 3)$.

Solution: Let $\mathbf{b} = (1, 3)$. Then $\|\mathbf{b}\| = (1^2 + 3^2)^{1/2} = \sqrt{10}$. The vector $\mathbf{a} = (a_1, a_2) = (1/\sqrt{10}, 3/\sqrt{10})$ is a vector with length 1 and with the same direction as the vector $\mathbf{b}$. Now, $f_1'(x, y) = 2x + 2y$ and $f_2'(x, y) = 2x + 3y^2$, so that $f_1'(1, 1) = 4$, $f_2'(1, 1) = 5$. According to (7),

$$f_\mathbf{a}'(1, 1) = f_1'(1, 1)a_1 + f_2'(1, 1)a_2 = 4\frac{1}{\sqrt{10}} + 5\frac{3}{\sqrt{10}} = \frac{19}{10}\sqrt{10}$$

By introducing φ as the angle between the vectors $\nabla f(\mathbf{x})$ and $\mathbf{a}$ (see (1.1.40)), we have

$$f_\mathbf{a}'(\mathbf{x}) = \|\nabla f(\mathbf{x})\| \|\mathbf{a}\| \cos \varphi \tag{8}$$

Remember that $\cos \varphi \leq 1$ for all φ and $\cos 0 = 1$. So when $\|\mathbf{a}\| = 1$, it follows that at points where $\nabla f(\mathbf{x}) \neq \mathbf{0}$, the number $f_\mathbf{a}'(\mathbf{x})$ is largest when $\varphi = 0$, i.e. when $\mathbf{a}$ points in the same direction as $\nabla f(\mathbf{x})$, while $f_\mathbf{a}'(\mathbf{x})$ is smallest when $\varphi = \pi$ (and hence $\cos \varphi = -1$), i.e. when $\mathbf{a}$ points in the opposite direction to $\nabla f(\mathbf{x})$. Moreover, it follows that the length of $\nabla f(\mathbf{x})$ equals the magnitude of the maximum directional derivative.

The most important observations about the gradient are gathered in this theorem:

---

[1] Interior points, open sets, neighbourhoods, and related topological concepts are reviewed in Section 13.1.

THEOREM 2.1.1 (PROPERTIES OF THE GRADIENT)

Suppose that $f(\mathbf{x}) = f(x_1, \ldots, x_n)$ is C^1 in an open set A. Then, at points $\mathbf{x}$ where $\nabla f(\mathbf{x}) \neq \mathbf{0}$, the gradient $\nabla f(\mathbf{x}) = (f_1'(\mathbf{x}), f_2'(\mathbf{x}), \ldots, f_n'(\mathbf{x}))$ satisfies:

(a) $\nabla f(\mathbf{x})$ is orthogonal to the level surface through $\mathbf{x}$.

(b) $\nabla f(\mathbf{x})$ points in the direction of maximal increase of f.

(c) $\|\nabla f(\mathbf{x})\|$ measures how fast the function increases in the direction of maximal increase.

We assumed above that $\nabla f(\mathbf{x}) \neq \mathbf{0}$. Points $\mathbf{x}$ where $\nabla f(\mathbf{x}) = \mathbf{0}$ are called *stationary* points for f. If f is C^1, it follows from (7) that all directional derivatives are equal to 0 at a stationary point.

The Mean-Value Theorem

The mean-value theorem for functions of one variable (see e.g. EMEA) can easily be generalized to functions of several variables. Suppose that $\mathbf{x}$ and $\mathbf{y}$ both lie in $\mathbb{R}^n$. Then define the *closed and open line segments between* $\mathbf{x}$ *and* $\mathbf{y}$ respectively, as the sets

$$[\mathbf{x}, \mathbf{y}] = \{\lambda\mathbf{x} + (1 - \lambda)\mathbf{y} : \lambda \in [0, 1]\} \ \text{ and } \ (\mathbf{x}, \mathbf{y}) = \{\lambda\mathbf{x} + (1 - \lambda)\mathbf{y} : \lambda \in (0, 1)\}$$

THEOREM 2.1.2 (THE MEAN-VALUE THEOREM)

Suppose that $f : \mathbb{R}^n \to \mathbb{R}$ is C^1 in an open set containing $[\mathbf{x}, \mathbf{y}]$. Then there exists a point $\mathbf{w} \in (\mathbf{x}, \mathbf{y})$ such that

$$f(\mathbf{x}) - f(\mathbf{y}) = \nabla f(\mathbf{w}) \cdot (\mathbf{x} - \mathbf{y}) \tag{9}$$

Proof: Define $\varphi(\lambda) = f(\lambda\mathbf{x} + (1 - \lambda)\mathbf{y})$. Then $\varphi'(\lambda) = \nabla f(\lambda\mathbf{x} + (1 - \lambda)\mathbf{y}) \cdot (\mathbf{x} - \mathbf{y})$. According to the mean-value theorem for functions of one variable, there exists a number λ_0 in $(0, 1)$ such that $\varphi(1) - \varphi(0) = \varphi'(\lambda_0)$. Putting $\mathbf{w} = \lambda_0\mathbf{x} + (1 - \lambda_0)\mathbf{y}$, we get (9). ∎

PROBLEMS FOR SECTION 2.1

1. Compute the gradients of the following functions at the given points.

    (a) $f(x, y) = y^2 + xy$ at $(2, 1)$ (b) $g(x, y, z) = xe^{xy} - z^2$ at $(0, 0, 1)$

2. Let $f(t)$ be a C^1 function of t with $f'(t) \neq 0$.

    (a) Put $F(x, y) = f(x^2 + y^2)$. Find the gradient ∇F at an arbitrary point and show that it is parallel to the straight line which joins the point and the origin.

    (b) Put $G(x, y) = f(y/x)$. Find ∇G at an arbitrary point where $x \neq 0$, and show that it is orthogonal to the straight line joining the point and the origin.

3. Compute the directional derivatives of the following functions at the given points and in the given directions.

(a) $f(x, y) = 2x + y - 1$ at $(2,1)$, in the direction given by $(1,1)$.

(b) $g(x, y, z) = xe^{xy} - xy - z^2$ at $(0,1,1)$, in the direction given by $(1,1,1)$.

4. Let $f(x_1, \ldots, x_n) = x_1^2 + x_2^2 + \cdots + x_n^2$. Find the directional derivative of f in the direction given by the vector $\mathbf{a} = (a_1, a_2, \ldots, a_n)$ by using definition (6). Check the result by using (7). (Suppose that $\|\mathbf{a}\| = 1$.)

5. (a) Find the directional derivative of $f(x, y, z) = xy \ln(x^2+y^2+z^2)$ at the point $(1,1,1)$ in the direction given by the vector from the point $(3,2,1)$ to the point $(-1, 1, 2)$.

(b) Determine also the direction of maximal increase from the point $(1,1,1)$.

6. Suppose that $f(x, y)$ has continuous partial derivatives, that the maximum directional derivative of f at $(0,0)$ is equal to 4, and that it is attained in the direction given by the vector from the origin to the point $(1,3)$. Find $\nabla f(0, 0)$.

7. Let $\mathbf{b} = (b_1, \ldots, b_n)$ be a given vector and define the function $f(\mathbf{x}) = f(x_1, \ldots, x_n) = \mathbf{b} \cdot \mathbf{x}$. Show that the derivative of f along the vector $\mathbf{a} = (a_1, \ldots, a_n)$ is $\mathbf{b} \cdot \mathbf{a}$.

8. Let $f(\mathbf{v}) = f(v_1, \ldots, v_n)$ denote a positive valued differentiable function of n variables defined whenever $v_i > 0, i = 1, 2, \ldots, n$. The **directional elasticity** of f at the point $\mathbf{v}$ along the vector $\mathbf{v}/\|\mathbf{v}\| = \mathbf{a}$, hence in the direction from the origin to $\mathbf{v}$, is denoted by $\mathrm{El}_{\mathbf{a}} f(\mathbf{v})$ and is, by definition,

$$\mathrm{El}_{\mathbf{a}} f(\mathbf{v}) = \frac{\|\mathbf{v}\|}{f(\mathbf{v})} f_{\mathbf{a}}'(\mathbf{v}), \qquad \mathbf{a} = \frac{\mathbf{v}}{\|\mathbf{v}\|}$$

where $f_{\mathbf{a}}'(\mathbf{v})$ is the directional derivative of f in the direction given by $\mathbf{a}$. Use (7) to show that

$$\mathrm{El}_{\mathbf{a}} f(\mathbf{v}) = \sum_{i=1}^{n} \mathrm{El}_i f(\mathbf{v})$$

where $\mathrm{El}_i f(\mathbf{v})$ denotes the partial elasticity of f w.r.t. v_i. (When $f(\mathbf{v})$ is a production function, $\mathrm{El}_{\mathbf{a}} f(\mathbf{v})$ is called the **scale elasticity**.)

9. Prove that if F is C^2, then by differentiating the formula for y' in (1) w.r.t. x one has

$$y'' = -\frac{1}{(F_2')^3}[F_{11}''(F_2')^2 - 2F_{12}''F_1'F_2' + F_{22}''(F_1')^2] = \frac{1}{(F_2')^3}\begin{vmatrix} 0 & F_1' & F_2' \\ F_1' & F_{11}'' & F_{12}'' \\ F_2' & F_{21}'' & F_{22}'' \end{vmatrix} \quad (10)$$

2.2 Convex Sets

Convexity plays an important role in theoretical economics. In this book we shall see many examples of its importance.

A set S in the plane is called **convex** if each pair of points in S can be joined by a line segment lying entirely within S. Examples are given in Fig. 1. In (d) the non-convex set is the union $S_1 \cup S_2$ of two ovals, each of which is convex on its own.

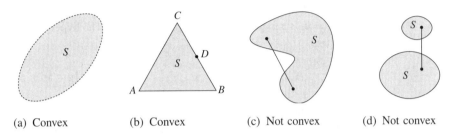

| (a) Convex | (b) Convex | (c) Not convex | (d) Not convex |

Figure 1 Convex and non-convex sets.

This definition of a convex set can be extended to sets in $\mathbb{R}^n$. Let $\mathbf{x}$ and $\mathbf{y}$ be any two points in $\mathbb{R}^n$. The closed **line segment** between $\mathbf{x}$ and $\mathbf{y}$ is the set

$$[\mathbf{x}, \mathbf{y}] = \{\mathbf{z} : \text{there exists } \lambda \in [0, 1] \text{ such that } \mathbf{z} = \lambda\mathbf{x} + (1 - \lambda)\mathbf{y}\} \tag{1}$$

whose members are the **convex combinations** $\mathbf{z} = \lambda\mathbf{x} + (1 - \lambda)\mathbf{y}$, with $0 \leq \lambda \leq 1$, of the two points $\mathbf{x}$ and $\mathbf{y}$. See Fig. 2. If $\lambda = 0$, then $\mathbf{z} = \mathbf{y}$. Moreover, $\lambda = 1$ gives $\mathbf{z} = \mathbf{x}$, and $\lambda = 1/2$ gives $\mathbf{z} = \frac{1}{2}\mathbf{x} + \frac{1}{2}\mathbf{y}$, the midpoint between $\mathbf{x}$ and $\mathbf{y}$. Note that if we let λ run through *all* real values, then $\mathbf{z}$ describes the whole of the straight line L through $\mathbf{x}$ and $\mathbf{y}$. This line passes through $\mathbf{y}$ and has the direction determined by $\mathbf{x} - \mathbf{y}$. (See Fig. 3 and (1.1.42).)

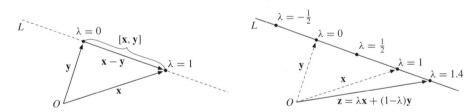

Figure 2 The closed segment $[\mathbf{x}, \mathbf{y}]$.   **Figure 3** The straight line through $\mathbf{x}$ and $\mathbf{y}$.

The definition of a convex set in $\mathbb{R}^n$ is now easy to formulate.

DEFINITION OF A CONVEX SET

A set S in $\mathbb{R}^n$ is called **convex** if $[\mathbf{x}, \mathbf{y}] \subseteq S$ for all $\mathbf{x}, \mathbf{y}$ in S, or equivalently, if

$$\lambda\mathbf{x} + (1 - \lambda)\mathbf{y} \in S \text{ for all } \mathbf{x}, \mathbf{y} \text{ in } S \text{ and all } \lambda \text{ in } [0, 1] \tag{2}$$

Note in particular that the empty set and also any set consisting of one single point are convex. Intuitively speaking, a convex set must be "connected" without any "holes", and its boundary must not "bend inwards" at any point.

EXAMPLE 1   The set H of all points $\mathbf{x} = (x_1, x_2, \ldots, x_n)$ in $\mathbb{R}^n$ that satisfy

$$\mathbf{p} \cdot \mathbf{x} = p_1 x_1 + p_2 x_2 + \cdots + p_n x_n = m \qquad (*)$$

where $\mathbf{p} \neq \mathbf{0}$, is a hyperplane in $\mathbb{R}^n$. (See (1.1.43).) The hyperplane H divides $\mathbb{R}^n$ into two convex sets,

$$H_+ = \{\mathbf{x} \in \mathbb{R}^n : \mathbf{p} \cdot \mathbf{x} \geq m\} \quad \text{and} \quad H_- = \{\mathbf{x} \in \mathbb{R}^n : \mathbf{p} \cdot \mathbf{x} \leq m\}$$

These two sets are called *half spaces*. To show that H_+ is convex, take two arbitrary points $\mathbf{x}^1$ and $\mathbf{x}^2$ in H_+. Then $\mathbf{p} \cdot \mathbf{x}^1 \geq m$ and $\mathbf{p} \cdot \mathbf{x}^2 \geq m$. For each λ in $[0, 1]$, we have to show that $\lambda \mathbf{x}^1 + (1 - \lambda)\mathbf{x}^2 \in H_+$, i.e. that $\mathbf{p} \cdot (\lambda \mathbf{x}^1 + (1 - \lambda)\mathbf{x}^2) \geq m$. It follows easily from the rules for the dot product (1.1.36) that

$$\mathbf{p} \cdot (\lambda \mathbf{x}^1 + (1 - \lambda)\mathbf{x}^2) = \mathbf{p} \cdot \lambda \mathbf{x}^1 + \mathbf{p} \cdot (1 - \lambda)\mathbf{x}^2$$
$$= \lambda \mathbf{p} \cdot \mathbf{x}^1 + (1 - \lambda)\mathbf{p} \cdot \mathbf{x}^2 \geq \lambda m + (1 - \lambda)m = m$$

(Where did we use the assumption that $\lambda \in [0, 1]$?) Convexity of H_- is shown in the same way, and it is equally easy to show that the hyperplane H itself is convex. (Convexity of H also follows from (3) below, since $H = H_+ \cap H_-$.)

If S and T are two convex sets in $\mathbb{R}^n$, then their intersection $S \cap T$ is also convex (see Fig. 4). More generally:

$$S_1, \ldots, S_m \text{ are convex sets in } \mathbb{R}^n \implies S_1 \cap \cdots \cap S_m \text{ is convex} \qquad (3)$$

Proof: (One of the world's simplest.) Suppose that $\mathbf{x}$ and $\mathbf{y}$ both lie in $S = S_1 \cap \cdots \cap S_m$. Then $\mathbf{x}$ and $\mathbf{y}$ both lie in S_i for each $i = 1, \ldots, m$. Because S_i is convex, the line segment $[\mathbf{x}, \mathbf{y}]$ must lie in S_i for each $i = 1, \ldots, m$ and hence in the intersection $S_1 \cap \cdots \cap S_m = S$. This means that S is convex.   ∎

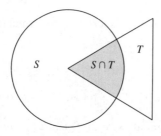

Figure 4 $S \cap T$ is convex, but $S \cup T$ is not.

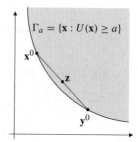

Figure 5 Γ_a is a convex set.

The union of convex sets is usually not convex. See Fig. 4 again, as well as Fig. 1 (d).

EXAMPLE 2   Let $U(\mathbf{x}) = U(x_1, \ldots, x_n)$ denote the utility function of an individual. If $U(\mathbf{x}^0) = a$, then the **upper level set** or **upper contour set** $\Gamma_a = \{\mathbf{x} : U(\mathbf{x}) \geq a\}$ consists of all commodity vectors $\mathbf{x}$ that the individual values at least as much as $\mathbf{x}^0$. In consumer theory, Γ_a is often assumed to be a convex set for every a. (The function U is then called *quasiconcave*.) Figure 5 shows a typical upper level set for the case of two goods.

EXAMPLE 3   Let $\mathbf{x} = (x_1, \ldots, x_n)$ represent a commodity vector as in Example 2 and let $\mathbf{p} = (p_1, \ldots, p_n)$ be the corresponding price vector. Then $\mathbf{p} \cdot \mathbf{x} = p_1 x_1 + \cdots + p_n x_n$ is the cost of buying $\mathbf{x}$. A consumer who has m dollars to spend on the commodities, has a *budget set* $\mathcal{B}(\mathbf{p}, m)$, defined by the inequalities

$$\mathbf{p} \cdot \mathbf{x} = p_1 x_1 + \cdots + p_n x_n \leq m \quad \text{and} \quad x_1 \geq 0, \ldots, x_n \geq 0$$

The budget set $\mathcal{B}(\mathbf{p}, m)$ consists of all commodity vectors that the consumer can afford. Let $\mathbb{R}_+^n$ denote the set of all $\mathbf{x}$ for which $x_1 \geq 0, \ldots, x_n \geq 0$. Then $\mathcal{B} = H_- \cap \mathbb{R}_+^n$, using the notation from Example 1. It is easy to see that $\mathbb{R}_+^n$ is a convex set. (If $\mathbf{x} \geq 0$ and $\mathbf{y} \geq 0$ and $\lambda \in [0, 1]$, then evidently $\lambda \mathbf{x} + (1 - \lambda)\mathbf{y} \geq 0$.) Hence $\mathcal{B}(\mathbf{p}, m)$ is convex according to (3), since we showed in Example 1 that H_- is convex. Note that this means that if the consumer can afford each of the commodity vectors $\mathbf{x}$ and $\mathbf{y}$, she can also afford any convex combination of these commodity vectors.

PROBLEMS FOR SECTION 2.2

1. Determine (in a rough way) which of the following four sets are convex:

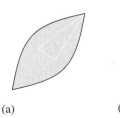   

        (a)   (b)   (c)   (d)

2. Determine which of the following sets are convex by drawing each in the xy-plane.

    (a) $\{(x, y) : x^2 + y^2 < 2\}$ (b) $\{(x, y) : x \geq 0, \ y \geq 0\}$

    (c) $\{(x, y) : x^2 + y^2 > 8\}$ (d) $\{(x, y) : x \geq 0, \ y \geq 0, \ xy \geq 1\}$

    (e) $\{(x, y) : xy \leq 1\}$ (f) $\{(x, y) : \sqrt{x} + \sqrt{y} \leq 2\}$

3. Let S be the set of all points $(x_1, \ldots, x_n)$ in $\mathbb{R}^n$ that satisfy all the m inequalities

$$a_{11}x_1 + a_{12}x_2 + \cdots + a_{1n}x_n \leq b_1$$
$$a_{21}x_1 + a_{22}x_2 + \cdots + a_{2n}x_n \leq b_2$$
$$\cdots\cdots\cdots\cdots\cdots\cdots\cdots\cdots\cdots\cdots\cdots$$
$$a_{m1}x_1 + a_{m2}x_2 + \cdots + a_{mn}x_n \leq b_m$$

and moreover are such that $x_1 \geq 0, \ldots, x_n \geq 0$. Show that S is a convex set.

4. If S and T are two sets in $\mathbb{R}^n$ and a and b are scalars, let $aS + bT$ denote the set of all points of the form $a\mathbf{x} + b\mathbf{y}$, where $\mathbf{x} \in S$ and $\mathbf{y} \in T$. Prove that if S and T are both convex, then so is $aS + bT$.

5. If S and T are any two sets, the **Cartesian product** $S \times T$ of S and T is defined by $S \times T = \{(s, t) : s \in S, t \in T\}$, as illustrated in the figure for the case when S and T are intervals of the real line. Prove that if S and T are a convex sets in $\mathbb{R}^n$ and $\mathbb{R}^m$, respectively, then $S \times T$ is also convex (in $\mathbb{R}^{n+m}$).

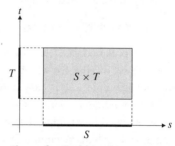

Figure for Problem 5

6. Let $S = \{\mathbf{x} \in \mathbb{R}^n : \|\mathbf{x}\| \leq r\}$ be the closed n-dimensional ball centred at the origin and with radius $r > 0$.

   (a) Prove that S is convex. (Use the fact that if $\mathbf{x}$ and $\mathbf{y}$ are points in $\mathbb{R}^n$ and a and b are real numbers, then $\|a\mathbf{x} + b\mathbf{y}\| \leq \|a\mathbf{x}\| + \|b\mathbf{y}\| \leq |a| \|\mathbf{x}\| + |b| \|\mathbf{y}\|$.)

   (b) If we replace $\leq$ with $<$, $=$, or $\geq$ in the definition of S, we get three new sets S_1, S_2, and S_3. Which of them is/are convex?

HARDER PROBLEMS

7. (a) Let S be a set of real numbers with the property that if $x_1, x_2 \in S$, then the midpoint $\frac{1}{2}(x_1 + x_2)$ also belongs to S. Show by an example that S is not necessarily convex.

   (b) Does it make any difference if S is closed?

8. Show that if a convex subset S of $\mathbb{R}$ contains more than one point, it must be an interval. (*Hint:* Show first that if S is bounded, then S must be an interval with endpoints inf S and sup S. See Section A.2.)

2.3 Concave and Convex Functions I

Recall that a C^2 function of one variable $y = f(x)$ is called concave on the interval I if $f''(x) \leq 0$ for all x in I—the graph then turns its hollow side downwards: ∩.

We need a definition that is valid more generally and preferably for functions of n variables that may not even be differentiable. Here is our first geometric attempt.

The function f is called **concave (convex)** *if it is defined on a convex set and the line segment joining any two points on the graph is never above (below) the graph.*

For concave functions of two variables the definition is illustrated in Fig. 1.

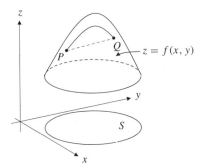

Figure 1 $f(x, y)$ is concave; for all points P and Q on the graph of f, the line segment PQ lies below the graph.

Figure 2 $TR' = f(\lambda \mathbf{x} + (1 - \lambda)\mathbf{x}^0) \geq TR = \lambda f(\mathbf{x}) + (1 - \lambda) f(\mathbf{x}^0)$.

This definition is difficult to use directly. After all, for a function that is specified by a complicated formula, it is far from evident whether the condition is satisfied or not.

The two points P and Q in Fig. 2 correspond to points $\mathbf{x}^0$ and $\mathbf{x}$ in the domain of f such that $P = (\mathbf{x}^0, f(\mathbf{x}^0))$ and $Q = (\mathbf{x}, f(\mathbf{x}))$. An arbitrary point R on the line segment PQ has the coordinates $\lambda Q + (1 - \lambda)P = (\lambda \mathbf{x} + (1 - \lambda)\mathbf{x}^0, \lambda f(\mathbf{x}) + (1 - \lambda) f(\mathbf{x}^0))$ for a suitable λ in [0, 1]. This point lies directly above the point $\lambda \mathbf{x} + (1 - \lambda)\mathbf{x}^0$ on the line segment between $\mathbf{x}$ and $\mathbf{x}^0$ in the "$\mathbf{x}$-plane". The corresponding point on the graph of f can be expressed as $R' = (\lambda \mathbf{x} + (1 - \lambda)\mathbf{x}^0, f(\lambda \mathbf{x} + (1 - \lambda)\mathbf{x}^0))$. The fact that R lies below, or in any case not above R', can be expressed by the following inequality:

$$f(\lambda \mathbf{x} + (1 - \lambda)\mathbf{x}^0) \geq \lambda f(\mathbf{x}) + (1 - \lambda) f(\mathbf{x}^0)$$

This motivates the following algebraic definition:

DEFINITION OF A CONCAVE FUNCTION

A function $f(\mathbf{x}) = f(x_1, \ldots, x_n)$ defined on a convex set S is **concave** on S if

$$f(\lambda \mathbf{x} + (1 - \lambda)\mathbf{x}^0) \geq \lambda f(\mathbf{x}) + (1 - \lambda) f(\mathbf{x}^0) \tag{1}$$

for all $\mathbf{x}$ and $\mathbf{x}^0$ in S and all λ in (0, 1).

$f(\mathbf{x})$ is **convex** if (1) holds with $\geq$ replaced by $\leq$.

Note that for $\lambda = 0$ and for $\lambda = 1$, we always have equality in (1).

If we have *strict* inequality in (1) whenever $\mathbf{x} \neq \mathbf{x}^0$, then f is **strictly concave**. The function whose graph is drawn in Fig. 1 is, therefore, strictly concave.

The function f is **convex** on S if $-f$ is concave. Hence, f is convex if (1) is valid with $\geq$ replaced by $\leq$. Furthermore, f is **strictly convex** if $-f$ is strictly concave.

The inequality in (1) is written in vector form. Representing the vectors by their components, we have an equivalent version of (1):

$$f\left(\lambda x_1 + (1 - \lambda)x_1^0, \ \ldots, \ \lambda x_n + (1 - \lambda)x_n^0\right) \geq \lambda f(x_1, \ldots, x_n) + (1 - \lambda)f(x_1^0, \ldots, x_n^0)$$

It is usually impractical to apply definition (1) directly to show that a function is concave or convex in a certain set. We shall later develop a number of theorems that often help us to decide concavity/convexity with ease. Let us still consider two examples in which we rely on definition (1).

EXAMPLE 1   Use definition (1) to show that the function f defined for all (x, y) by

$$f(x, y) = 1 - x^2 \qquad \text{(so y does not appear in the formula for f)}$$

is concave. Is it strictly concave?

Solution: Let (x, y) and (x^0, y^0) be arbitrary points in the plane. We must show that for all λ in $(0, 1)$,

$$f(\lambda x + (1 - \lambda)x^0, \ \lambda y + (1 - \lambda)y^0) \geq \lambda f(x, y) + (1 - \lambda)f(x^0, y^0) \qquad \text{(i)}$$

Using the definition of f, we see that (i) is equivalent to $1 - [\lambda x + (1 - \lambda)x^0]^2 \geq \lambda(1 - x^2) + (1 - \lambda)[1 - (x^0)^2]$. Expanding and collecting all terms on the left-hand side yields

$$\lambda(1 - \lambda)\left[x^2 - 2xx^0 + (x^0)^2\right] = \lambda(1 - \lambda)(x - x^0)^2 \geq 0 \qquad \text{(ii)}$$

This inequality is obviously satisfied for all λ in $(0, 1)$. Thus $f(x, y)$ is concave.

When $x = x^0$, we have equality in (ii), and thus equality in (i) for all values of y and y^0. But then f cannot be strictly concave.

NOTE 1   The one-variable function $g(x) = 1 - x^2$ is concave. Example 1 showed that it is also concave considered as a function of two variables, x and y. In general, it follows directly from the definitions that if $g(x_1, \ldots, x_p)$ is concave (convex) in $(x_1, \ldots, x_p)$, then for $n > p$, $f(x_1, \ldots, x_p, x_{p+1}, \ldots, x_n) = g(x_1, \ldots, x_p)$ is concave (convex) in $(x_1, \ldots, x_n)$,

Figure 3 shows a portion of the graph of a function of the form $f(x, y) = g(x)$. Here $g(x)$ is concave, and therefore so is $f(x, y)$. Through each point on the graph there is a straight line parallel to the y-axis which lies *in* the graph. This shows that f cannot be strictly concave, even though g is.

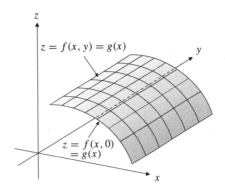

Figure 3 g is strictly concave; f is concave,
but not strictly concave.

EXAMPLE 2   Show that the linear function $f(\mathbf{x}) = \mathbf{a} \cdot \mathbf{x} = a_1 x_1 + \cdots + a_n x_n$, where $\mathbf{a} = (a_1, \ldots, a_n)$
is constant, is both concave and convex.

Solution: From the rules for the dot product, $f(\lambda \mathbf{x} + (1-\lambda)\mathbf{x}^0) = \mathbf{a} \cdot (\lambda \mathbf{x} + (1-\lambda)\mathbf{x}^0) =$
$\lambda \mathbf{a} \cdot \mathbf{x} + (1 - \lambda)\mathbf{a} \cdot \mathbf{x}^0 = \lambda f(\mathbf{x}) + (1 - \lambda)f(\mathbf{x}^0)$. Inequality (1) is satisfied with equality,
and f is both concave and convex, but not strictly concave or strictly convex. (For $n = 2$
the graph of f is a plane in 3-space, and we have shown that all points on the line segment
between (x_1, x_2) and (x_1^0, x_2^0) lie in the plane.)

Concavity/Convexity for C^2 Functions

Recall that a C^2 function $f(x)$ of one variable is concave in the interval I if and only if
$f''(x) \leq 0$ in I, whereas $f''(x) < 0$ in I is sufficient, but not necessary for $f(x)$ to be
strictly concave. (See e.g. EMEA.) For functions of two variables, there is a corresponding
characterization. (It is a special case of the next two theorems which are proved at the end
of this section.)

THEOREM 2.3.1

Let $z = f(x, y)$ be a C^2 function defined on an open convex set S in the plane.
Then (all inequalities must hold throughout S):

(a) f is convex $\iff$ $f_{11}'' \geq 0$, $f_{22}'' \geq 0$, and $f_{11}'' f_{22}'' - (f_{12}'')^2 \geq 0$

(b) f is concave $\iff$ $f_{11}'' \leq 0$, $f_{22}'' \leq 0$, and $f_{11}'' f_{22}'' - (f_{12}'')^2 \geq 0$

(c) $f_{11}'' > 0$ and $f_{11}'' f_{22}'' - (f_{12}'')^2 > 0$ $\implies$ f is strictly convex

(d) $f_{11}'' < 0$ and $f_{11}'' f_{22}'' - (f_{12}'')^2 > 0$ $\implies$ f is strictly concave

NOTE 2   The implications in parts (c) and (d) cannot be reversed. For example, $f(x, y) =$
$-x^4 - y^4$ is strictly concave in the whole plane, even though $f_{11}''(0, 0) = 0$.

NOTE 3 From the two inequalities specified in part (c), it follows that $f_{22}''(x, y) > 0$ as well. (In fact, the second inequality implies $f_{11}'' f_{22}'' > (f_{12}'')^2 \geq 0$. Thus if $f_{11}'' > 0$, then also $f_{22}'' > 0$.) In a similar way, from the two inequalities in part (d), it follows that $f_{22}''(x, y) < 0$. (Compare Note 1.8.1.)

EXAMPLE 3   Let $f(x, y) = 2x - y - x^2 + 2xy - y^2$ for all (x, y). Is f concave/convex?

Solution: We find that $f_{11}'' = -2$, $f_{12}'' = f_{21}'' = 2$, and $f_{22}'' = -2$. Hence $f_{11}'' f_{22}'' - (f_{12}'')^2 = 0$. We see that the conditions in part (b) in Theorem 2.3.1 are satisfied, so f is concave for all (x, y).

EXAMPLE 4   Let $f(x, y) = x^2 - y^2 - xy - x^3$ for all (x, y). Find the largest domain S in which f is concave.

Solution: We find that $f_{11}'' = 2 - 6x$, $f_{12}'' = f_{21}'' = -1$, and $f_{22}'' = -2$. Hence $f_{11}'' \leq 0$ iff $2 - 6x \leq 0$, i.e. $x \geq 1/3$. Moreover, $f_{11}'' f_{22}'' - (f_{12}'')^2 = 12x - 5 \geq 0$ iff $x \geq 5/12$. Since $5/12 > 1/3$, we conclude that the set S consists of all (x, y) where $x \geq 5/12$.

EXAMPLE 5   Check the concavity/convexity of the Cobb–Douglas function

$$f(x, y) = x^a y^b, \qquad a + b \leq 1, \ a \geq 0, \ b \geq 0$$

defined on the set $S = \{(x, y) : x > 0, \ y > 0\}$.

Solution: We find that

$$f_{11}'' = a(a-1)x^{a-2}y^b, \quad f_{12}'' = abx^{a-1}y^{b-1}, \quad \text{and} \quad f_{22}'' = b(b-1)x^a y^{b-2}$$

Since a and b belong to $[0,1]$, one has $f_{11}'' \leq 0$ and $f_{22}'' \leq 0$. Moreover, $f_{11}'' f_{22}'' - (f_{12}'')^2 = abx^{2a-2}y^{2b-2}(1-a-b) \geq 0$ in S. Thus the conditions in part (b) of Theorem 2.3.1 are satisfied and $f(x, y)$ is concave in S. If a and b are positive and $a + b < 1$, then $f_{11}'' < 0$ and $f_{11}'' f_{22}'' - (f_{12}'')^2 > 0$, so f is strictly concave according to (d) in Theorem 2.3.1.

The results in Theorem 2.3.1 on concavity/convexity of functions of two variables can be generalized to functions of n variables. Suppose that $z = f(\mathbf{x}) = f(x_1, \ldots, x_n)$ is a C^2 function in a open convex set S in $\mathbb{R}^n$. The matrix

$$\mathbf{f}''(\mathbf{x}) = (f_{ij}''(\mathbf{x}))_{n \times n} \tag{2}$$

is called the *Hessian (matrix)* of f at $\mathbf{x}$, and the n determinants

$$D_r(\mathbf{x}) = \begin{vmatrix} f_{11}''(\mathbf{x}) & f_{12}''(\mathbf{x}) & \cdots & f_{1r}''(\mathbf{x}) \\ f_{21}''(\mathbf{x}) & f_{22}''(\mathbf{x}) & \cdots & f_{2r}''(\mathbf{x}) \\ \vdots & \vdots & \ddots & \vdots \\ f_{r1}''(\mathbf{x}) & f_{r2}''(\mathbf{x}) & \cdots & f_{rr}''(\mathbf{x}) \end{vmatrix}, \quad r = 1, 2, \ldots, n \tag{3}$$

are the *leading principal minors* of $\mathbf{f}''(\mathbf{x})$—see Section 1.8.

Theorem 2.3.1 (c) and (d) can then be generalized as follows:

THEOREM 2.3.2 (STRICT CONVEXITY/CONCAVITY: SUFFICIENT CONDITIONS)

Suppose that $f(\mathbf{x}) = f(x_1, \ldots, x_n)$ is a C^2 function defined on an open, convex set S in $\mathbb{R}^n$. Let $D_r(\mathbf{x})$ be defined by (3). Then:

(a) $D_r(\mathbf{x}) > 0$ for all $\mathbf{x}$ in S and all $r = 1, \ldots, n$ $\implies$ f is strictly convex.

(b) $(-1)^r D_r(\mathbf{x}) > 0$ for all $\mathbf{x}$ in S and all $r = 1, \ldots, n$ $\implies$ f is strictly concave.

When $n = 2$ and $\mathbf{x} = (x, y)$, then $D_1(\mathbf{x}) = f_{11}''(\mathbf{x})$ and $D_2(\mathbf{x}) = \begin{vmatrix} f_{11}''(\mathbf{x}) & f_{12}''(\mathbf{x}) \\ f_{21}''(\mathbf{x}) & f_{22}''(\mathbf{x}) \end{vmatrix}$.

Hence the conditions in (a) in Theorem 2.3.2 reduce to those in part (c) of Theorem 2.3.1, and the conditions in (b) reduce to those in part (d) of Theorem 2.3.1.

Parts (a) and (b) of Theorem 2.3.1 can also be generalized. To do so, however, we must consider the signs of *all* the principal minors of the Hessian matrix $\mathbf{f}''(\mathbf{x}) = (f_{ij}''(\mathbf{x}))_{n \times n}$. Recall from Section 1.8 that a principal minor $\Delta_r(\mathbf{x})$ of order r in $\mathbf{f}''(\mathbf{x}) = (f_{ij}''(\mathbf{x}))_{n \times n}$ is obtained by deleting all but r rows and all but the r columns with the same numbers. (Proofs of Theorems 2.3.2 and 2.3.3 are given at the end of this section.)

THEOREM 2.3.3 (CONVEXITY/CONCAVITY: NECESSARY/SUFFICIENT CONDITIONS)

Suppose that $f(\mathbf{x}) = f(x_1, \ldots, x_n)$ is a C^2 function defined on an open, convex set S in $\mathbb{R}^n$. Let $\Delta_r(\mathbf{x})$ denote a generic principal minor of order r in the Hessian matrix. Then:

(a) f is convex in S $\iff$ $\Delta_r(\mathbf{x}) \geq 0$ for all $\mathbf{x}$ in S and all $\Delta_r(\mathbf{x}), r = 1, \ldots, n$.

(b) f is concave in S $\iff$ $(-1)^r \Delta_r(\mathbf{x}) \geq 0$ for all $\mathbf{x}$ in S and all $\Delta_r(\mathbf{x})$, $r = 1, \ldots, n$.

EXAMPLE 6   Examine the convexity/concavity of the function f defined for all x, y, and z by
$f(x, y, z) = 100 - 2x^2 - y^2 - 3z - xy - e^{x+y+z}$.

Solution: The Hessian of f is $\mathbf{f}''(x, y, z) = \begin{pmatrix} -4 - e^u & -1 - e^u & -e^u \\ -1 - e^u & -2 - e^u & -e^u \\ -e^u & -e^u & -e^u \end{pmatrix}$, where

$u = x + y + z$. The three leading principal minors are $D_1 = f_{11}'' = -4 - e^u$ and

$$D_2 = \begin{vmatrix} -4 - e^u & -1 - e^u \\ -1 - e^u & -2 - e^u \end{vmatrix} = 7 + 4e^u, \quad D_3 = \begin{vmatrix} -4 - e^u & -1 - e^u & -e^u \\ -1 - e^u & -2 - e^u & -e^u \\ -e^u & -e^u & -e^u \end{vmatrix} = -7e^u.$$

Thus $D_1 < 0$, $D_2 > 0$, and $D_3 < 0$. By Theorem 2.3.2 (b), f is strictly concave.

NOTE 4 For any fixed open convex set S in $\mathbb{R}^n$, if we combine the statements in Theorems 2.3.2 and 2.3.3 with Theorem 1.8.1, we get the following results:

The Hessian matrix $\mathbf{f}''(\mathbf{x})$ is positive definite in $S \implies f(\mathbf{x})$ is strictly convex in S (4)

The Hessian matrix $\mathbf{f}''(\mathbf{x})$ is negative definite in $S \implies f(\mathbf{x})$ is strictly concave in S (5)

$f(\mathbf{x})$ is convex in $S \iff$ the Hessian matrix $\mathbf{f}''(\mathbf{x})$ is positive semidefinite in S (6)

$f(\mathbf{x})$ is concave in $S \iff$ the Hessian matrix $\mathbf{f}''(\mathbf{x})$ is negative semidefinite in S (7)

Useful Results

Using Theorems 2.3.2 and 2.3.3 to decide convexity/concavity can be quite hard, although easier than relying directly on the definitions. The following two theorems can sometimes ease the task of establishing concavity/convexity.

THEOREM 2.3.4

If f and g are functions defined on a convex set S in $\mathbb{R}^n$, then:

(a) f and g are concave and $a \geq 0, b \geq 0$ $\implies$ $af + bg$ is concave

(b) f and g are convex and $a \geq 0, b \geq 0$ $\implies$ $af + bg$ is convex

Proof: We prove (a). The proof of (b) is similar.
(a) Put $G(\mathbf{x}) = af(\mathbf{x}) + bg(\mathbf{x})$. For λ in $(0, 1)$ and $\mathbf{x}, \mathbf{x}^0$ in S we have

$$\begin{aligned}
G(\lambda\mathbf{x} + (1 - \lambda)\mathbf{x}^0) &= af(\lambda\mathbf{x} + (1 - \lambda)\mathbf{x}^0) + bg(\lambda\mathbf{x} + (1 - \lambda)\mathbf{x}^0) \\
&\geq a\big[\lambda f(\mathbf{x}) + (1 - \lambda)f(\mathbf{x}^0)\big] + b\big[\lambda g(\mathbf{x}) + (1 - \lambda)g(\mathbf{x}^0)\big] \\
&= \lambda\big[af(\mathbf{x}) + bg(\mathbf{x})\big] + (1 - \lambda)\big[af(\mathbf{x}^0) + bg(\mathbf{x}^0)\big] \\
&= \lambda G(\mathbf{x}) + (1 - \lambda)G(\mathbf{x}^0)
\end{aligned}$$

Here we use the definition of G first, and then the definition of concavity of f and g together with $a \geq 0, b \geq 0$. The implied inequality says that G is concave.   ∎

The results in Theorem 2.3.4 can obviously be generalized. For instance,

$f_1, \ldots, f_m$ concave and $a_1 \geq 0, \ldots, a_m \geq 0 \implies a_1 f_1 + \cdots + a_m f_m$ concave   (8)

The composition of two concave functions is not necessarily concave. If for example, $f(x) = -x^2$ and $F(u) = -e^u$, then f and F are both (strictly) concave, but the composite function $F(f(x)) = -e^{-x^2}$ is actually convex in an interval about the origin.

But if we also require the exterior function to be *increasing*, then the composite function is concave. In general we have the following important result:

THEOREM 2.3.5

Suppose that $f(\mathbf{x})$ is defined for all $\mathbf{x}$ in a convex set S in $\mathbb{R}^n$ and that F is defined over an interval in $\mathbb{R}$ that contains $f(\mathbf{x})$ for all $\mathbf{x}$ in S. Then:

(a) $f(\mathbf{x})$ is concave and $F(u)$ is concave and increasing $\Rightarrow U(\mathbf{x}) = F(f(\mathbf{x}))$ is concave

(b) $f(\mathbf{x})$ is convex and $F(u)$ is convex and increasing $\Rightarrow U(\mathbf{x}) = F(f(\mathbf{x}))$ is convex

(c) $f(\mathbf{x})$ is concave and $F(u)$ is convex and decreasing $\Rightarrow U(\mathbf{x}) = F(f(\mathbf{x}))$ is convex

(d) $f(\mathbf{x})$ is convex and $F(u)$ is concave and decreasing $\Rightarrow U(\mathbf{x}) = F(f(\mathbf{x}))$ is concave

Proof: (a) Let $\mathbf{x}, \mathbf{x}^0 \in S$ and let $\lambda \in (0, 1)$. Then

$$U(\lambda\mathbf{x} + (1-\lambda)\mathbf{x}^0) = F\big(f(\lambda\mathbf{x} + (1-\lambda)\mathbf{x}^0)\big) \geq F\big(\lambda f(\mathbf{x}) + (1-\lambda)f(\mathbf{x}^0)\big)$$
$$\geq \lambda F(f(\mathbf{x})) + (1-\lambda)F(f(\mathbf{x}^0)) = \lambda U(\mathbf{x}) + (1-\lambda)U(\mathbf{x}^0)$$

The first inequality uses the concavity of f and the fact that F is increasing. The second inequality is due to the concavity of F.

The statement in (b) is shown in the same way. We then obtain (c) and (d) from (a) and (b) by replacing F with $-F$. ∎

NOTE 5 Suppose the functions f and F in (a) are C^2 functions of *one* variable. With $U(x) = F(f(x))$, then $U'(x) = F'(f(x)) \cdot f'(x)$ and $U''(x) = F''(f(x)) \cdot (f'(x))^2 + F'(f(x)) \cdot f''(x)$. Because F is concave and increasing and f is concave, $F'' \leq 0$, $F' \geq 0$, and $f'' \leq 0$. It follows immediately that $U''(x) \leq 0$. This "calculus" proof of (a) is valid for C^2 functions of one variable.

If f is a C^2 function of n variables, it is possible to prove (a) partly relying on Theorem 2.3.3(b), but such a proof would be rather complicated. After attempting it, however, you might come to appreciate the extreme simplicity of the proof above, which needs no differentiability assumptions at all.

If we drop the requirement in (a) that F be concave, then $U(\mathbf{x})$ is not necessarily concave. If for example $f(x) = \sqrt{x}$ and $F(u) = u^3$, then f is concave for $x \geq 0$ and F is increasing, but $U(x) = F(f(x)) = x^{3/2}$ is *convex* rather than concave.

NOTE 6 The results in Theorem 2.3.5 can easily be generalized to the case $U(\mathbf{x}) = F(f_1(\mathbf{x}), \ldots, f_m(\mathbf{x}))$, where the functions $f_1(\mathbf{x}), \ldots, f_m(\mathbf{x})$ are all concave (convex) and $F(u_1, \ldots, u_m)$ is concave (convex) and moreover increasing in each variable.

If $f(\mathbf{x}) = \mathbf{a} \cdot \mathbf{x} + b$, so that f is an affine function of $\mathbf{x}$, then in (a) and (b), the assumption that F is increasing can be dropped. Indeed, in the proof of (a), the first inequality used the concavity of f and the fact that F is increasing. When f is affine, this inequality becomes an equality, and the rest of the argument is as before. Thus:

A concave (convex) function of an affine function is concave (convex)   (9)

EXAMPLE 7   Examine the concavity/convexity of the following functions:

(a) $f(x, y, z) = ax^2 + by^2 + cz^2$ (a, b, and c are nonnegative)

(b) $g(x, y, z) = e^{ax^2 + by^2 + cz^2}$ (a, b, and c are nonnegative)

(c) $h(x_1, \ldots, x_n) = (a_1 x_1 + \cdots + a_n x_n)^2$

Solution: The function f is convex as a sum of convex functions. The function g is also convex. In fact, $g(x, y, z) = e^u$, with $u = f(x, y, z) = ax^2 + by^2 + cz^2$. Here the transformation $u \mapsto e^u$ is convex and increasing, and u is convex, so by Theorem 2.3.5(b), g is convex. Finally, h is a convex function ($u \mapsto u^2$) of a linear function, and thus convex according to (9).

EXAMPLE 8   Define the function G on $S = \{(x, y) : x^2 + y^2 < a^2\}$ by

$$G(x, y) = Ax + By + \ln[a^2 - (x^2 + y^2)]$$

Show that G is concave in S. (A, B, and a are constants. The domain of G is S, because $\ln u$ is defined only when $u > 0$.)

Solution: The function $g(x, y) = Ax + By$ is linear and hence concave by Example 2. Define $h(x, y) = \ln[a^2 - (x^2 + y^2)]$. If we put $f(x, y) = a^2 - x^2 - y^2$ and $F(u) = \ln u$, then $h(x, y) = F(f(x, y))$. As a sum of concave functions, $f(x, y)$ is concave. Moreover, $F'(u) = 1/u$ and $F''(u) = -1/u^2$, so F is increasing and concave. According to (a) in Theorem 2.3.5, the function $h(x, y)$ is concave, so $G(x, y) = g(x, y) + h(x, y)$ is concave as a sum of concave functions.

We end this section by proving Theorems 2.3.3 and 2.3.2.

Proof of Theorem 2.3.3: (a) Let us first show $\Leftarrow$. Take two points $\mathbf{x}$, $\mathbf{x}^0$ in S and let $t \in [0, 1]$. Define $g(t) = f(\mathbf{x}^0 + t(\mathbf{x} - \mathbf{x}^0)) = f(t\mathbf{x} + (1 - t)\mathbf{x}^0)$. The chain rule for functions of several variables gives $g'(t) = \sum_{i=1}^{n} f_i'(\mathbf{x}^0 + t(\mathbf{x} - \mathbf{x}^0))(x_i - x_i^0)$. Using the chain rule again, we get

$$g''(t) = \sum_{i=1}^{n} \sum_{j=1}^{n} f_{ij}''(\mathbf{x}^0 + t(\mathbf{x} - \mathbf{x}^0))(x_i - x_i^0)(x_j - x_j^0) \tag{i}$$

By the assumption in (a) that $\Delta_r(\mathbf{y}) \geq 0$ for all $\mathbf{y}$ in S and all $r = 1, \ldots, n$, Theorem 1.8.1 (b) implies that the quadratic form in (i) is ≥ 0 for t in $[0, 1]$. This shows that g is convex. In particular,

$$\begin{aligned} g(t) = g(t \cdot 1 + (1 - t) \cdot 0) &\leq tg(1) + (1 - t)g(0) \\ &= tf(\mathbf{x}) + (1 - t)f(\mathbf{x}^0) \end{aligned} \tag{ii}$$

But this shows that f is convex, since the inequality in (1) is satisfied with $\leq$.

To prove that $\Rightarrow$ is valid in case (a), suppose f is convex in S. According to Theorem 1.8.1 (b), it suffices to show that for all $\mathbf{x}$ in S and all $h_1, \ldots, h_n$ we have

$$Q = \sum_{i=1}^{n} \sum_{j=1}^{n} f_{ij}''(\mathbf{x}) h_i h_j \geq 0 \tag{iii}$$

Now S is an open set, so if $\mathbf{x} \in S$ and $\mathbf{h} = (h_1, \ldots, h_n)$ is an arbitrary vector, there exists a positive number a such that $\mathbf{x} + t\mathbf{h} \in S$ for all t with $|t| < a$. Let $I = (-a, a)$. Define the function p on I by $p(t) = f(\mathbf{x} + t\mathbf{h})$. According to (9), p is convex in I. Hence $p''(t) \geq 0$ for all t in I. But

$$p''(t) = \sum_{i=1}^{n} \sum_{j=1}^{n} f_{ij}''(\mathbf{x} + t\mathbf{h}) h_i h_j \tag{iv}$$

Putting $t = 0$, we get inequality (iii).

Proof of Theorem 2.3.2: Define the function g as in the proof of Theorem 2.3.3. We will also need formulas (i) and (ii) in that proof.

(a) If the specified conditions are satisfied, the Hessian matrix $\mathbf{f}''(\mathbf{x})$ is positive definite according to Theorem 1.8.1(a). So for $\mathbf{x} \neq \mathbf{x}^0$ the sum in (i) is > 0 for all t in $[0, 1]$. It follows that g is strictly convex. The inequality in (ii) of the proof above is then strict for t in $(0, 1)$, so f is strictly convex.

(b) Follows from (a) by replacing f with $-f$.   ∎

PROBLEMS FOR SECTION 2.3

1. Which of the functions whose graphs are shown in the figure below are (presumably) convex/concave, strictly concave/strictly convex?

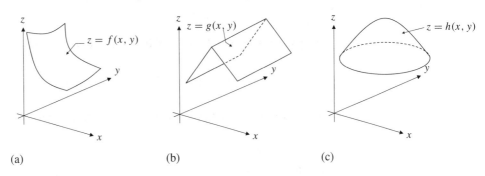

(a)   (b)   (c)

2. Let f be defined for all x, y by $f(x, y) = x - y - x^2$.

   (a) Show that f is concave (i) by using Theorem 2.3.1, (ii) by using Theorem 2.3.4.

   (b) Show that $-e^{-f(x,y)}$ is concave.

3. (a) Show that $f(x, y) = ax^2 + 2bxy + cy^2 + px + qy + r$ is strictly concave if $ac - b^2 > 0$ and $a < 0$, whereas it is strictly convex if $ac - b^2 > 0$ and $a > 0$.

   (b) Find necessary and sufficient conditions for $f(x, y)$ to be concave/convex.

4. For which values of the constant a is the following function concave/convex?

$$f(x, y) = -6x^2 + (2a + 4)xy - y^2 + 4ay$$

5. Examine the convexity/concavity of the following functions:

   (a) $z = x + y - e^x - e^{x+y}$ (b) $z = e^{x+y} + e^{x-y} - \frac{1}{2}y$ (c) $w = (x + 2y + 3z)^2$

6. Suppose $y = f(\mathbf{x})$ is a production function determining output y as a function of the vector $\mathbf{x}$ of nonnegative factor inputs, with $f(\mathbf{0}) = 0$. Show that:

   (a) If f is concave, then $f_{ii}''(\mathbf{x}) \leq 0$ (so each marginal product $f_i'(\mathbf{x})$ decreasing).

   (b) If f is concave, then $f(\lambda\mathbf{x})/\lambda$ is decreasing as a function of λ.

   (c) If f is homogeneous of degree 1 (constants returns to scale), then f is not strictly concave.

HARDER PROBLEMS

7. Let f be defined for all $\mathbf{x}$ in $\mathbb{R}^n$ by

$$f(\mathbf{x}) = \|\mathbf{x}\| = \sqrt{x_1^2 + \cdots + x_n^2}$$

   Prove that f is convex. Is f strictly convex? (*Hint:* Use the properties of the norm in Section 1.1.)

8. Show by using Theorem 2.3.1 that the CES function f defined for $K > 0, L > 0$ by

$$f(K, L) = A\left[\delta K^{-\rho} + (1 - \delta)L^{-\rho}\right]^{-1/\rho} \qquad (A > 0, \ \rho \neq 0, \ 0 \leq \delta \leq 1)$$

   is concave for $\rho \geq -1$ and convex for $\rho \leq -1$. (See also Example 2.5.6.)

9. Consider the Cobb–Douglas function $z = f(\mathbf{x}) = x_1^{a_1} x_2^{a_2} \cdots x_n^{a_n}$ $(a > 0, \ldots, a_n > 0)$ defined for all $x_1 > 0, \ldots, x_n > 0$.

   (a) Prove that the kth leading principal minor of the Hessian $\mathbf{f}''(\mathbf{x})$ is

$$D_k = \frac{a_1 \cdots a_k}{(x_1 \cdots x_k)^2} z^k \begin{vmatrix} a_1 - 1 & a_1 & \cdots & a_1 \\ a_2 & a_2 - 1 & \cdots & a_2 \\ \vdots & \vdots & \ddots & \vdots \\ a_k & a_k & \cdots & a_k - 1 \end{vmatrix}$$

   (b) Prove that $D_k = (-1)^{k-1}(\sum_{i=1}^k a_i - 1)z^k \dfrac{a_1 \cdots a_k}{(x_1 \cdots x_k)^2}$. (*Hint:* Add all the other rows to the first row, extract the common factor $\sum_{i=1}^k a_i - 1$, and then subtract the first column in the new determinant from all the other columns.)

   (c) Prove that the function is strictly concave if $a_1 + \cdots + a_n < 1$.

2.4 Concave and Convex Functions II

We continue our discussion of concave/convex functions. Our first result has a geometric interpretation. Consider Fig. 2.3.1. The tangent plane at any point on the graph will obviously lie above the graph. The following algebraic version of this geometric statement is important in both static and dynamic optimization theory.

THEOREM 2.4.1 CONCAVITY FOR DIFFERENTIABLE FUNCTIONS

Suppose that $f(\mathbf{x})$ is a C^1 function defined on an open, convex set S in $\mathbb{R}^n$. Then:

(a) f is concave in S if and only if

$$f(\mathbf{x}) - f(\mathbf{x}^0) \le \nabla f(\mathbf{x}^0) \cdot (\mathbf{x} - \mathbf{x}^0) = \sum_{i=1}^{n} \frac{\partial f(\mathbf{x}^0)}{\partial x_i}(x_i - x_i^0) \tag{1}$$

for all $\mathbf{x}$ and $\mathbf{x}^0$ in S.

(b) f is strictly concave iff the inequality (1) is always strict when $\mathbf{x} \ne \mathbf{x}^0$.

(c) The corresponding result for convex (strictly convex) functions is obtained by changing $\le$ to $\ge$ ($<$ to $>$) in the inequality (1).

Proof: (a) Suppose f is concave, and let $\mathbf{x}^0, \mathbf{x} \in S$. According to definition (2.3.1),

$$f(\mathbf{x}) - f(\mathbf{x}^0) \le \frac{f(\mathbf{x}^0 + \lambda(\mathbf{x} - \mathbf{x}^0)) - f(\mathbf{x}^0)}{\lambda} \tag{$*$}$$

for all λ in $(0, 1)$. Let $\lambda \to 0$. The right-hand side of ($*$) then approaches the right-hand side in (1) (see the argument for formula (2.1.7)). Because the weak inequality is preserved when passing to the limit, we have shown inequality (1).

To prove the reverse implication let $\mathbf{x}, \mathbf{x}^0 \in S$ and $\lambda \in (0, 1)$. Put $\mathbf{z} = \lambda\mathbf{x} + (1 - \lambda)\mathbf{x}^0$. Then $\mathbf{z}$ belongs to S, and according to (1),

$$f(\mathbf{x}) - f(\mathbf{z}) \le \nabla f(\mathbf{z}) \cdot (\mathbf{x} - \mathbf{z}), \quad f(\mathbf{x}^0) - f(\mathbf{z}) \le \nabla f(\mathbf{z}) \cdot (\mathbf{x}^0 - \mathbf{z}) \tag{ii}$$

where we used the gradient notation from Section 2.1.

Multiply the first inequality in (ii) by $\lambda > 0$ and the second by $1 - \lambda > 0$, and add the resulting inequalities. This gives

$$\lambda(f(\mathbf{x}) - f(\mathbf{z})) + (1 - \lambda)(f(\mathbf{x}^0) - f(\mathbf{z}))$$
$$\le \nabla f(\mathbf{z}) \cdot \left[\lambda(\mathbf{x} - \mathbf{z}) + (1 - \lambda)(\mathbf{x}^0 - \mathbf{z})\right] \tag{iii}$$

Here $\lambda(\mathbf{x} - \mathbf{z}) + (1 - \lambda)(\mathbf{x}^0 - \mathbf{z}) = \lambda\mathbf{x} + (1 - \lambda)\mathbf{x}^0 - \mathbf{z} = \mathbf{0}$, so the right-hand side of (iii) is 0. Then rearranging (iii) we see that f is concave.

(b) Suppose that f is strictly concave in S. Then inequality ($*$) is strict for $\mathbf{x} \ne \mathbf{x}^0$. With $\mathbf{z} = \mathbf{x}^0 + \lambda(\mathbf{x} - \mathbf{x}^0)$, we have

$$f(\mathbf{x}) - f(\mathbf{x}^0) < \frac{f(\mathbf{z}) - f(\mathbf{x}^0)}{\lambda} \le \frac{\nabla f(\mathbf{x}^0) \cdot (\mathbf{z} - \mathbf{x}^0)}{\lambda} = \nabla f(\mathbf{x}^0) \cdot (\mathbf{x} - \mathbf{x}^0)$$

where we used inequality (1), which we have already proved, and the fact that $\mathbf{z} - \mathbf{x}^0 = \lambda(\mathbf{x} - \mathbf{x}^0)$. This shows that (1) holds with strict inequality.

On the other hand, if (1) holds with strict inequality for $\mathbf{x} \ne \mathbf{x}^0$, then (ii) and (iii) hold with $\le$ replaced by $<$, and thus f is strictly concave. ∎

The next theorem lists several interesting properties of concave/convex functions.

THEOREM 2.4.2

Let $f(\mathbf{x}) = f(x_1, \ldots, x_n)$ and $g(\mathbf{x}) = g(x_1, \ldots, x_n)$ be defined on a convex set S in $\mathbb{R}^n$. Then:

(a) If f is concave, the set $P_a = \{\mathbf{x} \in S : f(\mathbf{x}) \geq a\}$ is convex for each number a.

(b) If f is convex, the set $P^a = \{\mathbf{x} \in S : f(\mathbf{x}) \leq a\}$ is convex for each number a.

(c) f is concave $\iff M_f = \{(\mathbf{x}, y) : \mathbf{x} \in S \text{ and } y \leq f(\mathbf{x})\}$ is convex.

(d) f is convex $\iff M^f = \{(\mathbf{x}, y) : \mathbf{x} \in S \text{ and } y \geq f(\mathbf{x})\}$ is convex.

(e) f and g are concave $\implies h(\mathbf{x}) = \min(f(\mathbf{x}), g(\mathbf{x}))$ is concave.

(f) f and g are convex $\implies H(\mathbf{x}) = \max(f(\mathbf{x}), g(\mathbf{x}))$ is convex.

Proof: (a) Let $\mathbf{x}$ and $\mathbf{y}$ be points in P_a. Then $\mathbf{x}$ and $\mathbf{y}$ belong to S, while $f(\mathbf{x}) \geq a$ and $f(\mathbf{y}) \geq a$. If $\lambda \in [0, 1]$, then $\lambda\mathbf{x} + (1-\lambda)\mathbf{y}$ also belongs to S (since S is convex). Because f is concave,

$$f(\lambda\mathbf{x} + (1-\lambda)\mathbf{y}) \geq \lambda f(\mathbf{x}) + (1-\lambda)f(\mathbf{y}) \geq \lambda a + (1-\lambda)a = a$$

This shows that $\lambda\mathbf{x} + (1-\lambda)\mathbf{y} \in P_a$, which confirms that P_a is convex. (If P_a is empty, P_a is convex by definition.)

Part (b) is shown in the same way. Parts (c) and (d) follow easily from the definitions, and are left to the reader.

(e) The function h maps $\mathbf{x}$ to the smaller of the numbers $f(\mathbf{x})$ and $g(\mathbf{x})$. Using the notation from part (c), $M_h = M_f \cap M_g$. The hypothesis that f and g are concave implies that M_f and M_g are convex, by part (c). Since the intersection of convex sets is convex, it follows from (c) that M_h is convex and so h is concave. Part (f) is shown in the same way. ∎

The result in part (c) is illustrated in Fig. 1, while Fig. 2 illustrates part (e).

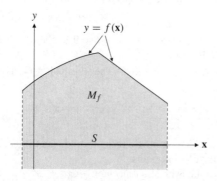

Figure 1 $M_f = \{(\mathbf{x}, y) : \mathbf{x} \in S, \ y \leq f(\mathbf{x})\}$

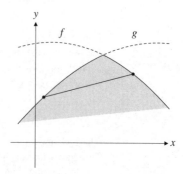

Figure 2 $M_{\min(f,g)} = M_f \cap M_g$

If the concave function f in Theorem 2.4.1 is not C^1, we still have the following result:

THEOREM 2.4.3 EXISTENCE OF A SUPERGRADIENT

Let f be concave on a convex set $S \subseteq \mathbb{R}^n$, and let $\mathbf{x}^0$ be an interior point in S. Then there exists a vector $\mathbf{p}$ in $\mathbb{R}^n$ such that

$$f(\mathbf{x}) - f(\mathbf{x}^0) \leq \mathbf{p} \cdot (\mathbf{x} - \mathbf{x}^0) \quad \text{for all } \mathbf{x} \text{ in } S \tag{2}$$

A vector $\mathbf{p}$ that satisfies (2) is called a **supergradient** for f at $\mathbf{x}^0$. Symmetrically, if f is convex, there exists a vector $\mathbf{q}$ in $\mathbb{R}^n$ such that (2) is valid with $\leq$ replaced by $\geq$ and $\mathbf{p}$ by $\mathbf{q}$. Such a vector is called a **subgradient** for f.

Proof: Let $M_f = \{(\mathbf{x}, y) : \mathbf{x} \in S \text{ and } y \leq f(\mathbf{x})\}$. According to Theorem 2.4.2(c), M_f is convex. The point $\mathbf{z}^0 = (\mathbf{x}^0, f(\mathbf{x}^0)) \in M_f$ is a boundary point of M_f, since $(\mathbf{x}^0, f(\mathbf{x}^0) + \gamma) \notin M_f$ for all $\gamma > 0$. By the supporting hyperplane theorem (Theorem 13.6.2) there exists a vector $\mathbf{q}^0 = (\mathbf{p}^0, r) \neq (\mathbf{0}, 0)$, with $\mathbf{p}^0 \in \mathbb{R}^n$ and $r \in \mathbb{R}$, such that

$$(\mathbf{p}^0, r) \cdot \mathbf{z} \leq (\mathbf{p}^0, r) \cdot (\mathbf{x}^0, f(\mathbf{x}^0)) \quad \text{for all } \mathbf{z} \text{ in } M_f \tag{$*$}$$

Given any $\nu > 0$, one has $\mathbf{z} = (\mathbf{x}^0, f(\mathbf{x}^0) - \nu) \in M_f$, so $\mathbf{p}^0 \cdot \mathbf{x}^0 + r f(\mathbf{x}^0) - r\nu \leq \mathbf{p}^0 \cdot \mathbf{x}^0 + r f(\mathbf{x}^0)$ by ($*$). Hence $-r\nu \leq 0$ for all $\nu > 0$. It follows that $r \geq 0$.

We want to prove that $r \neq 0$. To this end note that for all $\mathbf{x}$ in S, $\mathbf{z} = (\mathbf{x}, f(\mathbf{x})) \in M_f$, and so from ($*$), $(\mathbf{p}^0, r) \cdot (\mathbf{x}, f(\mathbf{x})) \leq (\mathbf{p}^0, r) \cdot (\mathbf{x}^0, f(\mathbf{x}^0))$. That is

$$\mathbf{p}^0 \cdot \mathbf{x} + r f(\mathbf{x}) \leq \mathbf{p}^0 \cdot \mathbf{x}^0 + r f(\mathbf{x}^0) \quad \text{for all } \mathbf{x} \in S \tag{$**$}$$

Suppose $r = 0$. Then $\mathbf{p}^0 \neq \mathbf{0}$. Since $\mathbf{x}^0$ is an interior point of S, for some $\lambda > 0$ one has $\mathbf{x}^0 + \lambda \mathbf{p}^0 \in S$. Substituting $\mathbf{x} = \mathbf{x}^0 + \lambda \mathbf{p}^0$ in ($**$) yields $\mathbf{p}^0 \cdot \mathbf{x}^0 + \lambda \mathbf{p}^0 \cdot \mathbf{p}^0 \leq \mathbf{p}^0 \cdot \mathbf{x}^0$. This reduces to $\lambda \mathbf{p}^0 \cdot \mathbf{p}^0 \leq 0$, implying that $\lambda \leq 0$ because $\mathbf{p}^0 \neq \mathbf{0}$, a contradiction. Thus $r = 0$ is inconsistent with the hypothesis that $\mathbf{x}^0$ is an interior point of S.

So $r > 0$. If we define $\mathbf{p} = -\mathbf{p}^0/r$, and divide ($**$) by r, we get inequality (2). ∎

NOTE 1 If f is defined on a set $S \subseteq \mathbb{R}^n$, and if $\mathbf{x}^0$ is an interior point in S at which f is differentiable and if $\mathbf{p}$ is a vector that satisfies (2), then $\mathbf{p} = \nabla f(\mathbf{x}^0)$. This result follows from the observation that $\varphi(\mathbf{x}) = f(\mathbf{x}) - f(\mathbf{x}^0) - \mathbf{p} \cdot (\mathbf{x} - \mathbf{x}^0)$ has a maximum at $\mathbf{x}^0$, so $\nabla \varphi(\mathbf{x}^0) = \mathbf{0}$.

Jensen's Inequality

Suppose we put $\mathbf{x} = \mathbf{x}_1$, $\mathbf{x}^0 = \mathbf{x}_2$, $\lambda_1 = \lambda$ and $\lambda_2 = 1 - \lambda$ in the definition (2.3.1) of a concave function. This leads to the equivalent definition: f is concave on S if and only if

$$f(\lambda_1 \mathbf{x}_1 + \lambda_2 \mathbf{x}_2) \geq \lambda_1 f(\mathbf{x}_1) + \lambda_2 f(\mathbf{x}_2)$$

for all $\mathbf{x}_1$ and $\mathbf{x}_2$ in S and for all $\lambda_1 \geq 0$ and $\lambda_2 \geq 0$ with $\lambda_1 + \lambda_2 = 1$.

Jensen's inequality is a generalization of this characterization of a concave function.

THEOREM 2.4.4 (JENSEN'S INEQUALITY, DISCRETE VERSION)

A function f is concave on the convex set S in $\mathbb{R}^n$ if and only if

$$f(\lambda_1 \mathbf{x}_1 + \cdots + \lambda_n \mathbf{x}_n) \geq \lambda_1 f(\mathbf{x}_1) + \cdots + \lambda_n f(\mathbf{x}_n) \tag{3}$$

holds for all $\mathbf{x}_1, \ldots, \mathbf{x}_n$ in S, and for all $\lambda_1 \geq 0, \ldots, \lambda_n \geq 0$ with $\lambda_1 + \cdots + \lambda_n = 1$.

The corresponding result for convex functions is obtained by reversing the inequality sign in (3).

It is obvious that if (3) holds, then f is concave: With $n = 2$ and $\lambda = \lambda_1 = 1 - \lambda_2$, (3) reduces to the inequality in the definition of a concave function. Problem 3 suggests an argument showing that the inequality (3) holds for any concave function.

EXAMPLE 1   **(Production Smoothing)**   Consider a manufacturing firm producing a single commodity. The cost of maintaining an output level y per year for a fraction λ of a year is $\lambda C(y)$, where $C'(y) > 0$ and $C''(y) \geq 0$ for all $y \geq 0$. In fact, the firm's output level can fluctuate over the year. Show that, given the total output Y that the firm produces over the whole year, the firm's total cost per year is minimized by choosing a constant flow of output.

Solution: Suppose the firm chooses different output levels $y_1, \ldots, y_n$ per year for fractions of the year $\lambda_1, \ldots, \lambda_n$, respectively. Then the total output is $\sum_{i=1}^{n} \lambda_i y_i = Y$, which is produced at total cost $\sum_{i=1}^{n} \lambda_i C(y_i)$. Applying Jensen's inequality to the convex function C gives the inequality $\sum_{i=1}^{n} \lambda_i C(y_i) \geq C\left(\sum_{i=1}^{n} \lambda_i y_i\right) = C(Y)$. The right-hand side is the cost of maintaining the constant output level Y over the whole year, and this is the minimum cost.

There is also a continuous version of Jensen's inequality that involves integrals. We restrict our attention to functions of one real variable. A proof of the next theorem is indicated in Problem 4.

THEOREM 2.4.5 (JENSEN'S INEQUALITY, CONTINUOUS VERSION)

Let $x(t)$ and $\lambda(t)$ be continuous functions in the interval $[a, b]$, with $\lambda(t) \geq 0$ and $\int_a^b \lambda(t)\,dt = 1$. If f is a concave function defined on the range of $x(t)$, then

$$f\left(\int_a^b \lambda(t) x(t)\,dt\right) \geq \int_a^b \lambda(t) f(x(t))\,dt \tag{4}$$

NOTE 2   Jensen's inequality is important in statistics. One application is this: If f is concave in an interval I and if X is a random variable with finite expectation $E(X)$, then $f(E(X)) \geq E(f(X))$.

EXAMPLE 2   **(Consumption Smoothing in Continuous Time)**   Suppose that a consumer expects to live from now (time $t = 0$) until time T. Let $c(t)$ denote consumption expenditure flow at time t, and $y(t)$ the given income flow. Let w_0 be wealth at time 0. Assume that the consumer would like to choose $c(t)$ so as to maximize the *lifetime intertemporal utility function*

$$\int_0^T e^{-\alpha t} u(c(t))\,dt \tag{i}$$

where $\alpha > 0$ is the *rate of impatience or of utility discount*, and $u(c)$ is a strictly increasing concave utility function (such as $\ln c$ or $-c^{-2}$). Suppose that r is the instantaneous rate of interest on savings, and that the consumer is not allowed to pass time T in debt. The initial wealth together with the present discounted value (PDV) of future income is $w_T = w_0 + \int_0^T e^{-rt} y(t)\,dt$.

The *intertemporal budget constraint* is expressed by the requirement that the PDV of consumption cannot exceed w_T:

$$\int_0^T e^{-rt} c(t)\, dt \le w_T \qquad \text{(for all admissible } c(t)) \tag{ii}$$

Finding an optimal time path of consumption for a problem like this generally involves techniques from optimal control theory. (See Example 9.4.2.) In the special case when $r = \alpha$, however, an optimal time path can easily be found by means of Jensen's inequality. Let $\bar{c}$ be the (constant) level of consumption that satisfies the equation

$$\int_0^T e^{-rt}\bar{c}\, dt = w_T = w_0 + \int_0^T e^{-rt} y(t)\, dt \tag{iii}$$

Note how $\bar{c} = \bar{y}$ in the special case when $w_0 = 0$ and $y(t) = \bar{y}$ for all t. Our claim is that an optimal path is to choose $c(t) = \bar{c}$ for all t, which we call "consumption smoothing" because all fluctuations in income are smoothed out through saving and borrowing in a way that leaves consumption constant over time.

To establish this claim, define the constant $\bar{\alpha} = \int_0^T e^{-rt}\, dt$. Then (iii) implies $\bar{c} = w_T/\bar{\alpha}$. Now apply Jensen's inequality to the concave function u with weights $\lambda(t) = (1/\bar{\alpha})e^{-rt}$. This yields

$$u\left(\int_0^T (1/\bar{\alpha})e^{-rt} c(t)\, dt \right) \ge \int_0^T (1/\bar{\alpha})e^{-rt} u(c(t))\, dt = (1/\bar{\alpha}) \int_0^T e^{-rt} u(c(t))\, dt \tag{iv}$$

Inequalities (iv) and (ii), together with the fact that $\bar{c} = w_T/\bar{\alpha}$ and the definition of $\bar{\alpha}$, respectively, imply that

$$\int_0^T e^{-rt} u(c(t))\, dt \le \bar{\alpha} u\left(\frac{1}{\bar{\alpha}} \int_0^T e^{-rt} c(t)\, dt \right) \le \bar{\alpha} u\left(\frac{w_T}{\bar{\alpha}} \right) = \bar{\alpha} u(\bar{c}) = \int_0^T e^{-rt} u(\bar{c})\, dt \tag{v}$$

This proves that no other consumption plan satisfying budget constraint (ii) can yield a higher value of lifetime utility, given by (i), than does the "smoothed consumption" path with $c(t) = \bar{c}$ for all t.[2]

PROBLEMS FOR SECTION 2.4

1. Use Theorem 2.4.1 to prove that $f(x, y) = 1 - x^2 - y^2$ defined in $\mathbb{R}^2$ is concave.

2. Give a direct proof for the following special case of Theorem 2.4.1: If $f''(x) \le 0$ for all x in an interval I and x_0 is an interior point in I, then $f(x) - f(x_0) \le f'(x_0)(x - x_0)$ for all x in I. (*Hint:* Study the function g given by $g(x) = f(x) - f'(x_0)(x - x_0)$.)

HARDER PROBLEMS

3. Prove Jensen's inequality (3) for $n = 3$. (*Hint:* If $n = 3$ and $\lambda_3 = 1$, the inequality in (3) is trivial. If $\lambda_3 \ne 1$, then $\lambda_1 + \lambda_2 \ne 0$, and

$$f(\lambda_1 \mathbf{x}_1 + \lambda_2 \mathbf{x}_2 + \lambda_3 \mathbf{x}_3) = f\left((\lambda_1 + \lambda_2)\left(\frac{\lambda_1}{\lambda_1 + \lambda_2}\mathbf{x}_1 + \frac{\lambda_2}{\lambda_1 + \lambda_2}\mathbf{x}_2 \right) + \lambda_3 \mathbf{x}_3 \right) \tag{*}$$

Show how (3) can now be derived from the result for $n = 2$. The general proof of (3) is based on mathematical induction.)

---

[2] This is actually quite an important topic in economics. The level of consumption that can be sustained without change is how J. R. Hicks defined "income." M. Friedman called a similar measure "permanent income," and enunciated the "permanent income hypothesis" according to which a measure of "permanent consumption" equals permanent income.

4. Prove Jensen's inequality (4) for the case in which f is C^1 by using the following idea: By (1), concavity of f implies that $f(x(t)) - f(z) \leq f'(z)(x(t) - z)$. Multiply both sides of this inequality by $\lambda(t)$ and integrate w.r.t. t. Then let $z = \int_a^b \lambda(t) x(t)\, dt$.

5. Suppose S is a convex subset of $\mathbb{R}^n$ and the function $f: S \to \mathbb{R}^n$ has a supergradient at every point of S. Prove that f is concave.

2.5 Quasiconcave and Quasiconvex Functions

Let $f(\mathbf{x})$ be a function defined over a convex set S in $\mathbb{R}^n$. For each real number a, define the subset P_a of S by

$$P_a = \left\{ \mathbf{x} \in S : f(\mathbf{x}) \geq a \right\} \tag{1}$$

Then P_a is called an **upper level set** for f. It consists of those points in S which have values of f which are greater than or equal to a. Figure 1 shows the graph of a function of two variables and Figure 2 one of its upper level sets. In fact, the function is a typical example of a quasiconcave function.

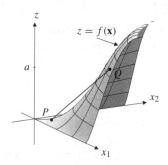

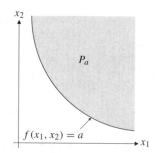

Figure 1 A quasiconcave function of two variables.

Figure 2 An upper level set for the function in Fig. 1.

DEFINITION OF QUASICONCAVE AND QUASICONVEX FUNCTIONS

A function f, defined over a convex set $S \subseteq \mathbb{R}^n$, is **quasiconcave** if the upper level set $P_a = \{\mathbf{x} \in S : f(\mathbf{x}) \geq a\}$ is convex for each number a.

We say that f is **quasiconvex** if $-f$ is quasiconcave. So f is quasiconvex iff the **lower level set** $P^a = \{\mathbf{x} : f(\mathbf{x}) \leq a\}$ is convex for each number a.

$$(2)$$

EXAMPLE 1   The function f defined for all (x, y) by $f(x, y) = e^{-x^2 - y^2}$ is proportional to the bivariate normal distribution function in statistics. (Its graph is often called "bell-shaped".) Show that it is quasiconcave.

Solution: Note that $f(x, y) \leq 1$ for all (x, y) and that $f(0, 0) = 1$. For each number a, let $P_a = \{(x, y) : e^{-x^2 - y^2} \geq a\}$. If $a > 1$, P_a is empty, and thus convex. If $a = 1$, the set P_a consists only of the point $(0, 0)$, which is convex. If $a \leq 0$, P_a is the whole xy-plane, which again is convex. Suppose $a \in (0, 1)$. Then $e^{-x^2 - y^2} \geq a$ iff $-x^2 - y^2 \geq \ln a$ iff $x^2 + y^2 \leq -\ln a$. The points (x, y) satisfying the last inequality are those on or inside the circle centred at the origin with radius $\sqrt{-\ln a}$. (Since $a \in (0, 1)$, $-\ln a$ is positive.) This is a convex set, so all upper level sets of f are convex, and thus f is quasiconcave.

EXAMPLE 2   Let $y = f(x)$ be any function of one variable that is either increasing or decreasing on an interval. Explain why f is quasiconcave as well as quasiconvex. (In particular, it follows that a quasiconcave function is not necessarily "bell-shaped".)

Solution: The level sets are either intervals or empty. Figure 3 shows a typical case.

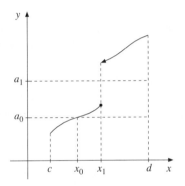
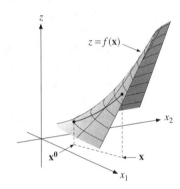

Figure 3 $P_{a_0} = [x_0, d]$, $P_{a_1} = (x_1, d]$ **Figure 4**

The function in Fig. 1 is not concave. For example, the line segment joining points P and Q on the graph lies *above* the graph of f, not below. On the other hand, according to Theorem 2.4.2 (a), a concave function has convex upper level sets. Likewise, a convex function has convex lower level sets.

Thus:

$$\text{If } f(\mathbf{x}) \text{ is concave, then } f(\mathbf{x}) \text{ is quasiconcave.}$$
$$\text{If } f(\mathbf{x}) \text{ is convex, then } f(\mathbf{x}) \text{ is quasiconvex.}$$
$$(3)$$

Theorem 2.3.4 implies that a sum of concave (convex) functions is again concave (convex). The corresponding result is not valid for quasiconcave (quasiconvex) functions (see Problem 6):

WARNING

A sum of quasiconcave functions need not be quasiconcave.

Some useful properties of quasiconcave functions, illustrated in Fig. 4, are these:

THEOREM 2.5.1

Let f be a function of n variables defined on a convex set S in $\mathbb{R}^n$. Then f is quasiconcave if and only if either of the following equivalent conditions is satisfied for all $\mathbf{x}$ and $\mathbf{x}^0$ in S and all λ in $(0, 1)$:

$$f(\lambda \mathbf{x} + (1 - \lambda)\mathbf{x}^0) \geq \min\{f(\mathbf{x}), f(\mathbf{x}^0)\} \tag{4}$$

$$f(\mathbf{x}) \geq f(\mathbf{x}^0) \implies f(\lambda \mathbf{x} + (1 - \lambda)\mathbf{x}^0) \geq f(\mathbf{x}^0) \tag{5}$$

Proof: Suppose that f is quasiconcave. Let $\mathbf{x}$, $\mathbf{x}^0 \in S$, $\lambda \in (0, 1)$, and define $a = \min(f(\mathbf{x}), f(\mathbf{x}^0))$. Then $\mathbf{x}$ and $\mathbf{x}^0$ both belong to the set $P_a = \{\mathbf{u} \in S : f(\mathbf{u}) \geq a\}$. Since P_a is convex, the vector $\lambda \mathbf{x} + (1 - \lambda)\mathbf{x}^0$ is also in P_a, meaning that $f(\lambda \mathbf{x} + (1 - \lambda)\mathbf{x}^0) \geq a$. So (4) is satisfied.

Suppose on the other hand that (4) is valid and let a be an arbitrary number. We must show that P_a is convex. If P_a is empty or consists only of one point, P_a is evidently convex. If P_a contains more than one point, take two arbitrary points $\mathbf{x}$ and $\mathbf{x}^0$ in P_a. Then $f(\mathbf{x}) \geq a$ and $f(\mathbf{x}^0) \geq a$. Also, for all λ in $(0, 1)$, (4) implies that $f(\lambda \mathbf{x} + (1 - \lambda)\mathbf{x}^0) \geq \min(f(\mathbf{x}), f(\mathbf{x}^0)) \geq a$, i.e. $\lambda \mathbf{x} + (1 - \lambda)\mathbf{x}^0$ lies in P_a. Hence P_a is convex.

Finally, it is easy to prove that (4) holds for all $\mathbf{x}, \mathbf{x}^0 \in S$ and all $\lambda \in (0, 1)$ iff (5) holds for all such $\mathbf{x}, \mathbf{x}^0, \lambda$. ∎

The following result is useful in utility theory.

THEOREM 2.5.2

Let $f(\mathbf{x})$ be defined on a convex set S in $\mathbb{R}^n$ and let F be a function of one variable whose domain includes $f(S)$.

(a) If $f(\mathbf{x})$ is quasiconcave (quasiconvex) and F is increasing, then $F(f(\mathbf{x}))$ is quasiconcave (quasiconvex).

(b) If $f(\mathbf{x})$ is quasiconcave (quasiconvex) and F is decreasing, then $F(f(\mathbf{x}))$ is quasiconvex (quasiconcave).

Proof: (a) We need the following simple observation (draw a picture): If F is increasing,

$$F(\min\{a, b\}) = \min\{F(a), F(b)\} \quad \text{and} \quad F(\max\{a, b\}) = \max\{F(a), F(b)\} \tag{$*$}$$

for all a and b in the domain of F. Consider first the case where f is quasiconcave. Let $\mathbf{x}$ and $\mathbf{x}^0$ be points in S and let λ be a number in $(0, 1)$. According to (4) in Theorem 2.5.1, $f(\lambda \mathbf{x} + (1 - \lambda)\mathbf{x}^0) \geq \min\{f(\mathbf{x}), f(\mathbf{x}^0)\}$. Then, since F is increasing, $(*)$ implies

$$F(f(\lambda \mathbf{x} + (1 - \lambda)\mathbf{x}^0)) \geq F(\min\{f(\mathbf{x}), f(\mathbf{x}^0)\}) = \min\{F(f(\mathbf{x})), F(f(\mathbf{x}^0))\}$$

It follows from (4) that the composite function $\mathbf{x} \mapsto F(f(\mathbf{x}))$ is quasiconcave. The argument in the quasiconvex case is entirely similar, replacing $\geq$ with $\leq$ and min with max.

Statement (b) is shown in the same way as (a), using the facts that if F is decreasing, then $F(\min\{a, b\}) = \max\{F(a), F(b)\}$ and $F(\max\{a, b\}) = \min\{F(a), F(b)\}$.   ∎

EXAMPLE 3   In Example 1 we showed that $f(x, y) = e^{-x^2-y^2}$ is quasiconcave. Because of Theorem 2.5.2 we can give a simpler argument. The function $-x^2 - y^2$ is concave, and therefore quasiconcave. The function $u \mapsto e^u$ is increasing, so $f(x, y)$ is quasiconcave.

EXAMPLE 4   Economists usually think of an individual's utility function as a means of describing preferences, rather than as a numerical measurement of "happiness" associated with a certain commodity bundle. So economists are more concerned with the level sets of the utility function than with the numerical values taken by the function. Given a utility function, any increasing transformation of that function represents the same level sets, although the numerical values assigned to the level curves are different. Note that according to Theorem 2.5.2, the property of quasiconcavity is preserved by an arbitrary increasing transformation. (This is not the case for the property of concavity, as Example 3 shows.)

A set K in $\mathbb{R}^n$ is called a **cone** if $x \in K$ and $t > 0$ implies $tx \in K$. Recall that a function f defined on a cone K is called *homogeneous of degree q* if $f(tx) = t^q f(x)$ for all x in K and all $t > 0$.

THEOREM 2.5.3

Let $f(x)$ be a function defined on a convex cone K in $\mathbb{R}^n$. Suppose that f is quasiconcave and homogeneous of degree q, where $0 < q \le 1$, that $f(0) = 0$, and that $f(x) > 0$ for all $x \ne 0$ in K. Then f is concave.

Proof: Consider first the case when $q = 1$. We need to show that if x and y are points in K and $\lambda \in (0, 1)$, then

$$f(\lambda x + (1 - \lambda)y) \ge \lambda f(x) + (1 - \lambda)f(y) \tag{$*$}$$

If $x = 0$, then $f(x) = 0$, and $(*)$ is satisfied with equality since f is homogeneous of degree 1. The same is true if $y = 0$. Suppose next that $x \ne 0$ and $y \ne 0$. Then $f(x) > 0$ and $f(y) > 0$, by hypothesis. Given any $\lambda \in (0, 1)$, put $\alpha = f(x)/f(y)$, $\beta = \alpha\lambda + (1 - \lambda)$, $\mu = \alpha\lambda/\beta$, and let $x' = (\beta/\alpha)x$, $y' = \beta y$. Note that $\mu \in (0, 1)$. Also, $\mu x' + (1-\mu)y' = \lambda x + (\beta - \alpha\lambda)y = \lambda x + (1-\lambda)y$. Moreover, $f(x') = (\beta/\alpha)f(x) = \beta f(y) = f(y')$. Since f is quasiconcave,

$$f(\lambda x + (1 - \lambda)y) = f(\mu x' + (1 - \mu)y') \ge f(x') = f(y') = \mu f(x') + (1 - \mu)f(y')$$
$$= (\mu\beta/\alpha)f(x) + (\beta - \beta\mu)f(y) = \lambda f(x) + (1 - \lambda)f(y)$$

This proves the theorem in the case when $q = 1$.

Finally, suppose that $q \in (0, 1)$, and define a new function g by $g(x) = (f(x))^{1/q}$ for all x in K. Then g is quasiconcave and homogeneous of degree 1, and $g(x) > 0$ for $x \ne 0$. According to the argument above, g is concave. Theorem 2.3.5 (a) shows that $f = g^q$ is also concave.   ∎

EXAMPLE 5   The Cobb–Douglas function is defined for all $x_1 > 0, \ldots, x_n > 0$ by

$$z = A x_1^{a_1} x_2^{a_2} \cdots x_n^{a_n} \qquad (a_1, a_2, \ldots, a_n, \text{ and } A \text{ are positive constants}) \qquad (*)$$

Taking the natural logarithm of each side yields

$$\ln z = \ln A + a_1 \ln x_1 + \cdots + a_n \ln x_n$$

As a sum of concave functions, $\ln z$ is concave, and hence quasiconcave. Now, $z = e^{\ln z}$, and the function $u \mapsto e^u$ is increasing. But then z is quasiconcave.

For $a_1 + \cdots + a_n < 1$, the Cobb–Douglas function is strictly concave. (See Problem 2.3.9.) For $a_1 + \cdots + a_n > 1$, it is not concave. (Along the ray $x_1 = \cdots = x_n = x$, one has $z = A x^{a_1 + \cdots + a_n}$, which is strictly convex for $a_1 + \cdots + a_n > 1$.)

If $a_1 + \cdots + a_n = 1$, Theorem 2.5.3 shows that the function is concave. The following display sets out some of the most important properties of the Cobb–Douglas function.

PROPERTIES OF THE COBB—DOUGLAS FUNCTION

The Cobb–Douglas function $z = A x_1^{a_1} \cdots x_n^{a_n}$, defined for $x_1 > 0, \ldots, x_n > 0$, with A and $a_1, \ldots, a_n$ positive, is homogeneous of degree $a_1 + \cdots + a_n$, and:

(a) quasiconcave for all $a_1, \ldots, a_n$ (6)

(b) concave for $a_1 + \cdots + a_n \leq 1$

(c) strictly concave for $a_1 + \cdots + a_n < 1$

EXAMPLE 6   The generalized CES function is defined for $x_1 > 0, x_2 > 0, \ldots, x_n > 0$ by

$$z = A(\delta_1 x_1^{-\rho} + \delta_2 x_2^{-\rho} + \cdots + \delta_n x_n^{-\rho})^{-\mu/\rho}, \quad A > 0, \ \mu > 0, \ \rho \neq 0, \ \delta_i > 0, \ i = 1, \ldots, n$$

We have $z = A u^{-\mu/\rho}$ where $u = \delta_1 x_1^{-\rho} + \delta_2 x_2^{-\rho} + \cdots + \delta_n x_n^{-\rho}$. If $\rho \leq -1$, then u is quasiconvex (in fact convex as a sum of convex functions) and $u \mapsto A u^{-\mu/\rho}$ is increasing, so z is quasiconvex, according to Theorem 2.5.2 (a). If $\rho \in [-1, 0)$, then u is quasiconcave (in fact concave) and $u \mapsto A u^{-\mu/\rho}$ is increasing, so z is quasiconcave according to Theorem 2.5.2(a). If $\rho > 0$, then u is quasiconvex (in fact convex) and $u \mapsto A u^{-\mu/\rho}$ is decreasing, so z is quasiconcave according to Theorem 2.5.2 (b).

It is easy to see that z is homogeneous of degree μ. It follows from Theorem 2.5.3 that if $0 < \mu \leq 1$ and $\rho \geq -1$, then z is concave.

PROPERTIES OF THE GENERALIZED CES FUNCTION

The CES function $z = A(\delta_1 x_1^{-\rho} + \delta_2 x_2^{-\rho} + \cdots + \delta_n x_n^{-\rho})^{-\mu/\rho}$, $A > 0$, $\mu > 0$, $\rho \neq 0$, $\delta_i > 0$, $i = 1, \ldots, n$ is homogeneous of degree μ, and:

(a) quasiconvex for $\rho \leq -1$, quasiconcave for $\rho \geq -1$ (7)

(b) concave for $\mu \leq 1, \rho \geq -1$

A stronger property than quasiconcavity is strict quasiconcavity:

A function f defined on a convex set $S \subseteq \mathbb{R}^n$ is called **strictly quasiconcave** if

$$f(\lambda \mathbf{x} + (1 - \lambda)\mathbf{x}^0) > \min\{f(\mathbf{x}), f(\mathbf{x}^0)\} \tag{8}$$

for all $\mathbf{x}$ and $\mathbf{x}^0$ in S with $\mathbf{x} \neq \mathbf{x}^0$ and all λ in $(0, 1)$. The function f is **strictly quasiconvex** if $-f$ is strictly quasiconcave.

NOTE 1 Some authors use a weaker definition of strict quasiconcavity and only require (8) to hold when $f(\mathbf{x}) \neq f(\mathbf{x}^0)$. But then f is not necessarily quasiconcave. See Problem 7.

It follows from Theorem 2.5.1(4) that a strictly quasiconcave function is quasiconcave. (It suffices to check what happens if $\mathbf{x} = \mathbf{x}^0$.) We see from the definition that a strictly increasing (or decreasing) function of one variable is always strictly quasiconcave.

An important fact about strictly quasiconcave functions is that they cannot have more than one global maximum point: If $\mathbf{x}$ and $\mathbf{x}^0$ are two different points with $f(\mathbf{x}) = f(\mathbf{x}^0)$, then $f(\mathbf{z}) > f(\mathbf{x})$ for each $\mathbf{z}$ on the open line segment $(\mathbf{x}, \mathbf{x}^0)$.

Quasiconcave C^1 Functions

Theorem 2.4.1 implies that the graph of a concave C^1 function lies below its tangent hyperplane. We now consider a somewhat similar characterization of quasiconcave C^1 functions. The geometric idea is suggested in Fig. 5, where the upper level set $P_a = \{\mathbf{x} : f(\mathbf{x}) \geq a\}$ is convex.

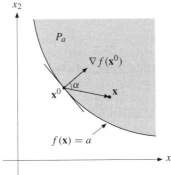

Figure 5 P_a is convex and $\nabla f(\mathbf{x}_0) \cdot (\mathbf{x} - \mathbf{x}_0) \geq 0$.

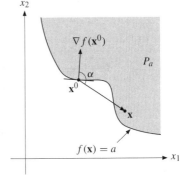

Figure 6 P_a is not convex and $\nabla f(\mathbf{x}_0) \cdot (\mathbf{x} - \mathbf{x}_0) < 0$.

Here $\mathbf{x} = (x_1, x_2)$ and $f(\mathbf{x}^0) = a$. The gradient $\nabla f(\mathbf{x}^0)$ of f at $\mathbf{x}^0$ is orthogonal to the level curve $f(\mathbf{x}) = a$ at $\mathbf{x}^0$, and points in the direction of maximal increase of f. (See Theorem 2.1.1.) Points $\mathbf{z}$ that satisfy $\nabla f(\mathbf{x}^0) \cdot (\mathbf{z} - \mathbf{x}^0) = 0$ are on the tangent hyperplane to the level curve at $\mathbf{x}^0$. If we choose an $\mathbf{x}$ in P_a, then $f(\mathbf{x}) \geq a = f(\mathbf{x}^0)$, and it seems that the angle α between the vectors $\mathbf{x} - \mathbf{x}^0$ and $\nabla f(\mathbf{x}^0)$ is always acute ($\leq 90°$), in the sense that $\nabla f(\mathbf{x}^0) \cdot (\mathbf{x} - \mathbf{x}^0) = \|\nabla f(\mathbf{x}^0)\| \, \|\mathbf{x} - \mathbf{x}^0\| \cos \alpha \geq 0$. (See formula (2.1.8).) Thus, points $\mathbf{x}$ in P_a all lie "above" the tangent hyperplane to the level surface. In that sense, the tangent hyperplane "supports" the upper level set. On the other hand, in Fig. 6 the level set P_a is not convex, and the tangent hyperplane does not support the level set.

THEOREM 2.5.4

Let f be a C^1 function of n variables defined on an open convex set S in $\mathbb{R}^n$. Then f is quasiconcave on S if and only if for all $\mathbf{x}$ and $\mathbf{x}^0$ in S

$$f(\mathbf{x}) \geq f(\mathbf{x}^0) \implies \nabla f(\mathbf{x}^0) \cdot (\mathbf{x} - \mathbf{x}^0) = \sum_{i=1}^{n} \frac{\partial f(\mathbf{x}^0)}{\partial x_i}(x_i - x_i^0) \geq 0 \tag{9}$$

Proof: We prove that if f is quasiconcave then (9) is valid. (The reverse implication is also true, but less useful.) Let $\mathbf{x}, \mathbf{x}^0 \in S$ and define the function g on $[0, 1]$ by $g(t) = f(\mathbf{x}^0 + t(\mathbf{x} - \mathbf{x}^0))$. Then $g'(t) = \nabla f(\mathbf{x}^0 + t(\mathbf{x} - \mathbf{x}^0)) \cdot (\mathbf{x} - \mathbf{x}^0)$. (See the argument for (2.1.7).) Suppose $f(\mathbf{x}) \geq f(\mathbf{x}^0)$. Then by (5) in Theorem 2.5.1, $g(t) \geq g(0)$ for all t in $[0, 1]$. This implies that $g'(0) = \nabla f(\mathbf{x}^0) \cdot (\mathbf{x} - \mathbf{x}^0) \geq 0$. ∎

A Determinant Criterion for Quasiconcavity

This section ends with a criterion for checking the quasiconcavity of a function by examining the signs of certain determinants, called **bordered Hessians**. The ordinary Hessians used in Section 2.3 to examine the concavity of a function (see Theorem 2.3.3) are "bordered" by an extra row and column consisting of the first-order partial derivatives of the function. For the case of two variables the result is this. (See also Problem 8.)

THEOREM 2.5.5

Let $f(x, y)$ be a C^2 function defined in an open, convex set S in the plane. Define the bordered Hessian determinant

$$B_2(x, y) = \begin{vmatrix} 0 & f_1'(x, y) & f_2'(x, y) \\ f_1'(x, y) & f_{11}''(x, y) & f_{12}''(x, y) \\ f_2'(x, y) & f_{21}''(x, y) & f_{22}''(x, y) \end{vmatrix} \tag{10}$$

Then:

(a) A necessary condition for f to be quasiconcave in S, is that $B_2(x, y) \geq 0$ for all (x, y) in S.

(b) A sufficient condition for f to be strictly quasiconcave in S, is that $f_1'(x, y) \neq 0$ and $B_2(x, y) > 0$ for all (x, y) in S.

EXAMPLE 7   We already know from Example 5 that the Cobb–Douglas function defined for all $x_1 > 0$, $\ldots, x_n > 0$ by $z = A x_1^{a_1} x_2^{a_2} \cdots x_n^{a_n}$ (with A and $a_1, \ldots, a_n$ all positive) is always quasiconcave. We can use Theorem 2.5.5 to confirm this result for $n = 2$. The first- and second-order partial derivatives can be expressed as $z_i' = a_i z / x_i$, $z_{ii}'' = a_i (a_i - 1) z / x_i^2$, $z_{ij}'' = a_i a_j z / x_i x_j$ (for $i \neq j$). Consider the case $n = 2$. Then the determinant $B_2 = B_2(x_1, x_2)$ is

$$
B_2 = \begin{vmatrix} 0 & \dfrac{a_1}{x_1} z & \dfrac{a_2}{x_2} z \\[2mm] \dfrac{a_1}{x_1} z & \dfrac{a_1(a_1 - 1)}{x_1^2} z & \dfrac{a_1 a_2}{x_1 x_2} z \\[2mm] \dfrac{a_2}{x_2} z & \dfrac{a_2 a_1}{x_2 x_1} z & \dfrac{a_2(a_2 - 1)}{x_2^2} z \end{vmatrix} = \dfrac{a_1 a_2}{(x_1 x_2)^2} z^3 \begin{vmatrix} 0 & 1 & 1 \\ a_1 & a_1 - 1 & a_1 \\ a_2 & a_2 & a_2 - 1 \end{vmatrix}
$$

where we have systematically removed all the common factors from each row and column. In the last determinant, subtract the first column from each of the others, and then add the last two rows to the first. Then we see that $B_2 = a_1 a_2 (a_1 + a_2) z^3 / (x_1 x_2)^2$. Because A, a_1, and a_2 are all positive, one has $B_2 > 0$. Moreover, $z_1' \neq 0$. We conclude from Theorem 2.5.5(b) that the Cobb–Douglas function $z = A x_1^{a_1} x_2^{a_2}$ is strictly quasiconcave. (This argument can easily be extended to be valid for a general value of n by using the next theorem.)

We go on to consider the general case. Define

$$
B_r(\mathbf{x}) = \begin{vmatrix} 0 & f_1'(\mathbf{x}) & \cdots & f_r'(\mathbf{x}) \\ f_1'(\mathbf{x}) & f_{11}''(\mathbf{x}) & \cdots & f_{1r}''(\mathbf{x}) \\ \vdots & \vdots & \ddots & \vdots \\ f_r'(\mathbf{x}) & f_{r1}''(\mathbf{x}) & \cdots & f_{rr}''(\mathbf{x}) \end{vmatrix}, \quad r = 1, \ldots, n \tag{11}
$$

THEOREM 2.5.6

Let f be a C^2 function defined in an open, convex set S in $\mathbb{R}^n$. Define the bordered Hessian determinants $B_r(\mathbf{x})$, by (11). Then:

(a) A necessary condition for f to be quasiconcave is that $(-1)^r B_r(\mathbf{x}) \geq 0$ for all $\mathbf{x}$ in S and all $r = 1, \ldots, n$.

(b) A sufficient condition for f to be strictly quasiconcave is that $(-1)^r B_r(\mathbf{x}) > 0$ for all $\mathbf{x}$ in S and all $r = 1, \ldots, n$.

Proof: We prove only (b). (The proof uses some results from Chapter 3.) Let $\mathbf{x}^*$ be an arbitrary point in S and consider the problem

$$
\max f(\mathbf{x}) \quad \text{subject to} \quad g(\mathbf{x}) = \nabla f(\mathbf{x}^*) \cdot (\mathbf{x} - \mathbf{x}^*) \leq 0, \quad \mathbf{x} \in S \tag{$*$}
$$

Let $\mathcal{L}(\mathbf{x}) = f(\mathbf{x}) - \lambda \nabla f(\mathbf{x}^*) \cdot (\mathbf{x} - \mathbf{x}^*) = f(\mathbf{x}) - \lambda(f_1'(\mathbf{x}^*)(x_1 - x_1^0) + \cdots + f_n'(\mathbf{x}^*)(x_n - x_n^0))$. Then $\nabla \mathcal{L}'(\mathbf{x}) = \nabla f(\mathbf{x}) - \lambda \nabla f(\mathbf{x}^*)$, and, in particular, $\mathcal{L}'(\mathbf{x}^*) = 0$ for $\lambda = 1$, so for this value of λ the first-order conditions for a local maximum at $\mathbf{x}^*$ are satisfied. Moreover, $g_i'(\mathbf{x}^*) = f_i'(\mathbf{x}^*)$ for all i and $\mathcal{L}_{ij}''(\mathbf{x}^*) = f_{ij}''(\mathbf{x}^*)$ for all i and j. Thus the condition in (b) evidently implies that the sufficient conditions for a strict local maximum of problem $(*)$ are satisfied at $\mathbf{x}^*$ (see Theorem 3.6.2). Then for $\mathbf{x} \neq \mathbf{x}^*$ and $\mathbf{x}$ close to $\mathbf{x}^*$, $f(\mathbf{x}) < f(\mathbf{x}^*)$ when $\nabla f(\mathbf{x}^*) \cdot (\mathbf{x} - \mathbf{x}^*) \leq 0$, or

$$\text{for } \mathbf{x} \neq \mathbf{x}^* \text{ close to } \mathbf{x}^*, \quad f(\mathbf{x}) \geq f(\mathbf{x}^*) \Rightarrow \nabla f(\mathbf{x}^*) \cdot (\mathbf{x} - \mathbf{x}^*) > 0 \qquad (**)$$

Let $\mathbf{x}' \neq \mathbf{x}''$ belong to S and assume that $f(\mathbf{x}'') \leq f(\mathbf{x}')$. Define $\mathbf{h}(t) = t\mathbf{x}' + (1-t)\mathbf{x}''$ with $t \in [0, 1]$. Consider the problem

$$\min_{s \in [0,1]} f(\mathbf{h}(s))$$

A minimum point t' must exist, and it can be assumed to belong to $[0, 1)$ because $f(\mathbf{x}'') \leq f(\mathbf{x}')$. We claim that $t' = 0$. Assume for a contradiction that $t' > 0$. Then, for t close to t', we have $f(\mathbf{h}(t)) \geq f(\mathbf{h}(t'))$, and so from $(**)$, $\nabla f(\mathbf{h}(t')) \cdot (\mathbf{h}(t) - \mathbf{h}(t')) = (t - t')\nabla f(\mathbf{h}(t')) \cdot (\mathbf{x}' - \mathbf{x}'') > 0$. But with t' as an interior point, the first order condition for a minimum is that $[(d/ds)f(\mathbf{h}(s))]_{s=t'} = \nabla f(\mathbf{h}(t')) \cdot (\mathbf{x}' - \mathbf{x}'') = 0$, so we have a contradiction. Hence $t' = 0$. Thus for all $s \in (0, 1)$, $f(\mathbf{h}(s)) \geq f(\mathbf{h}(0)) = f(\mathbf{x}'')$. But the equality $f(\mathbf{h}(t'')) = f(\mathbf{h}(0))$ cannot hold for any t'' in $(0, 1)$, because then t'' would be an interior minimum point. Thus $f(\mathbf{h}(s)) > f(\mathbf{x}'')$ for all s in $(0, 1)$, and by definition f is strictly quasiconcave. ∎

PROBLEMS FOR SECTION 2.5

1. Use (6) and (7) to classify as (quasi)concave or (quasi)convex each of the functions $z = F(x, y)$ defined for all $x > 0$, $y > 0$ by:

   (a) $z = 100x^{1/3}y^{1/4}$ (b) $z = x^2y^3$ (c) $z = 250x^{0.02}y^{0.98}$

   (d) $z = \sqrt{x^2 + y^2}$ (e) $z = (x^{1/3} + y^{1/3})^3$ (f) $z = (x^{-1/4} + y^{-1/4})^{-3/4}$

2. Determine if the following functions are quasiconcave:

   (a) $f(x) = 3x + 4$ (b) $f(x, y) = ye^x$, $y > 0$

   (c) $f(x, y) = -x^2y^3$ (d) $f(x) = x^3 + x^2 + 1$ if $x < 0$, $f(x) = 1$ if $x \geq 0$

3. (a) If $f(\mathbf{x})$ is concave, for which values of the constants a and b can one be sure that $af(\mathbf{x}) + b$ is concave?

   (b) If $f(\mathbf{x})$ is concave and positive valued, determine if the functions $g(\mathbf{x}) = \ln f(\mathbf{x})$ and $h(\mathbf{x}) = e^{f(\mathbf{x})}$ are concave/quasiconcave.

4. Consider the function $f(x) = -x^2/(1 + x^2)$. Sketch the graph of f and prove that f is quasiconcave by using the definition. Does Theorem 2.5.6 give the same result?

5. What does Theorem 2.5.6 (b) say about C^2 functions of one variable?

6. Show that, although the two functions $f(x) = -x$ and $g(x) = x^3$ are both quasiconcave and quasiconvex, their sum is neither.

HARDER PROBLEMS

7. Let $f : \mathbb{R} \to \mathbb{R}$ be defined by $f(0) = 0$ and $f(x) = 1$ if $x \neq 0$. Verify that f satisfies inequality (8) for all λ in $(0, 1)$ and all x and x^0 with $f(x) \neq f(x^0)$. But show that f is still not quasiconcave.

8. Suppose $F(x, y)$ is a C^2 function with $F'_2(x, y) > 0$. Let $y = \varphi(x)$ be defined implicitly by the equation $F(x, y) = C$. Prove that $\varphi(x)$ is convex if and only if $B_2(x, y) \geq 0$ (see (10)). (This convexity is equivalent to F being quasiconcave.) (*Hint:* You will need formula (2.1.10) from Problem 2.1.9.)

9. Let $f_1, \ldots, f_m$ be concave functions defined on a convex set S in $\mathbb{R}^n$. Define the function g over S by

$$g(\mathbf{x}) = F(f_1(\mathbf{x}), \ldots, f_m(\mathbf{x}))$$

where $F(u_1, \ldots, u_m)$ is quasiconcave and increasing in each variable. Prove that g is quasiconcave.

10. Modify the proof of Theorem 2.5.3 to show that if f is strictly quasiconcave and homogeneous of degree $q \in (0, 1)$, then f is strictly concave.

2.6 Taylor's Formula

When studying the behaviour of a complicated function f near a particular point of its domain, it is often useful to approximate f by a much simpler function.

Consider first the behaviour of a function f of one variable near a point a. The linear function $p(x) = f(a) + f'(a)(x - a)$ has $p(a) = f(a)$ and $p'(a) = f'(a)$, and so the two functions have same value and the same derivative at the point a. In fact, $y = f(a) + f'(a)(x - a)$ is the equation of the tangent to the graph of f at $x = a$. For x close to a we get the "first-order approximation"

$$f(x) \approx f(a) + f'(a)(x - a) \tag{1}$$

Suppose more generally that we seek an nth-order polynomial $p(x) = a_0 + a_1(x - a) + a_2(x - a)^2 + \cdots + a_n(x - a)^n$ with the same value and the same first n derivatives at a as f. Then $p(x)$ is the right-hand side of the approximation[3]

$$f(x) \approx f(a) + \frac{f'(a)}{1!}(x - a) + \frac{f''(a)}{2!}(x - a)^2 + \cdots + \frac{f^{(n)}(a)}{n!}(x - a)^n \quad (x \text{ close to } a) \tag{2}$$

---

[3] Recall that if n is a natural number, $n!$ (read as "n factorial") is defined as $n! = 1 \cdot 2 \cdot 3 \cdot \ldots \cdot (n-1) \cdot n$. By convention, $0! = 1$.

The two functions f and p have such a high degree of contact at $x = a$ that it is reasonable to expect the approximation in (2) to be good over some (possibly small) interval centred at $x = a$.

Nevertheless, the usefulness of such polynomial approximations is unclear unless something is known about the error that results. Taylor's formula, one of the main results in mathematical analysis, helps remedy this deficiency.

Consider the approximation in (2). Except at $x = a$, the function $f(x)$ and the polynomial $p(x)$ on the right-hand side of (2) are usually different. The difference between the two is called the *remainder after n terms*. We denote it by $R_{n+1}(x)$. Hence,

$$f(x) = f(a) + \frac{1}{1!} f'(a)(x - a) + \cdots + \frac{1}{n!} f^{(n)}(a)(x - a)^n + R_{n+1}(x)$$

The following theorem gives an explicit formula for the remainder (see e.g. EMEA)

THEOREM 2.6.1 (TAYLOR'S FORMULA)

Suppose f is $n + 1$ times differentiable in an interval that contains a and x. Then

$$f(x) = f(a) + \frac{f'(a)}{1!}(x - a) + \cdots + \frac{f^{(n)}(a)}{n!}(x - a)^n + \frac{f^{(n+1)}(c)}{(n + 1)!}(x - a)^{n+1} \qquad (3)$$

for some number c between a and x.

NOTE 1 The remainder term in (3) resembles the preceding terms in the sum. The only difference is that in the formula for the remainder, $f^{(n+1)}$ is evaluated at a point c, where c is some unspecified number between a and x, whereas in all the other terms, the derivatives are evaluated at a. The number c depends, in general, on x, a, and n, as well as the function f.

Putting $n = 1$, $a = 0$ in formula (3) gives

$$f(x) = f(0) + f'(0)x + \tfrac{1}{2}f''(c)x^2 \qquad \text{for some } c \text{ between } 0 \text{ and } x \qquad (4)$$

This formula tells us that $\tfrac{1}{2}f''(c)x^2$ is the error that results if we replace $f(x)$ with its linear approximation at $x = 0$.

Taylor's Formula for Functions of Two Variables

Let $z = f(x, y)$ be defined in a neighbourhood of (x_0, y_0) and let (h, k) be a given pair of numbers. With t as a real number, define the function g by $g(t) = f(x_0 + th, y_0 + tk)$. The function g records how $f(x, y)$ behaves along the straight line through (x_0, y_0) in the direction determined by the vector (h, k).

We see that $g(1) = f(x_0 + h, y_0 + k)$ and $g(0) = f(x_0, y_0)$. According to formula (3), there exists a number c in $(0, 1)$ such that

$$g(1) = g(0) + \frac{1}{1!}g'(0) + \cdots + \frac{1}{n!}g^{(n)}(0) + \frac{1}{(n + 1)!}g^{(n+1)}(c) \qquad (*)$$

If we find $g'(0)$, $g''(0)$ etc., and insert the results into $(*)$, we obtain the general Taylor's formula in two variables.

The formula is particularly useful for the case $n = 1$, when $(*)$ reduces to

$$g(1) = g(0) + g'(0) + \frac{1}{2}g''(c) \qquad (**)$$

Using the chain rule we find that $g'(t) = f_1'(x_0 + th, y_0 + tk)h + f_2'(x_0 + th, y_0 + tk)k$ and $g''(t) = f_{11}''(x_0 + th, y_0 + tk)h^2 + 2f_{12}''(x_0 + th, y_0 + tk)hk + f_{22}''(x_0 + th, y_0 + tk)k^2$. Thus $g'(0) = f_1'(x_0, y_0)h + f_2'(x_0, y_0)k$ and $g''(c) = f_{11}''(\bar{x}, \bar{y})h^2 + 2f_{12}''(\bar{x}, \bar{y})hk + f_{22}''(\bar{x}, \bar{y})k^2$, where $\bar{x} = x_0 + ch$, $\bar{y} = y_0 + ck$. Inserting these expressions into $(*)$ gives:

THEOREM 2.6.2 (TAYLOR'S FORMULA. LINEAR TERMS AND REMAINDER)

Suppose f is C^2 in a circle around (x_0, y_0) that contains $(x_0 + h, y_0 + k)$. Then

$$f(x_0 + h, y_0 + k) = f(x_0, y_0) + f_1'(x_0, y_0)h + f_2'(x_0, y_0)k$$
$$+ \frac{1}{2}\left[f_{11}''(\bar{x}, \bar{y})h^2 + 2f_{12}''(\bar{x}, \bar{y})hk + f_{22}''(\bar{x}, \bar{y})k^2\right]$$

where $\bar{x} = x_0 + ch$, $\bar{y} = y_0 + ck$ for some number c in $(0, 1)$.

In formula $(*)$, let us put $n = 2$, $x_0 = y_0 = 0$, and $h = x$, $k = y$. Disregarding the remainder, this gives the following quadratic approximation to $f(x, y)$ around $(0, 0)$:

$$f(x, y) \approx f(0, 0) + f_1'(0, 0)x + f_2'(0, 0)y$$
$$+ \frac{1}{2}\left(f_{11}''(0, 0)x^2 + 2f_{12}''(0, 0)xy + f_{22}''(0, 0)y^2\right) \qquad (5)$$

EXAMPLE 1   Find the quadratic approximation around $(0, 0)$ for $f(x, y) = e^x \ln(1 + y)$.

Solution: We find that $f_1'(x, y) = e^x \ln(1 + y)$, $f_2'(x, y) = e^x/(1 + y)$. Moreover, $f_{11}''(x, y) = e^x \ln(1 + y)$, $f_{12}''(x, y) = e^x/(1 + y)$, and $f_{22}''(x, y) = -e^x/((1 + y)^2$. It follows that $f(0, 0) = 0$, $f_1'(0, 0) = 0$, $f_2'(0, 0) = 1$, $f_{11}''(0, 0) = 0$, $f_{12}''(0, 0) = 1$, and $f_{22}''(0, 0) = -1$. From (5) we get

$$e^x \ln(1 + y) \approx y + xy - \frac{1}{2}y^2$$

Taylor's Formula with n Variables

We briefly explain how to derive Taylor's formula for a function of many variables.

Suppose we want to approximate $z = f(\mathbf{x}) = f(x_1, \ldots, x_n)$ near $\mathbf{x}^0 = (x_1^0, \ldots, x_n^0)$. Let $\mathbf{h} = (h_1, \ldots, h_n)$ and define the function g by $g(t) = f(x_1^0 + th_1, \ldots, x_n^0 + th_n) = f(\mathbf{x}^0 + t\mathbf{h})$. We use formula $(**)$ once again. According to the chain rule for functions of several variables, we have

$$g'(t) = f_1'(\mathbf{x}^0 + t\mathbf{h}) \cdot h_1 + \cdots + f_n'(\mathbf{x}^0 + t\mathbf{h}) \cdot h_n \qquad (6)$$

Differentiating w.r.t. t once more gives

$$g''(t) = \left[\frac{d}{dt} f_1'(\mathbf{x}^0 + t\mathbf{h})\right]h_1 + \cdots + \left[\frac{d}{dt} f_n'(\mathbf{x}^0 + t\mathbf{h})\right]h_n \qquad (*)$$

Here, for each $i = 1, 2, \ldots, n$, one has

$$\frac{d}{dt} f_i'(\mathbf{x}^0 + t\mathbf{h}) = f_{i1}''(\mathbf{x}^0 + t\mathbf{h})h_1 + f_{i2}''(\mathbf{x}^0 + t\mathbf{h})h_2 + \cdots + f_{in}''(\mathbf{x}^0 + t\mathbf{h})h_n$$

$$= \sum_{j=1}^{n} f_{ij}''(\mathbf{x}^0 + t\mathbf{h})h_j$$

using summation notation. Substituting back in $(*)$, we have

$$g''(t) = \sum_{i=1}^{n}\sum_{j=1}^{n} f_{ij}''(\mathbf{x}^0 + t\mathbf{h})h_i h_j \qquad (7)$$

Now use the formula $g(1) = g(0) + g'(0) + \frac{1}{2}g''(c)$, with $0 < c < 1$ and insert $t = 0$ into the expression for $g'(t)$ and $t = c$ into the expression for $g''(t)$. The result is:

THEOREM 2.6.3 (TAYLOR'S FORMULA FOR FUNCTIONS OF N VARIABLES)

Suppose f is C^2 in an open set containing the line segment $[\mathbf{x}^0, \mathbf{x}^0 + \mathbf{h}]$. Then

$$f(\mathbf{x}^0 + \mathbf{h}) = f(\mathbf{x}^0) + \sum_{i=1}^{n} f_i'(\mathbf{x}^0)h_i + \frac{1}{2}\sum_{i=1}^{n}\sum_{j=1}^{n} f_{ij}''(\mathbf{x}^0 + c\mathbf{h})h_i h_j \qquad (8)$$

for some c in $(0, 1)$.

If we include only one term, and let $\mathbf{x}^0 = (x_1^0, \ldots, x_n^0) = (0, \ldots, 0)$ and $\mathbf{h} = (h_1, \ldots, h_n) = (x_1, \ldots, x_n)$, we obtain the formula

$$f(\mathbf{x}) = f(\mathbf{0}) + \sum_{i=1}^{n} f_i'(\mathbf{0})x_i + \frac{1}{2}\sum_{i=1}^{n}\sum_{j=1}^{n} f_{ij}''(\mathbf{0})x_i x_j + R_3 \qquad (9)$$

The remainder R_3 can be expressed as a triple sum involving third order derivatives. It can also be expressed as $R_3 = \frac{1}{2}\sum_{i=1}^{n}\sum_{j=1}^{n}\left[f_{ij}''(c\mathbf{x}) - f_{ij}''(\mathbf{0})\right]x_i x_j$ for some c in $(0, 1)$.

PROBLEMS FOR SECTION 2.6

1. Find the quadratic approximations at $(0, 0)$ for

   (a) $f(x, y) = e^{x+y}(xy - 1)$ (b) $f(x, y) = e^{xe^y}$ (c) $f(x, y) = \ln(1 + x^2 + y^2)$

2. Write down formula (9) for $U(x_1, \ldots, x_n) = e^{-x_1} + \cdots + e^{-x_n}$.

2.7 Transformations

Many economic applications involve functions that map points (vectors) in $\mathbb{R}^n$ to points (vectors) in $\mathbb{R}^m$. Such functions are often called **transformations** or **mappings**. For example, we are often interested in how an m-vector $\mathbf{y}$ of endogenous variables depends on an n-vector $\mathbf{x}$ of exogenous variables.

Linear transformations constitute a simple but very important class. A transformation $\mathbf{f} : \mathbb{R}^n \to \mathbb{R}^m$ is called **linear** if

$$\mathbf{f}(\mathbf{x}_1 + \mathbf{x}_2) = \mathbf{f}(\mathbf{x}_1) + \mathbf{f}(\mathbf{x}_2), \qquad \mathbf{f}(\alpha\mathbf{x}_1) = \alpha\mathbf{f}(\mathbf{x}_1) \tag{1}$$

for all $\mathbf{x}_1$ and $\mathbf{x}_2$ in $\mathbb{R}^n$ and all scalars α. A well-known result from linear algebra states that for *every* linear transformation $\mathbf{f} : \mathbb{R}^n \to \mathbb{R}^m$ there is a unique $m \times n$ matrix $\mathbf{A}$ such that $\mathbf{f}(\mathbf{x}) = \mathbf{A}\mathbf{x}$ for all $\mathbf{x}$ in $\mathbb{R}^n$. The jth column $\mathbf{a}_j = (a_{1j}, \ldots, a_{mj})'$ of $\mathbf{A}$ is $\mathbf{f}(\mathbf{e}_j)$, where $\mathbf{e}_j = (0, \ldots, 1, \ldots, 0)'$ is the jth *standard unit vector* in $\mathbb{R}^n$, that is, the n-vector with 1 in the jth component and 0 elsewhere.

Conversely, it is clear that for any $m \times n$ matrix $\mathbf{A}$, the mapping $\mathbf{x} \mapsto \mathbf{A}\mathbf{x}$ is a linear transformation $\mathbb{R}^n \to \mathbb{R}^m$. Indeed, the rules for matrix multiplication show that

$$\mathbf{A}(\mathbf{x}_1 + \mathbf{x}_2) = \mathbf{A}\mathbf{x}_1 + \mathbf{A}\mathbf{x}_2, \qquad \mathbf{A}(\alpha\mathbf{x}_1) = \alpha\mathbf{A}\mathbf{x}_1 \tag{2}$$

This demonstrates a one-to-one correspondence between linear transformations $\mathbb{R}^n \to \mathbb{R}^m$ and $m \times n$ matrices. (When vectors are considered as matrices, they are usually taken to be column vectors—that is, matrices with a single column. The matrix product $\mathbf{A}\mathbf{x}$ then makes sense, and yields a column vector.)

Linear Approximations and Differentiability

Recall that if a one-variable function f is differentiable at a point a, then the *linear approximation* to f around a is given by

$$f(a + h) \approx f(a) + f'(a)h \qquad \text{(for small values of } h\text{)}$$

This is useful because the *approximation error* defined by

$$R(h) = \text{true value} - \text{approximate value} = f(a + h) - f(a) - f'(a)h$$

becomes negligible for sufficiently small h. Of course, $R(h)$ becomes small in the trivial sense that $R(h) \to 0$ as $h \to 0$. More importantly, however, $R(h)$ also becomes small *in comparison with h*—that is

$$\lim_{h \to 0} \frac{R(h)}{h} = \lim_{h \to 0} \left(\frac{f(a + h) - f(a)}{h} - f'(a) \right) = 0$$

In fact, f is differentiable at a if and only if there exists a number c such that

$$\lim_{h \to 0} \frac{f(a + h) - f(a) - ch}{h} = 0$$

If such a c exists, it is unique and $c = f'(a)$.

These one-dimensional concepts admit straightforward generalizations to many dimensions. In particular, a transformation $\mathbf{f}$ is *differentiable* at a point $\mathbf{a}$ if it admits a linear approximation around $\mathbf{a}$:

DEFINITION OF DIFFERENTIABILITY AND DERIVATIVES

If $\mathbf{f} : A \to \mathbb{R}^m$ is a transformation defined on a subset A of $\mathbb{R}^n$ and $\mathbf{a}$ is an interior point of A, then $\mathbf{f}$ is said to be **differentiable** at $\mathbf{a}$ if there exists an $m \times n$ matrix $\mathbf{C}$ such that

$$\lim_{\mathbf{h} \to 0} \frac{\|\mathbf{f}(\mathbf{a} + \mathbf{h}) - \mathbf{f}(\mathbf{a}) - \mathbf{C}\mathbf{h}\|}{\|\mathbf{h}\|} = 0 \tag{3}$$

If such a matrix $\mathbf{C}$ exists, it is called the **(total) derivative** of $\mathbf{f}$ at $\mathbf{a}$, and is denoted by $\mathbf{f}'(\mathbf{a})$. An alternative notation for $\mathbf{f}'(\mathbf{a})$ is $D\mathbf{f}(\mathbf{a})$.

If $\mathbf{f}$ has a derivative, then the derivative is unique (in fact, it must equal the Jacobian matrix of $\mathbf{f}$ at $\mathbf{a}$, see below), so we are justified in speaking of *the* derivative. As in the one-dimensional case, if $\mathbf{f}$ is differentiable at $\mathbf{a}$, then the linear transformation $\mathbf{h} \mapsto \mathbf{f}'(\mathbf{a})\mathbf{h}$ is a good approximation to $\mathbf{h} \mapsto \mathbf{f}(\mathbf{a}+\mathbf{h}) - \mathbf{f}(\mathbf{a})$ for sufficiently small $\mathbf{h}$, and the approximation $\mathbf{f}(\mathbf{a} + \mathbf{h}) \approx \mathbf{f}(\mathbf{a}) + \mathbf{f}'(\mathbf{a})\mathbf{h}$, or, equivalently,

$$\mathbf{f}(\mathbf{x}) \approx \mathbf{f}(\mathbf{a}) + \mathbf{f}'(\mathbf{a})(\mathbf{x} - \mathbf{a})$$

is called the **linear** (or **first-order**) **approximation to f around a**.

Several questions arise: How can we tell whether a transformation $\mathbf{f}$ is differentiable at a point $\mathbf{x}$; how do we find $\mathbf{f}'(\mathbf{x})$; what properties do derivatives have?

Consider first the special case $m = 1$, so f is an "ordinary" (one-dimensional) function of n variables. It turns out that if f is differentiable at $\mathbf{x}$, then f has a derivative $f'_{\mathbf{a}}(\mathbf{x})$ along every vector $\mathbf{a}$, and these derivatives are all determined by the derivative $f'(\mathbf{x})$ of f at $\mathbf{x}$.

THEOREM 2.7.1

If $f : A \to \mathbb{R}$ is defined on a subset A of $\mathbb{R}^n$ and f is differentiable at an interior point $\mathbf{x}$ of A, then f has a derivative $f'_{\mathbf{a}}(\mathbf{x})$ along every n-vector $\mathbf{a}$, and $f'_{\mathbf{a}}(\mathbf{x}) = f'(\mathbf{x})\mathbf{a}$. (Remember that $f'(\mathbf{x})$ is a $1 \times n$ matrix.)

Proof: From the definition in Section 2.1, the derivative along $\mathbf{a}$ is

$$f'_{\mathbf{a}}(\mathbf{x}) = \lim_{h \to 0} \left(\frac{f(\mathbf{x} + h\mathbf{a}) - f(\mathbf{x}) - f'(\mathbf{x})\mathbf{a}h}{h} + f'(\mathbf{x})\mathbf{a} \right) = \mathbf{0} + f'(\mathbf{x})\mathbf{a} \qquad ∎$$

In particular, if $\mathbf{e}_j = (0, \dots, 1, \dots, 0)'$ is the jth standard unit vector in $\mathbb{R}^n$, then $f'_{\mathbf{e}_j}(\mathbf{x}) = f'(\mathbf{x})\mathbf{e}_j$ is the partial derivative $f'_j(\mathbf{x})$ of f with respect to the jth variable. On the other hand, $f'(\mathbf{x})\mathbf{e}_j$ is the jth component of $f'(\mathbf{x})$. Hence, $f'(\mathbf{x})$ is the row vector

$$f'(\mathbf{x}) = (f'(\mathbf{x})\mathbf{e}_1, \ldots, f'(\mathbf{x})\mathbf{e}_n) = (f_1'(\mathbf{x}), \ldots, f_n'(\mathbf{x}))$$

which we recognize as the gradient $\nabla f(\mathbf{x})$ of f at $\mathbf{x}$.[4] (See Section 2.1.)
We are now prepared to tackle the case of transformations into $\mathbb{R}^m$.

THEOREM 2.7.2

A transformation $\mathbf{f} = (f_1, \ldots, f_m)'$ from a subset A of $\mathbb{R}^n$ into $\mathbb{R}^m$ is differentiable at an interior point $\mathbf{x}$ of A if and only if each component function $f_i : A \to \mathbb{R}$, $i = 1, \ldots m$, is differentiable at $\mathbf{x}$. Moreover,

$$\mathbf{f}'(\mathbf{x}) = \begin{pmatrix} f_1'(\mathbf{x}) \\ \vdots \\ f_m'(\mathbf{x}) \end{pmatrix}$$

is the $m \times n$ matrix whose ith row is $f_i'(\mathbf{x}) = \nabla f_i(\mathbf{x})$.

Proof: Let $\mathbf{C}$ be an $m \times n$ matrix and let $\mathbf{R}(\mathbf{h}) = \mathbf{f}(\mathbf{x}+\mathbf{h}) - \mathbf{f}(\mathbf{x}) - \mathbf{Ch}$. The ith component of $\mathbf{R}(\mathbf{h})$, $i = 1, \ldots, m$, is $R_i(\mathbf{h}) = f_i(\mathbf{x} + \mathbf{h}) - f_i(\mathbf{x}) - \mathbf{C}_i\mathbf{h}$, where $\mathbf{C}_i$ is the ith row of $\mathbf{C}$. For each i,

$$|R_i(\mathbf{h})| \le \|\mathbf{R}(\mathbf{h})\| \le |R_1(\mathbf{h})| + \cdots + |R_m(\mathbf{h})|$$

It follows that

$$\lim_{\mathbf{h}\to 0} \frac{\|\mathbf{R}(\mathbf{h})\|}{\|\mathbf{h}\|} = 0 \quad \Longleftrightarrow \quad \lim_{\mathbf{h}\to 0} \frac{|R_i(\mathbf{h})|}{\|\mathbf{h}\|} = 0 \text{ for all } i = 1, \ldots, m$$

Hence, f is differentiable at $\mathbf{x}$ if and only if each f_i is differentiable at $\mathbf{x}$. Also, the ith row of the matrix $\mathbf{C} = \mathbf{f}'(\mathbf{x})$ is the derivative of f_i, that is $\mathbf{C}_i = \nabla f_i(\mathbf{x})$. ∎

It follows that if $\mathbf{f}$ is differentiable at $\mathbf{x}$, then its derivative is the matrix

$$\mathbf{f}'(\mathbf{x}) = \begin{pmatrix} \dfrac{\partial f_1}{\partial x_1}(\mathbf{x}) & \dfrac{\partial f_1}{\partial x_2}(\mathbf{x}) & \cdots & \dfrac{\partial f_1}{\partial x_n}(\mathbf{x}) \\ \vdots & \vdots & & \vdots \\ \dfrac{\partial f_m}{\partial x_1}(\mathbf{x}) & \dfrac{\partial f_m}{\partial x_2}(\mathbf{x}) & \cdots & \dfrac{\partial f_m}{\partial x_n}(\mathbf{x}) \end{pmatrix}$$

This is called the **Jacobian matrix of f at x**. Its rows are the gradients of the component functions of $\mathbf{f}$.

---

[4] The gradient $\nabla f(\mathbf{x})$ of a function is thus an exception to the rule that vectors (regarded as matrices) are usually taken to be column vectors.

We know that if a function $f : \mathbb{R} \to \mathbb{R}$ is differentiable at a point x, then it is continuous at x. A similar result holds in the multidimensional case.

THEOREM 2.7.3

If a transformation $\mathbf{f}$ from $A \subseteq \mathbb{R}^n$ into $\mathbb{R}^m$ is differentiable at an interior point $\mathbf{a}$ of A, then $\mathbf{f}$ is continuous at $\mathbf{a}$.

Proof: Let $\mathbf{C} = \mathbf{f}'(\mathbf{x})$. Then for small but nonzero $\mathbf{h}$, the triangle inequality yields

$$\|\mathbf{f}(\mathbf{a}+\mathbf{h}) - \mathbf{f}(\mathbf{a})\| \leq \|\mathbf{f}(\mathbf{a}+\mathbf{h}) - \mathbf{f}(\mathbf{a}) - \mathbf{C}\mathbf{h}\| + \|\mathbf{C}\mathbf{h}\|$$

$$= \|\mathbf{h}\| \left(\frac{\|\mathbf{f}(\mathbf{a}+\mathbf{h}) - \mathbf{f}(\mathbf{a}) - \mathbf{C}\mathbf{h}\|}{\|\mathbf{h}\|} \right) + \|\mathbf{C}\mathbf{h}\|$$

Since $\mathbf{f}$ is differentiable at $\mathbf{a}$, the fraction in the parentheses tends to 0 as $\mathbf{h} \to \mathbf{0}$, and the term $\|\mathbf{C}\mathbf{h}\|$ also tends to 0. Hence, $\mathbf{f}(\mathbf{a}+\mathbf{h}) \to \mathbf{f}(\mathbf{a})$ as $\mathbf{h} \to \mathbf{0}$. ∎

If $\mathbf{f}$ and $\mathbf{g}$ are transformations from $A \subseteq \mathbb{R}^n$ into $\mathbb{R}^m$, and if they are both differentiable at a point $\mathbf{x}$ in A, then the following rules hold (α is a constant scalar):

$$(\alpha\mathbf{f})'(\mathbf{x}) = \alpha\mathbf{f}'(\mathbf{x}), \quad (\mathbf{f}+\mathbf{g})'(\mathbf{x}) = \mathbf{f}'(\mathbf{x}) + \mathbf{g}'(\mathbf{x})$$

There is also a *chain rule* for transformations.

THEOREM 2.7.4 (THE CHAIN RULE)

Suppose $\mathbf{f} : A \to \mathbb{R}^m$ and $\mathbf{g} : B \to \mathbb{R}^p$ are defined on $A \subseteq \mathbb{R}^n$ and $B \subseteq \mathbb{R}^m$, with $\mathbf{f}(A) \subseteq B$, and suppose that $\mathbf{f}$ and $\mathbf{g}$ are differentiable at $\mathbf{x}$ and $\mathbf{f}(\mathbf{x})$, respectively. Then the composite transformation $\mathbf{g} \circ \mathbf{f} : A \to \mathbb{R}^p$ defined by $(\mathbf{g} \circ \mathbf{f})(\mathbf{x}) = \mathbf{g}(\mathbf{f}(\mathbf{x}))$ is differentiable at $\mathbf{x}$, and

$$(\mathbf{g} \circ \mathbf{f})'(\mathbf{x}) = \mathbf{g}'(\mathbf{f}(\mathbf{x}))\,\mathbf{f}'(\mathbf{x}) \tag{4}$$

Proof: An heuristic derivation of formula (4) using linear approximations is obtained in this way:

$$(\mathbf{g} \circ \mathbf{f})(\mathbf{x}+\mathbf{h}) - (\mathbf{g} \circ \mathbf{f})(\mathbf{x}) = \mathbf{g}(\mathbf{f}(\mathbf{x}+\mathbf{h})) - \mathbf{g}(\mathbf{f}(\mathbf{x}))$$

$$\approx \mathbf{g}'(\mathbf{f}(\mathbf{x}))\,[\mathbf{f}(\mathbf{x}+\mathbf{h}) - \mathbf{f}(\mathbf{x})] \approx \mathbf{g}'(\mathbf{f}(\mathbf{x}))\,\mathbf{f}'(\mathbf{x})\mathbf{h}$$

To go beyond a heuristic explanation and prove the theorem, one must show that the error $\mathbf{e}(\mathbf{h}) = (\mathbf{g} \circ \mathbf{f})(\mathbf{x}+\mathbf{h}) - (\mathbf{g} \circ \mathbf{f})(\mathbf{x}) - \mathbf{g}'(\mathbf{f}(\mathbf{x}))\mathbf{f}'(\mathbf{x})\mathbf{h}$ involved in this approximation satisfies $\|\mathbf{e}(\mathbf{h})\|/\|\mathbf{h}\| \to 0$ as $\mathbf{h} \to \mathbf{0}$.

Define $\mathbf{k}(\mathbf{h}) = \mathbf{f}(\mathbf{x}+\mathbf{h}) - \mathbf{f}(\mathbf{x}) = \mathbf{f}'(\mathbf{x})\mathbf{h} + \mathbf{e_f}(\mathbf{h})$, where $\|\mathbf{e_f}(\mathbf{h})\|/\|\mathbf{h}\| \to 0$ as $\mathbf{h} \to \mathbf{0}$. Also $\mathbf{g}(\mathbf{f}(\mathbf{x}+\mathbf{k})) - \mathbf{g}(\mathbf{f}(\mathbf{x})) = \mathbf{g}'(\mathbf{f}(\mathbf{x}))\mathbf{k} + \mathbf{e_g}(\mathbf{k})$, where $\|\mathbf{e_g}(\mathbf{k})\|/\|\mathbf{k}\| \to 0$ as $\mathbf{k} \to \mathbf{0}$. Note that $\|\mathbf{k}(\mathbf{h})\| \leq$

$K\|\mathbf{h}\|$ for all small $\mathbf{h}$, with K some fixed constant. Observe also that for all $\varepsilon > 0$, $\|\mathbf{e_g}(\mathbf{k})\| < \varepsilon\|\mathbf{k}\|$, for $\mathbf{k}$ small, so $\|\mathbf{e_g}(\mathbf{k}(\mathbf{h}))\| < \varepsilon\|\mathbf{k}(\mathbf{h})\| \le \varepsilon K\|\mathbf{h}\|$ when $\mathbf{h}$ is small. Hence, $\|\mathbf{e_g}(\mathbf{k}(\mathbf{h}))\|/\|\mathbf{h}\| \to 0$ as $\mathbf{h} \to \mathbf{0}$. Then

$$\begin{aligned}
\mathbf{e}(\mathbf{h}) &= \mathbf{g}(\mathbf{f}(\mathbf{x}) + \mathbf{k}(\mathbf{h})) - \mathbf{g}(\mathbf{f}(\mathbf{x})) - \mathbf{g}'(\mathbf{f}(\mathbf{x}))\,\mathbf{f}'(\mathbf{x})\mathbf{h} \\
&= \mathbf{g}'(\mathbf{f}(\mathbf{x}))\mathbf{k}(\mathbf{h}) + \mathbf{e_g}(\mathbf{k}(\mathbf{h})) - \mathbf{g}'(\mathbf{f}(\mathbf{x}))\mathbf{f}'(\mathbf{x})\mathbf{h} \\
&= \mathbf{g}'(\mathbf{f}(\mathbf{x}))\mathbf{e_f}(\mathbf{h}) + \mathbf{e_g}(\mathbf{k}(\mathbf{h}))
\end{aligned}$$

and $\|\mathbf{e}(\mathbf{h})\|/\|\mathbf{h}\| \le \|\mathbf{g}'(\mathbf{f}(\mathbf{x}))\mathbf{e_f}(\mathbf{h})\|/\|\mathbf{h}\| + \|\mathbf{e_g}(\mathbf{k}(\mathbf{h}))\|/\|\mathbf{h}\|$. The right-hand side converges to zero as $\mathbf{h} \to \mathbf{0}$. ∎

The Jacobian matrices $\mathbf{g}'(\mathbf{f}(\mathbf{x})), \mathbf{f}'(\mathbf{x})$, and $(\mathbf{g} \circ \mathbf{f})'(\mathbf{x}_0)$ are $p \times m, m \times n$, and $p \times n$ matrices, respectively. Note that the chain rule relates composition of functions to multiplication of the Jacobian matrices representing their derivatives, and thus to compositions of the linear transformations given by these derivatives.

The chain rule (4) is written in a very compact form. The following example shows that it actually represents familiar formulas from calculus written in matrix form.

EXAMPLE 1   Suppose $\mathbf{f} : \mathbb{R}^3 \to \mathbb{R}^2$ and $\mathbf{g} : \mathbb{R}^2 \to \mathbb{R}^2$ are defined by

$$\begin{aligned}
y_1 &= f_1(x_1, x_2, x_3), & z_1 &= g_1(y_1, y_2) \\
y_2 &= f_2(x_1, x_2, x_3), & z_2 &= g_2(y_1, y_2)
\end{aligned}$$

Then $\mathbf{h} = \mathbf{g} \circ \mathbf{f}$ is defined by

$$\begin{aligned}
z_1 &= h_1(x_1, x_2, x_3) = g_1(f_1(x_1, x_2, x_3), f_2(x_1, x_2, x_3)) \\
z_2 &= h_2(x_1, x_2, x_3) = g_2(f_1(x_1, x_2, x_3), f_2(x_1, x_2, x_3))
\end{aligned}$$

According to the chain rule (4),

$$\begin{pmatrix} \dfrac{\partial h_1}{\partial x_1} & \dfrac{\partial h_1}{\partial x_2} & \dfrac{\partial h_1}{\partial x_3} \\[2ex] \dfrac{\partial h_2}{\partial x_1} & \dfrac{\partial h_2}{\partial x_2} & \dfrac{\partial h_2}{\partial x_3} \end{pmatrix} = \begin{pmatrix} \dfrac{\partial g_1}{\partial y_1} & \dfrac{\partial g_1}{\partial y_2} \\[2ex] \dfrac{\partial g_2}{\partial y_1} & \dfrac{\partial g_2}{\partial y_2} \end{pmatrix} \begin{pmatrix} \dfrac{\partial f_1}{\partial x_1} & \dfrac{\partial f_1}{\partial x_2} & \dfrac{\partial f_1}{\partial x_3} \\[2ex] \dfrac{\partial f_2}{\partial x_1} & \dfrac{\partial f_2}{\partial x_2} & \dfrac{\partial f_3}{\partial x_3} \end{pmatrix}$$

Evaluating the matrix product on the right, we get the familiar formula

$$\frac{\partial h_i}{\partial x_j} = \frac{\partial g_i}{\partial y_1}\frac{\partial f_1}{\partial x_j} + \frac{\partial g_i}{\partial y_2}\frac{\partial f_2}{\partial x_j}, \quad i = 1, 2, \quad j = 1, 2, 3$$

(The partial derivatives of g_i are evaluated at $\mathbf{y} = (y_1, y_2) = (f_1(\mathbf{x}), f_2(\mathbf{x}))$.)

We now know how to find the derivative of $\mathbf{f} = (f_1, \dots, f_m)$, if it exists, and we know some of its properties. But when does it exist? It is not sufficient that all the first-order partial derivatives $\partial f_i/\partial x_j$ exist. In fact, Problem 5 shows that $\mathbf{f}'(\mathbf{x})$ need not exist even if $\mathbf{f}$ has directional derivatives in all directions. But it turns out that *if the partial derivatives $\partial f_i/\partial x_j$ are all continuous at a point $\mathbf{a}$, then $\mathbf{f}$ is differentiable at $\mathbf{a}$.*

A function $f : \mathbb{R} \to \mathbb{R}$ is said to be of **class C^k** $(k = 1, 2, \dots)$ if all of its partial derivatives of order up to and including k exist and are continuous. Similarly a transformation $\mathbf{f} = (f_1, \dots, f_m)$ from (a subset of) $\mathbb{R}^n$ into $\mathbb{R}^m$ is said to be of **class C^k** if each of its component functions $f_1, \dots, f_m$ is C^k.

THEOREM 2.7.5 (C^1 FUNCTIONS ARE DIFFERENTIABLE)

If $\mathbf{f}$ is a C^1 transformation from an open set $A \subseteq \mathbb{R}^n$ into $\mathbb{R}^m$, then $\mathbf{f}$ is differentiable at every point $\mathbf{x}$ in A.

Proof: By Theorem 2.7.2, $\mathbf{f}$ is differentiable if each component f_i is differentiable. Hence, in the proof we can assume that $\mathbf{f}$ is real-valued, and written f. Define the error term by

$$R(\mathbf{h}) = f(\mathbf{x} + \mathbf{h}) - f(\mathbf{x}) - \sum_{i=1}^{n} f_i'(\mathbf{x}) h_i$$

and let $\mathbf{e}_j$ denote the jth unit vector in $\mathbb{R}^n$. Now,

$$f(\mathbf{x} + \mathbf{h}) - f(\mathbf{x}) = \sum_{i=1}^{n} [f(\mathbf{x} + \sum_{j=1}^{i} h_j \mathbf{e}_j) - f(\mathbf{x} + \sum_{j=1}^{i-1} h_j \mathbf{e}_j)] = \sum_{i=1}^{n} f_i'(\mathbf{x} + \sum_{j=1}^{i-1} h_j \mathbf{e}_j + \theta h_i \mathbf{e}_i) h_i$$

with $\theta_i \in (0, 1)$, where the mean-value theorem is used to obtain the last equality. Then $R(\mathbf{h}) = \sum_{i=1}^{n} f_i'(\mathbf{x} + \sum_{j=1}^{i-1} h_j \mathbf{e}_j + \theta h_i \mathbf{e}_i) - \sum_{i=1}^{n} f_i'(\mathbf{x}) h_i$. Because the derivatives $f_i'(\mathbf{x})$ are assumed to be continuous, and $(h_i / \|\mathbf{h}\|)[f_i'(\mathbf{x} + \sum_{j=1}^{i} h_j \mathbf{e}_j + \theta_i h_i \mathbf{e}_i) h_i - f_i'(\mathbf{x}) h_i] / h_i$ tends to 0 as $h_i \to 0$, it follows that $R(\mathbf{h}) / \|\mathbf{h}\| \to \mathbf{0}$ as $\mathbf{h} \to \mathbf{0}$. ∎

We next derive two useful inequalities. Let $\mathbf{f}$ be a C^1 function from $\mathbb{R}^n$ into $\mathbb{R}^m$. Then for all $\mathbf{x}$ and $\mathbf{y}$,

$$\|\mathbf{f}(\mathbf{y}) - \mathbf{f}(\mathbf{x})\| \leq \max_{\mathbf{z} \in [\mathbf{x}, \mathbf{y}]} \|\mathbf{f}'(\mathbf{z})(\mathbf{y} - \mathbf{x})\| \tag{5}$$

To prove this inequality, note first that $\|\mathbf{a}\| = \max_{\|\mathbf{b}\|=1} |\mathbf{b} \cdot \mathbf{a}|$. This is obvious if $\mathbf{a} = \mathbf{0}$. Suppose $\mathbf{a} \neq \mathbf{0}$. For $\|\mathbf{b}\| = 1$, by the Cauchy–Schwarz inequality, $|\mathbf{b} \cdot \mathbf{a}| \leq \|\mathbf{b}\| \|\mathbf{a}\| = \|\mathbf{a}\|$, with equality if $\mathbf{b} = \mathbf{a}/\|\mathbf{a}\|$. Hence, it suffices to prove $\|\mathbf{b} \cdot \mathbf{f}(\mathbf{y}) - \mathbf{b} \cdot \mathbf{f}(\mathbf{x})\| \leq \max_{\mathbf{z} \in [\mathbf{x}, \mathbf{y}]} \|\mathbf{b} \cdot \mathbf{f}'(\mathbf{z})(\mathbf{y} - \mathbf{x})\|$ for $\|\mathbf{b}\| = 1$. By the mean-value theorem (Theorem 2.1.2), for some $\mathbf{z} \in [\mathbf{x}, \mathbf{y}]$ we have $\mathbf{b} \cdot \mathbf{f}(\mathbf{y}) - \mathbf{b} \cdot \mathbf{f}(\mathbf{x}) = \mathbf{b} \cdot \mathbf{f}'(\mathbf{z})(\mathbf{y} - \mathbf{x})$, which concludes the proof.

By applying the inequality (5) to the function $\mathbf{y} \mapsto \mathbf{f}(\mathbf{y}) - \mathbf{f}'(\mathbf{w})\mathbf{y}$, with $\mathbf{w}$ as a fixed vector, the following inequality is obtained for all $\mathbf{x}$, $\mathbf{y}$, and $\mathbf{w}$ in $\mathbb{R}^n$:

$$\|\mathbf{f}(\mathbf{y}) - \mathbf{f}(\mathbf{x}) - \mathbf{f}'(\mathbf{w})(\mathbf{y} - \mathbf{x})\| \leq \max_{\mathbf{z} \in [\mathbf{x}, \mathbf{y}]} \|(\mathbf{f}'(\mathbf{z}) - \mathbf{f}'(\mathbf{w}))(\mathbf{y} - \mathbf{x})\| \tag{6}$$

The Inverse of a Transformation

Consider a transformation $\mathbf{f} : A \to B$ where $A \subseteq \mathbb{R}^n$ and $B \subseteq \mathbb{R}^m$. Suppose the range of $\mathbf{f}$ is the whole of B. Recall that $\mathbf{f}$ is *one-to-one* if $\mathbf{x}_1 \neq \mathbf{x}_2 \Rightarrow \mathbf{f}(\mathbf{x}_1) \neq \mathbf{f}(\mathbf{x}_2)$. In this case, for each point $\mathbf{y}$ in B there is exactly one point $\mathbf{x}$ in A such that $\mathbf{f}(\mathbf{x}) = \mathbf{y}$, and the **inverse** of $\mathbf{f}$ is the transformation $\mathbf{f}^{-1} : B \to A$ (note the order!) which maps each $\mathbf{y}$ in B to precisely that point $\mathbf{x}$ in A for which $\mathbf{f}(\mathbf{x}) = \mathbf{y}$.

When does a transformation $\mathbf{f}$ have an inverse? By definition, it has an inverse if and only if $\mathbf{f}$ is one-to-one, but this is often difficult to check directly. The problem is then to find useful conditions on $\mathbf{f}$ which ensure that the inverse exists.

Theorem 2.7.6 below gives a local solution to this problem. Global solutions are much harder to come by. See Section 2.10 for some results in this direction.

As a first step, note that if $\mathbf{f} : U \to V$ and $\mathbf{g} : V \to U$ are differentiable and mutually inverse transformations between open sets U and V in $\mathbb{R}^n$, then $\mathbf{g} \circ \mathbf{f}$ is the identity transformation on U, and therefore $(\mathbf{g} \circ \mathbf{f})'(\mathbf{x}) = \mathbf{I}_n$ for all $\mathbf{x}$ in U. The chain rule then gives $\mathbf{g}'(\mathbf{f}(\mathbf{x}))\mathbf{f}'(\mathbf{x}) = \mathbf{I}_n$. This means, in particular, that the Jacobian matrix $\mathbf{f}'(\mathbf{x})$ must be nonsingular, so $|\mathbf{f}'(\mathbf{x})| \neq 0$. Also, $\mathbf{g}'(\mathbf{f}(\mathbf{x}))$ is the inverse matrix $(\mathbf{f}'(\mathbf{x}))^{-1}$.

The determinant $|\mathbf{f}'(\mathbf{x})|$ is called the **Jacobian determinant** of $\mathbf{f}$, and is often written as $\partial(f_1, \ldots, f_n)/\partial(x_1, \ldots, x_n)$.

THEOREM 2.7.6 (INVERSE FUNCTION THEOREM)

Consider a transformation $\mathbf{f} = (f_1, \ldots, f_n)$ from $A \subseteq \mathbb{R}^n$ into $\mathbb{R}^n$ and assume that $\mathbf{f}$ is C^k $(k \geq 1)$ in an open set containing $\mathbf{x}^0 = (x_1^0, \ldots, x_n^0)$. Furthermore, suppose that

$$|\mathbf{f}'(\mathbf{x})| = \frac{\partial(f_1, \ldots, f_n)}{\partial(x_1, \ldots, x_n)} \neq 0 \quad \text{for} \quad \mathbf{x} = \mathbf{x}^0$$

Let $\mathbf{y}^0 = \mathbf{f}(\mathbf{x}^0)$. Then there exists an open set U around $\mathbf{x}^0$ such that $\mathbf{f}$ maps U one-to-one onto an open set V around $\mathbf{y}^0$, and there is an inverse mapping $\mathbf{g} = \mathbf{f}^{-1} : V \to U$ which is also C^k.

Moreover, for all $\mathbf{y}$ in V, we have

$$\mathbf{g}'(\mathbf{y}) = (\mathbf{f}'(\mathbf{x}))^{-1}, \quad \text{where } \mathbf{x} = \mathbf{g}(\mathbf{y}) \in U$$

A proof can be found in e.g. Marsden and Hoffman (1993) or Munkres (1991).

Because $\mathbf{f}$, generally, is one-to-one only in a (possibly small) neighbourhood of $\mathbf{x}^0$, we say that Theorem 2.7.6 gives sufficient conditions for the existence of a *local* inverse. Briefly formulated:

A C^k transformation $\mathbf{f}$ from $\mathbb{R}^n$ into $\mathbb{R}^n$ with nonzero Jacobian determinant at $\mathbf{x}^0$ has a local inverse transformation around $\mathbf{f}(\mathbf{x}^0)$, and this inverse is also C^k. $\qquad$ (7)

One implication of the theorem is that if $\mathbf{f}$ is C^1 in an open set around $\mathbf{x}^0$ and $\mathbf{f}'(\mathbf{x}^0) \neq 0$, then $\mathbf{f}$ is one-to-one in an open ball around $\mathbf{x}^0$. If the Jacobian determinant is different from 0 for all $\mathbf{x}$ in a set A, will $\mathbf{f}$ then be one-to-one in the whole of A? If $n = 1$ and A is an interval in $\mathbb{R}$, this is true, but in general the answer is no, as shown by the next example.

EXAMPLE 2 $\quad$ Define the transformation $\mathbf{f}$ from $A = \{(x_1, x_2) : x_1^2 + x_2^2 \geq 1\} \subseteq \mathbb{R}^2$ into $\mathbb{R}^2$ by

$$\mathbf{f}(x_1, x_2) = (y_1, y_2), \quad \text{where} \quad y_1 = x_1^2 - x_2^2, \quad y_2 = x_1 x_2$$

(a) Compute the Jacobian determinant of $\mathbf{f}$ and show that it is $\neq 0$ in the whole of A.

(b) What does $\mathbf{f}$ do to the points $(1,1)$ and $(-1, -1)$?

(c) Comment on the results in (a) and (b).

Solution: (a) $\mathbf{f}'(x_1, x_2) = \begin{vmatrix} \partial y_1/\partial x_1 & \partial y_1/\partial x_2 \\ \partial y_2/\partial x_1 & \partial y_2/\partial x_2 \end{vmatrix} = \begin{vmatrix} 2x_1 & -2x_2 \\ x_2 & x_1 \end{vmatrix} = 2(x_1^2 + x_2^2) \neq 0$

for all (x_1, x_2) in A.

(b) Both $(x_1, x_2) = (1, 1)$ and $(x_1, x_2) = (-1, -1)$ are mapped into $(y_1, y_2) = (0, 1)$.

(c) Even though the Jacobian matrix of $\mathbf{f}$ is $\neq \mathbf{0}$ in all of A, $\mathbf{f}$ is not one-to-one in all of A.

Transformations from $\mathbb{R}^n$ to $\mathbb{R}^m$, where $m \leq n$

The theorem on inverse functions deals with transformations from a subset of $\mathbb{R}^n$ into $\mathbb{R}^n$. Now, consider a more general situation, in which $\mathbf{f}$ is a C^1 transformation from a subset of $\mathbb{R}^n$ into $\mathbb{R}^m$ with $m \leq n$, and let U be a neighbourhood of a point $\mathbf{x}^0$ in $\mathbb{R}^n$. Then U will contain a ball B centred at $\mathbf{x}^0$ with a positive radius r. The set $\mathbf{f}(U) = \{f(\mathbf{x}) : \mathbf{x} \in U\}$ will contain $\mathbf{f}(\mathbf{x}^0) = \mathbf{y}^0$. Is $\mathbf{y}^0$ an interior point of $\mathbf{f}(U)$? Not necessarily. For example, if $\mathbf{f} : \mathbb{R}^3 \to \mathbb{R}^2$ is defined by $\mathbf{f}(x, y, z) = (x + y + z, x + y + z)$, then $\mathbf{f}$ maps $\mathbb{R}^3$ into a straight line through $\mathbf{y}^0 = (0, 0)$, which certainly does not contain a neighbourhood of $\mathbf{y}^0$. Thus the mapping makes $\mathbb{R}^3$ collapse into a set of lower dimension than the target set (a straight line in this case). The final theorem of this section tells us that such a collapse is impossible if the Jacobian matrix of $\mathbf{f}$ has maximal rank at $\mathbf{x}^0$. (Note that the Jacobian of $\mathbf{f}(x, y) = (x + y + z, x + y + z)$ is the matrix $\begin{pmatrix} 1 & 1 & 1 \\ 1 & 1 & 1 \end{pmatrix}$, which has rank 1.)

THEOREM 2.7.7

Suppose $\mathbf{f}$ is a transformation from an open subset A of $\mathbb{R}^n$ into $\mathbb{R}^m$, and that $m \leq n$. If $\mathbf{f}$ is C^1 in a neighbourhood of $\mathbf{x}^0 \in A$, and the Jacobian matrix has rank m at $\mathbf{x}^0$, then $\mathbf{f}(\mathbf{x}^0)$ is an interior point of $\mathbf{f}(U)$ for any open neighbourhood U of $\mathbf{x}^0$.

A proof can be found in e.g. Marsden and Hoffman (1993) or Munkres (1991).

PROBLEMS FOR SECTION 2.7

1. Consider the transformation from $\mathbb{R}^2$ to $\mathbb{R}^2$ determined by $(x_1, x_2) \mapsto (y_1, y_2)$, where

$$y_1 = x_1 - x_1 x_2, \quad y_2 = x_1 x_2 \tag{$*$}$$

Compute the Jacobian determinant of this transformation, and find the inverse (where it exists) by solving the system of equations in $(*)$ for x_1 and x_2. Examine what the transformation does to the rectangle determined by $1 \leq x_1 \leq 2$, $1/2 \leq x_2 \leq 2/3$. Draw a figure!

2. Consider the linear transformation $T: (x, y) \mapsto (u, v)$ from $\mathbb{R}^2$ to $\mathbb{R}^2$ determined by $u = ax + by$, $v = cx + dy$, where a, b, c, and d are constants, not all equal to 0. Suppose the Jacobian determinant of T is 0. Then, show that T maps the whole of $\mathbb{R}^2$ onto a straight line through the origin of the uv-plane.

3. Consider the transformation $T : \mathbb{R}^2 \to \mathbb{R}^2$ defined by $T(r, \theta) = (r\cos\theta, r\sin\theta)$.

   (a) Compute the Jacobian determinant J of T.

   (b) Let A be the domain in the (r, θ) plane determined by $1 \le r \le 2$ and $\theta \in [0, k]$, where $k > 2\pi$. Show that $J \neq 0$ in the whole of A, yet T is not one-to-one in A.

4. Give sufficient conditions on f and g to ensure that the equations

$$u = f(x, y), \quad v = g(x, y)$$

   can be solved for x and y locally. Show that if the solutions are $x = F(u, v)$, $y = G(u, v)$, and J denotes the Jacobian determinant of f and g w.r.t. u and v, then

$$\frac{\partial F}{\partial u} = \frac{1}{J}\frac{\partial g}{\partial y}, \quad \frac{\partial G}{\partial u} = -\frac{1}{J}\frac{\partial g}{\partial x}$$

5. Let f be defined for all (x, y) by

$$f(x, y) = \frac{xy^2}{x^2 + y^4} \quad \text{and} \quad f(0, 0) = 0$$

   (a) Show that $f_1'(x, y)$ and $f_2'(x, y)$ exist for all (x, y).

   (b) Show that f has a directional derivative in every direction at every point.

   (c) Show that f is not continuous at $(0, 0)$. Is f differentiable at $(0, 0)$?

2.8 Implicit Function Theorems

Even elementary economics books consider the following problem: *If a system of equations defines some endogenous variables as functions of the remaining exogenous variables, what are the partial derivatives of these functions?* This section addresses the question whether these functions exist, and if they do exist, whether they are differentiable.

Consider first the simplest case, with *one* equation of the form

$$f(x, y) = 0 \tag{$*$}$$

Assuming that f is C^1 and that $(*)$ defines y as a differentiable function of x, implicit differentiation yields $f_1'(x, y) + f_2'(x, y)y' = 0$. If $f_2'(x, y) \neq 0$, then $y' = -f_1'(x, y)/f_2'(x, y)$.

Geometrically, (∗) represents a curve in the xy plane, which could be the curve illustrated in Fig. 1.

Studying the curve we observe that for $x > x_1$ there is no y such that (x, y) satisfies the equation. If $x_2 < x < x_1$, there are two values of y for which (x, y) satisfies the equation. (The curve has $x = x_2$ as a vertical asymptote.) Finally, for $x \leq x_2$, there is only one corresponding y. Note that the equation defines y as a function of x in any interval contained in $(-\infty, x_2]$. Consider on the other hand an interval contained in (x_2, x_1). The domain of y must be restricted in order for the equation to define y as a function of x in the interval. Now, consider the point (x_0, y_0). If the rectangle R is as in Fig. 1, the equation *does* define y as a function of x in this rectangle. The graph of this function is given in Fig. 2. The size of the rectangle R is constrained by the requirement that each straight line through R parallel to the y-axis must intersect the curve in one and only one point.

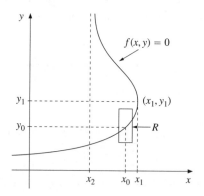

Figure 1 The graph of $f(x, y) = 0$

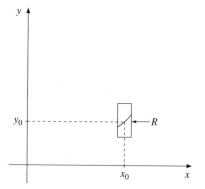

Figure 2 $f(x, y) = 0$ defines y as a function of x in the rectangle R.

Similar rectangles and corresponding solutions of the equation can be constructed for all other points on the curve, except one: the "easternmost" point (x_1, y_1). Regardless of the size of the chosen rectangle around (x_1, y_1) (with (x_1, y_1) as an interior point), for those x close to x_1 on the left there will be two values of y satisfying the equation. For those x to the right of x_1, there is no suitable y at all. Hence, the equation does not define y as a function of x in a neighbourhood of the point (x_1, y_1). Note that $f_2'(x_1, y_1) = 0$. (The curve $f(x, y) = 0$ is a level curve for $z = f(x, y)$, and at each point on the curve, the gradient of f, i.e. the vector (f_1', f_2'), is orthogonal to the level curve. At (x_1, y_1), the gradient is clearly parallel to the x-axis, and thus its y-component f_2' is equal to 0.)

As indicated in this example, the crucial condition for $f(x, y) = 0$ to define y as a function of x around (x_0, y_0) is that $f_2'(x_0, y_0) \neq 0$. In general, there are *implicit function theorems* which state when an equation or a system of equations defines some of the variables as functions of the remaining variables. For equation (∗), sufficient conditions for $f(x, y) = 0$ to define y as a function of x, are briefly indicated in the following:

If $f(x_0, y_0) = 0$ and $f'_2(x_0, y_0) \neq 0$, then the equation $f(x, y) = 0$ defines y as a function $y = \varphi(x)$ of x near x_0, with $y_0 = \varphi(x_0)$, and with its derivative given by $y' = -f'_1(x, y)/f'_2(x, y)$. (1)

THEOREM 2.8.1 (THE IMPLICIT FUNCTION THEOREM)

Suppose $f(x, y)$ is C^1 in an open set A containing (x_0, y_0), with $f(x_0, y_0) = 0$ and $f'_2(x_0, y_0) \neq 0$. Then there exist an interval $I_1 = (x_0 - \delta, x_0 + \delta)$ and an interval $I_2 = (y_0 - \varepsilon, y_0 + \varepsilon)$ (with $\delta > 0$ and $\varepsilon > 0$) such that $I_1 \times I_2 \subseteq A$ and:

(a) for every x in I_1 the equation $f(x, y) = 0$ has a unique solution in I_2 which defines y as a function $y = \varphi(x)$ in I_1;

(b) φ is C^1 in $I_1 = (x_0 - \delta, x_0 + \delta)$, with derivative

$$\varphi'(x) = -\frac{f'_1(x, \varphi(x))}{f'_2(x, \varphi(x))} \tag{2}$$

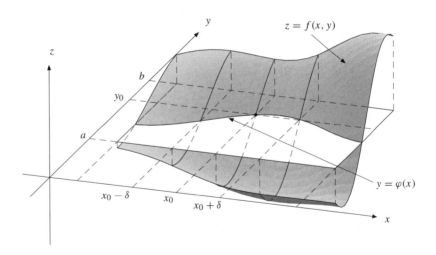

Figure 3 A section of the graph of $z = f(x, y)$ over the rectangle R.

To explain this theorem, consider Fig. 3 which shows the graph of $z = f(x, y)$. The graph intersects the xy-plane at the point (x_0, y_0), because $f(x_0, y_0) = 0$. Result (a) implies that the surface cuts the xy-plane in a curve which is the graph of a function $y = \varphi(x)$ in a neighbourhood of (x_0, y_0). The figure illustrates the case when $f'_2(x_0, y_0) > 0$. Because $f'_2(x, y)$ is continuous, in this case $f'_2(x, y)$ is positive in an open neighbourhood around

(x_0, y_0), and so for a fixed x, $f(x, y)$ becomes a strictly increasing function of y. Choose a and b so close to y_0 that if $a < y_0 < b$, then $f(x_0, a) < 0 < f(x_0, b)$. Then for x close to x_0, we have $f(x, a) < 0 < f(x, b)$, because of the continuity of f. According to the intermediate value theorem, for each such x there exists a point y in (a, b) with $f(x, y) = 0$. Because f is strictly increasing w.r.t. y in a neighbourhood of (x_0, y_0), the solution is unique. The solution y is a function $\varphi(x)$ of x and part (b) claims that it is C^1.

EXAMPLE 1   Show that the equation $x^2 e^y - 2y + x = 0$ defines y as a function of x in an interval around the point $(-1, 0)$. Find the derivative of this function at $x = -1$. (Observe that the equation cannot be solved explicitly for y.)

Solution: Put $f(x, y) = x^2 e^y - 2y + x$. Then $f_1'(x, y) = 2x e^y + 1$, $f_2'(x, y) = x^2 e^y - 2$, and f is C^1 everywhere. Furthermore, $f(-1, 0) = 0$ and $f_2'(-1, 0) = -1 \neq 0$. According to Theorem 2.8.1, the equation therefore defines y as a C^1 function of x in an interval around $(-1, 0)$. Because $f_1'(-1, 0) = -1$, equation (2) implies that $y' = -1$ at $x = -1$.

Theorem 2.8.1 gives *sufficient conditions* for $f(x, y) = 0$ to define y as a function of x in a neighbourhood of (x_0, y_0). The crucial condition is that $f_2'(x_0, y_0) \neq 0$. The next example shows that this condition is not *necessary*.

EXAMPLE 2   Let $f(x, y) = y^3 - x$. Then $f_2'(x, y) = 3y^2$, so that $f(0, 0) = 0$ and $f_2'(0, 0) = 0$. The equation $y^3 - x = 0$ still defines y as a function of x around $(0, 0)$. Here, $y^3 - x = 0 \iff y = x^{1/3}$, and $y = x^{1/3}$ is a function which is defined for all x. Note that its derivative at $x = 0$ does not exist.

The General Case

Theorem 2.8.1 can be generalized to systems of equations of the form

$$
\begin{aligned}
f_1(x_1, x_2, \ldots, x_n, y_1, y_2, \ldots, y_m) &= 0 \\
&\cdots\cdots\cdots\cdots\cdots\cdots\cdots\cdots\cdots\cdots\cdots\cdots\cdots\cdots \qquad\Longleftrightarrow\qquad \mathbf{f}(\mathbf{x}, \mathbf{y}) = \mathbf{0} \qquad (3)\\
f_m(x_1, x_2, \ldots, x_n, y_1, y_2, \ldots, y_m) &= 0
\end{aligned}
$$

with $\mathbf{f} = (f_1, \ldots, f_m)'$, $\mathbf{x} = (x_1, \ldots, x_n)$, and $\mathbf{y} = (y_1, \ldots, y_m)$. Here there are $n + m$ variables and m equations. Let $(\mathbf{x}^0, \mathbf{y}^0) = (x_1^0, \ldots, x_n^0, y_1^0, \ldots, y_m^0)$ be an "equilibrium solution" of (3). If $x_1, \ldots, x_n$ are the *exogenous* variables and $y_1, \ldots, y_m$ are the *endogenous* variables, then the problem is: Under what conditions will (3) define the endogenous variables as C^1 functions of the exogenous variables in a neighbourhood of $(\mathbf{x}^0, \mathbf{y}^0)$, and what happens to the endogenous variables when the exogenous variables are slightly changed? More specifically, what is the derivative of $\mathbf{y}$ w.r.t. $\mathbf{x}$? The answer is given by the following theorem. It is convenient to use the notation

$$
\frac{\partial \mathbf{f}(\mathbf{x}, \mathbf{y})}{\partial \mathbf{x}} = \begin{pmatrix} \partial f_1/\partial x_1 & \cdots & \partial f_1/\partial x_n \\ \cdots\cdots\cdots\cdots\cdots\cdots\cdots\cdots \\ \partial f_m/\partial x_1 & \cdots & \partial f_m/\partial x_n \end{pmatrix}
$$

or $\mathbf{f}_{\mathbf{x}}'(\mathbf{x}, \mathbf{y})$, for the Jacobian matrix of $\mathbf{f}(\mathbf{x}, \mathbf{y})$ w.r.t. $\mathbf{x}$. Similarly, $\partial \mathbf{f}/\partial \mathbf{y} = \mathbf{f}_{\mathbf{y}}'(\mathbf{x}, \mathbf{y})$ denotes the Jacobian matrix of $\mathbf{f}$ w.r.t. $\mathbf{y}$.

THEOREM 2.8.2 (THE IMPLICIT FUNCTION THEOREM, GENERAL VERSION)

Suppose $\mathbf{f} = (f_1, \ldots, f_m)$ is C^1 in an open set A in $\mathbb{R}^{n+m}$, and consider the vector equation $\mathbf{f}(\mathbf{x}, \mathbf{y}) = \mathbf{0}$, where $\mathbf{x} \in \mathbb{R}^n$ and $\mathbf{y} \in \mathbb{R}^m$. Let $(\mathbf{x}^0, \mathbf{y}^0)$ be an interior point of A satisfying $\mathbf{f}(\mathbf{x}, \mathbf{y}) = \mathbf{0}$. Suppose that the Jacobian determinant of $\mathbf{f}$ w.r.t. $\mathbf{y}$ is different from 0 at $(\mathbf{x}^0, \mathbf{y}^0)$—i.e.

$$\left| \frac{\partial \mathbf{f}(\mathbf{x}, \mathbf{y})}{\partial \mathbf{y}} \right| = \frac{\partial(f_1, \ldots, f_m)}{\partial(y_1, \ldots, y_m)} \neq 0 \quad \text{at} \quad (\mathbf{x}, \mathbf{y}) = (\mathbf{x}^0, \mathbf{y}^0) \tag{4}$$

Then there exist open balls B_1 and B_2 around $\mathbf{x}^0$ and $\mathbf{y}^0$, respectively, with $B_1 \times B_2 \subseteq A$, such that $|\partial \mathbf{f}(\mathbf{x}, \mathbf{y})/\partial \mathbf{y}| \neq 0$ in $B_1 \times B_2$, and such that for each $\mathbf{x}$ in B_1 there is a unique $\mathbf{y}$ in B_2 with $\mathbf{f}(\mathbf{x}, \mathbf{y}) = \mathbf{0}$. In this way $\mathbf{y}$ is defined on B_1 as a C^1 function $\mathbf{g}(\mathbf{x})$ of $\mathbf{x}$. The Jacobian matrix $\partial \mathbf{y}/\partial \mathbf{x} = \partial \mathbf{g}/\partial \mathbf{x} = (\partial g_i(\mathbf{x})/\partial x_j)$ can be found by implicit differentiation of (3), and

$$\frac{\partial \mathbf{g}}{\partial \mathbf{x}} = -\left(\frac{\partial \mathbf{f}}{\partial \mathbf{y}} \right)^{-1} \left(\frac{\partial \mathbf{f}}{\partial \mathbf{x}} \right) \tag{5}$$

NOTE 1 Let us show how to derive (5) by implicit differentiation of (3). Insert $y_1 = g_1(\mathbf{x})$, $\ldots, y_m = g_m(\mathbf{x})$ into (3). Then, for $j = 1, \ldots, n$, implicit differentiation w.r.t. x_j yields

$$\frac{\partial f_1}{\partial x_j} + \frac{\partial f_1}{\partial y_1} \frac{\partial y_1}{\partial x_j} + \cdots + \frac{\partial f_1}{\partial y_m} \frac{\partial y_m}{\partial x_j} = 0$$

$$\cdots\cdots\cdots\cdots\cdots\cdots\cdots\cdots\cdots\cdots\cdots \tag{6}$$

$$\frac{\partial f_m}{\partial x_j} + \frac{\partial f_m}{\partial y_1} \frac{\partial y_1}{\partial x_j} + \cdots + \frac{\partial f_m}{\partial y_m} \frac{\partial y_m}{\partial x_j} = 0$$

Move the first term in each equation to the right-hand side and use matrix notation to obtain

$$\begin{pmatrix} \dfrac{\partial f_1}{\partial y_1} & \cdots & \dfrac{\partial f_1}{\partial y_m} \\ \vdots & & \vdots \\ \dfrac{\partial f_m}{\partial y_1} & \cdots & \dfrac{\partial f_m}{\partial y_m} \end{pmatrix} \begin{pmatrix} \dfrac{\partial y_1}{\partial x_j} \\ \vdots \\ \dfrac{\partial y_m}{\partial x_j} \end{pmatrix} = - \begin{pmatrix} \dfrac{\partial f_1}{\partial x_j} \\ \vdots \\ \dfrac{\partial f_m}{\partial x_j} \end{pmatrix} \tag{7}$$

The coefficient matrix on the left-hand side is then $\partial \mathbf{f}/\partial \mathbf{y}$, and the right-hand side is minus the jth column of $\partial \mathbf{f}/\partial \mathbf{x}$. By multiplying (7) from the left by $(\partial \mathbf{f}/\partial \mathbf{y})^{-1}$, we get the jth column of $\partial \mathbf{g}/\partial \mathbf{x} = \partial \mathbf{y}/\partial \mathbf{x}$. Of course (7) holds for all $j = 1, \ldots, n$, and (5) just expresses these n simultaneous equations in matrix form.

NOTE 2 Suppose $f_1, \ldots, f_m$ are C^r functions ($r > 1$). Then it follows from (5) that g_1, $\ldots, g_m$ are also C^r functions.

PROBLEMS FOR SECTION 2.8

1. Show that the following equations define y implicitly as a function of x in an interval around x_0. Find y' when $x = x_0$.

   (a) $y^3 + y - x^3 = 0$, $x_0 = 0$ (b) $x^2 + y + \sin(xy) = 0$, $x_0 = 0$

2. Check if the following equations can be represented in the form $z = g(x, y)$ in a neighbourhood of the given point (x_0, y_0, z_0). Compute $g_1'(x_0, y_0)$ and $g_2'(x_0, y_0)$.

   (a) $x^3 + y^3 + z^3 - xyz - 1 = 0$, $(x_0, y_0, z_0) = (0, 0, 1)$

   (b) $e^z - z^2 - x^2 - y^2 = 0$, $(x_0, y_0, z_0) = (1, 0, 0)$

3. The point $P = (x, y, z, u, v, w) = (1, 1, 0, -1, 0, 1)$ satisfies all the equations

$$y^2 - z + u - v - w^3 = -1$$
$$-2x + y - z^2 + u + v^3 - w = -3$$
$$x^2 + z - u - v + w^3 = 3$$

   Find u_x', v_x', and w_x' at P.

4. The functions f and g are defined in $\mathbb{R}^2$ by $f(u, v) = e^u \cos v$, $g(u, v) = e^u \sin v$. Show that the Jacobian determinant $\partial(f, g)/\partial(u, v)$ of this transformation is different from 0 *everywhere*. How many solutions are there to the following two systems of equations?

   (a) $\begin{aligned} e^u \cos v &= 0 \\ e^u \sin v &= 0 \end{aligned}$ (b) $\begin{aligned} e^u \cos v &= 1 \\ e^u \sin v &= 1 \end{aligned}$

5. Suppose (x_0, y_0, u_0, v_0) satisfies the two equations

$$F(x, y, u, v) = x^2 - y^2 + uv - v^2 + 3 = 0$$
$$G(x, y, u, v) = x + y^2 + u^2 + uv - 2 = 0$$

   State conditions that are sufficient for this system to be represented by two equations $u = f(x, y)$, $v = g(x, y)$ in a neighbourhood of this point. Show that this condition is satisfied when $(x_0, y_0, u_0, v_0) = (2, 1, -1, 2)$, and compute $f_x'(2, 1)$, $f_y'(2, 1)$, $g_x'(2, 1)$ and $g_y'(2, 1)$.

2.9 Degrees of Freedom and Functional Dependence

A system of equations with more variables than equations will in general have many solutions. Usually, the larger is the difference between the number of variables and the number of equations, the larger is the set of solutions. In general, *a system of equations in n variables is said to have k* **degrees of freedom** *if there is a set of k variables that can be freely chosen, while the remaining n − k variables are uniquely determined once the k free variables have been assigned specific values.* Thus, the system must define $n - k$ of the variables as functions of the remaining k free variables. If the n variables are restricted to vary in a set A in $\mathbb{R}^n$, we say that the system has k *degrees of freedom in A*.

For an equation system to have k degrees of freedom, it suffices that there *exist* k variables that can be freely chosen. We do not require that *any* set of k variables can be chosen freely.

A rough rule can be used for a preliminary estimate of the number of degrees of freedom for a system of equation. This is called the "counting rule":

ROUGH COUNTING RULE

To find the number of degrees of freedom for a system of equations, count the
number of variables, n, and the number of "independent" equations, m. If $n > m$, $\qquad$ (1)
there are $n - m$ degrees of freedom in the system.

This rule lies behind the following economic proposition: "The number of independent targets that a government can pursue cannot possibly exceed the number of available policy instruments." For example, assuming that the targets of price stability, low unemployment, and stable exchange rates are independent, a government seeking to meet all three simultaneously, needs at least three independent policy instruments.

It is easy to give examples where the counting rule fails, and it is obvious that the word "independent" cannot be dropped from the statement of the counting rule. For instance, if we just add one equation which repeats one that has appeared before, the number of degrees of freedom will certainly not be reduced.

NOTE 1 If we have a *linear* system of m equations in n unknowns, $\mathbf{Ax} = \mathbf{b}$, then according to Theorem 1.5.1, the system has a solution iff the rank of the coefficient matrix $\mathbf{A}$ is equal to the rank of the augmented matrix. In this case, the counting rule gives the correct result iff the m row vectors in $\mathbf{A}$ are linearly independent, because then the rank of $\mathbf{A}$ is equal to m. (See Theorem 1.5.3.) So what is needed for the counting rule to apply in the case of linear systems is that the row vectors of the coefficient matrix be linearly independent.

The implicit function theorem gives us a precise local counting rule for the system

$$
\begin{aligned}
f_1(x_1, \ldots, x_n) &= 0 \\
&\cdots\cdots\cdots\cdots\cdots\cdots \qquad \Longleftrightarrow \qquad \mathbf{f}(\mathbf{x}) = \mathbf{0} \qquad (2) \\
f_m(x_1, \ldots, x_n) &= 0
\end{aligned}
$$

in the case $n > m$. Suppose that $f_1, \ldots, f_m$ are C^1 functions in a neighbourhood of a solution $\mathbf{x}^0$, and suppose that the Jacobian matrix $\mathbf{f}'(\mathbf{x})$ has rank m at $\mathbf{x}^0$. This implies that for some selection of m of the variables x_i, which we denote by $x_{i_1}, x_{i_2}, \ldots, x_{i_m}$, the Jacobian determinant

$$\frac{\partial(f_1, f_2, \ldots, f_m)}{\partial(x_{i_1}, x_{i_2}, \ldots, x_{i_m})}$$

is not 0 at $\mathbf{x}^0$. Then an easy modification of Theorem 2.8.2 shows that there exists a ball B around $\mathbf{x}^0$ so that system (1) defines $x_{i_1}, x_{i_2}, \ldots, x_{i_m}$ as functions of the other $n - m$ components x_i in B. Then system (1) has, by definition, $n - m$ degrees of freedom in B. Thus we have the following result:

CORRECT COUNTING RULE

If $\mathbf{x}^0$ is a solution of system (2) and the Jacobian matrix $\mathbf{f}'(\mathbf{x})$ has rank m at $\mathbf{x}^0$, then there exists a ball B around $\mathbf{x}^0$, such that the system has $n - m$ degrees of freedom in B. In this case the counting rule yields the correct result.   (3)

Functional Dependence

In formulating the counting rule we assumed that the equations were independent. Consider the system of equations (2) and suppose there exists a function G such that $f_m(\mathbf{x}) \equiv G(f_1(\mathbf{x}), \ldots, f_{m-1}(\mathbf{x}))$. Then $f_m(\mathbf{x})$ is *functionally dependent* on $f_1, \ldots, f_{m-1}$. More symmetrically, for the functions $f_1, \ldots, f_m$ to be functionally dependent in a set A, it is required that there exists a function F of m variables such that

$$F(f_1(\mathbf{x}), \ldots, f_m(\mathbf{x})) = 0 \quad \text{for all } \mathbf{x} \in A \tag{4}$$

If $F \equiv 0$, then (4) is satisfied regardless of the functions $f_1, \ldots, f_m$, so some additional requirements on F are needed. The following definition is the standard one:

DEFINITION OF FUNCTIONAL DEPENDENCE

The functions $f_1, \ldots, f_m$ are **functionally dependent in** A if there exists a C^1 function F on $\mathbb{R}^m$ which satisfies (4), and for some j, has $F'_j \neq 0$ everywhere.   (5)

With these conditions imposed on F, it is always possible (at least locally) to solve the equation $F(y_1, \ldots, y_m) = 0$ for y_j and get y_j as a function of the other variables y_i—i.e. $f_j(\mathbf{x})$ can be expressed as a function of the other $f_i(\mathbf{x})$ for $\mathbf{x} \in A$.

The concept of functional dependence is useful in connection with the discussion of superfluous equations. If F is a C^1 function such that $f_1, \ldots, f_m$ and F together satisfy (4) with

$A = \mathbb{R}^n$, $F(0, \ldots, 0) = 0$, and $F'_j \neq 0$ everywhere, then $F(0, \ldots, 0, f_j(\mathbf{x}), 0, \ldots, 0) = 0$ implies that $f_j(\mathbf{x}) = 0$—i.e. $f_i(\mathbf{x}) = 0$ for all $i \neq j$ implies that $f_j(\mathbf{x}) = 0$ also holds. In other words: If $\mathbf{x}$ satisfies all the equations except the jth, then $\mathbf{x}$ automatically also satisfies the jth equation. In this case, the jth equation is superfluous. Hence:

Suppose the equation system (2) has solutions and that $f_1(\mathbf{x}), \ldots, f_m(\mathbf{x})$ are functionally dependent. *Then the system contains at least one superfluous equation.*

NOTE 2 Consider system (2) and suppose the C^1 functions $f_1, \ldots, f_m$ are functionally dependent in $\mathbb{R}^n$ according to the definition (5). Because there is a superfluous equation, the counting rule fails. Then, according to (3), the Jacobian matrix $\mathbf{f}'(\mathbf{x})$ cannot have rank m at any solution point. By differentiation of (4) w.r.t. $\mathbf{x}$ it follows from the chain rule in matrix form that $\nabla F(\mathbf{f}(\mathbf{x}))\mathbf{f}'(\mathbf{x}) = \mathbf{0}$. Because $\nabla F(\mathbf{f}(\mathbf{x})) \neq \mathbf{0}$, the rows in the Jacobian matrix $\mathbf{f}'(\mathbf{x})$ are linearly dependent, and then $\mathbf{f}'(\mathbf{x})$ does *not* have rank m.

EXAMPLE 1   Show that $f(x, y) = e^y(1+x^2)$ and $g(x, y) = \ln(1+x^2) + y$ are functionally dependent in $\mathbb{R}^2$.

Solution: Put $F(y_1, y_2) = \ln y_1 - y_2$. Then $F(f(x, y), g(x, y)) = y + \ln(1 + x^2) - \ln(1+x^2) - y \equiv 0$ for all x, y. Moreover, $F'_2(y_1, y_2) = -1 \neq 0$, so f and g are functionally dependent.

Local Functional Dependence

A property implied by functional dependence is local functional dependence, defined as follows:

DEFINITION OF LOCAL FUNCTIONAL DEPENDENCE

The functions $f_1, \ldots, f_m$ are **locally functionally dependent** in an open set A if for each $\mathbf{x}_0$ in A there exist a ball $B(\mathbf{x}_0; r) \subseteq A$ and a C^1 function F such that $\nabla F(f_1(\mathbf{x}), \ldots, f_n(\mathbf{x})) \neq \mathbf{0}$ for all $\mathbf{x}$ in $B(\mathbf{x}_0; r)$ and $F(f_1(\mathbf{x}), \ldots, f_n(\mathbf{x})) = 0$ for all $\mathbf{x}$ in $B(\mathbf{x}_0; r)$. (6)

With this concept of local functional dependence the following two theorems hold.

THEOREM 2.9.1 (LOCAL FUNCTIONAL DEPENDENCE)

Let $\mathbf{f} = (f_1, \ldots, f_m)$ be a C^1 transformation defined in an open set A in $\mathbb{R}^n$. If the Jacobian matrix $\mathbf{f}'(\mathbf{x})$ has constant rank $< m$ in A, then $f_1, \ldots, f_m$ are locally functionally dependent.

Proof: Assume first that the Jacobian matrix has rank $m - 1$ in A. Let $\mathbf{x}^0 \in A$. For simplicity, assume that the submatrix $\mathbf{J}'(\mathbf{x}) = (\partial f_i(\mathbf{x})/\partial x_j)_{1 \le i \le m-1, 1 \le j \le m-1}$ has rank $m - 1$ at $\mathbf{x} = \mathbf{x}^0$. Then there exists a positive number r' such that this submatrix has rank $m - 1$ for all $\mathbf{x}$ in $B(\mathbf{x}^0; r')$. Write $(x_1, \ldots, x_{m-1}) = \mathbf{y}$, $(x_m, \ldots, x_n) = \mathbf{z}$, and consider the equation system

$$f_i(\mathbf{y}, \mathbf{z}) = v_i \ \text{ for } \ i < m, \quad x_i = x_i \ \text{ for } \ i \ge m$$

This system can be expressed as two vector equations,

$$\mathbf{v} = \mathbf{f}(\mathbf{y}, \mathbf{z}), \quad \mathbf{z} = \mathbf{z}$$

where $\mathbf{f} = (f_1, \ldots, f_{m-1})$, $\mathbf{v} = (v_1, \ldots, v_{m-1})$. This system evidently has a Jacobian determinant different from 0. Using the inverse function theorem, this equation system can be solved for $(\mathbf{y}, \mathbf{z})$ in terms of $\mathbf{v}$ and $\mathbf{z}$. We obtain $\mathbf{y} = \mathbf{y}(\mathbf{v}, \mathbf{z})$, $\mathbf{z} = \mathbf{z}$ for $(\mathbf{v}, \mathbf{z})$ in a ball $B((\mathbf{v}^0; \mathbf{z}^0); r'')$, where $\mathbf{v}^0 = (f_1(\mathbf{x}^0), \ldots, f_{m-1}(\mathbf{x}^0))$ and $\mathbf{z}^0 = (x_m^0, x_{m+1}^0, \ldots, x_n^0)$. Then $\{(\mathbf{y}(\mathbf{v}, \mathbf{z}), \mathbf{z}) : (\mathbf{v}, \mathbf{z}) \in B((\mathbf{v}^0, \mathbf{z}^0); r'')\} \subseteq A$, and an $r > 0$ can be found such that $B(\mathbf{x}^0; r)$ is contained in $\{(\mathbf{y}(\mathbf{v}, \mathbf{z}), \mathbf{z}) : (\mathbf{v}, \mathbf{z}) \in B((\mathbf{v}^0, \mathbf{z}^0); r'')\}$. Here $\mathbf{y}(\cdot, \cdot)$ is a C^1 function. We have $v_i = f_i(\mathbf{y}(\mathbf{v}, \mathbf{z}), \mathbf{z})$ for $i < m$, and we let $v_m = f_m(\mathbf{y}(\mathbf{v}, \mathbf{z}), \mathbf{z}) = h(\mathbf{v}, \mathbf{z})$. Differentiating these equations with respect to x_k, for a given $k \ge m$, we get $0 = \sum_{j < m}(\partial f_i/\partial x_j)(\partial x_j/\partial x_k) + (\partial f_i/\partial x_k)$ for $i < m$, $(\partial v_m/\partial x_k) = \sum_{j<m}(\partial f_m/\partial x_j)(\partial x_j/\partial x_k) + (\partial f_m/\partial x_k)$. Let us rewrite the equations as follows:

$$\sum_{j<m} \frac{\partial f_i}{\partial x_j}\frac{\partial x_j}{\partial x_k} = -\frac{\partial f_i}{\partial x_k} \quad \text{for} \quad i < m, \qquad \sum_{j<m} \frac{\partial f_m}{\partial x_j}\frac{\partial x_j}{\partial x_k} - \frac{\partial v_m}{\partial x_k} = -\frac{\partial f_m}{\partial x_k}$$

This is a linear equation system in the unknowns $\partial x_j/\partial x_m$ ($j < m$) and $\partial v_m/\partial x_k$. Using Cramer's rule, the numerator in this expression for $\partial v_m/\partial x_k$ is an $m \times m$ minor in the Jacobian matrix of $(f_1, \ldots, f_m)$, and it is therefore zero. The denominator has determinant $(-1)\det(\mathbf{J}'(\mathbf{y}(\mathbf{v}, \mathbf{z}), \mathbf{z})) \neq 0$. This means that v_m does not depend on $x_m, \ldots, x_n$, i.e. $v_m = f_m(\mathbf{y}(\mathbf{v}, \mathbf{z}), \mathbf{z}))$ is independent of $\mathbf{z}$. Hence, $v_m = f_m(\mathbf{y}(\mathbf{v}, \mathbf{z}), \mathbf{z})) = H(\mathbf{v})$ for some C^1 function H. Since $v_i = f_i(x_1, \ldots, x_n)$, we get $f_m(\mathbf{y}(\mathbf{v}, \mathbf{z}), \mathbf{z})) = H(f_1(\mathbf{y}(\mathbf{v}, \mathbf{z}), \mathbf{z}), \ldots, f_{m-1}(\mathbf{y}(\mathbf{v}, \mathbf{z}), \mathbf{z}))$. For every $(\mathbf{y}, \mathbf{z}) = (x_1, \ldots, x_n)$ in $B(\mathbf{x}^0; r)$, there exists a $\mathbf{v}$ such that $(\mathbf{y}, \mathbf{z}) = \mathbf{y}(\mathbf{v}, \mathbf{z}), \mathbf{z})$, i.e. $f_m(\mathbf{y}, \mathbf{z}) = H(f_1(\mathbf{y}, \mathbf{z}), \ldots, f_{m-1}(\mathbf{y}, \mathbf{z}))$ for all $(\mathbf{y}, \mathbf{z})$ in $B(\mathbf{x}^0; r)$. This means that f_m is functionally dependent on $f_1, \ldots, f_{m-1}$ in $B(\mathbf{x}^0; r)$. The case where the Jacobian matrix has constant rank $< m - 1$ follows from the next theorem. ∎

THEOREM 2.9.2 (THE RANK THEOREM)

Suppose that the m functions $f_1, \ldots, f_m$ are defined and C^1 in an open set A in $\mathbb{R}^n$. Assume that the Jacobian matrix of these functions has constant rank $p < m$ in A, and let $\mathbf{x}^0$ be a point in A. Then there exists an open ball $B(\mathbf{x}^0; r) \subseteq A$, functions $f_{i_1}, \ldots, f_{i_p}$, and $m - p$ functions H_j, $j \notin \{i_1, \ldots i_p\}$, that are all C^1, such that for all $\mathbf{x}$ in $B(\mathbf{x}^0; r)$ we have $f_j(\mathbf{x}) = H_j(f_{i_1}(\mathbf{x}), \ldots, f_{i_p}(\mathbf{x}))$ for every $j \notin \{i_1, \ldots i_p\}$.

Proof: (Sketch) Let $f_{i_1}, \ldots, f_{i_m}$ play the role of $f_1, \ldots, f_{m-1}$ in the preceding proof, and let each of the other f_j play the role of the function f_m. ∎

PROBLEMS FOR SECTION 2.9

1. Consider the macroeconomic model described by the system of equations

$$\text{(i) } Y = C + I + G, \quad \text{(ii) } C = f(Y - T), \quad \text{(iii) } I = h(r), \quad \text{(iv) } r = m(M)$$

where f, h, and m are given C^1 functions.

(a) According to the counting rule, how many degrees of freedom has this system?

(b) Give sufficient conditions for the system to determine Y, C, I, and r as functions of the exogenous policy variables M, T, and G in a neighbourhood of an equilibrium point.

2. Consider the functions $u = f(x, y)$, $v = g(x, y)$ given by

(i) $\quad u = e^{x+y}, \quad v = 2x^2 + 4xy + 2y^2 - x - y$

(ii) $\quad u = \dfrac{x}{y}, \quad v = \dfrac{y - x}{y + x}$

(iii) $u = \dfrac{x + y}{1 + xy}, \quad v = \dfrac{(x + y)(1 + xy)}{(1 - x^2)(1 - y^2)}$

(a) Show that in each case the Jacobian determinant $\partial(u, v)/\partial(x, y) = 0$ for all (x, y) where u and v are defined.

(b) Find a functional dependence between u and v in each case. (*Hint:* Solve the equation $u = f(x, y)$ for x and put the result into $v = g(x, y)$.)

3. Let $u = f(x, y)$, $v = g(x, y)$ and suppose that $\partial(u, v)/\partial(x, y) = 0$ for all (x, y) in A. Furthermore, suppose $\partial f/\partial x \neq 0$ at $(x_0, y_0) \in A$. Show that under suitable continuity conditions, f and g are functionally dependent in a ball around (x_0, y_0). (*Hint:* $u = f(x, y)$ yields $x = \varphi(y, u)$ because $\partial f/\partial x \neq 0$. Hence, $v = g(\varphi(y, u), y)$. Show that $\partial v/\partial y = 0$, so that $g(\varphi(y, u), y)$ is independent of y, and hence $v = g(\varphi(y, u), y) = \psi(u)$.)

4. (a) Show that $\partial(u, v, w)/\partial(x, y, z) = 0$ for all (x, y, z) where u, v, and w are defined, when

$$u = x + y - z, \quad v = x - y + z, \quad w = x^2 + y^2 + z^2 - 2yz$$

(b) Show that u, v, and w are functionally dependent.

5. Consider the system of equations

$$1 + (x + y)u - (2 + u)^{1+v} = 0$$
$$2u - (1 + xy)e^{u(x-1)} = 0$$

(a) Use Theorem 2.8.2 to show that the system defines u and v as functions of x and y in an open ball around $(x, y, u, v) = (1, 1, 1, 0)$. Find the values of the partial derivatives of the two functions w.r.t. x when $x = 1$, $y = 1$, $u = 1$, $v = 0$.

(b) Let a and b be arbitrary numbers in the interval $[0, 1]$. Use the intermediate value theorem to show that the equation

$$u - ae^{u(b-1)} = 0$$

has a solution in the interval $[0, 1]$. Is the solution unique?

(c) Show by using (b) that for any point (x, y), $x \in [0, 1]$, $y \in [0, 1]$, there exist solutions u and v of the system. Are u and v uniquely determined?

2.10 Existence and Uniqueness of Solutions of Systems of Equations

This section is concerned with the system of equations

$$f_1(x_1, \ldots, x_n) = y_1, \quad \ldots, \quad f_n(x_1, \ldots, x_n) = y_n \qquad \Longleftrightarrow \qquad \mathbf{f}(\mathbf{x}) = \mathbf{y} \qquad (1)$$

For given values of $y_1, \ldots, y_n$, when will system (1) have a solution $x_1, \ldots, x_n$? Also, when is the solution unique? Note that the number of equations is equal to the number of unknown variables x_i.

The inverse function theorem 2.7.6 tells us that *if* system (1) has a solution $\mathbf{y}^0 = \mathbf{f}(\mathbf{x}^0)$, and the Jacobian determinant is not 0 at $\mathbf{x}^0$, then (1) has a unique solution $\mathbf{x}$ for each $\mathbf{y}$ sufficiently close to $\mathbf{y}^0$. This result says nothing about the *existence* of a solution $\mathbf{x}^0$ of (1) for $\mathbf{y} = \mathbf{y}^0$.

General theorems on the existence and uniqueness of solutions to $\mathbf{f}(\mathbf{x}) = \mathbf{y}$ must involve strong restrictions on $\mathbf{f}$. This is clear even in the case $n = 1$. One can hardly claim that the equation $f(x) = 0$ usually has a unique solution. Think about the case where $f(x)$ is a quadratic polynomial, or more generally a polynomial of degree n.

Suppose f is a continuous function from $\mathbb{R}$ to $\mathbb{R}$ where either $f(x) \to \infty$ as $x \to \infty$ and $f(x) \to -\infty$ as $x \to -\infty$, or $f(x) \to -\infty$ as $x \to \infty$ and $f(x) \to \infty$ as $x \to -\infty$. Then by the intermediate value theorem, for any number y, the equation $f(x) = y$ has at least one solution. Of course, this solution will not necessarily be unique. However, suppose the following condition is satisfied:

$$\text{There exists a positive number } \gamma \text{ such that } f'(x) > \gamma \text{ for all } x \qquad (2)$$

Then $f(x) \to \infty$ as $x \to \infty$, and $f(x) \to -\infty$ as $x \to -\infty$, so there is a solution, and in addition, $f(x)$ is strictly increasing, so the solution is unique.

NOTE 1 The condition (2) cannot be replaced by the requirement that $f'(x) > 0$ for all x. For example, the function $f(x) = e^x$ has $f'(x) > 0$ for all x, but $e^x = -1$ has no solution.

The problem of existence and uniqueness of solutions to (1) becomes more complicated when $n \geq 2$. Let us present some arguments and results that sometimes are useful. We refer to Parthasarathy (1983) for proofs and more details.

For $n = 2$, we consider

$$f_1(x_1, x_2) = y_1, \quad f_2(x_1, x_2) = y_2 \quad \Longleftrightarrow \quad \mathbf{f}(\mathbf{x}) = \mathbf{y} \tag{3}$$

where f_1 and f_2 are C^1 functions. We seek sufficient conditions for system (3) to be uniquely solvable for x_1 and x_2, so that $x_1 = \varphi(y_1, y_2)$ and $x_2 = \psi(y_1, y_2)$.

Define

$$f_2(x_1, \infty) = \lim_{x_2 \to \infty} f_2(x_1, x_2), \qquad f_2(x_1, -\infty) = \lim_{x_2 \to -\infty} f_2(x_1, x_2)$$

When we write $f_2(x_1, \infty)$ or $f_2(x_1, -\infty)$, we implicitly assume that the corresponding limit exists or is $\pm\infty$. Suppose that for all x_1 either $f_2(x_1, \pm\infty) = \pm\infty$ or $f_2(x_1, \pm\infty) = \mp\infty$. Then for each x_1 the equation

$$f_2(x_1, x_2) = y_2$$

has a solution $x_2 = \tilde{x}_2(x_1, y_2)$, with $\partial\tilde{x}_2(x_1, y_2)/\partial x_1 = -(\partial f_2/\partial x_1)/(\partial f_2/\partial x_2)$. Suppose that $\tilde{x}_2(x_1, y_2)$ is uniquely determined as a C^1 function of x_1 and y_2. Insert this value of x_2 into the first equation in (3) to obtain

$$f_1(x_1, \tilde{x}_2(x_1, y_2)) = y_1 \tag{4}$$

Suppose that $\lim_{x_1 \to \pm\infty} f_1(x_1, \tilde{x}_2(x_1, y_2)) = f_1(\pm\infty, \tilde{x}_2(\pm\infty, y_2)) = \pm\infty$ (or $\mp\infty$). Then for all (y_1, y_2) the equation (4) has a solution $x_1 = x_1(y_1, y_2)$. If we put $x_2(y_1, y_2) = \tilde{x}_2(x_1(y_1, y_2), y_2)$, then $\mathbf{x} = (x_1(y_1, y_2), x_2(y_1, y_2))$ is a solution of $\mathbf{f}(\mathbf{x}) = \mathbf{y}$.

If there exists a constant $\alpha > 0$ such that the function $H(x_1, y_2) = f_1(x_1, \tilde{x}_2(x_1, y_2))$ has derivative $\partial H/\partial x_1 \geq \alpha > 0$ everywhere, then $H(\pm\infty, y_2) = \pm\infty$, which was a property we used above. Now,

$$\frac{\partial H}{\partial x_1} = \frac{\partial f_1(x_1, \tilde{x}_2(x_1, y_2))}{\partial x_1} + \frac{\partial f_1(x_1, \tilde{x}_2(x_1, y_2))}{\partial x_2} \frac{\partial\tilde{x}_2(x_1, y_2)}{\partial x_1}$$

$$= \frac{\partial f_1}{\partial x_1} + \frac{\partial f_1}{\partial x_2}\left(-\frac{\partial f_2/\partial x_1}{\partial f_2/\partial x_2}\right) = \frac{1}{\partial f_2/\partial x_2}\begin{vmatrix} \partial f_1/\partial x_1 & \partial f_1/\partial x_2 \\ \partial f_2/\partial x_1 & \partial f_2/\partial x_2 \end{vmatrix}$$

So if there exist positive constants k and h such that $0 < \partial f_2/\partial x_2 \leq k$ and the determinant is $\geq h$, then $\partial H/\partial x_1 \geq h/k > 0$. This is a loose motivation for the next theorem in the two-dimensional case.

THEOREM 2.10.1 (HADAMARD)

Let $\mathbf{f} : \mathbb{R}^n \to \mathbb{R}^n$ be a C^1 function, and suppose that there exist numbers h and k such that for all $\mathbf{x}$ and all $i, j = 1, \ldots, n$,

$$|\det(\mathbf{f}'(\mathbf{x}))| \geq h > 0 \quad \text{and} \quad |\partial f_i(\mathbf{x})/\partial x_j| \leq k \tag{5}$$

Then $\mathbf{f}$ has an inverse which is defined and C^1 on the whole of $\mathbb{R}^n$.

The theorem implies that for all $\mathbf{y}$ the equation $\mathbf{y} = \mathbf{f}(\mathbf{x})$ has a unique solution $\mathbf{x} = \mathbf{x}(\mathbf{y})$, and $\mathbf{x}'(\mathbf{y})$ is continuous.

In the two-dimensional case discussed above we postulated that when $|x_2|$ is large, so is $|f_2(x_1, x_2)|$, and hence also $\|\mathbf{f}(x_1, x_2)\|$. Furthermore, we also postulated that when $|x_1|$ is large, so is $|f_1(x_1, \tilde{x}_2(x_1, y_2))|$, and hence $\|\mathbf{f}(x_1, \tilde{x}_2(x_1, y_2))\|$. Provided $\det(\mathbf{f}'(\mathbf{x})) \neq 0$, we do get solutions of the equation $\mathbf{f}(\mathbf{x}) = \mathbf{y}$ if we require that $\|\mathbf{f}(\mathbf{x})\|$ is large when $\|\mathbf{x}\|$ is large.

THEOREM 2.10.2

Let $\mathbf{f} : \mathbb{R}^n \to \mathbb{R}^n$ be a C^1 function and suppose that $\det(\mathbf{f}'(\mathbf{x})) \neq 0$ for all $\mathbf{x}$. Then $\mathbf{f}(\mathbf{x})$ has an inverse which is defined and C^1 in $\mathbb{R}^n$, if and only if

$$\inf\{\|\mathbf{f}(\mathbf{x})\| : \|\mathbf{x}\| \geq n\} \to \infty \quad \text{as } n \to \infty \tag{6}$$

For proofs of the last theorems see Ortega and Rheinboldt (1970).

The results referred to so far deal with the existence and uniqueness of solutions to equations. We conclude with two results that are only concerned with uniqueness.

THEOREM 2.10.3 (GALE—NIKAIDO)

Let $\mathbf{f} : \mathbb{R}^n \to \mathbb{R}^n$ be C^1 and let Ω be the rectangle $\Omega = \{\mathbf{x} \in \mathbb{R}^n : \mathbf{a} \leq \mathbf{x} \leq \mathbf{b}\}$, where $\mathbf{a}$ and $\mathbf{b}$ are given vectors in $\mathbb{R}^n$. Then $\mathbf{f}$ is one-to-one in Ω if *one* of the following conditions is satisfied for all $\mathbf{x}$:

(a) $\mathbf{f}'(\mathbf{x})$ has only strictly positive principal minors.

(b) $\mathbf{f}'(\mathbf{x})$ has only strictly negative principal minors.

The last theorem in this section gives sufficient conditions for a function $\mathbf{f} : \mathbb{R}^n \to \mathbb{R}^n$ to be one-to-one on an arbitrarily given convex set Ω in $\mathbb{R}^n$. We need the following definition:

QUASIDEFINITE MATRICES

An $n \times n$ matrix $\mathbf{A}$ (not necessarily symmetric) is called **positive quasidefinite** in $S \subseteq \mathbb{R}^n$ if $\mathbf{x}'\mathbf{A}\mathbf{x} > 0$ for every n-vector $\mathbf{x} \neq \mathbf{0}$ in S. The matrix $\mathbf{A}$ is **negative quasidefinite** if $-\mathbf{A}$ is positive quasidefinite. (7)

THEOREM 2.10.4 (GALE—NIKAIDO)

Let $\mathbf{f} : \mathbb{R}^n \to \mathbb{R}^n$ be a C^1 function and suppose that the Jacobian matrix $\mathbf{f}'(\mathbf{x})$ is either positive quasidefinite everywhere in a convex set Ω, or negative quasidefinite everywhere in Ω. Then $\mathbf{f}$ is one-to-one in Ω.

Proof: Let $\mathbf{a} \neq \mathbf{b}$ be arbitrary points of Ω. Define $\mathbf{g}(t) = t\mathbf{a} + (1 - t)\mathbf{b}, t \in [0, 1]$. Let $\mathbf{h} = \mathbf{a} - \mathbf{b} \neq \mathbf{0}$, and define the function $w(t) = \mathbf{h}' \cdot \mathbf{f}(\mathbf{g}(t)) = h_1 f_1(\mathbf{g}(t)) + \cdots + h_n f_n(\mathbf{g}(t))$. Then $w'(t) = \left[h_1 f_1'(\mathbf{g}(t)) + \cdots + h_n f_n'(\mathbf{g}(t)) \right] \cdot \mathbf{g}'(t) = \left[h_1 f_1'(\mathbf{g}(t)) + \cdots + h_n f_n'(\mathbf{g}(t)) \right] \cdot \mathbf{h} = \mathbf{h}' \cdot \mathbf{f}'(\mathbf{g}(t)) \cdot \mathbf{h}$. If $\mathbf{f}'(\mathbf{x})$ is positive quasidefinite, then $w'(t) = \mathbf{h}' \cdot \mathbf{f}'(\mathbf{g}(t)) \cdot \mathbf{h} > 0$ for $\mathbf{h} \neq 0$ and so $w(1) > w(0)$. On the other hand, if $\mathbf{f}'(\mathbf{x})$ is negative quasidefinite, then $w(1) < w(0)$ In either case, therefore, $\mathbf{f}(\mathbf{a}) \neq \mathbf{f}(\mathbf{b})$, so $\mathbf{f}$ is one-to-one. ∎

NOTE 2 Theorem 1.8.1(a) states that when $\mathbf{A}$ is *symmetric*, $\mathbf{A}$ is positive (quasi-)definite iff the leading principal minors are all positive. Note that the Jacobian matrix $\mathbf{f}'(\mathbf{x})$ is not, in general, symmetric.

NOTE 3 Theorems about global uniqueness (univalence) are useful in several economic applications. For example, suppose that a national economy has n different industries each producing a single output under constant returns to scale, using other goods and scarce primary factors as inputs. Suppose the country is small, and faces a fixed price vector $\mathbf{p}$ in $\mathbb{R}^n_+$ at which it can import or export the n goods it produces. Suppose there are n primary factors whose prices are given by the vector $\mathbf{w}$ in $\mathbb{R}^n_+$. Equilibrium requires that $p_i = c_i(\mathbf{w})$ for each $i = 1, 2, \ldots, n$, where $c_i(\mathbf{w})$ is the minimum cost at prices $\mathbf{w}$ of producing one unit of good i. Then the vector equation $\mathbf{p} = \mathbf{c}(\mathbf{w})$, if it has a unique solution, will determine the factor price vector $\mathbf{w}$ as a function of $\mathbf{p}$. When different countries have the same unit cost functions, this leads to factor price equalization—because $\mathbf{p}$ is the same for all countries that trade freely, so is $\mathbf{w}$. See Parthasarathy (1983), Chapter IX, and its references.

PROBLEMS FOR SECTION 2.10

1. Show that $\mathbf{A} = \begin{pmatrix} 1 & 2 \\ 0 & 1 \end{pmatrix}$ has positive leading principal minors, but that $\mathbf{A}$ is not positive quasidefinite.

3

STATIC OPTIMIZATION

If, then, in Political Economy we have to deal with quantities and
complicated relations of quantities, we must reason
mathematically; we do not render the science less mathematical by
avoiding the symbols of algebra . . .
—Jevons (1871)

M uch of economic analysis relies on static optimization problems. For example, producers seek those combinations of inputs that maximize profits or minimize costs, whereas consumers seek commodity bundles that maximize utility subject to their budget constraints.

In most static optimization problems there is an **objective function** $f(x_1, \ldots, x_n) = f(\mathbf{x})$, a real-valued function of n variables whose value is to be optimized—i.e. maximized or minimized. There is also a **constraint set** or **admissible set** S that is some subset of $\mathbb{R}^n$, the Euclidean n-dimensional space. Then the problem is to find maximum or minimum points of f in S. Briefly formulated:

$$\max (\min) \; f(\mathbf{x}) \quad \text{subject to} \quad \mathbf{x} \in S$$

where max(min) indicates that we want to maximize or minimize f.

Depending on the set S, several different types of optimization problem can arise. If the optimum occurs at an interior point of S, we talk about the **classical case**. If S is the set of all points $\mathbf{x}$ that satisfy a given system of equations, we have the **Lagrange problem** of maximizing (or minimizing) a function subject to equality constraints. The general **nonlinear programming problem** arises when S consists of all points $\mathbf{x}$ in $\mathbb{R}^n$ that satisfy a given system of inequality constraints. Bounds on the availability of resources typically lead to inequality constraints.

The reader is assumed to have some prior understanding of the elementary theory of all these types of optimization problem, at least in the case of only a few variables and constraints. This chapter states and proves general results that are required in more advanced economic theory.

What happens to the optimum when the parameters change? The envelope theorem and other results in "comparative statics" address this question, which we discuss in connection with all the main types of optimization problem discussed.

3.1 Extreme Points

We begin by recalling some basic definitions and results. Let f be a function of n variables $x_1, \ldots, x_n$ defined on a set S in $\mathbb{R}^n$. Suppose that the point $\mathbf{x}^* = (x_1^*, \ldots, x_n^*)$ belongs to S and that the value of f at $\mathbf{x}^*$ is greater than or equal to the values attained by f at all other points $\mathbf{x} = (x_1, \ldots, x_n)$ of S. Thus, in symbols,

$$f(\mathbf{x}^*) \geq f(\mathbf{x}) \quad \text{for all } \mathbf{x} \text{ in } S \tag{$*$}$$

Then $\mathbf{x}^*$ is called a (global) **maximum point** for f in S and $f(\mathbf{x}^*)$ is called the **maximum value**. If the inequality in $(*)$ is strict for all $\mathbf{x} \neq \mathbf{x}^*$, then $\mathbf{x}^*$ is a **strict maximum point** for f in S. We define **(strict) minimum point** and **minimum value** by reversing the inequality sign in $(*)$. As collective names, we use **extreme points** and **extreme values** to indicate both maxima or minima.

A **stationary point** of f is a point where all the first-order partial derivatives are 0. We have the following well-known theorem:

THEOREM 3.1.1 (NECESSARY FIRST-ORDER CONDITIONS)

Let f be defined on a set S in $\mathbb{R}^n$ and let $\mathbf{x}^* = (x_1^*, \ldots, x_n^*)$ be an interior point in S at which f has partial derivatives. A necessary condition for $\mathbf{x}^*$ to be a maximum or minimum point for f is that $\mathbf{x}^*$ is a stationary point for f—that is, it satisfies the equations

$$f_i'(\mathbf{x}) = 0, \quad i = 1, \ldots, n \tag{1}$$

Interior stationary points for *concave* or *convex* functions are automatically extreme points:

THEOREM 3.1.2 (SUFFICIENT CONDITIONS WITH CONCAVITY/CONVEXITY)

Suppose that the function $f(\mathbf{x})$ is defined in a convex set S in $\mathbb{R}^n$ and let $\mathbf{x}^*$ be an interior point of S. Assume that f is C^1 in a ball around $\mathbf{x}^*$.

(a) If f is concave in S, then $\mathbf{x}^*$ is a (global) maximum point for f in S if and only if $\mathbf{x}^*$ is a stationary point for f.

(b) If f is convex in S, then $\mathbf{x}^*$ is a (global) minimum point for f in S if and only if $\mathbf{x}^*$ is a stationary point for f.

Proof: If f has a maximum or minimum at $\mathbf{x}^*$, then according to Theorem 3.1.1, the point $\mathbf{x}^*$ must be a stationary point.

Suppose on the other hand that $\mathbf{x}^*$ is stationary and that f is concave. We apply Theorem 2.4.1 with $\mathbf{x}^0 = \mathbf{x}^*$. Since $f_i'(\mathbf{x}^*) = 0$ for $i = 1, \ldots, n$, inequality (1) in Theorem 2.4.1 implies that $f(\mathbf{x}) \leq f(\mathbf{x}^*)$ for all $\mathbf{x}$ in S. This means that $\mathbf{x}^*$ is a maximum point.

The proof of (b) follows from that of (a), since $-f$ is concave. ∎

EXAMPLE 1   Find all (global) extreme points of $f(x, y, z) = x^2 + 2y^2 + 3z^2 + 2xy + 2xz$.

Solution: The only stationary point is $(0, 0, 0)$. The Hessian matrix is

$$\mathbf{f}''(x, y, z) = \begin{pmatrix} 2 & 2 & 2 \\ 2 & 4 & 0 \\ 2 & 0 & 6 \end{pmatrix}$$

The leading principal minors are $D_1 = 2$, $D_2 = 4$, and $D_3 = 8$. Hence, according to Theorem 2.3.2 (a), f is (strictly) convex, and we conclude from Theorem 3.1.2 (b) that $(0, 0, 0)$ is a (global) minimum point.

EXAMPLE 2   Let $x = F(\mathbf{v}) = F(v_1, \ldots, v_n)$ denote a firm's production function. If the nonnegative price of output is p and $q_1, \ldots, q_n$ are the nonnegative prices of the factors of production $v_1, \ldots, v_n$, then the firm's profit is given by

$$\pi = pF(v_1, \ldots, v_n) - q_1 v_1 - \cdots - q_n v_n \tag{*}$$

The first-order conditions for maximum profit are

$$\frac{\partial \pi}{\partial v_i} = pF_i'(v_1, \ldots, v_n) - q_i = 0, \quad i = 1, \ldots, n \tag{**}$$

Suppose that $(**)$ has a solution $\mathbf{v}^* = (v_1^*, \ldots, v_n^*)$, with $v_1^* > 0, \ldots, v_n^* > 0$. If F is concave, then π is also concave as the sum of the concave function $pF(v_1, \ldots, v_n)$ and the linear, hence concave, function $-q_1 v_1 - \cdots - q_n v_n$. It then follows from Theorem 3.1.2 (a) that the stationary point $(v_1^*, \ldots, v_n^*)$ really does maximize profit.

Suppose that F is the Cobb–Douglas function $F(v_1, \ldots, v_n) = A v_1^{a_1} \cdots v_n^{a_n}$, where A and $a_1, \ldots, a_n$ are positive, with $a_1 + \cdots + a_n < 1$. Then F is (strictly) concave (see (2.5.6)). In this case $(**)$ reduces to

$$pAa_i v_1^{a_1} \cdots v_i^{a_i - 1} \cdots v_n^{a_n} = q_i, \quad i = 1, \ldots, n \tag{***}$$

Dividing the first of these equations by each of the remaining $n - 1$ equations in turn, we get

$$\frac{a_1 v_2}{a_2 v_1} = \frac{q_1}{q_2}, \quad \frac{a_1 v_3}{a_3 v_1} = \frac{q_1}{q_3}, \quad \cdots, \quad \frac{a_1 v_n}{a_n v_1} = \frac{q_1}{q_n}$$

Hence, in general $v_i = (q_1 a_i / q_i a_1) v_1$, $i > 1$. Inserting these expressions for $v_2, \ldots, v_n$ into the first equation of $(***)$ yields

$$pAa_1 v_1^{a_1 - 1} \left(\frac{q_1 a_2}{q_2 a_1} \right)^{a_2} v_1^{a_2} \left(\frac{q_1 a_3}{q_3 a_1} \right)^{a_3} v_1^{a_3} \cdots \left(\frac{q_1 a_n}{q_n a_1} \right)^{a_n} v_1^{a_n} = q_1$$

This equation has v_1 as the only unknown. Putting $a = a_1 + \cdots + a_n$ and solving for v_1, we find an expression for v_1. Similar expressions for $v_2, \ldots, v_n$ are easily found. The result is

$$v_i = \left(\frac{a_i}{q_i} \right) (Ap)^{1/(1-a)} \left(\frac{a_1}{q_1} \right)^{a_1/(1-a)} \left(\frac{a_2}{q_2} \right)^{a_2/(1-a)} \cdots \left(\frac{a_n}{q_n} \right)^{a_n/(1-a)}, \quad i = 1, \ldots, n$$

This is the profit maximizing choice of input quantities of the different factors of production.

Theorem 3.1.2 requires concavity (convexity). Recall that maximizing (minimizing) a function $f(\mathbf{x})$ is equivalent to maximizing (minimizing) $F(f(\mathbf{x}))$, for any given strictly increasing function F. (See e.g. EMEA, Chapter 13.) If $f(\mathbf{x})$ is not concave (convex), then the transformed function $F(f(\mathbf{x}))$ may be concave for a suitably chosen strictly increasing F. Such a transformation makes it possible to apply Theorem 3.1.2.

EXAMPLE 3   Show that the function g be defined for all x, y, and z by

$$g(x, y, z) = (x^2 + 2y^2 + 3z^2 + 2xy + 2xz)^3$$

has a minimum at $(0, 0, 0)$.

Solution: Theorem 3.1.2 does not apply to g, because g is not convex. Nevertheless, note that $g(x, y, z) = (f(x, y, z))^3$, where f is the function studied in Example 1. Since g is a strictly increasing transformation of f, it too has $(0, 0, 0)$ as a minimum point.

The following theorem is an important result in optimization theory. (For a proof, see Section 13.3.)

THEOREM 3.1.3 (EXTREME-VALUE THEOREM)

Let $f(\mathbf{x})$ be a continuous function on a closed, bounded set S. Then f has both a maximum point and a minimum point in S.

NOTE 1 In most economic applications the set S referred to in Theorem 3.1.3 is specified using one or more inequalities. If the functions $g_j(\mathbf{x})$, $j = 1, \ldots, m$ are all continuous and $b_1, \ldots, b_m$ are given numbers, the set $S = \{\mathbf{x} : g_j(\mathbf{x}) \leq b_j, j = 1, \ldots, m\}$ is closed. If some (or all) of the inequalities are replaced by $\geq$ or $=$, the set is still closed. The set S is bounded if it is contained in some ball around the origin. (See Section 13.1 for general definitions and results on open sets, closed sets and related concepts.)

Suppose $f(\mathbf{x})$ is a C^1 function which we know has a maximum point $\mathbf{x}^*$ in a set S in $\mathbb{R}^n$—for instance, by appealing to Theorem 3.1.3. If $\mathbf{x}^*$ is an interior point of S, it must be a stationary point. (If $S = \{\mathbf{x} : g_j(\mathbf{x}) \leq b_j, j = 1, \ldots, m\}$, an interior point is one for which all the inequalities are strict.) If $\mathbf{x}^*$ is not an interior point of S, it must belong to the boundary of S. The following procedure can therefore be used to locate the maximum point:

(A) Record all interior stationary points of S. They are candidates for maximum.

(B) Find all maximum candidates on the boundary of S, where $g_j(x) = b_j$ for at least one j.

(C) Compute the value of f at all the candidates. Those that give f its largest value are the maximum points.

If we know that f has a minimum point, a completely analogous procedure will give us the minimum point or points. In EMEA this procedure was used to find extreme points for functions of two variables. Later we shall give more efficient methods for finding extreme points of such functions.

Envelope Theorems for Unconstrained Maxima

The objective function in economic optimization problems usually involves parameters like prices in addition to choice variables like quantities. Consider an objective function with a parameter vector $\mathbf{r}$ of the form $f(\mathbf{x}, \mathbf{r}) = f(x_1, \ldots, x_n, r_1, \ldots, r_k)$, where $\mathbf{x} \in S \subseteq \mathbb{R}^n$ and $\mathbf{r} \in \mathbb{R}^k$. For each fixed $\mathbf{r}$ suppose we have found the maximum of $f(\mathbf{x}, \mathbf{r})$ when $\mathbf{x}$ varies in S. The maximum value of $f(\mathbf{x}, \mathbf{r})$ usually depends on $\mathbf{r}$. We denote this value by $f^*(\mathbf{r})$ and call f^* the **value function**. Thus,

$$f^*(\mathbf{r}) = \max_{\mathbf{x} \in S} f(\mathbf{x}, \mathbf{r}) \qquad \text{(the value function)} \tag{2}$$

The vector $\mathbf{x}$ that maximizes $f(\mathbf{x}, \mathbf{r})$ depends on $\mathbf{r}$ and is denoted by $\mathbf{x}^*(\mathbf{r})$.[1] Then $f^*(\mathbf{r}) = f(\mathbf{x}^*(\mathbf{r}), \mathbf{r})$. How does $f^*(\mathbf{r})$ vary as the parameter r_j changes? Under certain conditions we have the following result:

$$\frac{\partial f^*(\mathbf{r})}{\partial r_j} = \left[\frac{\partial f(\mathbf{x}, \mathbf{r})}{\partial r_j} \right]_{\mathbf{x} = \mathbf{x}^*(\mathbf{r})}, \qquad j = 1, \ldots, k \tag{3}$$

where the partial derivative on the right-hand side is evaluated at $(\mathbf{x}^*(\mathbf{r}), \mathbf{r})$.

Note that when the parameter r_j changes, $f^*(\mathbf{r})$ changes for two reasons. First, a change in r_j changes $\mathbf{x}^*(\mathbf{r})$. Second, $f(\mathbf{x}^*(\mathbf{r}), \mathbf{r})$ changes directly because the variable r_j changes. Formula (3) claims that the first effect is zero. Assuming differentiability and interior solution, the reason is that, because $\mathbf{x} = \mathbf{x}^*(\mathbf{r})$ maximizes $f(\mathbf{x}, \mathbf{r})$ w.r.t. $\mathbf{x}$, all the partial derivatives $\partial f(\mathbf{x}^*(\mathbf{r}), \mathbf{r})/\partial x_i$ must be 0. Hence:

$$\frac{\partial f^*(\mathbf{r})}{\partial r_j} = \frac{\partial}{\partial r_j}\left(f(\mathbf{x}^*(\mathbf{r}), \mathbf{r}) \right) = \sum_{i=1}^{n} \frac{\partial f(\mathbf{x}^*(\mathbf{r}), \mathbf{r})}{\partial x_i} \frac{\partial x_i^*(\mathbf{r})}{\partial r_j} + \left[\frac{\partial f(\mathbf{x}, \mathbf{r})}{\partial r_j} \right]_{\mathbf{x} = \mathbf{x}^*(\mathbf{r})}$$

$$= \left[\frac{\partial f(\mathbf{x}, \mathbf{r})}{\partial r_j} \right]_{\mathbf{x} = \mathbf{x}^*(\mathbf{r})}$$

EXAMPLE 4   The profit function π in Example 2 depends on the input vector $\mathbf{v}$ and the parametric prices p and $\mathbf{q} = (q_1, \ldots, q_n)$. Specifically,

$$\pi = \pi(\mathbf{v}, p, \mathbf{q}) = pF(\mathbf{v}) - q_1 v_1 - \cdots - q_n v_n$$

Let $\pi^*(p, \mathbf{q})$ denote the value function in the problem of maximizing π w.r.t. $\mathbf{v}$, and let $\mathbf{v}^* = \mathbf{v}^*(p, \mathbf{q})$ be the associated $\mathbf{v}$ vector. Then according to (3),

$$\frac{\partial \pi^*(p, \mathbf{q})}{\partial p} = \frac{\partial \pi(\mathbf{v}^*, p, \mathbf{q})}{\partial p} = F(\mathbf{v}^*), \qquad \frac{\partial \pi^*(p, \mathbf{q})}{\partial q_j} = \frac{\partial \pi(\mathbf{v}^*, p, \mathbf{q})}{\partial q_j} = -v_j^* \qquad (*)$$

---

[1] There may be several choices of $\mathbf{x}$ that maximize $f(\mathbf{x}, \mathbf{r})$ for a given parameter vector $\mathbf{r}$. Then we let $\mathbf{x}(\mathbf{r})$ denote one of these choices, and try to select $\mathbf{x}$ for different values of $\mathbf{r}$ so that $\mathbf{x}(\mathbf{r})$ is a differentiable function of $\mathbf{r}$.

This is intuitively clear: When the price of the product increases by Δp, the optimal profit increases by approximately $F(\mathbf{v}^*)\Delta p$, since $F(\mathbf{v}^*)$ is the optimal number of units produced. If the price of the jth input factor q_j increases by Δq_j, the optimal profit decreases by about $v_j^* \Delta q_j$ units, since v_j^* is the amount of factor j used at the optimum.

The statement of and argument for (3) were not precise. We formulate and prove three "envelope theorems" that remedy this imprecision.

THEOREM 3.1.4 (ENVELOPE THEOREM 1)

In the problem $\max_{\mathbf{x} \in S} f(\mathbf{x}, \mathbf{r})$, where $S \subseteq \mathbb{R}^n$ and $\mathbf{r} = (r_1, \ldots, r_k)$, suppose that there is a maximum point $\mathbf{x}^*(\mathbf{r})$ in S for every $\mathbf{r}$ in some ball $B(\mathbf{r}^*; \delta)$, with $\delta > 0$. Furthermore, assume that the mappings $\mathbf{r} \mapsto f(\mathbf{x}^*(\mathbf{r}^*), \mathbf{r})$ and $\mathbf{r} \mapsto f^*(\mathbf{r})$ (defined in (2)) are both differentiable at $\mathbf{r}^*$. Then

$$\frac{\partial f^*(\mathbf{r}^*)}{\partial r_j} = \left[\frac{\partial f(\mathbf{x}, \mathbf{r})}{\partial r_j} \right]_{(\mathbf{x}=\mathbf{x}^*(\mathbf{r}^*),\, \mathbf{r}=\mathbf{r}^*)} \qquad j = 1, \ldots, k \qquad (4)$$

Proof: Define the function $\varphi(\mathbf{r}) = f(\mathbf{x}^*(\mathbf{r}^*), \mathbf{r}) - f^*(\mathbf{r})$. Because $\mathbf{x}^*(\mathbf{r}^*)$ is a maximum point of $f(\mathbf{x}, \mathbf{r})$ when $\mathbf{r} = \mathbf{r}^*$, one has $\varphi(\mathbf{r}^*) = 0$ and $\varphi(\mathbf{r}) \leq 0$ for all $\mathbf{r}$ in $B(\mathbf{r}^*; \delta)$. It follows that φ has an interior maximum at $\mathbf{r} = \mathbf{r}^*$. The equality in the theorem follows from the fact that $\mathbf{r} = \mathbf{r}^*$ must satisfy the first-order conditions $\varphi_j'(\mathbf{r}) = 0$ for $j = 1, \ldots, k$. ∎

In Theorem 3.1.4 it is *assumed* a priori that $f^*(\mathbf{r})$ is differentiable. The next theorem gives sufficient conditions for differentiability.

THEOREM 3.1.5 (ENVELOPE THEOREM 2)

Suppose $f(\mathbf{x}, \mathbf{r})$ is a C^2 function of $(\mathbf{x}, \mathbf{r})$ for all $\mathbf{x}$ in an open convex set $S \subseteq \mathbb{R}^n$ and all $\mathbf{r}$ in an open ball $B(\mathbf{r}^*; \delta) \subseteq \mathbb{R}^k$. Assume that for each $\mathbf{r}$ in $B(\mathbf{r}^*; \delta)$, the function $\mathbf{x} \mapsto f(\mathbf{x}, \mathbf{r})$ is concave, and that when $\mathbf{r} = \mathbf{r}^*$ it satisfies the sufficient second-order conditions for strict concavity in Theorem 2.3.2 (b). Moreover, assume that $\mathbf{x}^*$ is a maximum point for $\mathbf{x} \mapsto f(\mathbf{x}, \mathbf{r}^*)$ in S. Then $f^*(\mathbf{r}) = \max_{\mathbf{x} \in S} f(\mathbf{x}, \mathbf{r})$ is defined in an open ball around $\mathbf{r}^*$. Moreover, f^* is C^1 at $\mathbf{r}^*$, and (4) holds.

Proof: The first-order conditions for maximizing $f(\mathbf{x}, \mathbf{r})$ w.r.t. $\mathbf{x}$ can be written in the form $\nabla_{\mathbf{x}} f(\mathbf{x}, \mathbf{r}) = \mathbf{0}$, where $\nabla_{\mathbf{x}} f$ denotes the partial gradient vector w.r.t. $\mathbf{x}$, holding $\mathbf{r}$ fixed. The Jacobian matrix J of the mapping $\mathbf{x} \mapsto \nabla_{\mathbf{x}} f(\mathbf{x}, \mathbf{r})$ evaluated at $(\mathbf{x}^*, \mathbf{r}^*)$ is the Hessian matrix $\mathbf{f}_{\mathbf{xx}}''(\mathbf{x}^*, \mathbf{r}^*)$. By the sufficient conditions for strict concavity, this Hessian matrix is negative definite, hence nonsingular. Because f is a C^2 function, the Hessian matrix $\mathbf{f}_{\mathbf{xx}}''(\mathbf{x}, \mathbf{r})$ must still be negative definite in some open ball of $\mathbb{R}^{n+k}$ centred at $(\mathbf{x}^*, \mathbf{r}^*)$. By the implicit function theorem, it follows that the equation system $\nabla_{\mathbf{x}} f(\mathbf{x}, \mathbf{r}) = \mathbf{0}$ in the unknown vector $\mathbf{x}$ has a solution $\mathbf{x}(\mathbf{r})$ which is a C^1 function of $\mathbf{r}$ in some ball $B(\mathbf{r}^*; \varepsilon)$, with $\mathbf{x}(\mathbf{r}^*) = \mathbf{x}^*$. Provided that $\mathbf{r}$ lies in $B(\mathbf{r}^*; \varepsilon) \cap B(\mathbf{r}^*; \delta)$, the function $\mathbf{x} \mapsto f(\mathbf{x}, \mathbf{r})$ is concave, so $\mathbf{x}(\mathbf{r})$ is a maximum point of $\mathbf{x} \mapsto f(\mathbf{x}, \mathbf{r})$ for $\mathbf{x}$ in S. Evidently, $f^*(\mathbf{r}) = f(\mathbf{x}(\mathbf{r}), \mathbf{r})$ is differentiable at $\mathbf{r} = \mathbf{r}^*$. In particular, the preceding theorem applies. ∎

A crucial assumption in the previous theorem is that $\mathbf{x} \mapsto f(\mathbf{x}, \mathbf{r})$ is concave. The next theorem replaces this with the assumption that $\mathbf{r} \mapsto f^*(\mathbf{r})$ is concave.

THEOREM 3.1.6 (ENVELOPE THEOREM 3)

Suppose that $f^*(\mathbf{r}) = \sup_{\mathbf{x} \in S} f(\mathbf{x}, \mathbf{r})$ is finite and concave in $\mathbf{r} \in A$, where A is an open convex set in $\mathbb{R}^k$, and $S \subseteq \mathbb{R}^n$. Assume that the point $(\mathbf{x}^*, \mathbf{r}^*) \in S \times A$ satisfies $f(\mathbf{x}^*, \mathbf{r}^*) = f^*(\mathbf{r}^*)$ and that $f'_{\mathbf{r}}(\mathbf{x}, \mathbf{r})$ exists at $(\mathbf{x}^*, \mathbf{r}^*)$. Then $f^*(\mathbf{r})$ is differentiable at $\mathbf{r}^*$ and $\nabla f^*(\mathbf{r}^*) = \nabla_{\mathbf{r}} f(\mathbf{x}^*, \mathbf{r}^*)$, i.e. (4) holds.

Proof: Because A is open, Theorem 2.4.3 implies that f^* has a supergradient at $\mathbf{r}^*$, which we will denote by $\mathbf{a}$. From the definition of f^*, it follows that

$$f(\mathbf{x}^*, \mathbf{r}) - f(\mathbf{x}^*, \mathbf{r}^*) \le f^*(\mathbf{r}) - f^*(\mathbf{r}^*) \le \mathbf{a} \cdot (\mathbf{r} - \mathbf{r}^*) \quad \text{for all } \mathbf{r} \text{ in } A \qquad (*)$$

This implies that $\mathbf{a}$ is a supergradient of $\mathbf{r} \mapsto f(\mathbf{x}^*, \mathbf{r})$ at $\mathbf{r}^*$. By Note 2.4.1, we conclude that $\mathbf{a} = \nabla_{\mathbf{r}} f(\mathbf{x}^*, \mathbf{r}^*)$. Now,

$$\frac{f(\mathbf{x}^*, \mathbf{r}) - f(\mathbf{x}^*, \mathbf{r}^*) - \mathbf{a} \cdot (\mathbf{r} - \mathbf{r}^*)}{\|\mathbf{r} - \mathbf{r}^*\|} \le \frac{f^*(\mathbf{r}) - f^*(\mathbf{r}^*) - \mathbf{a} \cdot (\mathbf{r} - \mathbf{r}^*)}{\|\mathbf{r} - \mathbf{r}^*\|} \le 0 \quad \text{for all } \mathbf{r} \ne \mathbf{r}^*$$

But the first expression here $\to 0$ as $\mathbf{r} \to \mathbf{r}^*$. So $[f^*(\mathbf{r}) - f^*(\mathbf{r}^*) - \mathbf{a} \cdot (\mathbf{r} - \mathbf{r}^*)]/\|\mathbf{r} - \mathbf{r}^*\| \to 0$ also, which verifies that f^* is differentiable at $\mathbf{r}^*$, with $\nabla f^*(\mathbf{r}^*) = \mathbf{a} = \nabla_{\mathbf{r}} f(\mathbf{x}^*, \mathbf{r}^*)$.   ∎

PROBLEMS FOR SECTION 3.1

1. Consider the function g defined for all $x > 0$, $y > 0$ by

$$g(x, y) = x^3 + y^3 - 3x - 2y$$

Show that g is convex in its domain, and find its (global) minimum value.

2. (a) A firm produces two output goods, denoted by A and B. The cost per day is $C(x, y) = 0.04x^2 - 0.01xy + 0.01y^2 + 4x + 2y + 500$ when x units of A and y units of B are produced ($x > 0$, $y > 0$). The firm sells all it produces at prices 13 per unit of A and 8 per unit of B. Show that the profit function is

$$\pi(x, y) = 9x + 6y - 0.04x^2 + 0.01xy - 0.01y^2 - 500$$

   (b) Determine the values of x and y at which $\pi(x, y)$ attains its maximum.

3. (a) Referring to Example 2 above, solve the problem $\max p v_1^{1/3} v_2^{1/2} - q_1 v_1 - q_2 v_2$.

   (b) Let $\pi^*(p, q_1, q_2)$ denote the value function. Verify the three equalities in $(*)$ in Example 4 in this case.

4. Find the functions $x^*(r)$ and $y^*(r)$ such that $x = x^*(r)$ and $y = y^*(r)$ solve the problem

$$\max_{x,y} f(x, y, r) = \max_{x,y}(-x^2 - xy - 2y^2 + 2rx + 2ry)$$

where r is a parameter. Verify equation (3).

5. Find the solutions $x^*(r, s)$ and $y^*(r, s)$ of the problem

$$\max_{x, y} f(x, y, r, s) = \max_{x, y}(r^2 x + 3s^2 y - x^2 - 8y^2)$$

where r and s are parameters. Verify equation (3).

3.2 Local Extreme Points

Suppose one is trying to find the maximum of a function which is not concave, or a minimum of a function which is not convex. Then Theorem 3.1.2 cannot be used. Instead, one possible procedure is to identify *local* extreme points, and then compare the values of the function at different local extreme points in the hope of finding a global maximum (or minimum).

The point $\mathbf{x}^*$ is a **local maximum point** of f in S if $f(\mathbf{x}) \leq f(\mathbf{x}^*)$ for all $\mathbf{x}$ in S sufficiently close to $\mathbf{x}^*$. More precisely, the requirement is that there exists a positive number r such that

$$f(\mathbf{x}) \leq f(\mathbf{x}^*) \quad \text{for all } \mathbf{x} \text{ in } S \text{ with } \|\mathbf{x} - \mathbf{x}^*\| < r \qquad (*)$$

(Equivalently, if we let $B(\mathbf{x}^*; r) = \{\mathbf{x} \in \mathbb{R}^n : \|\mathbf{x} - \mathbf{x}^*\| < r\}$ denote the **open n-ball** centred at $\mathbf{x}^*$ and with radius r, then $\mathbf{x}^*$ is a local maximum point for f in S if there exists a positive number r such that $f(\mathbf{x}) \leq f(\mathbf{x}^*)$ for all $\mathbf{x}$ in $B(\mathbf{x}^*; r) \cap S$.) If the first inequality in $(*)$ is strict for $\mathbf{x} \neq \mathbf{x}^*$, then $\mathbf{x}^*$ is a **strict local maximum point** for f in S.

A **(strict) local minimum point** is defined in the obvious way, and it should be clear what is meant by **local maximum and minimum values**, **local extreme points**, and **local extreme values**. Of course, a global extreme point is also a local extreme point, but the converse is not always true.

In searching for maximum and minimum points, Theorem 3.1.1 on necessary first-order conditions is very useful. The same result applies to local extreme points as well: *A local extreme point in the interior of the domain of a differentiable function must be a stationary point.* (This observation follows because the proof of Theorem 3.1.1 considers the behaviour of the function only in a small neighbourhood of the optimal point.) A stationary point $\mathbf{x}^*$ of f that is neither a local maximum point nor a local minimum point is called a **saddle point** of f. Thus, arbitrarily close to a saddle point, there are points with both higher and lower values than the function value at the saddle point. We study next conditions allowing the stationary points of a function of n variables to be classified as local maximum points, local minimum points, and saddle points.

First recall the second-order conditions for local extreme points for functions of two variables. If $f(x, y)$ is a C^2 function with (x^*, y^*) as an interior stationary point, then

$$f_{11}''(x^*, y^*) > 0 \ \& \ \begin{vmatrix} f_{11}''(x^*, y^*) & f_{12}''(x^*, y^*) \\ f_{21}''(x^*, y^*) & f_{22}''(x^*, y^*) \end{vmatrix} > 0 \implies \text{local min. at } (x^*, y^*) \quad (1)$$

$$f_{11}''(x^*, y^*) < 0 \ \& \ \begin{vmatrix} f_{11}''(x^*, y^*) & f_{12}''(x^*, y^*) \\ f_{21}''(x^*, y^*) & f_{22}''(x^*, y^*) \end{vmatrix} > 0 \implies \text{local max. at } (x^*, y^*) \quad (2)$$

$$\begin{vmatrix} f_{11}''(x^*, y^*) & f_{12}''(x^*, y^*) \\ f_{21}''(x^*, y^*) & f_{22}''(x^*, y^*) \end{vmatrix} < 0 \implies \quad (x^*, y^*) \text{ is a saddle point} \tag{3}$$

In order to generalize these results to functions of n variables, we need to consider the n *leading principal minors* of the Hessian matrix $\mathbf{f}''(\mathbf{x}) = (f_{ij}''(\mathbf{x}))_{n \times n}$:

$$D_k(\mathbf{x}) = \begin{vmatrix} f_{11}''(\mathbf{x}) & f_{12}''(\mathbf{x}) & \cdots & f_{1k}''(\mathbf{x}) \\ f_{21}''(\mathbf{x}) & f_{22}''(\mathbf{x}) & \cdots & f_{2k}''(\mathbf{x}) \\ \vdots & \vdots & \ddots & \vdots \\ f_{k1}''(\mathbf{x}) & f_{k2}''(\mathbf{x}) & \cdots & f_{kk}''(\mathbf{x}) \end{vmatrix}, \quad k = 1, \dots, n \tag{4}$$

THEOREM 3.2.1 (SUFFICIENT CONDITIONS FOR LOCAL EXTREME POINTS)

Suppose that $f(\mathbf{x}) = f(x_1, \dots, x_n)$ is defined on a set S in $\mathbb{R}^n$ and that $\mathbf{x}^*$ is an interior stationary point. Assume also that f is C^2 in an open ball around $\mathbf{x}^*$. Let $D_k(\mathbf{x})$ be defined by (4). Then:

(a) $D_k(\mathbf{x}^*) > 0, \ k = 1, \dots, n \qquad \implies \quad \mathbf{x}^*$ is a local minimum point.

(b) $(-1)^k D_k(\mathbf{x}^*) > 0, \ k = 1, \dots, n \implies \quad \mathbf{x}^*$ is a local maximum point.

Proof: (a) A determinant is a continuous function of its elements. If $D_k(\mathbf{x}^*) > 0$ for all k, it is possible to find a ball $B(\mathbf{x}^*; r)$ with radius $r > 0$ so small that $D_k(\mathbf{x}) > 0$ for all $\mathbf{x}$ in $B(\mathbf{x}^*; r)$ and all $k = 1, \dots, n$. Hence, according to Theorem 1.8.1(a), the quadratic form $\sum_{i=1}^{n} \sum_{j=1}^{n} f_{ij}''(\mathbf{x})h_i h_j$ is positive definite for all $\mathbf{x}$ in $B(\mathbf{x}^*; r)$. It follows from (2.3.4) that f is (strictly) convex in $B(\mathbf{x}^*; r)$. But then Theorem 3.1.2 shows that the stationary point $\mathbf{x}^*$ is a minimum point for f in $B(\mathbf{x}^*; r)$, and therefore a local minimum point for f in S.

(b) follows from (a) by replacing f with $-f$ and noting rule (1.1.20) for evaluating determinants. ∎

Theorem 3.2.1 is often referred to as the **second-derivative test**. Check to see that for $n = 2$ the implications in (a) and (b) reduce to those in (1) and (2).

SADDLE POINT TEST

If $\mathbf{x}^*$ is a stationary point of f such that $D_n(\mathbf{x}^*) \neq 0$ and neither of the conditions in (a) and (b) of Theorem 3.2.1 are satisfied, then $\mathbf{x}^*$ is a saddle point. $\tag{5}$

By (5) and Theorem 3.2.1, stationary points $\mathbf{x}^*$ for f where $D_n(\mathbf{x}^*) \neq 0$, are now fully classified as either local maximum points, local minimum points, or saddle points. If $D_n(\mathbf{x}^*) = 0$, a closer examination is necessary in order to classify the stationary point. (Note the analogy with the one-variable case in which "anything can happen" at a stationary point where $f''(x^*) = 0$.)

EXAMPLE 1   The following function has stationary points $(-2, -2, -2)$ and $(0, 0, 0)$:

$$f(x, y, z) = x^3 + 3xy + 3xz + y^3 + 3yz + z^3$$

Classify these points by using Theorem 3.2.1 and (5).

Solution: The Hessian matrix is $\begin{pmatrix} f_{11}'' & f_{12}'' & f_{13}'' \\ f_{21}'' & f_{22}'' & f_{23}'' \\ f_{31}'' & f_{32}'' & f_{33}'' \end{pmatrix} = \begin{pmatrix} 6x & 3 & 3 \\ 3 & 6y & 3 \\ 3 & 3 & 6z \end{pmatrix}.$

At $(-2, -2 - 2)$ the leading principal minors are

$$6(-2) = -12, \quad \begin{vmatrix} -12 & 3 \\ 3 & -12 \end{vmatrix} = 135, \quad \begin{vmatrix} -12 & 3 & 3 \\ 3 & -12 & 3 \\ 3 & 3 & -12 \end{vmatrix} = -1350$$

According to part (b) in Theorem 3.2.1, $(-2, -2, -2)$ is a local maximum point.

At $(0, 0, 0)$ the leading principal minors are 0, -9, and 54. In this case neither the conditions in (a) nor the conditions in (b) are satisfied. Moreover, $D_3(0, 0, 0) = 54 \neq 0$. According to (5), $(0, 0, 0)$ is a saddle point.

Necessary Conditions for Local Extreme Points

Suppose the function $f(\mathbf{x}) = f(x_1, \ldots, x_n)$ is defined on a set S, and assume that $\mathbf{x}^* = (x_1^*, \ldots, x_n^*)$ is an interior stationary point of f in S. Consider the one-variable function $g(x_1) = f(x_1, x_2^*, \ldots, x_n^*)$. It has a stationary point at x_1^*, because $g'(x_1^*) = f_1'(\mathbf{x}^*) = 0$. Suppose $g''(x_1^*) = f_{11}''(\mathbf{x}^*) < 0$. Then $g(x_1)$ has a local maximum at x_1^*. Stated differently, the condition $f_{11}''(\mathbf{x}^*) < 0$ is sufficient for f to have a local maximum at the stationary point $\mathbf{x}^*$ in the direction parallel to the x_1-axis. (Note that in the notation of (4), $f_{11}''(\mathbf{x}^*) < 0$ is equivalent to $(-1)^1 D_1(\mathbf{x}^*) > 0$, which is condition (b) in Theorem 3.2.1 when $k = 1$.) In general, the condition $f_{ii}''(\mathbf{x}^*) < 0$ $(i = 1, \ldots, n)$ implies that f has a local maximum at the stationary point $\mathbf{x}^*$ in the direction of the x_i-axis. These conditions do not, however, tell much about whether f has a local maximum or minimum in directions through $\mathbf{x}^*$ other than those parallel to one of the coordinate axes.

To study the behaviour of f in an arbitrary direction, define the function g by

$$g(t) = f(\mathbf{x}^* + t\mathbf{h}) = f(x_1^* + th_1, \ldots, x_n^* + th_n) \qquad (6)$$

where $\mathbf{h} = (h_1, \ldots, h_n)$ is an arbitrary fixed vector in $\mathbb{R}^n$ with length 1, so $\|\mathbf{h}\| = 1$. The function g describes the behaviour of f along the straight line through $\mathbf{x}^*$ parallel to the vector $\mathbf{h}$, as suggested in Fig. 1.

Suppose that $\mathbf{x}^*$ is an interior local maximum point for f. Then if $r > 0$ is small enough, $B(\mathbf{x}^*; r) \subseteq S$, and $f(\mathbf{x}) \leq f(\mathbf{x}^*)$ for all $\mathbf{x}$ in $B(\mathbf{x}^*; r)$. If $t \in (-r, r)$, then $\mathbf{x}^* + t\mathbf{h} \in B(\mathbf{x}^*; r)$ because $\|(\mathbf{x}^* + t\mathbf{h}) - \mathbf{x}^*\| = \|t\mathbf{h}\| = |t| < r$. But then for all t in $(-r, r)$, we have $f(\mathbf{x}^* + t\mathbf{h}) \leq f(\mathbf{x}^*)$, or $g(t) \leq g(0)$. Thus the function g has an interior maximum at $t = 0$. From the theory of functions of one variable, $g'(0) = 0$ and $g''(0) \leq 0$

are necessary conditions for a maximum at $t = 0$. By the rules for differentiating composite functions of several variables, one has (see (2.6.6) and (2.6.7))

$$g'(t) = \sum_{i=1}^{n} f_i'(\mathbf{x}^* + t\mathbf{h})h_i, \qquad g''(t) = \sum_{i=1}^{n}\sum_{j=1}^{n} f_{ij}''(\mathbf{x}^* + t\mathbf{h})h_i h_j \qquad (7)$$

For all choices of $\mathbf{h}$ with $\|\mathbf{h}\| = 1$, it follows that $g'(0) = 0$ and $g''(0) \leq 0$. The condition $g''(0) \leq 0$ yields

$$\sum_{i=1}^{n}\sum_{j=1}^{n} f_{ij}''(\mathbf{x}^*)h_i h_j \leq 0 \quad \text{for all } \mathbf{h} = (h_1, \dots, h_n) \quad \text{with} \quad \|\mathbf{h}\| = 1 \qquad (8)$$

This is an equality if $\mathbf{h} = \mathbf{0}$, and if $\mathbf{h} = (h_1, \dots, h_n)$ is a vector with length $\neq 0$, the inequality holds for $\mathbf{h}/\|\mathbf{h}\|$, and so also for $\mathbf{h}$. Thus, in the terminology of Section 1.8,

A necessary condition for $f(\mathbf{x})$ to have a local minimum (maximum) at $\mathbf{x}^*$ is that the quadratic form in (8) is positive (negative) semidefinite. $\qquad (9)$

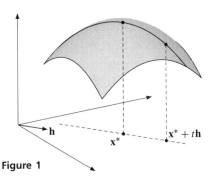

Figure 1

The results in (9) can be formulated by using Theorem 1.8.1. Recall that the *principal minors* of order k of the Hessian matrix are obtained by deleting $n - k$ rows in $|\mathbf{f}''(\mathbf{x})| = |(f_{ij}''(\mathbf{x}))_{n \times n}|$ and the $n - k$ columns with the same numbers.

THEOREM 3.2.2 (NECESSARY CONDITIONS FOR LOCAL EXTREME POINTS)

Suppose that $f(\mathbf{x}) = f(x_1, \dots, x_n)$ is defined on a set S in $\mathbb{R}^n$, and $\mathbf{x}^*$ is an interior stationary point in S. Assume that f is C^2 in a ball around $\mathbf{x}^*$. Let $\Delta_k(\mathbf{x})$ denote a generic principal minor of order k of the Hessian matrix. Then:

(a) $\mathbf{x}^*$ is a local minimum point $\implies$ $\begin{cases} \Delta_k(\mathbf{x}^*) \geq 0 \text{ for all principal minors} \\ \text{of order } k = 1, \dots, n. \end{cases}$

(b) $\mathbf{x}^*$ is a local maximum point $\implies$ $\begin{cases} (-1)^k \Delta_k(\mathbf{x}^*) \geq 0 \text{ for all principal} \\ \text{minors of order } k = 1, \dots, n. \end{cases}$

We have already formulated and proved sufficient conditions for local optimality (Theorem 3.2.1). Looking back at the function g in (6), with $\mathbf{h}$ as a fixed direction vector, the conditions $g'(0) = 0$ and $g''(0) < 0$ are *sufficient* for g to have a local maximum at $t = 0$. Thus we see that if $\mathbf{x}^*$ is a stationary point of f and the quadratic form $\sum_{i=1}^{n}\sum_{j=1}^{n} f''_{ij}(\mathbf{x}^*)h_ih_j$ is negative definite, then f has a strict local maximum at $\mathbf{x}^*$ in *each* direction through $\mathbf{x}^*$. It seems reasonable to guess that $\mathbf{x}^*$ is then a local maximum point for f. The proof of Theorem 3.2.1 established that this is correct. Thus we have:

A sufficient condition for $f(\mathbf{x})$ to have a local minimum (maximum) at $\mathbf{x}^*$ is that the quadratic form in (8) is positive (negative) definite. (10)

NOTE 1 Conclusions about local (or global) extreme points of functions of several variables cannot always be based only on what happens to the function along each straight line through the point. For instance, $f(x, y) = (y-x^2)(y-2x^2)$ has a saddle point at $(0, 0)$ even though the function has a local minimum along each straight line through the origin.

NOTE 2 The definiteness of a quadratic form can be determined from the signs of the eigenvalues of the corresponding matrix. Suppose that neither of the conditions in (a) and (b) of Theorem 3.2.1 are satisfied. Then the Hessian matrix $\mathbf{f}''(\mathbf{x}^*)$ is neither positive nor negative definite. According to Theorem 1.8.2, this means that it cannot have only positive or only negative eigenvalues. If, in addition, $D_n(\mathbf{x}^*) = |\mathbf{f}''(\mathbf{x}^*)| \neq 0$, then 0 is not an eigenvalue of the Hessian matrix $\mathbf{f}''(\mathbf{x}^*)$, so it must have both positive and negative eigenvalues. According to Theorem 1.8.2, the matrix $\mathbf{f}''(\mathbf{x}^*)$ cannot then be positive or negative semidefinite, so (9) shows that $\mathbf{x}^*$ is neither a local maximum nor a local minimum point. That is, $\mathbf{x}^*$ must be a saddle point. This proves the saddle point result in (5).

PROBLEMS FOR SECTION 3.2

1. The function

$$f(x_1, x_2, x_3) = x_1^2 + x_2^2 + 3x_3^2 - x_1x_2 + 2x_1x_3 + x_2x_3$$

defined on $\mathbb{R}^3$ has only one stationary point. Show that it is a local minimum point.

2. Classify the stationary points of

$$f(x, y, z) = -2x^3 + 15x^2 - 36x + 2y - 3z + \int_y^z e^{t^2}\, dt$$

3. (a) Let f be defined for all (x, y) by $f(x, y) = x^3 + y^3 - 3xy$. Show that $(0, 0)$ and $(1, 1)$ are the only stationary points, and compute the quadratic form in (8) for f at these stationary points.

   (b) What do (9) and (10) imply about the stationary points?

   (c) Classify the stationary points by using (1)–(3).

4. Classify the stationary points of

   (a) $f(x, y, z) = x^2 + 2y^2 + 3z^2 + 2xy + 2xz$

   (b) $f(x_1, x_2, x_3, x_4) = 20x_2 + 48x_3 + 6x_4 + 8x_1x_2 - 4x_1^2 - 12x_3^2 - x_4^2 - 4x_2^3$

HARDER PROBLEMS

5. Consider the function f defined for all (x, y) by

$$f(x, y) = (1 + y)^3 x^2 + y^2$$

Prove that f has a unique stationary point at $(0, 0)$ which is a local minimum, but f has no global minimum.

3.3 Equality Constraints: The Lagrange Problem

A general optimization problem with equality constraints is of the form

$$\max (\min) \; f(x_1, \ldots, x_n) \text{ subject to } \begin{cases} g_1(x_1, \ldots, x_n) = b_1 \\ \ldots\ldots\ldots\ldots\ldots \\ g_m(x_1, \ldots, x_n) = b_m \end{cases} (m < n) \qquad (1)$$

We assume that $m < n$ because otherwise there are usually no degrees of freedom.

In vector formulation, the problem is

$$\max (\min) \; f(\mathbf{x}) \quad \text{subject to} \quad g_j(\mathbf{x}) = b_j, \quad j = 1, \ldots, m \; (m < n) \qquad (2)$$

(If we define the vector function $\mathbf{g} = (g_1, g_2, \ldots, g_m)$ and let $\mathbf{b} = (b_1, b_2, \ldots, b_m)$, the constraints can be expressed as the vector equality $\mathbf{g}(\mathbf{x}) = \mathbf{b}$.)

The standard procedure for solving this problem is first to define the **Lagrange function**, or **Lagrangian**,

$$\mathcal{L}(\mathbf{x}) = f(\mathbf{x}) - \lambda_1 g_1(\mathbf{x}) - \cdots - \lambda_m g_m(\mathbf{x}) \qquad (3)$$

where $\lambda_1, \ldots, \lambda_m$ are called **Lagrange multipliers**. The necessary first-order conditions for optimality are then:

$$\frac{\partial \mathcal{L}(\mathbf{x})}{\partial x_i} = \frac{\partial f(\mathbf{x})}{\partial x_i} - \sum_{j=1}^{m} \lambda_j \frac{\partial g_j(\mathbf{x})}{\partial x_i} = 0, \quad i = 1, \ldots, n \qquad (4)$$

The n equations in (4) and the m equations in (1) are to be solved simultaneously for the $n + m$ variables $x_1, \ldots, x_n$ and $\lambda_1, \ldots, \lambda_m$. The resulting solution vectors $(x_1, \ldots, x_n)$ are then the candidates for optimality.

This recipe for finding possible solutions to problem (1) is valid subject to a condition given in the following theorem. The theorem also gives sufficient conditions for optimality. The proof is given at the end of this section. (We highly recommend that the reader at least studies the illuminating and simple proof of sufficiency.)

THEOREM 3.3.1 (NECESSARY CONDITIONS AND SUFFICIENT CONDITIONS)

(a) Suppose that the functions f and $g_1, \ldots, g_m$ are defined on a set S in $\mathbb{R}^n$, and that $\mathbf{x}^* = (x_1^*, \ldots, x_n^*)$ is an interior point of S that solves problem (1). Suppose further that f and $g_1, \ldots, g_m$ are C^1 in a ball around $\mathbf{x}^*$, and that

$$
\mathbf{g}'(\mathbf{x}^*) = \begin{pmatrix} \dfrac{\partial g_1(\mathbf{x}^*)}{\partial x_1} & \cdots & \dfrac{\partial g_1(\mathbf{x}^*)}{\partial x_n} \\ \vdots & & \vdots \\ \dfrac{\partial g_m(\mathbf{x}^*)}{\partial x_1} & \cdots & \dfrac{\partial g_m(\mathbf{x}^*)}{\partial x_n} \end{pmatrix} \quad \text{has rank } m \tag{5}
$$

Then there exist unique numbers $\lambda_1, \ldots, \lambda_m$ such that (4) is valid.

(b) If there exist numbers $\lambda_1, \ldots, \lambda_m$ and an admissible $\mathbf{x}^*$ which together satisfy the first-order conditions (4), and if the Lagrangian $\mathcal{L}(\mathbf{x})$ defined by (3) is concave (convex) in $\mathbf{x}$, then $\mathbf{x}^*$ solves the maximization (minimization) problem (1).

NOTE 1 Often the Lagrangian is written in the alternative form

$$
\mathcal{L}(\mathbf{x}) = f(\mathbf{x}) - \lambda_1(g_1(\mathbf{x}) - b_1) - \cdots - \lambda_m(g_m(\mathbf{x}) - b_m)
$$

but the extra terms $\lambda_1 b_1 + \cdots + \lambda_m b_m$ are completely irrelevant except possibly as a mnemonic device. In particular, some writers like to include the equations $\partial \mathcal{L}/\partial \lambda_j = 0$ or $g_j(\mathbf{x}) - b_j = 0$ among the first-order conditions.

NOTE 2 The condition on the rank of $\mathbf{g}'(\mathbf{x}^*)$ is called a *constraint qualification*. Using the gradient concept from Section 2.1, condition (4) can be expressed as:

$$
\nabla f(\mathbf{x}^*) = \lambda_1 \nabla g_1(\mathbf{x}^*) + \cdots + \lambda_m \nabla g_m(\mathbf{x}^*) \tag{6}
$$

The gradients $\nabla g_1(\mathbf{x}^*), \ldots, \nabla g_m(\mathbf{x}^*)$ are the row vectors of $\mathbf{g}'(\mathbf{x}^*)$. The constraint qualification is therefore equivalent to the condition that the gradients $\nabla g_1(\mathbf{x}^*), \ldots, \nabla g_m(\mathbf{x}^*)$ are linearly independent. (See Section 1.4.) Note that the sufficient conditions in Theorem 3.3.1(b) do not involve the constraint qualification.

NOTE 3 Let us give a geometric interpretation of (6) in the problem

$$
\max f(x, y, z) \quad \text{subject to} \quad g_1(x, y, z) = b_1, \ g_2(x, y, z) = b_2
$$

Each constraint represents (in general) a surface in 3-space, and the constraint set S is therefore, typically, a curve K in 3-space, the intersection of the two surfaces. The two gradients ∇g_1 and ∇g_2 are normals to their respective surfaces at a point $P = (x^*, y^*, z^*)$ on K, and therefore normals to K at P. If f has a maximum at P on K, then a level surface for f must touch K at P, but not cut it. Then, the gradient ∇f must be a normal to K

at P. Therefore, the three vectors ∇f, ∇g_1, and ∇g_2 all lie in the (two-dimensional) plane normal to K at P. If ∇g_1 and ∇g_2 are linearly independent, then ∇f can be expressed as a linear combination $\nabla f = \lambda_1 \nabla g_1 + \lambda_2 \nabla g_2$ of ∇g_1 and ∇g_2, for appropriate numbers λ_1 and λ_2. This is exactly in accordance with (6).

EXAMPLE 1   Use Theorem 3.3.1 to solve the problem

$$\max\ f(x, y, z) = x + 2z \quad \text{s.t.} \quad \begin{cases} g_1(x, y, z) = x + y + z = 1 \\ g_2(x, y, z) = x^2 + y^2 + z = 7/4 \end{cases}$$

(*Hint:* Eliminate the Lagrange multipliers from the first-order conditions to show that $y = 2x - 1/2$.)

Solution: Here $\mathcal{L}(x, y, z) = x + 2z - \lambda_1(x + y + z) - \lambda_2(x^2 + y^2 + z)$, so the first-order conditions are

(i) $\mathcal{L}_1' = 1 - \lambda_1 - 2\lambda_2 x = 0$ (ii) $\mathcal{L}_2' = -\lambda_1 - 2\lambda_2 y = 0$ (iii) $\mathcal{L}_3' = 2 - \lambda_1 - \lambda_2 = 0$

From equation (iii) we obtain $\lambda_2 = 2 - \lambda_1$, which inserted into (ii) gives $-\lambda_1 - 4y + 2\lambda_1 y = 0$, or $\lambda_1(2y - 1) = 4y$. This equation implies that $y \neq 1/2$, so $\lambda_1 = 4y/(2y - 1)$. Inserting this into (i) with $\lambda_2 = 2 - \lambda_1$ eventually yields

$$y = 2x - 1/2 \tag{iv}$$

Inserting (iv) into the constraints gives $3x + z = 3/2$ and $5x^2 - 2x + z = 3/2$. The first of these equations yields $z = -3x + 3/2$, which inserted into the second gives $5x(x - 1) = 0$. Hence, $x = 0$ or $x = 1$. For $x = 0$, we have $y = -1/2$ and $z = 3/2$. For $x = 1$, we have $y = 3/2$ and $z = -3/2$. Inserting these into the maximand shows that $f(0, -1/2, 3/2) = 3$ and $f(1, 3/2, -3/2) = -2$. We conclude that the only possible solution candidate is $(0, -1/2, 3/2)$. The associated values of the multipliers are $\lambda_1 = \lambda_2 = 1$.
    When $\lambda_1 = \lambda_2 = 1$ the Lagrangian is $-x^2 - y^2 - y$, which is a concave function of (x, y, z). We conclude that $(0, -1/2, 3/2)$ is a maximum point.

Lagrange Multipliers as Shadow Prices

The optimal values of $x_1, \ldots, x_n$ in problem (1) will depend on the vector $\mathbf{b} = (b_1, \ldots, b_m)$, in general. If $\mathbf{x}^*(\mathbf{b}) = (x_1^*(\mathbf{b}), \ldots, x_n^*(\mathbf{b}))$ denotes the vector of optimal values of the choice variables, then the corresponding value

$$f^*(\mathbf{b}) = f(x_1^*(\mathbf{b}), \ldots, x_n^*(\mathbf{b})) \qquad \text{(value function)} \tag{7}$$

of f is called the **(optimal) value function** for problem (1). The values of the Lagrange multipliers will also depend on $\mathbf{b}$; we write $\lambda_j = \lambda_j(\mathbf{b})$ for $j = 1, \ldots, m$. We have the following important result (precise conditions for (8) to hold are given in Section 3.8),

$$\frac{\partial f^*(\mathbf{b})}{\partial b_j} = \lambda_j(\mathbf{b}), \qquad j = 1, \ldots, m \tag{8}$$

The Lagrange multiplier $\lambda_j = \lambda_j(\mathbf{b})$ for the jth constraint is the rate at which the optimal value of the objective function changes w.r.t. changes in the constant b_j. In economics, the number $\lambda_j(\mathbf{b})$ is referred to as a **shadow price** (or **marginal value**) imputed to a unit of "resource" j.

Note that the Lagrange multipliers for problem (1) may well be negative, so that an increase in b_j can lead to a decrease in the value function.

If $db_1, \ldots, db_m$ are small in absolute value, then according to the linear approximation formula, $f^*(\mathbf{b}+d\mathbf{b}) - f^*(\mathbf{b}) \approx (\partial f^*(\mathbf{b})/\partial b_1) db_1 + \cdots + (\partial f^*(\mathbf{b})/\partial b_m) db_m$, and using (8),

$$f^*(\mathbf{b} + d\mathbf{b}) - f^*(\mathbf{b}) \approx \lambda_1(\mathbf{b}) db_1 + \cdots + \lambda_m(\mathbf{b}) db_m \tag{9}$$

This formula makes it possible to estimate the change in the value function when the components of the resource vector are slightly changed.

Proof of (8), assuming differentiability: Suppose $\mathbf{b}^*$ is any fixed resource vector and let $\boldsymbol{\lambda}^* = \boldsymbol{\lambda}(\mathbf{b}^*)$. Note that for any $\mathbf{b}$,

$$f^*(\mathbf{b}) = f(\mathbf{x}^*(\mathbf{b})) = f(\mathbf{x}^*(\mathbf{b})) - \sum_j \lambda_j^*(g_j(\mathbf{x}^*(\mathbf{b})) - b_j) = \mathcal{L}(\mathbf{x}^*(\mathbf{b})) + \sum_j \lambda_j^* b_j$$

where $\mathcal{L}(\mathbf{x}) = f(\mathbf{x}) - \sum_j \lambda_j^* g_j(\mathbf{x})$. Then

$$\frac{\partial f^*(\mathbf{b})}{\partial b_j} = \frac{\partial \mathcal{L}(\mathbf{x}^*(\mathbf{b}))}{\partial b_j} + \lambda_j^*$$

Using the first-order conditions $\partial \mathcal{L}(\mathbf{x}^*(\mathbf{b}))/\partial x_k = 0$, and assuming that $\mathbf{x}^*(\mathbf{b})$ is differentiable w.r.t. $\mathbf{b}$ at $\mathbf{b}^*$, one has

$$\frac{\partial f^*(\mathbf{b}^*)}{\partial b_j} = \sum_{k=1}^n \frac{\partial \mathcal{L}(\mathbf{x}^*(\mathbf{b}^*))}{\partial x_k} \frac{\partial x_k^*(\mathbf{b}^*)}{\partial b_j} + \lambda_j^* = \lambda_j^* \qquad \blacksquare$$

EXAMPLE 2   Consider Example 1 and suppose we change the first constraint to $x + y + z = 0.98$ and the second constraint to $x^2 + y^2 + z = 1.80$. Estimate the corresponding change in the value function by using (9). Then solve the constrained optimization problem with the new right-hand sides, and find the corresponding (exact) value of the value function.

Solution: Using the notation introduced above and the results in Example 1, we have $b_1 = 1$, $b_2 = 1.75$, $db_1 = -0.02$, $db_2 = 0.05$, $\lambda_1(1, 1.75) = \lambda_2(1, 1.75) = 1$, and $f^*(b_1, b_2) = f^*(1, 1.75) = 0 + 2(3/2) = 3$. Then (9) yields $f^*(1 - 0.02, 1.75 + 0.05) - f^*(1, 1.75) \approx \lambda_1(1, 1.75) db_1 + \lambda_2(1, 1.75) db_2 = 1 \cdot (-0.02) + 1 \cdot (0.05) = 0.03$. Thus, $f^*(0.98, 1.80) = f^*(1 - 0.02, 1.75 + 0.05) \approx 3 + 0.03 = 3.03$.

In the new optimization problem with the right-hand sides adjusted, equation (iv) in Example 1 can be derived exactly as before. Thus, we end up with the three equations $x + y + z = 0.98$, $x^2 + y^2 + z = 1.8$, and $y = 2x - 0.5$. The solutions are $(x_1, y_1, z_1) \approx (-0.0138, -0.5276, 1.5214)$ and $(x_2, y_2, z_2) \approx (1.0138, 1.5276, -1.5614)$. The first solution is optimal and the value function is 3.029. So using the approximation in (9) gave a very good estimate of the new value of the value function.

An Economic Interpretation of the Lagrange Multipliers

Consider a firm producing some final product by using n different intermediate goods. Those intermediate goods are using as inputs m different resources whose total supplies are $b_1, \ldots, b_m$. Given the quantities $x_1, \ldots, x_n$ of the intermediate goods, let $f(\mathbf{x}) = f(x_1, \ldots, x_n)$ denote the number of units of the final output, and let $g_j(\mathbf{x})$ be the corresponding number of units of resource number j required, $j = 1, \ldots, m$. Problem (1) can then be formulated as follows:

Find the amounts $x_1, \ldots, x_n$ of the intermediate goods that give the largest possible output of the final good, while making full use of all the resources.

Suppose the price of output is 1, and let p_j denote the price per unit of resource j, $j = 1, \ldots, m$. Then the net profit at these prices is

$$P(\mathbf{x}) = f(\mathbf{x}) - \sum_{j=1}^{m} p_j g_j(\mathbf{x}) \qquad (10)$$

Suppose that $P(\mathbf{x})$ is concave. A sufficient condition for P to have a maximum point with $x_1 > 0, \ldots, x_n > 0$, is that

$$\frac{\partial P(\mathbf{x})}{\partial x_i} = \frac{\partial f(\mathbf{x})}{\partial x_i} - \sum_{j=1}^{m} p_j \frac{\partial g_j(\mathbf{x})}{\partial x_i} = 0, \quad i = 1, \ldots, n \qquad (11)$$

For each resource price vector $\mathbf{p} = (p_1, \ldots, p_m)$, this system of equations determines optimal values of $x_1, \ldots, x_n$, and, in turn, the quantities $g_1(\mathbf{x}), \ldots, g_m(\mathbf{x})$ of the m resources needed.

Depending on the price vector $\mathbf{p}$, the quantity of resource j used at the optimum will be less than, equal to, or larger than the stock b_j available of that resource. Is it possible to choose prices for the resources so that the quantities actually used at the optimum are precisely equal to the available resources? Since (11) gives the first-order conditions for problem (1), we see that the answer is yes: Make resource prices equal to the Lagrange multipliers obtained from the first-order conditions for problem (1): *So, when the Lagrange multipliers are used as resource prices, maximizing the net profit in (10) leads to the available stock of each resource being used in full. The resulting quantities $x_1, \ldots, x_n$ are those that maximize production subject to the resource constraints.*

Envelope Result for Lagrange Problems

In economic optimization problems the objective function as well as the constraint functions will often depend on parameters. These parameters are held constant when optimizing, but can vary with the economic situation. What happens to the optimal value function when the parameters change? The envelope results of Section 3.1 and the interpretation of the Lagrange multipliers were results in this direction.

Consider the following general Lagrange problem

$$\max_{\mathbf{x}} (\min_{\mathbf{x}}) \ f(\mathbf{x}, \mathbf{r}) \ \text{s.t.} \ g_j(\mathbf{x}, \mathbf{r}) = 0, \ j = 1, \ldots, m \qquad (12)$$

where $\mathbf{r} = (r_1, \ldots, r_k)$ is a vector of parameters. Note that in problem (12) we maximize (minimize) w.r.t. $\mathbf{x}$, with $\mathbf{r}$ held constant.

The values of $x_1, \ldots, x_n$ that solve problem (12) will be functions of $\mathbf{r}$. (We assume a unique solution.) If we denote them by $x_1^*(\mathbf{r}), \ldots, x_n^*(\mathbf{r})$, then

$$f^*(\mathbf{r}) = f(x_1^*(\mathbf{r}), \ldots, x_n^*(\mathbf{r})) \tag{13}$$

is called the **value function**. Suppose that $\lambda_i = \lambda_i(\mathbf{r})$, $i = 1, \ldots, m$, are the Lagrange multipliers in the first-order conditions for problem (12) and let $\mathcal{L}(\mathbf{x}, \mathbf{r}) = f(\mathbf{x}, \mathbf{r}) - \sum_{j=1}^{m} \lambda_j g_j(\mathbf{x}, \mathbf{r})$ be the Lagrangian. Under certain conditions (see Theorem 3.8.4), we have the following relationship:

ENVELOPE RESULT

$$\frac{\partial f^*(\mathbf{r})}{\partial r_i} = \left(\frac{\partial \mathcal{L}(\mathbf{x}, \mathbf{r})}{\partial r_i} \right)_{\mathbf{x} = \mathbf{x}^*(\mathbf{r})}, \quad i = 1, \ldots, k \tag{14}$$

The expression on the right-hand side is obtained by differentiating $\mathcal{L}(\mathbf{x}, \mathbf{r})$ with respect to argument no. $n + i$, and then evaluating at $(\mathbf{x}^*(\mathbf{r}), \mathbf{r})$. This result generalizes the envelope results from Section 3.1. Note that if r_i is changed slightly, then $f^*(\mathbf{r})$ changes for two reasons: Firstly, $\mathbf{x}^*(\mathbf{r})$ will change, so $f(\mathbf{x}^*(\mathbf{r}), \mathbf{r})$ changes as a result. Secondly, $f(\mathbf{x}^*(\mathbf{r}), \mathbf{r})$ changes as a direct result of the change in its second argument. Formula (14) indicates, however, that the change in the first argument has a negligible influence on the value of $f(\mathbf{x}^*(\mathbf{r}), \mathbf{r})$.

EXAMPLE 3   Consider the standard utility maximization problem (see Examples 2.2.2 and 2.2.3)

$$\max \; U(\mathbf{x}) \quad \text{subject to} \quad \mathbf{p} \cdot \mathbf{x} = m \tag{*}$$

The maximum value of U will depend on the price vector $\mathbf{p}$ and income m: $U^* = U^*(\mathbf{p}, m)$, which is called the **indirect utility function**. Find expressions for $\partial U^* / \partial m$ and $\partial U^* / \partial p_i$.

Solution: The Lagrangian is $\mathcal{L} = U(\mathbf{x}) - \lambda \mathbf{p} \cdot \mathbf{x}$, and since $\partial \mathcal{L} / \partial m = \lambda$, (14) gives

$$\frac{\partial U^*}{\partial m} = \lambda$$

In this case λ measures the increase in maximal utility when revenue increases by one unit. Therefore, λ is often called the **marginal utility of money**. Moreover, equation (14) gives

$$\frac{\partial U^*}{\partial p_i} = \frac{\partial \mathcal{L}}{\partial p_i} = -\lambda x_i^*, \quad i = 1, \ldots, n \qquad \textbf{(Roy's identity)}$$

This formula has a nice interpretation: the marginal disutility of a price increase is the marginal utility of income (λ) multiplied by the quantity demanded (x_i^*). Intuitively, this is because, for a small price change, the loss of real income is approximately equal to the change in price multiplied by the quantity demanded.

Proof of Theorem 3.3.1:

(a) Since the $m \times n$ matrix in (5) is assumed to have rank m, there exists a nonsingular $m \times m$ submatrix. After renumbering the variables, if necessary, we can assume that it consists of the first m columns. By the implicit function theorem (Theorem 2.8.2) the m constraints in (1) define $x_1, \ldots, x_m$ as C^1 functions of $\tilde{\mathbf{x}} = (x_{m+1}, \ldots, x_n)$ in some ball B around $\mathbf{x}^*$, so we can write

$$x_j = h_j(x_{m+1}, \ldots, x_n) = h_j(\tilde{\mathbf{x}}), \quad j = 1, \ldots, m \tag{i}$$

Then $f(x_1, \ldots, x_n)$ reduces to a composite function

$$M(\tilde{\mathbf{x}}) = f(h_1(\tilde{\mathbf{x}}), \ldots, h_m(\tilde{\mathbf{x}}), \tilde{\mathbf{x}})$$

of $\tilde{\mathbf{x}}$ only. Since $\mathbf{x}^*$ is a local extreme point for f subject to the given constraints, M must have a (free) local extreme point at $\tilde{\mathbf{x}}^* = (x_{m+1}^*, \ldots, x_n^*)$. Hence the partial derivatives of M w.r.t. x_{m+1}, $\ldots, x_n$ must be 0:

$$\frac{\partial M}{\partial x_k} = \frac{\partial f}{\partial x_1} \frac{\partial h_1}{\partial x_k} + \cdots + \frac{\partial f}{\partial x_m} \frac{\partial h_m}{\partial x_k} + \frac{\partial f}{\partial x_k} = 0, \quad k = m+1, \ldots, n \tag{ii}$$

where the partial derivatives are evaluated at $\mathbf{x}^*$.

The next step is to make use of the constraints in order to express $\partial h_1/\partial x_k, \ldots, \partial h_m/\partial x_k$ in terms of the partial derivatives of the functions g_j. To do this, first insert (i) into the constraints to get

$$g_j(h_1(\tilde{\mathbf{x}}), \ldots, h_m(\tilde{\mathbf{x}}), \tilde{\mathbf{x}}) = b_j, \quad j = 1, \ldots, m \tag{iii}$$

for all $\tilde{\mathbf{x}} = (x_{m+1}, \ldots, x_n)$ in B. Differentiating (iii) w.r.t. x_k gives

$$\sum_{s=1}^{m} \frac{\partial g_j}{\partial x_s} \frac{\partial h_s}{\partial x_k} + \frac{\partial g_j}{\partial x_k} = 0, \quad k = m+1, \ldots, n, \quad j = 1, \ldots, m \tag{iv}$$

In particular, this is valid at $\mathbf{x}^*$. Now multiply each of the m equations in (iv) by a scalar λ_j, then add these equations over j, to obtain

$$\sum_{j=1}^{m} \lambda_j \sum_{s=1}^{m} \frac{\partial g_j}{\partial x_s} \frac{\partial h_s}{\partial x_k} + \sum_{j=1}^{m} \lambda_j \frac{\partial g_j}{\partial x_k} = 0, \quad k = m+1, \ldots, n \tag{v}$$

Next, subtract (v) from (ii),

$$\sum_{s=1}^{m} \left(\frac{\partial f}{\partial x_s} - \sum_{j=1}^{m} \lambda_j \frac{\partial g_j}{\partial x_s} \right) \frac{\partial h_s}{\partial x_k} + \frac{\partial f}{\partial x_k} - \sum_{j=1}^{m} \lambda_j \frac{\partial g_j}{\partial x_k} = 0, \quad k = m+1, \ldots, n \tag{vi}$$

These equations are valid for all choices of $\lambda_1, \ldots, \lambda_m$, when the partial derivatives are evaluated at $\mathbf{x}^*$. Suppose that we can prove the existence of numbers $\lambda_1, \ldots, \lambda_m$ such that

$$\frac{\partial f}{\partial x_s} - \sum_{j=1}^{m} \lambda_j \frac{\partial g_j}{\partial x_s} = 0, \quad s = 1, \ldots, m \tag{vii}$$

Then we see that the first m equations in (4) are satisfied, and if we substitute (vii) into (vi), the $n - m$ last equations in (4) are also satisfied.

It remains only to show that a solution $\lambda_1, \ldots, \lambda_m$ of (vii) exists. To do so, rewrite the system as

$$\begin{aligned} \frac{\partial g_1}{\partial x_1} \lambda_1 + \cdots + \frac{\partial g_m}{\partial x_1} \lambda_m &= \frac{\partial f}{\partial x_1} \\ &\cdots \cdots \cdots \cdots \cdots \cdots \cdots \cdots \cdots \cdots \\ \frac{\partial g_1}{\partial x_m} \lambda_1 + \cdots + \frac{\partial g_m}{\partial x_m} \lambda_m &= \frac{\partial f}{\partial x_m} \end{aligned} \tag{viii}$$

Here the coefficient matrix is nonsingular because it is the transpose of the matrix in (5). So (viii) has a *unique* solution $\lambda_1, \ldots, \lambda_m$. The proof of (a) is complete.

(b) To prove sufficiency, suppose that the Lagrangian $\mathcal{L}(\mathbf{x})$ is concave. Condition (4) means that the Lagrangian is stationary at $\mathbf{x}^*$. Then by Theorem 3.1.2,

$$\mathcal{L}(\mathbf{x}^*) = f(\mathbf{x}^*) - \sum_{j=1}^{m} \lambda_j g_j(\mathbf{x}^*) \geq f(\mathbf{x}) - \sum_{j=1}^{m} \lambda_j g_j(\mathbf{x}) = \mathcal{L}(\mathbf{x}) \quad \text{for all } \mathbf{x} \text{ in } S \qquad \text{(ix)}$$

But for all admissible $\mathbf{x}$, we have $g_j(\mathbf{x}) = b_j$ and, of course, $g_j(\mathbf{x}^*) = b_j$ for all j. Hence, all admissible $\mathbf{x}$ satisfy $\sum_{j=1}^{m} \lambda_j g_j(\mathbf{x}) = \sum_{j=1}^{m} \lambda_j g_j(\mathbf{x}^*)$, so (ix) implies that $f(\mathbf{x}^*) \geq f(\mathbf{x})$. Thus $\mathbf{x}^*$ solves problem (1). (Note that this proof of sufficiency does not require $\nabla g_1(\mathbf{x}^*), \ldots, \nabla g_m(\mathbf{x}^*)$ to be linearly independent.) ∎

NOTE 4 The argument used to prove sufficiency in Theorem 3.3.1(b) actually uses only the fact that $\mathcal{L}(\mathbf{x}^*) \geq \mathcal{L}(\mathbf{x})$ for all $\mathbf{x}$. So even when $\mathcal{L}$ is not concave, $\mathbf{x}^*$ solves (1) if it is a global (unconstrained) maximum point for $\mathcal{L}$ that happens to satisfy $\mathbf{g}(\mathbf{x}^*) = \mathbf{b}$ for the given $\lambda_1, \ldots, \lambda_m$.

NOTE 5 Theorem 3.3.1 is still valid if $\mathbf{x}$ is (also) restricted to some open set A, provided we add the requirement that A is convex in the sufficient condition of part (b).

PROBLEMS FOR SECTION 3.3

1. (a) Solve the problem $\max (100 - x^2 - y^2 - z^2)$ subject to $x + 2y + z = a$.

   (b) Compute the optimal value function $f^*(a)$ and verify that (8) holds.

2. (a) Solve the problem

   $$\max x + 4y + z \quad \text{subject to} \quad x^2 + y^2 + z^2 = 216 \quad \text{and} \quad x + 2y + 3z = 0$$

   (b) Change the first constraint to $x^2 + y^2 + z^2 = 215$ and the second to $x + 2y + 3z = 0.1$. Estimate the corresponding change in the maximum value by using (9).

3. (a) Solve the problem max $e^x + y + z$ subject to $\begin{cases} x + y + z = 1 \\ x^2 + y^2 + z^2 = 1 \end{cases}$.

   (b) Replace the constraints by $x + y + z = 1.02$ and $x^2 + y^2 + z^2 = 0.98$. What is the approximate change in optimal value of the objective function?

4. Consider the problem (assuming $m \geq 4$)

   $$\max U(x_1, x_2) = \tfrac{1}{2} \ln(1 + x_1) + \tfrac{1}{4} \ln(1 + x_2) \quad \text{subject to} \quad 2x_1 + 3x_2 = m$$

   (a) Let $x_1^*(m)$ and $x_2^*(m)$ denote the values of x_1 and x_2 that solve the problem. Find these functions and the corresponding Lagrange multiplier.

   (b) The optimal value U^* of $U(x_1, x_2)$ is a function of m. Find an explicit expression for $U^*(m)$, and show that $dU^*/dm = \lambda$.

5. (a) Solve the problem

$$\max x^2 + y^2 + z^2 \quad \text{subject to} \quad x^2 + y^2 + 4z^2 = 1 \quad \text{and} \quad x + 3y + 2z = 0$$

   (b) Suppose we change the first constraint to $x^2 + y^2 + 4z^2 = 1.05$ and the second constraint to $x + 3y + 2z = 0.05$. Estimate the corresponding change in the value function.

6. (a) In Example 3 let $U(\mathbf{x}) = \sum_{j=1}^{n} A_j \ln(x_j - a_j)$, where a_j and A_j are all positive constants with $\sum_{j=1}^{n} A_j = 1$, and with $R = m - \sum_{j=1}^{n} a_j p_j > 0$. Show that if $\mathbf{x} = \mathbf{x}^*$ solves problem (∗) in Example 3, then

$$x_j^* = a_j + RA_j/p_j, \quad j = 1, 2, \ldots, n$$

   (b) Let $U^*(\mathbf{p}, m) = U(\mathbf{x}^*)$ denote the indirect utility function. Verify Roy's identity.

HARDER PROBLEMS

7. (a) Find the solution of the following problem by solving the constraints for x and y:

$$\text{minimize} \ x^2 + (y - 1)^2 + z^2 \quad \text{subject to} \quad x + y = \sqrt{2} \text{ and } x^2 + y^2 = 1$$

   (b) Note that there are 3 variables and 2 constraints (z does not appear in the constraint functions). Show that the conditions in Theorem 3.3.1 are not satisfied, and that there are no Lagrange multipliers for which the Lagrangian is stationary at the solution point.

8. Let

$$Q(x_1, \ldots, x_n) = \sum_{i=1}^{n} \sum_{j=1}^{n} a_{ij} x_i x_j, \quad S = \{(x_1, \ldots, x_n) : x_1^2 + \cdots + x_n^2 = 1\}$$

Assume that the coefficient matrix $\mathbf{A} = (a_{ij})$ of the quadratic form Q is symmetric and prove that Q attains maximum and minimum values over the set S which are equal to the largest and smallest eigenvalues of $\mathbf{A}$. (*Hint:* Consider first the case $n = 2$. Write $Q(\mathbf{x})$ as $Q(\mathbf{x}) = \mathbf{x}'\mathbf{A}\mathbf{x}$. The first-order conditions give $\mathbf{A}\mathbf{x} = \lambda \mathbf{x}$.)

3.4 Local Second-Order Conditions

This section deals with local second-order conditions for the general optimization problem (3.3.1) with equality constraints. We begin by considering briefly the case with only one constraint, since this is the one that occurs most commonly in economics:

$$\text{local max (min)} \ f(\mathbf{x}) = f(x_1, \ldots, x_n) \quad \text{subject to} \quad g(\mathbf{x}) = g(x_1, \ldots, x_n) = b \quad (1)$$

The Lagrangian is $\mathcal{L} = f(\mathbf{x}) - \lambda g(\mathbf{x})$. Suppose $\mathbf{x}^*$ satisfies the first-order conditions in Theorem 3.3.1, so that the Lagrangian is stationary at $\mathbf{x}^*$. (The constraint qualification is that the gradient of g at $\mathbf{x}^*$ is not $\mathbf{0}$.) For each $r = 2, \ldots, n$, define the **bordered Hessian determinant**[2]

$$B_r(\mathbf{x}^*) = \begin{vmatrix} 0 & \frac{\partial g(\mathbf{x}^*)}{\partial x_1} & \cdots & \frac{\partial g(\mathbf{x}^*)}{\partial x_r} \\ \frac{\partial g(\mathbf{x}^*)}{\partial x_1} & \mathcal{L}_{11}''(\mathbf{x}^*) & \cdots & \mathcal{L}_{1r}''(\mathbf{x}^*) \\ \vdots & \vdots & \ddots & \vdots \\ \frac{\partial g(\mathbf{x}^*)}{\partial x_r} & \mathcal{L}_{r1}''(\mathbf{x}^*) & \cdots & \mathcal{L}_{rr}''(\mathbf{x}^*) \end{vmatrix} \tag{2}$$

Then we have the following results:

$$B_r(\mathbf{x}^*) < 0 \text{ for } r = 2, \ldots, n \implies \mathbf{x}^* \text{ solves the local min. problem in (1)} \tag{3}$$

$$(-1)^r B_r(\mathbf{x}^*) > 0 \text{ for } r = 2, \ldots, n \implies \mathbf{x}^* \text{ solves the local max. problem in (1)} \tag{4}$$

Consider next the general optimization problem with several equality constraints,

$$\text{local max(min) } f(\mathbf{x}) \quad \text{subject to} \quad g_j(\mathbf{x}) = b_j, \quad j = 1, \ldots, m \quad (m < n) \tag{5}$$

The Lagrangian is still $\mathcal{L}(\mathbf{x}) = f(\mathbf{x}) - \sum_{j=1}^m \lambda_j g_j(\mathbf{x})$. The general results that extend (3) and (4) use the following determinants, for $r = m+1, \ldots, n$:

$$B_r(\mathbf{x}^*) = \begin{vmatrix} 0 & \cdots & 0 & \frac{\partial g_1(\mathbf{x}^*)}{\partial x_1} & \cdots & \frac{\partial g_1(\mathbf{x}^*)}{\partial x_r} \\ \vdots & \ddots & \vdots & \vdots & & \vdots \\ 0 & \cdots & 0 & \frac{\partial g_m(\mathbf{x}^*)}{\partial x_1} & \cdots & \frac{\partial g_m(\mathbf{x}^*)}{\partial x_r} \\ \frac{\partial g_1(\mathbf{x}^*)}{\partial x_1} & \cdots & \frac{\partial g_m(\mathbf{x}^*)}{\partial x_1} & \mathcal{L}_{11}''(\mathbf{x}^*) & \cdots & \mathcal{L}_{1r}''(\mathbf{x}^*) \\ \vdots & & \vdots & \vdots & \ddots & \vdots \\ \frac{\partial g_1(\mathbf{x}^*)}{\partial x_r} & \cdots & \frac{\partial g_m(\mathbf{x}^*)}{\partial x_r} & \mathcal{L}_{r1}''(\mathbf{x}^*) & \cdots & \mathcal{L}_{rr}''(\mathbf{x}^*) \end{vmatrix} \tag{6}$$

NOTE 1 In order to apply the following theorem you may have to renumber the variables in order to make the *first m* columns in the matrix $(\partial g_i(\mathbf{x}^*)/\partial x_j)$ linearly independent. (See Theorem 1.9.1.)

---

[2] It is called the bordered Hessian because it is the determinant of the Hessian matrix of $\mathcal{L}$ with an extra row and column added as "borders".

THEOREM 3.4.1 (SECOND-DERIVATIVE TEST: GENERAL CASE)

Suppose the functions f and $g_1, \ldots, g_m$ are defined on a set S in $\mathbb{R}^n$, and let $\mathbf{x}^*$ be an interior point in S satisfying the necessary conditions in Theorem 3.3.1. Suppose that f and $g_1, \ldots, g_m$ are C^2 in a ball around $\mathbf{x}^*$. Define the determinant $B_r(\mathbf{x}^*)$ by (6). Then:

(a) If $(-1)^m B_r(\mathbf{x}^*) > 0$ for $r = m + 1, \ldots, n$, then $\mathbf{x}^*$ solves the local minimization problem in (1).

(b) If $(-1)^r B_r(\mathbf{x}^*) > 0$ for $r = m + 1, \ldots, n$, then $\mathbf{x}^*$ solves the local maximization problem in (1).

Check to see that if $m = 1$, the conditions in (a) and (b) reduce to those in (3) and (4). Note that the sign factor $(-1)^m$ is the same for all r in (a), while the sign factor in (b) varies with r. The conditions (a) and (b) on the signs of the determinants are referred to as the **(local) second-order conditions**. Note that these determinants are the last $n - m$ leading principal minors of the "full" determinant $B_n(\mathbf{x}^*)$ that we get in (6) when $r = n$. Note too that $n - m$ is the number of degrees of freedom remaining when m independent constraints are imposed on n variables.

EXAMPLE 1   It is easy to see that the only point that satisfies the first-order conditions for the problem

$$\text{local max (min) } f(x, y, z) = x^2 + y^2 + z^2 \quad \text{s.t.} \quad \begin{cases} g_1(x, y, z) = x + 2y + z = 30 \\ g_2(x, y, z) = 2x - y - 3z = 10 \end{cases}$$

is $P = (10, 10, 0)$. What has Theorem 3.4.1 to say about this point?

Solution: With $m = 2$ and $n = 3$, the conditions in (a) reduce to $(-1)^2 B_r(P) > 0$ for $r = 3$, i.e. $B_3(P) > 0$. On the other hand, (b) reduces to $(-1)^r B_r(P) > 0$ for $r = 3$, i.e. $B_3(P) < 0$. Thus, only the sign of $B_3(P)$ must be checked. This determinant is

$$B_3(P) = \begin{vmatrix} 0 & 0 & \partial g_1/\partial x & \partial g_1/\partial y & \partial g_1/\partial z \\ 0 & 0 & \partial g_2/\partial x & \partial g_2/\partial y & \partial g_2/\partial z \\ \partial g_1/\partial x & \partial g_2/\partial x & \mathcal{L}''_{xx} & \mathcal{L}''_{xy} & \mathcal{L}''_{xz} \\ \partial g_1/\partial y & \partial g_2/\partial y & \mathcal{L}''_{yx} & \mathcal{L}''_{yy} & \mathcal{L}''_{yz} \\ \partial g_1/\partial z & \partial g_2/\partial z & \mathcal{L}''_{zx} & \mathcal{L}''_{zy} & \mathcal{L}''_{zz} \end{vmatrix} = \begin{vmatrix} 0 & 0 & 1 & 2 & 1 \\ 0 & 0 & 2 & -1 & -3 \\ 1 & 2 & 2 & 0 & 0 \\ 2 & -1 & 0 & 2 & 0 \\ 1 & -3 & 0 & 0 & 2 \end{vmatrix}$$

Rather tedious computations show that this determinant is equal to 150. Therefore, P is a local minimum point.

Motivation and Proof of Theorem 3.4.1

To give some explanation for the conditions in the theorem above, suppose for the moment that $\mathbf{x}^*$ is a local extreme point for the Lagrange function $\mathcal{L}$ itself. If in addition $\mathbf{x}^*$ satisfies the m equality constraints, then $\mathbf{x}^*$ obviously solves problem (1). Hence, if $\mathbf{x}^*$ is a stationary point for the Lagrangian, then

$$\sum_{i=1}^{n}\sum_{j=1}^{n} \mathcal{L}_{ij}''(\mathbf{x}^*)h_ih_j \text{ is negative (positive) definite} \tag{$*$}$$

is a sufficient condition for $\mathcal{L}$ to have a local maximum (minimum) at $\mathbf{x}^*$. Therefore, when $(*)$ holds and $\mathbf{x}^*$ is a stationary point that satisfies the constraints in (1), then $\mathbf{x}^*$ solves the problem. Note that $(*)$ is "too sufficient" because it considers every vector $\mathbf{h} = (h_1, \ldots, h_n) \neq \mathbf{0}$, while it is enough that the quadratic form is negative (positive) only for variations in $\mathbf{h}$ that (roughly speaking) satisfy the restrictions imposed by the constraints. It turns out that it suffices to consider variations in $h_1, \ldots, h_n$ that cause $\mathbf{x}^* + \mathbf{h}$ to vary within the intersection of the tangent planes of the graphs of $g_1, \ldots, g_m$ at $\mathbf{x}^*$.

SUFFICIENT CONDITIONS FOR LOCAL OPTIMALITY

Suppose that $\mathbf{x}^*$ is a stationary point of the Lagrangian which satisfies the constraints, and that the quadratic form in $(*)$ is negative (positive) for all the $(h_1, \ldots, h_n) \neq (0, \ldots, 0)$ that satisfy the m linearly independent equations

$$\frac{\partial g_j(\mathbf{x}^*)}{\partial x_1}h_1 + \cdots + \frac{\partial g_j(\mathbf{x}^*)}{\partial x_n}h_n = 0, \quad j = 1, 2, \ldots, m \tag{7}$$

Then $\mathbf{x}^*$ is a solution to problem (1).

Proof of Theorem 3.4.1:   To prove part (a) we must show that $f(\mathbf{x}^* + \mathbf{h}) - f(\mathbf{x}^*) \geq 0$ for all vectors $\mathbf{x}^* + \mathbf{h}$ that are sufficiently close to $\mathbf{x}^*$ and satisfy $g_i(\mathbf{x}^* + \mathbf{h}) = b_i, i = 1, \ldots, m$.

We begin by expanding the Lagrangian $\mathcal{L}$ about $\mathbf{x}^*$ using Taylor's formula and including terms up to the second order. (As in Theorem 2.6.3.) With $\mathbf{h} = (h_1, \ldots, h_n)$, we get

$$\mathcal{L}(\mathbf{x}^* + \mathbf{h}) = \mathcal{L}(\mathbf{x}^*) + \sum_{i=1}^{n} \mathcal{L}_i'(\mathbf{x}^*)h_i + \frac{1}{2}\sum_{i=1}^{n}\sum_{j=1}^{n} \mathcal{L}_{ij}''(\mathbf{x}^* + c\mathbf{h})h_ih_j, \quad c \in (0, 1) \tag{i}$$

Because $\mathbf{x}^*$ satisfies all the constraints, $\mathcal{L}(\mathbf{x}^*) = f(\mathbf{x}^*) - \sum_{i=1}^{m} \lambda_i b_i$. Moreover, $\mathcal{L}_j'(\mathbf{x}^*) = 0$ for $j = 1, \ldots, n$. Therefore, (i) can be written as

$$f(\mathbf{x}^* + \mathbf{h}) - f(\mathbf{x}^*) = \sum_{k=1}^{m} \lambda_k(g_k(\mathbf{x}^* + \mathbf{h}) - b_k) + \frac{1}{2}\sum_{i=1}^{n}\sum_{j=1}^{n} \mathcal{L}_{ij}''(\mathbf{x}^* + c\mathbf{h})h_ih_j \tag{ii}$$

The first sum on the right-hand side is 0 when $\mathbf{x}^* + \mathbf{h}$ satisfies the constraints. Therefore, if the double sum in (ii) is positive for all such $\mathbf{x}^* + \mathbf{h} \neq \mathbf{x}^*$ sufficiently close to $\mathbf{x}^*$, then $\mathbf{x}^*$ is a local minimum point for problem (1).

By Theorem 1.9.1, the assumption in part (a) implies that

$$\sum_{i=1}^{n}\sum_{j=1}^{n} \mathcal{L}_{ij}''(\mathbf{x}^*)h_ih_j > 0 \text{ for all } \mathbf{h} \neq \mathbf{0} \text{ such that } \sum_{j=1}^{n} \frac{\partial g_k(\mathbf{x}^*)}{\partial x_j}h_j = 0, \quad k = 1, \ldots, m \tag{iii}$$

We proceed by expanding g_k about $\mathbf{x}^*$, this time retaining only terms of the first order:

$$g_k(\mathbf{x}^* + \mathbf{h}) - b_k = \sum_{j=1}^{n} \frac{\partial g_k(\mathbf{x}^* + c_k \mathbf{h})}{\partial x_j} h_j, \quad c_k \in (0, 1), \quad k = 1, \ldots, m \qquad \text{(iv)}$$

where we have used the fact that $g_k(\mathbf{x}^*) = b_k, \; k = 1, \ldots, m$.

Now consider the $(m + n) \times (m + n)$ bordered Hessian matrix

$$\mathbf{B}(\mathbf{x}^0, \mathbf{x}^1, \ldots, \mathbf{x}^m) = \begin{pmatrix} \mathbf{0} & \mathbf{G}(\mathbf{x}^1, \ldots, \mathbf{x}^m) \\ \mathbf{G}(\mathbf{x}^1, \ldots, \mathbf{x}^m)' & \mathcal{L}''(\mathbf{x}^0) \end{pmatrix}$$

where $\mathbf{G}(\mathbf{x}^1, \ldots, \mathbf{x}^m) = (\partial g_i(\mathbf{x}^i)/\partial x_j)_{m \times n}$ for arbitrary vectors $\mathbf{x}^1, \ldots, \mathbf{x}^m$ in some open ball around $\mathbf{x}^*$, and $\mathcal{L}''(\mathbf{x}^0)$ is the Hessian matrix of $\mathcal{L}$ evaluated at $\mathbf{x}^0$. For $r = m+1, \ldots, n$, let $\tilde{B}_r(\mathbf{x}^0, \mathbf{x}^1, \ldots, \mathbf{x}^m)$ be the $(m + r) \times (m + r)$ leading principal minor of this matrix. The determinants $\tilde{B}_1, \ldots, \tilde{B}_n$ are continuous functions of the collection of vectors $(\mathbf{x}^0, \mathbf{x}^1, \ldots, \mathbf{x}^m)$, viewed as a point of $\mathbb{R}^{(m+1)n}$. Moreover, $\tilde{B}_r(\mathbf{x}^*, \mathbf{x}^*, \ldots, \mathbf{x}^*) = B_r(\mathbf{x}^*)$. So, under the hypothesis that $(-1)^m B_r(\mathbf{x}^*) > 0$ for $r = m+1, \ldots, n$, there is an open ball U in $\mathbb{R}^n$ with centre at $\mathbf{x}^*$ such that $(-1)^m \tilde{B}_r(\mathbf{x}^0, \mathbf{x}^1, \ldots, \mathbf{x}^m) > 0$ for $r = m + 1, \ldots, n$ whenever the $m + 1$ vectors $\mathbf{x}^0, \mathbf{x}^1, \ldots, \mathbf{x}^m$ all belong to U. Now, if $\mathbf{x}^* + \mathbf{h}$ belongs to U, then so do all the vectors $\mathbf{x}^* + c\mathbf{h}$ and $\mathbf{x}^* + c_k \mathbf{h}, k = 1, \ldots, m$. By Theorem 1.9.1, if $\|\mathbf{h}\|$ is sufficiently small, then with $\mathbf{r} = (r_1, \ldots, r_n)$,

$$\sum_{i=1}^{n} \sum_{j=1}^{n} \mathcal{L}''_{ij}(\mathbf{x}^* + c\mathbf{h}) r_i r_j > 0 \text{ for all } \mathbf{r} \neq \mathbf{0} \text{ such that } \sum_{j=1}^{n} \frac{\partial g_k(\mathbf{x}^* + c_k \mathbf{h})}{\partial x_j} r_j = 0, \; k = 1, \ldots, m \quad \text{(v)}$$

Suppose now that $\mathbf{x}^* + \mathbf{h}$ is a point of U that satisfies all the constraints. Then according to (iv), $\sum_{j=1}^{n}(\partial g_k(\mathbf{x}^* + c_k \mathbf{h})/\partial x_j)h_j = 0$, for $k = 1, \ldots, m$. If we put $r_j = h_j, j = 1, \ldots, n$, it follows from (v) that the double sum in (ii) is > 0. Part (b) is shown in a similar way. ∎

PROBLEMS FOR SECTION 3.4

1. Consider the problem

$$\text{max (min)} \quad x^2 + y^2 \quad \text{subject to} \quad 4x^2 + 2y^2 = 4$$

   (a) Find the four points that satisfy the first-order conditions.

   (b) Compute $B_2(x, y)$ in (2) at the four points found in (a). What can you conclude?

   (c) Can you give a geometric interpretation of the problem?

2. Consider the problem

$$\text{max (min)} \quad x^2 + y^2 + z^2 \quad \text{subject to} \quad x + y + z = 1$$

   Compute B_2 and B_3 in (2). Show that the second-order conditions for a local minimum are satisfied.

3. Use Theorem 3.4.1 to classify the candidates for optimality in the problem

$$\text{local max (min)} \quad x + y + z \quad \text{s.t.} \quad x^2 + y^2 + z^2 = 1 \text{ and } x - y - z = 1$$

3.5 Inequality Constraints: Nonlinear Programming

A more general form of constrained optimization problem arises when we replace the equality constraints of (3.3.1) with inequality constraints. The result is the following **nonlinear programming problem**, which we will call the **standard problem**

$$\max \ f(x_1, \ldots, x_n) \ \text{ subject to } \ \begin{cases} g_1(x_1, \ldots, x_n) \leq b_1 \\ \ldots\ldots\ldots\ldots\ldots \\ g_m(x_1, \ldots, x_n) \leq b_m \end{cases} \tag{1}$$

A vector $\mathbf{x} = (x_1, \ldots, x_n)$ that satisfies all the constraints is called **admissible** (or **feasible**). The set of all admissible vectors is called the **admissible set** (or the **feasible set**). We assume that f and all the g_j functions are C^1.

Whereas in the case of equality constraints in Section 3.3 the number of constraints were assumed to be strictly less than the number of variables, in the present problem this restriction is not necessary. In fact, there can be many more constraints than variables.

Note that minimizing $f(\mathbf{x})$ is equivalent to maximizing $-f(\mathbf{x})$. Moreover, an inequality constraint of the form $g_j(\mathbf{x}) \geq b_j$ can be rewritten as $-g_j(\mathbf{x}) \leq -b_j$, whereas an equality constraint $g_j(\mathbf{x}) = b_j$ is equivalent to the pair of inequality constraints $g_j(\mathbf{x}) \leq b_j$ and $-g_j(\mathbf{x}) \leq -b_j$. In this way, most constrained optimization problems can be expressed in the form (1).

The standard procedure for solving problem (1) is similar to the recipe used to solve the corresponding problem with equality constraints in Section 3.3.[3] We define the Lagrangian exactly as before, $\mathcal{L}(\mathbf{x}) = f(\mathbf{x}) - \lambda_1 g_1(\mathbf{x}) - \cdots - \lambda_m g_m(\mathbf{x})$, where $\lambda_1, \ldots, \lambda_m$ are the Lagrange multipliers. Again the first-order partial derivatives of the Lagrangian are equated to 0:

$$\frac{\partial \mathcal{L}(\mathbf{x})}{\partial x_i} = \frac{\partial f(\mathbf{x})}{\partial x_i} - \sum_{j=1}^{m} \lambda_j \frac{\partial g_j(\mathbf{x})}{\partial x_i} = 0, \quad i = 1, \ldots, n \tag{2}$$

In addition, and this is the new feature, we introduce the **complementary slackness conditions**

$$\lambda_j \geq 0 \quad (\lambda_j = 0 \ \text{if} \ g_j(\mathbf{x}) < b_j), \quad j = 1, \ldots, m \tag{3}$$

Finally, of course, the constraints have to be satisfied.

In "normal cases" these are the *necessary conditions* for optimality in problem (1). Thus, if we find all vectors $\mathbf{x}$, with associated values of $\lambda_1, \ldots, \lambda_m$, that together satisfy all these conditions, we then have all the solution candidates, at least one of which solves the problem (assuming it has a solution).

Condition (3) is rather tricky. It requires that for each j, the number λ_j is nonnegative, and moreover that $\lambda_j = 0$ if $g_j(\mathbf{x}) < b_j$. Thus, if $\lambda_j > 0$, we must have $g_j(\mathbf{x}) = b_j$. An alternative formulation of this condition is:

$$\lambda_j \geq 0, \quad \lambda_j[g_j(\mathbf{x}) - b_j] = 0, \quad j = 1, \ldots, m \tag{4}$$

---

[3] If you have not been exposed to nonlinear programming before, it might be a good idea to study a somewhat more elementary treatment first, starting with the case $n = 2$, $m = 1$ as in, say, EMEA, Section 14.7.

Later in this section we shall see that even in nonlinear programming, the Lagrange multiplier λ_j can be interpreted as a "price" associated with increasing the right-hand side b_j of "resource constraint" j by one unit. With this interpretation, prices are nonnegative, and if the resource constraint is not **binding** (or not **active**) in the sense that $g_j(\mathbf{x}) < b_j$ at the optimum, then the price per unit associated with increasing b_j by a small amount is 0.

The two inequalities $\lambda_j \geq 0$ and $g_j(\mathbf{x}) \leq b_j$ are **complementarily slack** in the sense that at most one can be "slack"—that is, at most one can hold with strict inequality. Equivalently, at least one must be an equality.

Warning: It *is* possible to have *both* $\lambda_j = 0$ *and* $g_j(\mathbf{x}) = b_j$ in (3). See Problem 5.

Conditions (2) and (3) are often called the **Kuhn–Tucker conditions**. They are (essentially) *necessary* conditions for an admissible vector to solve problem (1). In general, they are definitely not sufficient on their own. Indeed, suppose one can find a point $\mathbf{x}^*$ at which f is stationary and $g_j(\mathbf{x}^*) < b_j$ for all j. Then the Kuhn–Tucker conditions will automatically be satisfied by $\mathbf{x}^*$ together with all the Lagrange multipliers $\lambda_j = 0$. Yet then $\mathbf{x}^*$ could be a local or global minimum or maximum, or some kind of saddle point.

The next theorem shows that with proper concavity conditions, the Kuhn–Tucker conditions are sufficient. Then, at least formally, no constraint qualification is needed. (But see Problem 3.6.1.)

THEOREM 3.5.1 (SUFFICIENT CONDITIONS I)

Consider the standard problem (1) and suppose that $\mathbf{x}^*$ is admissible and satisfies conditions (2)–(3). If the Lagrangian $\mathcal{L}(\mathbf{x}) = f(\mathbf{x}) - \sum_{j=1}^{m} \lambda_j g_j(\mathbf{x})$ (with the λ_j values obtained from the recipe) is concave, then $\mathbf{x}^*$ is optimal.

Proof: Since $\mathcal{L}(\mathbf{x})$ is concave and $\partial\mathcal{L}(\mathbf{x}^*)/\partial x_i = 0$ for $i = 1, \ldots, n$, then according to Theorem 3.1.2 (a), $\mathbf{x} = \mathbf{x}^*$ maximizes $\mathcal{L}(\mathbf{x})$. Hence, for all $\mathbf{x}$,

$$f(\mathbf{x}^*) - \sum_{j=1}^{m} \lambda_j g_j(\mathbf{x}^*) \geq f(\mathbf{x}) - \sum_{j=1}^{m} \lambda_j g_j(\mathbf{x})$$

Rearranging gives the equivalent inequality

$$f(\mathbf{x}^*) - f(\mathbf{x}) \geq \sum_{j=1}^{m} \lambda_j (g_j(\mathbf{x}^*) - g_j(\mathbf{x})) \qquad (*)$$

It suffices to show that the sum on the right-hand side is ≥ 0 for all admissible $\mathbf{x}$, because this will imply that $\mathbf{x}^*$ solves problem (1).

Suppose that $g_j(\mathbf{x}^*) < b_j$. Then (3) shows that $\lambda_j = 0$. For those terms in the sum in $(*)$ where $g_j(\mathbf{x}^*) = b_j$, we have $\lambda_j(g_j(\mathbf{x}^*) - g_j(\mathbf{x})) = \lambda_j(b_j - g_j(\mathbf{x})) \geq 0$, since $\mathbf{x}$ is admissible and $\lambda_j \geq 0$. The sum on the right-hand side of $(*)$ therefore consists partly of terms that are 0 (since $\lambda_j = 0$), and partly of terms that are ≥ 0. All in all, the sum is ≥ 0. ∎

EXAMPLE 1   Find the maximum of $\frac{1}{2}x - y$ subject to $x + e^{-x} + z^2 \le y$ and $x \ge 0$.

Solution: It is important first to write the problem in exactly the same form as (1), with all constraints as $\le$ inequalities:

$$\max\ f(x, y, z) = \tfrac{1}{2}x - y \quad \text{subject to} \quad \begin{cases} g_1(x, y, z) = x + e^{-x} + z^2 - y \le 0 \\ g_2(x, y, z) = -x \qquad\qquad\quad \le 0 \end{cases}$$

The Lagrangian is $\mathcal{L}(x, y, z) = \frac{1}{2}x - y - \lambda_1(x + e^{-x} + z^2 - y) - \lambda_2(-x)$. Then (2) and (3) take the form

$$\mathcal{L}'_x = \tfrac{1}{2} - \lambda_1(1 - e^{-x}) + \lambda_2 = 0 \tag{i}$$
$$\mathcal{L}'_y = -1 + \lambda_1 = 0 \tag{ii}$$
$$\mathcal{L}'_z = -2\lambda_1 z = 0 \tag{iii}$$
$$\lambda_1 \ge 0 \quad (\lambda_1 = 0 \text{ if } x + e^{-x} + z^2 < y) \tag{iv}$$
$$\lambda_2 \ge 0 \quad (\lambda_2 = 0 \text{ if } x > 0) \tag{v}$$

From (ii) we obtain $\lambda_1 = 1$, and then (iii) gives $z = 0$. Moreover, from (iv) and $z = 0$ we see that $x + e^{-x} = y$.

If $x = 0$, (i) gives $\frac{1}{2} + \lambda_2 = 0$, which would contradict $\lambda_2 \ge 0$. Thus $x > 0$, and (v) gives $\lambda_2 = 0$. From (i) we get $\frac{1}{2} - (1 - e^{-x}) = 0$, so $e^{-x} = \frac{1}{2}$ and $x = \ln 2$, which implies that $y = x + e^{-x} = \ln 2 + \frac{1}{2}$.

Thus only the point $(x, y, z) = (\ln 2, \ln 2 + \frac{1}{2}, 0)$ is admissible and also satisfies the Kuhn–Tucker conditions with $\lambda_1 = 1$, $\lambda_2 = 0$. The Lagrangian is therefore $\mathcal{L}(x, y, z) = -\frac{1}{2}x - e^{-x} - z^2$, which is concave as the sum of the concave functions $-\frac{1}{2}x$, $-e^{-x}$, and $-z^2$. Theorem 3.5.1 then tells us that $(x, y, z) = (\ln 2, \ln 2 + \frac{1}{2}, 0)$ solves the problem.

In more complicated nonlinear programming problems it is sometimes hard to know where to begin "attacking" the necessary conditions. A general method for finding all candidates for optimality in a nonlinear programming problem can be formulated as follows: First, examine the case in which all the constraints are active; then examine all cases in which all but one of the constraints are active; then all cases in which all but two are active; and so on. In the end, examine the case in which none of the constraints is active. At each step, we find all vectors **x**, with associated values of the Lagrange multipliers, that satisfy all the relevant conditions—if there are any. Then we calculate the value of the objective function for these values of **x**, and retain those **x** with the highest values. Except for perverse problems, we will have found the optimal solution. The procedure should become clearer once you have seen it in action.

EXAMPLE 2   Solve the problem $\max x^2 + 2y$ subject to $x^2 + y^2 \le 5$, $y \ge 0$.

Solution: To put the problem into the exact form (1), define $f(x, y) = x^2 + 2y$, $g_1(x, y) = x^2 + y^2$, $g_2(x, y) = -y$, and $b_1 = 5$, $b_2 = 0$. The Lagrangian is

$$\mathcal{L} = x^2 + 2y - \lambda_1(x^2 + y^2) - \lambda_2(-y)$$

and the conditions (2) and (3) reduce to

$$\mathcal{L}'_x = 2x - 2\lambda_1 x = 0 \tag{i}$$
$$\mathcal{L}'_y = 2 - 2\lambda_1 y + \lambda_2 = 0 \tag{ii}$$
$$\lambda_1 \geq 0 \quad (\lambda_1 = 0 \text{ if } x^2 + y^2 < 5) \tag{iii}$$
$$\lambda_2 \geq 0 \quad (\lambda_2 = 0 \text{ if } y > 0) \tag{iv}$$

We start the systematic procedure:

(I) *Both constraints are active.* Then $x^2 + y^2 = 5$ and $y = 0$. But with $y = 0$, (ii) gives $\lambda_2 = -2$, which contradicts (iv). So there are no solution candidates in this case.

(II) *Constraint 1 is active, 2 is inactive.* In this case $x^2 + y^2 = 5$ and $y > 0$. From (iv) we obtain $\lambda_2 = 0$, and (ii) gives $\lambda_1 y = 1$ while (i) implies $x(1 - \lambda_1) = 0$. From the last equality we conclude that *either $x = 0$ or $\lambda_1 = 1$, or both.*
 If $x = 0$, then $x^2 + y^2 = 5$ yields $y = \pm\sqrt{5}$. Since $y > 0$, only $y = \sqrt{5}$ is possible. Then $\lambda_1 = 1/\sqrt{5}$ and $\lambda_2 = 0$. Hence we have found that $(x, y) = (0, \sqrt{5})$, with $\lambda_1 = 1/\sqrt{5}$ and $\lambda_2 = 0$, satisfies (i)–(iv) and thus is one solution candidate.
 If $\lambda_1 = 1$, then $\lambda_1 y = 1$ implies $y = 1$ and from $x^2 + y^2 = 5$ we obtain $x = \pm 2$. Thus $(2, 1)$ and $(-2, 1)$ are two more solution candidates, with $\lambda_1 = 1$ and $\lambda_2 = 0$.

(III) *Constraint 1 is inactive, 2 is active.* Then $x^2 + y^2 < 5$ and $y = 0$. But then from (ii) it follows that $\lambda_2 = -2$, a contradiction. So no candidate arises in this case.

(IV) *Both constraints are inactive.* Then $x^2 + y^2 < 5$, $y > 0$, and $\lambda_1 = \lambda_2 = 0$. This contradicts (ii). So no candidate solution appears in this case.

Conclusion: There are three solution candidates, $(x, y) = (0, \sqrt{5})$, $(x, y) = (2, 1)$, and $(x, y) = (-2, 1)$. We see that $f(0, \sqrt{5}) = 2\sqrt{5}$, while $f(2, 1) = f(-2, 1) = 6$. Hence, the points $(2, 1)$ and $(-2, 1)$ give the largest value of $f(x, y)$ among the three candidates.

 The function $f(x, y) = x^2 + 2y$ is continuous, and the set S of admissible pairs (x, y) consists of the points on or inside the circle $x^2 + y^2 = 5$, with $y \geq 0$. Thus S is one half of a circular disk. It is evidently closed and bounded. According to the extreme value theorem (Theorem 3.1.3), $f(x, y)$ has a maximum in S. But then $(2, 1)$ and $(-2, 1)$ must be the solutions. (If one wants to be precise, the constraint qualification discussed in the next section should be checked.)

 It does not look promising to apply Theorem 3.5.1 in this case, because $f(x, y) = x^2 + 2y$ is convex. Still, with $\lambda_1 = 1$, and $\lambda_2 = 0$, the Lagrangian $\mathcal{L} = x^2 + 2y - (x^2 + y^2) - 0 \cdot (-y) = -y^2 + 2y$ is actually concave, and Theorem 3.5.1 shows that $(\pm 2, 1)$ both solve the maximization problem.

 The sufficient conditions in Theorem 3.5.1 require concavity of the Lagrangian. This *is* satisfied if $f(\mathbf{x})$ is concave and $\lambda_1 g_1(\mathbf{x}), \ldots, \lambda_m g_m(\mathbf{x})$ are all convex, since a sum of concave functions is concave. The next theorem gives an interesting generalization.

THEOREM 3.5.2 (SUFFICIENT CONDITIONS II)

In Theorem 3.5.1 concavity of $\mathcal{L}$ can be replaced by the following condition:

$f(\mathbf{x})$ is concave and $\lambda_j g_j(\mathbf{x})$, $j = 1, \ldots, m$, are all quasiconvex

Proof: We want to show that for all admissible $\mathbf{x}$, $f(\mathbf{x}) - f(\mathbf{x}^*) \leq 0$. Since $f(\mathbf{x})$ is concave, then according to Theorem 2.4.1,

$$f(\mathbf{x}) - f(\mathbf{x}^*) \leq \nabla f(\mathbf{x}^*) \cdot (\mathbf{x} - \mathbf{x}^*) = \sum_{j=1}^{m} \lambda_j \nabla g_j(\mathbf{x}^*) \cdot (\mathbf{x} - \mathbf{x}^*) \qquad \text{(i)}$$

where we also used (2) in vector form. (See (3.3.6).) It therefore suffices to show that for all $j = 1, \ldots, m$, and all admissible $\mathbf{x}$,

$$\lambda_j \nabla g_j(\mathbf{x}^*) \cdot (\mathbf{x} - \mathbf{x}^*) \leq 0 \qquad \text{(ii)}$$

The inequality in (ii) is satisfied for those j such that $g_j(\mathbf{x}^*) < b_j$, because then $\lambda_j = 0$. For those j such that $g_j(\mathbf{x}^*) = b_j$, we have $g_j(\mathbf{x}) \leq g_j(\mathbf{x}^*)$ (because $\mathbf{x}$ is admissible), and hence $-\lambda_j g_j(\mathbf{x}) \geq -\lambda_j g_j(\mathbf{x}^*)$. Since the function $-\lambda_j g_j$ is quasiconcave, it follows from Theorem 2.5.4 that $\nabla(-\lambda_j g_j(\mathbf{x}^*)) \cdot (\mathbf{x} - \mathbf{x}^*) \geq 0$, and hence $\lambda_j \nabla g_j(\mathbf{x}^*) \cdot (\mathbf{x} - \mathbf{x}^*) \leq 0$. ∎

NOTE 1   It is easy to see that the requirement that $\lambda_j g_j(\mathbf{x})$ is quasiconvex in Theorem 3.5.2 can be replaced by the weaker requirement that $\sum_{j=1}^{m} \lambda_j g_j(\mathbf{x})$ is quasiconvex. (Remember that a sum of quasiconvex functions is not necessarily quasiconvex.)

Properties of the Value Function

Consider again the standard nonlinear programming problem (1). The optimal value of the objective $f(\mathbf{x})$ obviously depends on $b_1, \ldots, b_m$. The function defined by [4]

$$f^*(\mathbf{b}) = \max\left\{ f(\mathbf{x}) : g_j(\mathbf{x}) \leq b_j, \ j = 1, \ldots, m \right\} \qquad \text{(5)}$$

assigns to each $\mathbf{b} = (b_1, \ldots, b_m)$ the optimal value $f^*(\mathbf{b})$ of f. It is called the **value function** for the problem.

Let the optimal choice for $\mathbf{x}$ in problem (5) be denoted by $\mathbf{x}^*(\mathbf{b})$, and assume that it is unique. Let $\lambda_j(\mathbf{b})$ for $j = 1, 2, \ldots, m$ be the corresponding Lagrange multipliers. Then, if $\partial f^*(\mathbf{b})/\partial b_j$ exists,

$$\frac{\partial f^*(\mathbf{b})}{\partial b_j} = \lambda_j(\mathbf{b}), \qquad j = 1, \ldots, m \qquad \text{(6)}$$

The value function f^* is not necessarily C^1. In Section 3.8 sufficient conditions for (6) to hold (and for $f^*(\mathbf{b})$ to be differentiable) are given. See also Problem 7.

---

[4] We assume that the maximum value always exists. This will be true, for example, in the common situation where the admissible set is bounded for all possible $\mathbf{b}$. Where the maximum does not exist, we have to replace max in (5) by sup.

EXAMPLE 3   A firm has L units of labour available and produces three goods whose values per unit of output are a, b, and c respectively. Producing x, y, and z units of the goods requires αx^2, βy^2, and γz^2 units of labour, respectively. Solve the problem

$$\max\ f(x, y, z) = ax + by + cz \quad \text{subject to} \quad g(x, y, z) = \alpha x^2 + \beta y^2 + \gamma z^2 \leq L$$

of maximizing the value of output that can be produced using L units of labour, where the coefficients a, b, c, α, β, and γ are all positive constants. Find the value function and verify (6) in this case.

Solution: The Lagrangian is $\mathcal{L}(x, y, z) = ax + by + cz - \lambda(\alpha x^2 + \beta y^2 + \gamma z^2)$. Necessary conditions for (x^*, y^*, z^*) to solve the problem are

$$a - 2\lambda\alpha x^* = 0, \quad b - 2\lambda\beta y^* = 0, \quad c - 2\lambda\gamma z^* = 0$$

$$\lambda \geq 0 \quad (\lambda = 0 \text{ if } \alpha(x^*)^2 + \beta(y^*)^2 + \gamma(z^*)^2 < L)$$

We see that λ, x^*, y^*, and z^* must all be positive. Moreover, $\lambda = a/2\alpha x^* = b/2\beta y^* = c/2\gamma z^*$. So

$$x^* = a/2\alpha\lambda, \quad y^* = b/2\beta\lambda, \quad z^* = c/2\gamma\lambda \qquad (*)$$

Because $\lambda > 0$, the complementary slackness condition implies that $\alpha(x^*)^2 + \beta(y^*)^2 + \gamma(z^*)^2 = L$. Inserting the expressions for x^*, y^*, and z^* into the resource constraint yields

$$\frac{a^2}{4\alpha\lambda^2} + \frac{b^2}{4\beta\lambda^2} + \frac{c^2}{4\gamma\lambda^2} = L$$

It follows that

$$\lambda = \tfrac{1}{2}L^{-1/2}\sqrt{a^2/\alpha + b^2/\beta + c^2/\gamma} \qquad (**)$$

The suggestion for a solution of the problem is therefore given by $(*)$, with λ as in $(**)$. The Lagrangian $\mathcal{L}$ is obviously concave, so we have found the solution.

The value function is

$$f^*(L) = ax^* + by^* + cz^* = (a^2/\alpha + b^2/\beta + c^2/\gamma)/2\lambda = \sqrt{L}\sqrt{a^2/\alpha + b^2/\beta + c^2/\gamma}$$

But then $df^*(L)/dL = \tfrac{1}{2}L^{-1/2}\sqrt{a^2/\alpha + b^2/\beta + c^2/\gamma}$, so (6) is confirmed.

Note that the value function $f^*(\mathbf{b})$ defined in (5) must be increasing in each variable $b_1, \ldots, b_m$. This is because as b_j increases with all the other variables held fixed, the admissible set becomes larger; hence, $f^*(\mathbf{b})$ cannot decrease. Thus if f^* *is* differentiable, $\partial f^*(\mathbf{b})/\partial b_j \geq 0$ and equation (6) confirms that $\lambda_j(\mathbf{b}) \geq 0$.

Here is another interesting result:

$$f(\mathbf{x}) \text{ is concave and } g_1(\mathbf{x}), \ldots, g_m(\mathbf{x}) \text{ are convex} \implies f^*(\mathbf{b}) \text{ is concave} \qquad (7)$$

Proof: Suppose that $\mathbf{b}'$ and $\mathbf{b}''$ are two arbitrary right-hand side vectors, and let $f^*(\mathbf{b}') = f(\mathbf{x}^*(\mathbf{b}'))$, $f^*(\mathbf{b}'') = f(\mathbf{x}^*(\mathbf{b}''))$, with $g_j(\mathbf{x}^*(\mathbf{b}')) \leq b'_j$, $g_j(\mathbf{x}^*(\mathbf{b}'')) \leq b''_j$ for $j = 1, \ldots, m$.

Let $t \in [0, 1]$. Corresponding to the right-hand side vector $t\mathbf{b}' + (1 - t)\mathbf{b}''$ there exists an optimal solution $\mathbf{x}^*(t\mathbf{b}' + (1 - t)\mathbf{b}'')$, and

$$f^*(t\mathbf{b}' + (1 - t)\mathbf{b}'') = f(\mathbf{x}^*(t\mathbf{b}' + (1 - t)\mathbf{b}''))$$

Define $\hat{\mathbf{x}} = t\mathbf{x}^*(\mathbf{b}') + (1 - t)\mathbf{x}^*(\mathbf{b}'')$. Then convexity of g_j for $j = 1, \ldots, m$ implies that

$$g_j(\hat{\mathbf{x}}) \le tg_j(\mathbf{x}^*(\mathbf{b}')) + (1 - t)g_j(\mathbf{x}^*(\mathbf{b}'')) \le tb_j' + (1 - t)b_j''$$

Thus $\hat{\mathbf{x}}$ is admissible in the problem where the right-hand side vector is $t\mathbf{b}' + (1 - t)\mathbf{b}''$, and in that problem $\mathbf{x}^*(t\mathbf{b}' + (1 - t)\mathbf{b}'')$ is optimal. It follows that

$$f(\hat{\mathbf{x}}) \le f(\mathbf{x}^*(t\mathbf{b}' + (1 - t)\mathbf{b}'')) = f^*(t\mathbf{b}' + (1 - t)\mathbf{b}'') \tag{$*$}$$

But concavity of f implies that

$$f(\hat{\mathbf{x}}) \ge tf(\mathbf{x}^*(\mathbf{b}')) + (1 - t)f(\mathbf{x}^*(\mathbf{b}'')) = tf^*(\mathbf{b}') + (1 - t)f^*(\mathbf{b}'') \tag{$**$}$$

From the inequalities $(*)$ and $(**)$ we conclude that $f^*(\mathbf{b})$ is concave. ∎

PROBLEMS FOR SECTION 3.5

1. Solve the problem $\max 1 - x^2 - y^2$ subject to $x \ge 2$ and $y \ge 3$ by a direct argument, and then by using Kuhn–Tucker.

2. Solve the problem $\max x^2 + y^2$ subject to $x \in [0, 1]$ and $y \in [0, 1]$ by a direct argument, and then by using Kuhn–Tucker.

3. (a) Reformulate the problem

$$\text{minimize } 4\ln(x^2 + 2) + y^2 \quad \text{subject to} \quad x^2 + y \ge 2, \quad x \ge 1$$

   as a standard Kuhn–Tucker maximization problem and write down the necessary Kuhn–Tucker conditions.

   (b) Find the solution of the problem. (Take it for granted that there is a solution.)

4. Solve the problem $\max xy + x + y$ subject to $x^2 + y^2 \le 2$, $x + y \le 1$.

5. Solve the problem $\max 1 - (x - 1)^2 - e^{y^2}$ subject to $x^2 + y^2 \le 1$.

6. (a) By using x and y units of two inputs, a firm produces $\sqrt{xy}$ units of a product. The input factor costs are w and p per unit, respectively. The firm wants to minimize the costs of producing at least q units, but it is required to use at least a units of the first input. Here w, p, a, and q are positive constants. Formulate the nonlinear

programming problem that emerges. Reformulate the problem as a maximization problem, and write down the Kuhn–Tucker conditions for (x^*, y^*) to solve the problem.

(b) Explain why $\sqrt{x^* y^*} = q$ if (x^*, y^*) is optimal, and solve the problem. (*Hint:* You need to consider two cases.)

7. (a) Solve the nonlinear programming problem (a and b are constants)

$$\text{maximize} \quad 100 - e^{-x} - e^{-y} - e^{-z} \quad \text{subject to } x + y + z \le a, \ x \le b$$

(b) Let $f^*(a, b)$ be the (optimal) value function. Compute the partial derivatives of f^* with respect to a and b, and relate them to the Lagrange multipliers.

(c) Put $b = 0$, and show that $F^*(a) = f^*(a, 0)$ is concave in a.

8. Consider the problem

$$\max_{x \in [-1,1]} (x - r)^2$$

For $r = 0$ the problem has two solutions, $x = \pm 1$. For $r \ne 0$, there is only one solution. Show that the value function $f^*(r)$ is not differentiable at $r = 0$.

3.6 Constraint Qualifications

In Section 3.5 we presented a recipe for solving the nonlinear programming problem

$$\max f(\mathbf{x}) \quad \text{subject to} \quad g_j(\mathbf{x}) \le b_j, \ j = 1, \ldots, m \tag{1}$$

We also mentioned that in some cases this recipe does not lead to the solution. To take care of some "pathological" cases, we introduce the following condition.

CONSTRAINT QUALIFICATION

The gradient vectors $\nabla g_j(\mathbf{x}^*)$ $(1 \le j \le m)$ corresponding to those constraints that are active at $\mathbf{x}^*$, are linearly independent. $\tag{2}$

An alternative formulation of this condition is: Delete all rows in the Jacobian matrix $\mathbf{g}'(\mathbf{x}^*)$ (see (3.3.5)) that correspond to constraints that are inactive at $\mathbf{x}^*$. Then the remaining matrix should have rank equal to the number of rows.

THEOREM 3.6.1 (KUHN—TUCKER NECESSARY CONDITIONS)

Suppose that $\mathbf{x}^* = (x_1^*, \ldots, x_n^*)$ solves problem (1) where f and $g_1, \ldots, g_m$ are C^1 functions. Suppose furthermore that the constraint qualification (2) holds. Then there exist unique numbers $\lambda_1, \ldots, \lambda_m$ such that the Kuhn–Tucker conditions (3.5.2)–(3.5.3) hold at $\mathbf{x} = \mathbf{x}^*$.

NOTE 1 If the constraint qualification fails at an optimal point, it may happen that this point does not satisfy the Kuhn–Tucker conditions. See Problem 1 for an example.

NOTE 2 Some textbooks are not very clear about how to use the constraint qualification. Let us explain how to apply Theorem 3.6.1 carefully when the constraint qualification is taken seriously. To solve the optimization problem two steps need to be carried out:

(I) Find all admissible points where the Kuhn–Tucker conditions are satisfied.

(II) Find also all the admissible points where the constraint qualification fails.

Among these two types of points (candidates), all possible optimum points must occur. If values of the objective function are calculated for all these candidates, the "best" candidates can be singled out: Those giving the objective function the highest value among all candidates. If the problem has optimal points, then these are the same as the best candidates.

An erroneous procedure is sometimes encountered: From the Kuhn–Tucker conditions one finds a unique candidate $\mathbf{x}^*$. The constraint qualification is then checked only at $\mathbf{x} = \mathbf{x}^*$. However, the constraint qualification may fail at other admissible points. These points will also be candidates.

Let us show what needs adding to our solution to the problem in Example 3.5.2 in order to take the constraint qualification into consideration. (Since the Lagrangian for that problem happens to be concave with appropriate Lagrange multipliers, the point we found before satisfies sufficient conditions for constrained optimality.)

EXAMPLE 1   Solve the problem max $x^2 + 2y$ subject to $x^2 + y^2 \leq 5$, $y \geq 0$.

Solution: Let $g_1(x, y) = x^2 + y^2$ and $g_2(x, y) = -y$. Then $\nabla g_1(x, y) = (2x, 2y)$ and $\nabla g_2(x, y) = (0, -1)$. Let us go through steps (I)–(IV) in Example 3.5.2 once again, this time also considering the constraint qualification.

(I) *Both constraints are active.* We found no admissible pair satisfying the Kuhn–Tucker conditions. We must now also check to see if there exist pairs satisfying the constraints with equality, and for which the constraint qualification fails. The two equations $x^2 + y^2 = 5$ and $y = 0$ have solutions $(-\sqrt{5}, 0)$ and $(\sqrt{5}, 0)$. But at both these points the gradients $(2x, 2y)$ and $(0, -1)$ are linearly independent. Hence, the constraint qualification *is* satisfied. We therefore obtain no additional candidates in this the case.

(II) *Constraint 1 is active, 2 is inactive.* Then $x^2 + y^2 = 5$ and $y > 0$. To see if the constraint qualification is satisfied for points satisfying the constraints in the present case, only $\nabla g_1(x, y) = (2x, 2y)$ needs to be checked. When $x^2 + y^2 = 5$, then $(x, y) \neq (0, 0)$ so that $\nabla g_1(x, y) \neq (0, 0)$, and hence linearly independent. (A single vector, $\mathbf{a} = (a_1, \ldots, a_n)$, is linearly independent iff $\mathbf{a}$ is not the zero vector.) Since the constraint qualification is satisfied for all points of the present type, no additional candidates are obtained (beyond the ones obtained in this step in Example 3.5.2).

(III) *Constraint 1 is inactive, 2 is active.* Here, $\nabla g_2(x, y) = (0, -1)$ is linearly independent for all pairs satisfying the constraints in the present case, so no additional candidates are obtained at this step.

(IV) *Both constraints are inactive.* Then the constraint qualification holds trivially, so no additional candidates are obtained.

Conclusion: The only points that satisfy the necessary conditions, are (as before) $(0, \sqrt{5})$, $(2, 1)$, and $(-2, 1)$. Here $f(2, 1) = f(-2, 1) > f(0, \sqrt{5})$. By the extreme-value theorem, $(2, 1)$ and $(-2, 1)$ are both solutions.

In Section 3.4 we formulated and proved sufficient conditions for local optimality in optimization problems with equality constraints. Here is the corresponding result for nonlinear programming.

THEOREM 3.6.2 (SUFFICIENT CONDITION FOR LOCAL MAXIMUM)

Assume that an admissible vector $\mathbf{x}^*$ and a set of multipliers $\lambda_1, \ldots, \lambda_m$ satisfy the necessary Kuhn–Tucker conditions (3.5.2)–(3.5.3) for problem (1). Define $J = \{j : g_j(\mathbf{x}^*) = b_j\}$, the set of active constraints, and assume that $\lambda_j > 0$ for all j in J. Consider the Lagrange problem

$$\max f(\mathbf{x}) \quad \text{subject to} \quad g_j(\mathbf{x}) = b_j, j \in J \qquad (3)$$

Evidently, $\mathbf{x}^*$ satisfies the necessary first-order conditions for this problem, for the given multipliers λ_j. If $\mathbf{x}^*$ also satisfies the sufficient second-order conditions for problem (3) (see Theorem 3.4.1) for these same λ_j, then $\mathbf{x}^*$ is a strict local maximum point for problem (1).

Proof: For simplicity assume that, after relabelling the constraints, $J = \{1, \ldots, m'\}$ with $m' \le m$. Consider the Lagrange problem

$$\max f(\mathbf{x}) \quad \text{subject to} \quad g_j(\mathbf{x}) + x_{n+j}^2 = b_j, \ j = 1, \ldots, m' \qquad (*)$$

in which the active inequality constraints have been replaced by equality constraints, each involving one extra variable. The new problem can be written as

$$\max \tilde{f}(\mathbf{y}) \quad \text{subject to} \quad \tilde{g}_j(\mathbf{y}) = b_j, j = 1, \ldots, m', \ \mathbf{y} = (x_1, \ldots, x_{n+m'}) \in \mathbb{R}^{n+m'} \qquad (**)$$

where $\tilde{g}_j = g_j + x_{n+j}^2$ and $\tilde{f}(\mathbf{y}) = f(\mathbf{x})$. Write $\mathbf{y}^* = (x_1^*, \ldots, x_n^*, 0, \ldots, 0) \in \mathbb{R}^{n+m'}$. Given the multipliers λ_j mentioned in the theorem, it is easily checked that $\mathbf{y}^*$ satisfies the necessary first-order conditions for problem $(**)$. Denote the determinants (3.4.6) pertaining to problem $(**)$ by $\tilde{B}_r(\mathbf{y})$ instead of $B_r(\mathbf{y})$, and those pertaining to problem (3) by $B_r(\mathbf{x})$. The second-order sufficient conditions referred to in the theorem imply that the determinants $B_r(\mathbf{x}^*)$ satisfy the conditions $(-1)^r B_r(\mathbf{x}^*) > 0$, for $r = m' + 1, \ldots, n$. Evidently, $(-1)^r \tilde{B}_r(\mathbf{y}^*) = (-1)^r B_r(\mathbf{x}^*)$ for $r = m' + 1, \ldots, n$. Also, for $r = n + 1, \ldots, n + m'$, the determinant $\tilde{B}_r(\mathbf{y}^*)$ is obtained from $B_n(\mathbf{x}^*)$ by adding $n - r$ rows and columns at the end, with the new diagonal elements equal to $-2\lambda_1, \ldots, -2\lambda_{n-r}$, while all the new off-diagonal elements are zero. It follows that $(-1)^r \tilde{B}_r(\mathbf{y}) = (-1)^r B_n(\mathbf{x}^*)(-2\lambda_1) \ldots (-2\lambda_{n-r}) = (-1)^n B_n(\mathbf{x}^*)(2\lambda_1) \ldots (2\lambda_{n-r}) > 0$ for $r = n + 1, \ldots, n + m'$. Hence $\mathbf{y}^*$ satisfies the sufficient conditions for a strict local maximum point in the Lagrange problem $(**)$. The original Kuhn–Tucker problem (1) has more constraints, so $\mathbf{x}^*$ is surely a strict local maximum point in that problem. ∎

Concave Programming Problems

The nonlinear programming problem (1) is said to be a **concave programming problem** (or just a **concave program**) in the case when f is concave and each g_j is a convex function. In this case, the set of admissible vectors satisfying the m constraints is convex. From now on, we write the concave program in the vector form

$$\max f(\mathbf{x}) \quad \text{subject to} \quad \mathbf{g}(\mathbf{x}) \le \mathbf{b} \tag{4}$$

where $\mathbf{g} = (g_1, \ldots, g_m)$ and $\mathbf{b} = (b_1, \ldots, b_m)$. When each component function g_j is convex, we say that the vector function $\mathbf{g}$ is convex also.

In the following results no differentiability requirements are imposed. Instead, however, we make use of the following constraint qualification.

THE SLATER CONDITION

There exists a vector $\mathbf{z}$ in $\mathbb{R}^n$ such that $\mathbf{g}(\mathbf{z}) \ll \mathbf{b}$, i.e. $g_j(\mathbf{z}) < b_j$ for all j. $\tag{5}$

So at least one vector in the constraint set simultaneously satisfies all the constraints with strict inequality.

THEOREM 3.6.3 (NECESSARY CONDITIONS FOR CONCAVE PROGRAMMING)

Suppose that (4) is a concave program satisfying the Slater constraint qualification. Then the optimal value function $f^*(\mathbf{c})$ is defined for (at least) all $\mathbf{c} \ge \mathbf{g}(\mathbf{z})$, and has a supergradient at $\mathbf{b}$. Furthermore, if $\boldsymbol{\lambda}$ is any supergradient of f^* at $\mathbf{b}$, then $\boldsymbol{\lambda} \ge \mathbf{0}$, and any solution $\mathbf{x}^*$ of problem (4) is an unconstrained maximum point of the Lagrangian $\mathcal{L}(\mathbf{x}, \boldsymbol{\lambda}) = f(\mathbf{x}) - \boldsymbol{\lambda} \cdot \mathbf{g}(\mathbf{x})$ which also satisfies $\boldsymbol{\lambda} \cdot (\mathbf{g}(\mathbf{x}^*) - \mathbf{b}) = 0$ (the complementary slackness condition).

Proof: We consider only the (usual) special case where, for all (finite) $\mathbf{c}$ in $\mathbb{R}^m$, the admissible set of points $\mathbf{x}$ that satisfy $\mathbf{g}(\mathbf{x}) \le \mathbf{c}$ is bounded, and so compact because of the assumption that the functions g_j are C^1. In this case $f^*(\mathbf{c})$ is defined as a maximum value whenever there exists at least one $\mathbf{x}$ satisfying $\mathbf{g}(\mathbf{x}) \le \mathbf{c}$, which is certainly true when $\mathbf{c} \ge \mathbf{z}$. (For a full proof allowing for the possibility that $f^*(\mathbf{c})$ may only be defined as a supremum for some values of $\mathbf{c}$, one first has to prove that f^* is concave in this case as well.) In this special case, f^* is obviously defined for all $\mathbf{c} \ge \mathbf{z}$. According to (3.5.7), f^* must be concave. Moreover, $f^*(\mathbf{g}(\mathbf{x}^*)) = f^*(\mathbf{b})$, by definition. Because of the Slater condition, $\mathbf{b}$ is an interior point in the domain of f^*. By Theorem 2.4.2, the concave function $f^*(\mathbf{c})$ has a supergradient $\boldsymbol{\lambda}$ at $\mathbf{b}$, so $f^*(\mathbf{c}) - f^*(\mathbf{b}) \le \boldsymbol{\lambda} \cdot (\mathbf{c} - \mathbf{b})$. If $\mathbf{c} \ge \mathbf{b}$, then $f^*(\mathbf{c}) \ge f^*(\mathbf{b})$, so $\boldsymbol{\lambda} \cdot (\mathbf{c} - \mathbf{b}) \ge 0$. This implies that $\boldsymbol{\lambda} \cdot \mathbf{d} \ge 0$ for all $\mathbf{d} \ge \mathbf{0}$, which implies that $\boldsymbol{\lambda} \ge \mathbf{0}$. Now, if $\mathbf{x}^*$ solves (4), then for every $\mathbf{x}$ in $\mathbb{R}^n$,

$$f(\mathbf{x}) \le f^*(\mathbf{g}(\mathbf{x})) \le f^*(\mathbf{b}) + \boldsymbol{\lambda} \cdot (\mathbf{g}(\mathbf{x}) - \mathbf{b}) \quad \text{or} \quad f(\mathbf{x}) - \boldsymbol{\lambda} \cdot \mathbf{g}(\mathbf{x}) \le f^*(\mathbf{b}) - \boldsymbol{\lambda} \cdot \mathbf{b} \le f(\mathbf{x}^*) - \boldsymbol{\lambda} \cdot \mathbf{g}(\mathbf{x}^*) \quad (*)$$

so $\mathbf{x}^*$ maximizes $f(\mathbf{x}) - \boldsymbol{\lambda} \cdot \mathbf{g}(\mathbf{x})$ for $\mathbf{x} \in \mathbb{R}^n$. Also, the inequalities $\boldsymbol{\lambda} \ge \mathbf{0}$ and $\mathbf{g}(\mathbf{x}) \le \mathbf{b}$ jointly imply that $\boldsymbol{\lambda} \cdot (\mathbf{g}(\mathbf{x}) - \mathbf{b}) \le 0$. But for $\mathbf{x} = \mathbf{x}^*$, when $f(\mathbf{x}) = f^*(\mathbf{b})$, the first part of $(*)$ implies that $\boldsymbol{\lambda} \cdot (\mathbf{g}(\mathbf{x}^*) - \mathbf{b}) \ge 0$. Hence $\boldsymbol{\lambda} \cdot (\mathbf{g}(\mathbf{x}^*) - \mathbf{b}) = 0$, which shows complementary slackness. ∎

NOTE 3 The complementary slackness condition $\lambda \cdot (\mathbf{g}(\mathbf{x}^*) - \mathbf{b}) = 0$ together with $\lambda \geq \mathbf{0}$ is equivalent to the complementary slackness condition (3.5.4). In fact, $0 = \lambda(\mathbf{g}(\mathbf{x}^*) - \mathbf{b}) = \sum_{i=1}^n \lambda_j(g_j(\mathbf{x}^*) - b_j^*)$, and each term in this sum must be 0, since a sum of nonnegative terms can only add up to 0 if each term is 0.

THEOREM 3.6.4 (SUFFICIENT CONDITIONS FOR CONCAVE PROBLEMS)

Consider problem (4) with f concave and $\mathbf{g}$ convex, and assume that there exist a vector $\lambda \geq \mathbf{0}$ and an admissible vector $\mathbf{x}^*$ which together have the property that $\mathbf{x}^*$ maximizes $f(\mathbf{x}) - \lambda \cdot \mathbf{g}(\mathbf{x})$ among all $\mathbf{x}$ in $\mathbb{R}^n$, and $\lambda \cdot (\mathbf{g}(\mathbf{x}^*) - \mathbf{b}) = 0$. Then $\mathbf{x}^*$ solves problem (4) and λ is a supergradient for f^* at $\mathbf{b}$.

Proof: By assumption, $f(\mathbf{x}) - \lambda \cdot \mathbf{g}(\mathbf{x}) \leq f(\mathbf{x}^*) - \lambda \cdot \mathbf{g}(\mathbf{x}^*)$ for all $\mathbf{x}$, and $\lambda \cdot \mathbf{g}(\mathbf{x}^*) = \lambda \cdot \mathbf{b}$, so $f(\mathbf{x}) - f(\mathbf{x}^*) \leq \lambda \cdot (\mathbf{g}(\mathbf{x}) - \mathbf{b}) \leq 0$ for all admissible $\mathbf{x}$. Thus $\mathbf{x}^*$ solves problem (4).

Take any vector $\mathbf{c}$ and let $\mathbf{g}(\mathbf{x}) \leq \mathbf{c}$. Then $f(\mathbf{x}) - f(\mathbf{x}^*) \leq \lambda \cdot \mathbf{g}(\mathbf{x}) - \lambda \cdot \mathbf{b} \leq \lambda \cdot (\mathbf{c} - \mathbf{b})$. This is valid for any $\mathbf{x}$ such that $\mathbf{g}(\mathbf{x}) \leq \mathbf{c}$, including any maximum point $\mathbf{x}$ such that $f(\mathbf{x}) = f^*(\mathbf{c})$. Because $f(\mathbf{x}^*) = f^*(\mathbf{b})$, it follows that $f^*(\mathbf{c}) - f^*(\mathbf{b}) \leq \lambda \cdot (\mathbf{c} - \mathbf{b})$. ∎

NOTE 4 In this proof concavity and convexity are not needed. What matters is that $\mathbf{x}^*$ should be a global (unconstrained) maximum of the Lagrangian expression $\mathcal{L}(\mathbf{x}, \lambda) = f(\mathbf{x}) - \lambda \cdot \mathbf{g}(\mathbf{x})$.

PROBLEMS FOR SECTION 3.6

1. Consider the problem

$$\max f(x, y) = xy \text{ subject to } g(x, y) = (x + y - 2)^2 \leq 0$$

Explain why the solution is $(x, y) = (1, 1)$. Verify that the Kuhn–Tucker conditions are not satisfied for any λ, and that the constraint qualification does not hold at $(1, 1)$.

2. (a) Show that $x = 0$, $y = 0$ is the solution to the problem

$$\max -x - y - x^2 - y^2 \text{ subject to } (x + y)^2 \leq 0$$

What do the Kuhn–Tucker conditions give you? (Note that $f(x, y) = -x - y - x^2 - y^2$ is concave and $g(x, y) = (x + y)^2$ is convex.)

(b) $x = 0$ is obviously the solution to the problem $\max -x$ s.t. $x^3 \geq 0$. What does the recipe give you? (Note that $f(x) = -x$ is concave and $g(x) = -x^3$ is quasiconvex.)

3.7 Nonnegativity Constraints

Often the variables involved in economic optimization problems are inherently nonnegative. Thus we frequently encounter the standard nonlinear programming problem with **nonnegativity constraints**:

$$\max \ f(\mathbf{x}) \quad \text{subject to} \quad \begin{cases} g_1(\mathbf{x}) \le b_1 \\ \cdots\cdots \\ g_m(\mathbf{x}) \le b_m \end{cases} \quad x_1 \ge 0, \ldots, x_n \ge 0 \qquad (1)$$

We introduce n new constraints in addition to the m original ones:

$$g_{m+1}(\mathbf{x}) = -x_1 \le 0, \quad \ldots, \quad g_{m+n}(\mathbf{x}) = -x_n \le 0 \qquad (2)$$

This converts (1) into a problem of the form (3.5.1). We introduce Lagrange multipliers μ_1, $\ldots$, μ_n to go with the new constraints and form the extended Lagrangian

$$\mathcal{L}_1(\mathbf{x}) = f(\mathbf{x}) - \sum_{j=1}^{m} \lambda_j g_j(\mathbf{x}) - \sum_{1=1}^{n} \mu_i(-x_i)$$

According to (3.5.2) and (3.5.3) the necessary conditions for $\mathbf{x}^*$ to solve the problem are

$$\frac{\partial f(\mathbf{x}^*)}{\partial x_i} - \sum_{j=1}^{m} \lambda_j \frac{\partial g_j(\mathbf{x}^*)}{\partial x_i} + \mu_i = 0, \qquad i = 1, \ldots, n \qquad (i)$$

$$\lambda_j \ge 0 \ (\lambda_j = 0 \text{ if } g_j(\mathbf{x}^*) < b_j), \qquad j = 1, \ldots, m \qquad (ii)$$

$$\mu_i \ge 0 \ (\mu_i = 0 \text{ if } x_i > 0), \qquad i = 1, \ldots, n \qquad (iii)$$

To reduce this collection of $m+n$ constraints and $m+n$ Lagrange multipliers, the necessary conditions for problem (1) are sometimes formulated slightly differently, as in Theorem 3.7.1 below. In fact, it follows from (i) that $\partial f(\mathbf{x}^*)/\partial x_i - \sum_{j=1}^{m} \lambda_j \partial g_j(\mathbf{x}^*)/\partial x_i = -\mu_i$. Since $\mu_i \ge 0$ and $-\mu_i = 0$ if $x_i > 0$, we see that (i) and (iii) together are equivalent to the condition

$$\frac{\partial f(\mathbf{x}^*)}{\partial x_i} - \sum_{j=1}^{m} \lambda_j \frac{\partial g_j(\mathbf{x}^*)}{\partial x_i} \le 0 \ (= 0 \text{ if } x_i^* > 0), \quad i = 1, \ldots, n$$

The relevant constraint qualification for problem (1), with $g_{m+1}, \ldots, g_{m+n}$ defined in (2), is:

CONSTRAINT QUALIFICATION

The gradient vectors $\nabla g_j(\mathbf{x}^*)$ $(j = 1, \ldots, m + n)$ corresponding to those constraints that are active at $\mathbf{x}^*$, are linearly independent. $\qquad (3)$

THEOREM 3.7.1 (KUHN—TUCKER NECESSARY CONDITIONS)

Suppose that $\mathbf{x}^* = (x_1^*, \ldots, x_n^*)$ solves problem (1). Suppose further that the constraint qualification (3) is satisfied. Then there exist unique numbers $\lambda_1, \ldots, \lambda_m$ such that:

(a) $\dfrac{\partial f(\mathbf{x}^*)}{\partial x_i} - \displaystyle\sum_{j=1}^{m} \lambda_j \dfrac{\partial g_j(\mathbf{x}^*)}{\partial x_i} \leq 0 \ \ (= 0 \text{ if } x_i^* > 0), \quad i = 1, \ldots, n$

(b) $\lambda_j \geq 0 \ \ (= 0 \text{ if } g_j(\mathbf{x}^*) < b_j), \quad j = 1, \ldots, m$

THEOREM 3.7.2 (SUFFICIENT CONDITIONS)

Consider problem (1) and suppose that $\mathbf{x}^*$ and $\lambda_1, \ldots, \lambda_m$ satisfy conditions (a) and (b) in Theorem 3.7.1. If the Lagrangian $\mathcal{L}(\mathbf{x}) = f(\mathbf{x}) - \sum_{j=1}^{m} \lambda_j g_j(\mathbf{x})$ is concave, then $\mathbf{x}^*$ is optimal.

Note that in the new formulation of the necessary/sufficient conditions we use the ordinary Lagrangian, not the extended Lagrangian $\mathcal{L}_1$ used above.

The proof of Theorem 3.7.2 is a simple modification of the proof of Theorem 3.5.1. Theorem 3.5.2 also holds for problem (1), with obvious modifications.

EXAMPLE 1   Solve the problem

$$\max \ 3 \ln(z + 1) - z - 2x - y \quad \text{subject to} \quad z^2 \leq x + y, \ x \geq 0, \ y \geq 0, \ z \geq 0$$

Solution: Let $\mathcal{L}(x, y, z) = 3 \ln(z+1) - z - 2x - y - \lambda(z^2 - x - y)$. The Kuhn–Tucker conditions are:

$$\mathcal{L}'_x = -2 + \lambda \leq 0 \quad (= 0 \text{ if } x^* > 0) \tag{i}$$

$$\mathcal{L}'_y = -1 + \lambda \leq 0 \quad (= 0 \text{ if } y^* > 0) \tag{ii}$$

$$\mathcal{L}'_z = \frac{3}{z^* + 1} - 1 - 2\lambda z^* \leq 0 \quad (= 0 \text{ if } z^* > 0) \tag{iii}$$

$$\lambda \geq 0 \quad (\lambda = 0 \text{ if } (z^*)^2 < x^* + y^*) \tag{iv}$$

From (ii) we get $\lambda \leq 1$, and (i) shows that we must have $x^* = 0$. (If $x^* > 0$, then $\lambda = 2$.)

Suppose first that $\lambda > 0$. Then it follows from (iv) that $(z^*)^2 = x^* + y^* = y^*$. If $y^* = 0$, then $z^* = 0$. Condition (iii) would then give $3 - 1 \leq 0$, which is impossible. Thus we must have $y^* > 0$. Then (ii) gives $\lambda = 1$. Moreover, $z^* = \sqrt{y^*} > 0$, so (iii) gives

$$\frac{3}{z^* + 1} - 1 - 2z^* = 0, \quad \text{i.e.} \quad (z^*)^2 + \tfrac{3}{2}z^* - 1 = 0$$

This quadratic equation has the roots $z = -2$ and $z = 1/2$. Since $z^* > 0$, the only possible solution is $z^* = 1/2$, and we see that the combination $x^* = 0$, $y^* = (z^*)^2 = \frac{1}{4}$, $z^* = \frac{1}{2}$, and $\lambda = 1$ satisfies all the Kuhn–Tucker conditions.

Suppose next that $\lambda = 0$. Then from (i) and (ii) we have $x^* = y^* = 0$, and since $0 \leq z^* \leq \sqrt{x^* + y^*}$, it follows that $z^* = 0$. This contradicts (iii).

The function $f(x, y, z) = 3 \ln(z + 1) - z - 2x - y$ is concave as a sum of concave functions, while $g(x, y, z) = z^2 - x - y$ is convex as a sum of convex functions. From Theorem 3.7.2 we conclude that $x^* = 0$, $y^* = 1/4$, $z^* = 1/2$ is the solution.

An Economic Interpretation

A general economic interpretation of (1) can be given in line with the interpretation of the Lagrange problem in Section 3.3. The only difference is that in the present case the inequalities $g_j(\mathbf{x}) \leq b_j$ reflect the fact that we no longer insist that all the resources are fully utilized. Thus Problem (1) can then be formulated as follows:

Find nonnegative activity levels at which to operate the production processes in order to obtain the largest possible output of the produced commodity, taking into account the impossibility of using more of any resource than its total supply.

For each resource j, specify a shadow price of λ_j per unit. To produce $f(\mathbf{x})$ units of the commodity requires $g_j(\mathbf{x})$ units of resource j at a shadow cost of $\lambda_j g_j(\mathbf{x})$. If we let the shadow price per unit of the produced commodity be 1, then the function $\pi(\mathbf{x})$ defined by

$$\pi(\mathbf{x}) = f(\mathbf{x}) - \sum_{j=1}^{m} \lambda_j g_j(\mathbf{x}) \tag{4}$$

indicates the *shadow profit* from running the processes at the vector $\mathbf{x}$ of activity levels. Suppose that we find an activity vector $\mathbf{x}^* = (x_1^*, \ldots, x_n^*)$ and nonnegative shadow prices $\lambda_1, \ldots, \lambda_m$ such that:

(A) $\mathbf{x}^*$ maximizes shadow profit among all nonnegative vectors of activity levels.

(B) $\mathbf{x}^*$ satisfies each resource constraint $g_j(\mathbf{x}^*) \leq b_j$, $j = 1, \ldots, m$.

(C) If the jth resource is not fully used because $g_j(\mathbf{x}^*) < b_j$, then the shadow price λ_j of that resource is 0.

Under these conditions $\mathbf{x}^*$ solves problem (1). The proof is an easy modification of the first part of the proof of Theorem 3.6.4. It follows from (C) that

$$\sum_{i=1}^{n} \lambda_j g_j(\mathbf{x}^*) = \sum_{i=1}^{n} \lambda_j b_j \tag{5}$$

Thus, at the given shadow prices for the resources, *the total value of the resources used at the optimum* $\mathbf{x}^*$ *is equal to the total shadow value of the initial stocks.*

The conditions (A)–(C) are not, in general, necessary for optimality, i.e. the appropriate prices do not necessarily exist. However, if the function π in (4) is concave, and if we impose the Slater condition on the constraint set, then one can prove the existence of such prices $\lambda_1, \ldots, \lambda_m$. The proof is an easy modification of the proof of Theorem 3.6.3.

PROBLEMS FOR SECTION 3.7

1. Solve the problem   max $1 - x^2 - y^2$ subject to $x \geq 0$, $y \geq 0$, by (a) a direct argument and (b) using the Kuhn–Tucker conditions.

2. Solve the following nonlinear programming problems:

   (a) max xy subject to $x + 2y \leq 2$, $x \geq 0$, $y \geq 0$

   (b) max $x^\alpha y^\beta$ subject to $x + 2y \leq 2$, $x > 0$, $y > 0$, where $\alpha > 0$, $\beta > 0$, and $\alpha + \beta \leq 1$.

3. (a) Write down the necessary Kuhn–Tucker conditions for the problem

$$\max \ln(1 + x) + y \quad \text{subject to} \quad px + y \leq m, \quad x \geq 0, \quad y \geq 0$$

   (b) Find the solution for p in $(0, 1]$ and $m > 1$.

4. A model for studying the export of gas from Russia to the rest of Europe involves the following optimization problem:

$$\max \left[x + y - \tfrac{1}{2}(x + y)^2 - \tfrac{1}{4}x - \tfrac{1}{3}y \right] \quad \text{s.t. } x \leq 5, \ y \leq 3, \ -x + 2y \leq 2, \ x \geq 0, \ y \geq 0$$

   Sketch the admissible set S in the xy-plane, and show that the maximum cannot occur at an interior point of S. Solve the problem.

HARDER PROBLEMS

5. Suppose that $\mathbf{x}^* = (x_1^*, \ldots, x_n^*) \geq \mathbf{0}$ and $\boldsymbol{\lambda} = (\lambda_1, \ldots, \lambda_m) \geq \mathbf{0}$ satisfy the sufficient conditions (A)–(C), so that $\mathbf{x}^*$ solves problem (1). Suppose that $\hat{\mathbf{x}} = (\hat{x}_1, \ldots, \hat{x}_n) \geq \mathbf{0}$ also solves the problem. Prove that, *for the same $\lambda_1, \ldots, \lambda_m$ as those associated with* $\mathbf{x}^*$, the vector $\hat{\mathbf{x}}$ will also satisfy (A)–(C), but with $\mathbf{x}^*$ replaced by $\hat{\mathbf{x}}$. (*Hint:* Use (A) to prove that $\sum_{j=1}^{m} \lambda_j g_j(\hat{\mathbf{x}}) \geq \sum_{j=1}^{m} \lambda_j g_j(\mathbf{x}^*)$. Then argue why the last inequality is an equality.)

6. With reference to problem (1), define $\widehat{\mathcal{L}}(\mathbf{x}, \boldsymbol{\lambda}) = f(\mathbf{x}) - \sum_{j=1}^{m} \lambda_j (g_j(\mathbf{x}) - b_j)$. We say that $\widehat{\mathcal{L}}$ has a **saddle point** at $(\mathbf{x}^*, \boldsymbol{\lambda}^*)$, with $\mathbf{x}^* \geq \mathbf{0}$, $\boldsymbol{\lambda}^* \geq \mathbf{0}$, if

$$\widehat{\mathcal{L}}(\mathbf{x}, \boldsymbol{\lambda}^*) \leq \widehat{\mathcal{L}}(\mathbf{x}^*, \boldsymbol{\lambda}^*) \leq \widehat{\mathcal{L}}(\mathbf{x}^*, \boldsymbol{\lambda}) \quad \text{for all } \mathbf{x} \geq \mathbf{0} \text{ and all } \boldsymbol{\lambda} \geq \mathbf{0} \qquad (*)$$

   (a) Show that if $\widehat{\mathcal{L}}$ has a saddle point at $(\mathbf{x}^*, \boldsymbol{\lambda}^*)$, then $\mathbf{x}^*$ solves problem (1). (*Hint:* Use the second inequality in $(*)$ to show that $g_j(\mathbf{x}^*) \leq b_j$ for $j = 1, \ldots, m$. Show next that $\sum_{j=1}^{m} \lambda_j^* (g_j(\mathbf{x}^*) - b_j) = 0$. Then use the first inequality in $(*)$ to finish the proof.)

   (b) Suppose that there exist $\mathbf{x}^* \geq \mathbf{0}$ and $\boldsymbol{\lambda}^* \geq \mathbf{0}$ satisfying both $g_j(\mathbf{x}^*) \leq b_j$ and $g_j(\mathbf{x}^*) = b_j$ whenever $\lambda_j^* > 0$ for $j = 1, \ldots, m$, as well as $\widehat{\mathcal{L}}(\mathbf{x}, \boldsymbol{\lambda}^*) \leq \widehat{\mathcal{L}}(\mathbf{x}^*, \boldsymbol{\lambda}^*)$ for all $\mathbf{x} \geq \mathbf{0}$. Show that $\widehat{\mathcal{L}}(\mathbf{x}, \boldsymbol{\lambda})$ has a saddle point at $(\mathbf{x}^*, \boldsymbol{\lambda}^*)$ in this case.

3.8 Other Topics

Quasiconcave Programming

The following theorem is important for economists, because in many economic optimization problems the objective function is assumed to be quasiconcave, rather than concave.

THEOREM 3.8.1 (SUFFICIENT CONDITIONS FOR QUASICONCAVE PROGRAMS)

Consider the standard problem (3.5.1) (or the standard problem with nonnegativity constraints (3.7.1)), where the objective function f is C^1 and quasiconcave. Assume that there exist numbers $\lambda_1, \ldots, \lambda_m$ and a vector $\mathbf{x}^*$ such that

(a) $\mathbf{x}^*$ is admissible and satisfies the Kuhn–Tucker conditions (3.5.2)–(3.5.3) (or (a) and (b) in Theorem 3.7.1).

(b) $\nabla f(\mathbf{x}^*) \neq \mathbf{0}$.

(c) $\lambda_j g_j(\mathbf{x})$ is quasiconvex for $j = 1, \ldots, m$.

Then $\mathbf{x}^*$ is optimal.

Proof: Consider any admissible vector $\mathbf{x}$ such that $g_j(\mathbf{x}) \leq b_j$ for $j = 1, \ldots, m$. For $g_j(\mathbf{x}^*) = b_j$ we have $\lambda_j g_j(\mathbf{x}) \leq \lambda_j g_j(\mathbf{x}^*)$, and this inequality is valid also if $g_j(\mathbf{x}) < b_j$, because then $\lambda_j = 0$. Since the function $-\lambda_j g_j$ is quasiconcave, Theorem 2.5.4 implies that $-\lambda_j \nabla g_j(\mathbf{x}^*) \cdot (\mathbf{x} - \mathbf{x}^*) \geq 0$ for all j, or $\lambda_j \nabla g_j(\mathbf{x}^*) \cdot (\mathbf{x} - \mathbf{x}^*) \leq 0$ for all j. Hence, $0 \geq \sum_{j=1}^{m} \lambda_j \nabla g_j(\mathbf{x}^*) \cdot (\mathbf{x} - \mathbf{x}^*) = \nabla f(\mathbf{x}^*) \cdot (\mathbf{x} - \mathbf{x}^*)$. By inequality (2.5.9) in Theorem 2.5.4, this implies that $f(\mathbf{x}) \leq f(\mathbf{x}^*)$. Hence $\mathbf{x}^*$ is optimal. ∎

NOTE 1 If we consider the problem max $f(x)$ subject to $x \geq 0$, condition (a) in Theorem 3.8.1 reduces to $f'(x^*) \leq 0$ and $x^* f'(x^*) = 0$, which is certainly not sufficient for a quasiconcave function to have a maximum at x^*. Thus condition (b) cannot be dropped. (Example: The quasiconcave function $f(x) = x^3$ has no maximum at $x = 0$.)

EXAMPLE 1   Consider the following problem in consumer theory (see Example 3.3.3),

$$\max U(\mathbf{x}) \quad \text{subject to } \mathbf{p} \cdot \mathbf{x} \leq m, \ \mathbf{x} \geq \mathbf{0}$$

assuming that the utility function U is C^1 and quasiconcave. Suppose $\mathbf{x}^* = (x_1^*, \ldots, x_n^*)$ is admissible and satisfies conditions (a) and (b) in Theorem 3.7.1:

$$U_i'(\mathbf{x}^*) \leq \lambda p_i \quad (U_i'(\mathbf{x}^*) = \lambda p_i \ \text{ if } \ x_i^* > 0), \quad i = 1, \ldots, n \tag{i}$$

$$\lambda \geq 0 \ (\lambda = 0 \ \text{ if } \ \mathbf{p} \cdot \mathbf{x}^* < m) \tag{ii}$$

Suppose too that $\nabla U(\mathbf{x}^*) \neq \mathbf{0}$, i.e. not all the partial derivatives $U_1'(\mathbf{x}^*), \ldots, U_n'(\mathbf{x}^*)$ are zero. Then $\mathbf{x}^*$ solves the problem. If we assume in addition that $U_i'(\mathbf{x}^*) \geq 0$ for all i, then at least one $U_i'(\mathbf{x}^*) > 0$, and (i) implies that $\lambda > 0$, so $\mathbf{p} \cdot \mathbf{x}^* = m$, i.e. all income is spent.

Kuhn–Tucker Necessary Conditions with Mixed Constraints

In some optimization problems equality constraints and inequality constraints occur simultaneously. Necessary conditions for such problems are given in the following theorem:

THEOREM 3.8.2 (NECESSARY CONDITIONS WITH MIXED CONSTRAINTS)

Suppose that $\mathbf{x}^* = (x_1^*, \ldots, x_n^*)$ solves the problem

$$\max f(\mathbf{x}) \text{ s.t. } g_j(\mathbf{x}) \leq b_j, \quad j = 1, \ldots, m', \quad g_j(\mathbf{x}) = b_j, \ j = m'+1, \ldots, m$$

where f and $g_1, \ldots, g_m$ are C^1 functions and $m - m' < n$. Suppose further that the constraint qualification (3.6.2) holds for $g_1, \ldots, g_m$. Then there exist unique numbers $\lambda_1, \ldots, \lambda_m$ such that

(a) $\nabla f(\mathbf{x}^*) = \sum_{j=1}^{m} \lambda_j \nabla g_j(\mathbf{x}^*)$

(b) $\lambda_j \geq 0 \ (\lambda_j = 0 \text{ if } g_j(\mathbf{x}^*) < b_j), \quad j = 1, \ldots, m'$

The proofs of this theorem and the rest of the results in this section are available on the book's website.

NOTE 2 Conditions (a) and (b) in the theorem are the same as (3.5.2) and (3.5.3), except that the complementary slackness conditions in (b) pertain only to $j \leq m'$, i.e. to the inequality constraints.

Envelope Theorems for Mixed Constraints

Consider the following general problem

$$\max_{\mathbf{x}} f(\mathbf{x}, \mathbf{r}) \text{ s.t. } g_j(\mathbf{x}, \mathbf{r}) \leq b_j, \ j = 1, \ldots, m', \ g_j(\mathbf{x}, \mathbf{r}) = b_j, \ j = m'+1, \ldots, m \quad (1)$$

where $\mathbf{r} = (r_1, \ldots, r_k)$ is a vector of parameters. Note that in problem (1) we maximize w.r.t. $\mathbf{x}$, with $\mathbf{r}$ held constant.

The maximum value of $f(\mathbf{x}, \mathbf{r})$ will depend on $\mathbf{r}$, and we denote it by $f^*(\mathbf{r})$. If we let $\Gamma(\mathbf{r})$ denote the set of admissible points in (1), i.e.

$$\Gamma(\mathbf{r}) = \{\mathbf{x} : g_j(\mathbf{x}, \mathbf{r}) \leq b_j, \ j = 1, \ldots, m', \ g_j(\mathbf{x}, \mathbf{r}) = b_j, \ j = m'+1, \ldots, m\}$$

we define the (maximum) value function by

$$f^*(\mathbf{r}) = \sup_{\mathbf{x} \in \Gamma(\mathbf{r})} f(\mathbf{x}, \mathbf{r}) \quad (2)$$

We use sup (supremum) to cover the case where the maximum value does not exist. The domain of f^* is the set of all $\mathbf{r}$ for which $\Gamma(\mathbf{r})$ is nonempty.

The values of $x_1, \ldots, x_n$ that solve problem (1) will be functions of $\mathbf{r}$. (We assume for the moment a unique solution.) If we denote them by $x_1^*(\mathbf{r}), \ldots, x_n^*(\mathbf{r})$, then

$$f^*(\mathbf{r}) = f(x_1^*(\mathbf{r}), \ldots, x_n^*(\mathbf{r})) \tag{3}$$

Suppose that $\lambda_i = \lambda_i(\mathbf{r}^*)$, $i = 1, \ldots, m$, are the Lagrange multipliers in the first-order conditions for the problem (1) when $\mathbf{r}$ equals a certain given vector $\mathbf{r}^*$, and let $\mathcal{L}(\mathbf{x}, \mathbf{r}) = f(\mathbf{x}, \mathbf{r}) - \sum_{j=1}^m \lambda_j g_j(\mathbf{x}, \mathbf{r})$ be the Lagrangian. Under certain conditions (see Theorem 3.8.4 below), we have the following relationship, which generalizes the envelope results from Sections 3.1 and 3.3:

ENVELOPE RESULT

$$\frac{\partial f^*(\mathbf{r}^*)}{\partial r_i} = \left[\frac{\partial \mathcal{L}(\mathbf{x}, \mathbf{r})}{\partial r_i} \right]_{\mathbf{x}=\mathbf{x}^*(\mathbf{r}^*),\ \mathbf{r}=\mathbf{r}^*}, \quad i = 1, \ldots, k \tag{4}$$

We state more precise results for two different cases, first when the vector $\mathbf{b} = (b_1, \ldots, b_m)$ varies with $\mathbf{r}$ fixed, and second when $\mathbf{r}$ varies with $\mathbf{b}$ fixed. Because each constraint $g_j(\mathbf{x}, \mathbf{r}) \leq b_j$ (or $g_j(\mathbf{x}, \mathbf{r}) = b_j$) is equivalent to the constraint $\tilde{g}_j(\mathbf{x}, \mathbf{r}, b_j) \leq 0$ (or $\tilde{g}_j(\mathbf{x}, \mathbf{r}, b_j) = 0$) where $\tilde{g}_j(\mathbf{x}, \mathbf{r}, b_j)$ is defined as $g_j(\mathbf{x}, \mathbf{r}) - b_j$, the second case actually includes the first.

THEOREM 3.8.3 (INTERPRETATION OF LAGRANGE MULTIPLIERS)

Consider the problem

$$\max f(\mathbf{x}) \text{ s.t. } g_j(\mathbf{x}) \leq b_j, j = 1, \ldots, m', \quad g_j(\mathbf{x}) = b_j, \ j = m' + 1, \ldots, m$$

and let $f^*(\mathbf{b})$ be maximum value function for the problem. Suppose that:

(a) For $\mathbf{b} = \mathbf{b}^*$ the problem has a unique solution $\mathbf{x}^* = \mathbf{x}(\mathbf{b}^*)$.

(b) There exist an open ball $B(\mathbf{b}^*; r)$ and a constant K such that for every $\mathbf{b}$ in $B(\mathbf{b}^*; r)$, the problem has an optimal solution $\mathbf{x}'$ in $B(\mathbf{x}^*; K)$.

(c) The functions f and $g_1, \ldots, g_m$ are C^1 in some open ball around $\mathbf{x}(\mathbf{b}^*)$.

(d) The gradient vectors $\nabla g_j(\mathbf{x}^*)$ corresponding to those constraints that are active when $\mathbf{b} = \mathbf{b}^*$, are linearly independent.

Then $f^*(\mathbf{b})$ is differentiable at $\mathbf{b}^*$ and $\partial f^*(\mathbf{b}^*)/\partial b_i = \lambda_i(\mathbf{b}^*)$, $i = 1, \ldots, m$.

NOTE 3 This follows from Corollary 2, page 242 in Clarke (1983). The assumptions in the theorem imply that a maximum point exists for every $\mathbf{b}$ in $B(\mathbf{b}^*; r)$. Hence $f^*(\mathbf{b})$ is defined in this ball, but perhaps not outside. Note also that f^* is C^1 near $\mathbf{b}^*$ if the solution $\mathbf{x}'$ in $B(\mathbf{x}^*; K)$ is unique for every $\mathbf{b}$ in $B(\mathbf{b}^*; r)$.

For the second case, one precise result is the following theorem.

THEOREM 3.8.4 (A GENERAL ENVELOPE THEOREM)

Consider problem (1) and suppose:

(a) For $\mathbf{r} = \mathbf{r}^*$ the problem has a unique solution $\mathbf{x}^* = \mathbf{x}(\mathbf{r}^*)$.

(b) There exist an open ball $B(\mathbf{r}^*; \alpha)$ and a constant K such that for every $\mathbf{r}$ in $B(\mathbf{r}^*; \alpha)$, problem (1) has at least one solution $\mathbf{x}'$ in $B(\mathbf{x}^*; K)$.

(c) The functions f and $g_1, \ldots, g_m$ are C^1 in some open ball around $(\mathbf{x}(\mathbf{r}^*), \mathbf{r}^*)$.

(d) The gradient vectors $\nabla_{\mathbf{x}} g_j(\mathbf{x}^*, \mathbf{r}^*)$ corresponding to those constraints that are active when $\mathbf{r} = \mathbf{r}^*$, are linearly independent.

Then $f^*(\mathbf{r})$ is differentiable at $\mathbf{r}^*$ and (4) is valid.

NOTE 4   If the appropriate Lagrangian is concave, condition (b) can be deleted in Theorems 3.8.3 and 3.8.4. (Formally, "max" must be replaced by sup, and f^* must be given the value $-\infty$ if the supremum is taken over an empty set.)

NOTE 5   Conditions (c) and (d) alone imply that $\mathbf{r}^*$ is an interior point of the domain of f^*.

NOTE 6   The conditions stated in Theorem 3.8.4 guarantee that the function $f^*(\mathbf{r})$ is defined for $\mathbf{r}$ in a neighbourhood of $\mathbf{r}^*$, but perhaps not outside this set. Moreover, $f^*(\mathbf{r})$ is C^1 near $\mathbf{r}^*$ if the solutions $\mathbf{x}'$ are unique for all $\mathbf{r}$ in $B(\mathbf{r}^*; \alpha)$.

Suppose from now on that f and $g_1, \ldots, g_m$ in problem (1) are C^2 functions, that the constraints are all equalities, and that the sufficient second-order conditions for a local maximum in Theorem 3.4.1(b), as well as the constraint qualification, are satisfied at $\mathbf{x}^* = \mathbf{x}(\mathbf{r}^*)$. Then there exist open balls U and V around $\mathbf{r}^*$ and $\mathbf{x}^*$, such that, for every $\mathbf{r}'$ in U, the equation system consisting of the first-order conditions and the constraints has a unique solution $(\mathbf{x}', \boldsymbol{\lambda}')$ with $\mathbf{x}'$ in V. (To see this, note that this system of equations has a nonzero Jacobian determinant with respect to the unknowns x_i, λ_j.)

Write $\mathbf{x}' = \mathbf{x}(\mathbf{r}')$, $\boldsymbol{\lambda}' = \boldsymbol{\lambda}(\mathbf{r}')$. The solutions $\mathbf{x}(\mathbf{r}')$, $\boldsymbol{\lambda}(\mathbf{r}')$ are C^1 functions of $\mathbf{r}'$ in an open ball around $\mathbf{r}^*$. Inserting these solutions in the system of equations described above and then differentiating w.r.t. r'_j gives a linear system of equations that determines $\partial x_i / \partial r'_j$ and $\partial \lambda_i / \partial r'_j$. We refrain from writing down the general system of equations that arises.

If the Lagrange multipliers are strictly positive for the active inequality constraints at $\mathbf{x}^*$, $\mathbf{r}^*$, then a similar method also works in the general case. Then only the active inequality constraints are included in the above procedure, and they are required to hold with equality.

It can be seen that the sufficient second-order conditions for a local maximum are also satisfied for $\mathbf{x}(\mathbf{r}')$ and $\boldsymbol{\lambda}(\mathbf{r}')$ when $\mathbf{r}'$ is close to $\mathbf{r}^*$.

PROBLEMS FOR SECTION 3.8

1. (a) Solve the problem max $x^2 + y^2 + z^2$ subject to $\begin{cases} 2x^2 + y^2 + z^2 \leq a^2 \\ x + y + z = 0 \end{cases}$.

   (b) Verify (4) in this case.

2. (a) Consider Problem 3.5.6 and compute $C^*(x^*, y^*) = -wx^* - py^*$, the value function in the (reformulated) maximization problem, in the case $pq^2/w < a^2$.

   (b) With the Lagrangian $\mathcal{L}(x, y, w, p, a, q) = -wx - py + \lambda(x - a) + \mu(\sqrt{xy} - q)$, verify (4) for all the four parameters w, p, a, and q.

3. Consider the problem

$$\max(\min) \ x^2 + y^2 \quad \text{subject to} \quad r^2 \leq 2x^2 + 4y^2 \leq s^2$$

   where $0 < r < s$.

   (a) Solve the maximization problem and verify (4) in this case.

   (b) Reformulate the minimization problem as a maximization problem, solve it, and verify (4) in this case.

   (c) Can you give a geometric interpretation of the problem and its solution?

4 TOPICS IN INTEGRATION

I don't know mathematics, therefore I have to think.
—Joan Robinson

This chapter considers some topics in the theory of integration. We presume that the reader has previously studied the elementary theory for functions of one variable, for instance in EMEA. Section 4.1 briefly reviews some of this material, and provides several problems that may help the reader recall material that is supposed to have been learned previously.

Leibniz's rule for differentiating definite integrals w.r.t. parameters is discussed in Section 4.2. Thereafter Section 4.3 contains a brief treatment of the gamma function. The main topic of this chapter is, however, multiple integration; in particular, the rule for changing variables in multiple integrals is considered in some detail.

4.1 Review of One-Variable Integration

Let $f(x)$ be a continuous function on an interval I. Recall that an **indefinite integral** of $f(x)$ is a function $F(x)$ whose derivative is equal to $f(x)$ for all x in I. In symbols,

$$\int f(x)\,dx = F(x) + C \qquad \text{where} \qquad F'(x) = f(x)$$

For instance, if $a \neq -1$, then

$$\int x^a\,dx = \frac{1}{a+1}x^{a+1} + C \qquad \text{because} \qquad \frac{d}{dx}\left(\frac{1}{a+1}x^{a+1}\right) = x^a$$

Two other important indefinite integrals are

$$\text{(a)} \int \frac{1}{x}\,dx = \ln|x| + C, \qquad \text{(b)} \int e^{ax}\,dx = \frac{1}{a}e^{ax} + C \quad (a \neq 0)$$

Note that (a) has been expressed in a form that makes it valid even when x is negative.

Two useful ways to transform an integral involve **integration by parts,**

$$\int f(x)g'(x)\,dx = f(x)g(x) - \int f'(x)g(x)\,dx \tag{1}$$

and **integration by substitution,** or **by change of variable,**

$$\int f(x)\,dx = \int f(g(u))\,g'(u)\,du \qquad (\text{where } x = g(u)) \tag{2}$$

The **definite integral** of a continuous function $f(x)$ is given by

$$\int_a^b f(x)\,dx = \Big|_a^b F(x) = F(b) - F(a), \quad \text{where } F'(x) = f(x) \text{ for all } x \text{ in } (a, b) \tag{3}$$

Recall that if $f(x) \geq 0$ in the interval $[a, b]$, then $\int_a^b f(x)\,dx$ is the area under the graph of f over $[a, b]$.

For a definite integral the formula for integration by substitution is

$$\int_a^b f(x)\,dx = \int_{u_1}^{u_2} f(g(u))g'(u)\,du \qquad (x = g(u),\ g(u_1) = a,\ g(u_2) = b) \tag{4}$$

Note also the following implications of (3):

$$\frac{d}{dx}\int_a^x f(t)\,dt = f(x), \qquad \frac{d}{dx}\int_x^b f(t)\,dt = -f(x) \tag{5}$$

PROBLEMS FOR SECTION 4.1

Find the integrals in Problems 1–5.

1. (a) $\displaystyle\int (1 - 3x^2)\,dx$ (b) $\displaystyle\int x^{-4}\,dx$ (c) $\displaystyle\int (1 - x^2)^2\,dx$

2. (a) $\displaystyle\int_0^{10} (10t^2 - t^3)\,dt$ (b) $\displaystyle\int_0^{10} 4te^{-2t}\,dt$ (c) $\displaystyle\int_0^{10} \frac{10t^2 - t^3}{t + 1}\,dt$

3. (a) $\displaystyle\int_0^1 \frac{4x^3}{\sqrt{4 - x^2}}\,dx$ (b) $\displaystyle\int_1^8 \frac{1}{3 + \sqrt{t + 8}}\,dt$ (c) $\displaystyle\int_1^{e^2} \sqrt{x}\ln x\,dx$

4. (a) $\displaystyle\int \frac{(x^n - x^m)^2}{\sqrt{x}}\,dx$ (b) $\displaystyle\int_0^{1/3} \frac{dx}{e^x + 1}$ (c) $\displaystyle\int_1^5 x\sqrt{x - 1}\,dx$

5. (a) $\displaystyle\int_4^9 \frac{(\sqrt{x} - 1)^2}{x}\,dx$ (b) $\displaystyle\int_0^1 \ln(1 + \sqrt{x})\,dx$ (c) $\displaystyle\int_0^{27} \frac{x^{1/3}}{1 + x^{1/3}}\,dx$

4.2 Leibniz's Formula

Integrals appearing in economics often depend on parameters. How does the value of the integral change if the parameters change? We consider first a simple case.

Differentiation under the Integral Sign

Let f be a function of two variables and consider the function F defined by

$$F(x) = \int_c^d f(x, t)\, dt$$

where c and d are constants. We want to find $F'(x)$. Since the limits of integration do not depend on x, it is natural to guess that we have the following result:

$$F(x) = \int_c^d f(x, t)\, dt \implies F'(x) = \int_c^d \frac{\partial f(x, t)}{\partial x}\, dt \tag{1}$$

Thus we *differentiate the integral with respect to a parameter that occurs only under the integral sign, by differentiating under the integral sign.*

In order to prove (1) we have to rely on the definition of the derivative. We get

$$F'(x) = \lim_{h \to 0} \frac{F(x+h) - F(x)}{h} = \lim_{h \to 0} \int_c^d \frac{f(x+h, t) - f(x, t)}{h}\, dt$$

$$= \int_c^d \lim_{h \to 0} \frac{f(x+h, t) - f(x, t)}{h}\, dt = \int_c^d f'_x(x, t)\, dt$$

The only problematic step here is moving the limit inside the integral sign. (See Protter and Morrey (1991), Theorem 11.1.) A more precise formulation (in a more general case) is given in Theorem 4.2.1.

EXAMPLE 1   The present value of a continuous flow of income $f(t), t \in [0, T]$, at interest rate r, is

$$K = \int_0^T f(t) e^{-rt}\, dt$$

Find dK/dr. (The limits of integration are independent of r.)

Solution: Formula (1) implies that

$$\frac{dK}{dr} = \int_0^T f(t)(-t) e^{-rt}\, dt = -\int_0^T t f(t) e^{-rt}\, dt$$

The General Case

The general problem can be formulated as follows: Let $f(x, t)$, $u(x)$, and $v(x)$ be given functions, and define the function F by the formula

$$F(x) = \int_{u(x)}^{v(x)} f(x, t)\, dt \tag{2}$$

If x changes, then the limits of integration $v(x)$ and $u(x)$ both change, and in addition the integrand $f(x, t)$ changes for each t. What is the total effect on $F(x)$ from such a change in x? In particular, what is $F'(x)$?

The answer is given in Theorem 4.2.1.[1] (Recall that a function of n variables is a C^k function if it and all its partial derivatives up to and including order k are continuous.)

THEOREM 4.2.1 (LEIBNIZ'S FORMULA)

Suppose that $f(x, t)$ and $f'_x(x, t)$ are continuous over the rectangle determined by $a \le x \le b, c \le t \le d$, that $u(x)$ and $v(x)$ are C^1 functions over $[a, b]$, and that the ranges of u and v are contained in $[c, d]$. Then

$$F(x) = \int_{u(x)}^{v(x)} f(x, t)\, dt \implies$$

$$F'(x) = f\big(x, v(x)\big)v'(x) - f\big(x, u(x)\big)u'(x) + \int_{u(x)}^{v(x)} \frac{\partial f(x, t)}{\partial x}\, dt \qquad (3)$$

Proof: Let H be the following function of three variables:

$$H(x, u, v) = \int_u^v f(x, t)\, dt$$

Then $F(x) = H(x, u(x), v(x))$, and according to the chain rule

$$F'(x) = H'_x + H'_u u'(x) + H'_v v'(x) \qquad (*)$$

Here H'_x is the partial derivative of H w.r.t. x with u and v as constants. Because of (1), $H'_x = \int_u^v f'_x(x, t)\, dt$. Moreover, according to (4.1.5), $H'_v = f(x, v)$ and $H'_u = -f(x, u)$. Inserting these results into $(*)$ yields (3). ∎

EXAMPLE 2   Use (3) to compute $F'(x)$ when $F(x) = \int_x^{x^2} \frac{1}{2}t^2 x\, dt$. Check the answer by calculating the integral first and then differentiating.

Solution: We obtain

$$F'(x) = \frac{1}{2}(x^2)^2 x \cdot 2x - \frac{1}{2}x^2 x \cdot 1 + \int_x^{x^2} \frac{1}{2}t^2\, dt$$

$$= x^6 - \frac{1}{2}x^3 + \Big|_x^{x^2} \frac{1}{6}t^3 = x^6 - \frac{1}{2}x^3 + \frac{1}{6}\big((x^2)^3 - x^3\big) = \frac{7}{6}x^6 - \frac{2}{3}x^3$$

[1] In Richard Feynman's *Surely You're Joking, Mr. Feynman!* (Bantam Books, New York, 1986), the late Nobel laureate vividly describes the usefulness of this result to physicists; it is equally useful to economists.

In this case, the integral $F(x)$ is easy to calculate explicitly:

$$F(x) = \tfrac{1}{2}x \int_x^{x^2} t^2\, dt = \tfrac{1}{2}x \left. \tfrac{1}{3}t^3 \right|_x^{x^2} = \tfrac{1}{6}(x^7 - x^4)$$

Differentiating w.r.t x gives the same expression for $F'(x)$ as before.

EXAMPLE 3   In a growth model studied by N. Kaldor and J. A. Mirrlees, a function N is defined by

$$N(t) = \int_{t-T(t)}^t n(\tau)e^{-\delta(t-T(t))}\, d\tau$$

where $T = T(t)$ is a given function. Compute $\dot N(t)$ under appropriate conditions on the functions n and T.

Solution: If n is continuous and T is C^1, Leibniz's formula gives

$$\dot N(t) = n(t)e^{-\delta(t-T(t))} - n(t - T(t))\, e^{-\delta(t-T(t))}(1 - \dot T(t))$$
$$+ \int_{t-T(t)}^t n(\tau)(-\delta)(1 - \dot T(t))\, e^{-\delta(t-T(t))}\, d\tau$$
$$= \left[n(t) - (1 - \dot T(t))\, n(t - T(t)) \right] e^{-\delta(t-T(t))} - \delta(1 - \dot T(t))\, N(t)$$

EXAMPLE 4   Suppose that a small business earns a net profit stream $y(t)$ for $t \in [0, T]$. At time $s \in [0, T]$, the discounted value (DV) of future profits is

$$V(s, r) = \int_s^T y(t)e^{-r(t-s)}\, dt$$

where r is the constant rate of discount. Compute $V_s'(s, r)$ by means of Leibniz's rule.

Solution: We get

$$V_s'(s, r) = -y(s) + \int_s^T y(t)re^{-r(t-s)}\, dt = -y(s) + rV(s, r) \qquad (*)$$

where the last equality was obtained by moving the constant r outside the integral sign.

Solving equation $(*)$ for r yields

$$r = \frac{y(s) + V_s'(s, r)}{V(s, r)} \qquad (**)$$

This has an important interpretation. At time s, the business owner earns $y(s)$, and the DV of future profits is increasing at the instantaneous rate $V_s'(s, r)$. The ratio on the right-hand side of $(**)$ is known as the *proportional instantaneous rate of return* of the investment. Equation $(**)$ requires this ratio to be equal to r. In fact, if r were the proportional instantaneous rate of return on a (relatively) safe asset like government bonds, and if the left-hand side of $(**)$ were higher than the right-hand side, then the business owner would be better off selling the business for the amount $V(s, r)$, which it is worth at time s, and holding bonds instead. But if the left-hand side of $(**)$ were lower than the right-hand side, then existing bondholders would do better to sell their bonds and set up replicas of this small business.

Infinite Intervals of Integration

Leibniz's formula can be generalized to integrals with unbounded intervals of integration.

THEOREM 4.2.2

Suppose that $f(x, t)$ and $f'_x(x, t)$ are continuous for all $t \geq c$ and all x in $[a, b]$, and suppose that the integral

$$\int_c^\infty f(x, t)\, dt \tag{4}$$

converges for each x in $[a, b]$. Suppose further that $f'_x(x, t)$ is **integrably bounded** in the sense that there exists a function $p(t)$, independent of x, such that $|f'_x(x, t)| \leq p(t)$ for all $t \geq c$ and all x in $[a, b]$, and such that $\int_c^\infty p(t)\, dt$ converges. Then

$$\frac{d}{dx} \int_c^\infty f(x, t)\, dt = \int_c^\infty f'_x(x, t)\, dt \tag{5}$$

The existence of $p(t)$ can be replaced by the weaker condition that $\int_c^\infty f'_x(x, t)\, dt$ converges uniformly on $[a, b]$. We refer to Chapter 11 of Protter and Morrey (1991) for the definition of uniform convergence, and for the proof of Theorem 4.2.2.

Obvious changes to Theorem 4.2.2 yield similar theorems for integrals of the type $\int_{-\infty}^d f(x, t)\, dt$, and also for integrals of the type $\int_{-\infty}^{+\infty} f(x, t)\, dt$. Combining these results with Leibniz's formula gives conditions ensuring that the formula applies to integrals of the following kinds, $\int_{-\infty}^{v(x)} f(x, t)\, dt$ and $\int_{u(x)}^\infty f(x, t)\, dt$.

EXAMPLE 5   Let $K(t)$ denote the capital stock of some firm at time t, and let $p(t)$ be the price per unit of capital. Let $R(t)$ denote the rental price per unit of capital. In capital theory, one principle for the determining the correct price of the firm's capital is given by the equation

$$p(t)K(t) = \int_t^\infty R(\tau)K(\tau)e^{-r(\tau - t)}\, d\tau \qquad \text{(for all } t) \tag{$*$}$$

This says that the current cost of capital should equal the discounted present value of the returns from lending it. Find an expression for $R(t)$ by differentiating $(*)$ w.r.t. t.

Solution: We get $\dot{p}(t)K(t) + p(t)\dot{K}(t) = -R(t)K(t) + \int_t^\infty R(\tau)K(\tau)re^{-r(\tau - t)}\, d\tau$. The last integral is simply $rp(t)K(t)$, so solving the equation for $R(t)$ yields

$$R(t) = \left(r - \frac{\dot{K}(t)}{K(t)} \right) p(t) - \dot{p}(t)$$

Thus the rental price is equal to $rp(t)$, the interest cost of each unit of capital, minus $p\dot{K}/K$, which represents the loss from depreciation, minus $\dot{p}$, because increases in the price of the capital good reduce the cost of holding it.

PROBLEMS FOR SECTION 4.2

1. Find an expression for $F'(x)$ when

(a) $F(x) = \int_1^2 \frac{e^{xt}}{t} \, dt \quad (x \neq 0)$

(b) $F(x) = \int_1^e \ln(xt) \, dt \quad (x > 0)$

(c) $F(x) = \int_0^1 \frac{e^{-t} \, dt}{1 + xt} \quad (x > -1)$

(d) $F(x) = \int_3^8 \frac{t^2}{(1 - xt)^2} \, dt \quad (x > \frac{1}{3})$

(Do not try to evaluate the integrals you get in (c) and (d).)

2. Use formula (1) to find $F'(\alpha)$ when $F(\alpha) = \int_0^1 xe^{\alpha x^2} \, dx$. Check the result by finding an explicit expression for $F(\alpha)$ and differentiating.

3. Use (3) to find an expression for $F'(x)$ when

(a) $F(x) = \int_0^{2x} t^3 \, dt$

(b) $F(x) = \int_0^x \left(x^2 + t^3\right)^2 \, dt$

(c) $F(x) = \int_{\sqrt{x}}^{x^2} \cos(t^2 - x^4) \, dt$

(d) $F(x) = \int_{e^x}^{e^{2x}} \sin(t + x) \, dt$

4. Let f and g be C^1 functions. Find an expression for $I = \frac{d}{d\rho} \int_0^{g(\rho)} e^{-\rho t} f(t) \, dt$.

5. The **moment generating function** of a random variable X with density function f is $M(t) = \int_{-\infty}^{\infty} e^{tx} f(x) \, dx$. Prove (under suitable conditions on f and t) that $M'(0) = \int_{-\infty}^{\infty} xf(x) \, dx$, the expectation of X, and generally that the nth derivative $M^{(n)}(0) = \int_{-\infty}^{\infty} x^n f(x) \, dx$, which is the nth moment.

6. Find $\dot{x}(t)$ if $x(t) = \int_{-\infty}^t e^{-\delta(t-\tau)} y(\tau) \, d\tau$.

7. A model by J. Tobin involves the function $F(\sigma_k) = \int_{-\infty}^{+\infty} U(\mu_k + \sigma_k z) f(z, 0, 1) \, dz$, where μ_k is a function of σ_k. Under suitable restrictions on the functions U, μ_k, and f, find an expression for $dF(\sigma_k)/d\sigma_k$.

HARDER PROBLEMS

8. A vintage growth model due to L. Johansen involves the following definitions:

$$K(t) = \int_{-\infty}^t f(t - \tau)k(\tau) \, d\tau, \quad T(0) = \int_0^{\infty} f(\xi) \, d\xi, \quad V(t) = \frac{1}{T(0)} \int_{-\infty}^t G(\tau, t) \, d\tau$$

where $G(\tau, t) = k(\tau) \int_{t-\tau}^{\infty} f(\xi) \, d\xi$. With suitable restrictions on the functions involved, prove that $\dot{V}(t) = k(t) - K(t)/T(0)$.

9. Define

$$z(t) = \int_t^{2t} x(\tau) \exp\left(-\int_t^\tau r(s)\,ds\right) d\tau, \quad p(t) = \exp\left(-\int_t^{2t} r(s)\,ds\right)$$

where the functions $x(\tau)$ and $r(s)$ are both differentiable. Show that

$$\dot{z}(t) - r(t)z(t) = 2p(t)x(2t) - x(t)$$

10. A firm faces uncertain demand D and has existing inventory I. There are different costs per unit of having too much or too little stock. So the firm wants to choose its stock level Q so that it minimizes the function

$$g(Q) = c(Q - I) + h\int_0^Q (Q - D)f(D)\,dD + p\int_Q^a (D - Q)f(D)\,dD$$

where c, I, h, p, and a are positive constants, $p \geq c$, and f is a given nonnegative function that satisfies $\int_0^a f(D)\,dD = 1$ (which means that f can be interpreted as a probability distribution function).

(a) Compute $g'(Q)$ and $g''(Q)$, and show that g is convex.

(b) Define $F(Q^*) = \int_0^{Q^*} f(D)\,dD$, where Q^* is the minimum point of $g(Q)$. Use the first-order conditions for minimization of g to find an equation for $F(Q^*)$, the probability that demand D does not exceed Q^*. Use this equation to find the value of $F(Q^*)$.

4.3 The Gamma Function

Around 1725 the Swiss mathematician L. Euler asked the following question: Is there a "smooth" function defined on $(0, \infty)$ that maps each natural number n to the value $n! = 1 \cdot 2 \cdot \ldots \cdot n$. Euler thereby discovered one of the most studied functions in the whole of mathematical analysis, the **gamma function**. It is defined by

$$\Gamma(x) = \int_0^\infty e^{-t}t^{x-1}\,dt, \quad x > 0 \tag{1}$$

(Recall that Γ is the upper case Greek letter "gamma".) This function crops up in several areas of application, and there is a vast literature investigating its mathematical properties.[2] We shall just mention a few simple properties.

For definition (1) to make sense, it must be shown that the integral exists for each $x > 0$. Not only is the interval of integration unbounded, but for x in $(0, 1)$ the integrand $e^{-t}t^{x-1}$

----
[2] For example N. Nielsen: *Handbuch der Theorie der Gammafunktion*, Leipzig (1906), 326 pages.

tends to ∞ as $t \to 0$. In order to show that the integral converges, partition the interval $(0, \infty)$ into two parts:

$$\int_0^\infty e^{-t} t^{x-1} \, dt = \int_0^1 e^{-t} t^{x-1} \, dt + \int_1^\infty e^{-t} t^{x-1} \, dt \qquad (*)$$

Concerning the first integral on the right-hand side, note that $0 \le e^{-t} \le 1$ for $t \ge 0$, so $0 \le e^{-t} t^{x-1} \le t^{x-1}$ for all $t \ge 0$. Because $\int_0^1 t^{x-1} \, dt$ converges (to $1/x$), it follows that $\int_0^1 e^{-t} t^{x-1} \, dt$ converges. Convergence of the other integral is shown as follows: Because $e^{-t} t^b \to 0$ as $t \to \infty$ for every b, there exists a number t_0 such that $t \ge t_0$ implies $e^{-t} t^{x+1} < 1$. Hence $e^{-t} t^{x-1} < 1/t^2$ for $t \ge t_0$. But $\int_{t_0}^\infty (1/t^2) \, dt$ converges (to $1/t_0$), so we conclude that the second integral on the right-hand side of $(*)$ converges. Thus $\Gamma(x)$ is well-defined for all $x > 0$.

Let us compute some values of $\Gamma(x)$. For $x = 1$ it is easy:

$$\Gamma(1) = \int_0^\infty e^{-t} \, dt = 1$$

Further, integration by parts gives

$$\Gamma(x+1) = \int_0^\infty e^{-t} t^x \, dt = -\left.\vphantom{\int} e^{-t} t^x \right|_0^\infty + \int_0^\infty e^{-t} x t^{x-1} \, dt = x\Gamma(x) \quad \text{for } x > 0 \quad (2)$$

This is the so-called **functional equation** for the gamma function. This equation implies that $\Gamma(2) = \Gamma(1+1) = 1\Gamma(1) = 1$, $\Gamma(3) = 2\Gamma(2) = 2 \cdot 1$, $\Gamma(4) = 3\Gamma(3) = 3 \cdot 2 \cdot 1$. By induction,

$$\Gamma(n) = (n-1) \cdot (n-2) \cdot \ldots \cdot 3 \cdot 2 \cdot 1 = (n-1)!$$

for every natural number n.

It is more difficult to compute $\Gamma(x)$ if x is not a natural number. In order to compute $\Gamma(\tfrac{1}{2})$, for instance, we need the **Poisson integral formula**

$$\int_0^\infty e^{-t^2} \, dt = \frac{1}{2}\sqrt{\pi} \qquad (3)$$

This is proved in Example 4.8.2. By symmetry of the graph of e^{-t^2} about $t = 0$, it follows that $\int_{-\infty}^{+\infty} e^{-t^2} \, dt = \sqrt{\pi}$. Substituting $u = \sqrt{\lambda}\, t$ leads to

$$\int_{-\infty}^{+\infty} e^{-\lambda t^2} \, dt = \sqrt{\frac{\pi}{\lambda}} \qquad (\lambda > 0) \qquad (4)$$

Now (3) allows us to compute $\Gamma(\tfrac{1}{2})$. In fact, $\Gamma(\tfrac{1}{2}) = \int_0^\infty e^{-t} t^{-1/2} \, dt = 2\int_0^\infty e^{-u^2} \, du = \sqrt{\pi}$, using the substitution $t = u^2$.

Once the values of Γ in $(0, 1]$ are known, we can find $\Gamma(x)$ for every positive x by making use of the functional equation (2).

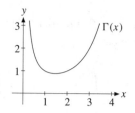

Figure 1 The gamma function

The gamma function is continuous in the interval $(0, \infty)$. It can be shown that it has a minimum ≈ 0.8856 at the point $x \approx 1.4616$. The graph is shown in Fig. 1.

PROBLEMS FOR SECTION 4.3

1. Compute

   (a) $\displaystyle\int_0^\infty e^{-ax^2}\,dx \qquad (a > 0)$

   (b) $\displaystyle\int_{-\infty}^{+\infty} \frac{1}{\sqrt{2\pi}} e^{-x^2/2}\,dx$

2. Use (2) to find $\Gamma(\tfrac{3}{2})$ and show by induction that for every natural number n,

$$\Gamma\left(n + \frac{1}{2}\right) = \frac{1 \cdot 3 \cdot 5 \cdot \ldots \cdot (2n - 1)}{2^n}\sqrt{\pi} = \frac{(2n-1)!}{2^{2n-1}(n-1)!}\sqrt{\pi}$$

3. One can show that for every $x > 0$ there exists a θ in $(0, 1)$ (where θ depends on x) such that

$$\Gamma(x) = \sqrt{2\pi}\,x^{x-1/2}e^{-x}e^{\theta/12x}$$

   Use this formula to show that if n is a natural number, then

$$n! \approx \sqrt{2\pi n}\,(n/e)^n \qquad \textbf{(Stirling's formula)}$$

4. Show that $\displaystyle\Gamma(x) = \int_0^1 \left(\ln\left(\frac{1}{z}\right)\right)^{x-1} dz$. (*Hint:* Substitute $t = -\ln z$ in (1).)

5. The **gamma distribution** with parameters $\lambda > 0$ and $\alpha > 0$ is given by

$$f(x) = \frac{\lambda^\alpha}{\Gamma(\alpha)}x^{\alpha-1}e^{-\lambda x}, \quad x > 0, \qquad f(x) = 0 \quad \text{for} \quad x \le 0$$

   (a) Prove that $\int_{-\infty}^\infty f(x)\,dx = 1$.

   (b) Compute the moment generating function $M(t)$ associated with f provided $t < \lambda$. (See Problem 4.2.5.) Compute also $M'(0)$, and in general, $M^{(n)}(0)$.

4.4 Multiple Integrals over Product Domains

The remainder of this chapter deals with multiple integrals. These arise in statistics when considering multidimensional continuous (probability) distributions. Double integrals also play a role in some interesting continuous time dynamic optimization problems. We start with the simplest case.

Double Integrals over Rectangles

The first topic is integration of functions of two variables defined over rectangles in the xy-plane. We begin with a geometric problem.

The Cartesian product of the two intervals $[a, b]$ and $[c, d]$ is the rectangle $R = [a, b] \times [c, d]$ in the xy-plane determined by the inequalities $a \leq x \leq b$ and $c \leq y \leq d$. Let f be a continuous function defined on R with $f(x, y) \geq 0$ for all (x, y) in R. Consider Fig. 1. The double integral over R will measure the volume of the "box" that has the rectangle R as its bottom and the graph of f as its curved "lid". This box consists of all points (x, y, z) such that $(x, y) \in R$ and $0 \leq z \leq f(x, y)$. This is also called the **ordinate set** of f over R.

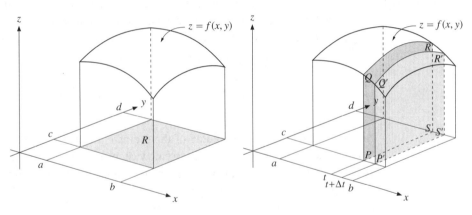

Figure 1   **Figure 2**

Let t be an arbitrary point in the interval $[a, b]$. Construct a plane parallel to the yz-plane intersecting the x-axis at $x = t$. This plane cuts the ordinate set of f into two parts. The intersection of this plane with the ordinate set is the shaded plane surface $PQRS$ in Fig. 2. The area of this shaded surface is a function of t, which we denote by $A(t)$. It is easy to find an expression for this area. In fact, $A(t)$ is the area under the curve connecting Q to R over the interval $[c, d]$. The relevant curve is the intersection between the graph of $z = f(x, y)$ and the plane $x = t$, so its equation is $z = \varphi(y) = f(t, y)$ with $y \in [c, d]$. Hence,

$$A(t) = \int_c^d f(t, y)\, dy \qquad (*)$$

Denote by $V(t)$ the volume of the ordinate set of f over the variable rectangle $[a, t] \times [c, d]$. In particular, $V(a) = 0$, and $V(b)$ is the total volume to be evaluated.

If we add Δt to t, the incremental volume is $V(t + \Delta t) - V(t)$. In Fig. 2 this is the volume of the slice that lies between the surface $PQRS$ and $P'Q'R'S'$. If Δt is small, then this volume is approximately equal to $A(t)\Delta t$. Therefore $V(t + \Delta t) - V(t) \approx A(t)\Delta t$, implying that

$$\frac{V(t + \Delta t) - V(t)}{\Delta t} \approx A(t)$$

This approximation, in general, improves as Δt gets smaller. In the limit as $\Delta t \to 0$ we can reasonably expect to obtain $V'(t) = A(t)$. Hence,

$$V(b) - V(a) = \int_a^b A(t)\, dt$$

Because $V(a) = 0$, if we put $V = V(b)$ and use (*), we get

$$V = \int_a^b \left(\int_c^d f(t, y)\, dy \right) dt \tag{**}$$

The preceding argument receives support from the next example and from Theorem 4.4.1. This makes (**) a natural definition of volume of the ordinate set of f over R.

EXAMPLE 1   If $f(x, y) = M$ for all (x, y) in R, where M is a positive constant, then the ordinate set of f over R is a rectangular box in the usual sense. The base area is $(b - a)(d - c)$ and its height is M, so its volume is $M(b - a)(d - c)$. Show that (**) gives the same result.

Solution: Letting $f(x, y) = M$ in (**) yields

$$\int_a^b \left(\int_c^d M\, dy \right) dt = \int_a^b \left(\Big|_c^d My \right) dt = \int_a^b M(d - c)\, dt = \Big|_a^b M(d - c)t = M(d - c)(b - a)$$

Suppose we try to find the volume of the ordinate set of f over $R = [a, b] \times [c, d]$ by using the argument above, except that we now choose t in $[c, d]$ and then let the intersecting plane be parallel to the xz-plane and pass through the point $y = t$ on the y-axis. The area of the plane surface in the intersection between the ordinate set and the plane $y = t$ is $\int_a^b f(x, t)\, dx$, so the formula for the volume becomes

$$\int_c^d \left(\int_a^b f(x, t)\, dx \right) dt \tag{***}$$

Because we are computing the same volume in both cases, we should get the same answer, provided our intuitive argument above is correct. The next theorem guarantees that the numbers obtained in (**) and (***) are indeed equal if f is continuous on R. (See Protter and Morrey (1991), Chapter 8, for a proof.)

THEOREM 4.4.1

Let f be a continuous function defined over the rectangle $R = [a, b] \times [c, d]$. Then

$$\int_a^b \left(\int_c^d f(t, y)\, dy \right) dt = \int_c^d \left(\int_a^b f(x, t)\, dx \right) dt$$

Now, let f be an arbitrary continuous function over the rectangle $R = [a, b] \times [c, d]$. We then define the **double integral of f over R**, denoted by $\iint_R f(x, y) \, dx \, dy$, as

$$\iint_R f(x, y) \, dx \, dy = \int_a^b \left(\int_c^d f(x, y) \, dy \right) dx = \int_c^d \left(\int_a^b f(x, y) \, dx \right) dy \quad (1)$$

We can take either of the two last expressions as the definition of the double integral, because they are equal according to Theorem 4.4.1.

Note that we calculate $\int_a^b (\int_c^d f(x, y) \, dy) \, dx$ in the following way:

(a) Keep x fixed and integrate $f(x, y)$ w.r.t. y from $y = c$ to $y = d$. This gives $\int_c^d f(x, y) \, dy$, a function of x.

(b) Now integrate $\int_c^d f(x, y) \, dy$ from $x = a$ to $x = b$ to obtain $\int_a^b (\int_c^d f(x, y) \, dy) \, dx$.

In (1) we do not require $f(x, y)$ to be nonnegative. It turns out that double integrals need not always be interpreted as volumes, just as single integrals need not always be interpreted as areas.

Let us now consider some applications of (1).

EXAMPLE 2   Compute $\iint_R (x^2 y + xy^2 + 2x) \, dx \, dy$, where $R = [0, 1] \times [-1, 3]$.

Solution: The integrand is continuous everywhere. Consider first

$$\int_0^1 \left(\int_{-1}^3 (x^2 y + xy^2 + 2x) \, dy \right) dx$$

Treating x as a constant, first evaluate the inner integral:

$$\int_{-1}^3 (x^2 y + xy^2 + 2x) \, dy = \left. (\tfrac{1}{2} x^2 y^2 + \tfrac{1}{3} xy^3 + 2xy) \right|_{y=-1}^{y=3} = 4x^2 + \tfrac{52}{3} x$$

Integrating a second time gives

$$\int_0^1 \left(\int_{-1}^3 (x^2 y + xy^2 + 2x) \, dy \right) dx = \int_0^1 (4x^2 + \tfrac{52}{3} x) \, dx = \left. (\tfrac{4}{3} x^3 + \tfrac{26}{3} x^2) \right|_0^1 = 10$$

Let us now perform the integration in the reverse order. Holding y constant, we get

$$\int_0^1 (x^2 y + xy^2 + 2x) \, dx = \left. (\tfrac{1}{3} x^3 y + \tfrac{1}{2} x^2 y^2 + x^2) \right|_0^1 = \tfrac{1}{3} y + \tfrac{1}{2} y^2 + 1$$

Therefore,

$$\int_{-1}^3 \left(\int_0^1 (x^2 y + xy^2 + 2x) \, dx \right) dy = \int_{-1}^3 (\tfrac{1}{3} y + \tfrac{1}{2} y^2 + 1) \, dy = 10$$

We reached the same result by both procedures. So Theorem 4.4.1 is confirmed in this case, and we can write with confidence

$$\iint_R (x^2 y + xy^2 + 2x) \, dx \, dy = 10 \quad \text{when } R = [0, 1] \times [-1, 3]$$

EXAMPLE 3   Compute $\int_1^b \left(\int_1^d \dfrac{y-x}{(y+x)^3} \, dy \right) dx$, where b and d are constants greater than 1.

Solution: By means of a little trick, the inner integral becomes

$$\int_1^d \frac{y-x}{(y+x)^3} \, dy = \int_1^d \frac{y+x-2x}{(y+x)^3} \, dy = \int_1^d \frac{1}{(y+x)^2} \, dy - 2x \int_1^d \frac{1}{(y+x)^3} \, dy$$

$$= \Big|_{y=1}^{y=d} \left(-\frac{1}{y+x} \right) - 2x \Big|_{y=1}^{y=d} \left(-\frac{1}{2} \frac{1}{(y+x)^2} \right) = -\frac{d}{(x+d)^2} + \frac{1}{(x+1)^2}$$

Hence

$$\int_1^b \left(\int_1^d \frac{y-x}{(y+x)^3} \, dy \right) dx = -\int_1^b \frac{d}{(x+d)^2} \, dx + \int_1^b \frac{1}{(x+1)^2} \, dx$$

$$= \Big|_1^b \frac{d}{x+d} - \Big|_1^b \frac{1}{x+1} = \frac{d}{b+d} - \frac{d}{d+1} - \frac{1}{b+1} + \frac{1}{2}$$

Choosing instead to integrate w.r.t. x first, we obtain

$$\int_1^b \frac{y-x}{(y+x)^3} \, dx = \frac{b}{(y+b)^2} - \frac{1}{(y+1)^2}$$

Then

$$\int_1^d \left(\int_1^b \frac{y-x}{(y+x)^3} \, dx \right) dy = -\frac{b}{b+d} + \frac{b}{b+1} + \frac{1}{d+1} - \frac{1}{2}$$

Simple algebra now shows that the two results are equal.

Multiple Integrals

Let Ω denote the Cartesian product $[a_1, b_1] \times \cdots \times [a_n, b_n]$ of the closed intervals $[a_1, b_1]$, ..., $[a_n, b_n]$, that is, the set of all n-vectors $(x_1, x_2, \ldots, x_n)$ in $\mathbb{R}^n$ such that $a_i \leq x_i \leq b_i$ for $i = 1, 2, \ldots, n$. We call Ω an **n-dimensional rectangle.**

If f is a continuous function defined over Ω, define the **multiple integral** of f over Ω as

$$\iint \cdots \int_\Omega f(x_1, \ldots, x_{n-1}, x_n) \, dx_1 \ldots dx_{n-1} \, dx_n$$

$$= \int_{a_n}^{b_n} \left(\int_{a_{n-1}}^{b_{n-1}} \cdots \left(\int_{a_1}^{b_1} f(x_1, \ldots, x_{n-1}, x_n) \, dx_1 \right) \ldots dx_{n-1} \right) dx_n \tag{2}$$

The meaning of the notation on the right-hand side of (2) is that integration is to be performed first w.r.t. x_1, all other variables being treated as constants, then w.r.t. x_2, treating the remainder of the variables $(x_3, \ldots, x_n)$ as constants, etc.

Definition (2) is a simple generalization of (1). In this general case one can still prove that the order of integration on the right-hand side is immaterial, provided that f is continuous in Ω.

PROBLEMS FOR SECTION 4.4

1. Evaluate the following double integrals:

(a) $\displaystyle\int_0^2 \int_0^1 (2x + 3y + 4)\, dx\, dy$ (b) $\displaystyle\int_0^a \int_0^b (x - a)(x - b)\, dx\, dy$

(c) $\displaystyle\int_1^3 \int_1^2 (x - y)/(x + y)\, dx\, dy$ (d) $\displaystyle\int_0^{1/2} \int_0^{2\pi} y^3 \sin(xy^2)\, dx\, dy$

2. Find $I = \displaystyle\int_1^a \Big(\int_0^b \frac{1}{x^3} e^{y/x}\, dy \Big)\, dx$ $(a > 1,\ b > 0)$

3. Consider the function $f(x, y) = \dfrac{2k}{(x + y + 1)^3}$ (k constant). Let R be the rectangle $R = [0, a] \times [0, 1]$, where $a > 0$ is a constant. Determine the value k_a of k such that $\iint_R f(x, y)\, dx\, dy = 1$. Show that $k_a > 2$ for all $a > 0$.

4. Compute the double integral $I = \displaystyle\int_0^2 \Big(\int_{-2}^1 (x^2 y^3 - (y + 1)^2)\, dy \Big)\, dx$.

HARDER PROBLEMS

5. Find $I = \displaystyle\iint \cdots \int_\Omega (x_1^2 + x_2^2 + \cdots + x_n^2)\, dx_1\, dx_2 \ldots dx_n$ where Ω is the region in $\mathbb{R}^n$ determined by the inequalities $0 \le x_i \le 1$ for $i = 1, 2, \ldots, n$.

4.5 Double Integrals over General Domains

Consider the set A in the xy-plane indicated in Fig. 1. The boundary of A consists of segments of the lines $x = a$ and $x = b$ and the graphs of the continuous functions $u(x)$ and $v(x)$, where $u(x) \le v(x)$ for all x in $[a, b]$.

Suppose that $f(x, y)$ is a continuous function defined over A, and that $f(x, y) \ge 0$ for all (x, y) in A. Then the graph of f above the set A determines a three-dimensional solid indicated in Fig. 2. The intersection of the solid with the plane at distance x from the yz-plane is the shaded plane region indicated in Fig. 2. The area of this region can be described as the area under the graph of $f(x, y)$ (x fixed) over the interval $[u(x), v(x)]$. If we denote the resulting function of x by F, we have

$$F(x) = \int_{u(x)}^{v(x)} f(x, y)\, dy$$

Here we have integrated w.r.t. y while keeping x fixed. One can prove that $F(x)$ is a continuous function of x. As for the case in which A is rectangular, a geometrically plausible argument supports the conclusion that the volume V of the solid must be given by

$$V = \int_a^b F(x)\,dx = \int_a^b \left(\int_{u(x)}^{v(x)} f(x,y)\,dy \right) dx \tag{1}$$

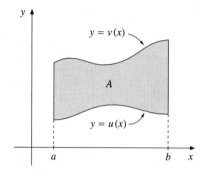

Figure 1

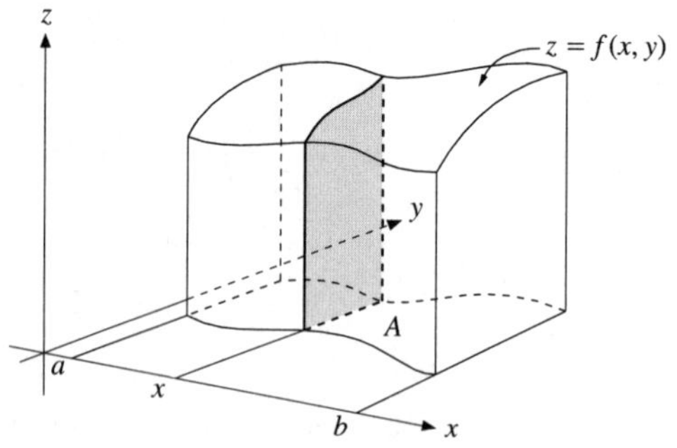

Figure 2

Briefly formulated the argument is this: Let $V(x)$ denote the volume of that part of the solid in Fig. 2 which lies to left of the shaded region. Thus $V(a) = 0$ and $V(b) = V$, and $F(x)$ is the area of the shaded region. Let x be incremented by Δx. Then the volume of the associated slice of thickness Δx is approximately $F(x)\Delta x$. The exact volume of this slice is $V(x+\Delta x) - V(x)$, which is therefore approximately equal to $F(x)\Delta x$. This approximation will, in general, be better for smaller Δx, so in the limit we expect to have $V'(x) = F(x)$. Hence, $V(b) - V(a) = \int_a^b F(x)\,dx$, implying that $V = \int_a^b F(x)\,dx$ (because $V(b) = V$ and $V(a) = 0$).

Formally, we could *define* the volume V by (1). Note that if $u(x) = c$ and $v(x) = d$, so that A is a rectangle, then definition (1) reduces to (∗∗) in Section 4.4. Let us illustrate with an example.

EXAMPLE 1   Let A be the set in the xy-plane bounded by the straight lines $x = 0$ and $x = 1$ and the graphs of $y = x$ and $y = x^2+1$. The set A is indicated in Fig. 3. The function $f(x, y) = xy^2$ is continuous and ≥ 0 over A. Find the volume V under the graph of f.

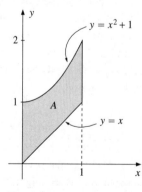

Figure 3

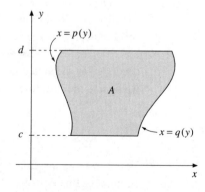

Figure 4

Solution: In this case

$$V = \int_0^1 \left(\int_x^{x^2+1} xy^2 \, dy \right) dx$$

Here

$$\int_x^{x^2+1} xy^2 \, dy = x \left. \frac{1}{3} y^3 \right|_x^{x^2+1} = \frac{1}{3} x \left[(x^2+1)^3 - x^3 \right] = \frac{1}{3} x^7 + x^5 - \frac{1}{3} x^4 + x^3 + \frac{1}{3} x$$

because x is kept constant when integrating w.r.t. y. Hence

$$V = \int_0^1 \left(\frac{1}{3} x^7 + x^5 - \frac{1}{3} x^4 + x^3 + \frac{1}{3} x \right) dx = \left. \left(\frac{1}{24} x^8 + \frac{1}{6} x^6 - \frac{1}{15} x^5 + \frac{1}{4} x^4 + \frac{1}{6} x^2 \right) \right|_0^1 = \frac{67}{120}$$

It is possible to derive similar expressions for volumes in space when the base A is determined in other ways. For example, if the set A is as indicated in Fig. 4, and $f(x, y) \geq 0$ in A, then the volume V under the graph of f over A is given by

$$\int_c^d \left(\int_{p(y)}^{q(y)} f(x, y) \, dx \right) dy \tag{2}$$

It is a worthwhile exercise to go through the argument leading to this formula after the same pattern as for equation (1) above.

In Fig. 5, we see that every straight line parallel to the x-axis or y-axis intersects the boundary of the shaded set in at most two points. Let the functions u and v depicted in Fig. 5 be continuous. Since they are strictly increasing, they have continuous inverse functions u^{-1} and v^{-1}. If f is a continuous nonnegative function defined over this set, the volume under the graph of f can be computed in two different ways. Under the given conditions one can prove that

$$\int_0^b \left(\int_{u(x)}^{v(x)} f(x, y) \, dy \right) dx = \int_0^d \left(\int_{v^{-1}(y)}^{u^{-1}(y)} f(x, y) \, dx \right) dy \tag{3}$$

On the left-hand side we have integrated first w.r.t. y and then w.r.t. x, and on the right-hand side we have integrated in the reverse order. If the set is of the type indicated, and f is continuous, the two expressions are always equal. Nevertheless, it is sometimes important to choose the right order of integration in order to have simple integrals. (See Problem 4.)

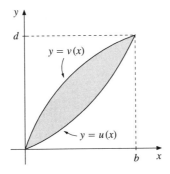

Figure 5

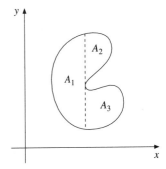

Figure 6

How do we define the double integral over more complicated domains of integration, such as the set in Fig. 6? The obvious solution is to partition the set into smaller parts, each of which is one of the types considered above. (One such partition is indicated in Fig. 6.) We then define the double integral over the entire set as the sum of the double integrals over each of its parts. If the set is a union of finitely many sets of the types we have considered, one can prove that the double integral is independent of how this subdivision is done.

Let A be an arbitrary set in the xy-plane of one of the types considered above, and f a continuous function defined on A (not necessarily ≥ 0). **The double integral of f over A,**

$$\iint_A f(x, y) \, dx \, dy \tag{4}$$

is defined as in (1) provided A is as in Fig. 1, by (2) if A is of the form in Fig. 4, and so on. If $f(x, y) \geq 0$, the number obtained from (4) can be interpreted as the volume of a solid in space. It turns out, however, that the double integral as defined here can be given a number of other interpretations of greater interest to economists. In statistics, for example, probability is calculated using double integrals of two-dimensional density functions, and in the theory of production, multiple integrals of capacity distributions are considered.

A Useful Formula

Let $f(x, y)$ be a continuous function over the rectangle $[a, b] \times [c, d]$. We shall prove that

$$\frac{\partial^2 F(x, y)}{\partial x \partial y} = f(x, y) \quad \text{for all } (x, y) \text{ in } [a, b] \times [c, d] \implies$$

$$\int_c^d \left(\int_a^b f(x, y) \, dx \right) dy = F(b, d) - F(a, d) - F(b, c) + F(a, c) \tag{5}$$

Indeed, if y in $[c, d]$ is fixed, then $\partial F/\partial y$ is a function of x whose derivative w.r.t. x is $\partial^2 F/\partial x \partial y = f(x, y)$. Hence, for each y in $[c, d]$,

$$\int_a^b f(x, y) \, dx = \left. \frac{\partial F(x, y)}{\partial y} \right|_{x=a}^{x=b} = \frac{\partial F(b, y)}{\partial y} - \frac{\partial F(a, y)}{\partial y}$$

so that

$$\int_c^d \left(\int_a^b f(x, y) \, dx \right) dy = \int_c^d \left(\frac{\partial F(b, y)}{\partial y} - \frac{\partial F(a, y)}{\partial y} \right) dy = \left. \Big(F(b, y) - F(a, y) \Big) \right|_c^d$$

$$= F(b, d) - F(a, d) - F(b, c) + F(a, c)$$

PROBLEMS FOR SECTION 4.5

1. (a) Sketch the domain of integration and compute the integral $\int_0^1 \left(\int_{x^2}^x (x^2 + xy) \, dy \right) dx$.

   (b) Change the order of integration and verify that you obtain the same result as in (a).

2. Compute the integral in Example 1 by first integrating w.r.t. x. (*Hint:* The set in Fig. 3 must be subdivided into two parts.)

3. What is the geometric interpretation of $\iint_A 1 \, dx \, dy$, where A is a set in the xy-plane?

4. Let $f(x, y) = e^{x^2}$ be defined over the triangle $A = \{(x, y) : x \in [0, 1], \ 0 \le y \le x\}$. Find the volume V under the graph of f over A. (*Hint:* Integrate first w.r.t. y. If you try to integrate w.r.t. x first, there is no expression for the relevant integral in terms of elementary functions.)

5. Compute the integral $\displaystyle\int_0^3 \left(\int_{4x/3}^{\sqrt{25-x^2}} 2x \, dy \right) dx$ by reversing the order of integration.

6. Calculate $\displaystyle\int_0^1 \int_0^1 |x - y| \, dx \, dy$. Can you confirm your result by a geometric argument?

HARDER PROBLEMS

7. Sketch the set $A = \{(x, y) : 0 \le x \le 2\pi, \ -x \le y \le \sin x\}$ in the xy-plane. Then compute the double integral $\displaystyle\iint_A 2y \cos x \, dx \, dy$.

8. A model by J.E. Meade on savings, inheritance and economic growth involves the double integral

$$I = \int_0^F \left(\int_0^{F-\theta} e^{a\theta} e^{bT} \, dT \right) d\theta, \quad a \ne 0, \ b \ne 0, \ a \ne b.$$

   (a) Show that $I = \big(\varphi(a) - \varphi(b)\big)/(a - b)$, where $\varphi(u) = (e^{uF} - 1)/u$.

   (b) Sketch the domain of integration in the θT-plane and write down the expression for I when we first integrate w.r.t. θ. Test the answer in (a) by computing this new double integral (if you have the energy).

9. (From Johansen (1972).) For fixed positive values of q_1 and q_2, consider the set $G(q_1, q_2)$ in the $\xi_1 \xi_2$-plane given by (draw a sketch!)

$$G(q_1, q_2) = \big\{ (\xi_1, \xi_2) : q_1\xi_1 + q_2\xi_2 \le 1, \ \xi_1 \ge 0, \ \xi_2 \ge 0 \big\}$$

   Let $f(\xi_1, \xi_2)$ be a continuous function defined over $G(q_1, q_2)$.

   (a) Write down the double integral of f over $G(q_1, q_2)$ when integrating first w.r.t. ξ_2.

   (b) Write down the corresponding expression, integrating first w.r.t. ξ_1.

   (c) The value of the double integral in (a) and in (b) will depend on q_1 and q_2, denote it by $g(q_1, q_2)$. Compute $\partial g/\partial q_1$.

4.6 Riemann's Definition of Multiple Integrals

We consider next how to define multiple integrals in a way that corresponds to Riemann's definition of the usual single integral. (See for example Chapter 9 in EMEA.) We need this definition in order to explain the rule for changing variables in multiple integrals.

Let f be a bounded function defined on a closed and bounded set A in the plane, and let R be a rectangle containing A. Subdivide the rectangle into a number of smaller rectangles as indicated in Fig. 1.

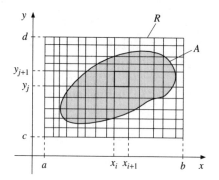

Figure 1   **Figure 2**

Let R_{ij} denote the typical subrectangle $[x_i, x_{i+1}] \times [y_j, y_{j+1}]$. Some of these rectangles R_{ij} will lie inside A, others will be entirely or partly outside A. For each R_{ij} inside A, choose an arbitrary point (x_i^*, y_j^*) in R_{ij}. The product $f(x_i^*, y_j^*)\Delta x_i \Delta y_j$, where $\Delta x_i = x_{i+1} - x_i$, $\Delta y_j = y_{j+1} - y_j$, can be interpreted geometrically as the volume of the rectangular column suggested in Fig. 2. Form the sum of all these products corresponding to rectangles R_{ij} inside A:

$$\sum_{R_{ij} \subseteq A} f(x_i^*, y_j^*) \, \Delta x_i \, \Delta y_j \tag{1}$$

Suppose this sum tends to a limit as the number of rectangles increases in such a way that the diameter of the largest approaches 0. Suppose further that this limit is independent of the particular sequence of subdivisions that we choose and also independent of which points (x_i^*, y_j^*) we choose in R_{ij}. Then the limit is called the **double integral of f over A**. (The limit process here is more complicated than those we have used before. For technical details, see e.g. Protter and Morrey (1991), Chapter 8, or Munkres (1991).)

When A is one of the types of set described in Section 4.5 (in connection with Figs. 4.5.1, 4.5.4, and 4.5.6), one can prove that the limit in (1) exists and is equal to the double integral as defined in Section 4.5.

EXAMPLE 1   Compute $\int_0^1 \int_0^1 (x + xy) \, dx \, dy$ from the definition associated with (1).

Solution: Subdivide the rectangle $R = [0, 1] \times [0, 1]$ into n^2 subrectangles by putting $x_i = i/n$, $y_j = j/n$ for $i, j = 0, \ldots, n$. Then $\Delta x_i = x_{i+1} - x_i = 1/n$, $\Delta y_j = y_{j+1} - y_j =$

$1/n$. Put $x_i^* = i/n$, $y_j^* = j/n$. Then $(x_i^* + x_i^* y_j^*) \Delta x_i \Delta y_j = (i/n + ij/n^2)1/n^2 = i/n^3 + ij/n^4$, so that the sum in (1) becomes

$$\sum_{j=0}^{n-1} \sum_{i=0}^{n-1} \left(\frac{1}{n^3} i + \frac{1}{n^4} i \cdot j \right) = \frac{1}{n^3} \sum_{j=0}^{n-1} \left(\sum_{i=0}^{n-1} i \right) + \frac{1}{n^4} \left(\sum_{j=0}^{n-1} j \right) \left(\sum_{i=0}^{n-1} i \right)$$

$$= \frac{1}{n^3} n \frac{(n-1)n}{2} + \frac{1}{n^4} \frac{(n-1)n}{2} \cdot \frac{(n-1)n}{2} = \frac{1}{2} \left(1 - \frac{1}{n} \right) + \frac{1}{4} \left(1 - \frac{1}{n} \right)^2$$

As $n \to \infty$, the number of subrectangles will increase, and at the same time their (equal) diameters will tend to 0. The expression above clearly tends to $1/2 + 1/4 = 3/4$, so we finally obtain

$$\int_0^1 \int_0^1 (x + xy) \, dx \, dy = \frac{3}{4}$$

To confirm this result, compute the integral in the usual way.

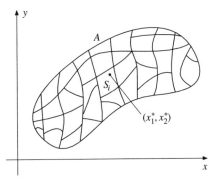

Figure 3

The definition associated with (1) involved subdividing the given set in the xy-plane into rectangles. But we could equally well have used other kinds of subdivision. Let us consider this briefly without going into technical details. Imagine that the closed and bounded set A is subdivided into n subsets $S_1, \ldots, S_n$, with areas $\Delta s_1, \ldots, \Delta s_n$ (see Fig. 3). Choose a point (x_i^*, y_i^*) in S_i, $i = 1, \ldots, n$, and form the sum

$$f(x_1^*, y_1^*) \Delta s_1 + \cdots + f(x_n^*, y_n^*) \Delta s_n = \sum_{i=1}^{n} f(x_i^*, y_i^*) \Delta s_i$$

Suppose we construct a whole sequence of such subdivisions with associated sums, in such a way that the greatest diameter of any subset tends to 0. The limit of these sums will then equal the double integral of $f(x, y)$ over A, as defined before. This limit is independent of how we subdivide A. Moreover, it is independent of which points (x_i^*, y_i^*) are chosen in each S_i. Briefly formulated,

$$\iint_A f(x, y) \, dx \, dy = \lim_{\text{diam}(S_i) \to 0} \sum_{i=1}^{n} f(x_i^*, y_i^*) \Delta s_i \qquad (2)$$

Riemann's definition of the double integral makes it possible to prove a number of properties that correspond to similar ones for the one-dimensional integral.

For instance, suppose f and g are continuous functions over a set A in the xy-plane, and that the double integrals of f and g over A are defined. Then

$$\iint_A [f(x, y) + g(x, y)]\, dx\, dy = \iint_A f(x, y)\, dx\, dy + \iint_A g(x, y)\, dx\, dy \qquad (3)$$

$$\iint_A cf(x, y)\, dx\, dy = c \iint_A f(x, y)\, dx\, dy \quad (c \text{ constant}) \qquad (4)$$

$$\iint_A f(x, y)\, dx\, dy = \iint_{A_1} f(x, y)\, dx\, dy + \iint_{A_2} f(x, y)\, dx\, dy \qquad (5)$$

In the last formula, we assume that $A = A_1 \cup A_2$, $A_1 \cap A_2 = \varnothing$, and $\iint_{A_1}$ and $\iint_{A_2}$ are defined.

Let f still be defined over A and suppose that there exist numbers m and M such that $m \leq f(x, y) \leq M$ for all (x, y) in A. Then there exists a number ξ in $[m, M]$ such that

$$\iint_A f(x, y)\, dx\, dy = \xi \cdot \iint_A dx\, dy = \xi \cdot \text{area}(A) \qquad (6)$$

The number ξ is called the **average value** of f in A, and (6) is called the **mean value theorem for double integrals**. If S is a *connected set* (i.e. not the union of two or more disjoint closed sets), and f is continuous, then there exists a point $(\bar{x}, \bar{y})$ in A such that ξ given by (6) is equal to $f(\bar{x}, \bar{y})$. In this case (6) takes the form

$$\iint_A f(x, y)\, dx\, dy = f(\bar{x}, \bar{y}) \cdot \text{area}(A) \qquad \text{for some } (\bar{x}, \bar{y}) \text{ in } A \qquad (7)$$

This section has dealt with double integrals. It should be clear that the theory associated with (1) and (2) can be generalized to triple integrals and multiple integrals in general. One can also obtain formulas that correspond to (3)–(7), but we shall not pursue this matter any further.

PROBLEMS FOR SECTION 4.6

1. Compute the double integral

$$\int_0^2 \left(\int_0^1 (2x - y + 1)\, dx \right) dy$$

(a) by the method in Example 1 above,

(b) by integrating in the usual way.

4.7 Change of Variables

One of the most important methods of integration for single integrals is rule (4.1.4) for integration by substitution:

$$\int_a^b f(x)\,dx = \int_{u_1}^{u_2} f(g(u))g'(u)\,du \qquad (x = g(u),\; g(u_1) = a,\; g(u_2) = b) \qquad (1)$$

It turns out that there is a similar rule for changing variables in multiple integrals. Let us look at this problem for double integrals first.

Change of Variables in Double Integrals

Consider the double integral $\iint_A f(x, y)\,dx\,dy$. We want to introduce new variables u and v together with functions h and g such that

$$x = g(u, v), \qquad y = h(u, v) \qquad (2)$$

With suitable restrictions on the integrands and the domains of integration, we have

$$\iint_A f(x, y)\,dx\,dy = \iint_{A'} f(g(u, v))\,h(u, v)\left|\frac{\partial(g, h)}{\partial(u, v)}\right|\,du\,dv \qquad (3)$$

where

$$\frac{\partial(g, h)}{\partial(u, v)} = \begin{vmatrix} \dfrac{\partial g}{\partial u} & \dfrac{\partial g}{\partial v} \\[2ex] \dfrac{\partial h}{\partial u} & \dfrac{\partial h}{\partial v} \end{vmatrix} \qquad \text{is the } \textbf{Jacobian determinant} \qquad (4)$$

and where A' is the set in the uv-plane "corresponding to" the given set A in the xy-plane. Precise conditions for (3) to be true are stated in Theorem 4.7.1.

Comparing the two formulas (1) and (3), we see that introducing new variables causes two things to happen. First, the domain of integration is changed in each case. Second, a new factor appears under the integral sign. In (1) it is $g'(u)$, whereas in (3) it is the *absolute value of the Jacobian determinant* of the transformation (2). The main problem in the proof of (3) is to show why we need to take the absolute value of $\partial(g, h)/\partial(u, v)$. Before taking a closer look at this problem, let us see how this formula can be applied to a simple example.

EXAMPLE 1   Compute $I = \iint_A (x^2 + y^2 - 1)\,dx\,dy$ where A is the set in the xy-plane bounded by the straight lines $x + y = 1$, $x + y = 5$, $x - y = -1$, and $x - y = 1$. The set is shown in Fig. 1.

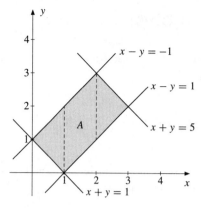

Figure 1   **Figure 2**

Solution: By subdividing the set A in a suitable way, one can compute the given integral. For example, if we use the vertical lines $x = 1$ and $x = 2$ to divide A into three parts (see Fig. 1), we can see that I is equal to

$$\int_0^1 \Big(\int_{1-x}^{1+x} (x^2 + y^2 - 1)\,dy\Big)\,dx + \int_1^2 \Big(\int_{x-1}^{x+1} (x^2 + y^2 - 1)\,dy\Big)\,dx + \int_2^3 \Big(\int_{x-1}^{5-x} (x^2 + y^2 - 1)\,dy\Big)\,dx$$

After a fair amount of calculation, we can find the value $I = 52/3$. In this case, however, A is a rotated rectangle. This suggests that it might be easier to introduce $u = x - y$ and $v = x + y$ as new variables. Note that this transformation transforms the boundary lines $x - y = -1$ and $x - y = 1$ of A into the straight lines $u = -1$ and $u = 1$, and the straight lines $x + y = 1$ and $x + y = 5$ into $v = 1$ and $v = 5$. Let A' be the rectangle in the uv-plane shown in Fig. 2. The transformation transforms the boundary lines of A in xy-plane into the boundary lines of A' in the uv-plane. Moreover, the interior of A is mapped in a one-to-one fashion onto the interior of A'. From $u = x - y$ and $v = x + y$ it follows that

$$x = \tfrac{1}{2}(u + v), \quad y = \tfrac{1}{2}(-u + v) \tag{i}$$

which, in a similar way, maps A' onto A. The transformation given by (i) corresponds to the transformation (2), and in this case the Jacobian is

$$\begin{vmatrix} \partial x/\partial u & \partial x/\partial v \\ \partial y/\partial u & \partial y/\partial v \end{vmatrix} = \begin{vmatrix} 1/2 & 1/2 \\ -1/2 & 1/2 \end{vmatrix} = \frac{1}{4} + \frac{1}{4} = \frac{1}{2}$$

With x and y given by (i), the integrand becomes

$$x^2 + y^2 - 1 = \tfrac{1}{4}(u + v)^2 + \tfrac{1}{4}(-u + v)^2 - 1 = \tfrac{1}{2}u^2 + \tfrac{1}{2}v^2 - 1$$

Therefore, through simple calculations formula (3) yields

$$I = \iint_A (x^2 + y^2 - 1)\,dx\,dy = \iint_{A'} \big(\tfrac{1}{2}u^2 + \tfrac{1}{2}v^2 - 1\big)\tfrac{1}{2}\,du\,dv$$

$$= \tfrac{1}{2}\int_1^5 \Big(\int_{-1}^1 \big(\tfrac{1}{2}u^2 + \tfrac{1}{2}v^2 - 1\big)\,du\Big)\,dv = \tfrac{52}{3}$$

Provided (3) is applicable in this case, it simplifies the computational work considerably.

Consider next the general double integral of $f(x, y)$ over some set A in the plane and assume that we introduce the new variables u and v, where

$$x = g(u, v), \quad y = h(u, v) \tag{$*$}$$

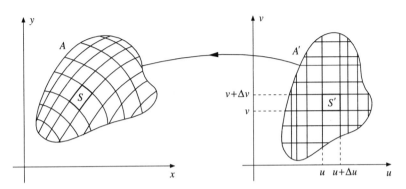

Figure 3 A curvilinear grid

We shall give the main lines of reasoning in an argument that can be extended into a full proof of formula (3). Assume that g and h are C^1 functions that together map the set A' into A, and that each point (x, y) in A is the image of a unique point (u, v) in A'. The sets A and A' might be as indicated in Fig. 3.

The definition (4.6.2) of the double integral of f over A allows any sequence of subdivisions of A into subsets, provided the diameter of the largest subset converges to 0. We shall make use of this fact and employ a subdivision of A that is "induced" by the transformation ($*$) in the following way. Take a point in A with coordinates (x, y). The unique point (u, v) in A' that corresponds to (x, y) is given implicitly by ($*$). The numbers u and v are called the *curvilinear coordinates* of (x, y) w.r.t. the given transformation. Keep u fixed at $u = u_0$. A number of points in A will have curvilinear coordinates with this special value of u, namely those points (x, y) of A for which $x = g(u_0, v)$, $y = h(u_0, v)$. By choosing different fixed values of u, we obtain a family of curves in A. These curves cannot intersect because the correspondence between the points of A and A' is one-to-one. Similarly, by choosing different fixed values of v, we get another family of curves in A, characterized by the fact that along any particular curve, v has a fixed value. Some of the curves in the curvilinear grid obtained in this way are indicated in the set A in Fig. 3. Through the transformation ($*$), this curvilinear grid corresponds to the rectangular grid drawn in the set A'. If we "refine" the rectangular grid in A', the curvilinear grid in A will also be "refined".

Consider next the rectangle S' indicated in A' in Fig. 3. Its area $\Delta S'$ is equal to $\Delta u \Delta v$, and the transformation ($*$) maps it to a curvilinear "rectangle" S in A. If we denote the area of S by ΔS, we obtain an approximation to the double integral by f over A as the sum

$$\sum f(x, y) \Delta S \tag{$**$}$$

where (x, y) is an arbitrary point in S, and we sum over all the curvilinear rectangles in A. We drop from the sum in ($**$) those rectangles that have points in common with the boundary of A. The joint contribution to the sum in (∗∗) from all these boundary rectangles will tend to 0 as the subdivision is refined.

To proceed further we need another expression for the sum in (∗∗). First, let us find an approximate value of ΔS by using the fact that S is the image of the rectangle S' under the transformation (∗). The relationship between S and S' is indicated in more detail in Fig. 4.

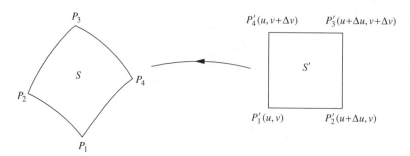

Figure 4

The point P_1 is the image of P_1' under (∗), so P_1 has coordinates $(g(u, v), h(u, v))$. The point P_2 is the image of P_2', so P_2 has coordinates $(g(u + \Delta u, v), h(u + \Delta u, v))$. In the same way the coordinates of P_3 and P_4 are $(g(u + \Delta u, v + \Delta v), h(u + \Delta u, v + \Delta v))$ and $(g(u, v + \Delta v), h(u, v + \Delta v))$, respectively. If Δu and Δv are small, we obtain good approximations to these coordinates by using Taylor's formula and including only first-order terms.

If the coordinates of P_i are (x_i, y_i), $i = 1, \ldots, 4$, we get

$$P_1 : x_1 = g(u, v), \quad y_1 = h(u, v)$$

$$P_2 : x_2 = g(u + \Delta u, v) \approx g(u, v) + \frac{\partial g}{\partial u} \Delta u, \quad y_2 = h(u + \Delta u, v) \approx h(u, v) + \frac{\partial h}{\partial u} \Delta u$$

$$P_3 : x_3 = g(u + \Delta u, v + \Delta v) \approx g(u, v) + \frac{\partial g}{\partial u} \Delta u + \frac{\partial g}{\partial v} \Delta v,$$

$$y_3 = h(u + \Delta u, v + \Delta v) \approx h(u, v) + \frac{\partial h}{\partial u} \Delta u + \frac{\partial h}{\partial v} \Delta v$$

$$P_4 : x_4 = g(u, v + \Delta v) \approx g(u, v) + \frac{\partial g}{\partial v} \Delta v, \quad y_4 = h(u, v + \Delta v) \approx h(u, v) + \frac{\partial h}{\partial v} \Delta v$$

For small values of Δu and Δv the curvilinear rectangle $P_1 P_2 P_3 P_4$ is approximately a parallelogram. Therefore, its area is approximately twice the area of the triangle $P_1 P_2 P_3$ with vertices (x_1, y_1), (x_2, y_2), (x_3, y_3). But this triangular area is given by half the absolute value of the determinant (see Problem 2)

$$\begin{vmatrix} 1 & x_1 & y_1 \\ 1 & x_2 & y_2 \\ 1 & x_3 & y_3 \end{vmatrix} = \begin{vmatrix} 1 & x_1 & y_1 \\ 0 & x_2 - x_1 & y_2 - y_1 \\ 0 & x_3 - x_1 & y_3 - y_1 \end{vmatrix} = (x_2 - x_1)(y_3 - y_1) - (x_3 - x_1)(y_2 - y_1)$$

With the approximate expressions for the coordinates obtained above, the determinant is

$$\frac{\partial g}{\partial u} \Delta u \left(\frac{\partial h}{\partial u} \Delta u + \frac{\partial h}{\partial v} \Delta v \right) - \left(\frac{\partial g}{\partial u} \Delta u + \frac{\partial g}{\partial v} \Delta v \right) \frac{\partial h}{\partial u} \Delta u = \left(\frac{\partial g}{\partial u} \frac{\partial h}{\partial v} - \frac{\partial g}{\partial v} \frac{\partial h}{\partial u} \right) \Delta u \Delta v$$

Hence ΔS is approximately equal to the absolute value of $\begin{vmatrix} \partial g/\partial u & \partial g/\partial v \\ \partial h/\partial u & \partial h/\partial v \end{vmatrix} \Delta u \Delta v$. The

determinant here is the Jacobian of the transformation (*), so

$$\Delta S \approx \left| \frac{\partial(g, h)}{\partial(u, v)} \right| \Delta u \Delta v \qquad\qquad (***)$$

It is reasonable to expect that this approximation will be better for smaller Δu and Δv.

We observed above that $\sum f(x, y)\Delta S$ is an approximation to the double integral of f over A when we sum over all the curvilinear rectangles in A that have no points in common with the boundary of A. By using (*) and (***), we therefore obtain

$$\sum f(x, y)\Delta S \approx \sum f(g(u, v), h(u, v)) \left| \frac{\partial(g, h)}{\partial(u, v)} \right| \Delta u \Delta v \qquad\qquad (5)$$

There is a one-to-one correspondence between curvilinear rectangles S in A and rectangles S' in A'. It follows that the last sum is an approximation to the double integral of the function $f(g(u, v), h(u, v)) \left| \partial(g, h)/\partial(u, v) \right|$ over the set A': If the subdivision of A' is refined in such a way that the diameter of the largest rectangle tends to 0, then passing to the limit in (5) gives (3).

Without going into details about the finer points of the proof, we formulate the precise result as follows. (See Protter and Morrey (1991) or Munkres (1991) for a more precise treatment.)

THEOREM 4.7.1 (CHANGE OF VARIABLES IN DOUBLE INTEGRALS)

Suppose that
$$x = g(u, v), \quad y = h(u, v)$$

defines a one-to-one C^1 transformation from an open, bounded set A' in the uv-plane onto an open bounded set A in the xy-plane, and assume that the Jacobian determinant $\partial(g, h)/\partial(u, v)$ is bounded on A'. Let f be a bounded, continuous function defined on A. Then

$$\iint_A f(x, y)\, dx\, dy = \iint_{A'} f(g(u, v), h(u, v)) \left| \frac{\partial(g, h)}{\partial(u, v)} \right| du\, dv$$

NOTE 1   A set in the plane is said to have *area* (or *measure*) 0 if it can be covered by a sequence of rectangles whose total area is arbitrarily small. (A set consisting of a finite number of points or of a finite number of curves with finite lengths will have measure 0.) It turns out that we can always remove a subset of measure 0 from the domain of integration without affecting the value of the integral. *It is therefore sufficient if the conditions in the theorem are satisfied after suitable subsets of measure 0 are removed from A and A'.*

The condition in the theorem that the transformation be one-to-one is sometimes difficult to check. Note that it is not sufficient to assume that the Jacobian determinant is different from 0 throughout A'. (See Example 2.7.2.)

Polar Coordinates

When a double integral is difficult to compute in the usual way, it is natural to search for a suitable substitution so that one can use Theorem 4.7.1. The choice of the new variables must take into account the form of the integrand as well as the domain of integration. One substitution that is often helpful is that of introducing *polar coordinates*. In that case we usually denote u and v by r and θ, and we define the transformation by

$$x = r \cos\theta, \quad y = r \sin\theta \tag{6}$$

The Jacobian is then equal to r (see Problem 2.7.3). If we assume that $r > 0$ and that θ lies in an interval of the form $[\theta_0, \theta_0 + 2\pi)$, then (6) defines a one-to-one C^1 transformation. (From Problem 2.7.3 we see that the transformation need not be one-to-one over an arbitrary set in the $r\theta$-plane.) In this case (3) takes the form

$$\iint_A f(x, y)\, dx\, dy = \iint_{A'} f(r \cos\theta, r \sin\theta) r\, dr\, d\theta \tag{7}$$

The introduction of polar coordinates is particularly convenient if r or θ is constant along the boundary of the domain of integration, and/or when the integrand is particularly simple when expressed in polar coordinates. Consider the following illustrative example.

EXAMPLE 2   Find $\iint_A \sqrt{x^2 + y^2}\, dx\, dy$, with $A = \{(x, y) : 4 \le x^2 + y^2 \le 9,\ \frac{1}{3}\sqrt{3}\,x \le y \le \sqrt{3}\,x\}$.

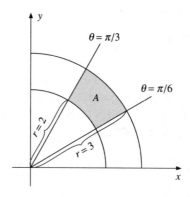

Figure 5

Solution: Figure 5 shows the set A, which is bounded by the circles $x^2 + y^2 = 4$ and $x^2 + y^2 = 9$ and the straight lines $y = \sqrt{3}\,x/3$ and $y = \sqrt{3}\,x$. The straight lines in question form angles $\pi/6$ and $\pi/3$ respectively with the x-axis. Hence, in polar coordinates A is determined by $2 \le r \le 3,\ \pi/6 \le \theta \le \pi/3$. The conditions in Theorem 4.7.1 are satisfied. Because $\sqrt{x^2 + y^2} = \sqrt{r^2 \cos^2\theta + r^2 \sin^2\theta} = r$, we get

$$\iint_A \sqrt{x^2 + y^2}\, dx\, dy = \int_{\pi/6}^{\pi/3} \left(\int_2^3 r \cdot r\, dr \right) d\theta = \int_{\pi/6}^{\pi/3} \left(\Big|_2^3 \frac{r^3}{3} \right) d\theta = \frac{19\pi}{18}$$

To find this answer by direct integration would be quite cumbersome.

Changing Variables in Multiple Integrals

Theorem 4.7.1 can be generalized to n-dimensional integrals. We just state the result.

THEOREM 4.7.2 (CHANGE OF VARIABLES IN MULTIPLE INTEGRALS)

Suppose that $\mathbf{x} = (x_1, \ldots, x_n) = \mathbf{g}(\mathbf{u}) = (g_1(\mathbf{u}), \ldots, g_n(\mathbf{u}))$, where $\mathbf{u} = (u_1, \ldots, u_n)$, defines a one-to-one C^1 transformation $\mathbf{g}$ from an open, bounded set A' in "$\mathbf{u}$-space" onto an open, bounded set A in "$\mathbf{x}$-space". Suppose that the Jacobian determinant

$$J = \frac{\partial(g_1, \ldots, g_n)}{\partial(u_1, \ldots, u_n)}$$

is bounded on A'. Let f be a bounded, continuous function defined on A. Then

$$\int \cdots \int_A f(x_1, \ldots x_n) \, dx_1 \ldots dx_n = \int \cdots \int_{A'} f(g_1(\mathbf{u}), \ldots, g_n(\mathbf{u})) \, |J| \, du_1 \ldots du_n$$

Note 4.7.1 (appropriately generalized) applies equally well to the present theorem.

PROBLEMS FOR SECTION 4.7

1. Consider the double integral $\iint_A (x+xy) \, dx \, dy$ where A is the rectangle in the xy-plane with vertices at the points $(2,0)$, $(4,2)$, $(2,4)$ and $(0,2)$.

   (a) Compute the integral directly.

   (b) What integral do we obtain if we introduce new variables u and v, where $u = x - y$ and $v = x + y$? Compute its value.

2. Show that the area of a triangle with vertices at (x_1, y_1), (x_2, y_2), and (x_3, y_3) in the xy-plane is given by half the absolute value of the determinant

$$\begin{vmatrix} 1 & x_1 & y_1 \\ 1 & x_2 & y_2 \\ 1 & x_3 & y_3 \end{vmatrix}$$

   (*Hint:* Draw the normals from each of the three points to the x-axis.)

3. (a) Compute the following double integral by introducing polar coordinates:

$$\iint_A x^2 \, dx \, dy, \quad \text{where } A = \{(x, y) : x^2 + y^2 \le 1/4\}$$

   (b) What is the value of the double integral if $A = \{(x, y) : x^2 + (y - 1)^2 \le 1/4\}$?

4. Consider the linear transformation $T : \mathbb{R}^2 \rightarrow \mathbb{R}^2$ given by

$$x = au + bv, \quad y = cu + dv$$

(a) Find the Jacobian J of T. Show that T maps the unit square $[0, 1] \times [0, 1]$ in the uv-plane onto a parallelogram in the xy-plane whose area is $|J|$. (Make use of Problem 2.)

(b) If A' is an arbitrary bounded set in the uv-plane and the boundary of A' has measure 0, then one can prove that in general

$$\text{area}(T(A')) = |J| \cdot \text{area}(A')$$

Verify that this formula holds if T is given by (i) in Example 1 and A' is the set in Fig. 2. (See Note 4.7.1 for the definition of sets of measure 0, and Chapter 14 for the definition of the boundary of a set.)

5. Let A_1 be the set $\{(x, y) : x^2 + y^2 \leq 1\}$ and let A_2 be the set in $\mathbb{R}^2$ bounded by the lines $y - 2x = -1$, $y - 2x = 1$, $y + 3x = 4$, and $y + 3x = 8$. Compute the following integrals by introducing suitable substitutions.

(a) $\displaystyle\iint_{A_1} (1 - x^2 - y^2)\, dx\, dy$ (b) $\displaystyle\iint_{A_2} (x + y)\, dx\, dy$

4.8 Generalized Double Integrals

So far, the treatment of multiple integrals in this chapter has dealt with integrals of bounded, continuous functions over bounded sets. We now consider briefly the problem of defining double integrals when the domain of integration is infinite and/or the integrand is unbounded. We begin by considering a type of double integral frequently encountered in statistics,[3]

$$F(x, y) = \int_{-\infty}^{x} \int_{-\infty}^{y} f(u, v)\, dv\, du \tag{1}$$

The definition of this double integral is straightforward if we recall the standard way of defining integrals of one variable functions on unbounded intervals. We let $F(x, y) = \int_{-\infty}^{x} G(u, y)\, du$, where $G(u, y) = \int_{-\infty}^{y} f(u, v)\, dv$. The latter integral is, by definition, $\int_{-\infty}^{y} f(u, v)\, dv = \lim_{N \to \infty} \int_{-N}^{y} f(u, v)\, dv$, provided the limit exists. Then $F(x, y) = \int_{-\infty}^{x} G(u, y)\, du = \lim_{M \to \infty} \int_{-M}^{x} G(u, y)\, du$, provided this limit also exists.

---

[3] If the two random variables X and Y have a joint distribution determined by the probability density function $f(x, y)$, then $F(x, y)$ is the cumulative distribution function. For f to be a valid density function, and F a valid distribution function, one requires $f \geq 0$ and $F(\infty, \infty) = 1$.

EXAMPLE 1   Evaluate the integral (1) for $x \geq 0$, $y \geq 0$ if $f(u, v) = \frac{1}{4}e^{-|u|-|v|}$.

Solution: Since $e^{-|u|-|v|} = e^{-|u|}e^{-|v|}$, we get $F(x, y) = \frac{1}{4}\int_{-\infty}^{x}\int_{-\infty}^{y} e^{-|u|}e^{-|v|}\, dv\, du = \frac{1}{4}\int_{-\infty}^{x} e^{-|u|}\, du \int_{-\infty}^{y} e^{-|v|}\, dv$. Since $|u| = u$ if $u \geq 0$ and $|u| = -u$ if $u < 0$, we find that $\int_{-\infty}^{x} e^{-|u|}\, du = \int_{-\infty}^{0} e^{u}\, du + \int_{0}^{x} e^{-u}\, du = \big|_{-\infty}^{0} e^{u} + \big|_{0}^{x} -e^{-u} = 1 + (-e^{-x} + 1) = 2 - e^{-x}$. Similarly, $\int_{-\infty}^{y} e^{-|v|}\, dv = 2 - e^{-y}$, and so

$$F(x, y) = \frac{1}{4}\int_{-\infty}^{x}\int_{-\infty}^{y} e^{-|u|-|v|}\, dv\, du = \frac{1}{4}(2 - e^{-x})(2 - e^{-y})$$

Note that if $x \to \infty$ and $y \to \infty$, then $F(x, y) \to 1$.

In the last example it is natural to define $\int_{-\infty}^{\infty}\int_{-\infty}^{\infty} f(u, v)\, dv\, du = 1$. In general, if we integrate $f(x, y) \geq 0$ over $A = \mathbb{R}^2 = (-\infty, \infty) \times (-\infty, \infty)$, it turns out that we can define

$$\int_{-\infty}^{\infty}\int_{-\infty}^{\infty} f(x, y)\, dx\, dy = \lim_{n \to \infty} \iint_{A_n} f(x, y)\, dx\, dy \tag{2}$$

where $A_n = [-n, n] \times [-n, n]$. (Check that this definition gives the correct result in Example 1.) Problem 5 shows what can go wrong if we remove the assumption that $f(x, y) \geq 0$.

Consider more generally a bounded, continuous function f defined on an unbounded set A in the plane. We assume that $f(x, y) \geq 0$, since this simplifies matters somewhat. Our problem is to find a sensible definition of the double integral of $f(x, y)$ over A. Our point of departure is the fact that we already *have* defined the double integral of $f(x, y)$ over each closed, bounded subset of A. Let $A_1, A_2, \ldots$ be an *increasing* sequence of closed, bounded subsets of A, so that

$$A_1 \subseteq A_2 \subseteq \cdots \subseteq A_n \subseteq \cdots \subseteq A$$

We shall say that A_n *converges to* A if for each closed, bounded subset A' of A there exists a number N such that for each $n \geq N$ we have $A' \subseteq A_n$. If this is the case, we define

$$\iint_{A} f(x, y)\, dx\, dy = \lim_{n \to \infty} \iint_{A_n} f(x, y)\, dx\, dy \tag{3}$$

if the limit exists. One can prove that if the limit exists for one such sequence $\{A_n\}$ converging to A, then it will also exist and have the same value for any other sequence of this type. One can try, in each case, to choose a convenient sequence of the required type. If the limit in (3) exists, we say that the double integral of f over A *converges*. If not, we say that it *diverges*. In order to show that the double integral of f over A diverges, it is obviously enough to find *one* such sequence $\{A_n\}$ as described above for which the limit in (3) does not exist.

EXAMPLE 2   Compute $\iint_{A} e^{-(x^2+y^2)}\, dx\, dy$ when A is the whole xy-plane ($A = \mathbb{R}^2$), (i) by using $A_n = \{(x, y) : x^2 + y^2 \leq n^2\}$; (ii) by using $B_n = [-n, n] \times [-n, n]$. Use the results to prove the Poisson integral formula (formula (4.3.3)).

Solution: (i) The conditions for using (3) are satisfied and, using polar coordinates,

$$I_n = \iint_{A_n} e^{-(x^2+y^2)}\,dx\,dy = \int_0^{2\pi}\left(\int_0^n e^{-r^2}r\,dr\right)d\theta$$

$$= \int_0^{2\pi}\left[\Big|_0^n\left(-\tfrac{1}{2}e^{-r^2}\right)\right]d\theta = \tfrac{1}{2}(1 - e^{-n^2})\int_0^{2\pi}d\theta = \pi(1 - e^{-n^2}) \xrightarrow[n\to\infty]{} \pi$$

It follows that the given double integral is convergent, with value π.

(ii) The integral over B_n is $J_n = \iint_{B_n} e^{-(x^2+y^2)}\,dx\,dy = \int_{-n}^n\left(\int_{-n}^n e^{-x^2}e^{-y^2}\,dx\right)dy$. Since the integrand is separable, $J_n = \left(\int_{-n}^n e^{-x^2}\,dx\right)\left(\int_{-n}^n e^{-y^2}\,dy\right) = \left(\int_{-n}^n e^{-x^2}\,dx\right)^2$. And since $A_n \subseteq B_n \subseteq A_{2n}$ for all n and $e^{-(x^2+y^2)} > 0$ everywhere, $\pi(1 - e^{-n^2}) \le \left(\int_{-n}^n e^{-x^2}\,dx\right)^2 \le \pi(1 - e^{-4n^2})$. Taking limits as $n \to \infty$, we get $\pi = \left(\int_{-\infty}^\infty e^{-x^2}\,dx\right)^2$, so $\int_{-\infty}^\infty e^{-x^2}\,dx = \sqrt{\pi}$. By symmetry, $\int_0^\infty e^{-x^2}\,dx = \tfrac{1}{2}\sqrt{\pi}$, the Poisson integral formula.

Unbounded Functions

This section concludes with just one example indicating how to extend the definition of double integrals to certain unbounded functions defined over bounded sets. The idea resembles the one associated with the definition (3) above. For more details, see Protter and Morrey (1991).

EXAMPLE 3   The function $f(x, y) = (x^2 + y^2)^{-p}$, $p > 0$, is not bounded over the set A determined by $0 < x^2 + y^2 \le 1$, because $f(x, y) \to \infty$ as $(x, y) \to (0, 0)$. The double integral

$$\iint_A \frac{1}{(x^2 + y^2)^p}\,dx\,dy$$

is therefore so far not defined. For $n = 1, 2, \ldots$, let A_n be the circular ring (or *annulus*) defined by $1/n^2 \le x^2 + y^2 \le 1$. Then $A_1, A_2, \ldots$ form an increasing sequence of sets $A_1 \subseteq A_2 \subseteq \cdots \subseteq A_n \subseteq \cdots$, and as n increases, A_n will "tend to" the set $A = \{(x, y) : 0 < x^2 + y^2 \le 1\}$, because $\bigcup_{n=1}^\infty A_n = A$. The double integral of f is defined over the set A_n for each $n = 1, 2, \ldots$. Indeed, by introducing polar coordinates, we obtain

$$I_n = \iint_{A_n} \frac{1}{(x^2 + y^2)^p}\,dx\,dy = \int_0^{2\pi}\left(\int_{1/n}^1 \frac{1}{r^{2p}}r\,dr\right)d\theta = \int_0^{2\pi}\left(\int_{1/n}^1 r^{1-2p}\,dr\right)d\theta$$

It follows that $I_n = 2\pi \ln n$ for $p = 1$, while $I_n = \pi(1 - n^{2(p-1)})/(1 - p)$ for $p \ne 1$. If $p < 1$, then $n^{2(p-1)} \to 0$ as $n \to \infty$, and $I_n \to \pi/(1 - p)$. If $p \ge 1$, we see that I_n does not tend to any limit. On the basis of this observation, if $0 < p < 1$, we say that the integral is convergent, with a value $\pi/(1 - p)$, whereas we say that it is divergent if $p \ge 1$.

PROBLEMS FOR SECTION 4.8

1. (a) Compute the value of the double integral $\iint_{x^2+y^2\geq1} \dfrac{1}{(x^2+y^2)^3} \, dx \, dy$.

   (b) Discuss the convergence (for different values of p) if we replace the integrand in (a) with $(x^2+y^2)^{-p}$, but keep the same domain of integration.

2. If $I(z) = \int_{-\infty}^{\infty} \left(\int_{-\infty}^{z-x} f(x,y) \, dy \right) dx$ then, under appropriate conditions on $f(x,y)$, compute $I'(z)$ by using Leibniz's rule.

3. (a) Let $f(x,y) = k\sqrt{1-x^2-y^2}$. Find a value of k such that $\iint_{x^2+y^2\leq1} f(x,y) \, dx \, dy = 1$. (Then $f(x,y)$ is a joint density function for two stochastic variables X and Y.)

   (b) With the value of k from part (a), find the marginal density of X, which is defined as $f_X(x) = \int_{x^2+y^2\leq1} f(x,y) \, dy$.

4. Let $I(b,d)$ denote the double integral in Example 4.4.3. Find the two limits

$$\lim_{b\to\infty} [\, \lim_{d\to\infty} I(b,d)\,] \quad \text{and} \quad \lim_{d\to\infty} [\, \lim_{b\to\infty} I(b,d)\,]$$

What do your answers tell you about $\displaystyle\int_{1}^{\infty} \int_{1}^{\infty} (y-x)(y+x)^{-3} \, dx \, dy$?

5. (a) Prove that if the function F is defined by (1), then under appropriate conditions, $F''_{12}(x,y) = f(x,y)$. (*Hint:* Use Leibniz's rule.)

   (b) Verify this equality for the function in Example 1.

HARDER PROBLEMS

6. Compute

   (a) $\displaystyle\iint_{\mathbb{R}^2} (x^2+y^2+1)^{-3/2} \, dx \, dy$

   (b) $\displaystyle\iint_{\mathbb{R}^2} \dfrac{e^{-(x-y)^2}}{1+(x+y)^2} \, dx \, dy$

7. Check whether the following double integrals converge and, if they do, find their values.

   (a) $\displaystyle\iint_{0<x^2+y^2\leq1} \dfrac{x^2}{(x^2+y^2)^{3/2}} \, dx \, dy$

   (b) $\displaystyle\iint_{A} \dfrac{-\ln(x^2+y^2)}{\sqrt{x^2+y^2}} \, dx \, dy$

   In (b) let $A = \{(x,y) : 0 < x^2+y^2 \leq 1, \ x \geq 0, \ y \geq 0\}$.

5 DIFFERENTIAL EQUATIONS I:
FIRST-ORDER EQUATIONS IN ONE VARIABLE

...the task of the theory of ordinary differential equations is
to reconstruct the past and predict the future of the process from
a knowledge of this local law of evolution.
—V. I. Arnold (1973)

Economists often study the changes over time in economic variables like national income, the interest rate, the money supply, oil production, or the price of wheat. The laws of motion governing these variables are usually expressed in terms of one or more equations.

If time is regarded as continuous and the equations involve unknown functions and their derivatives, we find ourselves considering *differential equations*. In macroeconomic theory especially but also in many other areas of economics, a certain knowledge of differential equations is essential. Another example is finance theory, where the pricing of options now requires quite advanced methods in the theory of differential equations.

The systematic study of differential equations was initiated by Newton and Leibniz in the seventeenth century, and this topic is still one of the most important in mathematics. The simplest kind of differential equation involves only first-order derivatives of a single variable. Such differential equations are the subject of this chapter.

5.1 Introduction

What is a differential equation? As the name suggests, it is an equation. Unlike ordinary algebraic equations, in a differential equation:

A. The unknown is a function, not a number.

B. The equation includes one or more of the derivatives of the function.

An *ordinary* differential equation is one for which the unknown is a function of only one variable. *Partial differential equations* are equations where the unknown is a function of two or more variables, and one or more of the partial derivatives of the function are included.

In this chapter we restrict attention to first-order (ordinary) differential equations—that is, equations where only the first-order derivatives of the unknown functions of one variable are included. Three typical examples are:

$$\dot{x} = ax, \qquad \dot{x} + ax = b, \qquad \dot{x} + ax = bx^2$$

With suitably chosen constants, these describe natural growth, growth towards a limit, and logistic growth, respectively. (Recall that we often use dot notation for the derivative, $\dot{x} = dx/dt$, especially when the independent variable is time t.) Other examples of first-order differential equations are

$$\text{(a)} \ \dot{x} = x + t \qquad \text{(b)} \ \dot{K} = \alpha \sigma K + H_0 e^{\mu t} \qquad \text{(c)} \ \dot{k} = s f(k) - \lambda k$$

In Examples 5.4.3 and 5.7.3, respectively, we shall give equations (b) and (c) interesting economic interpretations, both concerning the evolution of an economy's capital stock.

Solving equation (a), for instance, means finding all functions $x(t)$ such that, for every value of t, the derivative $\dot{x}(t)$ of $x(t)$ is equal to $x(t) + t$. In equation (b), $K(t)$ is the unknown function, whereas α, σ, H_0, and μ are constants. In equation (c), $f(k)$ is a given function, whereas s and λ are constants. The unknown function is $k = k(t)$.

NOTE 1 We often use t to denote the independent variable. This is because most differential equations that appear in economics have time as their independent variable. The following theory is valid even if the independent variable is not time, however.

A first-order differential equation is written

$$\dot{x} = F(t, x) \tag{1}$$

where F is a given function of two variables, and $x = x(t)$ is the unknown function. A **solution** of (1) in an interval I of the real line is any differentiable function φ defined on I such that $x = \varphi(t)$ satisfies (1), that is $\dot{\varphi}(t) = F(t, \varphi(t))$ for all t in I.[1] The graph of a solution is called a **solution curve** or an **integral curve**.

The equations (a), (b), and (c) are all of the form (1). For example, (a) becomes $dx/dt = F(t, x)$ with $F(t, x) = x + t$.

EXAMPLE 1   Consider the differential equation

$$\dot{x} = x + t \tag{$*$}$$

(a) Show that both $x = -t - 1$ and $x = e^t - t - 1$ are particular solutions of the equation over the entire real line.

(b) More generally, show that $x = Ce^t - t - 1$ is a solution of ($*$) for all t, whatever the choice of the constant C.

(c) Show that $x = e^t - 1$ is not a solution of ($*$).

---

[1] Usually we assume that the interval I is open, but sometimes it is useful to allow closed (or half-open) intervals. If I is a closed interval, a solution is required to be continuous on I and to satisfy (1) in the interior of I.

Solution:

(a) If $x = -t - 1$, then $\dot{x} = -1$ and $x + t = (-t - 1) + t = -1$. Hence, $\dot{x} = x + t$ for all t in this case. If $x = e^t - t - 1$, then $\dot{x} = e^t - 1$ and $x + t = (e^t - t - 1) + t = e^t - 1$. Again we see that $(*)$ is satisfied for all t.

(b) When $x = Ce^t - t - 1$, we have $\dot{x} = Ce^t - 1 = x + t$ for all t.

(c) If $x = e^t - 1$, then $\dot{x} = e^t$ and $x + t = e^t + t - 1$. In this case, $\dot{x}$ is only equal to $x + t$ for $t = 1$, so $x = e^t - 1$ is *not* a solution of equation $(*)$ on any interval.

Example 1 illustrates the fact that a differential equation usually has infinitely many solutions. We found that $x = Ce^t - t - 1$ was a solution of $\dot{x} = x + t$ for each choice of the constant C. The answer to Problem 5.4.3 shows that no other function satisfies the equation.

The set of all solutions of a differential equation is called its **general solution**, while any specific function that satisfies the equation is called a **particular solution**.

A first-order differential equation usually has a general solution that depends on *one* constant. (Problem 5 shows why we must use the word "usually" in this statement.) If we require the solution to pass through a given point in the tx-plane, then the constant is determined uniquely, except in special cases.

EXAMPLE 2   Assuming that the general solution is $x(t) = Ce^t - t - 1$, find the solution of $\dot{x} = x + t$ that passes through the point $(t, x) = (0, 1)$.

Solution: To make the solution $x(t) = Ce^t - t - 1$ pass through $(t, x) = (0, 1)$, we must have $x(0) = 1$. Hence $1 = Ce^0 - 0 - 1$, implying that $C = 2$. The required solution, therefore, is $x(t) = 2e^t - t - 1$.

The problem in Example 2 is this: Find the unique function $x(t)$ such that

$$\dot{x}(t) = x(t) + t \qquad \text{and} \qquad x(0) = 1 \qquad\qquad (*)$$

If $t = 0$ denotes the initial time, then $x(0) = 1$ is called an **initial condition** and we call $(*)$ an **initial-value problem**.

Such initial-value problems arise naturally in many economic models. For instance, suppose an economic growth model involves a first-order differential equation for the accumulation of capital over time. The initial stock of capital is historically given, and therefore helps to determine the unique solution of the equation.

Qualitative Theory

When the theory of differential equations was first developed, mathematicians primarily tried to find explicit solutions for some special types of equation. It became increasingly obvious, however, that only very few equations could be solved this way. In many cases, moreover, explicit formulas for the solutions are not really needed. Instead, the main interest is in a few important properties of the solution. As a result, the theory of differential equations includes many results concerning the general behaviour of the solutions. This is the so-called *qualitative theory*. Its main results include existence and uniqueness theorems, sensitivity analysis, and investigations of the stability of equilibria. Such topics are of both theoretical interest and practical importance, and will be discussed in some detail.

Along with this qualitative theory, much work has been put into developing useful numerical methods for finding approximate solutions of differential equations. Computers are playing an increasingly important role here, but these developments are not discussed in this book.

PROBLEMS FOR SECTION 5.1

1. Show that $x(t) = Ce^{-t} + \frac{1}{2}e^t$ is a solution of the differential equation $\dot{x}(t) + x(t) = e^t$ for all values of the constant C.

2. Show that $x = Ct^2$ is a solution of the differential equation $t\dot{x} = 2x$ for all choices of the constant C. Find in particular the integral curve through $(1, 2)$.

3. Show that any function $x = x(t)$ that satisfies the equation $xe^{tx} = C$ is a solution of the differential equation $(1 + tx)\dot{x} = -x^2$. (*Hint:* Differentiate $xe^{tx} = C$ implicitly w.r.t. t.)

4. In each of the following cases, show that any function $x = x(t)$ that satisfies the equation on the left is a solution of the corresponding differential equation on the right.

   (a) $x^2 = 2at$, $\qquad 2x\dot{x} = 2t\dot{x}^2 + a$ $\quad$ (*a* is a constant)

   (b) $\frac{1}{2}e^{t^2} + e^{-x}(x + 1) + C = 0$, $\qquad x\dot{x} = te^{t^2+x}$

   (c) $(1 - t)x^2 = t^3$, $\qquad 2t^3\dot{x} = x(x^2 + 3t^2)$

5. Show that $x = Ct - C^2$ is a solution of the differential equation $\dot{x}^2 = t\dot{x} - x$, for all values of the constant C. Then show that it is not the general solution because $x = \frac{1}{4}t^2$ is also a solution.

HARDER PROBLEMS

6. The function $x = x(t)$ satisfies $x(0) = 0$ and the differential equation $\dot{x} = (1 + x^2)t$, for all t. Prove that $t = 0$ is a global minimum point for $x(t)$, and that the function $x(t)$ is convex for all t. (*Hint:* You do not have to solve the equation.)

5.2 The Direction Is Given: Find the Path!

Consider again the differential equation $\dot{x} = x + t$, which was studied in Examples 5.1.1 and 5.1.2. If $x = x(t)$ is a solution, then the slope of the tangent to the graph (or integral curve) at the point (t, x) is equal to $x + t$. At the point $(t, x) = (0, 0)$ the slope is therefore equal to 0, whereas at $(1, 2)$ the slope is 3, and so on. In Fig. 1, we have drawn small straight-line segments with slopes $x + t$ through several points in the (t, x)-plane. This gives us a so-called **direction diagram** (or **slope field**) for the differential equation $\dot{x} = x + t$. If an integral curve passes through one of these points, it will have the corresponding line segment as its tangent. This allows us to sketch curves that follow the direction of the line segments, and get a general impression of what the integral curves of $\dot{x} = x + t$ must look like.

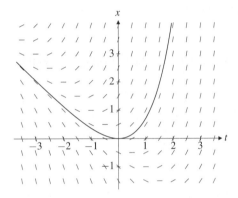

Figure 1   A direction diagram for $\dot{x} = x + t$.
The integral curve through $(0, 0)$ is shown.

A direction diagram like this can be drawn for any differential equation of the form $\dot{x} = F(t, x)$. (Computer programs like *Maple* and *Mathematica* enable us to draw direction diagrams and solution curves with ease.) Whether or not it is possible to solve the equation explicitly, a direction diagram can give a rough but useful indication of how the integral curves behave. In a nutshell, the problem of solving the differential equation $\dot{x} = F(t, x)$ can be put like this: The direction is given, find the path!

PROBLEMS FOR SECTION 5.2

1. Draw a direction diagram for the differential equation $\dot{x} = x/t$ and draw some integral curves.

2. Draw a direction diagram for the differential equation $\dot{x} = -t/x$ and draw the integral curve through $(2, 0)$.

5.3 Separable Equations

Suppose that $\dot{x} = F(t, x)$, where $F(t, x)$ can be written as a product of two functions, one of which depends only on t and the other only on x. Specifically, suppose that

$$\dot{x} = f(t)g(x) \tag{1}$$

We say that this differential equation is **separable**. For instance, $\dot{x} = -2tx^2$ is obviously separable, whereas $\dot{x} = t^2 + x$ is not.

It is important to learn to distinguish between separable and nonseparable equations, because separable equations are among those that can be solved in terms of integrals of known functions.

EXAMPLE 1   Decide which of the following differential equations are separable:

(a) $\dot{x} = x^2 - 1$ (b) $\dot{x} = xt + t$ (c) $\dot{x} = xt + t^2$

(d) $x\dot{x} = e^{x+t}\sqrt{1 + t^2}$ (e) $\dot{x} = \sqrt[4]{t^2 + x}$ (f) $\dot{x} = F(t) + G(x)$

Solution:

(a) Separable. Let $f(t) = 1$ and $g(x) = x^2 - 1$.

(b) Separable, because $xt + t = t(x + 1)$.

(c) Not separable. It is impossible to write the sum $xt + t^2$ in the form $f(t)g(x)$. Note that $t(x + t)$ does not count as a separation because both factors would then depend on t.

(d) Separable. Because $e^{x+t} = e^x e^t$, we can put $f(t) = e^t\sqrt{1 + t^2}$ and $g(x) = e^x/x$.

(e) Not separable. It is impossible to write $\sqrt[4]{t^2 + x}$ in the form $f(t)g(x)$.

(f) Not separable in general. (The equation looks simple, but no method is known for solving this equation, except numerically or in special cases such as when G is a linear function of x.)

Note that a particular solution of (1) arises if $g(x)$ has a zero at $x = a$, so that $g(a) = 0$. In fact, $x(t) \equiv a$ will be a solution of the equation in this case, because the right- and left-hand sides of the equation are both 0 for all t. For instance, $\dot{x} = (x + 1)(x - 3)$ has the two particular solutions $x(t) \equiv -1$ and $x(t) \equiv 3$. (In addition it has $x = -1 + 4/(1 - Ce^{4t})$ as a solution of all values of the constant C. See Example 5.)

Using differential notation, a general method for solving (1) can be expressed in the following way:

METHOD FOR SOLVING SEPARABLE DIFFERENTIAL EQUATIONS:

A. Write equation (1) as

$$\frac{dx}{dt} = f(t)g(x) \qquad\qquad (*)$$

B. Separate the variables:

$$\frac{dx}{g(x)} = f(t)\, dt$$

C. Integrate each side:

$$\int \frac{dx}{g(x)} = \int f(t)\, dt$$

D. Evaluate the two integrals (if possible) and you obtain a solution of $(*)$ (possibly in implicit form). Solve for x, if possible.

E. In addition, every zero $x = a$ of $g(x)$ gives the constant solution $x(t) \equiv a$.

To justify the method, suppose that $x = \varphi(t)$ is a function defined in an interval I such that $g(\varphi(t)) \neq 0$ throughout I. Then $x = \varphi(t)$ will solve (1) iff

$$\frac{\dot{\varphi}(t)}{g(\varphi(t))} = f(t)$$

for all t in I. But these two functions are equal in I iff

$$\int \frac{\dot{\varphi}(t)}{g(\varphi(t))}\, dt = \int f(t)\, dt$$

Suppose we substitute $x = \varphi(t)$, so that $dx = \dot{\varphi}(t)\, dt$ in the integral on the left-hand side. Then according to the rule of integration by substitution, the last equation is equivalent to

$$\int \frac{dx}{g(x)} = \int f(t)\, dt$$

Thus,

$$G(x) = F(t) + C$$

where $G'(x) = 1/g(x)$, $F'(t) = f(t)$, and C is a constant.

NOTE 1   This solution is valid in any interval I throughout which $g(x) \neq 0$. If g is also continuous in I, it can never change sign, so that $G'(x) = 1/g(x)$ has the same sign for all x in I. Then G itself is either strictly increasing or strictly decreasing in I, hence invertible. It follows that $G(x) = F(t) + C$ has a solution $x = G^{-1}(F(t) + C)$.

EXAMPLE 2   Solve the differential equation

$$\frac{dx}{dt} = -2tx^2$$

and find the integral curve that passes through $(t, x) = (1, -1)$.

Solution: We observe first that $x(t) \equiv 0$ is one (trivial) solution. But this does not go through $(1, -1)$, so we follow the recipe:

Separate:
$$-\frac{dx}{x^2} = 2t\, dt$$

Integrate:
$$-\int \frac{dx}{x^2} = \int 2t\, dt$$

Evaluate:
$$\frac{1}{x} = t^2 + C$$

It follows that the general solution is

$$x = \frac{1}{t^2 + C} \qquad\qquad (*)$$

To find the integral curve through $(1, -1)$, we must determine the correct value of C. Because we require $x = -1$ for $t = 1$, it follows from $(*)$ that $-1 = 1/(1 + C)$, so $C = -2$. Thus, the integral curve passing through $(1, -1)$ is $x = 1/(t^2 - 2)$.

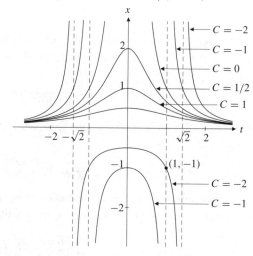

Figure 1 The solution curves $x = 1/(t^2 + C)$ for particular values of C.

Figure 1 shows integral curves of the form $(*)$ for five different values of C. The constant of integration crucially affects the shape of the curve as well as its position. (Note that when $C < 0$, we do not get solutions defined over the entire real line.)

EXAMPLE 3   Solve the differential equation $\dfrac{dx}{dt} = \dfrac{t^3}{x^6 + 1}$.

Solution: We use the previous method, with $f(t) = t^3$ and $g(x) = 1/(x^6 + 1)$. Because $g(x)$ is never 0, there are no constant solutions. We proceed as follows:

Separate:
$$(x^6 + 1)\, dx = t^3\, dt$$

Integrate:
$$\int (x^6 + 1)\, dx = \int t^3\, dt$$

Evaluate:
$$\tfrac{1}{7}x^7 + x = \tfrac{1}{4}t^4 + C$$

The desired functions $x = x(t)$ are those that satisfy the last equation for all t.

NOTE 2 We usually say that we have solved a differential equation even if the unknown function (as shown in Example 3) cannot be expressed explicitly. The important point is that we have found an equation involving the unknown function where the derivative of that function does not appear.

EXAMPLE 4   **(Economic Growth)** Let $X = X(t)$ denote the national product, $K = K(t)$ the capital stock, and $L = L(t)$ the number of workers in a country at time t. Suppose that, for all $t \geq 0$,

$$\text{(a) } X = AK^{1-\alpha}L^{\alpha} \qquad \text{(b) } \dot{K} = sX \qquad \text{(c) } L = L_0 e^{\lambda t}$$

where A, α, s, L_0, and λ are all positive constants, with $0 < \alpha < 1$. Derive from these equations a single differential equation to determine $K = K(t)$, and find the solution of that equation when $K(0) = K_0 > 0$. (This is a special case of the Solow model discussed in Example 5.7.3. In (a) we have a Cobb–Douglas production function, (b) says that aggregate investment is proportional to output, whereas (c) implies that the labour force grows exponentially.)

Solution: From (a) to (c), we derive the single differential equation

$$\dot{K} = \frac{dK}{dt} = sAK^{1-\alpha}L^{\alpha} = sAL_0^{\alpha}e^{\alpha\lambda t}K^{1-\alpha}$$

This is clearly separable. Using the recipe yields:

$$K^{\alpha-1}\,dK = sAL_0^{\alpha}e^{\alpha\lambda t}\,dt$$

$$\int K^{\alpha-1}\,dK = \int sAL_0^{\alpha}e^{\alpha\lambda t}\,dt$$

$$\frac{1}{\alpha}K^{\alpha} = \frac{1}{\alpha\lambda}sAL_0^{\alpha}e^{\alpha\lambda t} + C$$

If we put $C_1 = \alpha C$, we get $K^{\alpha} = (s/\lambda)AL_0^{\alpha}e^{\alpha\lambda t} + C_1$. If $K = K_0$ for $t = 0$, we get $C_1 = K_0^{\alpha} - (s/\lambda)AL_0^{\alpha}$. Therefore the solution is

$$K = \left[K_0^{\alpha} + (s/\lambda)AL_0^{\alpha}(e^{\alpha\lambda t} - 1)\right]^{1/\alpha}$$

See Problem 8 for a closer examination of this model.

EXAMPLE 5   Solve the following differential equation when $a \neq b$:

$$\frac{dx}{dt} = B(x - a)(x - b)$$

In particular, find the solution when $B = -1/2$, $a = -1$, and $b = 2$, and draw some integral curves in this case.

Solution: Observe that both $x \equiv a$ and $x \equiv b$ are trivial solutions of the equation. In order to find the other solutions, separate the variables as follows. First, put all terms involving x on the left-hand side, and all terms involving t on the right-hand side. Then integrate, to get

$$\int \frac{1}{(x-a)(x-b)} \, dx = \int B \, dt$$

The next step is to transform the integrand on the left. We find that

$$\frac{1}{(x-a)(x-b)} = \frac{1}{b-a} \left(\frac{1}{x-b} - \frac{1}{x-a} \right)$$

(Verify this by expanding the right-hand side.) Hence,

$$\int \frac{1}{(x-a)(x-b)} \, dx = \frac{1}{b-a} \left(\int \frac{1}{x-b} \, dx - \int \frac{1}{x-a} \, dx \right)$$

Except for an additive constant, the last expression equals

$$\frac{1}{b-a} \left(\ln |x-b| - \ln|x-a| \right) = \frac{1}{b-a} \ln \frac{|x-b|}{|x-a|}$$

So, for some constant C_1, the solution is

$$\frac{1}{b-a} \ln \frac{|x-b|}{|x-a|} = Bt + C_1 \qquad \text{or} \qquad \ln \left| \frac{x-b}{x-a} \right| = B(b-a)t + C_2$$

with $C_2 = C_1(b-a)$. So

$$\left| \frac{x-b}{x-a} \right| = e^{B(b-a)t+C_2} = e^{B(b-a)t} e^{C_2} \quad \text{or} \quad \frac{x-b}{x-a} = \pm e^{C_2} e^{B(b-a)t} = C e^{B(b-a)t} \qquad (*)$$

after defining the new constant $C = \pm e^{C_2}$. Solving this last equation for x finally gives

$$\frac{dx}{dt} = B(x-a)(x-b) \iff x = \frac{b - aCe^{B(b-a)t}}{1 - Ce^{B(b-a)t}} = a + \frac{b-a}{1 - Ce^{B(b-a)t}} \qquad (2)$$

For $B = -1/2$, $a = -1$, and $b = 2$, the differential equation is $\dot{x} = -\frac{1}{2}(x+1)(x-2)$. Note that $\dot{x}$ is positive for x between -1 and 2. Hence, the integral curves rise with t in the horizontal strip between lines $x = -1$ and $x = 2$. In the same way, we can see directly from the differential equation that the integral curves are falling above and below this strip. In addition to the constant solutions $x = -1$ and $x = 2$, indicated by dashed horizontal lines in Fig. 2, we see that the general solution of the equation $\dot{x} = -\frac{1}{2}(x+1)(x-2)$ is

$$x = -1 + \frac{3}{1 - Ce^{-3t}}$$

Some of the associated integral curves are shown in Fig. 2.

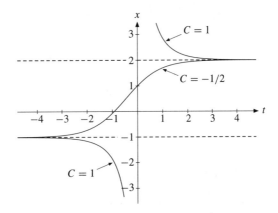

Figure 2 Some solution curves for $\dot{x} = -\frac{1}{2}(x+1)(x-2)$.

NOTE 3   In the second part of ($*$) we removed the absolute value sign around the fraction $(x - b)/(x - a)$, and replaced the factor e^{C_2} by $\pm e^{C_2}$, where we use $+$ if the fraction is positive, $-$ if it is negative. We claim that we must use the same sign for all t in the interval where the solution $x = x(t)$ is defined: The argument leading to ($*$) assumed that x is different from a and b everywhere. Moreover, x is a continuous function. Therefore, $(x - b)/(x - a)$ is continuous and different from 0 in the whole domain of x. If follows that the fraction has the same sign everywhere—if not, the intermediate value theorem would imply that the fraction must be zero for some t. Hence the factor $\pm e^{C_2}$ has the same value for all relevant values of t, i.e. it is a constant factor (denoted by C in ($*$)).

EXAMPLE 6   **(Compound Interest)** Suppose that $w = w(t) > 0$ is the wealth held in an investment account at time t, and that $r(t)$ is the interest rate, with interest compounded continuously. Then

$$\dot{w} = r(t)w \qquad (*)$$

which is a separable equation. Separating the variables and integrating yields

$$\int \frac{dw}{w} = \int r(t)\,dt$$

Therefore, $\ln w = R(t) + C_1$ where $R(t) = \int r(t)\,dt$. So the solution is

$$w(t) = e^{R(t)+C_1} = e^{C_1}e^{R(t)} = Ce^{R(t)} \qquad (**)$$

after introducing the new constant $C = e^{C_1}$. Suppose the initial value of the account is $w(0)$. Then ($**$) implies that $w(0) = Ce^{R(0)}$, so $C = w(0)e^{-R(0)}$ and ($**$) becomes $w(t) = w(0)e^{R(t)-R(0)}$. But $R(t) - R(0) = \int_0^t r(s)\,ds$, and so

$$w(t) = w(0)e^{\int_0^t r(s)\,ds} = w(0) \exp \int_0^t r(s)\,ds$$

This is the unique solution of ($*$) with $w(0)$ as the size of the account at time $t = 0$.

PROBLEMS FOR SECTION 5.3

1. Solve the equation $x^2\dot{x} = t + 1$. Find the integral curve through $(t, x) = (1, 1)$.

2. Solve the following differential equations:

   (a) $\dot{x} = t^3 - t$ (b) $\dot{x} = te^t - t$ (c) $e^x\dot{x} = t + 1$

3. Find the general solutions of the following differential equations. Also find the integral curves through the indicated points.

   (a) $t\dot{x} = x(1 - t)$, $(t_0, x_0) = (1, 1/e)$ (b) $(1 + t^3)\dot{x} = t^2x$, $(t_0, x_0) = (0, 2)$

   (c) $x\dot{x} = t$, $(t_0, x_0) = (\sqrt{2}, 1)$ (d) $e^{2t}\dot{x} - x^2 - 2x = 1$, $(t_0, x_0) = (0, 0)$

4. Find the general solution of $\dot{x} + a(t)x = 0$. In particular, when $a(t) = a + bc^t$ (a, b, and c are positive; $c \neq 1$) show that the solution of the equation can be written in the form $x = Cp^t q^{c^t}$, where p and q are constants determined by a, b, and c, whereas C is an arbitrary constant. (This is Gompertz–Makeham's law of mortality.)

5. Explain why biological populations that develop as suggested in the figures A and B below *cannot* be described by differential equations of the form $\dot{N}/N = f(N)$, no matter how the function f is chosen. ($N(t)$ is the size of the population at time t.)

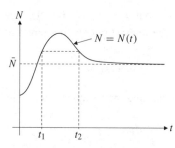

Figure A

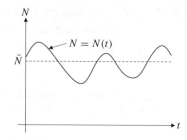

Figure B

6. Find $x = x(t)$ when $\text{El}_t\, x = t\dot{x}/x$, the elasticity of $x(t)$ w.r.t. t, satisfies the following equations for all t:

   (a) $\text{El}_t\, x = a$ (b) $\text{El}_t\, x = at + b$ (c) $\text{El}_t\, x = ax + b$

7. The following differential equations have been studied in economics. Solve them.

   (a) $\dot{K} = (An_0^a a^b)K^{b-c}e^{(av+\varepsilon)t}$, $b - c \neq 1, \alpha v + \varepsilon \neq 0$

   (b) $\dot{x} = \dfrac{(\beta - \alpha x)(x - a)}{x}$, $\alpha > 0, \beta > 0, a > 0, \alpha a \neq \beta$

   (Hint for (b): $\dfrac{x}{(\beta - \alpha x)(x - a)} = \dfrac{1}{\beta - \alpha a}\left(\dfrac{\beta}{\beta - \alpha x} + \dfrac{a}{x - a}\right)$.)

HARDER PROBLEMS

8. (a) With reference to Example 4, show that K/L tends to $(sA/\lambda)^{1/\alpha}$ as $t \to \infty$. Compute the limit for X/L as $t \to \infty$.

 (b) Replace equation (c) in Example 4 by (c′) $L = b(t + a)^p$, where a, b, and p are positive constants. From (a), (b), and (c′), derive a differential equation for $K = K(t)$. Solve the equation when $K(0) = K_0$, and examine the behaviour of K/L as $t \to \infty$.

9. In connection with their study of CES (constant elasticity of substitution) production functions, Arrow, Chenery, Minhas, and Solow were led to consider the differential equation

$$\frac{dy}{dx} = \frac{y(1 - \alpha y^\varrho)}{x} \qquad (\alpha \text{ and } \varrho \text{ are constants}, \varrho \neq 0, x > 0, y > 0) \qquad (*)$$

Use the identity $1/y + \alpha y^{\varrho - 1}/(1 - \alpha y^\varrho) = 1/y(1 - \alpha y^\varrho)$ to show that the general solution is

$$y = (\beta x^{-\varrho} + \alpha)^{-1/\varrho} \qquad (**)$$

(Suppose we let $x = K/L$, $y = Y/L$, and define new constants A and a by $A = (\alpha + \beta)^{-1/\varrho}$ and $a = \beta/(\alpha + \beta)$. Then $1 - a = \alpha/(\alpha + \beta)$ and $\alpha + \beta = A^{-\varrho}$, so $\alpha = (1 - a)A^{-\varrho}$ and $\beta = aA^{-\varrho}$. Now it follows that $Y = A\big[aK^{-\varrho} + (1 - a)L^{-\varrho}\big]^{-1/\varrho}$, which is a special form of the CES production function.)

5.4 First-Order Linear Equations

A **first-order linear differential equation** is one that can be written in the form

$$\dot{x} + a(t)x = b(t) \qquad (1)$$

where $a(t)$ and $b(t)$ denote continuous functions of t in a certain interval, and $x = x(t)$ is the unknown function. Equation (1) is called "linear" because the left-hand side is a linear function of x and $\dot{x}$.

The following are all examples of first-order linear equations:

(a) $\dot{x} + x = t$ (b) $\dot{x} + 2tx = 4t$ (c) $(t^2 + 1)\dot{x} + e^t x = t \ln t$

The first two equations are obviously of the form (1). The last one can be put into this form if we divide each term by $t^2 + 1$ to get $\dot{x} + [e^t/(t^2 + 1)]x = t \ln t/(t^2 + 1)$.

The Simplest Case

Consider the following equation with a and b as constants, where $a \neq 0$:

$$\dot{x} + ax = b \qquad (2)$$

Let us multiply this equation by the positive factor e^{at}, called an **integrating factor**. We then get the equivalent equation

$$\dot{x}e^{at} + axe^{at} = be^{at} \qquad (*)$$

It may not be obvious why we came up with this idea, but it turns out to be a good one because the left-hand side of $(*)$ happens to be the derivative of the product xe^{at}. Thus $(*)$ is equivalent to

$$\frac{d}{dt}(xe^{at}) = be^{at} \qquad (**)$$

According to the definition of the indefinite integral, equation $(**)$ holds for all t in an interval iff $xe^{at} = \int be^{at}\, dt = (b/a)e^{at} + C$ for some constant C. Multiplying this equation by e^{-at} gives the solution for x. Briefly formulated:

$$\dot{x} + ax = b \iff x = Ce^{-at} + \frac{b}{a} \qquad (C \text{ is a constant}) \qquad (3)$$

If we let $C = 0$ in (3), we obtain the constant solution $x(t) = b/a$. We say that $x = b/a$ is an *equilibrium state*, or a *stationary state*, for the equation. Observe how this solution can be obtained from $\dot{x} + ax = b$ by letting $\dot{x} = 0$ and then solving the resulting equation for x. If the constant a is positive, then the solution $x = Ce^{-at} + b/a$ converges to b/a as $t \to \infty$. In this case, the equation is said to be *stable*, because every solution of the equation converges to an equilibrium as t approaches infinity. See Section 5.7 for more on stability.

EXAMPLE 1   Find the general solution of

$$\dot{x} + 2x = 8$$

and determine whether the equation is stable.

Solution: By (3), the solution is $x = Ce^{-2t} + 4$. Here the equilibrium state is $x = 4$, and the equation is stable because $a = 2 > 0$, so $x \to 4$ as $t \to \infty$.

EXAMPLE 2   **(Price Adjustment Mechanism)** Let $D(P) = a - bP$ denote the demand and $S(P) = \alpha + \beta P$ the supply of a certain commodity when the price is P. Here a, b, α, and β are positive constants. Assume that the price $P = P(t)$ varies with time, and that $\dot{P}$ is proportional to excess demand $D(P) - S(P)$. Thus,

$$\dot{P} = \lambda[D(P) - S(P)]$$

where λ is a positive constant. Inserting the expressions for $D(P)$ and $S(P)$ into this equation gives $\dot{P} = \lambda(a - bP - \alpha - \beta P)$. Rearranging, we then obtain

$$\dot{P} + \lambda(b + \beta)P = \lambda(a - \alpha)$$

According to (3), the solution is

$$P = Ce^{-\lambda(b+\beta)t} + \frac{a - \alpha}{b + \beta}$$

Because $\lambda(b + \beta)$ is positive, as t tends to infinity, P converges to the equilibrium price $P^e = (a - \alpha)/(b + \beta)$, for which $D(P^e) = S(P^e)$. Thus, the equation is stable.

Variable Right-Hand Side

The method used to find the solution of (2) can immediately be applied to the following case of a variable right-hand side:

$$\dot{x} + ax = b(t)$$

Without further comment, after multiplying by the integrating factor e^{at}, we find:

$$\dot{x}e^{at} + axe^{at} = b(t)e^{at}, \quad \text{or equivalently} \quad \frac{d}{dt}(xe^{at}) = b(t)e^{at}, \text{ so}$$

$$xe^{at} = \int b(t)e^{at}\, dt + C$$

Multiplying the last equation by e^{-at} yields the solution for x:

$$\dot{x} + ax = b(t) \iff x = Ce^{-at} + e^{-at}\int e^{at}b(t)\, dt \tag{4}$$

EXAMPLE 3   **(Economic Growth)** Consider the following model of economic growth in a developing country:

(a) $X(t) = \sigma K(t)$ (b) $\dot{K}(t) = \alpha X(t) + H(t)$ (c) $N(t) = N_0 e^{\rho t}$

Here $X(t)$ is total domestic product per year, $K(t)$ is capital stock, $H(t)$ is the net inflow of foreign investment per year, and $N(t)$ is the size of the population, all measured at time t. In (a) we assume that the volume of production is simply proportional to the capital stock, with the factor of proportionality σ being called the *average productivity of capital*. In (b) we assume that the total growth of capital per year is equal to internal savings plus net foreign investment. We assume that savings are proportional to production, with the factor of proportionality α being called the *savings rate*. Finally, (c) tells us that population increases at a constant proportional rate of growth ρ.

Derive from these equations a differential equation for $K(t)$. Assume that $H(t) = H_0 e^{\mu t}$, and find the solution of the differential equation in this case, given that $K(0) = K_0$ and $\alpha\rho \neq \mu$. Find an expression for $x(t) = X(t)/N(t)$, which is domestic product per capita.

Solution: From (a) and (b), it follows that $K(t)$ must satisfy the linear equation

$$\dot{K}(t) - \alpha\sigma K(t) = H(t)$$

Put $H(t) = H_0 e^{\mu t}$ and use (4) to obtain

$$K(t) = Ce^{\alpha\sigma t} + e^{\alpha\sigma t}\int e^{-\alpha\sigma t}H_0 e^{\mu t}\, dt = Ce^{\alpha\sigma t} + e^{\alpha\sigma t}H_0\int e^{(\mu-\alpha\sigma)t}\, dt$$

$$= Ce^{\alpha\sigma t} + e^{\alpha\sigma t}\frac{H_0}{\mu - \alpha\sigma}e^{(\mu-\alpha\sigma)t} = Ce^{\alpha\sigma t} + \frac{H_0}{\mu - \alpha\sigma}e^{\mu t}$$

For $t = 0$, we obtain $K(0) = K_0 = C + H_0/(\mu - \alpha\sigma)$, so $C = K_0 - H_0/(\mu - \alpha\sigma)$. Thus, the solution is

$$K(t) = \left(K_0 - \frac{H_0}{\mu - \alpha\sigma}\right)e^{\alpha\sigma t} + \frac{H_0}{\mu - \alpha\sigma}e^{\mu t} \tag{*}$$

Per capita production is equal to $x(t) = X(t)/N(t) = \sigma K(t)/N_0 e^{\rho t}$. If we use the expression for $K(t)$ in (*), an easy calculation shows that

$$x(t) = x(0)e^{(\alpha\sigma - \rho)t} + \left(\frac{\sigma}{\alpha\sigma - \mu}\right)\frac{H_0}{N_0}e^{(\alpha\sigma - \rho)t}\left[1 - e^{(\mu - \alpha\sigma)t}\right] \tag{**}$$

Problem 11 asks you to study this model more closely.

The General Case

We proceed to find the solution of the general linear equation (1). The trick used to solve $\dot{x} + ax = b(t)$ must be modified. We first multiply equation (1) by a suitably chosen integrating factor $e^{A(t)}$, to obtain

$$\dot{x}e^{A(t)} + a(t)xe^{A(t)} = b(t)e^{A(t)} \tag{5}$$

Now we need to find an $A(t)$ such that the left-hand side of this equation equals the derivative of $xe^{A(t)}$. But the derivative of $xe^{A(t)}$ is equal to $\dot{x}e^{A(t)} + x\dot{A}(t)e^{A(t)}$. We therefore make $A(t)$ satisfy $\dot{A}(t) = a(t)$ by choosing $A(t) = \int a(t)\, dt$; this makes (5) equivalent to the equation

$$\frac{d}{dt}(xe^{A(t)}) = b(t)e^{A(t)}$$

Thus $xe^{A(t)}$ is an indefinite integral of $b(t)e^{A(t)}$, so there exists a constant C such that $xe^{A(t)} = \int b(t)e^{A(t)}\, dt + C$. Multiplying by $e^{-A(t)}$ we obtain

$$x = Ce^{-A(t)} + e^{-A(t)}\int b(t)e^{A(t)}\, dt, \quad \text{where} \quad A(t) = \int a(t)\, dt$$

To summarize, we have shown that:

$$\dot{x} + a(t)x = b(t) \iff x = e^{-\int a(t)\, dt}\left(C + \int e^{\int a(t)\, dt}b(t)\, dt\right) \tag{6}$$

EXAMPLE 4 Find the general solution of $\dot{x} + 2tx = 4t$ and the integral curve through $(t, x) = (0, -2)$.

Solution: The formula in (6) can be used with $a(t) = 2t$ and $b(t) = 4t$. Then $\int a(t)\, dt = \int 2t\, dt = t^2 + C_1$. We choose $C_1 = 0$ so that $\int a(t)\, dt = t^2$ (choosing another value for C_1 instead gives the same general solution). Then (6) gives

$$x = e^{-t^2}\left(C + \int e^{t^2}4t\, dt\right) = Ce^{-t^2} + e^{-t^2}2e^{t^2} = Ce^{-t^2} + 2$$

If $x = -2$ for $t = 0$, then $-2 = Ce^0 + 2$, and so $C = -4$. The integral curve through $(0, -2)$ has the equation $x = 2 - 4e^{-t^2}$.

The solution when x(t₀) = x₀ is given

Assume that the value of $x(t)$ is known for $t = t_0$. Then the constant C in (6) is determined. We derive here the formula for the corresponding solution of the equation, which is sometimes useful.

Define $F(t)$ as an indefinite integral of $b(t)e^{A(t)}$, where $A(t) = \int a(t)\, dt$ and so $A(t) - A(s) = \int_s^t a(\xi)\, d\xi$. The solution in (6) then becomes

$$x(t) = Ce^{-A(t)} + e^{-A(t)} F(t)$$

Now let $t = t_0$ and solve for C to get $C = x(t_0)e^{A(t_0)} - F(t_0)$. Hence,

$$x(t) = x(t_0)e^{-[A(t)-A(t_0)]} + e^{-A(t)}[F(t) - F(t_0)]$$

By definition of $F(t)$, we have $F(t) - F(t_0) = \int_{t_0}^t b(s)e^{A(s)}\, ds$. So

$$e^{-A(t)}[F(t) - F(t_0)] = e^{-A(t)}\int_{t_0}^t b(s)e^{A(s)}\, ds = \int_{t_0}^t b(s)e^{-[A(t)-A(s)]}\, ds$$

(We can include $e^{-A(t)}$ in the integrand, because we are integrating w.r.t. s.) Finally, therefore, we have the following result:

$$\dot{x} + a(t)x = b(t), \; x(t_0) = x_0 \iff x = x_0 e^{-\int_{t_0}^t a(\xi)\,d\xi} + \int_{t_0}^t b(s)e^{-\int_s^t a(\xi)\,d\xi}\, ds \tag{7}$$

Wealth Accumulation

As in Example 5.3.6, suppose that the amount of savings in an account at time t is $w = w(t)$. Suppose now that there are deposits and withdrawals at the rates $y(t)$ and $c(t)$, respectively. If there is continuous compounding of interest at the rate $r(t)$, then wealth at time t follows the differential equation

$$\dot{w} = r(t)w + y(t) - c(t) \tag{8}$$

This is clearly a first-order linear differential equation. According to (7), the solution is

$$w(t) = w(0)e^{\int_0^t r(s)\,ds} + \int_0^t [y(\tau) - c(\tau)]e^{\int_\tau^t r(s)\,ds}\, d\tau \tag{9}$$

Since $\int_\tau^t r(s)\,ds = \int_0^t r(s)\,ds - \int_0^\tau r(s)\,ds$, and since $\int_0^t r(s)\,ds$ is independent of τ, equation (9) can be written as:

$$w(t)e^{-\int_0^t r(s)\,ds} = w(0) + \int_0^t [y(\tau) - c(\tau)]e^{-\int_0^\tau r(s)\,ds}\, d\tau \tag{10}$$

This equation states that the present discounted value (PDV) of assets at time t is the sum of the initial assets $w(0)$ and the total PDV of all deposits, minus the total PDV of all withdrawals. Note that the discount factor to be applied to wealth at time τ is $e^{-\int_0^\tau r(s)\,ds}$.

If there are no deposits to or withdrawals from the account, then $y(t) = c(t) = 0$ and so (8) reduces to the separable equation $\dot{w} = r(t)w$. The general solution is $w = Ae^{\int r(t)\,dt}$.

PROBLEMS FOR SECTION 5.4

1. Find the general solution of $\dot{x} + \frac{1}{2}x = \frac{1}{4}$. Determine the equilibrium state of the equation, and examine whether it is stable. Also draw some typical integral curves.

2. Find the general solutions of the following linear differential equations:

   (a) $\dot{x} + x = 10$ (b) $\dot{x} - 3x = 27$ (c) $4\dot{x} + 5x = 100$

3. Find the general solution of $\dot{x} = x + t$. (See Example 5.1.1.)

4. Find the general solutions of the following differential equations, and in each case, find the integral curve through $(t, x) = (0, 1)$:

   (a) $\dot{x} - 3x = 5$ (b) $3\dot{x} + 2x + 16 = 0$ (c) $\dot{x} + 2x = t^2$

5. In a macroeconomic model $C(t)$, $I(t)$, and $Y(t)$ denote respectively the consumption, investment, and national income in a country at time t. Assume that, for all t:

   (i) $C(t) + I(t) = Y(t)$ (ii) $I(t) = k\dot{C}(t)$ (iii) $C(t) = aY(t) + b$

   where a, b, and k are positive constants, with $a < 1$.

   (a) Derive the following differential equation for $Y(t)$: $\dot{Y}(t) = \dfrac{1-a}{ka}Y(t) - \dfrac{b}{ka}$.

   (b) Solve this equation when $Y(0) = Y_0$, and then find the corresponding $I(t)$.

   (c) Compute $\lim_{t \to \infty}[Y(t)/I(t)]$ for $Y_0 \neq b/(1-a)$.

6. The equation in (3) is separable. Solve it as a separable differential equation, and show that you obtain the same solution as that given in (3).

7. Find the general solutions of the following differential equations:

   (a) $t\dot{x} + 2x + t = 0$ $(t \neq 0)$ (b) $\dot{x} - \dfrac{1}{t}x = t$ $(t > 0)$

   (c) $\dot{x} - \dfrac{t}{t^2 - 1}x = t$ $(t > 1)$ (d) $\dot{x} - \dfrac{2}{t}x + \dfrac{2a^2}{t^2} = 0$ $(t > 0)$

8. For the differential equation $\dot{x} = 2tx + t(1 + t^2)$, show that the solution $x(t)$ that passes through $(t, x) = (0, 0)$ has a local minimum at $t = 0$.

9. Prove that if $x(T) = x_T$, the solution to (1) can be expressed as

$$x(t) = x_T e^{\int_t^T a(\xi)\, d\xi} - \int_t^T b(\tau) e^{-\int_\tau^t a(\xi)\, d\xi}\, d\tau$$

HARDER PROBLEMS

10. Let $N = N(t)$ denote the size of a certain population, $X = X(t)$ the total product, and $x(t) = X(t)/N(t)$ the product per capita at time t. T. Haavelmo (1954) studied the model described by the equations:

$$\text{(i)} \quad \frac{\dot{N}}{N} = \alpha - \beta \frac{N}{X} \qquad \text{(ii)} \quad X = AN^a$$

where α, β, and a are positive constants, with $a \neq 1$. Show that this leads to a differential equation of the form (3) for $x = x(t)$. Solve this equation and then find expressions for $N = N(t)$ and $X = X(t)$. Examine the limits for $x(t)$, $N(t)$, and $X(t)$ as $t \to \infty$ in the case $0 < a < 1$.

11. Consider the model in Example 3.

(a) Let $H_0 = 0$ and then find the condition for the production per capita to increase with time. A common estimate for σ in developing countries is 0.3. If the population increases at the rate 3% per year ($\rho = 0.03$), how high must the savings rate α be for $x(t)$ to increase with time?

(b) Show that $x(t)$ given by (∗∗) is greater than $x(0)e^{(a\sigma - \rho)t}$ for all $t > 0$. (Look at the two cases $\alpha\sigma - \mu > 0$ and $\alpha\sigma - \mu < 0$ separately.) Why was this to be expected?

(c) Assume that $\alpha\sigma < \rho$. Find a necessary and sufficient condition to obtain *sustained* growth in production per capita. Give an economic interpretation.

5.5 Exact Equations and Integrating Factors

We started this chapter by studying the differential equation $\dot{x} = F(t, x)$. Only in very special cases can we find explicit analytical solutions—for example, when the equation is separable or when it is linear in x. In this section we study first-order equations of the form

$$f(t, x) + g(t, x)\dot{x} = 0 \tag{1}$$

where f and g are C^1 functions. (Of course, $\dot{x} = F(t, x)$ can be written in this form: $F(t, x) + (-1)\dot{x} = 0$.) Suppose we happen to find a function $h(t, x)$ such that

$$h'_t(t, x) = f(t, x) \qquad \text{and} \qquad h'_x(t, x) = g(t, x) \tag{2}$$

Note that $\frac{d}{dt}h(t, x) = h'_t(t, x) + h'_x(t, x)\dot{x}$. So if (2) is satisfied, equation (1) is equivalent to $\frac{d}{dt}h(t, x) = 0$, which is satisfied if and only if $h(t, x) = C$ for some constant C. The solutions of (1) are therefore those functions $x = x(t)$ that satisfy

$$h(t, x) = C, \qquad \text{for some constant } C \tag{3}$$

EXAMPLE 1   The differential equation

$$1 + tx^2 + t^2 x \dot{x} = 0 \qquad (*)$$

is neither separable nor linear. But we might just notice that the function $h(t, x) = t + \frac{1}{2} t^2 x^2$ has partial derivatives $h'_t(t, x) = 1 + tx^2$ and $h'_x(t, x) = t^2 x$. Then we see that the solution of $(*)$ is any differentiable function x defined implicitly by the equation $t + \frac{1}{2} t^2 x^2 = C$, for some constant C.

The key step in finding the solution of equation (1) having the form (3) is to determine an appropriate function h. Note first a necessary condition for the existence of such a function h. In fact, if $f(t, x) = h'_t(t, x)$ and $g(t, x) = h'_x(t, x)$, then $f'_x(t, x) = h''_{tx}(t, x)$ and $g'_t(t, x) = h''_{xt}(t, x)$. Hence, by Young's theorem on the equality of second-order cross derivatives,

$$f'_x(t, x) = g'_t(t, x) \qquad (4)$$

We shall show in a moment that (4) is also sufficient for the existence of a function h satisfying (2). Equation (1) is called **exact** if (4) is satisfied.

In Example 1, $f(t, x) = 1 + tx^2$ and $g(t, x) = t^2 x$, and we see that (4) is satisfied because $f'_x(t, x) = g'_t(t, x) = 2tx$, so the equation is exact. Note also that if we write the separable equation (5.3.1) as $f(t) - \dot{x}/g(x) = 0$, then condition (4) holds trivially.

Now, consider equation (1) and suppose that condition (4) is satisfied. Motivated by the first equation in (2), define the function h by

$$h(t, x) = \int_{t_0}^{t} f(\tau, x) \, d\tau + \alpha(x) \qquad (5)$$

where we need to choose $\alpha(x)$ appropriately. Differentiating (5) w.r.t. x and using (4) yields

$$h'_x(t, x) = \int_{t_0}^{t} f'_x(\tau, x) \, d\tau + \alpha'(x) = \int_{t_0}^{t} g'_t(\tau, x) \, d\tau + \alpha'(x) \qquad (6)$$

Now $\int_{t_0}^{t} g'_t(\tau, x) \, d\tau = g(t, x) - g(t_0, x)$. To make (6) easy to solve let us put

$$\alpha'(x) = g(t_0, x) \quad \text{with} \quad \alpha(x_0) = 0, \quad \text{so that} \quad \alpha(x) = \int_{x_0}^{x} g(t_0, \xi) \, d\xi \qquad (7)$$

Together (5) and (7) imply that the left-hand side of equation (3) takes the form

$$h(t, x) = \int_{t_0}^{t} f(\tau, x) \, d\tau + \int_{x_0}^{x} g(t_0, \xi) \, d\xi \qquad (8)$$

EXAMPLE 2   For equation $(*)$ in Example 1, $f(t, x) = 1 + tx^2$ and $g(t, x) = t^2 x$, so formula (8) yields

$$h(t, x) = \int_{t_0}^{t} (1 + \tau x^2) \, d\tau + \int_{x_0}^{x} t_0^2 \xi \, d\xi = \left. (\tau + \tfrac{1}{2} \tau^2 x^2) \right|_{t_0}^{t} + \tfrac{1}{2} \left. t_0^2 \xi^2 \right|_{x_0}^{x}$$

$$= t + \tfrac{1}{2} t^2 x^2 - t_0 - \tfrac{1}{2} t_0^2 x^2 + \tfrac{1}{2} t_0^2 x^2 - \tfrac{1}{2} t_0^2 x_0^2 = t + \tfrac{1}{2} t^2 x^2 - t_0 - \tfrac{1}{2} t_0^2 x_0^2$$

Except for the constant $t_0 - \frac{1}{2} t_0^2 x_0^2$, equation (3) gives the same answer as in Example 1.

Consider equation (1) again. If the equation is not already exact, one might wonder if it can be made so by multiplying it by a suitable function $\beta(t, x)$. In fact, the equation $\beta(t, x) f(t, x)$ $+ \beta(t, x) g(t, x) \dot{x} = 0$ is exact provided that $\dfrac{\partial}{\partial x}[\beta(t, x) f(t, x)] = \dfrac{\partial}{\partial t}[\beta(t, x) g(t, x)]$, or equivalently,

$$\beta'_x(t, x) f(t, x) + \beta(t, x) f'_x(t, x) = \beta'_t(t, x) g(t, x) + \beta(t, x) g'_t(t, x) \tag{9}$$

A function $\beta(t, x)$ satisfying (9) is called an **integrating factor** for the differential equation (1). In general it is hard to find such an integrating factor, even when one exists. But in two special cases it is relatively easy.

Case I: Suppose $(f'_x - g'_t)/g$ is a function of t alone. Then we can let $\beta(t, x) = \beta(t)$. In this case (9) reduces to $\beta(t) f'_x = \beta(t) g'_t + \beta'(t) g$. So

$$\beta'(t) = \beta(t)\frac{f'_x - g'_t}{g}, \quad \text{and hence} \quad \beta(t) = \exp\left(\int \frac{f'_x - g'_t}{g}\, dt\right) \tag{10}$$

Case II: Suppose $(g'_t - f'_x)/f$ is a function of x alone. Then we can let $\beta(t, x) = \beta(x)$. In this case (9) reduces to $f\beta'(x) + \beta(x) f'_x = \beta(x) g'_t$. So

$$\beta'(x) = \beta(x)\frac{g'_t - f'_x}{f}, \quad \text{and hence} \quad \beta(x) = \exp\left(\int \frac{g'_t - f'_x}{f}\, dx\right) \tag{11}$$

EXAMPLE 3   Solve the differential equation $1 - (t + 2x)\dot{x} = 0, t > 0, x > 0$.

Solution: (The equation is clearly equivalent to $\dot{x} = 1/(t + 2x)$, which is neither separable nor linear.) With $f(t, x) = 1$ and $g(t, x) = -t - 2x$ we get $(g'_t - f'_x)/f = -1$, which does not depend on t, so Case II applies. By (11), $\beta(x) = \exp(\int(-1)\, dx) = e^{-x}$ is an integrating factor. Hence, $e^{-x} - e^{-x}(t + 2x)\dot{x} = 0$ is exact, and (8) takes the form

$$h(t, x) = \int_{t_0}^{t} e^{-x}\, d\tau - \int_{x_0}^{x} e^{-\xi}(t_0 + 2\xi)\, d\xi = \left.t e^{-x}\right|_{t_0}^{t} + \left.e^{-\xi}(t_0 + 2\xi)\right|_{x_0}^{x} - \int_{x_0}^{x} 2e^{-\xi}\, d\xi$$

$$= t e^{-x} + 2x e^{-x} - e^{-x_0}(t_0 + 2x_0) + 2(e^{-x} - e^{-x_0})$$

where we have integrated by parts. The solution of the differential equation is then any differentiable function $x = x(t)$ that satisfies $h(t, x) = C$ for some constant C, or the equation $t e^{-x} + 2x e^{-x} + 2e^{-x} = C_1$ for some constant C_1.

PROBLEMS FOR SECTION 5.5

1. Solve the differential equation $2t + 3x^2\dot{x} = 0$, first as a separable equation, and second by considering it as an exact equation.

2. Solve the differential equation $1 + (2 + t/x)\dot{x} = 0, t > 0, x > 0$.

5.6   Transformation of Variables

Only very special types of differential equation have solutions given by explicit formulas. However, transforming the variables sometimes converts a seemingly insoluble differential equation into one of a familiar type that we already know how to solve.

One example is **Bernoulli's equation** which has the form

$$\dot{x} + a(t)x = b(t)x^r \tag{1}$$

where the exponent r is a fixed real number, and where $a(t)$ and $b(t)$ are given continuous functions.

If $r = 0$, the equation is linear, and if $r = 1$, it is separable, since $\dot{x} = (b(t) - a(t))x$. Suppose that $r \neq 1$, and let us look for a solution with $x(t) > 0$ for all t, so that the power x^r is always well defined. If we divide (1) by x^r, we obtain

$$x^{-r}\dot{x} + a(t)x^{1-r} = b(t) \tag{*}$$

Now introduce the transformation

$$z = x^{1-r} \tag{2}$$

of the variable x. Then $\dot{z} = (1 - r)x^{-r}\dot{x}$. Substituting this into (*) gives

$$\frac{1}{1-r}\dot{z} + a(t)z = b(t) \tag{3}$$

which is a linear differential equation for $z = z(t)$. Once $z(t)$ has been found, we can use (2) to determine $x(t) = z(t)^{1/(1-r)}$, which then becomes the solution of (1).

EXAMPLE 1   Solve the differential equation $\dot{x} = -tx + t^3 x^3$.

Solution: This is a Bernoulli equation with $r = 3$. As suggested by (2), we introduce the transformation $z = x^{1-3} = x^{-2}$. After rearranging, equation (3) then takes the form

$$\dot{z} - 2tz = -2t^3$$

This is a linear differential equation, and we can use formula (5.4.6) with $a(t) = -2t$. Because $\int a(t)\, dt = \int -2t\, dt = -t^2$, we get

$$z = Ce^{t^2} - 2e^{t^2} \int t^3 e^{-t^2}\, dt \tag{*}$$

If we substitute $u = -t^2$ in the last integral, then $du = -2t\, dt$ and we have

$$\int t^3 e^{-t^2}\, dt = \frac{1}{2}\int ue^u\, du = \frac{1}{2}ue^u - \frac{1}{2}e^u = -\frac{1}{2}t^2 e^{-t^2} - \frac{1}{2}e^{-t^2}$$

where we have used integration by parts. Now (*) yields

$$z = Ce^{t^2} - 2e^{t^2}\left(-\frac{1}{2}t^2 e^{-t^2} - \frac{1}{2}e^{-t^2}\right) = Ce^{t^2} + t^2 + 1$$

It follows that the original equation has the solutions

$$x = \pm z^{-1/2} = \pm \frac{1}{\sqrt{Ce^{t^2} + t^2 + 1}}$$

Here are two other examples of successful substitutions.

EXAMPLE 2   The differential equation

$$y' - 1 + 2x(y - x)^2 = 0 \qquad (*)$$

evidently has $y = x$ as one solution. Define $y = x + 1/z$, where z is a function of x, and show that this substitution leads to a separable differential equation for z. Solve this equation and then find the solution of $(*)$ that passes through the point $(x, y) = (0, -1/2)$. (Note that in this example x is the free variable and y is the unknown function, and we write y' for dy/dx.)

Solution: If $z \neq 0$, differentiating $y = x + 1/z$ w.r.t. x gives $y' = 1 - z'/z^2$. When we insert this into $(*)$ and reorganize, we obtain an equation that reduces to $z' = 2x$, with general solution $z = x^2 + C$. We are looking for the solution with $y = -1/2$ when $x = 0$. This gives $z = -2$ when $x = 0$, so $C = -2$. Hence the required solution is $y = x + 1/(x^2 - 2)$ (defined for $-\sqrt{2} < x < \sqrt{2}$).

EXAMPLE 3   Show that the substitution $z = x + t^2$ transforms the differential equation

$$\dot{x} = \frac{2t}{x + t^2} \qquad (*)$$

into a separable differential equation for z, and use this to find the general solution.

Solution: The suggested substitution implies that $\dot{x} = \dot{z} - 2t$. Inserting this into $(*)$ gives $\dot{z} - 2t = 2t/z$, hence

$$\dot{z} = 2t\left(1 + \frac{1}{z}\right) = 2t\frac{z + 1}{z}$$

This is a separable equation, and we use the recipe from Section 5.3. First we note the constant solution $z \equiv -1$. The other solutions are found in the usual way by separating the variables:

$$\int \frac{z}{z + 1} \, dz = \int 2t \, dt$$

Since $z/(z + 1) = (z + 1 - 1)/(z + 1) = 1 - 1/(z + 1)$, we obtain $z - \ln|z + 1| = t^2 + C_1$. If we now use $z = x + t^2$ and reorganize, we get $\ln|x + t^2 + 1| = x - C_1$, which gives

$$|x + t^2 + 1| = e^{-C_1}e^x, \quad \text{i.e.} \quad x + t^2 + 1 = \pm e^{-C_1}e^x$$

Hence, with $C = \pm e^{-C_1}$, these solutions are given implicitly by

$$x = Ce^x - t^2 - 1$$

The constant solution $z = -1$ gives $x = -t^2 - 1$, which corresponds to $C = 0$.

PROBLEMS FOR SECTION 5.6

1. Solve the following Bernoulli equations assuming $t > 0$, $x > 0$:

   (a) $t\dot{x} + 2x = tx^2$ (b) $\dot{x} = 4x + 2e^t \sqrt{x}$ (c) $t\dot{x} + x = x^2 \ln t$

2. Solve the differential equation $(1 + tx)\dot{x} = -x^2$. (*Hint:* Try the substitution $w = tx$.)

3. An economic growth model leads to the Bernoulli equation

   $$\dot{K} = \alpha A(n_0)^a e^{(av+\varepsilon)t} K^b - \alpha\delta K \quad (A, n_0, a, b, v, \alpha, \delta, \text{ and } \varepsilon \text{ are positive constants})$$

   Find the general solution of the equation when $av + \varepsilon + \alpha\delta(1 - b) \neq 0$ and $b \neq 1$.

4. An economic growth model by T. Haavelmo (1954) leads to the differential equation

   $$\dot{K} = \gamma_1 bK^\alpha + \gamma_2 K$$

   where γ_1, γ_2, b and α are positive constants, $\alpha \neq 1$ and $K = K(t)$ is the unknown function. The equation is separable, but solve it as a Bernoulli equation.

5. (a) Consider the equation

   $$t\dot{x} = x - f(t)x^2, \qquad t > 0 \tag{$*$}$$

   where f is a given continuous function, and $x = x(t)$ is the unknown function. Show that the substitution $x = tz$ transforms it into a separable equation in $z = z(t)$.

   (b) Let $f(t) = t^3/(t^4 + 2)$ and find the solution curve through the point $(1, 1)$.

6. Differential equations of the form $\dot{x} = g(x/t)$, where the right-hand side depends only on the ratio x/t, are called **projective**. Prove that if we substitute $z = x/t$, a projective equation becomes a separable equation with z as the unknown function. Use this method to solve the equation $3tx^2\dot{x} = x^3 + t^3$.

7. Find the general solution of the projective equation $\dot{x} = 1 + x/t - (x/t)^2$.

HARDER PROBLEMS

8. In general, differential equations of the form

   $$\dot{x} = P(t) + Q(t)x + R(t)x^2 \qquad \textbf{(Riccati's equation)}$$

   can only be solved numerically. But if we know a particular solution $u = u(t)$, the substitution $x = u + 1/z$ will transform the equation into a linear differential equation for z as a function of t. Prove this, and apply it to $t\dot{x} = x - (x - t)^2$.

5.7 Qualitative Theory and Stability

It is convenient when economic models involve differential equations that can be solved explicitly. In such cases, it is usually easy to study the properties of the solution. Because most kinds of differential equation do not have this nice property, however, many models involve equations whose solutions cannot be expressed in terms of elementary functions.

The theory we have discussed so far is insufficient for another reason. Any economic model is based on a number of assumptions. It is often desirable to make these assumptions as weak as possible without losing the essential aspects of the problem. If a differential equation appears in the model, it therefore typically contains unspecified parameters.

As a result, when a differential equation is used to describe some particular economic phenomenon, the typical situation is as follows:

A. It is impossible to obtain an explicit solution of the equation.

B. The equation contains unspecified parameters (or even unspecified functions).

Even so, there is often much that can be said about the nature of any solution to the differential equation. In this section, we discuss, in particular, the stability of any solution.

Autonomous Equations. Phase Diagrams

Many differential equations in economics can be expressed in the form

$$\dot{x} = F(x) \tag{1}$$

This is a special case of the equation $\dot{x} = F(t, x)$, in which t does not explicitly appear on the right-hand side. For this reason, the equation in (1) is called **autonomous**.

To examine the properties of the solutions to (1), it is useful to study its **phase diagram**. This is obtained by putting $y = \dot{x}$ and drawing the curve $y = F(x)$ in the xy-plane (or $x\dot{x}$-plane). An example is indicated in Fig. 1.

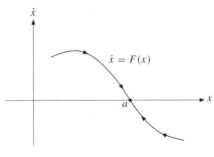

Figure 1

Any solution $x = x(t)$ of (1) has an associated $\dot{x} = \dot{x}(t)$. For every t, the pair $(x(t), \dot{x}(t))$ is a point on the curve in the phase diagram. What can be said generally about this point when t increases? If we consider a point on the curve lying above the x-axis, then $F(x(t)) > 0$ and therefore $\dot{x}(t) = F(x(t)) > 0$, so that $x(t)$ increases with t. *It follows from this observation* *that the point $(x(t), \dot{x}(t))$ moves from left to right in the diagram if we are above the x-axis. On the other hand, if we are at a point on the graph below the x-axis, then $\dot{x}(t) < 0$, and $x(t)$ decreases with t, so we move from right to left.* These movements are indicated by arrows in Fig. 1.

Stability

One of the most important properties of a differential equation is whether it has any *equilibrium* or *stationary states*. These correspond to solutions of the equation that do not change over time. In many economic applications, it is also very important to know whether an equilibrium state is *stable*. This can often be determined even if we cannot find explicit solutions of the equation. In physics, the rest position of a pendulum (hanging downward and motionless) is stable; if it is slightly disturbed while in this position, it will swing back and forth until it gradually approaches the equilibrium state of rest. To use a common analogy, we do not expect to encounter an unstable equilibrium in the real world for the same reason that a pin will not balance on its point.

In general, we say that a point a represents an **equilibrium state** or a **stationary state** for equation (1) if $F(a) = 0$. In this case, $x(t) \equiv a$ is a solution of the equation. If $x(t_0) = a$ for some value t_0 of t, then $x(t)$ is equal to a for all t.

The example of Fig. 1 has one equilibrium state, a. It is called **globally asymptotically stable**, because if $x(t)$ is a solution to $\dot{x} = F(x)$ with $x(t_0) = x_0$, then $x(t)$ will always converge to the point on the x-axis with $x = a$ for any start point (t_0, x_0).

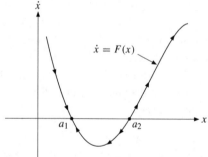

Figure 2 a_1 is a locally stable equilibrium state for $\dot{x} = F(x)$, whereas a_2 is unstable.

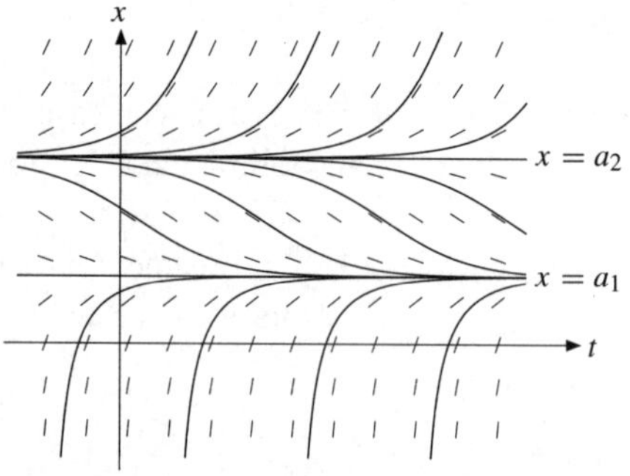

Figure 3   A corresponding directional diagram and some solution curves for $\dot{x} = F(x)$.

In Fig. 2 there are two equilibrium states, a_1 and a_2. If we are in either of these states, then we will remain there. However, there is an important difference between the two. If $x(t)$ starts close to a_1, but not at a_1, then $x(t)$ will approach a_1 as t increases. On the other hand, if $x(t)$ starts close to, but not at a_2, then $x(t)$ will move away from a_2 as t increases. We say that a_1 is a **locally asymptotically stable equilibrium state,** whereas a_2 is **unstable.**

Look at Fig. 2 again. Note that at the stable point a_1, the graph of $\dot{x} = F(x)$ has a negative slope, whereas the slope is positive at a_2. Suppose that a is an equilibrium state for $\dot{x} = F(x)$, so that $F(a) = 0$. If $F'(a) < 0$, then $F(x)$ is positive to the left of $x = a$, and negative to the right. The situation around a is then similar to that around a_1, and a is therefore stable. On the other hand, if $F'(a) > 0$, then the situation around a is similar to the situation around a_2 in the figure. Hence, a is unstable. We have the following result:

(a) $F(a) = 0$ and $F'(a) < 0 \Rightarrow a$ is a locally asymptotically stable equilibrium.

(b) $F(a) = 0$ and $F'(a) > 0 \Rightarrow a$ is an unstable equilibrium.

$$(2)$$

If $F(a) = 0$ and $F'(a) = 0$, then (2) is inconclusive. You should now give two different examples showing that a can be locally stable or locally unstable in this case.

EXAMPLE 1   The following equation, which was studied in Section 5.4,

$$\dot{x} + ax = b \qquad (a \neq 0)$$

is a special case of (1), with $F(x) = b - ax$. In this case, there is *one* equilibrium state, at $x = b/a$, where $F'(x) = -a$. According to (2), $x = b/a$ is locally asymptotically stable if $a > 0$, but unstable if $a < 0$. Compare this result with the remarks following equation (5.4.3).

EXAMPLE 2   **(Price Adjustment Mechanism)** We generalize Example 5.4.2 and assume that the price $P = P(t)$ satisfies the nonlinear differential equation

$$\dot{P} = H(D(P) - S(P)) \qquad (*)$$

As before, $\dot{P}$ is a function of the excess demand $D(P) - S(P)$. We assume that the function H satisfies $H(0) = 0$ and $H' > 0$, so that H is strictly increasing. If demand is greater than supply when the price is P, then $D(P) - S(P) > 0$, so $\dot{P} > 0$, and the price increases. On the other hand, the price decreases when $D(P) - S(P) < 0$. Equation $(*)$ therefore represents what can be called a *price adjustment mechanism*.

Assume P^e is an equilibrium price for $(*)$, so that $H(D(P^e) - S(P^e)) = 0$, and hence $D(P^e) - S(P^e) = 0$. At the equilibrium price P^e, demand is equal to supply. If we put $F(P) = H(D(P) - S(P))$, then $F'(P) = H'(D(P) - S(P))(D'(P) - S'(P))$. Because $H' > 0$, we see that $F'(P)$ has the same sign as $D'(P) - S'(P)$. If we use (2), we see that the equilibrium price P^e is *stable* if $D'(P^e) - S'(P^e) < 0$. This condition is usually satisfied because we expect that $D' < 0$ and $S' > 0$.

EXAMPLE 3   **(Solow's Growth Model)** This "neoclassical" growth model is based on the differential equation

$$\dot{k} = sf(k) - \lambda k \qquad (3)$$

Here the unknown function $k = k(t)$ denotes capital per worker, $s > 0$ denotes the constant rate of saving, f is a production function (national product per worker as a function of capital per worker), and $\lambda > 0$ denotes the constant proportional rate of growth of the number of workers.

Note that (3) is a separable equation. But because f is not specified, we still cannot find an explicit solution of the equation. Assume that the phase diagram for equation (3) is as shown in Fig. 4. Then there is a unique equilibrium state with $k^* > 0$. It is given by

$$sf(k^*) = \lambda k^* \tag{4}$$

By studying Fig. 4 we see that k^* is stable. No matter what the initial capital per worker $k(0)$ has been, $k(t) \to k^*$ as $t \to \infty$.

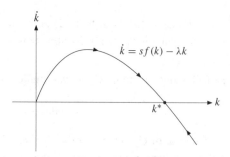

Figure 4 Phase diagram for (3), with appropriate conditions on f.

Here is a more detailed model that leads to equation (3). Let $X(t)$ denote national income, $K(t)$ capital, and $L(t)$ the number of workers in a country at time t. Assume that

(i) $X(t) = F(K(t), L(t))$ (ii) $\dot{K}(t) = sX(t)$ (iii) $L(t) = L_0 e^{\lambda t}$

where F is a production function, and s is the rate of savings. Assume that F is homogeneous of degree 1, so that $F(K, L) = LF(K/L, 1)$ for all K and L. Define $k(t) = K(t)/L(t) = $ capital per worker, and $f(k) = F(k, 1) = F(K/L, 1) = F(K, L)/L = $ output per worker. Then $\dot{k}/k = (d/dt)(\ln k) = (d/dt)(\ln K - \ln L)$, and so

$$\frac{\dot{k}}{k} = \frac{\dot{K}}{K} - \frac{\dot{L}}{L} = \frac{sF(K, L)}{K} - \lambda = \frac{sLf(k)}{K} - \lambda = \frac{sf(k)}{k} - \lambda \tag{iv}$$

from which (3) follows at once.

NOTE 1   Let us briefly discuss sufficient conditions for the existence and uniqueness of an equilibrium in the Solow model. It is usual to assume that $f(0) = 0$, as well as that $f'(k) > 0$ and $f''(k) < 0$ for all $k > 0$. It is also common to postulate the so-called *Inada conditions*,[2] according to which $f'(k) \to \infty$ as $k \to 0$ and also $f'(k) \to 0$ as $k \to \infty$.

To see why these conditions are sufficient, define $G(k) = sf(k) - \lambda k$. Then $G'(k) = sf'(k) - \lambda$, and equation (3) changes to $\dot{k} = G(k)$. The assumptions on f imply that $G(0) = 0$, $G'(k) \to \infty$ as $k \to 0$, $G'(k) \to -\lambda < 0$ as $k \to \infty$, and $G''(k) = sf''(k) < 0$ for all $k > 0$. So G has a unique stationary point $\hat{k} > 0$ at which $G'(\hat{k}) = 0$. Obviously, $G(\hat{k}) > 0$. But $G'(k) < -\frac{1}{2}\lambda < 0$ for all large enough k. It follows that $G(k) \to -\infty$ as $k \to \infty$, so there is a unique point $k^* > 0$ with $G(k^*) = 0$. In addition, $G'(k^*) < 0$. According to (2), this is a sufficient condition for the local asymptotic stability of k^*.

---

[2] Named after the Japanese economist K.-I. Inada, who introduced them into growth theory.

General Results on Autonomous Equations

Figure 3 shows some solution curves for $\dot{x} = F(x)$ graphed in Fig. 2. It seems that given the graph of one solution curve, the others are obtained by shifting that curve horizontally to the right or to the left. This is confirmed by the following: If $x = \varphi(t)$ is a solution of $\dot{x} = F(x)$, so is $x = \varphi(t + c)$ for any constant c, because $\dot{x} = \dot{\varphi}(t + c) = F(\varphi(t + c))$.

Note how Fig. 3 displays two constant (equilibrium) solutions, corresponding to the zeros a_1 and a_2 of the function F, while all the other solutions seem to be either strictly increasing or strictly decreasing in the intervals where they are defined. This behaviour of the solutions of $\dot{x} = F(x)$ turns out to be typical provided F is a C^1 function. To prove this result we use Theorem 5.8.1 in the next section, which says that when F is C^1, there is one and only one solution curve passing through a given point (t_0, x_0) in the tx-plane.

THEOREM 5.7.1

If F is a C^1 function, every solution of the autonomous differential equation $\dot{x} = F(x)$ is either constant or strictly monotone on the interval where it is defined.

Proof: Suppose first that x is a solution such that $\dot{x}(t_0) = 0$ for some t_0, and put $a = x(t_0)$. Then $F(a) = F(x(t_0)) = \dot{x}(t_0) = 0$, so a is a zero of F. The constant function $x_a(t) \equiv a$ is then another solution. Because both $x(t)$ and $x_a(t)$ pass through the same point (t_0, a) in the tx-plane, it follows that $x(t) = x_a(t) = a$ for all t. Hence x is a constant function. (See Note 5.8.2.)

If x is not a constant solution, then $\dot{x}(t) \neq 0$ for all t in the domain of x. Because x is differentiable and F is continuous, the derivative $\dot{x}(t) = F(x(t))$ is a continuous function of t. It follows that $\dot{x}$ must have the same sign everywhere in its domain, otherwise the intermediate value theorem would give us a zero for $\dot{x}$. Hence $\dot{x}$ is either positive everywhere or negative everywhere, and x itself must be either strictly increasing everywhere or strictly decreasing everywhere. ∎

Assume still that F is C^1. Then two different solution curves for $\dot{x} = F(x)$ cannot have common points (Theorem 5.8.1). (This holds also in the nonautonomous case.) In the present autonomous case, all solution curves crossing any given line parallel to the t axis have the same slope at the crossing points.

Let us return to the example illustrated in Fig. 2. The straight lines $x = a_1$ and $x = a_2$ in the phase diagram of Fig. 3 are solution curves. Hence no other solution curve can cross either of these lines. Consider a solution $x = \varphi(t)$ that passes through a point (t_0, x_0) where $a_1 < x_0 < a_2$. Then $\varphi(t)$ must lie in the interval (a_1, a_2) for *all* t, so φ is strictly decreasing with lower bound a_1. This implies that $\varphi(t)$ must approach a limit as t approaches infinity. It is reasonable to expect (and it follows from Theorem 5.7.2 below) that the limit $a = \lim_{t \to \infty} \varphi(t)$ must be an equilibrium state for the equation $\dot{x} = F(x)$. Since there are no equilibrium states in the open interval (a_1, a_2), we must actually have $a = a_1$. Similarly we see that a solution that lies below a_1 will grow towards a_1 in the limit as $t \to \infty$. A solution with $x > a_2$ will tend to infinity, unless there are other equilibrium states larger than a_2.

THEOREM 5.7.2 (A CONVERGENT SOLUTION CONVERGES TO AN EQUILIBRIUM)

Suppose that $x = x(t)$ is a solution of $\dot{x} = F(x)$, where the function F is continuous. Suppose that $x(t)$ approaches a (finite) limit a as t approaches ∞. Then a must be an equilibrium state for the equation—i.e. $F(a) = 0$.

Proof: For a contradiction, suppose $F(a) > 0$. Since F is continuous, there exists a $\delta > 0$ such that $|F(x) - F(a)| < \frac{1}{2}F(a)$ for all x in $(a - \delta, a + \delta)$. In particular, $F(x) > \frac{1}{2}F(a)$ for all x in this interval. Since $\lim_{t \to \infty} x(t) = a$, there must exist a T such that $x(t)$ lies in $(a - \delta, a + \delta)$ for all $t > T$. For $t > T$ we then have $\dot{x}(t) = F(x(t)) > \frac{1}{2}F(a)$. Hence, $x(t) - x(T) = \int_T^t \dot{x}(\tau)\,d\tau > \frac{1}{2}F(a)(t - T)$. But the last expression tends to ∞ as $t \to \infty$. It follows that $x(t)$ also tends to ∞ as $t \to \infty$, contrary to $x(t)$ being in the interval $(a - \delta, a + \delta)$. Therefore we cannot have $F(a) > 0$. A similar argument shows that we cannot have $F(a) < 0$ either. Hence, $F(a) = 0$. ∎

PROBLEMS FOR SECTION 5.7

1. Draw phase diagrams associated with the differential equations and determine the nature of the possible equilibrium states.

   (a) $\dot{x} = x - 1$ (b) $\dot{x} + 2x = 24$ (c) $\dot{x} = x^2 - 9$

2. Determine the nature of the possible equilibrium states for:

   (a) $\dot{x} = x^3 + x^2 - x - 1$ (b) $\dot{x} = 3x^2 + 1$ (c) $\dot{x} = xe^x$

3. Consider the differential equation $\dot{x} = \frac{1}{2}(x^2 - 1)$, $x(0) = x_0$.

   (a) Find the solution of this separable differential equation, and draw some integral curves in the tx-plane. What happens to the solution as $t \to \infty$ for different initial points x_0?

   (b) Draw the phase diagram for the equation. Find the two equilibrium states. Decide whether they are stable or unstable. Compare with the results in part (a).

HARDER PROBLEMS

4. (a) The stationary state k^* defined by (4) in Example 3 depends on s and λ. Find expressions for $\partial k^*/\partial s$ and $\partial k^*/\partial \lambda$ and determine the signs of these derivatives when f is strictly concave. (Show that in this case $sf'(k^*) < \lambda$.) Give an economic interpretation of the result. Prove that $F_K'(K, L) = f'(k)$.

   (b) Consumption per worker c is defined by $c = (X - \dot{K})/L$. Show that when $k = k^*$, then $c = f(k^*) - \lambda k^*$. Use this to show that if consumption per worker in the stationary state is to be maximized, it is necessary that $f'(k^*) = \lambda$, that is, $\partial F/\partial K = \lambda$. Thus, the marginal product of capital $\partial F/\partial K$ must equal the relative rate of growth of the number of workers. (This is often called "the golden rule of accumulation.")

   (c) Show that in the stationary state, $\dot{K}/K$ is equal to λ.

5.8 Existence and Uniqueness

For an economic model to be consistent, the equations in that model must have a solution. This is no less true when the model involves one or more differential equations. Also, if a solution does exist that satisfies the relevant initial conditions, we want to know whether the solution is unique.

Answers to such questions are provided by existence and uniqueness theorems. For first-order equations, one has the following result (which is implied by the more general Theorem 5.8.2 below).

THEOREM 5.8.1 (EXISTENCE AND UNIQUENESS I)

Consider the first-order differential equation

$$\dot{x} = F(t, x)$$

and suppose that both $F(t, x)$ and $F'_x(t, x)$ are continuous in an open set A in the tx-plane. Let (t_0, x_0) be an arbitrary point in A. Then there exists exactly one "local" solution of the equation that passes through the point (t_0, x_0).

In order to focus attention on the main points of the theorem, it has been stated rather loosely. Let us be more specific.

NOTE 1 If the conditions in the theorem are met, and (t_0, x_0) is an arbitrary point in A, then there exist an interval (a, b) around t_0, and a function $x(t)$ defined in (a, b), such that $x(t)$ is a solution of the equation in (a, b) with $x(t_0) = x_0$ and $(t, x(t)) \in A$ for all t in (a, b). Note that the theorem guarantees only the *existence* of an interval as described; the length of the interval could be very small. For this reason Theorem 5.8.1 is a *local* existence theorem; it ensures the existence of a solution only in a small neighbourhood of t_0.

NOTE 2 As for uniqueness, one can prove that if $x(t)$ and $y(t)$ are solutions of the equation lying in A with $x(t_0) = y(t_0)$, then $x(t) = y(t)$ for all t at which both solutions are defined.

EXAMPLE 1   If $F(t, x) = ax$, the equation in the theorem is $\dot{x} = ax$. In this case, the functions $F(t, x) = ax$ and $F'_x(t, x) = a$ are continuous everywhere. Theorem 5.8.1 implies that there is a unique solution curve passing through each point (t_0, x_0). In fact, the required solution is $x(t) = x(t_0)e^{a(t-t_0)}$.

EXAMPLE 2   Let $F(t, x) = f(t)g(x)$. It follows from Theorem 5.8.1 that existence and uniqueness are ensured if $f(t)$ is continuous and $g(x)$ is continuously differentiable.

As pointed out in Note 1, Theorem 5.8.1 gives no information about the length of the interval on which the solution is defined. One factor which can limit this interval is that $x = x(t)$ can grow so fast that the solution "explodes" to infinity even while t remains bounded.

EXAMPLE 3   Find the largest interval on which there is a solution of $\dot{x} = x^2$ with $x(0) = 1$.

Solution: Any nonzero solution of this separable equation is of the form $x = -1/(t+C)$. Because $x(0) = 1$ gives $C = -1$, the solution is $x = 1/(1 - t)$, defined on $(-\infty, 1)$. The solution curve is shown in Fig. 1. The graph "runs off to ∞" as t approaches 1 from the left, and this solution cannot be extended beyond $(-\infty, 1)$. (The function $x = 1/(1 - t)$ also satisfies $\dot{x} = x^2$ for $t > 1$, but this is not part of the solution satisfying $x(0) = 1$.)

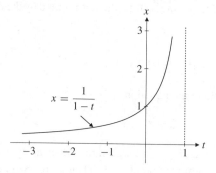

Figure 1   **Figure 2**

The following more precise result specifies an interval on which a solution is defined. A proof is given in Section 14.3.

THEOREM 5.8.2 (EXISTENCE AND UNIQUENESS II)

Consider the initial value problem

$$\dot{x} = F(t, x), \qquad x(t_0) = x_0 \tag{1}$$

Suppose that $F(t, x)$ and $F'_x(t, x)$ are continuous over the rectangle

$$\Gamma = \{ (t, x) : |t - t_0| \le a, \; |x - x_0| \le b \}$$

and let

$$M = \max_{(t,x)\in\Gamma} |F(t, x)|, \qquad r = \min(a, b/M) \tag{2}$$

Then (1) has a unique solution $x(t)$ on $(t_0 - r, t_0 + r)$, and $|x(t) - x_0| \le b$ in this interval.

NOTE 3 It may well be that the solution in Theorem 5.8.2 can be extended to a larger interval than that described in the theorem. Note that the length of this interval is determined by the number r, the smaller of the numbers a and b/M. Of course, we cannot expect r to be larger than a, and the inequality $r \le b/M$ ensures that the solution $x(t)$ will stay inside the rectangle Γ. Because $-M \le \dot{x} \le M$ as long as $(t, x) \in \Gamma$, the part of any solution curve through (t_0, x_0) that is contained in Γ must lie between the two straight lines through (t_0, x_0) with slopes $\pm M$, as illustrated in Fig. 2.

EXAMPLE 4   Prove that

$$\dot{x} = 3t^2 - te^{-x^2}, \qquad x(0) = 0$$

has a unique solution on the interval $(-\frac{1}{2}, \frac{1}{2})$, and that $|x(t)| \le 1$ in this interval.

Solution: We use the notation of Theorem 5.8.2 with $a = \frac{1}{2}$ and $b = 1$. The rectangle Γ is $\Gamma = \{(t, x) : |t| \le \frac{1}{2}, |x| \le 1\}$. Note that $|F(t, x)| = |3t^2 - te^{-x^2}| \le 3t^2 + |t|e^{-x^2} \le 3/4 + 1/2 = 5/4$ for all (t, x) in Γ. The desired conclusion follows from Theorem 5.8.2, with $M = 5/4$ and $r = \min\{1/2, 1/(5/4)\} = 1/2$.

EXAMPLE 5   Consider the initial value problem $\dot{x} = F(t, x)$, $x(t_0) = x_0$ in Theorem 5.8.2, and suppose that F and F'_x are continuous everywhere. Assume too that F is uniformly bounded—i.e. there exists a number M such that $|F(t, x)| \le M$ for all (t, x). Then Theorem 5.8.2 applies with $r = \min(a, b/M)$. But under these assumptions r can be made arbitrarily large by choosing a and b sufficiently large. Hence, there exists a unique solution $x(t)$ defined on the whole of $(-\infty, \infty)$—i.e. we have **global** existence.

Picard's Method of Successive Approximations

Here is a brief indication of how to prove Theorem 5.8.2 which simultaneously suggests a method to construct an approximate solution of $\dot{x} = F(t, x)$ with $x(t_0) = x_0$.

Define the sequence of functions $\{x_n(t)\}$, $n = 0, 1, 2, \ldots$, by letting $x_0(t) \equiv x_0$, and

$$x_n(t) = x_0 + \int_{t_0}^{t} F(s, x_{n-1}(s)) \, ds, \qquad n = 1, 2, \ldots \tag{$*$}$$

Assuming that F and F'_x are continuous, one can show that under the hypotheses of Theorem 5.8.2, the sequence $x_n(t)$ is well defined and converges uniformly[3] to a function $x(t)$ satisfying $|x(t) - x_0| \le b$ for all t in $(t_0 - r, t_0 + r)$. As $n \to \infty$, the left-hand side of $(*)$ converges to $x(t)$ for each t in $(t_0 - r, t_0 + r)$, whereas it can be shown that the right-hand side converges to $x_0 + \int_{t_0}^{t} F(s, x(s)) \, ds$. So $x(t) = \int_{t_0}^{t} F(s, x(s)) \, ds$ for all t in $(t_0 - r, t_0 + r)$. Differentiating this equation w.r.t. t yields $\dot{x}(t) = F(t, x(t))$. Moreover, $x(t_0) = x_0$, so $x(t)$ *is* a solution of (1).

EXAMPLE 6   Use Picard's method to solve the initial value problem

$$\dot{x} = t + x, \qquad x(0) = 0 \tag{$*$}$$

Solution: Here $F(t, x) = t + x$, so $x_0(t) \equiv 0$ and then

$$x_1(t) = 0 + \int_0^t F(s, x_0(s)) \, ds = \int_0^t (s + 0) \, ds = \frac{1}{2}t^2$$

$$x_2(t) = 0 + \int_0^t F(s, x_1(s)) \, ds = \int_0^t \left(s + \frac{1}{2}s^2\right) ds = \frac{1}{2!}t^2 + \frac{1}{3!}t^3$$

$$x_3(t) = 0 + \int_0^t F(s, x_2(s)) \, ds = \int_0^t \left(s + \frac{1}{2!}s^2 + \frac{1}{3!}s^3\right) ds = \frac{1}{2!}t^2 + \frac{1}{3!}t^3 + \frac{1}{4!}t^4$$

---

[3] See Protter and Morrey (1991), Section 9.3 for the definition of uniform convergence.

By induction on n one can verify that the general expression for $x_n(t)$ is

$$x_n(t) = \frac{1}{2!}t^2 + \frac{1}{3!}t^3 + \cdots + \frac{1}{(n+1)!}t^{n+1} \qquad (**)$$

But $e^t = 1 + \frac{1}{1!}t + \frac{1}{2!}t^2 + \frac{1}{3!}t^3 + \cdots$ (see e.g. EMEA). So as $n \to \infty$, we get

$$x_n(t) \to e^t - 1 - t$$

The required solution of $(*)$ is therefore $x(t) = \lim_{n\to\infty} x_n(t) = e^t - 1 - t$. (Check this solution by verifying directly that $(*)$ is satisfied.)

Global Existence

In many dynamic economic models one is interested in establishing the existence of a solution of a differential equation in a prescribed interval. For example, in the standard Solow growth model that leads to the differential equation $\dot{k} = sf(k) - \lambda k$ for capital per worker (see Example 5.7.3), we would like to know whether there is a solution defined on the whole interval $[0, \infty)$.[4] Example 5 supplied a set of sufficient conditions for global existence, but the following result is much more powerful. (See Hartman (1982).)

THEOREM 5.8.3 (GLOBAL EXISTENCE AND UNIQUENESS)

Consider the initial value problem

$$\dot{x} = F(t, x), \qquad x(t_0) = x_0$$

Suppose that $F(t, x)$ and $F'_x(t, x)$ are continuous for all (t, x). Suppose too that there exist continuous functions $a(t)$ and $b(t)$ such that

$$|F(t, x)| \le a(t)|x| + b(t) \quad \text{for all } (t, x) \tag{3}$$

Given an arbitrary point (t_0, x_0), there exists a unique solution $x(t)$ of the initial value problem, defined on $(-\infty, \infty)$. If (3) is replaced by the condition

$$xF(t, x) \le a(t)|x|^2 + b(t) \quad \text{for all } x \text{ and for all } t \ge t_0 \tag{4}$$

then the initial value problem has a unique solution defined on $[t_0, \infty)$.

NOTE 4   Condition (3) implies that $|\dot{x}|$ is bounded by a linear function of $|x|$. The requirement in (4) is more sophisticated. It is related to the fact that the problem of $x(t)$ "exploding" is only relevant if the product $xF(t, x) = x\dot{x}$ is large and positive: If $x(t)$ is large and $\dot{x}(t) = F(t, x(t))$ is also large, then we are in trouble. However, if $x(t)$ is large and $\dot{x}(t) = F(t, x(t))$ is negative, then $x(t)$ decreases as t increases.

Condition (3) really is stronger than (4). To see why, note first that $|x| \le 1 + |x|^2$ for all x (because $u \le 1 + u^2$ for all u). Suppose that (3) holds. Then

$$xF(t, x) \le |x|\,|F(t, x)| \le a(t)|x|^2 + b(t)|x|$$
$$\le a(t)|x|^2 + b(t)(1 + |x|^2) = (a(t) + b(t))|x|^2 + b(t)$$

---

[4] In fact, the behaviour of a solution as $t \to \infty$ has been studied extensively in the economic literature, but the existence problem is usually ignored.

which is precisely an inequality of the type (4). Example 7 presents a case where (4) is satisfied, but not (3).

NOTE 5 Here is a brief explanation of why the weaker condition (4) ensures global existence for $t \geq t_0$: Any solution must satisfy $(d/dt)(x(t)^2) = 2x(t)\dot{x}(t) \leq 2a(t)x(t)^2 + 2b(t)$. But by (5.4.6), the linear equation $\dot{y}(t) = 2a(t)y(t) + 2b(t)$ with $y(t_0) = x(t_0)^2$ has a solution for all $t \geq t_0$. Because $(d/dt)(x(t)^2) \leq \dot{y}(t)$ and $x(t_0)^2 = y(t_0)$, it follows that $(d/dt)[x(t)^2 - y(t)] \leq 0$, and so $x(t)^2 \leq y(t)$ for all $t \geq t_0$. Therefore $[x(t)]^2$ does not explode. This makes it plausible that $x(t)$ is defined for all t.

NOTE 6 Condition (3) will be satisfied if for all (t, x),

$$|F'_x(t, x)| \leq c(t) \quad \text{for some continuous function } c(t) \tag{5}$$

According to the mean-value theorem (see e.g. Theorem 2.1.2), $F(t, x) - F(t, 0) = F'_x(t, \theta)x$ for some θ in $[0, x]$. Hence, $|F(t, x)| = |F'_x(t, \theta)x + F(t, 0)| \leq |F'_x(t, \theta)| |x| + |F(t, 0)| \leq a(t)|x| + b(t)$ if we let $a(t) = c(t)$ and $b(t) = |F(t, 0)|$.

EXAMPLE 7 Examine whether Theorem 5.8.3 applies to the problem $\dot{x} = -x^3$, $x(1) = 1$.

Solution: Clearly (3) is not satisfied. But $xF(t, x) = x(-x^3) = -x^4 \leq 0$, so (4) is satisfied with $a(t) \equiv b(t) \equiv 0$. Hence, there exists a solution on $[1, \infty)$. (In fact, this separable equation has the unique solution $x(t) = (2t - 1)^{-1/2}$. This solution is valid only for $t > 1/2$, not for all of $(-\infty, \infty)$.)

EXAMPLE 8 Consider once again the Solow model of Example 5.7.3, with

$$\dot{k} = sf(k) - \lambda k, \qquad k(0) = k_0 > 0 \tag{*}$$

Suppose that $f'(0) < \infty$, $f(0) = 0$, $f'(k) \to 0$ as $k \to \infty$, and $f''(k) \leq 0$ for all $k \geq 0$. This implies that $f'(k) \leq f'(0)$ for all $k \geq 0$, and the phase diagram is as in Figure 5.7.4 with two equilibrium states, 0 and k^*. Define $F(k)$ for all k by

$$F(k) = \begin{cases} sf(k) - \lambda k, & k \geq 0 \\ sf'(0)k - \lambda k, & k < 0 \end{cases}$$

Note that for $k \geq 0$, $F(k)$ equals $\dot{k}$, as given by (*). Also, for $k \geq 0$, we have $F'(k) = sf'(k) - \lambda \leq sf'(0) - \lambda$, and for $k < 0$, we have $F'(k) = sf'(0) - \lambda$. Furthermore, $F'(k) \geq -\lambda$ for all k. Therefore the equation $\dot{k} = F(k)$ satisfies condition (5) with $c(t) = \max(\lambda, sf'(0) - \lambda)$. We conclude that the equation has a unique solution on $(-\infty, \infty)$.

The functions $k_1(t) \equiv 0$ and $k_2(t) \equiv k^*$ are both solutions of (*). If $k(t)$ is any solution with $k(0) = k_0 \in (0, k^*)$, then because these curves cannot intersect, $k(t)$ will always lie in the interval $(0, k^*)$, as in the discussion that follows Theorem 5.7.1.

NOTE 7 Suppose we drop the requirement in Theorems 5.8.1 to 5.8.3 that $F'_x(t, x)$ be continuous, but retain all the other conditions. Then a solution will still exist, but may not be unique. To ensure uniqueness, the following weaker requirement is sufficient: $F(t, x)$ is *locally Lipschitz continuous* w.r.t. x in A in the sense that, for each (t, x) in A, there exists a neighbourhood N of (t, x) in $\mathbb{R}^2$ and a constant L such that $|F(t, x') - F(t, x'')| \leq L|x' - x''|$ whenever (t, x') and (t, x'') belong to N.

Dependence of Solutions on Parameters

Assume that the conditions of Theorem 5.8.1 or 5.8.2 are met. The unique solution will obviously depend on the initial values t_0 and x_0. One can prove that the solution depends continuously on t_0 and x_0, so that small changes in t_0 and x_0 cause small changes in the solution. In fact, the solution will even be differentiable as a function of (t_0, x_0). For a precise formulation in a more general setting, see Section 7.6.

Differential equations appearing in economic models often involve a number of parameters in addition to the initial values. These parameters are often inferred imperfectly from empirical observations and so are subject to uncertainty. This gives a reason to prefer models whose solutions are not very sensitive to small perturbations of the parameters. In fact, under rather mild restrictions placed on the differential equation, one can prove that the solution depends continuously on the parameters. Again see Section 7.6.

PROBLEMS FOR SECTION 5.8

1. Show that $x = Ct^2$ satisfies the differential equation $t\dot{x} = 2x$ for all values of the constant C. But all the corresponding solution curves pass through the point $(0, 0)$. How do you reconcile this observation with Theorem 5.8.1?

2. Use Theorem 5.8.3 to show that $\dot{x} = t^2 + e^{-x^2}$, $x(0) = 0$, has a unique solution on the interval $(-\infty, \infty)$.

3. Use Picard's method of successive approximations to solve the equation $\dot{x} = x$ with $x(0) = 1$. (*Hint:* Consider the Taylor expansion of e^x. See e.g. EMEA.)

4. Find the unique solution of $\dot{x} = x(1 - x)$, $x(0) = 1/2$, defined on $(-\infty, \infty)$. Show that neither of the conditions (3) or (4) in Theorem 5.8.3 is satisfied.

5. Let a and b be arbitrary constants, $a < b$, and define the function φ by

$$\varphi(t) = \begin{cases} -(t-a)^2 & \text{if } t \leq a \\ 0 & \text{if } a < t < b \\ (t-b)^2 & \text{if } t \geq b \end{cases}$$

Sketch the graph of φ when $a = -2$ and $b = 3$. Use the definition of the derivative to show that φ is differentiable at $t = a$ and $t = b$. For all choices of a and b prove that $x = \varphi(t)$ is a solution of the differential equation $\dot{x} = 2\sqrt{|x|}$ on the whole real line. Explain why this shows that the requirement in Theorem 5.8.1 that $F(t, x)$ is differentiable w.r.t. x cannot be dropped.

6

DIFFERENTIAL EQUATIONS II:
SECOND-ORDER EQUATIONS AND SYSTEMS IN THE PLANE

Understanding of mathematics cannot be transmitted by painless
entertainment any more than education in music can be brought by
the most brilliant journalism to those who have never listened
intensively. Actual contact with the content of living mathematics
is necessary.
—Richard Courant (1941)

I n Chapter 5 we studied only first-order differential equations. Yet many economic models
are based on differential equations in which second- or higher-order derivatives appear. For
example, in an important area of dynamic optimization called the *calculus of variations*, the
first-order condition for optimality involves a second-order differential equation. (See Section
8.2.) Sections 6.1–6.4 treat the standard theory of second-order linear equations. Next, Sections
6.5 and 6.6 are devoted to systems of two simultaneous differential equations in two variables.
When there are two variables, the phase plane techniques covered in Section 6.7 provide useful
insights concerning the form of the solutions, and especially their long-run (asymptotic) behaviour. Section 6.8 discusses stability properties for nonlinear systems in the plane, which are
important in macroeconomic theory. Saddle points, which occur in a large number of economic
models, are the topic of Section 6.9.

6.1 Introduction

Second-order differential equations can usually be written in the form

$$\ddot{x} = F(t, x, \dot{x}) \tag{1}$$

where F is a given fixed function, $x = x(t)$ is the unknown function, and $\dot{x} = dx/dt$.
Compared with Chapter 5, the new feature is the presence of $\ddot{x} = d^2x/dt^2$. A **solution** of
(1) on an interval I is a twice differentiable function that satisfies the equation.

The simplest type of second-order equation appears in the following example.

EXAMPLE 1   Find all solutions of

$$\ddot{x} = k \qquad (k \text{ is a constant})$$

Solution: Because $\ddot{x} = (d/dt)\dot{x}$, direct integration implies that the equation is equivalent to $\dot{x} = \int k\,dt = kt + A$, for some constant A. After integrating once more, we see that
the equation is satisfied iff $x = \frac{1}{2}kt^2 + At + B$. Geometrically, the solution represents for
$k \neq 0$ a collection of parabolas in the tx-plane whose axes are all parallel to the x-axis.

Differential Equations Where x or t Is Missing

In two special cases the solution of equation (1) can be reduced to the solution of first-order
equations. The two cases are

$$\text{(a) } \ddot{x} = F(t, \dot{x}) \qquad \text{(b) } \ddot{x} = F(x, \dot{x}) \tag{2}$$

In case 2(a), x is missing. We introduce the new variable $u = \dot{x}$. Then (a) becomes $\dot{u} = F(t, u)$, which is a first-order equation. If we find the general solution $u(t)$ of this first-order
equation, then integrating $\dot{x}(t) = u(t)$ will yield the general solution $x(t)$ of (a).

EXAMPLE 2   Solve the equation $\ddot{x} = \dot{x} + t$.

Solution: Substituting $u = \dot{x}$ yields $\dot{u} = u + t$. This first-order equation has the general
solution $u = Ae^t - t - 1$, where A is a constant (see Problem 5.4.3). Hence, $\dot{x} = Ae^t - t - 1$.
Integrating this equation yields $x = \int (Ae^t - t - 1)\,dt = Ae^t - \frac{1}{2}t^2 - t + B$, where B is a
second arbitrary constant.

In case 2(b), t is not explicitly present in the equation, and the equation is called **autonomous**.
The equation cannot be solved explicitly, except in special cases.

A standard trick which, in principle, can be used to solve equation 2(b), is to let x be the independent
variable instead of t. Letting $'$ denote differentiation w.r.t. x, we have

$$\dot{x} = \frac{dx}{dt} = \frac{1}{dt/dx} = \frac{1}{t'}$$

and moreover,

$$\ddot{x} = \frac{dx^2}{dt^2} = \frac{d}{dt}\left(\frac{dx}{dt}\right) = \frac{d}{dt}\left(\frac{1}{t'}\right) = \frac{d}{dx}\left(\frac{1}{t'}\right)\frac{dx}{dt} = -\frac{t''}{(t')^2}\frac{1}{t'} = -\frac{t''}{(t')^3}$$

Inserting these expressions for $\dot{x}$ and $\ddot{x}$ into $\ddot{x} = F(x, \dot{x})$, then simplifying, yields

$$t'' = -(t')^3 F(x, 1/t') \tag{3}$$

In this equation t does not appear explicitly, so the method used to solve 2(a) works, in principle.

EXAMPLE 3   Solve the equation $\ddot{x} = -x\dot{x}^3$.

Solution: Obviously, $x(t) = C$ is a solution for any constant C. Equation (3) becomes $t'' = -(t')^3(-x)(1/t'^3) = x$, or $d^2t/dx^2 = x$. Integrating yields $dt/dx = \frac{1}{2}x^2 + A$, and further integration
results in $t = \frac{1}{6}x^3 + Ax + B$, where A and B are arbitrary constants. A solution of the equation is
therefore given implicitly by the equation $x^3 + A_1x + B_1 = 6t$.

Solving equation (1) becomes even more difficult if the right-hand side includes t, the unknown function x, and its derivative $\dot{x}$. In fact, only rather special cases have explicit solutions; generally, one has to resort to numerical solutions for given initial conditions. Even so, it turns out that the *existence* of a solution of (1) can be established for almost all the equations that are likely to appear in applications. In fact, the general solution of the equation will depend on two arbitrary constants, as it did in Examples 1–3; that is, the solution is of the form $x = x(t; A, B)$. If we require that the solution passes through a given point (t_0, x_0), and that the slope $\dot{x}(t)$ has a given value a at $t = t_0$, then A and B are usually uniquely determined by the two requirements $x(t_0; A, B) = x_0$ and $\dot{x}(t_0; A, B) = a$.

If the constants are determined in this way by the values of $x(t)$ and $\dot{x}(t)$ at an "initial" point of time t_0, we have an *initial value problem*.

EXAMPLE 4   Solve the initial value problem $\ddot{x} = \dot{x} + t, \quad x(0) = 1, \; \dot{x}(0) = 2.$

Solution: According to Example 2, the general solution of this second-order equation is $x = Ae^t - \frac{1}{2}t^2 - t + B$. Letting $x(0) = 1$ yields $1 = A + B$. Moreover, $\dot{x} = Ae^t - t - 1$, so $\dot{x}(0) = 2$ implies that $2 = A - 1$. Thus, $A = 3$ and $B = -2$, so the unique solution of the problem is $x = 3e^t - \frac{1}{2}t^2 - t - 2$.

PROBLEMS FOR SECTION 6.1

1. Find the general solutions of the following differential equations:

   (a) $\ddot{x} = t$ (b) $\ddot{x} = \sin t$ (c) $\ddot{x} = e^t + t^2$

2. Solve the initial value problem $\quad \ddot{x} = t^2 - t, \; x(0) = 1, \; \dot{x}(0) = 2.$

3. Solve the problem (see Example 2) $\quad \ddot{x} = \dot{x} + t, \; x(0) = 1, \; x(1) = 2.$ (In this case the constants are determined by the value of $x(t)$ at two different points of time.)

4. Solve the following differential equations:

   (a) $\ddot{x} + 2\dot{x} = 8$ (b) $\ddot{x} - 2\dot{x} = 2e^{2t}$ (c) $\ddot{x} - \dot{x} = t^2$

5. If $u(y)$ is a utility function and $y > 0$ denotes wealth, the fraction $R_A = -u''(y)/u'(y)$ is called the **degree of absolute risk aversion**, and $R_R = yR_A$ is called the **degree of relative risk aversion.**

   (a) Find an expression for $u(y)$ if $R_A = \lambda$, where λ is a constant.

   (b) Find an expression for $u(y)$ if $R_R = k$, where k is a constant. Distinguish between the cases $k = 1$ and $k \neq 1$.

HARDER PROBLEMS

6. (a) Solve the equation $\ddot{x} = \dot{x}^2/x$ by using the method leading to (3).

   (b) In Section 6.3 we shall give a simple method for solving equations of the type $\ddot{x} = ax + b\dot{x}$. Show that in this case (3) is a complicated differential equation.

7. The partial differential equation $u''_{xx}(t, x) = u'_t(t, x)$ (the "diffusion equation") appears in modern finance theory.

   (a) Show that for every α, the function $u(t, x) = e^{t\alpha^2} e^{\alpha x}$ is a solution of the equation.

   (b) Suppose that the equation has a solution of the form $u(x, t) = g(y)$, where $y = x/\sqrt{t}$. Show that $g(y)$ then satisfies the equation $g''(y)/g'(y) = -\frac{1}{2}y$. Show that the solution of this equation is $g(y) = A \int e^{-\frac{1}{4}y^2} dy + B$, where A and B are constants.

6.2 Linear Differential Equations

The general second-order linear differential equation is

$$\ddot{x} + a(t)\dot{x} + b(t)x = f(t) \tag{1}$$

where $a(t)$, $b(t)$, and $f(t)$ are all continuous functions of t on some interval I. In contrast to first-order linear equations, there is no explicit solution of (1) in the general case. However, something useful can be said about the structure of the general solution.

Let us begin with the **homogeneous** equation obtained from (1) by replacing $f(t)$ by 0:

$$\ddot{x} + a(t)\dot{x} + b(t)x = 0 \tag{2}$$

We claim that if $u_1 = u_1(t)$ and $u_2 = u_2(t)$ both satisfy (2), then $x = Au_1 + Bu_2$ also satisfies (2) for all choices of constants A and B. In fact, we get $\dot{x} = A\dot{u}_1 + B\dot{u}_2$ and $\ddot{x} = A\ddot{u}_1 + B\ddot{u}_2$. Inserting these expressions for $\dot{x}$ and $\ddot{x}$ into the left-hand side of (2) yields

$$\ddot{x} + a(t)\dot{x} + b(t)x = A\ddot{u}_1 + B\ddot{u}_2 + a(t)(A\dot{u}_1 + B\dot{u}_2) + b(t)(Au_1 + Bu_2)$$
$$= A[\ddot{u}_1 + a(t)\dot{u}_1 + b(t)u_1] + B[\ddot{u}_2 + a(t)\dot{u}_2 + b(t)u_2]$$

It was assumed that u_1 and u_2 satisfy (2), so this last expression is 0. Thus, we have proved that the function $x = Au_1 + Bu_2$ satisfies (2) for all values of constants A and B.

Suppose then that we have somehow managed to find two solutions u_1 and u_2 of (2). Then $x = Au_1 + Bu_2$ satisfies (2) for all values of A and B. Is this the general solution? No, in order to be sure that $Au_1 + Bu_2$ is the general solution of (2), we must require u_1 and u_2 not to be constant multiples of each other—that is, they must not be proportional. (For a proof, see Section 7.1.)

Equation (1) is called a **nonhomogeneous equation**, and (2) is the homogeneous equation associated with it. Suppose we are able to find *some particular solution* $u^* = u^*(t)$ of (1). If $x(t)$ is an arbitrary solution of (1), then it is easy to see that the difference $x(t) - u^*(t)$ is a solution of the homogeneous equation (2). In fact, if $v = v(t) = x(t) - u^*(t)$, then $\dot{v} = \dot{x} - \dot{u}^*$ and $\ddot{v} = \ddot{x} - \ddot{u}^*$, so

$$\ddot{v} + a(t)\dot{v} + b(t)v = \ddot{x} - \ddot{u}^* + a(t)(\dot{x} - \dot{u}^*) + b(t)(x - u^*)$$
$$= \ddot{x} + a(t)\dot{x} + b(t)x - [\ddot{u}^* + a(t)\dot{u}^* + b(t)u^*]$$
$$= f(t) - f(t) = 0$$

Thus, $x(t) - u^*(t)$ is a solution of the homogeneous equation. But then, according to the argument above, $x(t) - u^*(t) = Au_1(t) + Bu_2(t)$, where $u_1(t)$ and $u_2(t)$ are two nonproportional solutions of (2), and A and B are arbitrary constants. Conversely, if x is a function such that $x - u^*$ is a solution of the homogeneous equation, then x is a solution of the nonhomogeneous equation. All in all we arrive at the following result:

THEOREM 6.2.1

(a) The homogeneous differential equation

$$\ddot{x} + a(t)\dot{x} + b(t)x = 0$$

has the **general solution**

$$x = Au_1(t) + Bu_2(t)$$

where $u_1(t)$ and $u_2(t)$ are two solutions that are not proportional, and A and B are arbitrary constants.

(b) The nonhomogeneous differential equation

$$\ddot{x} + a(t)\dot{x} + b(t)x = f(t)$$

has the **general solution**

$$x = Au_1(t) + Bu_2(t) + u^*(t)$$

where $Au_1(t) + Bu_2(t)$ is the general solution of the associated homogeneous equation (with $f(t)$ replaced by zero), and $u^*(t)$ is any **particular solution** of the nonhomogeneous equation.

EXAMPLE 1   Find the general solutions of   (a) $\ddot{x} - x = 0$ and   (b) $\ddot{x} - x = t$.

Solution: (a) The problem is to find those functions that do not change when differentiated twice. You probably recall that $x = e^t$ has this property, as does $x = 2e^t$. But these two functions are proportional. So we need to find another function with the property that differentiating it twice leaves it unchanged. After some thought, you might come up with the idea of trying $x = e^{-t}$. In fact, $\dot{x} = -e^{-t}$, and so $\ddot{x} = e^{-t}$. Because e^t and e^{-t} are not proportional, the general solution is $x = Ae^t + Be^{-t}$, with A and B arbitrary constants.

(b) (In the next section we shall give a general method for solving such equations.) We need only find a particular solution of the equation. By trial and error we find that $u(t) = -t$ satisfies the equation. The general solution is therefore

$$x = Ae^t + Be^{-t} - t \qquad (A \text{ and } B \text{ are arbitrary constants})$$

There is no general method of discovering the two solutions of (2) that are needed for the general solution of the equation. However, in the special case when the coefficients $a(t)$ and $b(t)$ are both constants, it is always possible to find the two solutions required. The next section shows how to do this.

PROBLEMS FOR SECTION 6.2

1. (a) Prove that $u_1 = e^t$ and $u_2 = te^t$ both satisfy $\ddot{x} - 2\dot{x} + x = 0$. Show that u_1 and u_2 are not proportional, and use this to find the general solution of the equation.

   (b) Find the general solution of $\ddot{x} - 2\dot{x} + x = 3$.

2. Show that $u_1 = \sin t$ and $u_2 = \cos t$ both are solutions of $\ddot{x} + x = 0$. What is the general solution of the equation?

3. (a) Prove that both $u_1 = e^{2t}$ and $u_2 = e^{-3t}$ are solutions of $\ddot{x} + \dot{x} - 6x = 0$. What is the general solution?

   (b) Find the general solution of $\ddot{x} + \dot{x} - 6x = 6t$. (*Hint:* The equation has a particular solution of the form $Ct + D$.)

4. A study of the optimal exhaustion of a natural resource uses the equation

$$\ddot{x} - \frac{2 - \alpha}{1 - \alpha} a\, \dot{x} + \frac{a^2}{1 - \alpha} x = 0 \qquad (\alpha \neq 0,\ \alpha \neq 1,\ a \neq 0)$$

Prove that $u_1 = e^{at}$ and $u_2 = e^{at/(1-\alpha)}$ are both solutions. What is the general solution?

HARDER PROBLEMS

5. Let $a \neq b$ be two real numbers. Prove that the differential equation

$$(t + a)(t + b)\ddot{x} + 2(2t + a + b)\dot{x} + 2x = 0$$

has two solutions of the form $(t + k)^{-1}$ for appropriate choices of k. Find the general solution of the equation. (*Hint:* Let $x = (t + k)^{-1}$ and then adjust k until the function satisfies the differential equation.)

6.3 Constant Coefficients

Consider the *homogeneous* equation

$$\ddot{x} + a\dot{x} + bx = 0 \tag{1}$$

where a and b are arbitrary constants, and $x = x(t)$ is the unknown function. According to Theorem 6.2.1, finding the general solution of (1) requires us to discover two solutions $u_1(t)$ and $u_2(t)$ that are not proportional. Because the coefficients in (1) are constants, it seems a good idea to try possible solutions x with the property that x, $\dot{x}$, and $\ddot{x}$ are all constant multiples of each other. The exponential function $x = e^{rt}$ has this property, because $\dot{x} = re^{rt} = rx$ and $\ddot{x} = r^2 e^{rt} = r^2 x$. So we try adjusting the constant r in order that $x = e^{rt}$ satisfies (1). This requires us to arrange that $r^2 e^{rt} + are^{rt} + be^{rt} = 0$. Cancelling the positive factor e^{rt} tells us that e^{rt} satisfies (1) iff r satisfies

$$r^2 + ar + b = 0 \tag{2}$$

This is the **characteristic equation** of the differential equation (1). It is a quadratic equation whose roots are real iff $\frac{1}{4}a^2 - b \geq 0$. Solving (2) by the quadratic formula in this case yields the two **characteristic roots**

$$r_1 = -\tfrac{1}{2}a + \sqrt{\tfrac{1}{4}a^2 - b}, \qquad r_2 = -\tfrac{1}{2}a - \sqrt{\tfrac{1}{4}a^2 - b} \tag{3}$$

Generally, there are three different cases to consider that are summed up in the following theorem.

THEOREM 6.3.1

The **general solution** of
$$\ddot{x} + a\dot{x} + bx = 0$$
is as follows:

(I) If $\frac{1}{4}a^2 - b > 0$ (when the characteristic equation has two distinct real roots):

$$x = Ae^{r_1 t} + Be^{r_2 t}, \quad \text{where} \quad r_{1,2} = -\tfrac{1}{2}a \pm \sqrt{\tfrac{1}{4}a^2 - b}$$

(II) If $\frac{1}{4}a^2 - b = 0$ (when the characteristic equation has one real double root):

$$x = (A + Bt)e^{rt}, \quad \text{where} \quad r = -\tfrac{1}{2}a$$

(III) If $\frac{1}{4}a^2 - b < 0$ (when the characteristic equation has no real roots):

$$x = e^{\alpha t}(A \cos \beta t + B \sin \beta t), \quad \alpha = -\tfrac{1}{2}a, \ \beta = \sqrt{b - \tfrac{1}{4}a^2}$$

(I): The case $\frac{1}{4}a^2 - b > 0$ is the simplest, because it gives real and distinct characteristic roots r_1 and r_2. The functions $e^{r_1 t}$ and $e^{r_2 t}$ both satisfy (1). These functions are not proportional when $r_1 \neq r_2$, so the general solution in this case is $Ae^{r_1 t} + Be^{r_2 t}$.

(II): If $\frac{1}{4}a^2 - b = 0$, then $r = -\frac{1}{2}a$ is a double root of (2), and $u_1 = e^{rt}$ satisfies (1). Problem 6 is devoted to this case. We claim that $u_2 = te^{rt}$ also satisfies (1). This is because $\dot{u}_2 = e^{rt} + tre^{rt}$ and $\ddot{u}_2 = re^{rt} + re^{rt} + tr^2 e^{rt}$, which inserted into the left-hand side of (1) gives

$$\ddot{u}_2 + a\dot{u}_2 + bu_2 = e^{rt}(a + 2r) + te^{rt}(r^2 + ar + b)$$

after simplifying. But the last expression is 0 because $r = -\frac{1}{2}a$ and $r^2 + ar + b = 0$. Thus, e^{rt} and te^{rt} are indeed both solutions of equation (1). These two solutions are not proportional, so the general solution is $Ae^{rt} + Bte^{rt}$ in this case.

(III): If $\frac{1}{4}a^2 - b < 0$, the characteristic equation has no real roots. An example is the equation $\ddot{x} + x = 0$, which occurred in Problem 6.2.2; here $a = 0$ and $b = 1$, so $\frac{1}{4}a^2 - b = -1$. The general solution was $A \sin t + B \cos t$. It should, therefore, come as no surprise that when $\frac{1}{4}a^2 - b < 0$, the solution of (1) involves trigonometric functions.

Define the two functions $u_1(t) = e^{\alpha t} \cos \beta t$ and $u_2(t) = e^{\alpha t} \sin \beta t$, where α and β are defined in (III). We claim that both these functions satisfy (1). Since they are not proportional, the general solution of equation (1) in this case is as exhibited in (III).

Let us show that $u_1(t) = e^{\alpha t} \cos \beta t$ satisfies (1). We find that $\dot{u}_1(t) = \alpha e^{\alpha t} \cos \beta t - \beta e^{\alpha t} \sin \beta t$. Furthermore, $\ddot{u}_1(t) = \alpha^2 e^{\alpha t} \cos \beta t - \alpha\beta e^{\alpha t} \sin \beta t - \alpha\beta e^{\alpha t} \sin \beta t - \beta^2 e^{\alpha t} \cos \beta t$. Hence, $\ddot{u}_1 + a\dot{u}_1 + bu_1 = e^{\alpha t}[(\alpha^2 - \beta^2 + \alpha a + b) \cos \beta t - \beta(2\alpha + a) \sin \beta t]$. By using the values of α and β given in (III), we see that $2\alpha + a = 0$ and $\alpha^2 - \beta^2 + \alpha a + b = \frac{1}{4}a^2 - (b - \frac{1}{4}a^2) - \frac{1}{2}a^2 + b = 0$. This shows that $u_1(t) = e^{\alpha t} \cos \beta t$ satisfies equation (1). A similar argument shows that $u_2(t) = e^{\alpha t} \sin \beta t$ satisfies (1) as well.

NOTE 1 When $\frac{1}{4}a^2 - b < 0$, i.e. in case III, an alternative form of the solution is $x = Ce^{\alpha t} \cos(\beta t + D)$. (See Problem 5.)

NOTE 2 If we use complex numbers (see Section B.3), when $\frac{1}{4}a^2 < b$ the solutions of the characteristic equation $r^2 + ar + b = 0$ can be written as $r_{1,2} = \alpha \pm i\beta$, where $\alpha = -\frac{1}{2}a$ and $\beta = \sqrt{b - \frac{1}{4}a^2}$ are precisely the real numbers occurring in the solution in case III.

With $r_{1,2} = \alpha \pm i\beta$, the two complex exponential functions $e^{r_1 t} = e^{\alpha t}(\cos \beta t + i \sin \beta t)$ and $e^{r_2 t} = e^{\alpha t}(\cos \beta t - i \sin \beta t)$ both satisfy (1). But so does any linear combination of these solutions. In particular, $(e^{r_1 t} + e^{r_2 t})/2 = e^{\alpha t} \cos \beta t$ and $(e^{r_1 t} - e^{r_2 t})/2i = e^{\alpha t} \sin \beta t$ both satisfy (1), and these are precisely the two functions given as solutions before.

EXAMPLE 1   Find the general solutions of the following equations:

$$\text{(a)} \quad \ddot{x} - 3x = 0 \qquad \text{(b)} \quad \ddot{x} - 4\dot{x} + 4x = 0 \qquad \text{(c)} \quad \ddot{x} - 6\dot{x} + 13x = 0$$

Solution: (a) The characteristic equation $r^2 - 3 = 0$ has two real roots $r_1 = -\sqrt{3}$ and $r_2 = \sqrt{3}$. The general solution is

$$x = Ae^{-\sqrt{3}t} + Be^{\sqrt{3}t}$$

(b) The characteristic equation $r^2 - 4r + 4 = (r - 2)^2 = 0$ has the double root $r = 2$. Hence, the general solution is

$$x = (A + Bt)e^{2t}$$

(c) The characteristic equation $r^2 - 6r + 13 = 0$ has no real roots. According to case (III), $\alpha = -a/2 = -(-6)/2 = 3$ and $\beta = \sqrt{13 - \frac{1}{4}(-6)^2} = 2$, so the general solution is

$$x = e^{3t}(A \cos 2t + B \sin 2t)$$

The Nonhomogeneous Equation

Consider next the *nonhomogeneous* equation

$$\ddot{x} + a\dot{x} + bx = f(t) \tag{4}$$

where $f(t)$ is an arbitrary continuous function. According to Theorem 6.2.1(b), the general solution of (5) is given by

$$x = x(t) = Au_1(t) + Bu_2(t) + u^*(t) \tag{5}$$

We have explained how to find the term $Au_1(t) + Bu_2(t)$ by solving the corresponding homogeneous equation. But how do we find a particular solution $u^* = u^*(t)$ of (4)? In fact, there is a simple *method of undetermined coefficients* that works in many cases.

If $b = 0$ in (4), then the term in x is missing and the substitution $u = \dot{x}$ transforms the equation into a linear equation of the first order (see Example 6.1.2). So we may assume $b \neq 0$. Consider the following special forms of $f(t)$:

(A) $f(t) = A$ (constant)

In this case we check to see if (4) has a solution that is constant, $u^* = c$. Then $\dot{u}^* = \ddot{u}^* = 0$, so the equation reduces to $bc = A$. Hence, $c = A/b$. Thus, for $b \neq 0$:

$$\ddot{x} + a\dot{x} + bx = A \quad \text{has a particular solution} \quad u^* = A/b \tag{6}$$

(B) $f(t)$ is a polynomial

Suppose $f(t)$ is a polynomial of degree n. Then a reasonable guess is that (4) has a particular solution that is also a polynomial of degree n, of the form $u^* = A_n t^n + A_{n-1} t^{n-1} + \cdots + A_1 t + A_0$. We determine the undetermined coefficients $A_n, A_{n-1}, \ldots, A_0$ by requiring u^* to satisfy (4) and equating coefficients of like powers of t.

EXAMPLE 2   Find a particular solution of

$$\ddot{x} - 4\dot{x} + 4x = t^2 + 2 \tag{$*$}$$

Solution: The right-hand side is a polynomial of degree 2. So we let $u^* = At^2 + Bt + C$ and try adjusting A, B, and C to give a solution. We obtain $\dot{u}^* = 2At + B$, and so $\ddot{u}^* = 2A$. Inserting these expressions for u^*, $\dot{u}^*$, and $\ddot{u}^*$ into ($*$) yields the equation $2A - 4(2At + B) + 4(At^2 + Bt + C) = t^2 + 2$. Collecting like terms on the left-hand side gives $4At^2 + (4B - 8A)t + (2A - 4B + 4C) = t^2 + 2$. Equating coefficients of like powers of t yields $4A = 1$, $4B - 8A = 0$, and $2A - 4B + 4C = 2$. Solving these three equations gives $A = \frac{1}{4}$, $B = \frac{1}{2}$, and $C = \frac{7}{8}$. Hence, a particular solution of equation ($*$) is

$$u^* = \tfrac{1}{4}t^2 + \tfrac{1}{2}t + \tfrac{7}{8}$$

Note that the right-hand side of ($*$) is $t^2 + 2$, without any t term. Yet no function of the form $Ct^2 + D$ will satisfy it; any solution must include the term $\frac{1}{2}t$.

EXAMPLE 3   The theory of options involves differential equations, in some of which the independent variable is not time. One problem that typically arises requires solving the differential equation

$$f''(x) + af'(x) + bf(x) = \alpha x + \beta \tag{$*$}$$

Here $f(x)$ denotes the value of a stock option when the stock price is x. For the case of a "call option", offering the right to buy a stock at a fixed "strike price", the constant b is usually negative. Solve the equation in this case.

Solution: The homogeneous equation has characteristic equation $r^2 + ar + b = 0$ with the roots $r_{1,2} = -\frac{1}{2}a \pm \sqrt{\frac{1}{4}a^2 - b}$. With $b < 0$ we have $\frac{1}{4}a^2 - b > 0$, and the roots are real and different. The homogeneous equation therefore has the solution

$$f(x) = Ae^{r_1 x} + Be^{r_2 x} \qquad (A \text{ and } B \text{ are constants})$$

In order to find a particular solution of $(*)$, we try $u(x) = Px + Q$. Then $u'(x) = P$ and $u''(x) = 0$. Inserting these into $(*)$ gives $aP + b(Px + Q) = \alpha x + \beta$ or $bPx + (aP + bQ) = \alpha x + \beta$. Hence $P = \alpha/b$ and $Q = (\beta b - \alpha a)/b^2$, so that a particular solution is $u(x) = \alpha x/b + (\beta b - \alpha a)/b^2$. The general solution of $(*)$ is therefore (assuming $b < 0$)

$$f(x) = Ae^{r_1 x} + Be^{r_2 x} + \frac{\alpha}{b}x + \frac{\beta b - \alpha a}{b^2}, \qquad r_{1,2} = -\frac{1}{2}a \pm \sqrt{\frac{1}{4}a^2 - b}$$

(C) $f(t) = pe^{qt}$

A natural choice of particular solution would seem to be $u^* = Ae^{qt}$. Then $\dot{u}^* = Aqe^{qt}$, $\ddot{u}^* = Aq^2 e^{qt}$, and substitution into (4) yields $Ae^{qt}(q^2 + aq + b) = pe^{qt}$. Hence, if $q^2 + aq + b \neq 0$,

$$\ddot{x} + a\dot{x} + bx = pe^{qt} \quad \text{has the particular solution} \quad u^* = \frac{p}{q^2 + aq + b}e^{qt} \tag{7}$$

The condition $q^2 + aq + b \neq 0$ means that q is not a solution of the characteristic equation (2)—that is, that e^{qt} is not a solution of (1). If q is a simple root of $q^2 + aq + b = 0$, we look for a constant B such that Bte^{qt} is a solution. If q is a double root, then $Ct^2 e^{qt}$ is a solution for some constant C.

(D) $f(t) = p \sin rt + q \cos rt$

Again the method of undetermined coefficients works. Let $u^* = A \sin rt + B \cos rt$ and adjust the constants A and B so that the coefficients of $\sin rt$ and $\cos rt$ match. If $f(t)$ is itself a solution of the homogeneous equation, then $u^* = At \sin rt + Bt \cos rt$ will be a particular solution for suitable choices of constants A and B.

EXAMPLE 4   Find a particular solution of $\ddot{x} - 4\dot{x} + 4x = 2 \cos 2t$.

Solution: In this case, it might seem natural to suggest a particular solution of the form $u = A \cos 2t$. Note, however, that the term $-4\dot{u}$ gives us a $\sin 2t$ term on the left-hand side, and no matching term occurs on the right-hand side of the equation. So we try $u^* = A \sin 2t + B \cos 2t$ instead, and adjust constants A and B appropriately. We have $\dot{u}^* = 2A \cos 2t - 2B \sin 2t$ and $\ddot{u}^* = -4A \sin 2t - 4B \cos 2t$. Inserting these expressions into the equation and rearranging, we get $8B \sin 2t - 8A \cos 2t = 2 \cos 2t$. Thus, letting $B = 0$ and $A = -1/4$, we see that the given equation is satisfied for all t. So $u^* = (-1/4) \sin 2t$ is a particular solution of the equation.

The technique for obtaining particular solutions described above also applies if $f(t)$ is a sum, difference, or product of polynomials, exponential functions, or trigonometric functions of the type mentioned. For instance, if $f(t) = (t^2 + 1)e^{3t} + \sin 2t$, let $u^* = (At^2 + Bt + C)e^{3t} + D \sin 2t + E \cos 2t$. On the other hand, if $f(t)$ is an entirely different type of function such as $t \ln t$, the method of undetermined coefficients does not work.

Euler's Differential Equation

One type of equation that occasionally occurs in economics is **Euler's differential equation**,

$$t^2\ddot{x} + at\dot{x} + bx = 0, \quad (t > 0) \tag{8}$$

The easiest way of solving such equations is to introduce a new independent variable s by putting $t = e^s$, i.e. $s = \ln t$. Then $\dot{x} = dx/dt = (dx/ds)(ds/dt) = (1/t)(dx/ds)$, and differentiating $\dot{x}$ with respect to t yields

$$\ddot{x} = \frac{d}{dt}\dot{x} = \frac{d}{dt}\left(\frac{1}{t}\frac{dx}{ds}\right) = -\frac{1}{t^2}\frac{dx}{ds} + \frac{1}{t}\frac{d}{dt}\left(\frac{dx}{ds}\right) = -\frac{1}{t^2}\frac{dx}{ds} + \frac{1}{t}\frac{d^2x}{ds^2}\frac{1}{t}$$

because

$$\frac{d}{dt}\left(\frac{dx}{ds}\right) = \frac{d}{ds}\left(\frac{dx}{ds}\right)\frac{ds}{dt} = \frac{d^2x}{ds^2}\cdot\frac{1}{t}$$

Inserting these expressions into (8) yields

$$\frac{d^2x}{ds^2} + (a-1)\frac{dx}{ds} + bx = 0 \tag{9}$$

This is an ordinary second-order equation with constant coefficients.

EXAMPLE 5   Solve the equation $t^2\ddot{x} + t\dot{x} - x = 0$.

Solution: With $s = \ln t$, equation (9) is here $\dfrac{d^2x}{ds^2} - x = 0$, with general solution $x = Ae^s + Be^{-s} = At + Bt^{-1}$.

EXAMPLE 6   In the theory of options one encounters the equation

$$x^2 f''(x) + axf'(x) + bf(x) = \alpha x + \beta$$

where $f(x)$ denotes the value of a stock option when the price of the stock is x. If $(a-1)^2 > 4b$ (which is often the case in option models), the homogeneous equation has the solution

$$f(x) = Ax^{r_1} + Bx^{r_2}$$

where $r_{1,2} = -\frac{1}{2}(a-1) \pm \frac{1}{2}\sqrt{(a-1)^2 - 4b}$. We easily find $u^*(x) = \alpha x/(a+b) + \beta/b$ as a particular solution.

PROBLEMS FOR SECTION 6.3

Find the general solutions of the equations in Problems 1 and 2.

1. (a) $\ddot{x} - 3x = 0$ (b) $\ddot{x} + 4\dot{x} + 8x = 0$ (c) $3\ddot{x} + 8\dot{x} = 0$

   (d) $4\ddot{x} + 4\dot{x} + x = 0$ (e) $\ddot{x} + \dot{x} - 6x = 8$ (f) $\ddot{x} + 3\dot{x} + 2x = e^{5t}$

2. (a) $\ddot{x} - x = \sin t$ (b) $\ddot{x} - x = e^{-t}$ (c) $3\ddot{x} - 30\dot{x} + 75x = 2t + 1$

3. Solve the following differential equations for the specific initial conditions:

   (a) $\ddot{x} + 2\dot{x} + x = t^2$, $x(0) = 0,\ \dot{x}(0) = 1$

   (b) $\ddot{x} + 4x = 4t + 1$, $x(\pi/2) = 0,\ \dot{x}(\pi/2) = 0$

4. Find a particular solution of the differential equation

$$\ddot{L} + \gamma[\beta + \alpha(1-\beta)]\dot{L} - \gamma\delta^* L = -\gamma\delta^* kt - \gamma\delta^* L_0 \qquad (\gamma\delta^* \neq 0)$$

   and then discuss when the general solution oscillates.

5. Prove that the general solution of $\ddot{x} + a\dot{x} + bx = 0$ in the case $\frac{1}{4}a^2 - b < 0$ can be written as $x = Ce^{\alpha t}\cos(\beta t + D)$, where C and D are arbitrary constants, $\alpha = -\frac{1}{2}a$, and $\beta = \frac{1}{2}\sqrt{4b - a^2}$.

6. Consider the equation $\ddot{x} + a\dot{x} + bx = 0$ when $\frac{1}{4}a^2 - b = 0$, so that the characteristic equation has a double root $r = -a/2$. Let $x(t) = u(t)e^{rt}$ and prove that this function is a solution if and only if $\ddot{u} = 0$. Conclude that the general solution is $x = (A + Bt)e^{rt}$.

7. Find the general solutions of the following equations for $t > 0$:

   (a) $t^2\ddot{x} + 5t\dot{x} + 3x = 0$ (b) $t^2\ddot{x} - 3t\dot{x} + 3x = t^2$

8. Solve the differential equation $\ddot{x} + 2a\dot{x} - 3a^2x = 100e^{bt}$ for all values of the constants a and b.

9. A business cycle model due to F. Dresch incorporates the equation

$$\dot{p}(t) = a \int_{-\infty}^{t} \left[D(p(\tau)) - S(p(\tau)) \right] d\tau \qquad (a > 0) \qquad\qquad (*)$$

where $p(t)$ denotes a price index at time t, and $D(p)$ and $S(p)$ are aggregate demand and supply, respectively. Thus, $(*)$ says that the rate of price increase is proportional to the accumulated total of all past excess demand. In the case when $D(p) = d_0 + d_1 p$ and $S(p) = s_0 + s_1 p$, where $d_1 < 0$ and $s_1 > 0$, differentiate $(*)$ w.r.t. t in order to deduce a second-order differential equation for $p(t)$. Then find the general solution of this equation.

6.4 Stability for Linear Equations

Suppose the variables of an economic model change over time according to some differential equation (or system of differential equations). If appropriate initial conditions are imposed, there is a unique solution of the system. Also, if one or more initial conditions are changed, the solution changes. An important question is this: Will small changes in the initial conditions have any effect on the long-run behaviour of the solution, or will the effect "die out" as $t \to \infty$? In the latter case the system is called **asymptotically stable**. On the other hand, if small changes in the initial conditions might lead to significant differences in the behaviour of the solution in the long run, then the system is **unstable**.

Consider in particular the second-order nonhomogeneous differential equation

$$\ddot{x} + a(t)\dot{x} + b(t)x = f(t) \qquad\qquad (1)$$

Recall that the general solution of (1) is $x = Au_1(t) + Bu_2(t) + u^*(t)$, where $Au_1(t) + Bu_2(t)$ is the general solution of the associated homogeneous equation (with $f(t)$ replaced by zero), and $u^*(t)$ is a particular solution of the nonhomogeneous equation.

Equation (1) is called **globally asymptotically stable** *if every solution* $Au_1(t) + Bu_2(t)$ *of the associated homogeneous equation tends to 0 as* $t \to \infty$ *for all values of A and B. Then the effect of the initial conditions "dies out" as* $t \to \infty$.

If $Au_1(t) + Bu_2(t)$ tends to 0 as $t \to \infty$ for all values of A and B, then in particular $u_1(t) \to 0$ as $t \to \infty$ (choose $A = 1$, $B = 0$), and $u_2(t) \to 0$ as $t \to \infty$ (choose $A = 0$, $B = 1$). On the other hand, the condition that $u_1(t)$ and $u_2(t)$ both tend 0 as t tends to infinity is obviously sufficient for $Au_1(t) + Bu_2(t)$ to tend to 0 as $t \to \infty$.

EXAMPLE 1   Study the stability of

(a) $t^2\ddot{x} + 3t\dot{x} + \frac{3}{4}x = 3$ (b) $\ddot{x} + 2\dot{x} + 5x = e^t$ (c) $\ddot{x} + \dot{x} - 2x = 3t^2 + 2$

Solution:

(a) This is an Euler equation whose general solution is $x(t) = At^{-1/2} + Bt^{-3/2} + 4$. The equation is clearly globally asymptotically stable and $x(t) \to 4$ as $t \to \infty$.

(b) The corresponding characteristic equation is $r^2 + 2r + 5 = 0$, with complex roots $r_1 = -1 + 2i$, $r_2 = -1 - 2i$, so $u_1 = e^{-t} \cos 2t$ and $u_2 = e^{-t} \sin 2t$ are linearly independent solutions of the homogeneous equation. (See (III) in Theorem 6.3.1 and Note 6.3.2.) As $t \to \infty$, both u_1 and u_2 tend to 0, since $\cos 2t$ and $\sin 2t$ are both less than or equal to 1 in absolute value and $e^{-t} \to 0$ as $t \to \infty$. The equation is therefore globally asymptotically stable.

(c) Here $u_1 = e^t$ is one solution of the homogeneous equation. Since $u_1 = e^t$ does not tend to 0 as $t \to \infty$, the equation is *not* globally asymptotically stable.

A Useful Characterization of Stability

In the case of second-order linear equations with constant coefficients there is a simple characterization of global asymptotic stability:

$$\ddot{x} + a\dot{x} + bx = f(t) \text{ is globally asymptotically stable} \iff a > 0 \text{ and } b > 0 \qquad (2)$$

Proof: The equation in (2) is stable iff two linearly independent solutions u_1 and u_2 of the associated homogeneous equation tend to 0 as $t \to \infty$.

If the characteristic equation $r^2 + ar + b = 0$ has different real roots r_1 and r_2, then the solutions $u_1 = e^{r_1 t}$ and $u_2 = e^{r_2 t}$ are linearly independent. Both of these functions tend to 0 as $t \to \infty$ iff $r_1 < 0$ and $r_2 < 0$.

If the characteristic equation has a double root r, then $u_1 = e^{rt}$ and $u_2 = te^{rt}$ are linearly independent solutions. These functions both tend to 0 as $t \to \infty$ iff $r < 0$. (Remember that when $r < 0$, then $te^{rt} = t/e^{-rt} \to 0$ as $t \to \infty$.)

From the theory of quadratic equations, we know that if $r^2 + ar + b = 0$ has real roots r_1 and r_2 (possibly equal), then $r_1 + r_2 = -a$ and $r_1 r_2 = b$. If r_1 and r_2 are both negative, then it follows that a and b must both be positive. Conversely, if a and b are both positive, then $r_1 + r_2 = -a$ shows that at least one of the roots is negative, and $r_1 r_2 = b$ shows that both are negative.

It remains to show (2) when the characteristic equation $r^2 + ar + b = 0$ has no real roots, i.e. when $\frac{1}{4}a^2 - b < 0$. In this case, $b > \frac{1}{4}a^2$, so b will always be positive. Moreover, we know from part (III) of Theorem 6.3.1 that two linearly independent solutions of the corresponding homogeneous equation are $u_1 = e^{\alpha t} \cos \beta t$ and $u_2 = e^{\alpha t} \sin \beta t$, where $\alpha = -a/2$ and $\beta = \frac{1}{2}\sqrt{4b - a^2}$. It is clear that u_1 and u_2 tend to 0 as $t \to \infty$ iff $\alpha < 0$, i.e. iff $a > 0$. This concludes the proof of (2). ∎

Recall that in the complex number $r = \alpha + i\beta$, α is the real part, and that the real part of a real number is the number itself. With these concepts (2) can be formulated in an alternative way that is easier to generalize:

The equation $\ddot{x} + a\dot{x} + bx = f(t)$ is globally asymptotically stable iff both roots of the characteristic equation $r^2 + ar + b = 0$ have negative real parts. $\qquad (3)$

EXAMPLE 2   For the last two equations in Example 1, it follows immediately from (2) that (b) is stable, whereas (c) is unstable.

EXAMPLE 3   In a paper on growth theory, the following equation is studied:

$$\ddot{v} + (\mu - \frac{\lambda}{a})\dot{v} + \lambda\gamma v = -\frac{\lambda}{a}\dot{b}(t)$$

where μ, λ, γ, and a are constants, and $\dot{b}(t)$ is a fixed function. Examine the stability.

Solution: This is a second-order linear equation with constant coefficients. According to (2), the equation is stable iff $\mu > \lambda/a$ and $\lambda\gamma > 0$.

NOTE 1 (**Asymptotically stable equilibrium states**)   Consider the differential equation $\ddot{x} + a\dot{x} + bx = c$ where $b \neq 0$. Then $x^* = c/b$ is an equilibrium state, since $x(t) = c/b$ is a constant solution of the equation. All solutions of the equation will tend to the equilibrium state as $t \to \infty$ iff $a > 0$ and $b > 0$. We then say that the **equilibrium state $x^* = c/b$ is globally asymptotically stable**.

PROBLEMS FOR SECTION 6.4

1. Determine which of the equations in Problem 6.3.1 are globally asymptotically stable, and verify (2) in this case.

2. A model by T. Haavelmo leads to an equation of the type

$$\ddot{p}(t) = \gamma(a - \alpha)p(t) + k \qquad (\alpha, \gamma, a, \text{ and } k \text{ are constants})$$

Solve the equation. Can the constants be chosen to make the equation globally asymptotically stable?

6.5 Simultaneous Equations in the Plane

So far we have considered finding one unknown function to satisfy a single differential equation. Many dynamic economic models, especially in macroeconomics, involve several unknown functions that satisfy a number of simultaneous differential equations.

Consider the important special case with two unknowns and two equations:

$$\dot{x} = f(t, x, y)$$
$$\dot{y} = g(t, x, y)$$

(1)

We assume that f, g, f_x', f_y', g_x', and g_y' are continuous.

In economic models that lead to systems of this type, $x = x(t)$ and $y = y(t)$ are state variables characterizing the economic system at a given time t. Usually, the state of the system $(x(t_0), y(t_0))$ is known at some initial time t_0 and the future development of the system is then uniquely determined. The rate of change of each variable depends not only on t and the variable itself, but on the other variable as well. In this sense, the two variables $x(t)$ and $y(t)$ "interact". Systems of this type may exhibit very complicated behaviour.

A **solution** of (1) is a pair of differentiable functions $(x(t), y(t))$ which is defined on some interval I, and which satisfies both equations. With the assumptions imposed on f and g, if t_0 is a point in I, and x_0 and y_0 are given numbers, there will be one and only one pair of functions $(x(t), y(t))$ that satisfies (1) and has $x(t_0) = x_0$, $y(t_0) = y_0$.

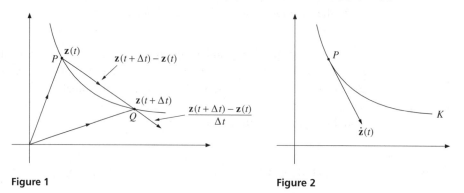

Figure 1   **Figure 2**

NOTE 1 If $(x(t), y(t))$ is a solution of (1), at time t the system is at the point $(x(t), y(t))$ in the xy-plane. When t varies, then $(x(t), y(t))$ traces out a curve K in the xy-plane. In Fig. 1 the vector $\mathbf{z}(t) = (x(t), y(t))$ points from the origin to the point $P = (x(t), y(t))$ and $\mathbf{z}(t + \Delta t) = (x(t + \Delta t), y(t + \Delta t))$ points from the origin to the point Q. The vector $\mathbf{z}(t + \Delta t) - \mathbf{z}(t)$ points from P to Q, and $[\mathbf{z}(t + \Delta t) - \mathbf{z}(t)]/\Delta t$ points in the same direction if $\Delta t > 0$ (and in the opposite direction if $\Delta t < 0$). If t is kept fixed and Δt tends to 0, the point Q will tend to P, and the vector $[\mathbf{z}(t + \Delta t) - \mathbf{z}(t)]/\Delta t$ will tend to the **tangent vector** to the curve K at P. We see that

$$\frac{\mathbf{z}(t + \Delta t) - \mathbf{z}(t)}{\Delta t} = \left(\frac{x(t + \Delta t) - x(t)}{\Delta t}, \frac{y(t + \Delta t) - y(t)}{\Delta t}\right) \to (\dot{x}(t), \dot{y}(t)) \text{ as } t \to 0$$

Thus the vector $\dot{\mathbf{z}}(t) = (\dot{x}(t), \dot{y}(t))$, which describes how quickly $x(t)$ and $y(t)$ change when t is changed, is a tangent vector to the curve K at P, as illustrated in Fig. 2.

The general solution of (1) usually depends on two arbitrary constants A and B, and can then be written as $x = \Phi_1(t; A, B)$, $y = \Phi_2(t; A, B)$. The two constants are determined if we specify an initial condition for each variable—for example, $x(t_0) = x_0$, $y(t_0) = y_0$.

How can one find the general solution of (1)? Of course, one cannot expect exact methods to work in complete generality, but explicit solutions can be found in some important cases.

One method is to reduce (1) to a second-order differential equation in only one unknown: Use the first equation in (1) to express y as a function $y = h(t, x, \dot{x})$ of t, x, and $\dot{x}$. Differentiate this equation w.r.t. t and substitute the expressions for y and $\dot{y}$ into the second equation in (1). We then obtain a second-order differential equation to determine $x = x(t)$. When $x(t)$ is determined, we find $y(t) = h(t, x(t), \dot{x}(t))$.

EXAMPLE 1   Find the general solution of the system

$$\dot{x} = 2x + e^t y - e^t$$
$$\dot{y} = 4e^{-t}x + y$$

Find also the solution that gives $x = y = 0$ for $t = 0$.

Solution: Solving the first equation for y gives $y = \dot{x}e^{-t} - 2xe^{-t} + 1$. Differentiating w.r.t. t yields $\dot{y} = \ddot{x}e^{-t} - \dot{x}e^{-t} - 2\dot{x}e^{-t} + 2xe^{-t}$. Inserting these expressions for y and $\dot{y}$ into the second equation gives $\ddot{x}e^{-t} - 3\dot{x}e^{-t} + 2xe^{-t} = 4xe^{-t} + \dot{x}e^{-t} - 2xe^{-t} + 1$, or

$$\ddot{x} - 4\dot{x} = e^t$$

Using the methods of Section 6.3, we find that the general solution for x is

$$x = A + Be^{4t} - \tfrac{1}{3}e^t$$

From $y = \dot{x}e^{-t} - 2xe^{-t} + 1 = (4Be^{4t} - \tfrac{1}{3}e^t)e^{-t} - 2(A + Be^{4t} - \tfrac{1}{3}e^t)e^{-t} + 1$ we get

$$y = -2Ae^{-t} + 2Be^{3t} + \tfrac{4}{3}$$

If $x = y = 0$ for $t = 0$, then $A + B - \tfrac{1}{3} = 0$ and $-2A + 2B + \tfrac{4}{3} = 0$. Solving these equations yields $A = \tfrac{1}{2}$, $B = -\tfrac{1}{6}$.

Recursive Systems

Suppose that the two differential equations take the special form

$$\dot{x} = f(t, x, y), \quad \dot{y} = g(t, y)$$

so that one of the two variables varies independently of the other. Then the system can be solved recursively in two steps:

(i) first solve $\dot{y} = g(t, y)$ as an ordinary first-order differential equation to get $y(t)$;

(ii) second, substitute this value of $y = y(t)$ in the equation $\dot{x} = f(t, x, y)$ to get another first-order differential equation in $x(t)$.

Of course, one can use a similar approach to the pair of equations $\dot{x} = f(t, x)$, $\dot{y} = g(t, x, y)$.

Solution Method for Autonomous Systems

When system (1) is of the form $dx/dt = f(x, y)$, $dy/dt = g(x, y)$, so that f and g do not depend explicitly on t, there is an alternative solution procedure: Around a point where $\dot{x} \neq 0$, we can view y as a function of x with $dy/dx = \dot{y}/\dot{x} = g(x, y)/f(x, y)$. Solve this equation to give $y = \varphi(x)$. Then $x(t)$ is found by solving $\dot{x} = f(x, \varphi(x))$. Finally, $y(t) = \varphi(x(t))$.

EXAMPLE 2   Use the method described above to find the solution of the system

$$\dot{x} = y$$
$$\dot{y} = y^2/x \qquad (x > 0, \; y > 0)$$

that has $x(1) = 1$ and $y(1) = 2$.

Solution: We see that $dy/dx = \dot{y}/\dot{x} = y^2/xy = y/x$, which is a separable differential equation whose solution is $y = Ax$. Then $\dot{x} = y = Ax$, with solution $x = Be^{At}$. This gives $y = Ax = ABe^{At}$. If $x(1) = 1$ and $y(1) = 2$, then $1 = Be^{A}$ and $2 = ABe^{A}$. We find $A = 2$ and $B = e^{-2}$, so the required solution is $x = e^{2t-2}$, $y = 2e^{2t-2}$.

Linear Systems with Constant Coefficients

Consider the linear system

$$\dot{x} = a_{11}x + a_{12}y + b_1(t)$$
$$\dot{y} = a_{21}x + a_{22}y + b_2(t) \qquad (2)$$

Suppose $a_{12} \neq 0$. (If $a_{12} = 0$, the first equation is a simple linear differential equation in only one unknown.) Let us derive a second-order equation by modifying the method used in Example 1. Differentiating the first equation w.r.t. t, then substituting $\dot{y}$ from the second equation in (2), we obtain $\ddot{x} = a_{11}\dot{x} + a_{12}(a_{21}x + a_{22}y + b_2(t)) + \dot{b}_1(t)$. Substituting $a_{12}y = \dot{x} - a_{11}x - b_1(t)$ from the first equation in (2), then simplifying, we have

$$\ddot{x} - (a_{11} + a_{22})\dot{x} + (a_{11}a_{22} - a_{12}a_{21})x = a_{12}b_2(t) - a_{22}b_1(t) + \dot{b}_1(t) \qquad (3)$$

This is a second-order differential equation with constant coefficients. The general solution is of the form $x(t) = Au_1(t) + Bu_2(t) + u^*(t)$, where A and B are arbitrary constants.

The solution for $y(t)$ is found from $a_{12}y = \dot{x} - a_{11}x - b_1(t)$, and it depends on the same two constants. In fact, we obtain the following explicit formulas for the solution of system (2):

$$x(t) = Au_1(t) + Bu_2(t) + u^*(t)$$
$$y(t) = P(A, B)u_1(t) + Q(A, B)u_2(t) + \frac{1}{a_{12}}[\dot{u}^*(t) - a_{11}u^*(t) - b_1(t)] \qquad (4)$$

where the functions $P(A, B)$ and $Q(A, B)$ are defined as follows: If λ_1 and λ_2 denote the roots of the characteristic polynomial of equation (3), then:

(a) If λ_1 and λ_2 are real and different and $u_1(t) = e^{\lambda_1 t}$, $u_2(t) = e^{\lambda_2 t}$, then $P(A, B) = A(\lambda_1 - a_{11})/a_{12}$ and $Q(A, B) = B(\lambda_2 - a_{11})/a_{12}$.

(b) If $\lambda_1 = \lambda_2$ is a real double root and $u_1(t) = e^{\lambda_1 t}$, $u_2(t) = te^{\lambda_1 t}$, then $P(A, B) = (\lambda_1 A + B - a_{11}A)/a_{12}$ and $Q(A, B) = B(\lambda_1 - a_{11})/a_{12}$.

(c) If $\lambda_1 = \alpha + i\beta$ and $\lambda_2 = \alpha - i\beta$, $\beta \neq 0$, and $u_1(t) = e^{\alpha t}\cos\beta t$, $u_2(t) = e^{\alpha t}\sin\beta t$, then $P(A, B) = [\alpha A + \beta B - a_{11}A]/a_{12}$ and $Q(A, B) = [\alpha B - \beta A - a_{11}B]/a_{12}$.

An argument similar to the above shows that y must satisfy the differential equation

$$\ddot{y} - (a_{11} + a_{22})\dot{y} + (a_{11}a_{22} - a_{12}a_{21})y = a_{21}b_1(t) - a_{11}b_2(t) + \dot{b}_2(t) \qquad (5)$$

Note that (3) and (5) have the same associated homogeneous equation, so that their characteristic equations are identical.[1]

We have seen how the problem of solving (most) first-order systems of the form (1) can be transformed into the problem of solving one second-order equation in only one of the variables. On the other hand, any second-order differential equation $\ddot{x} = F(t, x, \dot{x})$ can be converted into a system of the form (1) simply by defining a new variable $y = \dot{x}$. Then $\dot{y} = \ddot{x} = F(t, x, \dot{x}) = F(t, x, y)$, and the system becomes

$$\dot{x} = y, \qquad \dot{y} = F(t, x, y) \tag{6}$$

Solutions Based on Eigenvalues

With $b_1(t) = b_2(t) = 0$, system (2) reduces to the homogeneous system

$$\begin{matrix} \dot{x} = a_{11}x + a_{12}y \\ \dot{y} = a_{21}x + a_{22}y \end{matrix} \quad \Longleftrightarrow \quad \begin{pmatrix} \dot{x} \\ \dot{y} \end{pmatrix} = \begin{pmatrix} a_{11} & a_{12} \\ a_{21} & a_{22} \end{pmatrix} \begin{pmatrix} x \\ y \end{pmatrix} \tag{7}$$

Let us see if by an appropriate choice of numbers v_1, v_2, and λ we can make $(x, y) = (v_1 e^{\lambda t}, v_2 e^{\lambda t})$ a solution of (7). Inserting $\dot{x} = v_1 \lambda e^{\lambda t}$ and $\dot{y} = v_2 \lambda e^{\lambda t}$ into (7) yields

$$\begin{pmatrix} v_1 \lambda e^{\lambda t} \\ v_2 \lambda e^{\lambda t} \end{pmatrix} = \begin{pmatrix} a_{11} & a_{12} \\ a_{21} & a_{22} \end{pmatrix} \begin{pmatrix} v_1 e^{\lambda t} \\ v_2 e^{\lambda t} \end{pmatrix}$$

Cancelling the factor $e^{\lambda t}$ gives the equation

$$\begin{pmatrix} a_{11} & a_{12} \\ a_{21} & a_{22} \end{pmatrix} \begin{pmatrix} v_1 \\ v_2 \end{pmatrix} = \lambda \begin{pmatrix} v_1 \\ v_2 \end{pmatrix}$$

In the terminology of Chapter 1, $\begin{pmatrix} v_1 \\ v_2 \end{pmatrix}$ is an eigenvector of the matrix $\mathbf{A} = \begin{pmatrix} a_{11} & a_{12} \\ a_{21} & a_{22} \end{pmatrix}$, with eigenvalue λ. The eigenvalues are the solutions of the equation

$$\begin{vmatrix} a_{11} - \lambda & a_{12} \\ a_{21} & a_{22} - \lambda \end{vmatrix} = \lambda^2 - (a_{11} + a_{22})\lambda + (a_{11}a_{22} - a_{12}a_{21}) = 0 \tag{8}$$

The case in which $\mathbf{A}$ has different real eigenvalues, λ_1 and λ_2, is the simplest. Then $\mathbf{A}$ has two linearly independent eigenvectors $\begin{pmatrix} v_1 \\ v_2 \end{pmatrix}$ and $\begin{pmatrix} u_1 \\ u_2 \end{pmatrix}$, and the general solution of (7) is

$$\begin{pmatrix} x \\ y \end{pmatrix} = Ae^{\lambda_1 t} \begin{pmatrix} v_1 \\ v_2 \end{pmatrix} + Be^{\lambda_2 t} \begin{pmatrix} u_1 \\ u_2 \end{pmatrix} \tag{9}$$

where A and B are arbitrary constants.

---

[1] If we solve equations (3) and (5) separately, we end up with 4 constants. But these 4 constants cannot all be chosen independently of one another. Once we have chosen the constants for x, say, the constants for y are already completely determined, since (2) gives $y = (1/a_{12})(\dot{x} - a_{11}x - b_1(t))$.

EXAMPLE 3   Solve the system $\dot{x} = 2y$, $\dot{y} = x + y$ by the eigenvalue method.

Solution: The system can be written as

$$\begin{pmatrix} \dot{x} \\ \dot{y} \end{pmatrix} = \mathbf{A} \begin{pmatrix} x \\ y \end{pmatrix} \quad \text{with} \quad \mathbf{A} = \begin{pmatrix} 0 & 2 \\ 1 & 1 \end{pmatrix} \tag{*}$$

The characteristic polynomial of $\mathbf{A}$ is $\begin{vmatrix} 0 - \lambda & 2 \\ 1 & 1 - \lambda \end{vmatrix} = \lambda^2 - \lambda - 2 = (\lambda + 1)(\lambda - 2)$.

Hence the eigenvalues are $\lambda_1 = -1$ and $\lambda_2 = 2$. Corresponding eigenvectors are $\begin{pmatrix} -2 \\ 1 \end{pmatrix}$ and $\begin{pmatrix} 1 \\ 1 \end{pmatrix}$, respectively. According to (9), the general solution of (*) is therefore

$$\begin{pmatrix} x \\ y \end{pmatrix} = Ae^{-t} \begin{pmatrix} -2 \\ 1 \end{pmatrix} + Be^{2t} \begin{pmatrix} 1 \\ 1 \end{pmatrix} = \begin{pmatrix} -2Ae^{-t} + Be^{2t} \\ Ae^{-t} + Be^{2t} \end{pmatrix}$$

Consider a nonhomogeneous system of the form

$$\begin{aligned} \dot{x} &= a_{11}x + a_{12}y + b_1 \\ \dot{y} &= a_{21}x + a_{22}y + b_2 \end{aligned} \tag{10}$$

where b_1 and b_2 are constants. This can be transformed into a homogeneous system by introducing new variables. The method is illustrated in the next example.

EXAMPLE 4   Find the solutions of the system

$$\begin{aligned} \dot{x} &= 2y + 6 \\ \dot{y} &= x + y - 3 \end{aligned} \tag{*}$$

First note that the equilibrium point (where $\dot{x} = \dot{y} = 0$) is $(6, -3)$. Introduce new variables $z = x - 6$ and $w = y + 3$ that measure the deviation of x and y from their equilibrium values. Then $\dot{z} = \dot{x}$ and $\dot{w} = \dot{y}$, so the system (*) is transformed into

$$\begin{aligned} \dot{z} &= 2(w - 3) + 6 = 2w \\ \dot{w} &= (z + 6) + (w - 3) - 3 = z + w \end{aligned}$$

According to the preceding example the general solution of the system is $z = -2Ae^{-t} + Be^{2t}$ and $w = Ae^{-t} + Be^{2t}$. The general solution of (*) is therefore $x = z + 6 = -2Ae^{-t} + Be^{2t} + 6$ and $y = w - 3 = Ae^{-t} + Be^{2t} - 3$.

PROBLEMS FOR SECTION 6.5

1. Find the general solutions of the following systems:

(a)
$$\begin{aligned} \dot{x} &= y \\ \dot{y} &= x + t \end{aligned}$$

(b)
$$\begin{aligned} \dot{x} &= x + y \\ \dot{y} &= x - y \end{aligned}$$

(c)
$$\begin{aligned} \dot{x} &= 2x - 3y \\ \dot{y} &= -x + t \end{aligned}$$

2. Find the unique solutions of the given systems that satisfy the given initial conditions.

    (a) $\dot{x}(t) = a(x(t) + y(t))$, $\dot{y}(t) = b(x(t) + y(t))$, $x(0) = \frac{1}{2}$, $y(0) = \frac{1}{2}$

    (b) $\dot{x} = 2tx + y$, $\dot{y} = -2(t + x)$, $x(0) = 1$, $y(0) = 1$

    (c) $\dot{x} = -2y + \sin t$, $\dot{y} = 2x + 1 - \cos t$, $x(0) = 0$, $y(0) = 0$

3. (a) Find the general solution of the differential equation $\ddot{x} - 2\dot{x} - x = 0$.

    (b) Find the general solution of the system

    $$\dot{x} = x + e^{2t} p$$
    $$\dot{p} = 2e^{-2t} x - p$$

4. In a model by M.J. Beckmann and H.E. Ryder the following system of differential equations is encountered:

    $$\dot{\pi}(t) = \alpha \pi(t) - \sigma(t), \quad \dot{\sigma}(t) = \pi(t) - \frac{1}{\beta}\sigma(t)$$

    Find the general solution when $\alpha + 1/\beta > 2$.

5. Find the solution curve passing through $(t, x, y) = (1, 1, \sqrt{2})$ for the system

    $$\dot{x} = \frac{ty^2}{1 + x^2}, \quad \dot{y} = \frac{txy}{1 + x^2} \qquad (t > 0)$$

    (*Hint:* See Example 2.)

6.6 Equilibrium Points for Linear Systems

Consider the linear system with constant coefficients

$$\dot{x} = a_{11}x + a_{12}y + b_1 \qquad \Longleftrightarrow \qquad \begin{pmatrix} \dot{x} \\ \dot{y} \end{pmatrix} = A \begin{pmatrix} x \\ y \end{pmatrix} + \begin{pmatrix} b_1 \\ b_2 \end{pmatrix} \tag{1}$$
$$\dot{y} = a_{21}x + a_{22}y + b_2$$

The equilibrium points for this system are determined by the equations

$$\begin{array}{cc} a_{11}x + a_{12}y + b_1 = 0 & \qquad a_{11}x + a_{12}y = -b_1 \\ & \text{or} \\ a_{21}x + a_{22}y + b_2 = 0 & \qquad a_{21}x + a_{22}y = -b_2 \end{array} \tag{2}$$

which result from putting $\dot{x} = \dot{y} = 0$ in (1). If $|A| \neq 0$, this system has a unique solution (x^*, y^*), which is called an **equilibrium point** (or an **equilibrium state**) for the system (1). Cramer's rule tells us that the equilibrium point is

$$x^* = \frac{a_{12}b_2 - a_{22}b_1}{|A|}, \quad y^* = \frac{a_{21}b_1 - a_{11}b_2}{|A|} \tag{3}$$

The pair $(x(t), y(t)) = (x^*, y^*)$ with $(\dot{x}(t), \dot{y}(t)) = (0, 0)$ will then be a solution of (1). Since $\dot{x} = \dot{y} = 0$ at the equilibrium point, it follows that if the system is at (x^*, y^*), it has always been there and will always stay there.

EXAMPLE 1   Find the equilibrium point for the system

$$\begin{array}{l} \dot{x} = -2x + y + 2 \\ \dot{y} = -2y + 8 \end{array} \quad \Longleftrightarrow \quad \begin{pmatrix} \dot{x} \\ \dot{y} \end{pmatrix} = \begin{pmatrix} -2 & 1 \\ 0 & -2 \end{pmatrix} \begin{pmatrix} x \\ y \end{pmatrix} + \begin{pmatrix} 2 \\ 8 \end{pmatrix}$$

Find also the general solution, and examine what happens when t tends to infinity.

Solution: We easily see that $|A| \neq 0$ and that $(x^*, y^*) = (3, 4)$ is the equilibrium point. The solution of the system is found by using the methods explained in the previous section. The general solution turns out to be $x(t) = Ae^{-2t} + Bte^{-2t} + 3$, $y(t) = Be^{-2t} + 4$. As t tends to infinity, $(x(t), y(t))$ tends to the equilibrium point $(3, 4)$.

In general, an equilibrium point (x^*, y^*) for (1) is called **globally asymptotically stable** if every solution tends to the equilibrium point as $t \to \infty$. Thus the equilibrium point $(3, 4)$ in Example 1 is globally asymptotically stable.

We showed in Section 6.5 (see (6.5.3) and (6.5.5)) that a solution $(x(t), y(t))$ of (1) must satisfy the two second-order equations ($\text{tr}(A)$ denotes the trace of A, see Section 1.6)

$$\ddot{x} - \text{tr}(A)\dot{x} + |A|x = a_{12}b_2 - a_{22}b_1, \qquad \ddot{y} - \text{tr}(A)\dot{y} + |A|y = a_{21}b_1 - a_{11}b_2 \qquad (4)$$

If $|A| \neq 0$, these equations have x^* and y^* given in (3) as their respective equilibrium points. Moreover, the characteristic equation of each of the equations in (4) is the same as the eigenvalue equation of A. (See (6.5.8).) Using (6.4.2) and (6.4.3), we obtain the following result:

THEOREM 6.6.1

Suppose that $|A| \neq 0$. Then the equilibrium point (x^*, y^*) for the linear system

$$\begin{array}{l} \dot{x} = a_{11}x + a_{12}y + b_1 \\ \dot{y} = a_{21}x + a_{22}y + b_2 \end{array} \quad \Longleftrightarrow \quad \begin{pmatrix} \dot{x} \\ \dot{y} \end{pmatrix} = A \begin{pmatrix} x \\ y \end{pmatrix} + \begin{pmatrix} b_1 \\ b_2 \end{pmatrix}$$

is globally asymptotically stable if and only if

$$\text{tr}(A) = a_{11} + a_{22} < 0 \quad \text{and} \quad \det(A) = a_{11}a_{22} - a_{12}a_{21} > 0$$

or equivalently, if and only if both eigenvalues of A have negative real parts.

EXAMPLE 2   Examine the stability of the equilibrium point $(0, 0)$ for the system

$$\begin{array}{l} \dot{x} = y \\ \dot{y} = -2x - y \end{array} \quad \Longleftrightarrow \quad \begin{pmatrix} \dot{x} \\ \dot{y} \end{pmatrix} = \begin{pmatrix} 0 & 1 \\ -2 & -1 \end{pmatrix} \begin{pmatrix} x \\ y \end{pmatrix}$$

Solution: The coefficient matrix has trace -1 and determinant 2, so according to Theorem 6.6.1 the system is globally asymptotically stable. In this case all solutions converge to the equilibrium point $(0, 0)$ as $t \to \infty$. It is easy to confirm this statement by finding the general solution of the system. The methods explained in Section 6.5 lead to a second-order equation in x,

$$\ddot{x} + \dot{x} + 2x = 0, \quad \text{with the solution} \quad x = e^{-t/2}\left(A \cos \tfrac{1}{2}\sqrt{7}\,t + B \sin \tfrac{1}{2}\sqrt{7}\,t\right)$$

By using $y = \dot{x}$, we find a similar expression for y. We see from the formulas obtained that $x(t)$ and $y(t)$ both tend to 0 as $t \to \infty$.

Alternative Behaviour Around Equilibrium Points

In this subsection we give a brief survey of how system (1) behaves when the equilibrium point is not necessarily globally asymptotically stable.

According to equation (6.5.4), the general solution of (1) is

$$\begin{aligned} x(t) &= Au_1(t) + Bu_2(t) + x^* \\ y(t) &= P(A, B)u_1(t) + Q(A, B)u_2(t) + y^* \end{aligned} \tag{5}$$

where $u_1(t)$ and $u_2(t)$ are described in (a)–(c) following equation (6.5.4) and (x^*, y^*) is the equilibrium point.

Disregarding the cases where one or both eigenvalues are 0, we have the follow results:

(A) If both eigenvalues of **A** have negative real parts, then (x^*, y^*) is globally asymptotically stable (a **sink**). All solution curves converge to the equilibrium point as $t \to \infty$.

(B) If both eigenvalues of **A** have positive real parts, then (x^*, y^*) is a **source**. In this case all solution curves starting away from the equilibrium point explode as t increases, i.e. $\|(x(t), y(t))\| \to \infty$ as $t \to \infty$. See Example 3(a).

(C) If the eigenvalues are real with opposite signs, $\lambda_1 < 0$ and $\lambda_2 > 0$, then (x^*, y^*) is a so-called **saddle point**. (The eigenvalues are real and of opposite signs iff the determinant of **A** is negative. See Note 6.9.1.) In this case only solutions of the form $x(t) = Ae^{\lambda_1 t} + x^*$, $y(t) = A(\lambda_1 - a_{11})e^{\lambda_1 t}/a_{12} + y^*$ converge to the equilibrium point as $t \to \infty$. All other solution curves move away from the equilibrium point as $t \to \infty$. (See Section 6.9 for further discussions.)

(D) If the eigenvalues are purely imaginary ($\lambda_{1,2} = \pm i\beta$), then (x^*, y^*) is a so-called **centre**. Then all solution curves are periodic with the same period. The solution curves are ellipses, or circles. See Example 3(b).

EXAMPLE 3   Examine the character of the equilibrium points for the following systems:

$$\text{(a)} \quad \begin{aligned} \dot{x} &= 2y \\ \dot{y} &= -x + 2y \end{aligned} \qquad \text{(b)} \quad \begin{aligned} \dot{x} &= -y \\ \dot{y} &= x \end{aligned}$$

Solution: In both cases the equilibrium point is $(0, 0)$.

(a) The eigenvalues are $\lambda_{1,2} = 1 \pm i$, and the general solution is $x(t) = Ae^t \cos t + Be^t \sin t$, $y(t) = \tfrac{1}{2}(A + B)e^t \cos t + \tfrac{1}{2}(-A + B)e^t \sin t$. Both $x(t)$ and $y(t)$ exhibit explosive oscillations unless $A = B = 0$.

(b) Here the eigenvalues are $\lambda_{1,2} = \pm i$ and the general solution is $x(t) = A \cos t + B \sin t$, $y(t) = A \sin t - B \cos t$. For all t we find that $x(t)^2 + y(t)^2 = A^2 + B^2$, so that the solution curves in the xy-plane are circles with centre at the equilibrium point $(0, 0)$.

PROBLEMS FOR SECTION 6.6

1. Check (if possible) the stability of the following systems by using Theorem 6.6.1:

(a) $\begin{aligned} \dot{x} &= x - 8y \\ \dot{y} &= 2x - 4y \end{aligned}$

(b) $\begin{aligned} \dot{x} &= x - 4y + 2 \\ \dot{y} &= 2x - y - 5 \end{aligned}$

(c) $\begin{aligned} \dot{x} &= -x - 3y + 5 \\ \dot{y} &= 2x - 2y + 2 \end{aligned}$

2. For what values of the constant a are the following systems globally asymptotically stable?

(a) $\begin{aligned} \dot{x} &= ax - y \\ \dot{y} &= x + ay \end{aligned}$

(b) $\begin{aligned} \dot{x} &= ax - (2a - 4)y \\ \dot{y} &= x + 2ay \end{aligned}$

3. Find the general solution of the system

$$\begin{aligned} \dot{x} &= x + 2y + 1 \\ \dot{y} &= -y + 2 \end{aligned}$$

(i) by using the same method as in Example 6.5.1, (ii) by using the eigenvalue method. Is the system globally asymptotically stable?

6.7 Phase Plane Analysis

The solution procedures studied in this chapter give explicit answers only for quite restrictive and exceptional classes of differential equations. In this section we shall indicate how, even when explicit solutions are unavailable, geometric arguments can still shed light on the structure of the solutions of autonomous systems of differential equations in the plane. System (6.5.1) is called **autonomous** (time independent) if f and g do not depend explicitly on t, so the equations become

$$\begin{aligned} \dot{x} &= f(x, y) \\ \dot{y} &= g(x, y) \end{aligned} \qquad \textbf{(autonomous system)} \qquad (1)$$

A solution $(x(t), y(t))$ of (1) describes a curve or *path* in the xy-plane. It consists of all points $\{(x(t), y(t)) : t \in I\}$, where I is the interval of definition. If $(x(t), y(t))$ is a solution of (1), then so is $(x(t + a), y(t + a))$ for any constant a. Hence $(x(t), y(t))$ and $(x(t + a), y(t + a))$ have the same path. (This is only valid for autonomous systems.) For the autonomous system (1), $(\dot{x}(t), \dot{y}(t))$ is uniquely determined at the point $(x(t), y(t))$, and two paths in the xy-plane cannot intersect.

Phase plane analysis is concerned with the technique of studying the behaviour of paths in the "phase plane" based on information obtained directly from (1).

From (1) it follows that the rates of change of $x(t)$ and $y(t)$ are given by $f(x(t), y(t))$ and $g(x(t), y(t))$, respectively. In particular, if, say, $f(x(t), y(t)) > 0$ and $g(x(t), y(t)) < 0$ at a point $P = (x(t), y(t))$, then as t increases, the system will move from the point P down and to the right. In fact the direction of motion is given by the tangent vector $(\dot{x}(t), \dot{y}(t))$ to the path at P as illustrated in Fig. 1, and the speed of motion is given by the length of the vector $(\dot{x}(t), \dot{y}(t))$.

To illustrate the dynamics of system (1), we can, in principle, draw such vectors from every point in the plane. Such a family of vectors is called a **vector field**. Of course, in practice, one can draw only a small representative sample of these vectors. On the basis of the vector field one can draw paths for the system and thereby exhibit the **phase portrait** or **phase diagram** of the system.

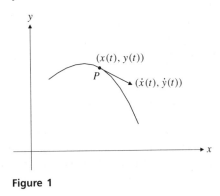

Figure 1

EXAMPLE 1   Figure 2 shows a vector field for the system

$$\dot{x} = y, \qquad \dot{y} = -2x - y \qquad (*)$$

which we studied in Example 6.6.2. The lengths of the vectors have been proportionally reduced, so as not to interfere with each other. But the length of a vector still suggests the speed of motion. Note that $(\dot{x}, \dot{y}) = (0, 0)$ only at the point $(0, 0)$, which is the *equilibrium point*.

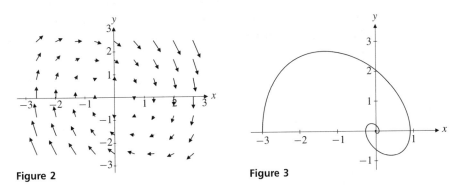

Figure 2   **Figure 3**

A closer study of the vector field seems to indicate that the paths spiral towards the equilibrium point $(0, 0)$. The speed of motion decreases as one gets closer to the origin. Figure 3 shows the particular path that starts at the point $(-3, 0)$, and spirals towards $(0, 0)$. We know from Example 6.6.2 that since $(0, 0)$ is globally asymptotically stable, *all* paths for this linear system, wherever they start, tend to the equilibrium point $(0, 0)$ as $t \to \infty$.

In general, a point (a, b) where $f(a, b) = g(a, b) = 0$ is called an **equilibrium point** (or **stationary point**) for system (1). Because $\dot{x} = \dot{y} = 0$ at an equilibrium point E, if the system is at E, then it always will be (and always was) at E.

The equilibrium points of (1) are the points of intersection of the two curves $f(x, y) = 0$ and $g(x, y) = 0$, which are called the **nullclines** of the system.

To draw a phase diagram of (1), begin by drawing the two nullclines. At each point on the nullcline $f(x, y) = 0$, the $\dot{x}$ component is zero and the velocity vector is vertical. It points up if $\dot{y} > 0$, down if $\dot{y} < 0$.

At each point on the nullcline $g(x, y) = 0$, the $\dot{y}$ component is 0, and the velocity vector is horizontal. It points to the right if $\dot{x} > 0$, to the left if $\dot{x} < 0$.

EXAMPLE 2   Draw a phase diagram for system $(*)$ in Example 1.

Solution: The nullclines and the direction of motion on paths crossing the nullclines are shown in Fig. 4. Note that the nullclines for $(*)$ divide the phase plane into four *regions* or *sectors*, denoted by (I), (II), (III), and (IV) in Fig. 4.

In sectors (I) and (II), $y > 0$, so $\dot{x} > 0$, whereas in Sectors (III) and (IV), $y < 0$ and so $\dot{x} < 0$. On the other hand, in sectors (I) and (IV), $2x + y > 0$ and so $\dot{y} < 0$, whereas in Sectors (II) and (III), $2x + y < 0$ and so $\dot{y} > 0$. (A convenient check that you have determined the direction of the arrows correctly is this: Pick a point in each of the four sectors, and calculate $(\dot{x}, \dot{y})$ at each of these points. For example, $(2, 2)$ is in sector (I) and $(\dot{x}, \dot{y}) = (2, -6)$. The point $(-2, 2)$ is in sector (II) and $(\dot{x}, \dot{y}) = (2, 2)$. In sector (III) the point $(-2, -2)$ has $(\dot{x}, \dot{y}) = (-2, 6)$. Finally, at $(2, -2)$ in sector (IV) we have $(\dot{x}, \dot{y}) = (-2, -2)$.)

In Fig. 5, the direction of motion on a path at a point in each of the four sectors is indicated by arrows. In accordance with common practice, at each of these points one arrow for each of the x and y directions is given. We usually draw the arrows with the same length. (If the arrows are given with their correct lengths, then they correspond to the vectors $(\dot{x}, 0)$ and $(0, \dot{y})$. It follows that the actual direction of the path through the point corresponds to the sum of these two vectors.)

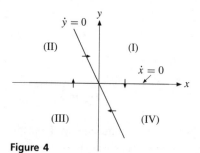

Figure 4   Figure 5

EXAMPLE 3   In a model of economic growth, capital $K = K(t)$ and consumption $C = C(t)$ satisfy
the pair of differential equations

$$\dot{K} = aK - bK^2 - C, \quad \dot{C} = w(a - 2bK)C \qquad (*)$$

Here $a, b,$ and w are positive constants. Construct a phase diagram for this system, assuming
that $K \geq 0$ and $C \geq 0$.

Solution: The nullcline $\dot{K} = 0$ is the parabola $C = aK - bK^2$, and the two other
nullclines are $C = 0$ and $K = a/2b$, which are both part of $\dot{C} = 0$. In Fig. 6 the three
nullclines are drawn. There are three equilibrium points, $(0, 0)$, $(a/b, 0)$, and $(a/2b, a^2/4b)$.

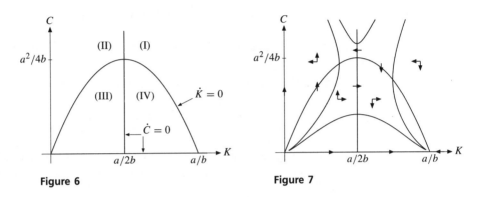

Figure 6   **Figure 7**

In sector (I), $C > aK - bK^2$ and $K > a/2b$, so $\dot{K} < 0$ and $\dot{C} < 0$. In sectors (II), (III),
and (IV), we have $\dot{K} < 0$, $\dot{C} > 0$, then $\dot{K} > 0$, $\dot{C} > 0$, and $\dot{K} > 0$, $\dot{C} < 0$, respectively.
The appropriate arrows have been drawn in Fig. 7. Some paths consistent with the arrows
are indicated.

These examples indicate that useful information about the solution paths is obtained by
partitioning the phase plane into regions where we know the direction of increase or decrease
of each variable. In particular, the partition will often indicate whether or not a certain
equilibrium point is stable, in the sense that paths starting near the equilibrium point tend to
that point as $t \to \infty$. However, to determine whether an equilibrium point is stable or not,
a phase diagram analysis should be supplemented with tests based on analytical methods
like those set out in the subsequent sections.

PROBLEMS FOR SECTION 6.7

1. Perform a phase plane analysis of the following systems and then find their explicit
   solutions.

   (a)
   $$\dot{x} = y$$
   $$\dot{y} = x$$

   (b)
   $$\dot{x} = x + y$$
   $$\dot{y} = x - y$$

   (c)
   $$\dot{x} = x - 4y$$
   $$\dot{y} = 2x - 5y$$

2. Perform a phase plane analysis of the system

$$\dot{x} = x(k - ay), \quad \dot{y} = y(-h + bx), \quad x > 0, \, y > 0$$

where a, b, h, and k are positive constants. This is the famous Lotka–Volterra model from mathematical biology. See Example 7.5.2.

3. In an economic model, $K = K(t)$ denotes capital, $C = C(t)$ consumption, while α, A, and r are positive constants, with $\alpha < 1$. Assume that

$$\dot{K} = AK^\alpha - C$$
$$\dot{C} = C\left(\alpha AK^{\alpha-1} - r\right)$$

Perform a phase plane analysis of this system when $A = 2$, $\alpha = 0.5$, and $r = 0.05$.

4. (a) Draw a phase diagram and some typical paths for the autonomous system

$$\dot{x} = -x, \quad \dot{y} = -xy - y^2$$

(b) Solve the system with $x(0) = -1$, $y(0) = 1$. (*Hint:* You will need to solve a Bernoulli equation. See Section 5.6. One of the integrals cannot be evaluated.) Find the limit $\lim_{t \to \infty} (x(t), y(t))$.

5. Consider the system

$$\dot{x} = -x, \quad \dot{y} = -x^2 y$$

Here is $(0, 0)$ an equilibrium point. (In fact, $(0, b)$ is an equilibrium point for every value of b.) Find the unique solution of the system that passes through the point $(1, 1)$ for $t = 0$. Show that the corresponding path does not converge to $(0, 0)$.

6. (a) Perform a phase plane analysis of the following system, where $x > 0$ and $y > 0$.

$$\dot{x} = x(y - x - \ln x - 1), \quad \dot{y} = 1 - x \qquad (*)$$

(b) Introduce the transform $z = y - \ln x$, and show that $(*)$ becomes

$$\dot{z} = 2 - z, \quad \dot{y} = 1 - e^{y-z} \qquad (**)$$

Perform a phase plane analysis of this system. (Whereas stability of the equilibrium point $(\bar{x}, \bar{y}) = (1, 2)$ is not clear from the diagram in (a), the corresponding equilibrium point $(\bar{z}, \bar{y}) = (2, 2)$ is "clearly" stable in the diagram in (b). This example is due to Conlisk and Ramanathan, *Review of Economic Studies* (1970).)

6.8 Stability for Nonlinear Systems

In this section we study the stability theory for the autonomous system

$$\dot{x} = f(x, y)$$
$$\dot{y} = g(x, y) \tag{1}$$

An equilibrium point (a, b) of the system (where $f(a, b) = g(a, b) = 0$) is called **locally asymptotically stable** if any path starting near (a, b) tends to (a, b) as $t \to \infty$. An equilibrium point (a, b) is called **globally asymptotically stable** if *any* solution of (1) (wherever it starts) converge to (a, b) as $t \to \infty$. (A more precise definition of stability is given in Section 7.5.)

To examine whether (a, b) is locally asymptotically stable, we have to consider how solutions of the system behave in a neighbourhood of (a, b). To this end, consider the linear approximation of the functions $f(x, y)$ and $g(x, y)$ about (a, b). If (x, y) is sufficiently close to (a, b), then (see Section 2.6),

$$f(x, y) \approx f(a, b) + f_1'(a, b)(x - a) + f_2'(a, b)(y - b)$$
$$g(x, y) \approx g(a, b) + g_1'(a, b)(x - a) + g_2'(a, b)(y - b)$$

Because $f(a, b) = 0$ and $g(a, b) = 0$,

$$f(x, y) \approx f_1'(a, b)x + f_2'(a, b)y + b_1$$

and

$$g(x, y) \approx g_1'(a, b)x + g_2'(a, b)y + b_2$$

where $b_1 = -f_1'(a, b)a - f_2'(a, b)b$ and $b_2 = -g_1'(a, b)a - g_2'(a, b)b$. It is therefore reasonable to expect that in a neighbourhood of (a, b), system (1) "behaves" approximately like the linear system

$$\dot{x} = f_1'(a, b)x + f_2'(a, b)y + b_1$$
$$\dot{y} = g_1'(a, b)x + g_2'(a, b)y + b_2 \tag{$*$}$$

Note that the definitions of b_1 and b_2 imply that (a, b) is also an equilibrium point of system ($*$). According to Theorem 6.6.1, for this linear system (a, b) is globally asymptotically stable if and only if the eigenvalues of the matrix

$$\mathbf{A} = \begin{pmatrix} f_1'(a, b) & f_2'(a, b) \\ g_1'(a, b) & g_2'(a, b) \end{pmatrix} \tag{2}$$

both have negative real parts, or equivalently, if and only if $\mathbf{A}$ has negative trace and positive determinant. Since ($*$) "behaves" approximately like (1) near (a, b), we conjecture that in this case (a, b) is a *locally* asymptotically stable equilibrium point for system (1). This conjecture is indeed correct. The first proof was given by the Russian mathematician A.M. Lyapunov, who in his doctoral thesis from 1892 laid much of the foundation for the stability theory for differential equations. (For a proof, see Coddington and Levinson (1955).)

THEOREM 6.8.1 (LYAPUNOV)

Suppose that f and g are C^1 functions and let (a, b) be an equilibrium point for the system

$$\dot{x} = f(x, y), \qquad \dot{y} = g(x, y)$$

Let $\mathbf{A}$ be the Jacobian matrix $\mathbf{A} = \begin{pmatrix} f_1'(a, b) & f_2'(a, b) \\ g_1'(a, b) & g_2'(a, b) \end{pmatrix}$.

If

$$\operatorname{tr}(\mathbf{A}) = f_1'(a, b) + g_2'(a, b) < 0$$

and

$$\det(\mathbf{A}) = f_1'(a, b)g_2'(a, b) - f_2'(a, b)g_1'(a, b) > 0$$

i.e. if both eigenvalues of $\mathbf{A}$ have negative real parts, then (a, b) is locally asymptotically stable.

NOTE 1   If the eigenvalues λ_1 and λ_2 of $\mathbf{A}$ in Theorem 6.8.1 are real with $\lambda_1 < \lambda_2 < 0$, then all the solution paths that converge to (a, b) as $t \to \infty$, become "tangent in the limit" to the line through (a, b) with the same direction as the eigenvector corresponding to λ_2. See Theorem 6.9.1 for the case $\lambda_1 < 0 < \lambda_2$.

EXAMPLE 1   The system

$$\dot{x} = f(x, y) = -3x - 2y + 8x^2 + y^3$$
$$\dot{y} = g(x, y) = 3x + y - 3x^2y^2 + y^4$$

has $(0, 0)$ as an equilibrium point. Prove that it is locally asymptotically stable.

Solution: Here $f_1'(0, 0) = -3$, $f_2'(0, 0) = -2$, $g_1'(0, 0) = 3$, and $g_2'(0, 0) = 1$, so $\operatorname{tr}(\mathbf{A}) = -3 + 1 = -2 < 0$ and $\det(\mathbf{A}) = -3 - (-6) = 3 > 0$. By Theorem 6.8.1, the equilibrium point $(0, 0)$ is locally asymptotically stable.

EXAMPLE 2   **(Price Adjustment Mechanism)** Consider the following system of differential equations (generalizing Example 5.7.2),

$$\dot{p} = H_1(D_1(p, q) - S_1(p, q)), \qquad \dot{q} = H_2(D_2(p, q) - S_2(p, q)) \qquad (*)$$

Here p and q denote prices of two different commodities, $D_i(p, q)$ and $S_i(p, q)$, $i = 1, 2$ are demand and supply for the two commodities, while H_1 and H_2 are fixed functions of one variable. Assume that $H_1(0) = H_2(0) = 0$ and that $H_1' > 0$, $H_2' > 0$, so that H_1 and H_2 are both strictly increasing. This implies that if there is excess demand for commodity 1, so that $D_1(p, q) - S_1(p, q) > 0$, then $\dot{p} > 0$, and thus the price of commodity 1 will increase. The corresponding property holds for commodity 2.

Suppose (p^0, q^0) is an equilibrium point for system $(*)$. By our assumptions on H_1 and H_2, we have $D_1(p^0, q^0) = S_1(p^0, q^0)$, $D_2(p^0, q^0) = S_2(p^0, q^0)$. Thus, at prices p^0 and q^0, demand is equal to supply for each commodity. The stability properties of the equilibrium can be examined by appealing to Theorem 6.8.1: *The equilibrium point (p^0, q^0) is asymptotically stable for system* (∗) *provided*

$$H_1'(0)\left(\frac{\partial D_1}{\partial p} - \frac{\partial S_1}{\partial p}\right) + H_2'(0)\left(\frac{\partial D_2}{\partial q} - \frac{\partial S_2}{\partial q}\right) < 0 \qquad (a)$$

and

$$\left(\frac{\partial D_1}{\partial p} - \frac{\partial S_1}{\partial p}\right)\left(\frac{\partial D_2}{\partial q} - \frac{\partial S_2}{\partial q}\right) > \left(\frac{\partial D_1}{\partial q} - \frac{\partial S_1}{\partial q}\right)\left(\frac{\partial D_2}{\partial p} - \frac{\partial S_2}{\partial p}\right) \qquad (b)$$

All the partial derivatives are evaluated at (p^0, q^0), and in (b) we have cancelled the positive factor $H_1'(0) H_2'(0)$. Normally, $\partial D_1/\partial p$ and $\partial D_2/\partial q$ are negative, while $\partial S_1/\partial p$ and $\partial S_2/\partial q$ are positive. (If the price of some commodity increases, then the demand goes down while supply goes up.) Because $H_1' > 0$ and $H_2' > 0$, we conclude that (a) is "normally" satisfied. In order to determine the sign in (b), the functions involved must be further specified. However, the left-hand side depends on "own" price effects—how p affects D_1 and S_1, and how q affects D_2 and S_2—whereas the right-hand side depends on "cross" price effects.

Olech's Theorem

We end this section with a brief look at a special result on *global* stability of an autonomous system of differential equations in the plane. (See Olech (1963).)

THEOREM 6.8.2 (OLECH)

Consider the following system, where f and g are C^1 functions in $\mathbb{R}^2$,

$$\dot{x} = f(x, y), \quad \dot{y} = g(x, y)$$

and let (a, b) be an equilibrium point. Let $\mathbf{A}(x, y) = \begin{pmatrix} f_1'(x, y) & f_2'(x, y) \\ g_1'(x, y) & g_2'(x, y) \end{pmatrix}$, and assume that the following three conditions are all satisfied:

(a) $\operatorname{tr}(\mathbf{A}(x, y)) = f_1'(x, y) + g_2'(x, y) < 0$ in all of $\mathbb{R}^2$

(b) $\det(\mathbf{A}(x, y)) = f_1'(x, y)g_2'(x, y) - f_2'(x, y)g_1'(x, y) > 0$ in all of $\mathbb{R}^2$

(c) $f_1'(x, y)g_2'(x, y) \neq 0$ in all of $\mathbb{R}^2$ or $f_2'(x, y)g_1'(x, y) \neq 0$ in all of $\mathbb{R}^2$

Then (a, b) is globally asymptotically stable.

In contrast to the Lyapunov theorem, which gives local stability, conditions (a), (b), and (c) in Olech's theorem are required to hold throughout $\mathbb{R}^2$, not only at the equilibrium point. But then these stronger conditions give global stability.

EXAMPLE 3   Use Theorem 6.8.2 to prove that $(0, 0)$ is a globally asymptotically stable equilibrium for

$$\dot{x} = f(x, y) = 1 - e^{x-y}, \quad \dot{y} = g(x, y) = -y$$

Solution: Here $f_1'(x, y) = -e^{x-y}$, $f_2'(x, y) = e^{x-y}$, $g_1'(x, y) = 0$, and $g_2'(x, y) = -1$. It follows immediately that conditions (a), (b), and (c) in Theorem 6.8.2 are all satisfied, so the equilibrium point $(0, 0)$ is globally asymptotically stable.

PROBLEMS FOR SECTION 6.8

1. Determine (if possible) the local asymptotic stability of the following systems at the given stationary points by using Theorem 6.8.1:

(a) $\begin{aligned}\dot{x} &= -x + \tfrac{1}{2}y^2 \\ \dot{y} &= 2x - 2y\end{aligned}$ at $(0, 0)$

(b) $\begin{aligned}\dot{x} &= x - 3y + 2x^2 + y^2 - xy \\ \dot{y} &= 2x - y - e^{x-y}\end{aligned}$ at $(1, 1)$

(c) $\begin{aligned}\dot{x} &= -x^3 - y \\ \dot{y} &= x - y^3\end{aligned}$ at $(0, 0)$

(d) $\begin{aligned}\dot{x} &= 2x + 8 \sin y \\ \dot{y} &= 2 - e^x - 3y - \cos y\end{aligned}$ at $(0, 0)$

2. Use Theorem 6.8.2 to show that $(0, 0)$ is a globally asymptotically stable equilibrium point for the system

$$\dot{x} = y, \quad \dot{y} = -ky - w^2 x \quad (k > 0, \, w \neq 0)$$

3. G. Heal studies the system

$$\dot{q} = a\big(p - c(q)\big), \qquad \dot{p} = b\big(D(p) - q\big)$$

where q is the amount sold of a commodity, p is its price per unit, $c(q)$ is the average cost function, and $D(p)$ is the demand function. Here a and b are positive constants and $D'(p) < 0$. Prove that an equilibrium point (q^*, p^*) (where $p^* = c(q^*)$ and $D(p^*) = q^*$) is locally asymptotically stable provided $c'(q^*) > 0$.

4. A model of the business cycle by N. Kaldor uses the system

$$\dot{Y} = \alpha(I(Y, K) - S(Y, K)), \quad \dot{K} = I(Y, K) \quad (\alpha > 0) \tag{$*$}$$

where Y is national income, K is capital stock, $I(Y, K)$ is an investment function and $S(Y, K)$ is a savings function. Assume that $I'_Y > 0$, $I'_K < 0$, $S'_Y > 0$, $S'_K < 0$, and $I'_K - S'_K < 0$. Use Olech's theorem to prove that an equilibrium point for $(*)$ is globally asymptotically stable provided $\alpha(I'_Y - S'_Y) + I'_K < 0$ and $I'_K S'_Y < S'_K I'_Y$.

5. (a) In a model of pollution, $K = K(t)$ denotes the capital stock of the economy and $P = P(t)$ denotes the level of pollution at time t. The development of the economy is described by the system

$$\dot{K} = K(sK^{\alpha-1} - \delta), \quad \dot{P} = K^\beta - \gamma P \tag{$*$}$$

The constants satisfy the conditions $s \in (0, 1)$, $\alpha \in (0, 1)$, $\delta > 0$, $\gamma > 0$, and $\beta > 1$. Find the equilibrium point (K^*, P^*) in the open first quadrant, and check (if possible) the stability of the point by using Theorem 6.8.1.

(b) Find an explicit expression for $K(t)$ when $K(0) = K_0 \geq 0$, and examine its limit as $t \to \infty$.

6.9 Saddle Points

Dynamic economic models often have equilibria that are not asymptotically stable. In some cases a different type of behaviour near an equilibrium is encountered: Two paths approach the equilibrium point from opposite directions as $t \to \infty$. All other paths move away from the equilibrium point. The precise result is this:.

THEOREM 6.9.1 (LOCAL SADDLE POINT)

Suppose that f and g are C^1 functions and let (a, b) be an equilibrium point for the system

$$\dot{x} = f(x, y), \qquad \dot{y} = g(x, y)$$

Let $\mathbf{A} = \begin{pmatrix} f_1'(a, b) & f_2'(a, b) \\ g_1'(a, b) & g_2'(a, b) \end{pmatrix}$ be the Jacobian matrix, and suppose that

$$\det(\mathbf{A}) = f_1'(a, b)g_2'(a, b) - f_2'(a, b)g_1'(a, b) < 0$$

or, equivalently, that the eigenvalues of $\mathbf{A}$ are nonzero real numbers of opposite signs. Then, for any given start point t_0, there exist exactly two solution paths $(x_1(t), y_1(t))$ and $(x_2(t), y_2(t))$ defined on $[t_0, \infty)$ that converge towards (a, b) from opposite directions in the phase plane. As $t \to \infty$, both paths become "tangent in the limit" to the line through (a, b) with the same direction as the eigenvector corresponding to the negative eigenvalue of $\mathbf{A}$. Such an equilibrium is called a **local saddle point**.

NOTE 1 The characteristic equation of $\mathbf{A}$ is $r^2 - \text{tr}(\mathbf{A})r + \det(\mathbf{A}) = 0$. The quadratic equation $r^2 + ar + b = 0$ has the two roots $r_{1,2} = -\frac{1}{2}a \pm \frac{1}{2}\sqrt{a^2 - 4b}$. If $b < 0$, both roots are real and nonzero, and moreover $r_1 r_2 = b < 0$, so the roots are of opposite signs. On the other hand, if r_1 and r_2 are real and of opposite signs, then $b = r_1 r_2 < 0$. This explains the equivalence in the theorem.

NOTE 2 It is important to realize that the trajectories of the solutions guaranteed by Theorem 6.9.1 could have their starting points very close to the equilibrium although their solutions are defined on an infinite time interval. This is why we refer to the theorem as a local saddle point result. In many economic models one needs a global version of the theorem. (For a global version of Theorem 6.9.1, see e.g. Seierstad and Sydsæter (1987), Theorem 19 page 256.) [2]

NOTE 3 If the system is linear with constant coefficients,

$$\dot{x} = a_{11}x + a_{12}y + b_1 \quad \text{with} \quad \begin{vmatrix} a_{11} & a_{12} \\ a_{21} & a_{22} \end{vmatrix} < 0$$
$$\dot{y} = a_{21}x + a_{22}y + b_2$$

---

[2] The paths of the system resemble the paths taken by a drop of water falling on a horse saddle. The drop of water will converge to the centre of the saddle if it hits precisely on the ridge of the saddle, but will fall to the ground if it hits in a different place.

then there is a unique equilibrium point, which is a *global* saddle point. In this case the paths that approach the equilibrium point will run along the straight line corresponding to the eigenvector associated with the negative eigenvalue. (See the next example.)

EXAMPLE 1   Consider the following system with equilibrium $(0, 0)$:

$$\dot{x} = 2y, \quad \dot{y} = 3x - y$$

With $f(x, y) = 2y$ and $g(x, y) = 3x - y$, the matrix $\mathbf{A}$ in Theorem 6.9.1 is $\begin{pmatrix} 0 & 2 \\ 3 & -1 \end{pmatrix}$. Because the determinant of $\mathbf{A}$ is equal to -6, the equilibrium is a local saddle point. The characteristic polynomial of $\mathbf{A}$ is $\lambda^2 + \lambda - 6 = (\lambda - 2)(\lambda + 3)$, so the eigenvalues are -3 and 2. An eigenvector associated with the negative eigenvalue -3 is $\begin{pmatrix} -2 \\ 3 \end{pmatrix}$. Figure 1 shows a phase diagram in which the two paths converging to the equilibrium point are indicated by dashed lines. Both lines are in the direction of the eigenvector.

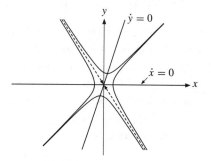

Figure 1

EXAMPLE 2   Consider system $(*)$ in Example 6.7.3, with

$$\dot{K} = aK - bK^2 - C, \quad \dot{C} = w(a - 2bK)C$$

One equilibrium point is $P = (a/2b, a^2/4b)$. Here the matrix $\mathbf{A}$ evaluated at P is

$$\mathbf{A} = \begin{pmatrix} a - 2bK & -1 \\ -2wbC & w(a - 2bK) \end{pmatrix} = \begin{pmatrix} 0 & -1 \\ -wa^2/2 & 0 \end{pmatrix}$$

Thus $\det(\mathbf{A}) = -wa^2/2 < 0$, so $(a/2b, a^2/4b)$ is a local saddle point.

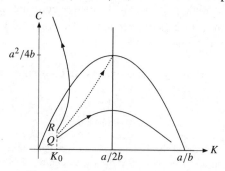

Figure 2

The evolution of the system depends drastically on the values of $K(0) = K_0$ and $C(0) = C_0$. In Fig. 2 we assume that $K_0 < a/2b$.

If $C(0) = C_0$ is small, the path starts at a point like Q in Figure 2. Then, as t increases, $K(t)$ steadily increases. On the other hand, $C(t)$ is increasing until $K(t)$ has reached the level $a/2b$, then $C(t)$ starts decreasing. If $C(0) = C_0$ is bigger, so that the path starts at R, then consumption increases, whereas capital first increases and then decreases. It is not hard to imagine that, for some start point between Q and R, the path converges to the equilibrium point P. This behaviour is confirmed by Theorem 6.9.1.

Other Types of Equilibrium Point

Lyapunov's Theorem 6.8.1 and the saddle point theorem 6.9.1 show that in some important cases the limiting behaviour of a nonlinear system near an equilibrium point is similar to behaviour of the linearized system. In the two theorems the eigenvalues of the Jacobian matrix both had negative real parts, or were real with opposite signs, respectively.

If the eigenvalues have positive real parts, solutions that start close to the equilibrium point move away from it, and the equilibrium point is a "source".

If the eigenvalues are purely imaginary, or 0, no definite statement about the limiting character of the solution can be made. For details we refer to the literature.

PROBLEMS FOR SECTION 6.9

1. (a) Show that the equilibrium point of the following system is a local saddle point:

$$\dot{x} = -\tfrac{1}{2}x + y, \qquad \dot{y} = y - 2$$

   Find also the eigenvalues of the associated matrix $\mathbf{A}$ in Theorem 6.9.1, and an eigenvector corresponding to the negative eigenvalue.

   (b) Draw a phase diagram in which the two paths converging to the equilibrium point are indicated. Find explicit expressions for these two paths.

2. Find the equilibrium point and check if it is a saddle point:

$$\dot{k} = f(k) - \delta k - c, \qquad \dot{c} = -c(r + \delta - f'(k))$$

   Assume that δ and r are positive constants, $f(0) = 0$, $f'(k) > 0$, $f''(k) < 0$, $f'(0) > r + \delta$, and $f'(\infty) < \delta$.

3. Consider the following system of differential equations:

$$\dot{x} = x\left(y - \frac{x}{2} - 2\right), \qquad \dot{y} = y\left(1 - \frac{y}{2x}\right)$$

   (a) Find the unique equilibrium point (x_0, y_0) in $S = \{(x, y) : x > 0, \ y > 0\}$. Is the equilibrium point (x_0, y_0) asymptotically stable? Is it a saddle point?

   (b) Draw a phase diagram for the system and indicate the behaviour of some integral curves in the region S.

4. Consider the following system of first-order differential equations:

$$\dot{x} = y^2 - x$$
$$\dot{y} = \frac{25}{4} - y^2 - \left(x - \frac{1}{4}\right)^2$$

(a) Find all equilibrium points of the system and classify them, if possible (i.e. determine for each of them if it is locally asymptotically stable, a local saddle point, or neither).

(b) Draw a phase diagram for the system, and indicate some possible integral curves.

7 DIFFERENTIAL EQUATIONS III:
HIGHER-ORDER EQUATIONS

Teach a parrot the terms "supply and demand" and you've got an economist.
—Carlyle

This chapter discusses generalizations and extensions of the theory in the two preceding chapters. Many of these generalizations are simple extensions of the theory developed in Chapter 6 for second-order equations or for two-variable systems, and in such cases the treatment is brief. The method of constructing Lyapunov functions to decide stability of autonomous systems of differential equations is one new topic briefly discussed in Section 7.5.

Only a few types of differential equation can be solved explicitly. Some theoretical issues concerning existence and uniqueness for first-order equations were discussed in Section 5.8. We generalize and extend these results in Section 7.1 for linear equations and in Section 7.6 for nonlinear equations.

The last section gives an introduction to some types of partial differential equations with applications to economics.

7.1 Linear Differential Equations

A differential equation of the n-th order can usually be written in the form

$$\frac{d^n x}{dt^n} = F\left(t, x, \frac{dx}{dt}, \ldots, \frac{d^{n-1}x}{dt^{n-1}}\right) = F\left(t, x, \dot{x}, \ldots, x^{(n-1)}\right) \tag{1}$$

Here is F a given function of $n+1$ variables and $x = x(t)$ is the unknown function. We use the notation $x^{(n-1)}$ for $d^{n-1}x/dt^{n-1}$.

If F is a *linear function* of x and of its derivatives w.r.t. t up to and including those of order $n-1$, we usually write the equation as

$$\frac{d^n x}{dt^n} + a_1(t)\frac{d^{n-1}x}{dt^{n-1}} + \cdots + a_{n-1}(t)\frac{dx}{dt} + a_n(t)x = f(t) \tag{2}$$

where $a_1(t), \ldots, a_n(t)$, and $f(t)$ are fixed continuous functions.

The associated **homogeneous equation** is obtained when the right-hand side is 0:

$$\frac{d^n x}{dt^n} + a_1(t)\frac{d^{n-1}x}{dt^{n-1}} + \cdots + a_{n-1}(t)\frac{dx}{dt} + a_n(t)x = 0 \tag{3}$$

Suppose that $u_1(t), \ldots, u_n(t)$ are n different solutions of (3). Then it is easy to verify that any linear combination $C_1 u_1(t) + \cdots + C_n u_n(t)$ also satisfies (3), for all values of the constants $C_1, \ldots, C_n$. (For $n = 2$ this was verified in Section 6.2.) Already for the case $n = 2$, however, we know that this is not necessarily the general solution.

The m functions $u_1(t), \ldots, u_m(t)$ are **linearly dependent** if there exist constants $C_1, \ldots, C_m$, not all 0, such that

$$C_1 u(t) + \cdots + C_m u_m(t) = 0 \quad \text{for all } t \tag{$*$}$$

If $u_1(t), \ldots, u_m(t)$ are not linearly dependent, they are called **linearly independent**. Then equation ($*$) is satisfied for all t only if $C_1 = \cdots = C_m = 0$. If $n = 2$, the assumption of linear independence is equivalent to the assumption that the two functions are not proportional.

There is no general method for finding the general solution to (3). The following theorem exhibits the structure of the general solutions to equations (2) and (3). (For the case $n = 2$ these results were discussed in Section 6.2.)

THEOREM 7.1.1

(a) The homogeneous equation (3) has the **general solution**

$$x = x(t) = C_1 u_1(t) + \cdots + C_n u_n(t) \tag{4}$$

where $u_1(t), \ldots, u_n(t)$ are any n linearly independent solutions of (3) and $C_1, \ldots, C_n$ are arbitrary constants.

(b) The nonhomogeneous equation (2) has the **general solution**

$$x = x(t) = C_1 u_1(t) + \cdots + C_n u_n(t) + u^*(t) \tag{5}$$

where $C_1 u_1(t) + \cdots + C_n u_n(t)$ is the general solution of the corresponding homogeneous equation (3) and $u^*(t)$ is some particular solution of the nonhomogeneous equation (2).

The proof of Theorem 7.1.1 relies on the following *existence and uniqueness* theorem. (See Theorem 7.6.2 for a generalization.)

THEOREM 7.1.2 (EXISTENCE AND UNIQUENESS FOR LINEAR EQUATIONS)

Suppose that $a_1(t), \ldots, a_n(t)$, and $f(t)$ are all continuous functions on an open interval (α, β) ($\alpha = -\infty$ and/or $\beta = \infty$ are not excluded). Let $x_0, x_0^{(1)}, \ldots, x_0^{(n-1)}$ be n given numbers and suppose $t_0 \in (\alpha, \beta)$. Then the differential equation (2) has one and only one solution $x(t)$ on the interval (α, β) that satisfies the conditions

$$x(t_0) = x_0, \quad \frac{dx(t_0)}{dt} = x_0^{(1)}, \quad \ldots, \quad \frac{d^{n-1}x(t_0)}{dt^{n-1}} = x_0^{(n-1)}$$

Proof of Theorem 7.1.1: (a) Suppose that $u_1(t), \ldots, u_n(t)$ are n linearly independent solutions of (3) and let $x(t)$ be an arbitrary solution. We have to prove the existence of constants $C_1, \ldots, C_n$ such that $x(t) = C_1 u_1(t) + \cdots + C_n u_n(t)$.

Assume that the solution curve for $x = x(t)$ passes through (t_0, x_0), and let $x_0^{(1)}, x_0^{(2)}, \ldots, x_0^{(n-1)}$ be given numbers. Suppose we could prove the existence of constants $C_1, \ldots, C_n$ such that

$$
\begin{aligned}
C_1 u_1(t_0) + \cdots + C_n u_n(t_0) &= x_0 \\
C_1 \dot{u}_1(t_0) + \cdots + C_n \dot{u}_n(t_0) &= x_0^{(1)} \\
&\cdots\cdots\cdots\cdots\cdots \\
C_1 u_1^{(n-1)}(t_0) + \cdots + C_n u_n^{(n-1)}(t_0) &= x_0^{(n-1)}
\end{aligned}
\qquad (*)
$$

Then the functions $C_1 u_1(t) + \cdots + C_n u_n(t)$ and $x(t)$ would have the same value at t_0 and, moreover, they would have the same values for the first $n - 1$ derivatives at t_0. By Theorem 7.1.2 the two solutions would coincide and the proof would be complete.

By Cramer's rule, $(*)$ has a unique solution $C_1, \ldots, C_n$ provided the **Wronskian** determinant

$$
W(t_0) =
\begin{vmatrix}
u_1(t_0) & \cdots & u_n(t_0) \\
\dot{u}_1(t_0) & \cdots & \dot{u}_n(t_0) \\
\vdots & & \vdots \\
u_1^{(n-1)}(t_0) & \cdots & u_n^{(n-1)}(t_0)
\end{vmatrix}
$$

is $\neq 0$. We shall prove that $W(t_0) \neq 0$ when the functions $u_1(t), \ldots, u_n(t)$ are indeed linearly independent.

Suppose $W(t_0) = 0$. Then the columns of the Wronskian are linearly dependent according to Theorem 1.3.1. Therefore there exist numbers $\lambda_1, \ldots, \lambda_m$, not all equal to 0, such that

$$
\begin{aligned}
\lambda_1 u_1(t_0) + \cdots + \lambda_n u_n(t_0) &= 0 \\
\lambda_1 \dot{u}_1(t_0) + \cdots + \lambda_n \dot{u}_n(t_0) &= 0 \\
&\cdots\cdots\cdots\cdots\cdots \\
\lambda_1 u_1^{(n-1)}(t_0) + \cdots + \lambda_n u_n^{(n-1)}(t_0) &= 0
\end{aligned}
\qquad (**)
$$

Put $\hat{x}(t) = \lambda_1 u_1(t) + \cdots + \lambda_n u_u(t)$. Then $\hat{x}(t)$ satisfies (3) because all the functions $u_i(t)$ do. Moreover, the equations $(**)$ imply that $\hat{x}(t_0) = 0, \hat{x}^{(1)}(t_0) = 0, \ldots, \hat{x}^{(n-1)}(t_0) = 0$. By Theorem 7.1.2 there is only one solution of (3) that satisfies these requirements for all t. The function that is equal to 0 for all t has this property, and therefore $\lambda_1 u_1(t) + \cdots + \lambda_n u_n(t) = 0$ for all t. This contradicts the hypothesis that $u_1(t), \ldots, u_n(t)$ are linearly independent. Thus $W(t_0) \neq 0$, and the proof is complete.

To prove (b), let $x(t)$ be an arbitrary solution of (2) and let $u^*(t)$ be a particular solution of (2). Then it is easy to see (by substitution) that $x(t) - u^*(t)$ satisfies the homogeneous equation (3). So there must exist constants $C_1, \ldots, C_n$ and a set of linearly independent solutions $u_1(t), \ldots, u_n(t)$ of (3) such that $x(t) - u^*(t) = C_1 u_1(t) + \cdots + C_n u_n(t)$. The result follows immediately. ∎

Variation of Parameters

We briefly describe a method for finding the solution of a nonhomogeneous linear equation once the general solution of the homogeneous equation is known. The good news is that it works (in principle) whatever is the function $f(t)$ in (2). The bad news is that it usually quite laborious.

Suppose that $u_1, u_2, \ldots, u_n$ are n linearly independent solutions of the homogeneous equation (3). Let

$$x = C_1(t)u_1 + \cdots + C_n(t)u_n \qquad (*)$$

where the functions $C_1(t), \ldots, C_n(t)$ are chosen to satisfy the $n-1$ equations

$$\dot{C}_1(t)u_1 + \cdots + \dot{C}_n(t)u_n = 0$$
$$\dot{C}_1(t)\dot{u}_1 + \cdots + \dot{C}_n(t)\dot{u}_n = 0$$
$$\cdots\cdots\cdots\cdots\cdots\cdots\cdots$$
$$\dot{C}_1(t)u_1^{(n-2)} + \cdots + \dot{C}_n(t)u_n^{(n-2)} = 0$$

By repeated differentiation and substitution, one verifies eventually that the function defined by $(*)$ satisfies the nonhomogeneous equation (2) provided that

$$\dot{C}_1(t)u_1^{(n-1)} + \cdots + \dot{C}_n(t)u_n^{(n-1)} = f(t)$$

Thus we have n equations which, because the functions $u_1, \ldots, u_n$ are linearly independent, can be used to determine $\dot{C}_1(t), \ldots, \dot{C}_n(t)$. By integration we find $C_1(t), \ldots, C_n(t)$, and x given in $(*)$ is the solution of (2).

EXAMPLE 1   Use the method above to find the solutions of $\ddot{x} - 3\dot{x} + 2x = t$.

Solution: In this case $n = 2$. We easily find the two linearly independent solutions $u_1 = e^t$ and $u_2 = e^{2t}$ of the corresponding homogeneous equation, and therefore want to choose $C_1(t)$ and $C_2(t)$ such that $x = C_1(t)e^t + C_2(t)e^{2t}$ is a solution. The relevant equations for determining $C_1(t)$ and $C_2(t)$ are here

$$\dot{C}_1(t)e^t + \dot{C}_2(t)e^{2t} = 0$$
$$\dot{C}_1(t)e^t + \dot{C}_2(t)2e^{2t} = t$$

The first of these equations gives $\dot{C}_1(t) = -e^t\dot{C}_2(t)$, which inserted into the second equation gives $\dot{C}_2(t)e^{2t} = t$, or $\dot{C}_2(t) = te^{-2t}$. Integrating by parts, $C_2(t) = \int te^{-2t}\,dt = -\frac{1}{2}te^{-2t} - \frac{1}{4}e^{-2t} + B$. Then $\dot{C}_1(t) = -e^t\dot{C}_2(t) = -te^{-t}$, so $C_1(t) = -\int te^{-t}\,dt = te^{-t} + e^{-t} + A$. Inserting these expressions for $C_1(t)$ and $C_2(t)$ into $(*)$, we obtain the general solution

$$x = Ae^t + Be^{2t} + \tfrac{1}{2}t + \tfrac{3}{4}$$

PROBLEMS FOR SECTION 7.1

1. Find the general solution of $\dddot{x} - 2\ddot{x} - \dot{x} + 2x = 10$. (*Hint:* e^t, e^{-t}, and e^{2t} are solutions of the homogeneous equation.)

2. Use variation of parameters to solve $\ddot{x} - x = e^{-t}$.

3. Solve the equation $\ddot{x} + x = 1/t, t > 0$. (The integrals cannot be evaluated.)

7.2 Constant Coefficients

The general linear differential equation of order n with constant coefficients takes the form

$$\frac{d^n x}{dt^n} + a_1 \frac{d^{n-1} x}{dt^{n-1}} + \cdots + a_{n-1} \frac{dx}{dt} + a_n x = f(t) \tag{1}$$

The associated homogeneous equation is

$$\frac{d^n x}{dt^n} + a_1 \frac{d^{n-1} x}{dt^{n-1}} + \cdots + a_{n-1} \frac{dx}{dt} + a_n x = 0 \tag{2}$$

According to Theorem 7.1.1, the general solution of (1) is of the form

$$x = x(t) = C_1 u_1(t) + \cdots + C_n u_n(t) + u^*(t)$$

where the functions $u_1(t), \ldots, u_n(t)$ are n linearly independent solutions of (2), the numbers $C_1, \ldots, C_n$ are n arbitrary constants, and $u^*(t)$ is some particular solution of (1).

Solutions of the Homogeneous Equation

Guided by the results in Chapter 6 for the case $n = 2$, we try to find solutions of (2) of the form $x = e^{rt}$ for appropriate values of r. Substituting $x = e^{rt}$ into (2) and cancelling the positive factor e^{rt}, we obtain the **characteristic equation** of (2) (or (1)):

$$r^n + a_1 r^{n-1} + \cdots + a_{n-1} r + a_n = 0 \tag{3}$$

Also, $p(r) = r^n + a_1 r^{n-1} + \cdots + a_{n-1} r + a_n$ is the **characteristic polynomial**. By the fundamental theorem of algebra, equation (3) has exactly n roots, real or complex, provided that each root is counted according to its multiplicity.

Suppose first that equation (3) has n distinct real roots $r_1, r_2, \ldots, r_n$. Then $e^{r_1 t}, e^{r_2 t}, \ldots, e^{r_n t}$ all satisfy (2), and one can prove that these n functions are linearly independent. So the general solution of (2) is

$$x(t) = C_1 e^{r_1 t} + C_2 e^{r_2 t} + \cdots + C_n e^{r_n t}$$

The *general* method for finding n linearly independent solutions of (2) can be described as follows. First, find all roots of (3) and notice the multiplicity of each of them. A real root r with multiplicity 1 (i.e. a simple root) gives the solution

$$e^{rt}$$

A real root r with multiplicity p yields the p linearly independent solutions

$$e^{rt}, te^{rt}, \ldots, t^{p-1} e^{rt}$$

A pair of complex roots $r = \alpha + i\beta, \bar{r} = \alpha - i\beta$ with multiplicity 1 yields the two solutions

$$e^{\alpha t} \cos \beta t, \quad e^{\alpha t} \sin \beta t$$

(Complex solutions of (3) appear in complex conjugate pairs.)

A pair of complex roots $r = \alpha + i\beta$, $\bar{r} = \alpha - i\beta$, each with multiplicity q, yields the $2q$ linearly independent solutions

$$e^{\alpha t} \cos \beta t, \ e^{\alpha t} \sin \beta t, \ \ldots, \ t^{q-1} e^{\alpha t} \cos \beta t, \ t^{q-1} e^{\alpha t} \sin \beta t$$

This procedure always finds n solutions of (2) that are linearly independent. It is illustrated in the following example.

EXAMPLE 1   Find the general solution of the equation

$$\frac{d^5 x}{dt^5} + 5 \frac{d^4 x}{dt^4} + 12 \frac{d^3 x}{dt^3} + 16 \frac{d^2 x}{dt^2} + 12 \frac{dx}{dt} + 4x = 0$$

Solution: The characteristic polynomial is here (in this constructed example),

$$p(r) = r^5 + 5r^4 + 12r^3 + 16r^2 + 12r + 4 = (r^2 + 2r + 2)^2 (r + 1)$$

The polynomial has the simple real root $r_1 = -1$, and the complex roots $r_2 = -1 + i$, $r_3 = -1 - i$, both with multiplicity 2. The general solution of the given equation is therefore

$$x = Ae^{-t} + D_1 e^{-t} \cos t + D_2 e^{-t} \sin t + D_3 t e^{-t} \cos t + D_4 t e^{-t} \sin t$$

where A and $D_1, \ldots, D_4$ are arbitrary constants.

Finding a Particular Solution

In order to find the general solution of the nonhomogeneous equation (1), it remains to find a particular solution $u^* = u^*(t)$ of (1). If $f(t)$ is a linear combination of terms of the form

$$e^{at}, \ t^m, \ \cos bt \ \text{ or } \ \sin bt \tag{$*$}$$

or products of such terms, then the method of undetermined coefficients developed in Section 6.3 for the case $n = 2$ will lead us to a particular solution. Consider a simple example.

EXAMPLE 2   Find the general solution of

$$\frac{d^5 x}{dt^5} + 5 \frac{d^4 x}{dt^4} + 12 \frac{d^3 x}{dt^3} + 16 \frac{d^2 x}{dt^2} + 12 \frac{dx}{dt} + 4x = t^2 + t - 1$$

Solution: The corresponding homogeneous equation was solved in Example 1. It remains to find a particular solution. The form of the right-hand side of the given equation suggests putting $u^* = At^2 + Bt + C$. We then try to adjust the coefficients appropriately. We get $\dot{u}^* = 2At + B$, $\ddot{u}^* = 2A$, and higher order derivatives are 0. Substituting into the given equation yields $32A + 24At + 12B + 4At^2 + 4Bt + 4C = t^2 + t - 1$, or after collecting terms,

$$4At^2 + (24A + 4B)t + (32A + 12B + 4C) = t^2 + t - 1$$

This equation is satisfied for all t when $4A = 1$, $24A + 4B = 1$, and $32A + 12B + 4C = -1$. Hence $A = \frac{1}{4}$, $B = -\frac{5}{4}$, $C = \frac{3}{2}$, and so $u^*(t) = \frac{1}{4}t^2 - \frac{5}{4}t + \frac{3}{2}$ is a particular solution of the equation.

The method of undetermined coefficients depends on our ability to guess the general form of a particular solution. The method usually fails if the right-hand side is of a type different from those mentioned above. However, variation of parameters, as discussed in Section 7.1, may still work.

PROBLEMS FOR SECTION 7.2

1. Find the general solutions of the following equations:

   (a) $\dddot{x} + 3\ddot{x} + 3\dot{x} + x = 3$ (b) $\dfrac{d^4x}{dt^4} - 3\dfrac{d^3x}{dt^3} + \dfrac{d^2x}{dt^2} + 4x = 2t - 1$

   (Hint for (b): $r^4 - 3r^3 + r^2 + 4 = (r^2 + r + 1)(r - 2)^2$.)

2. Find $x = x(t)$ if $x(0) = 0$, $\dot{x}(0) = 1$, $\ddot{x}(0) = 0$ and

   $$\dddot{x} - \ddot{x} - \dot{x} + x = 8te^{-t}$$

3. In a model due to T. Haavelmo, a function $K = K(t)$ satisfies the equation

   $$\ddot{K} = (\gamma_1 \kappa + \gamma_2)\dot{K} + (\gamma_1 \sigma + \gamma_3)\mu_0 e^{\mu t} \int_0^t e^{-\mu \tau} \dot{K}(\tau) d\tau$$

   where γ_1, γ_2, γ_3, κ, σ, μ_0, and μ are constants.

   (a) Deduce a third-order differential equation for $K = K(t)$.

   (b) Find the conditions for the characteristic equation of the third-order equation to have three different real roots. Prove that the solution in that case has the structure

   $$K(t) = C_1 e^{r_1 t} + C_2 e^{r_2 t} + C_3$$

4. Suppose that $u_1(t), \ldots, u_n(t)$ are $n - 1$ times differentiable. Let $W(t)$ denote the Wronskian $W(t)$ defined in the proof of Theorem 7.1.1. Prove that if $W(t) \neq 0$ for all t, then $u_1(t), \ldots, u_n(t)$ are linearly independent. (*Hint:* Study the proof of Theorem 7.1.1.)

7.3   Stability of Linear Differential Equations

Global asymptotic stability for general second-order linear equations was defined in Section 6.4. As a direct generalization we say that equation (7.1.2) is **globally asymptotically stable** if the general solution $C_1 u_1(t) + \cdots + C_n u_n(t)$ of the corresponding homogeneous equation tends to 0 as $t \to \infty$, regardless of the values of the constants $C_1, \ldots, C_n$. Thus the "effect of the initial conditions" dies out as t approaches ∞.

If we put $C_j = 1$ and $C_i = 0$ for $i \neq j$, we see, in particular, that $u_j(t) \to 0$ as $t \to \infty$, and this holds for all $j = 1, \ldots, n$. On the other hand, these requirements are surely sufficient for the equation to be globally asymptotically stable.

Constant Coefficients

Consider the case with constant coefficients

$$\frac{d^n x}{dt^n} + a_1 \frac{d^{n-1} x}{dt^{n-1}} + \cdots + a_n x = f(t) \tag{1}$$

and let $u_1(t), \ldots, u_n(t)$ be the n linearly independent solutions of the associated homogeneous equation obtained by the procedure described in Section 7.2. Each $u_j(t)$ corresponds to a root r_j of the characteristic equation. To simplify notation, put $r_j = \alpha + i\beta$. According to whether r_j is real ($\beta = 0$) with multiplicity 1 or multiplicity > 1, or complex ($\beta \neq 0$) with multiplicity 1 or > 1, the corresponding solution u_j is one of the following functions:

$$e^{\alpha t}, \quad t^k e^{\alpha t}, \quad e^{\alpha t} \cos \beta t, \quad e^{\alpha t} \sin \beta t, \quad t^k e^{\alpha t} \cos \beta t, \quad \text{or} \quad t^k e^{\alpha t} \sin \beta t$$

In each case it follows that $u_j \to 0$ as $t \to \infty$ if and only if $\alpha < 0$. Here is a detailed argument for the case $u_j = t^r e^{\alpha t} \cos \beta t$, where r is a natural number, while α and β are real numbers. As $t \to \infty$, $t^r \to \infty$. Because $\cos \beta t$ does not approach 0 as $t \to \infty$ for any value of β, the condition $\alpha < 0$ is *necessary* for u_j to approach 0 as $t \to \infty$. On the other hand, if $\alpha < 0$, then $e^\alpha < 1$ and thus $a = e^{-\alpha} > 1$. Hence, $t^r e^{\alpha t} = t^r / a^t \to 0$ as $t \to \infty$. (See e.g. EMEA.) Because $|\cos \beta t| \leq 1$, we conclude that $u_j \to 0$ as $t \to \infty$. The condition $\alpha < 0$ is therefore necessary as well as sufficient for u_j to approach 0 as $t \to \infty$.

THEOREM 7.3.1

A necessary and sufficient condition for

$$\frac{d^n x}{dt^n} + a_1 \frac{d^{n-1} x}{dt^{n-1}} + \cdots + a_n x = f(t)$$

to be globally asymptotically stable is that every root of the characteristic equation $r^n + a_1 r^{n-1} + \cdots + a_n = 0$ has a negative real part.

To check if (1) is globally asymptotically stable therefore, it suffices to find the roots of the characteristic equation. These roots are again functions of the coefficients $a_1, a_2, \ldots, a_n$ alone.

The case $n = 1$ is easy. The characteristic equation of $\dot{x} + a_1 x = f(t)$ is $r + a_1 = 0$, so the characteristic root is $r = -a_1$. Thus the equation is globally asymptotically stable if and only if $a_1 > 0$. For $n = 2$ it was proved in (6.4.2) that $\ddot{x} + a\dot{x} + bx = f(t)$ is globally asymptotically stable if and only if $a > 0$ and $b > 0$. On the basis of these results it is easy to find a *necessary* condition for (1) to be globally asymptotically stable:

$$\text{If (1) is globally asymptotically stable, then } a_1, \ldots, a_n \text{ are all positive} \qquad (2)$$

The characteristic polynomial $p(r) = r^n + a_1 r^{n-1} + \cdots + a_n$ can be decomposed into its first and second degree factors—i.e. factors of the form $r + c$ for real zeros and $r^2 + ar + b$ for complex conjugate pairs of zeros. If all zeros of $p(r)$ have negative real parts, then those of $r + c$ and $r^2 + ar + b$ must have negative real parts. So c, a, and b must be positive. As a product of polynomials with positive coefficients, $p(r)$ has positive coefficients only.

Except for the cases $n = 1$ and $n = 2$, the condition that $a_1, \ldots, a_n$ are all positive is not sufficient for stability of (1) (see Example 2 below). We state a theorem that, in conjunction with Theorem 7.3.1, provides necessary and sufficient conditions for equation (1) to be globally asymptotically stable.[1]

THEOREM 7.3.2 (HURWITZ—ROUTH)

Let

$$a_0 r^n + a_1 r^{n-1} + \cdots + a_n \qquad (a_0 > 0)$$

be a polynomial of degree n with real coefficients. A necessary and sufficient condition for all zeros of the polynomial to have negative real parts is that all the leading principal minors in the following $n \times n$ matrix are all positive:

$$\mathbf{A} = \begin{pmatrix} a_1 & a_3 & a_5 & \cdots & 0 & 0 \\ a_0 & a_2 & a_4 & \cdots & 0 & 0 \\ 0 & a_1 & a_3 & \cdots & 0 & 0 \\ \vdots & \vdots & \vdots & \ddots & \vdots \\ 0 & 0 & 0 & \cdots & a_{n-1} & 0 \\ 0 & 0 & 0 & \cdots & a_{n-2} & a_n \end{pmatrix}$$

The kth column of the matrix $\mathbf{A}$ is a vector of the form

$$\left(0, \ldots, 0, 0, a_{k+2}, a_{k+1}, a_k, a_{k-1}, a_{k-2}, \ldots, a_1, a_0, 0, \ldots, 0\right)'$$

where a_k is on the main diagonal. An element a_{k+j} with $k + j$ negative or greater than n is 0. For $n = 1, 2, 3, 4$, with $a_0 = 1$, the matrix $\mathbf{A}$ is given respectively by

$$(a_1), \quad \begin{pmatrix} a_1 & 0 \\ 1 & a_2 \end{pmatrix}, \quad \begin{pmatrix} a_1 & a_3 & 0 \\ 1 & a_2 & 0 \\ 0 & a_1 & a_3 \end{pmatrix}, \quad \begin{pmatrix} a_1 & a_3 & 0 & 0 \\ 1 & a_2 & a_4 & 0 \\ 0 & a_1 & a_3 & 0 \\ 0 & 1 & a_2 & a_4 \end{pmatrix} \qquad (*)$$

---

[1] Leading principal minors are defined in Section 1.8. For a proof, see Obreschkoff (1963).

By combining Theorems 7.3.1 and 7.3.2 we obtain:

(a) $\dot{x} + a_1 x = f(t)$ is globally asymptotically stable $\iff a_1 > 0$

(b) $\ddot{x} + a_1 \dot{x} + a_2 x = f(t)$ is globally asymptotically stable

$$\iff a_1 > 0 \text{ and } a_2 > 0 \qquad (3)$$

(c) $\dddot{x} + a_1 \ddot{x} + a_2 \dot{x} + a_3 x = f(t)$ is globally asymptotically stable

$$\iff a_1 > 0, \ a_3 > 0, \text{ and } a_1 a_2 - a_3 > 0$$

These equivalences are in accordance with our earlier results for $n = 1$ and $n = 2$. For $n = 3$ the requirements in Theorem 7.3.2 are:

$$a_1 > 0, \quad \begin{vmatrix} a_1 & a_3 \\ 1 & a_2 \end{vmatrix} = a_1 a_2 - a_3 > 0, \quad \begin{vmatrix} a_1 & a_3 & 0 \\ 1 & a_2 & 0 \\ 0 & a_1 & a_3 \end{vmatrix} = (a_1 a_2 - a_3)a_3 > 0$$

From this we see that the last equivalence in (3) is indeed correct.

EXAMPLE 1   Prove that the third-order equation $\dddot{x} + 3\ddot{x} + 7\dot{x} + 5x = e^{3t}$ is globally asymptotically stable.

Solution: Here $a_1 = 3 > 0$, $a_3 = 5 > 0$, and $a_1 a_2 - a_3 = 21 - 5 = 16 > 0$, so that the equation is globally asymptotically stable.

EXAMPLE 2   Prove that the fourth-order equation $\ddddot{x} + \dddot{x} + \ddot{x} + \dot{x} + x = \sin t$ is not globally asymptotically stable.

Solution: This equation is globally asymptotically stable if and only if all the leading principal minors of the last matrix in (∗) are positive. But we find that

$$\begin{vmatrix} a_1 & a_3 \\ 1 & a_2 \end{vmatrix} = \begin{vmatrix} 1 & 1 \\ 1 & 1 \end{vmatrix} = 0$$

Hence the equation is not globally asymptotically stable.

PROBLEMS FOR SECTION 7.3

1. Check global asymptotic stability for problem 7.2.1(a).

2. Show that the equation $\dddot{x} + 4\ddot{x} + 5\dot{x} + 2x = 0$ is globally asymptotically stable by using (3). Confirm the result by finding the general solution of the equation. (*Hint:* Recall that integer zeros of the characteristic polynomial divide the constant term 2.)

7.4 Systems of Differential Equations

By introducing new variables, a system of ordinary differential equations can usually be transformed into a system of first-order equations in many variables of the form

$$\frac{dx_1}{dt} = f_1(t, x_1, \ldots, x_n)$$

$$\ldots\ldots\ldots\ldots\ldots\ldots \tag{1}$$

$$\frac{dx_n}{dt} = f_n(t, x_1, \ldots, x_n)$$

This is called a **normal system**.

EXAMPLE 1   Transform the following system into the form (1)

$$\ddot{x}_1 = F_1(t, x_1, \dot{x}_1, x_2, \dot{x}_2), \quad \ddot{x}_2 = F_2(t, x_1, \dot{x}_1, x_2, \dot{x}_2)$$

Solution: Introduce new unknowns $u_1, u_2, u_3,$ and u_4 defined by $u_1 = x_1, u_2 = \dot{x}_1,$ $u_3 = x_2,$ and $u_4 = \dot{x}_2$. Then the system is transformed into the first-order system

$$\dot{u}_1 = u_2, \quad \dot{u}_2 = F_1(t, u_1, u_2, u_3, u_4), \quad \dot{u}_3 = u_4, \quad \dot{u}_4 = F_2(t, u_1, u_2, u_3, u_4)$$

which is in the form (1).

EXAMPLE 2   Prove that the differential equation $\dfrac{d^n x}{dt^n} = F\left(t, x, \dfrac{dx}{dt}, \ldots, \dfrac{d^{n-1}x}{dt^{n-1}}\right)$ can be transformed into a normal system.

Solution: Define $y_1 = x, y_2 = dx/dt, \ldots, y_n = d^{n-1}x/dt^{n-1}$. Then the given equation takes the form

$$\dot{y}_1 = y_2, \quad \dot{y}_2 = y_3, \quad \ldots, \quad \dot{y}_{n-1} = y_n, \quad \dot{y}_n = F(t, y_1, y_2, \ldots, y_n)$$

This is normal system of n first-order equations.

The examples above indicate that systems of differential equations usually can be reduced to the normal form (1). Therefore, in studying systems of differential equations, not much is lost if we restrict attention to normal systems.

A **solution** of (1) is a set of functions $x_1 = x_1(t), \ldots, x_n = x_n(t)$ that satisfy all the equations. Geometrically, such a solution describes a **curve** in $\mathbb{R}^n$. The parameter t usually denotes time, and as t varies, we say that the system "moves along" the curve. The vector $\dot{\mathbf{x}}(t) = (\dot{x}_1(t), \ldots, \dot{x}_n(t))$ is the *velocity vector* associated with $\mathbf{x}(t) = (x_1(t), \ldots, x_n(t))$. The space with coordinates $x_1, \ldots, x_n$ is called the **phase space** associated with system (1).

In the case $n = 3$, as t varies, the vector $\mathbf{x}(t) = (x_1(t), x_2(t), x_3(t))$ traces out a curve in $\mathbb{R}^3$, and

$$\frac{\mathbf{x}(t + \Delta t) - \mathbf{x}(t)}{\Delta t} = \left(\frac{x_1(t + \Delta t) - x_1(t)}{\Delta t}, \frac{x_2(t + \Delta t) - x_2(t)}{\Delta t}, \frac{x_3(t + \Delta t) - x_1(t)}{\Delta t}\right)$$

tends to the vector $\dot{\mathbf{x}}(t) = (\dot{x}_1(t), \dot{x}_2(t), \dot{x}_3(t))$ as a limit as $\Delta t \to 0$. As in the case $n = 2$ in Section 6.5 (see Fig. 6.5.1), we realize that $\dot{\mathbf{x}}(t)$ is a tangent vector to the curve.

Let $\mathbf{F}(t, \mathbf{x}(t))$ denote the vector with components $f_i(t, \mathbf{x}(t)) = f_i(t, x_1(t), \ldots, x_n(t))$, $i = 1, \ldots, n$. Then (1) can be written in the concise form

$$\dot{\mathbf{x}} = \mathbf{F}(t, \mathbf{x}) \tag{2}$$

In economic models that lead to systems of the type (1), the functions $x_1(t), \ldots, x_n(t)$ are state variables characterizing the given economic system at time t. Usually the state of the system at some definite time t_0 is known, so $\mathbf{x}(t_0) = (x_1(t_0), \ldots, x_n(t_0))$ is given. Now, according to the existence and uniqueness theorem for (1), *if f_i and $\partial f_i / \partial x_j$ are continuous for all $i = 1, \ldots, n, j = 1, \ldots, n$, then there is one and only one vector of functions $x_1(t), \ldots, x_n(t)$ that satisfies (1) and has the prescribed values for $t = t_0$ (see Theorem 7.6.1).*

In the case of (1), the general solution usually depends on n arbitrary constants,

$$x_1 = \Phi_1(t; C_1, \ldots, C_n), \quad \ldots, \quad x_n = \Phi_n(t; C_1, \ldots, C_n)$$

For each choice of $C_1, \ldots, C_n$ the solution describes a curve in $\mathbb{R}^n$.

In Example 2 we showed that an nth-order differential equation can be transformed into a system of first-order equations. Sometimes one can find the solution of system (1) by going the other way around. The method was illustrated for the case $n = 2$ in Section 6.5.

Linear Systems

In some models the functions $f_1, \ldots, f_n$ appearing in (1) are linear, or it may be an acceptable approximation to treat them as linear. Then the system is

$$\dot{x}_1 = a_{11}(t)x_1 + \cdots + a_{1n}(t)x_n + b_1(t)$$
$$\cdots\cdots\cdots\cdots\cdots\cdots\cdots\cdots\cdots\cdots\cdots\cdots \tag{3}$$
$$\dot{x}_n = a_{n1}(t)x_1 + \cdots + a_{nn}(t)x_n + b_n(t)$$

By a method similar to that applied to the case $n = 2$ in Section 6.5, the problem of solving (3) can be transformed into the problem of solving one linear differential equation in one unknown function, say x_1.

Let $\mathbf{x}, \dot{\mathbf{x}}$ and $\mathbf{b}(t)$ be the three column vectors with components $x_1, \ldots, x_n, \dot{x}_1, \ldots, \dot{x}_n$, and $b_1(t), \ldots, b_n(t)$, respectively. Let $\mathbf{A}$ denote the matrix $(a_{ij}(t))_{(n \times n)}$. Then (3) can be written in the matrix form

$$\dot{\mathbf{x}} = \mathbf{A}(t)\mathbf{x} + \mathbf{b}(t) \tag{4}$$

A particularly important case occurs when all the functions $a_{ij}(t)$ are constants. Then

$$\dot{\mathbf{x}} = \mathbf{A}\mathbf{x} + \mathbf{b}(t) \quad \Longleftrightarrow \quad \dot{x}_i = a_{i1}x_1 + \cdots + a_{in}x_n + b_i(t), \quad i = 1, \ldots, n \tag{5}$$

Applied to (5) the transformation referred to above will lead to an nth-order linear equation with constant coefficients. Such equations can always be solved explicitly. Their characteristic equations coincide with the eigenvalue equation for the matrix $\mathbf{A}$, as we saw in Section 6.5 for the case $n = 2$. On the basis of Theorem 7.3.1 we deduce the following result:

$$\dot{\mathbf{x}} = \mathbf{A}\mathbf{x} + \mathbf{b}(t) \text{ is globally asymptotically stable} \Longleftrightarrow$$

$$\text{all the eigenvalues of } \mathbf{A} \text{ have negative real parts} \tag{6}$$

Global asymptotic stability of $\dot{\mathbf{x}} = \mathbf{A}\mathbf{x} + \mathbf{b}(t)$ means, in particular, that the general solution of $\dot{\mathbf{x}} = \mathbf{A}\mathbf{x}$ tends to the zero vector $\mathbf{0}$ as $t \to \infty$, regardless of the initial conditions.

Solutions Based on Eigenvalues

The system

$$\dot{\mathbf{x}} = \mathbf{A}\mathbf{x} + \mathbf{b} \tag{7}$$

can alternatively be solved by using methods from linear algebra, as shown for $n = 2$ in Section 6.5. Suppose first that $\mathbf{b} = \mathbf{0}$. We search for numbers λ and $v_1, v_2, \ldots, v_n$ such that the vector function $\mathbf{x} = \mathbf{v}e^{\lambda t} = (v_1 e^{\lambda t}, v_2 e^{\lambda t}, \ldots, v_n e^{\lambda t})$ satisfies $\dot{\mathbf{x}} = \mathbf{A}\mathbf{x}$. With $\mathbf{x} = \mathbf{v}e^{\lambda t}$ we have $\dot{\mathbf{x}} = \lambda e^{\lambda t}\mathbf{v}$, so $\lambda e^{\lambda t}\mathbf{v} = \mathbf{A}(\mathbf{v}e^{\lambda t}) = e^{\lambda t}\mathbf{A}\mathbf{v}$. Cancelling the common factor $e^{\lambda t}$ yields

$$\mathbf{A}\mathbf{v} = \lambda\mathbf{v} \tag{8}$$

Hence any nonzero solution $\mathbf{v}$ is an eigenvector of the matrix $\mathbf{A}$ with eigenvalue λ.

The case where $\mathbf{A}$ has n different real eigenvalues, $\lambda_1, \lambda_2, \ldots, \lambda_n$, is the simplest. Then $\mathbf{A}$ has n linearly independent eigenvectors $\mathbf{v}_1, \mathbf{v}_2, \ldots, \mathbf{v}_n$, and the general solution of $\dot{\mathbf{x}} = \mathbf{A}\mathbf{x}$ is

$$\mathbf{x}(t) = C_1 e^{\lambda_1 t}\mathbf{v}_1 + \cdots + C_n e^{\lambda_n t}\mathbf{v}_n$$

Suppose that $\mathbf{x}^0$ is an equilibrium point for (7) in the sense that $\mathbf{A}\mathbf{x}^0 + \mathbf{b} = \mathbf{0}$. If we define $\mathbf{w} = \mathbf{x} - \mathbf{x}^0$, then $\mathbf{w}$ measures the deviation of $\mathbf{x}$ from the equilibrium state $\mathbf{x}^0$. Then $\dot{\mathbf{w}} = \dot{\mathbf{x}}$, which inserted into (7) gives $\dot{\mathbf{w}} = \dot{\mathbf{x}} = \mathbf{A}\mathbf{x} + \mathbf{b} = \mathbf{A}(\mathbf{w} + \mathbf{x}^0) + \mathbf{b} = \mathbf{A}\mathbf{w} + \mathbf{A}\mathbf{x}^0 + \mathbf{b} = \mathbf{A}\mathbf{w}$. In this way the nonhomogeneous system (7) can be reduced to a homogeneous system.

NOTE 1 The solution of the scalar initial value problem $\dot{x} = ax$, $x(t_0) = x^0$, is $x = e^{a(t-t_0)}x^0$. It is tempting to conjecture that the more general initial value problem $\dot{\mathbf{x}} = \mathbf{A}\mathbf{x}$, $\mathbf{x}(t_0) = \mathbf{x}^0$ has the solution $\mathbf{x} = e^{\mathbf{A}(t-t_0)}\mathbf{x}^0$. This is correct if e to the power of a matrix is properly defined. In fact, if $\mathbf{A}$ is an $n \times n$-matrix and t is any number, we define

$$e^{\mathbf{A}t} = \mathbf{I} + t\mathbf{A} + \frac{t^2}{2!}\mathbf{A}^2 + \frac{t^3}{3!}\mathbf{A}^3 + \cdots \tag{9}$$

One can show that this series converges for all t, and that $(d/dt)e^{\mathbf{A}t} = \mathbf{A}e^{\mathbf{A}t}$. Since $(d/dt)(e^{\mathbf{A}t}\mathbf{c}) = \mathbf{A}e^{\mathbf{A}t}\mathbf{c} = \mathbf{A}(e^{\mathbf{A}t}\mathbf{c})$, it follows that $e^{\mathbf{A}t}\mathbf{c}$ is a solution to $\dot{\mathbf{x}} = \mathbf{A}\mathbf{x}$ for every constant vector $\mathbf{c}$, and this is the only possible solution.

Moreover, one can show that $(e^{\mathbf{A}t})^{-1} = e^{-\mathbf{A}t}$ and that $e^{\mathbf{A}(t+s)} = e^{\mathbf{A}t}e^{\mathbf{A}s}$, but $e^{\mathbf{A}t+\mathbf{B}t}$ is not equal to $e^{\mathbf{A}t}e^{\mathbf{B}t}$ unless $\mathbf{A}\mathbf{B} = \mathbf{B}\mathbf{A}$.

The Resolvent

We shall explain how one can (in principle) solve equation (4). Consider first the homogeneous system

$$\dot{\mathbf{x}} = \mathbf{A}(t)\mathbf{x} \tag{*}$$

For any t_0, this equation has n unique solutions $\mathbf{p}_j(t) = (p_{1j}(t), \ldots, p_{nj}(t))'$, $t \in \mathbb{R}$, satisfying $\mathbf{p}_j(t_0) = \mathbf{e}_j$, $j = 1, \ldots, n$, where $\mathbf{e}_j$ is the jth standard unit vector in $\mathbb{R}^n$. (The existence and uniqueness of the solutions follows from Theorem 7.6.2 below.) The **resolvent** of $(*)$ is the $n \times n$ matrix

$$\mathbf{P}(t, t_0) = \begin{pmatrix} p_{11}(t) & \cdots & p_{1n}(t) \\ \vdots & \ddots & \vdots \\ p_{n1}(t) & \cdots & p_{nn}(t) \end{pmatrix} \tag{10}$$

whose columns are the solutions $\mathbf{p}_j(t)$. Evidently, it satisfies $\dot{\mathbf{P}}(t, t_0) = (d/dt)\mathbf{P}(t, t_0) = \mathbf{A}(t)\mathbf{P}(t, t_0)$ and $\mathbf{P}(t_0, t_0) = \mathbf{I}_n$, where $\mathbf{I}_n$ is the unit matrix of order n. The solution of $(*)$ with $\mathbf{x}(t_0) = \mathbf{x}^0$ is obviously $\mathbf{x}(t) = \mathbf{P}(t, t_0)\mathbf{x}^0$.

For the nonhomogeneous equation (4), one can then derive the following:

$$\dot{\mathbf{x}} = \mathbf{A}(t)\mathbf{x} + \mathbf{b}(t), \quad \mathbf{x}(t_0) = \mathbf{x}^0 \iff \mathbf{x} = \mathbf{P}(t, t_0)\mathbf{x}^0 + \int_{t_0}^t \mathbf{P}(t, s)\mathbf{b}(s)\,ds \tag{11}$$

To show that $\mathbf{x}(t)$ is a solution, we observe from Leibniz's formula that

$$\dot{\mathbf{x}}(t) = \dot{\mathbf{P}}(t, t_0)\mathbf{x}^0 + \mathbf{P}(t, t)\mathbf{b}(t) + \int_{t_0}^t \dot{\mathbf{P}}(t, s)\mathbf{b}(s)\,ds$$

$$= \mathbf{A}(t)\mathbf{P}(t, t_0)\mathbf{x}^0 + \int_{t_0}^t \mathbf{A}(t)\mathbf{P}(t, s)\mathbf{b}(s)\,ds + \mathbf{b}(t) = \mathbf{A}(t)\mathbf{x}(t) + \mathbf{b}(t)$$

The matrix $\mathbf{P}(t, s)$ denotes the resolvent at time t when the initial point of time is s. By the uniqueness of the $\mathbf{p}_j(t)$'s, it follows that $\mathbf{P}(t, t_0) \cdot \mathbf{P}(t_0, t) = \mathbf{I}$, so $\mathbf{P}(t, t_0)$ has an inverse. More generally (also by uniqueness), $\mathbf{P}(t, s) = \mathbf{P}(t, \tau) \cdot \mathbf{P}(\tau, s)$ for all t, s, and τ. In particular, $\mathbf{P}(t, s) = \mathbf{P}(t, t_0)(\mathbf{P}(s, t_0))^{-1}$.

If $\mathbf{A}(t)$ is the constant matrix $\mathbf{A}$, then $\mathbf{P}(t, s) = \mathbf{P}(t - s, 0) = e^{\mathbf{A}(t-s)}$ for all t and s. Hence

$$\dot{\mathbf{x}} = \mathbf{A}\mathbf{x} + \mathbf{b}(t), \quad \mathbf{x}(t_0) = \mathbf{x}^0 \iff \mathbf{x} = \mathbf{P}(t, t_0)\mathbf{x}^0 + \int_{t_0}^t \mathbf{P}(t - s, 0)\mathbf{b}(s)\,ds \tag{12}$$

Note finally that if $\mathbf{P}(t, s)$ is the resolvent of $\dot{\mathbf{x}} = \mathbf{A}(t)\mathbf{x}$, then $t \mapsto \mathbf{P}(s, t)'$ (the transpose of $\mathbf{P}(s, t)$) is the resolvent of the equation

$$\dot{\mathbf{z}}(t) = -\mathbf{A}(t)'\,\mathbf{z}(t) \tag{13}$$

To prove that $t \mapsto \mathbf{P}(s, t)'$ satisfies (13), differentiate $\mathbf{P}(t, s)\mathbf{P}(s, t) = \mathbf{I}_n$ w.r.t. t to obtain

$$((\partial/\partial t)\mathbf{P}(t, s))\mathbf{P}(s, t) + \mathbf{P}(t, s)(\partial/\partial t)\mathbf{P}(s, t) = \mathbf{0}$$

which implies that $\mathbf{A}(t)\mathbf{P}(t, s)\mathbf{P}(s, t) + \mathbf{P}(t, s)(\partial/\partial t)\mathbf{P}(s, t) = \mathbf{0}$, or $(\partial/\partial t)\mathbf{P}(s, t) = -\mathbf{P}(t, s)^{-1}\mathbf{A}(t)$ $= -\mathbf{P}(s, t)\mathbf{A}(t)$, i.e. $(\partial/\partial t)\mathbf{P}(s, t)' = -\mathbf{A}(t)'\mathbf{P}(s, t)'$.

PROBLEMS FOR SECTION 7.4

1. Find the general solution of the following system

$$\dot{x}_1 = -x_1 + x_2 + x_3, \quad \dot{x}_2 = x_1 - x_2 + x_3, \quad \dot{x}_3 = x_1 + x_2 + x_3$$

(*Hint:* Derive a third-order differential equation for x_1.)

2. Use Theorem 7.6.2 below on the linear equation $\dot{\mathbf{x}} = \mathbf{A}\mathbf{x}$ to prove that if $\mathbf{x}(t)$ is not identically 0, then $\mathbf{x}(t) \neq \mathbf{0}$ for all t.

7.5 Stability for Nonlinear Systems

This section generalizes the stability theory of autonomous systems in the plane to the more general autonomous system

$$\dot{x}_1 = f_1(x_1, \ldots, x_n)$$

$$\ldots\ldots\ldots\ldots\ldots\ldots\ldots$$ (1)

$$\dot{x}_n = f_n(x_1, \ldots, x_n)$$

in n dimensions. We assume that $f_1, \ldots, f_n$ are all C^1 functions.

A point $\mathbf{a} = (a_1, \ldots, a_n)$ is called an **equilibrium point** for (1) if

$$f_1(a_1, \ldots, a_n) = 0, \quad \ldots, \quad f_n(a_1, \ldots, a_n) = 0$$

Note that $x_1 = x_1(t) = a_1, \ldots, x_n = x_n(t) = a_n$ is then a solution of the system. If $x_1, \ldots, x_n$ are state variables for some economic (or biological or physical) system, and (1) is satisfied, then $\mathbf{a}$ is an **equilibrium state**.

An equilibrium point $\mathbf{a}$ is *stable* if all nearby solution curves remain nearby. But the integral curves that are near a stable equilibrium point do not necessarily have to converge to the equilibrium point. We now define precisely the concepts of stable and locally asymptotically stable equilibrium points:

DEFINITION OF STABILITY

The equilibrium state $\mathbf{a} = (a_1, \ldots, a_n)$ for system (1) is **stable** if for each $\varepsilon > 0$ there exists a $\delta > 0$ (that generally depends on ε) such that, if $\|\mathbf{x} - \mathbf{a}\| < \delta$, then every solution $\boldsymbol{\varphi}(t) = (\varphi_1(t), \ldots, \varphi_n(t))$ of (1) that satisfies $\boldsymbol{\varphi}(0) = \mathbf{x}$ is defined for all $t > 0$ and satisfies the inequality

$$\|\boldsymbol{\varphi}(t) - \mathbf{a}\| < \varepsilon \quad \text{for all } t > 0$$

If $\mathbf{a}$ is stable and, in addition, there exists a $\delta_0 > 0$ such that

$$\|\mathbf{x} - \mathbf{a}\| < \delta_0 \implies \lim_{t \to \infty} \|\boldsymbol{\varphi}(t) - \mathbf{a}\| = 0$$

then $\mathbf{a}$ is called **locally asymptotically stable**.

Note that $\mathbf{a}$ is locally asymptotically stable if solutions that come near $\mathbf{a}$ not only remain nearby, but also converge to $\mathbf{a}$.

An equilibrium that is not stable is called **unstable**. If $\mathbf{a}$ is unstable, then for every $\varepsilon > 0$ and for every $\delta > 0$ there exists at least one solution $\boldsymbol{\varphi}(t)$ such that $\boldsymbol{\varphi}(0) = \mathbf{x}$ and $\|\mathbf{x} - \mathbf{a}\| \geq \delta$ for some $t > 0$. These definitions are illustrated in Fig. 1. For an example of an equilibrium state that is stable, but not asymptotically stable, see the Lotka–Volterra model in Example 2 below.

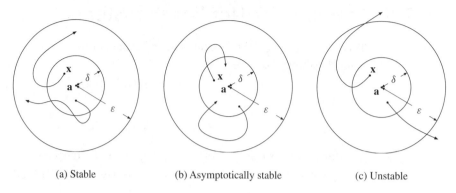

(a) Stable   (b) Asymptotically stable   (c) Unstable

Figure 1

Theorem 6.8.1, on locally asymptotically stable equilibrium points for systems of autonomous equations in the plane, has a natural extension to n dimensions (see Hirsch and Smale (1974)):

THEOREM 7.5.1 (LYAPUNOV)

Let $\mathbf{a} = (a_1, \ldots, a_n)$ be an equilibrium point for system (1) and let $\mathbf{A}$ be the Jacobian matrix

$$\mathbf{A} = \begin{pmatrix} \dfrac{\partial f_1(\mathbf{a})}{\partial x_1} & \cdots & \dfrac{\partial f_1(\mathbf{a})}{\partial x_n} \\ \vdots & \ddots & \vdots \\ \dfrac{\partial f_n(\mathbf{a})}{\partial x_1} & \cdots & \dfrac{\partial f_n(\mathbf{a})}{\partial x_n} \end{pmatrix} \tag{2}$$

If all the eigenvalues of $\mathbf{A}$ have negative real parts, then $\mathbf{a}$ is locally asymptotically stable. If at least one eigenvalue of $\mathbf{A}$ has positive real part, then $\mathbf{a}$ is unstable.

NOTE 1   The condition that all the eigenvalues of $\mathbf{A}$ have negative real parts is sufficient but not necessary for $\mathbf{a}$ to be locally asymptotically stable. For instance, $a = 0$ is a locally asymptotically stable point for $\dot{x} = -x^3$, but the matrix $\mathbf{A}$ has the eigenvalue $f'(0) = 0$.

NOTE 2   Let us apply the theorem to the scalar equation $\dot{x} = F(x)$. Assume that $x = a$ is an equilibrium point. The matrix $\mathbf{A}$ in (2) is then the 1×1 matrix $F'(a)$, and the only eigenvalue of $\mathbf{A}$ is $\lambda = F'(a)$. Thus, we conclude from the theorem that $x = a$ is locally asymptotically stable provided $F'(a) < 0$, and $x = a$ is unstable provided $F'(a) > 0$. This accords with the results in (5.7.2).

Lyapunov Functions

Let $\mathbf{a} = (a_1, \ldots, a_n)$ be an equilibrium point for system (1) and let $V(\mathbf{x}) = V(x_1, \ldots, x_n)$ be a C^1 function defined in an open neighbourhood Ω of $\mathbf{a}$. We call $V(\mathbf{x})$ **positive definite** in Ω if

$$V(\mathbf{a}) = 0 \quad \text{and} \quad V(\mathbf{x}) > 0 \quad \text{for all } \mathbf{x} \text{ in } \Omega, \ \mathbf{x} \neq \mathbf{a}$$

Thus, $V(\mathbf{x})$ is positive definite in Ω if it has a unique minimum at $\mathbf{a}$, with minimum value 0.

Let $\mathbf{x}(t) = (x_1(t), \ldots, x_n(t))$ be a solution of (1). Then V becomes a function of t "along" the solution $\mathbf{x}(t)$, and its derivative w.r.t. t is

$$\dot{V}(\mathbf{x}(t)) = \sum_{i=1}^{n} \frac{\partial V(\mathbf{x}(t))}{\partial x_i} \frac{dx_i}{dt} = \sum_{i=1}^{n} \frac{\partial V(\mathbf{x}(t))}{\partial x_i} f_i(\mathbf{x}(t)) = \nabla V(\mathbf{x}(t)) \cdot \mathbf{f}(\mathbf{x}(t)) \qquad (3)$$

If $V(\mathbf{x})$ is positive definite and $\dot{V}(\mathbf{x})$ given by (3) is ≤ 0 for all $\mathbf{x}$ in Ω, then $V(\mathbf{x})$ is called a **Lyapunov function** for system (1). If $\dot{V}(\mathbf{x})$ is < 0 for all $\mathbf{x} \neq \mathbf{a}$ in Ω, then $V(\mathbf{x})$ is called a **strong Lyapunov function** for the system.

THEOREM 7.5.2 (LYAPUNOV)

Let $\mathbf{a} = (a_1, \ldots, a_n)$ be an equilibrium point for system (1). If there is a Lyapunov function for the system in an open neighbourhood Ω of $\mathbf{a}$, then $\mathbf{a}$ is a stable equilibrium point. If there is a strong Lyapunov function for the system, then $\mathbf{a}$ is locally asymptotically stable.

Proof: Choose $\varepsilon > 0$ so small that $\bar{B} = \{\mathbf{x} : \|\mathbf{x} - \mathbf{a}\| \leq \varepsilon\} \subseteq \Omega$. Let $V(\mathbf{x})$ be a Lyapunov function. The boundary $A = \{\mathbf{x} : \|\mathbf{x} - \mathbf{a}\| = \varepsilon\}$ of $\bar{B}$ is compact, and since V is continuous, V has a minimum value α over A. Because $V(\mathbf{x})$ is positive definite, $\alpha > 0$. By continuity of V, we can choose a $\delta > 0$ such that $V(\mathbf{x}) < \alpha$ for all $\mathbf{x}$ in the ball $C = \{\mathbf{x} : \|\mathbf{x} - \mathbf{a}\| < \delta\}$. Then $C \subseteq \bar{B}$, and we see that if a solution curve for (1) starts at a point $\mathbf{x}_0$ in C, then that solution curve cannot meet A, because V is decreasing along solution curves. Hence any solution starting in C never leaves $\bar{B}$. Thus $\mathbf{a}$ is stable.

Now suppose that V is a *strong* Lyapunov function. We want to prove that if $\mathbf{x}(t)$ is a solution starting at a point $\mathbf{x}(0) = \mathbf{x}_0$ in C, then $\mathbf{x}(t) \to \mathbf{a}$ as $t \to \infty$. Evidently, $V(\mathbf{x}(t))$ converges to some limit $V^* \geq 0$. By the mean value theorem, there exist points t_k in $(k, k+1)$ such that $\dot{V}(\mathbf{x}(t_k)) = V(\mathbf{x}(k+1)) - V(\mathbf{x}(k))$, $k = 1, 2, \ldots$. By compactness of $\bar{B}$, a subsequence $\mathbf{x}(t_{k_j})$ converges to some point $\mathbf{x}^*$ in $\bar{B}$. Taking limits in the last equality, we get $\dot{V}(\mathbf{x}^*) = V^* - V^* = 0$. But then $\mathbf{x}^* = \mathbf{a}$ ($\mathbf{a}$ is the only point where $\dot{V} = 0$). Hence, $0 = V(\mathbf{a}) = V(\mathbf{x}^*) = \lim_j V(\mathbf{x}(t_{k_j})) = \lim_{t \to \infty} V(\mathbf{x}(t)) = V^*$. For a contradiction, assume that $\mathbf{x}(t)$ does not converge to $\mathbf{a}$. Then for some ε there exists a sequence $\{t^k\}$ such that $\|\mathbf{x}(t^k) - \mathbf{a}\| \geq \varepsilon$. By compactness of $\bar{B}$ the sequence $\{t^k\}$ has a subsequence $\{s_j\} = \{t^{k_j}\}$ such that $\{\mathbf{x}(s_j)\}$ converges to a point $\mathbf{x}_*$ in $\bar{B}$. Then $V(\mathbf{x}_*) = \lim_{j \to \infty} V(\mathbf{x}(s_j)) = 0$, so $\mathbf{x}_* = \mathbf{a}$, contradicting $\|\mathbf{x}(s_j) - \mathbf{a}\| \geq \varepsilon$ for all j. ∎

NOTE 3 Actually, a proof is needed of the fact that a solution starting at $\mathbf{x}_0$ at $t = 0$ can be extended to a solution defined for all $t > 0$. (See e.g. Hirsch and Smale (1974), Section 9.4.)

According to our previous terminology, an equilibrium point for (1) is **globally asymptotically stable** if *any* solution of (1) (wherever it starts) converges to $\mathbf{a}$ as t tends to ∞. One can prove the following additional result (see LaSalle and Lefschetz (1961)):

THEOREM 7.5.3

Let $\mathbf{a} = (a_1, \ldots, a_n)$ be an equilibrium point for system (1), and assume that there exists a Lyapunov function $V(\mathbf{x})$ for (1) that is defined in all of $\mathbb{R}^n$. Suppose

$$V(\mathbf{x}) \to \infty \quad \text{as} \quad \|\mathbf{x} - \mathbf{a}\| \to \infty \tag{4}$$

Then $\mathbf{a}$ is globally asymptotically stable.

EXAMPLE 1   Prove that $V(x, y) = x^2 + y^2$ is a Lyapunov function for the system

$$\dot{x} = -x - y, \quad \dot{y} = x - y$$

with equilibrium point $(0, 0)$. Prove that $(0, 0)$ is globally asymptotically stable.

Solution: $V(x, y)$ is clearly positive definite, and $\dot{V} = 2x\dot{x} + 2y\dot{y} = 2x(-x - y) + 2y(x - y) = -2x^2 - 2y^2 < 0$ for all $(x, y) \neq (0, 0)$. According to Theorem 7.5.2 the equilibrium point $(0, 0)$ is locally asymptotically stable. In fact, because $V(x, y) = x^2 + y^2 \to \infty$ as $\|(x, y)\| = \sqrt{x^2 + y^2} \to \infty$, the equilibrium is globally asymptotically stable by Theorem 7.5.3.

EXAMPLE 2   Consider the celebrated *Lotka–Volterra predator-prey model*

$$\dot{x} = x(k - ay), \quad \dot{y} = y(-h + bx) \tag{i}$$

with a, b, h, and k all positive constants. Here x is the population of prey (say rabbits) and y is the population of predators (say foxes). The rate of rabbit population growth is a decreasing function of the fox population, but the rate of fox population growth is an increasing function of the rabbit population.

Note that there are two equilibrium points, $(0, 0)$ and $(x_0, y_0) = (h/b, k/a)$. By studying a phase diagram it is easy to see that $(0, 0)$ is not stable. (See Problem 6.7.3.)

To check for stability of (x_0, y_0), consider the function

$$H(x, y) = b(x - x_0 \ln x) + a(y - y_0 \ln y) \tag{ii}$$

We claim that $L(x, y) = H(x, y) - H(x_0, y_0)$ is a Lyapunov function for (i). (To understand how to arrive at this function, see Problem 4). Note that $L'_x = b(1 - x_0/x)$ and $L'_y = a(1 - y_0/y)$, so (x_0, y_0) is a stationary point for L. Moreover, $L''_{xx} = bx_0/x^2 > 0$, $L''_{yy} = ay_0/y^2 > 0$, and $L''_{xy} = 0$, so L is strictly convex for all $x > 0$, $y > 0$. It follows that (x_0, y_0) is the unique minimum point for L. But $L(x_0, y_0) = 0$, so $L(x, y)$ is positive definite. Moreover, with $x_0 = h/b$, $y_0 = k/a$, we obtain for all $x > 0$, $y > 0$,

$$\dot{L} = b(1 - x_0/x)\dot{x} + a(1 - y_0/y)\dot{y} = b(1 - x_0/x)x(k - ay) + a(1 - y_0/y)y(-h + bx) = 0 \tag{iii}$$

We conclude from Theorem 7.5.2 that (x_0, y_0) is a stable equilibrium point.

In fact, (iii) implies that $L(x, y)$ is constant along solution curves for (i). One can prove that the curves $L(x, y) = $ constant are closed curves, so that the populations of predator and prey will oscillate cyclically. For further discussion of this model see Hirsch and Smale (1974), Chapter 2.

PROBLEMS FOR SECTION 7.5

1. Prove that $(0, 0)$ is an asymptotically stable point for each of the following systems.

   (a) $\dot{x} = -y - x^3$, $\dot{y} = x - y^3$.   (Put $V(x, y) = x^2 + y^2$.)

   (b) $\dot{x} = -\frac{7}{4}x + \frac{1}{4}y$, $\dot{y} = \frac{3}{5}x - \frac{5}{4}y$.   (Put $V(x, y) = 12x^2 + 12xy + 20y^2$.)

   (c) Test the stability of (b) by using Theorem 7.5.1 as well.

2. Consider the following differential equation for $p > 0$:

   $$\dot{p} = a\left(\frac{b}{p} - c\right), \quad \text{where } a, b \text{ and } c \text{ are positive constants}$$

   Find the equilibrium point and prove that it is locally asymptotically stable by using Theorem 7.5.2. (*Hint:* $V(p) = (p - b/c)^2$.)

3. Consider the system of differential equations

   $$\dot{x}_i = u_i'(x_1, \ldots, x_n), \quad i = 1, \ldots, n$$

   where $u(\mathbf{x}) = u(x_1, \ldots, x_n)$ is C^1 in an open set Ω about $\mathbf{0} = (0, \ldots, 0)$. Suppose $u(\mathbf{x})$ has a global maximum at $\mathbf{0}$ and that $\nabla u(\mathbf{x}) \neq \mathbf{0}$ when $\mathbf{x} \neq \mathbf{0}$. Prove that $\mathbf{0}$ is locally asymptotically stable. (*Hint:* Put $V(\mathbf{x}) = u(\mathbf{0}) - u(\mathbf{x})$ and use Theorem 7.5.2.)

4. (a) Consider a system of differential equations of the form

   $$\dot{x} = f_1(x)f_2(y), \quad \dot{y} = g_1(x)g_2(y)$$

   Eliminate t from the system to obtain

   $$\frac{dy}{dx} = \frac{\dot{y}}{\dot{x}} = \frac{g_1(x)g_2(y)}{f_1(x)f_2(y)} \quad \text{at points where } \dot{x} \neq 0 \tag{$*$}$$

   Deduce that $H(x, y) = \int (g_1(x)/f_1(x))\, dx - \int (f_2(y)/g_2(y))\, dy$ is constant along each solution curve.

   (b) Show that for the Lotka–Volterra system (i) in Example 2, $H(x, y)$ is given by (ii) in Example 2.

5. Consider the following generalization of the Lotka–Volterra system:

   $$\dot{x} = kx - axy - \varepsilon x^2, \quad \dot{y} = -hy + bxy - \delta y^2$$

   where a, b, h, k, δ, and ε are positive constants, with $bk > h\varepsilon$. (In particular, there is logistic growth of the rabbit population in the absence of foxes.) Verify that $x_0 = (ah + k\delta)/(ab + \delta\varepsilon)$, $y_0 = (bk - h\varepsilon)/(ab + \delta\varepsilon)$ is an equilibrium point. Prove that $L(x, y)$ defined in Example 2, with (x_0, y_0) as given in the present case, is a Lyapunov function with $\dot{L} = -\varepsilon b(x - x_0)^2 - a\delta(y - y_0)^2$ along a solution curve. Conclusion?

7.6 Qualitative Theory

The local and global existence and uniqueness theorems of Section 5.8 can be generalized to vector differential equations in n dimensions. The motivation and the examples that were presented for the scalar case are important aids towards understanding the general theorems.

THEOREM 7.6.1 (LOCAL EXISTENCE AND UNIQUENESS)

Consider the initial value problem

$$\dot{\mathbf{x}} = \mathbf{F}(t, \mathbf{x}), \qquad \mathbf{x}(t_0) = \mathbf{x}_0 \tag{1}$$

Suppose that the elements of the vector $\mathbf{F}(t, \mathbf{x})$ and the matrix $\mathbf{F}'_{\mathbf{x}}(t, x)$ are continuous over the $(n + 1)$-dimensional rectangle $\Gamma = \{ (t, \mathbf{x}) : |t - t_0| \leq a, \ \|\mathbf{x} - \mathbf{x}_0\| \leq b \}$, and let

$$M = \max_{(t,\mathbf{x}) \in \Gamma} \|\mathbf{F}(t, \mathbf{x})\|, \qquad r = \min(a, b/M) \tag{2}$$

Then (1) has a unique solution $\mathbf{x}(t)$ on $(t_0 - r, t_0 + r)$ and $\|\mathbf{x}(t) - \mathbf{x}_0\| \leq b$ in this interval.

THEOREM 7.6.2 (GLOBAL EXISTENCE AND UNIQUENESS)

Consider the initial value problem (1). Suppose that the elements of the vector $\mathbf{F}(t, \mathbf{x})$ and the matrix $\mathbf{F}'_{\mathbf{x}}(t, \mathbf{x})$ are continuous functions for all $(t, \mathbf{x})$, and suppose that there exist continuous scalar functions $a(t)$ and $b(t)$ such that

$$\|\mathbf{F}(t, \mathbf{x})\| \leq a(t)\|\mathbf{x}\| + b(t) \quad \text{for all } (t, \mathbf{x}) \tag{3}$$

Given an arbitrary point $(t_0, \mathbf{x}_0)$, there exists a unique solution $\mathbf{x}(t)$ of (1), defined on $(-\infty, \infty)$. If (3) is replaced by the requirement

$$\mathbf{x} \cdot \mathbf{F}(t, \mathbf{x}) \leq a(t)\|\mathbf{x}\|^2 + b(t) \quad \text{for all } \mathbf{x} \text{ and all } t \geq t_0 \tag{4}$$

then the initial value problem (1) has a unique solution defined on $[t_0, \infty)$.

The notes to Theorems 5.8.2 and 5.8.3 for the scalar case are relevant also for Theorems 7.6.1 and 7.6.2. (For proofs of these theorems and of Theorem 7.6.3 below, see Hartman (1982).)

NOTE 1 Condition (3) is satisfied if, for all $(t, \mathbf{x})$,

$$\sup_{\|\mathbf{y}\|=1} \|\mathbf{F}'_{\mathbf{x}}(t, \mathbf{x}) \, \mathbf{y}\| \leq c(t) \quad \text{for some continuous function } c(t) \tag{5}$$

Dependence on Initial Conditions

How does the solution of a differential equation change when the initial conditions change? A precise result is formulated in the next theorem. We need to spell out some crucial assumptions:

(A) $\mathbf{F}(t, \mathbf{x})$ is defined and continuous on an open set A in $\mathbb{R}^{n+1}$.

(B) For each $(t, \mathbf{x})$ in A there exist a number $r > 0$ and an interval (a, b) that contains t, with $(a, b) \times B(\mathbf{x}; r) \subseteq A$, and a constant L such that for all $\mathbf{y}, \mathbf{y}'$ in $B(\mathbf{x}; r)$ and for all t in (a, b) we have

$$\|\mathbf{F}(t, \mathbf{y}) - \mathbf{F}(t, \mathbf{y}')\| \leq L \|\mathbf{y} - \mathbf{y}'\| \tag{6}$$

The function $\mathbf{F}$ is called **Lipschitz continuous** in $\mathbf{x}$ if it satisfies (6).

THEOREM 7.6.3 (CONTINUOUS DEPENDENCE ON INITIAL CONDITIONS)

Consider the vector differential equation $\dot{\mathbf{x}} = \mathbf{F}(t, \mathbf{x})$, where $\mathbf{F}(t, \mathbf{x})$ satisfies both (A) and the Lipschitz condition (B). Suppose that $\tilde{\mathbf{x}}(t)$ is a solution of the equation on an interval (a, b) with $(t, \tilde{\mathbf{x}}(t))$ in A, and let $\tilde{t}_0 \in (a, b)$, $\tilde{\mathbf{x}}^0 = \tilde{\mathbf{x}}(\tilde{t}_0)$. Then there exists a neighbourhood $N = (\tilde{t}_0 - \alpha, \tilde{t}_0 + \alpha) \times B(\tilde{\mathbf{x}}^0; r)$ with $r > 0$ and $\alpha > 0$, such that for every $(t_0, \mathbf{x}^0)$ in N there exists a unique solution through $(t_0, \mathbf{x}^0)$ defined on $[a, b]$ whose graph lies in A. If this solution is denoted by $\mathbf{x}(t; t_0, \mathbf{x}^0)$, then for every t in $[a, b]$ the function $(t_0, \mathbf{x}^0) \mapsto \mathbf{x}(t; t_0, \mathbf{x}^0)$ is continuous in N. If F is C^1 in A, then $\mathbf{x}(t; t_0, \mathbf{x}^0)$ is a C^1 function of $(t_0, \mathbf{x}^0)$ in N, and

$$\frac{\partial \mathbf{x}(t; \tilde{t}_0, \tilde{\mathbf{x}}^0)}{\partial \mathbf{x}^0} = \mathbf{P}(t, \tilde{t}_0) \tag{7}$$

$$\frac{\partial \mathbf{x}(t; \tilde{t}_0, \tilde{\mathbf{x}}^0)}{\partial t_0} = -\mathbf{P}(t, \tilde{t}_0) \cdot \mathbf{F}(\tilde{t}_0, \tilde{\mathbf{x}}^0) \tag{8}$$

where the $n \times n$ matrix $\mathbf{P}(t, \tilde{t}_0)$ is the resolvent of the linear differential equation

$$\dot{\mathbf{z}} = \mathbf{F}'_\mathbf{x}(t, \tilde{\mathbf{x}}(t))\mathbf{z} \tag{9}$$

Let us test Theorem 7.6.3 on a simple example.

EXAMPLE 1   Consider the system $\dot{x}_1 = 2x_2$, $\dot{x}_2 = x_1 + x_2$, which can be written as $\dot{\mathbf{x}} = \mathbf{F}(t, \mathbf{x})$ if we put

$$\mathbf{x} = \begin{pmatrix} x_1 \\ x_2 \end{pmatrix}, \qquad \mathbf{F}(t, \mathbf{x}) = \begin{pmatrix} 2x_2 \\ x_1 + x_2 \end{pmatrix}$$

Conditions (A) and (B) in Theorem 7.6.3 are satisfied everywhere for this linear system.
The general solution of $\dot{\mathbf{x}} = \mathbf{F}(t, \mathbf{x})$ with $x_1(t_0) = x_1^0$ and $x_2(t_0) = x_2^0$ is

$$\begin{aligned} x_1 &= \tfrac{2}{3}(x_1^0 - x_2^0)e^{t_0}e^{-t} + \tfrac{1}{3}(x_1^0 + 2x_2^0)e^{-2t_0}e^{2t} \\ x_2 &= -\tfrac{1}{3}(x_1^0 - x_2^0)e^{t_0}e^{-t} + \tfrac{1}{3}(x_1^0 + 2x_2^0)e^{-2t_0}e^{2t} \end{aligned} \tag{i}$$

We see that x_1 and x_2 are C^1 functions of (t_0, x_1^0, x_2^0).
In the present case, the left-hand side of (7) is the following 2×2 matrix (evaluated at (x_1^0, x_2^0, t_0) rather than at $(\tilde{x}_1^0, \tilde{x}_2^0, \tilde{t}_0)$),

$$\begin{pmatrix} \partial x_1/\partial x_1^0 & \partial x_1/\partial x_2^0 \\ \partial x_2/\partial x_1^0 & \partial x_2/\partial x_2^0 \end{pmatrix} = \begin{pmatrix} \tfrac{2}{3}e^{t_0}e^{-t} + \tfrac{1}{3}e^{-2t_0}e^{2t} & -\tfrac{2}{3}e^{t_0}e^{-t} + \tfrac{2}{3}e^{-2t_0}e^{2t} \\ -\tfrac{1}{3}e^{t_0}e^{-t} + \tfrac{1}{3}e^{-2t_0}e^{2t} & \tfrac{1}{3}e^{t_0}e^{-t} + \tfrac{2}{3}e^{-2t_0}e^{2t} \end{pmatrix} \tag{ii}$$

Notice that because $\mathbf{F}(t, \mathbf{x})$ is linear in $\mathbf{x}$, the differential equation in (9) is identical to $\dot{\mathbf{x}} = \mathbf{F}(t, \mathbf{x})$. Thus we see that the right-hand side of (7) is the resolvent of $\dot{\mathbf{x}} = \mathbf{F}(\mathbf{x}, t)$. According to (7.4.10), the two columns of $\mathbf{P}(t, t_0)$ are obtained from (i) by putting $x_1^0 = x_1(t_0) = 1$, $x_2^0 = x_2(t_0) = 0$, and $x_1^0 = x_1(t_0) = 0$, $x_2^0 = x_2(t_0) = 1$, respectively. Hence

$$\mathbf{P}(t, t_0) = \begin{pmatrix} \frac{2}{3}e^{t_0}e^{-t} + \frac{1}{3}e^{-2t_0}e^{2t} & -\frac{2}{3}e^{t_0}e^{-t} + \frac{2}{3}e^{-2t_0}e^{2t} \\ -\frac{1}{3}e^{t_0}e^{-t} + \frac{1}{3}e^{-2t_0}e^{2t} & \frac{1}{3}e^{t_0}e^{-t} + \frac{2}{3}e^{-2t_0}e^{2t} \end{pmatrix} \tag{iii}$$

Because the matrices in (ii) and (iii) are identical, (7) is confirmed.

Using (i), the left-hand side of (8) evaluated at (t_0, x_1^0, x_2^0) is

$$\begin{pmatrix} \partial x_1/\partial t_0 \\ \partial x_2/\partial t_0 \end{pmatrix} = \begin{pmatrix} \frac{2}{3}(x_1^0 - x_2^0)e^{t_0}e^{-t} - \frac{2}{3}(x_1^0 + 2x_2^0)e^{-2t_0}e^{2t} \\ -\frac{1}{3}(x_1^0 - x_2^0)e^{t_0}e^{-t} - \frac{2}{3}(x_1^0 + 2x_2^0)e^{-2t_0}e^{2t} \end{pmatrix} \tag{iv}$$

The right-hand side of (8) is $-\mathbf{P}(t, t_0) \cdot \mathbf{F}(t_0, \mathbf{x}^0) = -\mathbf{P}(t, t_0) \cdot \begin{pmatrix} 2x_2^0 \\ x_1^0 + x_2^0 \end{pmatrix}$. Using (iii) we see that this matrix product is equal to the column vector in (iv). Thus (8) is confirmed.

7.7 A Glimpse at Partial Differential Equations

In an ordinary differential equation, the unknown function depends on a single variable, and the equation involves the ordinary derivative of that function. In a partial differential equation, however, the unknown function depends on two or more variables, and the equation involves the partial derivatives of that function. When such an equation involves only derivatives of the first order, it is said to be of first order. For example, the general partial differential equation of first order in two variables has the form

$$F(x, y, z, \partial z/\partial x, \partial z/\partial y) = 0 \tag{1}$$

where $z = z(x, y)$ is the unknown function. Here are two simple examples.

EXAMPLE 1   Find the most general function $z = z(x, y)$ satisfying $\partial z/\partial y = 3x^2y - y^2$.

Solution: First, we keep x constant, and integrate $3x^2y - y^2$ w.r.t. y. The most general function of x and y whose derivative w.r.t. y equals $3x^2y - y^2$, is $3x^2\frac{1}{2}y^2 - \frac{1}{3}y^3 + C$. But when x is variable, note that C could be an arbitrary function of x. Thus, the general solution is $z = \frac{3}{2}x^2y^2 - \frac{1}{3}y^3 + \varphi(x)$, where $\varphi(x)$ is any differentiable function of x.

EXAMPLE 2   Find the solutions of $z'_x + az'_y = 0$.

Solution: One might guess that there are solutions with $z'_x = \alpha$ and $z'_y = \beta$ for suitable constants α and β. Indeed, this is a solution provided that $\alpha + a\beta = 0$. Thus, $z = -a\beta x + \beta y + C$ is a solution for all real β and C. But there are many other solutions as well. Indeed, provided that $z'_y \neq 0$, the equation can be rewritten as $z'_x/z'_y = -a$. Economists should recognize this as saying that the marginal rate of substitution between x and y is equal to the constant $-a$. This suggests that the level curves of $z(x, y)$ should be straight lines of slope a, and so that the general solution is $z = g(ax - y)$ for an arbitrary differentiable function g. Indeed, using the chain rule, $z'_x = ag'(ax - y)$ and $z'_y = -g'(ax - y)$, so $z'_x + az'_y \equiv 0$, so any such function does satisfy the equation. The technique set out below shows that this is the general solution.

These examples indicate that the set of solutions of a given partial differential equation is often enormous. For ordinary differential equations the general solution depends on one or more arbitrary constants, according to whether the equation is of first or higher order. However, for any such equation, the different solutions are all functions of the same type. *For partial differential equations of the type (1), typically the general solution depends on an arbitrary differentiable function.*

Quasi-linear Equations of First Order

Consider the general *quasi-linear differential equation* of first order,

$$P(x, y, z)\frac{\partial z}{\partial x} + Q(x, y, z)\frac{\partial z}{\partial y} = R(x, y, z) \tag{2}$$

where $P = P(x, y, z)$, $Q = Q(x, y, z)$ and $R = R(x, y, z)$ are all defined in an open set Ω in 3-space, and we assume that $P \neq 0$ in Ω.

The problem is to find all functions $z = z(x, y)$ that satisfy (2). The graph of such a function is called a solution surface or an **integral surface** for (2).

In order to find the general solution of (2), Lagrange proposed the following recipe:

RECIPE FOR SOLVING (2)

(A) Solve the following pair of ordinary differential equations, called the *characteristic equations:*

$$\frac{dy}{dx} = \frac{Q}{P}, \qquad \frac{dz}{dx} = \frac{R}{P} \tag{3}$$

where x is the independent variable. The solutions of this simultaneous system can be written in the form $y = \varphi_1(x, C_1, C_2)$, $z = \varphi_2(x, C_1, C_2)$, where C_1 and C_2 are constants of integration. Solving these equations for C_1 and C_2 yields

$$u(x, y, z) = C_1, \qquad v(x, y, z) = C_2 \tag{4}$$

(B) Then the general solution $z = \varphi(x, y)$ of (2) is given implicitly by the equation

$$\Phi\big(u(x, y, z), v(x, y, z)\big) = 0 \tag{5}$$

where Φ is any differentiable function of two variables, provided that z occurs in equation (5) (otherwise the equation cannot define z as a function of x and y).

If $P = 0$ somewhere, one can use $dx/dy = P/Q$ and $dz/dy = R/Q$ as characteristic equations instead. The recipe usually gives all solutions of (2), but problems arise when $P(x, y, z) = 0$ and $Q(x, y, z) = 0$ simultaneously.

EXAMPLE 3   (a) Find the general solution of $\dfrac{\partial z}{\partial x} + \dfrac{y}{x}\dfrac{\partial z}{\partial y} = \dfrac{y}{z}$ $(x \neq 0, z \neq 0)$.

(b) Find the only solution satisfying the *boundary condition* $z(3, y) = y$.

Solution: The equations in (A) are, with $P = 1$, $Q = y/x$, and $R = y/z$,

$$\frac{dy}{dx} = \frac{y}{x}, \qquad \frac{dz}{dx} = \frac{y}{z}$$

The first equation is separable, with solution $y = C_1 x$. Inserting this expression into the second equation gives $dz/dx = C_1 x/z$, so $z\, dz = C_1 x\, dx$, and hence $\frac{1}{2}z^2 = \frac{1}{2}C_1 x^2 + \frac{1}{2}C_2$. (We use $\frac{1}{2}C_2$ rather than C_2 to simplify our expressions.)

Solving $y = C_1 x$ and $\frac{1}{2}z^2 = \frac{1}{2}C_1 x^2 + \frac{1}{2}C_2$ for C_1 and C_2 yields

$$C_1 = y/x, \qquad C_2 = z^2 - xy$$

The general solution $z(x, y)$ of the given equation is then defined implicitly by the equation

$$\Phi(y/x, z^2 - xy) = 0$$

where Φ is an arbitrary differentiable function.

If $\Phi'_2 \neq 0$, we can express $z^2 - xy$ as a C^1 function φ of y/x, so that $z^2 - xy = \varphi(y/x)$, or

$$z^2 = xy + \varphi(y/x) \tag{*}$$

Any function $z = z(x, y)$ that satisfies the latter equation for some C^1 function φ is a solution of the given equation.

(b) The boundary condition requires, geometrically, that the integral surface intersects the plane $x = 3$ along the curve $z = y$. When $z(3, y) = y$, then $z(3, y)^2 = y^2$ and (*) for $x = 3$ yields $y^2 = 3y + \varphi(y/3)$, or $\varphi(y/3) = y^2 - 3y$, i.e. $\varphi(u) = (3u)^2 - 3(3u) = 9u^2 - 9u$, where $u = y/3$. Hence, a solution $z(x, y)$ that satisfies the boundary condition must satisfy the equation $z(x, y)^2 = xy + 9(y/x)^2 - 9y/x$.

EXAMPLE 4   Suppose $z = z(x, y)$ has constant elasticity a w.r.t. x, i.e.

$$\frac{x}{z}\frac{\partial z}{\partial x} = a, \qquad (x \neq 0, \ z \neq 0) \tag{i}$$

What does the method above tell us about $z(x, y)$?

Solution: If we compare (i) with (2), we see that $P = x/z$, $Q = 0$, $R = a$. So the equations in (A) take the form

$$\frac{dy}{dx} = 0, \qquad \frac{dz}{dx} = a\frac{z}{x}$$

Hence $y = C_1$, $z = C_2 x^a$, or $C_1 = y$, $C_2 = zx^{-a}$. The solution of (i) is therefore $\Phi(y, zx^{-a}) = 0$. If $\Phi'_2 \neq 0$, we get $zx^{-a} = \varphi(y)$, i.e.

$$z = \varphi(y)x^a \tag{ii}$$

where φ is an arbitrary differentiable function. (Because the elasticity of x^a w.r.t. x is a and $\varphi(y)$ is independent of x, it is clear that when z is given by (ii), it has elasticity a w.r.t. x.)

Let us give a brief explanation of why the recipe works. The functions P, Q, and R in (2) can be regarded as the components of a vector in $\mathbb{R}^3$. As (x, y, z) varies, the function

$$(x, y, z) \mapsto (P, Q, R) = (P(x, y, z), Q(x, y, z), R(x, y, z)) \qquad (*)$$

is called the **vector field of the differential equation** (2). For simplicity, we shall assume that P, Q, and R are C^1 functions defined throughout $\mathbb{R}^3$, and that $(P, Q, R) \neq (0, 0, 0)$ everywhere. The (direction of the) vector (P, Q, R) at a point in $\mathbb{R}^3$ is called the **characteristic direction** at that point.

If $z = \varphi(x, y)$ is the equation of a surface in $\mathbb{R}^3$, then the vector $(\partial z/\partial x, \partial z/\partial y, -1)$ is orthogonal to its tangent plane (see Note 2.1.1). The scalar product of this vector and (P, Q, R) is

$$\left(\frac{\partial z}{\partial x}, \frac{\partial z}{\partial y}, -1\right) \cdot (P, Q, R) = P\frac{\partial z}{\partial x} + Q\frac{\partial z}{\partial y} - R \qquad (**)$$

Hence $z = \varphi(x, y)$ is a solution of equation (2) if and only if the characteristic direction (P, Q, R) is tangent to the graph of φ at every point.

If $t \mapsto (x(t), y(t), z(t))$ is a parametric representation of a curve γ in $\mathbb{R}^3$, then the tangent vector to γ is $(\dot{x}(t), \dot{y}(t), \dot{z}(t))$. (See Section 7.4.) The curve γ is called a **characteristic** for equation (2) if the tangent to γ at every point has the same direction as the vector (P, Q, R), i.e. if there is a nonzero function α such that

$$(\dot{x}(t), \dot{y}(t), \dot{z}(t)) = \alpha(t)\big(P(x(t), y(t), z(t)),\; Q(x(t), y(t), z(t)),\; R(x(t), y(t), z(t))\big)$$

for all t. After a suitable change in the parameter t, we can assume $\alpha(t) \equiv 1$, so that $(\dot{x}, \dot{y}, \dot{z}) = (P, Q, R)$.

It follows from the existence and uniqueness theorem (Theorem 7.6.1) that every point of $\mathbb{R}^3$ has exactly one characteristic for (2) passing through it. Furthermore, if $z = \varphi(x, y)$ is a solution of (2) and $\mathbf{x}^0 = (x_0, y_0, z_0)$ is a point on the graph of φ, then the entire characteristic through $\mathbf{x}^0$ lies in the graph of φ. To see why, let $\gamma : t \mapsto (x(t), y(t), z(t))$ be a parametric representation of the characteristic through $\mathbf{x}^0$. We can assume that $\gamma(0) = \mathbf{x}^0$. Let $V(t) = z(t) - \varphi(x(t), y(t))$. Then $V(0) = z_0 - \varphi(x_0, y_0) = 0$, and the derivative of V is

$$\dot{V}(t) = \dot{z}(t) - \varphi_1'(x(t), y(t))\dot{x}(t) - \varphi_2'(x(t), y(t))\dot{y}(t)$$
$$= R(x, y, z) - \varphi_1'(x, y)P(x, y, z) - \varphi_2'(x, y)Q(x, y, z) = 0$$

where we have suppressed the parameter t in the second line. But then V must be a constant function with $V(t) = V(0) = 0$ for all t. So $\gamma(t)$ belongs to the graph of φ for all t.

Hence, the graph of a solution of (2) is a union of characteristics for the equation. For example, if $\varphi(x, y)$ solves (2) and we find all characteristics through the points $(x_0, y, \varphi(x, y))$, then the graph of φ consists of the union of these as y varies over $\mathbb{R}$. On the other hand, if $\psi(x, y)$ is a function whose graph $z = \psi(x, y)$ is a union of characteristics for (2), then at every point on the graph, the characteristic direction is tangent to the graph, and therefore ψ is a solution of (2).

To find the characteristics of (2), we need to solve the differential equations

$$\dot{x} = P(x, y, z), \quad \dot{y} = Q(x, y, z), \quad \dot{z} = R(x, y, z) \qquad (6)$$

If $P \neq 0$, we can eliminate t and use x as a free variable instead. Then $dy/dx = \dot{y}/\dot{x} = Q/P$ and $dz/dx = \dot{z}/\dot{x} = R/P$, precisely the equations (3) in the recipe. For every pair of constants C_1 and C_2, each of the two equations in (4) is the equation of a surface, and the intersection of these surfaces is a characteristic of equation (2). At each point $\mathbf{x}^0 = (x_0, y_0, z_0)$ of this characteristic the vector $(P(\mathbf{x}^0), Q(\mathbf{x}^0), R(\mathbf{x}^0))$ is tangent to the curve, and therefore tangent to each of the surfaces $u(x, y, z) = C_1$ and $v(x, y, z) = C_2$. This implies that

$$(P(\mathbf{x}^0), Q(\mathbf{x}^0), R(\mathbf{x}^0)) \cdot \nabla u(\mathbf{x}^0) = (P(\mathbf{x}^0), Q(\mathbf{x}^0), R(\mathbf{x}^0)) \cdot \nabla v(\mathbf{x}^0) = 0$$

since the gradients of u and v are orthogonal to the respective surfaces.

If we keep C_2, say, fixed and vary the constant C_1 in a "smooth" way, we would expect the resulting family of characteristic curves to make up a surface, which would then be a solution surface for (2). More generally, we could vary C_1 and C_2 simultaneously in a proper manner. One way to do so is to demand that they satisfy an equation $\Phi(C_1, C_2) = 0$, where Φ is a C^1 function with a nonzero gradient. This leads to the equation (5).

Suppose $\Phi(u, v)$ is such a function, and let $F(x, y, z) = \Phi(u(x, y, z), v(x, y, z))$. Then (5) is equivalent to the equation $F(x, y, z) = 0$. Straightforward calculations give

$$\nabla F(x, y, z) = \Phi'_1(u, v)\nabla u(x, y, z) + \Phi'_2(u, v)\nabla v(x, y, z)$$

Hence

$$(P, Q, R) \cdot \nabla F(x, y, z) = 0$$

which means that the surface $F(x, y, z) = 0$ is the graph of a solution of (2), provided $F'_3(x, y, z) \neq 0$. This shows that the recipe does indeed lead to solutions of the partial differential equation (2).

It can be shown that the recipe yields *all* solutions of (2), provided that P and Q are not simultaneously equal to 0.

A More General Case

Consider the more general problem of finding all functions $z = z(x_1, \ldots, x_n)$ of n variables satisfying the general quasi-linear partial differential equation

$$P_1 \frac{\partial z}{\partial x_1} + P_2 \frac{\partial z}{\partial x_2} + \cdots + P_n \frac{\partial z}{\partial x_n} = Q \tag{7}$$

Here $P_1, \ldots, P_n$, and Q are functions of $x_1, \ldots x_n$ and z.

It turns out that the method used above for solving (2) can be generalized. We solve (7) in the following way: Assume that $P_1 \neq 0$ and find the general solution of the system

$$\frac{dx_2}{dx_1} = \frac{P_2}{P_1}, \quad \cdots, \quad \frac{dx_n}{dx_1} = \frac{P_n}{P_1}, \quad \frac{dz}{dx_1} = \frac{Q}{P_1} \tag{8}$$

in the form

$$x_2 = \psi_2(x_1; C_1, \ldots, C_n)$$

$$\ldots\ldots\ldots\ldots\ldots\ldots\ldots$$

$$x_n = \psi_n(x_1; C_1, \ldots, C_n)$$

$$z = \psi_{n+1}(x_1; C_1, \ldots, C_n)$$

Solving (if possible) for $C_1, \ldots, C_n$, we obtain

$$u_1(x_1, x_2, \ldots, x_n, z) = C_1, \quad \ldots, \quad u_n(x_1, x_2, \ldots, x_n, z) = C_n$$

If φ is an arbitrary differential function of n variables, and at least one of the functions $u_1, \ldots, u_n$ involves z, then the general solution of (7) is given implicitly by

$$\Phi\big(u_1(x_1, \ldots, x_n, z), \ldots, u_n(x_1, \ldots, x_n, z)\big) = 0 \tag{9}$$

i.e., a solution $z = z(x_1, \ldots, x_n)$ of this equation is a solution of (7).

EXAMPLE 5   Solve the equation

$$x_1 \frac{\partial z}{\partial x_1} + x_2 \frac{\partial z}{\partial x_2} + x_3 \frac{\partial z}{\partial x_3} = x_1 x_2 x_3 \qquad (x_1 \neq 0) \tag{i}$$

Solution: Here

$$\frac{dx_2}{dx_1} = \frac{x_2}{x_1}, \qquad \frac{dx_3}{dx_1} = \frac{x_3}{x_1}, \qquad \frac{dz}{dx_1} = \frac{x_1 x_2 x_3}{x_1} = x_2 x_3$$

The first two equations give us

$$(\text{ii}) \quad x_2 = C_1 x_1 \qquad \text{and} \qquad (\text{iii}) \quad x_3 = C_2 x_1$$

Inserting these into the third equation in (i) yields $dz = C_1 C_2 x_1^2 \, dx_1$. Hence, $z + C_3 = \frac{1}{3} C_1 C_2 x_1^3$, where C_3 is an arbitrary constant. Putting $C_4 = 3C_3$, we obtain

$$3z + C_4 = C_1 C_2 x_1^3 \tag{iv}$$

Solving (ii), (iii) and (iv) for C_1, C_2, and C_4, we obtain

$$C_1 = x_2/x_1, \qquad C_2 = x_3/x_1, \qquad C_4 = x_1 x_2 x_3 - 3z \tag{v}$$

The general solution of the given equation is therefore $\Phi(x_2/x_1, x_3/x_1, x_1 x_2 x_3 - 3z) = 0$, or, if $\Phi_3' \neq 0$,

$$z = \frac{1}{3} x_1 x_2 x_3 - \varphi\left(\frac{x_2}{x_1}, \frac{x_3}{x_1}\right)$$

where φ is an arbitrary C^1 function of two variables.

For further discussions about quasi-linear partial differential equations, see e.g. Zauderer (1989).

PROBLEMS FOR SECTION 7.7

1. Find the general solutions of

    (a) $\dfrac{\partial z}{\partial x} = x^3 + xy^2 - e^x y$ (b) $\dfrac{\partial z}{\partial x} + 2 \dfrac{\partial z}{\partial y} = 3$ (c) $x^2 \dfrac{\partial z}{\partial x} + y^2 \dfrac{\partial z}{\partial y} = z^2$

2. Find the general solution of the partial differential equation

$$y^2 \frac{\partial z}{\partial x} + y \frac{\partial z}{\partial y} = \frac{1}{2} z, \qquad y > 0, \ z > 0$$

3. (a) Find the general solution of the partial differential equation

$$x \frac{\partial z}{\partial x} - y \frac{\partial z}{\partial y} = x, \qquad x > 0, \ y > 0, \ z > 0 \tag{$*$}$$

    (b) Find a solution $z = f(x, y)$ of ($*$) such that $f(x, 1) = x^2$ for all x.

4. Find all functions $z = z(x, y)$ that satisfy $\text{El}_x\, z - \text{El}_y\, z = x$. (Here $\text{El}_x\, z$ denotes the partial elasticity of z w.r.t. x when y is constant, and likewise for $\text{El}_y\, z$.)

5. In utility theory we encounter the following problem: Find all functions $U = U(x_1, x_2)$ with the property that the ratio between the marginal utilities w.r.t. x_1 and x_2 depends on (say) x_1 only. Thus we must solve the equation

$$\frac{\partial U}{\partial x_1} - f(x_1)\frac{\partial U}{\partial x_2} = 0$$

where f is a given function. Solve this problem.

6. A result in the theory of homogeneous functions states that $z = z(x, y)$ satisfies the equation

$$x\frac{\partial z}{\partial x} + y\frac{\partial z}{\partial y} = nz$$

if and only if $z(x, y)$ is homogeneous of degree n. (See e.g. EMEA.) Make use of the method described above to confirm the "only if part" of this result.

7. In a problem in the theory of production, McElroy studies the equation

$$v_1\frac{\partial x}{\partial v_1} + v_2\frac{\partial x}{\partial v_2} = x\varepsilon(x)$$

where $\varepsilon(x)$ is a given positive function and v_1, v_2, and x are positive. Prove that the solution of the equation can be written in the form $x = F(g(v_1, v_2))$ where g is homogeneous of degree 1, while F is an increasing function. (Thus x is a homothetic function of v_1, v_2, see e.g. EMEA.)

8. A model by W. Leontief requires finding the most general function $z = F(x_1, x_2, x_3)$ satisfying the differential equation

$$\frac{\partial z}{\partial x_1} = f(x_1, x_2)\frac{\partial z}{\partial x_2} \quad (f \text{ a given function})$$

Prove that the general solution is $z = G(\varphi(x_1, x_2), x_3)$, where G is an arbitrary differentiable function of two variables, and $\varphi(x_1, x_2)$ is a certain differentiable function of x_1 and x_2.

8

CALCULUS OF VARIATIONS

We are usually convinced more easily by reasons we have found ourselves than by those which have occurred to others.
—Pascal (1670)

This chapter gives a brief introduction to the classical calculus of variations. The next two chapters deal with optimal control theory, which is a modern generalization of the classical theory that offers a unified method for treating very general dynamic optimization problems in continuous time. This new theory is now used by a large number of economists, even when they face a problem that can be solved with the calculus of variations. Economics students interested in dynamic optimization problems should therefore make a serious effort to learn the basic facts of optimal control theory. It is considerably easier to understand the modern methods, however, if one has some prior knowledge of the classical theory.

The calculus of variations actually has a rather long history. Some of its main results were established by Euler and Lagrange as early as in the 18th century. Since then the subject has formed an important part of applied mathematics. In economics, some of its first applications were by Ramsey (1928) to an optimal savings problem (see Example 8.1.1), and by Hotelling (1931) to a problem of how to extract a natural resource (see Example 9.1.2).

8.1 The Simplest Problem

We begin by introducing a problem from optimal growth theory that is closely related to Ramsey's pioneering discussion of optimal saving. It forms the basis of much recent work in macroeconomic theory, as discussed in the textbooks by Blanchard and Fischer (1989) and Barro and Sala-i-Martin (1995).

EXAMPLE 1   **(How much should a nation save?)** Consider an economy evolving over time where $K = K(t)$ denotes the capital stock, $C = C(t)$ consumption, and $Y = Y(t)$ net national product at time t. Suppose that

$$Y = f(K), \qquad \text{where } f'(K) > 0 \text{ and } f''(K) \leq 0 \qquad \text{(i)}$$

Thus net national product is a strictly increasing, concave function of the capital stock alone. For each t assume that

$$f(K(t)) = C(t) + \dot{K}(t) \tag{ii}$$

which means that output, $Y(t) = f(K(t))$, is divided between consumption, $C(t)$, and investment, $\dot{K}(t)$. Moreover, let $K(0) = K_0$ be the historically given capital stock existing "today" at $t = 0$, and suppose that there is a fixed planning period $[0, T]$. Now, for each choice of investment function $\dot{K}(t)$ on the interval $[0, T]$, capital is fully determined by $K(t) = K_0 + \int_0^t \dot{K}(\tau)d\tau$, and (ii) in turn determines $C(t)$. The question Ramsey and his followers have addressed is how much investment would be desirable. High consumption today is in itself preferable, but equation (ii) tells us that it leads to a low rate of investment. This in turn results in a lower capital stock in the future, thus reducing the possibilities for future consumption. One must somehow find a way to reconcile the conflict between consuming in the present and investing for the future.

To this end, assume that the society has a utility function U, where $U(C)$ is the utility (flow) the country enjoys when the total consumption is C. Suppose too that

$$U'(C) > 0, \qquad U''(C) < 0$$

so that U is strictly increasing and strictly concave. (This assumption implies that when society has a high level of consumption, it enjoys a lower increase in satisfaction from a given increase in consumption than when there is a low level of consumption.) Now, as is common in this literature, introduce a discount rate r to reflect the idea that the present may matter more than the future. That is, for each $t \geq 0$ we multiply $U(C(t))$ by the discount factor e^{-rt}. However, Ramsey himself criticized such "impatience", so he put $r = 0$, in effect. Anyway, assume that the goal of investment policy is to choose $K(t)$ for t in $[0, T]$ in order to make the total discounted utility over the period $[0, T]$ as large as possible. Another way of formulating the problem is: Find the path of capital $K = K(t)$, with $K(0) = K_0$, that maximizes

$$\int_0^T U(C(t))e^{-rt} dt = \int_0^T U(f(K(t)) - \dot{K}(t))e^{-rt} dt \tag{1}$$

Usually, some "terminal condition" on $K(T)$ is imposed—for example, that $K(T) = K_T$, where K_T is given. One possibility is $K_T = 0$, with no capital left for times after T. This problem is studied in Example 8.4.1.

Example 1 is a special case of the simplest general problem in the calculus of variations. This takes the form

$$\max \int_{t_0}^{t_1} F(t, x, \dot{x}) dt \quad \text{subject to} \quad x(t_0) = x_0, \quad x(t_1) = x_1 \tag{2}$$

Here F is a given "well-behaved" function of three variables, whereas t_0, t_1, x_0, and x_1 are given numbers. More precisely: Among all well-behaved functions $x(t)$ that satisfy $x(t_0) = x_0$ and $x(t_1) = x_1$, find one making the integral in (2) as large as possible.

Geometrically, the problem is illustrated in Fig. 1. The two end points $A = (t_0, x_0)$ and $B = (t_1, x_1)$ are given in the tx-plane. For each smooth curve that joins the points A and B, the integral in (2) has a definite value. Find the curve that makes the integral as large as possible.

So far the integral in (2) has been maximized. Because minimizing the integral of $F(t, x, \dot{x})$ leads to the same function $x = x(t)$ as maximizing the integral of $-F(t, x, \dot{x})$, there is an obvious relationship between the maximization and minimization problems.

The first known application of the calculus of variations was to the "brachistochrone problem".[1] Given two points A and B in a vertical plane, the time required for a particle to slide along a curve from A to B under the sole influence of gravity will depend on the shape of the curve. The problem is to find the curve along which the particle goes from A to B as quickly as possible. (See Fig. 2.)

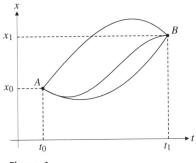

Figure 1

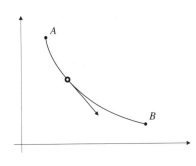

Figure 2

One's first reaction to the problem might be that it is easy, because the straight line joining A to B must be the solution. This is not correct. (Actually, the straight line between A and B solves another variational problem: Find the shortest curve joining A and B. See Problem 8.2.6.) In 1696, the Swiss mathematician John Bernoulli proved that the solution is a part of a curve called a *cycloid*. This starts out steeply so that the particle can accelerate rapidly, acquiring momentum in both the vertical and horizontal directions, before the curve flattens out as it approaches B. Using elementary physics one can show that the brachistochrone problem reduces to the problem of minimizing an integral of the type appearing in (2).

PROBLEMS FOR SECTION 8.1

1. The graphs of the following functions pass through the points $(0, 0)$ and $(1, e^2 - 1)$ in the tx-plane.

$$\text{(i) } x = (e^2 - 1)t \qquad \text{(ii) } x = x(t) = e^{1+t} - e^{1-t}$$

Compute the value of $J(x) = \int_0^1 (x^2 + \dot{x}^2)\, dt$ in both cases. Which of them gives the lesser value to $J(x)$?

[1] The word "brachistochrone" is derived from two Greek roots meaning "shortest" and "time".

8.2 The Euler Equation

The simplest variational problem is this:[2]

$$\max \int_{t_0}^{t_1} F(t, x, \dot{x})\, dt \qquad \text{subject to} \qquad x(t_0) = x_0, \quad x(t_1) = x_1 \qquad (1)$$

Already in 1744 the Swiss mathematician L. Euler proved that a function $x(t)$ can only solve problem (1) if $x(t)$ satisfies the differential equation

$$\frac{\partial F}{\partial x} - \frac{d}{dt}\left(\frac{\partial F}{\partial \dot{x}} \right) = 0 \qquad (2)$$

called the **Euler equation**. Here $\partial F/\partial x$ denotes the derivative $F_2'(t, x, \dot{x})$ of $F(t, x, \dot{x})$ w.r.t. the second variable, whereas $\partial F/\partial \dot{x}$ denotes $F_3'(t, x, \dot{x})$.

Replacing F with $-F$ does not change (2), so the Euler equation also represents a necessary condition for solving the corresponding minimization problem.

Note that in equation (2), the term $(d/dt)(\partial F(t, x, \dot{x})/\partial \dot{x})$ denotes the *total derivative* of $\partial F/\partial \dot{x}$ w.r.t. t, allowing for the dependence of $\partial F/\partial \dot{x}$ on all three variables which depend on t. Assuming that $x = x(t)$ is C^2, one finds that[3]

$$\frac{d}{dt}\left(\frac{\partial F(t, x, \dot{x})}{\partial \dot{x}} \right) = \frac{\partial^2 F}{\partial t\, \partial \dot{x}} + \frac{\partial^2 F}{\partial x\, \partial \dot{x}} \cdot \dot{x} + \frac{\partial^2 F}{\partial \dot{x}\, \partial \dot{x}} \cdot \ddot{x} \qquad (*)$$

Inserting this into (2) and rearranging, the Euler equation becomes

$$\frac{\partial^2 F}{\partial \dot{x}\, \partial \dot{x}} \cdot \ddot{x} + \frac{\partial^2 F}{\partial x\, \partial \dot{x}} \cdot \dot{x} + \frac{\partial^2 F}{\partial t\, \partial \dot{x}} - \frac{\partial F}{\partial x} = 0 \qquad (3)$$

Alternatively, equation (3) can be written as $F_{33}''\ddot{x} + F_{32}''\dot{x} + F_{31}'' - F_2' = 0$, and we see that the Euler equation is a differential equation of the second order (if $F_{33}'' \neq 0$).

The Euler equation gives a *necessary condition* for optimality. It is not, in general, sufficient. By analogy with static optimization problems, it is natural to expect that appropriate concavity (convexity) requirements on $F(t, x, \dot{x})$ will ensure optimality. In the next section we shall prove that for the maximization problem (1), concavity of $F(t, x, \dot{x})$ w.r.t. $(x, \dot{x})$ is sufficient, while convexity of $F(t, x, \dot{x})$ w.r.t. $(x, \dot{x})$ is sufficient for the corresponding minimization problem.

EXAMPLE 1   Solve the problem:

$$\max \int_0^2 (4 - 3x^2 - 16\dot{x} - 4\dot{x}^2)e^{-t}\, dt, \quad x(0) = -8/3, \quad x(2) = 1/3$$

---

[2] In the next section we specify the regularity conditions to be imposed on F and $x(t)$.

[3] According to the chain rule we have $\frac{d}{dt}G(u(t), v(t), w(t)) = G_1'\dot{u} + G_2'\dot{v} + G_3'\dot{w}$. Equation (*) follows by letting $G = F_{\dot{x}}'$, $u = t$, $v = x$, and $w = \dot{x}$.)

Solution: Here $F(t, x, \dot{x}) = (4 - 3x^2 - 16\dot{x} - 4\dot{x}^2)e^{-t}$, so $\partial F/\partial x = -6xe^{-t}$ and $\partial F/\partial \dot{x} = (-16 - 8\dot{x})e^{-t}$. Using Equation (2) requires finding $(d/dt)[(-16 - 8\dot{x})e^{-t}]$. The product rule for differentiation gives

$$(d/dt)[(-16 - 8\dot{x})e^{-t}] = 16e^{-t} - 8\ddot{x}e^{-t} + 8\dot{x}e^{-t}$$

so the Euler equation reduces to $-6xe^{-t} - 16e^{-t} + 8\ddot{x}e^{-t} - 8\dot{x}e^{-t} = 0$. Cancelling the nonzero common factor $8e^{-t}$ yields

$$\ddot{x} - \dot{x} - \tfrac{3}{4}x = 2 \tag{*}$$

This is a linear differential equation of the second order with constant coefficients (see Section 6.3). The characteristic equation is $r^2 - r - \tfrac{3}{4} = 0$, with roots $r_1 = -1/2$ and $r_2 = 3/2$. The nonhomogeneous equation (*) has a particular solution $-8/3$, so the general solution is $x = x(t) = Ae^{-\frac{1}{2}t} + Be^{\frac{3}{2}t} - 8/3$ where A and B are arbitrary constants. The boundary conditions $x(0) = -8/3$ and $x(2) = 1/3$ imply that $0 = A + B$ and $Ae^{-1} + Be^3 = 3$. It follows that $A = -3/(e^3 - e^{-1})$ and $B = -A$, and so

$$x = x(t) = \frac{-3}{e^3 - e^{-1}}e^{-\frac{1}{2}t} + \frac{3}{e^3 - e^{-1}}e^{\frac{3}{2}t} - \frac{8}{3} \tag{**}$$

This is the only solution of the Euler equation that satisfies the given boundary conditions. The function $F(t, x, \dot{x}) = (4 - 3x^2 - 16\dot{x} - 4\dot{x}^2)e^{-t}$ is concave in $(x, \dot{x})$, as a sum of concave functions. We conclude that we have found the solution of the problem.

EXAMPLE 2   Consider the simple macroeconomic problem of trying to steer the state $y(t)$ of the economy over the course of a planning period $[0, T]$ toward the desired level $\hat{y}$, independent of t, by means of the control $u(t)$, where $\dot{y}(t) = u(t)$. Because using the control is costly, the objective is to minimize the integral $\int_0^T \left[(y(t) - \hat{y})^2 + c(u(t))^2\right] dt$ with $y(T) = \hat{y}$, where c is a positive constant.

It is more convenient to define $x(t)$ as the difference between the original state variable and the target level $\hat{y}$, so that the target value of x is 0. Then $u(t) = \dot{x}(t)$. This leads to the following variational problem:

$$\min \int_0^T (x^2 + c\dot{x}^2)\, dt, \quad x(0) = x_0, \quad x(T) = 0$$

where x_0 is the initial deviation from the target level. Find the optimal solution $x^*(t)$.

Solution: In this case the integrand is $F(t, x, \dot{x}) = x^2 + c\dot{x}^2$, so $\partial F/\partial x = 2x$ and $\partial F/\partial \dot{x} = 2c\dot{x}$. The Euler equation is $2x - (d/dt)(2c\dot{x}) = 0$, or

$$\ddot{x} - (1/c)x = 0$$

The general solution is

$$x = Ae^{rt} + Be^{-rt}, \quad \text{where } r = 1/\sqrt{c}$$

The initial condition $x(0) = x_0$ and the terminal condition $x(T) = 0$ yield the two equations $A + B = x_0$ and $Ae^{rT} + Be^{-rT} = 0$. These two equations in A and B have the solution $A = -x_0 e^{-rT}/(e^{rT} - e^{-rT})$ and $B = x_0 e^{rT}/(e^{rT} - e^{-rT})$. It follows that the only possible solution is

$$x^*(t) = \frac{x_0}{e^{rT} - e^{-rT}} \left[e^{r(T-t)} - e^{-r(T-t)} \right]$$

The function $F = x^2 + c\dot{x}^2$ is convex in $(x, \dot{x})$ (as a sum of convex functions), so the solution to the problem has been found.

Important Special Cases

If the integrand $F(t, x, \dot{x})$ in (1) does not depend on x, then the Euler equation reduces to $(d/dt)F'_{\dot{x}}(t, x, \dot{x}) = 0$, so $F'_{\dot{x}}(t, x, \dot{x}) = C$ for some constant C. This is a first-order differential equation.

In many variational problems in economics the integrand $F(t, x, \dot{x})$ in (1) is of the form $F(x, \dot{x})$, so that t does not enter explicitly. It is then possible to reduce the Euler equation to a first-order equation. The trick is to calculate the total derivative of the expression $F(x, \dot{x}) - \dot{x}\partial F(x, \dot{x})/\partial \dot{x}$ as follows:

$$\frac{d}{dt}\left[F(x, \dot{x}) - \dot{x}\frac{\partial F(x, \dot{x})}{\partial \dot{x}} \right] = \dot{x}\frac{\partial F}{\partial x} + \ddot{x}\frac{\partial F}{\partial \dot{x}} - \ddot{x}\frac{\partial F}{\partial \dot{x}} - \dot{x}\frac{d}{dt}\frac{\partial F}{\partial \dot{x}} = \dot{x}\left[\frac{\partial F}{\partial x} - \frac{d}{dt}\left(\frac{\partial F}{\partial \dot{x}} \right) \right] \quad (*)$$

It follows that if the Euler equation is satisfied for all t in $[t_0, t_1]$, then the expression in $(*)$ is 0. That is, the derivative of $F - \dot{x}\partial F/\partial \dot{x}$ must be 0 for all t. In this case the Euler equation implies that

$$F - \dot{x}\frac{\partial F}{\partial \dot{x}} = C \quad (C \text{ constant}) \tag{4}$$

for some constant C. This is a first-order differential equation which, in general, is easier to handle than the (second-order) Euler equation. Because of the possibility that $\dot{x} = 0$, the Euler equation is not quite equivalent to (4). Every solution of the Euler equation is clearly a solution to (4) for some constant C. On the other hand, for each value of C, any solution of (4) that is not constant on any interval is a solution of the Euler equation. But if $\dot{x} = 0$ on some interval, then x may not solve the Euler equation.

It follows from (3) that the Euler equation associated with $F(x, \dot{x})$ has a constant solution $x = k$ on some interval if and only if $F'_x(k, 0) = 0$. Hence, if $F'_x(x, 0) \neq 0$ for all x, then the Euler equation is equivalent to equation (4). Equation (4) is then called a **first integral** of the Euler equation.

EXAMPLE 3   Consider Example 8.1.1 with no discounting, so that $r = 0$. The objective (1) then becomes $\int_0^T U(C(t)) \, dt = \int_0^T U(f(K(t)) - \dot{K}(t)) \, dt$. In this case the integrand is $F = U(C) = U(f(K) - \dot{K})$, so $F'_{\dot{K}} = -U'(C)$. Hence equation (4) reduces to

$$U(C) + \dot{K}U'(C) = c \quad (c \text{ is a constant}) \tag{$*$}$$

One usually assumes that $f' > 0$ and $U' > 0$, so $F'_K = U'(C)f'(K) > 0$, and $(*)$ is equivalent to the Euler equation.

PROBLEMS FOR SECTION 8.2

1. Solve the problem $\max \int_0^1 (4xt - \dot{x}^2)\, dt$, $x(0) = 2$, $x(1) = 2/3$.

2. Solve the problem $\min \int_0^1 (t\dot{x} + \dot{x}^2)\, dt$, $x(0) = 1$, $x(1) = 0$.

3. Find the Euler equation associated with $J(x) = \int_{t_0}^{t_1} F(t, x, \dot{x})\, dt$ when

   (a) $F(t, x, \dot{x}) = x^2 + \dot{x}^2 + 2xe^t$ (b) $F(t, x, \dot{x}) = -e^{\dot{x} - ax}$

   (c) $F(t, x, \dot{x}) = [(x - \dot{x})^2 + x^2]e^{-at}$ (d) $F(t, x, \dot{x}) = 2tx + 3x\dot{x} + t\dot{x}^2$

4. Solve the problem $\min \int_0^1 (x^2 + 2tx\dot{x} + \dot{x}^2)\, dt$, $x(0) = 1$, $x(1) = 2$.

5. Solve the problem $\min \int_0^1 (x^2 + tx + tx\dot{x} + \dot{x}^2)\, dt$, $x(0) = 0$, $x(1) = 1$.

6. The part of the graph of the function $x = x(t)$ that joins the points (t_0, x_0) and (t_1, x_1) has length given by $L = \int_{t_0}^{t_1} \sqrt{1 + \dot{x}^2}\, dt$. Find the $x(t)$ that minimizes L. Comment on the answer.

7. Solve the problem $\min \int_1^2 (x^2 + tx\dot{x} + t^2\dot{x}^2)\, dt$, $x(1) = 0$, $x(2) = 1$.

8. H.Y. Wan considers the problem of finding a function $x = x(t)$ which maximizes

$$\int_0^T \left[N(\dot{x}(t)) + \dot{x}(t) f(x(t)) \right] e^{-rt}\, dt$$

where N and f are given C^1 functions, r and T are positive constants, $x(0) = x_0$, and $x(T) = x_T$. Deduce the Euler equation, $\frac{d}{dt} N'(\dot{x}) = r[N'(\dot{x}) + f(x)]$.

8.3 Why the Euler Equation is Necessary

In the previous section we showed how to use the Euler equation to find solution candidates to variational problems. In this section we formulate and prove a precise result in which the regularity conditions on F and x are specified.

The Euler equation plays a similar role in the calculus of variations as the familiar first-order conditions in static optimization. The main result is summed up in the following theorem. The proof is very instructive and should be studied carefully by students who want insight into dynamic optimization.[4]

---

[4] We assume in the proof that the admissible functions are C^2. By using a more elaborate argument (see Gelfand and Fomin (1963)), one can prove the result assuming only that the admissible functions are C^1.

THEOREM 8.3.1 (NECESSARY CONDITIONS)

Suppose that F is a C^2 function of three variables. Suppose that $x^*(t)$ maximizes or minimizes

$$J(x) = \int_{t_0}^{t_1} F(t, x, \dot{x})\, dt \tag{1}$$

among all **admissible** functions $x(t)$ i.e.—all C^1 functions $x(t)$ defined on $[t_0, t_1]$ that satisfy the boundary conditions

$$x(t_0) = x_0, \quad x(t_1) = x_1, \qquad (x_0 \text{ and } x_1 \text{ given numbers})$$

Then $x^*(t)$ is a solution of the Euler equation

$$\frac{\partial F(t, x, \dot{x})}{\partial x} - \frac{d}{dt}\left(\frac{\partial F(t, x, \dot{x})}{\partial \dot{x}}\right) = 0 \tag{2}$$

If $F(t, x, \dot{x})$ is concave (convex) in $(x, \dot{x})$, an admissible $x^*(t)$ that satisfies the Euler equation solves the maximization (minimization) problem.

Proof: To prove the Euler equation we need only compare the optimal solution with members of a special class of functions. Suppose $x^* = x^*(t)$ is an optimal solution to the maximization problem, and let $\mu(t)$ be any C^2 function that satisfies $\mu(t_0) = \mu(t_1) = 0$. For each real number α, define a *perturbed* function $x(t)$ by $x(t) = x^*(t) + \alpha\mu(t)$. (See Fig. 1.)

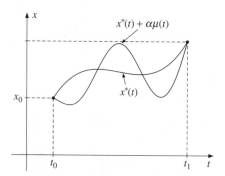

Figure 1

Note that if α is small, the function $x(t)$ is "near" the function $x^*(t)$. Clearly, $x(t)$ is admissible, because it is C^2 with $x(t_0) = x^*(t_0) + \alpha\mu(t_0) = x_0 + \alpha \cdot 0 = x_0$ and $x(t_1) = x^*(t_1) + \alpha\mu(t_1) = x_1 + \alpha \cdot 0 = x_1$. Because of the hypothesis that $x^*(t)$ is optimal, $J(x^*) \geq J(x^* + \alpha\mu)$ for all α. If the function $\mu(t)$ is kept fixed, then $J(x^* + \alpha\mu)$ is a function $I(\alpha)$ of only the single scalar α, given by

$$I(\alpha) = \int_{t_0}^{t_1} F\big(t, \, x^*(t) + \alpha\mu(t), \, \dot{x}^*(t) + \alpha\dot{\mu}(t)\big)\, dt \tag{3}$$

Obviously $I(0) = J(x^*)$ and $I(\alpha) \leq I(0)$ for all α. Hence the function I has a maximum at $\alpha = 0$. Because I is a differentiable function and $\alpha = 0$ is an interior point in the domain of I, one must have $I'(0) = 0$. (Obviously, this equation must hold for the minimization problem as well.) This condition allows one to deduce the Euler equation.

Looking at (3), note that to calculate $I'(\alpha)$ requires differentiating under the integral sign. We apply Leibniz's formula (Theorem 4.2.1) to obtain:

$$I'(\alpha) = \int_{t_0}^{t_1} \frac{\partial}{\partial \alpha} F(t, x^*(t) + \alpha \mu(t), \dot{x}^*(t) + \alpha \dot{\mu}(t)) \, dt$$

According to the chain rule,

$$\frac{\partial}{\partial \alpha} F(t, x^*(t) + \alpha \mu(t), \dot{x}^*(t) + \alpha \dot{\mu}(t)) = F_2' \cdot \mu(t) + F_3' \cdot \dot{\mu}(t)$$

where F_2' and F_3' are both evaluated at $(t, x^*(t) + \alpha \mu(t), \dot{x}^*(t) + \alpha \dot{\mu}(t))$. For $\alpha = 0$ this point is $(t, x^*(t), \dot{x}^*(t))$, so

$$I'(0) = \int_{t_0}^{t_1} \left[F_2'(t, x^*(t), \dot{x}^*(t)) \cdot \mu(t) + F_3'(t, x^*(t), \dot{x}^*(t)) \cdot \dot{\mu}(t) \right] dt$$

or, in more compact notation,

$$I'(0) = \int_{t_0}^{t_1} \left[\frac{\partial F^*}{\partial x} \mu(t) + \frac{\partial F^*}{\partial \dot{x}} \dot{\mu}(t) \right] dt \qquad \text{(i)}$$

where the asterisks indicate that the derivatives are evaluated at $(t, x^*, \dot{x}^*)$.

To proceed further, integrate the second term of the integrand by parts to obtain

$$\int_{t_0}^{t_1} \frac{\partial F^*}{\partial \dot{x}} \dot{\mu}(t) \, dt = \left. \left(\frac{\partial F^*}{\partial \dot{x}} \right) \mu(t) \right|_{t_0}^{t_1} - \int_{t_0}^{t_1} \frac{d}{dt} \left(\frac{\partial F^*}{\partial \dot{x}} \right) \mu(t) \, dt$$

Inserting this result into (i) and rearranging the terms gives

$$I'(0) = \int_{t_0}^{t_1} \left[\frac{\partial F^*}{\partial x} - \frac{d}{dt} \left(\frac{\partial F^*}{\partial \dot{x}} \right) \right] \mu(t) \, dt + \left(\frac{\partial F^*}{\partial \dot{x}} \right)_{t=t_1} \mu(t_1) - \left(\frac{\partial F^*}{\partial \dot{x}} \right)_{t=t_0} \mu(t_0) \qquad \text{(4)}$$

However, the function μ satisfies $\mu(t_0) = \mu(t_1) = 0$, so the last two terms of (4) are zero. Hence, the first-order condition $I'(0) = 0$ reduces to

$$\int_{t_0}^{t_1} \left[\frac{\partial F^*}{\partial x} - \frac{d}{dt} \left(\frac{\partial F^*}{\partial \dot{x}} \right) \right] \mu(t) \, dt = 0 \qquad \text{(ii)}$$

In the argument leading to this result, $\mu(t)$ was a *fixed* function. But (ii) must be valid for *all* functions $\mu(t)$ that are C^2 on $[t_0, t_1]$ and that are 0 at t_0 and at t_1. It stands to reason then that the bracketed expression in (ii) must be 0 for all t in $[t_0, t_1]$. (See the argument in the subsection below.) It follows that $x^*(t)$ satisfies the Euler equation.

Suppose then that $F(t, x, \dot{x})$ is concave in $(x, \dot{x})$ and suppose that $x^* = x^*(t)$ satisfies the Euler equation as well as the boundary conditions $x^*(t_0) = x_0$ and $x^*(t_1) = x_1$. Let $x = x(t)$ be an arbitrary admissible function in the problem. Because $F(t, x, \dot{x})$ is concave in $(x, \dot{x})$, Theorem 2.4.1 implies that

$$F(t, x, \dot{x}) - F(t, x^*, \dot{x}^*) \leq \frac{\partial F(t, x^*, \dot{x}^*)}{\partial x}(x - x^*) + \frac{\partial F(t, x^*, \dot{x}^*)}{\partial \dot{x}}(\dot{x} - \dot{x}^*) \qquad \text{(iii)}$$

Using the Euler equation, reversing the inequality (iii) yields (with simplified notation)

$$
\begin{aligned}
F^* - F &\geq \frac{\partial F^*}{\partial x}(x^* - x) + \frac{\partial F^*}{\partial \dot{x}}(\dot{x}^* - \dot{x}) \\
&= \left[\frac{d}{dt} \left(\frac{\partial F^*}{\partial \dot{x}} \right) \right](x^* - x) + \frac{\partial F^*}{\partial \dot{x}}(\dot{x}^* - \dot{x}) = \frac{d}{dt} \left[\frac{\partial F^*}{\partial \dot{x}}(x^* - x) \right]
\end{aligned}
\qquad \text{(iv)}
$$

Because (iv) is valid for all t in $[t_0, t_1]$, integrating yields

$$\int_{t_0}^{t_1} (F^* - F)\, dt \geq \int_{t_0}^{t_1} \frac{d}{dt}\left[\frac{\partial F^*}{\partial \dot{x}}(x^* - x)\right] dt = \left.\frac{\partial F^*}{\partial \dot{x}}(x^* - x)\right|_{t_0}^{t_1} \tag{5}$$

However, both $x^*(t)$ and $x(t)$ satisfy $x^*(t_0) = x(t_0) (= x_0)$ and $x^*(t_1) = x(t_1) (= x_1)$. So the last expression in (5) is equal to 0. It follows that

$$\int_{t_0}^{t_1} \left[F(t, x^*, \dot{x}^*) - F(t, x, \dot{x})\right] dt \geq 0$$

for every admissible function $x = x(t)$. This confirms that $x^*(t)$ solves the maximization problem. The corresponding result for the minimization problem is easily derived.   ∎

The Fundamental Lemma

For the interested reader we now show how equation (ii) in the proof above implies the Euler equation. First we need:

THEOREM 8.3.2   (THE FUNDAMENTAL LEMMA)

Suppose that f is a continuous function on $[t_0, t_1]$, and that $\int_{t_0}^{t_1} f(t)\mu(t)\, dt = 0$ for every function $\mu = \mu(t)$ which is C^2 in this interval and satisfies $\mu(t_0) = \mu(t_1) = 0$. Then $f(t) = 0$ for all t in $[t_0, t_1]$.

Proof: Suppose there exists a number s in (t_0, t_1) such that $f(s) > 0$. We show that this yields a contradiction. Indeed, because f is continuous, there must be an interval (α, β) with s in $(\alpha, \beta) \subseteq (t_0, t_1)$ such that $f(t) > 0$ for all t in (α, β). For all t in $[t_0, t_1]$ define (see Fig. 2)

$$\mu(t) = \begin{cases} 0 & \text{if } t \notin (\alpha, \beta) \\ (t - \alpha)^3(\beta - t)^3 & \text{if } t \in (\alpha, \beta) \end{cases}$$

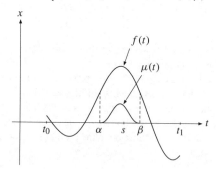

Figure 2

Because $(\alpha, \beta) \subseteq (t_0, t_1)$, we have $\mu(t_0) = \mu(t_1) = 0$. Also, because $\mu(t) = \mu'(t) = \mu''(t) = 0$ at $t = \alpha$ and $t = \beta$, it is obvious that $\mu(t)$ is C^2 everywhere. Now $f(t) \cdot \mu(t) > 0$ in (α, β), while $f(t) \cdot \mu(t) = 0$ outside (α, β). Therefore $\int_{t_0}^{t_1} f(t)\mu(t)\, dt = \int_{\alpha}^{\beta} f(t)\mu(t)\, dt > 0$, which gives a contradiction. In the same way one can show that it is also impossible to have $f(t) < 0$ for some t in (t_0, t_1). Therefore, $f(t) = 0$ for all t in (t_0, t_1). By continuity it follows that $f(t) = 0$ for all t in $[t_0, t_1]$.   ∎

To apply this theorem to (ii) above, put $f(t) = (\partial F^*/\partial x) - (d/dt)(\partial F^*/\partial \dot{x})$. With our assumptions on F and $x = x(t)$, the function f is continuous on $[t_0, t_1]$, and so $f(t) = 0$ for all t in $[t_0, t_1]$, which reduces to the Euler equation.

NOTE 1   Suppose that in the standard variational problem the requirement

$$h(t, x, \dot{x}) > 0 \qquad\qquad (*)$$

is imposed as an extra condition, where h is a given C^1 function of three variables. In order to be admissible a function $x(t)$ must then satisfy $h(t, x(t), \dot{x}(t)) > 0$ for all t in $[t_0, t_1]$. A simple case is one in which it is assumed that $x > 0$. If $x^*(t)$ solves problem with $(*)$ imposed, then $x^*(t)$ has to satisfy the Euler equation. In fact, because of the continuity assumption, $h(t, x(t), \dot{x}(t))$ must be positive for all $x(t)$ sufficiently close to $x^*(t)$, and the result follows because the Euler equation was derived by comparing the value of the criterion functional only with functions close to $x^*(t)$. Note that in this case the function F in (1) only has to be defined and C^2 for triples $(t, x, \dot{x})$ that satisfy $h(t, x, \dot{x}) > 0$.

Suppose that for all t in $[t_0, t_1]$ the function $F(t, x, \dot{x})$ is concave in $(x, \dot{x})$ for all $(x, \dot{x})$ satisfying $h(t, x, \dot{x}) > 0$, with $h(t, x, \dot{x})$ quasi-concave in $(x, \dot{x})$. Then an admissible $x^*(t)$ satisfying the Euler equation is optimal.

NOTE 2   A variational problem does not necessarily have a solution. For example, in the Ramsey model of Example 8.1.1, it is obvious that with realistic production functions the required terminal capital stock at the end of the planning period can be set so high that there is no admissible solution. Problem 3 includes another example where an optimal solution does not exist.

Note that the existence of a solution to a variational problem can often be established even if the concavity or convexity conditions in Theorem 8.3.1 are not satisfied. (By analogy, many non-concave functions of one variable have a maximum.) We refer to Section 10.4.

PROBLEMS FOR SECTION 8.3

1. Show that there is no solution to the problem

$$\max \int_0^1 (x^2 + \dot{x}^2)\, dt, \quad x(0) = 0, \quad x(1) = 0$$

   (*Hint:* Let $x(t) = a(t - t^2)$, compute the integral, and let $a \to \infty$.)

2. (a) Write down the Euler equation associated with the problem

$$\max \int_0^T U(\bar{c} - \dot{x}e^{rt})\, dt, \quad x(0) = x_0, \quad x(T) = 0$$

   where $x = x(t)$ is the unknown function, $T, \bar{c}, r,$ and x_0 are positive constants, and U is a given C^1 function of one variable.

   (b) Put $U(c) = -e^{vc}/v$, where v is a positive constant. Write down and solve the Euler equation in this case, then explain why you have solved the problem.

HARDER PROBLEMS

3. Show that the problem min $\int_a^1 t\dot{x}^2\, dt$, $x(a) = 0$, $x(1) = 1$ has a solution if $a \in (0, 1)$, but not if $a = 0$.

4. R.M. Goodwin considers the problem of maximizing the integral

$$\int_0^1 \ln\left[y - \sigma\dot{y} - \bar{z}l(t)\right] dt$$

w.r.t. the function $y = y(t)$. Here σ and $\bar{z}$ are positive constants and $l(t)$ is a given positive function.

(a) Find the Euler equation in this case.

(b) Suppose that $l(t) = l_0 e^{\alpha t}$ and then find the solution of the equation when $\alpha\sigma \neq 1$.

8.4 Optimal Savings

This section considers in more detail the finite horizon optimal savings problem of Example 8.1.1.

EXAMPLE 1   Find the Euler equation for the Ramsey problem in Example 8.1.1:

$$\max \int_0^T U(f(K(t)) - \dot{K}(t))e^{-rt}\, dt, \qquad K(0) = K_0, \qquad K(T) = K_T$$

Deduce an expression for the corresponding relative rate of change of consumption, $\dot{C}/C$, where $C = f(K) - \dot{K}$. Also, show that the concavity condition in Theorem 8.3.1 is satisfied if $f'(K) > 0$, $f''(K) \leq 0$, $U'(C) > 0$, and $U''(C) < 0$.

Solution: Let $F(t, K, \dot{K}) = U(C)e^{-rt}$ with $C = f(K) - \dot{K}$. Then we find that $\partial F/\partial K = U'(C)f'(K)e^{-rt}$ and $\partial F/\partial \dot{K} = -U'(C)e^{-rt}$, so that the Euler equation reduces to $U'(C)f'(K)e^{-rt} - \frac{d}{dt}\left(-U'(C)e^{-rt}\right) = 0$. Both $U'(C)$ and e^{-rt} depend on t, so by the product rule for differentiation, $\frac{d}{dt}\left(U'(C)e^{-rt}\right) = U''(C)\dot{C}e^{-rt} - rU'(C)e^{-rt}$. Multiplying by e^{rt} and rearranging, it follows that

$$U'(C)(f'(K) - r) + U''(C)\dot{C} = 0 \tag{$*$}$$

and so we obtain

$$\frac{\dot{C}}{C} = \frac{U'(C)}{CU''(C)}(r - f'(K)) = \frac{r - f'(K)}{\check{\omega}} \tag{1}$$

where $\check{\omega} = \mathrm{El}_C\, U'(C) = CU''(C)/U'(C)$ is the **elasticity of marginal utility** with respect to consumption. Note that $\check{\omega} < 0$ because it is assumed that $U'(C) > 0$ and $U''(C) < 0$. (An estimate sometimes used for $\check{\omega}$ is -0.6.) It follows that

$$\frac{\dot{C}}{C} > 0 \iff f'(K) > r \tag{2}$$

Hence, consumption increases if and only if the marginal productivity of capital exceeds the discount rate.

On the other hand, if $f'(K) < r$, there is so much impatience to consume that consumption starts off high, then declines over time.

If we use the fact that $\dot{C} = f'(K)\dot{K} - \ddot{K}$ in equation $(*)$, and divide it by $U''(C)$, we get

$$\ddot{K} - f'(K)\dot{K} + \frac{U'(C)}{U''(C)}(r - f'(K)) = 0 \tag{3}$$

Because f is concave ($f''(K) \leq 0$), it follows that $f(K) - \dot{K}$ is also concave in $(K, \dot{K})$, as a sum of concave functions. The function U is increasing and concave, so $U(f(K) - \dot{K})e^{-rt}$ is also concave in $(K, \dot{K})$. (Theorem 2.3.5(a).) Any solution of (3) which satisfies the boundary conditions must therefore be a solution of the problem.

Equation (3) is a complicated second-order differential equation. Explicit solutions are obtainable only in special cases. But note how interesting economic conclusions have been obtained anyway.

EXAMPLE 2   Solve Example 1 when $f(K) = bK$ and $U(C) = C^{1-v}/(1 - v)$, where $b > 0$, $v > 0$, $v \neq 1$, and $b \neq (b - r)/v$.

Solution: Equation (3) yields

$$\ddot{K} - \left(b - \frac{r-b}{v}\right)\dot{K} + \frac{b-r}{v}bK = 0$$

For $b \neq (b - r)/v$, this second-order differential equation has the general solution

$$K(t) = Ae^{bt} + Be^{(b-r)t/v} \tag{$*$}$$

The constants A and B are determined by the equations $K_0 = A + B$, $K_T = Ae^{bT} + Be^{(b-r)T/v}$. Because $f(K)$ is concave and U is increasing and concave, the function $K(t)$ given by $(*)$, with the constants determined by these two equations, solves the problem.

PROBLEMS FOR SECTION 8.4

1. Find the Euler equation for the variational problem

$$\max \int_0^T e^{-t/4} \ln(2K - \dot{K})\, dt, \qquad K(0) = K_0, \quad K(T) = K_T$$

and solve the problem.

2. (a) Solve the problem

$$\max \int_0^T e^{-t/10}\left(\frac{1}{100}tx - \dot{x}^2\right) dt, \qquad x(0) = 0, \quad x(T) = S$$

(b) Let $T = 10$ and $S = 20$ and find the solution in this case.

3. We generalize Example 1. Let $Y(t) = f(K(t), t)$ and replace $U(C)e^{-rt}$ by $U(C, t)$. Assume also that capital depreciates at the proportional rate δ, so that $C = f(K, t) - \dot{K} - \delta K$. The problem then becomes

$$\max \int_0^T U(f(K, t) - \dot{K} - \delta K, \, t) \, dt, \quad K(0) = K_0, \quad K(T) = K_T$$

What is the Euler equation in this case? Find an expression for $\dot{C}/C$.

4. A monopolist's production of a commodity per unit of time is $x = x(t)$. Suppose $b(x)$ is the associated cost function. At time t, let $D(p(t), \dot{p}(t))$ be the demand for the commodity per unit of time when the price is $p(t)$. If production at any time is adjusted to meet demand, the monopolist's total profit in the time interval $[0, T]$ is given by

$$\int_0^T \left[pD(p, \dot{p}) - b(D(p, \dot{p})) \right] dt$$

Suppose that $p(0)$ is given and there is a terminal condition on $p(T)$. The monopolist's natural problem is to find a price function $p(t)$ which maximizes his total profit.

(a) Find the Euler equation associated with this problem.

(b) Let $b(x) = \alpha x^2 + \beta x + \gamma$ and $x = D(p, \dot{p}) = Ap + B\dot{p} + C$, where $\alpha, \beta, \gamma, B,$ and C are positive constants, while A is negative. Solve the Euler equation in this case.

8.5 More General Terminal Conditions

So far in our variational problems, the initial and terminal values of the unknown function have all been fixed. In economic applications the initial point is usually fixed because it represents a historically given initial situation. On the other hand, in many models the terminal value of the unknown function can be free, or subject to more general restrictions. This section considers two of the most common terminal conditions that appear in economic models.

The problems we study are briefly formulated as

$$\max \int_{t_0}^{t_1} F(t, x, \dot{x}) \, dt, \quad x(t_0) = x_0, \quad \text{(a) } x(t_1) \text{ free} \quad \text{or} \quad \text{(b) } x(t_1) \geq x_1 \qquad (1)$$

In case the terminal condition is (a), any C^1 function is admissible if its graph joins the fixed point (t_0, x_0) to any point on the vertical line $t = t_1$, as illustrated in Fig. 1. We simply don't care where on the line $t = t_1$ the graph ends.

In case (b) any C^1 function is admissible if its graph joins the fixed point (t_0, x_0) to any point on or above the level x_1 on the vertical line $t = t_1$, as illustrated in Fig. 2. Terminal conditions of this type are often encountered in economics. For instance, in the optimal savings model of the previous section it makes sense to replace the terminal condition $K(T) = K_T$ by $K(T) \geq K_T$.

The inequality sign in (b) sometimes needs to be reversed. For example, if $x(t)$ denotes the total stock of a pollutant in a lake, then $x(t_1) \leq x_1$ means that at the end of the planning period pollution should not exceed a prescribed level x_1.

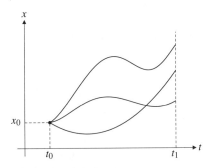

Figure 1: $x(t_1)$ free   **Figure 2:** $x(t_1) \geq x_1$

An important observation concerning (1) is that an optimal solution to either of the two problems must satisfy the Euler equation: Suppose $x^*(t)$ solves either problem, and let $x^*(t_1) = \bar{x}$. Then, in particular, $x^*(t)$ solves the corresponding variational problem with fixed terminal point $(t_1, \bar{x})$. According to Theorem 8.3.1, the function $x^*(t)$ must then satisfy the Euler equation. The condition $x^*(t_0) = x_0$ places one restriction on the constants in the general solution of the Euler equation. A so called *transversality condition* is needed to determine the other constant. The relevant transversality condition is spelled out in the next theorem.

THEOREM 8.5.1 (TRANSVERSALITY CONDITIONS)

If $x^*(t)$ solves problem (1) with either (a) or (b) as the terminal condition, then $x^*(t)$ must satisfy the Euler equation (8.2.2). With the terminal condition (a), the **transversality condition** is

$$\left(\frac{\partial F^*}{\partial \dot{x}} \right)_{t=t_1} = 0 \tag{2}$$

With the terminal condition (b), the **transversality condition** is

$$\left(\frac{\partial F^*}{\partial \dot{x}} \right)_{t=t_1} \leq 0 \quad \left(\left(\frac{\partial F^*}{\partial \dot{x}} \right)_{t=t_1} = 0 \quad \text{if} \quad x^*(t_1) > x_1 \right) \tag{3}$$

If $F(t, x, \dot{x})$ is concave in $(x, \dot{x})$, then an admissible $x^*(t)$ that satisfies both the Euler equation and the appropriate transversality condition will solve problem (1).

Proof: We already know that the Euler equation must be satisfied. To derive the transversality conditions, we define the function J by $J(x) = \int_{t_0}^{t_1} F(t, x, \dot{x})\, dt$, and we compare its value at $x^*(t)$ with its value at the perturbed function $x(t) = x^*(t) + \alpha\mu(t)$. In both cases we require that $\mu(t_0) = 0$.

Suppose the terminal condition is (a). The value of $x(t_1)$ is unconstrained, so the perturbed function $x(t)$ is admissible whatever the value of $\mu(t_1)$. Defining $I(\alpha)$ by (8.3.3), once again $I'(0)$ is given by (8.3.4). But the Euler equation is satisfied and $\mu(t_0) = 0$, so the condition that $I'(0) = 0$ reduces to

$$\left(\frac{\partial F^*}{\partial \dot{x}}\right)_{t=t_1} \mu(t_1) = 0$$

Because $\mu(t_1)$ can be chosen different from 0, the conclusion is that (2) must hold.

Suppose that $F(t, x, \dot{x})$ is concave in $(x, \dot{x})$. The argument leading to (8.3.5) holds as before. Evaluating the last expression in (8.3.5) at the upper limit yields 0 because of the transversality condition (2). Evaluating it at the lower limit also yields 0, because $x^*(t_0) = x(t_0) = x_0$. Again we conclude that $x^*(t)$ solves the maximization problem.

Suppose the terminal condition is (b). For $x = x^* + \alpha\mu$ to be admissible, μ must be chosen so that $\mu(t_0) = 0$ and $x^*(t_1) + \alpha\mu(t_1) \geq x_1$. There are two cases to consider:

(I) $x^*(t_1) > x_1$. In this case the optimal candidate "overshoots" the target. Choose $|\mu(t_1)|$ and $|\alpha|$ small enough so that $|\mu(t_1)| \cdot |\alpha| < x^*(t_1) - x_1$. Define $I(\alpha)$ as before by (8.3.3). Then $I(\alpha)$ must have a local maximum for $\alpha = 0$, so that $I'(0) = 0$, where $I'(0)$ is given in (8.3.4). Because the Euler equation is satisfied for $x^* = x^*(t)$ and $\mu(t_0) = 0$, we find as in the proof of (2) that $(\partial F/\partial \dot{x})_{t=t_1} \mu(t_1) = 0$. Choosing $\mu(t_1)$ different from 0 yields $(\partial F/\partial \dot{x})_{t=t_1} = 0$.

(II) $x^*(t_1) = x_1$. The requirement $x^*(t_1) + \alpha\mu(t_1) \geq x_1$ gives $\alpha\mu(t_1) \geq 0$ in this case. Choose $\mu(t)$ such that $\mu(t_0) = 0$ and $\mu(t_1) > 0$. Then $x^*(t) + \alpha\mu(t)$ is admissible for all $\alpha \geq 0$, and therefore $I(\alpha) \leq I(0)$ for all $\alpha \geq 0$. This implies that $I'(0) \leq 0$, and so $I'(0) = (\partial F/\partial \dot{x})_{t=t_1} \mu(t_1) \leq 0$. Because $\mu(t_1) > 0$, this yields $(\partial F/\partial \dot{x})_{t=t_1} \leq 0$.

Taken together, the conclusions in (I) and (II) reduce to (3), because $\mu(t_1) > 0$

If $F(t, x, \dot{x})$ is concave in $(x, \dot{x})$, the argument leading up to (8.3.5) is again valid, and the last expression in (8.3.5) is now equal to

$$\left(\frac{\partial F^*}{\partial \dot{x}}\right)_{t=t_1} \left[x^*(t_1) - x(t_1)\right] \tag{$*$}$$

If $x^*(t_1) > x_1$, then $(\partial F^*/\partial \dot{x})_{t=t_1} = 0$ and the expression in ($*$) is equal to 0. If $x^*(t_1) = x_1$, then $x^*(t_1) - x(t_1) = x_1 - x(t_1) \leq 0$, since $x(t_1) \geq x_1$. Because $(\partial F^*/\partial \dot{x})_{t=t_1}$ is ≤ 0 according to (3), the product in ($*$) is ≥ 0. Thus the expression in (8.3.5) is always ≥ 0, so the conclusion follows. ∎

NOTE 1 Condition (3) is a little tricky. It says that $\partial F/\partial \dot{x}_{t=t_1}$ is always less than or equal to 0, but equal to 0 if $x^*(t_1)$ overshoots, in the sense that it is greater than x_1.

NOTE 2 If we minimize the integral in (1), the theorem is still valid if (3) is replaced by

$$\left(\frac{\partial F}{\partial \dot{x}}\right)_{t=t_1} \geq 0 \quad \left(\text{and } \left(\frac{\partial F}{\partial \dot{x}}\right)_{t=t_1} = 0 \text{ if } x^*(t_1) > x_1\right) \tag{4}$$

and we require $F(t, x, \dot{x})$ to be convex.

NOTE 3 If the inequality sign in (1)(b) is reversed, so is the inequality sign $\leq$ in (3).

EXAMPLE 1   Find the solutions to the following problems:

$$\max \int_0^1 (1 - x^2 - \dot{x}^2)\, dt, \quad x(0) = 1, \quad \text{with} \quad \text{(a) } x(1) \text{ free} \quad \text{or} \quad \text{(b) } x(1) \geq 2$$

Solution: The Euler equation is easily seen to be $\ddot{x} - x = 0$, with general solution $x(t) = Ae^t + Be^{-t}$. The condition $x(0) = 1$ gives $1 = A + B$, so an optimal solution to either problem must be of the form $x^*(t) = Ae^t + (1 - A)e^{-t}$, and thus $\dot{x}^*(t) = Ae^t - (1 - A)e^{-t}$. Furthermore, $\partial F / \partial \dot{x} = -2\dot{x}$.

With (a) as the terminal condition, (2) requires $\dot{x}^*(1) = 0$, so $Ae^1 - (1 - A)e^{-1} = 0$, and hence $A = 1/(e^2 + 1)$. The only possible solution is therefore

$$x^*(t) = \frac{1}{e^2 + 1}(e^t + e^2 e^{-t})$$

Because $F(t, x, \dot{x}) = 1 - x^2 - \dot{x}^2$ is concave in $(x, \dot{x})$, the solution has been found.

With (b) as the terminal condition, we require $x^*(1) = Ae + (1 - A)e^{-1} \geq 2$, so $A \geq (2e - 1)/(e^2 - 1)$. Suppose $x^*(1) > 2$. Then condition (3) gives $\dot{x}^*(1) = 0$, and so again $A = 1/(e^2 + 1)$. But then the inequality $A \geq (2e - 1)/(e^2 - 1)$ is not satisfied. We conclude that $x^*(1) = 2$, or $A = (2e - 1)/(e^2 - 1)$. With this value of A, $\partial F^*/\partial \dot{x} = -2\dot{x}^*$ is ≤ 0, so the only possible solution is therefore

$$x^*(t) = \frac{1}{e^2 - 1}((2e - 1)e^t + (e^2 - 2e)e^{-t})$$

Because $F(t, x, \dot{x}) = 1 - x^2 - \dot{x}^2$ is concave in $(x, \dot{x})$, the solution has been found.

EXAMPLE 2   Consider the macro economic problem of Example 8.2.2, but now assume that $x(T)$ is unrestricted. Find the optimal solution $x^*(t)$, and discuss what happens to the terminal state $x^*(T)$ as the horizon $T \to \infty$ and also as $c \to 0$.

Solution: Again the Euler equation is $\ddot{x} - x/c = 0$, and the general solution satisfying the initial condition is $x = Ae^{rt} + (x_0 - A)e^{-rt}$ where $r = 1/\sqrt{c}$. The transversality condition (2) reduces to $\dot{x}(T) = 0$. Because $\dot{x}(t) = rAe^{rt} - r(x_0 - A)e^{-rt}$, this implies that $rAe^{rT} - r(x_0 - A)e^{-rT} = 0$. It follows that the only possible solution to the problem is

$$x^*(t) = \frac{x_0}{e^{rT} + e^{-rT}}\left[e^{r(T-t)} + e^{-r(T-t)}\right]$$

Note that $x^*(T) = 2x_0/(e^{rT} + e^{-rT}) \to 0$ as $T \to \infty$. Also, as $c \to 0$, so $r \to \infty$ and therefore $x^*(T) \to 0$. In fact, because

$$\frac{e^{r(T-t)} + e^{-r(T-t)}}{e^{rT} + e^{-rT}} = \frac{e^{-rt} + e^{-r(2T-t)}}{1 + e^{-2rT}} \to 0 \quad \text{as} \quad r \to \infty$$

it follows that $x^*(t) \to 0$ even with T fixed. This is not surprising. As c becomes small, the costs become negligible, so $x^*(t)$ gets adjusted to 0 almost immediately.

Because $F = x^2 + \dot{x}^2$ is convex in $(x, \dot{x})$, the optimal solution has been found.

EXAMPLE 3   Let $A(t)$ denote a pensioner's wealth at time t, and let w be the (constant) pension income per unit of time. Suppose that the person can borrow and save at the same constant rate of interest r. Consumption per unit of time at time t is then given by $C(t) = rA(t) + w - \dot{A}(t)$. Suppose the pensioner plans consumption from now, $t = 0$, until the expected time of death T, so as to maximize

$$\int_0^T U(C(t))e^{-\rho t}\, dt = \int_0^T U(rA(t) + w - \dot{A}(t))e^{-\rho t}\, dt$$

where U is a utility function with $U' > 0$, $U'' < 0$, and ρ is a discount rate. Suppose that present wealth is A_0, and the minimum desired legacy is A_T, so that an admissible wealth function must satisfy $A(0) = A_0$ and $A(T) \geq A_T$. Characterize the possible solutions. (This model has been studied by Atkinson (1971).)

Solution: The criterion function is $F(t, A, \dot{A}) = U(rA + w - \dot{A})e^{-\rho t}$. The Euler equation is easily shown to be

$$\ddot{A} - r\dot{A} + (\rho - r)U'/U'' = 0 \tag{$*$}$$

Because $U' > 0$, one has $\partial F/\partial \dot{A} = -U'(C)e^{-\rho t} < 0$ everywhere. Therefore (3) implies that $A^*(T) = A_T$. Hence, any optimal solution $A^*(t)$ of the problem must satisfy $(*)$ with $A^*(0) = A_0$ and $A^*(T) = A_T$. Because of the requirement imposed on U, the function $F(t, A, \dot{A})$ *is* concave in $(A, \dot{A})$ (for the same reason as in Example 8.4.1). Note that we have not proved that $(*)$ really has a solution which satisfies the boundary conditions. See Problem 4 for a special case.

PROBLEMS FOR SECTION 8.5

1. Solve the problem

$$\min \int_0^1 (t\dot{x} + \dot{x}^2)\, dt, \quad x(0) = 1, \quad \text{(i) with } x(1) \text{ free}, \quad \text{(ii) with } x(1) \geq 1$$

2. (a) Solve the variational problem

$$\max \int_0^1 \left(10 - \dot{x}^2 - 2x\dot{x} - 5x^2\right) e^{-t}\, dt, \quad x(0) = 0, \quad x(1) = 1$$

   (b) What is the optimal solution if (i) $x(1)$ free?   (ii) $x(1) \geq 2$?

3. J.K. Sengupta has considered the problem

$$\min \int_0^T (\alpha_1 \bar{Y}^2 + \alpha_2 G^2)\, dt, \quad \dot{\bar{Y}} = r_1 \bar{Y} - r_2 G, \quad \bar{Y}(0) = Y_0, \quad \bar{Y}(T) \text{ free}$$

   where $\alpha_1, \alpha_2, r_1, r_2, T$, and Y_0 are given positive constants. Formulate this as a variational problem with $\bar{Y} = \bar{Y}(t)$ as the unknown function. Find the corresponding Euler equation, and solve the problem.

4. Solve the problem in Example 3 when $U(C) = a - e^{-bC}$, with $a > 0$ and $b > 0$.

5. (a) A community wants to plant trees on a piece of land over a period of 5 years. Let $x(t)$ be the number of acres that have been planted at time t, and let $u(t)$ be the rate of planting, so that $\dot{x}(t) = u(t)$. Let the cost per unit of time of planting be given by the function $C(t, u)$. The total discounted cost of planting in the period from $t = 0$ to $t = 5$, when the rate of interest is r, is then $\int_0^5 C(t, u)e^{-rt}\, dt$. Write down the necessary conditions for the problem

$$\min \int_0^5 C(t, \dot{x})e^{-rt}\, dt, \quad x(0) = 0, \quad x(5) \geq 1500$$

(b) Solve the problem when $r = 0$, and $C(t, u) = g(u)$, with $g(0) = 0$, $g'(u) > 0$, and $g''(u) > 0$.

8.6 Generalizations

In this concluding section of the chapter we mention very briefly some generalizations and some further developments.

Variable Final Time

In the problems considered so far the time period $[t_0, t_1]$ has been fixed. In some variational problems in economics t_1 (which could be the end of the planning period) is not fixed but subject to choice. Variable final time problems will be studied in a more general control theory setting in Section 9.8.

Infinite Horizon

Growth theory has been one of the main areas of applications of the calculus of variations to economics. Most of the models in the literature have an infinite horizon. Such problems will be dealt with in some detail in a more general control theory setting in Section 9.11.

Several Unknown Functions

The theory presented so far has been restricted to the case when each $x(t)$ is a single real variable. It can easily be generalized to the case where the unknown is a vector function $\mathbf{x}(t)$, i.e. we study variational problems where there are several unknown functions of t. It is easy to show that the Euler equation, regarded as a vector differential equation, is still valid. That is, one must have

$$\frac{\partial F}{\partial x_i} - \frac{d}{dt}\left(\frac{\partial F}{\partial \dot{x}_i}\right) = 0 \tag{1}$$

for each component $x_i(t)$ of the vector $\mathbf{x}(t)$. The transversality conditions can also be generalized in a straightforward manner.

The Integrand Depends on Higher Order Derivatives

Consider a variational problem where the integrand depends on higher order derivatives of the unknown function. With appropriate requirements on F, the problem is to maximize or minimize

$$\int_{t_0}^{t_1} F\left(t, x, \frac{dx}{dt}, \frac{d^2x}{dt^2}, \ldots, \frac{d^nx}{dt^n}\right) dt \qquad (2)$$

where $x(t)$ and its first $n - 1$ derivatives have given values at t_0 and t_1. One can show that a necessary condition for $x^* = x^*(t)$ to solve this problem is that it satisfies the following **generalized Euler equation**

$$\frac{\partial F}{\partial x} - \frac{d}{dt}\left(\frac{\partial F}{\partial \dot{x}}\right) + \frac{d^2}{dt^2}\left(\frac{\partial F}{\partial \ddot{x}}\right) - \cdots + (-1)^n \frac{d^n}{dt^n}\left(\frac{\partial F}{\partial x^{(n)}}\right) = 0 \qquad (3)$$

We refer to Gelfand and Fomin (1963) and Hestenes (1966) for further details.

The Unknown Function Depends on Two Variables

Suppose the variable function has two arguments t and s. With appropriate requirements on F, the problem is to maximize or minimize

$$\iint_R F\left(t, s, x, \frac{\partial x}{\partial t}, \frac{\partial x}{\partial s}\right) dt\, ds \qquad (4)$$

where R is a closed domain in the plane and $x = x(t, s)$ is the unknown function. In addition, require that $x(t, s)$ takes prescribed values on the boundary of R. One can then prove that a necessary condition for $x^* = x^*(t, s)$ to solve the problem is that it satisfies the following partial differential equation (see Gelfand and Fomin (1963)):

$$\frac{\partial F}{\partial x} - \frac{\partial}{\partial t}\left(\frac{\partial F}{\partial x_t'}\right) - \frac{\partial}{\partial s}\left(\frac{\partial F}{\partial x_s'}\right) = 0 \qquad (5)$$

PROBLEMS FOR SECTION 8.6

1. Consider the problem of maximizing $J(x)$, subject to the given conditions.

$$J(x) = \int_0^{\pi/2} (\ddot{x}^2 - x^2 + t^2)\, dt, \qquad \begin{array}{ll} x(0) = 1, & x(\pi/2) = 0, \\ \dot{x}(0) = 0, & \dot{x}(\pi/2) = -1 \end{array}$$

Find the associated Euler equation and its solution.

2. Consider the problem of maximizing $J(y)$ w.r.t $y(x)$, subject to the given conditions.

$$J(y) = \int_{-1}^{1} (\tfrac{1}{2}\mu y''^2 + \rho y)\, dx, \qquad y(-1) = 0, \; y'(-1) = 0, \; y(1) = 0, \; y'(1) = 0$$

where μ and ρ are constants. Find the associated Euler equation and its solution.

9

CONTROL THEORY: BASIC TECHNIQUES

A person who insists on understanding every tiny step before going to the next is liable to concentrate so much on looking at his feet that he fails to realize he is walking in the wrong direction.
—I. Stewart (1975)

Optimal control theory is a modern extension of the classical calculus of variations. Whereas the Euler equation, the main result of the latter theory, dates back to 1744, the main result in optimal control theory, called the **maximum principle**, was developed in the 1950s by a group of Russian mathematicians. (See Pontryagin et al. (1962).) The maximum principle gives necessary conditions for optimality in a wide range of dynamic optimization problems. It includes all the necessary conditions that emerge from the classical theory, but can also be applied to a significantly wider range of problems.

Since 1960, thousands of papers in economics literature have used control theory. It has been applied to, for instance, economic growth, inventory control, taxation, extraction of natural resources, irrigation, and the theory of regulation under asymmetric information.

This chapter contains some important results based on reasoning that appears widely in economics literature. ("What every economist should know about optimal control theory.") It concentrates on the case where there is a single control variable and a single state variable.

9.1 The Basic Problem

Consider a system whose state at time t is characterized by a number $x(t)$, the **state variable**. The process that causes $x(t)$ to change can be controlled, at least partially, by a **control function** $u(t)$. We assume that the rate of change of $x(t)$ depends on t, $x(t)$, and $u(t)$. The state at some initial point t_0 is typically known, $x(t_0) = x_0$. Hence the evolution of $x(t)$ is described by a controlled differential equation

$$\dot{x}(t) = g(t, x(t), u(t)), \quad x(t_0) = x_0 \tag{1}$$

Suppose we choose some control function $u(t)$ defined for $t \geq t_0$. Inserting this function into (1) gives a first-order differential equation for $x(t)$ alone. Because the initial point is fixed, a unique solution of (1) is usually obtained.

By choosing different control functions $u(t)$, the system can be steered along many different paths, not all of which are equally desirable. As usual in economic analysis, assume that it is possible to measure the benefits associated with each path. More specifically, assume that the benefits can be measured by means of the integral

$$J = \int_{t_0}^{t_1} f(t, x(t), u(t)) \, dt \tag{2}$$

where f is a given function. Here, J is called the **objective function** or the **criterion function**. Certain restrictions are often placed on the final state $x(t_1)$. Moreover, the time t_1 at which the process stops is not necessarily fixed. The fundamental problem that we study is:

Among all pairs $(x(t), u(t))$ that obey the differential equation in (1) with $x(t_0) = x_0$ and that satisfy the constraints imposed on $x(t_1)$, find one that maximizes (2).

EXAMPLE 1   **(Economic Growth)** Consider the control problem

$$\max \int_0^T (1 - s) f(k) \, dt, \quad \dot{k} = sf(k), \quad k(0) = k_0, \quad k(T) \geq k_T, \quad 0 \leq s \leq 1$$

Here $k = k(t)$ is the real capital stock of a country and $f(k)$ is its production function. Moreover, $s = s(t)$, the control variable, is the rate of investment, and it is natural to require that $s \in [0, 1]$. The quantity $(1-s)f(k)$ is the flow of consumption per unit of time. We wish to maximize the integral of this quantity over $[0, T]$, i.e. to maximize total consumption over the period $[0, T]$. The constant k_0 is the initial capital stock, and the condition $k(T) \geq k_T$ means that we wish to leave a capital stock of at least k_T to those who live after time T. (Example 9.6.3(b) studies a special case of this model.)

EXAMPLE 2   **(Oil Extraction)** Let $x(t)$ denote the amount of oil in a reservoir at time t. Assume that at $t = 0$ the field contains K barrels of oil, so that $x(0) = K$. If $u(t)$ is the rate of extraction, then[1]

$$\dot{x}(t) = -u(t), \quad x(0) = K \tag{*}$$

Suppose that the market price of oil at time t is known to be $q(t)$, so that the sales revenue per unit of time at t is $q(t)u(t)$. Assume further that the cost C per unit of time depends on t, x and u, so that $C = C(t, x, u)$. The instantaneous rate of profit at time t is then

$$\pi(t, x(t), u(t)) = q(t)u(t) - C(t, x(t), u(t))$$

If the discount rate is r, the total discounted profit over the interval $[0, T]$ is

$$\int_0^T [q(t)u(t) - C(t, x(t), u(t))] e^{-rt} \, dt \tag{**}$$

---

[1] Integrating each side of (*) yields $x(t) - x(0) = - \int_0^t u(\tau) \, d\tau$, or $x(t) = K - \int_0^t u(\tau) \, d\tau$. This equation just says that the amount of oil left at time t is equal to the initial amount K, minus the total amount that has been extracted during the time span $[0, t]$, namely $\int_0^t u(\tau) \, d\tau$.

It is natural to assume that $u(t) \geq 0$, and that $x(T) \geq 0$.

Problem I: Find the rate of extraction $u(t) \geq 0$ that maximizes (**) subject to (*) and $x(T) \geq 0$ over a fixed extraction period $[0, T]$.

Problem II: Find the rate of extraction $u(t) \geq 0$ and also the optimal terminal time T that maximizes (**) subject to (*) and $x(T) \geq 0$.

These two problems are *optimal control problems*. Problem I has a fixed terminal time T, whereas Problem II is referred to as a free terminal time problem. See Example 9.8.1.

9.2 A Simple Case

We begin by studying a control problem with no restrictions on the control variable and no restrictions on the terminal state—that is, no restrictions are imposed on the value of $x(t)$ at $t = t_1$. Given the fixed times t_0 and t_1, our problem is

$$\text{maximize} \int_{t_0}^{t_1} f(t, x(t), u(t)) \, dt, \quad u(t) \in (-\infty, \infty) \tag{1}$$

subject to

$$\dot{x}(t) = g(t, x(t), u(t)), \quad x(t_0) = x_0, \ x_0 \text{ fixed}, \ x(t_1) \text{ free} \tag{2}$$

Given any control function $u(t)$ defined on $[t_0, t_1]$, the associated solution of the differential equation in (2) with $x(t_0) = x_0$ will usually be uniquely determined on the whole of $[t_0, t_1]$. A pair $(x(t), u(t))$ that satisfies (2) is called an **admissible pair**. Among all admissible pairs we search for an **optimal pair**, i.e. a pair of functions that maximizes the integral in (1).

Notice that the problem is to maximize an objective function (or integral) w.r.t. u subject to the constraint (2). Because this constraint is a differential equation on the interval $[t_0, t_1]$, it can be regarded as an infinite number of equality constraints, one for each time t in $[t_0, t_1]$.

Economists usually incorporate equality constraints in their optimization problems by forming a Lagrangian function, with a Lagrange multiplier corresponding to each constraint. Here, by an analogy, the necessary conditions for the problem associate a number $p(t)$ with the constraint (2) for each t in $[t_0, t_1]$. The resulting function $p = p(t)$ is called the **adjoint function** (or **co-state variable**) associated with the differential equation. Corresponding to the Lagrangian function in the present problem is the **Hamiltonian** H. For each time t in $[t_0, t_1]$ and each possible triple (x, u, p), of the state, control, and adjoint variables, the Hamiltonian is defined by

$$H(t, x, u, p) = f(t, x, u) + pg(t, x, u) \tag{3}$$

A set of necessary conditions for optimality is given in the following theorem. (Some regularity conditions required are discussed in the next section.)

THEOREM 9.2.1 (THE MAXIMUM PRINCIPLE)

Suppose that $(x^*(t), u^*(t))$ is an optimal pair for problem (1)–(2). Then there exists a continuous function $p(t)$ such that, for all t in $[t_0, t_1]$,

$$u = u^*(t) \text{ maximizes } H(t, x^*(t), u, p(t)) \text{ for } u \in (-\infty, \infty) \tag{4}$$

$$\dot{p}(t) = -H'_x(t, x^*(t), u^*(t), p(t)), \quad p(t_1) = 0 \tag{5}$$

NOTE 1   The requirement that $p(t_1) = 0$ in (5) is called a **transversality condition**. So condition (5) tells us that in the case where $x(t_1)$ is free, the adjoint variable vanishes at t_1.

The conditions in Theorem 9.2.1 are necessary, but not sufficient for optimality. The following theorem gives sufficient conditions.

THEOREM 9.2.2 (MANGASARIAN)

If the requirement

$$H(t, x, u, p(t)) \quad \text{is concave in } (x, u) \text{ for each } t \text{ in } [t_0, t_1] \tag{6}$$

is added to the requirements in Theorem 9.2.1, then we obtain *sufficient* conditions. Thus, if we find a triple $(x^*(t), u^*(t), p(t))$ that satisfies (2), (4), (5), and (6), then $(x^*(t), u^*(t))$ is optimal.

NOTE 2   Changing $u(t)$ on a small interval causes $f(t, x, u)$ to change immediately. Moreover, at the end of this interval $x(t)$ has changed and this change is transmitted throughout the remaining time interval. In order to steer the process optimally, the choice of $u(t)$ at each instant of time must anticipate the future changes in $x(t)$. In short, we have to plan ahead. In a certain sense, the adjoint function $p(t)$ takes care of this need for forward planning. Equation (5) implies that $p(t) = \int_t^{t_1} H'_x(s, x^*(s), u^*(s), p^*(s)) \, ds$.

NOTE 3   If the problem is to minimize the objective in (1), then we can rewrite the problem as one of maximizing the negative of the original objective function. Alternatively, we could reformulate the maximum principle for the minimization problem: An optimal control will minimize the Hamiltonian, and convexity of $H(t, x, u, p(t))$ w.r.t. (x, u) is the relevant sufficient condition.

Since the control region is $(-\infty, \infty)$, a *necessary* condition for (4) is that

$$H'_u(t, x^*(t), u^*(t), p(t)) = 0 \tag{7}$$

If $H(t, x(t), u, p(t))$ is concave in u, condition (7) is also sufficient for the maximum condition (4) to hold, because we recall that an interior stationary point for a concave function is (globally) optimal.

It is helpful to see how these conditions allow some simple examples to be solved.

EXAMPLE 1   Solve the problem

$$\max \int_0^T \left[1 - tx(t) - u(t)^2\right] dt, \qquad \dot{x}(t) = u(t), \ x(0) = x_0, \ x(T) \text{ free}, \ u \in \mathbb{R}$$

where x_0 and T are positive constants.

Solution: The Hamiltonian is $H(t, x, u, p) = 1 - tx - u^2 + pu$, and the control $u = u^*(t)$ maximizes $H(t, x^*(t), u, p(t))$ w.r.t. u only if it satisfies $H'_u = -2u + p(t) = 0$. Thus $u^*(t) = \frac{1}{2}p(t)$. Because $H'_x = -t$, the conditions in (5) reduce to $\dot{p}(t) = t$ and $p(T) = 0$. Integrating gives $p(t) = \frac{1}{2}t^2 + C$ with $\frac{1}{2}T^2 + C = 0$, so

$$p(t) = -\tfrac{1}{2}(T^2 - t^2) \quad \text{and then} \quad u^*(t) = -\tfrac{1}{4}(T^2 - t^2)$$

Because $\dot{x}^*(t) = u^*(t) = -\frac{1}{4}(T^2 - t^2)$, integrating $\dot{x}^*(t) = u^*(t)$ and imposing $x^*(0) = x_0$ gives

$$x^*(t) = x_0 - \tfrac{1}{4}T^2 t + \tfrac{1}{12}t^3$$

Thus, there is only one pair $(x^*(t), u^*(t))$ that, together with $p(t)$, satisfies both necessary conditions (4) and (5). We have therefore found the only possible pair which could solve the problem. Because $H(t, x, u, p) = 1 - tx - u^2 + pu$ is concave in (x, u) (it is a sum of concave functions), $(x^*(t), u^*(t))$ is indeed optimal.

EXAMPLE 2   **(A Macroeconomic Control Problem)**   Consider once again the macroeconomic model of Example 8.2.2. If we drop the terminal constraint at the end of the planning period, we face the following control problem

$$\min_{u(t)} \int_0^T [x(t)^2 + cu(t)^2] dt, \quad \dot{x}(t) = u(t), \ x(0) = x_0, \ x(T) \text{ free}$$

where $u(t) \in \mathbb{R}$ and $c > 0$. Use the maximum principle to solve the problem.

Solution: We maximize $-\int_0^T [x(t)^2 + cu(t)^2] dt$. The Hamiltonian is

$$H(t, x, u, p) = -x^2 - cu^2 + pu$$

So $H'_x = -2x$ and $H'_u = -2cu + p$. A necessary condition for $u^*(t)$ to maximize the Hamiltonian is that $H'_u = 0$ at $u = u^*(t)$, or that $-2cu^*(t) + p(t) = 0$. Therefore $u^*(t) = p(t)/2c$. The differential equation for $p(t)$ is

$$\dot{p}(t) = -H'_x(t, x^*(t), u^*(t), p(t)) = 2x^*(t) \tag{$*$}$$

From $\dot{x}^*(t) = u^*(t)$ and $u^*(t) = p(t)/2c$, we have

$$\dot{x}^*(t) = p(t)/2c \tag{$**$}$$

The two first-order differential equations $(*)$ and $(**)$ can be used to determine the functions p and x^*. Differentiate $(*)$ w.r.t. t and then use $(**)$ to obtain $\ddot{p}(t) = 2\dot{x}^*(t) = p(t)/c$, whose general solution is

$$p(t) = Ae^{rt} + Be^{-rt}, \quad \text{where } r = 1/\sqrt{c}$$

Imposing the boundary conditions $p(T) = 0$ and $\dot{p}(0) = 2x^*(0) = 2x_0$ implies that $Ae^{rT} + Be^{-rT} = 0$ and $r(A - B) = 2x_0$. These two equations determine A and B, which must be $A = 2x_0e^{-rT}/[r(e^{rT} + e^{-rT})]$ and $B = -2x_0e^{rT}/[r(e^{rT} + e^{-rT})]$. Therefore

$$p(t) = \frac{2x_0}{r(e^{rT} + e^{-rT})}\left[e^{-r(T-t)} - e^{r(T-t)}\right] \quad \text{and} \quad x^*(t) = \tfrac{1}{2}\dot{p}(t) = x_0\frac{e^{r(T-t)} + e^{-r(T-t)}}{e^{rT} + e^{-rT}}$$

The Hamiltonian $H = -x^2 - cu^2 + pu$ is concave in (x, u), which confirms that this is the solution to the problem. (The same result was obtained in Example 8.5.2.)

PROBLEMS FOR SECTION 9.2

Solve the control problems 1–5:

1. $\displaystyle\max_{u(t)\in(-\infty,\infty)} \int_0^2 [e^t x(t) - u(t)^2]\, dt, \quad \dot{x}(t) = -u(t), \quad x(0) = 0, \quad x(2)$ free

2. $\displaystyle\max_{u(t)\in(-\infty,\infty)} \int_0^1 [1 - u(t)^2]\, dt, \quad \dot{x}(t) = x(t) + u(t), \quad x(0) = 1, \quad x(1)$ free

3. $\displaystyle\min_{u(t)\in(-\infty,\infty)} \int_0^1 [x(t) + u(t)^2]\, dt, \quad \dot{x}(t) = -u(t), \quad x(0) = 0, \quad x(1)$ free

4. $\displaystyle\max_{u\in(-\infty,\infty)} \int_0^{10} \left[1 - 4x(t) - 2u(t)^2\right] dt, \quad \dot{x}(t) = u(t), \quad x(0) = 0, \quad x(10)$ free

5. $\displaystyle\max_{u(t)\in(-\infty,\infty)} \int_0^T (x - u^2)\, dt, \quad \dot{x} = x + u, \quad x(0) = 0, \quad x(T)$ free

6. (a) Write down conditions (7) and (5) for the problem

$$\max_{I\in(-\infty,\infty)} \int_0^T [qf(K) - c(I)]\, dt, \quad \dot{K} = I - \delta K, \quad K(0) = K_0, \quad K(T) \text{ free}$$

($K = K(t)$ denotes the capital stock of a firm, $f(K)$ is the production function, q is the price per unit of output, $I = I(t)$ is investment, $c(I)$ is the cost of investment, δ is the rate of depreciation of capital, K_0 is the initial capital stock, and T is the planning horizon.)

   (b) Let $f(K) = K - 0.03K^2$, $q = 1$, $c(I) = I^2$, $\delta = 0.1$, $K_0 = 10$, and $T = 10$. Derive a second-order differential equation for K, and explain how to find the solution.

9.3 Regularity Conditions

In most applications of control theory to economics, the control functions are explicitly or implicitly restricted in various ways. For instance, in the oil extraction problem of Section 9.1, $u(t) \geq 0$ was a natural restriction, because it means that you cannot pump oil back into the reservoir.

In general, assume that $u(t)$ takes values in a fixed subset U of the reals, called the **control region**. In the oil extraction problem, then, $U = [0, \infty)$, and $u(t)$ can take the value 0. Actually, an important aspect of control theory is that the control region can be closed, so that $u(t)$ can take values at the boundary of U. (In the classical calculus of variation, by contrast, one usually considered open control regions, although developments in the theory around 1930–1940 paved the way for the modern theory.)

What regularity conditions is it natural to impose on the control function $u(t)$? Among the many papers in economics literature that use control theory, the majority assume implicitly or explicitly that the control functions are continuous. Consequently, many of our examples and problems will deal with continuous controls. Yet in some applications, continuity is too restrictive. For example, the control variable $u(t)$ could be the fraction of investment in one plant, with the remaining fraction $1 - u(t)$ allocated to a second plant. Then it is natural to allow control functions that suddenly switch all the investment from one plant to the other. Because they alternate between extremes, such functions are often called **bang-bang** controls. A simple example of such a control is

$$u(t) = \begin{cases} 1 & \text{for } t \text{ in } [t_0, t'] \\ 0 & \text{for } t \text{ in } (t', t_1] \end{cases}$$

which involves a single shift at time t'. In this case $u(t)$ is *piecewise continuous*, with a jump discontinuity at $t = t'$.

By definition, a function has a **finite jump** at a point of discontinuity if it has (finite) one-sided limits at the point. A function is **piecewise continuous** if it has at most a finite number of discontinuities on each finite interval, with finite jumps at each point of discontinuity. (The value of a control $u(t)$ at a point of discontinuity will not be of any importance, but let us agree to choose the value of $u(t)$ at a point of discontinuity t' as the left-hand limit of $u(t)$ at t'. Then $u(t)$ will be **left-continuous** as illustrated in Fig. 1.) Moreover, if the control problem concerns the time interval $[t_0, t_1]$, we shall assume that $u(t)$ is continuous at both end points of this interval.

What is meant by a "solution" of $\dot{x} = g(t, x, u)$ when $u = u(t)$ has discontinuities? A **solution** is a **continuous** function $x(t)$ that has a derivative that satisfies the equation, except at points where $u(t)$ is discontinuous. The graph of $x(t)$ will, in general, have "kinks" at the points of discontinuity of $u(t)$, and it will usually not be differentiable at these kinks. It is, however, still continuous at the kinks.

For the oil extraction problem in Example 9.1.2, Fig. 1 shows one possible control function, whereas Fig. 2 shows the corresponding development of the state variable. The rate of extraction is initially a constant u_0 on the interval $[0, t']$, then a different constant u_1 (with $u_1 < u_0$) on (t', t''). Finally, on $(t'', T]$, the rate of extraction $u(t)$ gradually declines from a level lower than u_1 until the field is exhausted at time T. Observe that the graph of $x(t)$ is connected, but has kinks at t' and t''.

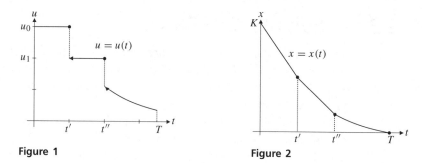

Figure 1   **Figure 2**

So far no restrictions have been placed on the functions $g(t, x, u)$ and $f(t, x, u)$. For the analysis presented in this chapter, it suffices to assume that f, g, and their first-order partial derivatives w.r.t. x and u are continuous in (t, x, u). These continuity assumptions will be implicitly assumed from now on.

Necessary Conditions, Sufficient Conditions, and Existence

In static optimization theory there are three main types of result that can be used to find possible global solutions: Theorems giving necessary conditions for optimality (typically, first-order conditions), theorems giving sufficient conditions (typically, first-order conditions supplemented by appropriate concavity/convexity requirements), and finally existence theorems (typically, the extreme value theorem).

In control theory the situation is similar. The maximum principle, in different versions, gives *necessary* conditions for optimality, i.e. conditions which a possible optimal control *must* satisfy. These conditions do not guarantee that the maximization problem has a solution.

The second type of theorem consists of sufficiency results, of the kind originally developed by Mangasarian. Theorems of this type impose certain concavity/convexity requirements on the functions involved. If a control function $u^*(t)$ (with corresponding state variable $x^*(t)$ and adjoint variable $p(t)$) satisfies the stated sufficient conditions, then $(x^*(t), u^*(t))$ solves the maximization problem. But these sufficient conditions are rather demanding, and in many problems there are optimal solutions although the sufficient conditions are not satisfied.

Existence theorems give conditions which ensure that an optimal solution of the problem really exists. The conditions needed for existence are less stringent than the sufficient conditions. Existence theorems are used (in principle) in the following way: One finds, by using the necessary conditions, all the "candidates" for a solution of the problem. If the existence of an optimal solution is assured, then an optimal solution can be found by simply examining which of the candidates gives the largest values of the objective function. (This direct comparison of different candidates is unnecessary if we use sufficient conditions.)

9.4 The Standard Problem

Section 9.2 studied a control problem with no restriction on the control function at any time, and also no restriction on the state variable at the terminal time; $x(t_1)$ was free. These features are unrealistic in many economic models, as has already been pointed out.

This section considers the **"standard end constrained problem"**

$$\max \int_{t_0}^{t_1} f(t, x, u)\, dt, \quad u \in U \subseteq \mathbb{R} \tag{1}$$

$$\dot{x}(t) = g(t, x(t), u(t)), \quad x(t_0) = x_0 \tag{2}$$

with one of the following terminal conditions imposed

$$\text{(a) } x(t_1) = x_1 \quad \text{(b) } x(t_1) \geq x_1 \quad \text{or} \quad \text{(c) } x(t_1) \text{ free} \tag{3}$$

Again, t_0, t_1, x_0, and x_1 are fixed numbers and U is the fixed control region. A pair $(x(t), u(t))$ that satisfies (2) and (3) is called an **admissible pair**. Among all admissible pairs we seek an **optimal pair**, i.e. a pair of functions that maximizes the integral in (1).

In order to formulate correct necessary conditions, we need to define the Hamiltonian as

$$H(t, x, u, p) = p_0 f(t, x, u) + p g(t, x, u) \tag{4}$$

The new feature is the constant number p_0 in front of $f(t, x, u)$. If $p_0 \neq 0$, we can divide by p_0 to get a new Hamiltonian in which $p_0 = 1$, in effect. But if $p_0 = 0$, this normalization is impossible.[2]

THEOREM 9.4.1 (THE MAXIMUM PRINCIPLE. STANDARD END CONSTRAINTS)

Suppose that $(x^*(t), u^*(t))$ is an optimal pair for the standard end constrained problem (1)–(3). Then there exists a continuous function $p(t)$ and a number p_0, which is either 0 or 1, such that for all t in $[t_0, t_1]$ we have $(p_0, p(t)) \neq (0, 0)$ and, moreover:

(A) The control $u^*(t)$ maximizes the Hamiltonian $H(t, x^*(t), u, p(t))$ w.r.t. $u \in U$, i.e.

$$H(t, x^*(t), u, p(t)) \leq H(t, x^*(t), u^*(t), p(t)) \quad \text{for all } u \text{ in } U \tag{5}$$

(B) $\dot{p}(t) = -H_x'(t, x^*(t), u^*(t), p(t))$ \hfill (6)

(C) Corresponding to each of the terminal conditions (b) and (c) in (3) there is a **transversality condition** on $p(t_1)$:

(b') $p(t_1) \geq 0$ (with $p(t_1) = 0$ if $x^*(t_1) > x_1$) \hfill (7)

(c') $p(t_1) = 0$

[In case (a) there is no condition on $p(t_1)$.]

---

[2] For a proof see Fleming and Rishel (1975).

NOTE 1 In some "bizarre" problems the conditions in the theorem are only satisfied with $p_0 = 0$. (See Problem 10.) Note that in this case the conditions in the maximum principle do not change at all if f is replaced by any arbitrary function. In fact, when $p_0 = 0$, then (5) takes the form $pg(t, x^*(t), u, p(t)) \leq pg(t, x^*(t), u^*(t), p(t))$ for all u in U.

In the examples and problems to follow we shall assume without proof that $p_0 = 1$, except in Example 4 where we show the type of argument needed to prove that $p_0 = 1$. (Almost all papers in economic literature using control theory assume that the problem is "normal" in the sense that $p_0 = 1$.)

If $x(t_1)$ is free, then according to (7)(c'), $p(t_1) = 0$. Since $(p_0, p(t_1))$ cannot be $(0, 0)$, we conclude that in this case $p_0 = 1$ and Theorem 9.2.1 is correct as stated.

NOTE 2 If the inequality sign in (3)(b) is reversed, so are the inequality signs in (7)(b').

NOTE 3 The derivative $\dot{p}(t)$ in (6) does not necessarily exist at the discontinuity points of $u^*(t)$, and (6) need hold only wherever $u^*(t)$ is continuous.

NOTE 4 If U is a convex set and the function H is strictly concave in u, one can show that an optimal control $u^*(t)$ must be continuous.

The conditions in the maximum principle are necessary, but generally not sufficient for optimality. The following theorem gives sufficient conditions.

THEOREM 9.4.2 (MANGASARIAN)

Suppose that $(x^*(t), u^*(t))$ is an admissible pair with corresponding adjoint function $p(t)$ such that the conditions (A)–(C) in Theorem 9.4.1 are satisfied with $p_0 = 1$. Suppose further that the control region U is convex and that $H(t, x, u, p(t))$ is concave in (x, u) for every t in $[t_0, t_1]$. Then $(x^*(t), u^*(t))$ is an optimal pair.

In general, it is not easy to apply Theorems 9.4.1 and 9.4.2. In principle one can use the following approach:

(a) For each triple (t, x, p), maximize $H(t, x, u, p)$ w.r.t. $u \in U$. In many cases, this maximization occurs at a unique maximum point $u = \hat{u}(t, x, p)$.

(b) Insert this function into the differential equations (2) and (6) to obtain

$$\dot{x}(t) = g(t, x(t), \hat{u}(t, x(t), p(t))) \quad \text{and} \quad \dot{p}(t) = -H_x'(t, x(t), \hat{u}(t, x(t), p(t)), p(t))$$

This gives two differential equations to determine the functions $x(t)$ and $p(t)$.

(c) The constants in the general solution $(x(t), p(t))$ of these differential equations are determined by combining the initial condition $x(t_0) = x_0$ with the terminal conditions and the transversality conditions (7). The state variable obtained in this way is denoted by $x^*(t)$, and the corresponding control variable is $u^*(t) = \hat{u}(t, x^*(t), p(t))$. The pair $(x^*(t), u^*(t))$ is then a candidate for optimality.

This sketch suggests that the maximum principle may contain enough information to give only one or perhaps a few solution candidates, and in fact the procedure (a)–(c) is useful in many problems.

EXAMPLE 1   Solve the problem

$$\max \int_0^1 x(t)\,dt, \quad \dot{x}(t) = x(t) + u(t), \quad x(0) = 0, \quad x(1) \text{ free}, \quad u \in [-1, 1]$$

Solution: Looking at the objective function, we see that it pays to have $x(t)$ as large as possible all the time, and from the differential equation it follows that this is obtained by having u as large as possible all the time, i.e. $u(t) = 1$ for all t. So this must be the optimal control. Let us confirm this by using the maximum principle.

The Hamiltonian function with $p_0 = 1$ is $H(t, x, u, p) = x + px + pu$, which is linear and hence concave in (x, u), so Theorem 9.4.2 applies. The differential equation (6) together with $p(1) = 0$ (see (7)(c')) gives

$$\dot{p} = -1 - p, \qquad p(1) = 0$$

This differential equation is especially simple because it is linear with constant coefficients. According to (5.4.3), the general solution is $p(t) = Ae^{-t} - 1$, where A is determined by $0 = p(1) = Ae^{-1} - 1$, which gives $A = e$. Hence, $p(t) = e^{1-t} - 1$, and we see that $p(t) > 0$ for all t in $[0, 1)$. Since the optimal control should maximize $H(t, x^*(t), u, p(t))$, we see from the expression for H that we must have $u^*(t) = 1$ for all t in $[0, 1]$. The corresponding path $x^*(t)$ for the state variable x satisfies the equation $\dot{x}^*(t) = x^*(t) + 1$, with general solution $x^*(t) = Be^t - 1$. Since $x^*(0) = 0$, we obtain $B = 1$, and so

$$x^*(t) = e^t - 1$$

We see now that $u^*(t)$, $x^*(t)$, and $p(t)$ satisfy all the requirements in Theorem 9.4.2. We conclude that we have found the solution to the problem.

EXAMPLE 2   **(Optimal Consumption)**   Consider a consumer who expects to live from the present time, when $t = 0$, until time T. Let $c(t)$ denote his consumption expenditure at time t and $y(t)$ his predicted income. Let $w(t)$ denote his wealth at time t. Then

$$\dot{w}(t) = r(t)w(t) + y(t) - c(t) \tag{$*$}$$

where $r(t)$ is the instantaneous rate of interest at time t. Suppose the consumer wants to maximize the "lifetime intertemporal utility function"

$$\int_0^T e^{-\alpha t} u\big(c(t)\big)\,dt$$

where $\alpha > 0$, and $u'(c) > 0$, $u''(c) < 0$ for all $c > 0$. The dynamic constraint is (*) above. In addition, $w(0) = w_0$ is given, and there is the terminal constraint $w(T) \geq 0$ preventing the consumer from dying in debt.

This is an optimal control problem with $w(t)$ as the state variable and $c(t)$ as the control variable. We assume that $c(t) > 0$ so that the control region is $(0, \infty)$. We will try to characterize the optimal consumption path, and look at some special cases.

The Hamiltonian for this problem is $H(t, w, c, p) = e^{-\alpha t}u(c) + p[r(t)w + y - c]$, with $p_0 = 1$ and with $p = p(t)$ as the adjoint function. Let $c^* = c^*(t)$ be an optimal solution. Then $H'_c = 0$ at c^*, i.e.

$$e^{-\alpha t}u'(c^*(t)) = p(t) \tag{i}$$

Hence, the adjoint variable is equal to the discounted value of marginal utility. Also,

$$\dot{p}(t) = -H'_w = -p(t)r(t) \tag{ii}$$

so that the adjoint variable decreases at a proportional rate equal to the rate of interest. Notice that (ii) is a separable differential equation whose solution is (see Example 5.3.6)

$$p(t) = p(0) \exp\left[-\int_0^t r(s)\,ds\right] \tag{iii}$$

A more explicit formula is not possible, except in special cases. One such is when $r(t) = r$, independent of time, and $r = \alpha$. Then (iii) reduces to $p(t) = p(0)e^{-rt}$, and (i) becomes $e^{-rt}u'(c^*(t)) = p(0)e^{-rt}$, or $u'(c^*(t)) = p(0)$. It follows that $c^*(t)$ is a constant, $c^*(t) = \bar{c}$, independent of time. Then (*) becomes $\dot{w} = rw + y(t) - \bar{c}$, whose solution is

$$w^*(t) = e^{rt}\left[w_0 + \int_0^t e^{-rs}y(s)\,ds - \frac{\bar{c}}{r}(1 - e^{-rt})\right] \tag{iv}$$

Because of (7)(b'), the terminal constraint $w^*(T) \geq 0$ implies that

$$p(T) \geq 0 \text{ (with } p(T) = 0 \text{ if } w^*(T) > 0)$$

It follows that if $w^*(T) > 0$, then $p(T) = 0$, which contradicts (i). Thus $w^*(T) = 0$, so it is optimal for the consumer to leave no legacy after time T. The condition $w^*(T) = 0$ determines the optimal level of $\bar{c}$, which is [3]

$$\bar{c} = \frac{r}{1 - e^{-rT}}\left[w_0 + \int_0^T e^{-rs}y(s)\,ds\right]$$

It is interesting to consider the special cases where the utility function u is

$$u(c) = \frac{(c - \underline{c})^{1-\varepsilon}}{1 - \varepsilon} \quad (\varepsilon > 0;\ \varepsilon \neq 1) \quad \text{or} \quad u(c) = \ln(c - \underline{c}) \tag{v}$$

---

[3] This is the same answer as that derived in Example 2.4.2, equation (iii).

Then $u'(c) = (c - \underline{c})^{-\varepsilon}$ in both cases, with $\varepsilon = 1$ when $u(c) = \ln(c - \underline{c})$. Note that when $\underline{c} = 0$, the *elasticity of marginal utility* is $\mathrm{El}_c u'(c) = cu''(c)/u'(c) = -\varepsilon$.

When $\underline{c} > 0$, the level $\underline{c}$ of consumption can be regarded as minimum subsistence, below which consumption should never be allowed to fall, if possible. With utility given by (v), equation (i) can be solved explicitly for $c^*(t)$. In fact

$$c^*(t) = \underline{c} + \left[e^{\alpha t} p(t) \right]^{-1/\varepsilon} \tag{vi}$$

In order to keep the algebra manageable, restrict attention once again to the case when $r(t) = r$, independent of time, but now $r \neq \alpha$ is allowed. Still, $p(t) = p(0)e^{-rt}$ and so (vi) implies that

$$c^*(t) = \underline{c} + \left[e^{(\alpha - r)t} p(0) \right]^{-1/\varepsilon} = \underline{c} + Ae^{\gamma t}$$

where $A = p(0)^{-1/\varepsilon}$ and $\gamma = (r - \alpha)/\varepsilon$. Then (∗) becomes

$$\dot{w} = rw + y - \underline{c} - Ae^{\gamma t}$$

Multiplying this first-order equation by the integrating factor e^{-rt} leads to

$$\frac{d}{dt}\left(e^{-rt} w \right) = e^{-rt}\left(\dot{w} - rw \right) = e^{-rt}\left(y - \underline{c} - Ae^{\gamma t} \right)$$

Integrating each side from 0 to t gives

$$e^{-rt} w(t) - w_0 = \int_0^t e^{-rs} y(s)\, ds - \frac{\underline{c}}{r}\left(1 - e^{-rt}\right) - \frac{A}{r - \gamma}\left[1 - e^{-(r-\gamma)t}\right]$$

In particular,

$$w(T) = e^{rT} w_0 + \int_0^T e^{r(T-t)} y(t)\, dt - \frac{\underline{c}}{r}\left(e^{rT} - 1\right) - \frac{A}{r - \gamma}\left(e^{rT} - e^{\gamma T}\right)$$

Again $p(T) > 0$ and thus $w^*(T) = 0$, so the optimal path involves choosing $p(0)$ such that $A = p(0)^{-1/\varepsilon}$ has the value

$$A = \frac{r - \gamma}{e^{rT} - e^{\gamma T}}\left[e^{rT} w_0 + \int_0^T e^{r(T-t)} y(t)\, dt - \frac{\underline{c}}{r}\left(e^{rT} - 1\right) \right]$$

There are two significantly different cases involved here. The first is when $r > \alpha$ and so $\gamma > 0$. Then consumption grows over time starting from the level $\underline{c} + A$. But if $r < \alpha$ and so $\gamma < 0$, then optimal consumption shrinks over time. This makes sense because $r < \alpha$ is the case when the agent discounts future utility at a rate α that exceeds the rate of interest.

The previous case with constant consumption is when $\gamma = 0$. The same solution emerges in the limit as $\varepsilon \to \infty$, which represents the case when the consumer is extremely averse to fluctuations in consumption.

In the next example the optimal control is bang-bang.

EXAMPLE 3   Solve the following control problem:

$$\max \int_0^1 (2x - x^2)\, dt, \quad \dot{x} = u, \quad x(0) = 0, \quad x(1) = 0, \quad u \in [-1, 1]$$

Solution: The Hamiltonian is $H = 2x - x^2 + pu$, which is concave in (x, u). The optimal control $u^*(t)$ must maximize $2x^*(t) - (x^*(t))^2 + p(t)u$ subject to $u \in [-1, 1]$. Only the term $p(t)u$ depends on u, so

$$u^*(t) = \begin{cases} 1 & \text{if } p(t) > 0 \\ -1 & \text{if } p(t) < 0 \end{cases} \tag{$*$}$$

The differential equation for $p(t)$ is

$$\dot{p}(t) = -H_x'(t, x^*(t), u^*(t), p(t)) = 2x^*(t) - 2 = 2(x^*(t) - 1) \tag{$**$}$$

Note that $\dot{x}^*(t) = u^*(t) \le 1$. Because $x^*(0) = 0$, it follows that $x^*(t) < 1$ for all t in $[0, 1)$. Then $(**)$ implies that $p(t)$ is strictly decreasing in $[0, 1]$.

Suppose there could be a solution with $p(1) \ge 0$. Because $p(t)$ is strictly decreasing in $[0, 1]$, one would have $p(t) > 0$ in $[0, 1)$, and then $(*)$ would imply that $u^*(t) = 1$ for all t. In this case, $\dot{x}^*(t) = 1$ for all t in $[0, 1]$. With $x^*(0) = 0$ we get $x^*(t) \equiv t$ and thus $x^*(1) = 1$, which is incompatible with the terminal condition $x^*(1) = 0$. Thus any solution must satisfy $p(1) < 0$. Suppose $p(t) < 0$ for all t in $(0, 1]$. Then from $(*)$, $u^*(t) = -1$ for all such t, so $x^*(t) \equiv -t$ with $x^*(1) = -1$, violating the terminal condition. Hence, for some t^* in $(0, 1)$, the function $p(t)$ switches from being positive to being negative, with $p(t^*) = 0$. A possible path for $p(t)$ is shown in Fig. 1.

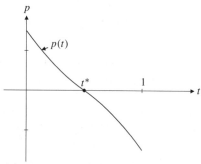

Figure 1

It follows that $u^*(t) = 1$ in $[0, t^*]$[4] and $u^*(t) = -1$ in $(t^*, 1]$. On $[0, t^*)$, therefore, $\dot{x}^*(t) = 1$, and with $x^*(0) = 0$ this yields $x^*(t) = t$. Since $x^*(t)$ is required to be continuous at t^*, $x^*(t^*) = x^*(t^{*-}) = t^*$. In $(t^*, 1]$, $\dot{x}^*(t) = -1$ so $x^*(t) = -t + C$ for some constant C.

---

[4] Recall our convention to let $u^*(t)$ be left-continuous.

Because $x^*(t)$ is continuous at t^*, $x^*(t^{*+}) = t^*$, so $C = 2t^*$. Hence, $x^*(t) = -t + 2t^*$. Then $x^*(1) = 0$ implies that $t^* = 1/2$. We conclude that the optimal solution is

$$u^*(t) = \begin{cases} 1 & \text{in } [0, 1/2] \\ -1 & \text{in } (1/2, 1] \end{cases} \qquad x^*(t) = \begin{cases} t & \text{in } [0, 1/2] \\ 1-t & \text{in } (1/2, 1] \end{cases}$$

To find $p(t)$, note that $\dot{p}(t) = 2x^*(t) - 2 = 2t - 2$ in $[0, 1/2]$. Because $p(1/2) = 0$, one has $p(t) = t^2 - 2t + 3/4$. In the interval $(1/2, 1]$, (**) implies that $\dot{p}(t) = -2t$, and because $p(t)$ is continuous with $p(1/2) = 0$, the adjoint function is $p(t) = -t^2 + 1/4$. For this function $p(t)$ the maximum condition (*) is satisfied.

The last example shows a typical kind of argument needed to prove that $p_0 \neq 0$.

EXAMPLE 4   Consider Example 3 again. Including the multiplier p_0, the Hamiltonian function (4) is $H = p_0(2x - x^2) + pu$, and the differential equation (6) for p is $\dot{p} = -H'_x = -p_0(2 - 2x^*(t))$. Suppose $p_0 = 0$. Then $\dot{p} = 0$ and so p is a constant, $\bar{p}$. Because $(p_0, p(t)) = (p_0, \bar{p}) \neq (0, 0)$, that constant $\bar{p}$ is not 0. Now, an optimal control must maximize $pu = \bar{p}u$ subject to $u \in [-1, 1]$. If $\bar{p} > 0$, then obviously $u^*(t) = 1$ for all t in $[0, 1]$. This means that $\dot{x}^*(t) \equiv 1$, with $x^*(0) = 0$, so $x^*(t) \equiv t$. This violates the terminal condition $x^*(1) = 0$. If $\bar{p} < 0$, then obviously $u^*(t) \equiv -1$, and $\dot{x}^*(t) \equiv -1$ for all t in $[0, 1]$, with $x^*(0) = 0$, so $x^*(t) \equiv -t$. This again violates the terminal condition. We conclude that $p_0 = 0$ is impossible, so $p_0 = 1$.

PROBLEMS FOR SECTION 9.4

1. What is the obvious solution to the problem

$$\max \int_0^T x(t)\, dt, \quad \dot{x}(t) = u(t), \quad x(0) = 0, \quad x(T) \text{ free}, \quad u(t) \in [0, 1]$$

where T is a fixed positive constant? Compute the associated value, $V(T)$, of the objective function. Find the solution also by using Theorem 9.4.2.

2. Solve the problem: $\max \int_0^1 (1 - x^2 - u^2)\, dt, \quad \dot{x} = u, \quad x(0) = 0, \quad x(1) \geq 1, \quad u \in \mathbb{R}.$

3. Consider the problem in Example 9.2.1.

    (a) Replace $u \in \mathbb{R}$ by $u \in [0, 1]$ and find the optimal solution.

    (b) Replace $u \in \mathbb{R}$ by $u \in [-1, 1]$ and find the optimal solution, provided $T > 2$.

4. Solve the following problems. Also compute the corresponding value of the objective function.

    (a) $\max_{u \in [0,1]} \int_0^{10} x\, dt, \quad \dot{x} = u, \quad x(0) = 0, \quad x(10) = 2$

    (b) $\max_{u \in [0,1]} \int_0^T x\, dt, \quad \dot{x} = u, \quad x(0) = x_0, \quad x(T) = x_1$ (with $x_0 < x_1 < x_0 + T$)

5. (a) Given the fixed positive number T, write down the conditions in Theorem 9.4.1 for the problem

$$\max \int_0^T -(u^2 + x^2)\, dt, \quad \dot{x} = au, \quad x(0) = 1, \quad x(T) \text{ free}, \quad u(t) \in [0, 1]$$

and find the solution when $a \geq 0$.

(b) Find the solution if $a < 0$. (*Hint:* Try $u^*(t) \in (0, 1)$ for all t.)

6. Solve the following special case of Problem I in Example 9.1.2:

$$\max \int_0^5 [10u - (u^2 + 2)]e^{-0.1t}\, dt, \quad \dot{x} = -u, \quad x(0) = 10, \quad x(5) \geq 0, \quad u \geq 0$$

7. (From Kamien and Schwartz (1991).) A firm has an order of B units of a commodity to be delivered at time T. Let $x(t)$ be the stock at time t. We assume that the cost per unit of time of storing $x(t)$ units is $ax(t)$. The increase in $x(t)$, which equals production per unit of time, is $u(t) = \dot{x}(t)$. Assume that the total cost of production per unit of time is equal to $b(u(t))^2$. Here a and b are positive constants. So the firm's natural problem is

$$\min \int_0^T \left[ax(t) + bu(t)^2\right] dt, \quad \dot{x}(t) = u(t), \quad x(0) = 0, \quad x(T) = B, \quad u(t) \geq 0$$

(a) Write down the necessary conditions implied by Theorem 9.4.1.

(b) Find the only possible solution to the problem and explain why it really is a solution. (*Hint:* Distinguish between the cases $B \geq aT^2/4b$ and $B < aT^2/4b$.)

8. Find the only possible solution to the problem

$$\max \int_0^2 (x^2 - 2u)\, dt, \quad \dot{x} = u, \quad x(0) = 1, \quad x(2) \text{ free}, \quad u \in [0, 1]$$

(*Hint:* Show that $p(t)$ is strictly decreasing.)

9. Consider the problem $\max \int_0^2 u\, dt$, $\dot{x} = u$, $x(0) = 0$, $x(2) \leq 1$, $u \in [-1, 1]$.

(a) Prove that the associated adjoint variable $p(t)$ is a constant, and show that this constant has to be -1. But then $H \equiv 0$, and $u^*(t)$ is not determined by the maximum condition (5).

(b) Show that *any* control which implies that $x^*(2) = 1$ solves the problem.

10. Consider the problem $\max \int_0^1 -u\, dt$, $\dot{x} = u^2$, $x(0) = x(1) = 0$, $u \in \mathbb{R}$.

(a) Explain why $u^*(t) = x^*(t) = 0$ solves the problem.

(b) Show that the conditions in the maximum principle are satisfied only for $p_0 = 0$.

9.5 The Maximum Principle and the Calculus of Variations

The introduction to this chapter claimed that optimal control theory extends the classical calculus of variations. Consider what the maximum principle has to say about the standard variational problem

$$\max \int_{t_0}^{t_1} F(t, x, \dot{x}) \, dt, \qquad x(t_0) = x_0, \qquad \begin{cases} \text{(a)} \ x(t_1) = x_1 \\ \text{(b)} \ x(t_1) \geq x_1 \\ \text{(c)} \ x(t_1) \ \text{free} \end{cases} \tag{1}$$

To transform this to a control problem, simply let $\dot{x}(t)$ be a control variable with $\dot{x}(t) = u(t)$. Because there are no restrictions on $\dot{x}(t)$ in the variational problem, there are no restrictions on the control function $u(t)$. Hence, $U = \mathbb{R}$.

The control problem has the particularly simple differential equation $\dot{x}(t) = u(t)$. The Hamiltonian is $H(t, x, u, p) = p_0 F(t, x, u) + pu$. The maximum principle states that if $u^*(t)$ solves the problem, then H as a function of u must be maximized at $u^*(t)$. Because $U = \mathbb{R}$, a necessary condition for this maximum is

$$H'_u(t, x, u, p(t)) = p_0 F'_u(t, x, u) + p(t) = 0 \tag{*}$$

Since $(p_0, p(t)) \neq (0, 0)$, equation $(*)$ implies that $p_0 \neq 0$, so $p_0 = 1$. The differential equation for $p(t)$ is

$$\dot{p}(t) = -H'_x(t, x, u, p) = -F'_x(t, x, u) \tag{**}$$

Differentiating $(*)$ with respect to t yields

$$\frac{d}{dt}\left(F'_u(t, x, u) \right) + \dot{p}(t) = 0 \tag{***}$$

Since $u = \dot{x}$, it follows from $(**)$ and $(***)$ that

$$F'_x(t, x, \dot{x}) - \frac{d}{dt}\left(F'_{\dot{x}}(t, x, \dot{x}) \right) = 0 \tag{2}$$

which is the Euler equation. Moreover, $(*)$ implies that

$$p(t) = -F'_{\dot{x}}(t, x, \dot{x}) \tag{3}$$

Using (3) it is easy to check that the transversality conditions in (9.4.7) are precisely those set out in Section 8.5. Note also that concavity of the Hamiltonian with respect to (x, u) is equivalent to concavity of $F(t, x, \dot{x})$ with respect to $(x, \dot{x})$.

Thus the maximum principle confirms all the main results found in Chapter 8. Actually, it contains more information about the solution of the optimization problem. For instance, according to the maximum principle, for every t in $[t_0, t_1]$ the Hamiltonian attains its maximum at $u^*(t)$. Assuming that F is a C^2 function, not only is $H'_u = 0$, but also $H''_{uu} \leq 0$, implying that $F''_{\dot{x}\dot{x}} \leq 0$. This is the so-called **Legendre condition** in the calculus of variations. (Also, continuity of $p(t)$ and (3) together give the **Weierstrass–Erdmann corner condition**, requiring $F'_{\dot{x}}$ to be continuous. This is a well known result in the classical theory.)

PROBLEMS FOR SECTION 9.5

1. Find the only possible solution to the following problem by using both the calculus of variations and control theory:

$$\max \int_0^1 (2xe^{-t} - 2x\dot{x} - \dot{x}^2)\, dt, \quad x(0) = 0, \ x(1) = 1$$

2. Solve the following problem by using both the calculus of variations and control theory:

$$\max \int_0^2 (3 - x^2 - 2\dot{x}^2)\, dt, \quad x(0) = 1, \ x(2) \geq 4$$

3. Solve the following problem by using both the calculus of variations and control theory:

$$\max \int_0^1 (-2\dot{x} - \dot{x}^2)e^{-t/10}\, dt, \quad x(0) = 1, \ x(1) = 0$$

4. At time $t = 0$ an oil field contains $\bar{x}$ barrels of oil. It is desired to extract all of the oil during a given time interval $[0, T]$. If $x(t)$ is the amount of oil left at time t, then $-\dot{x}$ is the extraction rate (which is ≥ 0 when $x(t)$ is decreasing). Assume that the world market price per barrel of oil is given and equal to $ae^{\alpha t}$. The extraction costs per unit of time are assumed to be $\dot{x}(t)^2 e^{\beta t}$. The profit per unit of time is then $\pi = -\dot{x}(t)ae^{\alpha t} - \dot{x}(t)^2 e^{\beta t}$. Here a, α, and β are constants, $a > 0$. This leads to the variational problem

$$\max \int_0^T \left[-\dot{x}(t)ae^{\alpha t} - \dot{x}(t)^2 e^{\beta t} \right] e^{-rt}\, dt, \qquad x(0) = \bar{x}, \ x(T) = 0, \qquad (**)$$

where r is a positive constant. Find the Euler equation for problem $(**)$, and show that at the optimum $\partial \pi / \partial \dot{x} = ce^{rt}$ for some constant c. Derive the same result by using control theory.

5. S. Strøm considers the problem

$$\max_x \int_0^T \{U(x(t)) - b(x(t)) - gz(t)\}\, dt, \quad \dot{z}(t) = ax(t), \ z(0) = z_0, \ z(T) \text{ free}$$

Here $U(x)$ is the utility enjoyed by society consuming x, whereas $b(x)$ is total cost and $z(t)$ is the stock of pollution at time t. Assume that U and b satisfy $U' > 0$, $U'' < 0$, $b' > 0$, and $b'' > 0$. The control variable is $x(t)$, whereas $z(t)$ is the state variable. The constants a and g are positive.

(a) Write down the conditions implied by the maximum principle. Show that the adjoint function is given by $p(t) = g(t - T)$, $t \in [0, T]$, and prove that if $x^*(t) > 0$ solves the problem, then

$$U'(x^*(t)) = b'(x^*(t)) + ag(T - t) \qquad (*)$$

(b) Prove that a solution of $(*)$ with $x^*(t) > 0$ must solve the problem. Show that $x^*(t)$ is strictly increasing. (*Hint:* Differentiate $(*)$ with respect to t.)

9.6 Adjoint Variables as Shadow Prices

Like the Lagrange multipliers used to solve static constrained optimization problems in Chapter 3, the adjoint function $p(t)$ in the maximum principle can be given an interesting price interpretation.

Consider the standard endconstrained problem (9.4.1)–(9.4.3). Suppose that it has a unique optimal solution $(x^*(t), u^*(t))$ with unique corresponding adjoint function $p(t)$. The corresponding value of the objective function will depend on x_0, x_1, t_0, and t_1. So it is denoted by

$$V(x_0, x_1, t_0, t_1) = \int_{t_0}^{t_1} f(t, x^*(t), u^*(t))\, dt \tag{1}$$

We call V the **(optimal) value function**. (When $x(t_1)$ is free, x_1 is not an argument of V.)

Suppose x_0 is changed slightly. In general, both $u^*(t)$ and $x^*(t)$ will change over the whole interval $[t_0, t_1]$. For typical problems in control theory, there is no guarantee that V is differentiable at a particular point. But at any point where it is differentiable,

$$\frac{\partial V(x_0, x_1, t_0, t_1)}{\partial x_0} = p(t_0) \tag{2}$$

The number $p(t_0)$ therefore measures the marginal change in the optimal value function as x_0 increases.

EXAMPLE 1   In Example 9.2.1 the objective function was $\int_0^T \left[1 - tx(t) - u(t)^2\right] dt$, and the solution was $u^*(t) = -\frac{1}{4}(T^2 - t^2)$, $x^*(t) = x_0 - \frac{1}{4}T^2 t + \frac{1}{12}t^3$, with $p(t) = -\frac{1}{2}(T^2 - t^2)$. So the value function is

$$V(x_0, T) = \int_0^T \left[1 - tx^*(t) - (u^*(t))^2\right] dt = \int_0^T \left[1 - x_0 t + \frac{1}{4}T^2 t^2 - \frac{1}{12}t^4 - \frac{1}{16}(T^2 - t^2)^2\right] dt$$

This last integral could be evaluated exactly, but fortunately we do not need to. Instead, simply differentiating V w.r.t. x_0 under the integral sign using formula (4.2.1) gives

$$\frac{\partial V(x_0, T)}{\partial x_0} = \int_0^T (-t)\, dt = -\frac{1}{2}T^2$$

On the other hand, $p(0) = -\frac{1}{2}T^2$, so (2) is confirmed.

Formula (2) interprets $p(t)$ at time $t = t_0$. What about $p(t)$ at an arbitrary $t \in (t_0, t_1)$? We want an interpretation that relates to the value function for the problem defined over the whole interval $[t_0, t_1]$, not only the subinterval $[t, t_1]$. Consider again problem (9.4.1)–(9.4.3), but assume that all admissible $x(t)$ are forced to have a jump equal to v at $t \in (t_0, t_1)$, so that $x(t^+) - x(t^-) = v$. Suppose all admissible $x(t)$ are continuous elsewhere. The optimal value function V for this problem will depend on v. Suppose that $(x^*(t), u^*(t))$ is the optimal solution of the problem for $v = 0$. Then, under certain conditions, it can be shown that V as a function of v is defined in a neighbourhood of $v = 0$, that V is differentiable w.r.t. v at $v = 0$, and that

$$\left(\frac{\partial V}{\partial v}\right)_{v=0} = p(t) \tag{3}$$

The adjoint variable $p(t)$ is approximately the change in the value function (1) due to a unit increase in $x(t)$.[5]

A General Economic Interpretation

Consider a firm that seeks to maximize its profit over a planning period $[t_0, t_1]$. The state of the firm at time t is described by its capital stock $x(t)$. At each time t the firm can partly influence its immediate profit, as well as the change in its future capital stock. Let the firm's decision or control variable at time t be $u(t)$. Let the rate of profit at time t be $f(t, x(t), u(t))$, so that the total profit in the time period $[t_0, t_1]$ is

$$\int_{t_0}^{t_1} f(t, x(t), u(t)) \, dt$$

The firm can choose $u(t)$ within certain limits, so that $u(t) \in U = [u_0, u_1]$, but it cannot directly influence $x(t)$. The rate of change in the capital stock depends on the present capital stock as well as on the value chosen for $u(t)$ at time t. Thus,

$$\dot{x}(t) = g(t, x(t), u(t)), \qquad x(t_0) = x_0$$

where x_0 is the given capital stock at time $t = t_0$. The control variable $u(t)$ not only influences the immediate profit but also, via the differential equation, influences the rate of change of the capital stock and thereby the future capital stock, which again changes the total profit.

Suppose we have found the solution to this problem, with corresponding adjoint function $p(t)$. According to (3), $p(t)$ is a "**shadow price**" of the capital stock, since $p(t)$ measures the marginal profit of capital. The Hamiltonian is $H = f(t, x, u) + p(t)g(t, x, u)$. Consider a small time interval $[t, t + \Delta t]$. Over this time interval, $\Delta x \approx g(t, x, u) \Delta t$ and so

$$H \, \Delta t = f(t, x, u) \, \Delta t + p(t)g(t, x, u) \, \Delta t \approx f(t, x, u) \, \Delta t + p(t) \, \Delta x$$

Hence $H \, \Delta t$ is the sum of the instantaneous profit $f(t, x, u) \, \Delta t$ earned in the time interval $[t, t + \Delta t]$ and the contribution $p(t) \, \Delta x$ to the total profit produced by the extra capital Δx at the end of this time period. The maximum principle requires choosing at each time the value of u that maximizes H, and hence $H \, \Delta t$.

---

[5] Economists have realized for a long time that the adjoint can be interpreted as a shadow price. Dorfman (1969) has an illuminating discussion on the economic interpretations, extending the material in the next subsection.

Other Sensitivity Results

Consider once again the standard end constrained problem (9.4.1)–(9.4.3) and its optimal value function (1). It turns out that, provided V is differentiable, the effects on V of small changes in x_1, t_0, and t_1 can also be expressed very simply. Define

$$H^*(t) = H(t, x^*(t), u^*(t), p(t)) \tag{4}$$

Then

$$\frac{\partial V}{\partial x_0} = p(t_0), \quad \frac{\partial V}{\partial x_1} = -p(t_1), \quad \frac{\partial V}{\partial t_0} = -H^*(t_0), \quad \frac{\partial V}{\partial t_1} = H^*(t_1) \tag{5}$$

The first of these equations was discussed above. As for the second, it is like the first, except that requiring the state x_1 to be larger at time t_1, has an effect that is opposite of allowing x_0 to be larger at time t_0. For example, in the capital accumulation interpretation in the previous subsection, increasing the initial capital stock x_0 by one unit increases the total profit by approximately $p(t_0)$. On the other hand, increasing the capital which must be left at the end of the planning period t_1 decreases the total profit earned by approximately $p(t_1)$. The third equality is similar to the fourth except for the change of sign. In the capital accumulation interpretation, increasing t_1 makes the planning period longer and the total profit increases (if it is positive). On the other hand, increasing t_0 makes the planning period shorter, so the total profit decreases. The last equality is illustrated in the next example.

NOTE 1   Consider the standard end constrained problem with $x(t_1)$ free. If $(x^*(t), u^*(t))$ is an optimal pair with corresponding adjoint function $p(t)$, then according to condition (9.4.7)(c'), $p(t_1) = 0$. This makes sense in light of the second formula in (5): The pair $(x^*(t), u^*(t))$ will solve the problem with terminal condition $x(t_1) = x^*(t_1) = x_1$, and the optimal value function V is given in (1). Since the optimal path in the problem with $x(t_1)$ free ends at $x^*(t_1)$, small changes in $x_1 = x^*(t_1)$ will not change V, and therefore $p(t_1) = -\partial V/\partial x_1 = 0$. With the economic interpretation given above the result is also natural: If there is no reason to care about the capital stock at the end of the planning period, its shadow price should be equal to 0.

EXAMPLE 2   Verify the last equality in (5) for the problem in Example 1.

Solution: Differentiating the value function $V(x_0, T)$ from Example 1 w.r.t. T, using the Leibniz rule (4.2.3) yields

$$\frac{\partial V}{\partial T} = 1 - x_0 T + \tfrac{1}{4}T^4 - \tfrac{1}{12}T^4 + \int_0^T \left[\tfrac{1}{2}t^2 T - \tfrac{1}{8}(T^2 - t^2)2T \right] dt$$

Integrating and simplifying gives

$$\frac{\partial V}{\partial T} = 1 - x_0 T + \tfrac{1}{6}T^4$$

Now, $H^*(T) = 1 - Tx^*(T) - (u^*(T))^2 + p(T)u^*(T) = 1 - x_0 T + \tfrac{1}{6}T^4$, because $u^*(T) = 0$ and $x^*(T) = x_0 - \tfrac{1}{6}T^3$. Thus the last result in (5) is confirmed.

EXAMPLE 3   **(Economic Growth)**   Consider the following problem in economic growth theory due to Shell (1967):

$$\max \int_0^T (1 - s(t))e^{\rho t} f(k(t))e^{-\delta t}\, dt$$

$$\dot{k}(t) = s(t)e^{\rho t} f(k(t)) - \lambda k(t), \quad k(0) = k_0, \quad k(T) \geq k_T > k_0, \quad 0 \leq s(t) \leq 1$$

Here $k(t)$ is the capital stock (a state variable), $s(t)$ is the savings rate (a control variable) and $f(k)$ is a production function. Suppose that $f(k) > 0$ whenever $k \geq k_0 e^{-\lambda T}$, that $f'(k) > 0$, and that ρ, δ, λ, T, k_0, and k_T are all positive constants.

(a) Suppose $(k^*(t), s^*(t))$ solves the problem. Write down the conditions in the maximum principle in this case. What are the possible values of $s^*(t)$?

(b) Put $\rho = 0$, $f(k) = ak$, $a > 0$, $\delta = 0$ and $\lambda = 0$. Suppose that $T > 1/a$ and that $k_0 e^{aT} > k_T$. Try to find the only possible solution to the problem.

(c) Compute the value function for the problem in (b) and then verify the relevant equalities in (5).

Solution: (a) The Hamiltonian is $H = (1 - s)e^{\rho t} f(k)e^{-\delta t} + p(se^{\rho t} f(k) - \lambda k)$. If $(k^*(t), s^*(t))$ solves the problem, then in particular, $s^*(t)$ must solve

$$\max (1 - s)e^{\rho t} f(k^*(t))e^{-\delta t} + p(t)\big[se^{\rho t} f(k^*(t)) - \lambda k^*(t)\big] \text{ subject to } s \in [0, 1]$$

Disregarding the terms that do not depend on s, $s^*(t)$ must maximize the expression $e^{\rho t} f(k^*(t))\big(-e^{-\delta t} + p(t)\big)s$ for $s \in [0, 1]$. Hence we must choose

$$s^*(t) = \begin{cases} 1 & \text{if } p(t) > e^{-\delta t} \\ 0 & \text{if } p(t) < e^{-\delta t} \end{cases} \tag{i}$$

A possible optimal control can therefore only take the values 1 and 0 (except if $p(t) = e^{-\delta t}$). Except where $s^*(t)$ is discontinuous,

$$\dot{p}(t) = -(1 - s^*(t))e^{\rho t} f'(k^*(t))e^{-\delta t} - p(t)s^*(t)e^{\rho t} f'(k^*(t)) + \lambda p(t) \tag{ii}$$

The transversality condition (9.4.7)(b′) gives

$$p(T) \geq 0 \quad (p(T) = 0 \text{ if } k^*(T) > k_T) \tag{iii}$$

For more extensive discussion of the model, see Shell (1967).

(b) Briefly formulated, the problem reduces to

$$\max \int_0^T (1 - s)ak\, dt, \qquad \dot{k} = ask, \quad k(0) = k_0, \quad k(T) \geq k_T > k_0$$

with $s \in [0, 1]$, $a > 0$, $T > 1/a$, and $k_0 e^{aT} > k_T$.

The Hamiltonian is $H = (1 - s)ak + pask$. The differential equation (ii) is now

$$\dot{p}(t) = -a + s^*(t)a(1 - p(t)) \tag{iv}$$

whereas (i) implies that

$$s^*(t) = \begin{cases} 1 & \text{if } p(t) > 1 \\ 0 & \text{if } p(t) < 1 \end{cases} \qquad \text{(v)}$$

From (iv) and (v) it follows that

$$\dot{p}(t) = -a < 0 \quad \text{if} \quad p(t) < 1, \text{while } \dot{p}(t) = -ap(t) \quad \text{if} \quad p(t) > 1 \qquad \text{(vi)}$$

In all cases $\dot{p}(t) < 0$, so $p(t)$ is strictly decreasing.

Suppose $p(0) < 1$, which implies that $p(t) < 1$ throughout $(0, T]$. Then by (v), $s^*(t) \equiv 0$, and so $k^*(t) \equiv k_0$, which contradicts $k^*(T) \geq k_T > k_0$. Hence $p(0) > 1$. Then there are two possible paths for $p(t)$, which are shown in Fig. 1. In the first case $p(T) = 0$; in the second case, $p(T) > 0$.

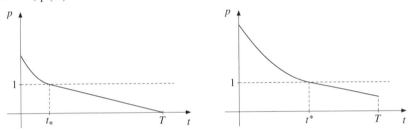

Figure 1: Two possible paths for $p(t)$.

Case I: $p(T) = 0$. Since $p(t)$ is continuous and strictly decreasing with $p(0) > 1$ and $p(T) = 0$, there is a unique $t_* \in (0, T)$ such that $p(t_*) = 1$, with $p(t) > 1$ in $[0, t_*)$ and $p(t) < 0$ in $(t_*, T]$. Then $s^*(t) = 1$ in $[0, t_*)$ and $s^*(t) = 0$ in $(t_*, T]$. By (vi), $\dot{p}(t) = -ap(t)$ in $[0, t_*)$ and $\dot{p}(t) = -a$ in $(t_*, T]$. On $(t_*, T]$, we have $p(t) = -a(t - T)$, because we have assumed $p(T) = 0$. But $p(t_*) = 1$, so $1 = -a(t_* - T)$, implying that $t_* = T - 1/a$. Furthermore, $p(t) = e^{a(T-t)-1}$ on $[0, T - 1/a]$. This gives the following solution candidate:

For $t \in [0, T - 1/a]$, $\quad s^*(t) = 1, \; k^*(t) = k_0 e^{at}, \quad$ and $p(t) = e^{a(T-t)-1} \qquad$ (vii)

For $t \in (T - 1/a, T]$, $\quad s^*(t) = 0, \; k^*(t) = k_0 e^{aT-1}, \quad$ and $p(t) = -a(t - T) \qquad$ (viii)

To verify all the conditions in the maximum principle, it remains to check that $k(T) \geq k_T$. Here this reduces to $k_0 e^{aT-1} \geq k_T$, or $e^{aT-1} \geq k_T / k_0$, or

$$t_* = T - \frac{1}{a} \geq \frac{1}{a} \ln\left(\frac{k_T}{k_0}\right) \qquad \text{(ix)}$$

If this inequality holds, then (vii)–(ix) give a possible solution to the problem.

Case II: $p(T) > 0$. In this case, by (iii), $k^*(T) = k_T$. If it were true that $p(T) \geq 1$, then one would have $p(t) > 1$ and so $s^*(t) = 1$ for all t in $[0, T)$, implying that $k^*(T) = k_0 e^{aT} > k_T$, a contradiction. So there exists a unique t^* in $[0, T)$ such that $p(t^*) = 1$. Similar arguments to those for case I suggest the following as an optimal solution:

For $t \in [0, t^*]$, $\quad s^*(t) = 1, \; k^*(t) = k_0 e^{at}, \quad$ and $p(t) = e^{a(t^*-t)} \qquad$ (x)

For $t \in (t^*, T]$, $\quad s^*(t) = 0, \; k^*(t) = k_0 e^{at^*}, \quad$ and $p(t) = 1 - a(t - t^*) \qquad$ (xi)

From $k^*(T) = k_T$ it follows that $e^{at^*} = k_T/k_0$, so

$$t^* = \frac{1}{a} \ln\left(\frac{k_T}{k_0}\right) \tag{xii}$$

We note that $t^* < T$ is equivalent to $k_0 e^{aT} > k_T$, as assumed. All of this was derived under the assumption that $p(T) > 0$, i.e. $1 - a(T - t^*) > 0$, which gives

$$T - \frac{1}{a} < \frac{1}{a} \ln\left(\frac{k_T}{k_0}\right) = t^* \tag{xiii}$$

Putting the two cases together, there is only one solution candidate, with

$$s^*(t) = 1 \ \text{ in } \ [0, \bar{t}], \qquad s^*(t) = 0 \ \text{ in } \ (\bar{t}, T] \tag{xiv}$$

where $\bar{t} = \max\{T - 1/a, \ (1/a)\ln(k_T/k_0)\}$.

Example 9.7.3 proves that we have found the optimal solution.

(c) For case I in (b) we have

$$V(k_0, k_T, T) = \int_{T-1/a}^{T} ak_0 e^{aT-1}\, dt = ak_0 e^{aT-1}[T - (T - 1/a)] = k_0 e^{aT-1}$$

so $\partial V/\partial k_0 = e^{aT-1} = p(0)$, using (vii). Also $\partial V/\partial k_T = 0 = -p(T)$. Finally, $H^*(T) = (1 - s^*(T))ak^*(T) + p(T)as^*(T)k^*(T) = ak^*(T) = ak_0 e^{aT-1} = \partial V/\partial T$.

For case II,

$$V(k_0, k_T, T) = \int_{t^*}^{T} ak_0 e^{at^*}\, dt = ak_0 e^{at^*}(T - t^*) = ak_T\left(T - \frac{1}{a}\ln k_T + \frac{1}{a}\ln k_0\right)$$

Hence $\partial V/\partial k_0 = k_T/k_0$, and we see that $p(0) = e^{at^*} = k_T/k_0$ also. Moreover, $\partial V/\partial k_T = a\left(T - \frac{1}{a}\ln k_T + \frac{1}{a}\ln k_0\right) - 1 = a(T - t^*) - 1$, and $-p(T) = a(T - t^*) - 1$ also. Finally, $\partial V/\partial T = ak_T$ and $H^*(T) = ak^*(T) = ak_0 e^{at^*} = ak_0(k_T/k_0) = ak_T$.

PROBLEMS FOR SECTION 9.6

1. (a) Solve the control problem

$$\max \int_0^T (x - \tfrac{1}{2}u^2)\, dt, \quad \dot{x} = u, \ \ x(0) = x_0, \ \ x(T) \text{ free}, \ \ u(t) \in \mathbb{R}$$

   (b) Compute the optimal value function $V(x_0, T)$, and verify the first and the last equalities in (5).

2. Verify that $V'(T) = H^*(T)$ for Problem 9.4.1.

3. Verify (5) for Problem 9.4.4(b).

HARDER PROBLEMS

4. (a) Given the positive constant T, find the only possible solution to the problem:

$$\max \int_0^T (2x^2 e^{-2t} - ue^t)\, dt, \quad \dot{x} = ue^t, \quad x(0) = 1, \quad x(T) \text{ free}, \quad u \in [0, 1]$$

   (b) Compute the value function $V(T)$ and verify that $V'(T) = H^*(T)$.

5. Consider the problem $\max \int_0^1 ux\, dt$, $\dot{x} = 0$, $x(0) = x_0$, $x(1)$ free, $u \in [0, 1]$.

   (a) Prove that if $x_0 < 0$, then the optimal control is $u^* = 0$, and if $x_0 > 0$, then the optimal control is $u^* = 1$.

   (b) Show that the value function $V(x_0)$ is not differentiable at $x_0 = 0$.

9.7 Sufficient Conditions

The maximum principle provides necessary conditions for optimality. Only solution candidates fulfilling these necessary conditions can possibly solve the problem. However, the maximum principle by itself cannot tell us whether a given candidate is optimal or not, nor does it tell us whether or not an optimal solution exists.

The following result, originally due to Mangasarian, has been referred to before. In fact, it is quite easy to prove.

THEOREM 9.7.1 (MANGASARIAN)

Consider the standard end constrained problem (9.4.1)–(9.4.3) with U an interval of the real line. Suppose the admissible pair $(x^*(t), u^*(t))$ satisfies all the conditions (9.4.5)–(9.4.7) of the maximum principle, with the associated adjoint function $p(t)$, and with $p_0 = 1$. Then, if

$$H(t, x, u, p(t)) \quad \text{is concave w.r.t. } (x, u) \text{ for all } t \text{ in } [t_0, t_1] \tag{1}$$

the pair $(x^*(t), u^*(t))$ solves the problem.

If $H(t, x, u, p(t))$ is strictly concave w.r.t. (x, u), then the pair $(x^*(t), u^*(t))$ is the unique solution to the problem.

NOTE 1 Suppose that U is an open interval (u_0, u_1). Then the concavity of $H(t, x, u, p(t))$ in u implies that the maximization condition (A) in Theorem 9.4.1 is equivalent to the first-order condition $\partial H^*/\partial u = \partial H(t, x^*(t), u^*(t), p(t))/\partial u = 0$. (See Theorem 3.1.2.) The concavity of $H(t, x, u, p(t))$ in (x, u) is satisfied, for example, if f and g are concave in (x, u) and $p(t) \geq 0$, or if f is concave whereas g is linear in (x, u).

Suppose that $U = [u_0, u_1]$. If $u^*(t) \in (u_0, u_1)$, then $\partial H^*/\partial u = 0$. If the lower limit $u^*(t) = u_0$ maximizes the Hamiltonian, then $\partial H^*/\partial u \leq 0$, because otherwise if $\partial H^*/\partial u > 0$, then the Hamiltonian would be increasing to the right of u_0. If the upper limit $u^*(t) = u_1$ maximizes the Hamiltonian, then we see in a similar way that $\partial H^*/\partial u \geq 0$. Because the Hamiltonian is concave in u, it follows that if $U = [u_0, u_1]$, then the maximum condition (9.4.5) is *equivalent* to the conditions:

$$\frac{\partial H^*}{\partial u} \begin{cases} \leq 0 & \text{if } u^*(t) = u_0 \\ = 0 & \text{if } u^*(t) \in (u_0, u_1) \\ \geq 0 & \text{if } u^*(t) = u_1 \end{cases} \tag{2}$$

These conditions are illustrated in Fig. 1.

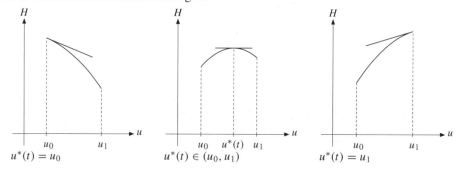

Figure 1

If the Hamiltonian is concave in u, the maximization condition in (9.4.5) can be *replaced* by the inequality

$$\frac{\partial H^*}{\partial u}(u^*(t) - u) \geq 0 \quad \text{for all} \quad u \in [u_0, u_1] \tag{3}$$

If $u^*(t) \in (u_0, u_1)$, condition (3) reduces to $\partial H^*/\partial u = 0$. If $u^*(t) = u_0$, then $u^*(t) - u = u_0 - u \leq 0$ for all $u^*(t) \in [u_0, u_1]$, so (3) is equivalent to $\partial H^*/\partial u \leq 0$. On the other hand, if $u^*(t) = u_1$, then $u^*(t) - u = u_1 - u \geq 0$ for all $u^*(t) \in [u_0, u_1]$, so (3) is equivalent to $\partial H^*/\partial u \geq 0$.

Proof of Theorem 9.7.1: Suppose that $(x, u) = (x(t), u(t))$ is an arbitrary alternative admissible pair. We must show that

$$D_u = \int_{t_0}^{t_1} f(t, x^*(t), u^*(t)) \, dt - \int_{t_0}^{t_1} f(t, x(t), u(t)) \, dt \geq 0$$

First, simplify notation by writing H^* instead of $H(t, x^*(t), u^*(t), p(t))$ and H instead of $H(t, x(t), u(t), p(t))$, etc. Then, using the definition of the Hamiltonian and the fact that $\dot{x}^*(t) = g(t, x^*(t), u^*(t))$ and $\dot{x}(t) = g(t, x(t), u(t))$, we have $f^* = H^* - p\dot{x}^*$ and $f = H - p\dot{x}$. Therefore

$$D_u = \int_{t_0}^{t_1} (H^* - H) \, dt + \int_{t_0}^{t_1} p(\dot{x} - \dot{x}^*) \, dt \tag{$*$}$$

Because H is concave in (x, u), Theorem 2.4.1 implies that

$$H - H^* \leq \frac{\partial H^*}{\partial x}(x - x^*) + \frac{\partial H^*}{\partial u}(u - u^*) \qquad (**)$$

Now, $\dot{p} = -\partial H^*/\partial x$, so $(*)$ and $(**)$ together imply that

$$D_u \geq \int_{t_0}^{t_1} \left[\dot{p}(x - x^*) + p(\dot{x} - \dot{x}^*) \right] dt + \int_{t_0}^{t_1} \frac{\partial H^*}{\partial u}(u^* - u)\, dt$$

Because of (3), the second integral is ≥ 0. Moreover, according to the rule for differentiating a product, $\dot{p}(x - x^*) + p(\dot{x} - \dot{x}^*) = (d/dt)(p(x - x^*))$. Hence,

$$D_u \geq \int_{t_0}^{t_1} \frac{d}{dt}[p(x - x^*)]\, dt = \Big|_{t_0}^{t_1} p(t)[x(t) - x^*(t)] = p(t_1)(x(t_1) - x^*(t_1)) \qquad (***)$$

where the last equality holds because the contribution from the lower limit of integration is 0 because $x(t_0) - x^*(t_0) = x_0 - x_0 = 0$.

Now one can use the terminal condition (9.4.3) and the transversality condition (9.4.7) to show that the last term in $(***)$ is always ≥ 0. Indeed, if (9.4.3)(a) holds, then $x(t_1) - x^*(t_1) = x_1 - x_1 = 0$. But if (9.4.3)(b) holds, then $p(t_1) \geq 0$ and so if $x^*(t_1) = x_1$, then $p(t_1)(x(t_1) - x^*(t_1)) = p(t_1)[x(t_1) - x_1] \geq 0$ because $x(t_1) \geq x_1$. Alternatively, if $x^*(t_1) > x_1$, then $p(t_1) = 0$, and the term is 0. Finally, if (9.4.3)(c) holds, then $p(t_1) = 0$, and the term is 0. In all cases, therefore, one has $D_u \geq 0$.

If H is strictly concave in (x, u), then the inequality $(**)$ is strict for $(x, u) \neq (x^*, u^*)$, and so $D_u > 0$ unless $x(t) = x^*(t)$ and $u(t) = u^*(t)$ for all t. Hence (x^*, u^*) is the unique solution to the problem. ∎

Most of the control problems presented so far can be solved by using Mangasarian's sufficient conditions. However, in many important economic models the Hamiltonian is not concave. Arrow has suggested a weakening of this concavity condition. Define

$$\widehat{H}(t, x, p) = \max_{u \in U} H(t, x, u, p) \qquad (4)$$

assuming that the maximum value is attained. The function $\widehat{H}(t, x, p)$ is called the **maximized Hamiltonian**. Then one can show:

THEOREM 9.7.2 (ARROW'S SUFFICIENT CONDITIONS)

Suppose that $(x^*(t), u^*(t))$ is an admissible pair in the standard end constrained problem (9.4.1)–(9.4.3) that satisfies all the requirements in the maximum principle, with $p(t)$ as the adjoint function, and with $p_0 = 1$. Suppose further that

$$\widehat{H}(t, x, p(t)) \text{ is concave in } x \text{ for every } t \in [t_0, t_1] \qquad (5)$$

Then $(x^*(t), u^*(t))$ solves the problem.

A proof and further discussion of this result is postponed to Section 10.1.

NOTE 2   Here is an important generalization of the theorem: Suppose the problem imposes the constraint that $x(t)$ belongs to a convex set $A(t)$ for all t. Suppose also that $x^*(t)$ is an interior point of $A(t)$ for every t. Then Theorem 9.7.2 is still valid, and $x \mapsto \widehat{H}(t, x, p(t))$ need only be concave for x in $A(t)$.

EXAMPLE 1   Consider the problem

$$\max \int_0^2 (u^2 - x)\, dt, \quad \dot{x} = u, \quad x(0) = 0, \quad x(2) \text{ free}, \quad 0 \le u \le 1$$

(a) Find the only possible solution candidate by using the maximum principle.

(b) Use Theorem 9.7.2 to prove that the pair found in (a) is optimal.

Solution: (a) The Hamiltonian with $p_0 = 1$ is $H(t, x, u, p) = u^2 - x + pu$. Because $H'_x = -1$, the differential equation for $p = p(t)$ becomes $\dot{p} = -H'_x = 1$. The solution of this equation with $p(2) = 0$ is $p(t) = t - 2$. According to the maximum condition (9.4.5), for each t in $[0, 2]$, an optimal control $u^*(t)$ must maximize $u^2 - x^*(t) + (t - 2)u = -x^*(t) + u^2 + tu - 2u$ subject to $u \in [0, 1]$. The term $-x^*(t)$ is independent of u, so $u^*(t)$ must maximize $g(u) = u^2 + tu - 2u$ subject to $u \in [0, 1]$. Note that $g(u)$ is a strictly convex function, so its maximum cannot occur at an interior point of $[0, 1]$. At the end points, $g(0) = 0$ and $g(1) = t - 1$. Thus the maximum of g depends on the value of t. Clearly, if $t < 1$ the maximum of g occurs at $u = 0$, and if $t > 1$, the maximum occurs at $u = 1$. Thus the only possible optimal control which is continuous on the left at $t = 1$ is the bang-bang control

$$u^*(t) = \begin{cases} 0 & \text{if } t \in [0, 1] \\ 1 & \text{if } t \in (1, 2] \end{cases}$$

In the interval $[0, 1]$ one has $\dot{x}^*(t) = u^*(t) = 0$ and $x^*(0) = 0$, so $x^*(t) = 0$. In the interval $(1, 2]$ one has $\dot{x}^*(t) = u^*(t) = 1$ and $x^*(1) = 0$, so $x^*(t) = t - 1$. We have found the only possible pair that can solve the problem.

(b) The Hamiltonian with $p(t) = t - 2$ is $H(t, x, u, p) = u^2 - x + (t - 2)u$, which is convex in u. The maximized Hamiltonian is seen to be

$$\widehat{H}(t, x, p(t)) = \max_{u \in [0,1]} u^2 - x + (t - 2)u = \begin{cases} -x & \text{if } t \in [0, 1] \\ -x + t - 1 & \text{if } t \in (1, 2] \end{cases}$$

For each t in $[0, 2]$, the maximized Hamiltonian is linear in x, hence concave. The conclusion follows from Theorem 9.7.2.

The following example illustrates an important aspect of Theorem 9.7.2: It suffices to show that the maximized Hamiltonian is concave as a function of x with $p(t)$ as the adjoint function derived from the maximum principle.

EXAMPLE 2   Use Theorem 9.7.2 to prove that for the problem

$$\max \int_0^1 3u\, dt, \quad \dot{x} = u^3, \quad x(0) = 0, \quad x(1) \le 0, \quad u \in [-2, \infty)$$

$u^*(t) = 1$ in $[0, 8/9]$ and $u^*(t) = -2$ in $(8/9, 1]$ is an optimal control with $p(t) \equiv -1$.

Solution: The Hamiltonian with $p(t) \equiv -1$ is $H(t, x, u, p) = 3u - u^3$, which is not concave in (x, u). (See Fig. 2.) However, the maximized Hamiltonian is $\widehat{H}(t, x, p(t)) = \max_{u \in [-2, \infty)} (3u - u^3) \equiv 2$, which *is* concave. Note that $p(t) \equiv -1$ satisfies $\dot{p} = -\partial H^* / \partial x = 0$. Moreover, both $u^*(t) = 1$ and $u^*(t) = -2$ maximize $3u - u^3$ for $u \in [-2, \infty)$ (see Fig. 2). Because $p(1) = -1$, the result in Note 9.4.2 implies that $x^*(1) = 0$. The function $x^*(t)$ must satisfy the equation $\dot{x}^*(t) = (u^*(t))^3$ for each t, and also have $x^*(0) = 0$ and $x^*(1) = 0$. One possibility is $x^*(t) = t$ in $[0, 8/9]$, with $u^*(t) = 1$, and $x^*(t) = 8 - 8t$ in $(8/9, 1]$, with $u^*(t) = -2$. Because all the conditions in Theorem 9.7.2 are satisfied, this is a solution. (But the solution is not unique. One could also have, for example, $x^*(t) = -8t$ in $[0, 1/9]$ with $u^*(t) = -2$, and $x^*(t) = t - 1$ in $(1/9, 1]$ with $u^*(t) = 1$.)

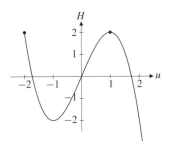

Figure 2

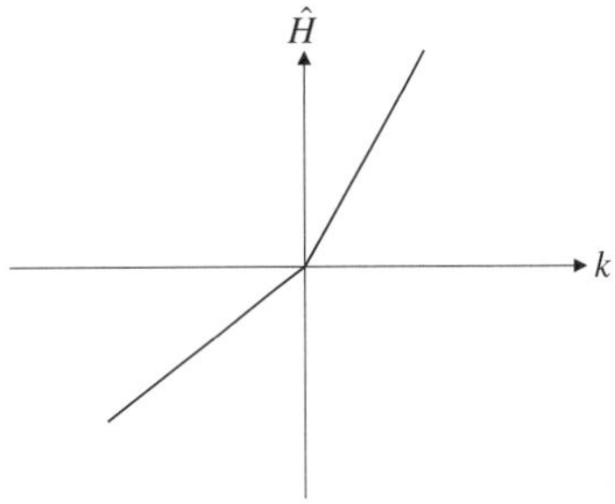

Figure 3

Our final example makes use of Note 2.

EXAMPLE 3   Consider the capital accumulation model of Example 9.6.3(b). Prove that the proposed solution candidate is optimal.

Solution: The Hamiltonian is $H(t, k, s, p) = (1 - s)ak + pask = ak[1 + (p - 1)s]$. This function is not concave in (k, s) for $p \neq 1$, because $H''_{kk} H''_{ss} - (H''_{ks})^2 = -a^2(p - 1)^2$. The function $\widehat{H}$ defined in (4) is

$$\widehat{H}(t, k, p(t)) = ak \max_{s \in [0,1]} [1 + (p(t) - 1)s]$$

Given $\bar{t}$ defined as in the solution to Example 9.6.3(b), we found that for $t \in [0, \bar{t})$, the adjoint variable is $p(t) > 1$. It follows that $\widehat{H}(t, k, p(t)) = ap(t)k$ for $k \geq 0$, while $\widehat{H}(t, k, p(t)) = ak$ for $k \leq 0$. For $t \in (\bar{t}, T)$, however, the adjoint variable is $p(t) < 1$, and it follows that $\widehat{H}(t, k, p(t)) = ak$ for $k \geq 0$, while $\widehat{H}(t, k, p(t)) = ap(t)k$ for $k \leq 0$. It is tempting to suggest that because $\widehat{H}$ is linear in each case, $\widehat{H}$ concave in k. But the graph in Fig. 3 shows that $\widehat{H}$ is convex, and not concave.

Define $A(t) = \{k : k \geq 0\}$. Certainly, the optimal $k^*(t)$ is positive for all t, so $k^*(t)$ is an interior point of $A(t)$ for every t. For $k \geq 0$,

$$\widehat{H}(t, k, p(t)) = \begin{cases} akp(t) & \text{if } p(t) > 1 \\ ak & \text{if } p(t) \leq 1 \end{cases}$$

Thus for each t, $\widehat{H}(t, k, p(t))$ is concave as a function of $k \in A = [0, \infty)$. According to Theorem 9.7.2 and Note 2, the suggested candidate in Example 9.6.3(b) is optimal.

NOTE 3 To give a complete solution of an optimal control problem using the Mangasarian (or Arrow) sufficiency results, it is necessary to prove that there is a pair $(x^*(t), u^*(t))$ satisfying all the requirements. In problems where it is impossible to find explicit solutions for $x^*(t)$ and $u^*(t)$, this means that we must prove that there exist admissible solutions of the differential equations which are valid for the whole interval $[t_0, t_1]$. (This is almost never done in economics literature.)

NOTE 4 (**What to do if the Arrow condition fails**)   If the maximized Hamiltonian is not concave, then the Mangasarian condition also fails. For the corresponding case in static optimization problems we turned next to the extreme value theorem, which promises that under certain conditions, there exists an optimal solution. In Section 10.4 we discuss analogous existence theorems for control problems.

PROBLEMS FOR SECTION 9.7

1. (a) Solve the control problem

$$\max \int_0^1 (100 - x - \tfrac{1}{2}u^2)\, dt, \quad \dot{x} = u, \ x(0) = x_0, \ x(1) = x_1, \ u \in (-\infty, \infty)$$

(b) Verify that $\partial V/\partial x_0 = p(0)$ and $\partial V/\partial x_1 = -p(1)$, where V is the optimal value function.

2. (a) Find the only possible solution to

$$\max \int_0^{10} (1 - s)\sqrt{k}\, dt, \quad \dot{k} = s\sqrt{k}, \quad k(0) = 1, \quad k(10) \text{ free}, \quad s \in [0, 1]$$

(b) Use Theorem 9.7.2 to prove that the solution candidate in (a) is optimal.

3. Solve the problem (where T, α, and β are positive constants, $\alpha \neq 2\beta$)

$$\max \int_0^T e^{-\beta t}\sqrt{u}\, dt \ \text{ when } \dot{x}(t) = \alpha x(t) - u(t), \ x(0) = 1, \ x(T) = 0, \ u(t) \geq 0$$

What happens if the terminal condition $x(T) = 0$ is changed to $x(T) \geq 0$?

4. Let f be a C^1-function defined on a set A in $\mathbb{R}^n$, and let S be a convex set in the interior of A. Show that if $\mathbf{x}^0$ maximizes $f(\mathbf{x})$ in S, then $\nabla f(\mathbf{x}^0) \cdot (\mathbf{x}^0 - \mathbf{x}) \geq 0$ for all $\mathbf{x}$ in S. (*Hint:* Define the function $g(t) = f(t\mathbf{x} + (1 - t)\mathbf{x}^0)$ for t in $[0, 1]$. Then $g(0) \geq g(t)$ for all t in $[0, 1]$.)

9.8 Variable Final Time

In the optimal control problems studied so far the time interval has been fixed. Yet for some control problems in economics, the final time is a variable to be chosen optimally, along with the path $u(t)$, $t \in [t_0, t_1]$. One instance is the optimal extraction problem of Example 9.1.2, in which it is natural to have the length of the extraction period as a variable (in addition to the rate of extraction). Another important case is the minimal time problem in which the objective is to steer a system from its initial state to a desired state as quickly as possible.

The **variable final time problem** considered here can be briefly formulated as follows (note that the choice variables u and t_1 are indicated below the max instruction):

$$\max_{u, t_1} \int_{t_0}^{t_1} f(t, x, u)\, dt, \quad \dot{x} = g(t, x, u), \quad x(t_0) = x_0, \quad \begin{cases} \text{(a)} & x(t_1) = x_1 \\ \text{(b)} & x(t_1) \geq x_1 \\ \text{(c)} & x(t_1) \text{ free} \end{cases} \quad (1)$$

The only difference from the standard end constrained problem is that t_1 can now be chosen. Thus, the problem is to maximize the integral in (1) over all admissible control functions $u(t)$ that, over the time interval $[t_0, t_1]$, bring the system from x_0 to a point satisfying the terminal conditions. In contrast to the previous problems, the admissible control function can be defined on different time intervals.

Suppose $(x^*(t), u^*(t))$ is an optimal solution defined on $[t_0, t_1^*]$. Then the conditions (9.4.5)–(9.4.7) in the maximum principle are still valid on the interval $[t_0, t_1^*]$, because the pair $(x^*(t), u^*(t))$ must be optimal for the corresponding fixed time problem with $t_1 = t_1^*$. In fact, the result is this[6]:

THEOREM 9.8.1 (THE MAXIMUM PRINCIPLE WITH VARIABLE FINAL TIME)

Let $(x^*(t), u^*(t))$ be an admissible pair defined on $[t_0, t_1^*]$ which solves problem (1) with t_1 free ($t_1 \in (t_0, \infty)$). Then all the conditions in the maximum principle (Theorem 9.4.1) are satisfied on $[t_0, t_1^*]$, and, in addition,

$$H(t_1^*, x^*(t_1^*), u^*(t_1^*), p(t_1^*)) = 0 \quad (2)$$

Compared with a fixed final time problem there is one additional unknown t_1^*. Fortunately, (2) is one extra condition.

One method for solving variable final time problems is first to solve the problem with t_1 fixed for every $t_1 > t_0$. The optimal final time t_1^* must then maximize the optimal value function V as a function of t_1. According to (9.6.5), if V is differentiable, then $\partial V / \partial t_1 = H^*(t_1) = H^*(t_1^*, x^*(t_1^*), u^*(t_1^*), p(t_1^*))$. Thus, condition (2) is precisely as expected.

---

[6] For a proof see Hestenes (1966).

NOTE 1 (**A common misunderstanding**)   Concavity of the Hamiltonian in (x, u) is *not* sufficient for optimality when t_1 is free. For sufficiency results when the final time is variable, see Seierstad and Sydsæter (1987), Sections 2.9 and 6.7.

EXAMPLE 1   Consider Problem II in Example 9.1.2 for the special case when the cost function $C = C(t, u)$ is independent of x and convex in u, with $C_{uu}'' > 0$. Thus, the problem is

$$\max_{u, T} \int_0^T \left[q(t)u(t) - C(t, u(t))\right]e^{-rt}\, dt, \quad \dot{x}(t) = -u(t), \quad x(0) = K, \quad x(T) \geq 0, \quad u(t) \geq 0$$

What does the maximum principle imply for this problem?

Solution: Suppose $(x^*(t), u^*(t))$, defined on $[0, T^*]$, solves this problem. The Hamiltonian with $p_0 = 1$ is $H(t, x, u, p) = [q(t)u - C(t, u)]e^{-rt} + p(-u)$, and the maximum principle states that there exists a continuous function $p(t)$ such that

$$u^*(t) \text{ maximizes } \left[q(t)u - C(t, u)\right]e^{-rt} - p(t)u \text{ subject to } u \geq 0 \tag{i}$$

$$\dot{p}(t) = -\frac{\partial H}{\partial x} = 0, \quad p(T^*) \geq 0 \; (p(T^*) = 0 \text{ if } x^*(T^*) > 0) \tag{ii}$$

$$\left[q(T^*)u^*(T^*) - C(T^*, u^*(T^*))\right]e^{-rT^*} = p(T^*)u^*(T^*) \tag{iii}$$

Because $p(t)$ is continuous, (ii) implies that $p(t) = \bar{p} \geq 0$, where $\bar{p}$ is a constant.

Put $g(u) = \left[q(t)u - C(t, u)\right]e^{-rt} - \bar{p}u$. Because $C(t, u)$ is convex in u and the other terms are linear in u, the function $g(u)$ is concave. According to (i), $u^*(t)$ maximizes $g(u)$ subject to $u \geq 0$. If $u^*(t) = 0$, then $g'(u^*(t)) = g'(0) \leq 0$. If $u^*(t) > 0$, then $g'(u^*(t)) = 0$. Therefore (i) implies that

$$\left[q(t) - C_u'(t, u^*(t))\right]e^{-rt} - \bar{p} \leq 0 \quad (= 0 \text{ if } u^*(t) > 0) \tag{iv}$$

Because g is concave, this condition is also sufficient for (i) to hold.

At any time t where $u^*(t) > 0$, equation (iv) implies that

$$q(t) - C_u'(t, u^*(t)) = \bar{p}e^{rt} \tag{v}$$

The left hand side is the marginal profit from extraction, $\partial \pi / \partial u$. Therefore, whenever it is optimal to have positive extraction, we have the following rule that was discovered by Hotelling (1931).

(HOTELLING'S RULE)

Positive optimal extraction requires the marginal profit to increase exponentially at a rate equal to the discount factor r. (3)

Putting $t = T^*$ in (v), and using (iii), we deduce that if $u^*(T^*) > 0$, then

$$C_u'(T^*, u^*(T^*)) = \frac{C(T^*, u^*(T^*))}{u^*(T^*)} \tag{vi}$$

Terminate extraction at a time when the marginal cost of extraction is equal to average cost!

If the problem has a solution with $u^*(t) > 0$, then (v) and (vi) both hold. If $C(T^*, 0) > 0$, then $u^*(T^*) > 0$, because $u^*(T^*) = 0$ contradicts (iii).

We have not proved that there exists an optimal solution. (For a more thorough discussion of this problem, see Seierstad and Sydsæter (1987), Section 2.9, Example 11.)

PROBLEMS FOR SECTION 9.8

1. Find the only possible solution to the following variable final time problems:

   (a) $\max\limits_{u,\,T} \displaystyle\int_0^T (x - t^3 - \tfrac{1}{2}u^2)\,dt, \qquad \dot{x} = u, \quad x(0) = 0, \quad x(T) \text{ free}, \quad u \in \mathbb{R}$

   (b) $\max\limits_{u,\,T} \displaystyle\int_0^T (-9 - \tfrac{1}{4}u^2)\,dt, \qquad \dot{x} = u, \quad x(0) = 0, \quad x(T) = 16, \quad u \in \mathbb{R}$

2. Solve problem 9.4.7 with T free.

3. Consider the optimal extraction problem over a fixed extraction period,

   $$\max_{u(t)\geq 0} \int_0^T \big[ae^{\alpha t}u(t) - (u(t))^2 e^{\beta t} - c\big]e^{-rt}\,dt, \quad \dot{x}(t) = -u(t), \quad x(0) = K, \quad x(T) = 0$$

   Here $x(t)$ and $u(t)$ have the same interpretation as in Example 1, with $q(t) = ae^{\alpha t}$ as the world market price, and $(u(t))^2 e^{\beta t} - c$ as the cost of extraction, with $c > 0$.

   (a) One can prove that if $u^*(t)$ is optimal, then $u^*(t) > 0$ for all t. (You are not required to show this.) The adjoint function is a constant $\bar{p}$. Find $u^*(t)$ expressed in terms of $\bar{p}$. Then find $x^*(t)$ and $\bar{p}$ for the case $\alpha = \beta = 0$, $r \neq 0$.

   (b) Let $T > 0$ be subject to choice (keeping the assumptions $\alpha = \beta = 0$, $r \neq 0$). Prove that the necessary conditions lead to an equation for determining the optimal T^* which has a unique positive solution. Assume that $\max_u (au - u^2 - c) > 0$, i.e. $a^2 > 4c$.

9.9 Current Value Formulations

Many control problems in economics literature have the following structure:

$$\max_{u \in U \subseteq \mathbb{R}} \int_{t_0}^{t_1} f(t, x, u)e^{-rt}\,dt, \quad \dot{x} = g(t, x, u), \quad x(t_0) = x_0, \quad \begin{cases} \text{(a)} \;\; x(t_1) = x_1 \\ \text{(b)} \;\; x(t_1) \geq x_1 \\ \text{(c)} \;\; x(t_1) \text{ free} \end{cases} \quad (1)$$

The new feature is the explicit appearance of the discount factor e^{-rt}. For such problems it is often convenient to formulate the maximum principle in a slightly different form. The ordinary Hamiltonian is $H = p_0 f(t, x, u)e^{-rt} + pg(t, x, u)$. Multiply it by e^{rt} to obtain the **current value Hamiltonian** $H^c = He^{rt} = p_0 f(t, x, u) + e^{rt} pg(t, x, u)$. Introducing $\lambda = e^{rt} p$ as the **current value shadow price** for the problem, one can write H^c in the form (where we put $p_0 = \lambda_0$)

$$H^c(t, x, u, \lambda) = \lambda_0 f(t, x, u) + \lambda g(t, x, u) \tag{2}$$

Note that if $\lambda = e^{rt} p$, then $\dot{\lambda} = re^{rt}p + e^{rt}\dot{p} = r\lambda + e^{rt}\dot{p}$ and so $\dot{p} = e^{-rt}(\dot{\lambda} - r\lambda)$. Also, $H^c = He^{rt}$ implies that $\partial H^c/\partial x = e^{rt}(\partial H/\partial x)$. So $\dot{p} = -\partial H/\partial x$ takes the form $\dot{\lambda} - r\lambda = -\partial H^c/\partial x$. In fact, one can prove the following:

THEOREM 9.9.1 (THE MAXIMUM PRINCIPLE. CURRENT VALUE FORMULATION)

Suppose that the admissible pair $(x^*(t), u^*(t))$ solves problem (1) and let H^c be the current value Hamiltonian (2). Then there exists a continuous function $\lambda(t)$ and a number λ_0, either 0 or 1, such that for all $t \in [t_0, t_1]$ we have $(\lambda_0, \lambda(t)) \neq (0, 0)$, and:

(A) $u = u^*(t)$ maximizes $H^c(t, x^*(t), u, \lambda(t))$ for $u \in U$ $\qquad\qquad$ (3)

(B) $\dot{\lambda}(t) - r\lambda(t) = -\dfrac{\partial H^c(t, x^*(t), u^*(t), \lambda(t))}{\partial x}$ $\qquad$ (4)

(C) Finally, the transversality conditions are:

$\quad$ (a′) $\lambda(t_1)$ no condition

$\quad$ (b′) $\lambda(t_1) \geq 0$ $\;(\lambda(t_1) = 0$ if $x^*(t_1) > x_1)$ $\qquad\qquad$ (5)

$\quad$ (c′) $\lambda(t_1) = 0$

The Mangasarian and Arrow sufficiency results from Section 9.7 have immediate extensions to problem (1). The conditions in Theorem 9.9.1 are sufficient for optimality if $\lambda_0 = 1$ and

$$H^c(t, x, u, \lambda(t)) \text{ is concave in } (x, u) \qquad\qquad \text{(Mangasarian)} \qquad (6)$$

or (more generally)

$$\widehat{H}^c(t, x, \lambda(t)) = \max_{u \in U} H^c(t, x, u, \lambda(t)) \text{ is concave in } x \qquad \text{(Arrow)} \qquad (7)$$

EXAMPLE 1 $\qquad$ Solve the following problem using the current value formulation.

$$\max_{u \geq 0} \int_0^{20} (4K - u^2)e^{-0.25t}\, dt, \quad \dot{K} = -0.25K + u, \quad K(0) = K_0, \quad K(20) \text{ is free}$$

Economic interpretation: $K(t)$ is the value of a machine, $u(t)$ is the repair effort, $4K - u^2$ is the instantaneous net profit at time t, and $e^{-0.25t}$ is the discount factor.

Solution: The current value Hamiltonian is $H^c = 4K - u^2 + \lambda(-0.25K + u)$ (with $\lambda_0 = 1$), and so $\partial H^c/\partial u = -2u + \lambda$ and $\partial H^c/\partial K = 4 - 0.25\lambda$. Assuming that $u^*(t) > 0$ (we try this assumption in the following), $\partial(H^c)^*/\partial u = 0$, so $u^*(t) = 0.5\lambda(t)$. The adjoint function λ satisfies

$$\dot{\lambda} - 0.25\lambda = -\partial(H^c)^*/\partial K = -4 + 0.25\lambda, \qquad \lambda(20) = 0$$

It follows that

$$\lambda(t) = 8(1 - e^{0.5t-10}) \quad \text{and} \quad u^*(t) = 0.5\lambda = 4(1 - e^{0.5t-10})$$

Note that $u^*(t) > 0$ in $[0, 20]$. The time path of $K^*(t)$ is found from $\dot{K}^* = -0.25K^* + u^* = -0.25K^* + 4(1 - e^{0.5t-10})$. Solving this linear differential equation with $K^*(0) = K_0$, we get

$$K^*(t) = (K_0 - 16 + \tfrac{16}{3}e^{-10})e^{-0.25t} + 16 - \tfrac{16}{3}e^{0.5t-10}$$

Here $H^c = (4K - u^2) + \lambda(-0.25K + u)$ is concave in (K, u), so we have found the complete solution.

Note that the pair $(K^*(t), \lambda(t))$ must satisfy the system

$$\dot{\lambda} = 0.5\lambda - 4, \quad \lambda(20) = 0$$
$$\dot{K} = -0.25K + 0.5\lambda, \quad K(0) = K_0$$

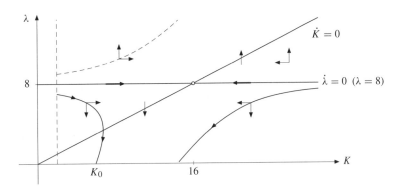

Figure 1 Phase diagram for Example 1.

Figure 1 shows a phase diagram for this system. When $K_0 < 16$ as in the figure, the curve drawn with a solid line is consistent with the indicated arrows. Initially the value of the machine increases, and the repair effort is reduced. Then, after the curve hits the line $\dot{K} = 0$, the value decreases and the repair effort is reduced till it eventually is 0. The dotted curve is also consistent with the arrows, but there is no way the curve can satisfy $\lambda(20) = 0$—the required repair effort is too high to lead to an optimal solution. (When λ is large, so is $u = 0.5\lambda$, and the integrand $4K - u^2$ becomes large negative.)

The diagrammatic analysis related to Fig. 1 in the last example is in a way superfluous since the solution has already been completely specified. But it is very useful in some problems where explicit solutions are unobtainable. See Section 9.12.

1. Find the solution to the following problem using the current value formulation:

$$\max_{u(t)\in\mathbb{R}} \int_0^T \left(-x^2 - \tfrac{1}{2}u^2\right)e^{-2t}\, dt, \quad \dot{x} = x + u, \quad x(0) = 1, \quad x(T) \text{ free}$$

2. Find the solution of Problem 9.4.6 using the current value formulation.

3. Find the solution of Problem 9.5.3 using the current value formulation.

9.10 Scrap Values

In some economic optimization problems it is natural to include within the optimality criterion an additional function representing the value or utility associated with the terminal state. This gives the typical problem

$$\max_{u(t)\in U} \left\{ \int_{t_0}^{t_1} f(t, x(t), u(t))\, dt + S(x(t_1)) \right\}, \quad \dot{x}(t) = g(t, x(t), u(t)), \quad x(t_0) = x_0 \quad (1)$$

The function $S(x)$ is called a **scrap value function**, and we shall assume that it is C^1.

Suppose that $(x^*(t), u^*(t))$ solves this problem (with no additional condition on $x(t_1)$). Then, in particular, that pair is a solution to the corresponding problem with fixed terminal point $(t_1, x^*(t_1))$. For all admissible pairs in this new problem, the scrap value function $S(x^*(t_1))$ is constant. But then $(x^*(t), u^*(t))$ must satisfy all the conditions in the maximum principle, except the transversality conditions. Then the correct transversality condition for "normal" problems is

$$p(t_1) = S'(x^*(t_1)) \quad (2)$$

This is quite natural if we use the general economic interpretation explained in Section 9.6. In fact, if $x(t)$ denotes the capital stock of a firm, then according to (2), the shadow price of capital at the end of the planning period is equal to the marginal scrap value of the terminal stock.

NOTE 1 If $S(x) \equiv 0$, then (2) reduces to $p(t_1) = 0$, which is precisely as expected in a problem with no restrictions on $x(t_1)$.

One way to show that (2) is the correct transversality condition involves transforming problem (1) into one studied before. Indeed, suppose that $(x(t), u(t))$ is an admissible pair for the problem (1). Then $\frac{d}{dt}S(x(t)) = S'(x(t))\dot{x}(t) = S'(x(t))g(t, x(t), u(t))$. So by integration,

$$S(x(t_1)) - S(x(t_0)) = \int_{t_0}^{t_1} S'(x(t))g(t, x(t), u(t))\, dt$$

Here $S(x(t_0)) = S(x_0)$ is a constant, so if the objective function in (1) is replaced by

$$\int_{t_0}^{t_1} [f(t, x(t), u(t)) + S'(x(t))g(t, x(t), u(t))] \, dt \tag{3}$$

then the new problem is of a type studied previously with no scrap value, still with $x(t_1)$ free. Let the Hamiltonian for this new problem be $H_1 = f + S'(x)g + qg = f + (q + S'(x))g$, with adjoint variable q. An optimal pair $(x^*(t), u^*(t))$ for this problem must have the properties:

(a) $u^*(t)$ maximizes $H_1(t, x^*(t), u, q(t))$ for $u \in U$

(b) $\dot{q}(t) = -\partial H_1^*/\partial x, \quad q(t_1) = 0$

Define $p(t) = q(t) + S'(x^*(t))$. Problem 7 asks you to prove that, if $H = f + pg$ is the ordinary Hamiltonian associated with problem (1), then $u^*(t)$ maximizes $H(x^*(t), u, p(t))$ for $u \in U$ and $\dot{p}(t) = -\partial H^*/\partial x$, with $p(t_1) = 0$.

Appropriate concavity conditions again ensure optimality as shown in the next theorem.

THEOREM 9.10.1 (SUFFICIENT CONDITIONS WITH SCRAP VALUE)

Suppose $(x^*(t), u^*(t))$ is an admissible pair for the scrap-value problem (1) and suppose there exists a continuous function $p(t)$ such that for all t in $[t_0, t_1]$,

(A) $u^*(t)$ maximizes $H(t, x^*(t), u, p(t))$ w.r.t. $u \in U$

(B) $\dot{p}(t) = -H_x'(t, x^*(t), u^*(t), p(t)), \quad p(t_1) = S'(x^*(t_1))$

(C) $H(t, x, u, p(t))$ is concave in (x, u) and $S(x)$ is concave

Then $(x^*(t), u^*(t))$ solves the problem.

Proof: Suppose that $(x, u) = (x(t), u(t))$ is an arbitrary admissible pair. We must show that

$$D_u = \int_{t_0}^{t_1} f(t, x^*(t), u^*(t)) \, dt + S(x^*(t_1)) - \int_{t_0}^{t_1} f(t, x(t), u(t)) \, dt - S(x(t_1)) \geq 0$$

Because $S(x)$ is C^1 and concave, $S(x^*(t_1)) - S(x(t_1)) \geq S'(x(t_1))[x^*(t_1) - x(t_1)]$. Combining this with the inequality $\int_{t_0}^{t_1}(f^* - f) \, dt \geq p(t_1)(x(t_1 - x^*(t_1)))$ that was derived in the proof of the Theorem 9.7.1, we get

$$D_u \geq [p(t_1) - S'(x^*(t_1))](x(t_1) - x^*(t_1)) = 0$$

where the last equality follows from (B). So $D_u \geq 0$. ∎

NOTE 2 The theorem still holds if the concavity of H in (x, u) is replaced by the Arrow condition requiring $\widehat{H}(t, x, p(t))$ to exist and be concave in x.

EXAMPLE 1   Solve the problem

$$\max_{u\in(-\infty,\infty)}\left\{\int_0^1 -\tfrac{1}{2}u^2\,dt + \sqrt{x(1)}\right\}, \quad \dot{x} = x + u, \quad x(0) = 0, \quad x(1) \text{ free}$$

Solution: We have $H = -\tfrac{1}{2}u^2 + p(x+u)$ and $S(x) = \sqrt{x} = x^{1/2}$. Hence $H_u' = -u + p$ and $H_x' = p$. Since $u \in (-\infty, \infty)$, $H_u' = 0$, which gives $u = p$, and we have the following differential equations, $\dot{x} = x + u = x + p$, $\dot{p} = -H_x' = -p$. The latter has the solution $p(t) = Ae^{-t}$. Then $\dot{x} = x + p = x + Ae^{-t}$, and this linear differential equation has the solution $x = Be^t - \tfrac{1}{2}Ae^{-t}$, where the constant B is determined by $x(0) = B - \tfrac{1}{2}A = 0$. Hence, $B = \tfrac{1}{2}A$, so that $x(t) = \tfrac{1}{2}A(e^t - e^{-t})$. The constant A is determined by the transversality condition $p(1) = Ae^{-1} = S'(x(1)) = \tfrac{1}{2}(x(1))^{-1/2} = \tfrac{1}{2}[\tfrac{1}{2}A(e^1 - e^{-1})]^{-1/2}$. Solving for A we find $A = e[2(e^2 - 1)]^{-1/3}$. Thus we have the following candidate for an optimal solution:

$$u(t) = p(t) = Ae^{-t}, \quad x(t) = \tfrac{1}{2}A(e^t - e^{-t}), \quad A = e[2(e^2 - 1)]^{-1/3}$$

Because the Hamiltonian is concave in (x, u) and the scrap value function is concave in x, this is the solution.

Current Value Formulation

Many control problems in economics literature have the following structure:

$$\max_{u\in U\subseteq\mathbb{R}}\left\{\int_{t_0}^{t_1} f(t, x, u)e^{-rt}\,dt + S(x(t_1))e^{-rt_1}\right\}, \quad \dot{x} = g(t, x, u), \quad x(t_0) = x_0 \quad (4)$$

$$\text{(a) } x(t_1) = x_1 \quad \text{(b) } x(t_1) \geq x_1 \quad \text{or} \quad \text{(c) } x(t_1) \text{ free} \quad (5)$$

The new features compared to problem (1) are the discount factor (or interest rate) r, and the reintroduction of the alternative terminal conditions in the standard problem. (If $x(t_1)$ is fixed as in 5(a), the scrap value function is a constant.)

The current value Hamiltonian for the problem is

$$H^c(t, x, u, \lambda) = \lambda_0 f(t, x, u) + \lambda g(t, x, u) \quad (6)$$

and the correct necessary conditions are as follows:

THEOREM 9.10.2 (CURRENT VALUE MAXIMUM PRINCIPLE WITH SCRAP VALUE)

Suppose that the admissible pair $(x^*(t), u^*(t))$ solves problem (4)–(5). Then there exists a continuous function $\lambda(t)$ and a number λ_0, either 0 or 1, such that for all $t \in [t_0, t_1]$ we have $(\lambda_0, \lambda(t)) \neq (0, 0)$, and:

(A) $u = u^*(t)$ maximizes $H^c(t, x^*(t), u, \lambda(t))$ for $u \in U$

(B) $\dot{\lambda}(t) - r\lambda(t) = -\dfrac{\partial H^c(t, x^*(t), u^*(t), \lambda(t))}{\partial x}$

(C) Finally, the transversality conditions are:

    (a') $\lambda(t_1)$ no condition

    (b') $\lambda(t_1) \geq \lambda_0 \dfrac{\partial S(x^*(t_1))}{\partial x}$ (with = if $x^*(t_1) > x_1$)

    (c') $\lambda(t_1) = \lambda_0 \dfrac{\partial S(x^*(t_1))}{\partial x}$

The following sufficiency result is a straightforward extension of Theorem 9.10.1:

THEOREM 9.10.3 (SUFFICIENT CONDITIONS)

The conditions in Theorem 9.10.2 with $\lambda_0 = 1$ are sufficient if U is convex, $H^c(t, x, u, \lambda(t))$ is concave in (x, u), and $S(x)$ is concave in x.

EXAMPLE 2   Consider the following problem:

$$\max\left\{ \int_0^T (x - u^2)e^{-0.1t} \, dt + ax(T)e^{-0.1T} \right\}$$

$$\dot{x} = -0.4x + u, \quad x(0) = 1, \quad x(T) \text{ is free}, \quad u \in \mathbb{R}$$

where a is a positive constant. Solve the problem.

Solution: The current value Hamiltonian, with $\lambda_0 = 1$, is $H^c(t, x, u, \lambda) = x - u^2 + \lambda(-0.4x + u)$, which is concave in (x, u). Moreover, $S(x) = ax$ is linear, and hence concave in x. The conditions in the maximum principle are therefore sufficient. Because H^c is concave in u and $u \in \mathbb{R}$, the maximum of the Hamiltonian occurs when

$$\frac{\partial H^c(t, x^*(t), u^*(t), \lambda(t))}{\partial u} = -2u^*(t) + \lambda(t) = 0 \tag{i}$$

Next, the differential equation for λ is

$$\dot{\lambda}(t) - 0.1\lambda(t) = -\frac{\partial H^c}{\partial x} = -1 + 0.4\lambda(t) \tag{ii}$$

Because $x(T)$ is free and $S(x) = ax$, condition (C)(c') yields

$$\lambda(T) = a \tag{iii}$$

By integrating the linear differential equation (ii), using (iii), we obtain

$$\lambda(t) = (a - 2)e^{-0.5(T-t)} + 2$$

From (i), $u^*(t) = \frac{1}{2}\lambda(t)$. Because $x^*(t)$ satisfies the linear differential equation $\dot{x}^* = -0.4x^* + u^* = -0.4x^* + \frac{1}{2}(a - 2)e^{-0.5(T-t)} + 1$, with $x^*(0) = 1$, one has

$$x^*(t) = \frac{5}{2} + \frac{5}{9}(a - 2)e^{-0.5(T-t)} - \left(\frac{3}{2} + \frac{5}{9}(a - 2)e^{-0.5T}\right)e^{-0.4t}$$

All the sufficient conditions are satisfied, so this is the solution.

EXAMPLE 3   **(Optimal Feeding of Fish)** Let $x(t)$ be the weight of a fish at time t and let $P(t, x)$ be the price per kilogram of a fish whose weight is x at time t. Furthermore, let $u(t)$ denote the amount of fish food per unit of time measured as a proportion of the weight of a fish, and let c be a cost of a kilogram of fish food. If the interest rate is r, then the present value of the profit from feeding the fish and then catching it at the fixed time T is

$$x(T)P(T, x(T))e^{-rT} - \int_0^T cx(t)u(t)e^{-rt}\, dt \tag{i}$$

Suppose that

$$\dot{x}(t) = x(t)g(t, u(t)), \quad x(0) = x_0 > 0 \tag{ii}$$

so that the proportional rate of growth in the weight of the fish is a known function $g(t, u(t))$. Assuming that $u(t) \geq 0$, the natural problem is to find the feeding function $u^*(t)$ and the corresponding weight function $x^*(t)$ that maximize (i) subject to the constraint (ii) and $u(t) \geq 0$.

(a) Write down necessary conditions for $(x^*(t), u^*(t))$, with corresponding adjoint function $\lambda(t)$, to solve the problem. Deduce an equation that $u^*(t)$ must satisfy if $u^*(t) > 0$.

(b) Suppose $c(t) = c$, $P(t, x) = a_0 + a_1 x$, and $g(t, u) = a - be^{st}/u$, where all the constants are positive, with $s > r$. Characterize the only possible solution.

Solution: (a) The current value Hamiltonian is $H^c(t, x, u, \lambda) = -cxu + \lambda xg(t, u)$, and the scrap value function is $S(x) = xP(t, x)$. Thus $\partial H^c/\partial x = -cu + \lambda g(t, u)$, $\partial H^c/\partial u = x(-c + \lambda g_u'(t, u))$, and $S_x'(t, x) = P(t, x) + x P_x'(t, x)$.

According to the maximum principle, there exists a continuous function $\lambda(t)$ such that

$$u^*(t) \text{ maximizes } x^*(t)(-cu + \lambda(t)g(t, u)) \text{ for } u \geq 0 \tag{iii}$$

and

$$\dot{\lambda}(t) - r\lambda(t) = -\frac{\partial (H^c)^*}{\partial x} = cu^*(t) - \lambda(t)g(t, u^*(t)) \tag{iv}$$

Furthermore, condition (C)(c′) takes the form

$$\lambda(T) = P(T, x^*(T)) + x^*(T)P'_x(T, x^*(T)) \tag{v}$$

From (iii) it follows that if $u^*(t) > 0$, then $\partial(H^c)^*/\partial u = 0$. If $x^*(t)$ is not 0 then

$$\lambda(t)g'_u(t, u^*(t)) = c \tag{vi}$$

(b) We have $g'_u(t, u) = be^{st}/u^2$, so (vi) yields $\lambda(t)be^{st}/(u^*(t))^2 = c$. Then $\lambda(t) > 0$, and with $u^*(t) > 0$, we obtain

$$u^*(t) = \sqrt{b/c}\ e^{\frac{1}{2}st}(\lambda(t))^{1/2}$$

Equation (iv) is now $\dot{\lambda}(t) - r\lambda(t) = cu^*(t) - \lambda(t)[a - be^{st}/u^*(t)]$, which reduces to

$$\dot{\lambda}(t) = (r - a)\lambda(t) + 2\sqrt{bc}\ e^{\frac{1}{2}st}(\lambda(t))^{1/2} \tag{vii}$$

Finally, (v) reduces to

$$\lambda(T) = a_0 + a_1 x^*(T) + a_1 x^*(T) = a_0 + 2a_1 x^*(T) \tag{viii}$$

The standard trick for solving the Bernoulli equation (vii) is to introduce a new variable z defined by $z = \lambda^{1/2}$. (See (5.6.2).) Then $\lambda = z^2$, so $\dot{\lambda} = 2z\dot{z}$, and (vii) yields

$$2z\dot{z} = (r - a)z^2 + 2\sqrt{bc}\ e^{\frac{1}{2}st}z, \quad \text{or} \quad \dot{z} = \tfrac{1}{2}(r - a)z + \sqrt{bc}\ e^{\frac{1}{2}st}$$

According to (5.4.4) this has the solution

$$z = Ae^{\frac{1}{2}(r-a)t} + \sqrt{bc}\ e^{\frac{1}{2}(r-a)t}\int e^{\frac{1}{2}(s-r+a)t}\ dt = Ae^{\frac{1}{2}(r-a)t} + \frac{2\sqrt{bc}}{s - r + a}e^{\frac{1}{2}st}$$

where A is a constant. Since $u^*(t) = \sqrt{b/c}e^{\frac{1}{2}st}z$, we get

$$u^*(t) = A\sqrt{b/c}\ e^{\frac{1}{2}(s+r-a)t} + \frac{2b}{s - r + a}e^{st} \tag{ix}$$

Inserting $u^*(t)$ into (ii) yields a separable differential equation for $x^*(t)$, with a unique solution satisfying $x^*(0) = x_0$. The constant A is finally determined by equation (viii).

PROBLEMS FOR SECTION 9.10

1. Find the solution to the control problem

$$\max\left\{\int_0^1 (1 - tu - u^2)\,dt + 2x(1) + 3\right\}, \quad \dot{x} = u, \quad x(0) = 1, \quad u \in (-\infty, \infty)$$

2. In a study of savings and inheritance, Atkinson (1971) considers the problem

$$\max\left\{\int_0^T U(rA(t) + w - u(t))e^{-\rho t}\,dt + e^{-\rho T}\varphi(A(T))\right\}, \quad \dot{A} = u, \quad A(0) = A_0$$

An economic interpretation is given in Example 8.5.3, except that the objective function now includes an extra term which measures the individual's discounted benefit from bequeathing $A(T)$. Suppose that $\varphi' > 0$, $\varphi'' < 0$. Give a set of sufficient conditions for the solution of this problem.

3. Solve the following control problem from economic growth theory:

$$\max\left\{\int_0^{10}(1-s)\sqrt{k}\,dt + 10\sqrt{k(10)}\right\}, \qquad \dot{k} = s\sqrt{k}, \quad k(0) = 1, \quad s \in [0,1]$$

where $k = k(t)$ is the capital stock, and $s = s(t)$ is the savings ratio. (See Problem 9.7.2.)

4. (a) Solve the problem

$$\max\left\{\int_0^1(x-u)\,dt + \tfrac{1}{2}x(1)\right\}, \qquad \dot{x} = u, \quad x(0) = \tfrac{1}{2}, \quad x(1) \text{ free}, \quad u \in [0,1]$$

(b) Solve the problem with the objective function $\int_0^1(x-u)\,dt - \tfrac{1}{4}(x(1)-2)^2$.

5. Consider the problem:

$$\max\left\{\int_0^T -u^2\,dt - x(T)^2\right\}, \qquad \dot{x} = -x + u, \quad x(0) = x_0, \quad u \in \mathbb{R}$$

(a) Solve the problem using Theorem 9.10.3.

(b) Compute the optimal value function, $V(x_0, T)$, and show that $\partial V/\partial x_0 = p(0)$ and $\partial V/\partial T = H^*(T)$.

6. Solve the following problem using the current value formulation

$$\max_{u\in\mathbb{R}}\left\{\int_0^T -e^{-rt}(x-u)^2\,dt - e^{-rT}x(T)^2\right\} \text{ s.t. } \dot{x} = u - x + a, \quad x(0) = 0, \quad x(T) \text{ free}$$

The constants r, a, and T are all positive.

7. Consider the control problem

$$\max \int_{t_0}^{t_1}[f(t,x,u) + S'(x)g(t,x,u)]\,dt, \qquad \dot{x} = g(t,x,u), \quad x(t_0) = x_0, \quad u \in U$$

(See (3).) Let the Hamiltonian be $H_1 = f + S'(x)g + qg = f + (q + S'(x))g$, with q as the adjoint variable. Then an optimal pair (x^*, u^*) for this problem must satisfy conditions (a) and (b) above Theorem 9.10.1. Define $p = q + S'(x^*)$ and let $H = f + pg$. Prove that properties (a) and (b) imply that u^* maximizes $H(t, x^*, u, p)$ for $u \in U$, while $\dot{p} = -\partial H^*/\partial x$, with $p(t_1) = S'(x^*(t_1))$. Thus conditions (A)–(C) in Theorem 9.10.1 are satisfied.

9.11 Infinite Horizon

Most of the optimal growth models appearing in literature have an infinite time horizon. The Nobel laureate Ragnar Frisch (1970) has the following to say about infinite horizon growth models:

> Questions of convergence under an infinite time horizon will depend so much on epsilontic refinements in the system of assumptions—and on the infinite constancy of these refinements—that we are humanly speaking absolutely certain of getting infinite time horizon results which have no relevance to concrete reality. And in particular we are absolutely certain of getting irrelevant results if such epsilontic exercises are made under the assumption of a constant technology. "In the long run we are all dead". These words by Keynes ought to be engraved in marble and put on the desk of all epsilontologists in growth theory under an infinite horizon.

Clearly, choosing an infinite horizon makes sense in economic models only if the distant future has no significant influence on the optimal path for the near future in which we are most interested. Nevertheless, the infinite horizon assumption often does simplify formulas and conclusions, though at the expense of some new mathematical problems that need to be sorted out.

A typical infinite horizon optimal control problem in economics literature takes the following form:

$$\max \int_{t_0}^{\infty} f(t, x(t), u(t)) e^{-rt} \, dt, \quad \dot{x}(t) = g(t, x(t), u(t)), \ x(t_0) = x_0, \ u(t) \in U \quad (1)$$

Often no condition is placed on $x(t)$ as $t \to \infty$, but many problems do impose the constraint

$$\lim_{t \to \infty} x(t) \geq x_1 \qquad (x_1 \text{ is a fixed number}) \tag{2}$$

The pair $(x(t), u(t))$ is *admissible* if it satisfies $\dot{x}(t) = g(t, x(t), u(t))$, $x(t_0) = x_0$, $u(t) \in U$, along with (2) when this is imposed. Suppose the integral (1) converges whenever the pair $(x(t), u(t))$ is admissible. For example, the integral will converge for all admissible $(x(t), u(t))$ if r is a positive constant, and if there exists a number M such that $|f(t, x, u)| \leq M$ for all (x, u).

One can then show (Halkin (1974)) that all the necessary conditions in the maximum principle hold, except the transversality conditions. With no transversality condition we get too many solution candidates.

NOTE 1 It is tempting to assume that all results for finite horizon problems can be carried over in a simple way to the infinite horizon case. This is wrong. For example, in a finite horizon problem with $x(t_1)$ free, the transversality condition is $p(t_1) = 0$. However, with no terminal condition, the "natural" transversality condition, $p(t) \to 0$ as $t \to \infty$, is not correct. A well known counterexample is due to Halkin (1974). This example also shows that the condition $p(t)x(t) \to 0$ is *not* a necessary condition for optimality, contrary to a widespread belief in economic literature, including some popular textbooks.

However, in economic models with $x(\infty)$ free, it is in most cases a sensible working hypothesis that $p(t)$ does tend to 0 as t tends to ∞. But ultimately, this must be confirmed.

Because of the presence of the discount factor e^{-rt} in the problem above, it is convenient to use the current value formulation with the current value Hamiltonian

$$H^c(t, x, u, \lambda) = \lambda_0 f(t, x, u) + \lambda g(t, x, u)$$

and with λ as the current value shadow price.

THEOREM 9.11.1 (SUFFICIENT CONDITIONS WITH AN INFINITE HORIZON)

Suppose that an admissible pair $(x^*(t), u^*(t))$ for problem (1), with or without terminal condition (2), satisfies the following conditions for some $\lambda(t)$ for all $t \geq t_0$, with $\lambda_0 = 1$:

(a) $u^*(t)$ maximizes $H^c(t, x^*(t), u, \lambda(t))$ w.r.t. $u \in U$

(b) $\dot{\lambda}(t) - r\lambda = -\partial H^c(t, x^*(t), u^*(t), \lambda(t))/\partial x$

(c) $H^c(t, x, u, \lambda(t))$ is concave w.r.t. (x, u)

(d) $\lim_{t \to \infty} \lambda(t)e^{-rt}[x(t) - x^*(t)] \geq 0$ for all admissible $x(t)$

Then $(x^*(t), u^*(t))$ is optimal.

Proof: For any admissible pair $(x(t), u(t))$ and for all $t \geq t_0$, define

$$D_u(t) = \int_{t_0}^{t} f(\tau, x^*(\tau), u^*(\tau))e^{-r\tau}\, d\tau - \int_{t_0}^{t} f(\tau, x(\tau), u(\tau))e^{-r\tau}\, d\tau = \int_{t_0}^{t} (f^* - f)e^{-r\tau}\, d\tau$$

in simplified notation. Now, $f^* = (H^c)^* - \lambda g^* = (H^c)^* - \lambda \dot{x}^*$ and $f = H^c - \lambda \dot{x}$, so

$$D_u(t) = \int_{t_0}^{t} [(H^c)^* - H^c]e^{-r\tau}\, d\tau + \int_{t_0}^{t} \lambda e^{-r\tau}(\dot{x} - \dot{x}^*)\, d\tau$$

By concavity of H^c, one has

$$(H^c)^* - H^c \geq -\frac{\partial(H^c)^*}{\partial x}(x - x^*) + \frac{\partial(H^c)^*}{\partial u}(u^* - u)$$

$$= (\dot{\lambda} - r\lambda)(x - x^*) + \frac{\partial(H^c)^*}{\partial u}(u^* - u)$$

so

$$D_u(t) \geq \int_{t_0}^{t} e^{-r\tau}[(\dot{\lambda} - r\lambda)(x - x^*) + \lambda(\dot{x} - \dot{x}^*)]\, d\tau + \int_{t_0}^{t} \frac{\partial(H^c)^*}{\partial u}(u^* - u)\, d\tau$$

As in the proof of Theorem 9.7.1, we see that the second integral is ≥ 0 and so

$$D_u(t) \geq \int_{t_0}^{t} \frac{d}{d\tau}[e^{-r\tau}\lambda(\tau)(x(\tau) - x^*(\tau))]\, d\tau = \Big|_{t_0}^{t} e^{-r\tau}\lambda(\tau)(x(\tau) - x^*(\tau))$$

The contribution from the lower limit of integration is 0 because $x^*(t_0) - x(t_0) = x_0 - x_0 = 0$, so $D_u(t) \geq e^{-rt}\lambda(t)(x(t) - x^*(t))$. Passing to the limit as $t \to \infty$ in this inequality and using (d), one concludes that $(x^*(t), u^*(t))$ is optimal. ∎

NOTE 2   Condition (d) is well known in economics literature, but is often not properly checked. Note that the inequality (d) must be shown for *all* admissible $x(t)$, which is often problematic. Suppose for example that $\lim_{t\to\infty} \lambda(t)e^{-rt} \geq 0$, $\lim_{t\to\infty} \lambda(t)e^{-rt}x^*(t) = 0$, and $x(t) \geq 0$ for all t. Do these conditions ensure that (d) is satisfied? The answer is no. For a counterexample consider what happens when $\lambda(t) = -1$, $r = 1$, $x(t) = e^t$, and $x^*(t) = 1$. Then $\lambda(t)e^{-t}[x(t) - x^*(t)] = -e^{-t}(e^t - 1) = e^{-t} - 1 \to -1$ as $t \to \infty$.

NOTE 3   Suppose the terminal condition is $\lim_{t\to\infty} x(t) \geq x_1$. Rewrite the bracketed expression in (d) as

$$\lambda(t)e^{-rt}(x(t) - x_1) + \lambda(t)e^{-rt}(x_1 - x^*(t)) \tag{*}$$

We claim that, provided the following three conditions are all satisfied, then condition (d) *is* satisfied.

(A) $\lim_{t\to\infty} \lambda(t)e^{-rt}(x_1 - x^*(t)) \geq 0$

(B) There exists a number M such that $|\lambda(t)e^{-rt}| \leq M$ for all $t \geq t_0$

(C) There exists a number t' such that $\lambda(t) \geq 0$ for all $t \geq t'$

Because of (A), in order to prove (d), it suffices to show that the first term in (*) tends to a number ≥ 0. If $\lim_{t\to\infty} x(t) = x_1$, then $x(t) - x_1$ tends to 0 as t tends to ∞, so because of (B), the first term in (*) tends to 0. If $\lim_{t\to\infty} x(t) > x_1$, then $x(t) - x_1 > 0$ for t sufficiently large. Then, because of (C), $\lambda(t)e^{-rt}(x(t) - x_1)$ tends to a number ≥ 0. We conclude that, if (A)–(C) are all satisfied for all admissible pairs, then (d) holds.

NOTE 4   Suppose that we introduce additional conditions for admissibility in Theorem 9.11.1. Then the inequality in Theorem 9.11.1(d) needs to hold only for pairs satisfying the additional conditions.

In particular, if it is required that $x(t) \geq x_1$ for all t, then it suffices to check conditions (A) and (C) in Note 3. This result is referred to as the **Malinvaud transversality conditions**.

EXAMPLE 1   Consider the problem

$$\max \int_0^\infty -u^2 e^{-rt}\, dt, \quad \dot{x} = ue^{-at}, \quad x(0) = 0, \quad \lim_{t\to\infty} x(t) \geq K, \quad u \in \mathbb{R}$$

The constants r, a, and K are positive, with $a > r/2$. Find the optimal solution.

Solution: The current value Hamiltonian is $H^c = -u^2 + \lambda u e^{-at}$, which is obviously concave in x and u. We find $\partial H^c/\partial x = 0$ and $\partial H^c/\partial u = -2u + \lambda e^{-at}$. It follows that $u = \frac{1}{2}\lambda e^{-at}$. The differential equation for λ is $\dot{\lambda} - r\lambda = -\partial H^c/\partial x = 0$, with the solution $\lambda = Ae^{rt}$, where A is a constant. Thus $u = \frac{1}{2}Ae^{(r-a)t}$. The differential equation for x then becomes

$$\dot{x} = ue^{-at} = \tfrac{1}{2}Ae^{(r-2a)t}, \quad x(0) = 0, \quad \text{with solution} \quad x(t) = \frac{A}{2(2a - r)}(1 - e^{(r-2a)t})$$

Thus $x(t)$ converges to $A/2(2a-r)$ as t approaches ∞. Hence we must have $A/2(2a-r) \geq K$, or $A \geq 2K(2a-r)$. In particular, $A \geq 0$, and (B) and (C) in Note 3 are satisfied. To check condition (A) requires considering

$$\lambda(t)e^{-rt}\left(K - x(t)\right) = Ae^{rt}e^{-rt}\left[K - \frac{A}{2(2a-r)}(1 - e^{(r-2a)t})\right]$$

which tends to $A[K - A/2(2a-r)]$ as t tends to ∞. We conclude that if we choose $A = 2K(2a-r)$, all the conditions in Theorem 9.11.1 are satisfied and we have found the optimal solution. Note that $p(t) = \lambda e^{-rt} = 2K(2a-r)$, which does not tend to 0 as t tends to ∞. Nor does $p(t)x^*(t)$.

EXAMPLE 2   Consider the following version of Example 8.5.3:

$$\max \int_0^\infty \frac{1}{1-\delta}[rA(t) + w - u(t)]^{1-\delta}e^{-\rho t}\, dt$$

$$\dot{A}(t) = u(t), \quad A(0) = A_0 > 0, \quad \lim_{t\to\infty} A(t) \geq -w/r, \quad u \in \mathbb{R}$$

Assume that $0 < \delta < 1$ and $0 < r < \rho$, and then solve the problem.

Solution: The current value Hamiltonian is $H^c = \frac{1}{1-\delta}(rA + w - u)^{1-\delta} + \lambda u$, and the differential equation for $\lambda(t)$ is

$$\dot{\lambda}(t) - \rho\lambda(t) = -\frac{\partial(H^c)^*}{\partial A} = -r\left[rA^*(t) + w - u^*(t)\right]^{-\delta} \tag{i}$$

The control function $u^*(t)$ maximizes

$$\varphi(u) = \frac{1}{1-\delta}[rA^*(t) + w - u]^{1-\delta} + \lambda u \quad \text{for} \quad u \in \mathbb{R} \tag{ii}$$

Now the function H^c is concave in (A, u), as a concave function of a linear function. (Alternatively, look at the Hessian.) In particular, $\varphi(u)$ is concave in u, so $u^*(t)$ maximizes $\varphi(u)$ provided $\varphi'(u^*(t)) = 0$, or if

$$-[rA^*(t) + w - u^*(t)]^{-\delta} + \lambda(t) = 0, \quad \text{or} \quad u^*(t) = rA^*(t) + w - \lambda(t)^{-1/\delta} \tag{iii}$$

Combining (i) and (iii), it follows that $\dot{\lambda}(t) - \rho\lambda(t) = -r\lambda(t)$, so $\dot{\lambda} = (\rho - r)\lambda(t)$, with solution

$$\lambda(t) = C_1 e^{(\rho-r)t} \tag{iv}$$

for some constant C_1. Because $\dot{A}^* = u^*$, it follows that

$$\dot{A}^*(t) - rA^*(t) = w - C_1^{-1/\delta}e^{-at} \quad \text{where} \quad a = (\rho - r)/\delta$$

The general solution of this linear differential equation is

$$A^*(t) = C_2 e^{rt} - w/r + C_1^{-1/\delta}e^{-at}/(a + r)$$

We must now find suitable values of the constants C_1 and C_2. It seems reasonable to assume that $\lim_{t\to\infty} A^*(t) = -w/r$. This is only possible if $C_2 = 0$. Then C_1 is determined by the initial condition $A^*(0) = A_0$, which gives $A_0 = -w/r + C_1^{-1/\delta}/(a+r)$. Hence we find that $C_1^{-1/\delta}/(a+r) = A_0 + w/r$. We therefore have the following candidate for an optimum:

$$A^*(t) = (A_0 + w/r)e^{-at} - w/r, \quad u^*(t) = -a(A_0 + w/r)e^{-at}, \quad \lambda(t) = \bar{\lambda}e^{(\rho-r)t} \quad \text{(v)}$$

where $\bar{\lambda} = \big((a+r)(A_0 + w/r)\big)^{-\delta}$.

It remains to verify (d) in Theorem 9.11.1. According to Note 3 it suffices to show that conditions (A), (B), and (C) are satisfied. In our case (A) holds because

$$\lim_{t\to\infty} \lambda(t)(w/r + A^*(t)) = \bar{\lambda}(A_0 + w/r)\lim_{t\to\infty} e^{-(r+a)t} = 0$$

and (B) and (C) are evidently satisfied. Hence we have shown that $(A^*(t), u^*(t))$ solves the problem.

Many economists seem to believe that for problems with an infinite horizon, no necessary transversality conditions are generally valid. This is wrong. But certain growth conditions are needed for such conditions to hold. A special result of this type is given in the next theorem. (See Seierstad and Sydsæter (1987), Section 3.9, Theorem 16 for a more general result. Please correct a misprint in that theorem: Replace $b > k$ by $b > (n-m)k$.)

THEOREM 9.11.2 (NECESSARY CONDITION FOR AN INFINITE HORIZON)

Assume that $(x^*(t), u^*(t))$ is optimal in problem (1), with no condition on the limiting behaviour of $x(t)$ as $t \to \infty$. Assume that $\int_{t_0}^{\infty} |f(t, x(t), u(t))|dt < \infty$ for all admissible $(x(t), u(t))$. Suppose too that there exist positive constants A and k with $r > k$ such that

$$|\partial f(t, x, u^*(t))/\partial x| \le A \text{ for all } x \tag{3}$$

and

$$\partial g(t, x, u^*(t))/\partial x \le k \text{ for all } x \tag{4}$$

Then there exists a continuous function $\lambda(t)$ such that, with $\lambda_0 = 1$,

$$H^c(t, x^*(t), u, \lambda(t)) \le H^c(t, x^*(t), u^*(t), \lambda(t)) \text{ for all } u \in U \tag{5}$$

The function $\lambda(t)$ equals $\lim_{T\to\infty} \lambda(t, T)$, where $\lambda(t, T)$ is the solution of

$$\dot{\lambda} - r\lambda = -\partial H(t, x^*(t), u^*(t), \lambda)/\partial x, \quad \lambda(T, T) = 0 \tag{6}$$

NOTE 5 In fact, if $G(t)$ is a set containing $x(t)$ for all admissible $x(t)$, and N is some positive number, then, for any t, (3) need only hold for $x \in B(x^*(t), 2Ne^{kt}) \cap G(t)$ and (4) need only hold for $|x| \ge N, x \in G(t)$.

1. Solve the problem

$$\max \int_0^\infty (\ln u)\, e^{-0.2t}\, dt, \quad \dot{x} = 0.1x - u, \quad x(0) = 10, \quad \lim_{t \to \infty} x(t) \geq 0, \quad u > 0$$

using Theorem 9.11.1 and Note 3.

2. Find the only possible solution to the problem

$$\max \int_0^\infty x(2 - u)e^{-t}\, dt, \quad \dot{x} = uxe^{-t}, \quad x(0) = 1, \quad x(\infty) \text{ is free}, \quad u \in [0, 1]$$

3. Compute the optimal value V of the objective function in Example 2. How does V change when ρ increases and when w increases? Show that $\partial V / \partial A_0 = \lambda(0)$.

4. Solve the problem

$$\max \int_{-1}^\infty (x - u)e^{-t}\, dt, \quad \dot{x} = ue^{-t}, \quad x(-1) = 0, \quad x(\infty) \text{ is free}, \quad u \in [0, 1]$$

9.12 Phase Diagrams

Consider the following problem

$$\max \int_{t_0}^{t_1} f(x, u)e^{-rt}\, dt, \quad \dot{x} = g(x, u), \quad x(t_0) = x_0, \quad u \in U \subseteq \mathbb{R} \tag{1}$$

with the standard end constraints, and with t_1 finite or ∞. In this case the functions f and g do not depend explicitly on t. Nor, therefore, does the current value Hamiltonian H^c.

Suppose that $u = u(x, \lambda)$ maximizes $H^c = f(x, u) + \lambda g(x, u)$ w.r.t. u for $u \in U$. Replacing u by $u = u(x, \lambda)$ in the differential equations for x and λ gives

$$\begin{aligned} \dot{x} &= F(x, \lambda) \\ \dot{\lambda} &= G(x, \lambda) \end{aligned} \tag{2}$$

This is an *autonomous* system that is simpler to handle than one in which $\dot{x}$ and $\dot{\lambda}$ depend explicitly on t as well as on x and λ. In particular, *phase plane analysis* (see Section 6.7) can be used to shed light on the evolution of an autonomous system even when explicit solutions are not obtainable. Example 9.9.1 showed a simple case.

We study two examples.

EXAMPLE 1   Write down the system of equations (2), and draw a phase diagram for the problem

$$\max \int_0^\infty (x - u^2)e^{-0.1t}\, dt, \quad \dot{x} = -0.4x + u, \quad x(0) = 1, \quad x(\infty) \text{ is free}, \quad u \in (0, \infty)$$

Try to find the solution of the problem. (See Example 9.10.2.)

Solution: In this case the Hamiltonian $H^c(t, x, u, \lambda) = (x - u^2) + \lambda(-0.4x + u)$ is concave in (x, u). The maximization of H^c w.r.t. u gives $u = 0.5\lambda$, assuming that λ is > 0. (We try this assumption in the following.) Hence, $\dot{x} = -0.4x + 0.5\lambda$. System (2) is here

$$\dot{x} = -0.4x + 0.5\lambda, \quad x(0) = 1$$
$$\dot{\lambda} = 0.5\lambda - 1 \tag{$*$}$$

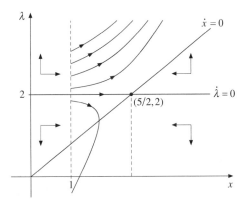

Figure 1: Phase diagram for system ($*$) in Example 1.

Figure 1 shows a phase diagram for ($*$). Any path $(x(t), \lambda(t))$ that solves the problem must start at some point on the vertical line $x = 1$, but no restrictions are imposed on $x(t)$ as $t \to \infty$. If we start above or below the line $\lambda = 2$, it appears that $(x(t), \lambda(t))$ will "wander off to infinity", which makes it difficult to satisfy requirement (d) in Theorem 9.11.1.

In fact, the general solution of ($*$) is $x^*(t) = \frac{5}{9}Ae^{0.5t} + \frac{5}{2} - (\frac{5}{9}A + \frac{3}{2})e^{-0.4t}$ and $\lambda(t) = Ae^{0.5t} + 2$. The expression we need to consider in Theorem 9.11.1(d) is the difference of the two terms, $\lambda(t)e^{-0.1t}x(t)$ and $\lambda(t)e^{-0.1t}x^*(t)$. For large values of t, the latter product is dominated by the term $\frac{5}{9}A^2e^{0.9t}$, which tends to infinity as t tends to infinity when $A \neq 0$; and that does not seem promising. It approaches 0 as t approaches infinity if $A = 0$ (then $\lambda \equiv 2$), and then the product is equal to $5e^{-0.1t} - 3e^{-0.5t}$, which does approach 0 as t approaches infinity. It is easy to see that $x(t) > 0$ for all $t \geq 0$ so $\lambda(t)e^{-0.1t}x(t)$ is > 0 for all $t \geq 0$. It follows that condition (d) in Theorem 9.11.1 is satisfied, and $x^*(t) = -\frac{3}{2}e^{-0.4t} + \frac{5}{2}$ is therefore optimal.

Coming back to the phase diagram, if we start at the point $(x, \lambda) = (1, 2)$, then $\lambda(t) \equiv 2$, while $x(t)$ converges to the value $\frac{5}{2}$, which is x-coordinate of the point of intersection between the curves $\dot{\lambda} = 0$ and $\dot{x} = 0$. The phase diagram therefore suggests the optimal solution to the problem.

The point $(\frac{5}{2}, 2)$ is an equilibrium point for system ($*$). Let us see what Theorem 6.9.1 says about this equilibrium point. Defining $f(x, \lambda) = -0.4x + 0.5\lambda$ and $g(x, \lambda) = 0.5\lambda - 1$, we find that the determinant of the Jacobian matrix in Theorem 6.9.1 is

$$\begin{vmatrix} -0.4 & 0.5 \\ 0 & 0.5 \end{vmatrix} = -0.2 < 0$$

so $(\frac{5}{2}, 2)$ really is a saddle point.

EXAMPLE 2   Consider an economy with capital stock $K = K(t)$ and production per unit of time $Y = Y(t)$, where $Y = aK - bK^2$, with a and b as positive constants. Consumption is $C > 0$, whereas $Y - C = aK^2 - bK - C$ is investment. Over the period $[0, \infty)$, the objective is to maximize total discounted utility. Specially, the problem is

$$\int_0^\infty \frac{1}{1-v} C^{1-v} e^{-rt} dt, \quad \dot{K} = aK - bK^2 - C, \quad K(0) = K_0 > 0$$

where $a > r > 0$ and $v > 0$, and C is the control variable. We require that

$$\lim_{t \to \infty} K(t) \geq 0$$

The current value Hamiltonian is $H^c = \frac{1}{1-v} C^{1-v} + \lambda(aK - bK^2 - C)$. An interior maximum of H^c requires $\partial H^c / \partial c = 0$, i.e.

$$C^{-v} = \lambda \tag{i}$$

The differential equation for $\lambda = \lambda(t)$ is $\dot{\lambda} = -\lambda(a - 2bK) + r\lambda$, or

$$\dot{\lambda} = \lambda(r - a + 2bK) = 2b\lambda\left(K - \frac{a-r}{2b}\right) \tag{ii}$$

Now (i) implies that $C = \lambda^{-1/v}$, which inserted into the differential equation for K yields

$$\dot{K} = aK - bK^2 - \lambda^{-1/v} \tag{iii}$$

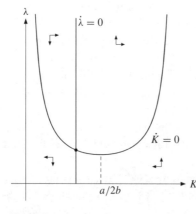

Figure 2

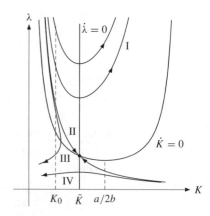

Figure 3

Figure 2 presents a phase diagram for the system given by (ii) and (iii). We see that $\dot{K} = 0$ for $\lambda = \left(aK - bK^2\right)^{-v}$, with $v > 0$. Here $z = aK - bK^2$ represents a concave parabola with $z = 0$ for $K = 0$ and for $K = a/b$. For $z = 0$, one has $\lambda = \infty$. The graph of $\dot{K} = 0$ is symmetrical about $K = a/2b$. Note that $\dot{\lambda} = 0$ when $K = (a - r)/2b$, which gives a straight line parallel to the λ-axis. Because $0 < (a - r)/2b < a/2b$, the graph of $\dot{\lambda} = 0$ will be as suggested in the figure. The equilibrium point $(\bar{K}, \bar{\lambda})$ is given by $\bar{K} = (a - r)/2b$, $\bar{\lambda} = \left[(a^2 - r^2)/4b\right]^{-v}$.

Figure 2 shows the $K\lambda$-plane divided into four parts. The arrows indicate the directions of the integral curves in each of these four parts. From (ii) we see that $K > (a - r)/2b$ implies $\dot{\lambda} > 0$, whereas $K < (a - r)/2b$ implies $\dot{\lambda} < 0$. Also, the right-hand side of (iii), $aK - bK^2 - \lambda^{-1/v}$, increases as λ increases for each fixed K, so that $\dot{K} > 0$ above the curve $\dot{K} = 0$, and $\dot{K} < 0$ below this curve.

Figure 3 shows some integral curves that $(K(t), \lambda(t))$ could follow as t increases. In this figure we have assumed that $K_0 < \bar{K}$. Of particular interest are paths that start at $K = K_0$, but other curves, which start with larger values of K, are also drawn. Note that, although K_0 is known, the quantity $\lambda(0)$ must be regarded as an unknown parameter. In this particular problem $\lambda(0)$ can be determined as follows: If $\lambda(0)$ is large, the point $(K(t), \lambda(t))$ starts high up on the line $K = K_0$ and moves along a curve like that marked I in Figure 3. If $\lambda(0)$ is small, then $(K(t), \lambda(t))$ starts low down on the line $K = K_0$ and moves along a the curve like III in the figure. If $\lambda(0)$ is even smaller, and $(K_0, \lambda(0))$ lies below the curve $\dot{K} = 0$, then $(K(t), \lambda(t))$ moves steadily "southwest", like curve IV. At some point on the line $K = K_0$, continuity suggests that there should be some particular value $\lambda^*(0)$ of $\lambda(0)$ such that the resultant curve is of type II, which converges to the stationary point $(\bar{K}, \bar{\lambda})$.

Here is a more precise argument: Curve I was obtained using a high initial value for $\lambda(0)$. Along curve I the point $(K(t), \lambda(t))$ moves down to the right until it reaches a minimum point where it crosses the line $\dot{\lambda} = 0$. Let $\lambda(0)$ decrease. Then curve I shifts downwards. Its minimum point on the line $\dot{\lambda} = 0$ will then shift downwards to the equilibrium point $(\bar{K}, \bar{\lambda})$. Actually, $\lambda^*(0)$ is precisely that value of $\lambda(0)$ which makes this minimum occur at the point $(\bar{K}, \bar{\lambda})$. This initial value $\lambda^*(0)$ leads to a special path $(K^*(t), \lambda^*(t))$. Both $\dot{K}^*(t)$ and $\dot{\lambda}^*(t)$ approach zero as $t \to \infty$. For all finite t, the path $(K^*(t), \lambda^*(t))$ never reaches the point $(\bar{K}, \bar{\lambda})$, but $(K^*(t), \lambda^*(t)) \to (\bar{K}, \bar{\lambda})$ as $t \to \infty$.

So far we have argued that the conditions of the maximum principle are satisfied along a curve $(K^*(t), \lambda^*(t))$ of type II in Figure 3, where $K^*(t) \to \bar{K}$ and $\lambda^*(t) \to \bar{\lambda}$ as $t \to \infty$. Let us prove that this candidate solution is optimal.

The present value Hamiltonian H^c is concave as a function of (K, C). With $\lambda(t)$ given and $C^*(t) = (\lambda(t))^{-1/v}$, the first-order condition for a maximum of H^c is satisfied, and because H^c is concave in C, it reaches a maximum at $C^*(t)$. Moreover, (A) in Note 9.11.3 is also satisfied: $\lambda(t)e^{-rt}K^*(t) \to 0$ as $t \to \infty$ and $\lim_{t\to\infty} \lambda(t)e^{-rt}K(t) \geq 0$ as $\lim_{t\to\infty} K(t) \geq 0$, because $\lambda(t)e^{-rt}$ is positive and bounded (it even approaches 0). These properties imply that

$$\lim_{t\to\infty} \lambda(t)e^{-rt}[K(t) - K^*(t)] \geq 0$$

for all admissible $K(t)$. This verifies all the sufficient conditions, so $(K^*(t), C^*(t))$ is optimal.[7]

Any solution of the system (ii) and (iii) will depend on K_0 and on $\lambda(0) = \lambda^0$, so it can be denoted by $K(t) = K(t; K_0, \lambda^0)$ and $\lambda(t) = \lambda(t; K_0, \lambda^0)$. In this problem, K_0 is given, whereas λ^0 is determined by the requirement that $\lim_{t\to\infty} \lambda(t; K_0, \lambda^0) = \bar{\lambda}$. Figure 3 actually shows *two* curves of type II that converge to $(\bar{K}, \bar{\lambda})$. The alternative solution of the differential equations converges to $(\bar{K}, \bar{\lambda})$ from the "southeast". This path does not solve

---

[7] We did not formally require $K(t) \geq 0$ for all t, but it is indeed a natural requirement. Then we need to check only conditions (A) and (C) in Note 9.11.3.

the optimization problem, however, because it must start from the wrong value of K at time $t = 0$. (It *does* solve the problem when $K_0 > \bar{K}$, however.)

The equilibrium point $(\bar{K}, \bar{\lambda}) = \left((a - r)/2b, \left[(a^2 - r^2)/4b\right]^{-v}\right)$ is an example of a *saddle point* (see Section 6.9). We show this by applying Theorem 6.9.1. To do so, define the functions $f(K, \lambda) = aK - bK^2 - \lambda^{-1/v}$ and $g(K, \lambda) = 2b\lambda(K - (a-r)/2b)$ corresponding to the right-hand sides of (iii) and (ii) respectively. Then at the point $(\bar{K}, \bar{\lambda})$ one has $\partial f/\partial K = a - 2b\bar{K} = r$, $\partial f/\partial \lambda = (1/v)\bar{\lambda}^{-1/v-1}$, $\partial g/\partial K = 2b\bar{\lambda}$ and $\partial g/\partial \lambda = 2b(\bar{K} - (a-r)/2b) = 0$. The determinant of the matrix $\mathbf{A}$ in Theorem 6.9.1 is therefore

$$\begin{vmatrix} r & (1/v)\bar{\lambda}^{-1/v-1} \\ 2b\bar{\lambda} & 0 \end{vmatrix} = -\frac{2b}{v}\bar{\lambda}^{-1/v} < 0$$

This confirms that $(\bar{K}, \bar{\lambda})$ really *is* a saddle point.

PROBLEMS FOR SECTION 9.12

1. (a) Consider the problem

$$\max \int_0^\infty (ax - \tfrac{1}{2}u^2)e^{-rt}\, dt, \qquad \dot{x} = -bx + u, \quad x(0) = x_0, \quad x(\infty) \text{ free}, \quad u \in \mathbb{R}$$

where a, r, and b are all positive. Write down the current value Hamiltonian H^c for this problem, and determine the system (2). What is the equilibrium point?

(b) Draw a phase diagram for $(x(t), \lambda(t))$ and show that for the two solutions which converge to the equilibrium point, $\lambda(t)$ is a constant.

(c) Use sufficient conditions to solve the problem.

(d) Show that $\partial V/\partial x_0 = \lambda(0)$, where V is the optimal value function.

2. In Problem 9.9.1 we studied a problem closely related to

$$\max \int_0^T \left(-x^2 - \tfrac{1}{2}u^2\right)e^{-2t}\, dt, \quad \dot{x} = x + u, \quad x(0) = 1, \quad x(T) \geq 0, \quad u \in \mathbb{R}$$

Solve this problem in the case $T = \infty$. (*Hint:* $\lim_{t\to\infty} p(t) = 0$.)

3. (a) Consider the problem

$$\max \int_0^T e^{-rt} \ln c(t)\, dt$$

$$\dot{K}(t) = A(K(t))^\alpha - c(t), \quad K(0) = K_0, \quad K(T) = K_T$$

where the constants A and r are positive, and $\alpha \in (0, 1)$. Here $K(t)$ denotes the capital stock of an economy and the control variable $c(t)$ denotes consumption at time t. The horizon T is fixed and finite. Prove that if $K = K^*(t) > 0$ and $c = c^*(t) > 0$ solve the problem, then

$$\dot{K} = AK^\alpha - c$$
$$\dot{c} = c(\alpha AK^{\alpha-1} - r)$$

(b) Suppose $A = 2$, $\alpha = 1/2$, and $r = 0.05$. Prove that the equilibrium is a saddle point. In Problem 6.7.3 you were asked to draw a phase diagram of the system.

(c) Indicate in the diagram for Problem 6.7.3 a possible integral curve for the case $K_0 = 100$ and $K_T = 600$? What is the solution when $K_0 = 100$ and $T = \infty$, with $K(T) > 0$ for all t?

4. Consider the problem

$$\max_{u \in \mathbb{R}} \int_0^\infty [-(x-1)^2 - \tfrac{1}{2}u^2]e^{-t}\, dt, \quad \dot{x} = x - u, \; x(0) = \tfrac{1}{2}, \; x(\infty) \text{ free}$$

(a) Solve the problem qualitatively by a saddle point argument.

(b) Find an explicit solution.

10

CONTROL THEORY WITH MANY VARIABLES

To be sure, mathematics can be extended to any branch of
knowledge, including economics, provided the concepts are so
clearly defined as to permit accurate symbolic representation.
That is only another way of saying that in some branches of
discourse it is desirable to know what you are talking about.
—D. MacDouglas (1956)

This chapter begins by extending the optimal control theory developed in the previous chapter to problems with several state and control variables. In the first section the main emphasis is on appropriate generalizations of results from Chapter 9. There is not too much discussion because the essential motivation was given in Chapter 9. However, we give a proof of the Arrow sufficiency theorem in the case of several state and control variables.

Section 10.2 deals with examples illustrating the theory.

Section 10.3 extends the infinite horizon theory of Section 9.11. In fact, the majority of the control models that appear in economics literature assume an infinite horizon.

Section 10.4 begins with a discussion of the existence of optimal controls. Then we present precise sensitivity results which are seldom spelled out except in specialized literature.

Section 10.5 offers a heuristic proof of the maximum principle, which, at least in the case of a free end, is close to a proper proof. In economics literature necessary conditions for optimality are often obtained by using the "Lagrangian method". This consists of introducing a suitable Lagrangian and equating its "derivatives" to 0. There is no justification for this method, but it might serve as a mnemonic device.

The chapter concludes with a short discussion of control problems with mixed constraints of the type $h(t, \mathbf{x}, \mathbf{u}) \geq \mathbf{0}$, as well as pure state constraints of the type $h(t, \mathbf{x}) \geq \mathbf{0}$. Many of the control problems that economists have considered involve additional constraints of these types.

10.1 Several Control and State Variables

Chapter 9 studied control problems with only one state and one control variable. In this section most of the results from Chapter 9 are generalized to control problems with an arbitrary number of state and control variables.

The **standard end constrained problem** is to find, for fixed values of t_0 and t_1, a pair of vector functions $(\mathbf{x}(t), \mathbf{u}(t)) = (x_1(t), \ldots, x_n(t), u_1(t), \ldots, u_r(t))$ defined on $[t_0, t_1]$ which

$$\text{maximizes} \quad \int_{t_0}^{t_1} f(t, \mathbf{x}(t), \mathbf{u}(t)) \, dt \tag{1}$$

subject to the dynamic constraints

$$\frac{dx_1(t)}{dt} = g_1(t, \mathbf{x}(t), \mathbf{u}(t))$$
$$\ldots\ldots\ldots\ldots\ldots\ldots \quad \text{or} \quad \dot{\mathbf{x}} = \mathbf{g}(t, \mathbf{x}(t), \mathbf{u}(t)) \tag{2}$$
$$\frac{dx_n(t)}{dt} = g_n(t, \mathbf{x}(t), \mathbf{u}(t))$$

the initial conditions

$$x_i(t_0) = x_i^0, \quad i = 1, \ldots, n \qquad (\mathbf{x}^0 = (x_1^0, \ldots, x_n^0) \text{ is a given point in } \mathbb{R}^n) \tag{3}$$

the terminal conditions

$$\begin{aligned}
&\text{(a)} \quad x_i(t_1) = x_i^1, &&i = 1, \ldots, l \\
&\text{(b)} \quad x_i(t_1) \geq x_i^1, &&i = l+1, \ldots, m \\
&\text{(c)} \quad x_i(t_1) \text{ free}, &&i = m+1, \ldots, n
\end{aligned} \tag{4}$$

and the control variable restrictions

$$\mathbf{u}(t) = (u_1(t), \ldots, u_r(t)) \in U \subseteq \mathbb{R}^r, \qquad (U \text{ is a given set in } \mathbb{R}^r) \tag{5}$$

In (2) the system of differential equations is also written as a vector differential equation, where $\dot{\mathbf{x}} = (dx_1/dt, dx_2/dt, \ldots, dx_n/dt)$, and $\mathbf{g} = (g_1, g_2, \ldots, g_n)$ is a vector function.

The pair $(\mathbf{x}(t), \mathbf{u}(t))$ is **admissible** if $u_1(t), \ldots, u_r(t)$ are all piecewise continuous, $\mathbf{u}(t)$ takes values in U and $\mathbf{x}(t) = (x_1(t), \ldots, x_n(t))$ is the corresponding continuous and piecewise differentiable vector function that satisfies (2), (3), and (4). The functions f and $g_1, \ldots, g_n$ and their partial derivatives w.r.t. the x_i's are assumed to be continuous in all the $n + r + 1$ variables.

There are n differential equations in (2) describing the rate of growth of each of the n state variables. By analogy with the single variable problem in Section 9.4, associate n adjoint functions $p_1(t), \ldots, p_n(t)$ with the n differential equations. The Hamiltonian $H = H(t, \mathbf{x}, \mathbf{u}, \mathbf{p})$, with $\mathbf{p} = (p_1, \ldots, p_n)$, is then defined by

$$H(t, \mathbf{x}, \mathbf{u}, \mathbf{p}) = p_0 f(t, \mathbf{x}, \mathbf{u}) + \mathbf{p} \cdot \mathbf{g}(t, \mathbf{x}, \mathbf{u}) = p_0 f(t, \mathbf{x}, \mathbf{u}) + \sum_{i=1}^{n} p_i g_i(t, \mathbf{x}, \mathbf{u}) \tag{6}$$

The Maximum Principle

The maximum principle for the problem gives *necessary* conditions for optimality, but the conditions are far from sufficient. For a proof see Fleming and Rishel (1975).

THEOREM 10.1.1 (THE MAXIMUM PRINCIPLE. STANDARD END CONSTRAINTS)

Suppose that $(\mathbf{x}^*(t), \mathbf{u}^*(t))$ is an optimal pair for the standard end constrained problem (1)–(5). Then there exist a constant p_0, with $p_0 = 0$ or $p_0 = 1$, and a continuous and piecewise differentiable function $\mathbf{p}(t) = (p_1(t), \ldots, p_n(t))$ such that for all t in $[t_0, t_1]$, $(p_0, \mathbf{p}(t)) \neq (0, \mathbf{0})$, and:

(A) The control function $\mathbf{u}^*(t)$ maximizes the Hamiltonian $H(t, \mathbf{x}^*(t), \mathbf{u}, \mathbf{p}(t))$ for $\mathbf{u} \in U$, i.e.

$$H(t, \mathbf{x}^*(t), \mathbf{u}, \mathbf{p}(t)) \leq H(t, \mathbf{x}^*(t), \mathbf{u}^*(t), \mathbf{p}(t)) \quad \text{for all } \mathbf{u} \text{ in } U \qquad (7)$$

(B) Wherever $\mathbf{u}^*(t)$ is continuous, the adjoint variables satisfy

$$\dot{p}_i(t) = -\frac{\partial H(t, \mathbf{x}^*(t), \mathbf{u}^*(t), \mathbf{p}(t))}{\partial x_i}, \quad i = 1, \ldots, n \qquad (8)$$

(C) Corresponding to the terminal conditions (a), (b), and (c) in (4), one has the transversality conditions:

(a') $p_i(t_1)$ no condition, $\qquad\qquad\qquad\qquad i = 1, \ldots, l$

(b') $p_i(t_1) \geq 0$ ($p_i(t_1) = 0$ if $x_i^*(t_1) > x_1^i$), $\qquad i = l+1, \ldots, m \qquad (9)$

(c') $p_i(t_1) = 0$, $\qquad\qquad\qquad\qquad\qquad i = m+1, \ldots, n$

NOTE 1 If some of the inequalities in (4) (b) are reversed, the corresponding inequalities in (9)(b') are reversed as well.

NOTE 2 One can show the following additional properties:

(a) The Hamiltonian

$$H(t, \mathbf{x}^*(t), \mathbf{u}^*(t), \mathbf{p}(t)) \quad \text{is continuous for all } t \qquad (10)$$

(b) If the partial derivatives $\partial f/\partial t$ and $\partial g_i/\partial t$, $i = 1, \ldots, n$, exist and are continuous, then

$$\frac{d}{dt}H(t, \mathbf{x}^*(t), \mathbf{u}^*(t), \mathbf{p}(t)) = \frac{\partial H(t, \mathbf{x}^*(t), \mathbf{u}^*(t), \mathbf{p}(t))}{\partial t} \qquad (11)$$

at all points of continuity of $\mathbf{u}^*(t)$. (See Problem 2.)

(c) Moreover,

$$U \text{ convex and } H \text{ strictly concave in } \mathbf{u} \implies \mathbf{u}^*(t) \text{ continuous for all } t \qquad (12)$$

NOTE 3 Suppose that the terminal condition is that $x_i(t_1)$ is free for $i = 1, \ldots, n$. Then (9)(c') yields $\mathbf{p}(t_1) = \mathbf{0}$, and then $p_0 = 1$.

NOTE 4 The adjoint variables in Theorem 10.1.1 can be given price interpretations corresponding to the price interpretations in Section 9.6 for the case $n = r = 1$. Indeed, let

$\mathbf{x}^1 = (x_1^1, \ldots, x_m^1)$ and define the value function V associated with the standard problem as

$$V(\mathbf{x}^0, \mathbf{x}^1, t_0, t_1) = \max \left\{ \int_{t_0}^{t_1} f(t, \mathbf{x}(t), \mathbf{u}(t))\, dt \ : \ (\mathbf{x}(t), \mathbf{u}(t)) \text{ admissible} \right\} \tag{13}$$

Then for $i = 1, 2, \ldots, n$ (for precise assumptions, see Section 10.4),

$$\frac{\partial V}{\partial x_i^0} = p_i(t_0), \qquad \frac{\partial V}{\partial x_i^1} = -p_i(t_1), \qquad \frac{\partial V}{\partial t_0} = -H^*(t_0), \qquad \frac{\partial V}{\partial t_1} = H^*(t_1) \tag{14}$$

Here H^* denotes the Hamiltonian evaluated along the optimal path.

Sufficient Conditions

The simplest general sufficiency theorem is the following:

THEOREM 10.1.2 (MANGASARIAN)

Consider the standard end constrained problem (1)–(5) with U convex, and suppose that the partial derivatives $\partial f / \partial u_j$ and $\partial g_i / \partial u_j$ all exist and are continuous. If the pair $(\mathbf{x}^*(t), \mathbf{u}^*(t))$ satisfies all the conditions in Theorem 10.1.1 with $p_0 = 1$, and if

$$H(t, \mathbf{x}, \mathbf{u}, \mathbf{p}(t)) \text{ is concave in } (\mathbf{x}, \mathbf{u}) \text{ for all } t \text{ in } [t_0, t_1] \tag{15}$$

then $(\mathbf{x}^*(t), \mathbf{u}^*(t)$ solves the problem.

If the function $H(t, \mathbf{x}, \mathbf{u}, \mathbf{p}(t))$ is strictly concave in $(\mathbf{x}, \mathbf{u})$, then $(\mathbf{x}^*(t), \mathbf{u}^*(t))$ is the unique solution to the problem.

NOTE 5   Because a sum of concave functions is concave, the concavity condition (15) is satisfied if f and $p_1(t)g_1, \ldots, p_n(t)g_n$ are all concave in $(\mathbf{x}, \mathbf{u})$.

At this point the reader might want to study Example 10.2.1 and then do problem 10.2.1.

The proof of Theorem 10.1.2 is very similar to the proof of Theorem 9.6.1, so we skip it. Instead, we take a closer look at Arrow's proposed generalization of the Mangasarian theorem. (See Arrow and Kurz (1970).) Define

$$\widehat{H}(t, \mathbf{x}, \mathbf{p}) = \max_{\mathbf{u} \in U} H(t, \mathbf{x}, \mathbf{u}, \mathbf{p}) \tag{16}$$

assuming that the maximum value is attained. Then the appropriate generalization of Theorem 9.7.2 is this:

THEOREM 10.1.3 (ARROW)

Suppose that $(\mathbf{x}^*(t), \mathbf{u}^*(t))$ is an admissible pair in the standard end constrained problem (1)–(5) that, together with the continuous and piecewise differentiable adjoint (vector) function $\mathbf{p}(t)$, satisfies all the conditions in Theorem 10.1.1 with $p_0 = 1$. Suppose further that

$$\widehat{H}(t, \mathbf{x}, \mathbf{p}(t)) \text{ is concave in } \mathbf{x} \text{ for all } t \text{ in } [t_0, t_1] \tag{17}$$

Then $(\mathbf{x}^*(t), \mathbf{u}^*(t))$ solves the problem.

Proof: Let $(\mathbf{x}, \mathbf{u}) = (\mathbf{x}(t), \mathbf{u}(t))$ be an arbitrary admissible pair. We must show that $D_{\mathbf{u}} = \int_{t_0}^{t_1} f(t, \mathbf{x}^*(t), \mathbf{u}^*(t)) \, dt - \int_{t_0}^{t_1} f(t, \mathbf{x}(t), \mathbf{u}(t)) \, dt \geq 0$. Let us simplify the notation by letting f^* denote $f(t, \mathbf{x}^*(t), \mathbf{u}^*(t))$, f denote $f(t, \mathbf{x}(t), \mathbf{u}(t))$, H^* denote $H(t, \mathbf{x}^*(t), \mathbf{u}^*(t), \mathbf{p}(t))$, etc. As in the proof of Theorem 9.7.1, it is easy to see that

$$D_{\mathbf{u}} = \int_{t_0}^{t_1} (H^* - H) \, dt + \int_{t_0}^{t_1} \mathbf{p}(t) \cdot (\dot{\mathbf{x}}(t) - \dot{\mathbf{x}}^*(t)) \, dt \tag{i}$$

Integration by parts yields

$$\int_{t_0}^{t_1} \mathbf{p}(t) \cdot (\dot{\mathbf{x}}(t) - \dot{\mathbf{x}}^*(t)) \, dt = \Big|_{t_0}^{t_1} \mathbf{p}(t) \cdot (\mathbf{x}(t) - \mathbf{x}^*(t)) - \int_{t_0}^{t_1} \dot{\mathbf{p}}(t) \cdot (\mathbf{x}(t) - \mathbf{x}^*(t)) \, dt$$
$$\geq - \int_{t_0}^{t_1} \dot{\mathbf{p}}(t) \cdot (\mathbf{x}(t) - \mathbf{x}^*(t)) \, dt \tag{ii}$$

To explain the last inequality, note first that because $\mathbf{x}(t_0) = \mathbf{x}^*(t_0)$ we get

$$\Big|_{t_0}^{t_1} \mathbf{p}(t) \cdot (\mathbf{x}(t) - \mathbf{x}^*(t)) = \mathbf{p}(t_1) \cdot (\mathbf{x}(t_1) - \mathbf{x}^*(t_1)) = \sum_{i=1}^{n} p_i(t_1)(x_i(t_1) - x_i^*(t_1)) \tag{iii}$$

We claim that this sum is ≥ 0, which will imply the inequality in (ii). In fact, for $i = 1, 2, \ldots, l$, we have $x_i(t_1) = x_i^*(t_1) = x_i^1$, so the corresponding terms are 0. Also for $i = m + 1, \ldots, n$ the corresponding terms in the sum in (iii) are 0 because by (9)(c'), $p_i(t_1) = 0$. If $i = l + 1, \ldots, m$ and $x_i^*(t_1) > x_i^1$, the corresponding terms are 0 because by (9)(b'), $p_i(t_1) = 0$. Finally, if $x_i^*(t_1) = x_i^1$, then $x_i(t_1) - x_i^*(t_1) \geq 0$ and by (9)(b'), $p_i(t_1) \geq 0$ so the corresponding terms are ≥ 0. All in all, this proves that the sum in (iii) is ≥ 0.

To proceed, note that by the definition of $\widehat{H}$,

$$H^* = \widehat{H}^* \quad \text{and} \quad H \leq \widehat{H} \tag{iv}$$

It follows from (i)–(iv) that

$$D_{\mathbf{u}} \geq \int_{t_0}^{t_1} [\widehat{H}^* - \widehat{H} - \dot{\mathbf{p}}(t) \cdot (\mathbf{x}(t) - \mathbf{x}^*(t))] \, dt \tag{v}$$

But (8) implies that $-\dot{\mathbf{p}}(t)$ is the (partial) gradient vector $\nabla_{\mathbf{x}} H^*$, which must equal $\nabla_{\mathbf{x}} \widehat{H}^*$ by the envelope Theorem 3.1.6. Because $\widehat{H}$ is concave w.r.t. $\mathbf{x}$, it follows from Theorem 2.4.1 that

$$\widehat{H} - \widehat{H}^* \leq -\dot{\mathbf{p}}(t)(\mathbf{x}(t) - \mathbf{x}^*(t)), \quad \text{or} \quad \widehat{H}^* - \widehat{H} \geq \dot{\mathbf{p}}(t)(\mathbf{x}(t) - \mathbf{x}^*(t))$$

This means that the integral on the right hand of (v) is nonnegative for all t in $[t_0, t_1]$, so $D_{\mathbf{u}} \geq 0$ as required. ∎

NOTE 6   The result in Problem 3 shows that condition (15) implies (17). Thus Theorem 10.1.3 generalizes Theorem 10.1.2.

NOTE 7   Suppose that in the standard end constrained problem (1)–(5) one requires that $\mathbf{x}(t) \in A(t)$ for all t, where $A(t)$ for each t is a given convex set in $\mathbb{R}^n$. Suppose also that $\mathbf{x}^*(t)$ is an interior point of $A(t)$ for each t. Theorem 10.1.3 is then valid, and $\mathbf{x} \mapsto \widehat{H}(t, \mathbf{x}, \mathbf{p}(t))$ need only be concave in the set $A(t)$.

Variable Final Time

Consider problem (1)–(5) with variable final time t_1. The problem is among all control functions $\mathbf{u}(t)$ that during the time interval $[t_0, t_1]$ steer the system from $\mathbf{x}^0$ along a time path satisfying (2) to a point where the boundary conditions in (4) are satisfied, to find one which maximizes the integral in (1). The time t_1 at which the process stops is not fixed, because the different admissible control functions can be defined on different time intervals. Theorem 9.8.1 has then the following immediate generalization:

THEOREM 10.1.4   (THE MAXIMUM PRINCIPLE. VARIABLE FINAL TIME)

Suppose that $(\mathbf{x}^*(t), \mathbf{u}^*(t))$ is an admissible pair defined on $[t_0, t_1^*]$ that solves problem (1)–(5) with t_1 free, $(t_1 \in (t_0, \infty))$. Then all the conditions in the maximum principle (Theorem 10.1.1) are satisfied on $[t_0, t_1^*]$, and, in addition,

$$H(t_1^*, \mathbf{x}^*(t_1^*), \mathbf{u}^*(t_1^*), \mathbf{p}(t_1^*)) = 0 \qquad (18)$$

For a proof, see Hestenes (1966). Neither the Mangasarian nor the Arrow theorems apply to variable final time problems. For sufficiency results, see Seierstad and Sydsæter (1987).

Current Value Formulations with Scrap Values

The theorems in Section 9.10 on current value formulations of optimal control problems with scrap value functions can easily be generalized to the following problem involving several state and control variables.

$$\max_{\mathbf{u} \in U \subseteq \mathbb{R}^r} \left\{ \int_{t_0}^{t_1} f(t, \mathbf{x}, \mathbf{u}) e^{-rt}\, dt + S(\mathbf{x}(t_1)) e^{-rt_1} \right\}, \quad \dot{\mathbf{x}} = \mathbf{g}(t, \mathbf{x}, \mathbf{u}), \quad \mathbf{x}(t_0) = \mathbf{x}^0 \qquad (19)$$

$$\begin{align}
\text{(a)} \quad & x_i(t_1) = x_i^1, && i = 1, \ldots, l \\
\text{(b)} \quad & x_i(t_1) \geq x_i^1, && i = l+1, \ldots, m \qquad (20) \\
\text{(c)} \quad & x_i(t_1) \text{ free}, && i = m+1, \ldots, n
\end{align}$$

Here r denotes a discount factor (or an interest rate). The current value Hamiltonian is by definition

$$H^c(t, \mathbf{x}, \mathbf{u}, \boldsymbol{\lambda}) = \lambda_0 f(t, \mathbf{x}, \mathbf{u}) + \boldsymbol{\lambda} \cdot \mathbf{g}(t, \mathbf{x}, \mathbf{u}) \qquad (21)$$

and the maximum principle is as follows:

THEOREM 10.1.5 (THE MAXIMUM PRINCIPLE)

Suppose that $(\mathbf{x}^*(t), \mathbf{u}^*(t))$ is an optimal pair for the problem (19)–(20). Then there exist a continuous and piecewise continuously differentiable vector function $\boldsymbol{\lambda}(t) = (\lambda_1(t), \ldots, \lambda_n(t))$ and a constant λ_0, with $\lambda_0 = 0$ or $\lambda_0 = 1$, such that $(\lambda_0, \boldsymbol{\lambda}(t)) \neq (0, \mathbf{0})$ for all t in $[t_0, t_1]$, and such that:

(A) For all t in $[t_0, t_1]$,

$$\mathbf{u} = \mathbf{u}^*(t) \text{ maximizes } H^c(t, \mathbf{x}^*(t), \mathbf{u}, \boldsymbol{\lambda}(t)) \text{ for } \mathbf{u} \in U \tag{22}$$

(B) Wherever $\mathbf{u}^*(t)$ is continuous,

$$\dot{\lambda}_i(t) - r\lambda_i(t) = -\frac{\partial H^c(t, \mathbf{x}^*(t), \mathbf{u}^*(t), \boldsymbol{\lambda}(t))}{\partial x_i}, \qquad i = 1, \ldots, n \tag{23}$$

(C) Finally, corresponding to the terminal conditions (20) (a), (b), and (c), one has the transversality conditions:

(a') $\lambda_i(t_1)$ no condition, $\hspace{5cm} i = 1, \ldots, l$

(b') $\lambda_i(t_1) \geq \lambda_0 \dfrac{\partial S^*(\mathbf{x}^*(t_1))}{\partial x_i}$ (with $=$ if $x_i^*(t_1) > x_i^1$), $\quad i = l+1, \ldots, m \hspace{1cm}$ (24)

(c') $\lambda_i(t_1) = \lambda_0 \dfrac{\partial S^*(\mathbf{x}^*(t_1))}{\partial x_i},$ $\hspace{4cm} i = m+1, \ldots, n$

THEOREM 10.1.6 (SUFFICIENT CONDITIONS. ARROW)

The conditions in Theorem 10.1.5 are sufficient (with $\lambda_0 = 1$) if

$$\widehat{H}^c(t, \mathbf{x}, \boldsymbol{\lambda}(t)) = \max_{\mathbf{u} \in U} H^c(t, \mathbf{x}, \mathbf{u}, \boldsymbol{\lambda}(t)) \text{ is concave in } \mathbf{x} \tag{25}$$

and

$$S(\mathbf{x}) \text{ is concave in } \mathbf{x}. \tag{26}$$

The problems for this section are of a theoretical nature. Non-theoretical exercises are found at the end of the next section.

PROBLEMS FOR SECTION 10.1

1. Consider the variational problem with an integral constraint

$$\max \int_{t_0}^{t_1} F(t, x, \dot{x}) \, dt, \quad x(t_0) = x^0, \; x(t_1) = x^1, \; \int_{t_0}^{t_1} G(t, x, \dot{x}) \, dt = K$$

Transform the problem to a control problem with one control variable ($u = \dot{x}$) and two state variables $x = x(t)$ and $y(t) = \int_{t_0}^{t} G(\tau, x(\tau), \dot{x}(\tau)) \, d\tau$.

2. Prove (11) assuming that $\mathbf{u}^*(t)$ is differentiable and $\mathbf{u}^*(t)$ belongs to the interior of U. (*Hint:* Differentiate $H(t, \mathbf{x}^*(t), \mathbf{u}^*(t), \mathbf{p}(t))$ totally w.r.t. t.)

3. Let S and U be convex sets in $\mathbb{R}^n$ and $\mathbb{R}^r$, respectively, and let $F(\mathbf{x}, \mathbf{u})$ be a real-valued concave function of $(\mathbf{x}, \mathbf{u})$, $\mathbf{x} \in S$, $\mathbf{u} \in U$. Define

$$f(\mathbf{x}) = \max_{\mathbf{u} \in U} F(\mathbf{x}, \mathbf{u}) \tag{$*$}$$

where we assume that the maximum value exists for each $\mathbf{x} \in S$. Prove that f is concave in S. (*Hint:* Let $\mathbf{x}_1, \mathbf{x}_2 \in S$, $\lambda \in (0, 1)$ and choose $\mathbf{u}_1, \mathbf{u}_2 \in U$ such that $f(\mathbf{x}_1) = F(\mathbf{x}_1, \mathbf{u}_1)$, $f(\mathbf{x}_2) = F(\mathbf{x}_2, \mathbf{u}_2)$.) Let B be a convex set in $\mathbb{R}^n \times \mathbb{R}^r$ and define the set $U_{\mathbf{x}} = \{\mathbf{u} : (\mathbf{x}, \mathbf{u}) \in B\}$. Prove that $g(\mathbf{x}) = \max_{\mathbf{u} \in U_{\mathbf{x}}} F(\mathbf{x}, \mathbf{u})$ is concave.

4. Rewrite the following problem as one of the type (1)–(5),

$$\max \int_{t_0}^{t_1} f(t, x, u)\, dt, \quad \dot{x} = g(t, x, u), \quad x(t_0) = x^0, u \in U, \quad \int_{t_0}^{t_1} h(t, x, u)\, dt = K$$

Here t_0, t_1, x^0, and K are given numbers, f, g, and h are given functions, and U is a subset of $\mathbb{R}$.

10.2 Some Examples

In this section the theory from the previous section is used to solve some multidimensional control problems. The first is intended to be simple enough for you to be able to make a real effort to solve it before looking at the suggested solution.

EXAMPLE 1   Solve the problem

$$\max_{u(t) \in \mathbb{R}} \int_0^T \left(x(t) + y(t) - \tfrac{1}{2}(u(t))^2 \right) dt, \quad \begin{cases} \dot{x}(t) = y(t), & x(0) = 0, & x(T) \text{ is free} \\ \dot{y}(t) = u(t), & y(0) = 0, & y(T) \text{ is free} \end{cases}$$

Verify that the last equality in (14) is satisfied.

Solution: Suppose that $(x^*(t), y^*(t), u^*(t))$ solves the problem. With the two adjoint variables p_1 and p_2, the Hamiltonian is $H = x + y - \tfrac{1}{2}u^2 + p_1 y + p_2 u$, which is clearly concave in (x, y, u). (Because $x(T)$ and $y(T)$ are free, Note 10.1.3 implies $p_0 = 1$.) We see that $H'_x = 1$, $H'_y = 1 + p_1$, and $H'_u = -u + p_2$.

The differential equations for p_1 and p_2 are $\dot{p}_1(t) = -1$ with $p_1(T) = 0$, and $\dot{p}_2(t) = -1 - p_1(t)$ with $p_2(T) = 0$. It follows that $p_1(t) = T - t$. Hence, $\dot{p}_2(t) = -1 + t - T$ and therefore $p_2(t) = -t + \tfrac{1}{2}t^2 - Tt + A$. The requirement $p_2(T) = 0$ implies that $A = \tfrac{1}{2}T^2 + T$. Thus

$$p_1(t) = T - t, \qquad p_2(t) = \tfrac{1}{2}(T - t)^2 + T - t$$

H is concave in u and $u \in \mathbb{R}$, so H has its maximum when $H'_u = 0$. This gives $u^*(t) = p_2(t) = \frac{1}{2}(T-t)^2 + T - t$. Since $\dot{y}^*(t) = u^*(t) = \frac{1}{2}(T-t)^2 + T - t$, we find by integration that $y^*(t) = -\frac{1}{6}(T-t)^3 + Tt - \frac{1}{2}t^2 + B$. The initial condition $y^*(0) = 0$ gives $B = \frac{1}{6}T^3$. From $\dot{x}^*(t) = y^*(t)$ we get $x^*(t) = \frac{1}{24}(T-t)^4 + \frac{1}{2}Tt^2 - \frac{1}{6}t^3 + \frac{1}{6}T^3t + C$. The requirement $x^*(0) = 0$ gives $C = -\frac{1}{24}T^4$. Hence the optimal choices for x^* and y^* are

$$x^*(t) = \tfrac{1}{24}(T-t)^4 + \tfrac{1}{2}Tt^2 - \tfrac{1}{6}t^3 + \tfrac{1}{6}T^3t - \tfrac{1}{24}T^4, \quad y^*(t) = -\tfrac{1}{6}(T-t)^3 + Tt - \tfrac{1}{2}t^2 + \tfrac{1}{6}T^3$$

Mangasarian's theorem shows that we have found the optimal solution.

The value function is $V(T) = \int_0^T \left(x^*(t) + y^*(t) - \frac{1}{2}(u^*(t))^2 \right) dt$, and a rather tedious computation (using Leibniz's formula) yields that $V'(T) = \frac{1}{2}T^2 + \frac{1}{2}T^3 + \frac{1}{8}T^4$. On the other hand, $H^*(T) = x^*(T) + y^*(T) - \frac{1}{2}(u^*(T))^2 + p_1(T)y^*(T) + p_2(T)u^*(T)$ is easily seen to equal $\frac{1}{2}T^2 + \frac{1}{2}T^3 + \frac{1}{8}T^4$, so confirming (10.1.14).

EXAMPLE 2 **(Two-sector Model)** This model is related to a model of Mahalanobis.) Consider an economy which is divided into two sectors. Sector 1 produces investment goods, while sector 2 produces consumption goods. Define

$$x_i(t) = \text{output in sector } i \text{ per unit of time, } i = 1, 2$$

$$u(t) = \text{the fraction of investment allocated to sector 1}$$

Assume that $\dot{x}_1 = aux_1$ and $\dot{x}_2 = a(1-u)x_1$, where a is a positive constant, so that the increase in production per unit of time in each sector is proportional to the fraction of investment allocated to that sector. By definition, $0 \le u(t) \le 1$, and if the planning period starts at time $t = 0$, then $x_1(0)$ and $x_2(0)$ are historically given.

We consider the problem of maximizing total consumption in a given planning period $[0, T]$. The problem is then, with a, T, x_1^0, and x_2^0 as positive constants:

$$\max_{u(t) \in [0,1]} \int_0^T x_2(t)\, dt, \quad \begin{cases} \dot{x}_1(t) = au(t)x_1(t), & x_1(0) = x_1^0, \quad x_1(T) \text{ is free} \\ \dot{x}_2(t) = a(1-u(t))x_1(t), & x_2(0) = x_2^0, \quad x_2(T) \text{ is free} \end{cases}$$

The Hamiltonian is $H = x_2 + p_1 aux_1 + p_2 a(1-u)x_1$, where p_1 and p_2 are the adjoint variables associated with the two differential equations. (Because both terminal stocks are free, Note 10.1.3 implies $p_0 = 1$.)

Suppose that $(x_1^*(t), x_2^*(t))$ and $u^*(t)$ solve the problem. According to Theorem 10.1.1 there exists a continuous vector function $(p_1(t), p_2(t))$ such that for all t in $[0, T]$, $u^*(t)$ is the value of u in $[0, 1]$ which maximizes $x_2^*(t) + p_1(t)aux_1^*(t) + p_2(t)a(1-u)x_1^*(t)$. Collecting the terms in H which depend on u, note that $u^*(t)$ must be chosen as that value of u in $[0, 1]$ which maximizes $a(p_1(t) - p_2(t))x_1^*(t)u$. Now, $x_1^*(0) = x_1^0 > 0$, and because $\dot{x}_1^*(t) = au^*(t)x_1^*(t)$, it follows that $x_1^*(t) > 0$ for all t. The maximum condition therefore implies that $u^*(t)$ should be chosen as

$$u^*(t) = \begin{cases} 1 & \text{if } p_1(t) > p_2(t) \\ 0 & \text{if } p_1(t) < p_2(t) \end{cases} \tag{i}$$

The function $p_2(t)$ satisfies $\dot{p}_2(t) = -\partial H^*/\partial x_2 = -1$ with $p_2(T) = 0$. Hence

$$p_2(t) = T - t$$

The function $p_1(t)$ satisfies $\dot{p}_1(t) = -\partial H^*/\partial x_1 = -p_1(t)au^*(t) - p_2(t)a(1 - u^*(t))$, with $p_1(T) = 0$. Because $p_1(T) = p_2(T) = 0$, one has $\dot{p}_1(T) = 0$. From $\dot{p}_2(t) = -1$, it follows that $p_1(t) < p_2(t)$ in an interval to the left of T. (See Fig. 1.) Let t^* be the largest value of t in $[0, T]$ for which $p_1(t) \geq p_2(t) = T - t$. (Possibly, $t^* = 0$.) Using (i) it follows that $u^*(t) = 0$ in (t^*, T). Hence $\dot{p}_1(t) = -ap_2(t) = -a(T - t)$ in (t^*, T). Integration yields $p_1(t) = -aTt + \frac{1}{2}at^2 + C_1$. But $p_1(T) = 0$, so $C_1 = \frac{1}{2}aT^2$ and hence

$$p_1(t) = -aTt + \tfrac{1}{2}at^2 + \tfrac{1}{2}aT^2 = \tfrac{1}{2}a(T - t)^2, \qquad t \in [t^*, T]$$

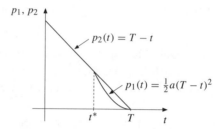

Figure 1 The behaviour of p_1 and p_2.

Unless $p_1(t) < p_2(t)$ for all t in $[0, T]$, the number t^* is determined by the requirement $p_1(t^*) = p_2(t^*)$. Using the expressions found for $p_1(t)$ and $p_2(t)$, it follows that

$$t^* = T - 2/a \ \text{ if } \ T > 2/a, \ \text{ otherwise } \ t^* = 0$$

Consider the case when $T > 2/a$, so $t^* > 0$. How does $p_1(t)$ behave in the interval $[0, t^*)$? Note first that

$$\dot{p}_1(t) = \begin{cases} -ap_1(t) & \text{if } p_1(t) > p_2(t) \\ -ap_2(t) & \text{if } p_1(t) \leq p_2(t) \end{cases}$$

If $p_1(t) > p_2(t)$, then $-ap_1(t) < -ap_2(t)$. Whatever is the relationship between $p_1(t)$ and $p_2(t)$, we always have

$$\dot{p}_1(t) \leq -ap_2(t) = a(t - T)$$

In particular, if $t < t^*$, then $\dot{p}_1(t) \leq a(t - T) < a(t^* - T) = -2$. Because $\dot{p}_2(t) = -1$ for all t and $p_1(t^*) = p_2(t^*)$, we conclude that $p_1(t) > p_2(t)$ for $t < t^*$. Hence, $u^*(t) = 1$ for t in $[0, t^*]$. The maximum principle therefore yields the following candidate for an optimal control, in the case when $T > 2/a$:

$$u^*(t) = \begin{cases} 1 & \text{if } t \in [0, T - 2/a] \\ 0 & \text{if } t \in (T - 2/a, T] \end{cases} \qquad (T > 2/a) \qquad \text{(ii)}$$

In $[0, T - 2/a]$, $u^*(t) = 1$ and so $\dot{p}_1 = -ap_1$, i.e. $p_1(t) = Ce^{-at}$. Because $p_1(t^*) = p_2(t^*) = T - t^* = 2/a$, this yields

$$p_1(t) = (2/a)e^{-a(t-T+2/a)}, \qquad t \in [0, T - 2/a)$$

It is easy to find explicit expressions for $x_1^*(t)$ and $x_2^*(t)$. (See Problem 2.)

In the other case, when $T \leq 2/a$, one has $t^* = 0$, so the candidate for an optimal control is

$$u^*(t) = 0 \quad \text{for all } t \text{ in } [0, T] \qquad (T \leq 2/a)$$

In this example the maximum principle yields only one candidate for an optimal control (in each of the cases $T > 2/a$ and $T \leq 2/a$).

The Hamiltonian is not concave in (x_1, x_2, u) (because of the product ux_1). Thus the Mangasarian theorem does not apply. The maximized Hamiltonian $\widehat{H}$ defined in (10.1.16) is for $x_1 \geq 0, x_2 \geq 0$,

$$\widehat{H}(t, x_1, x_2, p_1, p_2) = \begin{cases} x_2 + ap_1x_1 & \text{if } p_1 > p_2 \\ x_2 + ap_2x_1 & \text{if } p_1 \leq p_2 \end{cases}$$

For each t in $[0, T]$, the function $\widehat{H}$ is linear in (x_1, x_2). It is therefore concave in the set $A = \{(x_1, x_2) : x_1 \geq 0, \ x_2 \geq 0\}$. According to Theorem 10.1.3 and Note 10.1.7, the solution to the two-sector problem has been found.

PROBLEMS FOR SECTION 10.2

1. Solve the problem

$$\max_{u \in [-1,1]} \int_0^4 (10 - x_1 + u)\, dt, \qquad \begin{cases} \dot{x}_1(t) = x_2(t), & x_1(0) = 2, & x_1(4) \text{ is free} \\ \dot{x}_2(t) = u(t), & x_2(0) = 4, & x_2(4) \text{ is free} \end{cases}$$

2. In Example 2, for the case when $T > 2/a$, find the functions $x_1^*(t)$ and $x_2^*(t)$ corresponding to the control function given in (ii).

3. (a) Solve the problem

$$\max \int_0^T (\tfrac{1}{2}x_1 + \tfrac{1}{5}x_2 - u_1 - u_2)\, dt, \qquad \begin{cases} \dot{x}_1(t) = u_1(t), & x_1(0) = 0, & x_1(T) \text{ is free} \\ \dot{x}_2(t) = u_2(t), & x_2(0) = 0, & x_2(T) \text{ is free} \end{cases}$$

   with $0 \leq u_1(t) \leq 1, 0 \leq u_2(t) \leq 1$, and with T as a fixed number greater than 5.

   (b) Replace the objective functional by $\int_0^T (\tfrac{1}{2}x_1 + \tfrac{1}{5}x_2 - u_1 - u_2)\, dt + 3x_1(T) + 2x_2(T)$ and find the solution in this case.

4. Solve the problem

$$\max \int_0^T (x_2(t) + c(1 - u_1 - u_2))\, dt$$

$$\dot{x}_1(t) = au_1(t), \qquad\qquad x_1(0) = x_1^0, \quad x_1(T) \text{ free}$$

$$\dot{x}_2(t) = au_2(t) + bx_1(t), \qquad x_2(0) = x_2^0, \quad x_2(T) \text{ free}$$

$$0 \leq u_1, \quad 0 \leq u_2, \quad u_1 + u_2 \leq 1$$

where T, a, b, and c are positive constants and $T - c/a > T - 2/b > 0$. (Compared with Example 2, an extra flow of income amounting to one unit (say 1 billion per year) can be divided between extra capital investment in either the investment or consumption goods sectors, or consumed directly.)

5. Solve the problem

$$\max_{u\in[0,u^0]} \int_0^T (x_1 - cx_2 + u^0 - u)\,dt, \qquad \begin{cases} \dot{x}_1 = u, & x_1(0) = x_1^0, & x_1(t) \text{ is free} \\ \dot{x}_2 = bx_1, & x_2(0) = x_2^0, & x_1(t) \text{ is free} \end{cases}$$

where T, b, c, and u^0 are positive constants. (Economic interpretation: Oil is produced at the rate of u^0 per unit of time. The proceeds can be used to increase the capacity x_1 in the sector producing consumption goods. By adjusting the physical units, assume $\dot{x}_1 = u$. The production of consumption goods is proportional to x_1, and by adjusting the time unit, the constant of proportionality is chosen as 1. The production of consumption goods increases the stock of pollution, x_2, at a constant rate per unit. This subtracts cx_2 from utility per unit of time.)

6. Consider the problem:

$$\max \int_0^T U(c(t))e^{-rt}\,dt, \qquad \begin{cases} \dot{K}(t) = f(K(t), u(t)) - c(t), & K(0) = K_0, & K(T) = K_T \\ \dot{x}(t) = -u(t), & x(0) = x_0, & x(T) = 0 \end{cases}$$

where $u(t) \geq 0$, $c(t) \geq 0$. Here $K(t)$ denotes capital stock, $x(t)$ is the stock of a natural resource, $c(t)$ is consumption, and $u(t)$ is the rate of extraction. Moreover, U is a utility function and f is the production function. The constants T, K_0, K_T, and x_0 are positive. Assume that $U' > 0$, $U'' \leq 0$, $f_K' > 0$, $f_u' > 0$, and that $f(K, u)$ is concave in (K, u). This problem has two state variables (K and x) and two control variables (u and c).

(a) Write down the conditions in Theorem 10.1.1, assuming that $u(t) > 0$ and $c(t) > 0$ at the optimum.

(b) Derive from these conditions that

$$\frac{\dot{c}}{c} = \frac{r - f_K'(K, u)}{\check{\omega}}, \qquad \frac{d}{dt}(f_u'(K, u)) = f_K'(K, u)f_u'(K, u)$$

where $\check{\omega}$ is the elasticity of the marginal utility. See Section 8.4.

7. Solve the problem

$$\max_{u\in[0,1]} \int_0^2 (x - \tfrac{1}{2}u)\,dt, \qquad \begin{cases} \dot{x} = u, & x(0) = 1, & x(2) \text{ is free} \\ \dot{y} = u, & y(0) = 0, & y(2) \leq 1 \end{cases}$$

10.3 Infinite Horizon

Infinite horizon control problems were introduced in Section 9.11. This section extends the analysis in several directions. Consider as a point of departure the problem

$$\max_{\mathbf{u}(t) \in U} \int_{t_0}^{\infty} f(t, \mathbf{x}(t), \mathbf{u}(t))\, dt, \quad \dot{\mathbf{x}}(t) = \mathbf{g}(t, \mathbf{x}(t), \mathbf{u}(t)), \quad \mathbf{x}(t_0) = \mathbf{x}^0, \quad \lim_{t \to \infty} \mathbf{x}(t) = \mathbf{x}^1 \quad (1)$$

where $\mathbf{x}^1$ is a fixed vector in $\mathbb{R}^n$. Suppose the integral converges whenever $(\mathbf{x}(t), \mathbf{u}(t))$ satisfies the differential equation and $\mathbf{x}(t)$ tends to the limit $\mathbf{x}^1$ as t tends to ∞. For this problem the maximum principle holds. If we replace the condition $\lim_{t \to \infty} \mathbf{x}(t) = \mathbf{x}^1$ with $\lim_{t \to \infty} \mathbf{x}(t) \geq \mathbf{x}^1$ or $\lim_{t \to \infty} \mathbf{x}(t)$ free, then the maximum principle again holds, except for the transversality conditions.

When the integral in (1) does not converge for all admissible pairs, what is a reasonable optimality criterion? Suppose $(\mathbf{x}(t), \mathbf{u}(t))$ is an arbitrary admissible pair, and $(\mathbf{x}^*(t), \mathbf{u}^*(t))$ is a pair we wish to test for optimality. Define

$$D_{\mathbf{u}}(t) = \int_{t_0}^{t} f(\tau, \mathbf{x}^*(\tau), \mathbf{u}^*(\tau))\, d\tau - \int_{t_0}^{t} f_0(\tau, \mathbf{x}(\tau), \mathbf{u}(\tau))\, d\tau \quad (2)$$

There are several optimality criteria in economics literature which differ in how $D_{\mathbf{u}}(t)$ behaves for large values of t. The simplest of these criteria is:

OVERTAKING OPTIMAL

The pair $(\mathbf{x}^*(t), \mathbf{u}^*(t))$ is **OT optimal** if for each admissible pair $(\mathbf{x}(t), \mathbf{u}(t))$ there exists a number $T_{\mathbf{u}}$ such that $D_{\mathbf{u}}(t) \geq 0$ for all $t \geq T_{\mathbf{u}}$. $\quad (3)$

More important than overtaking optimality is the next criterion:

CATCHING-UP OPTIMAL

The pair $(\mathbf{x}^*(t), \mathbf{u}^*(t))$ is **CU optimal** if for each admissible pair $(\mathbf{x}(t), \mathbf{u}(t))$ and every $\varepsilon > 0$ there exists a number $T_{\mathbf{u},\varepsilon}$ such that $D_{\mathbf{u}}(t) \geq -\varepsilon$ whenever $t \geq T_{\mathbf{u},\varepsilon}$. $\quad (4)$

NOTE 1   In general, let $f(t)$ be a function defined for all $t \geq t_0$. Define the function $F(t) = \inf\{f(\tau) : \tau \geq t\}$. Then $F(t)$ is an increasing function of t, and we define

$$\lim_{t \to \infty} f(t) = \lim_{t \to \infty} F(t) = \lim_{t \to \infty} \left(\inf\{f(\tau) : \tau \geq t\} \right) \quad (5)$$

Here we allow $\lim_{t \to \infty} F(t) = \infty$. The following characterization is useful and quite straightforward to prove.

$$\lim_{t \to \infty} f(t) \geq a \iff \begin{cases} \text{For each } \varepsilon > 0 \text{ there exists a } t' \\ \text{such that } f(t) \geq a - \varepsilon \text{ for all } t \geq t' \end{cases} \quad (6)$$

With this definition the requirement in (4) can be formulated as:

$(\mathbf{x}^*(t), \mathbf{u}^*(t))$ is CU optimal $\iff$ $\lim_{t \to \infty} D_{\mathbf{u}}(t) \geq 0$ for all admissible pairs $(\mathbf{x}(t), \mathbf{u}(t))$

We turn next to the behaviour of $\mathbf{x}(t)$ as t approaches infinity. The requirement that $\mathbf{x}(t)$ tends to a limit as t approaches infinity is often too restrictive. So is the alternative requirement that $\lim_{t \to \infty} \mathbf{x}(t) \geq \mathbf{x}^1$ because it excludes paths where $\mathbf{x}(t)$ oscillates indefinitely. Among many possible terminal conditions consider the following:

$$\lim_{t \to \infty} x_i(t) \text{ exists and is equal to } x_i^1, \qquad\qquad i = 1, \dots, l \qquad (7a)$$

$$\underline{\lim}_{t \to \infty} x_i(t) \geq x_i^1, \qquad\qquad i = l+1, \dots, m \qquad (7b)$$

$$\text{no conditions imposed on } x_i(t) \text{ as } t \to \infty, \qquad\qquad i = m+1, \dots, n \qquad (7c)$$

One can show the following theorem (Halkin (1974)):

THEOREM 10.3.1 (THE MAXIMUM PRINCIPLE. INFINITE HORIZON)

Suppose the pair $(\mathbf{x}^*(t), \mathbf{u}^*(t))$ satisfies the differential equation in (1), the initial condition $\mathbf{x}(t_0) = \mathbf{x}^0$, and the terminal conditions (7). If this pair is OT or CU optimal, then it must satisfy all the conditions in Theorem 10.1.1 except the transversality condition.

The problem with this theorem is that when $l < n$ it gives too many solution candidates, because it includes no transversality condition.

Here is a result that gives sufficient conditions for CU optimality.

THEOREM 10.3.2 (SUFFICIENT CONDITIONS FOR AN INFINITE HORIZON)

Consider problem (1) and (7) and suppose that U is convex. If $(\mathbf{x}^*(t), \mathbf{u}^*(t))$ for $p_0 = 1$ and for all $t \geq t_0$ satisfies the conditions in Theorem 10.1.1, except the transversality conditions, and if moreover

$$H(t, \mathbf{x}, \mathbf{u}, \mathbf{p}(t)) \text{ is concave in } (\mathbf{x}, \mathbf{u}) \qquad (8)$$

and

$$\lim_{t \to \infty} [\mathbf{p}(t) \cdot (\mathbf{x}(t) - \mathbf{x}^*(t))] \geq 0 \text{ for all admissible } \mathbf{x}(t) \qquad (9)$$

then the pair $(\mathbf{x}^*(t), \mathbf{u}^*(t))$ is CU optimal.

Proof: Applying the arguments in the proof of Theorem 9.7.1 and putting $t_1 = t$, we obtain $D_{\mathbf{u}}(t) \geq \mathbf{p}(t) \cdot (\mathbf{x}(t) - \mathbf{x}^*(t))$. Taking $\underline{\lim}$ on both sides, it follows that $\underline{\lim}_{t \to \infty} D_{\mathbf{u}}(t) \geq 0$. ∎

The following conditions are *sufficient* for (9) to hold (see Seierstad and Sydsæter (1987), Section 3.7, Note 16). For all admissible $\mathbf{x}(t)$:

$$\lim_{t \to \infty} [p_i(t)(x_i^1 - x_i^*(t))] \geq 0 \qquad\qquad i = 1, \ldots, m \qquad\qquad (10a)$$

The exists a constant M such that

$|p_i(t)| \leq M$ for all $t \geq t_0$ $\qquad\qquad i = 1, \ldots, m \qquad\qquad (10b)$

Either there exists a number $t' \geq t_0$ such that $p_i(t) \geq 0$ for all $t \geq t'$, or there exists a number P such that $|x_i(t)| \leq P$ for all $t \geq t_0$ and $\lim_{t \to \infty} p_i(t) \geq 0$ $\qquad\qquad i = l+1, \ldots, m \qquad\qquad (10c)$

There exists a number Q such that $|x_i(t)| < Q$ for all $t \geq t_0$, and $\lim_{t \to \infty} p_i(t) = 0$ $\qquad\qquad i = m+1, \ldots, n \qquad\qquad (10d)$

NOTE 2 (**Malinvaud's transversality conditions**) If the terminal conditions 7(a)–(c) are replaced by the conditions $x_i(t) \geq x_i^1$ for all t and all $i = 1, \ldots, n$, then the inequalities $\mathbf{p}(t) \geq \mathbf{0}$ for all $t \geq t_0$ and 10(a) are sufficient for (9) to hold.

PROBLEMS FOR SECTION 10.3

1. Given $r \in (0, 1)$, solve the problem

$$\max \int_0^\infty (x - u)e^{-rt}\, dt, \quad \dot{x} = ue^{-t}, \quad x(0) = x_0 \geq 0, \quad u \in [0, 1]$$

2. (a) Solve the following problem when $r > a > 0$:

$$\max_{u \in [0,1]} \int_0^\infty x_2 e^{-rt}\, dt, \quad \begin{cases} \dot{x}_1 = aux_1, & x_1(0) = x_1^0 \geq 0 \\ \dot{x}_2 = a(1-u)x_1, & x_2(0) = x_2^0 = 0 \end{cases}$$

(b) Show that the problem has no solution when $r < a$.

10.4 Existence Theorems and Sensitivity

We mentioned at the end of Section 9.3 the role played by existence theorems in optimal control theory. Not every control problem has an optimal solution. For example, in most control problems in economics it is easy to impose requirements on the final state that are entirely unattainable. These are trivial examples of problems without optimal solutions. Moreover, when the control region U is open or unbounded, it is frequently the case that no optimal solution exists. Even if U is compact and there exist admissible pairs, there is no guarantee that an optimal pair exists.

As a practical control problem without an optimal solution, think of trying to keep a pan of boiling water at the constant temperature of 100°C for one hour when it is being heated on an electric burner whose only control is an on/off switch. If we disregard the cost of switching, there is no limit to the number of times we should turn the burner on and off.

In applications one often sees the argument that practical physical or economic considerations strongly suggest the existence of an optimum. Such considerations may be useful as heuristic arguments, but they can never replace a proper mathematical existence proof. In general, a necessary condition for a mathematical optimization problem to give a realistic representation of physical or economic reality is that the problem has a solution. If a practical problem appears to have no solution, the fault may lie with the mathematical description used to model it.

Consider the standard end constrained problem (10.1.1)–(10.1.5). For every $(t, \mathbf{x})$ in $\mathbb{R}^{n+1}$, define the set

$$N(t, \mathbf{x}) = \left\{ \left(f(t, \mathbf{x}, \mathbf{u}) + \gamma, \, g_1(t, \mathbf{x}, \mathbf{u}), \, \ldots, \, g_n(t, \mathbf{x}, \mathbf{u}) \right) : \gamma \leq 0, \, \mathbf{u} \in U \right\} \quad (1)$$

This is a set in $\mathbb{R}^{n+1}$ generated by letting γ take all values ≤ 0, while $\mathbf{u}$ varies in the control region U.

The next theorem requires the set $N(t, \mathbf{x})$ to be convex. This implies that if the system starts in position $\mathbf{x}$ at time t and can be driven at either of the two velocity vectors $\dot{\mathbf{x}}_1$ and $\dot{\mathbf{x}}_2$, then it can also be driven at any velocity vector which is a convex combination of $\dot{\mathbf{x}}_1$ and $\dot{\mathbf{x}}_2$. The "gain" obtained (measured in terms of the value of f) is no smaller than the convex combination of the gains associated with $\dot{\mathbf{x}}_1$ and $\dot{\mathbf{x}}_2$. (For a proof of the theorem see Cesari (1983).)

THEOREM 10.4.1 (FILIPPOV—CESARI'S EXISTENCE THEOREM)

Consider the standard end constrained problem (10.1.1)–(10.1.5). Suppose that there exists an admissible pair, and suppose further that:

(a) $N(t, \mathbf{x})$ in (1) is convex for every $(t, \mathbf{x})$.

(b) U is compact.

(c) There exists a number $b > 0$ such that $\|(\mathbf{x}(t)\| \leq b$ for all t in $[t_0, t_1]$ and all admissible pairs $(\mathbf{x}(t), \mathbf{u}(t))$.

Then there exists an optimal pair $(\mathbf{x}^*(t), \mathbf{u}^*(t))$ (where the control function $\mathbf{u}^*(t)$ is measurable).

NOTE 1 The condition (a) in Theorem 10.4.1 can be dropped if all the functions g_i are of the form $g_i(t, \mathbf{x}, \mathbf{u}) = h_i(t, \mathbf{x}) + k_i(t, \mathbf{u})$, where the h_i functions are linear in $\mathbf{x}$.

NOTE 2 Condition (c) in the theorem is implied by the following sufficient condition:

$$\text{There exist continuous functions } a(t) \text{ and } b(t) \text{ such that} \tag{2}$$
$$\|\mathbf{g}(t, \mathbf{x}, \mathbf{u})\| \le a(t)\|\mathbf{x}\| + b(t) \text{ for all } (\mathbf{x}, \mathbf{u}), \mathbf{u} \in U$$

NOTE 3 For an existence theorem for infinite horizon problems, see Seierstad and Sydsæter (1987), Section 3.7, Theorem 15.

NOTE 4 Consider problem (10.1.1)–(10.1.5) where t_1 is free to take values in an interval $[T_1, T_2]$ with $T_1 \ge t_0$. Then Theorem 10.4.1 is still valid if the requirements are satisfied for all t in $[t_0, T_2]$.

There is a technical problem with the Filippov–Cesari existence theorem which is suggested by the word "measurable". In order to ensure the existence of an optimal control, the class of admissible control functions must be enlarged to include "measurable" functions. These can be much "more discontinuous" than piecewise continuous functions. (For a brief survey, see Lee and Markus (1967), p. 55–56.) In almost all control problems encountered in applications one can assume that if there is a measurable control that solves the problem, then there exists a piecewise continuous control that solves the problem.

EXAMPLE 1   Consider the problem max $\int_0^1 x^2 dt$, $\dot{x} = 1 - u^2$, $x(0) = x(1) = 4$, $u \in [-1, 2] = U$. The Hamiltonian $H = x^2 + p(1 - u^2)$ is not concave in (x, u) and Arrow's sufficiency condition also fails. In Problem 3 you are asked to find a unique solution candidate by using the maximum principle. Use Theorem 10.4.1 to prove that this candidate is optimal.

Solution: Note first that $(x(t), u(t)) \equiv (4, 1)$ is an admissible pair. Also,

$$N(t, x) = \{(x^2 + \gamma, 1 - u^2) : \gamma \le 0, \ u \in [-1, 2]\}$$

which does not depend on t. As u varies in $[-1, 2]$, the second coordinate takes all values between 1 and -3. For fixed x, the first coordinate takes all values less than or equal to x^2. The set $N(t, x)$ is therefore as illustrated in Fig. 1.

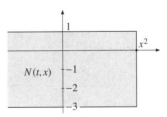

Figure 1 The set $N(t, x)$ in Example 1 is convex.

Obviously, $N(t, x)$ is convex as an "infinite rectangle", so (a) is satisfied. The set $U = [-1, 2]$ is compact. Since $|\dot{x}(t)| = |1 - u^2(t)| \le 3$ for all admissible $u(t)$, any admissible $x(t)$ satisfies $1 \le x(t) \le 7$ for all t in $[0, 1]$, which takes care of (c). We conclude that the unique pair satisfying the conditions in the maximum principle is optimal.

EXAMPLE 2   Show the existence of an optimal control for Example 10.2.2. (*Hint:* Use Note 2.)

Solution: Clearly, $u(t) \equiv 0$ gives an admissible solution, and the set $U = [0, 1]$ is compact. The set $N = N(t, \mathbf{x})$ is here

$$N(t, x_1, x_2) = \{ (x_2 + \gamma, \, aux_1, \, a(1 - u)x_1) \, : \, \gamma \leq 0, \, u \in [0, 1] \}$$

This is the set of points (ξ_1, ξ_2, ξ_3) in $\mathbb{R}^3$ with $\xi_1 \leq x_2$ and (ξ_2, ξ_3) lying on the line segment that joins $(0, ax_1)$ to $(ax_1, 0)$ in $\mathbb{R}^2$. Hence N is convex.

The inequality in (2) is also satisfied because

$$\|\mathbf{g}(t, x_1, x_2, u)\| = \|(aux_1, a(1 - u)x_1)\| = \sqrt{(aux_1)^2 + (a(1-u)x_1)^2}$$

$$= a|x_1|\sqrt{2u^2 - 2u + 1} \leq a|x_1| = a\sqrt{x_1^2} \leq a\sqrt{x_1^2 + x_2^2} = a\|(x_1, x_2)\|$$

using the fact that $2u^2 - 2u + 1 = 2u(u - 1) + 1 \leq 1$ for all u in $[0, 1]$. The existence of a (measurable) optimal control follows from Theorem 10.4.1.

Precise Sensitivity Results

We want to discuss briefly precise conditions for the sensitivity results in (10.1.14) to hold. Consider the standard end constrained problem (10.1.1)–(10.1.5) and assume that admissible pairs exist. Suppose one could compute the value of the objective functional in (10.1.1) for all admissible pairs $(\mathbf{x}(t), \mathbf{u}(t))$. Let $\mathbf{x}^1 = (x_1^1, \ldots, x_m^1)$ and define

$$V(\mathbf{x}^0, \mathbf{x}^1, t_0, t_1) = \sup \left\{ \int_{t_0}^{t_1} f(t, \mathbf{x}(t), \mathbf{u}(t)) \, dt \, : \, (\mathbf{x}(t), \mathbf{u}(t)) \text{ admissible} \right\} \quad (3)$$

(If $m = 0$, the right end point is free and V will not have $\mathbf{x}^1$ as an argument.) The function V is called the (optimal) **value function** of the problem. It is defined only for those $(\mathbf{x}^0, \mathbf{x}^1, t_0, t_1)$ for which admissible pairs exist. If for a given $(\mathbf{x}^0, \mathbf{x}^1, t_0, t_1)$ an *optimal* pair exists, then V is finite and equal to the integral in (10.1.1) evaluated along the optimal pair. (This was the case studied in Section 9.6.) If the set in (3) is not bounded above, then $V = \infty$.)

Suppose that $(\mathbf{x}^*(t), \mathbf{u}^*(t))$ solves problem (10.1.1)–(10.1.5) with $\mathbf{x}^0 = \bar{\mathbf{x}}^0, \mathbf{x}^1 = \bar{\mathbf{x}}^1$, $t_0 = \bar{t}_0, t_1 = \bar{t}_1$ for $p_0 = 1$, with corresponding adjoint function $\mathbf{p}(t)$. The next theorem gives sufficient conditions for V to be defined in a neighbourhood of $(\bar{\mathbf{x}}^0, \bar{\mathbf{x}}^1, \bar{t}_0, \bar{t}_1)$, and for V to be differentiable at $(\bar{\mathbf{x}}^0, \bar{\mathbf{x}}^1, \bar{t}_0, \bar{t}_1)$ with the following partial derivatives:

$$\frac{\partial V(\bar{\mathbf{x}}^0, \bar{\mathbf{x}}^1, \bar{t}_0, \bar{t}_1)}{\partial x_i^0} = p_i(\bar{t}_0), \qquad i = 1, \ldots, n \quad (4)$$

$$\frac{\partial V(\bar{\mathbf{x}}^0, \bar{\mathbf{x}}^1, \bar{t}_0, \bar{t}_1)}{\partial x_i^1} = -p_i(\bar{t}_1), \qquad i = 1, \ldots, n \quad (5)$$

$$\frac{\partial V(\bar{\mathbf{x}}^0, \bar{\mathbf{x}}^1, \bar{t}_0, \bar{t}_1)}{\partial t_0} = -H(\bar{t}_0, \mathbf{x}^*(\bar{t}_0), \mathbf{u}^*(\bar{t}_0), \mathbf{p}(\bar{t}_0)) \quad (6)$$

$$\frac{\partial V(\bar{\mathbf{x}}^0, \bar{\mathbf{x}}^1, \bar{t}_0, \bar{t}_1)}{\partial t_1} = H(\bar{t}_1, \mathbf{x}^*(\bar{t}_1), \mathbf{u}^*(\bar{t}_1), \mathbf{p}(\bar{t}_1)) \quad (7)$$

THEOREM 10.4.2

Consider the standard end constrained problem (10.1.1)–(10.1.5) with a compact control region U. Suppose that

(a) $(\mathbf{x}^*(t), \mathbf{u}^*(t))$ is a unique optimal solution.

(b) $\mathbf{p}(t)$ is uniquely determined by the necessary conditions given $\mathbf{x}^*(t)$, $\mathbf{u}^*(t)$, and $p_0 = 1$.

(c) There exist continuous functions $a(t)$ and $b(t)$ such that

$$\|f(t, \mathbf{x}, \mathbf{u})\| \leq a(t)\|\mathbf{x}\| + b(t) \quad \text{for all } (\mathbf{x}, \mathbf{u}) \text{ with } \mathbf{u} \in U \tag{8}$$

(d) The set $N(t, \mathbf{x})$ in (1) is convex for each $(t, \mathbf{x})$.

Then (4)–(7) are all valid.

For a proof of this theorem see Clarke (1983).

NOTE 5   Assume in this note that the uniqueness condition in (b) is replaced by the condition that the function $\mathbf{x} \mapsto \widehat{H}(t, \mathbf{x}, \mathbf{p}(t))$ is concave. Then the function V is defined for $t_0 = \bar{t}_0$, $t_1 = \bar{t}_0$, and $(\mathbf{x}^0, \mathbf{x}^1)$ in a neighbourhood of $(\bar{\mathbf{x}}^0, \bar{\mathbf{x}}^1)$, and the partial derivatives are given by (4) and (5) at $(\bar{\mathbf{x}}^0, \bar{\mathbf{x}}^1)$. If $l = n$ (and so the end point is fixed), or if $\mathbf{x} \mapsto \widehat{H}(t, \mathbf{x}, \mathbf{p}(t))$ is *strictly* concave, then *all* the partial derivatives (including those in (6) and (7)) exist. For further details see Seierstad and Sydsæter (1987).

PROBLEMS FOR SECTION 10.4

1. Show the existence of a optimal control and draw a picture of the set $N(t, x)$ for the problem

$$\max \int_0^1 x(t)\, dt, \qquad \dot{x}(t) = x(t) + u(t), \quad x(0) = 0, \quad x(1) \geq 1, \quad u \in [-1, 1]$$

2. Solve the problem: $\displaystyle \max_{u \in [0,1]} \int_0^1 (1-u)x^2\, dt, \quad \dot{x} = ux, \quad x(0) = x_0 > 0, \quad x(1)$ free.

3. Find the unique solution candidate in Example 1 using the maximum principle. (*Hint:* Argue why $u^*(t)$ can only take the values 0 and 2, and why any admissible $x(t)$ is > 0 in $[0, 1]$.)

10.5   A Heuristic Proof of the Maximum Principle

A full proof of the general maximum principle is quite demanding and draws on several advanced results in the theory of differential equations which are not in the toolkit of most economists. The heuristic arguments for the main results given below, although not precise, give a good indication of why the maximum principle is correct. We restrict our attention to problems with one state and one control variable.

Consider the following control problem with two alternative terminal conditions

$$\max_{u \in U} \int_{t_0}^{t_1} f(t, x, u)\, dt, \quad \dot{x} = g(t, x, u), \quad x(t_0) = x_0, \quad \begin{cases} x(t_1) \text{ free} \\ x(t_1) = x_1 \end{cases} \tag{i}$$

Think of $x = x(t)$ as a firm's capital stock and $\int_{t_0}^{t_1} f(t, x, u)\, dt$ as the total profit over the planning period $[t_0, t_1]$, in line with our general economic interpretation in Section 9.6. Define the value function by

$$V(t, x) = \max_{u \in U} \left\{ \int_t^{t_1} f(s, x(s), u(s))\, ds : \dot{x}(s) = g(s, x(s), u(s)), \; x(t) = x, \; \begin{cases} x(t_1) \text{ free} \\ x(t_1) = x_1 \end{cases} \right\} \tag{ii}$$

Thus $V(t, x)$ is the maximum profit obtainable if we start at time t with the capital stock x. Suppose the problem in (ii) has a unique solution, which we denote by $\tilde{u}(s; t, x), \tilde{x}(s; t, x)$, for $t_0 \leq t \leq s \leq t_1$. Then, by definition, $\tilde{x}(t; t, x) = x$.

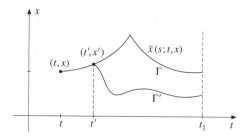

Figure 1   The case of $x(t_1)$ free.

Consider any starting point (t', x') which lies on the optimal path Γ defined by the original solution $\tilde{x}(s; t, x)$. If there were a better path Γ' starting at (t', x'), it would have been optimal for the solution starting at (t, x) to follow this improved path over the time interval $[t', t_1]$.[1] (See Fig. 1, which deals with the case when $x(t_1)$ is free.) For this reason, an optimal solution starting at (t, x) is automatically an optimal solution from (t', x') as well: *The "tail" of an optimal solution is optimal.* Using the uniqueness of $(\tilde{x}(s; t, x), \tilde{u}(s; t, x))$ for all (t, x), this implies the relations

$$\tilde{u}(s; t', x') = \tilde{u}(s; t, x), \quad \tilde{x}(s; t', x') = \tilde{x}(s; t, x)$$

whenever $t' \in [t, s]$ and $x' = \tilde{x}(t'; t, x)$. Hence,

$$V(t', \tilde{x}(t'; t, x)) = \int_{t'}^{t_1} f(s, \tilde{x}(s; t, x), \tilde{u}(s; t, x))\, ds$$

Differentiate this equation w.r.t. t' at $t' = t$. Because $d\tilde{x}(t'; t, x)/dt' = g(t', \tilde{x}(t'; t, x), \tilde{u}(t'; t, x))$, we have

$$V_t'(t, x) + V_x'(t, x) g(t, x, \tilde{u}(t; t, x)) = -f(t, x, \tilde{u}(t; t, x)) \tag{iii}$$

---

[1] "Better path" Γ' is intuitive language. It means that there exists an admissible pair $(x(s), u(s))$ (with corresponding path Γ') that gives a higher value to the integral of f over $[t', t_1]$ when $(x(s), u(s))$ is inserted, as compared with the value resulting from $(\tilde{x}(s; t, x), \tilde{u}(s; t, x))$.

Hence, if we define

$$\bar{p}(t, x) = V'_x(t, x)$$

and introduce the Hamiltonian function $H(t, x, u, p) = f(t, x, u) + p\, g(t, x, u)$, then equation (iii) can be written in the form

$$V'_t(t, x) + H(t, x, \tilde{u}(t; t, x), \bar{p}(t, x)) = 0 \qquad \text{(iv)}$$

Starting at the point (t, x), consider an alternative control which is a constant v on an interval $[t, t + \Delta t]$ and optimal thereafter. Let the corresponding state variable be $x^v(s)$ for s in $[t, t + \Delta t]$. Then

$$V(t, x) \geq \int_t^{t+\Delta t} f(s, x^v(s), v)\, ds + V(t + \Delta t, x^v(t + \Delta t))$$

and so

$$V(t + \Delta t, x^v(t + \Delta t)) - V(t, x) + \int_t^{t+\Delta t} f(s, x^v(s), v)\, ds \leq 0 \qquad \text{(v)}$$

Dividing this inequality by Δt and letting $\Delta t \to 0$, we get $\frac{d}{dt} V(t, x^v(t)) + f(t, x, v) \leq 0$. Now, $\frac{d}{dt} V(t, x) = V'_t(t, x(t)) + V'_x(t, x)\dot{x}^v$. Since $V'_x(t, x) = \bar{p}(t, x)$ and $\dot{x}^v(t) = g(t, x, v)$, we must have

$$V'_t(t, x) + \bar{p}(t, x)g(t, x, v) + f(t, x, v) \leq 0$$

Thus for all v in U,

$$V'_t(t, x) + H(t, x, v, \bar{p}(t, x)) \leq 0$$

Because of (iv), this implies that the optimal control $\tilde{u}(t; t, x)$ must maximize $H(t, x, u, \bar{p}(t, x))$ w.r.t. $u \in U$. In addition,

$$V'_t(t, x) + \max_{u \in U} H(t, x, u, V'_x(t, x)) = 0 \qquad \text{(vi)}$$

This is called the **Hamilton–Jacobi–Bellman equation**.

Next, define $x^*(t) = \tilde{x}(t; t_0, x_0)$ and $u^*(t) = \tilde{u}(t; t_0, x_0)$. These functions give the optimal solution to the original problem. Also, let $p(t) = \bar{p}(t, x^*(t))$. Then $\tilde{u}(t; t, x^*(t)) = u^*(t)$, and therefore

$$u = u^*(t) \text{ maximizes } H(t, x^*(t), u, p(t)) \text{ w.r.t. } u \in U \qquad \text{(vii)}$$

Finally, differentiating (iv) w.r.t. x and using the envelope theorem (see Section 3.8), we get

$$V''_{tx} + H'_x + H'_p \bar{p}'_x = 0$$

Because $p = V'_x$ and $H'_p = g$, this can be written as $\bar{p}'_t + \bar{p}'_x g = -H'_x$, where g is evaluated at $(t, x, \tilde{u}(t; t, x))$. If we let $x = x^*(t)$ and use $u^*(t) = \tilde{u}(t; t, x)$, then $\dot{p} = \bar{p}'_t + \bar{p}'_x \dot{x} = \bar{p}'_t + \bar{p}'_x g(t, x, u^*(t))$, so

$$\dot{p}(t) = -H'_x(t, x^*(t), u^*(t), p(t)) \qquad \text{(viii)}$$

By definition of V, if $x(t_1)$ is free, then $V(t_1, x) = 0$ for all x. Thus $\bar{p}(t_1, x) = 0$, and so we have the transversality condition

$$p(t_1) = 0 \qquad \text{(ix)}$$

Conditions (vii) to (ix) are the necessary conditions in the maximum principle (with t_1 fixed and $x(t_1)$ free). If $x(t_1)$ is fixed, condition (ix) is not valid (and not needed).

We have shown that

$$V'_{t_0} = -H^*(t_0), \qquad V'_{x_0} = p(t_0) \qquad \text{(x)}$$

In fact, the first equality follows from (iv) and the second one from the definitions of the function $\bar{p}$ and p. These are two of the formulas in (10.1.14). Reversing time gives the other two relations in (10.1.14):

$$V'_{t_1} = H^*(t_1), \qquad V'_{x_1} = -p(t_1) \qquad \text{(xi)}$$

Variable Final Time Problems

Consider problem (i) with t_1 free. Suppose $(x^*(t), u^*(t))$ is an optimal solution defined on $[t_0, t_1^*]$. Then conditions (vi)–(viii) must be valid on the interval $[t_0, t_1^*]$, because $(x^*(t), u^*(t))$ must be an optimal pair for the corresponding fixed time problem with $t_1 = t_1^*$. Moreover, at the terminal time t_1^* the value function's derivative w.r.t. t_1 must be 0. (As a function of t_1 it has a maximum at t_1^*.) Because of (xi), this means that

$$H^*(t_1^*) = H(t_1^*, x^*(t_1^*), u^*(t_1^*), p(t_1^*)) = V_{t_1}'(t_1^*, x^*(t_1^*)) = 0 \tag{xi}$$

This equation gives an extra condition for determining t_1^*, and is precisely condition (9.8.2).

NOTE 1 In the above heuristic "proof" of the maximum principle, differentiability of the function V was assumed without proof.

10.6 Mixed Constraints

This section describes control problems where the admissible pairs $(\mathbf{x}, \mathbf{u})$ are required to satisfy additional constraints of the form $\mathbf{h}(t, \mathbf{x}, \mathbf{u}) \geq \mathbf{0}$. Such restrictions often occur in economic models. If the control variable $\mathbf{u}$ as well as the state vector $\mathbf{x}$ appear in the function $\mathbf{h}$, the restriction is often referred to as a *"mixed constraint"*, while restrictions of the type $\mathbf{h}(t, \mathbf{x}) \geq \mathbf{0}$ are called *"pure state constraints"*.

Whether or not mixed constraints are present in a given control problem is partly a question of the form in which the problem is stated. Consider the following problem.

EXAMPLE 1   Consider the growth problem

$$\max_u \int_0^T U((1-u)f(K))\, dt, \quad \dot{K} = u, \ K(0) = K_0, \ K(T) = K_T, \ u \geq 0, \ f(K) - u \geq 0$$

Here there are two constraints for each t—namely, $h_1(t, K, u) = u \geq 0$ and $h_2(t, K, u) = f(K) - u \geq 0$. However, if we specify a control variable v so that $\dot{K} = vf(K)$, then the simple restriction $0 \leq v \leq 1$ replaces the mixed constraints. (If we require $f(K) - u \geq k > 0$, this trick does not work.)

We consider the **mixed constraints problem**

$$\max_{\mathbf{u}} \int_{t_0}^{t_1} f(t, \mathbf{x}, \mathbf{u})\, dt, \quad \dot{\mathbf{x}} = \mathbf{g}(t, \mathbf{x}, \mathbf{u}), \quad \mathbf{x}(t_0) = \mathbf{x}^0 \tag{1}$$

$$\mathbf{h}(t, \mathbf{x}, \mathbf{u}) \geq \mathbf{0} \quad \text{for all } t \tag{2}$$

with the terminal conditions

$$\begin{align}
&\text{(a)} \quad x_i(t_1) = x_i^1, &&i = 1, \ldots, l \\
&\text{(b)} \quad x_i(t_1) \geq x_i^1, &&i = l+1, \ldots, m \tag{3} \\
&\text{(c)} \quad x_i(t_1) \text{ free}, &&i = m+1, \ldots, n
\end{align}$$

As usual, $\mathbf{x}$ is n-dimensional and $\mathbf{u}$ is r-dimensional, while $\mathbf{h}$ is an s-dimensional vector function, so that the inequality $\mathbf{h}(t, \mathbf{x}, \mathbf{u}) \geq \mathbf{0}$ represents the s inequalities

$$h_k(t, \mathbf{x}(t), \mathbf{u}(t)) \geq 0, \qquad k = 1, \ldots, s \qquad (4)$$

All the restrictions on $\mathbf{u}(t)$ are assumed to have been incorporated into (2). Thus, no additional requirement of the form $\mathbf{u} \in U$ is imposed. In addition to the usual requirements on f and $\mathbf{g}$, it is assumed that $\mathbf{h}$ is a C^1 function in $(t, \mathbf{x}, \mathbf{u})$. The pair $(\mathbf{x}(t), \mathbf{u}(t))$ is **admissible** if $u_1(t), \ldots, u_r(t)$ are all piecewise continuous, and $\mathbf{x}(t) = (x_1(t), \ldots, x_n(t))$ is the corresponding continuous and piecewise differentiable vector function that satisfies $\dot{\mathbf{x}} = \mathbf{g}(t, \mathbf{x}, \mathbf{u})$, $\mathbf{x}(t_0) = \mathbf{x}^0$, (2), and (3). The theorem below gives sufficient conditions for the solution of the mixed constraints problem (1)–(3). To economists, it will come as no surprise that we associate multipliers $q_1(t), \ldots, q_s(t)$ with the constraints (2) and define the Lagrangian function, with $\mathbf{q} = (q_1, \ldots, q_s)$, as

$$\mathcal{L}(t, \mathbf{x}, \mathbf{u}, \mathbf{p}, \mathbf{q}) = H(t, \mathbf{x}, \mathbf{u}, \mathbf{p}) + \sum_{k=1}^{s} q_k h_k(t, \mathbf{x}, \mathbf{u}) \qquad (5)$$

where the Hamiltonian is as before $H(t, \mathbf{x}, \mathbf{u}, \mathbf{p}) = f(t, \mathbf{x}, \mathbf{u}) + \sum_{i=1}^{n} p_i g_i(t, \mathbf{x}, \mathbf{u})$ (with $p_0 = 1$).

In the following theorem $\mathcal{L}^*$ denotes evaluation of $\mathcal{L}$ at $(t, \mathbf{x}^*(t), \mathbf{u}^*(t), \mathbf{p}(t), \mathbf{q}(t))$.

THEOREM 10.6.1 (SUFFICIENT CONDITIONS)

Suppose $(\mathbf{x}^*(t), \mathbf{u}^*(t))$ is an admissible pair in the mixed constraints problem (1)–(3). Suppose further that there exist functions $\mathbf{p}(t) = (p_1(t), \ldots, p_n(t))$ and $\mathbf{q}(t) = (q_1(t), \ldots, q_s(t))$, where $\mathbf{p}(t)$ is continuous, while $\dot{\mathbf{p}}(t)$ and $\mathbf{q}(t)$ are piecewise continuous, such that the following requirements are satisfied:

$$\frac{\partial \mathcal{L}^*}{\partial u_j} = 0, \qquad\qquad\qquad\qquad j = 1, \ldots, r \qquad (6)$$

$$q_k(t) \geq 0 \quad (q_k(t) = 0 \text{ if } h_k(t, \mathbf{x}^*(t), \mathbf{u}^*(t)) > 0), \quad k = 1, \ldots, s \qquad (7)$$

$$\dot{p}_i(t) = -\frac{\partial \mathcal{L}^*}{\partial x_i} \text{ at all continuity points of } \mathbf{u}^*(t), \qquad i = 1, \ldots, n \qquad (8)$$

No conditions on $p_i(t_1)$, $\qquad\qquad\qquad\qquad i = 1, \ldots, l \qquad (9a)$

$p_i(t_1) \geq 0 \quad (p_i(t_1) = 0 \text{ if } x_i^*(t_1) > x_i^1), \qquad i = l+1, \ldots, m \qquad (9b)$

$p_i(t_1) = 0, \qquad\qquad\qquad\qquad\qquad i = m+1, \ldots, n \qquad (9c)$

$H(t, \mathbf{x}, \mathbf{u}, \mathbf{p}(t))$ is concave in $(\mathbf{x}, \mathbf{u})$ $\qquad\qquad\qquad\qquad (10)$

$h_k(t, \mathbf{x}, \mathbf{u})$ is quasiconcave in $(\mathbf{x}, \mathbf{u})$, $\qquad\qquad k = 1, \ldots, s \qquad (11)$

Then $(\mathbf{x}^*(t), \mathbf{u}^*(t))$ solves the problem.

A proof of this theorem is given in Seierstad and Sydsæter (1987), Section 4.3, which also discusses necessary conditions, generalizations, and examples, and has further references to other literature. A simpler treatment can be found in Léonard and Long (1992), Chapter 6. Note that as in nonlinear programming a constraint qualification is often needed to be able to find a pair $(x(t), u(t))$ of the type occurring in the theorem. The constraint qualification, more or less, requires that the control u appears in each constraint.

EXAMPLE 2   Solve the mixed constraints problem

$$\max \int_0^T u \, dt, \quad \dot{x} = ax - u, \quad x(0) = x^0, \quad x(T) \text{ free}, \quad \begin{cases} h_1(t, x, u) = u - c \geq 0 \\ h_2(t, x, u) = ax - u \geq 0 \end{cases}$$

Here x is the capital stock, u is consumption, and c is a subsistence level. The constants T, a, c, and x^0 are positive, with $T > 1/a$ and $ax^0 > c$.

Solution: The Hamiltonian and the Lagrangian are

$$H = u + p(ax - u), \qquad \mathcal{L} = H + q_1(u - c) + q_2(ax - u)$$

Here H as well as h_1 and h_2 are linear and hence concave in (x, u). The following conditions from Theorem 10.6.1 are therefore sufficient for optimality:

$$\frac{\partial \mathcal{L}^*}{\partial u} = 1 - p(t) + q_1(t) - q_2(t) = 0 \tag{i}$$

$$q_1(t) \geq 0 \qquad (q_1(t) = 0 \text{ if } u^*(t) > c) \tag{ii}$$

$$q_2(t) \geq 0 \qquad (q_2(t) = 0 \text{ if } ax^*(t) > u^*(t)) \tag{iii}$$

$$\dot{p}(t) = -\frac{\partial \mathcal{L}^*}{\partial x} = -ap(t) - aq_2(t), \quad p(T) = 0 \tag{iv}$$

$$u^*(t) \geq c, \qquad ax^*(t) - u^*(t) \geq 0 \tag{v}$$

Because $x^*(0) = x^0 > 0$ and $\dot{x}^*(t) = ax^*(t) - u^*(t) \geq 0$ for all t, one has $x^*(t) \geq x^0$ for all t. If $u^*(t) = c$, then $ax^*(t) - u^*(t) = ax^*(t) - c \geq ax^0 - c > 0$, and then from (iii), $q_2(t) = 0$. If $u^*(t) > c$, then (ii) implies $q_1(t) = 0$. Hence, for all t in $[0, T]$, either $q_1(t)$ or $q_2(t)$ is 0.

For $t < T$ close to T, because $p(T) = 0$, it follows that $p(t) < 1$. Define t^* as the latest time t in $[0, T]$ such that $p(t) \geq 1$, with $t^* = 0$ in case $p(t) < 1$ for all t in $[0, T]$. Then for all t in $(t^*, T]$, (i) implies that $q_2(t) = 1 - p(t) + q_1(t) > q_1(t)$ so $q_2(t) > 0$ and $\dot{p}(t) = -ap(t) - aq_2(t) = -ap(t) - a(1 - p(t) + q_1(t)) = -a$, since $q_1(t) = 0$. It follows that $p(t) = a(T - t)$ and so $q_2(t) = 1 - p(t) = 1 - a(T - t)$ for all t in $(t^*, T]$. Also, from (iii), $u^*(t) = ax^*(t)$ for all t in this interval.

From Problem 5.4.9 we see that the solution to (iv) is $p(t) = \int_t^T aq_2(\tau)e^{-a(t-\tau)} \, d\tau$, which is clearly ≥ 0. Moreover, $p(t)$ is continuous, so $p(t^*) = 1$ unless $t^* = 0$, and $\dot{p}(t^*) = -a - aq_2(t^*) < 0$. It follows from (iv) that $\dot{p}(t) \leq 0$, so that $p(t) > 1$ in $[0, t^*)$ and $p(t) < 1$ in $(t^*, T]$. Because $p(t) = a(T - t)$ for all t in $(t^*, T]$, unless $t^* = 0$, one has $1 = p(t^*) = a(T - t^*)$ and so $t^* = T - 1/a$. Then, because of the hypothesis that $T > 1/a$, the case $t^* = 0$ cannot arise.

In the interval $[0, t^*)$ one has $p(t) > 1$, so (i) implies that $q_1(t) > q_2(t)$ and, because either $q_1(t)$ or $q_2(t)$ is 0, in fact $q_2(t) = 0$. Then from (ii), $u^*(t) = c$ so that $\dot{x}^*(t) = ax^*(t) - c$, with $x^*(0) = x^0$. Solving this linear differential equation yields $x^*(t) = (x^0 - c/a)e^{at} + c/a$. The differential equation for $p(t)$ is $\dot{p} = -ap$ because $q_2 = 0$. Hence $p(t) = Ae^{-at}$ with $p(t^*) = 1$, so $p(t) = e^{-a(t-t^*)}$.

Since $x^*(t)$ is continuous also at t^*, and $\dot{x}^*(t) \equiv 0$ in $(t^*, T]$, $x^*(t)$ has the constant value $(x^0 - c/a)e^{at^*} + c/a$ in $(t^*, T]$.

We have found the following candidate for an optimal solution, with $t^* = T - 1/a$:

	$u^*(t)$	$x^*(t)$	$p(t)$	$q_1(t)$	$q_2(t)$
$[0, t^*]$	c	$(x^0 - c/a)e^{at} + c/a$	$e^{-a(t-t^*)}$	$e^{-a(t-t^*)} - 1$	0
$(t^*, T]$	$ax^*(t)$	$(x^0 - c/a)e^{at^*} + c/a$	$a(T - t)$	0	$1 - a(T - t)$

Mangasarian's theorem implies that this candidate is optimal. Note that in this example the multipliers $q_1(t)$ and $q_2(t)$ are continuous.

PROBLEMS FOR SECTION 10.6

1. (a) Write down the conditions in Theorem 10.6.1 for the problem

$$\max \int_0^2 (-\tfrac{1}{2}u^2 - x)\, dt, \quad \dot{x} = -u, \quad x(0) = 1, \quad x(2) \text{ free}, \quad x \geq u$$

(b) Solve the problem. (*Hint:* Guess that $u^*(t) = x^*(t)$ on some interval $[0, t^*]$, and $u^*(t) < x^*(t)$ on $(t^*, 2]$. Then $q(t^{*+}) = 0$, and $u^*(t^{*-}) = x^*(t^*) \geq u^*(t^{*+})$. We can use the following argument[2] to show that $q(t^{*-}) = 0$: From $\partial \mathcal{L}^*/\partial u = 0$ we get $q(t) = -p(t) - u^*(t)$. In particular, $q(t^{*-}) = -p(t^*) - u^*(t^{*-}) \leq -p(t^*) - u^*(t^{*+}) = q(t^{*+}) = 0$.)

2. Solve the problem

$$\max \int_0^2 (x - \tfrac{1}{2}u^2)\, dt, \quad \dot{x} = u, \quad x(0) = 1, \quad x(2) \text{ free}, \quad x \geq u$$

(*Hint:* Guess that $u^*(t) = x^*(t)$ on some interval $[0, t^*]$, and $u^*(t) < x^*(t)$ on $(t^*, 2]$. As in Problem 1, $q(t^{*-}) = 0$.)

3. Solve the following variant of Example 2.

$$\max \int_0^T u\, dt, \quad \dot{x} = ax - u, \quad x(0) = x^0 > 0, \quad x(T) \geq x_T, \quad c \leq u \leq ax$$

where $a > 0$, $c > 0$, $T > 1/a$, $ax^0 > c$, and $x^0 \leq x_T < (x^0 - c/a)e^{aT} + c/a$. (This model can be interpreted as a simple growth model with a subsistence level c.)

---

[2] The same argument is useful in other problems also, for example in Problem 2.

4. Solve the problem

$$\max \int_0^1 x\, dt, \quad \dot{x} = x + u, \quad x(0) = 0, \quad x(1) \text{ free}, \quad \begin{cases} h_1(t, x, u) = 1 - u \geq 0 \\ h_2(t, x, u) = 1 + u \geq 0 \\ h_3(t, x, u) = 2 - x - u \geq 0 \end{cases}$$

(*Hint:* See the solution to Example 9.4.1. Try with $u^*(t) = 1$, $x^*(t) = e^t - 1$ in the beginning.)

10.7 Pure State Constraints

This section briefly discusses a result giving sufficient conditions for a pure state constrained problem. It gives an indication of the type of results that can be proved, but we refer to literature for proofs, examples, and generalizations.

Consider the following **pure state constrained problem**,

$$\max \int_{t_0}^{t_1} f(t, \mathbf{x}, \mathbf{u})\, dt, \quad \dot{\mathbf{x}} = \mathbf{g}(t, \mathbf{x}, \mathbf{u}), \quad \mathbf{x}(t_0) = \mathbf{x}^0, \quad \mathbf{u}(t) \in U \subseteq \mathbb{R}^r \quad (1)$$

$$\mathbf{h}(t, \mathbf{x}) \geq \mathbf{0} \quad \text{for all } t \quad (2)$$

with the terminal conditions

$$\begin{array}{lll} \text{(a)} & x_i(t_1) = x_i^1, & i = 1, \ldots, l \\ \text{(b)} & x_i(t_1) \geq x_i^1, & i = l+1, \ldots, m \\ \text{(c)} & x_i(t_1) \text{ free}, & i = m+1, \ldots, n \end{array} \quad (3)$$

Note that in contrast to the mixed constraints case, we now allow a restriction of the form $u \in U$. The vector function $\mathbf{h}$ is s-dimensional, and the pure state constraint (2) can be written

$$h_k(t, \mathbf{x}(t)) \geq 0, \quad k = 1, \ldots, s \quad (4)$$

The sufficient conditions given in the next theorem are somewhat more complicated than those in Theorem 10.6.1. In particular, the adjoint functions may have jumps at the terminal time.

The Lagrangian associated with this problem is

$$\mathcal{L}(t, \mathbf{x}, \mathbf{u}, \mathbf{p}, \mathbf{q}) = H(t, \mathbf{x}, \mathbf{u}, \mathbf{p}) + \sum_{k=1}^{s} q_k h_k(t, \mathbf{x}) \quad (5)$$

with $H(t, \mathbf{x}, \mathbf{u}, \mathbf{p})$ as the usual Hamiltonian (with $p_0 = 1$).

THEOREM 10.7.1 (SUFFICIENT CONDITIONS)

Suppose $(\mathbf{x}^*(t), \mathbf{u}^*(t))$ is admissible in problem (1)–(3), and that there exist vector functions $\mathbf{p}(t)$ and $\mathbf{q}(t)$, where $\mathbf{p}(t)$ is continuous and $\dot{\mathbf{p}}(t)$ and $\mathbf{q}(t)$ are piecewise continuous in $[t_0, t_1)$, and numbers β_k, $k = 1, \ldots, s$, such that the following conditions are satisfied with $p_0 = 1$:

$$\mathbf{u} = \mathbf{u}^*(t) \text{ maximizes } H(t, \mathbf{x}^*(t), \mathbf{u}, \mathbf{p}(t)) \text{ for } \mathbf{u} \text{ in } U. \tag{6}$$

$$q_k(t) \geq 0 \quad (q_k(t) = 0 \text{ if } h_k(t, \mathbf{x}^*(t)) > 0), \qquad k = 1, \ldots, s \tag{7}$$

$$\dot{p}_i(t) = -\frac{\partial \mathcal{L}^*}{\partial x_i} \text{ at all continuity points of } \mathbf{u}^*(t), \qquad i = 1, \ldots, n \tag{8}$$

At t_1, $p_i(t)$ can have a jump discontinuity, in which case

$$p_i(t_1^-) - p_i(t_1) = \sum_{k=1}^{s} \beta_k \frac{\partial h_k(t_1, \mathbf{x}^*(t_1))}{\partial x_i}, \qquad i = 1, \ldots, n \tag{9}$$

$$\beta_k \geq 0 \quad (\beta_k = 0 \text{ if } h_k(t_1, \mathbf{x}^*(t_1)) > 0), \qquad k = 1, \ldots, s \tag{10}$$

$$\text{No conditions on } p_i(t_1), \qquad i = 1, \ldots, l \tag{11a}$$

$$p_i(t_1) \geq 0 \quad (p_i(t_1) = 0 \text{ if } x_i^*(t_1) > x_i^1), \qquad i = l+1, \ldots, m \tag{11b}$$

$$p_i(t_1) = 0, \qquad i = m+1, \ldots, n \tag{11c}$$

$$\widehat{H}(t, \mathbf{x}, \mathbf{p}(t)) = \max_{\mathbf{u} \in U} H(t, \mathbf{x}, \mathbf{u}, \mathbf{p}(t)) \text{ is concave in } \mathbf{x}. \tag{12}$$

$$h_k(t, \mathbf{x}) \text{ is quasiconcave in } \mathbf{x}, \qquad k = 1, \ldots, s \tag{13}$$

Then $(\mathbf{x}^*(t), \mathbf{u}^*(t))$ solves the problem.

Here $\mathbf{p}(t) = (p_1(t), \ldots, p_n(t))$ and $\mathbf{q}(t) = (q_1(t), \ldots, q_s(t))$, while $\mathcal{L}^*$ denotes evaluation of $\mathcal{L}$ at $(t, \mathbf{x}^*(t), \mathbf{u}^*(t), \mathbf{p}(t), \mathbf{q}(t))$.

NOTE 1 The conditions in this theorem are somewhat restrictive. In particular, sometimes one must allow $\mathbf{p}(t)$ to have discontinuities at interior points of $[t_0, t_1]$. For details and a proof, see Seierstad and Sydsaeter (1987).

EXAMPLE 1   Solve the problem

$$\max \int_0^4 (x - (u - 2)^2)\, dt, \quad \dot{x} = u \in \mathbb{R}, \quad x(0) = 0, \quad x(4) \text{ free}, \quad x(t) \leq 1$$

Solution: The Lagrangian is $\mathcal{L} = H + q(1 - x) = x - (u - 2)^2 + pu + q(1 - x)$. Here H is concave in (x, u) and $h(t, x) = 1 - x$ is quasiconcave, so the conditions (i)–(iv) below are therefore sufficient for optimality. Equation (i) results from the observation that H is concave in u and $u \in \mathbb{R}$, so condition (6) is equivalent to the condition $\partial H^*/\partial u = 0$.

$$u^*(t) = \tfrac{1}{2}p(t) + 2 \tag{i}$$

$$q(t) \geq 0 \quad (q(t) = 0 \text{ if } x^*(t) < 1) \tag{ii}$$

$$\dot{p}(t) = -\frac{\partial \mathcal{L}^*}{\partial x} = -1 + q(t), \quad p(4) = 0 \tag{iii}$$

$$p(4^-) - p(4) = -\beta \leq 0 \quad (\beta = 0 \text{ if } x^*(4) < 1) \tag{iv}$$

We can make guesses as to the behaviour of the solution as long as we verify that all the conditions in the theorem are satisfied. We guess that $x^*(t) < 1$ in an interval $[0, t^*)$ and that $x^*(t) = 1$ in $(t^*, 4]$. Then in $(t^*, 4)$, $u^*(t) = \dot{x}^*(t) = 0$, and from (i), $p(t) = -4$. But then from (iii) and (iv), $\beta = p(4) - p(4^-) = 4$. On $[0, t^*)$, from (ii) and (iii), $\dot{p}(t) = -1$. Since $p(t)$ is continuous at t^*, $p(t^{*-}) = -4$. Hence $p(t) = -4 + (t^* - t)$, and from (i), $u^*(t) = \frac{1}{2}(t^* - t)$. Integrating $\dot{x}^*(t) = \frac{1}{2}(t^* - t)$ yields $x^*(t) = -\frac{1}{4}(t^* - t)^2 + C$ on $[0, t^*)$. Since $x^*(t^*) = 1$, we get $x^*(t^*) = C = 1$. But $x^*(0) = 0$, so $t^* = 2$. Our suggestion is therefore:

In $[0, 2]$: $u^*(t) = 1 - \frac{1}{2}t$, $x^*(t) = 1 - \frac{1}{4}(2 - t)^2$, $p(t) = -t - 2$, and $q(t) = 0$.
In $(2, 4]$: $u^*(t) = 0$, $x^*(t) = 1$, $p(t) = -4$ (except that $p(4) = 0$), and $q(t) = 1$ with $\beta = 4$.
You should now verify that all the conditions (i)–(iv) are satisfied. Note that $p(t)$ has a jump at $t = 4$, from -4 to 0.

PROBLEMS FOR SECTION 10.7

1. Solve the problem

$$\min \int_0^5 (u + x)\, dt, \quad \dot{x} = u - t, \quad x(0) = 1, \quad x(5) \text{ free}, \quad x \geq 0, \quad u \geq 0$$

(*Hint:* See if it pays to keep $x(t)$ as low as possible all the time.)

2. Solve the problem

$$\max \int_0^2 (1 - x)\, dt, \quad \dot{x} = u, \quad x(0) = 1, \quad x(2) \text{ free}, \quad x \geq 0, \quad u \in [-1, 1]$$

(*Hint:* Start by reducing $x(t)$ as much as possible until $x(t) = 0$.)

3. Solve the problem

$$\max \int_0^{10} (-u^2 - x)\, dt, \quad \dot{x} = u, \quad x(0) = 1, \quad x(10) \text{ free}, \quad x \geq 0, \quad u \in \mathbb{R}$$

4. Consider the problem

$$\max \int_0^3 (4-t)u\,dt, \quad \dot{x}=u \in [0,2], \quad x(0)=1, \quad x(3)=3, \quad t+1-x \geq 0 \quad (*)$$

(a) Solve the problem when the constraint $t+1-x \geq 0$ is not imposed.

(b) Solve problem $(*)$.

10.8 Generalizations

In Chapter 9 and the previous sections of this chapter we have discussed some topics in optimal control theory. Many important economic problems cannot be treated using the methods described in this book.

More General Terminal Conditions

In some dynamical optimization problems the standard terminal conditions are replaced by the requirement that $\mathbf{x}(t)$ at time t_1 hits a **target** defined as a certain curve or surface in $\mathbb{R}^n$.

The optimal path in such a problem must end at some point $\mathbf{x}^1$ and therefore, in particular, will solve the corresponding control problem where *all* the admissible paths end at $\mathbf{x}^1$. The conditions in Theorem 10.1.1 must therefore still be valid, except the transversality conditions, which must be adjusted. See e.g. Seierstad and Sydsæter (1984), Chapter 3.

Markov Controls

The optimal solutions we have been looking for have been functions of time, $\mathbf{u}^*(t)$ and $\mathbf{x}^*(t)$. Such control functions are called "open-loop controls". Faced with the problem of steering an economic system optimally, such open-loop controls are often inadequate. The problem is that "disturbances" of many types will almost always occur, which will divert the system from the optimal path initially computed. If one still uses the "old" control $\mathbf{u}^*(t)$, one can end up with a development of the economy which is far from optimal, and which does not necessarily bring the economy to a desirable final state.

This problem is partly resolved if we are able to "synthesize" the optimal control, in the sense of expressing the optimal control as a function of the present time s and the present state $\mathbf{y}$. In this case, for each time s and each point $\mathbf{y}$ in the state space, we specify the optimal control $\tilde{\mathbf{u}} = \tilde{\mathbf{u}}_{s,\mathbf{y}}$ to use. Such controls are called **closed-loop** or **Markov controls**. We can find such Markov controls by solving the control problem with an arbitrary start point $(s, \mathbf{y})$, $s \in [t_0, t_1)$. The controls $\mathbf{u}^*(t)$ obtained will depend on the starting point $(s, \mathbf{y})$, $\mathbf{u}^*(t) = \mathbf{u}_{s,\mathbf{y}}^*(t)$. Of course, at time s, the control $\tilde{\mathbf{u}}(s, \mathbf{y}) = \mathbf{u}_{s,\mathbf{y}}^*(s)$ is used. Then $\tilde{\mathbf{u}}(s, \mathbf{y})$ is the required Markov control.

But these Markov controls are only conditionally optimal. They tell us which control to use after a disturbance has occurred, but they are optimal only in the absence of further disturbances.

If we stipulate the probability of future disturbances and then want to optimize the expected value of the objective functional, this gives a stochastic control problem, in which optimal Markov controls are determined by a different set of necessary conditions.

Jumps in State Variables

So far we have assumed that the control functions are piecewise continuous, and the state variables are continuous. In certain applications (e.g. in the theory of investment), the optimum may require sudden jumps in the state variables. See e.g. Seierstad and Sydsæter (1987), Chapter 3.

11

DIFFERENCE EQUATIONS

He (an economist) must study the present in the light of the past
for the purpose of the future.
—J. N. Keynes

M any of the quantities economists study (such as income, consumption, and savings) are
recorded at fixed time intervals (for example, each day, week, quarter, or year). Equations that relate such quantities at different discrete moments of time are called **difference equations**. For example, such an equation might relate the amount of national income in one period to the national income in one or more previous periods. In fact difference equations can be viewed as the discrete time counterparts of the differential equations in continuous time that were studied in Chapters 5–7.

11.1 First-Order Difference Equations

Let $t = 0, 1, 2, \ldots$ denote different discrete time periods or moments of time. We usually call $t = 0$ the *initial period*. If $x(t)$ is a function defined for $t = 0, 1, 2, \ldots$, we often use $x_0, x_1, x_2, \ldots$ to denote $x(0), x(1), x(2), \ldots$, and in general, we write x_t for $x(t)$.

Let $f(t, x)$ be a function defined for all positive integers t and all real numbers x. A first-order difference equation in x_t can usually be written in the form

$$x_{t+1} = f(t, x_t), \qquad t = 0, 1, 2, \ldots \tag{1}$$

This is a first-order equation because it relates the value of a function in period $t + 1$ to the value of the same function in the previous period t only.[1]

---

[1] It would be more appropriate to call (1) a "recurrence relation", and to reserve the term "difference equation" for an equation of the form $\Delta x_t = \tilde{f}(t, x_t)$, where Δx_t denotes the difference $x_{t+1} - x_t$. However, it is obvious how to transform a difference equation into an equivalent recurrence relation, and *vice versa*, so we make no distinction between the two kinds of equation.

Suppose x_0 is given. Then repeated application of equation (1) yields

$$x_1 = f(0, x_0)$$
$$x_2 = f(1, x_1) = f(1, f(0, x_0))$$
$$x_3 = f(2, x_2) = f(2, f(1, f(0, x_0)))$$

and so on. *For a given value of x_0, we can compute x_t for any value of t.* We call this the "insertion method" of solving (1).

Sometimes we can find a simple formula for x_t, but often this is not possible. A **general solution** of (1) is a function of the form $x_t = g(t; A)$ that satisfies (1) for every value of A, where A is an arbitrary constant. For each choice of x_0 there is usually one value of A such that $g(0, A) = x_0$.

EXAMPLE 1   A simple case of equation (1) is

$$x_{t+1} = 2x_t, \qquad t = 0, 1, \ldots \tag{$*$}$$

Suppose x_0 is given. Repeatedly applying (1) gives $x_1 = 2x_0$, $x_2 = 2x_1 = 2 \cdot 2x_0 = 2^2 x_0$, $x_3 = 2x_2 = 2 \cdot 2^2 x_0 = 2^3 x_0$ and so on. In general,

$$x_t = 2^t x_0, \qquad t = 0, 1, \ldots \tag{$**$}$$

The function $x_t = 2^t x_0$ satisfies $(*)$ for all t, as can be verified directly. For the given value of x_0, there is clearly no other function that satisfies the equation.

In general, for each choice of x_0, there is a corresponding unique solution of (1). Consequently, there are infinitely many solutions. When x_0 is given, the successive values of x_t can be computed for any natural number t. Does this not tell us the whole story?

In fact, we often need to know more. In economic applications, we are usually interested in establishing qualitative results. For example, we might be interested in the behaviour of the solution when t becomes very large, or in how the solution depends on some parameters that might influence the difference equation. Such questions are difficult or impossible to handle if we rely only on the above insertion method.

Actually, the insertion method suffers from another defect as a numerical procedure. For example, suppose that we have a difference equation like (1), and we want to compute x_{100}. A time-consuming process of successive insertions will finally yield an expression for x_{100}. However, computational errors can easily occur, and if we work with approximate numbers (as we are usually forced to do in serious applications), the approximation error might well explode and in the end give an entirely misleading answer. So there really is a need for a more systematic theory of difference equations. Ideally, the solutions should be expressed in terms of elementary functions. Unfortunately, this is possible only for rather restricted classes of equations.

A Simple First-Order Equation

Consider the difference equation

$$x_{t+1} = ax_t + b_t, \qquad t = 0, 1, \ldots \tag{2}$$

where a is a constant. The equation in Example 1 is a special case with $a = 2$, $b_t = 0$. Starting with a given x_0, we can calculate x_t algebraically for small t. Indeed

$$x_1 = ax_0 + b_0$$
$$x_2 = ax_1 + b_1 = a(ax_0 + b_0) + b_1 = a^2 x_0 + ab_0 + b_1$$
$$x_3 = ax_2 + b_2 = a(a^2 x_0 + ab_0 + b_1) + b_2 = a^3 x_0 + a^2 b_0 + ab_1 + b_2$$

and so on. This makes the pattern clear. In each case, the formula for x_t begins with the term $a^t x_0$, and then adds the terms $a^{t-1}b_0$, $a^{t-2}b_1$, ..., ab_{t-2}, b_{t-1} in turn. We thus arrive at the following general result:

$$x_{t+1} = ax_t + b_t \iff x_t = a^t x_0 + \sum_{k=1}^{t} a^{t-k} b_{k-1}, \qquad t = 0, 1, 2, \ldots \tag{3}$$

(Note that $a^{t-k} = a^0 = 1$ when $k = t$.) Indeed, to check that we have really found a solution to (2), substitute the expression suggested by (3) for x_t into the right-hand side of (2). This yields

$$ax_t + b_t = a\left(a^t x_0 + \sum_{k=1}^{t} a^{t-k} b_{k-1}\right) + b_t = a^{t+1} x_0 + \sum_{k=1}^{t} a^{t+1-k} b_{k-1} + b_t$$

$$= a^{t+1} x_0 + \sum_{k=1}^{t+1} a^{t+1-k} b_{k-1}$$

This matches our expression for x_{t+1}, so (3) does solve the difference equation.

Consider the special case when $b_k = b$ for all $k = 0, 1, 2, \ldots$. Then

$$\sum_{k=1}^{t} a^{t-k} b_{k-1} = b \sum_{k=1}^{t} a^{t-k} = b(a^{t-1} + a^{t-2} + \cdots + a + 1)$$

According to the summation formula for a geometric series, $1 + a + a^2 + \cdots + a^{t-1} = (1 - a^t)/(1 - a)$, for $a \neq 1$. Thus, for $t = 0, 1, 2, \ldots$,

$$x_{t+1} = ax_t + b \iff x_t = a^t\left(x_0 - \frac{b}{1-a}\right) + \frac{b}{1-a} \quad (a \neq 1) \tag{4}$$

For $a = 1$, we have $1 + a + \cdots + a^{t-1} = t$ and $x_t = x_0 + tb$ for $t = 1, 2, \ldots$.

EXAMPLE 2   Solve the following difference equations:

$$\text{(a)} \quad x_{t+1} = \tfrac{1}{2}x_t + 3, \qquad \text{(b)} \quad x_{t+1} = -3x_t + 4$$

Solution: (a) Using (4) we obtain the solution

$$x_t = \left(\tfrac{1}{2}\right)^t (x_0 - 6) + 6$$

(b) In this case, (4) gives

$$x_t = (-3)^t (x_0 - 1) + 1$$

EXAMPLE 3   **(A Multiplier–Accelerator Model of Growth)**   Let Y_t denote national income, I_t total investment, and S_t total saving—all in period t. Suppose that savings are proportional to national income, and that investment is proportional to the change in income from period t to $t + 1$. Then, for $t = 0, 1, 2, \ldots$,

$$S_t = \alpha Y_t$$
$$I_{t+1} = \beta(Y_{t+1} - Y_t)$$
$$S_t = I_t$$

The last equation is the familiar equilibrium condition that saving equals investment in each period. Here α and β are positive constants, and we assume that $\beta > \alpha > 0$. Deduce a difference equation determining the path of Y_t, given Y_0, and solve it.

Solution: From the first and third equations, $I_t = \alpha Y_t$, and so $I_{t+1} = \alpha Y_{t+1}$. Inserting these into the second equation yields $\alpha Y_{t+1} = \beta(Y_{t+1} - Y_t)$, or $(\alpha - \beta)Y_{t+1} = -\beta Y_t$. Thus,

$$Y_{t+1} = \frac{\beta}{\beta - \alpha}Y_t = \left(1 + \frac{\alpha}{\beta - \alpha}\right)Y_t, \qquad t = 0, 1, 2, \ldots \qquad (*)$$

Using (4) gives the solution

$$Y_t = \left(1 + \frac{\alpha}{\beta - \alpha}\right)^t Y_0, \qquad t = 0, 1, 2, \ldots$$

The difference equation $(*)$ constitutes an instance of the equation

$$Y_{t+1} = (1 + g)Y_t, \qquad t = 0, 1, 2, \ldots$$

which describes growth at the constant proportional rate g each period. The solution of the equation is $Y_t = (1 + g)^t Y_0$. Note that $g = (Y_{t+1} - Y_t)/Y_t$.

Equilibrium States and Stability

Consider the solution of $x_{t+1} = ax_t + b$ given in (4). If $x_0 = b/(1-a)$, then $x_t = b/(1-a)$ for all t. In fact, if $x_s = b/(1-a)$ for any $s \geq 0$, then $x_{s+1} = a(b/(1-a)) + b = b/(1-a)$, and again $x_{s+2} = b/(1-a)$, and so on. We conclude that if x_s ever becomes equal to $b/(1-a)$ at some time s, then x_t will remain at this constant level for each $t \geq s$. The constant $x^* = b/(1-a)$ is called an **equilibrium** (or **stationary**) state for $x_{t+1} = ax_t + b$.

NOTE 1   An alternative way of finding an equilibrium state x^* is to seek a solution of $x_{t+1} = ax_t + b$ with $x_t = x^*$ for all t. Such a solution must satisfy $x_{t+1} = x_t = x^*$ and so $x^* = ax^* + b$. Therefore, for $a \neq 1$, we get $x^* = b/(1-a)$ as before.

Suppose the constant a in (4) is less than 1 in absolute value—that is, $-1 < a < 1$. Then $a^t \to 0$ as $t \to \infty$, so (4) implies that

$$x_t \to x^* = \frac{b}{1-a} \qquad \text{as} \qquad t \to \infty$$

Hence, if $|a| < 1$, the solution converges to the equilibrium state as $t \to \infty$. The equation is then called **globally asymptotically stable**. Two kinds of stability are shown in Figs. 1 (a) and (b). In the first case, x_t converges monotonically down to the equilibrium state. In the second case, x_t exhibits decreasing fluctuations or **damped oscillations** around the equilibrium state.

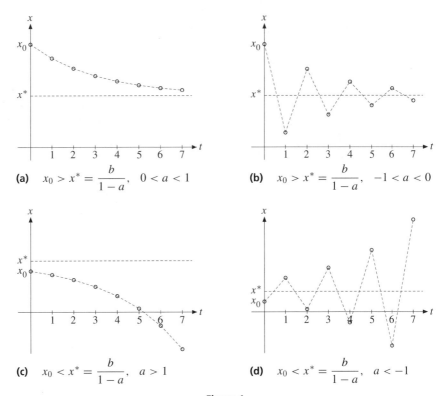

(a) $x_0 > x^* = \dfrac{b}{1-a}$, $0 < a < 1$ **(b)** $x_0 > x^* = \dfrac{b}{1-a}$, $-1 < a < 0$

(c) $x_0 < x^* = \dfrac{b}{1-a}$, $a > 1$ **(d)** $x_0 < x^* = \dfrac{b}{1-a}$, $a < -1$

Figure 1

If $|a| > 1$, then the absolute value of a^t tends to ∞ as $t \to \infty$. From (4), it follows that x_t moves farther and farther away from the equilibrium state, except when $x_0 = b/(1-a)$. Two versions of this phenomenon are illustrated in Figs. 1 (c) and (d). In the first case, x_t tends to $-\infty$, and in the second case, x_t exhibits increasing fluctuations or **explosive oscillations** around the equilibrium state.

EXAMPLE 4   Equation (a) in Example 2 is stable because $a = 1/2$. The equilibrium state is $b/(1-a) = 3/(1 - 1/2) = 6$. We see from the solution given in that example that $x_t \to 6$ as $t \to \infty$.

Equation (b) in Example 2 is not stable because $|a| = |-3| = 3 > 1$. The solution does *not* converge to the equilibrium state $x^* = 1$ as $t \to \infty$, except if $x_0 = 1$—in fact, there are explosive oscillations.

EXAMPLE 5   **(The Hog Cycle: A Cobweb Model)**   Assume that the total cost of raising q pigs is $C(q) = \alpha q + \beta q^2$. Suppose there are N identical pig farms. Let the demand function for pigs be given by $D(p) = \gamma - \delta p$, as a function of the price p, where the constants α, β, γ, and δ are all positive. Suppose, too, that each farmer behaves competitively, taking the price p as given and maximizing profits $\pi(q) = pq - C(q) = pq - \alpha q - \beta q^2$.

The quantity $q > 0$ maximizes profits only if

$$\pi'(q) = p - \alpha - 2\beta q = 0 \quad \text{and so} \quad q = (p - \alpha)/2\beta$$

It follows that $\pi'(q) > 0$ for $q < (p - \alpha)/2\beta$, and $\pi'(q) < 0$ for $q > (p - \alpha)/2\beta$. Thus, $q = (p - \alpha)/2\beta$ maximizes profits provided $p > \alpha$. In aggregate, the total supply of pigs from all N farms is the function

$$S = N(p - \alpha)/2\beta \qquad (p > \alpha)$$

of the price p. Now, suppose it takes one period to raise each pig, and that when choosing the number of pigs to raise for sale at time $t + 1$, each farmer remembers the price p_t at time t and expects p_{t+1} to be the same as p_t. Then the aggregate supply at time $t + 1$ will be $S(p_t) = N(p_t - \alpha)/2\beta$.

Equilibrium of supply and demand in all periods requires that $S(p_t) = D(p_{t+1})$, which implies that $N(p_t - \alpha)/2\beta = \gamma - \delta p_{t+1}, t = 0, 1, \ldots$. Solving for p_{t+1} in terms of p_t and the parameters gives the difference equation

$$p_{t+1} = -\frac{N}{2\beta\delta} p_t + \frac{\alpha N + 2\beta\gamma}{2\beta\delta}, \qquad t = 1, 2, \ldots \qquad (*)$$

The equilibrium price p^* with $p_{t+1} = p_t$ occurs at $p^* = (\alpha N + 2\beta\gamma)/(2\beta\delta + N)$. The solution of $(*)$ can be expressed as

$$p_t = p^* + (-a)^t (p_0 - p^*) \qquad (a = N/2\beta\delta)$$

Equation $(*)$ is stable if $|-a| < 1$, which happens when $N < 2\beta\delta$. In this case, $p_t \to p^*$ as $t \to \infty$. The solution in this case is illustrated in Fig. 2. Here, q_0 is the supply of pigs at time 0. The price at which all these can be sold is p_0. This determines the supply q_1 one period later. The resulting price at which they sell is p_1, and so on.

The resulting price cycles are damped, and both price and quantity converge to a steady-state equilibrium at (q^*, p^*). This is also an equilibrium of supply and demand. If $N > 2\beta\delta$, however, then the oscillations explode, and eventually p_t becomes less than α. Then the pig farms go out of business, and the solution has to be described in a different way. There is no convergence to a steady state in this case. A third, intermediate, case occurs when $N = 2\beta\delta$ and $a = 1$. Then the pair (q_t, p_t) oscillates perpetually between the two values $(\gamma - \delta p_0, p_0)$ and $(\delta(p_0 - \alpha), \alpha + \gamma/\delta - p_0)$ in even- and odd-numbered periods, respectively.

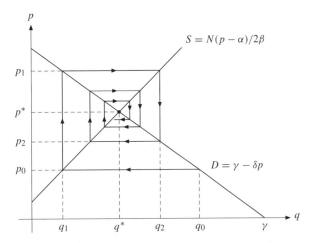

Figure 2 The cobweb model in Example 5—the stable case.

PROBLEMS FOR SECTION 11.1

1. Find the solutions of the following difference equations with the given values of x_0:

   (a) $x_{t+1} = 2x_t + 4$, $x_0 = 1$

   (b) $3x_{t+1} = x_t + 2$, $x_0 = 2$

   (c) $2x_{t+1} + 3x_t + 2 = 0$, $x_0 = -1$

   (d) $x_{t+1} - x_t + 3 = 0$, $x_0 = 3$

2. Consider the difference equation $x_{t+1} = ax_t + b$ in (4) and explain how its solution behaves in each of the following cases, with $x^* = b/(1-a)$ (for $a \neq 1$):

   (a) $0 < a < 1$, $x_0 < x^*$ (b) $-1 < a < 0$, $x_0 < x^*$ (c) $a > 1$, $x_0 > x^*$

   (d) $a < -1$, $x_0 > x^*$ (e) $a \neq 1$, $x_0 = x^*$ (f) $a = -1$, $x_0 \neq x^*$

   (g) $a = 1$, $b > 0$ (h) $a = 1$, $b < 0$ (i) $a = 1$, $b = 0$

3. (a) Consider the difference equation

$$y_{t+1}(a + by_t) = cy_t, \qquad t = 0, 1, \ldots$$

   where a, b, and c are positive constants, and $y_0 > 0$. Show that $y_t > 0$ for all t.

   (b) Define a new function x_t by $x_t = 1/y_t$. Show that by using this substitution, the new difference equation is of the type in (4). Next solve the difference equation $y_{t+1}(2 + 3y_t) = 4y_t$, assuming that $y_0 = 1/2$. What is the limit of y_t as $t \to \infty$?

4. By substituting $y_t = x_t - b/(1-a)$ transform equation (2) into a simple difference equation in y_t. Solve it and find a new confirmation of (4).

5. Consider the difference equation $x_t = \sqrt{x_{t-1} - 1}$ with $x_0 = 5$. Compute x_1, x_2, and x_3. What about x_4? (This problem illustrates the need to take care if the domain of the function f in (1) is restricted in any way.)

11.2 Present Discounted Values

The theory in the previous section can be applied to describe the changes over time in a savings account whose balance is subject to compound interest. Let a_t denote the value of the assets held in the account at the end of period t. Further, let c_t be the amount withdrawn for consumption and y_t the amount deposited as income during period t. If the interest rate per period is a constant r, the relevant difference equation is

$$a_{t+1} = (1+r)a_t + y_{t+1} - c_{t+1}, \qquad t = 0, 1, 2, \ldots \tag{1}$$

The result in (11.1.3) implies that the solution of (1) is

$$a_t = (1+r)^t a_0 + \sum_{k=1}^{t}(1+r)^{t-k}(y_k - c_k), \qquad t = 1, 2, \ldots \tag{2}$$

Let us multiply each term in (2) by $(1+r)^{-t}$, which is a factor of sufficient economic importance to have earned a standard name, namely the **discount factor**. The result is

$$(1+r)^{-t}a_t = a_0 + \sum_{k=1}^{t}(1+r)^{-k}(y_k - c_k) \tag{3}$$

If time 0 is now, then the left-hand side is the **present discounted value** (PDV) of the assets in the account at time t. Equation (3) says that this is equal to

(a) initial assets a_0

(b) plus the total PDV of all future deposits, $\sum_{k=1}^{t}(1+r)^{-k}y_k$

(c) *minus* the total PDV of all future withdrawals $\sum_{k=1}^{t}(1+r)^{-k}c_k$

If time t is now, the formula for a_t in (2) can be interpreted as follows: *Current assets a_t reflect the interest earned on initial assets a_0, with adjustments for the interest earned on all later deposits, or foregone because of later withdrawals.*

EXAMPLE 1   (**Mortgage Repayments**)   A particular case of the difference equation (1) occurs when a family borrows an amount K at time 0 as a home mortgage. Suppose there is a fixed interest rate r per period (usually a month rather than a year). Suppose, too, that there are equal repayments of amount a each period, until the mortgage is paid off after n periods (for example, 360 months = 30 years). The outstanding balance or *principal* b_t on the loan in period t satisfies the difference equation $b_{t+1} = (1+r)b_t - a$, with $b_0 = K$ and $b_n = 0$. This difference equation can be solved by using (11.1.4), which gives

$$b_t = (1+r)^t \left(K - \frac{a}{r} \right) + \frac{a}{r}$$

But $b_t = 0$ when $t = n$, so $0 = (1+r)^n (K - a/r) + a/r$. Solving for K yields

$$K = \frac{a}{r}[1 - (1+r)^{-n}] = a \sum_{t=1}^{n}(1+r)^{-t} \tag{*}$$

The original loan, therefore, is equal to the PDV of n equal repayments of amount a each period, starting in period 1. Solving for a instead yields

$$a = \frac{rK}{1 - (1+r)^{-n}} = \frac{rK(1+r)^n}{(1+r)^n - 1} \qquad (**)$$

Formulas $(*)$ and $(**)$ are the same as those derived by a more direct argument in EMEA, Chapter 10.

PROBLEMS FOR SECTION 11.2

1. Find the solution of (1) for $r = 0.2$, $a_0 = 1000$, $y_t = 100$, and $c_t = 50$.

2. Suppose that at time $t = 0$, you borrow \$100 000 at the fixed interest rate $r = 0.07$ per year. You are supposed to repay the loan in 30 equal annual repayments so that after $n = 30$ years, the mortgage is paid off. How much is each repayment?

3. A loan of amount \$$L$ is taken out on January 1 of year 0. Instalment payments for the principal and interest are paid annually, commencing on January 1 of year 1. Let the interest rate be $r < 2$, so that the interest amounts to rL for the first payment. The contract states that the principal share of the repayment will be half the size of the interest share.

   (a) Show that the debt after January 1 of year n is $(1 - r/2)^n L$.

   (b) Find r when it is known that exactly half the original loan is paid after 10 years.

   (c) What will the remaining payments be each year if the contract is not changed?

11.3 Second-Order Difference Equations

So far this chapter has considered first-order difference equations, in which each value x_{t+1} of a function is related to the value x_t of the function in the previous period only. Next we present a typical example from economics where it is necessary to consider second-order difference equations.

EXAMPLE 1   **(A Multiplier–Accelerator Growth Model)**   Let Y_t denote national income, C_t total consumption, and I_t total investment in a country at time t. Assume that for $t = 0, 1, \ldots$,

$$\text{(i) } Y_t = C_t + I_t \qquad \text{(ii) } C_{t+1} = aY_t + b \qquad \text{(iii) } I_{t+1} = c(C_{t+1} - C_t)$$

where a, b, and c are positive constants.

Equation (i) simply states that national income is divided between consumption and investment. Equation (ii) expresses the assumption that consumption in period $t + 1$ is a linear function of national income in the previous period. This is the "multiplier" part of the model. Finally, equation (iii) states that investment in period $t + 1$ is proportional to the change in consumption from the previous period. The idea is that the existing capital stock provides enough capacity for production to meet current consumption. So investment is only needed when consumption increases. This is the "accelerator" part of the model. The combined "multiplier–accelerator" model has been studied by several economists, notably P. A. Samuelson.

Assume that consumption C_0 and investment I_0 are known in the initial period $t = 0$. Then by (i), $Y_0 = C_0 + I_0$, and by (ii), $C_1 = aY_0 + b$. From (iii), we obtain $I_1 = c(C_1 - C_0)$, and then (i) in turn gives $Y_1 = C_1 + I_1$. Hence, Y_1, C_1, and I_1 are all known. Turning to (ii) again, we find C_2, then (iii) gives us the value of I_2, and (i) in turn produces the value of Y_2. Obviously, in this way, we can obtain expressions for C_t, Y_t, and I_t for all t in terms of C_0, Y_0, and the constants a, b, and c. However, the expressions derived get increasingly complicated.

Another method of studying the system is usually more enlightening. It consists of eliminating two of the unknown functions so as to end up with one difference equation in one unknown. Here we use this method to end up with a difference equation in Y_t. To do so, note that equations (i) to (iii) are valid for all $t = 0, 1, \ldots$. Replace t with $t + 1$ in (ii) and (iii), and t with $t + 2$ in (i) to obtain

$$\text{(iv)} \ C_{t+2} = aY_{t+1} + b \qquad \text{(v)} \ I_{t+2} = c(C_{t+2} - C_{t+1}) \qquad \text{(vi)} \ Y_{t+2} = C_{t+2} + I_{t+2}$$

Inserting (iv) and (ii) into (v) yields $I_{t+2} = ac(Y_{t+1} - Y_t)$. Inserting this result and (iv) into (vi) gives $Y_{t+2} = aY_{t+1} + b + ac(Y_{t+1} - Y_t)$. Rearranging gives

$$Y_{t+2} - a(1 + c)Y_{t+1} + acY_t = b, \qquad t = 0, 1, \ldots \tag{vii}$$

This is a second-order linear difference equation with Y_t as the unknown function. The next section sets out a general method for solving such equations. (See Problem 11.4.3.)

The typical second-order difference equation can be written in the form

$$x_{t+2} = f(t, x_t, x_{t+1}), \qquad t = 0, 1, \ldots \tag{1}$$

Suppose that f is defined for all possible values of the variables (t, x_t, x_{t+1}). Suppose x_0 and x_1 have fixed values. Letting $t = 0$ in (1), we see that $x_2 = f(0, x_0, x_1)$. Letting $t = 1$ yields $x_3 = f(1, x_1, f(0, x_0, x_1))$. By successively inserting $t = 2$, $t = 3$, $\ldots$ into (1), the values of x_t for *all* t are uniquely determined in terms of x_0 and x_1. Note in particular that there are infinitely many solutions, and that the solution of the equation is uniquely determined by its values in the first two periods. By definition, a **general** solution of (1) is a function of the form

$$x_t = g(t; A, B) \tag{2}$$

that satisfies (1) and has the property that every solution of (1) can be obtained from (2) by choosing appropriate values of A and B.

Linear Equations

The general second-order linear difference equation is

$$x_{t+2} + a_t x_{t+1} + b_t x_t = c_t \tag{3}$$

where a_t, b_t, and c_t are given functions of t. The associated **homogeneous** equation

$$x_{t+2} + a_t x_{t+1} + b_t x_t = 0 \tag{4}$$

is obtained from (3) by replacing c_t with 0. Compare these equations with the linear differential equations (6.2.1) and (6.2.2). By arguments which are much the same as for differential equations (but simpler), the following results are easy to establish:

THEOREM 11.3.1

The homogeneous difference equation

$$x_{t+2} + a_t x_{t+1} + b_t x_t = 0$$

has the **general solution**

$$x_t = A u_t^{(1)} + B u_t^{(2)}$$

where $u_t^{(1)}$ and $u_t^{(2)}$ are any two linearly independent solutions, and A and B are arbitrary constants.

THEOREM 11.3.2

The nonhomogeneous difference equation

$$x_{t+2} + a_t x_{t+1} + b_t x_t = c_t$$

has the **general solution**

$$x_t = A u_t^{(1)} + B u_t^{(2)} + u_t^*$$

where $A u_t^{(1)} + B u_t^{(2)}$ is the general solution of the associated homogeneous equation (with c_t replaced by zero), and u_t^* is any particular solution of the nonhomogeneous equation.

NOTE 1 In order to use these theorems, we need to know when two solutions of (4) are linearly independent. The following necessary and sufficient condition is easy to apply (and generalizes easily to the case of n functions):

$$\begin{vmatrix} u_0^{(1)} & u_0^{(2)} \\ u_1^{(1)} & u_1^{(2)} \end{vmatrix} \neq 0 \quad \Longleftrightarrow \quad u_t^{(1)} \text{ and } u_t^{(2)} \text{ are linearly independent} \tag{5}$$

See Problem 5 for a proof.

A General Solution

There is no universally applicable method of discovering the two linearly independent solutions of (4) that we need in order to find the general solution of the equation. But if we know two linearly independent solutions of (4) and thereby its general solution, then it is always possible to find the general solution of (3).

Consider the equation

$$x_{t+2} + a_t x_{t+1} + b_t x_t = c_t, \quad t = 0, 1, 2, \ldots \tag{6}$$

Suppose $u_t^{(1)}$ and $u_t^{(2)}$ are linearly independent solutions of the corresponding homogeneous equation and define

$$D_t = u_t^{(1)} u_{t+1}^{(2)} - u_{t+1}^{(1)} u_t^{(2)}$$

Then, if $D_t \neq 0$ for all $t = 1, 2, \ldots$, the general solution of (6) is given by

$$x_t = A u_t^{(1)} + B u_t^{(2)} - u_t^{(1)} \sum_{k=1}^{t} \frac{c_{k-1} u_k^{(2)}}{D_k} + u_t^{(2)} \sum_{k=1}^{t} \frac{c_{k-1} u_k^{(1)}}{D_k} \tag{7}$$

where A and B are arbitrary constants. (See Hildebrand (1968).)

When the coefficients a_t and b_t in (4) are constants independent of t, then it is always possible to find a simple formula for the general solution of (4). The next section shows how to do this.

PROBLEMS FOR SECTION 11.3

1. Prove by direct substitution that the following functions of t are solutions of the associated difference equation (A and B are constants):

   (a) $x_t = A + B\, 2^t, \qquad x_{t+2} - 3x_{t+1} + 2x_t = 0$

   (b) $x_t = A\, 3^t + B\, 4^t, \qquad x_{t+2} - 7x_{t+1} + 12x_t = 0$

2. Prove that $x_t = A + B\, t$ is the general solution of $x_{t+2} - 2x_{t+1} + x_t = 0$.

3. Prove that $x_t = A\, 3^t + B\, 4^t$ is the general solution of $x_{t+2} - 7x_{t+1} + 12x_t = 0$.

4. Prove that $x_t = A\, 2^t + B\, t 2^t + 1$ is the general solution of $x_{t+2} - 4x_{t+1} + 4x_t = 1$.

5. Prove the equivalence in (5). (*Hint:* If the determinant is zero, then the two columns are linearly dependent, and since both $u_t^{(1)}$ and $u_t^{(2)}$ are solutions of equation (4), this dependency will propagate to $u_t^{(1)}$ and $u_t^{(2)}$ for all t.)

11.4 Constant Coefficients

Consider the homogeneous equation

$$x_{t+2} + ax_{t+1} + bx_t = 0 \tag{1}$$

where a and b are arbitrary constants, $b \neq 0$, and x_t is the unknown function. According to Theorem 11.3.1, finding the general solution of (1) requires us to discover two solutions $u_t^{(1)}$ and $u_t^{(2)}$ that are linearly independent. On the basis of experience gained in some of the previous problems, it should come as no surprise that we try to find solutions to (1) of the form $x_t = m^t$. Then $x_{t+1} = m^{t+1} = m \cdot m^t$ and $x_{t+2} = m^{t+2} = m^2 \cdot m^t$. So inserting these expressions into (1) yields $m^t (m^2 + am + b) = 0$. If $m \neq 0$, then m^t satisfies (1) provided that

$$m^2 + am + b = 0 \tag{2}$$

This is the **characteristic equation** of the difference equation. Its solutions are

$$m_1 = -\tfrac{1}{2}a + \tfrac{1}{2}\sqrt{a^2 - 4b}, \qquad m_2 = -\tfrac{1}{2}a - \tfrac{1}{2}\sqrt{a^2 - 4b} \tag{3}$$

There are three different cases, which are summed up in the following theorem:

THEOREM 11.4.1

The **general solution** of

$$x_{t+2} + ax_{t+1} + bx_t = 0 \qquad (b \neq 0)$$

is as follows:

(I) If $a^2 - 4b > 0$ (the characteristic equation has two distinct real roots),

$$x_t = Am_1^t + Bm_2^t, \qquad m_{1,2} = -\tfrac{1}{2}a \pm \tfrac{1}{2}\sqrt{a^2 - 4b}$$

(II) If $a^2 - 4b = 0$ (the characteristic equation has one real double root),

$$x_t = (A + Bt)m^t, \qquad m = -\tfrac{1}{2}a$$

(III) If $a^2 - 4b < 0$ (the characteristic equation has no real roots),

$$x_t = r^t(A \cos \theta t + B \sin \theta t), \quad r = \sqrt{b}, \quad \cos \theta = -\frac{a}{2\sqrt{b}}, \quad \theta \in [0, \pi]$$

NOTE 1   If x_0 and x_1 are given numbers, then in all three cases the constants A and B are uniquely determined. For instance, in case (I), A and B are uniquely determined by the equations $x_0 = A + B$ and $x_1 = Am_1 + Bm_2$.

NOTE 2   The solution in case (III) can be expressed as

$$x_t = Cr^t \cos(\theta t + \omega) \tag{4}$$

where ω and C are arbitrary constants. (See the corresponding case for differential equations in Section 6.3.)

Proof of Theorem 11.4.1: (I): The case $a^2 - 4b > 0$ is the simplest. Then m_1 and m_2 are real and different, and m_1^t and m_2^t are both solutions of (1). The determinant in (11.3.5) has the value $m_2 - m_1 \neq 0$, so the two solutions are linearly independent, and the general solution is consequently as given in (I).

(II): If $a^2 - 4b = 0$, then $m = -\frac{1}{2}a$ is a double root of (2). This means that $m^2 + am + b = (m + \frac{1}{2}a)^2$. In addition to m^t, the function tm^t also satisfies (1) (see Problem 6). Moreover, these two functions are linearly independent because the determinant in (11.3.5) is equal to $m = -\frac{1}{2}a$. (Note that $a \neq 0$ because $b \neq 0$.) The general solution is, therefore, as indicated in (II).

(III): If $a^2 - 4b < 0$, the roots of (2) are complex. The two functions $u_t^{(1)} = r^t \cos \theta t$ and $u_t^{(2)} = r^t \sin \theta t$ are linearly independent. Indeed, the determinant in (11.3.5) is

$$\begin{vmatrix} 1 & 0 \\ r\cos\theta & r\sin\theta \end{vmatrix} = r\sin\theta = \sqrt{b}\sqrt{1-\cos^2\theta} = \sqrt{b}\sqrt{1-a^2/4b} = \tfrac{1}{2}\sqrt{4b-a^2} > 0$$

Moreover, direct substitution shows that both these functions satisfy (1).

Indeed, let us show that $u_t^{(1)} = r^t \cos \theta t$ satisfies (1). We find that $u_{t+1}^{(1)} = r^{t+1} \cos \theta(t+1)$ and $u_{t+2}^{(1)} = r^{t+2} \cos \theta(t+2)$. Hence, using the formula (B.1.8) for the cosine of a sum, we get

$$u_{t+2}^{(1)} + au_{t+1}^{(1)} + bu_t^{(1)} = r^{t+2}\cos\theta(t+2) + ar^{t+1}\cos\theta(t+1) + br^t\cos\theta t$$
$$= r^t[r^2(\cos\theta t\cos 2\theta - \sin\theta t\sin 2\theta) + ar(\cos\theta t\cos\theta - \sin\theta t\sin\theta) + b\cos\theta t]$$
$$= r^t[(r^2\cos 2\theta + ar\cos\theta + b)\cos\theta t - (r^2\sin 2\theta + ar\sin\theta)\sin\theta t]$$

Here the coefficients of $\cos \theta t$ and $\sin \theta t$ are both equal to 0 because $r^2\cos 2\theta + ar\cos\theta + b = r^2(2\cos^2\theta - 1) + ar\cos\theta + b = b(2a^2/4b - 1) + a\sqrt{b}(-a/2\sqrt{b}) + b = 0$, and likewise $r^2\sin 2\theta + ar\sin\theta = 2r^2\sin\theta\cos\theta + ar\sin\theta = 2r^2(-a/2r)\sin\theta + ar\sin\theta = 0$. This shows that $u_t^{(1)} = r^t\cos\theta t$ satisfies equation (1), and a similar argument shows that so does $u_t^{(2)} = r^t\sin\theta$. ∎

NOTE 3 An alternative argument for the solution in (III) relies on properties of the complex exponential function. In trigonometric form the roots in (3) are $m_1 = \alpha + i\beta = r(\cos\theta + i\sin\theta)$ and $m_2 = \alpha - i\beta = r(\cos\theta - i\sin\theta)$, with $\theta \in [0, \pi]$, $r = \sqrt{\alpha^2 + \beta^2} = \sqrt{b}$, $\cos\theta = \alpha/r = -a/2\sqrt{b}$, and $\sin\theta = \beta/r = (\sqrt{b - a^2/4})/\sqrt{b}$.

By de Moivre's formula, (B.3.8), $m_1^t = r^t(\cos\theta t + i\sin\theta t)$ and $m_2^t = r^t(\cos\theta t - i\sin\theta t)$. The complex functions m_1^t and m_2^t both satisfy (1), and so does every linear combination of them. In particular, $\frac{1}{2}(m_1^t + m_2^t) = r^t\cos\theta t$ and $\frac{1}{2i}(m_1^t - m_2^t) = r^t\sin\theta t$ both satisfy (1). The general solution of (1) is therefore as given in case (III).

We see that when the characteristic equation has complex roots, the solution of (1) involves oscillations. The number r is the **growth factor**. Note that when $|r| < 1$, then $|Ar^t| \to 0$ as $t \to \infty$ and the oscillations are **damped**. If $|r| > 1$, the oscillations are **explosive**, and in the case $|r| = 1$, we have undamped oscillations.

Let us now consider some examples of difference equations of the form (1).

EXAMPLE 1   Find the general solutions of

(a) $x_{t+2} - 3.9x_{t+1} + 3.78x_t = 0$ (b) $x_{t+2} - 6x_{t+1} + 9x_t = 0$ (c) $x_{t+2} - x_{t+1} + x_t = 0$

Solution: (a) The characteristic equation is $m^2 - 3.9m + 3.78 = 0$, whose roots are $m_1 = 1.8$ and $m_2 = 2.1$, so the general solution is

$$x_t = A(1.8)^t + B(2.1)^t$$

(b) The characteristic equation is $m^2 - 6m + 9 = (m-3)^2 = 0$, so $m = 3$ is a double root. The general solution is

$$x_t = (A + Bt)3^t$$

(c) The characteristic equation is $m^2 - m + 1 = 0$, with complex roots $m_1 = \frac{1}{2}(1 + i\sqrt{3})$ and $m_2 = \frac{1}{2}(1 - i\sqrt{3})$. Here $r = \sqrt{b} = 1$ and $\cos\theta = 1/2$, so $\theta = \frac{1}{3}\pi$. The general solution is

$$x_t = A\cos\frac{\pi}{3}t + B\sin\frac{\pi}{3}t$$

The frequency is $(\pi/3)/(2\pi) = 1/6$ and the growth factor is $\sqrt{b} = 1$, so the oscillations are undamped.

The Nonhomogeneous Case

Now consider the nonhomogeneous equation

$$x_{t+2} + ax_{t+1} + bx_t = c_t \qquad (b \neq 0) \tag{5}$$

According to Theorem 11.3.2, its general solution is

$$x_t = Au_t^{(1)} + Bu_t^{(2)} + u_t^* \tag{6}$$

where $Au_t^{(1)} + Bu_t^{(2)}$ is the general solution of the associated homogeneous equation (1), and u_t^* is a particular solution of (5). Theorem 11.4.1 tells us how to find $Au_t^{(1)} + Bu_t^{(2)}$. How do we find u_t^*? The general formula in (11.3.7) gives one answer, but it involves a lot of work, even when c_t is a simple function.

In some cases it is much easier. For example, suppose $c_t = c$, where c is a constant. Then (5) takes the form

$$x_{t+2} + ax_{t+1} + bx_t = c \qquad (c \text{ is a constant}) \tag{7}$$

We look for a solution of the form $x_t = C$, where C is a constant. Then $x_{t+1} = x_{t+2} = C$, so inserting $x_t = C$ into (7) gives $C + aC + bC = c$, that is, $C = c/(1 + a + b)$. Hence,

$$u_t^* = \frac{c}{1 + a + b} \qquad \text{is a particular solution of (7) when } 1 + a + b \neq 0 \tag{8}$$

(If $1 + a + b = 0$, no constant function satisfies (7). To handle this case, see Problem 4.)

Consider more generally the case in which c_t in (5) is a linear combination of terms of the form

$$a^t, \quad t^m, \quad \cos qt, \quad \text{or} \quad \sin qt$$

or products of such terms. Then the method of undetermined coefficients can be used to obtain a particular solution of (5). (If the function c_t in (5) happens to satisfy the homogeneous equation, the procedures described below must be modified.)[2]

EXAMPLE 2   Solve the equation $x_{t+2} - 5x_{t+1} + 6x_t = 4^t + t^2 + 3$.

Solution: The associated homogeneous equation has $m^2 - 5m + 6 = 0$ as its characteristic equation, with the two roots $m_1 = 2$ and $m_2 = 3$. Its general solution is, therefore, $A\, 2^t + B\, 3^t$. To find a particular solution we look for constants C, D, E, and F such that

$$u_t^* = C\, 4^t + D\, t^2 + E\, t + F$$

is a solution. (You cannot put $E = 0$.) This requires that

$$C4^{t+2} + D(t+2)^2 + E(t+2) + F - 5[C4^{t+1} + D(t+1)^2 + E(t+1) + F]$$
$$+ 6(C4^t + Dt^2 + Et + F) = 4^t + t^2 + 3$$

Expanding then rearranging yields $2C4^t + 2Dt^2 + (-6D + 2E)t + (-D - 3E + 2F) = 4^t + t^2 + 3$. For this to hold for all $t = 0, 1, \ldots$ one must have $2C = 1$, $2D = 1$, $-6D + 2E = 0$, and $-D - 3E + 2F = 3$. It follows that $C = 1/2$, $D = 1/2$, $E = 3/2$, and $F = 4$. The general solution of the equation is, therefore,

$$x_t = A\, 2^t + B\, 3^t + \tfrac{1}{2}4^t + \tfrac{1}{2}t^2 + \tfrac{3}{2}t + 4$$

Stability

Suppose an economy evolves according to some difference equation (or system of difference equations). If the right number of initial conditions are imposed, the system has a unique solution. Also, if one or more initial conditions are changed, the solution changes. An important question is this: Will small changes in the initial conditions have any effect on the long-run behaviour of the solution, or will the effect die out as $t \to \infty$? In the latter case, the system is called **stable**. On the other hand, if small changes in the initial conditions might lead to significant differences in the long run behaviour of the solution, then the system is **unstable**. Because an initial state cannot be pinpointed exactly, but only approximately, stability in the sense indicated above is sometimes a minimum requirement for a model to be economically meaningful.

Consider in particular the second-order nonhomogeneous difference equation (5) whose general solution is of the form $x_t = Au_t^{(1)} + Bu_t^{(2)} + u_t^*$. Equation (5) is called **globally asymptotically stable** if the general solution $Au_t^{(1)} + Bu_t^{(2)}$ of the associated homogeneous equation tends to 0 as $t \to \infty$, for all values of A and B. So the effect of the initial conditions dies out as $t \to \infty$.

If $Au_t^{(1)} + Bu_t^{(2)}$ tends to 0 as $t \to \infty$, for all values of A and B, then in particular $u_t^{(1)} \to 0$ as $t \to \infty$ (choose $A = 1$, $B = 0$), and $u_t^{(2)} \to 0$ as $t \to \infty$ (choose $A = 0$, $B = 1$). On the other hand, these two conditions are obviously sufficient for $Au_t^{(1)} + Bu_t^{(2)}$ to approach 0 as $t \to \infty$.

---

[2] For more details, we refer to Goldberg (1958) or Gandolfo (1980).

For the remainder of this section, $u_t^{(1)}$ and $u_t^{(2)}$ will denote the particular solutions of (1) that were used in the proof of Theorem 11.4.1.

We claim that $u_t^{(1)} \to 0$ and $u_t^{(2)} \to 0$ as $t \to \infty$ if and only if the moduli of the roots of $m^2 + am + b = 0$ are both less than 1.[3]

First, in the case when the characteristic polynomial has two distinct real roots, $m_1 \neq m_2$, the two solutions are $u_t^{(1)} = m_1^t$ and $u_t^{(2)} = m_2^t$. In this case, we see that $u_t^{(1)} \to 0$ and $u_t^{(2)} \to 0$ as $t \to \infty$ if and only if $|m_1| < 1$ and $|m_2| < 1$.

Second, when the characteristic polynomial has a double root, $m = -a/2$, then the two linearly independent solutions are m^t and tm^t. Again, $|m| < 1$ is a necessary and sufficient condition for these two solutions to approach 0 as $t \to \infty$.

Third, suppose the characteristic polynomial has complex roots $m = \alpha \pm i\beta$. Then $\alpha = -\frac{1}{2}a$ and $\beta = \frac{1}{2}\sqrt{4b - a^2}$. So the modulus of either root is equal to $|m| = \sqrt{\alpha^2 + \beta^2} = \sqrt{b}$. We argued before that the two solutions $r^t \cos\theta t$ and $r^t \sin\theta t$ tend to 0 as t tends to infinity if and only if $r = \sqrt{b} < 1$—that is, if and only if $b < 1$.

To summarize, we have the following result:

THEOREM 11.4.2

The equation

$$x_{t+2} + ax_{t+1} + bx_t = c_t$$

is globally asymptotically stable if and only if the following two equivalent conditions are satisfied:

(A) The roots of the characteristic equation $m^2 + am + b = 0$ have moduli strictly less than 1.

(B) $|a| < 1 + b$ and $b < 1$

It remains to prove that (B) is equivalent to (A). *Assume first that $b > a^2/4$.* Then the characteristic equation has complex roots $m_{1,2} = \alpha \pm i\beta$ and $|m_1| = |m_2| = \sqrt{b}$, and so (B) obviously implies (A). On the other hand, since $f(m) = m^2 + am + b$ is never zero, and since $f(0) = b$ is positive, the Intermediate Value Theorem tells us that $f(m)$ must be positive for all m. In particular $f(1) = 1 + a + b > 0$ and $f(-1) = 1 - a + b > 0$. But these conditions together are equivalent to $|a| < 1 + b$, so (A) implies (B) are also necessary. Problem 11 asks you to analyse the case of real roots.

EXAMPLE 3   Investigate the stability of the equation $x_{t+2} - \frac{1}{6}x_{t+1} - \frac{1}{6}x_t = c_t$.

Solution: In this case $a = -1/6$ and $b = -1/6$, so $|a| = 1/6$ and $1 + b = 5/6$. Thus, according to Theorem 11.4.2, the equation is stable. This conclusion can be confirmed by looking at the general solution of the associated homogeneous equation, which is $x_t = A(1/2)^t + B(-1/3)^t$. Clearly, $x_t \to 0$ irrespective of the values of A and B, so the given equation is globally asymptotically stable.

---

[3] See Section B.3. Note that if m is a real number, the modulus of m equals the absolute value of m.

EXAMPLE 4   Investigate the stability of equation (vii) in Example 11.3.1, where a and c are positive,

Solution: From Theorem 11.4.2 (B) it follows that the equation is stable if and only if $a(1+c) < 1 + ac$ and $ac < 1$—that is, if and only if $a < 1$ and $ac < 1$. (See also Problem 3.)

PROBLEMS FOR SECTION 11.4

Find the general solutions of the difference equations in Problems 1 and 2.

1. (a) $x_{t+2} - 6x_{t+1} + 8x_t = 0$ (b) $x_{t+2} - 8x_{t+1} + 16x_t = 0$

   (c) $x_{t+2} + 2x_{t+1} + 3x_t = 0$ (d) $3x_{t+2} + 2x_t = 4$

2. (a) $x_{t+2} + 2x_{t+1} + x_t = 9 \cdot 2^t$ (b) $x_{t+2} - 3x_{t+1} + 2x_t = 3 \cdot 5^t + \sin(\frac{1}{2}\pi t)$

3. Consider the difference equation (vii) in Example 11.3.1, with $a > 0, c > 0$, and $a \neq 1$.

   (a) Find a special solution of the equation.

   (b) Find the characteristic equation of the associated homogeneous equation and determine when it has two different real roots, or a double real root, or two complex roots.

4. Consider equation (7) and assume that $1 + a + b = 0$. If $a \neq -2$, find a constant D such that Dt satisfies (7). If $a = -2$, find a constant D such that Dt^2 satisfies (7).

5. A model of location uses the difference equation

$$D_{n+2} - 4(ab + 1)D_{n+1} + 4a^2b^2 D_n = 0, \qquad n = 0, 1, \ldots$$

where a and b are constants, and D_n is the unknown function. Find the solution of this equation assuming that $1 + 2ab > 0$.

6. Consider equation (1) assuming that $\frac{1}{4}a^2 - b = 0$, so that the characteristic equation has a real double root $m = -a/2$. Let $x_t = u_t(-a/2)^t$ and prove that x_t satisfies (1) provided that u_t satisfies the equation $u_{t+2} - 2u_{t+1} + u_t = 0$. Use the result in Problem 11.3.2 to find x_t.

7. Investigate the global asymptotic stability of the following equations:

   (a) $x_{t+2} - \frac{1}{3}x_t = \sin t$ (b) $x_{t+2} - x_{t+1} - x_t = 0$ (c) $x_{t+2} - \frac{1}{8}x_{t+1} + \frac{1}{6}x_t = t^2 e^t$

8. (a) A model due to B. J. Ball and E. Smolensky is based on the following system:

$$C_t = cY_{t-1}, \qquad K_t = \sigma Y_{t-1}, \qquad Y_t = C_t + K_t - K_{t-1}$$

Here C_t denotes consumption, K_t capital stock, Y_t net national product, whereas c and σ are positive constants. Give an economic interpretation of the equations.

(b) Derive a difference equation of the second order for Y_t. Find necessary and sufficient conditions for the solution of this equation to have explosive oscillations.

9. (a) A model by J. R. Hicks uses the following difference equation:

$$Y_{t+2} - (b+k)Y_{t+1} + kY_t = a(1+g)^t, \qquad t = 0, 1, \ldots$$

where a, b, g, and k are constants. Find a special solution Y_t^* of the equation.

(b) Give conditions for the characteristic equation to have two complex roots.

(c) Find the growth factor r of the oscillations when the conditions obtained in part (b) are satisfied, and determine when the oscillations are damped.

10. The authors Frisch, Haavelmo, Nørregaard-Rasmussen, and Zeuthen, in their study of the "wage-price spiral" of inflation, considered the following system for $t = 0, 1, \ldots$:

$$\text{(i)} \quad \frac{W_{t+2} - W_{t+1}}{W_{t+1}} = \frac{P_{t+1} - P_t}{P_t} \qquad \text{(ii)} \quad P_t = \gamma + \beta W_t$$

Here W_t denotes the wage level and P_t the price index at time t, whereas γ and β are constants. The first equation states that the proportional increase in wages is equal to the proportional increase in the price index one period earlier, whereas the second equation relates prices to current wages.

(a) Deduce from (i) and (ii) the following equation for W_t:

$$\frac{W_{t+2}}{\gamma + \beta W_{t+1}} = \frac{W_{t+1}}{\gamma + \beta W_t}, \qquad t = 0, 1, \ldots \qquad \text{(iii)}$$

(b) Use (iii) to prove that $W_{t+1} = c(\gamma + \beta W_t)$, $t = 0, 1, \ldots$, where $c = W_1/P_0$, and find a general expression for W_t when $c\beta \neq 1$. Under what conditions will the equation be globally asymptotically stable, and what is then the limit of W_t as $t \to \infty$?

HARDER PROBLEMS

11. Prove that the conditions in (B) in Theorem 11.4.2 are equivalent to the condition in (A) for the case when the characteristic polynomial has real roots, by studying the parabola $f(m) = m^2 + am + b$. (Consider the values of $f(-1)$, $f(1)$, $f'(-1)$, and $f'(1)$.)

11.5 Higher-Order Equations

In this section we briefly record some results for nth order difference equations,

$$x_{t+n} = f(t, x_t, x_{t+1}, \ldots, x_{t+n-1}), \qquad t = 0, 1, \ldots \qquad (1)$$

Suppose f is defined for all values of the variables. If we require that $x_0, x_1, \ldots, x_{n-1}$ have given fixed values by substituting $t = 0$ into (1), we find that $x_n = f(0, x_0, x_1, \ldots, x_{n-1})$ is uniquely determined. Then substituting $t = 1$ into (1) yields $x_{n+1} = f(1, x_1, x_2, \ldots, x_n) = f(1, x_1, x_2, \ldots, f(0, x_0, x_1, \ldots, x_{n-1}))$. And so on. Thus the solution of equation (1) is uniquely determined by the values x_t takes in the first n periods, $0, 1, \ldots, n - 1$.

The **general solution** of (1) is a function $x_t = g(t; C_1, \ldots, C_n)$ depending on n arbitrary constants, $C_1, \ldots, C_n$, that satisfies (1) and has the property that every solution of (1) can be obtained by giving $C_1, \ldots, C_n$ appropriate values.

Linear Equations

The general theory for second-order linear difference equations is easily generalized to nth order equations.

THEOREM 11.5.1

The general solution of the homogeneous difference equation

$$x_{t+n} + a_1(t)x_{t+n-1} + \cdots + a_{n-1}(t)x_{t+1} + a_n(t)x_t = 0$$

where $a_n(t) \neq 0$, is given by

$$x_t = C_1 u_t^{(1)} + \cdots + C_n u_t^{(n)}$$

where $u_t^{(1)}, \ldots, u_t^{(n)}$ are n linearly independent solutions of the equation and $C_1, \ldots, C_n$ are arbitrary constants.

THEOREM 11.5.2

The general solution of the nonhomogeneous difference equation

$$x_{t+n} + a_1(t)x_{t+n-1} + \cdots + a_{n-1}(t)x_{t+1} + a_n(t)x_t = b_t$$

where $a_n(t) \neq 0$, is given by

$$x_t = C_1 u_t^{(1)} + \cdots + C_n u_t^{(n)} + u_t^*$$

where $C_1 u_t^{(1)} + \cdots + C_n u_t^{(n)}$ is the general solution of the corresponding homogeneous equation, and u_t^* is a particular solution of the nonhomogeneous equation.

NOTE 1 In using the theorem we need the following generalization of (11.3.5): If $u_t^{(1)}, \ldots,$ $u_t^{(n)}$ are solutions of the homogeneous difference equation in Theorem 11.5.1, then

$$
\begin{vmatrix}
u_0^{(1)} & \cdots & u_0^{(n)} \\
u_1^{(1)} & \cdots & u_1^{(n)} \\
\cdots\cdots\cdots\cdots\cdots \\
u_{n-1}^{(1)} & \cdots & u_{n-1}^{(n)}
\end{vmatrix} \neq 0
\quad\Longleftrightarrow\quad
\begin{array}{l} u_t^{(1)}, \ldots, u_t^{(n)} \text{ are} \\ \text{linearly independent} \end{array}
\tag{2}
$$

Constant Coefficients

The general linear difference equation of nth order with constant coefficients takes the form

$$
x_{t+n} + a_1 x_{t+n-1} + \cdots + a_{n-1} x_{t+1} + a_n x_t = b_t, \qquad t = 0, 1, \ldots
\tag{3}
$$

The corresponding homogeneous equation is

$$
x_{t+n} + a_1 x_{t+n-1} + \cdots + a_{n-1} x_{t+1} + a_n x_t = 0, \qquad t = 0, 1, \ldots
\tag{4}
$$

We try to find solutions to (4) of the form $x_t = m^t$. Inserting this solution and cancelling the common factor m^t yields the **characteristic equation**

$$
m^n + a_1 m^{n-1} + \cdots + a_{n-1} m + a_n = 0
\tag{5}
$$

According to the fundamental theorem of algebra, this equation has exactly n roots, when each is counted according to its multiplicity.

Suppose first that equation (5) has n different real roots $m_1, m_2, \ldots, m_n$. Then $m_1^t, m_2^t,$ $\ldots, m_n^t$ all satisfy (4). These functions are moreover linearly independent, so the general solution of (4) in this case is

$$
x_t = C_1 m_1^t + C_2 m_2^t + \cdots + C_n m_n^t
$$

This is *not* the general solution of (4) if equation (5) has multiple roots and/or complex roots. The general method for finding n linearly independent solutions of (4) is as follows:

Find the roots of equation (5) together with their multiplicity.

(A) A real root m_i with multiplicity 1 gives the solution m_i^t.

(B) A real root m_j with multiplicity $p > 1$ gives the solutions $m_j^t, t m_j^t, \ldots, t^{p-1} m_j^t$.

(C) A pair of complex roots $\alpha \pm i\beta$, each with multiplicity 1, gives the solutions $r^t \cos \theta t$, $r^t \sin \theta t$, where $r = \sqrt{\alpha^2 + \beta^2}$, and $\theta \in [0, \pi]$ satisfies $\cos \theta = \alpha/r$, $\sin \theta = \beta/r$.

(D) A pair of complex roots $\alpha \pm i\beta$, each with multiplicity $q > 1$, gives the solutions $u, v,$ $tu, tv, \ldots, t^{q-1}u, t^{q-1}v$, with $u = r^t \cos \theta t$ and $v = r^t \sin \theta t$, where $r = \sqrt{\alpha^2 + \beta^2}$, and $\theta \in [0, \pi]$ satisfies $\cos \theta = \alpha/r$ and $\sin \theta = \beta/r$.

In order to find the general solution of the nonhomogeneous equation (3), it remains to find a particular solution u_t^* of (3). If b_t is a linear combination of products of terms of the form $a^t, t^m, \cos qt$ and $\sin qt$, as in Section 11.4, the method of undetermined coefficients again can be used.

Stability

Equation (3) is **globally asymptotically stable** if the general solution $C_1 u_t^{(1)} + \cdots + C_n u_t^{(n)}$ of the associated homogeneous equation (4) tends to 0 as $t \to \infty$, for all values of the constants $C_1, \ldots, C_n$. Then the effect of the initial conditions "dies out" as $t \to \infty$.

As in the case $n = 2$, equation (3) is globally asymptotically stable if and only if $u_i(t) \to 0$ as $t \to \infty$ for all $i = 1, \ldots, n$. Each u_i corresponds to a root, m_i, of the characteristic polynomial. Again, $u_i(t) \to 0$ as $t \to \infty$ if and only if modulus of the corresponding solution of the characteristic equation is < 1.

THEOREM 11.5.3

A necessary and sufficient condition for (3) to be global asymptotically stable is that all roots of the characteristic polynomial of the equation have moduli strictly less than 1.

The following result gives a stability condition based directly on the coefficients of the characteristic equation. (The dashed lines have been included to make it easier to see the structure of the determinants.) See Chipman (1950) for a discussion of this theorem.

THEOREM 11.5.4 (SCHUR)

Let

$$m^n + a_1 m^{n-1} + \cdots + a_{n-1} m + a_n$$

be a polynomial of degree n with real coefficients. A necessary and sufficient condition for all roots of the polynomial to have moduli less than 1 is that

$$\begin{vmatrix} 1 & a_n \\ a_n & 1 \end{vmatrix} > 0, \qquad \begin{vmatrix} 1 & 0 & a_n & a_{n-1} \\ a_1 & 1 & 0 & a_n \\ a_n & 0 & 1 & a_1 \\ a_{n-1} & a_n & 0 & 1 \end{vmatrix} > 0, \qquad \ldots,$$

$$\begin{vmatrix} 1 & 0 & \cdots & 0 & a_n & a_{n-1} & \cdots & a_1 \\ a_1 & 1 & \cdots & 0 & 0 & a_n & \cdots & a_2 \\ \vdots & \vdots & \ddots & \vdots & \vdots & \vdots & \ddots & \vdots \\ a_{n-1} & a_{n-2} & \cdots & 1 & 0 & 0 & \cdots & a_n \\ a_n & 0 & \cdots & 0 & 1 & a_1 & \cdots & a_{n-1} \\ a_{n-1} & a_n & \cdots & 0 & 0 & 1 & \cdots & a_{n-2} \\ \vdots & \vdots & \ddots & \vdots & \vdots & \vdots & \ddots & \vdots \\ a_1 & a_2 & \cdots & a_n & 0 & 0 & \cdots & 1 \end{vmatrix} > 0$$

Let us see what the theorem tell us in the case $n = 1$. When $n = 1$, Theorem 11.5.4 says that $m + a_1 = 0$ has a root with modulus < 1 if and only if $\begin{vmatrix} 1 & a_1 \\ a_1 & 1 \end{vmatrix} > 0$, i.e. if and only if $a_1^2 < 1$. (Of course, this is clear without using the theorem.) Now, $a_1^2 < 1 \Leftrightarrow |a_1| < 1$, so

$$x_{t+1} + a_1 x_t = c_t \text{ is globally asymptotically stable} \iff |a_1| < 1 \tag{6}$$

When $n = 2$, Theorem 11.5.4 says that both roots of $m^2 + a_1 m + a_2 = 0$ have moduli < 1 if and only if

$$D_1 = \begin{vmatrix} 1 & a_2 \\ \hline a_2 & 1 \end{vmatrix} > 0 \quad \text{and} \quad D_2 = \begin{vmatrix} 1 & 0 & a_2 & a_1 \\ a_1 & 1 & 0 & a_2 \\ \hline a_2 & 0 & 1 & a_1 \\ a_1 & a_2 & 0 & 1 \end{vmatrix} > 0 \tag{*}$$

Evaluating the determinants yields

$$D_1 = 1 - a_2^2 \quad \text{and} \quad D_2 = (1 - a_2)^2 (1 + a_1 + a_2)(1 - a_1 + a_2)$$

Here $D_1 > 0 \iff |a_2| < 1$. If $D_1 > 0$, then in particular $1 - a_2 \neq 0$, so that $D_2 > 0 \iff (1 + a_1 + a_2)(1 - a_1 + a_2) > 0 \iff |a_1| < 1 + a_2$. The product $(1 + a_1 + a_2)(1 - a_1 + a_2)$ is positive if and only if either both factors are positive or both are negative. If both are negative, $1 + a_1 + a_2 < 0$ and $1 - a_1 + a_2 < 0$. Adding these inequalities yields $2 + 2a_2 < 0$, i.e. $1 + a_2 < 0$, which contradicts $D_1 > 0$. Hence, if $D_1 > 0$ and $D_2 > 0$, then

$$1 + a_1 + a_2 > 0 \quad \text{and} \quad 1 - a_1 + a_2 > 0 \quad \text{and} \quad 1 - a_2 > 0 \tag{**}$$

On the other hand, if these inequalities are satisfied, then adding the first two implies that $2 + 2a_2 > 0$, i.e. $1 + a_2 > 0$. But then we see that (**) implies that D_1 and D_2 defined by (*) are both positive. Thus the conditions in (*) are equivalent to the conditions in (**). Since $1 + a_1 + a_2 > 0$ and $1 - a_1 + a_2 > 0$ are equivalent to $|a_1| < 1 + a_2$, we see that Theorem 11.4.2 is the particular case of Theorem 11.5.4 that holds when $n = 2$.

PROBLEMS FOR SECTION 11.5

1. Solve the following difference equations

   (a) $x_{t+3} - 3x_{t+1} + 2x_t = 0$ (b) $x_{t+4} + 2x_{t+2} + x_t = 8$

2. Examine the stability of the following difference equations:

   (a) $x_{t+2} - \frac{1}{3}x_t = \sin t$ (b) $x_{t+2} - x_{t+1} - x_t = 0$

   (c) $x_{t+2} - \frac{1}{8}x_{t+1} + \frac{1}{6}x_t = t^2 e^t$ (d) $x_{t+2} + 3x_{t+1} - 4x_t = t - 1$

3. In the $a_1 a_2$-plane, describe the domain defined by the inequalities (**).

4. Examine when the equation in problem 11.4.9 is globally asymptotically stable, assuming $k > 0$ and $b > 0$.

5. A paper by Akerlof and Stiglitz studies the equation

$$K_{t+2} + \left(\frac{\sigma\beta}{\alpha} - 2 \right) K_{t+1} + (1 - \sigma\beta) K_t = d$$

where the constants α, β, and σ are positive.

(a) Find a condition for both roots of the characteristic polynomial to be complex.

(b) Find a necessary and sufficient condition for stability.

11.6 Systems of Difference Equations

A first-order system of difference equations can usually be expressed in the **normal form**:[4]

$$x_1(t + 1) = f_1(t, x_1(t), \dots, x_n(t))$$
$$\dots\dots\dots\dots\dots\dots\dots\dots\dots\dots\dots\dots\dots , \qquad t = 0, 1, \dots \qquad (1)$$
$$x_n(t + 1) = f_n(t, x_1(t), \dots, x_n(t))$$

If $x_1(0), \dots, x_n(0)$ are specified, then $x_1(1), \dots, x_n(1)$ are found by substituting $t = 0$ in (1), next $x_1(2), \dots, x_n(2)$ are found by substituting $t = 1$, etc. Thus the values of $x_1(t)$, $\dots, x_n(t)$ are uniquely determined for all t (assuming that $f_1, \dots, f_n$ are defined for all values of the variables). Thus the solution of (1) is uniquely determined by the values of $x_1(0), \dots, x_n(0)$.

The **general solution** of (1) is given by n functions

$$x_1 = g_1(t; C_1, \dots, C_n), \dots, x_n = g_n(t; C_1, \dots, C_n) \qquad (**)$$

with the property that an arbitrary solution $(x_1(t), \dots, x_n(t))$ is obtained from $(**)$ by giving $C_1, \dots, C_n$ appropriate values.

Of course, there are no general methods that lead to explicit solutions of (1) in "closed" form. Only in some special cases can we find closed form solutions.

EXAMPLE 1   Find the general solution of the system

$$\text{(i)} \quad x_{t+1} = \tfrac{1}{2}x_t + \tfrac{1}{3}y_t, \qquad \text{(ii)} \quad y_{t+1} = \tfrac{1}{2}x_t + \tfrac{2}{3}y_t, \qquad t = 0, 1, \dots$$

---

[4] In this section, the argument t is often included in parentheses, when subscripts are needed to indicate different variables in the system.

Solution: Guided by the method we used to solve systems of two differential equations in Section 6.5, we try to derive a second-order difference equation with x_t as the only unknown. From (i) we obtain (iii) $y_t = 3x_{t+1} - \frac{3}{2}x_t$, which inserted into (ii) yields (iv) $y_{t+1} = 2x_{t+1} - \frac{1}{2}x_t$. Replacing t by $t+1$ in (i), we obtain (v) $x_{t+2} = \frac{1}{2}x_{t+1} + \frac{1}{3}y_{t+1}$. Inserting (iv) into (v), then rearranging, one obtains

$$x_{t+2} - \tfrac{7}{6}x_{t+1} + \tfrac{1}{6}x_t = 0$$

The characteristic equation is $m^2 - \frac{7}{6}m + \frac{1}{6} = 0$, with the roots $m_1 = 1$, $m_2 = \frac{1}{6}$. The general solution is then easily found. In turn, (iii) is used to find y_t. The result is

$$x_t = A + B\left(\tfrac{1}{6}\right)^t, \qquad y_t = \tfrac{3}{2}A - B\left(\tfrac{1}{6}\right)^t$$

Matrix Formulation of Linear Systems

If the functions $f_1, \ldots, f_n$ in (1) are linear, we obtain the system

$$x_1(t+1) = a_{11}(t)x_1(t) + \cdots + a_{1n}(t)x_n(t) + b_1(t)$$
$$\ldots\ldots\ldots\ldots\ldots\ldots\ldots\ldots\ldots\ldots\ldots\ldots\ldots\ldots\ldots , \qquad t = 0, 1, \ldots \qquad (2)$$
$$x_n(t+1) = a_{n1}(t)x_1(t) + \cdots + a_{nn}(t)x_n(t) + b_n(t)$$

Suppose we define

$$\mathbf{x}(t) = \begin{pmatrix} x_1(t) \\ \vdots \\ x_n(t) \end{pmatrix}, \qquad \mathbf{A}(t) = \begin{pmatrix} a_{11}(t) & \cdots & a_{1n}(t) \\ \vdots & \ddots & \vdots \\ a_{n1}(t) & \cdots & a_{nn}(t) \end{pmatrix}, \qquad \mathbf{b}(t) = \begin{pmatrix} b_1(t) \\ \vdots \\ b_n(t) \end{pmatrix}$$

Then (2) is equivalent to the matrix equation

$$\mathbf{x}(t+1) = \mathbf{A}(t)\mathbf{x}(t) + \mathbf{b}(t), \qquad t = 0, 1, \ldots \qquad (3)$$

The method suggested in Example 1 allows one, in general, to derive a linear nth order difference equation in one of the unknowns, say x_1. When all the coefficients $a_{ij}(t)$ are constants, $a_{ij}(t) = a_{ij}$, this method will lead to a linear difference equation with constant coefficients.

Alternatively, if $\mathbf{A}(t)$ is a constant matrix $\mathbf{A}$, then (3) reduces to

$$\mathbf{x}(t+1) = \mathbf{A}\mathbf{x}(t) + \mathbf{b}(t), \qquad t = 0, 1, \ldots \qquad (4)$$

Inserting $t = 0, 1, \ldots$, we get successively $\mathbf{x}(1) = \mathbf{A}\mathbf{x}(0) + \mathbf{b}(0)$, $\mathbf{x}(2) = \mathbf{A}\mathbf{x}(1) + \mathbf{b}(1) = \mathbf{A}^2\mathbf{x}(0) + \mathbf{A}\mathbf{b}(0) + \mathbf{b}(1)$, $\mathbf{x}(3) = \mathbf{A}\mathbf{x}(2) + \mathbf{b}(2) = \mathbf{A}^3\mathbf{x}(0) + \mathbf{A}^2\mathbf{b}(0) + \mathbf{A}\mathbf{b}(1) + \mathbf{b}(2)$, and in general,

$$\mathbf{x}(t) = \mathbf{A}^t\mathbf{x}(0) + \mathbf{A}^{t-1}\mathbf{b}(0) + \mathbf{A}^{t-2}\mathbf{b}(1) + \cdots + \mathbf{b}(t-1) \qquad (5)$$

If $\mathbf{b}(t) = \mathbf{0}$ for all t, then (with $\mathbf{A}^0 = \mathbf{I}$ as the identity matrix)

$$\mathbf{x}(t+1) = \mathbf{A}\mathbf{x}(t) \iff \mathbf{x}(t) = \mathbf{A}^t\mathbf{x}(0), \qquad t = 0, 1, \ldots \qquad (6)$$

Stability of Linear Systems

The linear system (4) is said to be **globally asymptotically stable** if, no matter what the initial conditions, the general solution of the corresponding homogeneous system $\mathbf{x}(t+1) = \mathbf{A}\mathbf{x}(t)$ tends to $\mathbf{0}$ as t tends to infinity. According to (6), the homogeneous system has the solution $\mathbf{x}(t) = \mathbf{A}^t \mathbf{x}(0)$. Hence we see that (4) is globally asymptotically stable if and only if $\mathbf{A}^t \mathbf{x}(0)$ tends to $\mathbf{0}$ as $t \to \infty$, for each choice of initial vector $\mathbf{x}(0) = \mathbf{x}_0$. From linear algebra it is known that

$$\mathbf{A}^t \mathbf{x}_0 \underset{t \to \infty}{\longrightarrow} \mathbf{0} \quad \text{for all } \mathbf{x}_0 \text{ in } \mathbb{R}^n \quad \Longleftrightarrow \quad \mathbf{A}^t \underset{t \to \infty}{\longrightarrow} \mathbf{0} \tag{7}$$

in the sense that every component of the $n \times n$ matrix $\mathbf{A}^t$ tends to 0. A necessary and sufficient condition for this is:

$$\mathbf{A}^t \underset{t \to \infty}{\longrightarrow} \mathbf{0} \quad \Longleftrightarrow \quad \text{all the eigenvalues of } \mathbf{A} \text{ have moduli less than 1} \tag{8}$$

The following result follows immediately:

THEOREM 11.6.1

A necessary and sufficient condition for system $\mathbf{x}(t + 1) = \mathbf{A}\mathbf{x}(t) + \mathbf{b}(t)$ to be globally asymptotically stable is that all the eigenvalues of the matrix $\mathbf{A}$ have moduli (strictly) less than 1.

Suppose in particular that the vector $\mathbf{b}(t)$ is independent of t, $\mathbf{b}(t) = \mathbf{b}$. According to (5) the solution of the system is

$$\mathbf{x}(t) = \mathbf{A}^t \mathbf{x}(0) + (\mathbf{A}^{t-1} + \mathbf{A}^{t-2} + \cdots + \mathbf{A} + \mathbf{I})\mathbf{b} \tag{9}$$

Suppose that the system is globally asymptotically stable so that all the eigenvalues of $\mathbf{A}$ have moduli less than 1. Now,

$$(\mathbf{I} + \mathbf{A} + \mathbf{A}^2 + \cdots + \mathbf{A}^{t-1})(\mathbf{I} - \mathbf{A}) = \mathbf{I} - \mathbf{A}^t \tag{10}$$

(Verify this by expanding the left-hand side.) Since $\lambda = 1$ is not an eigenvalue for $\mathbf{A}$ (it has modulus *equal to* 1), the determinant $|\mathbf{A} - \mathbf{I}|$ is not 0. But then $|\mathbf{I} - \mathbf{A}| \neq 0$, so $(\mathbf{I} - \mathbf{A})^{-1}$ exists. Multiplying (10) on the right by $(\mathbf{I} - \mathbf{A})^{-1}$ yields

$$\mathbf{I} + \mathbf{A} + \mathbf{A}^2 + \cdots + \mathbf{A}^{t-1} = (\mathbf{I} - \mathbf{A}^t)(\mathbf{I} - \mathbf{A})^{-1}$$

As $t \to \infty$, it follows from (8) that $\mathbf{A}^t \to \mathbf{0}$, and we conclude that

$$\mathbf{I} + \mathbf{A} + \mathbf{A}^2 + \cdots + \mathbf{A}^{t-1} \to (\mathbf{I} - \mathbf{A})^{-1} \quad \text{as } t \to \infty \tag{11}$$

We obtain therefore the following conclusion:

THEOREM 11.6.2

If all the eigenvalues of $A = (a_{ij})_{n \times n}$ have moduli (strictly) less than 1, the difference equation

$$x(t + 1) = Ax(t) + b, \quad t = 0, 1, \ldots$$

is globally asymptotically stable, and every solution $x(t)$ of the equation converges to the constant vector $(I - A)^{-1}b$.

The following theorem can often be used to show that a matrix has only eigenvalues with moduli less than 1:

THEOREM 11.6.3

Let $A = (a_{ij})$ be an arbitrary $n \times n$ matrix and suppose that

$$\sum_{j=1}^{n} |a_{ij}| < 1 \quad \text{for all } i = 1, \ldots, n$$

Then all the eigenvalues of A have moduli less than 1.

PROBLEMS FOR SECTION 11.6

1. Find the solutions of the following systems of difference equations with the given initial conditions (in each case $t = 0, 1, \ldots$):

(a) $\begin{aligned} x_{t+1} &= 2y_t \\ y_{t+1} &= \frac{1}{2}x_t \end{aligned}$, $\quad x_0 = y_0 = 1$

(b) $\begin{aligned} x_{t+1} &= -y_t - z_t + 1 \\ y_{t+1} &= -x_t - z_t + t \\ z_{t+1} &= -x_t - y_t + 2t \end{aligned}$, $\quad \begin{aligned} x_0 &= y_0 = 0 \\ z_0 &= 1 \end{aligned}$

2. Find the general solutions of the systems.

(a) $\begin{aligned} x_{t+1} &= ay_t \\ y_{t+1} &= bx_t \end{aligned}$

(b) $\begin{aligned} x_{t+1} &= ay_t + ck^t \\ y_{t+1} &= bx_t + dk^t \end{aligned}$ $\quad (k^2 \neq ab)$

3. A study of the US economy by R.J. Ball and E. Smolensky uses the system

$$y_t = 0.49y_{t-1} + 0.68i_{t-1}, \quad i_t = 0.032y_{t-1} + 0.43i_{t-1}$$

where y_t denotes production and i_t denotes investment at time t.

(a) Derive a difference equation of order 2 for y_t, and find its characteristic equation.

(b) Find approximate solutions of the characteristic equation, and indicate the general solution of the system.

11.7 Stability of Nonlinear Difference Equations

Stability of an equilibrium state for a first-order linear difference equation with constant coefficients was considered in Section 11.1. In the present section we take a brief look at the nonlinear case, and also the possibility of cycles of order 2.

Consider an autonomous first-order difference equation

$$x_{t+1} = f(x_t) \tag{1}$$

where $f : I \to I$ is defined on an interval I in $\mathbb{R}$. An **equilibrium** or **stationary state** for (1) is a number x^* such that $x^* = f(x^*)$, i.e. the constant function $x_t = x^*$ is a solution of (1). In the language of Chapter 14, x^* is a fixed point of f. As in the case of differential equations, equilibrium states for (1) may be stable or unstable.

An equilibrium state x^* for (1) is called **locally asymptotically stable** if every solution that starts close enough to x^* converges to x^*—i.e. there exists an $\varepsilon > 0$ such that if $|x_0 - x^*| < \varepsilon$, then $\lim_{t \to \infty} x_t = x^*$. The equilibrium state x^* is **locally unstable** if a solution that starts close to x^* tends to move away from x^*, at least to begin with. More precisely, x^* is locally unstable if there exists an $\varepsilon > 0$ such that for every x with $0 < |x - x^*| < \varepsilon$ one has $|f(x) - x^*| > |x - x^*|$.

The following result, analogous to (5.7.2), is an easy consequence of the mean-value theorem.

THEOREM 11.7.1

Let x^* be an equilibrium state for the difference equation (1), and suppose that f is C^1 in an open interval around x^*.

(a) If $|f'(x^*)| < 1$, then x^* is locally asymptotically stable.

(b) If $|f'(x^*)| > 1$, then x^* is locally unstable.

Proof: (a)   Since f' is continuous and $|f'(x^*)| < 1$, there exist an $\varepsilon > 0$ and a positive number $k < 1$ such that $|f'(x)| \le k$ for all x in $(x^* - \varepsilon, x^* + \varepsilon)$. Then, provided that $|x_0 - x^*| < \varepsilon$, the mean-value theorem tells us that

$$|x_1 - x^*| = |f(x_0) - f(x^*)| = |f'(c)(x_0 - x^*)| \le k|x_0 - x^*|$$

for some c between x_0 and x^*. By induction on t, it follows that $|x_t - x^*| \le k^t |x_0 - x^*|$ for all $t \ge 0$, and so $x_t \to x^*$ as $t \to \infty$.

(b)   Now suppose that $|f'(x^*)| > 1$. By continuity there exist an $\varepsilon > 0$ and a $K > 1$ such that $|f'(x)| > K$ for all x in $(x^* - \varepsilon, x^* + \varepsilon)$. Hence if $x_t \in (x^* - \varepsilon, x^* + \varepsilon)$, then

$$|x_{t+1} - x^*| = |f(x_t) - f(x^*)| \ge K|x_t - x^*|$$

Thus if x_t is close to but not equal to x^*, the distance between the solution x and the equilibrium x^* is magnified by a factor K or more at each step as long as x_t remains in $(x^* - \varepsilon, x^* + \varepsilon)$.   ∎

NOTE 1 If $|f'(x)| < 1$ for all x in I, then x^* is actually globally asymptotically stable in the obvious sense.

An equilibrium state x^* of equation (1) corresponds to a point (x^*, x^*) where the graph $y = f(x)$ of f intersects the straight line $y = x$. Figures 1 and 2 show two possible configurations around a stable equilibrium. In Fig. 1, $f'(x^*)$ is positive and the sequence $x_0, x_1, \ldots$ converges monotonically to x^*, whereas in Fig. 2, $f'(x^*)$ is negative and we get a cobweb-like behaviour with x_t alternating between values less than and greater than the equilibrium state $x^* = \lim_{t \to \infty} x_t$. In both cases the sequence of points $P_t = (x_t, x_{t+1}) = (x_t, f(x_t)), t = 0, 1, 2, \ldots$, on the graph of f converges towards the point (x^*, x^*).

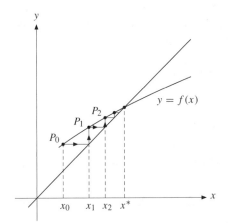

Figure 1 x^* stable, $f'(x^*) \in (0, 1)$.

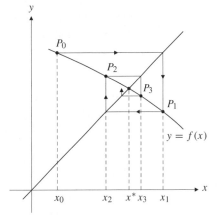

Figure 2 x^* stable, $f'(x^*) \in (-1, 0)$.

In Fig. 3, the graph of f near the equilibrium is too steep for convergence. Figure 4 shows that an equation of the form (1) may have solutions that exhibit cyclic behaviour, in this case a cycle of period 2. This is the topic of the next subsection.

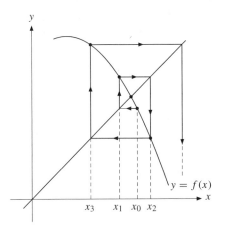

Figure 3 x^* unstable, $|f'(x^*)| > 1$.

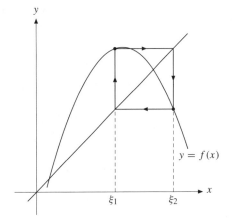

Figure 4 A cycle of period 2.

Cycles of Period 2

A **cycle** or **periodic solution** of (1) with period 2 is a solution x_t for which $x_{t+2} = x_t$ for all t, but $x_{t+1} \neq x_t$. In other words, $x_1 \neq x_0$, but $x_0 = x_2 = x_4 = \cdots$ and $x_1 = x_3 = x_5 = \cdots$.

Thus equation (1) admits a cycle of period 2 if and only if there exist distinct numbers ξ_1 and ξ_2 such that $f(\xi_1) = \xi_2$ and $f(\xi_2) = \xi_1$. If we let $F = f \circ f$, it is clear that ξ_1 and ξ_2 must be fixed points of F, i.e. they are equilibria of the difference equation

$$y_{t+1} = F(y_t) \equiv f(f(y_t)) \tag{2}$$

Such a cycle is said to be **locally asymptotically stable** if every solution of (1) that comes close to ξ_1 or ξ_2 converges to the cycle. Thus the cycle is locally asymptotically stable if and only if ξ_1 is a locally asymptotically stable equilibrium of equation (2), or equivalently, if and only if ξ_2 is such an equilibrium. The cycle is **locally unstable** if ξ_1 and ξ_2 are locally unstable equilibria of $f \circ f$. By the chain rule, $F'(x) = f'(f(x))f'(x)$, and so

$$F'(\xi_1) = f'(\xi_2)f'(\xi_1) = F'(\xi_2)$$

Theorem 11.7.2 implies the following.

If equation (1) admits a cycle of period 2, alternating between the values ξ_1 and ξ_2, then:

(a) If $|f'(\xi_1)f'(\xi_2)| < 1$, the cycle is locally asymptotically stable.

(b) If $|f'(\xi_1)f'(\xi_2)| > 1$, the cycle is locally unstable.

$$(3)$$

The Quadratic Case

A linear difference equation $x_{t+1} = ax_t + b$ with constant coefficients has no interesting cycles. The simplest nonlinear case is the case of a quadratic polynomial. So let $f(x) = ax^2 + bx + c$ (with $a \neq 0$) and consider the difference equation

$$x_{t+1} = f(x_t) = ax_t^2 + bx_t + c \tag{4}$$

The equilibrium states of (4), if any, are the solutions

$$x_1 = \frac{1 - b + \sqrt{(b-1)^2 - 4ac}}{2a}, \quad x_2 = \frac{1 - b - \sqrt{(b-1)^2 - 4ac}}{2a}$$

of the quadratic equation $x = f(x)$, i.e. $ax^2 + (b-1)x + c = 0$. These solutions exist if and only if $(b-1)^2 \geq 4ac$, and they are distinct if and only if $(b-1)^2 > 4ac$. The values of f' at these points are

$$f'(x_{1,2}) = 2ax_{1,2} + b = 1 \pm \sqrt{(b-1)^2 - 4ac}$$

It follows that if the equilibrium points exist and are distinct, then x_1 is always unstable, while x_2 is locally asymptotically stable if $(b-1)^2 - 4ac < 4$, and unstable if $(b-1)^2 - 4ac > 4$. (If $(b-1)^2 - 4ac = 4$, then x_2 is "locally asymptotically stable on one side" and unstable on the other side.)

Equation (4) admits a cycle of period 2 if there exist distinct numbers ξ_1 and ξ_2 such that $f(\xi_1) = \xi_2$ and $f(\xi_2) = \xi_1$. These numbers must be solutions of the equation $x = f(f(x))$. Since $f(f(x))$ is a polynomial of degree 4, it seems at first sight that we have to solve a rather difficult equation in order to find ξ_1 and ξ_2. Fortunately the equation simplifies because any solution of $x = f(x)$ is also a solution of $x = f(f(x))$, so $x - f(x)$ is a factor of the polynomial $x - f(f(x))$. A simple but tedious computation shows that $x - f(f(x)) = (x - f(x))g(x)$, where

$$g(x) = a^2 x^2 + a(b+1)x + ac + b + 1$$

The cycle points are the roots of the equation $g(x) = 0$, which are

$$\xi_1 = \frac{-(b+1) + \sqrt{(b-1)^2 - 4ac - 4}}{2a} , \quad \xi_2 = \frac{-(b+1) - \sqrt{(b-1)^2 - 4ac - 4}}{2a}$$

These roots exist and are distinct if and only if $(b-1)^2 > 4ac + 4$. Hence, if there is a cycle of period 2, the equilibrium points x_1 and x_2 also exist, and are both unstable. (See also Problem 1.)

Because $f'(\xi) = 2a\xi + b$, while $\xi_1 + \xi_2 = -(b+1)/a$ and $\xi_1\xi_2 = (ac + b + 1)/a^2$, a simple calculation shows that $f'(\xi_1)f'(\xi_2) = 4ac - (b-1)^2 + 5$. Then

$$|f'(\xi_1)f'(\xi_2)| < 1 \iff 4 < (b-1)^2 - 4ac < 6 \tag{5}$$

It follows that if the inequalities on the right are satisfied, then equation (4) admits a stable cycle of period 2. (The first inequality on the right is precisely the necessary and sufficient condition for a period 2 cycle to exist.)

PROBLEMS FOR SECTION 11.7

1. Show that if $f : I \to I$ is continuous and the difference equation $x_{t+1} = f(x_t)$ admits a cycle ξ_1, ξ_2 of period 2, it also has at least one equilibrium solution between ξ_1 and ξ_2. (*Hint:* Consider the function $f(x) - x$ over the interval with endpoints ξ_1 and ξ_2.)

2. A solution x^* of the equation $x = f(x)$ can be viewed as an equilibrium solution of the difference equation

$$x_{t+1} = f(x_t) \tag{*}$$

If this equilibrium is stable and x_0 is a sufficiently good approximation to x^*, then the solution $x_0, x_1, x_2, \ldots$ of (*) starting from x_0 will converge to x^*.

(a) Use this technique to determine the negative solution of $x = e^x - 3$ to at least three decimal places.

(b) The equation $x = e^x - 3$ also has a positive solution, but this is an unstable equilibrium of $x_{t+1} = e^{x_t} - 3$. Explain how nevertheless we can find the positive solution by rewriting the equation and using the same technique as above.

3. The function f in Fig. 4 is given by $f(x) = -x^2 + 4x - 4/5$. Find the values of the cycle points ξ_1 and ξ_2, and use (5) to determine whether the cycle is stable. It is clear from the figure that the difference equation $x_{t+1} = f(x_t)$ has two equilibrium states. Find these equilibria, show that they are both unstable, and verify the result in Problem 1.

DISCRETE TIME OPTIMIZATION

*In science, what is capable of proof
must not be believed without a proof.*[1]
—R. Dedekind (1887)

This chapter gives a brief introduction to *discrete time dynamic optimization problems*. The term *dynamic* refers to the fact that the problems involve systems evolving over time. Time is here measured by the number of whole periods (say weeks, quarters, or years) that have passed since time 0. So we speak of *discrete* time. In this case it is natural to study dynamic systems whose development is governed by difference equations.

If the horizon is finite, then such dynamic problems can be solved, in principle, using classical calculus methods. There are, however, special solution techniques described in the present chapter that take advantage of the special structure of discrete dynamic optimization problems.

Most of the chapter is concerned with dynamic programming. This is a general method for solving discrete time optimization problems that was formalized by R. Bellman in the late 1950s. There is also a brief introduction to discrete time control theory. The last two sections cover stochastic dynamic programming. (This is the only part of the book that relies on some knowledge of probability theory, though at a basic level.)

12.1 Dynamic Programming

Consider a system that is observed at times $t = 0, 1, \ldots, T$. Suppose the **state** of the system at time t is characterized by a real number x_t. For example, x_t might be the quantity of grain that is stockpiled at time t. Assume that the initial state x_0 is historically given, and that from then on the system evolves through time under the influence of a sequence of **controls** u_t, which can be chosen freely from a given set U, called the **control region**. For example, u_t might be the fraction of grain removed from the stock x_t during period t. The controls

---

[1] There is no ideal English translation of the German original: "Was beweisbar ist, soll in der Wissenschaft nicht ohne Beweis geglaubt werden."

influence the evolution of the system through a difference equation

$$x_{t+1} = g(t, x_t, u_t), \quad x_0 \text{ given}, \quad u_t \in U \tag{1}$$

where g is a *given* function. Thus, we assume that the state of the system at time $t + 1$ depends explicitly on the time t, on the state x_t in the preceding period t, and on u_t, the value chosen for the control at time t.

Suppose that we choose values for $u_0, u_1, \ldots, u_{T-1}$. Then (1) gives $x_1 = g(0, x_0, u_0)$. Since x_1 is now known, $x_2 = g(1, x_1, u_1)$, and next $x_3 = g(2, x_2, u_2)$, etc. In this way, (1) can be used to compute successively, or recursively, the values or states $x_1, x_2, \ldots, x_T$ in terms of the initial state, x_0, and the time path of the controls, $u_0, \ldots, u_{T-1}$. Each choice of $(u_0, u_1, \ldots, u_{T-1})$ gives rise to a sequence $(x_1, x_2, \ldots, x_T)$, for instance path 1 in Fig. 1. A different choice of $(u_0, u_1, \ldots, u_{T-1})$ gives another path, such as path 2 in the figure. Such controls u_t that depend only on time, are often called **open-loop controls**.

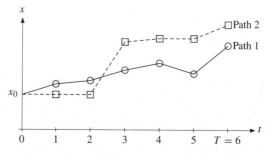

Figure 1 Different evolutions of system (1)

Different paths will usually have different utility or value. Assume that there is a function $f(t, x, u)$ of three variables such that the utility associated with a given path is represented by the sum

$$\sum_{t=0}^{T} f(t, x_t, u_t) \tag{*}$$

The sum is called the **objective function**, and it represents the sum of utilities (values) obtained at each point of time.

NOTE 1   The objective function is sometimes specified as $\sum_{t=0}^{T-1} f(t, x_t, u_t) + S(x_T)$, where S measures the net value associated with the terminal period. This is a special case of (*) in which $f(T, x_T, u_T) = S(x_T)$. (S is often called a **scrap value function**.)

Suppose that we choose values for $u_0, u_1, \ldots, u_{T-1}, u_T$, all from the set U. The initial state x_0 is given, and as explained above, (1) gives us $x_1, \ldots, x_T$. Let us denote corresponding pairs $(x_0, \ldots, x_T)$, $(u_0, \ldots, u_T)$ by $(\{x_t\}, \{u_t\})$, and call them **admissible sequence pairs**. For each admissible sequence pair the objective function has a definite value. We shall study the following problem:

Among all admissible sequence pairs $(\{x_t\}, \{u_t\})$ find one, $(\{x_t^*\}, \{u_t^*\})$, that makes the value of the objective function as large as possible. Such an admissible sequence pair is called an **optimal pair**, and the corresponding control sequence $\{u_t^*\}_{t=0}^T$ is called an **optimal control**. Briefly formulated, the problem is this:

$$\max \sum_{t=0}^T f(t, x_t, u_t) \quad \text{subject to} \quad x_{t+1} = g(t, x_t, u_t), \ x_0 \text{ given}, \ u_t \in U \qquad (2)$$

EXAMPLE 1   Let x_t be an individual's wealth at time t. At each point of time t, the individual has to decide the proportion u_t of x_t to consume, leaving the remaining proportion $1 - u_t$ for savings. Assume that wealth earns interest at the rate $\rho - 1 > 0$. After $u_t x_t$ is withdrawn for consumption, the stock of wealth is $(1 - u_t)x_t$. Because of interest, this grows to the amount $x_{t+1} = \rho(1 - u_t)x_t$ at the beginning of period $t + 1$. This goes for $t = 0, \ldots, T - 1$, with x_0 a positive constant. Suppose that the utility of consuming $c_t = u_t x_t$ is $U(t, c_t)$, where $U(t, c)$ is increasing and concave in c. Then the total utility over periods $t = 0, \ldots, T$ is $\sum_{t=0}^T U(t, u_t x_t)$. The problem facing the individual is therefore the following:

$$\max \sum_{t=0}^T U(t, u_t x_t) \quad \text{subject to} \quad x_{t+1} = \rho(1 - u_t)x_t, \ t = 0, \ldots, T - 1 \qquad (*)$$

with x_0 given and with u_t in $[0, 1]$ for $t = 0, \ldots, T$. Note that this is a standard dynamic optimization problem of the type described above. (See Problems 2, 3, and 8.)

The Value Function and its Properties

Return to the general problem described by (2). In order to find the optimal solution, we shall use a method that appears to solve a more general problem.

Suppose that at time $t = s$ the state of the system is x (any given real number). The best we can do in the remaining periods is to choose $u_s, u_{s+1}, \ldots, u_T$ (and thereby also $x_{s+1}, \ldots, x_T$) to maximize $\sum_{t=s}^T f(t, x_t, u_t)$ with $x_s = x$. We define the **(optimal) value function** for the problem at time s by[2]

$$J_s(x) = \max_{u_s, \ldots, u_T \in U} \sum_{t=s}^T f(t, x_t, u_t) \qquad (3)$$

where

$$x_s = x \quad \text{and} \quad x_{t+1} = g(t, x_t, u_t) \text{ for } t > s, \quad u_t \in U \qquad (4)$$

The controls $u_s^*, \ldots, u_T^*$ that give the maximum value in (3) subject to (4), will depend on x. In particular, the first control, u_s^*, will depend on $x \in \mathbb{R}$, $u_s^* = u_s^*(x_s) = u_s^*(x)$, where $x = x_s$ is the state at time s. Controls that depend on the state of the system in this way are called **closed-loop controls**, **feedback controls**, or **policies**.

Suppose that we have found the first control $u_s^*(x)$ for *each* $s = 0, 1, \ldots, T$. Then we have actually found the solution to the original problem (2). In particular, since the state at

---

[2] We assume that the maximum in (3) is attained. This is true if, for example, the functions f and g are continuous and U is compact.

$t = 0$ is x_0, the best choice of u_0 is $u_0^*(x_0)$. After $u_0^*(x_0)$ is found, the difference equation in (1) determines the corresponding x_1 as $x_1^* = g(0, x_0, u_0^*(x_0))$. Then $u_1^*(x_1^*)$ is the best choice of u_1 and this choice determines x_2^* by (1). Then again, $u_2^*(x_2^*)$ is the best choice of u_2, and so on.

We now prove an important property of the value function. At the terminal time $t = T$, we have $J_T(x) = \max_{u \in U} f(T, x, u)$. Suppose that at time $t = s\ (< T)$ we are in state $x_s = x$. What is the optimal choice for u_s? If we choose $u_s = u$, then at time $t = s$ we obtain the immediate reward $f(s, x, u)$, and according to (4), the state at time $s + 1$ will be $x_{s+1} = g(s, x, u)$. The highest total reward obtainable from time $s + 1$ to time T, starting from the state x_{s+1}, is $J_{s+1}(x_{s+1}) = J_{s+1}(g(s, x, u))$ according to definition (3). Hence the best choice of $u = u_s$ at time s must be a value of u that maximizes the sum

$$f(s, x, u) + J_{s+1}(g(s, x, u))$$

This leads to the following general result:

THEOREM 12.1.1 (FUNDAMENTAL EQUATIONS OF DYNAMIC PROGRAMMING)

Let $J_s(x)$ be the value function (3) for the problem

$$\max \sum_{t=0}^{T} f(t, x_t, u_t) \quad \text{subject to} \quad x_{t+1} = g(t, x_t, u_t), \quad u_t \in U \tag{5}$$

with x_0 given. Then $J_s(x)$ satisfies the equations

$$J_s(x) = \max_{u \in U} \left[f(s, x, u) + J_{s+1}(g(s, x, u)) \right], \quad s = 0, 1, \ldots, T - 1 \tag{6}$$

$$J_T(x) = \max_{u \in U} f(T, x, u) \tag{7}$$

NOTE 2 If we minimize rather than maximize the sum in (5), then Theorem 12.1.1 holds with "max" replaced by "min" in (6) and (7), because minimizing f is equivalent to maximizing $-f$.

NOTE 3 Let $X_t(x_0)$ denote the range of all possible values of the state x_t that can be generated by the difference equation (1) if we start in state x_0 and then go through all possible values of $u_0, \ldots, u_{t-1}$. Of course J_t need only be defined on $X_t(x_0)$.

Theorem 12.1.1 is the basic tool for solving dynamic optimization problems. It is used as follows: First find the function $J_T(x)$ by using (7). The maximizing value of u depends (usually) on x, and was denoted by $u_T^*(x)$ above. The next step is to use (6) to determine $J_{T-1}(x)$ and the corresponding $u_{T-1}^*(x)$. Then work backwards in this fashion to determine recursively all the value functions $J_T(x), \ldots, J_0(x)$ and the maximizers $u_T^*(x), \ldots, u_0^*(x)$. As explained above, this allows the solution to the original optimization problem to be constructed.

EXAMPLE 2   Use Theorem 12.1.1 to solve the problem

$$\max \sum_{t=0}^{3}(1 + x_t - u_t^2), \quad x_{t+1} = x_t + u_t, \quad t = 0, 1, 2, \quad x_0 = 0, \quad u_t \in \mathbb{R}$$

Solution: Here $T = 3$, $f(t, x, u) = 1 + x - u^2$, and $g(t, x, u) = x + u$. Consider first (7) and note that $J_3(x)$ is the maximum value of $1 + x - u^2$ for $u \in (-\infty, \infty)$. This maximum value is obviously attained for $u = 0$. Hence, in the notation introduced above,

$$J_3(x) = 1 + x, \quad \text{with } u_3^*(x) \equiv 0$$

For $s = 2$, the function to be maximized in (6) is $h_2(u) = 1 + x - u^2 + J_3(x + u)$. Of course, $J_3(x + u)$ is obtained by replacing x by $x + u$ in the formula for $J_3(x)$. Thus, $h_2(u) = 1 + x - u^2 + 1 + (x + u) = 2 + 2x + u - u^2$. The function $h_2(u)$ is concave in u, and $h_2'(u) = 1 - 2u = 0$ for $u = 1/2$, so this is the optimal choice of u. Then the maximum value of $h_2(u)$ is $h_2(1/2) = 2 + 2x + 1/2 - 1/4 = 9/4 + 2x$. Hence,

$$J_2(x) = \tfrac{9}{4} + 2x, \quad \text{with } u_2^*(x) \equiv \tfrac{1}{2}$$

For $s = 1$, the function to be maximized in (6) is given by $h_1(u) = 1 + x - u^2 + J_2(x + u) = 1 + x - u^2 + 9/4 + 2(x + u) = 13/4 + 3x + 2u - u^2$. Because h_1 is concave and $h_1'(u) = 2 - 2u = 0$ for $u = 1$, the maximum value of $h_1(u)$ is $13/4 + 3x + 2 - 1 = 17/4 + 3x$, so

$$J_1(x) = \tfrac{17}{4} + 3x, \quad \text{with } u_1^*(x) \equiv 1$$

Finally, for $s = 0$, the function to be maximized is $h_0(u) = 1 + x - u^2 + J_1(x + u) = 1 + x - u^2 + 17/4 + 3(x + u) = 21/4 + 4x + 3u - u^2$. The function h_0 is concave and $h_0'(u) = 3 - 2u = 0$ for $u = 3/2$, so the maximum value of $h_0(u)$ is $h_0(3/2) = 21/4 + 4x + 9/2 - 9/4 = 15/2 + 4x$. Thus,

$$J_0(x) = \tfrac{15}{2} + 4x, \quad \text{with } u_0^*(x) \equiv \tfrac{3}{2}$$

In this particular case the optimal choices of the controls are constants, independent of the states. The corresponding optimal values of the state variables are $x_1 = x_0 + u_0 = 3/2$, $x_2 = x_1 + u_1 = 3/2 + 1 = 5/2$, $x_3 = x_2 + u_2 = 5/2 + 1/2 = 3$. The maximum value of the objective function is 7.5.

Alternative solution: In simple cases like this, a dynamic optimization problem can be solved quite easily by ordinary calculus methods. By letting $t = 0$, 1, and 2 in the difference equation $x_{t+1} = x_t + u_t$, we get $x_1 = x_0 + u_0 = u_0$, $x_2 = x_1 + u_1 = u_0 + u_1$, and $x_3 = x_2 + u_2 = u_0 + u_1 + u_2$. Using these results, the objective function becomes the following function of u_0, u_1, u_2, and u_3:

$$I = (1 - u_0^2) + (1 + u_0 - u_1^2) + (1 + u_0 + u_1 - u_2^2) + (1 + u_0 + u_1 + u_2 - u_3^2)$$
$$= 4 + 3u_0 - u_0^2 + 2u_1 - u_1^2 + u_2 - u_2^2 - u_3^2$$

The problem has been reduced to that of maximizing I with respect to the control variables $u_0, u_1, u_2,$ and u_3. We see that I is a sum of concave functions and so is concave. Hence a stationary point will maximize I. The first-order derivatives of I are

$$\frac{\partial I}{\partial u_0} = 3 - 2u_0, \quad \frac{\partial I}{\partial u_1} = 2 - 2u_1, \quad \frac{\partial I}{\partial u_2} = 1 - 2u_2, \quad \frac{\partial I}{\partial u_3} = -2u_3$$

Equating these partial derivatives to zero yields the unique stationary point $(u_0, u_1, u_2, u_3) = (3/2, 1, 1/2, 0)$, which then solves our problem. We have the same solution as the one we obtained by using Theorem 12.1.1.

In principle, all finite dimensional dynamic programming problems can be solved this way using ordinary calculus, but the method becomes very unwieldy if the horizon T is large.

In the next example the terminal time is an arbitrarily given natural number and the optimal control turns out to depend on the state of the system.

EXAMPLE 3   Solve the following problem

$$\max\left(\sum_{t=0}^{T-1} -\tfrac{2}{3}u_t x_t + \ln x_T\right), \quad x_{t+1} = x_t(1 + u_t x_t), \quad x_0 \text{ positive constant}, \quad u_t \geq 0 \quad (*)$$

Solution: Because $x_0 > 0$ and $u_t \geq 0$, we have $x_t > 0$ for all t. Now, $f_0(T, x, u) = \ln x$ is independent of u, so $J_T(x) = \ln x$, and any u_T is optimal. Equation (6) with $s = T - 1$ yields

$$J_{T-1}(x) = \max_{u \geq 0}\left[-\tfrac{2}{3}ux + J_T(x(1 + ux))\right] = \max_{u \geq 0}\left[-\tfrac{2}{3}ux + \ln x + \ln(1 + ux)\right]$$

The maximum of the concave function $h(u) = -\tfrac{2}{3}ux + \ln x + \ln(1 + ux)$ is where its derivative is 0. This gives $h'(u) = -\tfrac{2}{3}x + x/(1 + ux) = 0$, or (since we can assume $x > 0$), $u = 1/(2x)$. Then $h(1/(2x)) = \ln x - 1/3 + \ln(3/2)$. Hence

$$J_{T-1}(x) = h(1/(2x)) = \ln x + C, \text{ with } C = -1/3 + \ln(3/2), \text{ and } u^*_{T-1}(x) = 1/(2x)$$

The next step is to use (6) for $s = T - 2$:

$$J_{T-2}(x) = \max_{u \geq 0}\left[-\tfrac{2}{3}ux + J_{T-1}(x(1 + ux))\right] = \max_{u \geq 0}\left[-\tfrac{2}{3}ux + \ln x + \ln(1 + ux) + C\right]$$

Again $u = u^*_{T-2}(x) = 1/(2x)$ gives the maximum because the first-order condition is the same, and we get

$$J_{T-2}(x) = \ln x + 2C, \text{ with } C = -1/3 + \ln(3/2), \text{ and } u^*_{T-2}(x) = 1/(2x)$$

This pattern continues and so, for $k = T, T - 1, \ldots, 1, 0$, we get

$$J_{T-k}(x) = \ln x + kC, \text{ with } C = -1/3 + \ln(3/2), \text{ and } u^*_{T-k}(x) = 1/(2x)$$

(or $J_t(x) = \ln x + (T - t)C$, $u^*_t = 1/(2x)$). Inserting $u^*_t = 1/(2x^*_t)$ in the difference equation gives $x^*_{t+1} = \left(\tfrac{3}{2}\right)x^*_t$, so $x^*_t = \left(\tfrac{3}{2}\right)^t x_0$, with $\bar{u}_t = \left(\tfrac{2}{3}\right)^t/(2x_0)$ as optimal control values.

NOTE 4   Consider the difference equation $x_{t+1} = g(t, x_t, u_t)$ and any given sequence of policies $u_0(x), \ldots, u_{T-1}(x)$, all taking values in a control region U. When the initial state x_0 is given, the evolution of the state x_t is then uniquely determined by the difference equation

$$x_{t+1} = g(t, x_t, u_t(x_t)), \quad x_0 \text{ given} \tag{*}$$

Let us write down the control values (numbers) $\bar{u}_t = u_t(x_t)$ given by this particular sequence of states $\{x_t\}$. Next insert these numbers $\bar{u}_t$ into the difference equation:

$$x_{t+1} = g(t, x_t, \bar{u}_t), \quad x_0 \text{ given} \tag{**}$$

This difference equation has the same solution as equation $(*)$. Hence, we get the same result whether we insert the functions $u_t(x)$, or the numbers $\bar{u}_t$.

Consider, for example, the case $x_{t+1} = x_t + u_t$, and choose $u_t(x) = 2x$ for all t. Then equation $(*)$ is $x_{t+1} = x_t + 2x_t = 3x_t$, and with x_0 given, the solution is $x_t = 3^t x_0$. The associated controls are $u_t = 2x_t = 2 \cdot 3^t x_0$, and equation $(**)$ is now $x_{t+1} = x_t + 2 \cdot 3^t x_0$. This equation is easily seen to have the solution $x_t = 3^t x_0$ as well. (Insert and check.)

Now, the dynamic programming method gives us the optimal control functions $u_t^*(x)$. Given the initial situation x_0, once we have calculated the values $\bar{u}_t$ using the optimal control functions $u_t^*(x)$, we can forget about these functions: At each point of time, we know that it is optimal to use $\bar{u}_t$ as the control variable.

It may nevertheless be useful not to forget entirely the form of each control function. Suppose that at time τ, there is an unexpected disturbance to the state x_τ^* obtained from the difference equation, which has the effect of changing the state to $\hat{x}_\tau$. Then $u_\tau^*(\hat{x}_\tau)$ still gives the optimal control to be used at that time, provided we know that no further disturbances will occur.

NOTE 5   Theorem 12.1.1 also holds if the control region is not fixed, but depends on (t, x), $U = U(t, x)$. Then the maximization in (2), (3), and (5) is carried out for u_t in $U(t, x_t)$. In (6) and (7), the maximization is carried out for $u \in U(s, x)$ and $u \in U(T, x)$, respectively. Frequently, the set $U(t, x)$ is determined by a set of inequalities, $\{u : h_i(t, x, u) \le 0, i = 1, \ldots, i^*\}$. If $U(t, x)$ is empty, then by convention, the maximum over $U(t, x)$ is set equal to $-\infty$.

NOTE 6   In the above formulation, the state x and the control u may well be vectors, in say $\mathbb{R}^n$ and $\mathbb{R}^r$, respectively. Then g must be a vector function as well, and the difference equation is a system of difference equations, one for each component of x. No changes are then needed in Theorem 12.1.1 (except that we would use boldface letters for x, u, and g).

EXAMPLE 4   Let x_t denote the value of an investor's assets at the start of period t, and u_t consumption during period t. Suppose that assets at the start of period $t + 1$ are proportional to savings $x_t - u_t$ in period t, with a factor of proportionality depending on t, i.e.

$$x_{t+1} = a_t(x_t - u_t), \quad a_t \text{ given positive numbers}$$

Assume that the initial assets, x_0, are positive. The utility associated with a level of consumption u during one period is supposed to be $u^{1-\gamma}$, while the utility of the assets at the end of period T is $Ax_T^{1-\gamma}$. Here A is a positive constant and $\gamma \in (0, 1)$. The investor wants to maximize the discounted value of the sum of utility from consumption and terminal assets. Define $\beta = 1/(1+r)$, where r is the rate of discount. Assume that no borrowing is allowed, with $0 < u_t < x_t$. The investor's problem is thus:

$$\max\left[\sum_{t=0}^{T-1} \beta^t u_t^{1-\gamma} + \beta^T Ax_T^{1-\gamma}\right], \quad x_{t+1} = a_t(x_t - u_t), \quad u_t \in (0, x_t) \tag{i}$$

Solution: Combined with Note 5, and with $U(t, x) = (0, x)$, Theorem 12.1.1 can be applied to the present problem. We then have $f(t, x, u) = \beta^t u^{1-\gamma}$ for $t = 0, 1, \ldots, T-1$, whereas $f(T, x, u) = \beta^T Ax^{1-\gamma}$. Since this function does not depend on u, (7) yields

$$J_T(x) = \max_{u \in (0,x)} \beta^T Ax^{1-\gamma} = \beta^T Ax^{1-\gamma} \tag{ii}$$

and any u_T in $(0, x)$ is optimal. Moreover, equation (6) yields

$$J_s(x) = \max_{u \in (0,x)}\left[\beta^s u^{1-\gamma} + J_{s+1}(a_s(x - u))\right] \tag{iii}$$

In particular, (ii) gives $J_T(a_{T-1}(x - u)) = \beta^T Aa_{T-1}^{1-\gamma}(x - u)^{1-\gamma}$, so

$$J_{T-1}(x) = \beta^{T-1} \max_{u \in (0,x)}\left[u^{1-\gamma} + \beta Aa_{T-1}^{1-\gamma}(x - u)^{1-\gamma}\right] \tag{iv}$$

Put $g(u) = u^{1-\gamma} + \beta Aa_{T-1}^{1-\gamma}(x - u)^{1-\gamma}$ for u in $(0, x)$. Computing $g'(u)$ and solving the equation $g'(u) = 0$ for u yields

$$u_{T-1} = u = x/C_{T-1}^{1/\gamma}, \quad \text{where} \quad C_{T-1}^{1/\gamma} = 1 + (\beta Aa_{T-1}^{1-\gamma})^{1/\gamma} \tag{v}$$

Because $\gamma \in (0, 1)$ and $\beta Aa_{T-1}^{1-\gamma} > 0$, g is easily seen to be concave over $(0, x)$. Then the value of u given in (v) does maximize $g(u)$. Now,

$$g\left(\frac{x}{C_{T-1}^{1/\gamma}}\right) = x^{1-\gamma}C_{T-1}^{(\gamma-1)/\gamma} + \beta Aa_{T-1}^{1-\gamma}\left(x - \frac{x}{C_{T-1}^{1/\gamma}}\right)^{1-\gamma}$$

$$= x^{1-\gamma}C_{T-1}^{(\gamma-1)/\gamma} + x^{1-\gamma}\left(C_{T-1}^{1/\gamma} - 1\right)^{\gamma} \cdot \frac{(C_{T-1}^{1/\gamma} - 1)^{1-\gamma}}{C_{T-1}^{(1-\gamma)/\gamma}} = x^{1-\gamma}C_{T-1}$$

Hence, by (iv),

$$J_{T-1}(x) = \beta^{T-1}C_{T-1}x^{1-\gamma} \tag{vi}$$

Notice that $J_{T-1}(x)$ has the same form as $J_T(x)$. Proceed by substituting $s = T - 2$ in (iii) to get:

$$J_{T-2}(x) = \beta^{T-2} \max_{u \in (0,x)}\left[u^{1-\gamma} + \beta C_{T-1}a_{T-2}^{1-\gamma}(x - u)^{1-\gamma}\right]$$

Comparing with (iv), we see that the maximum value is attained for

$$u_{T-2} = u = x/C_{T-2}^{1/\gamma}, \qquad \text{where} \quad C_{T-2}^{1/\gamma} = 1 + \left(\beta C_{T-1} a_{T-2}^{1-\gamma}\right)^{1/\gamma}$$

and that $J_{T-2}(x) = \beta^{T-2} C_{T-2} x^{1-\gamma}$. We can obviously go backwards repeatedly in this way, and obtain for every t,

$$J_t(x) = \beta^t C_t x^{1-\gamma} \tag{vii}$$

From (ii), $C_T = A$, while C_t for $t < T$ is determined recursively backwards by the following linear difference equation of the first order in $C_t^{1/\gamma}$:

$$C_t^{1/\gamma} = 1 + \left(\beta C_{t+1} a_t^{1-\gamma}\right)^{1/\gamma} = 1 + \left(\beta a_t^{1-\gamma}\right)^{1/\gamma} C_{t+1}^{1/\gamma} \tag{viii}$$

The optimal control is

$$u_t^*(x) = x/C_t^{1/\gamma}, \qquad t < T \tag{ix}$$

We find the optimal path by successively inserting $u_0^*, u_1^*, \dots$ into the difference equation (i) for x_t.

Suppose in particular that $a_t = a$ for all t. Then (viii) reduces to

$$C_{t+1}^{1/\gamma} - \frac{1}{\omega} C_t^{1/\gamma} = -\frac{1}{\omega}, \qquad \text{where} \quad \omega = \beta^{1/\gamma} a^{1/\gamma-1} \tag{x}$$

This is a first-order linear difference equation with constant coefficients. Using $C_T = A$, and solving the equation for $C_t^{1/\gamma}$, we obtain

$$C_t^{1/\gamma} = A^{1/\gamma} \omega^{T-t} + \frac{1 - \omega^{T-t}}{1 - \omega}, \qquad t = T, \, T-1, \, \dots, \, 0$$

PROBLEMS FOR SECTION 12.1

1. (a) Use Theorem 12.1.1 to solve the problem

$$\max \sum_{t=0}^{2} \left[1 - (x_t^2 + 2u_t^2)\right], \; x_{t+1} = x_t - u_t, \; t = 0, 1 \tag{$*$}$$

where $x_0 = 5$ and $u_t \in \mathbb{R}$. (Compute $J_s(x)$ and $u_s^*(x)$ for $s = 2, 1, 0$.)

(b) Use the difference equation in ($*$) to compute x_1 and x_2 in terms of u_0 and u_1 (with $x_0 = 5$), and find the sum in ($*$) as a function S of u_0, u_1, and u_2. Next, maximize this function as in Example 2.

2. Consider the problem

$$\max_{u_t \in [0,1]} \sum_{t=0}^{T} \left(\frac{1}{1+r}\right)^t \sqrt{u_t x_t}, \qquad x_{t+1} = \rho(1 - u_t)x_t, \; t = 0, \dots, T-1, \; x_0 > 0$$

where r is the rate of discount. Compute $J_s(x)$ and $u_s^*(x)$ for $s = T, T-1, T-2$.

3. (a) Replace the utility function in Problem 2 by $\sum_{t=0}^{T}(1+r)^{-t}u_t x_t$. Compute $J_T(x)$, $u_T^*(x)$, $J_{T-1}(x)$, and $u_{T-1}^*(x)$ for $x \geq 0$.

   (b) Prove that there exist constants P_s (depending on ρ and r) such that $J_s(x) = P_s x$ for $s = 0, 1, \ldots, T$.

   (c) Find $J_0(x)$ and optimal values of $u_0, u_1, \ldots, u_T$.

4. (a) Compute the value functions $J_T(x)$, $J_{T-1}(x)$, $J_{T-2}(x)$, and the corresponding control functions, $u_T^*(x)$, $u_{T-1}^*(x)$, and $u_{T-2}^*(x)$ for the problem

$$\max_{u_t \in [0,1]} \sum_{t=0}^{T}(3-u_t)x_t^2, \quad x_{t+1} = u_t x_t, \; t = 0, \ldots, T-1, \; x_0 \text{ is given}$$

   (b) Try to find a general expression for $J_{T-n}(x)$ for $n = 0, 1, 2, \ldots, T$, and the corresponding optimal controls.

5. Solve the problem:

$$\max_{u_t \in [0,1]} \left[\sum_{t=0}^{T-1}\left(-\tfrac{2}{3}u_t\right)+\ln x_T \right], \quad x_{t+1} = x_t(1+u_t), \; t = 0, \ldots, T-1, \; x_0 > 0 \text{ given}$$

6. (a) Write down the fundamental equations for the problem

$$\max_{u_t \in \mathbb{R}} \sum_{t=0}^{T}(x_t - u_t^2), \quad x_{t+1} = 2(x_t + u_t), \; t = 0, 1, \ldots, T-1, \; x_0 = 0$$

   (b) Prove that the value function for the problem is given by

$$J_{T-n}(x) = (2^{n+1}-1)x + \sum_{j=0}^{n}(2^j - 1)^2, \; n = 0, 1, \ldots, T$$

   Determine the optimal controls $u_t = u_t^*$ and the maximum value $V = J_0(0)$.

7. Consider the problem

$$\max_{u_t \in \mathbb{R}} \left[\sum_{t=0}^{T-1}(-e^{-\gamma u_t}) - \alpha e^{-\gamma x_T} \right], \quad x_{t+1} = 2x_t - u_t, \; t = 0, 1, \ldots, T-1, \; x_0 \text{ given}$$

   where α and γ are positive constants.

   (a) Compute $J_T(x)$, $J_{T-1}(x)$, and $J_{T-2}(x)$.

   (b) Prove that $J_t(x)$ can be written in the form

$$J_t(x) = -\alpha_t e^{-\gamma x}$$

   and find a difference equation for α_t.

8. Consider the following special case of Problem 2, where $r = 0$:

$$\max_{u_t \in [0,1]} \sum_{t=0}^{T} \sqrt{u_t x_t}, \quad x_{t+1} = \rho(1 - u_t)x_t, \quad t = 0, \ldots, T-1, \quad x_0 > 0$$

(a) Compute $J_T(x)$, $J_{T-1}(x)$, $J_{T-2}(x)$. (*Hint:* Prove that $\max_{u \in [0,1]} \left[\sqrt{u} + A\sqrt{1-u}\right] = \sqrt{1+A^2}$ with $u = 1/(1+A^2)$.)

(b) Show that the optimal control function is $u_s(x) = 1/(1 + \rho + \rho^2 + \cdots + \rho^{T-s})$, and find the corresponding $J_s(x)$, $s = 1, 2, \ldots, T$.

12.2 The Euler Equation

Economics literature sometimes considers the following "control variable free" formulation of the basic dynamic programming problem (e.g. Stokey et al. (1989))

$$\max \sum_{t=0}^{T} F(t, x_t, x_{t+1}), \quad x_0 \text{ given and } x_1, x_2, \ldots, x_{T+1} \text{ vary freely in } \mathbb{R} \qquad (1)$$

In this formulation the instantaneous reward $F(t, x_t, x_{t+1})$ at time t depends on t and on the values of the state variable in the periods t and $t + 1$.

If we define $u_t = x_{t+1}$, then (1) becomes a standard dynamic programming problem with $U = \mathbb{R}$. On the other hand, the dynamic optimization problem (12.1.2) can usually be formulated as a problem of the type (1). Suppose, in particular, that the equation $x_{t+1} = g(t, x_t, u_t)$ for each choice of x_t and x_{t+1} has a unique solution u_t in U, with $u_t = \varphi(t, x_t, x_{t+1})$. If we define the function F by $F(t, x_t, x_{t+1}) = f(t, x_t, \varphi(t, x_t, x_{t+1}))$ for $t < T$, and $F(T, x_T, x_{T+1}) = \max_{u \in U} f(T, x_T, u)$, then problem (12.1.2) is the same as problem (1). (If there is more than one value of u such that $g(t, x_t, u) = x_{t+1}$, let u_t be a value of u that maximizes $f(t, x_t, u)$, i.e. choose the best u that leads from x_t to x_{t+1}. Then, in any case, $F(t, x_t, x_{t+1}) = \max\{f(t, x_t, u) : u \in U, x_{t+1} = g(t, x_t, u)\}$.)

Let $\{x_0^*, \ldots, x_{T+1}^*\}$ be an optimal solution to problem (1). For each given t, the derivative of the expression in (1) w.r.t. x_{t+1} must be zero. If we define $F(T + 1, x_{T+1}, x_{T+2}) = 0$, then $\{x_0^*, \ldots, x_{T+1}^*\}$ satisfies[3]

$$F_2'(t + 1, x_{t+1}, x_{t+2}) + F_3'(t, x_t, x_{t+1}) = 0, \quad t = 0, 1, \ldots, T \quad \textbf{(Euler equation)} \qquad (2)$$

This is a second-order difference equation analogous to the Euler equation in the classical calculus of variations. (See Section 8.2.) Note carefully that the partial derivatives in (2) are evaluated at different triples.

---

[3] Only the two terms $F(t, x_t, x_{t+1}) + F(t + 1, x_{t+1}, x_{t+2})$ in the sum in (1) depend on x_{t+1}. Alternatively, we can require the derivative w.r.t. x_t to be 0. This gives the same equation.

A solution procedure for the Euler equation is as follows: First, for $t = T$, (2) reduces to $F_3'(T, x_T, x_{T+1}) = 0$. This equation is solved for x_{T+1}, yielding the function $x_{T+1} = x_{T+1}(x_T)$. Next, this function is inserted into (2) for $t = T - 1$, and (2) is then solved for x_T, yielding $x_T = x_T(x_{T-1})$. Then this function is inserted into (2) for $t = T - 2$ and (2) is then solved for x_{T-1} yielding the function $x_{T-1}(x_{T-2})$. In this manner we work backwards until the function $x_1(x_0)$ has been constructed. Since x_0 is given, the value of x_1 is determined, and then x_2 is determined, and so on.

EXAMPLE 1   Write down the Euler equation for the problem

$$\max \left[\sum_{t=0}^{2} [1 + x_t - (x_{t+1} - x_t)^2] + (1 + x_3) \right], \quad x_0 = 0, \ x_1, x_2, x_3 \in \mathbb{R} \qquad (*)$$

and find the solution of the problem. Show that the problem is equivalent to the problem in Example 12.1.2.

Solution: Define $F(t, x_t, x_{t+1}) = 1 + x_t - (x_{t+1} - x_t)^2$ for $t = 0$, 1, and 2, and let $F(3, x_3, x_4) = 1 + x_3$. Then the problem is of the type (1). For $t = 0$, 1, 2, we get $F_2'(t, x_t, x_{t+1}) = 1 + 2(x_{t+1} - x_t)$, and hence $F_2'(t + 1, x_{t+1}, x_{t+2}) = 1 + 2(x_{t+2} - x_{t+1})$. Moreover, $F_3'(t, x_t, x_{t+1}) = -2(x_{t+1} - x_t)$, so that the Euler equation for $t = 0$, 1 becomes $1 + 2(x_{t+2} - x_{t+1}) - 2(x_{t+1} - x_t) = 0$, or

$$x_{t+2} - 2x_{t+1} + x_t = -\tfrac{1}{2}, \quad t = 0, 1 \qquad (**)$$

For $t = 2$ the Euler equation is $F_2'(3, x_3, x_4) + F_3'(2, x_2, x_3) = 0$. With $F(3, x_3, x_4) = 1 + x_3$, this gives $1 + (-2)(x_3 - x_2) = 0$, or

$$x_3 - x_2 = \tfrac{1}{2} \qquad (***)$$

Let us solve the problem backwards. As x_4 does not appear in the Euler equation for $t = 3$, there is nothing to determine as regards x_4. The equation $(***)$ gives $x_3 = 1/2 + x_2$. Inserting this into $(**)$ for $t = 1$, gives $1/2 + x_2 - 2x_2 + x_1 = -1/2$, i.e. $x_2 = x_1 + 1$. Inserting this into $(**)$ for $t = 0$, gives $x_1 + 1 - 2x_1 + x_0 = -1/2$, i.e. $x_1 = x_0 + 3/2$. Since $x_0 = 0$, then $x_1 = 3/2$, and so $x_2 = 5/2$ and $x_3 = 3$.

Look back at Example 12.1.2. From the difference equation there we obtained $u_t = x_{t+1} - x_t$, so that if we define $F(t, x_t, x_{t+1}) = 1 + x_t - (x_{t+1} - x_t)^2$ for $t = 0$, 1 and 2, and $F(3, x_3, x_4) = \max_{u \in \mathbb{R}}(1 + x_3 - u^2) = 1 + x_3$, the problem in Example 12.1.2 is equivalent to problem $(*)$. Note how the two approaches yield the same optimal solution.

PROBLEMS FOR SECTION 12.2

1. (a) Transform Problem 12.1.1 to the form (1).

   (b) Derive the corresponding Euler equation, and find its solution. Compare with the answer to Problem 12.1.1.

2. (a) Transform the problem in Example 12.1.3 to the form (1).

   (b) Derive the corresponding Euler equation, and find its solution. Compare with the answer in Example 12.1.3.

12.3 Infinite Horizon

Economists often study dynamic optimization problems over an infinite horizon. This avoids specifying what happens after the finite horizon is reached. It also avoids having the horizon as an extra exogenous variable that features in the solution. This section considers how dynamic programming methods can be used to study the following infinite horizon problem:

$$\max \sum_{t=0}^{\infty} \beta^t f(x_t, u_t), \ x_{t+1} = g(x_t, u_t), \ t = 0, 1, 2, \ldots, \ x_0 \text{ given}, \ u_t \in U \subseteq \mathbb{R} \quad (1)$$

Here f and g are given functions of two variables, $\beta \in (0, 1)$ is a constant discount factor, and x_0 is a given number in $\mathbb{R}$. Having a discount factor $\beta < 1$ plays an important role in our subsequent analysis of this problem.

The sequence pair $(\{x_t\}, \{u_t\})$ is called **admissible** provided $u_t \in U$, x_0, and the difference equation in (1) is satisfied for all $t = 0, 1, 2, \ldots$. Note that neither f nor g depends explicitly on t. For this reason, problem (1) is called **autonomous**.

Assume that f satisfies the boundedness condition

$$M_1 \leq f(x, u) \leq M_2 \text{ for all } (x, u), u \in U, \text{ where } M_1 \text{ and } M_2 \text{ are given numbers} \quad (2)$$

Because $0 < \beta < 1$, the sum in (1) will always converge. Take any control sequence $\pi = (u_s, u_{s+1}, \ldots)$, where $u_{s+k} \in U$ for $k = 0, 1, \ldots$, and let $x_{t+1} = g(x_t, u_t)$ for $t = s$, $s + 1, \ldots$, with $x_s = x$. The total utility (or benefit) obtained during the periods $s, s + 1$, $\ldots$, is then

$$V_s(x, \pi) = \sum_{t=s}^{\infty} \beta^t f(x_t, u_t) = \beta^s V^s(x, \pi), \text{ where } \quad V^s(x, \pi) = \sum_{t=s}^{\infty} \beta^{t-s} f(x_t, u_t) \quad (3)$$

Moreover, let

$$J_s(x) = \max_{\pi} V_s(x, \pi) = \beta^s J^s(x), \quad \text{where} \quad J^s(x) = \max_{\pi} V^s(x, \pi) \quad (4)$$

and where the maximum is taken over all sequences $\pi = (u_s, u_{s+1}, \ldots)$ with $u_{s+k} \in U$.[4] Thus, $J_s(x)$ is the maximum total utility (or benefit) that can be obtained in all the periods from $t = s$ to ∞, given that the system is in state x at $t = s$. We call $J_s(x)$ the **(optimal) value function** for problem (1).

---

[4] The existence of this maximum is discussed later in Note 2.

The function $J^s(x)$ satisfies the following property:

$$J^0(x) = J^s(x) \tag{5}$$

Intuitively, this equality is rather obvious. When maximizing $V^s(x, \pi)$ and $V^0(x, \pi)$, we obtain the same value in both cases, since the future looks exactly the same at time 0 as at time s. Equation (5) implies that

$$J_s(x) = \beta^s J^0(x), \quad s = 0, 1, \ldots \tag{6}$$

Define

$$J(x) = J_0(x) = J^0(x) \tag{7}$$

From (6) it follows that if we know $J_0(x) = J(x)$, then we know $J_s(x)$ for all s. The main result in this section is the following:

THEOREM 12.3.1 (FUNDAMENTAL EQUATION FOR INFINITE HORIZON)

The value function $J_0(x) = J(x)$ in (4) for problem (1) satisfies the equation

$$J(x) = \max_{u \in U}\left[f(x, u) + \beta J(g(x, u)) \right] \quad \textbf{(the Bellman equation)} \tag{8}$$

A rough argument for (8) resembles the argument for Theorem 12.1.1: Suppose we are in state x at time $t = 0$. If we choose the control u, the immediate reward is $\beta^0 f(x, u) = f(x, u)$, and at time $t = 1$ we end up in state $x_1 = g(x, u)$. Choosing an optimal control sequence from $t = 1$ on gives a total reward over all subsequent periods that equals $J_1(g(x, u)) = \beta J(g(x, u))$. Hence, the best choice of u at $t = 0$ is one that maximizes the sum $f(x, u) + \beta J(g(x, u))$. The maximum of this sum is therefore $J(x)$.

Equation (8) is a "functional equation", in which the unknown function $J(x)$ appears on both sides. *Under the boundedness condition (2) and the assumptions that the maximum in (8) is attained and that $0 < \beta < 1$, this equation always has one and only one bounded solution $\hat{J}(x)$, and this solution is automatically the optimal value function for the problem. The control $u(x)$ that maximizes the right-hand side of (8) is the optimal control, which is therefore independent of t.*

In general it is difficult to use equation (8) to find $J(x)$. The problem is that maximizing the right-hand side of (8) requires knowledge of the function $J(x)$.

EXAMPLE 1   Consider the following infinite horizon analogue of problem (i) in Example 12.1.4 in the case $a_t = a$, and where we have introduced a new control v defined by $u = vx$. The former constraint $u \in (0, x)$ is then replaced by $v \in (0, 1)$:

$$\max \sum_{t=0}^{\infty} \beta^t (x_t v_t)^{1-\gamma}, \quad x_{t+1} = a(1 - v_t)x_t, \quad t = 0, 1, \ldots, \quad v_t \in (0, 1) \tag{i}$$

where a and x_0 are positive constants, $\beta \in (0, 1)$, $\gamma \in (0, 1)$, and $\beta a^{1-\gamma} < 1$. Because the horizon is infinite, we may think of x_t as the assets of some timeless institution like a university, corporation, or government.

In the notation of problem (1), $f(x, v) = (xv)^{1-\gamma}$ and $g(x, v) = a(1 - v)x$. With $J_0(x) = J(x)$, equation (8) yields

$$J(x) = \max_{v \in (0,1)} \left[(xv)^{1-\gamma} + \beta J(a(1 - v)x) \right] \tag{ii}$$

In the closely related problem in Example 12.1.4, the value function was proportional to $x^{1-\gamma}$. A reasonable guess in the present case is that $J(x) = kx^{1-\gamma}$ for some constant k. We try this as a solution. Then, cancelling the factor $x^{1-\gamma}$, (ii) reduces to

$$k = \max_{v \in (0,1)} \left[v^{1-\gamma} + \beta k a^{1-\gamma} (1 - v)^{1-\gamma} \right] \tag{iii}$$

Put $\varphi(v) = v^{1-\gamma} + \beta k a^{1-\gamma} (1 - v)^{1-\gamma}$. Then the first-order condition is

$$\varphi'(v) = (1 - \gamma) v^{-\gamma} - \beta(1 - \gamma) k a^{1-\gamma} (1 - v)^{-\gamma} = 0$$

implying that $v^{-\gamma} = \beta k a^{1-\gamma} (1 - v)^{-\gamma}$. Raising each side to the power $-1/\gamma$ and solving for v yields

$$v = \frac{1}{1 + \rho k^{1/\gamma}}, \quad \text{where } \rho = \left(\beta a^{1-\gamma} \right)^{1/\gamma} \tag{iv}$$

Note that $v \in (0, 1)$ and it is easy to verify that $\varphi(v)$ is concave. Thus we have shown that if $J(x) = kx^{1-\gamma}$, then the value of v that solves the maximization problem in (iii) is given by (iv). Then equation (iii) implies that k satisfies the equation

$$k = \frac{1}{(1 + \rho k^{1/\gamma})^{1-\gamma}} + \beta k a^{1-\gamma} \frac{\rho^{1-\gamma} k^{(1-\gamma)/\gamma}}{(1 + \rho k^{1/\gamma})^{1-\gamma}}$$

Recalling that $\beta a^{1-\gamma} = \rho^{\gamma}$, simple algebra reduces this equation to

$$k = \left(1 + \rho k^{1/\gamma} \right)^{\gamma - 1} [1 + k \rho^{\gamma} \rho^{1-\gamma} k^{(1-\gamma)/\gamma}] = \left(1 + \rho k^{1/\gamma} \right)^{\gamma}$$

Raise each side to the power $1/\gamma$, and solve for $k^{1/\gamma}$ to obtain $k^{1/\gamma} = 1/(1 - \rho)$, or $k = (1 - \rho)^{-\gamma}$. Then (iv) implies $v = 1 - \rho$. Because $J(x) = kx^{1-\gamma}$, we have

$$J(x) = (1 - \rho)^{-\gamma} x^{1-\gamma}, \quad \text{with} \quad v = 1 - \rho, \quad \rho = (\beta a^{1-\gamma})^{1/\gamma} \tag{v}$$

In this example the boundedness assumption (2) is not valid until one makes a simple transformation of the problem. Define the new state variable $y_t = x_t / a^t$. Then y_t satisfies the equation $y_{t+1} = (1 - v_t) y_t$. The objective function is now $\sum_{t=0}^{\infty} \hat{\beta}^t (y_t v_t)^{1-\gamma}$, where $\hat{\beta} = \beta a^{1-\gamma}$ and so $0 < \hat{\beta} < 1$. It is easy to verify that the function $\hat{J}(y) = J(ay)$ satisfies the Bellman equation for this new problem (the optimal v is the same). In the new problem the condition in Note 3 below is satisfied with $\bigcup_t \mathcal{X}_t(x_0) \subseteq (0, y_0)$ because the state y_t remains within the interval $(0, y_0)$ for all t, and so $0 < (y_t v_t)^{1-\gamma} < y_0^{1-\gamma}$ for all t and all v_t

in $(0, 1)$. Therefore v defined in (iv) *is* optimal and the problem is solved. According to (v), the optimal v_t is constant, $v_t = 1 - \rho$. The corresponding optimal x_t satisfies the difference equation $x_{t+1} = a(1 - v_t)x_t = a\rho x_t$. With $x_0 = x$, the solution is $x_t = x(a\rho)^t$. The value of the objective function in (i) is then

$$\sum_{t=0}^{\infty} \beta^t \left(x(a\rho)^t\right)^{1-\gamma}(1 - \rho)^{1-\gamma} = (1 - \rho)^{1-\gamma}x^{1-\gamma}\sum_{t=0}^{\infty}\left(\beta(a\rho)^{1-\gamma}\right)^t$$

$$= (1 - \rho)^{1-\gamma}x^{1-\gamma}\sum_{t=0}^{\infty}\rho^t = (1 - \rho)^{-\gamma}x^{1-\gamma}$$

where we have used the fact that $\beta(a\rho)^{1-\gamma} = (\beta a^{1-\gamma})\rho^{1-\gamma} = \rho^\gamma \rho^{1-\gamma} = \rho$ and that $\sum_{t=0}^{\infty}\rho^t = 1/(1 - \rho)$. The value of the objective function is therefore precisely equal to $J(x)$, as given by (v).

NOTE 1 As pointed out in Note 12.1.6, the same theory applies without change when x_t, u_t, and g are vector functions. Moreover U may depend on the state, $U = U(x)$ (but not explicitly on time).

NOTE 2 Whenever we wrote "max" above, it was implicitly assumed that the maximum exists. Of course, without further conditions on the system, this may not be true. Under assumptions (2), the same conditions as in the finite horizon case (f and g are continuous and U is compact) ensure that the maxima in (4) and (8) do exist. Meanwhile, we prove that (8) has a unique solution, which must therefore be the optimal value function. This is done using the result in Section A.4 on iterated suprema.

$$J_0(x_0) = \sup_{u_0,u_1,\dots}\sum_{t=0}^{\infty}\beta^t f(x_t, u_t) = \sup_{u_0\in U}\left[f(x_0, u_0) + \sup_{u_1,u_2,\dots}\sum_{t=1}^{\infty}\beta^t f(x_t, u_t)\right]$$

$$= \sup_{u_0\in U}\left[f(x_0, u_0) + J_1(g(x_0, u_0))\right] = \sup_{u_0\in U}\left[f(x_0, u_0) + \beta J_0(g(x_0, u_0))\right]$$

Next, the contraction mapping theorem 14.3.1 is used to prove that the Bellman equation (8) has a unique solution. Indeed, define the operator T on the space of bounded functions $I(x)$ so that $T(I)(x) = \sup_u[f(x, u) + \beta I(g(x, u))]$ for all x. For any bounded functions $\tilde{J}$ and $\bar{J}$, define $d(\tilde{J}, \bar{J}) = \sup_z|\tilde{J}(z) - \bar{J}(z)|$. Then

$$T(\tilde{J})(x) = \sup_u\left[f(x, u) + \beta\bar{J}(g(x, u)) + \beta\left(\tilde{J}(g(x, u)) - \bar{J}(g(x, u))\right)\right]$$

$$\leq \sup_u\left[f(x, u) + \beta\bar{J}(g(x, u)) + \beta d(\tilde{J}, \bar{J})\right] = T(\bar{J})(x) + \beta d(\tilde{J}, \bar{J})$$

Symmetrically, $T(\bar{J})(x) \leq T(\tilde{J})(x) + \beta d(\tilde{J}, \bar{J})$. So $|T(\tilde{J})(x) - T(\bar{J})(x)| \leq \beta d(\tilde{J}, \bar{J})$ for all x. This verifies that T is a contraction mapping, and the proof is complete.

Finally, it is easily seen that the control $u = u(x)$ yielding maximum in the Bellman equation is optimal: Defining $J^u(x_0) = \sum_{t=0}^{\infty} f(x_t, u(x_t))$, we have

$$J^u(x_0) = f(x_0, u(x_0)) + \beta\sum_{t=1}^{\infty}\beta^{t-1}f(x_t, u(x_t)) = f(x_0, u(x_0)) + \beta J^u(g(x_0, u(x_0)))$$

(The sum from $t = 1$ to infinity, is similar to the sum defining J^u, but the sequence x_t in the former sum starts at $g(x_0, u(x_0))$, hence the term $J^u(g(x_0, u(x_0)))$.) Since also $J(x_0) = f(x_0, u(x_0)) +$

$\beta J(g(x_0, u(x_0))$, then from the last equalities, we get $J^u(x_0) - J(x_0) = \beta[J^u(x_0) - J(x_0)]$, implying $J^u(x_0) - J(x_0) = 0$.

Suppose we replace max with sup in (12.1.3), (12.1.5), (12.1.6), (12.1.7), (12.3.4), and (12.3.8). Then equations (12.1.6), (12.1.7), and (12.3.8) still hold, even if no maximum exists. Moreover, (12.3.8) still has a unique solution, which is the optimal value function. Only if the suprema in (12.1.6), (12.1.7), and (12.3.8) are attained by a closed-loop control do optimal controls exist, and these optimal controls are those closed-loop controls.

NOTE 3 It suffices to assume that the boundedness condition (2) holds for all x in $\mathcal{X}(x_0) = \bigcup_{t=0}^{\infty} \mathcal{X}_t(x_0)$, where $\mathcal{X}_t(x_0)$ is defined in Note 12.1.3.

PROBLEMS FOR SECTION 12.3

1. Consider the following problem with $\beta \in (0, 1)$:

$$\max_{u_t \in (-\infty, \infty)} \sum_{t=0}^{\infty} \beta^t(-\tfrac{2}{3}x_t^2 - u_t^2), \qquad x_{t+1} = x_t + u_t, \quad t = 0, 1, \dots, \quad x_0 \text{ given}$$

(a) Suppose that $J(x) = -\alpha x^2$. Find a third degree equation for α. Find the associated value of u^*. (Disregard condition (2).)

(b) Given a start value x_0. By looking at the objective function, show that it is reasonable to assume that $|x_t| \leq |x_{t-1}|$ and that $u_t \leq |x_{t-1}|$. Does (2) then apply?

2. Consider the problem

$$\max_{u_t \in (0, \infty)} \left[\sum_{t=0}^{\infty} \beta^t(-e^{-u_t} - \tfrac{1}{2}e^{-x_t})\right], \qquad x_{t+1} = 2x_t - u_t, \; t = 0, 1, \dots, \; x_0 \text{ is given}$$

where $\beta \in (0, 1)$. Suppose that $J(x) = -\alpha e^{-x}, \alpha > 0$. Determine α. Disregard condition (2).

12.4 The Maximum Principle

Dynamic programming is the most frequently used method for solving discrete time dynamic optimization problems. An alternative solution technique is based on the so called maximum principle. The actual calculations needed are often rather similar. However, when there are terminal restrictions on the state variables, the maximum principle is often preferable. The corresponding principle for optimization problems in continuous time is studied in more detail in Chapters 9 and 10, because for such problems it is the most important method.

Consider first the discrete time dynamic optimization problem with one state, one control variable and a free right-hand side:

$$\max_{u_t \in U \subseteq \mathbb{R}} \sum_{t=0}^{T} f(t, x_t, u_t), \quad x_{t+1} = g(t, x_t, u_t), \quad t = 0, \ldots, T-1, \quad x_0 \text{ is given}, \quad x_T \text{ free} \quad (1)$$

Here we assume that the control region U is convex, i.e. an interval. The state variable x_t evolves from the initial state x_0 according to the law of motion (1), with u_t as a control that is chosen at each $t = 0, \ldots, T$. Define the **Hamiltonian** by

$$H(t, x, u, p) = \begin{cases} f(t, x, u) + pg(t, x, u) & \text{for } t < T \\ f(t, x, u) & \text{for } t = T \end{cases} \quad (2)$$

where p is called an **adjoint function (or co-state variable)**.

THEOREM 12.4.1 (THE MAXIMUM PRINCIPLE. NECESSARY CONDITIONS)

Suppose $(\{x_t^*\}, \{u_t^*\})$ is an optimal sequence pair for problem (1), and let H be defined by (2). Then there exist numbers p_t, with $p_T = 0$, such that for all $t = 0, \ldots, T$,

$$H_u'(t, x_t^*, u_t^*, p_t)(u - u_t^*) \leq 0 \quad \text{for all } u \in U \quad (3)$$

(Note that if u_t^* is an interior point of U, (3) implies that $H_u'(t, x_t^*, u_t^*, p_t) = 0$.) Furthermore, p_t is a solution to the difference equation

$$p_{t-1} = H_x'(t, x_t^*, u_t^*, p_t), \quad t = 1, \ldots, T \quad (4)$$

NOTE 1 For a proof see Arkin and Evstigneev (1987). A closer analogy with the continuous time maximum principle comes from writing the equation of motion as $x_{t+1} - x_t = g(t, x_t, u_t)$. If we redefine the Hamiltonian accordingly, then (4) is replaced by $p_t - p_{t-1} = -H_x'(t, x_t^*, u_t^*, p_t)$, which corresponds to equation (9.2.5).

Sufficient conditions are given in following theorem. The proof is similar to the proof of the corresponding theorem in continuous time.

THEOREM 12.4.2 (SUFFICIENT CONDITIONS)

Suppose that the sequence triple $(\{x_t^*\}, \{u_t^*\}, \{p_t\})$ satisfies all the conditions in Theorem 12.4.1, and suppose further that $H(t, x, u, p_t)$ is concave with respect to (x, u) for every t. Then the sequence triple $(\{x_t^*\}, \{u_t^*\}, \{p_t\})$ is optimal.

NOTE 2 Suppose that admissible pairs are also required to satisfy $(x_t, u_t) \in A_t$, $t = 0, \ldots, T$, where A_t is a convex set for all t. Then Theorem 12.4.2 is still valid, and H need only be concave in A_t.

NOTE 3 If U is compact and f and g are continuous, there will always exist an optimal solution. (This result can be proved by using the extreme value theorem.)

EXAMPLE 1 Apply Theorem 12.4.2 to the problem in Example 12.1.2,

$$\max \sum_{t=0}^{3}(1 + x_t - u_t^2), \quad x_{t+1} = x_t + u_t, \ x_0 = 0, \ t = 0, 1, 2, \ u_t \in \mathbb{R}$$

Solution: For $t < 3$, the Hamiltonian is $H = 1 + x - u^2 + p(x + u)$, so $H'_u = -2u + p$ and $H'_x = 1 + p$. For $t = 3$, $H = 1 + x - u^2$, so $H'_u = -2u$ and $H'_x = 1$. Note that the Hamiltonian is concave in (x, u). The control region is open, so (3) implies that $(H'_u)^* = 0$, i.e. $-2u_t^* - p_t = 0$ for $t = 0, 1, 2$, and $-2u_3^* = 0$ for $t = 3$. Thus $u_0^* = \frac{1}{2}p_0$, $u_1^* = \frac{1}{2}p_1$, and $u_2^* = \frac{1}{2}p_2$,

The difference equation (4) for p_t is $p_{t-1} = 1 + p_t$ for $t = 1, 2$, and so $p_0 = 1 + p_1$, $p_1 = 1 + p_2$. Moreover, (5) yields $p_2 = 1 + p_3$, and because x_3 is free, $p_3 = 0$. It follows that $p_2 = 1$, $p_1 = 1 + p_2 = 2$, and $p_0 = 1 + p_1 = 3$. This results in the following optimal choices for the controls, $u_0^* = 3/2$, $u_1^* = 1$, $u_2^* = 1/2$, and $u_3^* = 0$, which is the same result as in Example 12.1.2.

EXAMPLE 2 Consider an oil field in which $x_0 > 0$ units of extractable oil remain at time $t = 0$. Let $u_t \geq 0$ be the quantity of oil extracted in period t, and let x_t be the remaining stock at time t. Then $u_t = x_t - x_{t+1}$. Let $C(t, x_t, u_t)$ denote the cost of extracting u_t units in period t when the stock is x_t. Let p be the price per unit of oil and let r be the discount rate, with $\beta = 1/(1 + r) \in (0, 1)$ the corresponding discount factor. If T is the fixed end of the planning period, the problem of maximizing total discounted profit can be written as

$$\max_{u_t \geq 0} \sum_{t=0}^{T} \beta^t [pu_t - C(t, x_t, u_t)], \quad t = 0, 1, \ldots, T-1, \quad x_{t+1} = x_t - u_t, \quad x_0 > 0 \quad \text{(i)}$$

assuming also that

$$u_t \leq x_t, \quad t = 0, 1, \ldots, T \quad \text{(ii)}$$

because the amount extracted cannot exceed the stock.

Because of restriction (ii), this is not a dynamic optimization problem of the type described by (1). However, if we define a new control v_t by $u_t = v_t x_t$, then restriction (ii) combined with $u_t \geq 0$ reduces to the control restriction $v_t \in [0, 1]$, and we have a standard dynamic optimization problem. Assuming that $C(t, x, u) = u^2/x$, $0 < p < 1$, and $\beta \in (0, 1)$, apply the maximum principle to the problem

$$\max_{v_t \in [0,1]} \sum_{t=0}^{T} \beta^t (pv_t x_t - v_t^2 x_t), \quad x_{t+1} = x_t(1 - v_t), \quad x_0 > 0, \quad v_t \in [0, 1] \quad \text{(iii)}$$

with x_T free.

Solution: We denote the adjoint function by λ_t. We know that $\lambda_T = 0$. The Hamiltonian is $H = \beta^t(pvx - v^2x) + \lambda x(1-v)$. (This is valid also for $t = T$, because then $\lambda = \lambda_T = 0$.) Then $H'_v = \beta^t(px - 2vx) - \lambda x$ and $H'_x = \beta^t(pv - v^2) + \lambda(1 - v)$. So (3) implies that, for $(\{x_t^*\}, \{v_t^*\})$ to solve the problem, there must exist numbers λ_t, with $\lambda_T = 0$, such that, for all $t = 0, \ldots, T$,

$$[\beta^t x_t^*(p - 2v_t^*) - \lambda_t x_t^*](v - v_t^*) \leq 0 \quad \text{for all } v \text{ in } [0, 1] \tag{iv}$$

For $t = T$, with $\lambda_T = 0$, this condition reduces to

$$\beta^T x_T^*(p - 2v_T^*)(v - v_T^*) \leq 0 \quad \text{for all } v \text{ in } [0, 1] \tag{v}$$

Having $v_T^* = 0$ would imply that $pv \leq 0$ for all v in $[0, 1]$, which is impossible because $p > 0$. Suppose instead that $v_T^* = 1$. Then (v) reduces to $\beta^T x_T^*(p - 2)(v - 1) \leq 0$ for all v in $[0, 1]$, which is impossible because $p - 2 < 0$ (put $v = 0$). Hence, $v_T^* \in (0, 1)$. For $t = T$, condition (v) then reduces to $\beta^T x_T^*(p - 2v_T^*) = 0$, and so

$$v_T^* = \tfrac{1}{2}p \tag{vi}$$

According to (4), for $t = 1, \ldots, T$,

$$\lambda_{t-1} = \beta^t v_t^*(p - v_t^*) + \lambda_t(1 - v_t^*) \tag{vii}$$

For $t = T$, because $\lambda_T = 0$ and $v_T^* = \tfrac{1}{2}p$, this equation reduces to

$$\lambda_{T-1} = \beta^T v_T^*(p - v_T^*) = \tfrac{1}{4}p^2\beta^T \tag{viii}$$

For $t = T - 1$, the term within square brackets in (iv) is

$$\beta^{T-1}x_{T-1}^*(p - 2v_{T-1}^*) - \lambda_{T-1}x_{T-1}^* = \beta^{T-1}x_{T-1}^*[p(1 - \tfrac{1}{4}\beta p) - 2v_{T-1}^*] \tag{ix}$$

Because $0 < p < 1$ and $\beta \in (0, 1)$, one has $1 > \tfrac{1}{4}\beta p$. It follows that both $v_{T-1}^* = 0$ and $v_{T-1}^* = 1$ are impossible as optimal choices in (iv), so $v_{T-1}^* \in (0, 1)$ can only be the maximizer in (iv) provided the square bracket in the last line of (ix) is 0. Hence

$$v_{T-1}^* = \tfrac{1}{2}p(1 - \tfrac{1}{4}\beta p)$$

Let us now go k periods backwards in time. Define $q_{T-k} = \lambda_{T-k}/\beta^{T-k}$. We prove by backward induction that at each time $T - k$ we have an interior maximum point v_{T-k}^* in (iv). Then $v_{T-k}^* = \tfrac{1}{2}(p - q_{T-k})$, which belongs to $(0,1)$ if $q_{T-k} \in (2 - p, p)$. Using (vii) and the definition of q_{T-k}, we find that $q_{T-(k+1)} = F(q_{T-k})$ where $F(q) = \beta[\tfrac{1}{4}(p - q)^2 + q] \geq 0$. Note that $q \mapsto F(q)$ is a strictly convex function, and by the assumptions on the parameters, we have $0 < F(q) \leq \max\{F(0), F(p)\} = \max\{\beta p^2/4, \beta p\} < p$ for all q in $[0, p]$. Because $q_T = 0$, it follows that q_{T-k} does belong to $(0, p)$ for all $k \geq 1$. Thus the solution of the problem is given by $v_{T-k}^* = (1/2)(p - q_{T-k})$, where q_{T-k} is determined by $q_{T-(k+1)} = \beta^{-(T-k)}\lambda_{T-(k+1)} = F(q_{T-k})$, with $q_T = 0$.

1. Consider Problem 12.1.1.

    (a) Write down the Hamiltonian, condition (3), and the difference equation for p_t.

    (b) Use the maximum principle to find a unique solution candidate.

    (c) Solve the problem by using Theorem 12.4.2.

2. (Boltyanski) Consider the problem

$$\max_{u_t \in [-1,1]} \sum_{t=0}^{T} (u_t^2 - 2x_t^2) \quad \text{s.t.} \quad x_{t+1} = u_t, \quad t = 0, 1, \ldots, T-1, \quad x_0 = 0$$

    (a) Prove that $u_t^* = 0$ for $t = 0, 1, \ldots, T-1$, and $u_T^* = 1$ (or -1) are optimal controls. (Express the objective function as a function of $u_0, u_1, \ldots, u_T$ only.)

    (b) Verify that the conditions in Theorem 12.4.2 are satisfied.

    (c) Verify that u_t^* does not maximize $H(t, x_t^*, u, p_t)$ for $u \in [-1, 1]$.

12.5 More Variables

Consider the following problem with n state and r control variables:

$$\max \sum_{t=0}^{T} f(t, \mathbf{x}_t, \mathbf{u}_t), \quad \mathbf{x}_{t+1} = \mathbf{g}(t, \mathbf{x}_t, \mathbf{u}_t), \quad \mathbf{x}_0 \text{ is given}, \quad u_t \in U \subseteq \mathbb{R}^r \tag{1}$$

Here $\mathbf{x}_t$ is a state variable in $\mathbb{R}^n$ that evolves from the initial state $\mathbf{x}_0$ according to the law of motion (1), with $\mathbf{u}_t$ as a control that is chosen at each $t = 0, \ldots, T$. We put $\mathbf{x}_t = (x_t^1, \ldots, x_t^n)$, $\mathbf{u}_t = (u_t^1, \ldots, u_t^r)$, and $\mathbf{g} = (g^1, \ldots, g^n)$. We assume that the control region U is convex.

The terminal conditions are

$$\begin{align} \text{(a)} \quad & x_T^i = \bar{x}^i \quad \text{for } i = 1, \ldots, l \\ \text{(b)} \quad & x_T^i \geq \bar{x}^i \quad \text{for } i = l+1, \ldots, m \\ \text{(c)} \quad & x_T^i \text{ free} \quad \text{for } i = m+1, \ldots, n \end{align} \tag{2}$$

Define the **Hamiltonian** by

$$H(t, \mathbf{x}, \mathbf{u}, \mathbf{p}) = \begin{cases} q_0 f(t, \mathbf{x}, \mathbf{u}) + \sum_{i=1}^{n} p^i g_i(t, \mathbf{x}, \mathbf{u}) & \text{for } t < T \\ f(t, \mathbf{x}, \mathbf{u}) & \text{for } t = T \end{cases}$$

where $\mathbf{p} = (p^1, \ldots, p^n)$ is called an **adjoint function (or co-state variable)**. (For a proof of the following theorem, see Arkin and Evstigneev (1987).)

THEOREM 12.5.1 (THE MAXIMUM PRINCIPLE AND SUFFICIENCY)

Suppose that $(\{\mathbf{x}_t^*\}, \{\mathbf{u}_t^*\})$ is an optimal path for problem (1)–(2). Then there exist vectors $\mathbf{p}_t$ in $\mathbb{R}^n$ and a number q_0, with $(q_0, \mathbf{p}_T) \neq (0, \mathbf{0})$ and with $q_0 = 0$ or 1, such that for $t = 0, \ldots, T$,

$$\sum_{i=1}^{r} H'_{u^i}(t, \mathbf{x}_t^*, \mathbf{u}_t^*, \mathbf{p}_t)\,(u_t^i - (u_t^*)^i) \leq 0 \quad \text{for all } \mathbf{u} \in U \tag{3}$$

Also, the vector $\mathbf{p}_t = (p_t^1, \ldots, p_t^n)$ is a solution of

$$p_{t-1}^i = H'_{x^i}(t, \mathbf{x}_t^*, \mathbf{u}_t^*, \mathbf{p}_t), \qquad t = 1, \ldots, T-1 \tag{4}$$

Moreover,

$$p_{T-1}^i = q_0 \frac{\partial f(T, \mathbf{x}_T^*, \mathbf{u}_T^*)}{\partial x_T^i} + p_T^i \tag{5}$$

where the vector $\mathbf{p}_T = (p_T^1, \ldots, p_T^n)$ satisfies

(a') p_T^i no conditions $\qquad\qquad\qquad\qquad\qquad i = 1, \ldots, l$

(b') $p_T^i \geq 0$ $(p_T^i = 0$ if $x_T^{*i} > \bar{x}^i)$ $\qquad\qquad i = l+1, \ldots, m \tag{6}$

(c') $p_T^i = 0$ $\qquad\qquad\qquad\qquad\qquad\qquad i = m+1, \ldots, n$

If the conditions above are satisfied with $q_0 = 1$ and $H(t, \mathbf{x}, \mathbf{u}, \mathbf{p})$ is concave in $(\mathbf{x}, \mathbf{u})$, then $(\{\mathbf{x}_t^*\}, \{\mathbf{u}_t^*\})$ is optimal.

NOTE 1 If $m = 0$ (so that there are no restrictions on the terminal state $\mathbf{x}_T$), then $\mathbf{p}_T = \mathbf{0}$ and it follows from Theorem 12.5.1 that $q_0 = 1$.

NOTE 2 If $\mathbf{u}_t^*$ is an interior point of U, then (3) implies that $H'_{u^i}(t, \mathbf{x}_t^*, \mathbf{u}_t^*, \mathbf{p}_t) = 0$ for all $i = 1, \ldots, r$.

Infinite Horizon

We consider briefly the following infinite horizon version of problem (1)–(2),

$$\max \sum_{t=0}^{\infty} f(t, \mathbf{x}_t, \mathbf{u}_t), \qquad \mathbf{x}_t \in \mathbb{R}^n, \quad \mathbf{u}_t \in U \subseteq \mathbb{R}^r, \quad U \text{ convex} \tag{7}$$

where we maximize over all sequences $(\mathbf{x}_t, \mathbf{u}_t)$ satisfying

$$\mathbf{x}_{t+1} = \mathbf{g}(t, \mathbf{x}_t, \mathbf{u}_t), \quad t = 1, 2, \ldots, \qquad \mathbf{x}_0 \text{ given} \tag{8}$$

and the terminal conditions

(a) $\lim_{T \to \infty} x_i(T) = \hat{x}_i, \qquad i = 1, \ldots, m'$

(b) $\lim_{T \to \infty} x_i(T) \geq \hat{x}_i, \qquad i = m'+1, \ldots, m \tag{9}$

Note that f and $\mathbf{g} = (g_1, \ldots, g_n)$ can now depend explicitly on t. Assume that the sum in (7) exists for all admissible sequences. The functions f and $\mathbf{g}$ are assumed to be C^1 with respect to all x_i and u_j.

We do no more that state a sufficient condition for such problems:[6]

THEOREM 12.5.2 (SUFFICIENT CONDITIONS)

Suppose that the sequence $(\{\mathbf{x}_t^*\}, \{\mathbf{u}_t^*\}, \{\mathbf{p}_t\})$ satisfies the conditions (3)–(6) and for $q_0 = 1$. Suppose further that the Hamiltonian $H(t, \mathbf{x}, \mathbf{u}, \mathbf{p}_t)$ is concave in $(\mathbf{x}, \mathbf{u})$ for every t. Then $(\{\mathbf{x}_t^*\}, \{\mathbf{u}_t^*\})$ is optimal provided that the following transversality condition is satisfied: For all admissible sequences $(\{\mathbf{x}_t\}, \{\mathbf{u}_t\})$,

$$\lim_{t \to \infty} \mathbf{p}_t(\mathbf{x}_t - \mathbf{x}_t^*) \geq 0 \tag{10}$$

NOTE 3 Suppose there are additional conditions for a sequence $\{\mathbf{x}_t, \mathbf{u}_t\}$ to be admissible. Then (10) needs only to be tested for such sequences.

PROBLEMS FOR SECTION 12.5

1. Consider the problem

$$\max_{u,v \in \mathbb{R}} \sum_{t=0}^{2} \left[1 + x_t - y_t - 2u_t^2 - v_t^2 \right] \quad \text{s.t.} \quad \begin{cases} x_{t+1} = x_t - u_t, \ x_0 = 5 \\ y_{t+1} = y_t + v_t, \ y_0 = 2 \end{cases}, \quad t = 0, 1$$

(a) Solve the problem by using the difference equations to express the objective function I as a function only of $u_0, u_1, u_2, v_0, v_1,$ and v_2, and then optimize.

(b) Solve the problem by using dynamic programming. (Find $J_2(x, y), J_1(x, y),$ and $J_0(x, y)$ and the corresponding optimal controls.)

(c) Solve the problem by using Theorem 12.5.1.

2. Solve the problem

$$\max \sum_{t=0}^{T} (-x_t^2 - u_t^2) \quad \text{subject to} \quad x_{t+1} = y_t, \ y_{t+1} = y_t + u_t, \ t = 0, 1, \ldots, T-1$$

where $x_0 = x^0$ and $y_0 = y^0$ are given numbers and $u_t \in \mathbb{R}$.

---

[6] For the definition of $\underline{\lim}$ see Section 10.3.

3. Solve the problem

$$\max \sum_{t=0}^{\infty} \beta^t (x_t - u_t)] \quad \text{subject to} \quad x_{t+1} = u_t, \quad x_0 > 0, \quad u_t > 0$$

where $\beta \in (0, 1)$. Verify that $x_t^* > u_t^*$ for all t.

12.6 Stochastic Optimization

What is the best way of controlling a dynamic system subject to random disturbances? Stochastic dynamic programming is a central tool for tackling this problem.

In deterministic dynamic programming the state develops according to a difference equation $\mathbf{x}_{t+1} = \mathbf{g}(t, \mathbf{x}_t, \mathbf{u}_t)$, controlled by appropriate choices of the control variables $\mathbf{u}_t$. In this section, the state $\mathbf{x}_t$ is influenced by random disturbances, so that $\mathbf{x}_t$ is a stochastic variable. Following common practice, we often use capital letters instead of lower case letters for stochastic quantities, e.g. $\mathbf{X}_t$ instead of $\mathbf{x}_t$. We assume that $\mathbf{x}_t$ belongs to $\mathbb{R}^n$, that $\mathbf{u}_t$ is required to belong to a given subset U of $\mathbb{R}^r$, and that $t = 0, \ldots, T$.

Suppose now that the state equation takes the new form

$$\mathbf{X}_{t+1} = \mathbf{g}(t, \mathbf{X}_t, \mathbf{u}_t, \mathbf{V}_{t+1}), \quad \mathbf{X}_0 = \mathbf{x}_0, \mathbf{V}_0 = \mathbf{v}_0, \text{ with } \mathbf{x}_0 \text{ and } \mathbf{v}_0 \text{ given}, \quad \mathbf{u}_t \in U \quad (1)$$

We consider two cases. In the first, $\mathbf{V}_{t+1}$ is a random variable that takes values in a finite set $\mathcal{V}$. It is assumed that the probability that $\mathbf{V}_{t+1} = \mathbf{v} \in \mathcal{V}$ may depend on the outcome $\mathbf{v}_t$ at time t, as well as explicitly on time t. Then we consider the **conditional** probability that $\mathbf{V}_{t+1} = v$, given v_t, which is denoted by $P_t(v|v_t)$. In the second case, $\mathbf{V}_{t+1}$ may take values anywhere in a Euclidean space. Then the distribution of $\mathbf{V}_{t+1}$ is assumed to be described by a conditional density $p_t(\mathbf{v}|\mathbf{v}_t)$ that is a continuous function of $\mathbf{v}$ and $\mathbf{v}_t$ together.

EXAMPLE 1   Suppose that $Z_1, Z_2, \ldots$ are independently distributed stochastic variables which take positive values with specified probabilities independent of both the state and the control. Thus, at each time $t = 0, \ldots, T$, either there is a discrete distribution $P_t(Z_t)$, or a continuous density function $p_t(z_t)$. The state X_t is assumed to evolve according to the stochastic difference equation

$$X_{t+1} = Z_{t+1}(X_t - u_t), \quad u_t \in [0, \infty) \quad (i)$$

Here u_t is consumption, $X_t - u_t$ is investment, and Z_{t+1} is the return per invested dollar. Moreover, the utility of the terminal state x_T is $S(T, x_T, u) = \beta^T B x_T^{1-\gamma}$ and the utility of the current consumption is $\beta^t u_t^{1-\gamma}$ for $t < T$, where β is a discount factor and $0 < \gamma < 1$. The paths of the state x_t and of the control u_t are now uncertain (stochastic). The objective function to be maximized is the sum of expected discounted utility, given by

$$E\left[\sum_{t=0}^{T-1} \beta^t u_t^{1-\gamma} + \beta^T B X_T^{1-\gamma} \right] \quad (ii)$$

This problem will be studied in Example 3. In the discrete variable case, the expectation will be a sum, but in the continuous variable case it will be an integral.

Consider first a two-stage decision problem with one state and one control variable. Assume that one wants to maximize the objective function

$$E\big[f(0, X_0, u_0) + f(1, X_1, u_1)\big] = f(0, X_0, u_0) + Ef(1, X_1, u_1)$$

where E denotes expectation and f is some given function. Here the initial state $X_0 = x_0$ and an initial outcome v_0 are given, while X_1 is determined by the difference equation (1), i.e. $X_1 = g(0, x_0, u_0, V_1)$. We can find the maximum by first maximizing with respect to u_1, and then with respect to u_0. When choosing u_1, we simply maximize $f(1, X_1, u_1)$, assuming that X_1 is known before the maximization is carried out. The maximum point u_1^* becomes a function $u_1^*(X_1)$ of X_1. Insert this function instead of u_1 in the objective function, and replace the two occurrences of X_1 by $g(0, x_0, u_0, V_1)$. Then u_0 occurs in both terms of the objective function. A maximizing value of u_0 is then chosen, taking both these occurrences into account.

To see why it matters that we can observe X_1 before choosing u_1, the following example is illuminating: Consider the simple two stage decision problem with $f(0, X_0, u_0) = 0$, $f(1, X_1, u_1) = X_1 u_1$, and $X_1 = V_1$, where V_1 takes the values 1 and -1 with probabilities $1/2$, and where u must equal one of the two values 1 and -1. Then $E[X_1 u_1] = 0$ if we have to choose u_1 before observing X_1, hence a constant u_1. But if we can first observe X_1, then we can let u_1 depend on X_1. If we choose $u_1 = u_1(X_1) = X_1$, then $E[X_1 u_1] = 1$, which yields a better value of the objective. In all that follows we shall assume that X_t (in fact, both X_t and V_t), can be observed before choosing u_t.

Let us turn to the general problem. The process determined by (1) and the values of the random variables $\mathbf{V}_1, \mathbf{V}_2, \ldots$ is to be controlled in the best possible manner by appropriate choices of the variables $\mathbf{u}_t$. The objective function is now the expectation

$$E\left[\sum_{t=0}^{T} f(t, \mathbf{X}_t, \mathbf{u}_t(\mathbf{X}_t, \mathbf{V}_t))\right] \tag{2}$$

Here several things have to be explained. Each control $\mathbf{u}_t$, $t = 0, 1, 2, \ldots, T$ should be a function $\mathbf{u}_t(\mathbf{x}_t, \mathbf{v}_t)$ of the current state $\mathbf{x}_t$ and the outcome $\mathbf{v}_t$. Such functions are called "policies", or more specifically **Markov policies** or **Markov controls**. For many stochastic optimization problems, including those studied here, this is the natural class of policies to consider in order to achieve an optimum. The policies that occur in (2) are of this type. The letter E, as before, denotes expectation. To compute it requires specifying the probabilities that lie behind the calculation of the expectation. Recall that in the discrete random variable case the probability for the events $\mathbf{V}_1 = \mathbf{v}_1$ and $\mathbf{V}_2 = \mathbf{v}_2$ to occur jointly, given $\mathbf{V}_0 = \mathbf{v}_0$, equals the conditional probability for $\mathbf{V}_2 = \mathbf{v}_2$ to occur given $\mathbf{V}_1 = \mathbf{v}_1$, times the probability for $\mathbf{V}_1 = \mathbf{v}_1$ to occur given $\mathbf{V}_0 = \mathbf{v}_0$. That is, the joint probability equals $P_1(\mathbf{v}_2 \mid \mathbf{v}_1)$ times $P_0(\mathbf{v}_1 \mid \mathbf{v}_0)$. Similarly, the probability of the joint event $\mathbf{V}_1 = \mathbf{v}_1, \mathbf{V}_2 = \mathbf{v}_2, \ldots, \mathbf{V}_t = \mathbf{v}_t$, is given by

$$P^t(\mathbf{v}_1, \ldots, \mathbf{v}_t) = P_0(\mathbf{v}_1 \mid \mathbf{v}_0) \cdot P_1(\mathbf{v}_2 \mid \mathbf{v}_1) \cdots P_{t-1}(\mathbf{v}_t \mid \mathbf{v}_{t-1}) \tag{3}$$

In the continuous random variable case, the same formula is valid in determining the joint density $p^t(\mathbf{v}_1, \ldots, \mathbf{v}_t)$ provided each P_t is replaced by p_t.

Now, given the policies $\mathbf{u}_t(\mathbf{x}_t, \mathbf{v}_t)$, the sequence $\mathbf{X}_t$, $t = 1, \ldots, T$ in (2) is the solution of (1) when $\mathbf{V}_1, \ldots, \mathbf{V}_t$ and $\mathbf{u}_t = \mathbf{u}_t(\mathbf{X}_t, \mathbf{V}_t)$, $t = 0, \ldots, T-1$ are inserted successively. Hence, $\mathbf{X}_t$ depends on $\mathbf{V}_1, \ldots, \mathbf{V}_t$ and, for each t, the expectation $Ef(t, \mathbf{X}_t, \mathbf{u}_t(\mathbf{X}_t, \mathbf{V}_t))$ is calculated by means of the probabilities (or densities) specified in (3). We can write (2) as $\sum_{t=0}^{T} Ef(t, \mathbf{X}_t, \mathbf{u}_t(\mathbf{X}_t, \mathbf{V}_t))$, so we have now explained how the expectation in (2) is calculated.

Though not always necessary, we shall assume that f and $\mathbf{g}$ are continuous in $\mathbf{x}$, $\mathbf{u}$ (or in $\mathbf{x}$, $\mathbf{u}$, and $\mathbf{v}$ in the continuous random variable case).

The optimization problem is to find a sequence of policies $\mathbf{u}_0^*(\mathbf{x}_0, \mathbf{v}_0), \ldots, \mathbf{u}_T^*(\mathbf{x}_T, \mathbf{v}_T)$, that gives the expression in (2) the largest possible value.

We now define

$$J(t, \mathbf{x}_t, \mathbf{v}_t) = \max E\left[\sum_{s=t}^{T} f(s, \mathbf{X}_s, \mathbf{u}_s(\mathbf{X}_s, \mathbf{V}_s)) \mid \mathbf{x}_t, \mathbf{v}_t\right] \tag{4}$$

where the maximum is taken over all policy sequences $\mathbf{u}_s = \mathbf{u}_s(\mathbf{x}_s, \mathbf{v}_s)$, $s = t, \ldots, T$, given $\mathbf{v}_t$ and given that we "start" equation (1) in state $\mathbf{x}_t$ at time t, as indicated by "$\mid \mathbf{x}_t, \mathbf{v}_t$" in (4). The computation of the expectation in (4) is now based on conditional probabilities of the form $P(\mathbf{v}_{t+1}, \ldots, \mathbf{v}_s \mid \mathbf{v}_t) = P_t(\mathbf{v}_{t+1} \mid \mathbf{v}_t) \cdots P_{s-1}(\mathbf{v}_s \mid \mathbf{v}_{s-1})$ in the discrete case, and conditional densities in the continuous case.

The central tool in solving optimization problems of the type (1)–(2) is the following **dynamic programming equation** or **optimality equation**:

$$J(t-1, \mathbf{x}_{t-1}, \mathbf{v}_{t-1}) = \max_{\mathbf{u}_{t-1}}\left\{f(t-1, \mathbf{x}_{t-1}, \mathbf{u}_{t-1}) + E\left[J(t, \mathbf{X}_t, \mathbf{V}_t) \mid \mathbf{x}_{t-1}, \mathbf{v}_{t-1}\right]\right\} \tag{5}$$

where $\mathbf{X}_t = \mathbf{g}(t-1, \mathbf{x}_{t-1}, \mathbf{u}_{t-1}, \mathbf{V}_t)$. The "$\mathbf{x}_{t-1}$" in the symbol "$\mid \mathbf{x}_{t-1}, \mathbf{v}_{t-1}$" is just a reminder that inserting this value of $\mathbf{X}_t$ makes the expectation depend on $\mathbf{X}_{t-1}$, as well as on $\mathbf{V}_{t-1}$. After this insertion, equation (5) becomes

$$J(t-1, \mathbf{x}_{t-1}, \mathbf{v}_{t-1}) =$$
$$\max_{\mathbf{u}_{t-1}}\left\{f(t-1, \mathbf{x}_{t-1}, \mathbf{u}_{t-1}) + E\left[J(t-1, \mathbf{g}(t, \mathbf{x}_{t-1}, \mathbf{u}_{t-1}, \mathbf{V}_t), \mathbf{V}_t) \mid \mathbf{v}_{t-1}\right]\right\}$$

Moreover, when $t = T$ we have

$$J(T, \mathbf{x}_T, \mathbf{v}_T) = J(T, \mathbf{x}_T) = \max_{\mathbf{u}_T} f(T, \mathbf{x}_T, \mathbf{u}_T) \tag{6}$$

As in the deterministic case, first (6) is used to find $\mathbf{u}_T^*(\mathbf{x}_T, \mathbf{v}_T)$. Then (5) is used repeatedly to find $\mathbf{u}_{T-1}^*(\mathbf{x}_{T-1}, \mathbf{v}_{T-1})$, $\mathbf{u}_{T-2}^*(\mathbf{x}_{T-2}, \mathbf{v}_{T-2})$, etc.

Equations (5) and (6) are, essentially, both necessary and sufficient. They are sufficient in the sense that if $\mathbf{u}_{t-1}^*(\mathbf{x}_{t-1}, \mathbf{v}_{t-1})$ with $t = 1, \ldots, T$ maximizes the right-hand side of (5) (or (6) for $t = T + 1$), then $\mathbf{u}_{t-1}^*(\mathbf{x}_{t-1}, \mathbf{v}_{t-1})$, $t = 1, \ldots, T + 1$, are optimal policies. On the other hand, they are necessary in the sense that, for every $\mathbf{x}_{t-1}$, an optimal control

$\mathbf{u}_{t-1}^*(\mathbf{x}_{t-1}, \mathbf{v}_{t-1})$, $t = 1, \ldots, T$, yields a maximum on the right-hand side of (5), and, for $t = T + 1$, on the right–hand side of (6). To be a little more precise, it is necessary that the optimal control $\mathbf{u}_{t-1}^*(\mathbf{x}_{t-1}, \mathbf{v}_{t-1})$ yields a maximum on the right-hand side of (5) (or (6)) for all values of $\mathbf{x}_{t-1}$ and $\mathbf{v}_{t-1}$ that can occur with positive probability (positive probability density in the continuous case).

The intuitive argument for (5) is as follows: Suppose the system is in state $\mathbf{x}_{t-1}$. For a given $\mathbf{u}_{t-1}$, the "instantaneous" reward is $f(t - 1, \mathbf{x}_{t-1}, \mathbf{u}_{t-1})$. In addition, the maximal expected sum of rewards at all later times is $E[J(t, \mathbf{X}_t, \mathbf{V}_t) \mid \mathbf{x}_{t-1}, \mathbf{v}_{t-1}]$ provided $\mathbf{X}_t = \mathbf{g}(t - 1, \mathbf{x}_{t-1}, \mathbf{u}_{t-1}, \mathbf{V}_t)$. When using $\mathbf{u}_{t-1}$, the total expected maximum value gained over all future time points (now including even $t - 1$) is the sum in (5). The largest expected gain comes from choosing $\mathbf{u}_{t-1}$ to maximize the right-hand side of (5).

Note that when $P_t(\mathbf{v} \mid \mathbf{v}_t)$ (or $p_t(\mathbf{v} \mid \mathbf{v}_t)$) does not depend on $\mathbf{v}_t$, then $\mathbf{v}_t$ can be dropped from the functions $J_t(\mathbf{x}_t, \mathbf{v}_t)$, $\mathbf{u}_t(\mathbf{x}_t, \mathbf{v}_t)$ and in (5) and (6). (Intuitively, this is because in (5) the conditioning on $\mathbf{v}_{t-1}$ drops out, so $J(t - 1, \mathbf{x}_{t-1}, \mathbf{v}_{t-1})$ and the maximizing vector $\mathbf{u}_{t-1} = \mathbf{u}_{t-1}(\mathbf{x}_{t-1}, \mathbf{v}_{t-1})$ will not depend on $\mathbf{v}_{t-1}$.) Some examples below employ this simplification.

NOTE 1 The argument above also holds if the control region is a closed set that depends on t and $\mathbf{x}$—for example, if $U = U(t, \mathbf{x}) = \{\mathbf{u} : h_i(t, \mathbf{x}, \mathbf{u}) \leq 0\}$ where the functions h_i are continuous in $(\mathbf{x}, \mathbf{u})$. Thus it is here required that $\mathbf{u}_t \in U(t, \mathbf{x}_t)$. In this case the comments in Note 12.1.5 carry over.

EXAMPLE 2   Suppose that a gambler chooses to bet a certain fraction u of his wealth at even odds. Because of his skill, he wins this fraction with probability $p \geq 1/2$. Thus, if his wealth at time $t - 1$ is x_{t-1}, then x_t is equal to $x_{t-1} + ux_{t-1}$ with probability p, and x_t is equal to $x_{t-1} - ux_{t-1}$ with probability $1 - p$. (Formally, $X_t = X_{t-1} + u_{t-1}V_t X_{t-1}$, where $V_t \in \{-1, 1\}$, $\Pr[V_t = 1] = p$, and $\Pr[V_t = -1] = 1 - p$.) Suppose that he is going to play T times, and that the utility of terminal wealth x_T is $f(T, x_T) = \ln x_T = J(T, x_T)$ (note that $f(T, x_T)$ is independent of u_T). We also have $f(t, x_t) \equiv 0$ for $t < T$.

If the gambler's wealth at time $T - 1$ is x_{T-1} and he then bets ux_{T-1}, he will get $\ln(x_{T-1} + ux_{T-1})$ with probability p and $\ln(x_{T-1} - ux_{T-1})$ with probability $q = 1 - p$. Thus, the expected utility of his terminal wealth is

$$p \ln(x_{T-1} + ux_{T-1}) + q \ln(x_{T-1} - ux_{T-1}) = \ln x_{T-1} + A(u)$$

where $A(u) = p \ln(1 + u) + q \ln(1 - u)$ (because $p + q = 1$). At time $T - 1$ the optimality equation is therefore

$$J(T - 1, x_{T-1}) = \ln x_{T-1} + \max_{0 \leq u \leq 1} A(u)$$

The function $A(u)$ is concave, so the maximum is attained where

$$A'(u) = p \frac{1}{1 + u} - q \frac{1}{1 - u} = 0$$

This implies $p(1 - u) = q(1 + u)$, or $p - q = u(p + q) = u$, so $u^*_{T-1} = p - q$. Inserting this expression for u into the right-hand side gives the maximum value. This is $J(T - 1, x) = \ln x + B$, where $B = p \ln[1 + (p - q)] + q \ln[1 - (p - q)] = p \ln(2p) + q \ln(2q) = \ln 2 + p \ln p + q \ln q$.

Starting from x_{T-2}, we end up at $x_{T-1} = x_{T-2} + u x_{T-2}$ with probability p, and then obtain $J(T - 1, x_{T-1}) = \ln(x_{T-2} + u_{T-2} x_{T-2}) + B$; with probability q we end up at $x_{T-1} = x_{T-2} - u_{T-2} x_{T-2}$ and obtain $J(T - 1, x_{T-1}) = \ln(x_{T-2} - u x_{T-2}) + B$. Therefore,

$$J(T - 2, x_{T-2}) = \max_{0 \le u \le 1} \left(p \left[\ln(x_{T-2} + u x_{T-2}) + B \right] + q \left[\ln(x_{T-2} - u x_{T-2}) + B \right] \right)$$

$$= \ln x_{T-2} + B + \max_{0 \le u \le 1} A(u)$$

Once again, the maximum value in the latter maximization problem is B, with $u = p - q$. Hence

$$J(T - 2, x_{T-2}) = \ln x_{T-2} + 2B \qquad (u^*_{T-2} = p - q)$$

Continuing in this manner, for $k = 3, 4, \ldots$ gives

$$J(T - k, x_{T-k}) = \ln x_{T-k} + kB \qquad (u^*_{T-k} = p - q)$$

To conclude, we see that in every round it is optimal for the gambler to bet the same fraction $u = p - q = 2p - 1$ of his wealth. (If the objective function were $f(T, x_T) = x_T$ and $p > 1/2$, it is easy to see that he would bet all his wealth at every stage.)

The *strict concavity* of the utility function $\ln x_T$ means that a decline in wealth reduces utility more than a corresponding rise in wealth increases utility. Therefore the gambler is careful and bets only a fraction each time. This is what economists call risk aversion.

EXAMPLE 3   Solve the problem in Example 1,

$$\max E \left[\sum_{t=0}^{T-1} \beta^t u_t^{1-\gamma} + \beta^T B X_T^{1-\gamma} \right], \qquad X_{t+1} = Z_{t+1}(X_t - u_t), \quad x_0 > 0 \quad u_t \in (0, x_t)$$

where $0 < \gamma < 1$, $0 < \beta < 1$, $B > 0$, and $\{Z_t\}_{t=0}^{T-1}$ is a sequence of independently distributed non-negative random variables with $EZ_t^{1-\gamma} < \infty$ for all t.

Solution: Here $J(T, x_T) = \beta^T B x_T^{1-\gamma}$. To find $J(T - 1, x_{T-1})$, we use the optimality equation

$$J(T - 1, x_{T-1}) = \max_u \left(\beta^{T-1} u^{1-\gamma} + E \left[\beta^T B(Z_T(x_{T-1} - u))^{1-\gamma} \right] \right) \qquad (*)$$

The expectation must be calculated by using the probability distribution for Z_T. In fact, the expectation term in $(*)$ is equal to $\beta^T B D_T (x_{T-1} - u)^{1-\gamma}$, where $D_t = E[Z_t^{1-\gamma}]$. Hence, the expression to be maximized in $(*)$ is $\beta^{T-1} u^{1-\gamma} + \beta^T B D_T (x_{T-1} - u)^{1-\gamma}$. Define $C_T = B$, $C_{T-1}^{1/\gamma} = 1 + (\beta B D_T)^{1/\gamma}$, and generally $C_t^{1/\gamma} = 1 + (\beta C_{t+1} D_{t+1})^{1/\gamma}$. The same calculations as in Example 12.1.4 show that, in general, maximizing the expression $(1 - \gamma)u_t + \beta C_{t+1} a_t^{1-\gamma} (x - u)^{1-\gamma}$ for $u_t \in (0, x_t)$ gives $u_t = x/C_t^{1/\gamma}$, with maximum value equal to $C_t x^{1-\gamma}$, where $C_t^{1/\gamma} = 1 + (\beta C_{t+1} a_t^{1-\gamma})^{1/\gamma}$. Applying this for $D_t = a_{t-1}^{1-\gamma}$ gives $J_{T-1}(x) = \beta^{T-1} C_{T-1} x^{1-\gamma}$, $u_{T-1} = x/C_{T-1}^{1/\gamma}$, $J_{T-2}(x) = \beta^{T-2} C_{T-2} x^{1-\gamma}$, $u_{T-2} = x/C_{T-2}^{1/\gamma}$, and generally $J_t = \beta^t C_t x^{1-\gamma}$, $u_t = x/C_t^{1/\gamma}$.

We conclude this section with the following formal result:

THEOREM 12.6.1 (SUFFICIENCY OF THE OPTIMALITY EQUATIONS)

The sequence of policies $\pi = \{\mathbf{u}_t(\mathbf{x}_t, \mathbf{v}_t)\}_{t=0}^T$ solves the problem of maximizing (2) subject to (1) if, together with a sequence of functions $\{J(t, \mathbf{x}_t, \mathbf{v}_t)\}_{t=0}^T$, it satisfies the optimality equations (5) (for $t = 1, 2, \ldots, T$) as well as (6).

Proof: Let $\pi = \{\mathbf{u}_t(\mathbf{x}_t, \mathbf{v}_t)\}_{t=0}^T$ be an arbitrary control sequence. Define

$$J^\pi(t, \mathbf{x}_t, \mathbf{v}_t) = E\left[\sum_{s=t}^T f(s, \mathbf{X}_s, \mathbf{u}_s(\mathbf{X}_s, \mathbf{V}_s))|\mathbf{x}_t, \mathbf{v}_t\right]$$

which is the conditionally expected value in state $(\mathbf{x}_t, \mathbf{v}_t)$ at time t of following π from that state. Trivially, $J^\pi(T, \mathbf{x}_T, \mathbf{v}_T) \leq J(T, \mathbf{x}_T, \mathbf{v}_T)$, with equality if $\mathbf{u}_T(\mathbf{x}_T, \mathbf{v}_T)$ satisfies (6). By backwards induction, let us prove that $J^\pi(t, \mathbf{x}_t, \mathbf{v}_t) \leq J(t, \mathbf{x}_t, \mathbf{v}_t)$, with equality if π is such that $\mathbf{u}_s(\mathbf{x}_s, \mathbf{v}_s)$ satisfies (5) for $s = t, t+1, \ldots, T-1$, and $\mathbf{u}_T(\mathbf{x}_T, \mathbf{v}_T)$ satisfies (6). As the induction hypothesis, assume that this is true for t. Replacing t by $t-1$ in the above definition gives

$$J^\pi(t-1, \mathbf{x}_{t-1}, \mathbf{v}_{t-1}) = f(t-1, \mathbf{x}_{t-1}, \mathbf{u}_{t-1}(\mathbf{x}_{t-1}, \mathbf{v}_{t-1})) + E\left[\sum_{s=t}^T f(s, \mathbf{X}_s, \mathbf{u}_s(\mathbf{X}_s, \mathbf{V}_s))|\mathbf{x}_{t-1}, \mathbf{v}_{t-1}\right]$$

But the law of iterated expectations and the induction hypothesis together imply that

$$E\left[\sum_{s=t}^T f(s, \mathbf{X}_s, \mathbf{u}_s(\mathbf{X}_s, \mathbf{V}_s))|\mathbf{x}_{t-1}, \mathbf{v}_{t-1}\right] = E\left[E\left[\sum_{s=t}^T f(s, \mathbf{X}_s, \mathbf{u}_s(\mathbf{X}_s, \mathbf{V}_s))|\mathbf{X}_t, \mathbf{V}_t\right]|\mathbf{x}_{t-1}, \mathbf{v}_{t-1}\right]$$

$$= E[J^\pi(t, \mathbf{X}_t, \mathbf{V}_t)|\mathbf{x}_{t-1}, \mathbf{v}_{t-1}] \leq E[J(t, \mathbf{X}_t, \mathbf{V}_t)|\mathbf{x}_{t-1}, \mathbf{v}_{t-1}]$$

where $\mathbf{X}_t = \mathbf{g}(t, \mathbf{x}_{t-1}, \mathbf{u}_{t-1}(\mathbf{x}_{t-1}, \mathbf{v}_{t-1}), \mathbf{V}_t)$, with equality if $\mathbf{u}_s(\mathbf{x}_s, \mathbf{v}_s)$ satisfies (5) for $s = t$, $t+1, \ldots, T-1$, and $\mathbf{u}_T(\mathbf{x}_T, \mathbf{v}_T)$ satisfies (6). Hence

$$J^\pi(t-1, \mathbf{x}_{t-1}, \mathbf{v}_{t-1}) \leq f(t-1, \mathbf{x}_{t-1}, \mathbf{u}_{t-1}(\mathbf{x}_{t-1}, \mathbf{v}_{t-1})) + E[J(t, \mathbf{X}_t, \mathbf{V}_t)|\mathbf{x}_{t-1}, \mathbf{v}_{t-1}]$$

$$\leq \max_{\mathbf{u}}\{f(t-1, \mathbf{x}_{t-1}, \mathbf{u}) + E[J(t, \mathbf{g}(t, \mathbf{x}_{t-1}, \mathbf{u}, \mathbf{V}_t), \mathbf{V}_t)|\mathbf{v}_{t-1}]\}$$

$$= J(t-1, \mathbf{x}_{t-1}, \mathbf{v}_{t-1})$$

with equalities if $\mathbf{u}_s(\mathbf{x}_s, \mathbf{v}_s)$ satisfies (5) for $s = t-1, t, t+1, \ldots, T-1$, and $\mathbf{u}_T(\mathbf{x}_T, \mathbf{v}_T)$ satisfies (6). This verifies the induction hypothesis for $t-1$, and so completes the proof. ∎

In the discrete variable case, the above proof is easily adapted to show that a policy π^* is optimal only if the optimality equations hold at every time t ($t = 0, 1, 2, \ldots, T$) in any state $(\mathbf{x}_t, \mathbf{v}_t)$ which is reached with positive probability given π^*. In the continuous variable case these necessary conditions become a little bit more complicated: essentially, the optimality equations must hold at every time t ($t = 0, 1, 2, \ldots, T$) in almost every state $(\mathbf{x}_t, \mathbf{v}_t)$ which has a positive conditional probability density given π^*.

The Stochastic Euler Equation

In the formulation of problem (12.2.1) leading to the Euler equation, let the function F in the criterion contain a stochastic variable $V_{t+1} = v$, governed as before, by a conditional probability distribution $P_t(v, |v_t)$ or a conditional density $p_t(v|v_t)$. Hence, consider the problem

$$\max E \sum_{t=0}^{T} F(t, X_t, X_{t+1}, V_{t+1}), \quad x_0 \text{ given}, \quad x_t, \ldots, x_{T+1} \text{ free}$$

Now, we allow x_t to be a function of v_t and x_{t-1}. Hence we decide the value of x_t after observing v_t. Then the Euler equations takes the form

$$F_3'(T, x_T, x_{T+1}(x_T, v_{T+1}), v_{T+1}) = 0 \qquad (*)$$

and for $t = 0, \ldots, T - 1$,

$$E[F_2'(t+1, x_{t+1}, x_{t+2}(x_{t+1}, V_{t+2}), V_{t+2})|v_{t+1}] + F_3'(t, x_t, x_{t+1}(x_t, v_{t+1}), v_{t+1}) = 0 \quad (**)$$

First, $(*)$ is solved for x_{T+1}, yielding the function $x_{T+1} = x_{T+1}(x_T, v_{T+1})$. Next, this function is inserted into $(**)$ for $t = T - 1$, and $(**)$ is then solved for x_T, yielding $x_T = x_T(x_{T-1}, v_T)$. Then this function is inserted into $(**)$ for $t = T - 2$ and $(**)$ is then solved for x_{T-1} yielding the function $x_{T-1}(x_{T-2}, v_{T-1})$. In this manner we work backwards until the function $x_1(x_0, v_1)$ has been constructed. Since x_0 is given, the value of x_1 is determined once we have observed v_1. Then the value of $x_2 = x_2(x_1, v_2)$ is determined once we have observed v_2 and so on.

PROBLEMS FOR SECTION 12.6

1. Consider the stochastic dynamic programming problem

$$\max E\left[-\delta \exp(-\gamma X_T) + \sum_{t=0}^{T-1} -\exp(-\gamma u_t)\right], \quad X_{t+1} = 2X_t - u_t + V_{t+1}, \quad x_0 \text{ given}$$

where u_t are controls taking values anywhere in $\mathbb{R}$, $\delta > 0$ and $\gamma > 0$. Here V_{t+1}, $t = 0, 1, 2, \ldots, T - 1$, are identically and independently distributed. Moreover, $K = E[\exp(-\gamma V_{t+1})] < \infty$. Show that the optimal value function $J(t, x)$ can be written $J(t, x) = -\alpha_t \exp(-\gamma x)$, and find a backwards difference equation for α_t. What is α_T?

2. (Blanchard and Fischer (1989)) Solve the problem

$$\max E\left[\sum_{t=0}^{T-1}(1 + \theta)^{-t} \ln C_t + k(1 + \theta)^{-T} \ln A_T\right]$$

where w_t and C_t are controls, k and θ are positive constants, and

$$A_{t+1} = (A_t - C_t)[(1 + r_t)w_t + (1 + V_{t+1})(1 - w_t)]$$

where r_t is a given sequence. The stochastic variables V_t are independently and identically distributed.

3. Solve the problem

$$\max E\left[\sum_{t<T} 2u_t^{1/2} + aX_T\right], \quad a > 0, \quad x_0 > 0, \quad T \text{ fixed}, \quad u_t \geq 0$$

where $X_{t+1} = X_t - u_t$ with probability 1/2 and $X_{t+1} = 0$ with probability 1/2.

4. Solve the problem

$$\max E\sum_{t=0}^{T-1} -u_t^2 - X_T^2 \quad \text{subject to} \quad X_{t+1} = X_t V_{t+1} + u_t, \quad V_{t+1} \in \{0, 1\}$$

with $\Pr[V_{t+1} = 1 | V_t = 1] = 3/4$, $\Pr[V_{t+1} = 1 | V_t = 0] = 1/4$. (*Hint:* Try $J(t, x_t, 1) = -a_t x_t^2$, $J(t, x_t, 0) = -b_t x_t^2$.)

5. Solve the dynamic programming problem

$$\max E\sum_{t=0}^{T}(1 - u_t)X_t, \quad X_{t+1} = X_t + u_t X_t + V_{t+1}, \quad x_0 = 1, \quad u_t \in [0, 1]$$

where $V_{t+1} \geq 0$ is exponentially distributed with parameter λ (i.e. the density of V_{t+1} is $\varphi(v) = \lambda e^{-\lambda v}$).

6. (Hakansson) Let x_t denote capital, y_t income, c_t consumption (a control), and z_t investment with uncertain return (another control). The balance $x_t - c_t - z_t$ is placed in a bank, where it earns a return r equal to 1 plus the interest rate. Let the gross rate of return on the uncertain investment (i.e. z) be β_t (so β_t equals 1 plus an uncertain net rate of return). Assume the random variables β_t are independent and identically distributed. Then

$$X_{t+1} = (\beta_t - r)z_t + r(X_t - c_t) + y_t$$

Assume that $E\beta_t > r$. Let $K > 0$, $\gamma \in (0, 1)$ be given numbers. The maximization problem is

$$\max E\left[\sum_{t=1}^{T-1}(\alpha^t/\gamma)c_t^\gamma + K(\alpha^T/\gamma)X_T^\gamma\right]$$

where $c_t \geq 0$, $z_t \geq 0$.

(a) Solve the problem, i.e. find the optimal controls. Assume that $c_t > 0$ and $x_{t+1} > 0$ in optimum. (*Hint:* When maximizing w.r.t. (c, z), first maximize w.r.t. z. When maximizing w.r.t. z, use the fact that for an arbitrarily given number $b > 0$, one has

$$\max_{z \geq 0} E[\{rb + (\beta - r)z\}^\gamma] = b^\gamma a, \quad \text{where } a = \max_{s \geq 0} E[\{r + (\beta - r)s\}^\gamma] \qquad (*)$$

Don't try to find a, use it as a known parameter in the solution of the problem. Formally, we let $w^\gamma = -\infty$ when $w < 0$. Write expressions of the form $\{y + r(x - c) + (\beta - r)z\}^\gamma$ as $\{r(\frac{1}{r}y + x - c) + (\beta - r)z\}^\gamma$ when using $(*)$.)

(b) Discuss dependence on parameters in the problem, including the distribution of β. Show $(*)$.

7. Consider the problem

$$\max E\left[\sum_{t=0}^{T-1}((1-u_t)X_t^2 - u_t) + 2X_T^2\right] \quad \text{s. t.} \quad X_{t+1} = u_t X_t V_{t+1}, \quad u_t \in U = [0, 1]$$

where $V_{t+1} = 2$ with probability 1/4 and $V_{t+1} = 0$ with probability 3/4.

(a) Find $J(T, x)$, $J(T-1, x)$, and $J(T-2, x)$. (Note that the maximand will be convex in the control u, so any maximum will be situated at an endpoint of U.)

(b) Find $J(t, x)$ for general t.

8. Solve the problem

$$\max E\left[\sum_{1 \leq t \leq T-1} u_t^{1/2} + aX_t^{1/2}\right] \quad \text{subject to} \quad X_{t+1} = (X_t - u_t)V_{t+1}$$

where a and T are given positive numbers, and where $V_{t+1} = 0$ with probability 1/2, $V_{t+1} = 1$ with probability 1/2. (*Hint:* Try $J(t, x) = 2a_t x^{1/2}, a_t > 0$.)

9. Solve the gambler's problem in Example 2 when $f(T, x_T) = (x_T)^{1-\alpha}/(1-\alpha)$, where $\alpha > 0, \alpha \neq 1$.

10. (Bertsekas (1976)) A farmer annually produces X_k units of a certain crop and stores $(1 - u_k)X_k$ units of his production, where $0 \leq u_k \leq 1$. He invests the remaining $u_k X_k$ units, thus increasing next year's accumulated output to a level X_{k+1} given by

$$X_{k+1} = X_k + w_k u_k X_k, \quad k = 0, 1, \ldots, N-1$$

The scalars W_k are independent random variables with an identical probability distribution that depends neither on x_k nor u_k. Furthermore, $E[W_k] = \overline{w} > 0$. The problem is to find the optimal policy that maximizes the expected output accumulated over N years,

$$E\left[X_N + \sum_{k=0}^{N-1}(1 - u_k)X_k\right]$$

Show that one optimal control is given by:

(i) If $\overline{w} > 1$, then $u_0^*(x_0) = \cdots = u_{N-1}^*(x_{N-1}) = 1$.

(ii) If $0 < \overline{w} < 1/N$, then $u_0^*(x_0) = \cdots = u_{N-1}^*(x_{N-1}) = 0$.

(iii) If $1/N \leq \overline{w} \leq 1$, then

$$u_0^*(x_0) = \cdots = u_{N-\bar{k}-1}^*(x_{N-\bar{k}-1}) = 1$$

$$\vdots$$

$$u_{N-\bar{k}}^*(x_{N-\bar{k}}) = \cdots = u_{N-1}^*(x_{N-1}) = 0$$

where $\bar{k}$ is such that $1/(\bar{k}+1) \leq \overline{w} < 1/\bar{k}$. Note that this control consists of constant functions.

11. Use the stochastic Euler equation to solve the problem

$$\max E \sum_{t=0}^{2} [1 - (v_{t+1} + X_{t+1} - X_t)^2 + (1 + v_3 + X_3)], \quad X_0 = 0, X_1, X_2, X_3 \in \mathbb{R}$$

where all v_t are identically and independently distributed, with $Ev_t = 1/2$.

12.7 Infinite Horizon Stationary Problems

We consider an infinite horizon version of the problem in the previous section. Suppose that both $P_t(\mathbf{v}_{t+1} \mid \mathbf{v}_t)$ (or $p_t(\mathbf{v}_{t+1} \mid \mathbf{v}_t)$) and $\mathbf{g}$ are independent of t, and that the instantaneous reward is $\beta^t f(\mathbf{x}, \mathbf{u})$ with $\beta \in (0, 1]$. The problem is then often called **stationary** or **autonomous**. We focus on the discrete variable case, which takes the form

$$\max_{\pi} E \sum_{t=0}^{\infty} \beta^t f(\mathbf{X}_t, \mathbf{u}_t(\mathbf{X}_t, \mathbf{V}_t)), \quad \mathbf{u}_t(\mathbf{X}_t, \mathbf{V}_t) \in U, \qquad \Pr[\mathbf{V}_{t+1} = \mathbf{v} \mid \mathbf{v}_t] = P(\mathbf{v} \mid \mathbf{v}_t) \quad (1)$$

where $\mathbf{X}_t$ is governed by the stochastic difference equation

$$\mathbf{X}_{t+1} = \mathbf{g}(\mathbf{X}_t, \mathbf{u}_t(\mathbf{X}_t, \mathbf{V}_t), \mathbf{V}_{t+1}) \tag{2}$$

with $\mathbf{X}_0$ and $\mathbf{V}_0$ given. The functions f and $\mathbf{g}$ are continuous. The control functions $\mathbf{u}_t$ take values in a fixed control region U. Among all sequences $\pi = (\mathbf{u}_0(\mathbf{x}_0, \mathbf{v}_0), \mathbf{u}_1(\mathbf{x}_1, \mathbf{v}_1), \dots)$ of Markov controls, we seek one that maximizes the objective function in (1).

We introduce the following *boundedness condition*:

$$M_1 \leq f(\mathbf{x}, \mathbf{u}) \leq M_2 \text{ for all } (\mathbf{x}, \mathbf{u}) \in \mathbb{R}^n \times U, \text{ where } M_1 \text{ and } M_2 \text{ are given numbers} \quad (3)$$

For a given sequence π, let us write

$$J_\pi(s, \mathbf{x}_s, \mathbf{v}_s) = E\left[\sum_{t=s}^{\infty} \beta^t f(\mathbf{X}_t, \mathbf{u}_t(\mathbf{X}_t, \mathbf{V}_t)) \mid \mathbf{x}_s, \mathbf{v}_s \right] \tag{4}$$

and define $J(s, \mathbf{x}_s, \mathbf{v}_s) = \sup_\pi J_\pi(s, \mathbf{x}_s, \mathbf{v}_s)$. We claim that $J(1, \mathbf{x}_0, \mathbf{v}_0) = \beta J(0, \mathbf{x}_0, \mathbf{v}_0)$. The intuitive argument is as follows. Let $J_\pi^k(\mathbf{x}, \mathbf{v}) = \sum_{t=k}^{\infty} E[\beta^{t-k} f(\mathbf{X}_t, \mathbf{u}_t(\mathbf{X}_t, \mathbf{V}_t)) \mid \mathbf{x}, \mathbf{v}]$ and let $J^k(\mathbf{x}, \mathbf{v}) = \sup_\pi J_\pi^k(\mathbf{x}, \mathbf{v})$. Then $J^k(\mathbf{x}, \mathbf{v})$ is the maximal expected present value of future rewards discounted back to $t = k$, given that the process starts at $(\mathbf{x}, \mathbf{v})$ at time $t = k$. When starting at $(\mathbf{x}, \mathbf{v})$ at time $t = 0$, and discounting back to $t = 0$, the corresponding maximal expected value is $J^0(\mathbf{x}, \mathbf{v}) = J(0, \mathbf{x}, \mathbf{v})$. Because time does not enter explicitly in $P(\mathbf{v} \mid \mathbf{v}_t)$, $\mathbf{g}$, or f, the future looks exactly the same at time $t = k$ as it does at time $t = 0$. Hence $J^k(\mathbf{x}, \mathbf{v}) = J^0(\mathbf{x}, \mathbf{v})$. But $J(k, \mathbf{x}_0, \mathbf{v}_0) = \beta^k J^k(\mathbf{x}_0, \mathbf{v}_0)$ because, in the definition of $J_\pi(k, \mathbf{x}_0, \mathbf{v}_0)$, we discount back to $t = 0$. Hence $\beta^k J(0, \mathbf{x}_0, \mathbf{v}_0) = J(k, \mathbf{x}_0, \mathbf{v}_0)$, and in particular $\beta J(0, \mathbf{x}_0, \mathbf{v}_0) = J(1, \mathbf{x}_0, \mathbf{v}_0)$.

The heuristic argument for the optimality equation (12.6.5) works just as well in the infinite horizon case. When $t = 0$, if we write $\mathbf{x}$ and $\mathbf{v}$ instead of $\mathbf{x}_0$ and $\mathbf{v}_0$, define $J(\mathbf{x}, \mathbf{v}) = J(0, \mathbf{x}, \mathbf{v})$, then recognize that $J(1, \mathbf{x}, \mathbf{v}) = \beta J(0, \mathbf{x}, \mathbf{v})$, we derive from (12.6.5) the following **optimality equation** or **Bellman equation**

$$J(\mathbf{x}, \mathbf{v}) = \max_{\mathbf{u}} \left\{ f(\mathbf{x}, \mathbf{u}) + \beta E[J(\mathbf{X}_1, \mathbf{V}_1) \mid \mathbf{x}, \mathbf{v}] \right\} \tag{5}$$

where $\mathbf{X}_1 = \mathbf{g}(\mathbf{x}, \mathbf{u}, \mathbf{V}_1)$.

Observe that (5) is a "functional equation" which (we hope) determines the unknown function J that occurs on both sides of the equality sign. Once J is known, the optimal Markov control is obtained from the maximization in the optimality equation. The maximization seems to yield an optimal control function $\mathbf{u}(\mathbf{x}, \mathbf{v})$ not dependent on t. This is to be expected: Whether we observe $(\mathbf{x}, \mathbf{v})$ at time 0 or at time t does not matter; the optimal choice of control should be the same in the two situations, because the future looks exactly the same at both these times.

When the boundedness condition (3) is satisfied, it can be shown that the optimal value function is defined and satisfies the optimality equation. Moreover, the optimality equation has a unique bounded solution $J(\mathbf{x}, \mathbf{v})$. (At least this is so when "max" is replaced by "sup" in the Bellman equation.). Furthermore, $J(\mathbf{x}, \mathbf{v})$ is automatically the optimal value function in the problem, and any control $\mathbf{u}(\mathbf{x}, \mathbf{v})$ that maximizes the right-hand side of (5), given the function $J(\mathbf{x}, \mathbf{v})$, is optimal.

NOTE 1 (**Alternative Boundedness Conditions**) Complications arise when the boundedness condition (3) fails. First, the Bellman equation might then have more than one solution, or perhaps none. Even if it has one or more solutions, it might be that none of them is the optimal value function.

We consider two cases where some results can be obtained. In both cases we must allow infinite values for the optimal value function $J(\mathbf{x})$, $+\infty$ in case A, and $-\infty$ in case B. (Of course, $J(\mathbf{x}, \mathbf{v}) \equiv \infty$ and $J(\mathbf{x}, \mathbf{v}) \equiv -\infty$ in a sense satisfy the Bellman equation, being perhaps "false" solutions.)

A *Either $f(\mathbf{x}, \mathbf{u}) \geq 0$ for all $(\mathbf{x}, \mathbf{u}) \in \mathbb{R}^n \times U$ and $\beta \in (0, 1]$, or for some negative number γ, $f(\mathbf{x}, \mathbf{u}) \geq \gamma$ for all $(\mathbf{x}, \mathbf{u}) \in \mathbb{R}^n \times U$ and $\beta \in (0, 1)$.*

In this case if $\mathbf{u}(\mathbf{x}, \mathbf{v})$ yields the maximum in the Bellman equation with $J^{\mathbf{u}}(\mathbf{x}, \mathbf{v})$ inserted, then $\mathbf{u}(\mathbf{x}, \mathbf{v})$ is optimal. Here $J^{\mathbf{u}}(\mathbf{x}, \mathbf{v})$ is the value function arising from using $\mathbf{u}(\mathbf{x}, \mathbf{v})$ all the time.

Sometimes it is useful to know the fact that if $J^{\mathbf{u}}(s, \mathbf{x}, \mathbf{v}, T)$ is the value function arising from using $\mathbf{u} = \mathbf{u}(\mathbf{x}, \mathbf{v})$ all the time from s until $t = T$, then $J^{\mathbf{u}}(0, \mathbf{x}, \mathbf{v}, T) \to J^{\mathbf{u}}(\mathbf{x}, \mathbf{v})$ as $T \to \infty$.

B *Either $f(\mathbf{x}, \mathbf{u}) \leq 0$ for all $(\mathbf{x}, \mathbf{u}) \in \mathbb{R}^n \times U$ and $\beta \in (0, 1]$, or for some positive number γ, $f(\mathbf{x}, \mathbf{u}) \leq \gamma$ for all $(\mathbf{x}, \mathbf{u}) \in \mathbb{R}^n \times U$ and $\beta \in (0, 1)$.*

In this case it is known that if $\mathbf{u}(\mathbf{x}, \mathbf{v})$ satisfies the Bellman equation (i.e. yields maximum) with the optimal value function inserted, then $\mathbf{u}(\mathbf{x}, \mathbf{v})$ is optimal. If we are able to prove that the Bellman equation has one and only one solution $\hat{J}(\mathbf{x}, \mathbf{v}) > -\infty$, then this is the optimal value function $J(\mathbf{x}, \mathbf{v})$ provided we know that $J(\mathbf{x}, \mathbf{v}) > -\infty$. (Recall that $J(\mathbf{x}, \mathbf{v})$ is known to satisfy the Bellman equation, both in case A and B.) Another possibility is the following: Suppose we have solved the finite horizon problem, with horizon T. Assume that U is compact, and that $f(\mathbf{x}, \mathbf{u})$ and $\mathbf{g}(\mathbf{x}, \mathbf{u}, \mathbf{v})$ are continuous in $(\mathbf{x}, \mathbf{u})$. Denote the optimal value function in this problem by $J(0, \mathbf{x}, \mathbf{v}, T)$. If we now find the limit $\lim_{T \to \infty} J(0, \mathbf{x}, \mathbf{v}, T)$, then this is the optimal value function. (As $T \to \infty$, $J(0, \mathbf{x}, \mathbf{v}, T)$ converges to the optimal value function in this case, as well as in the cases A and (3).) For the results in this note see Bertsekas (1976) and Hernández-Lerma and Lasserre (1996).

To sum up, what do we do after we have found a pair $(\mathbf{u}(\mathbf{x}, \mathbf{v}), \hat{J}(\mathbf{x}, \mathbf{v}))$ satisfying the Bellman equation? In case A, we try to check if $J^{\mathbf{u}} = \hat{J}$ holds. If it does, $(\mathbf{u}(\mathbf{x}, \mathbf{v}), \hat{J}(\mathbf{x}, \mathbf{v}))$ is optimal ($\hat{J}$ is then the optimal value function). In case B with $\hat{J} > -\infty$, we either try to show that $\hat{J}$ is the only solution greater than $-\infty$ satisfying the Bellman equation and that $J > -\infty$, or we try to check that $J(0, \mathbf{x}, \mathbf{v}, T) \to \hat{J}(\mathbf{x}, \mathbf{v})$ as $T \to \infty$. If either of these tests comes out positive, $(\mathbf{u}(\mathbf{x}, \mathbf{v}), \hat{J}(\mathbf{x}, \mathbf{v}))$ is optimal.

NOTE 2   The boundedness condition (3), or the alternatives in Note 1, need only hold for $\mathbf{x}$ in $\mathcal{X}(\mathbf{x}_0) = \bigcup_t \mathcal{X}_t(\mathbf{x}_0)$ for all t, where $\mathcal{X}_t(\mathbf{x}_0)$ is the set of states that can be reached at time t when starting at $\mathbf{x}_0$ at time 0, considering all controls and all outcomes that can occur with positive probability. The conclusions drawn in the case where (3) is satisfied are also valid if the following weaker condition holds: There exist positive constants M, M^*, α, and δ such that for all $\mathbf{x} \in \mathcal{X}(\mathbf{x}_0)$ and $\mathbf{u} \in U$, one has $|f(\mathbf{x}, \mathbf{u})| \leq M^*(1 + \|\mathbf{x}\|^\alpha)$ and $\|\mathbf{g}(\mathbf{x}, \mathbf{u})\| \leq M + \delta\|\mathbf{x}\|$, with $\beta\delta^\alpha < 1$ and $\beta \in (0, 1)$.

EXAMPLE 1   Consider the following stochastic version of Example 12.3.1:

$$\max_{w_t \in (0,1)} E\left[\sum_{t=0}^{\infty} \beta^t X_t^{1-\gamma} w_t^{1-\gamma}\right] \tag{i}$$

$$X_{t+1} = V_{t+1}(1 - w_t)X_t, \quad x_0 \text{ is a positive constant}, \quad 0 < \gamma < 1 \tag{ii}$$

Here, $V_1, V_2, \ldots$ are identically and independently distributed nonnegative stochastic variables, with $D = EV^{1-\gamma} < \infty$, where V is any of the V_t. Now, $w \in (0, 1)$ is the control. It is assumed that

$$\beta \in (0, 1), \quad \gamma \in (0, 1), \quad \rho = (\beta D)^{1/\gamma} < 1 \tag{iii}$$

In the notation of problem (1)–(3), $f(x, w) = x^{1-\gamma}w^{1-\gamma}$ and $g(x, w, V) = V(1 - w)x$. The optimality equation (5) yields

$$J(x) = \max_{w \in (0,1)} \left[x^{1-\gamma}w^{1-\gamma} + \beta E J(V(1 - w)x)\right] \tag{iv}$$

We guess that $J(x)$ has the form $J(x) = kx^{1-\gamma}$ for some constant k. (The optimal value function had a similar form in the finite horizon version of this problem discussed in the previous section, as well as in the deterministic infinite horizon version of Example 12.3.1.) Then, cancelling the factor $x^{1-\gamma}$, (iv) reduces to

$$k = \max_{w \in (0,1)} \left[w^{1-\gamma} + \beta k D (1-w)^{1-\gamma} \right] \tag{v}$$

where $D = E[V^{1-\gamma}]$. Note that equation (v) is the same as equation (iii) in Example 12.3.1, except that $a^{1-\gamma}$ is replaced by D. It follows that $J(x) = (1-\rho)^{-\gamma} x^{1-\gamma}$, with $w = 1-\rho$, where $\rho = (\beta D)^{1/\gamma}$.

In this example the boundedness condition (3) is not satisfied for $x \in \bigcup_t \mathcal{X}_t(x_0)$.

One way to tackle this problem is to use the transformation $y_t = x_t / V_t$ with y_t satisfying $y_{t+1} = (1-w_t) z_t y_t$, $z_{t+1} = V_{t+1}$. Taking the expectation of the objective function inside the sum, and using the so-called monotone convergence theorem, the problem can be transformed into one in which the new discount factor is $\hat{\beta} = \beta E V^{1-\gamma} < 1$ and where $g = g(y, w) = y^{1-\gamma} w^{1-\gamma}$, with g satisfying (3) in $\bigcup_t \mathcal{X}_t(x_0)$. Yet another way out is the following: Let us use A in the note above. Then we need to know that $J^{w^*}(x) = J(x)$. It is fairly easy to carry out the explicit calculation of $J^{w^*}(x)$ ($W = w^*$ as in (vi)), by taking the expectation inside the sum in the objective and summing the resulting geometric series. But we don't need to do that. Noting that $x_t = x_0 \rho^t Z_1 \cdot \ldots \cdot Z_t$, evidently, we must have that $J^{w^*}(x_0) = k x_0^{1-\gamma}$ for some k. We must also have that $J^{w^*}(x_0)$ satisfies the equilibrium optimality equation with $w = w^*$ and the maximization deleted (in the problem where $U = w^*$, w^* is optimal !). But the only value of k which satisfies this equation were found above. Thus the test in A works and w^* as specified is optimal.

Counterexamples

The Bellman equation may have "false" solutions. Two examples will be given.

Consider the problem $\sum_{t=0}^{\infty} \beta^t (1 - u_t)$, subject to $x_{t+1} = (1/\beta)(x_t + u_t)$, $u_t \in [0, 1]$, x_0 given, $\beta \in (0, 1]$. The Bellman equation is satisfied by $J(x) = \gamma + x$, where $\gamma = 1/(1-\beta)$, with any $u = \bar{u} \in [0, 1]$ yielding the maximum in the Bellman equation, let, say, $\bar{u} = 1/2$. (The Bellman equation is then $\gamma + x = \max_u \{1 - u + \beta(\gamma + (1/\beta)(x+u))\} = 1 + \beta\gamma + x$ and γ equals $1 + \beta\gamma$.) Is then $u_t \equiv 1/2$ the optimal control, and $J(x) = \gamma + x$, the optimal value function? The first thing we note is that $J^{\bar{u}}(x)$ is independent of x, so $J^{\bar{u}}(x) \neq \gamma + x$. Neither $u_t \equiv 1/2$ nor $J(x_0) = \gamma + x_0$ are optimal entities, it is trivial that $u_t \equiv 0$ is optimal, with a criterion value independent of x_0 and strictly greater than the criterion value of $u_t \equiv 1/2$.

What about cases where we have $J^u(\mathbf{x}, \mathbf{v}) = J(\mathbf{x}, \mathbf{v})$, where $(\mathbf{u}(\mathbf{x}, \mathbf{v}), J(\mathbf{x}, \mathbf{v}))$ satisfies the Bellman equation? Consider the problem of maximizing $\sum_{t=0}^{\infty} \beta^t x_t (u_t - \alpha)$ subject to $x_{t+1} = x_t u_t$ and $0 \leq u_t \leq \alpha$, where $x_0 > 0$ is given, and α, β are positive constants satisfying $\alpha\beta = 1$, $\beta \in (0, 1]$.

Note that, regardless of which $u_t \in [0, \alpha]$ is chosen in each period, one has $x_t \geq 0$ for all t, so $\mathcal{X}(x_0) \subseteq [0, \infty)$.

The Bellman equation is

$$J(x) = \max_{u \in [0, \alpha]} \{x(u - \alpha) + \beta J(xu)\}$$

We look for solutions of the form $J(x) = \gamma x$, where γ is a constant. The condition for this to be a solution when $x > 0$ is that

$$\gamma = \max_{u \in [0, \alpha]} \{u - \alpha + \beta\gamma u\}$$

and we see that $\gamma = -1/\beta$ works. In this case any $u \in [0, \alpha]$ yields maximum in the Bellman equation. If we choose the same $u \in [0, \alpha)$ in each period, then $J^u = \sum_{t=0}^{\infty} \beta^t x_t(u - \alpha)$ where $x_t = u^t x_0$. Hence $J^u(x_0) = x_0(u - \alpha) \sum_{t=0}^{\infty} (\beta u)^t = x_0(u - \alpha)/(1 - \beta u) = -x_0/\beta = \gamma x_0$. So the function $J(x) \equiv -x/\beta = \gamma x$ solves the Bellman equation, and is the criterion value of a corresponding stationary policy $u_t \equiv$ constant $\in [0, \alpha)$. However, $J(x) = \gamma x$ is not equal to the criterion value of $u_t \equiv \alpha$.

Now, as x_t is always ≥ 0, $x_t(u_t - \alpha) \leq 0$, so $u_t \equiv \alpha$ is obviously optimal, with criterion value $= 0$, and $J(x) \equiv 0$ solves also the Bellman equation, with $u = \alpha$ as a maximizing control.

A necessary condition for optimality of a policy $\mathbf{u}(\mathbf{x}, \mathbf{v})$ is that it satisfies the Bellman equation for J^u inserted. (It is necessary that $\mathbf{u}(\mathbf{x}, \mathbf{v})$ satisfies the Bellman equation for the optimal value function $J(\mathbf{x}, \mathbf{v})$. It is also necessary that $J^u(\mathbf{x}, \mathbf{v}) = J(\mathbf{x}, \mathbf{v})$, hence the assertion follows.) It is a necessary and sufficient condition in case A, but not in Case B. In the first example (which is of type A), the Bellman equation is not satisfied by $\bar{u} = 1/2$, it is sufficient to note that $J^u(x)$ is a constant to see this. This condition is not sufficient in problems of type B, as we saw in the last example, which was of this type.

The first example was actually of the type (3), so in that case the Bellman equation can have unbounded (and hence "false" solutions), in addition to the unique (correct) bounded one.

Iterative Methods

In this subsection, we describe two new methods yielding approximate solutions to infinite horizon dynamic programming problems. One approximation result has already been mentioned: Under certain conditions, $J(0, \mathbf{x}, \mathbf{v}, T) \to J(\mathbf{x}, \mathbf{v})$ when $T \to \infty$. Another method is the **successive approximation method** that can be formulated as follows.

For any real-valued bounded function $h(\mathbf{x}, \mathbf{v})$, for any function $\mathbf{u} = \mathbf{u}(\mathbf{x}, \mathbf{v})$, define $\Psi^{\mathbf{u}}(h)$, which denotes a function of $(\mathbf{x}, \mathbf{v})$, by the formula

$$\Psi^{\mathbf{u}}(h)(\mathbf{x}, \mathbf{v}) = \{ f(\mathbf{x}, \mathbf{u}(\mathbf{x}, \mathbf{v})) + \beta E[h(\mathbf{g}(\mathbf{x}, \mathbf{u}(\mathbf{x}, \mathbf{v}), \mathbf{V}), \mathbf{V}) \mid \mathbf{x}, \mathbf{v}] \}$$

Then define the function $\Psi(h)$ by

$$\Psi(h)(\mathbf{x}, \mathbf{v}) = \max_{\mathbf{u}} \Psi^{\mathbf{u}}(h)(\mathbf{x}, \mathbf{v}) = \max_{\mathbf{u} \in U} \{ f(\mathbf{x}, \mathbf{u}) + \beta E[h(\mathbf{g}(\mathbf{x}, \mathbf{u}, \mathbf{V}), \mathbf{V}) \mid \mathbf{x}, \mathbf{v}] \}$$

Let $\Psi^2(h) = \Psi(\Psi h)$, $\Psi^3(h) = \Psi(\Psi^2(h))$, and so on. Choose in particular $h = 0$ and calculate successively $\Psi^1(0) = \Psi(0)$, $\Psi^2(0) = \Psi(\Psi^1(0))$, ... Let the control $\mathbf{u}_k(\mathbf{x}, \mathbf{v})$ be the one that yields a maximum at step k. (When $\Psi^{k-1}(0)$ is known, a maximization is carried out to find $\Psi^k(0)$, and we assume that all maxima are attained.) Provided that (3) is satisfied, the controls $\mathbf{u}_k(\mathbf{x}, \mathbf{v})$ are approximately optimal for k large.

The second method is called **policy improvement**. It works as follows. Choose an initial stationary policy $\mathbf{u}_0 = \mathbf{u}_0(\mathbf{x}, \mathbf{v})$. Calculate $J^{\mathbf{u}_0}(\mathbf{x}, \mathbf{v})$, the expected value of the objective when starting at $\mathbf{x}$ at time 0, and using $\mathbf{u}_0(\mathbf{x}, \mathbf{v})$ all the time. For each $(\mathbf{x}, \mathbf{v})$ find the control $\mathbf{u}_1(\mathbf{x}, \mathbf{v})$ that yields a maximum when calculating $\Psi(J^{\mathbf{u}_0})(\mathbf{x}, \mathbf{v})$. Next calculate $J^{\mathbf{u}_1}(\mathbf{x}, \mathbf{v})$, and find the control $\mathbf{u}_2(\mathbf{x}, \mathbf{v})$ that maximizes $\Psi(J^{\mathbf{u}_1})(\mathbf{x}, \mathbf{v})$, and so on. Since for any i, $J^{\mathbf{u}_i}(\mathbf{x}, \mathbf{v}) = f(\mathbf{x}, \mathbf{u}_i(\mathbf{x}, \mathbf{v})) + E[\beta J^{\mathbf{u}_i}(\mathbf{g}(\mathbf{x}, \mathbf{u}_i(\mathbf{x}, \mathbf{v}), \mathbf{V}))|\mathbf{x}, \mathbf{v}]$, it is clear that $\Psi(J^{\mathbf{u}_i}) \geq J^{\mathbf{u}_i}$. Then $\Psi^{\mathbf{u}_{i+1}}(\Psi(J^{\mathbf{u}_i})) \geq \Psi^{\mathbf{u}_{i+1}}(J^{\mathbf{u}_i}) = \Psi(J^{\mathbf{u}_i}) \geq J^{\mathbf{u}_i}$, $\Psi^{\mathbf{u}_{i+1}}(\Psi^{\mathbf{u}_{i+1}}(\Psi(J^{\mathbf{u}_i}))) \geq \Psi^{\mathbf{u}_{i+1}}(J^{\mathbf{u}_i}) = \Psi(J^{\mathbf{u}_i}) \geq J^{\mathbf{u}_i}$, and generally $(\Psi^{\mathbf{u}_{i+1}})^k(\Psi(J^{\mathbf{u}_i})) \geq J^{\mathbf{u}_i}$. By a contraction argument, $(\Psi^{\mathbf{u}_{i+1}})^k(\Psi(J^{\mathbf{u}_i})) \to J^{\mathbf{u}_{i+1}}$ when $k \to \infty$, and it follows that $J^{\mathbf{u}_{i+1}} \geq J^{\mathbf{u}_i}$. In fact, $J^{\mathbf{u}_i}(\mathbf{x}, \mathbf{v})$ increases monotonically to the optimal value function $J(\mathbf{x}, \mathbf{v})$ when (3) holds, and so for i large, $\mathbf{u}_i(\mathbf{x}, \mathbf{v})$ is approximately optimal. At each step $J^{\mathbf{u}_{i+1}}$ can be calculated approximately by using $(\Psi^{\mathbf{u}_{i+1}})^k(\Psi(J^{\mathbf{u}_i})) \to J^{\mathbf{u}_{i+1}}$.

PROBLEMS FOR SECTION 12.7

1. Consider the problem

$$\max E \sum_{t=0}^{\infty} \beta^t (-u_t^2 - X_t^2), \quad \beta \in (0, 1), \quad u_t \in \mathbb{R}$$

$$X_{t+1} = X_t + u_t + V_t, \quad E(V_{t+1}) = 0, \quad E(V_{t+1}^2) = d$$

(a) Guess that $J(x)$ is of the form $ax^2 + b$, and insert it into (5) to determine a and b.

(b) Solve the corresponding finite horizon problem assuming $J(t, x) = J(t, x, T) = \beta^t(a_t x^2 + b_t)$. (We now sum only up to time T.) Find $J(0, x_0, T)$, let $T \to \infty$ and prove that the solution in (a) is optimal (we are in case B).

2. Solve the problem

$$\max E \sum_{t=0}^{\infty} \alpha^t (\ln u_t + \ln X_t), \quad X_{t+1} = (X_t - u_t)V_{t+1}, \quad x_0 > 0, \quad u_t \in (0, x_t)$$

where $\alpha \in (0, 1)$, $V_t > 0$, and all the V_t are independent and identically distributed with $|E \ln V_t| < \infty$.

TOPOLOGY AND SEPARATION

*We could, of course, dismiss the rigorous proof as being
superfluous: if a theorem is geometrically obvious why prove it?
This was exactly the attitude taken in the eighteenth century. The
result, in the nineteenth century, was chaos and confusion: for
intuition, unsupported by logic, habitually assumes that
everything is much nicer behaved than it really is.*
—I. Stewart (1975)

This chapter concentrates on a few topics of a theoretical nature that turn out to be useful in some parts of economics, notably general equilibrium and its applications to modern macroeconomic theory. Section 13.1 takes a closer look at open and closed sets in $\mathbb{R}^n$, together with closely associated concepts such as the neighbourhood of a point, as well as the interior and boundary of a set. Next, Sections 13.2 and 13.3 cover the associated concepts of convergence, compactness, and continuity in $\mathbb{R}^n$. These concepts play an important part in mathematical analysis. Their systematic study belongs to *general* or *analytic topology*, an important branch of mathematics that saw a period of rapid development early in the 20th century. The precise definitions and carefully formulated arguments we provide may strike many readers as rather formal. Their primary purpose is not to give solution methods for concrete problems, but to equip the reader with the theoretical basis needed to understand why solutions may not even exist, as well as their regularity properties when they do exist. In the case of optimization problems, these ideas lead to the versions of the maximum theorem that are the subject of Section 13.4.

Another main theme of this chapter is separation theorems, which are useful in both general equilibrium and optimization theory. A discussion of "productive economies" and a discussion of Frobenius roots of square matrices wind up the chapter.

13.1 Point Set Topology in $\mathbb{R}^n$

This section begins by reviewing some basic facts concerning the n-dimensional Euclidean space $\mathbb{R}^n$, whose elements, or points, are n-vectors $\mathbf{x} = (x_1, \ldots, x_n)$. The **Euclidean distance** $d(x, y)$ between any two points $\mathbf{x} = (x_1, \ldots, x_n)$ and $\mathbf{y} = (y_1, \ldots, y_n)$ in $\mathbb{R}^n$ is the norm $\|\mathbf{x} - \mathbf{y}\|$ of the vector difference between $\mathbf{x}$ and $\mathbf{y}$. (See (1.1.37).) Thus,

$$d(\mathbf{x}, \mathbf{y}) = \|\mathbf{x} - \mathbf{y}\| = \sqrt{(x_1 - y_1)^2 + \cdots + (x_n - y_n)^2} \tag{1}$$

Note that $d(\mathbf{x}, \mathbf{y}) \geq \sqrt{(x_j - y_j)^2} = |x_j - y_j|$ for each j and that $d(\mathbf{x}, \mathbf{y}) \leq \sum_{j=1}^{n} |x_j - y_j|$. (See Problem 3.) Moreover, if $\mathbf{x}$, $\mathbf{y}$, and $\mathbf{z}$ are points in $\mathbb{R}^n$, then

$$d(\mathbf{x}, \mathbf{z}) \leq d(\mathbf{x}, \mathbf{y}) + d(\mathbf{y}, \mathbf{z}) \qquad \textbf{(triangle inequality)} \qquad (2)$$

which follows immediately from (1.1.39).

Recall that if $\mathbf{a}$ is a point in $\mathbb{R}^n$ and r is a positive real number, then the set of all points $\mathbf{x}$ in $\mathbb{R}^n$ whose distance from $\mathbf{a}$ is less than r, is called the **open ball** around $\mathbf{a}$ with radius r. This open ball is denoted by $B_r(\mathbf{a})$ or $B(\mathbf{a}; r)$. Thus,

$$B_r(\mathbf{a}) = B(\mathbf{a}; r) = \{\, \mathbf{x} \in \mathbb{R}^n : d(\mathbf{x}, \mathbf{a}) < r \,\} \qquad (3)$$

On the real line $\mathbb{R} = \mathbb{R}^1$, with $\mathbf{a} = a_1$, the set $B_r(\mathbf{a})$ is the open interval $(a_1 - r, a_1 + r)$. If $n = 2$, then $B_r(\mathbf{a})$ is an open disk in the plane. In three-dimensional space $\mathbb{R}^3$, $B_r(\mathbf{a})$ is the set of all points strictly inside the surface of a sphere with centre $\mathbf{a}$ and radius r, as indicated in Fig. 1.

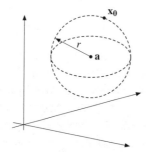

Figure 1 The open ball around $\mathbf{a}$ with radius r.

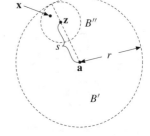

Figure 2 $B_r(\mathbf{a})$ is an open set.

Let S be any subset of $\mathbb{R}^n$. A point $\mathbf{a}$ in S is called an **interior point** of S if there is an open ball $B_r(\mathbf{a})$ centred at $\mathbf{a}$ which lies entirely within S. Thus, an interior point of S is completely surrounded by other points of S. The set of all interior points of S is called the **interior** of S, and is denoted by int(S) or S°.

A set S is called a **neighbourhood** of $\mathbf{a}$ if $\mathbf{a}$ is an interior point of S, that is, if S contains some open ball $B_r(\mathbf{a})$ around $\mathbf{a}$.

A set S in $\mathbb{R}^n$ is called **open** if all its members are interior points. On the real line $\mathbb{R}$, the simplest type of open set is an open interval.

EXAMPLE 1   Prove that the open ball $B' = B_r(\mathbf{a})$ is an open set.

Solution: Take any point $\mathbf{z}$ in B' and let $s = d(\mathbf{a}, \mathbf{z})$. Then $s < r$. Consider the open ball $B'' = B_{r-s}(\mathbf{z})$ with centre $\mathbf{z}$ and radius $r - s$. (See Fig. 2, which illustrates the proof when $n = 2$.) We claim that any point in B'' is also in B', which will show that B' is open. Indeed, if $\mathbf{x} \in B''$, then the triangle inequality implies that

$$d(\mathbf{a}, \mathbf{x}) \leq d(\mathbf{a}, \mathbf{z}) + d(\mathbf{z}, \mathbf{x}) < s + (r - s) = r$$

Hence $\mathbf{x} \in B'$.

EXAMPLE 2   Show that $A = \{(x, y) : x > y\}$ is an open set in $\mathbb{R}^2$.

Solution: Take any point (x_0, y_0) in A. Then $r = x_0 - y_0 > 0$. We claim that the open disk $B = B((x_0, y_0); r/2)$ with centre (x_0, y_0) and radius $r/2$ is contained in A, which will show that A is open. Take any point (x, y) in B. Then both $|x - x_0| < r/2$ and $|y - y_0| < r/2$. Hence $x > x_0 - r/2$ and $y < y_0 + r/2$. It follows that $x - y > x_0 - y_0 - r = 0$, and so $(x, y) \in A$ as claimed.

From the definition of an open set, together with Example 1 above, it follows that the interior of any set is open. Indeed, the interior of a set is its largest open subset (see Problem 10(a)). Also, $S = \text{int}(S)$ if and only if S is open.

Some important properties of open sets are summarized in the following theorem.

THEOREM 13.1.1 (PROPERTIES OF OPEN SETS)

(a) The whole space $\mathbb{R}^n$ and the empty set $\emptyset$ are both open.

(b) Arbitrary unions of open sets are open.

(c) The intersection of finitely many open sets is open.

Proof: (a) It is clear that $B_1(\mathbf{a}) \subseteq \mathbb{R}^n$ for all $\mathbf{a}$ in $\mathbb{R}^n$, so $\mathbb{R}^n$ is open. The empty set $\emptyset$ is open because the set has no element, so every member is an interior point.

(b) Let $\{U_i\}_{i \in I}$ be an arbitrary family of open sets in $\mathbb{R}^n$, and let $U^* = \bigcup_{i \in I} U_i$ be the union of the whole family. For each $\mathbf{x}$ in U^* there is at least one i in I such that $\mathbf{x} \in U_i$. Since U_i is open, there exists an open ball $B_r(\mathbf{x})$ with centre $\mathbf{x}$ such that $B_r(\mathbf{x}) \subseteq U_i \subseteq U^*$. Hence, $\mathbf{x}$ is an interior point of U^*. This shows that U^* is open.

(c) Let $\{U_i\}_{i=1}^{m}$ be a finite collection of open sets in $\mathbb{R}^n$, and let $U_* = \bigcap_{i=1}^{m} U_i$ be the intersection of all these sets. Let $\mathbf{x}$ be any point of U_*. Then for each $i = 1, \ldots, m$, the point $\mathbf{x}$ belongs to U_i, and because U_i is open, there exists an open ball $B_i = B_{r_i}(\mathbf{x})$ with centre $\mathbf{x}$ and radius $r_i > 0$ such that $B_i \subseteq U_i$. Let $B_* = B_r(\mathbf{x})$, where r is the smallest of the numbers $r_1, \ldots, r_m$. Then $\mathbf{x} \in B_* = \bigcap_{i=1}^{m} B_i \subseteq \bigcap_{i=1}^{m} U_i = U_*$, and it follows that U_* is open.   ∎

NOTE 1 The intersection of an infinite number of open sets need not be open. For instance, the intersection of the infinite family $B_{1/k}(\mathbf{0})$, $k = 1, 2, \ldots$, of open balls centred at $\mathbf{0}$ is the one-element set $\{\mathbf{0}\}$. The set $\{\mathbf{0}\}$ is not open, because $B_r(\mathbf{0})$ is not a subset of $\{\mathbf{0}\}$ for any positive r.

Recall that the **complement** of a set $S \subseteq \mathbb{R}^n$ is the set $\complement S = \mathbb{R}^n \setminus S$ of all points in $\mathbb{R}^n$ that do not belong to S. A point $\mathbf{x}_0$ in $\mathbb{R}^n$ is called a **boundary point** of the set $S \subseteq \mathbb{R}^n$ if *every* ball centred at $\mathbf{x}_0$ contains at least one point in S and at least one point in $\complement S$. Note that a boundary point of S is also a boundary point of $\complement S$, and vice versa. For instance, the point $\mathbf{x}_0$ in Fig. 1 is a boundary point of $B_r(\mathbf{a})$, as well as a boundary point of the complement of $B_r(\mathbf{a})$. In this particular case $\mathbf{x}_0$ does not belong to the set. In general, a set may include none, some, or all of its boundary points. An open set, however, contains none of its boundary points.

Each point in a set is either an interior point or a boundary point of the set. The set of all boundary points of a set S is called the **boundary** of S and is denoted by ∂S or bd(S). In Fig. 1, the boundary $\partial B_r(\mathbf{a})$ of the open ball $B_r(\mathbf{a})$ is the sphere consisting of all $\mathbf{x}$ with $d(\mathbf{x}, \mathbf{a}) = r$. The boundary of the open interval (a, b) in the real line consists of the two points a and b.

Note that, given any set $S \subseteq \mathbb{R}^n$, there is a corresponding partition of $\mathbb{R}^n$ into three mutually disjoint sets (some of which may be empty), namely:

(i) the interior of S, which consists of all points $\mathbf{x}$ in $\mathbb{R}^n$ such that $N \subseteq S$ for some neighbourhood N of $\mathbf{x}$.

(ii) the **exterior** of S, which consists of all points $\mathbf{x}$ in $\mathbb{R}^n$ for which there exists some neighbourhood N of $\mathbf{x}$ such that $N \subseteq \mathbb{R}^n \setminus S$;

(iii) the boundary of S, which consists of all points $\mathbf{x}$ in $\mathbb{R}^n$ with the property that every neighbourhood N of $\mathbf{x}$ intersects both S and its complement $\mathbb{R}^n \setminus S$.

A set S in $\mathbb{R}^n$ is said to be **closed** if it contains all its boundary points. The union $S \cup \partial S$ of S and its boundary is called the **closure** of S, denoted by $\overline{S}$ or cl(S). A point $\mathbf{a}$ belongs to $\overline{S}$ if and only if every open ball $B_r(\mathbf{a})$ around $\mathbf{a}$ intersects S. The closure $\overline{S}$ of any set S is indeed closed (see Problem 9(b)). In fact, $\overline{S}$ is the smallest closed set containing S (see Problem 10(b)). It follows that S is closed if and only if $S = \overline{S}$.

We noted above that S and $\complement S$ have the same boundary points. Furthermore, a set is open if and only if every point in the set is an interior point, i.e. if and only if it contains none of its boundary points. On the other hand, a set is closed if and only if it contains all its boundary points. It easily follows that the following statement is true.

$$\text{A set in } \mathbb{R}^n \text{ is closed if and only if its complement is open.} \tag{4}$$

Here are the most important properties of closed sets.

THEOREM 13.1.2 (PROPERTIES OF CLOSED SETS)

(a) The whole space $\mathbb{R}^n$ and the empty set $\emptyset$ are both closed.

(b) Arbitrary intersections of closed sets are closed.

(c) The union of finitely many closed sets is closed.

Proof: Part (a) is obvious. For (b) and (c), see Problem 12. ∎

NOTE 2 Infinite unions of closed sets need not be closed. (See Problem 11.)

One should be careful to note the technical meaning of the words open and closed. In everyday usage these words are opposites. (A café is either open or closed!) In topology, however, any set containing some of its boundary points but not all of them, is neither open nor closed. The half-open intervals $[a, b)$ and $(a, b]$, for example, are neither open nor closed in $\mathbb{R}$.

Another example is indicated in Fig. 3. Here, **a** is a boundary point that belongs to S, whereas **b** is a boundary point that does not belong to S. The set S is neither open nor closed in $\mathbb{R}^2$. By contrast, the empty set, $\emptyset$, and the whole space, $\mathbb{R}^n$, are both open and closed. These are the only two sets in $\mathbb{R}^n$ that are both open and closed. (See Problem 14.)

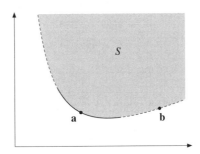

Figure 3

Economic analysis often involves sets defined in quite complicated ways. It may be difficult to see the practical relevance of knowing whether a given set includes or excludes a particular boundary point. Yet such knowledge can determine which mathematical tools are applicable.

PROBLEMS FOR SECTION 13.1

1. Show that if the points $\mathbf{x}$ and $\mathbf{y}$ in $\mathbb{R}^n$ satisfy $d(\mathbf{x}, \mathbf{y}) < r$, then $-r < x_j - y_j < r$ for all $j = 1, 2, \ldots, n$.

2. Show that if $\mathbf{x}$, $\mathbf{y}$, and $\mathbf{z}$ are points in $\mathbb{R}^n$, then $|d(\mathbf{z}, \mathbf{x}) - d(\mathbf{z}, \mathbf{y})| \leq d(\mathbf{x}, \mathbf{y})$.

3. Show that if $\mathbf{x} = (x_1, \ldots, x_n)$ and $\mathbf{y} = (y_1, \ldots, y_n)$ are points in $\mathbb{R}^n$, then $d(\mathbf{x}, \mathbf{y}) \leq \sum_{j=1}^{n} |x_j - y_j|$.

4. The figures below suggest five different sets in the plane. Which of them are open and/or closed? (Since the sets are imprecisely defined, the answer can only be rough.)

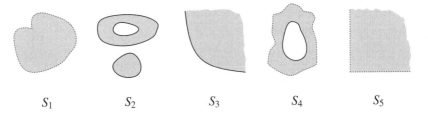

S_1 S_2 S_3 S_4 S_5

5. Sketch the set $S = \{ (x, y) \in \mathbb{R}^2 : x > 0, \ y \geq 1/x \}$ in the plane. Is S closed?

6. (a) Let E be the subset in $\mathbb{R}^2$ consisting of the point $(0, 0)$ and all points of the form $(1/n, 1/m)$ for $n = 1, 2, \ldots$ and $m = 1, 2, \ldots$. Is E closed?

   (b) Let F be the subset in $\mathbb{R}^2$ defined by $F = \{(0, 0) \cup \{(1/n, 1/n) : n = 1, 2, \ldots\}$. Is F closed?

7. Consider the following three subsets of $\mathbb{R}^2$:

$$A = \{(x, y) : y = 1, \ x \in \bigcup_{n=1}^{\infty}(2n, 2n + 1)\}$$
$$B = \{(x, y) : y \in (0, 1), \ x \in \bigcup_{n=1}^{\infty}(2n, 2n + 1)\}$$
$$C = \{(x, y) : y = 1, \ x \in \bigcup_{n=1}^{\infty}[2n, 2n + 1]\}$$

For each of these sets determine whether it is open, closed, or neither.

8. Show that the boundary ∂S of any set S in $\mathbb{R}^n$ is closed.

9. (a) Show that, if S and T are subsets of $\mathbb{R}^n$ such that $S \subseteq T$, then

$$\text{int}(S) \subseteq \text{int}(T) \quad \text{and} \quad \text{cl}(S) \subseteq \text{cl}(T)$$

   (b) Show that for any set S in $\mathbb{R}^n$, the closure $\text{cl}(S)$ is a closed set.

10. Let S be a subset of $\mathbb{R}^n$, and let $\mathcal{U} = \{U \subseteq \mathbb{R}^n : U \subseteq S$ and U is open$\}$ be the family of all open subsets of S. Similarly, let $\mathcal{F} = \{F \subseteq \mathbb{R}^n : F \supseteq S$ and F is closed$\}$ be the family of all closed supersets of S.

    (a) Show that $\text{int}(S) = \bigcup_{U \in \mathcal{U}} U$. Thus $\text{int}(S)$ is the largest open subset of S.

    (b) Show that $\text{cl}(S) = \bigcap_{F \in \mathcal{F}} F$. Thus $\text{cl}(S)$ is the smallest closed set containing S.

11. Show by an example that the union of infinitely many closed sets need not be closed. (*Hint:* Look at $\bigcup_{i=1}^{\infty} A_i$, where $A_i = \{1/i\} \subseteq \mathbb{R}$ for $i = 1, 2, \ldots$.)

12. Use De Morgan's laws (A.1.10) and the results of Theorem 13.1.1 to prove properties (b) and (c) in Theorem 13.1.2.

HARDER PROBLEMS

13. Let $\mathbb{Q}$ be the set of rational numbers. Prove that $\overline{\mathbb{Q}} = \mathbb{R}$ and $\partial\mathbb{Q} = \mathbb{R}$. What is the interior of $\mathbb{Q}$?

14. Prove that the empty set $\emptyset$ and the whole space $\mathbb{R}^n$ are the only sets in $\mathbb{R}^n$ that are both open and closed.

15. Which of the following statements are true for all subsets S and T of $\mathbb{R}^n$?

    (a) $\text{int}(\overline{S}) = \text{int}(S)$ (b) $\overline{S \cup T} = \overline{S} \cup \overline{T}$

    (c) $\partial S \subseteq S$ (d) S is open $\Longrightarrow S \cap T \subseteq \overline{S \cap T}$

13.2 Topology and Convergence

A **sequence** $\{\mathbf{x}_k\} = \{\mathbf{x}_k\}_{k=1}^{\infty} = \{\mathbf{x}_k\}_k$ in $\mathbb{R}^n$ is a function that for each natural number k yields a corresponding point $\mathbf{x}_k$ in $\mathbb{R}^n$. (See Section A.3.) The point $\mathbf{x}_k$ is called the *kth term* or *kth element* of the sequence. Note that the terms of a sequence need not all be distinct.

CONVERGENCE OF A SEQUENCE

A sequence $\{\mathbf{x}_k\}$ in $\mathbb{R}^n$ **converges** to a point $\mathbf{x}$ if for each $\varepsilon > 0$ there exists a natural number N such that $\mathbf{x}_k \in B_\varepsilon(\mathbf{x})$ for all $k > N$, or equivalently, if $\qquad\qquad$ (1) $d(\mathbf{x}_k, \mathbf{x}) \to 0$ as $k \to \infty$.

In other words, each open ball around $\mathbf{x}$, however small its radius ε, must contain $\mathbf{x}_k$ for all sufficiently large k. Geometrically speaking, as k increases, the points $\mathbf{x}_k$ must eventually all become concentrated around $\mathbf{x}$. Note that $\mathbf{x}_k$ need not approach $\mathbf{x}$ from any fixed direction, and the distance $d(\mathbf{x}_k, \mathbf{x})$ need not decrease monotonically as k increases.

If $\{\mathbf{x}_k\}$ converges to $\mathbf{x}$ we write

$$\mathbf{x}_k \to \mathbf{x} \quad \text{as} \quad k \to \infty, \quad \text{or} \quad \lim_{k\to\infty} \mathbf{x}_k = \mathbf{x}$$

and call $\mathbf{x}$ the **limit** of the sequence.

It follows from the definition of convergence that a sequence can have at most one limit (Problem 2). If a sequence is not convergent, it is **divergent**.

The definitions of limits and convergence generalize the corresponding definitions in Section A.3 for sequences of real numbers. The following result states that a sequence $\{\mathbf{x}_k\}$ in $\mathbb{R}^n$ will converge to a vector $\mathbf{x}$ if and only if each of its n component sequences converges (in $\mathbb{R}$) to the corresponding component of $\mathbf{x}$.

THEOREM 13.2.1 (CONVERGENCE OF EACH COMPONENT)

Let $\{\mathbf{x}_k\}$ be a sequence in $\mathbb{R}^n$. Then $\{\mathbf{x}_k\}$ converges to the vector $\mathbf{x}$ in $\mathbb{R}^n$ if and only if for each $j = 1, \ldots, n$, the real number sequence $\{x_k^{(j)}\}_{k=1}^{\infty}$, consisting of the jth component of each vector $\mathbf{x}_k$, converges to $x^{(j)}$, the jth component of $\mathbf{x}$.

Proof: For every k and every j one has $d(\mathbf{x}_k, \mathbf{x}) = \|\mathbf{x}_k - \mathbf{x}\| \geq \left| x_k^{(j)} - x^{(j)} \right|$. It follows that if $\mathbf{x}_k \to \mathbf{x}$, then $x_k^{(j)} \to x^{(j)} = x^{(j)}$.

Suppose on the other hand that $x_k^{(j)} \to x^{(j)}$ for $j = 1, 2, \ldots, n$. Then, given any $\varepsilon > 0$, for each $j = 1, \ldots, n$ there exists a number N_j such that $|x_k^{(j)} - x^{(j)}| < \varepsilon/\sqrt{n}$ for all $k > N_j$. It follows that

$$d(\mathbf{x}_k, \mathbf{x}) = \sqrt{\left| x_k^{(1)} - x^{(1)} \right|^2 + \cdots + \left| x_k^{(n)} - x^{(n)} \right|^2} < \sqrt{\varepsilon^2/n + \cdots + \varepsilon^2/n} = \sqrt{\varepsilon^2} = \varepsilon$$

for all $k > \max\{N_1, \ldots, N_n\}$. Therefore $\mathbf{x}_k \to \mathbf{x}$ as $k \to \infty$. $\blacksquare$

This characterization makes it easy to translate theorems about sequences of numbers into theorems about sequences in $\mathbb{R}^n$.

Let $\{\mathbf{x}_k\}$ be a sequence in $\mathbb{R}^n$. Consider a strictly increasing sequence $k_1 < k_2 < k_3 < \cdots$ of natural numbers, and let $\mathbf{y}_j = \mathbf{x}_{k_j}$ for $j = 1, 2, \ldots$. The sequence $\{\mathbf{y}_j\}_{j=1}^{\infty}$ is called a **subsequence** of $\{\mathbf{x}_k\}$, and is often denoted by $\{\mathbf{x}_{k_j}\}_{j=1}^{\infty}$. All terms of the subsequence $\{\mathbf{x}_{k_j}\}_j$ are present in the original sequence $\{\mathbf{x}_k\}_k$, but some or even most terms of the original sequence may be omitted as long as infinitely many remain. (See Section A.3.)

Cauchy Sequences

Cauchy sequences of real numbers are studied in Section A.3. There is a natural generalization to $\mathbb{R}^n$.

CAUCHY SEQUENCES

A sequence $\{\mathbf{x}_k\}$ in $\mathbb{R}^n$ is called a **Cauchy sequence** if for every $\varepsilon > 0$ there exists a number N such that

$$d(\mathbf{x}_k, \mathbf{x}_m) < \varepsilon \quad \text{for all } k > N \text{ and all } m > N \tag{2}$$

The main results in Section A.3 on Cauchy sequences in $\mathbb{R}$ carry over without difficulty to sequences in $\mathbb{R}^n$. In particular:

THEOREM 13.2.2 (CAUCHY'S CONVERGENCE CRITERION)

A sequence $\{\mathbf{x}_k\}$ in $\mathbb{R}^n$ is convergent if and only if it is a Cauchy sequence.

Proof: The proof that a convergent sequence is a Cauchy sequence is left to the reader as Problem 3. As for the converse, let $\{\mathbf{x}_k\}$ be a Cauchy sequence in $\mathbb{R}^n$. For each $j = 1, \ldots,$ n, the jth component sequence $\{x_k^{(j)}\}_k$ satisfies $|x_k^{(j)} - x_m^{(j)}| \leq \|\mathbf{x}_k - \mathbf{x}_m\|$, and so it is a Cauchy sequence in $\mathbb{R}$. Thus, according to Theorem A.3.5, for each j the component sequence $\{x_k^{(j)}\}_k$ must converge to a limit $\bar{x}^{(j)}$ in $\mathbb{R}$. But then Theorem 13.2.1 implies that $\{\mathbf{x}_k\}$ converges to the point $\bar{\mathbf{x}} = (\bar{x}^{(1)}, \ldots, \bar{x}^{(n)})$. ∎

Convergent sequences can be used to characterize very simply the closure of any set in $\mathbb{R}^n$.

THEOREM 13.2.3 (CLOSURE AND CONVERGENCE)

(a) For any set $S \subseteq \mathbb{R}^n$, a point $\mathbf{a}$ in $\mathbb{R}^n$ belongs to $\overline{S}$ if and only if $\mathbf{a}$ is the limit of a sequence $\{\mathbf{x}_k\}$ in S.

(b) A set $S \subseteq \mathbb{R}^n$ is closed if and only if every convergent sequence of points in S has its limit in S.

Proof: (a) Let $\mathbf{a} \in \bar{S}$. For each natural number k, the open ball $B(\mathbf{a}; 1/k)$ must intersect S, so we can choose an $\mathbf{x}_k$ in $B(\mathbf{a}; 1/k) \cap S$. Then $\mathbf{x}_k \to \mathbf{a}$ as $k \to \infty$.

On the other hand, assume that $\mathbf{a} = \lim_{k \to \infty} \mathbf{x}_k$ for some sequence $\{\mathbf{x}_k\}$ in S. We claim that $\mathbf{a} \in \bar{S}$. For any $r > 0$, we know that $\mathbf{x}_k \in B(\mathbf{a}; r)$ for all large enough k. Since $\mathbf{x}_k$ also belongs to S, it follows that $B(\mathbf{a}; r) \cap S \neq \emptyset$. Hence $\mathbf{a} \in \bar{S}$.

(b) Assume that S is closed, and let $\{\mathbf{x}_k\}$ be a convergent sequence such that $\mathbf{x}_k \in S$ for all k. By part (a), $\mathbf{x} = \lim_k \mathbf{x}_k$ belongs to $\bar{S} = S$.

Conversely, suppose that every convergent sequence of points from S has its limit in S. Let $\mathbf{a}$ be a point in $\bar{S}$. By (a), $\mathbf{a} = \lim_k \mathbf{x}_k$ for some sequence $\mathbf{x}_k$ in S, and therefore $\mathbf{a} \in S$, by hypothesis. This shows that $\bar{S} \subseteq S$, hence S is closed. ∎

Boundedness in $\mathbb{R}^n$

A set S in $\mathbb{R}^n$ is **bounded** if there exists a number M such that $\|\mathbf{x}\| \leq M$ for all $\mathbf{x}$ in S. In other words, no point of S is at a distance greater than M from the origin. A set that is not bounded is called **unbounded**. Similarly, a sequence $\{\mathbf{x}_k\}$ in $\mathbb{R}^n$ is **bounded** if the set $\{\mathbf{x}_k : k = 1, 2, \ldots\}$ is bounded.

It is easy to see that *any convergent sequence is bounded*. For if $\mathbf{x}_k \to \mathbf{x}$, then only finitely many terms of the sequence can lie outside the ball $B_1(\mathbf{x})$. The ball $B_1(\mathbf{x})$ is bounded and any finite set of points is bounded, so $\{\mathbf{x}_k\}$ must be bounded. On the other hand, a bounded sequence $\{\mathbf{x}_k\}$ in $\mathbb{R}^n$ is not necessarily convergent. In fact, a sequence $\{\mathbf{x}_k\}$ in a bounded set S may well "jump around" in S and not converge to any point.

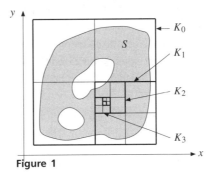

Figure 1

Suppose $\{\mathbf{x}_k\}$ is an arbitrary sequence in a bounded subset S of $\mathbb{R}^n$. Even though $\{\mathbf{x}_k\}$ is not necessarily convergent, we shall argue that it must contain a convergent subsequence.

Consider first the case where $n = 2$, so that S is a bounded set in the plane, as illustrated in Fig. 1. Then there exists a square K_0 so large that S is contained in K_0. Let L denote the length of each side of K_0. All terms of $\{\mathbf{x}_k\}$ will then belong to K_0. Divide K_0 into four equal squares, each of which has sides of length $L/2$. At least one of these four squares, say K_1, must contain $\mathbf{x}_k$ for infinitely many k. Pick one of these terms, say $\mathbf{x}_{k_1}$. Next, divide K_1 into four equal squares, each of which has sides of length $L/4$. In at least one of them, say K_2, there will still be an infinite number of terms from the sequence. Take one of them, $\mathbf{x}_{k_2}$, with $k_2 > k_1$. Continue in this way, dividing each successive square into smaller and smaller "subsquares" $K_2, K_3, \ldots$, as indicated in Fig. 1, to obtain a subsequence $\{\mathbf{x}_{k_j}\}$ of

$\{\mathbf{x}_k\}$ with $\mathbf{x}_{k_j}$ in K_j for $j = 1, 2, \dots$. It seems intuitively obvious that this subsequence converges to a unique point which is the intersection of all the squares K_j.

For the general case where n may not equal 2, suppose S is a bounded set in $\mathbb{R}^n$ and let K_0 be an n-dimensional cube containing S whose sides are all of length L. We can then divide this cube into 2^n equal parts, each having sides of length $L/2$, just as we divided the square into four equal parts when $n = 2$. This gives us a sequence $\{K_j\}$ of cubes, each lying inside its predecessor and having sides of length $L/2^j$ and a diagonal of length $\sqrt{n}L/2^j$, $j = 1, 2, \dots$. As in the two-dimensional case, we can find a subsequence $\{\mathbf{x}_{k_j}\}$ such that $\mathbf{x}_{k_j} \in K_j$ for $j = 1, 2, \dots$. Then whenever $i, j \geq m$, the points $\mathbf{x}_{k_i}$ and $\mathbf{x}_{k_j}$ both belong to K_m and therefore $d(\mathbf{x}_{k_i}, \mathbf{x}_{k_j}) \leq \sqrt{n}L/2^m$. Hence the subsequence $\{\mathbf{x}_{k_j}\}$ is a Cauchy sequence in $\mathbb{R}^n$, and is therefore convergent.

It is both unsurprising and easy to prove that, if S is unbounded, then there is a sequence in S without any convergent subsequence (see Problem 4). Hence, to summarize:

THEOREM 13.2.4

A subset S of $\mathbb{R}^n$ is bounded if and only if every sequence of points in S has a convergent subsequence.

Compactness

A set S in $\mathbb{R}^n$ is called **compact** if it is closed and bounded. For instance, the closed ball with centre $\mathbf{a}$ and radius r (> 0), defined as $\overline{B}(\mathbf{a}; r) = \{\mathbf{x} : d(\mathbf{x}, \mathbf{a}) \leq r\}$, is a compact set in $\mathbb{R}^n$. (The closed ball $\overline{B}(\mathbf{a}; r)$ is the closure of the open ball $B(\mathbf{a}; r) = \{\mathbf{x} : d(\mathbf{x}, \mathbf{a}) < r\}$.)

Compactness is a central concept in mathematical analysis. It also plays an important role in mathematical economics, for example in proving existence of solutions to maximization problems. Compact sets in $\mathbb{R}^n$ can be given the following very useful characterization.

THEOREM 13.2.5 (BOLZANO—WEIERSTRASS)

A subset S of $\mathbb{R}^n$ is compact (i.e. closed and bounded) if and only if every sequence of points in S has a subsequence that converges to a point in S.

Proof: Suppose S is compact and let $\{\mathbf{x}_k\}$ be a sequence in S. By Theorem 13.2.4, $\{\mathbf{x}_k\}$ contains a convergent subsequence. Since S is closed, it follows from Theorem 13.2.3 that the limit of the subsequence must be in S.

On the other hand, suppose that every sequence of points in S has a subsequence converging to a point of S. We must prove that S is closed and bounded. Boundedness follows from Theorem 13.2.4. To prove that S is closed, let $\mathbf{x}$ be any point in its closure $\overline{S}$. By Theorem 13.2.3 there is a sequence $\{\mathbf{x}_k\}$ in S with $\lim_{k\to\infty} \mathbf{x}_k = \mathbf{x}$. By assumption $\{\mathbf{x}_k\}$ has a subsequence $\{\mathbf{x}_{k_j}\}$ that converges to a limit $\mathbf{x}'$ in S. But $\{\mathbf{x}_{k_j}\}$ also converges also to $\mathbf{x}$. Hence, $\mathbf{x} = \mathbf{x}' \in S$. ∎

1. Examine the convergence of the following sequences in $\mathbb{R}^2$.

   (a) $\mathbf{x}_k = (1/k, 1 + 1/k)$ (b) $\mathbf{x}_k = (1 + 1/k, (1 + 1/k)^k)$

   (c) $\mathbf{x}_k = (k, 1 + 3/k)$ (d) $\mathbf{x}_k = ((k + 2)/3k, (-1)^k/2k)$

2. Prove that a sequence in $\mathbb{R}^n$ cannot converge to more than one point.

3. Prove that every convergent sequence in $\mathbb{R}^n$ is a Cauchy sequence. (*Hint:* See the proof of Theorem A.3.5.)

4. Prove that if every sequence of points from a set S in $\mathbb{R}^n$ contains a convergent subsequence, then S is bounded. (*Hint:* If S is unbounded, then for each natural number k there exists an $\mathbf{x}_k$ in S with $\|\mathbf{x}_k\| > k$.)

13.3 Continuous Functions

Section 2.7 dealt with some properties of transformations from $\mathbb{R}^n$ to $\mathbb{R}^m$. In particular, the notion of differentiability was introduced. This section takes a closer look at continuous transformations. (Logically, this discussion should have preceded Section 2.7.)

Consider first a real-valued function $z = f(\mathbf{x}) = f(x_1, \ldots, x_n)$ of n variables. Roughly speaking, f is continuous if small changes in the independent variables cause only small changes in the function value. The precise "ε–δ" definition is as follows:

CONTINUITY OF REAL-VALUED FUNCTIONS

A function f with domain $S \subseteq \mathbb{R}^n$ is **continuous** at a point $\mathbf{a}$ in S if for every $\varepsilon > 0$ there exists a $\delta > 0$ such that

$$|f(\mathbf{x}) - f(\mathbf{a})| < \varepsilon \quad \text{for all } \mathbf{x} \text{ in } S \text{ with } \|\mathbf{x} - \mathbf{a}\| < \delta \tag{1}$$

If f is continuous at every point $\mathbf{a}$ in a set S, we say that f is continuous on S.

As in the one-variable case, we have the following useful rule:

Any function of n variables that can be constructed from continuous functions by combining the operations of addition, subtraction, multiplication, division, and composition of functions, is continuous wherever it is defined.   (2)

Note that if $f(x_1, \ldots, x_n) = g(x_i)$, so that f depends on x_i alone, then continuity of the function g with respect to x_i implies continuity of f with respect to $(x_1, \ldots, x_n)$.

Consider next the general case of vector-valued functions introduced in Section 2.7.

CONTINUITY OF VECTOR-VALUED FUNCTIONS

A function $\mathbf{f} = (f_1, \ldots, f_m)$ from a subset S of $\mathbb{R}^n$ to $\mathbb{R}^m$ is said to be **continuous** at $\mathbf{x}^0$ in S if for every $\varepsilon > 0$ there exists a $\delta > 0$ such that $d(\mathbf{f}(\mathbf{x}), \mathbf{f}(\mathbf{x}^0)) < \varepsilon$ for all $\mathbf{x}$ in S with $d(\mathbf{x}, \mathbf{x}^0) < \delta$, or equivalently, such that $\mathbf{f}(B_\delta(\mathbf{x}^0) \cap S) \subseteq B_\varepsilon(\mathbf{f}(\mathbf{x}^0))$.   (3)

Intuitively, continuity of $\mathbf{f}$ at $\mathbf{x}^0$ means that $\mathbf{f}(\mathbf{x})$ is close to $\mathbf{f}(\mathbf{x}^0)$ when $\mathbf{x}$ is close to $\mathbf{x}^0$.

Frequently, the easiest way to show that a vector function is continuous, is to show that each component is continuous. To show the latter property we can use (2).

THEOREM 13.3.1   (CONTINUITY OF EACH COMPONENT)

A function $\mathbf{f} = (f_1, \ldots, f_m)$ from $S \subseteq \mathbb{R}^n$ to $\mathbb{R}^m$ is continuous at a point $\mathbf{x}^0$ in S if and only if each component function $f_j : S \to \mathbb{R}$, $j = 1, \ldots, m$, is continuous at $\mathbf{x}^0$.

Proof: Suppose $\mathbf{f}$ is continuous at $\mathbf{x}^0$. Then, for every $\varepsilon > 0$ there exists a $\delta > 0$ such that

$$|f_j(\mathbf{x}) - f_j(\mathbf{x}^0)| \leq d(\mathbf{f}(\mathbf{x}), \mathbf{f}(\mathbf{x}^0)) < \varepsilon$$

for every $\mathbf{x}$ in S with $d(\mathbf{x}, \mathbf{x}^0) < \delta$. Hence f_j is continuous at $\mathbf{x}^0$ for $j = 1, \ldots, m$.

Suppose on the other hand that each component f_j is continuous at $\mathbf{x}^0$. Then, for every $\varepsilon > 0$ and every $j = 1, \ldots, m$, there exists a $\delta_j > 0$ such that $|f_j(\mathbf{x}) - f_j(\mathbf{x}^0)| < \varepsilon/\sqrt{m}$ for every point $\mathbf{x}$ in S with $d(\mathbf{x}, \mathbf{x}^0) < \delta_j$. Let $\delta = \min\{\delta_1, \ldots, \delta_m\}$. Then $\mathbf{x} \in B_\delta(\mathbf{x}^0) \cap S$ implies that

$$d(\mathbf{f}(\mathbf{x}), \mathbf{f}(\mathbf{x}^0)) = \sqrt{|f_1(\mathbf{x}) - f_1(\mathbf{x}^0)|^2 + \cdots + |f_m(\mathbf{x}) - f_m(\mathbf{x}^0)|^2} < \sqrt{\tfrac{\varepsilon^2}{m} + \cdots + \tfrac{\varepsilon^2}{m}} = \varepsilon$$

This proves that $\mathbf{f}$ is continuous at $\mathbf{x}^0$.   ∎

Continuity and Sequences

Continuity of a function can be characterized by means of convergent sequences. In theoretical arguments this is often the easiest way to check if a function is continuous.

THEOREM 13.3.2

A function $\mathbf{f}$ from $S \subseteq \mathbb{R}^n$ into $\mathbb{R}^m$ is continuous at a point $\mathbf{x}^0$ in S if and only if $\mathbf{f}(\mathbf{x}_k) \to \mathbf{f}(\mathbf{x}^0)$ for every sequence $\{\mathbf{x}_k\}$ of points in S that converges to $\mathbf{x}^0$.

Proof of "only if": Suppose that $\mathbf{f}$ is continuous at $\mathbf{x}^0$, and let $\{\mathbf{x}_k\}$ be a sequence in S that converges to $\mathbf{x}^0$. Let $\varepsilon > 0$ be given. Then there exists a $\delta > 0$ such that $d(\mathbf{f}(\mathbf{x}), \mathbf{f}(\mathbf{x}^0)) < \varepsilon$ whenever $\mathbf{x} \in B_\delta(\mathbf{x}^0) \cap S$. Because $\mathbf{x}_k \to \mathbf{x}^0$, there exists a number N such that $d(\mathbf{x}_k, \mathbf{x}^0) < \delta$ for all $k > N$. But then $\mathbf{x}_k \in B_\delta(\mathbf{x}^0) \cap S$, and so $d(\mathbf{f}(\mathbf{x}_k), \mathbf{f}(\mathbf{x}^0)) < \varepsilon$ for all $k > N$, which implies that $\{\mathbf{f}(\mathbf{x}_k)\}$ converges to $\mathbf{f}(\mathbf{x}^0)$.

The proof of the reverse implication is left to the reader as Problem 6. ∎

The following property of continuous functions is often useful:

THEOREM 13.3.3 (CONTINUOUS FUNCTIONS PRESERVE COMPACTNESS)

Let $S \subseteq \mathbb{R}^n$ and let $\mathbf{f} : S \to \mathbb{R}^m$ be continuous. Then $\mathbf{f}(K) = \{f(\mathbf{x}) : \mathbf{x} \in K\}$ is compact for every compact subset K of S.

Proof: Let $\{\mathbf{y}_k\}$ be any sequence in $\mathbf{f}(K)$. By definition, for each k there is a point $\mathbf{x}_k$ in K such that $\mathbf{y}_k = \mathbf{f}(\mathbf{x}_k)$. Because K is compact, the sequence $\{\mathbf{x}_k\}$ has a subsequence $\{\mathbf{x}_{k_j}\}$ converging to a point $\mathbf{x}_0$ in K (by the Bolzano–Weierstrass theorem, Theorem 13.2.5). Because $\mathbf{f}$ is continuous, $\mathbf{f}(\mathbf{x}_{k_j}) \to \mathbf{f}(\mathbf{x}_0)$ as $j \to \infty$, where $\mathbf{f}(\mathbf{x}_0) \in \mathbf{f}(K)$ because $\mathbf{x}_0 \in K$. But then $\{\mathbf{y}_{k_j}\}$ is a subsequence of $\{\mathbf{y}_k\}$ that converges to a point $\mathbf{f}(\mathbf{x}_0)$ in $\mathbf{f}(K)$. So we have proved that any sequence in $\mathbf{f}(K)$ has a subsequence converging to a point of $\mathbf{f}(K)$. By Theorem 13.2.5, it follows that $\mathbf{f}(K)$ is compact. ∎

Theorem 13.3.3 can be used to prove the extreme value theorem, Theorem 3.1.3:

Proof of Theorem 3.1.3: By Theorem 13.3.3, $f(S)$ is compact. In particular, $f(S)$ is bounded, so $-\infty < a = \inf f(S)$ and $b = \sup f(S) < \infty$. Clearly, a and b are boundary points of $f(S)$. Because $f(S)$ is closed, a and b belong to $f(S)$. Hence there must exist points $\mathbf{c}$ and $\mathbf{d}$ in S such that $f(\mathbf{c}) = a$ and $f(\mathbf{d}) = b$. Obviously $\mathbf{c}$ is a minimum point and $\mathbf{d}$ is a maximum point. ∎

A Characterization of Continuity

Suppose that $\mathbf{f}$ is a continuous function from $\mathbb{R}^n$ to $\mathbb{R}^m$. If V is an open set in $\mathbb{R}^n$, the image $\mathbf{f}(V) = \{\mathbf{f}(\mathbf{x}) : \mathbf{x} \in V\}$ of V need not be open in $\mathbb{R}^m$. Nor need $\mathbf{f}(C)$ be closed if C is closed. (See Problem 3.) Nevertheless, the **inverse image** (or **preimage**) $\mathbf{f}^{-1}(U) = \{\mathbf{x} : \mathbf{f}(\mathbf{x}) \in U\}$ of an open set U under a continuous function $\mathbf{f}$ is always open. Similarly, the inverse image of any closed set must be closed. In fact, we have the following result:

THEOREM 13.3.4 (CHARACTERIZATION OF CONTINUITY)

Let $\mathbf{f}$ be any function from $\mathbb{R}^n$ to $\mathbb{R}^m$. Then $\mathbf{f}$ is continuous if and only if either of the following equivalent conditions is satisfied:

(a) $\mathbf{f}^{-1}(U)$ is open for each open set U in $\mathbb{R}^m$.

(b) $\mathbf{f}^{-1}(F)$ is closed for each closed set F in $\mathbb{R}^m$.

This theorem is a straightforward consequence of Theorem 13.3.5 below, which deals with the more general case in which **f** is not necessarily defined on all of $\mathbb{R}^n$.

EXAMPLE 1   In Examples 13.1.1 and 13.1.2 we used the definition of openness directly in order to prove that two particular sets were open. Such proofs become much easier once we understand how the above test can be applied.

For example, to show that the set $B' = B(\mathbf{x}; r) = \{\mathbf{x} : d(\mathbf{x}, \mathbf{a}) < r\}$ in Example 13.1.1 is open, define the function $f : \mathbb{R}^n \to \mathbb{R}$ by $f(\mathbf{x}) = d(\mathbf{x}, \mathbf{a})$. Then f is continuous (see Problem 4), $(-\infty, r)$ is open, and $B' = f^{-1}((-\infty, r))$. By Theorem 13.3.4, B' is open.

To prove that the set $A = \{(x, y) : x > y\}$ in Example 13.1.2 is open, define the continuous function g from $\mathbb{R}^2$ into $\mathbb{R}$ by $g(x, y) = x - y$. Note that $(x, y) \in A$ if and only if $g(x, y) > 0$. Hence $A = g^{-1}((0, \infty))$, and so A is open.

EXAMPLE 2   Let $U(\mathbf{x}) = U(x_1, \ldots, x_n)$ be a household's real-valued utility function, where **x** denotes its commodity vector and U is defined on the whole of $\mathbb{R}^n$. Recall from Example 2.2.2 that, for any real number a, the set $\Gamma_a = \{\mathbf{x} \in \mathbb{R}^n : U(\mathbf{x}) \geq a\}$ is an upper level set (or upper contour set) for U. If $U(\mathbf{x}^0) = a$, then Γ_a consists of all vectors that the household values at least as much as $\mathbf{x}^0$. (See Fig. 2.2.5.)

Let F be the closed interval $[a, \infty)$. Then

$$\Gamma_a = \{\mathbf{x} \in \mathbb{R}^n : U(\mathbf{x}) \geq a\} = \{\mathbf{x} \in \mathbb{R}^n : U(\mathbf{x}) \in F\} = U^{-1}(F)$$

According to Theorem 13.3.4, if U is continuous, then the set Γ_a is closed for each value of a. Hence, *continuous functions generate closed upper level sets*. They also generate closed lower level sets, which are sets of the form $\{\mathbf{x} \in \mathbb{R}^n : U(\mathbf{x}) \leq a\}$.

In standard microeconomic theory the set $\{\mathbf{x} \in \mathbb{R}^n : U(\mathbf{x}) = a\}$ is called an **indifference surface** for U. The subset of $\mathbb{R}$ consisting of the single point $\{a\}$ is a closed set. The indifference surface corresponding to a is the set $U^{-1}(\{a\})$. We conclude that if U is continuous, then the indifference surfaces are all closed sets.

Relative Topology

Sometimes we are concerned only with a given subset S of $\mathbb{R}^n$. For example, S might be the domain of a function which, like a Cobb–Douglas production function, is not defined on the whole of $\mathbb{R}^n$ (see Example 2.5.5). Subsets of S may be open or closed relative to S in a sense that we shall now define. These definitions will be useful in giving a characterization of continuity that applies to functions whose domain is not the whole of $\mathbb{R}^n$.

Given a set S in $\mathbb{R}^n$, we define the **relative open ball** with radius r around a point **a** in S as $B_r^S(\mathbf{a}) = B^S(\mathbf{a}; r) = B(\mathbf{a}; r) \cap S$. Once we have defined relative open balls, concepts like relative interior point, relative boundary point, relatively open set, and relatively closed set are defined in the same way as the ordinary versions of these concepts, except for the fact that $\mathbb{R}^n$ is replaced by S and balls by relative balls. Thus, given a subset A of S, a relative interior point of A is a point **a** in A such that $B^S(\mathbf{a}; r) \subseteq A$ for some $r > 0$. A point **a** is a relative boundary point of A if $\mathbf{a} \in S$ and all relative balls around **a** intersect both A and $S \setminus A$. By definition, a relatively open set consists only of relative interior points, and a relatively closed set contains all its relative boundary points. Note that $A \subseteq S$ is relatively closed in S if and only if $S \setminus A$ is relatively open in S.

Sometimes the word "relative(ly)" is replaced by the expression "in the relative topology of", e.g. "A is open in the relative topology of S". Note the following result:

(a) A is relatively open in S $\iff$ $A = U \cap S$ for some open set U in $\mathbb{R}^n$.

(b) A is relatively closed in S $\iff$ $A = F \cap S$ for some closed set F in $\mathbb{R}^n$.

(4)

Proof: Suppose first that A is relatively open in S. By definition, for each $\mathbf{a}$ in A there exists a ball $B(\mathbf{a}; r_{\mathbf{a}})$ such that $B(\mathbf{a}; r_{\mathbf{a}}) \cap S \subseteq A$. Then

$$A \subseteq \bigcup_{\mathbf{a} \in A} \left(B(\mathbf{a}; r_{\mathbf{a}}) \cap S \right) \subseteq A$$

and therefore

$$A = \bigcup_{\mathbf{a} \in A} \left(B(\mathbf{a}; r_{\mathbf{a}}) \cap S \right) = \left(\bigcup_{\mathbf{a} \in A} B(\mathbf{a}; r_{\mathbf{a}}) \right) \cap S$$

Let $U = \bigcup_{\mathbf{a} \in A} B(\mathbf{a}; r_{\mathbf{a}})$. Then U is an open set by Theorem 13.1.1 (b), and we have just shown that $A = U \cap S$.

On the other hand, suppose U is open in $\mathbb{R}^n$ and that $A = U \cap S$. If $\mathbf{a}$ is an arbitrary point in A, then $\mathbf{a} \in U$, so there exists an open ball $B(\mathbf{a}; r) \subseteq U$. It follows that $\mathbf{a} \in B(\mathbf{a}; r) \cap S \subseteq U \cap S = A$, so $\mathbf{a}$ is a relative interior point of A. Hence A is relatively open in S. This proves statement (a).

To prove (b), note that if A is relatively closed in S then $S \setminus A$ is relatively open, so $S \setminus A = U \cap S$ for some open set U in $\mathbb{R}^n$. But then $A = S \setminus (S \setminus A) = S \setminus (U \cap S) = S \setminus U = (\mathbb{R}^n \setminus U) \cap S$, and $F = \mathbb{R}^n \setminus U$ is closed in $\mathbb{R}^n$.

Conversely, if $A = F \cap S$ for some closed F in $\mathbb{R}^n$, then $S \setminus A = S \setminus (F \cap S) = (\mathbb{R}^n \setminus F) \cap S$. Since $\mathbb{R}^n \setminus F$ is open in $\mathbb{R}^n$, it follows from (a) that $S \setminus A$ is relatively open in $\mathbb{R}^n$, and so A is relatively closed. ∎

Note that we can choose $F = \bar{A}$ in (4)(b)—i.e. A is relatively closed in S if and only if $A = \bar{A} \cap S$. The following characterization of a relatively closed set is often useful. (The proof is left to the reader.)

A subset $F \subseteq S$ is **relatively closed** in S if and only if whenever a sequence $\{\mathbf{x}_k\}$ in F converges to a limit in S, this limit belongs to F.

(5)

Here is the promised characterization of continuous functions in terms of open or closed sets.

THEOREM 13.3.5

Let $\mathbf{f}$ be any function from $S \subseteq \mathbb{R}^n$ to $\mathbb{R}^m$. Then $\mathbf{f}$ is continuous if and only if either of the following conditions is satisfied:

(a) $\mathbf{f}^{-1}(U)$ is relatively open for each open set U in $\mathbb{R}^m$.

(b) $\mathbf{f}^{-1}(F)$ is relatively closed for each closed set F in $\mathbb{R}^m$.

Proof: (a) Let us first prove the "only if" part. Suppose $\mathbf{f}$ is continuous and U is an open set in $\mathbb{R}^m$. We want to show that $\mathbf{f}^{-1}(U)$ is open in the relative topology of S. Let $\mathbf{x}$ be any point in $\mathbf{f}^{-1}(U)$. Then

$f(x) \in U$, and since U is open, there is an $\varepsilon > 0$ such that $B(f(x); \varepsilon) \subseteq U$. Since f is continuous at x, there exists a $\delta > 0$ such that $f(x') \in B(f(x); \varepsilon) \subseteq U$ for all x' in $B(x; \delta) \cap S = B^S(x; \delta)$. Then $B^S(x; \delta) \subseteq f^{-1}(U)$, and so x is a relative interior point of $f^{-1}(U)$. It follows that $f^{-1}(U)$ is open.

   To prove the "if" part of (a), supposes that the inverse image of every open set in $\mathbb{R}^m$ is a relatively open set in S. Let x be any point in S. We shall show that f is continuous at x. Let ε be an arbitrary positive number. Then $U = B(f(x); \varepsilon)$ is an open set in $\mathbb{R}^m$, and $f^{-1}(U)$ is a relatively open set in S. Since $x \in f^{-1}(U)$, there is a relatively open ball $B^S(x; \delta)$ around x such that $B^S(x; \delta) \subseteq f^{-1}(U)$. Then for every x' in $B^S(x; \delta) = B(x; \delta) \cap S$, we have $f(x') \in U = B(f(x); \varepsilon)$. It follows that f is continuous at x.

   (b) Recall that a set F in $\mathbb{R}^m$ is closed if and only if its complement $\mathbb{R}^m \setminus F$ in $\mathbb{R}^m$ is open. Because

$$f^{-1}(\mathbb{R}^m \setminus F) = \{x \in S : f(x) \notin F\} = S \setminus f^{-1}(F)$$

the result for closed sets follows from that for open sets (and conversely).   ∎

PROBLEMS FOR SECTION 13.3

1. Prove that the set $S = \{(x, y) : 2x - y < 2 \text{ and } x - 3y < 5\}$ is open in $\mathbb{R}^2$.

2. Prove that the set $S = \{x \in \mathbb{R}^n : g_j(x) \leq 0, \ j = 1, \ldots, m\}$ is a closed set if the functions g_j are all continuous.

3. Give examples of subsets S of $\mathbb{R}$ and continuous functions $f : \mathbb{R} \to \mathbb{R}$ such that
   (a) S is closed, but $f(S)$ is not closed.
   (b) S is open, but $f(S)$ is not open.
   (c) S is bounded, but $f(S)$ is not bounded.

4. For a fixed a in $\mathbb{R}^n$, prove that the function $f : \mathbb{R}^n \to \mathbb{R}$ defined by $f(x) = d(x, a)$ is continuous. (*Hint:* See Problem 13.1.2.)

5. Let S be a closed set in $\mathbb{R}^n$ and y a fixed point in $\mathbb{R}^n$. Let $h(x) = d(x, y)$ for all x in S. Then $h(x)$ is a continuous function of x, by Problem 4. Use the extreme-value theorem to show that h attains a minimum at some point of S. (*Hint:* If x' is an arbitrary point in S, then any possible minimum point for $h(x)$ must lie in the intersection of S and the closed ball $\bar{B}(y; r)$ with radius $r = d(x', y)$.)

6. Prove the reverse implication in the proof of Theorem 13.3.2.

13.4 Maximum Theorems

Economic theory abounds with "comparative static" results. These describe what happens to an optimal solution in response to changes in exogenous parameters such as prices. In particular, will small changes in these parameters lead to only small changes in the criterion function? And to small changes in the optimal solution? The purpose of this section is to give some such results. Other results of this kind are presented in Chapter 14.

Suppose that $f(\mathbf{x}, \mathbf{y}) = f(x_1, \ldots, x_n, y_1, \ldots, y_m)$ is a continuous function defined for all $\mathbf{x}$ in X and all $\mathbf{y}$ in Y, where $X \subseteq \mathbb{R}^n$ and $Y \subseteq \mathbb{R}^m$. Suppose too that Y is *compact*. Then the extreme-value theorem (Theorem 3.1.3) implies that for every $\mathbf{x}$ in X the problem of maximizing $f(\mathbf{x}, \mathbf{y})$ subject to $\mathbf{y} \in Y$ has a solution. The maximum value of $f(\mathbf{x}, \mathbf{y})$ will depend on $\mathbf{x}$. Define the (**optimal**) **value function** $V : X \to \mathbb{R}$ for the problem by

$$V(\mathbf{x}) = \max_{\mathbf{y} \in Y} f(\mathbf{x}, \mathbf{y}) \tag{1}$$

The next theorem tells us that $V(\mathbf{x})$ is in fact continuous. For a given $\mathbf{x}$ in X there may be several $\mathbf{y}$ in Y that maximize $f(\mathbf{x}, \mathbf{y})$. However, it turns out that if for every $\mathbf{x}$ there is a *unique* $\mathbf{y} = \mathbf{y}(\mathbf{x})$ that solves problem (1), then $\mathbf{y}(\mathbf{x})$ varies continuously with $\mathbf{x}$.

THEOREM 13.4.1 (THE MAXIMUM THEOREM: THE SIMPLEST CASE)

Suppose that f is a continuous function from $X \times Y$ to $\mathbb{R}$, where $X \subseteq \mathbb{R}^n$, $Y \subseteq \mathbb{R}^m$, and Y is compact, with $X, Y \neq \emptyset$. Then:

(a) The value function $V(\mathbf{x}) = \max_{\mathbf{y} \in Y} f(\mathbf{x}, \mathbf{y})$ is a continuous function of $\mathbf{x}$.

(b) If the maximization problem has a unique solution $\mathbf{y} = \mathbf{y}(\mathbf{x})$ for every $\mathbf{x}$, then $\mathbf{y}(\mathbf{x})$ is continuous.

Proof: (a) We argue by contradiction. By the extreme-value theorem, $V(\mathbf{x})$ is defined for every $\mathbf{x}$ in X. Suppose V happens to be discontinuous at some $\mathbf{x}^0$ in X. By Theorem 13.3.2, there exists a sequence $\{\mathbf{x}_k\}$ converging to $\mathbf{x}^0$ such that $\{V(\mathbf{x}_k)\}$ does not converge to $V(\mathbf{x}^0)$. So there is an $\varepsilon > 0$ such that

$$|V(\mathbf{x}_k) - V(\mathbf{x}^0)| \geq \varepsilon \tag{$*$}$$

for infinitely many k. Hence there is a subsequence of $\{\mathbf{x}_k\}$ such that $(*)$ holds for every term of that subsequence. Replace the sequence $\{\mathbf{x}_k\}$ by this subsequence. Then we still have a sequence that converges to $\mathbf{x}^0$.

By the extreme-value theorem, for each k there is a $\mathbf{y}_k$ in Y such that $V(\mathbf{x}_k) = f(\mathbf{x}_k, \mathbf{y}_k)$. Use the Bolzano–Weierstrass theorem to choose a subsequence $\{\mathbf{y}_{k_j}\}_j$ that converges to some $\mathbf{y}^0$ in Y. For arbitrary $\mathbf{y}$ in Y, $f(\mathbf{x}_{k_j}, \mathbf{y}) \leq f(\mathbf{x}_{k_j}, \mathbf{y}_{k_j})$, so taking limits, we get $f(\mathbf{x}^0, \mathbf{y}) \leq f(\mathbf{x}^0, \mathbf{y}^0)$. Hence, $V(\mathbf{x}^0) = \max_{\mathbf{y}} f(\mathbf{x}^0, \mathbf{y}) \leq f(\mathbf{x}^0, \mathbf{y}^0)$. But by definition, $V(\mathbf{x}^0) \geq f(\mathbf{x}^0, \mathbf{y}^0)$, so $V(\mathbf{x}^0) = f(\mathbf{x}^0, \mathbf{y}^0)$. Then $V(\mathbf{x}^0) = \lim_j f(\mathbf{x}_{kj}, \mathbf{y}_{k_j}) = \lim_j V(\mathbf{x}_{k_j})$, contradicting $(*)$.

(b) Suppose that $\mathbf{y}(\mathbf{x})$ is not continuous at $\mathbf{x}^0$ in X. Then there exists a sequence $\{\mathbf{x}_k\}$ in X converging towards $\mathbf{x}^0$, such that $\{\mathbf{y}(\mathbf{x}_k)\}$ does not converge to $\mathbf{y}(\mathbf{x}^0)$. For some $\varepsilon > 0$ there exists a subsequence $\{\mathbf{x}_{k_j}\}$ such that $\|\mathbf{y}(\mathbf{x}_{k_j}) - \mathbf{y}(\mathbf{x}^0)\| \geq \varepsilon$ for all j. By compactness of Y, this sequence again has a subsequence $\{\tilde{\mathbf{x}}_i\}_i$ such that $\{\tilde{\mathbf{y}}_i\} = \{\mathbf{y}(\tilde{\mathbf{x}}_i)\}$ converges to some $\mathbf{y}' \neq \mathbf{y}(\mathbf{x}^0)$. Then $V(\mathbf{x}^0) = \lim_i V(\tilde{\mathbf{x}}_i) = \lim_i f(\tilde{\mathbf{x}}_i, \mathbf{y}(\tilde{\mathbf{x}}_i)) = f(\mathbf{x}^0, \mathbf{y}')$. This contradicts the hypothesis that the solution $\mathbf{y}(\mathbf{x})$ is unique. ∎

Note that the value function $V(\mathbf{x})$ in Theorem 13.4.1 is continuous even if $\mathbf{y}(\mathbf{x})$ is not unique. The theorem is illustrated (for the case $n = m = 1$) in Figs. 1 and 2.

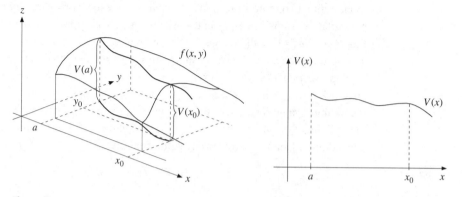

Figure 1   **Figure 2**

Figure 1 shows the graph of a function $f(x, y)$. For each x in X the function has a maximum value $V(x)$ w.r.t. y. The figure suggests that if the function $f(x, y)$ is continuous, then $V(x)$ is also likely to be a continuous function of x. The graph of V is shown in Fig. 2. Furthermore, if for each x there is only *one* value of y that maximizes $f(x, y)$, it seems plausible that this maximizing y will also vary continuously with x.

EXAMPLE 1   Let $X = \mathbb{R}$ and $Y = [-1, 2]$. Suppose that $f : X \times Y \to \mathbb{R}$ is defined by $f(x, y) = xy^2$. Consider the problem

$$\max f(x, y) \quad \text{subject to} \quad -1 \le y \le 2$$

For a fixed $x < 0$, $f(x, y) = xy^2$ is clearly maximized at $y = 0$, and the maximum value is 0. For a fixed $x > 0$, the function xy^2 is maximized at $y = 2$, and the maximum value is $4x$. Finally, for $x = 0$, all values of y in $[-1, 2]$ maximize xy^2, and the maximum value is 0. Thus, the value function $V(x)$ for the problem is

$$V(x) = \begin{cases} 0 & \text{if } x < 0 \\ 4x & \text{if } x \ge 0 \end{cases}$$

Hence, V is continuous for all x, and differentiable for $x \ne 0$. Note also that the maximum point $y(x)$ is unique for all $x \ne 0$, and is a continuous function of x in each of the two intervals $(-\infty, 0)$ and $(0, \infty)$.

EXAMPLE 2   Let $X = Y = \mathbb{R}$, and define $f : X \times Y \to \mathbb{R}$ by $f(x, y) = e^{-(xy-1)^2}$. It is easy to see that

$$V(x) = \max_{y \in \mathbb{R}} f(x, y) = \begin{cases} e^{-1} & \text{if } x = 0 \\ 1 & \text{if } x \ne 0 \end{cases}$$

Thus the value function is discontinuous at $x = 0$. The corresponding maximizing y is no longer a function of x, because at $x = 0$, any value of y is a maximizer. Note that in this example Y is not compact.

EXAMPLE 3   (**Maximum profit as a function of prices**.) Suppose the production of a commodity requires n different input factors. If $\mathbf{v} = (v_1, \ldots, v_n)$ is the vector of inputs, the number of units produced is $f(\mathbf{v})$. Assume that the production function f is defined and C^1 in $\mathbb{R}^n_+ = \{\mathbf{v} : \mathbf{v} \in \mathbb{R}^n, \ \mathbf{v} \geq \mathbf{0}\}$.[1] Assume moreover that for each positive number a there exists a number K_a such that if $\|\mathbf{v}\| \geq K_a$, then $\nabla f(\mathbf{v}) \cdot \mathbf{v}' < a$, where $\mathbf{v}' = \mathbf{v}/\|\mathbf{v}\|$. (Here $\mathbf{v}'$ is the unit vector with the same direction as $\mathbf{v}$, and $\nabla f(\mathbf{v}) \cdot \mathbf{v}' = f'_{\mathbf{v}'}(\mathbf{v})$ is the directional derivative of f at the point $\mathbf{v}$ in the direction $\mathbf{v}'$.)

If the selling price per unit of the product is p and the unit prices of the input factors are given by the vector $\mathbf{q} = (q_1, \ldots, q_n)$, then the profit as a function of the input vector $\mathbf{v}$ is $\pi(\mathbf{v}) = pf(\mathbf{v}) - \mathbf{q} \cdot \mathbf{v}$. The following facts can be established:

(a) For given prices $p > 0$ and $\mathbf{q} \gg \mathbf{0}$, the profit function $\pi(\mathbf{v})$ attains a maximum value $V(p, \mathbf{q})$ as $\mathbf{v}$ runs through $\mathbb{R}^n_+$.

(b) $V(p, \mathbf{q})$ is a continuous function of $(p, \mathbf{q})$ over $\mathbb{R}^{n+1}_{++} = \{(p, \mathbf{q}) : p > 0, \ \mathbf{q} \gg \mathbf{0}\}$.

To prove (a), choose positive numbers k and c such that $k > p$ and $(c, \ldots, c) \ll \mathbf{q}$. Define $a = c/(k\sqrt{n})$ and let K_a be as defined above. Then the set $D_a = \{\mathbf{v} \in \mathbb{R}^n : \mathbf{v} \geq \mathbf{0}, \ \|\mathbf{v}\| \leq K_a\}$ is a closed and bounded subset of $\mathbb{R}^n_+$. According to the extreme value theorem, $\pi(\mathbf{v})$ attains a maximum value $V(p, \mathbf{q})$ over D_a. To show that $V(p, \mathbf{q})$ is really the maximum value of $\pi(\mathbf{v})$ over the *whole* of $\mathbb{R}^n_+$, it suffices to show that for every vector $\mathbf{v}$ in $\mathbb{R}^n_+ \setminus D_a$ we can find a $\mathbf{v}_a$ in D_a with $\pi(\mathbf{v}_a) > \pi(\mathbf{v})$. Then $V(p, \mathbf{q}) \geq \pi(\mathbf{v}_a) > \pi(\mathbf{v})$.

Consider a ray S from the origin into $\mathbb{R}^n_+$, and let $\mathbf{v} \neq \mathbf{0}$ be a point of S. Then $\mathbf{v}' = \mathbf{v}/\|\mathbf{v}\|$ is a unit vector with the same direction as S, and the directional derivative of π at $\mathbf{v}$ in the direction $\mathbf{v}'$ is

$$\pi'_{\mathbf{v}'}(\mathbf{v}) = \nabla\pi(\mathbf{v}) \cdot \mathbf{v}' = p\nabla f(\mathbf{v}) \cdot \mathbf{v}' - \mathbf{q} \cdot \mathbf{v}'$$

Since $\|\mathbf{v}'\| = 1$ and $\mathbf{v}' \geq \mathbf{0}$, the vector $\mathbf{v}' = (v'_1, \ldots, v'_n)$ has at least one component $v'_i \geq 1/\sqrt{n}$, and then $\mathbf{q} \cdot \mathbf{v}' \geq q_i v'_i > c/\sqrt{n}$, by definition of c. If $\|\mathbf{v}\| \geq K_a$, then $\nabla f(\mathbf{v}) \cdot \mathbf{v}' < a$, so the directional derivative of π along S is

$$\pi'_{\mathbf{v}'}(\mathbf{v}) < pa - c/\sqrt{n} < ka - c/\sqrt{n} = 0$$

It follows that $\pi(\mathbf{v})$ is strictly decreasing along the ray S beyond the distance K_a from the origin, i.e. outside the compact the set D_a. If $\|\mathbf{v}\| > K_a$, then $\pi(\mathbf{v}) < \pi(\mathbf{v}_a)$, where $\mathbf{v}_a = (K_a/\|\mathbf{v}\|)\mathbf{v} \in D_a$ is the point on S at the distance K_a from the origin. This proves (a).

It remains to prove (b). Let c and k be positive numbers and let $a = c/(k\sqrt{n})$. Define D_a as before. From the proof of (a) we see that for all $(p, \mathbf{q})$ in the open set

$$U_{k,c} = \{(p, \mathbf{q}) \in \mathbb{R}^{n+1}_{++} : 0 < p < k, \ \mathbf{q} \gg (c, \ldots, c)\}$$

we have

$$V(p, \mathbf{q}) = \max_{\mathbf{v} \in D_a} \left(pf(\mathbf{v}) - \mathbf{q} \cdot \mathbf{v}\right)$$

Since D_a is compact, it follows from Theorem 13.4.1 that V is continuous in $U_{k,c}$. Since each point $(p, \mathbf{q}) \in \mathbb{R}^{n+1}_{++}$ is contained in such an open set $U_{k,c}$ for appropriate values of k and c, V is continuous everywhere in $\mathbb{R}^{n+1}_{++}$.

Let us now extend the scope of the maximum theorem by allowing the fixed set Y to be replaced with a set of the form

$$F(\mathbf{x}) = \{\mathbf{y} \in Y : g_i(\mathbf{x}, \mathbf{y}) \leq a_i, \quad i = 1, \ldots, l\}$$

---

[1] The inequality $\mathbf{v} \geq \mathbf{u}$ means $v_i \geq u_i$ for all $i = 1, \ldots, n$. If $v_i > u_i$ for all i, we write $\mathbf{v} \gg \mathbf{u}$.

that varies with $\mathbf{x}$. Here the functions g_i and the numbers a_i are given. The maximization problem becomes

$$\text{maximize } f(\mathbf{x}, \mathbf{y}) \quad \text{subject to} \quad \mathbf{y} \in F(\mathbf{x}) \tag{2}$$

Define the corresponding **value function**,

$$V(\mathbf{x}) = \sup_{\mathbf{y} \in F(\mathbf{x})} f(\mathbf{x}, \mathbf{y}) \tag{3}$$

Then the following theorem holds:

THEOREM 13.4.2 (THE MAXIMUM THEOREM: A MORE GENERAL CASE)

Suppose that $f(\mathbf{x}, \mathbf{y})$ and $g_i(\mathbf{x}, \mathbf{y})$, $i = 1, \ldots, l$, are continuous functions from $X \times Y$ into $\mathbb{R}$, where $X \subseteq \mathbb{R}^n$, $Y \subseteq \mathbb{R}^m$, and Y is compact. Suppose further that for every $\mathbf{x}$ in X, the set $F^\circ(\mathbf{x}) = \{\mathbf{y} \in Y : g_i(\mathbf{x}, \mathbf{y}) < a_i, i = 1, \ldots, l\}$ is nonempty and $\overline{F^\circ(\mathbf{x})} = F(\mathbf{x})$, where $F(\mathbf{x}) = \{\mathbf{y} \in Y : g_i(\mathbf{x}, \mathbf{y}) \leq a_i, i = 1, \ldots, l\}$. Then the value function $V(\mathbf{x})$ is continuous over X. Moreover, if the maximization problem has a unique maximum $\mathbf{y} = \mathbf{y}(\mathbf{x})$ for each $\mathbf{x}$ in X, then $\mathbf{y}(\mathbf{x})$ is continuous.

A proof can be obtained by combining Theorem 14.2.1 and Example 14.1.5 in the next chapter.

EXAMPLE 4   Let $f(x_1, y_1)$ and $g(x_2, y_2)$ be two continuous production functions that give the quantities produced of two commodities as functions of the input factors $x_1 \geq 0$, $y_1 \geq 0$, $x_2 \geq 0$, and $y_2 \geq 0$. Say x_i denotes labour and y_i energy. The sale prices are p and q, respectively. An entrepreneur wishes to choose x_1, x_2, y_1, and y_2 such that the revenue $pf(x_1, y_1) + qg(x_2, y_2)$ is maximized, given that the total outlays for the input factors do not exceed the budget constraint $m > 0$. Thus, the entrepreneur's problem is

$$\max \ pf(x_1, y_1) + qg(x_2, y_2) \quad \text{subject to} \quad r(x_1 + x_2) + s(y_1 + y_2) \leq m \tag{$*$}$$

where $r > 0$ and $s > 0$ are the prices of inputs. The set

$$F(r, s, m) = \{(x_1, x_2, y_1, y_2) \in \mathbb{R}_+^4 : r(x_1 + x_2) + s(y_1 + y_2) \leq m\}$$

is compact. (It is obviously closed, and it is also bounded, because if $(x_1, x_2, y_1, y_2) \in F(r, s, m)$ then $rx_i \leq m$ and $sy_i \leq m$, i.e. $x_i \in [0, m/r]$, $y_i \in [0, m/s]$). Theorem 13.4.2 implies that the maximum revenue is a continuous function of (p, q). If f and g are strictly concave, then $pf(x_1, y_1) + qg(x_2, y_2)$ is strictly concave. Since Y is convex and any maximum of a strictly concave function over a convex set is unique (if it exists), in this case there is a unique maximum point $(x_1^*, x_2^*, y_1^*, y_2^*)$, which must be a continuous function of (p, q).

Theorem 13.4.2 implies that for arbitrary chosen numbers m^* and k^*, the maximum profit is a continuous function of (p, q, r, s, m) for all $p > 0$, $q > 0$, $r, s \in [k^*, \infty)$, and $m \in (0, m^*]$. For such values of r, s, and m, we have $F(r, s, m) \subseteq F(k^*, k^*, m^*)$, the latter being a compact set. (In this case it is easy to see that $\overline{F^\circ(\mathbf{x})} = F(\mathbf{x})$.)

1. Let $f(x, y, z) = \ln(4 + y + z) + x^2 + e^z x^2 + e^{x^2 yz}$, let $S = \{(y, z) : y \geq 1, z \geq 1, y^2 + z^2 \leq 4\} \subseteq \mathbb{R}^2$, and define

$$v(x) = \max_{(y,z)\in S} f(x, y, z)$$

(a) Why is v continuous?

(b) Let $T = \{(y, z) : y > 0, z > 0, y^2 + z^2 \leq 4\} \subseteq \mathbb{R}^2$, and define

$$w(x) = \sup_{(y,z)\in T} f(x, y, z)$$

Why is w continuous? (*Hint:* With y and z positive, $f(x, y, z)$ is strictly increasing in y and in z.)

2. Use the theorems in this section to determine whether each of the following functions is continuous:

(a) $V_1(x) = \max_{u\in[0,1]} \left(e^{-xu^2} - (u - x)^2\right)$ (b) $V_2(x) = \max_{u\in(-\infty,\infty)} \left(e^{-xu^2} - (u - x)^2\right)$

13.5 Convex Sets

Section 2.2 gave the definition of convex sets and some of their basic properties. This section gives some further definitions and results that are occasionally useful in economics.

Linear Combinations of Sets

Let S and T be two arbitrary sets in $\mathbb{R}^n$. The **(vector) sum** of S and T is defined as

$$S + T = \{\mathbf{x} + \mathbf{y} : \mathbf{x} \in S \text{ and } \mathbf{y} \in T\} \tag{1}$$

Thus $S + T$ is the set of all possible sums $\mathbf{x} + \mathbf{y}$, when $\mathbf{x} \in S$ and $\mathbf{y} \in T$. For the case where S and T are subsets of $\mathbb{R}^2$, the construction is illustrated in Fig. 1. More generally, if a and b are any two scalars in $\mathbb{R}$, define $aS + bT$ as the set $\{a\mathbf{x} + b\mathbf{y} : \mathbf{x} \in S, \mathbf{y} \in T\}$. This definition does not require a and b to be nonnegative: indeed, taking $a = 1$ and $b = -1$ gives the **vector difference** $S - T$ of the two sets. Note that this is entirely different from the set-theoretic difference $S \setminus T = \{x : x \in S \text{ and } x \notin T\}$.

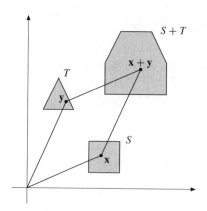

Figure 1 The sum of two sets.

EXAMPLE 1   Suppose that S is a firm's *production possibility set*, i.e. the set of all net output vectors that the firm can supply. If T is the corresponding set of a second firm, the set $S + T$ represents the *aggregate* net output vectors that the two firms can supply together.

If S and T are convex sets in $\mathbb{R}^n$, then $S + T$ is also convex, as Fig. 1 suggests. In fact, one has the following result:

$$S, T \text{ convex and } a, b \text{ real numbers} \implies aS + bT \text{ convex} \qquad (2)$$

Problem 1 asks you to prove (2), i.e. that any linear combination of two convex sets is convex. It is easy to extend this result to linear combinations of an arbitrary finite number of convex sets.

Convex Hulls

Suppose that $\mathbf{x}_1, \ldots, \mathbf{x}_m$ are vectors in $\mathbb{R}^n$. A point $\mathbf{x}$ that can be expressed in the form

$$\mathbf{x} = \lambda_1 \mathbf{x}_1 + \cdots + \lambda_m \mathbf{x}_m, \quad \text{with } \lambda_i \geq 0 \text{ for each } i \text{ and } \sum_{i=1}^{m} \lambda_i = 1 \qquad (3)$$

is called a **convex combination** of the points $\mathbf{x}_1, \ldots, \mathbf{x}_m$. The nonnegative scalars λ_i that sum to 1 are called **convex weights**. In particular, a convex combination of two points $\mathbf{x}_1$ and $\mathbf{x}_2$ takes the form $\lambda_1 \mathbf{x}_1 + \lambda_2 \mathbf{x}_2$ with $\lambda_1 \geq 0, \lambda_2 \geq 0$ and $\lambda_1 + \lambda_2 = 1$. Hence $\lambda_2 = 1 - \lambda_1$ and $\lambda_1 \mathbf{x}_1 + \lambda_2 \mathbf{x}_2 = \lambda_1 \mathbf{x}_1 + (1 - \lambda_1) \mathbf{x}_2$, with $\lambda_1 \in [0, 1]$. Thus a set S in $\mathbb{R}^n$ is convex if and only if it contains all convex combinations of each *pair* of points in S. An induction argument proves the following result (see Problem 7).

$$A \text{ convex set } S \text{ in } \mathbb{R}^n \text{ contains all convex combinations of finitely} \atop \text{many points from } S. \qquad (4)$$

If S is an *arbitrary* set in $\mathbb{R}^n$, the **convex hull** of S, denoted by co(S), is defined as

$$\text{co}(S) = \text{the set of all convex combinations of points from } S \qquad (5)$$

The convex hull is illustrated in Figs. 2 and 3.

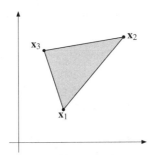

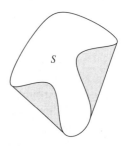

Figure 2 All convex combinations of $\mathbf{x}_1$, $\mathbf{x}_2$, $\mathbf{x}_3$.

Figure 3 If S is the unshaded set, then $\mathrm{co}(S)$ includes the shaded parts in addition.

A point in S is clearly a convex combination of itself, because $\mathbf{x} = 1 \cdot \mathbf{x}$. Hence $S \subseteq \mathrm{co}(S)$. In Problem 5 you are asked to prove that $\mathrm{co}(S)$ is always convex. Because (4) and (5) imply that any convex set containing S also contains $\mathrm{co}(S)$, the following must be true:

$$\mathrm{co}(S) \text{ is the smallest convex set containing } S \tag{6}$$

Carathéodory's Theorem

A **simplex** in $\mathbb{R}^n$ is a set $S = \mathrm{co}(V)$, where V is a set consisting of $n + 1$ points of $\mathbb{R}^n$, called the **vertices** of S, such that S has a nonempty interior. A particular example is the **unit simplex** T in $\mathbb{R}^n$, whose vertices are $\mathbf{0}$ and the n standard unit vectors $\mathbf{e}^1, \ldots, \mathbf{e}^n$, where $\mathbf{e}^i$ has its ith component equal to 1 and the other $n - 1$ components equal to 0. Obviously, any point in a simplex S can be expressed as a convex combination of at most $n + 1$ vertices. The following theorem shows that a similar result holds for all sets in $\mathbb{R}^n$.

THEOREM 13.5.1 (CARATHÉODORY)

If $S \subseteq \mathbb{R}^n$ and $\mathbf{x} \in \mathrm{co}(S)$, then $\mathbf{x}$ can be expressed as a convex combination of at most $n + 1$ points in S.

Proof: Suppose $\mathbf{x}$ equals the convex combination $\lambda_1 \mathbf{x}_1 + \cdots + \lambda_k \mathbf{x}_k$ of k points in $\mathbb{R}^n$, where $k > n + 1$. For $i = 1, \ldots, k$, let $\mathbf{y}_i = (\mathbf{x}_i, 1) \in \mathbb{R}^{n+1}$ denote the vector $\mathbf{x}_i$ augmented by an extra component equal to 1. The $k > n + 1$ vectors $\mathbf{y}_1, \ldots, \mathbf{y}_k$ in $\mathbb{R}^{n+1}$ are linearly dependent, so there exist scalars $\alpha_1, \ldots, \alpha_k$, not all 0, such that $\alpha_1 \mathbf{y}_1 + \cdots + \alpha_k \mathbf{y}_k = \mathbf{0} \in \mathbb{R}^{n+1}$, that is,

$$\alpha_1 \mathbf{x}_1 + \cdots + \alpha_k \mathbf{x}_k = \mathbf{0} \in \mathbb{R}^n \quad \text{and} \quad \alpha_1 + \cdots + \alpha_k = 0$$

Obviously, at least one α_j must be positive. Let $r = \max\{-\lambda_j / \alpha_j : \alpha_j > 0\}$. Then $r \leq 0$ and $\lambda_i + r\alpha_i \geq 0$ for all $i = 1, 2, \ldots, k$. This latter inequality is satisfied with equality for at least one index i. Hence,

$$\mathbf{x} = \mathbf{x} + r\mathbf{0} = \lambda_1 \mathbf{x}_1 + \cdots + \lambda_k \mathbf{x}_k + r(\alpha_1 \mathbf{x}_1 + \cdots + \alpha_k \mathbf{x}_k)$$
$$= (\lambda_1 + r\alpha_1)\mathbf{x}_1 + \cdots + (\lambda_k + r\alpha_k)\mathbf{x}_k$$

where $\lambda_i + r\alpha_i \geq 0$ for $i = 1, 2, \ldots, k$, and $(\lambda_1 + r\alpha_1) + \cdots + (\lambda_k + r\alpha_k) = 1$. Because $\lambda_i + r\alpha_i = 0$ for at least one i, $\mathbf{x}$ must be a convex combination of at most $k - 1$ of the points $\mathbf{x}_1, \ldots, \mathbf{x}_k$ in $\mathbb{R}^n$. Clearly, this process of eliminating points $\mathbf{x}_i$ can be repeated until $\mathbf{x}$ is expressed as a convex combination of at most $n + 1$ points. ∎

Extreme Points of Convex Sets

An **extreme point** of a convex set S in $\mathbb{R}^n$ is a point in S which does not lie "properly inside" any line segment in S. More precisely, $\mathbf{z}$ is an extreme point of S if $\mathbf{z} \in S$ and there are no $\mathbf{x}$ and $\mathbf{y}$ in S and λ in $(0, 1)$ such that $\mathbf{x} \neq \mathbf{y}$ and $\mathbf{z} = \lambda\mathbf{x} + (1 - \lambda)\mathbf{y}$. Equivalently, $\mathbf{z}$ is a point of S that cannot be expressed as a convex combination of other points of S. In $\mathbb{R}$, a compact interval has two extreme points, an open interval has no extreme points, and a half-open interval has one extreme point.

An extreme point of a convex set must be a boundary point (see Problem 6). Thus, an open ball $B_r(\mathbf{a}) \subseteq \mathbb{R}^n$ has no extreme points. For a closed ball $\overline{B_r(\mathbf{a})}$ every boundary point is an extreme point. But not all boundary points of every convex set are extreme points. To see why, look at Fig. 4, where A, B, and C are the only extreme points. The point D is a boundary point which is not an extreme point. (Why? Because D is a convex combination of B and C.)

The following theorem is stated without proof. (See Corollary 18.5.1 in Rockafellar (1970).)

THEOREM 13.5.2 (KREIN—MILMAN)

Every compact convex set in $\mathbb{R}^n$ is the convex hull of its extreme points.

This finite-dimensional result is actually due to Minkowski, and is therefore also known as Minkowski's theorem. Krein and Milman extended it to certain infinite-dimensional situations.

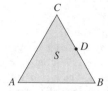

Figure 4 A, B, and C are extreme points, D is not.

Strictly Convex Sets

A **convex body** in $\mathbb{R}^n$ is a convex set with a nonempty interior. Suppose S is a convex body in $\mathbb{R}^n$ such that $\lambda\mathbf{x} + (1 - \lambda)\mathbf{y}$ is an interior point of S whenever $\mathbf{x}$ and $\mathbf{y}$ are distinct points in S and $\lambda \in (0, 1)$. In this case S is called a **strictly convex set**.

For example, a ball in n-space is a strictly convex set, whether it is open or closed. On the other hand, a closed pyramid in 3-space is convex, but not strictly convex.

It can be shown that a closed convex body S is strictly convex if and only if every boundary point of S is an extreme point. Generally, a convex body S is strictly convex if and only if every boundary point is an extreme point of the closure $\bar{S}$.

NOTE 1 Strict convexity can also be defined for sets S in $\mathbb{R}^n$ that contain no interior points. Call a point $\mathbf{z}$ in S a **relative interior point** if for every $\mathbf{c}$ in S there is a number $\mu > 1$ such that the point $\mu \mathbf{z} + (1 - \mu)\mathbf{c} = \mathbf{c} + \mu(\mathbf{z} - \mathbf{c}) \in S$, i.e. the line segment from $\mathbf{c}$ to $\mathbf{z}$ can be extended a little bit beyond $\mathbf{z}$ without leaving the set S.

The usual definition of strict convexity is this: S is *strictly convex* if for each pair of distinct points $\mathbf{x}$ and $\mathbf{y}$ in S, every point of the *open line segment* $(\mathbf{x}, \mathbf{y}) = \{\lambda \mathbf{x} + (1 - \lambda)\mathbf{y} : 0 < \lambda < 1\}$ is a relative interior point of S. For example, a circular disk (an infinitely thin coin) lying in $\mathbb{R}^3$ is strictly convex according to this definition. So is a line segment, or even a set consisting of a single point. When S has interior points, the two definitions are equivalent.

PROBLEMS FOR SECTION 13.5

1. Prove (2).

2. Construct the set $S + T$ in the cases shown in Figs. (a) and (b).

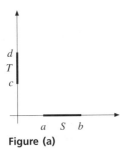

Figure (a)

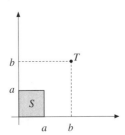

Figure (b)

3. Determine co(S) in the cases shown in Figs. (c) and (d). (In (d), S consists of the four dots.)

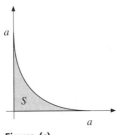

Figure (c)

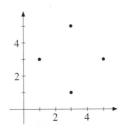

Figure (d)

4. Suppose that N units of a commodity (50 000 barrels of oil, for example) are spread out over points represented by a 2-dimensional coordinate system so that n_1 units are to be

found at the point $\mathbf{x}_1$, n_2 units are at $\mathbf{x}_2$, ..., n_m units are at $\mathbf{x}_m$, where $\sum_{i=1}^{m} n_i = N$. Explain why $\mathbf{z} = (1/N)(n_1\mathbf{x}_1 + n_2\mathbf{x}_2 + \cdots + n_m\mathbf{x}_m)$ is a convex combination of $\mathbf{x}_1$, $\mathbf{x}_2$, ..., $\mathbf{x}_m$. What is a common name for the point $\mathbf{z}$?

5. If S is an arbitrary set in $\mathbb{R}^n$, prove that the set co(S) in (5) is convex. (*Hint:* Let $\mathbf{x} = \lambda_1\mathbf{u}_1 + \cdots + \lambda_p\mathbf{u}_p$ and $\mathbf{y} = \mu_1\mathbf{v}_1 + \cdots + \mu_q\mathbf{v}_q$ be arbitrary points in co(S) with $\mathbf{u}_1, \ldots, \mathbf{u}_p$ and $\mathbf{v}_1, \ldots, \mathbf{v}_q$ all in S. Let $\lambda \in [0, 1]$ and prove by a direct argument that $\lambda\mathbf{x} + (1 - \lambda)\mathbf{y}$ is a convex combination of the points $\mathbf{u}_1, \ldots, \mathbf{u}_p, \mathbf{v}_1, \ldots, \mathbf{v}_q$.)

6. Show that an extreme point of a convex set must be a boundary point of the set. (*Hint:* Show that an interior point cannot be an extreme point.)

HARDER PROBLEMS

7. Prove (4). (*Hint:* The statement is true for $k = 2$ (and for $k = 1$). Suppose that it is true for $k = m$, where m is a positive integer, and let $\mathbf{x}_1, \ldots, \mathbf{x}_{m+1}$ be $m + 1$ points in S. Define $\mathbf{x} = \sum_{i=1}^{m} \lambda_i\mathbf{x}_i + \lambda_{m+1}\mathbf{x}_{m+1}$ with all $\lambda_i \geq 0$ and $\sum_{i=1}^{m+1} \lambda_i = 1$. If $\lambda_{m+1} = 1$, then $\mathbf{x} \in S$. Suppose next that $\lambda_{m+1} \neq 1$. Then

$$\mathbf{x} = (\lambda_1 + \cdots + \lambda_m)\left[\sum_{i=1}^{m} \frac{\lambda_i}{\lambda_1 + \cdots + \lambda_m}\mathbf{x}_i \right] + \lambda_{m+1}\mathbf{x}_{m+1}$$

is a convex combination of two points in S.)

8. Use Carathéodory's theorem to show that the convex hull of any compact set in $\mathbb{R}^n$ is compact. Give an example to show that co(S) need not be closed if S is closed but unbounded.

13.6 Separation Theorems

This section considers some theorems of a geometric nature with many applications in economic theory. The main result states that two disjoint convex sets in $\mathbb{R}^n$ can be separated by a hyperplane. In two dimensions, hyperplanes are straight lines, and the geometric content of the theorem in $\mathbb{R}^2$ is shown in Fig. 1.

Figure 2 shows an example of two disjoint sets in $\mathbb{R}^2$ that *cannot* be separated by a hyperplane; S is convex, but T is not. Of course, it may be possible to separate two sets even if either or both are not convex.

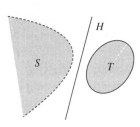

Figure 1 S and T are (strictly) separated by H.

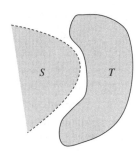

Figure 2 S and T cannot be separated by a hyperplane.

With its simple geometrical interpretation, the separation theorem in $\mathbb{R}^n$ is one of the most fundamental tools in modern optimization theory. In particular, it makes it possible to find optimality conditions without differentiability requirements in cases where the functions involved are either concave or convex, as appropriate.

Separation theorems are also useful in many other areas. An early economic application of separation theorems was to welfare economics, where they were used to prove, under suitable hypotheses, that a Pareto efficient allocation can be "decentralized" as a competitive equilibrium. (See Arrow (1951), or Mas-Colell et al. (1995).)

Recall from Example 2.2.1 (and (1.1.43)) that if $\mathbf{a}$ is a nonzero vector in $\mathbb{R}^n$ and α is a real number, then the set

$$H = \left\{\mathbf{x} : \mathbf{a} \cdot \mathbf{x} = \alpha\right\} \tag{1}$$

is a hyperplane in $\mathbb{R}^n$, with $\mathbf{a}$ as its normal. Moreover, the hyperplane H separates $\mathbb{R}^n$ into two closed half-spaces (see Example 2.2.1).

If S and T are subsets of $\mathbb{R}^n$, then H is said to **separate** S and T if S is contained in one of the closed half-spaces determined by H and T is contained in the other. In other words, S and T can be separated by a hyperplane if there exist a vector $\mathbf{a} \neq \mathbf{0}$ and a scalar α such that

$$\mathbf{a} \cdot \mathbf{x} \leq \alpha \leq \mathbf{a} \cdot \mathbf{y} \quad \text{for all } \mathbf{x} \text{ in } S \text{ and all } \mathbf{y} \text{ in } T \tag{$*$}$$

If both inequalities are strict, then the hyperplane $H = \{\mathbf{x} : \mathbf{a} \cdot \mathbf{x} = \alpha\}$ **strictly separates** S and T.

The first separation theorem we prove deals with the case where S is closed and convex, and T consists of only one point, $T = \{\mathbf{y}\}$. When a hyperplane separates a one-point set from another set, one often says (a little imprecisely) that the hyperplane separates the *point* from the other set, as in the theorem below.

THEOREM 13.6.1   (A SPECIAL SEPARATION THEOREM)

Let S be a closed, convex set in $\mathbb{R}^n$, and let $\mathbf{y}$ be a point in $\mathbb{R}^n$ that does not belong to S. Then there exists a nonzero vector $\mathbf{a}$ in $\mathbb{R}^n$ and a number α such that

$$\mathbf{a} \cdot \mathbf{x} < \alpha < \mathbf{a} \cdot \mathbf{y} \quad \text{for all } \mathbf{x} \text{ in } S \tag{2}$$

For every such α the hyperplane $H = \{\,\mathbf{x} : \mathbf{a} \cdot \mathbf{x} = \alpha\,\}$ *strictly separates* S and $\mathbf{y}$.

The geometric idea of the following proof is quite simple: Drop the "perpendicular" from **y** to the nearest point **w** of the set S. Let H' be the hyperplane through **w** with the vector **a** = **y** − **w** as a normal. Then H' will separate **y** and S because S is convex. Figure 3 illustrates the construction in the case $n = 2$. The desired hyperplane H is obtained by choosing α as any number strictly between **a** · **w** and **a** · **y**.

This argument sounds quite convincing in 2 or even 3 dimensions, but what about the general case? What is the perpendicular from a point to a convex set in $\mathbb{R}^n$? A rigorous proof is needed.

Proof: Because S is a closed set, among all the points of S there is one **w** = $(w_1, \ldots, w_n)$ that is closest to **y**. (For a precise argument, see Problem 13.3.5. Because S is convex, the point **w** is actually unique, but we do not need this fact in the proof.)

Let **a** = **y** − **w**, the vector from **w** to **y**. (See Fig. 3.) Since **w** $\in S$ and **y** $\notin S$, it follows that **a** $\neq$ **0**. Note that **a** · (**y** − **w**) = **a** · **a** > 0, and so **a** · **w** < **a** · **y**. Suppose we prove that

$$\mathbf{a} \cdot \mathbf{x} \le \mathbf{a} \cdot \mathbf{w} \qquad \text{for all } \mathbf{x} \text{ in } S \tag{i}$$

Then (2) will hold for every number α in the interval (**a** · **w**, **a** · **y**).

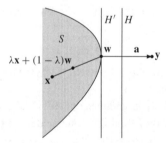

Figure 3 H' separates **y** from S, and H *strictly* separates **y** from S.

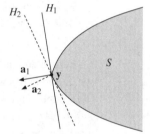

Figure 4 Two supporting hyperplanes to S at **y** are shown.

To prove (i), let **x** be any point in S. Since S is convex, $\lambda\mathbf{x} + (1 - \lambda)\mathbf{w} \in S$ for each λ in [0, 1]. Now define $g(\lambda)$ as the square of the distance from $\lambda\mathbf{x} + (1 - \lambda)\mathbf{w}$ to the point **y**:

$$g(\lambda) = \left\| \mathbf{y} - (\lambda\mathbf{x} + (1 - \lambda)\mathbf{w}) \right\|^2 = \left\| \mathbf{y} - \mathbf{w} + \lambda(\mathbf{w} - \mathbf{x}) \right\|^2$$

A little calculation shows that $g'(\lambda) = 2(\mathbf{y} - \mathbf{w} + \lambda(\mathbf{w} - \mathbf{x})) \cdot (\mathbf{w} - \mathbf{x})$. Also $g(0) = \|\mathbf{y} - \mathbf{w}\|^2$, the square of the distance between **y** and **w**. But **w** is the point in S that is closest to **y**, so $g(\lambda) \ge g(0)$ for all λ in [0, 1]. It follows that $0 \le g'(0) = 2(\mathbf{y} - \mathbf{w}) \cdot (\mathbf{w} - \mathbf{x}) = \mathbf{a} \cdot (\mathbf{w} - \mathbf{x})$, which proves (i). ∎

In the proof of Theorem 13.6.1 it was essential that **y** did not belong to S, and this gave the strict inequality in (2). If S is an arbitrary convex set (not necessarily closed), and if **y** is not an interior point of S, then it seems plausible that **y** can still be separated from S by a hyperplane. If **y** is a boundary point of S, such a hyperplane is called a **supporting hyperplane** to S at **y**. It passes through **y** and has the property that, for a suitable normal

$\mathbf{a} = (a_1, \ldots, a_n) \neq \mathbf{0}$ to it, $\mathbf{a} \cdot \mathbf{x} \leq \mathbf{a} \cdot \mathbf{y}$ for all $\mathbf{x} = (x_1, \ldots, x_n)$ in S (the vector $\mathbf{a}$ points away from S). Figure 4 shows two supporting hyperplanes to a set S at the same point $\mathbf{y}$, together with normals to these hyperplanes.

THEOREM 13.6.2 (SEPARATING HYPERPLANE)

Let S be a convex set in $\mathbb{R}^n$ and suppose $\mathbf{y} = (y_1, \ldots, y_n)$ is not an interior point of S. Then there exists a nonzero vector $\mathbf{a}$ in $\mathbb{R}^n$ such that

$$\mathbf{a} \cdot \mathbf{x} \leq \mathbf{a} \cdot \mathbf{y} \quad \text{for every } \mathbf{x} \text{ in } S \tag{3}$$

Proof: Let $\bar{S}$ be the closure of S. Because S is convex, so is $\bar{S}$ (see Problem 2). Because $\mathbf{y}$ is not an interior point of S and S is convex, $\mathbf{y}$ is not an interior point of $\bar{S}$ (see Problem 3). Hence there is a sequence $\{\mathbf{y}_k\}$ of points outside $\bar{S}$ that converges to $\mathbf{y}$. Now $\mathbf{y}_k \notin \bar{S}$ and $\bar{S}$ is closed and convex, so according to the preceding separation theorem, for each $k = 1, 2, \ldots$ there exists a vector $\mathbf{a}_k \neq \mathbf{0}$ such that $\mathbf{a}_k \cdot \mathbf{x} < \mathbf{a}_k \cdot \mathbf{y}_k$ for all $\mathbf{x}$ in $\bar{S}$. Without loss of generality, we can assume that $\|\mathbf{a}_k\| = 1$ for each k. Then $\{\mathbf{a}_k\}$ is a sequence of vectors in the unit sphere of $\mathbb{R}^n$. Because this sphere is compact, the Bolzano–Weierstrass theorem (Theorem 13.2.5) shows that $\{\mathbf{a}_k\}$ has a convergent subsequence $\{\mathbf{a}_{k_i}\}_i$. Let $\mathbf{a} = \lim_{i \to \infty} \mathbf{a}_{k_i}$. Then $\mathbf{a} \cdot \mathbf{x} = \lim_{i \to \infty}(\mathbf{a}_{k_i} \cdot \mathbf{x}) \leq \lim_{i \to \infty}(\mathbf{a}_{k_i} \cdot \mathbf{y}_{k_i}) = \mathbf{a} \cdot \mathbf{y}$ for every $\mathbf{x}$ in $\bar{S}$, as required. Moreover, $\mathbf{a} \neq \mathbf{0}$ because $\|\mathbf{a}\| = \lim_{i \to \infty} \|\mathbf{a}_{k_i}\| = 1$. ∎

The general separation property illustrated in Fig. 1 turns out to be a rather simple consequence of the last two theorems.

THEOREM 13.6.3 (MINKOWSKI'S SEPARATING HYPERPLANE THEOREM)

Let S and T be two disjoint nonempty convex sets in $\mathbb{R}^n$. Then there exists a nonzero vector $\mathbf{a}$ in $\mathbb{R}^n$ and a scalar α such that

$$\mathbf{a} \cdot \mathbf{x} \leq \alpha \leq \mathbf{a} \cdot \mathbf{y} \quad \text{for all } \mathbf{x} \text{ in } S \text{ and all } \mathbf{y} \text{ in } T \tag{4}$$

Thus S and T are separated by the hyperplane $H = \{\mathbf{z} \in \mathbb{R}^n : \mathbf{a} \cdot \mathbf{z} = \alpha\}$.

Proof: Let $W = S - T$ be the vector difference of the two convex sets S and T. Since S and T are disjoint, $\mathbf{0} \notin W$.

The set W is convex according to (13.5.2), so by Theorem 13.6.2 there exists an $\mathbf{a} \neq \mathbf{0}$ such that $\mathbf{a} \cdot \mathbf{w} \leq \mathbf{a} \cdot \mathbf{0} = 0$ for all $\mathbf{w}$ in W. Let $\mathbf{x}$ in S and $\mathbf{y}$ in T be any two points of these sets. Then $\mathbf{w} = \mathbf{x} - \mathbf{y} \in W$, so $\mathbf{a} \cdot (\mathbf{x} - \mathbf{y}) \leq 0$. Hence

$$\mathbf{a} \cdot \mathbf{x} \leq \mathbf{a} \cdot \mathbf{y} \quad \text{for all } \mathbf{x} \text{ in } S \text{ and all } \mathbf{y} \text{ in } T \tag{$*$}$$

From $(*)$ it follows, in particular, that the set $A = \{\mathbf{a} \cdot \mathbf{x} : \mathbf{x} \in S\}$ is bounded above by $\mathbf{a} \cdot \mathbf{y}$ for any $\mathbf{y}$ in T. Hence A has a supremum α, say. Since α is the least of all the upper bounds of A, it follows that $\alpha \leq \mathbf{a} \cdot \mathbf{y}$ for every $\mathbf{y}$ in T. Therefore $\mathbf{a} \cdot \mathbf{x} \leq \alpha \leq \mathbf{a} \cdot \mathbf{y}$ for all $\mathbf{x}$ in S and all $\mathbf{y}$ in T. Thus S and T are separated by the hyperplane $\{\mathbf{z} \in \mathbb{R}^n : \mathbf{a} \cdot \mathbf{z} = \alpha\}$. ∎

An even more general separation theorem for convex sets in $\mathbb{R}^n$ is the following. For a proof see Rockafellar (1970).

THEOREM 13.6.4 (GENERAL SEPARATING HYPERPLANE THEOREM)

Let S and T be two convex sets in $\mathbb{R}^n$ with no common relative interior points. Then S and T can be separated by a hyperplane, i.e. there exists a vector $\mathbf{a} = (a_1, \ldots, a_n) \neq \mathbf{0}$ and a scalar α such that

$$\mathbf{a} \cdot \mathbf{x} \leq \alpha \leq \mathbf{a} \cdot \mathbf{y} \quad \text{for all } \mathbf{x} \text{ in } S \text{ and all } \mathbf{y} \text{ in } T \tag{5}$$

NOTE 1 In many economic models in which one proves the existence of a set of prices with certain properties, those prices are closely related to the components of a normal to a suitable separating hyperplane.

PROBLEMS FOR SECTION 13.6

1. Let S be a nonempty, closed, convex set in $\mathbb{R}^n$ that does not contain the origin. Show that there exists a vector $\mathbf{a} = (a_1, \ldots, a_n)$ and a positive real number α such that

$$\sum_{i=1}^{n} a_i x_i > \alpha \qquad \text{for all } \mathbf{x} = (x_1, \ldots, x_n) \text{ in } S$$

2. Prove that if S is a convex set in $\mathbb{R}^n$, then its closure, $\bar{S}$, is also convex. (*Hint:* Assume $\mathbf{x}, \mathbf{y} \in \bar{S}$ and let $\mathbf{x}_k \to \mathbf{x}, \mathbf{y}_k \to \mathbf{y}$, where $\mathbf{x}_k, \mathbf{y}_k \in S$.)

3. Prove that if S is a convex set in $\mathbb{R}^n$, and $\mathbf{x}$ is not an interior point of S, then $\mathbf{x}$ is not an interior point of $\bar{S}$.

4. If S is a set in $\mathbb{R}^n$ and $\mathbf{y}$ is a boundary point of S, is $\mathbf{y}$ necessarily a boundary point of $\bar{S}$? (*Hint:* The irrational number $\sqrt{2}$ is a boundary point of the set $\mathbb{Q}$ of rational numbers, but what is $\overline{\mathbb{Q}}$? If S is *convex*, then it *is* true that a boundary point of S is also a boundary point of $\bar{S}$.)

5. Some books in economics have suggested the following generalization of Theorem 13.6.3: Two convex sets in $\mathbb{R}^n$ with only one point in common can be separated by a hyperplane. Is this statement correct? What about the assertion that two convex sets in $\mathbb{R}^n$ with disjoint interiors can be separated by a hyperplane?

13.7 Productive Economies and Frobenius's Theorem

The final section of this chapter will indicate how some of the rather abstract concepts and results discussed lead to some interesting insights in economic models.

Consider an economy with n commodities. Producing the commodity vector $\mathbf{x} = (x_1, \ldots, x_n)$ requires, in general, inputs of all goods. For $i = 1, \ldots, n$, let $f_i(\mathbf{x})$ denote the amount of good i needed to produce $\mathbf{x}$, so that $\mathbf{f}(\mathbf{x}) = (f_1(\mathbf{x}), \ldots, f_n(\mathbf{x}))$ is the commodity vector needed to produce $\mathbf{x}$. It is reasonable to assume that the function $\mathbf{f}$ is *increasing* in the sense that[2]

$$\mathbf{u} \leq \mathbf{v} \Rightarrow \mathbf{f}(\mathbf{u}) \leq \mathbf{f}(\mathbf{v})$$

The vector of net outputs left for consumption and investment, the **final supply**, is $\mathbf{y} = \mathbf{x} - \mathbf{f}(\mathbf{x})$.

Suppose that there exists a commodity vector $\mathbf{a} = (a^1, a^2, \ldots, a^n) \geq (0, 0, \ldots, 0)$ which can be produced, and for which the final supply $\mathbf{y} = \mathbf{a} - \mathbf{f}(\mathbf{a})$ is $\geq \mathbf{0}$. What other final supply vectors can be produced? A partial answer is given by the following theorem:

THEOREM 13.7.1

Let $\mathbf{f}$ be a continuous, increasing transformation from $\mathbb{R}^n_+$ into $\mathbb{R}^n_+$. Assume that there exists a vector $\mathbf{a} \geq \mathbf{0}$ such that $\mathbf{a} \geq \mathbf{f}(\mathbf{a})$. Then for every $\mathbf{y}$ such that $\mathbf{0} \leq \mathbf{y} \leq \mathbf{a} - \mathbf{f}(\mathbf{a})$, the equation $\mathbf{x} - \mathbf{f}(\mathbf{x}) = \mathbf{y}$ has a solution $\mathbf{x}$ with $\mathbf{y} \leq \mathbf{x} \leq \mathbf{a}$.

Proof: Suppose $\mathbf{y}$ satisfies $\mathbf{0} \leq \mathbf{y} \leq \mathbf{a} - \mathbf{f}(\mathbf{a})$. Let $\mathbf{x}_0 = \mathbf{y}$. Define $\mathbf{x}_1 = \mathbf{f}(\mathbf{x}_0) + \mathbf{y}$, and in general

$$\mathbf{x}_m = \mathbf{f}(\mathbf{x}_{m-1}) + \mathbf{y}, \qquad m = 1, 2, \ldots \tag{i}$$

We claim that

$$\mathbf{x}_m \leq \mathbf{a} \quad \text{for} \quad m = 0, 1, \ldots \tag{ii}$$

The inequality $\mathbf{x}_0 \leq \mathbf{a}$ follows because $\mathbf{x}_0 = \mathbf{y} \leq \mathbf{a} - \mathbf{f}(\mathbf{a})$ and $\mathbf{f}(\mathbf{a}) \geq \mathbf{0}$. Suppose $\mathbf{x}_k \leq \mathbf{a}$ for some k. Then $\mathbf{x}_{k+1} = \mathbf{f}(\mathbf{x}_k) + \mathbf{y} \leq \mathbf{f}(\mathbf{a}) + \mathbf{y} \leq \mathbf{a}$, and (ii) follows by induction.

We prove next that the sequence $\{\mathbf{x}_m\}_m$ is monotone:

$$\mathbf{x}_{m-1} \leq \mathbf{x}_m \quad \text{for} \quad m = 1, 2, \ldots \tag{iii}$$

This is surely true for $m = 1$, because $\mathbf{x}_0 = \mathbf{y} = \mathbf{x}_1 - \mathbf{f}(\mathbf{x}_0) \leq \mathbf{x}_1$. Suppose that (iii) is valid for $m = k$, so that $\mathbf{x}_{k-1} \leq \mathbf{x}_k$. Because $\mathbf{f}$ is increasing, $\mathbf{f}(\mathbf{x}_{k-1}) \leq \mathbf{f}(\mathbf{x}_k)$, so $\mathbf{f}(\mathbf{x}_{k-1}) + \mathbf{y} \leq \mathbf{f}(\mathbf{x}_k) + \mathbf{y}$, implying that $\mathbf{x}_k \leq \mathbf{x}_{k+1}$. Hence (iii) follows by induction.

For all m we have $\mathbf{x}_m \geq \mathbf{y}$ because $\mathbf{f}(\mathbf{x}_{m-1}) \geq \mathbf{0}$. Define $\mathbf{x} = \sup_m \mathbf{x}_m$ (which means that $x^i = \sup_m x^i_m$ for $i = 1, \ldots, n$, where $\mathbf{x} = (x^1, \ldots, x^n)$). Then $x^i_m \to x^i$ as $m \to \infty$

---

[2] Recall that $\mathbf{u} \leq \mathbf{v}$ means that $u_i \leq v_i$ for all $i = 1, \ldots, n$. If the inequality is strict, $u_i < v_i$ for all i, we write $\mathbf{u} \ll \mathbf{v}$.

for every i, and therefore $\mathbf{x}_m \to \mathbf{x}$ as $m \to \infty$. Now, letting $m \to \infty$ in (i) and using the continuity of $\mathbf{f}$, it follows that $\mathbf{x}$ satisfies the equation

$$\mathbf{x} = \mathbf{f}(\mathbf{x}) + \mathbf{y} \tag{iv}$$

By letting $m \to \infty$ in (ii), we also see that $\mathbf{x} \leq \mathbf{a}$, while (iv) shows that $\mathbf{x} \geq \mathbf{y}$, because $\mathbf{f}(\mathbf{x}) \geq 0$. ∎

Consider in particular the **Leontief case** where $\mathbf{f}$ is linear and given by $\mathbf{f}(\mathbf{x}) = \mathbf{A}\mathbf{x}$ for some $n \times n$ matrix $\mathbf{A} = (a_{ij})_{n \times n}$ with nonnegative elements. If $\mathbf{v} \geq \mathbf{u}$, then $\mathbf{v} - \mathbf{u} \geq \mathbf{0}$ and $\mathbf{A}(\mathbf{v} - \mathbf{u}) \geq \mathbf{0}$, or $\mathbf{A}\mathbf{v} \geq \mathbf{A}\mathbf{u}$. This shows that the function $\mathbf{f}$ is increasing, as well as obviously continuous, so Theorem 13.7.1 applies.

Suppose, in particular, that $\mathbf{A}$ satisfies the following requirement:

$$\mathbf{A} = (a_{ij})_{n \times n} \geq \mathbf{0} \text{ is } \textbf{productive} \iff \begin{cases} \text{There exists a vector } \mathbf{a} \gg 0 \\ \text{such that } \mathbf{a} \gg \mathbf{A}\mathbf{a} \end{cases} \tag{1}$$

If $\mathbf{A}$ is productive, then it is possible to produce a commodity vector which gives positive final supply for each good because $\mathbf{y} = \mathbf{a} - \mathbf{A}\mathbf{a} \gg \mathbf{0}$. In this case Theorem 13.7.1 can be significantly sharpened:

$$\text{If } \mathbf{A} \text{ is productive, then for every } \mathbf{y} \geq \mathbf{0} \text{ the equation } \mathbf{x} - \mathbf{A}\mathbf{x} = \mathbf{y} \text{ has a unique solution, and the solution satisfies } \mathbf{x} \geq \mathbf{y}. \tag{2}$$

Proof: Suppose $\mathbf{A}$ is productive, let $\mathbf{a}$ be as in (1), and let $\mathbf{y} \geq \mathbf{0}$ be given. By Theorem 13.7.1, the equation $\mathbf{x} - \mathbf{A}\mathbf{x} = \mathbf{y}$ certainly has a solution for every $\mathbf{y} \leq \mathbf{a} - \mathbf{A}\mathbf{a}$. But replacing $\mathbf{a}$ by $\lambda\mathbf{a}$ for any $\lambda > 0$ yields $\lambda\mathbf{a} - \mathbf{A}(\lambda\mathbf{a}) \gg 0$. Moreover, each component of $\lambda\mathbf{a} - \mathbf{A}(\lambda\mathbf{a}) = \lambda(\mathbf{a} - \mathbf{A}\mathbf{a})$ can be made as large as we please. Therefore, by Theorem 13.7.1, there is a solution $\mathbf{x}$ of $\mathbf{x} - \mathbf{A}\mathbf{x} = \mathbf{y}$ for *all* $\mathbf{y} \geq \mathbf{0}$.

To prove uniqueness, let $\mathbf{x}_i$ satisfy $(\mathbf{I} - \mathbf{A})\mathbf{x}_i = \mathbf{e}_i$, $i = 1, \ldots, n$, where $\mathbf{e}_i$ is the ith standard unit vector. Then $(\mathbf{I} - \mathbf{A})\mathbf{X} = \mathbf{I}$, where $\mathbf{X}$ is the matrix with $\mathbf{x}_1, \ldots, \mathbf{x}_n$ as columns. Hence $\mathbf{I} - \mathbf{A}$ is invertible, so $(\mathbf{I} - \mathbf{A})\mathbf{x} = \mathbf{y}$ has the unique solution $\mathbf{x} = (\mathbf{I} - \mathbf{A})^{-1}\mathbf{y}$. ∎

If $\{\mathbf{B}_k\}_k$ is a sequence of matrices, then $\mathbf{B}_k \to \mathbf{B}$ as $k \to \infty$ means that for all i and j the element b_{ij}^k of $\mathbf{B}_k$ converges to the element b_{ij} of $\mathbf{B}$. For *nonnegative* square matrices $\mathbf{A}$ the following equivalences hold:

$$\mathbf{A} \text{ is productive} \iff \begin{cases} \text{(a)} & (\mathbf{I} - \mathbf{A})^{-1} \text{ exists and is nonnegative} \\ \text{(b)} & \mathbf{A}^m \to \mathbf{0} \text{ as } m \to \infty \\ \text{(c)} & (\mathbf{I} - \mathbf{A})^{-1} = \mathbf{I} + \mathbf{A} + \mathbf{A}^2 + \cdots \end{cases} \tag{3}$$

The claim is that each of the properties (a), (b), and (c) is equivalent to $\mathbf{A}$ being productive.

Proof: The $\Rightarrow$ part of (a) was proved above. To prove the $\Rightarrow$ part of (b), let $\mathbf{a} \gg \mathbf{A}\mathbf{a}$ for $\mathbf{a} \gg \mathbf{0}$. Each component of $\mathbf{a}$ is then strictly larger than the corresponding component of $\mathbf{A}\mathbf{a}$. So there must then exist a λ in $(0, 1)$ such that $\lambda\mathbf{a} \gg \mathbf{A}\mathbf{a} \gg \mathbf{0}$. Then $\lambda^2\mathbf{a} = \lambda(\lambda\mathbf{a}) \gg \lambda\mathbf{A}\mathbf{a} =$

$\mathbf{A}(\lambda\mathbf{a}) \geqq \mathbf{A}(\mathbf{Aa}) = \mathbf{A}^2\mathbf{a} \gg \mathbf{0}$, and by induction we get $\lambda^m\mathbf{a} \gg \mathbf{A}^m\mathbf{a} \gg \mathbf{0}$ for $m = 1, 2,$ $\ldots$. If we let $m \to \infty$, then $\lambda^m\mathbf{a} \to \mathbf{0}$, because $\lambda \in (0, 1)$. Hence $\mathbf{A}^m\mathbf{a} \to \mathbf{0}$ as $m \to \infty$. But for each $j = 1, 2, \ldots, n$, we have $\mathbf{A}^m\mathbf{a} = \mathbf{A}^m\left(\sum_{i=1}^n a_i\mathbf{e}_i\right) = \sum_{i=1}^n a_i\mathbf{A}^m\mathbf{e}_i \geqq a_j\mathbf{A}^m\mathbf{e}_j$, and so the jth column $\mathbf{A}^m\mathbf{e}_j$ of $\mathbf{A}^m$ tends to $\mathbf{0}$ as a limit as $m \to \infty$. Therefore, $\mathbf{A}^m \to 0$ as $m \to \infty$.

To prove the $\Rightarrow$ part of (c), note that $(\mathbf{I} + \mathbf{A} + \cdots + \mathbf{A}^{m-1})(\mathbf{I} - \mathbf{A}) = \mathbf{I} - \mathbf{A}^m$. Because of (a),

$$\mathbf{I} + \mathbf{A} + \cdots + \mathbf{A}^{m-1} = (\mathbf{I} - \mathbf{A}^m)(\mathbf{I} - \mathbf{A})^{-1}$$

Letting $m \to \infty$ yields the conclusion. To prove that (c) is a sufficient condition for $\mathbf{A}$ to be productive, choose any $\mathbf{y} \gg \mathbf{0}$, and let $\mathbf{x} = (\mathbf{I} - \mathbf{A})^{-1}\mathbf{y} = \mathbf{y} + \mathbf{Ay} + \mathbf{A}^2\mathbf{y} + \cdots \gg \mathbf{0}$. Then $(\mathbf{I} - \mathbf{A})\mathbf{x} = \mathbf{y} \gg \mathbf{0}$ so $\mathbf{x} \gg \mathbf{Ax}$. The remaining parts of the proof are left to the reader as Problem 2. ∎

NOTE 1 Suppose that the function $\mathbf{f}$ in Theorem 13.7.1 is *homogeneous of degree 1*, and that $\mathbf{a} \gg \mathbf{f}(\mathbf{a})$ for $\mathbf{a} \gg \mathbf{0}$. By using the same argument as for (2), we conclude that the equation $\mathbf{x} - \mathbf{fx} = \mathbf{y}$ has a solution for every $\mathbf{y} \geqq \mathbf{0}$.

The last result of this section has several applications to economics. (See e.g. Nikaido (1970), Chapter 3.)

THEOREM 13.7.2 (FROBENIUS)

Suppose that $\mathbf{A} = (a_{ij})_{n\times n} \geqq \mathbf{0}$, and define

$$M = \{(\mu, \mathbf{a}) : \mu > 0, \ \mathbf{a} \gg \mathbf{0}, \ \mu\mathbf{a} \gg \mathbf{Aa}\}$$
$$\lambda_{\mathbf{A}} = \inf\{\mu : (\mu, \mathbf{a}) \in M \text{ for some } \mathbf{a} \gg \mathbf{0}\}$$

Then $\lambda_{\mathbf{A}} \geq 0$ is the largest real eigenvalue of $\mathbf{A}$ and has an associated nonnegative eigenvector. The eigenvalue $\lambda_{\mathbf{A}}$ is called the **Frobenius root** of $\mathbf{A}$.

Proof: There exists a sequence $(\mu_m, \mathbf{a}_m)$ of points in M such that $\mu_m \to \lambda_{\mathbf{A}}$ as $m \to \infty$. (Cf. the result in Problem A.3.3.) For each m, $\mathbf{a}_m \gg (1/\mu_m)\mathbf{Aa}_m$, and therefore $(1/\mu_m)\mathbf{A}$ is productive. Then by 3(a), $\mathbf{I} - (1/\mu_m)\mathbf{A}$ has an inverse, and so therefore does $\mu_m[I - (1/\mu_m)\mathbf{A}] = \mu_m\mathbf{I} - \mathbf{A}$. Let $\mathbf{1}$ denote the $n \times 1$ matrix with all elements equal to 1, and define $\mathbf{x}_m = (\mu_m\mathbf{I} - \mathbf{A})^{-1}\mathbf{1}$, $m = 1, 2, \ldots$. Then

$$(\mu_m\mathbf{I} - \mathbf{A})\mathbf{x}_m = \mathbf{1} \tag{i}$$

We demonstrate by contradiction that $\|\mathbf{x}_m\| \to \infty$ as $m \to \infty$. Indeed, if it did not, then the sequence $\{\|\mathbf{x}_m\|\}_m$ would have a bounded subsequence. But then, according to Theorem 13.2.4, $\{\mathbf{x}_m\}_m$ would have a convergent subsequence $\{\mathbf{x}_{m_j}\}_j$, with limit $\mathbf{x}^0 \geqq \mathbf{0}$. Replace m by m_j in (i) and let $j \to \infty$. Then in the limit $(\lambda_{\mathbf{A}}\mathbf{I} - \mathbf{A})\mathbf{x}^0 = \mathbf{1}$, so $\lambda_{\mathbf{A}}\mathbf{x}^0 - \mathbf{Ax}^0 = \mathbf{1}$. Since $\lambda_{\mathbf{A}}\mathbf{x}^0 - \mathbf{Ax}^0$ is equal to 1 in each component, $\mu\mathbf{x}^0 - \mathbf{Ax}^0 \gg \mathbf{0}$ for some μ slightly less than $\lambda_{\mathbf{A}}$.

Then $(\mu, \mathbf{x}^0) \in M$, contradicting the definition of $\lambda_{\mathbf{A}}$. We conclude that $\|\mathbf{x}_m\| \to \infty$ as $m \to \infty$.

Put $\mathbf{y}_m = \mathbf{x}_m/\|\mathbf{x}_m\|$. Then $\|\mathbf{y}_m\| = 1$, and the sequence $\{\mathbf{y}_m\}$ has a convergent subsequence $\{\mathbf{y}_{m_k}\}_k$ converging as $k \to \infty$ to some $\mathbf{y}^0$ with $\|\mathbf{y}^0\| = 1$. Replacing m by m_k in (i) and dividing the equation by $\|\mathbf{x}_{m_k}\|$, we obtain

$$(\mu_{m_k}\mathbf{I} - \mathbf{A})\mathbf{y}_{m_k} = (1/\|\mathbf{x}_{m_k}\|)\mathbf{1}$$

Now let $k \to \infty$. It follows that $(\lambda_{\mathbf{A}}\mathbf{I} - \mathbf{A})\mathbf{y}^0 = \mathbf{0}$, or

$$\mathbf{A}\mathbf{y}^0 = \lambda_{\mathbf{A}}\mathbf{y}^0$$

This equation shows that $\lambda_{\mathbf{A}}$ is an eigenvalue for $\mathbf{A}$, with eigenvector $\mathbf{y}^0 \geqq \mathbf{0}$. Because $\mu_m > 0$ for each m and $\mu_m \to \lambda_{\mathbf{A}}$, we have $\lambda_{\mathbf{A}} \geq 0$.

To prove that $\lambda_{\mathbf{A}}$ is the largest real eigenvalue of $\mathbf{A}$, suppose $\mu > \lambda_{\mathbf{A}}$. Then $\mu\mathbf{I} - \mathbf{A} = \mu[\mathbf{I} - (1/\mu)\mathbf{A}]$ is invertible according to the definition of $\lambda_{\mathbf{A}}$. By definition of $\lambda_{\mathbf{A}}$, there exists a point $(\lambda, \mathbf{a}) \in M$ such that $\mu > \lambda$. But then the definition of M obviously implies that $(\mu, \mathbf{a}) \in M$, and so that $(1/\mu)\mathbf{A}$ is a productive matrix. By (3), $\mu I - \mathbf{A}$ must be invertible, so μ cannot be an eigenvalue of $\mathbf{A}$. ∎

PROBLEMS FOR SECTION 13.7

1. For a nonnegative matrix $\mathbf{A}$, by (3)(a),

$$\mathbf{A} \text{ is productive} \iff (\mathbf{I} - \mathbf{A})\mathbf{x} = \mathbf{1} \text{ has a solution } \mathbf{x} \gg \mathbf{0}$$

Show that $\mathbf{A} = \begin{pmatrix} 1/3 & 1/2 \\ 1/9 & 1/3 \end{pmatrix}$ is productive.

2. Complete the proof of (3).

14

CORRESPONDENCES AND FIXED POINTS

Mathematics is like an addiction, or a disease; you can never truly shake it off, even if you want to.
—I. Stewart (1989)

The concept of a function is one of the most important in mathematics and its applications. A function *f* from a set *A* to a set *B* requires each element *x* of *A* to be mapped to exactly one element $f(x)$ in *B*. Many economic applications require a generalized concept of function allowing any element in *A* to be mapped to a set consisting of several elements in *B*. Such "multivalued" functions are usually called **correspondences** by economists. For example, suppose that **p** denotes a vector of parameters such as prices faced by some economic agent. Then $F(\mathbf{p})$ might be the set of the agent's optimal decisions given these parameters—for example, the set of a consumer's utility maximizing demands, or of a firm's profit maximizing production plans. Because optimal decisions may not always be unique, economists need to generalize the concept of a function in this way. Section 14.1 studies correspondences and some of their main properties.

The maximum theorems of Section 13.4 have a natural generalization to correspondences. Section 14.2 deals with such generalizations and also includes some economic applications.

Another main focus of this chapter is on some mathematical results of a rather deep nature, namely fixed point theorems. The brief Section 14.3 formulates and proves the existence of a fixed point for a special type of contraction mapping. This result has important applications to problems in the theory of differential equations, control theory and to infinite horizon dynamic programming.

Next we study the fixed point theorems of Brouwer and Kakutani. In economics these results are widely used to prove that equilibrium exists in various models of perfectly competitive markets and in general strategic form games. These applications are regarded as major triumphs of mathematical economics. According to Scarf (1973), "This demonstration [of the existence of an equilibrium] has provided one of the rare instances in which abstract mathematical techniques are indispensable in order to solve a problem of central importance to economic theory".

14.1 Correspondences

This section considers correspondences and in particular introduces several continuity assumptions that have been found useful by economists. The rather intricate relationships between these different concepts are set out in some detail.

DEFINITION OF CORRESPONDENCES

A **correspondence** F from a set A into a set B is a rule that maps each x in A to a subset $F(x)$ of B. Then one writes $F : A \twoheadrightarrow B$ and $x \mapsto F(x)$ (with double arrows to distinguish a correspondence from a function). $\qquad$ (1)

The set $F(x)$ in the definition is allowed to be empty for some elements x in A. The **domain** of F is A, the set of all x for which $F(x)$ is defined; the **effective domain** is the set of all x in A at which $F(x)$ is nonempty.

Correspondences are also called **set-valued maps** or **multi-valued functions**. If the subset $F(x)$ always reduces to a single point, the correspondence is effectively the same as an ordinary function. The concept of a correspondence from $A \subseteq \mathbb{R}^3$ into $\mathbb{R}^2$ is illustrated in Fig. 1.

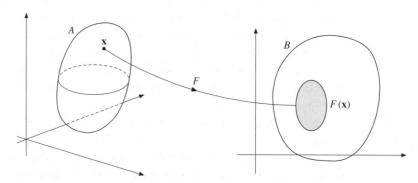

Figure 1 F is a correspondence from $A \subseteq \mathbb{R}^3$ to $\mathbb{R}^2$.

One familiar example of a correspondence is $y \mapsto f^{-1}(y)$ where f is an ordinary function from $\mathbb{R}$ to $\mathbb{R}$. Recall that $f^{-1}(y) = \{x : f(x) = y\}$, which may well be empty for some x, and may contain more than one element unless f is one-to-one.

EXAMPLE 1   Example 2.2.3 defines a consumer's **budget set**

$$\mathcal{B}(\mathbf{p}, m) = \{\mathbf{x} \in \mathbb{R}^n : \mathbf{p} \cdot \mathbf{x} \leq m, \ \mathbf{x} \geq \mathbf{0}\} \qquad (2)$$

for each price vector $\mathbf{p} \geq 0$ and income level $m \geq 0$. Thus, the budget set consists of all affordable nonnegative commodity vectors. Note that $(\mathbf{p}, m) \mapsto \mathcal{B}(\mathbf{p}, m)$ defines a correspondence from $\mathbb{R}_+^{n+1}$ into $\mathbb{R}_+^n$. See Fig. 2.

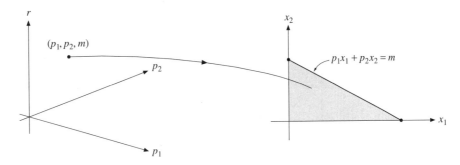

Figure 2 An individual's budget correspondence when there are two commodities.

EXAMPLE 2   Consider a firm producing a single commodity. Suppose that the total cost of production, as a function of output level Q, is given by

$$C(Q) = \begin{cases} 0 & \text{if } Q = 0 \\ F + aQ + cQ^2 & \text{if } Q > 0 \end{cases}$$

where F, a, and c are positive constants with $P > a$. Note that $C(Q) > F$ whenever $Q > 0$. In this sense, F is a "fixed" or "setup" cost that must be incurred in order to produce a positive level of output.

Suppose the firm faces the output price P. Then its profit, as a function of Q, is given by

$$\pi(Q) = PQ - C(Q) = \begin{cases} 0 & \text{if } Q = 0 \\ -F + (P - a)Q - cQ^2 & \text{if } Q > 0 \end{cases}$$

For $Q > 0$, one has $\pi'(Q) = P - a - 2cQ$ and $\pi''(Q) = -2c < 0$. Note that $\pi'(Q) = 0$ for $Q = Q^* = (P - a)/2c$, with $\pi(Q^*) = (P - a)^2/4c - F$. We see that $\pi(Q^*) \geq 0$ if and only if $(P - a)^2 \geq (2\sqrt{cF})^2$, i.e. if and only if $P \geq a + 2\sqrt{cF}$. It follows that the profit maximizing choice of output is

$$Q(P) = \begin{cases} 0 & \text{if } P \leq a + 2\sqrt{cF} \\ (P - a)/2c & \text{if } P \geq a + 2\sqrt{cF} \end{cases}$$

yielding the profit level

$$\pi(Q(P)) = \begin{cases} 0 & \text{if } P \leq a + 2\sqrt{cF} \\ (P - a)^2/4c - F & \text{if } P \geq a + 2\sqrt{cF} \end{cases}$$

Note that the producer's behaviour is described by a supply *correspondence* rather than a function because, when $P = a + 2\sqrt{cF}$, both 0 and $\sqrt{F/c}$ are quantities allowing the producer to earn zero profit. The supply correspondence is illustrated in Fig. 3 and also in Fig. 4, where the axes have been interchanged to conform with the standard convention in economics.

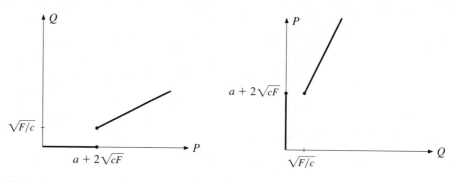

Figure 3   **Figure 4**

The **graph** of a correspondence $F : A \twoheadrightarrow B$ is defined as

$$\mathrm{graph}(F) = \{ (x, y) \in A \times B : x \in A \text{ and } y \in F(x) \} \tag{3}$$

If F is an ordinary function, its graph reduces to the familiar graph of a function.

Given a correspondence $F : A \mapsto B$ and any set $S \subseteq A$, the **range** or the **image** of S under F is defined as the set $F(S) = \bigcup_{x \in S} F(x)$.

EXAMPLE 3   Let F be the correspondence from $\mathbb{R}$ to $\mathbb{R}$ that maps every $x < 1$ to the interval $[1, 3]$, and every $x \geq 1$ to the set consisting only of the number 2. Hence

$$F(x) = \begin{cases} [1, 3], & x < 1 \\ \{2\}, & x \geq 1 \end{cases}$$

Draw the graph of F.

Solution: The graph of F is shown in Fig. 5. The dashed line indicates boundary points that are not part of the graph.

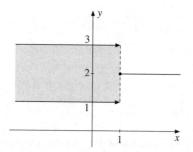

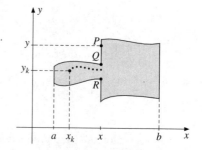

Figure 5 The correspondence F in Example 3 is lower hemicontinuous, but its graph is not closed.

Figure 6 This correspondence has a closed graph, but is not lower hemicontinuous.

Correspondences as relations

The graph of a correspondence from A to B is a subset of the Cartesian product $A \times B$. This subset can also be interpreted as a *relation* from A to B (see Appendix A). Indeed, for every correspondence $F : A \twoheadrightarrow B$ there is a unique relation R_F from A to B such that $a \, R_F \, b \iff b \in F(a)$. Similarly, to each relation R from a to B there is a correspondence $F_R : A \twoheadrightarrow B$ given by $F_R(a) = \{b \in B : a \, R \, b\}$.

The Closed Graph Property

Most of the rest of this section will deal with correspondences that map points in $\mathbb{R}^n$ to subsets of $\mathbb{R}^m$. Continuity is an important concept for ordinary functions. It ensures that small changes in the independent variable do not lead to large changes in the function values. For a correspondence F it is equally important to introduce certain continuity conditions ensuring that small changes in $\mathbf{x}$ do not change the image set $F(\mathbf{x})$ too drastically. However, unlike for (single-valued) functions, there are several different kinds of continuity for (multi-valued) correspondences. The distinctions between them are of some importance in economic theory. Of these different kinds of continuity, the simplest is the closed graph property:

CLOSED GRAPH PROPERTY OF A CORRESPONDENCE

A correspondence $F : X \subseteq \mathbb{R}^n \twoheadrightarrow \mathbb{R}^m$ has a **closed graph** at a point $\mathbf{x}^0$ in X if for every sequence $\{(\mathbf{x}_k, \mathbf{y}_k)\}$ of points in the graph of F that converges to a point $(\mathbf{x}^0, \mathbf{y}^0)$ in $\{\mathbf{x}^0\} \times \mathbb{R}^m \subseteq X \times \mathbb{R}^m$, one has $\mathbf{y}^0 \in F(\mathbf{x}^0)$.

The correspondence F has the **closed graph property** if it has a closed graph at every point in X, i.e. if for every convergent sequence $\{(\mathbf{x}_k, \mathbf{y}_k)\}$ in graph(F) whose limit is a point $(\mathbf{x}^0, \mathbf{y}^0)$ in $X \times \mathbb{R}^m$, one has $\mathbf{y}^0 \in F(\mathbf{x}^0)$.

(4)

If a correspondence F has a closed graph at $\mathbf{x}^0$, then in particular the set $F(\mathbf{x}^0)$ is closed. In the language of Section 13.3, $F : X \subseteq \mathbb{R}^n \twoheadrightarrow \mathbb{R}^m$ has the closed graph property if and only if graph(F) is relatively closed in $X \times \mathbb{R}^m$, i.e. if and only if graph(F) is the intersection of $X \times \mathbb{R}^m$ and a closed set in $\mathbb{R}^n \times \mathbb{R}^m$.

Figure 6 shows the graph of a correspondence $F : [a, b] \twoheadrightarrow \mathbb{R}$ which *does* have the closed graph property. It is clear from Fig. 5 that the correspondence F in Example 3 *does not* have the closed graph property.

EXAMPLE 4   Suppose that $g : \mathbb{R}^{n+m} \to \mathbb{R}$ is a continuous function. For all $\mathbf{x}$ in $\mathbb{R}^n$, define

$$\mathscr{P}(\mathbf{x}) = \{ \mathbf{y} \in \mathbb{R}^m : g(\mathbf{x}, \mathbf{y}) \le 0 \}$$

Show that the correspondence $\mathbf{x} \mapsto \mathscr{P}(\mathbf{x})$ has the closed graph property.

Solution: The domain of the correspondence is closed. The graph of the correspondence is the set $g^{-1}(-\infty, 0] = \{(\mathbf{x}, \mathbf{y}) : g(\mathbf{x}, \mathbf{y}) \le 0\}$. Because $(-\infty, 0]$ is closed and g is continuous, this inverse image is closed. But then $\mathbf{x} \mapsto \mathscr{P}(\mathbf{x})$ has the closed graph property.

Lower Hemicontinuity

Another frequently encountered continuity condition for correspondences is the following:

LOWER HEMICONTINUOUS CORRESPONDENCE

A correspondence $F : X \subseteq \mathbb{R}^n \to \mathbb{R}^m$ is **lower hemicontinuous** (or **l.h.c.**) at a point $\mathbf{x}^0$ in X if whenever $\mathbf{y}^0 \in F(\mathbf{x}^0)$ and $\{\mathbf{x}_k\}$ is a sequence in X that converges to $\mathbf{x}^0$, there exist a number k_0 and a sequence $\{\mathbf{y}_k\}_{k=k_0}^{\infty}$ in $\mathbb{R}^n$ that converges to $\mathbf{y}^0$ (5)
and satisfies $\mathbf{y}_k \in F(\mathbf{x}_k)$ for all $k \geq k_0$.

F is **lower hemicontinuous** (or **l.h.c.**) in X if it is l.h.c. at every point $\mathbf{x}$ in X.

Lower hemicontinuity requires a correspondence to be continuous in a sense that is almost the opposite of the closed graph property. For example, the correspondence shown in Fig. 5 is lower hemicontinuous, but does not have the closed graph property. But the opposite holds for the correspondence in Fig. 6. (To see why the correspondence in Fig. 6 is not lower hemicontinuous, consider the point P on the graph, and let the sequence $\{x_k\}$ be as suggested by the dots in the figure. In particular, suppose $\{x_k\}$ converges to x. It is obviously impossible to choose a sequence $y_k \in F(x_k)$ that converges to y, because the corresponding sequence $\{(x_k, y_k)\}$ can only converge to a point on the line segment RQ, and not to P.)

Roughly speaking, if a correspondence F has the closed graph property at a point $\mathbf{x}^0$ of its domain, then $F(\mathbf{x})$ cannot "explode" as $\mathbf{x}$ moves slightly away from $\mathbf{x}^0$, as happens at $x = 1$ in Fig. 5, but it may "implode", as happens at x in Fig. 6. For lower hemicontinuous correspondences the opposite is true: $F(\mathbf{x})$ cannot implode as $\mathbf{x}$ moves slightly away from $\mathbf{x}^0$, but it may explode.

EXAMPLE 5   Let $\mathbf{g} = (g_1, \ldots, g_l) : \mathbb{R}^{n+m} \to \mathbb{R}^l$ be continuous, let $\mathbf{b}$ be a given l-vector, let A be a given closed set in $\mathbb{R}^m$, and let X be a given set in $\mathbb{R}^n$. For each $\mathbf{x}$ in X, define the set $\mathcal{P}(\mathbf{x}) \subseteq \mathbb{R}^m$ by

$$\mathcal{P}(\mathbf{x}) = \{\mathbf{y} \in A : \mathbf{g}(\mathbf{x}, \mathbf{y}) \leqq \mathbf{b}\} = \{\mathbf{y} \in A : g_i(\mathbf{x}, \mathbf{y}) \leq b_i, \ i = 1, \ldots, l\}$$ (6)

Show that the correspondence $\mathbf{x} \mapsto \mathcal{P}(\mathbf{x})$ has the closed graph property. Show that it is also lower hemicontinuous if $\mathcal{P}(\mathbf{x}) = \overline{\mathcal{P}^{\circ}(\mathbf{x})}$ for every $\mathbf{x}$ in X, where $\mathcal{P}^{\circ}(\mathbf{x}) = \{\mathbf{y} \in A : g_i(\mathbf{x}, \mathbf{y}) < b_i, \ i = 1, \ldots, l\}$.

Solution: Proof of the closed graph property: Assume that $\mathbf{x}_k \to \mathbf{x}^0 \in X$ and $\mathbf{y}_k \to \mathbf{y}^0$ when $k \to \infty$, where $\mathbf{y}_k \in \mathcal{P}(\mathbf{x}_k)$ for all k. Then $\mathbf{y}_k \in A$ and $\mathbf{g}(\mathbf{x}_k, \mathbf{y}_k) \leq \mathbf{b}$. Because A is closed, $\mathbf{y}^0 \in A$. By continuity of $\mathbf{g}$, letting $k \to \infty$ in the inequality yields $\mathbf{g}(\mathbf{x}^0, \mathbf{y}^0) \leq \mathbf{b}$. It follows that $\mathbf{y}^0 \in \mathcal{P}(\mathbf{x}^0)$.

Proof of lower hemicontinuity: Let $\mathbf{y} \in \mathcal{P}(\mathbf{x})$ and let $\mathbf{x}_k \to \mathbf{x} \in X$. Because $\mathcal{P}(\mathbf{x}) = \overline{\mathcal{P}^{\circ}(\mathbf{x})}$, there exist vectors $\mathbf{y}^j$ in $\mathcal{P}^{\circ}(\mathbf{x})$ such that $\|\mathbf{y}^j - \mathbf{y}\| < 1/j$. Because $g_i(\mathbf{x}, \mathbf{y}^j) < b_i$ for $i = 1, \ldots, l$, there exists a strictly increasing sequence of numbers k_j such that for $k \geq k_j$, the inequality $g_i(\mathbf{x}_k, \mathbf{y}^j) \leq b_i$ holds for all i. Let $\mathbf{y}_k = \mathbf{y}^j$ for $k_j \leq k < k_{j+1}$. Then $\mathbf{y}_k$ belongs to $\mathcal{P}(\mathbf{x}_k)$ for $k \geq k_1$, and $\|\mathbf{y}_k - \mathbf{y}\| \leq 1/j$ for $k \geq k_j$, hence $\mathbf{y}_k \to \mathbf{y}$.

EXAMPLE 6   Show that the budget correspondence $\mathcal{B}(\mathbf{p}, m)$ defined in Example 1 has the closed graph property and is lower hemicontinuous at any point $(\mathbf{p}, m)$ where $m > 0$.

Solution: The closed graph property follows immediately from the previous example (with $A = \{\mathbf{x} : \mathbf{x} \geq \mathbf{0}\}$).

To prove that the correspondence is lower hemicontinuous when $m > 0$, it is enough to show that $\mathcal{B}(\mathbf{p}, m) = \overline{\mathcal{B}^{\circ}(\mathbf{p}, m)}$, where $\mathcal{B}^{\circ}(\mathbf{p}, m) = \{\mathbf{x} \geq \mathbf{0} : \mathbf{p} \cdot \mathbf{x} < m\}$. Given any $\mathbf{x} \in \mathcal{B}(\mathbf{p}, m)$, let $\alpha_k = (1 - 1/k)$, $k = 1, 2, \ldots$. Then $\alpha_k \mathbf{x} \to \mathbf{x}$ as $k \to \infty$. Moreover, as $\mathbf{p} \cdot \mathbf{x} \leq m$, $0 < \alpha_k < 1$, and $m > 0$, one has $\mathbf{p} \cdot \alpha_k \mathbf{x} \leq \alpha_k m < m$, so $\alpha_k \mathbf{x}$ belongs to $\mathcal{B}^{\circ}(\mathbf{p}, m)$, which proves the asserted equality.

Here is an alternative condition for lower hemicontinuity.

ALTERNATIVE CHARACTERIZATION OF LOWER HEMICONTINUITY

A correspondence $F : X \subseteq \mathbb{R}^n \twoheadrightarrow \mathbb{R}^m$ is lower hemicontinuous at $\mathbf{x}^0$ in X if and only if for each $\mathbf{y}^0$ in $F(\mathbf{x}^0)$ and each neighbourhood U of $\mathbf{y}^0$, there exists a neighbourhood N of $\mathbf{x}^0$ such that $F(\mathbf{x}) \cap U \neq \emptyset$ for all $\mathbf{x}$ in $N \cap X$.   (7)

Proof: Suppose that $F : X \twoheadrightarrow \mathbb{R}^m$ satisfies (7) at a point $\mathbf{x}^0$ in X, that $\mathbf{y}^0 \in F(\mathbf{x}^0)$, and that $\mathbf{x}_k \to \mathbf{x}^0$ as $k \to \infty$. Let $\{r_k\}$ be any sequence of positive numbers such that $r_k \to 0$ as $k \to \infty$. Given a neighbourhood $B(\mathbf{y}^0; r_k)$ of $\mathbf{y}^0$, condition (7) implies that there exists a neighbourhood N of $\mathbf{x}^0$ such that $F(\mathbf{x}) \cap B(\mathbf{y}^0; r_k) \neq \emptyset$ whenever $\mathbf{x} \in N \cap X$. But there exists a k^* such that $k \geq k^*$ implies $\mathbf{x}_k \in N \cap X$, so there exists a $\mathbf{y}_k$ in $F(\mathbf{x}_k)$ such that $\mathbf{y}_k \in B(\mathbf{y}^0; r_k)$. Clearly $\mathbf{y}_k \to \mathbf{y}^0$, so F satisfies (5) at $\mathbf{x}^0$.

On the other hand, suppose F does not satisfy (7) at a point $\mathbf{x}^0$ in X. Then there exist a point $\mathbf{y}^0 \in F(\mathbf{x}^0)$ and a neighbourhood U of $\mathbf{y}^0$ such that every neighbourhood N of $\mathbf{x}^0$ includes at least one point $\mathbf{x}_N$ satisfying $F(\mathbf{x}_N) \cap U = \emptyset$. Hence, there exists a sequence $\{\mathbf{x}_k\}$ in X such that $\mathbf{x}_k \to \mathbf{x}^0$ as $k \to \infty$ and $F(\mathbf{x}_k) \cap U = \emptyset$ for all $k \geq 1$. But then no sequence $\{\mathbf{y}_k\}$ with $\mathbf{y}_k \in F(\mathbf{x}_k)$, $k = 1, 2, \ldots$, can possibly converge to $\mathbf{y}^0$. So F cannot satisfy (5) at $\mathbf{x}^0$.   ∎

Comparing (7) with the corresponding topological condition for continuous functions leads immediately to the following important result:

THEOREM 14.1.1 (CONTINUOUS FUNCTIONS ARE L.H.C. CORRESPONDENCES)

A function $\mathbf{x} \mapsto \mathbf{f}(\mathbf{x})$ is continuous at a point $\mathbf{x}^0$ of its domain X if and only if the associated correspondence $\mathbf{x} \twoheadrightarrow \{\mathbf{f}(\mathbf{x})\}$ is lower hemicontinuous at $\mathbf{x}^0$.

Proof: Given any neighbourhood U of $\{\mathbf{f}(\mathbf{x}^0)\}$, one has $\{\mathbf{f}(\mathbf{x})\} \cap U \neq \emptyset \iff \mathbf{f}(\mathbf{x}) \in U$. So $\{\mathbf{f}(\mathbf{x})\} \cap U \neq \emptyset$ for all $\mathbf{x} \in N \cap X$ iff $\mathbf{f}(N \cap X) \subseteq U$, or iff $N \cap X \subseteq \mathbf{f}^{-1}(U)$. The result follows from (7) because the topological condition for $\mathbf{f}$ to be continuous at $\mathbf{x}^0$ is that $N \cap X \subseteq \mathbf{f}^{-1}(U)$ for some neighbourhood N of $\mathbf{x}^0$ whenever U is a neighbourhood of $\{\mathbf{f}(\mathbf{x}^0)\}$.   ∎

Upper Hemicontinuity

Now that lower hemicontinuity has been defined for correspondences, it is natural to ask whether there is a similar concept of upper hemicontinuity.

UPPER HEMICONTINUOUS CORRESPONDENCES

A correspondence $F : X \subseteq \mathbb{R}^n \twoheadrightarrow \mathbb{R}^m$ is said to be **upper hemicontinuous** (or **u.h.c.**) at a point $\mathbf{x}^0$ in X if $F(\mathbf{x}^0) \neq \emptyset$, and for every open set U that contains $F(\mathbf{x}^0)$, there exists a neighbourhood N of $\mathbf{x}^0$ such that $F(\mathbf{x}) \subseteq U$ for every $\mathbf{x}$ in $N \cap X$—i.e. such that $F(N \cap X) \subseteq U$.   (8)

 F is **upper hemicontinuous** (or **u.h.c.**) in X if it is u.h.c. at every $\mathbf{x}$ in X.

As was the case with l.h.c. correspondences, the following result is an immediate implication of definition (8):

THEOREM 14.1.2 (CONTINUOUS FUNCTIONS ARE U.H.C. CORRESPONDENCES)

The function $\mathbf{x} \mapsto \mathbf{f}(\mathbf{x})$ is continuous at a point $\mathbf{x}^0$ of its domain X if and only if the associated correspondence $\mathbf{x} \mapsto \{\mathbf{f}(\mathbf{x})\}$ is upper hemicontinuous at $\mathbf{x}^0$.

Proof: Let U be a open set containing $\mathbf{f}(\mathbf{x}^0)$ and let N be a neighbourhood of $\mathbf{x}^0$. Note that $\mathbf{f}(N \cap X) \subseteq U \iff N \cap X \subseteq \mathbf{f}^{-1}(U)$. The theorem follows from this equivalence.   ∎

NOTE 1 If $F : X \twoheadrightarrow \mathbb{R}^m$ is upper hemicontinuous at a point $\mathbf{x}^0$ in X and $F(\mathbf{x}^0)$ is a closed set, then $F(\mathbf{x})$ has the closed graph property at $\mathbf{x}^0$. (Proof: Let $\mathbf{x}_k \to \mathbf{x}^0$, $\mathbf{y}_k \to \mathbf{y}^0$, and $\mathbf{y}_k \in F(\mathbf{x}_k)$. Assume $\mathbf{y}^0 \notin F(\mathbf{x}^0)$. There is a closed ball B around $\mathbf{y}^0$ which is small enough not to intersect the closed set $F(\mathbf{x}^0)$. Applying (8) to the open set $\complement B = \mathbb{R}^m \setminus B$, there exists a neighbourhood N of $\mathbf{x}^0$ such that $F(N \cap X) \subseteq \complement B$. But for k large one has $\mathbf{x}_k \in N \cap X$ and so $\mathbf{y}_k \in F(\mathbf{x}_k) \subseteq \complement B$. It follows that $\mathbf{y}_k$ does not converge to $\mathbf{y}^0$.)

On the other hand, the following theorem also holds.

THEOREM 14.1.3

Suppose that the correspondence $F : X \subseteq \mathbb{R}^n \twoheadrightarrow \mathbb{R}^m$ has a closed graph at $\mathbf{x}^0$ and that F is locally bounded near $\mathbf{x}^0$ in the sense that there exists a neighbourhood N of $\mathbf{x}^0$ such that $F(N \cap X) = \bigcup_{\mathbf{x} \in N \cap X} F(\mathbf{x})$ is a bounded set. Then F is upper hemicontinuous at $\mathbf{x}^0$.

Proof: Let N be as in the theorem, and let $B(\mathbf{x}^0; \alpha) \subseteq N$. Suppose that F is not u.h.c. at $\mathbf{x}^0$ in X. Then there must exist an open set $U \supseteq F(\mathbf{x}^0)$ such that, given any ball $B(\mathbf{x}^0; \alpha/k)$, $k = 1, 2, \ldots$, there exists an $\mathbf{x}_k$ in $B(\mathbf{x}^0, \alpha/k) \cap X$ for which $F(\mathbf{x}_k) \not\subseteq U$. Choose vectors $\mathbf{y}_k$ in $F(\mathbf{x}_k) \cap U$. The boundedness property in the theorem implies that $\{\mathbf{y}_k\}$ has a subsequence $\{\mathbf{y}_{k_r}\}$ that converges to some point $\mathbf{y}^0$ in $F(\mathbf{x}^0)$ as $r \to \infty$. Because $\mathbb{R}^n \setminus U$ is closed and $\mathbf{y}_{k_r} \in \mathbb{R}^n \setminus U$, $\lim_{r\to\infty} \mathbf{y}_{k_r} = \mathbf{y}^0 \in \mathbb{R}^n \setminus U$, the limit $\mathbf{y}^0 \notin F(\mathbf{x}^0)$, a contradiction. ∎

The following result is an immediate consequence.

THEOREM 14.1.4 (COMPACT GRAPH TEST FOR UPPER HEMICONTINUITY)

If a correspondence F from $X \subseteq \mathbb{R}^n$ to $Y \subseteq \mathbb{R}^m$ has a compact graph, then it is upper hemicontinuous.

Problem 1 concerns an example of a (non-compact-valued) correspondence which has the closed graph property, but which is not upper hemicontinuous. Theorems 14.1.1 and 14.1.2 show that, if a correspondence is single-valued and so collapses to a function, then either upper or lower hemicontinuity (separately) implies that the function is continuous.

A correspondence that is both upper and lower hemicontinuous is called **continuous**. Of course, any constant-valued correspondence is continuous, as is any single-valued correspondence that collapses to a continuous function. But so are many others.

Composite Correspondences

If $f : A \to B$ and $g : B \to C$ are functions, then the composition $h = g \circ f$ is the function $h : A \to C$ given by $h(x) = g(f(x))$. Similarly, if $F : A \twoheadrightarrow B$ and $G : B \twoheadrightarrow C$ are correspondences, then the **composite correspondence** $H = G \circ F : A \twoheadrightarrow C$ is defined by

$$H(x) = G(F(x)) = \bigcup_{y \in F(x)} G(y)$$

Thus, $H(x)$ is the union of all the sets $G(y)$ that are obtained as y runs through $F(x)$. This means that $z \in H(x)$ if and only if $z \in G(y)$ for at least one y in $F(x)$.

Recall that the composition of two continuous functions is continuous. For correspondences between sets in Euclidean spaces we have the following results:

THEOREM 14.1.5

Let $F : X \subseteq \mathbb{R}^n \twoheadrightarrow Y \subseteq \mathbb{R}^m$ and $G : Y \twoheadrightarrow Z \subseteq \mathbb{R}^p$ be correspondences, and let $H = G \circ F : X \twoheadrightarrow Z$ be their composition. Then:

(a) If F and G have closed graphs and Y is compact, then H has the closed graph property.

(b) If F is upper hemicontinuous at $\mathbf{x}^0$ in X and G is upper hemicontinuous at every point of $F(\mathbf{x}^0)$, then H is upper hemicontinuous at $\mathbf{x}^0$.

(c) If F is lower hemicontinuous at $\mathbf{x}^0$ in X and G is lower hemicontinuous at every point of $F(\mathbf{x}^0)$, then H is lower hemicontinuous at $\mathbf{x}^0$.

Proof: (a) Suppose that $\{\mathbf{x}_k\}$ and $\{\mathbf{z}_k\}$ are convergent sequences in X and Z respectively, such that $\mathbf{z}_k \in H(\mathbf{x}_k)$ for all k, $\mathbf{x}^0 = \lim_k \mathbf{x}_k \in X$, and $\mathbf{z}^0 = \lim_k \mathbf{z}_k$. We must show that $\mathbf{z}^0 \in H(\mathbf{x}^0)$. The definition of a composite correspondence implies that for each k there exists a $\mathbf{y}_k$ in $F(\mathbf{x}_k)$ such that $\mathbf{z}_k \in G(\mathbf{y}_k)$. Because Y is compact, $\{\mathbf{y}_k\}$ has a convergent subsequence $\{\mathbf{y}_{k_r}\}$. Let $\mathbf{y}^0 = \lim_r \mathbf{y}_{k_r}$. The corresponding subsequences $\{\mathbf{x}_{k_r}\}$ and $\{\mathbf{z}_{k_r}\}$ of $\{\mathbf{x}_k\}$ and $\{\mathbf{z}_k\}$ converge to $\mathbf{x}^0$ and $\mathbf{z}^0$ respectively. Because $\mathbf{y}_{k_r} \in F(\mathbf{x}_{k_r})$ for all r, the closed graph properties of F and G imply that $\mathbf{y}^0 \in F(\mathbf{x}^0)$ and $\mathbf{z}^0 \in G(\mathbf{y}^0)$. It follows that $\mathbf{z}^0 \in H(\mathbf{x}^0)$.

(b) Let U be any open set containing $H(\mathbf{x}^0)$. Since $H(\mathbf{x}^0) = \bigcup_{\mathbf{y} \in F(\mathbf{x}^0)} G(\mathbf{y})$, the set U contains $G(\mathbf{y})$ for every $\mathbf{y} \in F(\mathbf{x}^0)$. Because G is u.h.c., for each such $\mathbf{y}$ there exists an open neighbourhood $N_{\mathbf{y}}$ of $\mathbf{y}$ such that $G(\mathbf{y}') \subseteq U$ whenever $\mathbf{y}' \in N_{\mathbf{y}} \cap Y$. Define $N^* = \bigcup_{\mathbf{y} \in F(\mathbf{x}^0)} N_{\mathbf{y}}$. As the union of open sets, this is an open set containing $F(\mathbf{x}^0)$. Because F is u.h.c. at $\mathbf{x}^0$, there must exist a neighbourhood N of $\mathbf{x}$ such that $F(\mathbf{x}) \subseteq N^* \cap Y$ whenever $\mathbf{x} \in N \cap X$. But then, for all such $\mathbf{x}$, one has

$$H(\mathbf{x}) = \bigcup_{\mathbf{y} \in F(\mathbf{x})} G(\mathbf{y}) \subseteq \bigcup_{\mathbf{y}' \in N^* \cap Y} G(\mathbf{y}') = \bigcup_{\mathbf{y} \in F(\mathbf{x}^0)} \left[\bigcup_{\mathbf{y}' \in N_{\mathbf{y}} \cap Y} G(\mathbf{y}') \right] \subseteq U$$

This confirms that H is u.h.c. at $\mathbf{x}^0$.

(c) This (much easier) proof is left to the reader—see Problem 11.   ∎

PROBLEMS FOR SECTION 14.1

1. Let $F(x) = \{1/x\}$ for $x \neq 0$, with $F(0) = \{0\}$. Prove that f has the closed graph property, but is not upper hemicontinuous.

2. Determine by a geometric argument whether or not the correspondences given by the following graphs have closed graphs and/or are lower hemicontinuous.

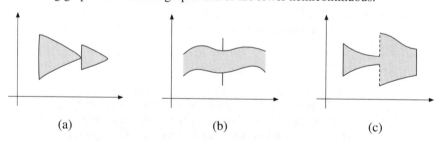

   (a)   (b)   (c)

3. Let the correspondence $F : \mathbb{R}_+ = [0, \infty) \twoheadrightarrow \mathbb{R}_+$ be given by $F(x) = [0, 1/x]$ for $x > 0$ and $F(0) = \mathbb{R}_+$. Prove that F has a closed graph and is lower hemicontinuous.

4. Let $X \subseteq \mathbb{R}^n$ and suppose the two correspondences $F : X \twoheadrightarrow \mathbb{R}^l$ and $G : X \twoheadrightarrow \mathbb{R}^m$ are upper hemicontinuous at a point $\mathbf{x}^0$ in X. Consider the product correspondence $H : X \twoheadrightarrow \mathbb{R}^{l+m}$ defined by $H(\mathbf{x}) = F(\mathbf{x}) \times G(\mathbf{x})$ for all $\mathbf{x}$ in X. Prove that H is upper hemicontinuous at $\mathbf{x}^0$. Similarly, prove that H is lower hemicontinuous at $\mathbf{x}^0$ if F and G are lower hemicontinuous at $\mathbf{x}^0$.

5. Suppose that the two compact-valued correspondences $F, G : X \subseteq \mathbb{R}^n \twoheadrightarrow \mathbb{R}^m$ are upper hemicontinuous at a point $\mathbf{x}^0$ in X. Consider the summation correspondence

$H : X \twoheadrightarrow \mathbb{R}^m$ defined by $H(\mathbf{x}) = F(\mathbf{x}) + G(\mathbf{x})$ for all $\mathbf{x}$ in X. Prove that H is upper hemicontinuous at $\mathbf{x}^0$. What may go wrong if F and G are not compact-valued?

6. Suppose $F : X \subseteq \mathbb{R}^n \twoheadrightarrow \mathbb{R}^m$ is lower hemicontinuous at a point $\mathbf{x}^0$ in X. Let $G : X \twoheadrightarrow \mathbb{R}^m$ be the correspondence whose value at each $\mathbf{x}$ in X is the convex hull $\mathrm{co}(F(\mathbf{x}))$. Prove that G is l.h.c. at $\mathbf{x}^0$.

7. Prove the following result: (**Sequence test for upper hemicontinuity.**) A compact-valued correspondence $F : X \subseteq \mathbb{R}^n \twoheadrightarrow \mathbb{R}^m$ is upper hemicontinuous at $\mathbf{x}^0$ in X if, whenever $\{(\mathbf{x}_k, \mathbf{y}_k)\}$ is a sequence of points in graph(F) for which $\mathbf{x}_k \to \mathbf{x}^0$ as $k \to \infty$, the corresponding sequence $\{\mathbf{y}_k\}$ has a convergent subsequence whose limit is a point of $F(\mathbf{x}^0)$. (The converse is also true.)

HARDER PROBLEMS

8. Let the functions $g_i(\mathbf{x}, \mathbf{y})$ in Example 5 be continuous in $(\mathbf{x}, \mathbf{y})$ and convex in $\mathbf{y}$. Furthermore, suppose that $\{\mathbf{y} : g_i(\mathbf{x}, \mathbf{y}) < b_i$ for $i = 1, \ldots, l\}$ is nonempty for all $\mathbf{x}$. Show that the correspondence $\mathcal{P}$ defined in Example 5 is then lower hemicontinuous. (*Hint:* Use the result in Example 5 and, for any $\mathbf{y}'$ in $\mathcal{P}(\mathbf{x})$, take $\mathbf{y}$ in $\mathcal{P}^\circ(\mathbf{x})$ and show that $\mathbf{y}'' = \lambda \mathbf{y} + (1 - \lambda)\mathbf{y}' \in \mathcal{P}^\circ(\mathbf{x})$ for λ in $(0, 1)$, then let $\lambda \to 0$.)

9. Let the functions $g_i(\mathbf{x}, \mathbf{y})$ in Example 5 be continuous, and have continuous partial derivatives w.r.t. $y_1, \ldots, y_m$. Furthermore, suppose that for all pairs $(\mathbf{x}, \mathbf{y})$ with $\mathbf{g}(\mathbf{x}, \mathbf{y}) \leqq \mathbf{b}$, the rank of the matrix with entries $\partial g_i(\mathbf{x}, \mathbf{y})/\partial x_j$, where $j = 1, \ldots, n$ and $i \in S(\mathbf{x}, \mathbf{y}) = \{i : g_i(\mathbf{x}, \mathbf{y}) = b_i\}$ is equal to the number of elements in the set $S(\mathbf{x}, \mathbf{y})$. Prove that the correspondence $\mathcal{P}(\mathbf{x})$ is then lower hemicontinuous. (*Hint:* Use Example 5.)

10. Let $a(x)$ and $b(x)$ be two continuous functions mapping $\mathbb{R}$ into $\mathbb{R}$, with $a(x) \leq b(x)$ for all x. Of all the different possible correspondences $F : \mathbb{R} \twoheadrightarrow \mathbb{R}$ that satisfy

$$(a(x), b(x)) \subseteq F(x) \subseteq [a(x), b(x)]$$

for all x, which are lower hemicontinuous, and which are upper hemicontinuous? (*Hint:* First examine the case when $a(x)$ and $b(x)$ are both constants.)

11. Prove part (c) of Theorem 14.1.5.

12. Suppose $F : X \subseteq \mathbb{R}^n \twoheadrightarrow \mathbb{R}^m$ is upper hemicontinuous at $\mathbf{x}^0$ in X. Let $G : X \twoheadrightarrow \mathbb{R}^m$ be the correspondence whose value at each $\mathbf{x}$ in X is the convex hull $\mathrm{co}(F(\mathbf{x}))$. Prove that G is upper hemicontinuous at $\mathbf{x}^0$. (*Hint:* Apply Carathéodory's theorem.)

14.2 A General Maximum Theorem

Assume that $F(\mathbf{x})$ is a correspondence from $X \subseteq \mathbb{R}^n$ into $Y \subseteq \mathbb{R}^m$, and let $f(\mathbf{x}, \mathbf{y})$ be a function from $X \times Y$ into $\mathbb{R}$. Consider the maximization problem

$$\text{maximize} \quad f(\mathbf{x}, \mathbf{y}) \quad \text{subject to} \quad \mathbf{y} \in F(\mathbf{x}) \tag{1}$$

Define the **choice** or **behaviour correspondence** Y^* from X into Y by

$$Y^*(\mathbf{x}) = \arg\max_{\mathbf{y} \in F(\mathbf{x})} f(\mathbf{x}, \mathbf{y}) = \left\{ \mathbf{y} \in F(\mathbf{x}) : f(\mathbf{x}, \mathbf{z}) \le f(\mathbf{x}, \mathbf{y}) \text{ for all } \mathbf{z} \text{ in } F(\mathbf{x}) \right\} \tag{2}$$

Thus for each $\mathbf{x}$ in X, the set $Y^*(\mathbf{x})$ consists of all the values of the argument $\mathbf{y}$ that maximize $f(\mathbf{x}, \mathbf{y})$ as $\mathbf{y}$ runs through the set $F(\mathbf{x})$.[1] Symbolically, we can illustrate the problem as in Fig. 1.

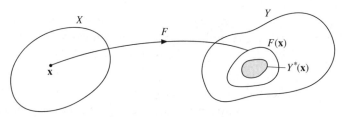

Figure 1

Also define the corresponding **value function**:

$$V(\mathbf{x}) = \sup_{\mathbf{y} \in F(\mathbf{x})} f(\mathbf{x}, \mathbf{y}) \tag{3}$$

The function V is well defined on the effective domain of F. If for some $\mathbf{x}$ the supremum is attained at some $\hat{\mathbf{y}}$, then $V(\mathbf{x}) = f(\mathbf{x}, \hat{\mathbf{y}}) = \max_{\mathbf{y} \in F(\mathbf{x})} f(\mathbf{x}, \mathbf{y})$. Note that if $\mathbf{x} \in X$ and $\mathbf{y} \in Y^*(\mathbf{x})$, then $V(\mathbf{x}) = f(\mathbf{x}, \mathbf{y})$. In fact, $Y^*(\mathbf{x}) = \left\{ \mathbf{y} \in F(\mathbf{x}) : f(\mathbf{x}, \mathbf{y}) = V(\mathbf{x}) \right\}$.

Here is a general (but somewhat vague) economic interpretation. First, $\mathbf{x}$ is a vector of exogenous parameters that jointly describe the "environment" faced by some maximizing economic agent. Given this vector $\mathbf{x}$, the **feasible set** $F(\mathbf{x})$ describes what options are available. Let $f(\mathbf{x}, \mathbf{y})$ measure the benefit to the economic agent from choosing the point $\mathbf{y}$ in $F(\mathbf{x})$ in situation $\mathbf{x}$. Then $Y^*(\mathbf{x})$ is the set of choices of $\mathbf{y}$ that maximize benefit.

In general, we are interested in finding the strongest possible continuity properties of $Y^*(\mathbf{x})$ and $V(\mathbf{x})$. Here is the main result.

---

[1] In general, for a function $\varphi : S \to \mathbb{R}$ the notation $\arg\max_{s \in S} \varphi(s)$ is used to denote the set of all values of the argument s in S that maximize $\varphi(s)$.

THEOREM 14.2.1 (THE MAXIMUM THEOREM)

Suppose that $\mathbf{x} \mapsto F(\mathbf{x})$ is a correspondence from $X \subseteq \mathbb{R}^n$ into $Y \subseteq \mathbb{R}^m$ that has nonempty compact values for all $\mathbf{x}$ in X and is continuous (i.e. both upper and lower hemicontinuous) at $\mathbf{x}^0$ in X. Let $f(\mathbf{x}, \mathbf{y})$ be a continuous function from $X \times Y$ into $\mathbb{R}$. Define

$$Y^*(\mathbf{x}) = \left\{ \mathbf{y} \in F(\mathbf{x}) : f(\mathbf{x}, \mathbf{z}) \le f(\mathbf{x}, \mathbf{y}) \text{ for all } \mathbf{z} \text{ in } F(\mathbf{x}) \right\}$$

Then $Y^*(\mathbf{x})$ is nonempty for all $\mathbf{x}$ in X. Moreover, the choice correspondence $\mathbf{x} \mapsto Y^*(\mathbf{x})$ is u.h.c. at $\mathbf{x}^0$, and the value function $V(\mathbf{x})$ is continuous at $\mathbf{x}^0$.

Proof: Because F has nonempty compact values for all $\mathbf{x}$ in X, the extreme-value theorem implies that $Y^*(\mathbf{x}) \ne \emptyset$ for all $\mathbf{x}$ in X.

Let W be an open bounded set containing $F(\mathbf{x}^0)$. Because F is assumed to be upper hemicontinuous, there is a ball U around $\mathbf{x}^0$ such that $F(\mathbf{x}) \subseteq W$ whenever $\mathbf{x} \in U$. Applying Theorem 14.1.4 (with $X = U$), upper hemicontinuity of $Y^*(\mathbf{x})$ at $\mathbf{x}^0$ will follow provided we can show that Y^* has the closed graph property at $\mathbf{x}^0$. Let $\{\mathbf{x}_k\}$ be any sequence of points in U that converges to $\mathbf{x}^0$ as $k \to \infty$ and let $\mathbf{y}_k \in Y^*(\mathbf{x}_k)$ converge to $\mathbf{y}^0$. We want to prove that $\mathbf{y}^0 \in Y^*(\mathbf{x}^0)$, and also that $V(\mathbf{x}_k) \to V(\mathbf{x}^0)$.

(1) Because F has the closed graph property at $\mathbf{x}^0$ and $\mathbf{y}_k \in Y^*(\mathbf{x}_k) \subseteq F(\mathbf{x}_k)$ for each k, we have $\mathbf{y}^0 \in F(\mathbf{x}^0)$.

(2) Take an arbitrary $\mathbf{z}^0$ in $F(\mathbf{x}^0)$. Because F is lower hemicontinuous at $\mathbf{x}^0$ and $\mathbf{x}_k \to \mathbf{x}^0$, there exists a sequence $\{\mathbf{z}_k\}$ with $\mathbf{z}_k \in F(\mathbf{x}_k)$ and $\mathbf{z}_k \to \mathbf{z}^0$. Now $\mathbf{y}_k \in Y^*(\mathbf{x}_k)$ and $\mathbf{z}_k \in F(\mathbf{x}_k)$, so the definition of Y^* implies that $f(\mathbf{x}_k, \mathbf{z}_k) \le f(\mathbf{x}_k, \mathbf{y}_k)$. Taking the limit as $k \to \infty$, continuity of f implies that $f(\mathbf{x}^0, \mathbf{z}^0) \le f(\mathbf{x}^0, \mathbf{y}^0)$. Because the choice of $\mathbf{z}^0$ in $F(\mathbf{x}^0)$ was arbitrary, it follows that $\mathbf{y}^0 \in Y^*(\mathbf{x}^0)$.

(3) The sequence $\{V(\mathbf{x}_k)\}_k$ of real numbers, even if it is unbounded, has a subsequence $\{V(\mathbf{x}_{k_r})\}_r$ which converges to a limit v, which may be infinite. Let $\mathbf{y}_k \in Y^*(\mathbf{x}_k)$ for each k. Because $\mathbf{x}_k \to \mathbf{x}^0$ and we have shown that $Y^*(\mathbf{x})$ is u.h.c. at $\mathbf{x}^0$, the subsequence $\{(\mathbf{x}_{k_r}, \mathbf{y}_{k_r})\}_r$ has a convergent "subsubsequence" $\{(\mathbf{x}'_m, \mathbf{y}'_m)\}_m$ whose limit must be a pair $(\mathbf{x}^0, \mathbf{y}')$ with $\mathbf{y}' \in Y^*(\mathbf{x}^0)$ and so $f(\mathbf{x}^0, \mathbf{y}') = V(\mathbf{x}^0)$. Obviously, $\mathbf{y}'_m \in Y^*(\mathbf{x}'_m)$ for each m, and so $V(\mathbf{x}'_m) = f(\mathbf{x}'_m, \mathbf{y}'_m)$. But f is continuous, so $f(\mathbf{x}'_m, \mathbf{y}'_m) \to f(\mathbf{x}^0, \mathbf{y}') = V(\mathbf{x}^0)$. Because $f(\mathbf{x}'_m, \mathbf{y}'_m) \to v$ as $m \to \infty$, this proves that any subsequence of $\{V(\mathbf{x}_k)\}_k$ that converges, even to infinity, must have the limit $v = V(\mathbf{x}^0)$. Hence $V(\mathbf{x}_k) \to V(\mathbf{x}^0)$. ∎

NOTE 1 Suppose there is a real-valued continuous function $\alpha(\mathbf{x})$ such that the correspondence $\mathbf{x} \mapsto F^+(\mathbf{x}) = \{\mathbf{y} \in Y : F(\mathbf{x}) \cap \{f(\mathbf{x}, \mathbf{y}) \ge \alpha(\mathbf{x})\}$ is nonempty and compact for all $\mathbf{x}$ in X, as well as upper hemicontinuous at $\mathbf{x}^0$. Then in Theorem 14.2.1, upper hemicontinuity of $F(\mathbf{x})$ at $\mathbf{x}^0$ and compactness of $F(\mathbf{x})$ can be dropped because $\emptyset \ne Y^*(\mathbf{x}) = \left\{ \mathbf{y} \in F^+(\mathbf{x}) : f(\mathbf{x}, \mathbf{z}) \le f(\mathbf{x}, \mathbf{y}) \text{ for all } \mathbf{z} \text{ in } F^+(\mathbf{x}) \right\}$, so one can replace $F(\mathbf{x})$ by $F^+(\mathbf{x})$.

EXAMPLE 1   In connection with Example 13.4.1 define the correspondence F for all x by $F(x) = [-1, 2]$. Then all the assumptions in Theorem 14.2.1 are satisfied and the set $Y^*(x)$ is $Y^*(x) = \{y \in [-1, 2] : xz^2 \leq xy^2 \text{ for all } z \in [-1, 2]\}$. It follows that

$$Y^*(x) = \begin{cases} \{0\} & \text{when } x < 0 \\ [-1, 2] & \text{when } x = 0 \\ \{2\} & \text{when } x > 0 \end{cases}$$

(For instance, if $x < 0$, then $Y^*(x)$ consists of all $y \in [-1, 2]$ such that $z^2 \geq y^2$ for all $z \in [-1, 2]$. In particular, $y^2 \leq 0$, so $y = 0$.) The correspondence $x \mapsto Y^*(x)$ is upper hemicontinuous. (Draw a figure!)

EXAMPLE 2   Let K be a nonempty compact convex set in $\mathbb{R}^n$. For all $\mathbf{x}$ in $\mathbb{R}^n$, define

$$\delta(\mathbf{x}, K) = \min_{\mathbf{y} \in K} d(\mathbf{x}, \mathbf{y}), \quad \psi(\mathbf{x}) = \arg\min_{\mathbf{y} \in K} d(\mathbf{x}, \mathbf{y})$$

where $d(\mathbf{x}, \mathbf{y})$ is the Euclidean distance. Thus $\delta(\mathbf{x}, K)$ can be interpreted as the minimum distance from $\mathbf{x}$ to K. Since $(d(\mathbf{x}, \mathbf{y}))^2$ is a strictly convex function of $\mathbf{y}$, it has a unique minimum over the convex set K of possible values of $\mathbf{y}$. Hence, $\psi(\mathbf{x})$ is single-valued—i.e. $\psi(\mathbf{x}) = \{\mathbf{y}^*(\mathbf{x})\}$ for some function $\mathbf{y}^*(\mathbf{x})$. In addition, the correspondence $\mathbf{x} \mapsto K$ is constant-valued, so continuous. Hence, the maximum theorem applies. The correspondence $\mathbf{x} \mapsto \psi(\mathbf{x})$ is therefore u.h.c., implying that the function $\mathbf{x} \mapsto \mathbf{y}^*(\mathbf{x})$ is continuous. In addition, $\mathbf{x} \mapsto \delta(\mathbf{x}, K) = d(\mathbf{x}, \mathbf{y}^*(\mathbf{x}))$ is also continuous.

EXAMPLE 3   (**Profit Maximization**) Suppose a firm produces a single output commodity using n different factors of production as inputs. Let the vector of strictly positive unit prices for the inputs be $\mathbf{w} = (w_1, \ldots, w_n) \gg \mathbf{0}$. Suppose that the firm's minimum cost, when faced with input prices $\mathbf{w} \gg \mathbf{0}$ and producing output $y \geq 0$, is given by the function $C(\mathbf{w}, y)$. One expects C to be increasing in $\mathbf{w}$ in the sense that $C(\mathbf{w}', y) \geq C(\mathbf{w}, y)$ whenever $\mathbf{w}' \geqq \mathbf{w}$, and that $C(\mathbf{w}, 0) = 0$. This will be assumed, as well as that $C(\mathbf{w}, y)$ is a continuous function. One also expects C to be increasing in y and homogeneous of degree one in $\mathbf{w}$, in the sense that $C(\lambda\mathbf{w}, y) = \lambda C(\mathbf{w}, y)$ for all $\lambda > 0$. All these properties are assumed here; that they are reasonable follows from the next example.

Finally, in order to ensure that profits remain bounded, assume that for each fixed $\mathbf{w} \gg \mathbf{0}$ the average cost $C(\mathbf{w}, y)/y$ tends to ∞ as $y \to \infty$.

Let $p > 0$ denote the price per unit of output. Consider the problem of maximizing the firm's profit $py - C(\mathbf{w}, y)$ by an appropriate choice of output y. We are interested in showing that the *supply correspondence* $(p, \mathbf{w}) \mapsto \eta(p, \mathbf{w}) = \arg\max_y\{py - C(\mathbf{w}, y)\}$ is u.h.c., and that the *profit function* $(p, \mathbf{w}) \mapsto \pi(p, \mathbf{w}) = \max_y\{py - C(\mathbf{w}, y)\}$ is continuous. It seems that the maximum theorem should be helpful, but there is a difficulty because the relevant feasible set $\{y : y \geq 0\}$ is not compact. However, define the set $F'(\mathbf{w}, p) = \{y \geq 0 : py - C(\mathbf{w}, y) \geq 0\}$. It is nonempty because $0 \in F'(\mathbf{w}, p)$. Choose any $\mathbf{w}^0 \gg 0$ and $p^0 > 0$. Because average cost $C(\mathbf{w}^0/2, y)/y \to \infty$ as $y \to \infty$, by hypothesis, a number y^* can be so chosen that $C(\mathbf{w}^0/2, y) > 2p^0y$ for all $y > y^*$. We claim that $F'(\mathbf{w}, p) \subseteq [0, y^*]$ for $\mathbf{w} \gg \mathbf{w}^0/2$, $p < 2p^0$. To see this, note that $y > y^*$ gives negative profits because $py - C(\mathbf{w}, y) < 2p^0y - C(\mathbf{w}^0/2, y) < 0$. Arguing as in Example 14.1.5, $F'(\mathbf{w}, p)$ has the closed graph property for $\mathbf{w} \gg \mathbf{w}^0$ and $p < p^0$. Because $[0, y']$ is bounded, Theorem 14.1.3 implies that $F'(\mathbf{w}, p)$ is upper hemicontinuous for all such $\mathbf{w}, p$. Finally, applying Note 1 with $F(\mathbf{w}, p) = [0, \infty)$ shows that $\pi(\mathbf{w}, p)$ is continuous and $\eta(\mathbf{w}, p)$ is upper hemicontinuous for $\mathbf{w} \gg \mathbf{w}^0/2$ and $p < 2p^0$. The same result extends to all $\mathbf{w} \gg 0$, $p^0 > 0$, since $\mathbf{w}^0$ and p^0 were arbitrary.

EXAMPLE 4 **(Cost Minimization)** Consider the same firm as in the previous example. Suppose that the level of output is determined by the production function $f(\mathbf{x})$, where $\mathbf{x} = (x_1, \ldots, x_n)$ is the input vector. Suppose also that f is defined and continuous on the set $\mathbb{R}^n_+ = \{\mathbf{x} \in \mathbb{R}^n : \mathbf{x} \geq \mathbf{0}\}$, that $f(\mathbf{0}) = 0$, and that f is also *monotone* in the sense that $f(\mathbf{x}') \geq f(\mathbf{x})$ whenever $\mathbf{x}' \geq \mathbf{x}$, with $f(\mathbf{x}') > f(\mathbf{x})$ whenever $\mathbf{x}' \gg \mathbf{x}$.

Consider the set $Y = f(\mathbb{R}^n_+) \subseteq \mathbb{R}$ of all possible output levels that the firm can produce. It must be an interval of the form $[0, \bar{y})$, where $\bar{y}$ may be $+\infty$. (There can be no $\bar{\mathbf{x}}$ such that $f(\bar{\mathbf{x}}) = \bar{y}$ because $f(\mathbf{x}) > f(\bar{\mathbf{x}})$ whenever $\mathbf{x} \gg \bar{\mathbf{x}}$. Given any input price vector $\mathbf{w} \gg \mathbf{0}$, the firm's (total) cost is given by $\mathbf{w} \cdot \mathbf{x}$. We shall now study the firm's **cost function**, which specifies the minimum cost of producing a given output level y in Y when the input price vector is $\mathbf{w}$. It is given by

$$C(\mathbf{w}, y) = \min_{\mathbf{x}} \{\mathbf{w} \cdot \mathbf{x} : f(\mathbf{x}) \geq y\}$$

In particular, we would like to apply Theorem 14.2.1 in order to demonstrate that $C(\mathbf{w}, y)$ is a continuous function, and the *input demand correspondence*, defined by

$$\xi(\mathbf{w}, y) = \arg \min_{\mathbf{x}} \{\mathbf{w} \cdot \mathbf{x} : f(\mathbf{x}) \geq y\}$$

is be upper hemicontinuous.

A difficulty here is that the constraint set $X(\mathbf{w}, y) = \{\mathbf{x} \in \mathbb{R}^n_+ : f(\mathbf{x}) \geq y\}$ is definitely unbounded. So, even though it is closed, it is not compact. So let us turn to Note 1. Given any $\widehat{\mathbf{w}} \gg \mathbf{0}$ and any $\hat{y}$ in $Y = [0, \bar{y})$, it is enough to prove continuity of C and upper hemicontinuity of ξ in a neighbourhood of $(\widehat{\mathbf{w}}, \hat{y})$ such as $W \times \check{Y}$, where $W = \{\mathbf{w} : \widehat{\mathbf{w}}/2 \ll \mathbf{w} \ll 2\widehat{\mathbf{w}}\}$ and $\check{Y} = [0, \check{y})$ for some point $\check{y}$ in $(\hat{y}, \bar{y})$. Let $\mathbf{1}$ be the vector whose components are all 1. Monotonicity guarantees that $f(\beta\mathbf{1})$ is a strictly increasing function of $\beta \geq 0$, with $f(0\mathbf{1}) = 0$ and $f(\beta\mathbf{1}) \geq f(\mathbf{x})$ when $f(\mathbf{x}) = \check{y}$ and β is so large that $\beta\mathbf{1} \geq \mathbf{x}$. Hence, there exists a $\check{\beta}$ such that $f(\check{\beta}\mathbf{1}) = \check{y}$. Given this $\check{\beta}$, define

$$\check{F}(\mathbf{w}, y) = \{\mathbf{x} \geq \mathbf{0} : f(\mathbf{x}) \geq y, \ \mathbf{w} \cdot \mathbf{x} \leq 2\widehat{\mathbf{w}} \cdot (\check{\beta}\mathbf{1})\}$$

Consider any fixed $(\mathbf{w}, y)$ in $W \times \check{Y}$. Note that $\check{\beta}\mathbf{1} \in \check{F}(\mathbf{w}, y)$. Also any $\mathbf{x}$ in $\check{F}(\mathbf{w}, y)$ must satisfy $\frac{1}{2}\widehat{\mathbf{w}} \cdot \mathbf{x} \leq \mathbf{w} \cdot \mathbf{x} \leq 2\widehat{\mathbf{w}} \cdot (\check{\beta}\mathbf{1})$, and so $\check{F}(\mathbf{w}, y) \subseteq A$, where $A = \{\mathbf{x} \in \mathbb{R}^n_+ : \frac{1}{2}\widehat{\mathbf{w}} \cdot \mathbf{x} \leq 2\widehat{\mathbf{w}} \cdot (\check{\beta}\mathbf{1})\}$, which is obviously a bounded set. Arguing as in Example 14.1.5, $\check{F}$ has a closed graph at every point of $W \times Y$, so Theorem 14.1.3 implies that $\check{F}$ is u.h.c. throughout $W \times Y$. Because f is monotonic, it is easy to see that $\check{F}(\mathbf{w}, y)$ is the closure of the set $\{\mathbf{x} \gg \mathbf{0} : f(\mathbf{x}) > y, \ \mathbf{w} \cdot \mathbf{x} < 2\widehat{\mathbf{w}} \cdot (\check{\beta}\mathbf{1})\}$. Then the result of Example 14.1.5 shows that $\check{F}$ is also l.h.c. throughout $W \times Y$. So Note 1 applies and gives continuity of $C(\mathbf{w}, y)$ and upper hemicontinuity of $\xi(\mathbf{w}, y)$ in $W \times Y$. Since $\widehat{\mathbf{w}}$ and $\hat{y}$ were arbitrary, these properties hold for all $\mathbf{w} \gg 0$, $y \geq 0$.

PROBLEMS FOR SECTION 14.2

1. Let $f(x, y) = -y^4 + x(y^2 - 1)$ for all x and $-1 \leq y \leq 1$, and consider the maximization problem $\max_{-1 \leq y \leq 1} f(x, y)$. Determine the value function for this problem, and describe the correspondence $Y^*(x) = \{y \in [-1, 1] : y \text{ maximizes } f(x, y) \text{ over } [-1, 1]\}$. Show that Y^* has the closed graph property.

2. Suppose that a consumer has a continuous and strictly quasiconcave utility function $U(\mathbf{x})$ defined on the set $\mathbb{R}^n_+$, which is maximized subject to the constraint $x \in \mathcal{B}(\mathbf{p}, m)$, where $(\mathbf{p}, m) \mapsto \mathcal{B}(\mathbf{p}, m)$ is the budget correspondence described in Example 14.1.1.

Explain why the consumer's (single-valued) demand function $\mathbf{x}(\mathbf{p}, m)$ and the associated indirect utility function $V(\mathbf{p}, m)$ are both continuous wherever $\mathbf{p} \gg \mathbf{0}$ and $m \geq 0$. What can go wrong if $p_i = 0$ for some i?

3. Suppose that the utility function of the consumer in Problem 2 is continuous but not even quasi-concave. What continuity properties can then be expected of the consumer's demand correspondence $(\mathbf{p}, m) \mapsto \xi(\mathbf{p}, m)$ and indirect utility function $V(\mathbf{p}, m)$? What difference would quasi-concavity make to the demand correspondence?

14.3 Fixed Points for Contraction Mappings

This brief section presents a so-called fixed point theorem with important applications to economics. In particular it is used in Section 12.3 in connection with the Bellman equation in infinite horizon dynamic programming.

A function F from a set S into $\mathbb{R}^m$ is called **bounded** on S if there exists a positive number M such that $\|F(\mathbf{x})\| \leq M$ for all $\mathbf{x}$ in S.

Let S be a subset of $\mathbb{R}^n$, and let $\mathcal{B}$ denote the set of all bounded functions from S into $\mathbb{R}^m$. We define the **distance** between two functions φ and ψ in $\mathcal{B}$ as

$$d(\varphi, \psi) = \sup_{\mathbf{x} \in S} \|\varphi(\mathbf{x}) - \psi(\mathbf{x})\|$$

Let $T : \mathcal{B} \to \mathcal{B}$ be a function (or "operator") that maps each function φ in $\mathcal{B}$ to a function $T(\varphi)$ in $\mathcal{B}$. Thus $T(\varphi)$ is also a bounded function $S \to \mathbb{R}^m$. We will write $T(\varphi)(\mathbf{x})$ for the value of $T(\varphi)$ at a point $\mathbf{x}$ in S. The function T called a **contraction mapping** if there exists a constant β in $(0, 1)$ such that for all φ and ψ in $\mathcal{B}$, one has

$$\|T(\varphi)(\mathbf{x}) - T(\psi)(\mathbf{x})\| \leq \beta d(\varphi, \psi) \quad \text{for all } \mathbf{x} \text{ in } S \tag{1}$$

or, equivalently,

$$d(T(\varphi), T(\psi)) \leq \beta d(\varphi, \psi) \tag{2}$$

For any two elements φ and ψ of $\mathcal{B}$, the distance between $T(\varphi)$ and $T(\psi)$ is then at most β times the distance between φ and ψ, hence the name contraction mapping.

THEOREM 14.3.1 (CONTRACTION MAPPING THEOREM)

Let S be a nonempty subset of $\mathbb{R}^n$ and let $\mathcal{B}$ be the set of all bounded functions from S into $\mathbb{R}^m$. Suppose that the operator $T : \mathcal{B} \to \mathcal{B}$ is a contraction mapping. Then there exists a unique function φ^* in $\mathcal{B}$ such that $\varphi^* = T(\varphi^*)$.

Proof: Since T is a contraction, there exists a β in $(0, 1)$ such that (2) is satisfied for all φ and ψ in $\mathcal{B}$. Choose an arbitrary function φ_0 in $\mathcal{B}$. Define $\varphi_1 = T(\varphi_0)$, and generally $\varphi_{n+1} = T(\varphi_n)$ for $n = 0, 1, 2, \ldots$. Let $\gamma_n = d(\varphi_{n+1}, \varphi_n)$. Then (2) implies that

$$\gamma_{n+1} = d(\varphi_{n+2}, \varphi_{n+1}) = d(T(\varphi_{n+1}), T(\varphi_n)) \leq \beta d(\varphi_{n+1}, \varphi_n) = \beta \gamma_n, \quad n \geq 0 \qquad \text{(i)}$$

An obvious induction argument shows that $\gamma_n \leq \beta^n \gamma_0$. We want to prove that for each point $\mathbf{x}$ in S, the sequence $\{\varphi_n(\mathbf{x})\}$ is a Cauchy sequence in $\mathbb{R}^m$. To this end note that

$$\varphi_{n+k} - \varphi_n = (\varphi_{n+k} - \varphi_{n+k-1}) + (\varphi_{n+k-1} - \varphi_{n+k-2}) + \cdots + (\varphi_{n+1} - \varphi_n)$$

Therefore, for every $\mathbf{x}$ in S, whenever $m > n$ it follows from the triangle inequality that

$$\|\varphi_m(\mathbf{x}) - \varphi_n(\mathbf{x})\| = \left\| \sum_{r=n}^{m-1} (\varphi_{r+1}(\mathbf{x}) - \varphi_r(\mathbf{x})) \right\| \leq \sum_{r=n}^{m-1} \|\varphi_{r+1}(\mathbf{x}) - \varphi_r(\mathbf{x})\|$$

$$\leq \sum_{r=n}^{m-1} \gamma_r \leq \sum_{r=n}^{m-1} \beta^r \gamma_0 = \beta^n \gamma_0 \frac{1 - \beta^{m-n}}{1 - \beta} \leq \frac{\beta^n \gamma_0}{1 - \beta} \qquad \text{(ii)}$$

The last expression is small when n is large. Hence $\varphi_n(\mathbf{x})$ is indeed a Cauchy sequence, with a limit $\varphi^*(\mathbf{x})$. Letting $m \to \infty$ in the inequalities (ii), with n fixed, we see that $\|\varphi^*(\mathbf{x}) - \varphi_n(\mathbf{x})\| \leq \beta^n \gamma_0 / (1 - \beta)$ for all $\mathbf{x}$ in S. Now,

$$\|T(\varphi^*)(\mathbf{x}) - \varphi_{n+1}(\mathbf{x})\| = \|T(\varphi^*)(\mathbf{x}) - T(\varphi_n(\mathbf{x}))\| \leq \beta^{n+1} \gamma_0 / (1 - \beta)$$

by (1). Letting $n \to \infty$ yields $\varphi^*(\mathbf{x}) = T(\varphi^*)(\mathbf{x})$ for all $\mathbf{x}$, and so $T(\varphi^*) = \varphi^*$. If another function φ^{**} satisfies $T(\varphi^{**}) = \varphi^{**}$, then by (2),

$$d(\varphi^*, \varphi^{**}) = d(T(\varphi^*), T(\varphi^{**})) \leq \beta d(\varphi^*, \varphi^{**})$$

Because $0 < \beta < 1$ and $d(\varphi^*, \varphi^{**}) \geq 0$, it follows that $d(\varphi^*, \varphi^{**}) = 0$, hence $\varphi^{**} = \varphi^*$. ∎

NOTE 1 The conclusion of the theorem remains true if $\mathcal{B}$ is restricted to only those bounded functions $\varphi : S \to \mathbb{R}^m$ that satisfy the inequality $\|\varphi(\mathbf{x}) - \mathbf{y}_0\| \leq A$ for a given point $\mathbf{y}_0$ in $\mathbb{R}^m$ and a given number A, i.e. every φ in $\mathcal{B}$ maps S into the closed ball of radius A around the point $\mathbf{y}_0$. It also remains true if we require that $\|\varphi(\mathbf{x}) - \varphi(\mathbf{x}')\| \leq M \|\mathbf{x} - \mathbf{x}'\|$ for all $\mathbf{x}$ and $\mathbf{x}'$ in S and a common given number M. It even remains true if both conditions are imposed on the elements of $\mathcal{B}$. To see this, note that if the relevant inequality or inequalities hold for each φ_n in the proof above, they still hold after passing to the limit (as $n \to \infty$).

EXAMPLE 1   As an example of how one can use the contraction mapping theorem, we prove Theorem 5.8.2 on the existence and uniqueness of solutions of differential equations.

Proof: We use the notation in Theorem 5.8.2. Further, let $K = \max_{(t,x)\in\Gamma} |F'_x(t,x)|$ and $k = \min\{a, b/M, 1/(2K)\}$. By the mean-value theorem, $|F(t,x) - F(t,x')| \le K|x - x'|$ for all t in $[t_0 - a, t_0 + a]$ and all x, x' in $[x_0 - b, x_0 + b]$.

We first prove the existence of a unique solution over the interval $I = [t_0 - k, t_0 + k]$ instead of $(t_0 - r, t_0 + r)$. A function x^* solves the initial value problem $\dot{x} = F(t,x), x(t_0) = x_0$ if and only if

$$x^*(t) = x_0 + \int_{t_0}^t F(s, x^*(s))\,ds$$

for all t in I. Suppose x^* is a solution. Then for t and t' in I we have

$$|x^*(t') - x^*(t)| = \left|\int_t^{t'} F(s, x^*(s))\,ds\right| \le M|t' - t|$$

since $|F(s,x)| \le M$ for all (s,x) in Γ. Let $\mathcal{B}$ be the set of all functions $x : I \to \mathbb{R}$ that satisfy $x(t_0) = x_0$ and $|x(t') - x(t)| \le M|t' - t|$ for all t, t' in I. The set $\mathcal{B}$ is nonempty, since it contains the constant function $x \equiv x_0$, and all functions that belong to $\mathcal{B}$ are continuous. Then the operator $T : \mathcal{B} \to \mathcal{B}$ defined by $T(x)(t) = x_0 + \int_{t_0}^t F(s, x(s))\,ds$ is well defined. (You should verify that $(s, x(s))$ lies in Γ.) For any two functions x and $\bar{x}$ in $\mathcal{B}$ and any s in I we have $|F(s, \bar{x}(s)) - F(s, x(s))| \le K|\bar{x}(s) - x(s)| \le Kd(\bar{x}, x)$, and so

$$|T(\bar{x})(t) - T(x)(t)| = \left|\int_{t_0}^t \big(F(s, \bar{x}(s)) - F(s, x(s))\big)\,ds\right| \le |t - t_0|Kd(\bar{x}, x) \le \tfrac{1}{2}d(\bar{x}, x)$$

since $|t - t_0| \le k \le 1/(2K)$. It follows that $d(T(\bar{x}), T(x)) = \sup_{t\in I} |T(\bar{x})(t) - T(x)(t)| \le \tfrac{1}{2}d(\bar{x}, x)$. Hence T is a contraction, and by Theorem 14.3.1 and the succeeding note, it has a unique fixed point x^*.

So far we have proved the existence of a unique solution over $[t_0 - k, t_0 + k]$. To extend this solution to all of $(t_0 - r, t_0 + r)$, note that we can use the same construction to show that there is a unique solution in a neighbourhood of any point in Γ. One can then splice together two solutions that agree on some common subinterval of their domains, and obtain a solution over the union of the domains. In this way, one can obtain a solution over all of $[t_0 - a, t_0 + a]$. We refrain from going into the details here. ∎

14.4 Brouwer's and Kakutani's Fixed Point Theorems

Consider a function $\mathbf{f}$ that maps each point $\mathbf{x}$ of a set K in $\mathbb{R}^n$ to a point $\mathbf{f}(\mathbf{x})$ of the same set K. We say that $\mathbf{f}$ maps the set K into itself. Usually, $\mathbf{x}$ and $\mathbf{f}(\mathbf{x})$ will be different. If $\mathbf{x}^*$ is a point such that $\mathbf{f}(\mathbf{x}^*) = \mathbf{x}^*$, that is, if the point $\mathbf{x}^*$ is mapped to itself, then $\mathbf{x}^*$ is called a **fixed point** of $\mathbf{f}$.

We would like to find conditions ensuring that any continuous function mapping K into itself has a fixed point. Note that some restrictions must be placed on K. For instance, the continuous mapping $f(x) = x + 1$ of the real line into itself has no fixed point; this is because $f(x^*) = x^*$ would imply that $x^* + 1 = x^*$, which is absurd.

The following result by L.E.J. Brouwer yields sufficient conditions for the existence of a fixed point. (See Ichiishi (1983) for a proof.)

THEOREM 14.4.1 (BROUWER'S FIXED POINT THEOREM)

Let K be a nonempty compact (closed and bounded) convex set in $\mathbb{R}^n$, and $\mathbf{f}$ a continuous function mapping K into itself. Then $\mathbf{f}$ has a fixed point $\mathbf{x}^*$, i.e. a point $\mathbf{x}^*$ in K such that $\mathbf{f}(\mathbf{x}^*) = \mathbf{x}^*$.

The function $\mathbf{f}$ in the theorem maps points $\mathbf{x}$ in $\mathbb{R}^n$ into points $\mathbf{y}$ in $\mathbb{R}^n$. It is therefore described by the system

$$y_1 = f_1(x_1, \ldots, x_n), \quad y_2 = f_2(x_1, \ldots, x_n), \quad \ldots, \quad y_n = f_n(x_1, \ldots, x_n)$$

So a fixed point $\mathbf{x}^* = (x_1^*, \ldots, x_n^*)$ of $\mathbf{f}$ must satisfy the equation system

$$x_1 = f_1(x_1, \ldots, x_n)$$
$$\ldots\ldots\ldots\ldots\ldots \tag{1}$$
$$x_n = f_n(x_1, \ldots, x_n)$$

This immediately shows how Brouwer's fixed point theorem can be used to establish the existence of a solution to a nonlinear system of equations. Note, however, that in order to apply the theorem one must establish the continuity of $\mathbf{f}$ and prove that $\mathbf{f}$ maps a suitable domain K into itself.

There are numerous applications of Brouwer's theorem in which the set K is the **standard unit simplex** Δ^{n-1} in $\mathbb{R}^n$ defined by [1]

$$\Delta^{n-1} = \left\{ \mathbf{x} = (x_1, \ldots, x_n) : x_1 \geq 0, \ \ldots, \ x_n \geq 0, \ \sum_{i=1}^{n} x_i = 1 \right\} \tag{2}$$

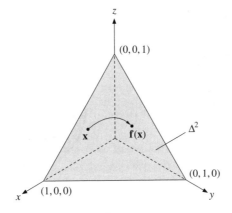

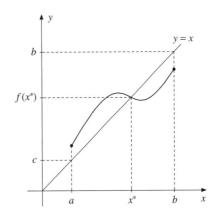

Figure 1 $\mathbf{f}$ maps Δ^2 into itself.

Figure 2 $f(x^*) = x^*$

For instance, $x_1, \ldots, x_n$ might denote the nonnegative prices of n different commodities, these prices being normalized by the convention that $x_1 + \cdots + x_n = 1$.

---

[1] Note that Δ^{n-1} is $(n-1)$-dimensional. For example, Δ^2 is contained in the (2-dimensional) plane $x_1 + x_2 + x_2 = 1$ in $\mathbb{R}^3$. See Fig. 1.

The set Δ^{n-1} is convex and compact. To see whether Brouwer's theorem applies to a given continuous function $\mathbf{f}$ defined on Δ^{n-1}, it is only necessary to check that $\mathbf{f}$ maps Δ^{n-1} into itself. If $\mathbf{f}$ is given by (1), then $\mathbf{f}$ will map Δ^{n-1} into itself provided that for all $(x_1, \ldots, x_n)$ in Δ^n, one has

$$f_1(x_1, \ldots, x_n) \geq 0, \quad \ldots, \quad f_n(x_1, \ldots, x_n) \geq 0, \quad \sum_{i=1}^{n} f_i(x_1, \ldots, x_n) = 1 \qquad (3)$$

The case when $n = 3$ is illustrated in Fig. 1. Brouwer's theorem implies that if $\mathbf{f}$ maps Δ^2 continuously into Δ^2, then there must be at least one point $\mathbf{x}^*$ in Δ^2 for which $\mathbf{f}(\mathbf{x}^*) = \mathbf{x}^*$.

In $\mathbb{R}^1$ (the real line), a nonempty compact convex set must be a closed and bounded interval $[a, b]$ (or a single point). So Brouwer's theorem asserts that a continuous function $f : [a, b] \to [a, b]$ must have a fixed point. But in this case, this follows from the intermediate value theorem. (Indeed, $g(x) = f(x) - x$ satisfies $g(a) \geq 0$, and $g(b) \leq 0$, so for some x^* in $[a, b]$, $g(x^*) = 0$.) The geometric content of this proposition is illustrated in Fig. 2. The graph of f must cross the diagonal $y = x$.

An Illustration

For the two-dimensional case the following illustration of the theorem might aid your intuition. Do not take the illustration too seriously, however!

Imagine an enormous flock of sheep crammed into a circular pen. Suppose that the flock suddenly starts moving and then stops after a certain time. At a given moment of time each sheep has a definite position in the pen, as shown in Fig. 3. Although each sheep can move, no sheep can move against or across the stream, so each sheep must stay close to its original neighbours.

Consider the mapping from the position originally occupied by each sheep to its final position after stopping. By the assumptions above, this is a continuous mapping (a dubious claim) of the pen into itself. Because the pen is a compact convex set, Brouwer's theorem applies. So there must be at least one "fixed sheep" which stops exactly where it started.

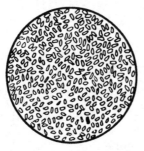

Figure 3   Figure 4

Now assume instead that the flock is enclosed in a circular ring, as indicated in Fig. 4. Suppose all the sheep move 90 degrees clockwise around the ring. Then each sheep will stop in an entirely new position. No "fixed sheep" exists in this case. As above, the movement indicated defines a continuous mapping of the pen into itself, but there is no fixed point. In fact, Brouwer's theorem does not apply since the ring of Fig. 4 is not a convex set.

The importance of this result for sheep farmers can hardly be underestimated, but it does indicate an important "topological difference" between a circular disc and a ring.

A Generalization

The convexity hypothesis in Theorem 14.4.1 can be relaxed. Let $L \subseteq \mathbb{R}^n$ be a **homeomorphic image** of K in the sense that there exists a one-to-one continuous mapping $\mathbf{g}$ of K onto L (i.e. $\mathbf{g}(K) = L$) whose inverse mapping $\mathbf{g}^{-1}$ is also continuous. Intuitively, homeomorphic images of a rubber ball are obtained by squashing or stretching, as long as we do not tear it apart, make any holes, or glue parts together. Note, in particular, that homeomorphic images of a convex set are not necessarily convex. The natural generalization of Brouwer's theorem is:

> Any homeomorphic image L of a nonempty compact convex set $K \subseteq \mathbb{R}^n$ has the fixed point property, i.e. any continuous function $\mathbf{f}$ mapping L into L has a fixed point. (4)

Proof: Let $\mathbf{f}$ be the continuous function mapping L into L, and let $\mathbf{g}$ be a homeomorphism—i.e. a continuous mapping of K onto L with a continuous inverse $\mathbf{g}^{-1}$. If $\mathbf{x} \in K$, then $\mathbf{g}(\mathbf{x}) \in L$, so $\mathbf{f}(\mathbf{g}(\mathbf{x})) \in L$, which implies that $\mathbf{g}^{-1}(\mathbf{f}(\mathbf{g}(\mathbf{x}))) \in K$. So the mapping $\mathbf{g}^{-1}\mathbf{f}\mathbf{g}$ must be a continuous function of K into itself. According to Theorem 14.4.1, there exists a fixed point $\mathbf{x}^*$ in K such that $\mathbf{g}^{-1}(\mathbf{f}(\mathbf{g}(\mathbf{x}^*))) = \mathbf{x}^*$. But then $\mathbf{g}(\mathbf{x}^*) = \mathbf{f}(\mathbf{g}(\mathbf{x}^*))$, and so $\mathbf{g}(\mathbf{x}^*)$ in L is a fixed point for $\mathbf{f}$. ∎

Brouwer's original motivation for his theorem was to examine the topological differences between various sets in $\mathbb{R}^n$. It was recognized only later that the theorem had interesting applications outside topology. The next section shows how Brouwer's theorem can be used to prove the existence of an equilibrium in a pure exchange economy. Although this type of economy is very simple and unrealistic, the existence proof contains many of the essential features that arise in richer general equilibrium models.

Kakutani's Fixed Point Theorem

Brouwer's theorem deals with fixed points of continuous functions on appropriate domains. Kakutani's theorem generalizes the theorem to correspondences. It is a reformulation of an existence theorem for saddle points proved by von Neumann in 1928 and used in his work on both game theory and growth theory. (For a proof, see Aubin and Frankowska (1990).)

THEOREM 14.4.2 (KAKUTANI'S FIXED POINT THEOREM)

Let K be a nonempty compact convex set in $\mathbb{R}^n$ and F a correspondence $K \twoheadrightarrow K$. Suppose that:

(a) $F(\mathbf{x})$ is a nonempty convex set in K for each $\mathbf{x}$ in K.

(b) F is upper hemicontinous.

Then F has a fixed point $\mathbf{x}^*$ in K, i.e. a point $\mathbf{x}^*$ such that $\mathbf{x}^* \in F(\mathbf{x}^*)$.

Notice that Brouwer's theorem is implied by Kakutani's because a continuous function $\mathbf{f}$ mapping the compact domain $K \subseteq \mathbb{R}^n$ into itself has an associated correspondence with non-empty convex values defined by $F(\mathbf{x}) = \{\mathbf{f}(\mathbf{x})\}$ for all $\mathbf{x}$ in K. This correspondence is upper hemicontinuous by Theorem 14.1.2, and so has the closed graph property.

In the one-dimensional case, Theorem 14.1.2 takes the form:

If the correspondence $F : [a, b] \to [a, b]$ has the closed graph property, where $F(x)$ is a nonempty closed interval for each x in $[a, b]$, then F has a fixed point. $\qquad$ (5)

Proof: For each x in $[a, b]$, the image of F is a closed interval depending on x, say $F(x) = [f(x), g(x)]$. Define $x^* = \sup\{x \in [a, b] : f(x) \geq x\}$. We claim that $f(x^*) \leq x^* \leq g(x^*)$, which means that $x^* \in F(x^*)$ and thus x^* is a fixed point.

To prove that $f(x^*) \leq x^*$, note that this is trivial if $x^* = b$, so assume $x^* < b$. Suppose contrary to the assumption that $f(x^*) > x^*$. Then also $f(x^*) > x^* + \varepsilon$ for some $\varepsilon > 0$. F is upper hemicontinuous at x^* (Theorem 14.1.3). According to definition (14.1.8), to the open set $U = (x^* + \varepsilon, \infty)$ containing $F(x^*) = [f(x^*), g(x^*)]$, there exists a neighbourhood N of x^* such that for z in $N \cap [a, b]$, we have $F(z) = [f(z), g(z)] \subseteq U$. Then, in particular, for z in $N \cap [a, b]$, $f(z) > x^* + \varepsilon$. If we choose N so small that all z in N satisfy $x^* < z < x^* + \varepsilon$, then $f(z) > x^* + \varepsilon > z$, contradicting the definition of x^*.

To prove that $g(x^*) \geq x^*$, note that this is trivial if $x^* = a$, so assume $x^* > a$. Suppose contrary to the assumption that $g(x^*) < x^*$. Then also $g(x^*) < x^* - \varepsilon$ for some $\varepsilon > 0$. Upper hemicontinuity of F at x^* implies that $F(z) \subseteq (-\infty, x^* - \varepsilon) \subseteq (-\infty, z)$ for all z close enough to x^*, with $z < x^*$ and $z > x^* - \varepsilon$. But then $f(z) \leq g(z) < x^* - \varepsilon < z$ for all $z < x^*$ close enough to x^*, contradicting the definition of x^*. ∎

The one-dimensional case is illustrated in Fig. 5. The fixed point is x^*. Figure 6 illustrates that in (5) one cannot drop the requirement that $F(x)$ be an interval (so convex).

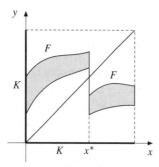

Figure 5 x^* is a fixed point for F.

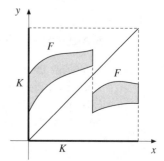

Figure 6 F has no fixed point.

PROBLEMS FOR SECTION 14.4

1. Consider the function f defined for all x in $(0, 1)$ by $f(x) = \frac{1}{2}(x + 1)$. Prove that f maps $(0, 1)$ into itself, but f has no fixed point. Why does Brouwer's theorem not apply?

2. Consider the continuous transformation $\mathbf{T} : (x, y) \mapsto (-y, x)$ from the xy-plane into itself, consisting of a 90° rotation around the origin. Define the sets

$$E = \{(x, y) : x^2 + y^2 = 1\}, \qquad B = \{(x, y) : x^2 + y^2 \leq 1\}$$

Are these sets compact? $\mathbf{T}$ induces continuous maps $\mathbf{T}_E : E \to E$ and $\mathbf{T}_B : B \to B$. Does either transformation have a fixed point? Explain the results in the light of Brouwer's theorem.

3. Let $\mathbf{A} = (a_{ij})$ be an $n \times n$ matrix whose elements all satisfy $a_{ij} \geq 0$. Assume that all column sums are 1, so that $\sum_{i=1}^{n} a_{ij} = 1$ $(j = 1, \ldots, n)$. Prove that if $\mathbf{x} \in \Delta^{n-1}$, then $\mathbf{Ax} \in \Delta^{n-1}$, where Δ^{n-1} is the unit simplex defined by (2). Hence, $\mathbf{x} \mapsto \mathbf{Ax}$ is a (linear) transformation of Δ^{n-1} into itself. What does Brouwer's theorem say in this case?

4. Consider the correspondence $F : [0, 2] \twoheadrightarrow [0, 2]$ that maps each x in $[0, 1)$ to $\{2\}$, maps $x = 1$ to $\{0, 2\}$, and finally maps each x in $(1, 2]$ to $\{0\}$. Draw the graph of F and determine whether F has a closed graph. Does Kakutani's theorem apply?

HARDER PROBLEMS

5. Assume that $f : [0, 1] \to [0, 1]$ satisfies $\overline{\lim}_{s \to x^-} f(s) \leq f(x) \leq \overline{\lim}_{s \to x^+} f(s)$ for all x in $[0, 1]$. (Only the right-hand (left-hand) inequality is required to hold for $x = 0$ $(x = 1)$.) Prove that f has a fixed point. (*Hint:* Consider $x^* = \sup A$, where $A = \{x \in [0, 1] : f(x) \geq x\}$.)

14.5 Equilibrium in a Pure Exchange Economy

Consider an economy with m consumers, each of whom is initially endowed with fixed quantities of n different commodities or goods. No production is possible, so the consumers merely engage in exchange. Trade takes place because each consumer wishes to acquire a bundle of commodities that is preferred to the initial endowment. This is described as a **pure exchange** economy.

As usual when discussing perfectly competitive markets, we assume that consumers can exchange their commodities at fixed price ratios. Specifically, we assume that a price vector $\mathbf{p} = (p_1, \ldots, p_n)$ is announced, where p_i is the nonnegative price per unit of commodity number i. Thus, any consumer can sell one unit of commodity j for the amount p_j, and use that amount to buy any other commodity i at the price p_i. In this way, the one unit of commodity j has the same value as p_j / p_i units of commodity i (assuming that $p_i > 0$).

The price vector $\mathbf{p}$ determines the market value $\mathbf{p} \cdot \mathbf{c} = \sum_{i=1}^{n} p_i c_i$ of any commodity bundle $\mathbf{c} = (c_1, \ldots, c_n)$, including any consumer's initial endowment. By exchanging at the fixed price ratios p_j / p_i, the consumer can achieve any commodity bundle whose market value equals that of the initial endowment. These are the *affordable* consumption bundles at which the consumer satisfies his or her *budget constraint*.

Among all affordable commodity bundles, each consumer selects one that is weakly preferred to all the others. In other words, each consumer's demands represent the choice of commodity bundle that maximizes a utility function subject to that consumer's own budget constraint. (We assume that there is a unique utility maximizing consumption bundle.)

Next, add the demands of all consumers for each commodity i and subtract the total initial endowment of i. The result is called the *excess demand* for that commodity. Because it depends on the price vector $\mathbf{p}$, the excess demand will be denoted by $g_i(\mathbf{p})$. When the price vector is $\mathbf{p}$, the sign of $g_i(\mathbf{p})$ indicates whether the total demand for commodity i is greater or less than the total endowment of that good.

The following question arises naturally in the minds of most economists. Is it possible to find prices of all commodities which ensure that the aggregate demand for each does not exceed the corresponding aggregate endowment? Prices with this property are called *equilibrium prices*. This is because, if all consumers do face such prices, then all their demands for every good can be satisfied simultaneously. So there are no unfulfilled demands that can force consumers to change their plans.

Let $\mathbf{p}^* = (p_1^*, \ldots, p_n^*)$ denote such an equilibrium price vector. By definition, it must satisfy the inequalities $g_i(\mathbf{p}^*) \leq 0$ for $i = 1, \ldots, n$. It will now be shown how Brouwer's fixed point theorem can be used to prove existence of an equilibrium price vector, provided suitable continuity conditions are imposed.

To proceed further requires a little extra notation. For each consumer j and commodity i, let w_i^j denote j's initial endowment of i, and $x_i^j(\mathbf{p})$ the same consumer's final demand when the price vector is $\mathbf{p}$. In addition, let

$$w_i = \sum_{j=1}^m w_i^j \quad \text{and} \quad x_i(\mathbf{p}) = \sum_{j=1}^m x_i^j(\mathbf{p}), \quad i = 1, \ldots, n$$

denote respectively the *total endowment* and *market demand* for each commodity i. The latter is equal to the total demand for commodity i by all consumers. The excess demand functions referred to above are then given by

$$g_i(\mathbf{p}) = x_i(\mathbf{p}) - w_i$$

Now, the total value of consumer j's initial endowment at the price vector $\mathbf{p}$ is $\sum_{i=1}^n p_i w_i^j$, so the budget constraint is

$$\sum_{i=1}^n p_i x_i^j(\mathbf{p}) = \sum_{i=1}^n p_i w_i^j \tag{1}$$

This is valid for each consumer, so summing (1) from $j = 1$ to $j = m$ and using the definitions of the aggregates w_i and $x_i(\mathbf{p})$, we obtain

$$\sum_{i=1}^n p_i x_i(\mathbf{p}) = \sum_{i=1}^n p_i w_i \quad \textbf{(Walras's Law)} \tag{2}$$

Thus, the value of the aggregate excess demand vector $g_i(\mathbf{p}) = \sum_{i=1}^n (x_i(\mathbf{p}) - w_i)$ at prices $\mathbf{p}$ is identically zero.

An equilibrium price vector $\mathbf{p}^*$ is characterized by the inequalities

$$x_i(\mathbf{p}^*) \leq w_i \quad \text{or} \quad g_i(\mathbf{p}^*) \leq 0 \quad \text{for all } i = 1, \ldots, n \tag{3}$$

so that the equilibrium market demand for each commodity does not exceed the total endowment of that commodity. Also, observe that because $\mathbf{p}^* \geq 0$ and $x_i(\mathbf{p}^*) \leq w_i$, each product $p_i^*(x_i(\mathbf{p}^*) - w_i)$ is ≤ 0. But the sum over $i = 1, \ldots, n$ of all these products is 0 because of Walras's Law (2). Consequently, it is impossible that $p_i^*(x_i(\mathbf{p}^*) - w_i) < 0$ for any i. Hence, we have proved that if $\mathbf{p}^*$ is an equilibrium price vector, then

$$x_i(\mathbf{p}^*) < w_i \quad \Rightarrow \quad p_i^* = 0, \qquad i = 1, \ldots, n \tag{4}$$

This is the *rule of free goods*: if any commodity is in excess supply in equilibrium, its price must be zero. In other words, *if there is a commodity for which the market demand is strictly less than the total stock, then the equilibrium price for that commodity must be 0.*

It is rather obvious that only price ratios, or relative prices, matter in this economy. For this reason, we can normalize by dividing the price vector $\mathbf{p}$ by the (positive) sum $p_1 + \cdots + p_n$ of the prices to ensure that this sum is equal to 1 (see Problem 1). Then all normalized price vectors will lie in the simplex Δ^{n-1} defined by (14.4.2).

Any existence proof requires continuity assumptions. It will be enough to assume that the market demand functions $\mathbf{p} \mapsto x_i(\mathbf{p})$, $i = 1, \ldots, n$, are continuous functions on the simplex Δ^{n-1} or, what amounts to the same thing, that the excess demand functions $g_1, \ldots, g_n$ are continuous on Δ^{n-1}. Our problem can now be stated as follows:

Suppose that $g_1, \ldots, g_n$ are continuous on Δ^{n-1} and assume that

$$\sum_{i=1}^{n} p_i g_i(\mathbf{p}) = 0 \quad \text{for all } \mathbf{p} \text{ in } \Delta^{n-1} \tag{5}$$

Is there a vector $\mathbf{p}^* = (p_i^*, \ldots, p_n^*)$ in Δ^n such that

$$g_1(\mathbf{p}^*) \leq 0, \quad \ldots, \quad g_n(\mathbf{p}^*) \leq 0 ?$$

(Note that (5) is a restatement of Walras's Law.)

We shall use Brouwer's theorem to prove existence. To do so, we construct a continuous mapping of Δ^{n-1} into itself for which any fixed point gives equilibrium prices. Consider first the mapping $(p_1, \ldots, p_n) \mapsto (p_1', \ldots, p_n')$ defined by

$$p_1' = p_1 + g_1(\mathbf{p}), \quad p_2' = p_2 + g_2(\mathbf{p}), \quad \ldots, \quad p_n' = p_n + g_n(\mathbf{p}) \tag{6}$$

This simple price adjustment mechanism has a certain economic appeal: it maps p_i, the "old" price of commodity i, to the new adjusted price $p_i' = p_i + g_i(\mathbf{p})$. If excess demand $g_i(\mathbf{p})$ is positive, so that the market demand exceeds the total available endowment, then the price is increased. The opposite is true if $g_i(\mathbf{p}) < 0$, when the price is lowered. So far, this is all very sensible. Note, however, that there is no guarantee that $p_i' \geq 0$. Moreover, the new prices p_i' usually will not sum to 1. Hence, the new price vector $(p_1', \ldots, p_n')$ will not necessarily belong to the simplex Δ^{n-1}. As a consequence, Brouwer's theorem does not apply to the mapping defined in (6). The mapping must be altered somewhat in order to work.

Before we present an alternative mapping, recall that if x is a real number, then $\max\{0, x\}$ denotes the larger of the two numbers 0 and x. Hence, if $x > 0$ then $\max\{0, x\} = x$, whereas

$\max\{0, x\} = 0$ if $x \le 0$. It is easy to check that $\max\{0, x\} = \frac{1}{2}(x + |x|)$, which shows that the function $x \mapsto \max\{0, x\}$ is continuous.

With this in mind, instead of (6) we define a mapping $(p_1, \ldots, p_n) \mapsto (p'_1, \ldots, p'_n)$ by

$$p'_i = \frac{1}{d(\mathbf{p})}\left(p_i + \max\{0, g_i(\mathbf{p})\}\right), \qquad i = 1, \ldots, n \tag{7}$$

where $d(\mathbf{p}) = 1 + \sum_{k=1}^{n}\max\{0, g_k(\mathbf{p})\} \ge 1$. It is difficult to provide a good economic motivation for this particular mapping. Nevertheless, it does what is needed. Note first that $p'_i \ge 0$ for all i. Also, the new prices p'_i sum to unity whenever the old prices p_i do. Hence, (7) defines a mapping of Δ^{n-1} into itself. We see, moreover, that each p'_i is a continuous function of $(p_1, \ldots, p_n)$. Thus Brouwer's theorem applies, and so there must exist a fixed point $\mathbf{p}^* = (p_1^*, \ldots, p_n^*)$ in Δ^{n-1}. At $\mathbf{p}^*$, for any $i = 1, \ldots, n$, one has

$$p_i^* = \frac{1}{d(\mathbf{p}^*)}\left(p_i^* + \max\{0, g_i(\mathbf{p}^*)\}\right)$$

This is easily seen to be equivalent to

$$(d(\mathbf{p}^*) - 1)p_i^* = \max\{0, g_i(\mathbf{p}^*)\} \tag{8}$$

The definition of $d(\mathbf{p})$ implies that $d(\mathbf{p}^*) \ge 1$. Suppose that $d(\mathbf{p}^*) > 1$. Then (8) implies that for those i with $p_i^* > 0$ one has $\max\{0, g_i(\mathbf{p}^*)\} > 0$, and so $g_i(\mathbf{p}^*) > 0$. Because $p_1^* + \cdots + p_n^* = 1$, however, at least one p_i^* is positive. It follows that $\sum_{i=1}^{n} p_i^* g_i(\mathbf{p}^*) > 0$, a contradiction of Walras's Law. Hence, we conclude that $d(\mathbf{p}*) = 1$. But then (8) implies that $\max\{0, g_i(\mathbf{p}^*)\} = 0$ for $i = 1, \ldots, n$, and so $g_i(\mathbf{p}^*) \le 0$ for $i = 1, \ldots, n$. This proves that $\mathbf{p}^*$ is an equilibrium price vector. The existence of an equilibrium in the pure exchange economy is thereby established.

Brouwer's fixed point theorem can only be used to prove existence. For the last example in particular, it does not by itself indicate any practical method for finding equilibrium prices.

The economic model considered above was one of pure exchange in the sense that there was no production of commodities. Moreover, consumer demand functions were single-valued. More realistic equilibrium models include producers as well as consumers, and allow (multi-valued) demand (and supply) correspondences. Obviously, existence of an equilibrium is an important issue in these more general models as well. It turns out that existence can still be established under suitable assumptions, making use of Kakutani's fixed point theorem for correspondences.

PROBLEMS FOR SECTION 14.5

1. In the pure exchange model studied above, suppose that each consumer j's demand functions $x_1^j(\mathbf{p}), \ldots, x_n^j(\mathbf{p})$ result from utility maximization subject to j's own budget constraint. Explain why the demand functions $x_i^j(\mathbf{p})$ are then all homogeneous of degree 0, and why this entitles us to normalize prices by setting $p_1 + \cdots + p_n = 1$.

APPENDIX

SETS, COMPLETENESS AND CONVERGENCE

If we can't imagine how something might fail to happen, we are
tempted to conclude that it must always happen. Of course,
according to this principle of reasoning, the poorer our
imagination the more facts we could establish!
—Loomis (1974)

This appendix considers a few selected topics from the foundations of mathematical analysis. Much of it is concerned with notation and definitions of concepts that appear repeatedly in the main part of the book.

A.1 Sets and Functions

A **set** is a "collection of objects". These objects are called the **elements** of the set. A finite set can be described by listing the objects: $\{a, b, c, \ldots, t\}$. Some infinite sets can be written in a similar way, like the set $\mathbb{N} = \{1, 2, 3, \ldots\}$ of all natural numbers, provided it is clear from the context precisely what the elements of the set are. We use the notation $x \in S$ to indicate that x is an element of S (or "belongs to S" or "is a member of S").

Two sets A and B are equal ($A = B$) if and only if they *have the same elements*. A consequence of this is that repetitions in the listing of a set have no effect: $\{1, 3, 5, 1, 5, 2, 1\} = \{1, 2, 3, 5\}$. This example also illustrates that the order of the elements in the listing makes no difference.

If A and B are two sets such that every element of A is also an element of B, then A is a **subset** of B and one writes $A \subseteq B$ (read as "A is a subset of B" or "A is included in B") or $B \supseteq A$ ("B includes A"). The set A is a **proper subset** of B if $A \subseteq B$ and $A \neq B$; sometimes one writes $A \subsetneq B$ in this case. The symbol $\subseteq$ is called the **inclusion** symbol.[1] It is clear that $A = B$ if and only if $A \subseteq B$ and $B \subseteq A$. It is also easy to see that if $A \subseteq B$ and $B \subseteq C$, then $A \subseteq C$.

The **empty set**, $\emptyset$, is a set with no elements at all. It is a subset of every set.

---

[1] Some authors use $\subset$ as the inclusion symbol, and some use $\subseteq$ for inclusion and reserve $\subset$ for proper inclusion. In this book we use $\subseteq$ for inclusion, whether proper or not.

There are several ways to build new sets from given sets. One very common construction is the creation of a subset of a given set by selecting those elements that have a certain property: If S is a set and $\alpha(x)$ is a condition that an element x of S may or may not satisfy, then $A = \{x \in S : \alpha(x)\}$ is the set of all those elements of S that satisfy the condition. For example, the set $A = \{1, 2, 3, 4\}$ of all natural numbers between 1 and 4 can be written as $\{x \in \mathbb{N} : 1 \leq x \leq 4\}$. If it is clear from the context exactly what the set S is, one often simply writes $\{x : \alpha(x)\}$ for the set $\{x \in S : \alpha(x)\}$.

If A and B are sets, then $A \cup B$, the **union** of A and B, is the set of all elements that belong to A or B (or both). The **intersection** $A \cap B$ of A and B is the set of the elements that belong to both A and B. If $A \cap B = \emptyset$, the sets A and B are **disjoint**. The set theoretic **difference** $A \setminus B$ ("A minus B") is the set of all elements in A that do not belong to B. The **symmetric difference** $A \triangle B = (A \setminus B) \cup (B \setminus A)$ is the set of all elements that belong to exactly one of the sets A and B.

The following are some important identities involving the operations defined above.

$$A \cup B = B \cup A, \quad (A \cup B) \cup C = A \cup (B \cup C), \quad A \cup \emptyset = A \tag{1}$$

$$A \cap B = B \cap A, \quad (A \cap B) \cap C = A \cap (B \cap C), \quad A \cap \emptyset = \emptyset \tag{2}$$

$$A \cup (B \cap C) = (A \cup B) \cap (A \cup C), \quad A \cap (B \cup C) = (A \cap B) \cup (A \cap C) \tag{3}$$

$$A \setminus (B \cup C) = (A \setminus B) \cap (A \setminus C), \quad A \setminus (B \cap C) = (A \setminus B) \cup (A \setminus C) \tag{4}$$

$$A \triangle B = B \triangle A, \quad (A \triangle B) \triangle C = A \triangle (B \triangle C), \quad A \triangle \emptyset = A \tag{5}$$

The formulas in (3) are called **distributive laws** and the formulas in (4) are known as **De Morgan's laws**.

In discussions involving sets, it is often the case that all the sets considered are subsets of some given "universal" set, Ω, say. When this is the case, the set difference $\Omega \setminus S$ is often written as A^c or $\complement S$, and called the **complement** of S. When we discuss subsets of $\mathbb{R}^n$, for instance, $\complement S = \mathbb{R}^n \setminus S$. With this notation, De Morgan's laws can be written as

$$\complement(B \cup C) = \complement B \cap \complement C, \qquad \complement(B \cap C) = \complement B \cup \complement C \tag{6}$$

(with A as the universal set).

The collection of all subsets of a set A is also a set, called the **power set** of A and denoted by $\mathcal{P}(A)$. Thus, $B \in \mathcal{P}(A) \iff B \subseteq A$.

We noted above that the order of the elements in a set specification such as $\{a, b, \ldots, t\}$ does not matter. Thus, in particular $\{a, b\} = \{b, a\}$. However, on many occasions one *is* interested in distinguishing between the first and the second elements of a pair. One such example is the coordinates of a point in the xy-plane. These coordinates are given as an **ordered pair** (a, b) of real numbers. The important property of ordered pairs is that $(a, b) = (c, d)$ if and only if $a = c$ and $b = d$. See Problem 1 for one possible way to define an ordered pair in set-theoretic terms. Once ordered pairs are available, ordered triples, quadruples, etc. are defined by $(a, b, c) = ((a, b), c)$, $(a, b, c, d) = ((a, b, c), d)$, etc. Of course, there is a natural one-to-one correspondence $((a, b), c) \leftrightarrow (a, (b, c))$, so it would not matter much if an ordered triple were defined as $(a, (b, c))$ instead of $((a, b), c)$. The important thing again is that $(a, b, c) = (d, e, f)$ if and only if $a = d$, $b = e$, and $c = f$.

If A and B are sets, their **Cartesian product** is the set $A \times B$ consisting of all ordered pairs (a, b) such that $a \in A$ and $b \in B$. Similarly, the Cartesian product of the sets A, B, and C is the set of all ordered triples (a, b, c) such that $a \in A$, $b \in B$, and $c \in C$. The natural one-to-one correspondence $((a, b), c) \leftrightarrow (a, (b, c))$ referred to above gives a one-to-one correspondence between $(A \times B) \times C$ and $A \times (B \times C)$, so one can well identify the two and write either product simply as $A \times B \times C$.

The Euclidean plane $\mathbb{R}^2$ is the Cartesian product $\mathbb{R} \times \mathbb{R}$. More generally, $\mathbb{R}^m = \mathbb{R} \times \cdots \times \mathbb{R}$ (m factors), and there is a natural identification between $\mathbb{R}^m \times \mathbb{R}^n$ and $\mathbb{R}^{m+n}$.

Indexed Sets

There is often a need to go beyond ordered pairs. Suppose that, for each i in some set I, we specify an object a_i (which can be a number, a set, or any other entity). Then these objects form an **indexed set** $\{a_i\}_{i \in I}$ with I as its **index set**. In formal terms, an indexed set is a function whose domain is the index set (see below).

There is an important difference between the indexed set $\{a_i\}_{i \in I}$, and the set of all the values a_i. For example, an n-vector $\mathbf{x} = (x_1, x_2, \ldots, x_n)$ is an indexed set with $\{1, 2, \ldots, n\}$ as its index set. Here the order of the elements does matter, and multiple occurrences of the same value will also matter. Thus the 5-dimensional *vector* $(3, -1, 3, 3, -2)$ is different from the vector $(3, -2, -1, 3, -1)$, whereas the *sets* $\{3, -1, 3, 3, -2\}$ and $\{3, -2, -1, 3, -1\}$ are equal (and equal to the set $\{-1, -2, 3\}$). Indexed sets make it possible to talk about sets whose elements appear in some specific order, and with possible repetitions. A **sequence** is an indexed set $\{a_k\}_{k \in \mathbb{N}}$ with the set $\mathbb{N}$ of natural numbers as its index set. Instead of $\{a_k\}_{k \in \mathbb{N}}$ one often writes $\{a_k\}_{k=1}^{\infty}$.

A set whose elements are sets is often called a **family** of sets, and so an indexed set of sets is also called an **indexed family** of sets.

Consider a nonempty indexed family $\{A_i\}_{i \in I}$ of sets (i.e. the index set I is nonempty). The **union** and the **intersection** of this family are the sets

$$\bigcup_{i \in I} A_i = \text{the set consisting of all } x \text{ that belong to } A_i \text{ for } at\ least\ one\ i \text{ in } I \qquad (7)$$

$$\bigcap_{i \in I} A_i = \text{the set consisting of all } x \text{ that belong to } A_i \text{ for } all\ i \text{ in } I \qquad (8)$$

The **distributive laws** in (3) can be generalized to

$$A \cup \left(\bigcap_{i \in I} B_i\right) = \bigcap_{i \in I} (A \cup B_i), \quad A \cap \left(\bigcup_{i \in I} B_i\right) = \bigcup_{i \in I} (A \cap B_i) \qquad (9)$$

and **De Morgan's laws** (4) to

$$A \setminus \left(\bigcup_{i \in I} B_i\right) = \bigcap_{i \in I} (A \setminus B_i), \quad A \setminus \left(\bigcap_{i \in I} B_i\right) = \bigcup_{i \in I} (A \setminus B_i) \qquad (10)$$

The union and the intersection of a sequence $\{A_n\}_{n \in \mathbb{N}} = \{A_n\}_{n=1}^{\infty}$ of sets is often written as $\bigcup_{n=1}^{\infty} A_n$ and $\bigcap_{n=1}^{\infty} A_n$. The meaning of notations like $\bigcup_{n=1}^{k} A_n$ should be obvious.

One can also form the Cartesian product of indexed families. If $\{A_i\}_{i \in I}$ is an indexed family, then $\prod_{i \in I} A_i$ is the set of all indexed sets $\{a_i\}_{i \in I}$ such that $a_i \in A_i$ for all $i \in I$. In particular,

$$\prod_{k=1}^{n} A_k = A_1 \times \cdots \times A_n = \{(a_1, \ldots, a_n) : a_k \in A_k \text{ for } k = 1, \ldots, n\}. \tag{11}$$

Relations

A **relation** from a set A to a set B is a subset of $A \times B$, that is, a set of ordered pairs (a, b) such that $a \in A$ and $b \in B$. If R is a relation, one often writes aRb instead of $(a, b) \in R$.

A relation from A to A is also called a (**binary**) **relation in** A. As an example of a relation in $\mathbb{R}$, consider the "less than" relation consisting of all ordered pairs of real numbers (x, y) with $x < y$.

The **domain** of a relation R from A to B is the set

$$\text{dom}(R) = \{a \in A : (a, b) \in R \text{ for some } b \text{ in } B\} = \{a \in A : aRb \text{ for some } b \text{ in } B\}$$

and the **range** of R is

$$\text{range}(R) = \{b \in B : (a, b) \in R \text{ for some } a \text{ in } A\} = \{b \in B : aRb \text{ for some } a \text{ in } A\}$$

The **inverse** of a relation R from A to B is the relation $R^{-1} = \{(b, a) \in B \times A : (a, b) \in R\}$ from B to A.

A relation R in X is **reflexive** if xRx for all x in X. It is **transitive** if xRy and yRz implies xRz, it is **symmetric** if xRy implies yRx, it is **anti-symmetric** if xRy and yRx implies $x = y$, and it is **complete** if for all x and y in X at least one of xRy or yRx holds. A **partial ordering** in X is a relation in X that is reflexive, transitive, and anti-symmetric. If a partial ordering is complete, it is called a **linear** (or **total**) **ordering**. The relation $\leq$ in $\mathbb{R}$ is a linear ordering.

For $n \geq 2$, the less-than-or-equal-to relation $\leq$ in $\mathbb{R}^n$ is defined by $(x_1, \ldots, x_n) \leq (y_1, \ldots, y_n) \Leftrightarrow x_k \leq y_k$ for $k = 1, \ldots, n$. The symbol $\leq$ is then usually taken to mean "$\leq$, but not $=$". (Some authors also use $<$ in this sense when comparing vectors. Caution is necessary!) There is also a strict inequality relation $\ll$, given by $(x_1, \ldots, x_n) \ll (y_1, \ldots, y_n) \Leftrightarrow x_k < y_k$ for all $k = 1, \ldots, n$. The relation $\leq$ is a partial ordering in $\mathbb{R}^n$.

An **equivalence relation** in X is a relation that is reflexive, transitive and symmetric. If R is an equivalence relation in X, then R induces a partitioning of X into disjoint **equivalence classes** $[x] = \{y \in X : yRx\}$. The union of all these equivalence classes is X.

Functions

A **function** (also called a **mapping**, **map** or **transformation**) $f : X \to Y$ from a set X to a set Y is a rule that assigns exactly one element $y = f(x)$ in Y to each x in X. In set-theoretic terms f is a *relation* from X to Y such that:

1. $\text{dom}(f) = X$.

2. For each x in X there is exactly one y in Y such that $x f y$.

Thus f is "single-valued" and "operates on" every x in X. One usually writes $f(x) = y$ instead of $x\, f\, y$. The set X is the **domain** and Y is the **codomain** of f. The **range** of f is the same as the range of f considered as a relation:

$$\text{range}(f) = \{y \in Y : y = f(x) \text{ for at least one } x \text{ in } X\} = \{f(x) : x \in X\}$$

The last formulation is an example of a somewhat sloppy notation that is often used when the meaning is clear from the context. The **graph** of f is the set

$$\text{graph}(f) = \{(x, y) \in X \times Y : y = f(x)\}$$

This is of course the same as the relation f as defined in the previous subsection.

The domain and range of a function can be determined from its graph. This makes it tempting to think that the graph holds all the information one will ever need about the function. Note, however, that in some applications one really needs to know the codomain, and not just the range.

If $f(x) = y$, one also writes $x \mapsto y$. The squaring function $s : \mathbb{R} \to \mathbb{R}$, for example, can then be written as $s : x \mapsto x^2$. Thus, $\mapsto$ indicates the effect of the function on an element of the domain. If the domain A of $f : A \to B$ is a subset of a set X, it is sometimes convenient to write $f : A \subseteq X \to B$, and maybe even $f : A \subseteq X \to B \subseteq Y$ if B is a subset of Y.

If $f : A \to B$ is a function and $S \subseteq A$, the **restriction** of f to S is the function $f|_S$ defined by $f|_S(x) = f(x)$ for every x in S.

A function $f : A \to B$ is **"one-to-one"** or **injective** if $f(a) \neq f(a')$ whenever $a \neq a'$, i.e. if f always maps distinct points in A to distinct points in B.

If the range of $f : A \to B$ is all of B, then f is called **surjective** or **onto**, and f is said to map A *onto* B.

When $f : A \to B$ is both injective and surjective (i.e., when it is both one-to-one and onto), it is called **bijective**.

If $f : A \to B$ is injective, then f has an inverse function $f^{-1} : \text{range}(f) \to A$, defined by $f^{-1}(b) = a \Leftrightarrow b = f(a)$. (Considered as a *relation*, f always has an inverse with range(f) as its domain, but this inverse relation is a *function* only when f is injective.)

The **composition** of a function $f : A \to B$ and a function $g : B \to C$ is the function $g \circ f : A \to C$ given by $(g \circ f)(a) = g(f(a))$ for all a in A. It is easy to check that this is the same as the composition of f and g as relations.

Direct and Inverse Images

Let $f : A \to B$ be a function. The **(direct) image** under f of a subset S of A is the set

$$f(S) = \{y \in B : y = f(x) \text{ for some } x \text{ in } A\}$$

and the **inverse image** under f of a set $T \subseteq B$ is

$$f^{-1}(T) = \{x \in A : f(x) \in T\}$$

Direct and inverse images satisfy a number of relations, among them the following (S_i and

T_i are subsets of A and B, respectively).

$$f(S_1 \cup S_2) = f(S_1) \cup f(S_2), \qquad\qquad f(\textstyle\bigcup_{i \in I} S_i) = \bigcup_{i \in I} f(S_i) \qquad (12)$$

$$f(S_1 \cap S_2) \subseteq f(S_1) \cap f(S_2), \qquad\qquad f(\textstyle\bigcap_{i \in I} S_i) \subseteq \bigcap_{i \in I} f(S_i) \qquad (13)$$

$$f^{-1}(T_1 \cup T_2) = f^{-1}(T_1) \cup f^{-1}(T_2), \qquad f^{-1}(\textstyle\bigcup_{i \in I} T_i) = \bigcup_{i \in I} f^{-1}(T_i) \qquad (14)$$

$$f^{-1}(T_1 \cap T_2) = f^{-1}(T_1) \cap f^{-1}(T_2), \qquad f^{-1}(\textstyle\bigcap_{i \in I} T_i) = \bigcap_{i \in I} f^{-1}(T_i) \qquad (15)$$

Note that inverse images preserve both unions and intersections, whereas direct images preserve only unions, not intersections (see Problem 3).

Some other properties of direct and inverse images are:

$$S \subseteq f^{-1}(f(S)), \quad f(f^{-1}(T)) \subseteq T, \quad f^{-1}(T) = f^{-1}(T \cap \text{range}(f)) \qquad (16)$$

$$S_1 \subseteq S_2 \implies f(S_1) \subseteq f(S_2) \text{ and } f(S_2) \setminus f(S_1) \subseteq f(S_2 \setminus S_1) \qquad (17)$$

$$T_1 \subseteq T_2 \implies f^{-1}(T_1) \subseteq f^{-1}(T_2) \text{ and } f^{-1}(T_2 \setminus T_1) = f^{-1}(T_2) \setminus f^{-1}(T_1) \qquad (18)$$

PROBLEMS FOR SECTION A.1

1. The ordered pair (a, b) is most commonly defined as the set $(a, b) = \{\{a\}, \{a, b\}\}$. Show that with this definition, $(a, b) = (c, d)$ if and only if $a = c$ and $b = d$.

2. Show the equalities $\text{dom}(R^{-1}) = \text{range}(R)$ and $\text{range}(R^{-1}) = \text{dom}(R)$ for a relation R from A to B.

3. Give an example to show that the inclusion signs in (13) cannot be replaced by equality signs.

4. Show that if R is a linear ordering in a set X, then the inverse relation R^{-1} is also a linear ordering.

5. Prove (16). Also, give examples to show that $\subseteq$ cannot always be replaced by $=$.

A.2   Least Upper Bound Principle

The real number system is fully characterized by a rather small number of axioms. The usual algebraic rules and the rules for inequalities are all well known. Here we consider briefly only the so-called *least upper bound principle*. An understanding of this principle is crucial for many of the arguments in this book. The need for this principle can be understood if we look at the problem of determining the area of a circle.

We know how to calculate the area of plane regions bounded by straight lines. Figure 1 shows a sequence of regular polygons inscribed in a circle. For $n \geq 3$, let A_n be the area

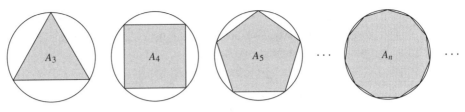

Figure 1

of a regular n-sided polygon inscribed in the circle. Thus, A_3 is the area of an equilateral triangle, A_4 is the area of a square, A_5 is the area of a regular pentagon, and so on.

The area of the circle must be greater than each of the numbers $A_3, A_4, A_5, \ldots$. On the other hand it seems clear that by choosing n sufficiently large, we can make the difference between the area of the circle and the area of an inscribed regular n-gon as small as we please. We now *define* the area of the circle as the smallest number greater than or equal to each of the numbers $A_3, A_4, A_5, \ldots$. This definition makes sense only if such a number exists. The existence of this number follows from a basic property of real numbers, called the principle of least upper bound.

Recall that a set S of real numbers is **bounded above** if there exists a real number b such that $b \geq x$ for all x in S. This number b is called an **upper bound** for S. A set that is bounded above has many upper bounds. A **least upper bound** for the set S is a number b^* that is an upper bound for S and is such that $b^* \leq b$ for every upper bound b.

The existence of a least upper bound is a basic and non-trivial property of the real number system.

LEAST UPPER BOUND PRINCIPLE

Any nonempty set of real numbers that is bounded above has a least upper bound.   (1)

A set S can have at most one least upper bound, because if b_1^* and b_2^* are both least upper bounds for S, then $b_1^* \leq b_2^*$ and $b_2^* \leq b_1^*$, and thus $b_1^* = b_2^*$. The least upper bound b^* of S is often called the **supremum** of S. We write $b^* = \sup S$ or $b^* = \sup_{x \in S} x$.

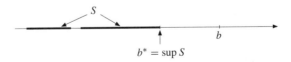

Figure 2 b is an upper bound for S, and $b^* = \sup S$ is the least upper bound for S.

EXAMPLE 1   The set $S = (0, 5)$, consisting of all x such that $0 < x < 5$, has many upper bounds, some of which are 100, 6.73, and 5. Clearly, no number smaller than 5 can be an upper bound, so 5 is the least upper bound. Thus $\sup S = 5$.

The set $T = \{x : x^2 < 2\} = (-\sqrt{2}, \sqrt{2})$ has many upper bounds, some of which are 9, 2, and $\sqrt{2}$. Clearly, no number smaller than $\sqrt{2}$ can be an upper bound of T, and so $\sqrt{2}$ is the least upper bound, $\sup T = \sqrt{2}$.

A set S is **bounded below** if there exists a real number a such that $x \geq a$ for all x in S. The number a is called a **lower bound** for S. A set S that is bounded below has a **greatest lower bound** a^*, with the property $a^* \leq x$ for all x in S, and $a^* \geq a$ for all lower bounds a. The number a^* is called the **infimum** of S and we write $a^* = \inf S$ or $a^* = \inf_{x \in S} x$. Thus,

$$\sup S = \text{the least number greater than or equal to all numbers in } S \qquad (2)$$
$$\inf S = \text{the greatest number less than or equal to all numbers in } S \qquad (3)$$

If S is not bounded below, we write $\inf S = -\infty$. If S is not bounded above, we write $\sup S = \infty$.

The following characterization of the supremum is easy to prove:

THEOREM A.2.1

Let S be a set of real numbers and b^* a real number. Then $\sup S = b^*$ if and only if the following two conditions are satisfied:

(a) $x \leq b^*$ for all x in S.

(b) For each $\varepsilon > 0$ there exists an x in S such that $x > b^* - \varepsilon$.

NOTE 1 The existence of a supremum of a set bounded above may seem to be "intuitively evident": Start with a nonempty set S of real numbers and an upper bound b for S, as in Fig. 2. Then move b to the left until it is "stopped" by the set S. The number b is still an upper bound for S, and it is the least of all the upper bounds.

The fact that the principle of least upper bound is a non-trivial property of the real number system is perhaps better appreciated if we realize that the principle does not hold within the set of rational numbers. For instance, let S be the set of all rational numbers r such that $r^2 < 2$. Within the rational number system, the set S has no least upper bound. All rational numbers larger than or equal to $\sqrt{2}$ are upper bounds for S, but there is not a smallest one among these numbers because $\sqrt{2}$ is irrational. (See Problem 2.)

PROBLEMS FOR SECTION A.2

1. Consider the three sets

$$A = (-3, 7], \qquad B = \left\{\frac{1}{n} : n = 1, 2, 3, \ldots\right\}, \qquad C = \{x : x > 0 \text{ and } x^2 > 3\}$$

Determine sup and inf for each of these three sets.

2. Suppose that r is a rational number with $r > \sqrt{2}$. Show that the rational number $s = (2 + r^2)/2r$ satisfies $\sqrt{2} < s < r$.

3. Show that $\sup S = \infty$ iff for every b in $\mathbb{R}$ there exists an x in S such that $x > b$.

A.3 Sequences of Real Numbers

Recall that a **sequence** is a function $k \mapsto x(k)$ whose domain is the set $\{1, 2, 3, \ldots\}$ of all positive integers. The **terms** $x(1)$, $x(2)$, $x(3)$, $\ldots$, $x(k)$, $\ldots$ of the sequence are usually denoted by using subscripts: $x_1, x_2, x_3, \ldots, x_k, \ldots$. We shall use the notation $\{x_k\}_{k=1}^{\infty}$, or simply $\{x_k\}_k$, or even just $\{x_k\}$, to indicate an arbitrary sequence of real numbers.

A sequence $\{x_k\}$ of real numbers is said to be

(a) **increasing** (or **nondecreasing**) if $x_k \leq x_{k+1}$ for $k = 1, 2, \ldots$

(b) **strictly increasing** if $x_k < x_{k+1}$ for $k = 1, 2, \ldots$

(c) **decreasing** (or **nonincreasing**) if $x_k \geq x_{k+1}$ for $k = 1, 2, \ldots$

(d) **strictly decreasing** if $x_k > x_{k+1}$ for $k = 1, 2, \ldots$

A sequence that is increasing or decreasing is called **monotone**.

EXAMPLE 1   Decide whether or not the three sequences of real numbers whose general terms are given below are monotone:

$$\text{(a) } x_k = 1 - 1/k \qquad \text{(b) } y_k = (-1)^k \qquad \text{(c) } z_k = \sqrt{k+1} - \sqrt{k}$$

Solution: The sequence $\{x_k\}$ is (strictly) increasing, because for $k = 1, 2, \ldots,$

$$x_{k+1} > x_k \iff 1 - 1/(1+k) > 1 - 1/k \iff 1/(k+1) < 1/k$$

And the last inequality clearly holds for all $k \geq 1$.

The sequence $\{y_k\}$ is not monotone. It is clearly neither increasing nor decreasing, because its terms are $-1, 1, -1, 1, -1, \ldots$.

The first three terms of the sequence $\{z_k\}$ are: $z_1 = \sqrt{2} - \sqrt{1} \approx 0.4142$, $z_2 = \sqrt{3} - \sqrt{2} \approx 0.3178$, and $z_3 = \sqrt{4} - \sqrt{3} \approx 0.2679$. Note that $z_1 > z_2 > z_3$. In fact, a standard trick shows that $\{z_k\}$ is indeed strictly decreasing:

$$z_k = \sqrt{k+1} - \sqrt{k} = \frac{(\sqrt{k+1} - \sqrt{k})(\sqrt{k+1} + \sqrt{k})}{\sqrt{k+1} + \sqrt{k}} = \frac{1}{\sqrt{k+1} + \sqrt{k}}$$

From the last fraction we see that z_k decreases when k increases.

A sequence $\{x_k\}$ is said to *converge* to a number x if x_k becomes arbitrarily close to x for all sufficiently large k. We write

$$\lim_{k\to\infty} x_k = x \qquad \text{or} \qquad x_k \to x \quad \text{as} \quad k \to \infty$$

The precise definition of convergence is as follows:

DEFINITION OF A CONVERGENT SEQUENCE

The sequence $\{x_k\}$ **converges** to x, and we write

$$\lim_{k\to\infty} x_k = x$$

(1)

if for every $\varepsilon > 0$ there exists a natural number N such that $|x_k - x| < \varepsilon$ for all $k > N$. The number x is called the **limit** of the sequence $\{x_k\}$. A **convergent** sequence is one that converges to some number.

Note that the limit of a convergent sequence is unique. (See Problem 7.) A sequence that does not converge to any real number is said to **diverge**.

In some cases we use the notation $\lim_{k\to\infty} x_k$ even if the sequence $\{x_k\}$ is divergent: If for each number M there exists a number N such that $x_k \geq M$ for all natural number $k \geq N$, then we say that x_k approaches ∞, and write $\lim_{k\to\infty} x_k = \infty$. In the same way we write $\lim_{k\to\infty} x_k = -\infty$ if for every number M there exists a number N such that $x_k \leq -M$ for all $k \geq N$.

In Example 1, the sequence $\{x_k\}$ converges to 1 because $1/k$ tends to 0 as k tends to ∞. (Using (1): Given $\varepsilon > 0$, we must find a number N such that for $k > N$ we have $|(1 - 1/k) - 1| < \varepsilon$, i.e. $1/k < \varepsilon$, or $k > 1/\varepsilon$. Clearly, this is accomplished by choosing an $N \geq 1/\varepsilon$.)

The sequence $\{y_k\}$ is divergent. If k is even, $y_k = 1$ and if k is odd, $y_k = -1$. So there is clearly no number y such that y_k tends to y as k tends to ∞.

The sequence $\{z_k\}$ is convergent, with $\lim_{k\to\infty} z_k = \lim_{k\to\infty} 1/\big(\sqrt{k+1} + \sqrt{k}\big) = 0$.

A sequence $\{x_k\}$ is **bounded** if there exists a number M such that $|x_k| \leq M$ for all $k = 1$, $2, \ldots$. It is easy to see that *every convergent sequence is bounded*: If $x_k \to x$, then by the definition of convergence, only finitely many terms of the sequence can lie outside the interval $I = (x - 1, x + 1)$. The set I is bounded and the finite set of points from the sequence that are not in I is bounded, so $\{x_k\}$ must be bounded. On the other hand, is every bounded sequence convergent? No. For example, the sequence $\{y_k\} = \{(-1)^k\}$ in Example 1 is bounded but not convergent. Suppose, however, that the sequence is monotone as well as bounded. Then it is convergent.

THEOREM A.3.1

Every bounded monotone sequence is convergent.

Proof: Suppose that $\{x_k\}$ is increasing and bounded. Let b^* be the least upper bound of the set $X = \{x_k : k = 1, 2, \ldots\}$, and let ε be an arbitrary positive number. Then $b^* - \varepsilon$ is not an upper bound of X, so there must be a term x_N of the sequence for which $x_N > b^* - \varepsilon$. Because the sequence is increasing, $b^* - \varepsilon < x_N \leq x_k$ for all $k > N$. But the x_k are all less than or equal to b^*, so $b^* - \varepsilon < x_k \leq b^*$. Thus, for any $\varepsilon > 0$ there exists a number N such that $|x_k - b^*| < \varepsilon$ for all $k > N$. Hence $\{x_k\}$ converges to b^*. If $\{x_k\}$ is decreasing and bounded, the argument is analogous. ∎

EXAMPLE 2   Consider the sequence $\{x_k\}$ defined by

$$x_1 = \sqrt{2}, \quad x_{k+1} = \sqrt{x_k + 2}, \quad k = 1, 2, \ldots \tag{*}$$

Use Theorem A.3.1 to prove that the sequence is convergent and find its limit. (*Hint:* Prove by induction that $x_k < 2$ for all k. Then prove that the sequence is (strictly) increasing.)

Solution: Note that $x_1 = \sqrt{2} < 2$, and if $x_k < 2$, then $x_{k+1} = \sqrt{x_k + 2} < \sqrt{2+2} = 2$, so by induction, $x_k < 2$ for all k. Moreover, because $x_k < 2$, one has

$$x_{k+1} = \sqrt{x_k + 2} > \sqrt{x_k + x_k} = \sqrt{2x_k} > \sqrt{x_k^2} = x_k$$

so $\{x_k\}$ is (strictly) increasing. By Theorem A.3.1 the sequence is convergent. If x is its limit, then letting $k \to \infty$ in (*) yields $x = \sqrt{x + 2}$, by the continuity of $\sqrt{x}$. This equation implies that $x^2 = x+2$, which has the two solutions -1 and $x = 2$. Because -1 is obviously not a solution of $x = \sqrt{x + 2}$, the only solution is $x = 2$, and thus $\lim_{k\to\infty} x_k = 2$.

Rules for Handling Convergent Sequences

Suppose that $\{x_k\}$ converges to x and $\{y_k\}$ converges to y as $k \to \infty$. For k sufficiently large, x_k is close to x and y_k is close to y. Then $x_k + y_k$ must be close to $x + y$, and it is therefore reasonable to believe that $x_k + y_k \to x + y$ as $k \to \infty$. Corresponding results hold for subtraction, multiplication, and division. In fact, we have the following result.

THEOREM A.3.2 (RULES FOR SEQUENCES)

Suppose that the sequences $\{x_k\}$ and $\{y_k\}$ converge to x and y, respectively. Then:
(a) $\lim_{k\to\infty}(x_k + y_k) = x + y$
(b) $\lim_{k\to\infty}(x_k - y_k) = x - y$
(c) $\lim_{k\to\infty}(x_k \cdot y_k) = x \cdot y$
(b) $\lim_{k\to\infty}(x_k/y_k) = x/y$, assuming that $y_k \neq 0$ for all k and $y \neq 0$.

Proof: (a) Here is a formal proof: Let ε be an arbitrary positive number. Since $\{x_k\}$ is convergent, there exists a number N_1 such that $|x_k - x| < \varepsilon/2$ for all $k > N_1$. In the same way there exists a number N_2 such that $|y_k - y| < \varepsilon/2$ for all $k > N_2$. Let N be the greater of the two numbers N_1 and N_2. Then for $k > N$,

$$|(x_k + y_k) - (x + y)| = |(x_k - x) + (y_k - y)| \le |x_k - x| + |y_k - y| < \varepsilon/2 + \varepsilon/2 = \varepsilon$$

But this means that $\lim_k (x_k + y_k) = x + y = \lim_k x_k + \lim_k y_k$.

The statement in (b) is proved in the same way. Proving (c) and (d) requires more complicated arguments to show that $|x_k y_k - xy|$ and $|x_k/y_k - x/y|$ are less than an arbitrary positive ε. For a precise proof we refer to e.g. Marsden and Hoffman (1993). ∎

Subsequences

Let $\{x_k\}$ be a sequence. Consider a strictly increasing sequence of natural numbers

$$k_1 < k_2 < k_3 < \cdots$$

and form a new sequence $\{y_j\}_{j=1}^{\infty}$, where $y_j = x_{k_j}$ for $j = 1, 2, \ldots$. The sequence $\{y_j\}_j = \{x_{k_j}\}_j$ is called a **subsequence** of $\{x_k\}$. Because the sequence $\{k_j\}$ is strictly increasing, $k_j \ge j$ for all j. The terms of the subsequence are all present in the original one. In fact, a subsequence can be viewed as the result of removing some (possibly none) of the terms of the original sequence. For example, $x_5, x_6, x_7, \ldots$ is the subsequence obtained by striking out the first four terms of the original sequence, and $x_2, x_4, x_6, \ldots$ is the subsequence obtained by removing all terms with an odd index. If $x_k = (-1)^k$ is the divergent sequence mentioned above, we may for example define the two subsequences $\{x_{2k}\}$ and $\{x_{2k-1}\}$. Here $x_{2k} = (-1)^{2k} = 1$, and $x_{2k-1} = (-1)^{2k-1} = -1$ for all k. Note that in this case the two particular subsequences considered are both convergent.

NOTE 1 Some proofs involve pairs of sequences $\{x_k\}_{k=1}^{\infty}$ and $\{x_{k^j}\}_{j=1}^{\infty}$ where $k^j \ge j$ for all j, but where the sequence $k^1, k^2, \ldots$ is not necessarily strictly increasing. Thus $\{x_{k^j}\}_j$ is "not quite" a subsequence of $\{x_k\}_k$. However, it is always possible to select terms from $\{x_{k^j}\}$ in such a way that we get a subsequence $\{x_{k_i}\}_i$ of $\{x_k\}_k$: Let $k_1 = k^1$, and generally $k_{i+1} = k^{k_i + 1}$. Then $k_{i+1} \ge k_i + 1 > k_i$.

The following important fact follows immediately from the definition of convergence:

THEOREM A.3.3

Every subsequence of a convergent sequence is itself convergent, and has the same limit as the original sequence.

The following result is less obvious but also useful.

THEOREM A.3.4

If the sequence $\{x_k\}$ is bounded, then it contains a convergent subsequence.

Proof: Suppose that $|x_k| \leq M$ for all $k = 1, 2, \ldots$ Let $y_n = \sup\{x_k : k \geq n\}$ for $n = 1, 2, \ldots$ Then $\{y_n\}$ is a decreasing sequence because the set $\{x_k : k \geq n\}$ shrinks as n increases. The sequence is also bounded because $y_n \in [-M, M]$. According to Theorem A.3.1, the sequence $\{y_n\}$ has a limit $x = \lim_{n \to \infty} y_n \in [-M, M]$. By the definition of y_n, we can choose a term x_{k^n} from the original sequence $\{x_k\}$ (with $k^n \geq n$) satisfying $|y_n - x_{k^n}| < 1/n$. (See Theorem A.2.1.) Then

$$|x - x_{k^n}| = |x - y_n + y_n - x_{k^n}| \leq |x - y_n| + |y_n - x_{k^n}| < |x - y_n| + 1/n \qquad (*)$$

This shows that $x_{k^n} \to x$ as $n \to \infty$. By using the construction in Note 1, we can extract from $\{x_{k^n}\}$ a subsequence of $\{x_k\}$ that converges to x. ∎

Cauchy Sequences

The definition (1) of a convergent sequence uses the value of the limit. If this limit is unknown, or inconvenient to calculate, the definition is not very useful because one cannot test all numbers to see if they meet the criterion. An important alternative necessary and sufficient condition for convergence is based on the following concept:

DEFINITION OF A CAUCHY SEQUENCE

A sequence $\{x_k\}$ of real numbers is called a **Cauchy sequence** if for every $\varepsilon > 0$, there exists a natural number N such that   (2)

$$|x_n - x_m| < \varepsilon \quad \text{for all } n > N \text{ and all } m > N$$

Note that the terms of a Cauchy sequence will eventually be close together, which need not be the case for an arbitrary sequence. In particular, the sequence $x_k = (-1)^k$, whose terms are alternatively -1 and 1, is clearly not a Cauchy sequence.

All the terms of a convergent sequence eventually cluster around the limit, so the sequence is a Cauchy sequence. The converse is also true, that is, every Cauchy sequence is convergent:

THEOREM A.3.5

A sequence is convergent if and only if it is a Cauchy sequence.

Proof: To prove the "only if part", suppose that $\{x_k\}$ converges to x. Given $\varepsilon > 0$, choose a natural number N such that $|x_k - x| < \varepsilon/2$ for all $k > N$. Then for $k > N$ and $m > N$,

$$|x_k - x_m| = |(x_k - x) + (x - x_m)| \leq |x_k - x| + |x - x_m| < \varepsilon/2 + \varepsilon/2 = \varepsilon$$

Therefore $\{x_k\}$ is a Cauchy sequence.

To prove the "if part", suppose $\{x_k\}$ is a Cauchy sequence. We first show that the sequence is bounded. By the Cauchy property, there is a number M such that $|x_k - x_M| < 1$ for $k > M$. This means that all points x_k with $k > M$ have a distance from x_M that is less than 1. Moreover, the finite set $\{x_1, x_2, \ldots, x_{M-1}\}$ is surely bounded. Hence $\{x_k\}$ is bounded. By Theorem A.3.4, it has a convergent subsequence $\{x_{k_j}\}$. Let $x = \lim_j x_{k_j}$. Because $\{x_k\}$ is a Cauchy sequence, for every $\varepsilon > 0$ there is a natural number N such that $|x_n - x_m| < \varepsilon/2$ for $n > N$ and $m > N$. Moreover, if J is sufficiently large, $|x_{k_j} - x| < \varepsilon/2$ for all $j > J$. Then for $k > N$ and $j > \max\{N, J\}$,

$$|x_k - x| \leq |x_k - x_{k_j}| + |x_{k_j} - x| < \varepsilon/2 + \varepsilon/2 = \varepsilon$$

Hence $x_k \to x$ as $k \to \infty$. ∎

EXAMPLE 3   Prove that the sequence $\{x_k\}$ with the general term $x_k = \dfrac{1}{1^2} + \dfrac{1}{2^2} + \dfrac{1}{3^2} + \cdots + \dfrac{1}{k^2}$ is a Cauchy sequence.

Solution: Let n and m be natural numbers with $m > n$, and define $p = m - n$. Then

$$|x_m - x_n| = |x_{n+p} - x_n| = \frac{1}{(n+1)^2} + \frac{1}{(n+2)^2} + \cdots + \frac{1}{(n+p)^2}$$
$$< \frac{1}{n(n+1)} + \frac{1}{(n+1)(n+2)} + \cdots + \frac{1}{(n+p-1)(n+p)}$$
$$= \left(\frac{1}{n} - \frac{1}{n+1}\right) + \left(\frac{1}{n+1} - \frac{1}{n+2}\right) + \cdots + \left(\frac{1}{n+p-1} - \frac{1}{n+p}\right)$$
$$= \frac{1}{n} - \frac{1}{n+p} < \frac{1}{n}$$

Thus, for any $\varepsilon > 0$, if we choose $n > 1/\varepsilon$, then $|x_m - x_n| < \varepsilon$ for all $m > n$. This proves that $\{x_k\}$ is a Cauchy sequence.

NOTE 2   The infinite series $\sum_{i=1}^{\infty} x_i$ is said to converge if the sequence $\{s_n\}$ of partial sums $s_n = x_1 + x_2 + \cdots + x_n$ is convergent. It follows from the previous example and Theorem A.3.5 that the infinite series

$$\sum_{i=1}^{\infty} x_i$$

is convergent. In fact, one can prove that this infinite series converges to $\pi^2/6$.

Upper and Lower Limits

Let $\{x_k\}$ be a sequence that is bounded above, and define $y_n = \sup\{x_k : k \geq n\}$ for $n = 1, 2,$ .... Each y_n is a finite number and $\{y_n\}_n$ is a decreasing sequence. Then either $\lim_{n\to\infty} y_n$ exists or is $-\infty$. We call this limit the **upper limit** (or **lim sup**) of the sequence $\{x_k\}$, and we introduce the following notation:

$$\limsup_{k\to\infty} x_k = \lim_{n\to\infty}\,(\sup\{x_k : k \geq n\}) \tag{3}$$

If $\{x_k\}$ is not bounded above, we write $\limsup_{k\to\infty} x_k = \infty$.

Similarly, if $\{x_k\}$ is bounded below, its **lower limit** (or **lim inf**), is defined as

$$\liminf_{k\to\infty} x_k = \lim_{n\to\infty}\,(\inf\{x_k : k \geq n\}) \tag{4}$$

If $\{x_k\}$ is not bounded below, we write $\liminf_{k\to\infty} x_k = -\infty$. The symbols lim sup and lim inf are often written as $\overline{\lim}$ and $\underline{\lim}$.

The following characterization of $\overline{\lim}$ is often useful.

A CHARACTERIZATION OF THE UPPER LIMIT

Let $\{x_k\}$ be a sequence of real numbers and b^* a (finite) real number. Then $\overline{\lim}_{k\to\infty} x_k = b^*$ if and only if the following two conditions are satisfied:

(a) For every $\varepsilon > 0$ there exists an integer N such that $x_k < b^* + \varepsilon$ for all $k > N$.

(b) For every $\varepsilon > 0$ and every integer M, there exists an integer $k > M$ such that $x_k > b^* - \varepsilon$. $\tag{5}$

A similar characterization holds for $\underline{\lim}$. Note that condition (a) means that ultimately *all* terms of the sequence lie to the left of $b^* + \varepsilon$ on the real line. Condition (b) means that for any $\varepsilon > 0$, however small, infinitely many terms lie to the right of $b^* - \varepsilon$.

EXAMPLE 4   Determine the $\overline{\lim}$ and $\underline{\lim}$ of the following sequences.

$$\text{(a) } \{x_k\} = \{(-1)^k\} \qquad \text{(b) } \{x_k\} = \left\{(-1)^k\left(2 + \frac{1}{k}\right) + 1\right\}$$

Solution: (a) For every n there exists a number $k \geq n$ with $(-1)^k = 1$. Hence $y_n = \sup\{(-1)^k : k \geq n\} = 1$, and so $\lim_{n\to\infty} y_n = 1$. Thus $\overline{\lim}_{k\to\infty} x_k = 1$. In the same way we see that $\underline{\lim}_{k\to\infty} x_k = -1$.

(b) Arguments similar to those in (a) yield: $\overline{\lim}_{k\to\infty} x_k = 3$, $\underline{\lim}_{k\to\infty} x_k = -1$.

It is not difficult to see that $\underline{\lim}_{k\to\infty} x_k \le \overline{\lim}_{k\to\infty} x_k$ for every sequence $\{x_k\}$. The following result is also rather easy and we leave the proof to the reader.

THEOREM A.3.6

If the sequence $\{x_k\}$ is convergent, then

$$\overline{\lim}_{k\to\infty} x_k = \underline{\lim}_{k\to\infty} x_k = \lim_{k\to\infty} x_k$$

On the other hand, if $\overline{\lim}_{k\to\infty} x_k = \underline{\lim}_{k\to\infty} x_k$, then $\{x_k\}$ is convergent.

PROBLEMS FOR SECTION A.3

1. Prove that the sequence $\{x_k\}$ defined by

$$x_1 = 1, \quad x_{k+1} = 2\sqrt{x_k}, \quad k = 1, 2, \ldots$$

converges, and find its limit. (*Hint:* Prove first by induction that $x_k < 4$ for all k.)

2. Prove that for the sequence $\{x_k\}$ in Example 2, $|x_{k+1} - 2| < \frac{1}{2}|x_k - 2|$, and use this to prove that $x_k \to 2$ as $k \to \infty$. (*Hint:* $x_{k+1} - 2 = (x_{k+1}^2 - 4)/(x_{k+1} + 2)$.)

3. Let S be a nonempty set of real numbers bounded above, and let $b^* = \sup S$. Show that there exists a sequence $\{x_n\}$, $x_n \in S$, such that $x_n \to b^*$. (*Hint:* For each n there exists a number x_n in S such that $x_n > b^* - 1/n$.)

4. Find all possible limits of subsequences of the two sequences defined by

$$x_k = 1 - \frac{1}{k} + (-1)^k, \qquad y_k = \left(1 + \frac{1}{k}\right) \sin k\frac{\pi}{3}$$

5. (a) Consider the two sequences with general terms

$$x_k = \frac{1}{2}(1 + (-1)^k), \qquad y_k = \frac{1}{2}(1 - (-1)^k)$$

Compute $\overline{\lim}_{k\to\infty}$ and $\underline{\lim}_{k\to\infty}$ of $\{x_k\}$, $\{y_k\}$, $\{x_k + y_k\}$, and $\{x_k y_k\}$.

(b) Prove that if the sequences $\{x_k\}$ and $\{y_k\}$ are bounded, then

(i) $\overline{\lim}_{k\to\infty} (x_k + y_k) \le \overline{\lim}_{k\to\infty} x_k + \overline{\lim}_{k\to\infty} y_k$

(ii) $\overline{\lim}_{k\to\infty} (x_k y_k) \le \overline{\lim}_{k\to\infty} x_k \cdot \overline{\lim}_{k\to\infty} y_k$ if $x_k \ge 0$ and $y_k \ge 0$ for all k

Note that the examples in (a) show that the inequality signs $\le$ in (i) and (ii) cannot be replaced by equality signs.

6. Let $\{x_k\}$ be a sequence such that $|x_{k+1} - x_k| < 1/2^k$ for all $k = 1, 2, \dots$. Prove that $\{x_k\}$ is a Cauchy sequence.

7. Prove that if $\{x_k\}$ converges to both x and y, then $x = y$.

HARDER PROBLEMS

8. Show that for every t in $(0, 1)$ the sequence $\{a_k\}$ defined by

$$a_0 = 0, \quad a_{k+1} = a_k + \frac{1}{2}(t - a_k^2), \quad k = 0, 1, \dots$$

is (strictly) increasing and converges to $\sqrt{t}$. (*Hint:* Use induction to prove that $\sqrt{t} - a_k \in (0, 1)$.)

9. Consider the two sequences $\{a_n\}$ and $\{b_n\}$ defined by

$$a_n = \left(1 + \frac{1}{n}\right)^n, \quad b_n = \left(1 + \frac{1}{n}\right)^{n+1}, \quad n = 1, 2, \dots$$

(a) Show that $a_1 < a_2 < a_3 < a_4$, and that $b_1 > b_2 > b_3 > b_4$.

(b) Use induction to prove *Bernoulli's inequality,*

$$(1 + x)^n \geq 1 + nx \quad \text{for } x \geq -1 \text{ and } n = 1, 2, 3, \dots$$

Show also that for $n > 1$ equality holds only for $x = 0$.

(c) Let $x = -1/n^2$ in the inequality in (b) and multiply by $(n/(n-1))^n$. Deduce that $a_n > a_{n-1}$, so $\{a_n\}$ is strictly increasing.

(d) Let $x = 1/(n^2 - 1)$ in the inequality in (b), and show that $(1 + 1/(n^2 - 1))^n > 1 + n/(n^2 - 1) > (n + 1)/n$. Then multiply by $((n + 1)/n)^n$ and show that $b_n < b_{n-1}$, so $\{b_n\}$ is strictly decreasing.

(e) Of course, $a_n < b_n$ for all n. Explain why the results in (c) and (d) show that $\{a_n\}$ and $\{b_n\}$ both converge. Because $b_n = a_n(1 + 1/n)$, the two sequences have the same limit. The common limit is e, and so $(1 + 1/n)^n < e < (1 + 1/n)^{n+1}$ for all n. For $n = 100$, we get $2.7048 < e < 2.7319$. As you surely know, the irrational number $e \approx 2.718281828$ is one of the most important numbers in mathematics.

10. Prove that every sequence of real numbers has a monotone subsequence.

A.4 Infimum and Supremum of Functions

Suppose that $f(\mathbf{x})$ is defined for all $\mathbf{x}$ in B, where $B \subseteq \mathbb{R}^n$. Using (A.2.2) and (A.2.3), we define the infimum and supremum of the function f over B by

$$\inf_{\mathbf{x} \in B} f(\mathbf{x}) = \inf\{\, f(\mathbf{x}) : \mathbf{x} \in B\,\}, \qquad \sup_{\mathbf{x} \in B} f(\mathbf{x}) = \sup\{\, f(\mathbf{x}) : \mathbf{x} \in B\,\} \tag{1}$$

EXAMPLE 1   Let $f(x) = e^{-x}$ be defined over $B = (-\infty, \infty)$. Find $\inf_{x \in B} f(x)$ and $\sup_{x \in B} f(x)$.

Solution: The range of $f(x)$ is the interval $(0, \infty)$. Therefore $\inf_{x \in B} f(x) = 0$, while $\sup_{x \in B} f(x) = \infty$.

Example 1 illustrates an important point: $\inf_{x \in B} f(x) = 0$, but for no number x is $f(x) = e^{-x} = 0$.

If a function f is defined over a set B, if $\inf_{\mathbf{x} \in B} f(\mathbf{x}) = y$, and if there exists a $\mathbf{c}$ in B such that $f(\mathbf{c}) = y$, then we say that the infimum is **attained** (at the point $\mathbf{c}$) in B. In this case the infimum y is called the **minimum** of f over B, and we often write min instead of inf. In the same way we write max instead of sup when the supremum of f over B is attained in B, and so becomes the maximum.

The following properties are sometimes useful. If the infimum and/or supremum value is attained, inf and sup can be replaced by min and max, respectively.

$$\text{(a)}\ \ \sup_{\mathbf{x} \in B}(-f(\mathbf{x})) = -\inf_{\mathbf{x} \in B} f(\mathbf{x}) \qquad \text{(b)}\ \ \inf_{\mathbf{x} \in B}(-f(\mathbf{x})) = -\sup_{\mathbf{x} \in B} f(\mathbf{x}) \tag{2}$$

$$\inf_{\mathbf{x} \in B}(f(\mathbf{x}) + g(\mathbf{x})) \geq \inf_{\mathbf{x} \in B} f(\mathbf{x}) + \inf_{\mathbf{x} \in B} g(\mathbf{x}) \tag{3}$$

$$\sup_{\mathbf{x} \in B}(f(\mathbf{x}) + g(\mathbf{x})) \leq \sup_{\mathbf{x} \in B} f(\mathbf{x}) + \sup_{\mathbf{x} \in B} g(\mathbf{x}) \tag{4}$$

$$\inf_{\mathbf{x} \in B}(\lambda f(\mathbf{x})) = \lambda \inf_{\mathbf{x} \in B} f(\mathbf{x}) \quad (\lambda \text{ is a positive real number}) \tag{5}$$

$$\sup_{\mathbf{x} \in B}(\lambda f(\mathbf{x})) = \lambda \sup_{\mathbf{x} \in B} f(\mathbf{x}) \quad (\lambda \text{ is a positive real number}) \tag{6}$$

Consider the inequality signs in (3) and (4). If $f(x) = x$ and $g(x) = -x$ in $(0, 1]$, then $\inf f(x) = 0$ and $\inf g(x) = -1$, whereas $\inf(f(x) + g(x)) = \inf 0 = 0$. In this case $\inf(f(x) + g(x)) = 0 > \inf f(x) + \inf g(x) = -1$. Illustrations of (2)(a) and (3) are given in Figs. 1 and 2, respectively.

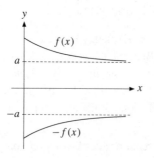

Figure 1 $\sup(-f(x)) = -\inf f(x) = -a$.

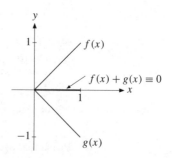

Figure 2 $\inf f(x) = 0$, $\inf g(x) = -1$, $\inf(f(x) + g(x)) = 0$.

We prove only (4): If $\sup f(\mathbf{x})$ or $\sup g(\mathbf{x})$ is ∞, then the inequality is surely satisfied. Suppose then that $\sup f(\mathbf{x}) = p$ and $\sup g(\mathbf{x}) = q$, where p and q are both finite numbers. In particular, $f(\mathbf{x}) \leq p$ and $g(\mathbf{x}) \leq q$ for all $\mathbf{x}$ in B, so $f(\mathbf{x}) + g(\mathbf{x}) \leq p + q$ for all $\mathbf{x}$ in B. But then $\sup(f(\mathbf{x}) + g(\mathbf{x})) \leq p + q = \sup f(\mathbf{x}) + \sup g(\mathbf{x})$, which proves (4).

If $f(\mathbf{x}, \mathbf{y})$ is a function defined on a Cartesian product $A \times B$, then

$$\sup_{(\mathbf{x},\mathbf{y}) \in A \times B} f(\mathbf{x}, \mathbf{y}) = \sup_{\mathbf{x} \in A} \left(\sup_{\mathbf{y} \in B} f(\mathbf{x}, \mathbf{y}) \right) \tag{7}$$

This equality expresses a very important fact: One way to find the supremum of $f(\mathbf{x}, \mathbf{y})$ over the set $A \times B$ is as follows: First find the supremum $\sup_{\mathbf{y}} f(\mathbf{x}, \mathbf{y})$ of $f(\mathbf{x}, \mathbf{y})$ for each given $\mathbf{x}$ as $\mathbf{y}$ varies over B. This supremum is a function of $\mathbf{x}$, and we take the supremum of this function as $\mathbf{x}$ runs through A.

The equality in (7) is also valid if sup is replaced by max, provided that the relevant suprema are attained, so that the maximum values exist.

Proof of (7): Let $p = \sup_{(\mathbf{x},\mathbf{y}) \in A \times B} f(\mathbf{x}, \mathbf{y})$ and $q = \sup_{\mathbf{x} \in A} \left(\sup_{\mathbf{y} \in B} f(\mathbf{x}, \mathbf{y}) \right)$. Then $f(\mathbf{x}, \mathbf{y}) \leq p$ for all $\mathbf{x}$ in A and $\mathbf{y}$ in B, so $\sup_{\mathbf{y} \in B} f(\mathbf{x}, \mathbf{y}) \leq p$ for all $\mathbf{x}$ in A. It follows that $q = \sup_{\mathbf{x} \in A} \left(\sup_{\mathbf{y} \in B} f(\mathbf{x}, \mathbf{y}) \right) \leq p$. Similarly, note that

$$f(\mathbf{x}, \mathbf{y}) \leq \sup_{\mathbf{y} \in B} f(\mathbf{x}, \mathbf{y}) \leq \sup_{\mathbf{x} \in A} \left(\sup_{\mathbf{y} \in B} f(\mathbf{x}, \mathbf{y}) \right) = q$$

for all $\mathbf{x}$ in A and all $\mathbf{y}$ in B, so $p = \sup_{(\mathbf{x},\mathbf{y}) \in A \times B} f(\mathbf{x}, \mathbf{y}) \leq q$. ∎

For infima, the obvious analogue of (7) is

$$\inf_{(\mathbf{x},\mathbf{y}) \in A \times B} f(\mathbf{x}, \mathbf{y}) = \inf_{\mathbf{x} \in A} \left\{ \inf_{\mathbf{y} \in B} f(\mathbf{x}, \mathbf{y}) \right\} \tag{8}$$

The result in (7) can be generalized. Let $f(x, y)$ be a real-valued function defined for all x in A, y in B (not necessarily subsets of Euclidean spaces), where A and B are given sets, and let C be a subset of $A \times B$. Then

$$\sup_{(x,y) \in C} f(x, y) = \sup_{x \in C_0} \left(\sup_{y \in C_x} f(x, y) \right) \tag{9}$$

where $C_0 = \{x \in A : (x, y) \in C \text{ for at least one } y \text{ in } B\}$ and $C_x = \{y \in B : (x, y) \in C\}$. The proof is an easy modification of the proof of (7).

On lim inf and lim sup of functions

This section concludes by defining some limit concepts that are needed in connection with infinite horizon dynamic economic models. They also help to understand the definitions of upper and lower hemicontinuous correspondences in Section 14.1.

Let f be a function defined on a set M in $\mathbb{R}^n$. Recall first the standard definition of a limit of a function of several variables. If $\mathbf{x}^0 \in \mathrm{cl}(M)$, the closure of M, we say that $f(\mathbf{x})$ converges to the number A as $\mathbf{x}$ tends to $\mathbf{x}^0$, if for each $\varepsilon > 0$, there exists a number $\delta > 0$ such that $\| f(\mathbf{x}) - f(\mathbf{x}^0)\| < \varepsilon$ for all $\mathbf{x}$ in M with $\mathbf{x} \neq \mathbf{x}^0$ and $\|\mathbf{x} - \mathbf{x}^0\| < \delta$.

Suppose now that $\mathbf{x}^0 \in \mathrm{cl}(M)$. We then define the **superior** and **inferior limits** of f at $\mathbf{x}^0$ as

$$\liminf_{\mathbf{x} \to \mathbf{x}^0} f(\mathbf{x}) = \lim_{r \to 0} \left(\inf\{ f(\mathbf{x}) : \mathbf{x} \in B(\mathbf{x}^0; r) \cap M, \ \mathbf{x} \neq \mathbf{x}^0 \} \right) \tag{10}$$

$$\limsup_{\mathbf{x} \to \mathbf{x}^0} f(\mathbf{x}) = \lim_{r \to 0} \left(\sup\{ f(\mathbf{x}) : \mathbf{x} \in B(\mathbf{x}^0; r) \cap M, \ \mathbf{x} \neq \mathbf{x}^0 \} \right) \tag{11}$$

Just as for sequences, we often write $\underline{\lim}$ and $\overline{\lim}$ for lim inf and lim sup. With these definitions we obtain the following rules, which are based on the corresponding rules for inf and sup:

$$\underline{\lim_{\mathbf{x} \to \mathbf{x}^0}} (f(\mathbf{x}) + g(\mathbf{x})) \geq \underline{\lim_{\mathbf{x} \to \mathbf{x}^0}} f(\mathbf{x}) + \underline{\lim_{\mathbf{x} \to \mathbf{x}^0}} g(\mathbf{x}) \qquad \text{(if the right-hand side is defined)} \tag{12}$$

$$\overline{\lim_{\mathbf{x} \to \mathbf{x}^0}} (f(\mathbf{x}) + g(\mathbf{x})) \leq \overline{\lim_{\mathbf{x} \to \mathbf{x}^0}} f(\mathbf{x}) + \overline{\lim_{\mathbf{x} \to \mathbf{x}^0}} g(\mathbf{x}) \qquad \text{(if the right-hand side is defined)} \tag{13}$$

$$\underline{\lim_{\mathbf{x} \to \mathbf{x}^0}} f(\mathbf{x}) \leq \overline{\lim_{\mathbf{x} \to \mathbf{x}^0}} f(\mathbf{x}), \quad \underline{\lim_{\mathbf{x} \to \mathbf{x}^0}} f(\mathbf{x}) = - \overline{\lim_{\mathbf{x} \to \mathbf{x}^0}} (-f)(\mathbf{x}), \quad \overline{\lim_{\mathbf{x} \to \mathbf{x}^0}} f(\mathbf{x}) = - \underline{\lim_{\mathbf{x} \to \mathbf{x}^0}} (-f)(\mathbf{x}) \tag{14}$$

Note that if $\lim_{\mathbf{x} \to \mathbf{x}^0} f(\mathbf{x})$ exists at a point $\mathbf{x}^0$, then $\underline{\lim}_{\mathbf{x} \to \mathbf{x}^0} f(\mathbf{x}) = \overline{\lim}_{\mathbf{x} \to \mathbf{x}^0} f(\mathbf{x}) = \lim_{\mathbf{x} \to \mathbf{x}^0} f(\mathbf{x})$. Conversely, if $\underline{\lim}_{\mathbf{x} \to \mathbf{x}^0} f(\mathbf{x}) = \overline{\lim}_{\mathbf{x} \to \mathbf{x}^0} f(\mathbf{x})$, then $\lim_{\mathbf{x} \to \mathbf{x}^0} f(\mathbf{x})$ exists and is equal to both.

A function f is called **upper semicontinuous** at a point $\mathbf{x}^0$ in M if $\overline{\lim}_{\mathbf{x} \to \mathbf{x}^0} f(\mathbf{x}) \leq f(\mathbf{x}^0)$. The function f is called **lower semicontinuous** at $\mathbf{x}^0$ if $\underline{\lim}_{\mathbf{x} \to \mathbf{x}^0} f(\mathbf{x}) \geq f(\mathbf{x}^0)$. An upper (lower) semicontinuous function defined on a compact nonempty set has a maximum (minimum) point.

APPENDIX

TRIGONOMETRIC FUNCTIONS

God created the integers, all else is the work of man.
—L. Kronecker

Many phenomena appear to repeat themselves with predictable regularity. Examples are alternating electric currents in physics, heartbeat and respiration in physiology, and seasonal variations in economics such as increased demand for heating fuel and warm clothing in winter, as opposed to air-conditioning and cool clothing in summer. Many economists have also looked for regular periodic patterns in macroeconomic variables like national output or interest rates. To describe such phenomena mathematically, one possibility is to use *trigonometric functions*. This appendix provides a brief review. The final Section B.3 gives a brief introduction to complex numbers.

B.1 Basic Definitions and Results

Consider the circle in Fig. 1 with radius 1 and centre at the origin in the uv-plane.

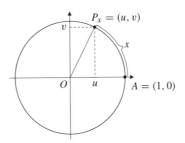

Figure 1 $\sin x = v$ and $\cos x = u$

Let A be the point on the circle with coordinates $(1, 0)$, and let P_x be the point on the circle for which the arc length between A and P_x is x. The point P_x has coordinates (u, v).

The arc x is measured in the same unit of length as the radius. Because the radius of the circle is $r = 1$, the circumference equals $2\pi r = 2\pi$. If $x = \pi/2$, we go one-quarter of the way round the circle in an anticlockwise direction to arrive at the point $P_{\pi/2}$, which has coordinates $(0, 1)$. For P_π, we go halfway round to the point with coordinates $(u, v) = (-1, 0)$; for $P_{3\pi/2}$, we get $(u, v) = (0, -1)$; for $P_0 = P_{2\pi}$, we have $(u, v) = (1, 0)$; and so on. For the point P_x shown in Fig. 1, we have $u \approx 0.45$ and $v \approx 0.9$. If x is negative, the length is measured clockwise around the circle.

In general, as x increases, so P_x moves round the unit circle, and the values of u and v oscillate up and down. They repeat themselves as P_x passes through points where it has been before. In particular, x, $x \pm 2\pi$, $x \pm 4\pi$, and so on, all define the same point on the circle. Thus, $P_x = P_{x+2n\pi}$ for $n = \pm1, \pm2, \ldots$. This procedure maps each real number x to a point P_x with coordinates (u, v).

> The **sine** function is the rule that maps x to the number v.

> The **cosine** function is the rule that maps x to the number u.

It is standard to abbreviate *sine* to sin and *cosine* to cos. So, referring to Fig. 1, we have

$$\sin x = v \qquad \text{and} \qquad \cos x = u \tag{1}$$

The circle in Fig. 1 has the equation $u^2 + v^2 = 1$. This implies the following important relationship:

$$(\sin x)^2 + (\cos x)^2 = 1 \tag{2}$$

The domains of the functions sin and cos are the set of all real numbers. The range of each is the closed interval $[-1, 1]$. Note also that a small change in x will change the point P_x only slightly, so the coordinates u and v will also change only slightly, and $v = \sin x$ and $u = \cos x$ are both continuous functions of x. (In fact, from Fig. 1, we see that a given change in x causes changes in u and v that are smaller in absolute value.)

If x is any number such that $\cos x \neq 0$, we define the **tangent** function by simply dividing $\sin x$ by $\cos x$. It is standard to abbreviate *tangent* to tan, so that

$$\tan x = \frac{\sin x}{\cos x} \qquad \text{(provided that } \cos x \neq 0) \tag{3}$$

The cotangent function, abbreviated cot, is defined by $\cot x = \cos x / \sin x$, for all x with $\sin x \neq 0$. It is clear that $\cot x = 1/\tan x$ when $\tan x$ and $\cot x$ are both defined.

Note that it is common practice to write $\sin^2 x$ for $(\sin x)^2$, $\cos^2 x$ for $(\cos x)^2$, and $\tan^2 x$ for $(\tan x)^2$. Similar notation is also used for higher powers of the trigonometric functions. For example, $\cos^3 x = (\cos x)^3$.

Measuring Angles in Radians

In trigonometry, it is common to define the sine, cosine, and tangent as functions of the *angles*, which is usually measured in degrees. Figure 1 shows how the arc length x can

be used instead to measure the angle AOP_x. Then it is said that the angle is measured in
radians. In elementary geometry it is common practice to operate with degrees, so one
must know how to convert degrees into radians and vice versa. In fact, $360° = 2\pi$ radians
because when $x = 2\pi$, the line OP_x has rotated through $360°$. So we have the following:

$$1° = \left(\frac{\pi}{180}\right) \text{ radians} \approx 0.017 \text{ radians}, \quad 1 \text{ radian} = \left(\frac{180}{\pi}\right)° \approx 57.3° \tag{4}$$

Figure 2 illustrates some particularly important angles measured in both degrees and radians.

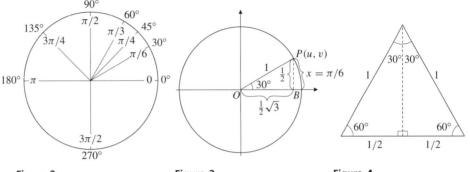

| Figure 2 | Figure 3 | Figure 4 |

The degree scale for measuring angles is built on an arbitrary choice of unit in that the
complete circle is divided into $360°$. This corresponds to the ancient Babylonian calendar
that divided the year into 360 days. From a mathematical point of view, the radian scale is
the most natural one for measuring angles. The reason is that calculus formulas are simpler
when angles are measured in radians rather than in degrees.

There is no method for finding exact numerical values of the trigonometric functions in
the general case. Approximations are available on most scientific calculators.

For certain special values of x, however, we can compute $\sin x$ and $\cos x$ exactly by
using elementary geometry. Consider Fig. 3. Here we have chosen $x = \pi/6$. Then angle
BOP is $30°$, and triangle BOP is half an equilateral triangle, as Fig. 4 shows more clearly.
So in Fig. 3, the length of PB is $\frac{1}{2}$. By Pythagoras' theorem, $(OB)^2 = (OP)^2 - (BP)^2 = 1 - \frac{1}{4} = \frac{3}{4}$, and so $OB = \frac{1}{2}\sqrt{3}$. The coordinates of P are therefore $u = \frac{1}{2}\sqrt{3}$ and $v = \frac{1}{2}$.
Hence,

$$\sin \frac{\pi}{6} = \frac{1}{2}, \qquad \cos \frac{\pi}{6} = \frac{1}{2}\sqrt{3}, \qquad \tan \frac{\pi}{6} = \frac{1}{3}\sqrt{3}$$

Similar geometric considerations establish the other entries in Table 1.

x	0	$\frac{\pi}{6} = 30°$	$\frac{\pi}{4} = 45°$	$\frac{\pi}{3} = 60°$	$\frac{\pi}{2} = 90°$	$\frac{3\pi}{4} = 135°$	$\pi = 180°$	$\frac{3\pi}{2} = 270°$	$2\pi = 360°$
$\sin x$	0	$\frac{1}{2}$	$\frac{1}{2}\sqrt{2}$	$\frac{1}{2}\sqrt{3}$	1	$\frac{1}{2}\sqrt{2}$	0	-1	0
$\cos x$	1	$\frac{1}{2}\sqrt{3}$	$\frac{1}{2}\sqrt{2}$	$\frac{1}{2}$	0	$-\frac{1}{2}\sqrt{2}$	-1	0	1
$\tan x$	0	$\frac{1}{3}\sqrt{3}$	1	$\sqrt{3}$	*	-1	0	*	0

* *Not defined.*

Table 1 Special values of the trigonometric functions

Graphs of the Trigonometric Functions

By definition of the point P_x in Fig. 1, $P_{x+2\pi} = P_x$ for all x, and therefore

$$\sin(x + 2\pi) = \sin x, \qquad \cos(x + 2\pi) = \cos x \tag{5}$$

We say that the functions sin and cos are **periodic** with **period** 2π. Also (see Problem 5),

$$\tan(x + \pi) = \tan x \tag{6}$$

so the tangent function is periodic with period π.

We noted before that the ranges of sin and cos are the interval $[-1, 1]$, so

$$-1 \le \sin x \le 1, \qquad -1 \le \cos x \le 1$$

The graphs of sin and cos are shown in Fig. 5. The cosine curve can be obtained by translating the sine curve $\pi/2$ units to the left. This follows from the first of the following formulas:

$$\sin(x + \pi/2) = \cos x, \qquad \cos(x + \pi/2) = -\sin x \tag{7}$$

(To prove these formulas, use Problem 4 and formula (8).)

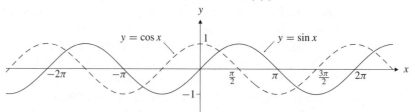

Figure 5

The graph of the tangent function is shown in Fig. 6. Note that its value is positive iff the sine and cosine functions have the same sign. Also $\tan x$ is undefined when $x = \frac{1}{2}\pi + n\pi$ for an integer n, because then $\cos x = 0$.

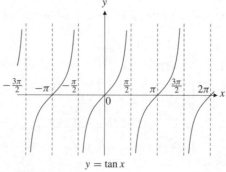

$y = \tan x$

Figure 6

Trigonometric Formulas

There is a plethora of trigonometric formulas that have pestered high school students (and their parents) for generations. Nevertheless, one particular formula really is useful:

$$\cos(x + y) = \cos x \cos y - \sin x \sin y \qquad (8)$$

(For a proof, see Problem 13.) By using this basic equation, similar formulas for $\cos(x - y)$, $\sin(x + y)$, and $\sin(x - y)$ are quite easy to prove (see Problems 3 and 4).

More Complicated Functions

We have discussed some important properties of the three basic trigonometric functions: sin, cos, and tan. In economics, they are mainly used in connection with periodic phenomena. Usually more complicated expressions must be used.

So far we have seen that $y = \sin x$ is periodic with period 2π. The graph of the function shows a wavelike curve that is said to have **period** (or **wavelength**) 2π. If, instead, we represent graphically the function given by $y = \sin(x/2)$, we still get a wavelike curve, but the period is now twice as long, namely 4π. When x increases from 0 to 4π, then $x/2$ increases from 0 to 2π, so $\sin(x/2)$ is periodic with period 4π. More generally, $y = \sin(ax)$ is periodic with period $2\pi/a$, because as x increases from 0 to $2\pi/a$, so ax increases from 0 to 2π. The value of $y = \sin(ax)$ will still oscillate between -1 and 1, and we say that the **amplitude** is equal to 1. To get a periodic function with amplitude A, just put $y = A \sin ax$, which varies between $-A$ and A. Hence,

$$y = A \sin(ax) \quad \text{has period } 2\pi/a \text{ and amplitude } A$$

The reciprocal, $a/2\pi$, of the period is called the **frequency**. It is the number of oscillations per radian.

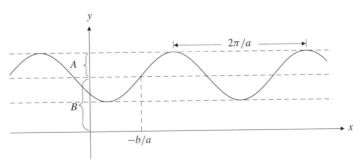

Figure 7

The graph of $y = A \sin(ax)$ intersects the x-axis at $x = 0$. To get a curve translated a certain distance in the x-direction, let $y = A \sin(ax + b)$. To get a curve translated in the y-direction, let

$$y = A \sin(ax + b) + B \qquad (9)$$

The graph of this function will be a sine curve with amplitude A and period $2\pi/a$. Relative to $y = A\sin(ax)$, it will be translated a distance $-b/a$ in the x-direction and a distance B in the y-direction. See Fig. 7 (in which $a > 0$ and $b < 0$).

PROBLEMS FOR SECTION B.1

1. Use a diagram like Fig. 3 to verify the values in Table 1 for $x = \pi/4$.

2. Verify that for all x, we have

$$\sin(-x) = -\sin x, \qquad \cos(-x) = \cos x, \qquad \tan(-x) = -\tan x$$

3. Write $\cos(x - y) = \cos[x + (-y)]$, then use the results in (8) and Problem 2 to verify that

$$\cos(x - y) = \cos x \cos y + \sin x \sin y \tag{10}$$

4. Show that $\cos(y - \pi/2) = \sin y$. From this, it follows that $\sin(y - \pi/2) = \cos(y - \pi) = -\cos y$. Then let $\sin(x + y) = \cos[x + (y - \pi/2)]$ and so prove that

$$\sin(x + y) = \sin x \cos y + \cos x \sin y, \qquad \sin(x - y) = \sin x \cos y - \cos x \sin y$$

5. Use the results in Problems 3 and 4 to prove (6) and (7).

6. Find the following values:
   (a) $\sin(\pi - \pi/6)$ (b) $\cos(\pi + \pi/6)$ (c) $\sin(-3\pi/4)$
   (d) $\cos(5\pi/4)$ (e) $\tan(7\pi/6)$ (f) $\sin(\pi/12)$

7. Simplify the following expressions:
   (a) $\sqrt{2}\sin(x + \frac{\pi}{4}) - \cos x$ (b) $\dfrac{\sin[\pi - (\alpha + \beta)]}{\cos[2\pi - (\alpha + \beta)]}$ (c) $\dfrac{\sin(a + x) - \sin(a - x)}{\cos(a + x) - \cos(a - x)}$

8. Prove that $\sin A - \sin B = 2\cos\dfrac{A + B}{2}\sin\dfrac{A - B}{2}$. (*Hint:* Put $x + y = A$ and $x - y = B$ in the two formulas in Problem 4, then subtract.)

9. Prove that for all real numbers x and y, $\sin(x + y)\sin(x - y) = \sin^2 x - \sin^2 y$.

10. Draw the graphs of the following functions. Then give their periods and amplitudes.
    (a) $f(x) = \sin(2x)$ (b) $g(x) = 3\sin(x/2)$ (c) $h(x) = 2\sin(3x + 4) + 2$

11. Explain why the following functions represent respectively an oscillation that dies out and an oscillation that explodes.   (a) $f(x) = (1/2)^x \sin x$ (b) $g(x) = 2^x \cos 2x$

12. Find functions whose graphs are shown in Figs. a to c. In Fig. c the dashed curves have the equations $y = \pm 2e^{-x/\pi}$.

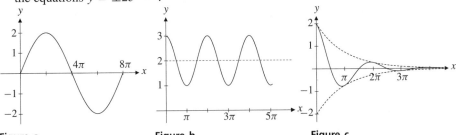

Figure a   Figure b   Figure c

13. In the figure below, the coordinates of the indicated points lying on the unit circle are respectively $A = (\cos y, -\sin y)$, $B = (1, 0)$, $C = (\cos x, \sin x)$, and $D = (\cos(x + y), \sin(x + y))$. Since the line segments AC and BD both subtend the angle $x + y$, they must have the same length. Use this fact together with (2) to prove the formula for $\cos(x + y)$ in (8).

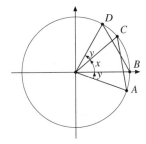

B.2 Differentiating Trigonometric Functions

Consider the graph of the sine function in Fig B.1.5. The slope of the graph of $f(x) = \sin x$ at $x = 0$ seems to be 1, as is the value of $\cos x$ at $x = 0$. Also the slope at $x = \pi/2$ is 0, as is $\cos \pi/2$. It is periodic, so its derivative must also be periodic. Therefore, it should not be surprising that (see also Problem 12)

$$y = \sin x \;\Rightarrow\; y' = \cos x \tag{1}$$

If u is a function of x, the chain rule for differentiation gives

$$y = \sin u, \;\; u = u(x) \;\Rightarrow\; y' = u' \cos u \tag{2}$$

Let $g(x) = \cos x$. According to (B.1.7), we have $g(x) = \sin(x + \pi/2)$, so (2) yields $g'(x) = \cos(x + \pi/2)$. But $\cos(x + \pi/2) = -\sin x$. Hence,

$$y = \cos x \;\Rightarrow\; y' = -\sin x \tag{3}$$

The quotient rule for differentiating $y = \tan x = \sin x / \cos x$ gives (see Problem 2)

$$y = \tan x \;\Rightarrow\; y' = \frac{1}{\cos^2 x} = 1 + \tan^2 x \qquad \text{(provided that } \cos x \neq 0) \qquad (4)$$

Combining these rules of differentiation with those developed earlier allows us to differentiate many expressions involving trigonometric functions.

EXAMPLE 1   Differentiate the following functions:

(a) $y = \sin 2x$ (b) $y = \sin^2 x + \cos^2 x$ (c) $y = \dfrac{\sin x}{\cos x + x}$ (d) $y = e^{ax} \sin bx$

Solution:

(a) Use (2) with $u = 2x$ to obtain $y' = 2 \cos u = 2 \cos 2x$.

(b) $y = (\sin x)^2 + (\cos x)^2 \;\Rightarrow\; y' = 2(\sin x) \cos x + 2(\cos x)(- \sin x) = 0$. (Note that $y' \equiv 0$, so that y must be constant. Since $y = 1$ when $x = 0$, this constant must be 1. Hence, we rediscover the relation $\sin^2 x + \cos^2 x = 1$.)

(c) Use the quotient rule for differentiation to obtain

$$\begin{aligned} y' &= \frac{(\cos x + x) \cos x - \sin x(- \sin x + 1)}{(\cos x + x)^2} \\ &= \frac{\cos^2 x + x \cos x + \sin^2 x - \sin x}{(\cos x + x)^2} = \frac{1 + x \cos x - \sin x}{(\cos x + x)^2} \end{aligned}$$

(d) The product rule yields $y' = ae^{ax} \sin bx + e^{ax} b \cos bx = e^{ax}(a \sin bx + b \cos bx)$.

Inverse Trigonometric Functions

Figure 1 illustrates the problem of solving the equation

$$\sin x = y \qquad (5)$$

for x. If $y > 1$ or $y < -1$, the equation $\sin x = y$ has no solution, whereas it has infinitely many solutions if $y \in [-1, 1]$.

However, suppose we require that $x \in [-\pi/2, \pi/2]$. In this interval, $\sin x$ is strictly increasing (because $(\sin x)' = \cos x > 0$ in $(-\pi/2, \pi/2)$).

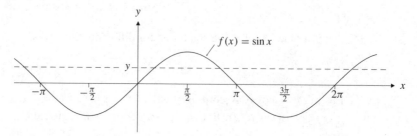

Figure 1

So equation (5) has a unique solution x in this interval for each y in $[-1, 1]$. We denote this solution by $x = \arcsin y$. According to standard terminology we have shown that the function $f(x) = \sin x$, with domain $[-\pi/2, \pi/2]$ and range $[-1, 1]$, has an inverse function g. We call this inverse the **arcsine** function. If we use x as the free variable,

$$g(x) = \arcsin x, \qquad x \in [-1, 1] \tag{6}$$

By definition, $\arcsin x$ is *that number in* $[-\pi/2, \pi/2]$ *whose sine is equal to* x ($\arcsin x$ is "the angle (arc) whose sine is x"). For instance, we have $\arcsin 1/2 = \pi/6$. The graph of $y = \arcsin x$ is shown in Fig. 2. Since the functions sin and arcsin are inverses of each other, the graphs of $y = \sin x$ and $y = \arcsin x$ are symmetric about the line $y = x$.

The derivative of $g(x) = \arcsin x$ is most easily found by implicit differentiation. From the definition of $g(x)$, it follows that $\sin g(x) = x$ for all $x \in (-1, 1)$. If we *assume* that $g(x)$ is differentiable, differentiating using the chain rule gives $\cos[g(x)] \cdot g'(x) = 1$. So $g'(x) = 1/\cos g(x) = 1/\sqrt{1 - \sin^2 g(x)} = 1/\sqrt{1 - x^2}$. Thus,

$$y = \arcsin x \;\Rightarrow\; y' = \frac{1}{\sqrt{1 - x^2}} \qquad (-1 < x < 1) \tag{7}$$

It can be shown in the same way that $y = \cos x$ defined on $[0, \pi]$ has an inverse function $y = \arccos x$ defined on $[-1, 1]$, and that

$$y = \arccos x \;\Rightarrow\; y' = -\frac{1}{\sqrt{1 - x^2}} \qquad (-1 < x < 1) \tag{8}$$

Consider, finally, $y = \tan x$ defined in the interval $(-\pi/2, \pi/2)$. Because $y' = 1/\cos^2 x > 0$, the function is strictly increasing, and the range is $(-\infty, \infty)$. The function, therefore, has an inverse function $y = \arctan x$ that is defined in $(-\infty, \infty)$ and has range $(-\pi/2, \pi/2)$. Using implicit differentiation again, this time in the equation $\tan y = x$ (so that $y = \arctan x$), one obtains

$$y = \arctan x \;\Rightarrow\; y' = \frac{1}{1 + x^2} \qquad (-\infty < x < \infty) \tag{9}$$

The graph of $y = \arctan x$ is shown in Fig. 3.

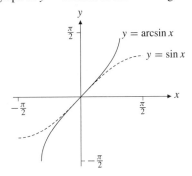

Figure 2

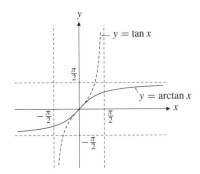

Figure 3

Calculators that have trigonometric functions usually also have their inverses. They are denoted by $\sin^{-1}$, $\cos^{-1}$, and $\tan^{-1}$. If one enters 0.5 and presses the $\boxed{\sin^{-1}}$ key, the answer is 30, because the calculator usually uses degrees. If radians are used, the calculator will give the answer $\pi/6$, or rather 0.5235988.

An Important Limit

The derivative of $f(x) = \sin x$ is the limit of the quotient $[\sin(x+h) - \sin x]/h$ as $h \to 0$. According to (1), at $x = 0$ we have $f'(0) = \cos 0 = 1$, so that $\lim_{h \to 0}(\sin h/h) = 1$. Changing the variable, we have the following useful limit result:

$$\lim_{x \to 0} \frac{\sin x}{x} = 1 \tag{10}$$

PROBLEMS FOR SECTION B.2

1. Find the derivatives of the following functions:

    (a) $y = \sin \frac{1}{2}x$ (b) $y = x \cos x$ (c) $y = \tan(x^2)$ (d) $y = e^{2x} \cos x$

2. Prove the differentiation rule in (4). (Remember that $\sin^2 x + \cos^2 x = 1$.)

3. Find the derivatives of the following functions:

    (a) $y = \sin x + \cos x$ (b) $y = x^5 \sin x + \sqrt{x} \cos x + 3$ (c) $y = \dfrac{\sqrt{x} \cos x}{x^2 + 1}$

4. Compute the following:

    (a) $\dfrac{d}{dx}(1 - \cos ax)$ (b) $\dfrac{d}{dt}(at \sin bt)$ (c) $\dfrac{d}{dt}(\sin\{\cos[\sin(at + b)]\})$

5. Use l'Hôpital's rule (see e.g. EMEA), if necessary, to compute

    (a) $\lim_{x \to 0} \dfrac{\sin 2x}{x}$ (b) $\lim_{t \to 0} \dfrac{\sin mt}{\sin nt}$ $(n \neq 0)$ (c) $\lim_{t \to 0} \dfrac{1 - \cos t}{t^2}$

6. Find the extreme points of $f(x) = (\sin x - x - 1)^3$ in the interval $I = [0, 3\pi/2]$.

7. Studies of economic cycles often use functions of the form

$$p(t) = C_0 + C_1 \cos \lambda t + C_2 \sin \lambda t$$

    Show that $p''(t) + \lambda^2 p(t)$ is a constant K, and find K.

8. Determine the following values:

    (a) $\arcsin \frac{1}{2}\sqrt{2}$ (b) $\arccos 0$ (c) $\arccos \frac{1}{2}\sqrt{3}$ (d) $\arctan \sqrt{3}$

9. Find the derivatives of the following:

    (a) $\arcsin 2x$ (b) $\arctan(x^2 + 1)$ (c) $\arccos \sqrt{x}$

10. Evaluate the following integrals (for the last two integrals, use integration by parts (4.1.1)):

    (a) $\displaystyle\int \sin x \, dx$ (b) $\displaystyle\int_0^{\pi/2} \cos x \, dx$ (c) $\displaystyle\int \sin^2 x \, dx$ (d) $\displaystyle\int_0^{\pi} x \cos x \, dx$

11. Evaluate the following integrals by introducing a suitable new variable (see (4.1.2)):

    (a) $\int \tan x \, dx = \int \dfrac{\sin x}{\cos x} \, dx$ (b) $\int \cos x e^{\sin x} \, dx$ (c) $\int \cos^5 x \sin x \, dx$

12. The derivative of $f(x) = \sin x$ is the limit of the quotient $[\sin(x + h) - \sin x]/h$ as $h \to 0$. From the figure below we see that this quotient is equal to $BC/\text{arc } BA$. If h is small, ACB is almost a right-angled triangle, because the arc BA is almost a straight line. Take the cosine of the angle CBA, which is approximately x. What do you see?

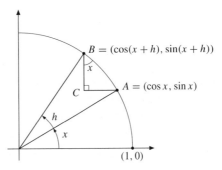

$B = (\cos(x + h), \sin(x + h))$

$A = (\cos x, \sin x)$

$(1, 0)$

B.3 Complex Numbers

We know how the concept of number can be extended from natural numbers via integers and rationals to real numbers. Each of these extensions expands the set of equations that have solutions. Now, simple quadratic equations like $x^2 + 1 = 0$ and $x^2 + 4x + 8 = 0$ have no solution within the real number system. By introducing complex numbers, however, all quadratic equations become soluble. In fact, within the complex number system, *any* polynomial equation $x^n + a_{n-1}x^{n-1} + \cdots + a_1 x + a_0 = 0$ has solutions.

The standard formula for solving the equation $x^2 + 4x + 8 = 0$ yields the expressions $-2 + \sqrt{-4}$ and $-2 - \sqrt{-4}$. So far, we have not given any meaning to these expressions. But if we take the liberty of writing $\sqrt{-4} = \sqrt{4}\sqrt{-1} = 2\sqrt{-1}$, we obtain the "solutions"

$$-2 + 2\sqrt{-1} \qquad \text{and} \qquad -2 - 2\sqrt{-1} \qquad\qquad (*)$$

Here -2 and 2 are well-known numbers, but $\sqrt{-1}$ is not. By pretending that $\sqrt{-1}$ is a number i whose square is -1, we make i satisfy the equation $i^2 = -1$.

By treating these expressions as if they satisfy the usual algebraic rules, with the additional provision that $\sqrt{-1}\sqrt{-1}$ means -1, expressions of the type $a + b\sqrt{-1}$ can be used to solve any quadratic equation without real roots.

The symbol $\sqrt{-1}$ can only be given a meaning in an extended system of "numbers". These new "numbers" are called **complex numbers**. They are two-component vectors (a, b) equipped with the standard addition rule, but with a new multiplication rule.

Informally, instead of writing (a, b), we usually write this complex number as $a + bi$, where i represents the (so far undefined) symbol $\sqrt{-1}$. Think of i as a symbol that simply identifies which is the second component in the complex number. The real number a is called the **real part**, and the real number b is called the **imaginary part** of the complex number (a, b). The operations of addition, subtraction and multiplication are defined by

$$(a + bi) + (c + di) = (a + c) + (b + d)i \tag{1}$$

$$(a + bi) - (c + di) = (a - c) + (b - d)i \tag{2}$$

$$(a + bi)(c + di) = (ac - bd) + (ad + bc)i \tag{3}$$

respectively. Formally, rule (1) should be written in the form $(a, b) + (c, d) = (a+b, c+d)$, and rule (3) should be written as $(a, b)(c, d) = (ac-bd, ad+bc)$. What makes the informal expressions $a+bi$ attractive is the fact that (3) is what results if we perform the multiplication $(a + bi)(c + di)$ according to the usual algebraic rules, thus obtaining the expression $ac + (ad + bc)i + bdi^2$, and then finally replace i^2 by -1. When multiplying complex numbers in practice, we usually perform the computation this way, rather than using rule (3) directly. The complex number $(1, 0)$ is a "unit" in the sense that $(1, 0)(a, b) = (a, b)$.

The way in which we divide two complex numbers can be motivated by the following calculations:

$$\frac{a + bi}{c + di} = \frac{(a + bi)(c - di)}{(c + di)(c - di)} = \frac{(ac + bd) + (bc - ad)i}{c^2 + d^2}$$

The division is defined when $c^2 + d^2 \neq 0$. The formal rule is this:

$$\frac{(a, b)}{(c, d)} = \left(\frac{ac + bd}{c^2 + d^2}, \frac{bc - ad}{c^2 + d^2} \right)$$

In particular, the inverse of $c + di$ is $1/(c + di) = (c - di)/(c^2 + d^2)$. Of course, we have to check that $(c - di)/(c^2 + d^2)$ deserves the name inverse—i.e., we have to check that $(c + di)[(c - di)/(c^2 + d^2)] = 1 + 0i$, which indeed is the case.

Consider now the problem of giving a meaning to the symbol $i = \sqrt{-1}$. We formally treat this as the problem of finding a complex number (a, b) with the property that $(a, b)(a, b) = (-1, 0)$. It is easy to see that there are two such complex numbers, $(0, 1)$ and $(0, -1)$, and we choose $(0, 1)$ as our i. Then we can formally interpret the symbol $a + bi$ as being $(a, 0)(1, 0) + (b, 0)(0, 1)$, where we simply omit $(1, 0)$ and write a and b instead of $(a, 0)$ and $(b, 0)$.

It is common practice to denote complex numbers by single letters near the end of the alphabet, such as $z = x + yi$ or $w = u + vi$. Two complex numbers, written in this manner, are equal iff both their real and their imaginary parts are equal—that is, $z = w$ iff $x = u$ and $y = v$. If the imaginary part of a complex number is 0, we let $x + 0i = x$. In fact, complex numbers of the form $x + 0i$ behave just like the corresponding real numbers with respect to addition and multiplication. In particular, the numbers $0 (= 0 + 0i)$ and $1 (= 1 + 0i)$ obey the same algebraic rules whether we regard them as complex or as real numbers. In addition, $(x, 0)(u, v) = (x + 0i)(u + vi) = (xu, xv) = x(u, v)$, where, for the moment, on the right-hand side, we revert to ordinary vector algebra and calculate a real number times a vector.

EXAMPLE 1   If $z = 3 + 4i$ and $w = 2 - 5i$, calculate   (a) $z + w$ (b) zw (c) z/w

Solution:

(a) $z + w = (3 + 4i) + (2 - 5i) = 5 - i$

(b) $zw = (3 + 4i)(2 - 5i) = 6 - 15i + 8i - 20i^2 = 26 - 7i$

(c) $\dfrac{z}{w} = \dfrac{3 + 4i}{2 - 5i} = \dfrac{(3 + 4i)(2 + 5i)}{(2 - 5i)(2 + 5i)} = \dfrac{6 + 15i + 8i - 20}{4 + 25} = \dfrac{-14 + 23i}{29}$

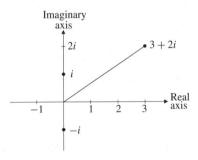

Figure 1 The complex plane   **Figure 2** Polar coordinates

Trigonometric Form of Complex Numbers

Each complex number $z = x + yi = (x, y)$ can be represented by a point in the plane. Figure 1 shows how to represent the three particular complex numbers i, $-i$, and $3 + 2i$.

Not surprisingly, the plane representing complex numbers is called the **complex plane**. The horizontal axis, representing numbers of the form $x + 0i$, is called the **real axis**, and the vertical axis, representing numbers of the form $0 + yi$, is called the **imaginary axis.**

Instead of representing a complex number $z = x + yi$ by the pair (x, y), we could use *polar coordinates.* As illustrated in Fig. 2, let θ be the angle (measured in radians) between the positive real axis and the vector from the origin to the point (x, y), and let r be the distance from the origin to the same point. Then $x = r \cos \theta$ and $y = r \sin \theta$, so

$$z = x + yi = r(\cos \theta + i \sin \theta) \qquad (4)$$

The last expression is the **trigonometric (or polar) form** of the complex number z. The angle θ is called the **argument** of the complex number z. Note that the distance from the origin to the point (x, y) is $r = \sqrt{x^2 + y^2}$. This is called the *modulus* of the complex number, denoted by $|z|$. Hence,

$$|z| = \sqrt{x^2 + y^2} \quad \text{is the **modulus** of } z = x + yi \qquad (5)$$

Multiplication and division of complex numbers have neat geometric interpretations if we represent the numbers in trigonometric form. Indeed, applying (3) gives

$$r_1(\cos\theta_1 + i\sin\theta_1)r_2(\cos\theta_2 + i\sin\theta_2) = r_1 r_2[\cos(\theta_1 + \theta_2) + i\sin(\theta_1 + \theta_2)] \quad (6)$$

because (B.1.8) and problem B.1.4 imply that $\cos(\theta_1 + \theta_2) = \cos\theta_1 \cos\theta_2 - \sin\theta_1 \sin\theta_2$ and $\sin(\theta_1 + \theta_2) = \sin\theta_1 \cos\theta_2 + \cos\theta_1 \sin\theta_2$. Thus, *the product of two complex numbers is that complex number whose modulus is the product of the moduli of the two factors, and whose argument is the sum of the arguments.*

Similarily, we can show that

$$\frac{r_1(\cos\theta_1 + i\sin\theta_1)}{r_2(\cos\theta_2 + i\sin\theta_2)} = \frac{r_1}{r_2}[\cos(\theta_1 - \theta_2) + i\sin(\theta_1 - \theta_2)] \quad (7)$$

If we let $r_1 = r_2 = 1$ and $\theta_1 = \theta_2 = \theta$ in (6), then we obtain $(\cos\theta + i\sin\theta)^2 = \cos 2\theta + i\sin 2\theta$. Similarly, one has

$$(\cos\theta + i\sin\theta)^3 = (\cos\theta + i\sin\theta)^2(\cos\theta + i\sin\theta)$$
$$= (\cos 2\theta + i\sin 2\theta)(\cos\theta + i\sin\theta) = \cos 3\theta + i\sin 3\theta$$

By induction, we find the famous result

$$(\cos\theta + i\sin\theta)^n = \cos n\theta + i\sin n\theta \quad \textbf{(de Moivre's formula)} \quad (8)$$

which is valid for all $n = 1, 2, 3, \ldots$

NOTE 1 This has been a very brief introduction to complex numbers. The need to extend the real number system arose in the sixteenth century when various Italian mathematicians derived analytic formulas for the solution to algebraic equations of degree 2, 3, and 4. For a long time, the complex numbers were regarded as "imaginary", mystical objects. Not any more. Actually, the extension of the number concept from the real numbers to the complex numbers is motivated by the same concern as the extension from the rationals to the reals. In both cases, we want certain equations to have solutions.

Nowadays complex numbers are indispensable in mathematics. Modern science just could not do without them. However, they do not play a very large role in economics. In this book, they allow a convenient description of the solutions to some higher-order difference and differential equations. That also makes them useful in stating results on the stability of solutions to differential equations.

PROBLEMS FOR SECTION B.3

1. If $z = 2 - 5i$ and $w = 3 + 3i$, compute the following expressions:

(a) $z + w$ (b) zw (c) $\dfrac{z}{w}$ (d) $|z|$

2. Represent the complex numbers $z = 2 - 2i$, $w = 1 + 3i$, and $z + w$ as points in the complex plane.

3. Write the following numbers in the form $x + yi$:

   (a) $\dfrac{3 + 2i}{1 - i}$ (b) $\dfrac{4 - 3i}{i}$ (c) $\dfrac{(3 - 2i)(2 - i)}{(-1 - i)(3 + 2i)}$ (d) $\left(\dfrac{1 - i}{1 + i}\right)^3$

4. Write the following numbers in trigonometric form:

   (a) $\sqrt{3} + 3i$ (b) -1 (c) $-2 - 2\sqrt{3}i$ (d) $1 - i$

ANSWERS TO ODD-NUMBERED PROBLEMS

Chapter 1

1.2

1. $\begin{pmatrix} a_{11}b_{11} + a_{12}b_{21} + a_{13}b_{31} & a_{11}b_{12} + a_{12}b_{22} + a_{13}b_{32} \\ a_{21}b_{11} + a_{22}b_{21} + a_{23}b_{31} & a_{21}b_{12} + a_{22}b_{22} + a_{23}b_{32} \\ a_{31}b_{11} + a_{32}b_{21} + a_{33}b_{31} & a_{31}b_{12} + a_{32}b_{22} + a_{33}b_{32} \end{pmatrix} = \begin{pmatrix} \mathbf{A}_{11}\mathbf{B}_{11} + \mathbf{A}_{12}\mathbf{B}_{21} \\ \mathbf{A}_{21}\mathbf{B}_{11} + \mathbf{A}_{22}\mathbf{B}_{21} \end{pmatrix}$

3. (a) $\begin{pmatrix} 1/2 & -1/2 & -1/2 & 0 & 1/2 \\ -1/2 & 1/2 & -1/2 & 0 & 1/2 \\ -1/2 & -1/2 & 1/2 & 0 & 1/2 \\ 0 & 0 & 0 & 1 & 0 \\ 1/2 & 1/2 & 1/2 & 0 & -1/2 \end{pmatrix}$ (b) $\begin{pmatrix} -2/11 & 3/11 & 0 & 0 \\ 5/11 & -2/11 & 0 & 0 \\ 0 & 0 & -2 & 3 \\ 0 & 0 & 3 & -4 \end{pmatrix}$ (c) $\begin{pmatrix} 1/2 & 0 & 0 & 0 \\ 0 & 0 & 0 & 1 \\ 0 & 0 & 1 & 0 \\ 0 & 1 & 0 & 0 \end{pmatrix}$

(In (a) use formula (4) with $\mathbf{A}_{11}$ as the 4×4 matrix in the upper left-hand corner. In (b) use formula (4) with $\mathbf{A}_{11}$ as the 2×2 matrix in the upper left-hand corner. In (c) use formula (5) with $\mathbf{A}_{22}$ as the 3×3 matrix in the lower right-hand corner.)

5. Show that $\begin{pmatrix} \mathbf{P} & \mathbf{R} \\ \mathbf{0} & \mathbf{Q} \end{pmatrix} \begin{pmatrix} \mathbf{P}^{-1} & -\mathbf{P}^{-1}\mathbf{R}\mathbf{Q}^{-1} \\ \mathbf{0} & \mathbf{Q}^{-1} \end{pmatrix} = \mathbf{I}$.

7. (a) Use the hint, the formula for the product of partitioned matrices, and (6) and (7).
(b) The determinant is $(a_1 - 1)(a_2 - 1) \cdots (a_n - 1)|\mathbf{F}|$. By using the results in (a), we get $|\mathbf{F}| = |\mathbf{I}_1 + \mathbf{BA}| = 1 + \sum_{i=1}^{n} 1/(a_i - 1)$, and the conclusion follows.

1.3

1. $\begin{pmatrix} 8 \\ 9 \end{pmatrix} = x \begin{pmatrix} 2 \\ 5 \end{pmatrix} + y \begin{pmatrix} -1 \\ 3 \end{pmatrix}$ requires $8 = 2x - y$ and $9 = 5x + 3y$, with solution $x = 3$ and $y = -2$.

3. The determinant of the matrix with the three vectors as columns is equal to 3, so the vectors are linearly independent.

5. Suppose $\alpha(\mathbf{a} + \mathbf{b}) + \beta(\mathbf{b} + \mathbf{c}) + \gamma(\mathbf{a} + \mathbf{c}) = \mathbf{0}$. Then $(\alpha + \gamma)\mathbf{a} + (\alpha + \beta)\mathbf{b} + (\beta + \gamma)\mathbf{c} = \mathbf{0}$. Because $\mathbf{a}$, $\mathbf{b}$, and $\mathbf{c}$ are linearly independent, $\alpha + \gamma = 0$, $\alpha + \beta = 0$, and $\beta + \gamma = 0$. It follows that $\alpha = \beta = \gamma = 0$, which means that $\mathbf{a} + \mathbf{b}$, $\mathbf{b} + \mathbf{c}$, and $\mathbf{a} + \mathbf{c}$ are linearly independent. The vectors $\mathbf{a} - \mathbf{b}$, $\mathbf{b} + \mathbf{c}$, and $\mathbf{a} + \mathbf{c}$ are linearly *dependent* because $(\mathbf{a} - \mathbf{b}) + (\mathbf{b} + \mathbf{c}) - (\mathbf{a} + \mathbf{c}) = \mathbf{0}$.

7. Both statements follow immediately from the definitions.

1.4

1. (a) 1. (The determinant of the matrix is 0, so the rank is less than 2. Because not all entries are 0, the rank is 1.)
(b) 2 (c) 2 (d) 3 (e) 2 (f) 3

3. $\mathbf{A} = \begin{pmatrix} 3 & 1 \\ 6 & 2 \end{pmatrix}$ and $\mathbf{B} = \begin{pmatrix} 1 & 2 \\ -3 & -6 \end{pmatrix}$. Here $r(\mathbf{AB}) = 0$ and $r(\mathbf{BA}) = 1$.

1.5

1. (a) $r(\mathbf{A}) = 1, r(\mathbf{A_b}) = 2$. No solutions.   (b) $x_1 = 1 + (2/3)t, x_2 = 1 + s - (5/3)t, x_3 = s$, and $x_4 = t$, with s, t arbitrary. Two degrees of freedom.   (c) $x_1 = (-1/3)s, x_2 = (5/3)s, x_3 = s$, and $x_4 = 1$, with s arbitrary. One degree of freedom.   (d) $r(\mathbf{A}) = 2, r(\mathbf{A_b}) = 3$. No solutions.

3. If $a \neq 0$ and $a \neq 7$, the system has a unique solution. If $a = 0$ and $b = 9/2$, or if $a = 7$ and $b = 10/3$, the system has infinitely many solutions, with one degree of freedom. For other values of the parameters, there are no solutions. (One way of solving the problem is by Gaussian elimination, where one ends up with the matrix
$$\begin{pmatrix} 1 & 2 & 3 & 1 \\ 0 & 1 & a-9 & b-3 \\ 0 & 0 & a(7-a) & -ab - 2b + 3a + 9 \end{pmatrix}.)$$

5. (a) Unique solution for $p \neq 3$. For $p = 3$ and $q = 0$, there are infinitely many solutions (1 degree of freedom). For $p = 3$ and $q \neq 0$, there are no solutions.   (b) For $p \neq 3$, only $\mathbf{z} = \mathbf{0}$ is orthogonal to the three vectors. For $p = 3$, the vector $\mathbf{z} = (-a, 0, a)$ is orthogonal to the three vectors for all values of a.

7. (a) $|\mathbf{A}_t| = (t-2)(t+3)$, so $r(\mathbf{A}_t) = 3$ if $t \neq 2$ and $t \neq -3$. Because $\begin{vmatrix} 1 & 3 \\ 2 & 5 \end{vmatrix} \neq 0, r(\mathbf{A}_2) = 2, r(\mathbf{A}_{-3}) = 2$.
   (b) $x_1 = -46 + 19t, x_2 = 19 - 7t, x_3 = t, t \in \mathbb{R}$
   (c) Any $\mathbf{z} \neq \mathbf{0}$ that satisfies $\mathbf{z}\mathbf{A}_2 = \mathbf{0}$ has this property. In particular, $\mathbf{z} = (10a, -7a, a)$ for $a \neq 0$.

1.6

1. (a) $-1, -5; \begin{pmatrix} 7 \\ 3 \end{pmatrix}, \begin{pmatrix} 1 \\ 1 \end{pmatrix}$ (b) No real eigenvalues.   (c) $5, -5; \begin{pmatrix} 1 \\ 1 \end{pmatrix}, \begin{pmatrix} -2 \\ 3 \end{pmatrix}$ (d) $2, 3, 4; \begin{pmatrix} 1 \\ 0 \\ 0 \end{pmatrix}, \begin{pmatrix} 0 \\ 1 \\ 0 \end{pmatrix}, \begin{pmatrix} 0 \\ 0 \\ 1 \end{pmatrix}$
   (e) $-1, 0, 2; \begin{pmatrix} 1 \\ -1 \\ 2 \end{pmatrix}, \begin{pmatrix} 1 \\ -1 \\ 1 \end{pmatrix}, \begin{pmatrix} 2 \\ 1 \\ 1 \end{pmatrix}$ (f) $0, 1, 3; \begin{pmatrix} 1 \\ 1 \\ 1 \end{pmatrix}, \begin{pmatrix} -1 \\ 0 \\ 1 \end{pmatrix}, \begin{pmatrix} 1 \\ -2 \\ 1 \end{pmatrix}$

3. Clearly, $\lambda = 0$ is an eigenvalue iff $|\mathbf{A}| = 0$. If $\lambda \neq 0$ is an eigenvalue of $\mathbf{A}$, then $\mathbf{A}$ has an inverse and $\mathbf{A}\mathbf{x} = \lambda\mathbf{x}$ implies $\mathbf{x} = \lambda\mathbf{A}^{-1}\mathbf{x}$, or $\mathbf{A}^{-1}\mathbf{x} = (1/\lambda)\mathbf{x}$, which shows that $1/\lambda$ is an eigenvalue of $\mathbf{A}^{-1}$.

5. $\mathbf{A}\mathbf{v}_1 = 3\mathbf{v}_1$ yields $a - c = 3, b - e = 0$, and $c - f = -3$. $\mathbf{A}\mathbf{v}_2 = \mathbf{v}_2$ yields $a + 2b + c = 1, b + 2d + e = 2$, and $c + 2e + f = 1$. Finally, $\mathbf{A}\mathbf{v}_3 = 4\mathbf{v}_3$ yields $a - b + c = 4, b - d + e = -4$, and $c - e + f = 4$. Solving these equations yields $\mathbf{A} = \begin{pmatrix} 3 & -1 & 0 \\ -1 & 2 & -1 \\ 0 & -1 & 3 \end{pmatrix}$.

7. The real eigenvalues are $\lambda_1 = 1$ and $\lambda_2 = 0$, with corresponding eigenvectors $\mathbf{v}_1 = (1, 1, 0, 0)'$ and $\mathbf{v}_2 = (0, 1, 0, 0)'$.

9. $|\mathbf{A} - \mathbf{I}| = \begin{vmatrix} a_{11} - 1 & a_{12} & \cdots & a_{1n} \\ a_{21} & a_{22} - 1 & \cdots & a_{2n} \\ \vdots & \vdots & \ddots & \vdots \\ a_{n1} & a_{n2} & \cdots & a_{nn} - 1 \end{vmatrix}$. Add all the last $n - 1$ rows to the first row. Because all the column sums in $\mathbf{A}$ are 1, all entries in the first row will be 0. Hence, $|\mathbf{A} - \mathbf{I}| = 0$, so 1 is an eigenvalue for $\mathbf{A}$.

1.7

1. (a) Eigenvalues are 1 and 3, with corresponding eigenvectors $\begin{pmatrix} 1 \\ -1 \end{pmatrix}$ and $\begin{pmatrix} 1 \\ 1 \end{pmatrix}$. Normalizing the eigenvectors, we choose $\mathbf{P} = \begin{pmatrix} 1/\sqrt{2} & 1/\sqrt{2} \\ -1/\sqrt{2} & 1/\sqrt{2} \end{pmatrix}$, and then $\mathbf{P}^{-1}\mathbf{A}\mathbf{P} = \text{diag}(1, 3)$.
   (b) $\mathbf{A}$ has only two eigenvalues, 0 and 2, with three linearly independent eigenvectors, $\begin{pmatrix} 1 \\ -1 \\ 0 \end{pmatrix}, \begin{pmatrix} 1 \\ 1 \\ 0 \end{pmatrix}, \begin{pmatrix} 0 \\ 0 \\ 1 \end{pmatrix}$.

Choose $\mathbf{P} = \begin{pmatrix} 1/\sqrt{2} & 1/\sqrt{2} & 0 \\ -1/\sqrt{2} & 1/\sqrt{2} & 0 \\ 0 & 0 & 1 \end{pmatrix}$, and then $\mathbf{P}^{-1}\mathbf{AP} = \text{diag}(0, 2, 2)$.

(c) $\mathbf{P} = \begin{pmatrix} 0 & \sqrt{2}/2 & -\sqrt{2}/2 \\ -4/5 & 3\sqrt{2}/10 & 3\sqrt{2}/10 \\ 3/5 & 2\sqrt{2}/5 & 2\sqrt{2}/5 \end{pmatrix}$, and then $\mathbf{P}^{-1}\mathbf{AP} = \text{diag}(1, 6, -4)$.

3. According to (1), $\mathbf{AB}$ and $\mathbf{A}^{-1}(\mathbf{AB})\mathbf{A} = \mathbf{BA}$ have the same eigenvalues. (Alternative argument: Because $\mathbf{A}^{-1}$ exists, $|\mathbf{A}| \neq 0$. So λ is an eigenvalue for $\mathbf{AB}$ $\iff$ $|\mathbf{AB} - \lambda\mathbf{I}| = 0$ $\iff$ $|\mathbf{A}(\mathbf{B} - \lambda\mathbf{A}^{-1})| = 0$ $\iff$ $|\mathbf{B} - \lambda\mathbf{A}^{-1}| = 0$ $\iff$ $|(\mathbf{B} - \lambda\mathbf{A}^{-1})\mathbf{A}| = 0$ $\iff$ $|\mathbf{BA} - \lambda\mathbf{I}| = 0$ $\iff$ λ is an eigenvalue for $\mathbf{BA}$.)

1.8

1. $a_{11}x_1^2 + 2a_{12}x_1x_2 + 2a_{13}x_1x_3 + a_{22}x_2^2 + 2a_{23}x_2x_3 + a_{33}x_3^2$

3. (a) Positive definite   (b) Positive definite   (c) Negative semidefinite   (d) Negative definite

5. (a) $Q(0, x_2, 0, \dots, 0) = a_{22}x_2^2$ is positive if $x_2 \neq 0$, so $a_{22} > 0$, etc.   (b) $Q(x_1, x_2, 0, \dots, 0) = a_{11}x_1^2 + 2a_{12}x_1x_2 + a_{22}x_2^2$ is a positive definite form in x_1, x_2, so the conditions in (b) are satisfied for $i, j = 1, 2$, etc.

7. By Theorem 1.7.2 all eigenvalues are real. If $\mathbf{A}$ is negative definite, then by Theorem 1.8.2(c) all the eigenvalues $\lambda_1, \dots, \lambda_n$ are negative. But then $\varphi(\lambda) = (\lambda - \lambda_1)(\lambda - \lambda_2)\cdots(\lambda - \lambda_n) = (\lambda + r_1)(\lambda + r_2)\cdots(\lambda + r_n)$, where r_i are all positive. Expanding this product obviously produces a polynomial with positive coefficients only. If, on the other hand, all the coefficients a_i in the eigenvalue polynomial are positive, then $\varphi(\lambda) \geq a_0 > 0$ for all $\lambda \geq 0$. So no positive number can be an eigenvalue.

1.9

1. Positive definite subject to the constraint. When $y = -x$, $x^2 - 2xy + y^2 = 4x^2$, which is positive except when $x = 0$. Using Theorem 1.9.1, $\begin{vmatrix} 0 & 1 & 1 \\ 1 & 1 & -1 \\ 1 & -1 & 1 \end{vmatrix} = -4 < 0$.)

3. Negative definite subject to the constraint. (Using Theorem 1.9.1, $\begin{vmatrix} 0 & 0 & 1 & 1 & 1 \\ 0 & 0 & 4 & -2 & 1 \\ 1 & 4 & -5 & 1 & 2 \\ 1 & -2 & 1 & -1 & 0 \\ 1 & 1 & 2 & 0 & -2 \end{vmatrix} = -180 < 0$.)

Chapter 2

2.1

1. (a) $\nabla f(x, y) = (y, 2y + x) = (1, 4)$ at $(2, 1)$.
(b) $\nabla g(x, y, z) = (e^{xy} + xye^{xy}, x^2e^{xy}, -2z) = (1, 0, -2)$ at $(0, 0, 1)$.

3. $3\sqrt{2}/2$ (b) $-2\sqrt{3}/3$ **5.** (a) $-(5\ln 3 + 8/3)/\sqrt{18}$ (b) $(\ln 3 + 2/3, \ln 3 + 2/3, 2/3)$

7. $f(\mathbf{x}) = b_1x_1 + \cdots + b_nx_n$, so $\nabla f(\mathbf{x}) = (b_1, \dots, b_n) = \mathbf{b}$, and $f_a'(\mathbf{x}) = \nabla f(\mathbf{x}) \cdot \mathbf{a} = \mathbf{b} \cdot \mathbf{a}$.

9. $y'' = -\dfrac{(F_{11}''(x, y) + F_{12}''(x, y)y')F_2'(x, y) - F_1'(x, y)(F_{21}''(x, y) + F_{22}''(x, y)y')}{[F_2'(x, y)]^2}$. Inserting $y' = -\dfrac{F_1'(x, y)}{F_2'(x, y)}$ and

rearranging yields $y'' = -\dfrac{1}{(F_2')^3}[F_{11}''(F_2')^2 - 2F_{12}''F_1'F_2' + F_{22}''(F_1')^2]$. Expanding the determinant according to the first row yields the same expression.

2.2

1. Only (a) and (d) are convex.

3. S is the intersection of $m + n$ convex sets (half spaces determined by the inequalities), and is therefore convex according to (3).

5. Suppose $(\mathbf{s}_1, \mathbf{t}_1)$ and $(\mathbf{s}_2, \mathbf{t}_2)$ both belong to $S \times T$, with $\mathbf{s}_1, \mathbf{s}_2 \in S$ and $\mathbf{t}_1, \mathbf{t}_2 \in T$. Now, $\lambda(\mathbf{s}_1, \mathbf{t}_1) + (1 - \lambda)(\mathbf{s}_2, \mathbf{t}_2) = (\lambda \mathbf{s}_1 + (1 - \lambda)\mathbf{s}_2, \lambda \mathbf{t}_1 + (1 - \lambda)\mathbf{t}_2)$. For $\lambda \in [0, 1]$, this belongs to $S \times T$ because $\lambda \mathbf{s}_1 + (1 - \lambda)\mathbf{s}_2 \in S$ and $\lambda \mathbf{t}_1 + (1 - \lambda)\mathbf{t}_2 \in T$, by the convexity of S and T. Hence, $S \times T$ is convex.

7. (a) The set $S = \mathbb{Q}$ of rational numbers has the property, but is not convex.   (b) If x, $y \in S$, then by repeated subdivision, $z_\lambda = \lambda x + (1 - \lambda)y \in S$, for $\lambda = 1/2$, and then also for $\lambda = 1/4, 3/4, \ldots$, and generally for $\lambda = k/2^i$, $k = 1, \ldots, 2^i - 1$, $i = 1, 2, \ldots$. The set T of points z_λ obtained by running through all such λ has the property that $\mathrm{cl}(T) = [x, y]$. Since S is closed, $[x, y] = \mathrm{cl}(T) \subseteq \mathrm{cl}(S) = S$. It follows that S is convex.

2.3

1. (a) Strictly convex.   (b) Concave, but not strictly concave.   (c) Strictly concave.

3. (a) $f_{11}'' = 2a$, $f_{12}'' = 2b$, $f_{22}'' = 2c$, and $f_{11}'' f_{22}'' - (f_{12}'')^2 = 2a2c - (2b)^2 = 4(ac - b^2)$. The result follows from Theorem 2.3.1.   (b) Using Theorem 2.3.1 again, f is concave iff $a \leq 0, b \leq 0$, and $ac - b^2 \geq 0$; f is convex iff $a \geq 0, b \geq 0$, and $ac - b^2 \geq 0$.

5. (a) $z_{11}''(x, y) = -e^x - e^{x+y}$, $z_{12}''(x, y) = -e^{x+y}$, and $z_{22}''(x, y) = -e^{x+y}$, so $z_{11}''(x, y) < 0$ and $z_{11}'' z_{22}'' - (z_{12}'')^2 = e^{2x+y} > 0$. Hence, z is strictly concave.   (b) z is strictly convex. $(z_{11}'' = e^{x+y} + e^{x-y} > 0$ and $z_{11}'' z_{22}'' - (z_{12}'')^2 = 4e^{2x} > 0.)$ (c) $w = u^2$, where $u = x + 2y + 3z$. So w is a convex function of an affine function, hence convex according to (9).

7. If $\mathbf{x}^0$, $\mathbf{x} \in \mathbb{R}^n$ and $\lambda \in (0, 1)$, then $f(\lambda \mathbf{x}^0 + (1-\lambda)\mathbf{x}) = \|\lambda \mathbf{x}^0 + (1-\lambda)\mathbf{x}\| \leq \|\lambda \mathbf{x}^0\| + \|(1-\lambda)\mathbf{x}\| = \lambda \|\mathbf{x}^0\| + (1-\lambda)\|\mathbf{x}\| = \lambda f(\mathbf{x}^0) + (1 - \lambda)f(\mathbf{x})$. Hence f is convex. But when $\mathbf{x} = \alpha \mathbf{x}^0$, then $f(\lambda \mathbf{x}^0 + (1 - \lambda)\mathbf{x}) = \|[\lambda + (1 - \lambda)\alpha]\mathbf{x}^0\| = \lambda \|\mathbf{x}^0\| + (1 - \alpha)\|\mathbf{x}\|$, so f is not strictly convex.

9. (a) First, note that $z_{ij}'' = a_i a_j z / x_i x_j$ for $i \neq j$, and $z_{ii}'' = a_i(a_i - 1)z/x_i^2$. By using rule (1.1.20) repeatedly, we obtain the formula for D_k.   (b) Use the hint.   (c) If $\sum_{i=1}^n a_i < 1$, then (because each a_i is positive) $\sum_{i=1}^k a_i < 1$ for all k, so the sign of D_k is that of $(-1)^k$. Then use Theorem 2.3.2(b).

2.4

1. Inequality (1) reduces to $1 - x^2 - y^2 - (1 - x_0^2 - y_0^2) \leq -2x_0(x - x_0) - 2y_0(y - y_0)$. Rearranging the terms yields the equivalent inequality $0 \leq x^2 - 2xx_0 + x_0^2 + y^2 - 2yy_0 + y_0^2$, or $0 \leq (x - x_0)^2 + (y - y_0)^2$, which is obviously true.

3. On the right-hand side of (∗), the coefficients $\lambda_1 + \lambda_2$ and λ_3 sum to 1, so definition (2.3.1) for $n = 2$ applies. Next note that $\lambda_1/(\lambda_1 + \lambda_2)$ and $\lambda_2/(\lambda_1 + \lambda_2)$ also sum to 1.

5. Let $\mathbf{x}, \mathbf{x}^0$ belong to S and let $\lambda \in (0, 1)$. Then $\mathbf{z} = \lambda \mathbf{x} + (1 - \lambda)\mathbf{y}$ belongs to S. By assumption a supergradient $\mathbf{p}$ exists at $\mathbf{z}$, so $f(\mathbf{x}) - f(\mathbf{z}) \leq \mathbf{p} \cdot (\mathbf{x} - \mathbf{z})$ and $f(\mathbf{x}^0) - f(\mathbf{z}) \leq \mathbf{p} \cdot (\mathbf{x}^0 - \mathbf{z})$. Multiplying the first inequality by λ, and the second one by $1 - \lambda$ then adding gives $\lambda[f(\mathbf{x}) - f(\mathbf{z})] + (1 - \lambda)[f(\mathbf{x}^0) - f(\mathbf{z})] \leq \mathbf{p} \cdot [\lambda \mathbf{x} + (1 - \lambda)\mathbf{x}^0 - \mathbf{z}] = 0$, by definition of $\mathbf{z}$. This is equivalent to the definition of concavity. Also, the sufficiency part of Theorem 2.4.1(a) holds because (1) says that $\nabla f(\mathbf{x}^0)$ must be a supergradient at $\mathbf{x}^0$.

2.5

1. According to (6): (a) F is strictly concave,   (b) F is quasiconcave,   (c) F is concave.   According to (7): (d) F is quasiconvex ($\rho = -2, \mu = 1$),   (e) F is concave ($\rho = -1/3, \mu = 1$),   (f) F is concave ($\rho = 1/4, \mu = 3/16$).

3. (a) $a \geq 0$ (b) $g(x)$ is concave according to Theorem 2.3.5 (a). h is quasiconcave according to Theorem 2.5.2 (a), because f is, in particular, quasiconcave.

5. $f'(x) \neq 0$ for all x implies that f is strictly quasiconcave. (In fact, even if f is only a C^1 function, $f'(x) \neq 0$ implies that either f is (strictly) increasing or (strictly) decreasing, and so is quasiconcave according to Example 2. It is then also strictly quasiconcave.

7. If $f(x) \neq f(x^0)$, then x or x^0 is 0, and the right-hand side of (8) is 0. For $\lambda \in (0, 1)$, the left-hand side is 1. The set $\{x : f(x) \geq 1/2\} = (-\infty, 0) \cup (0, \infty)$ is not convex, so f is not quasiconcave.

9. Use Theorem 2.5.1 (5). Assume $F(f_1(\mathbf{x}), \ldots, f_m(\mathbf{x})) \geq F(f_1(\mathbf{x}^0), \ldots, f_m(\mathbf{x}^0))$. Now, by concavity of each f_i,
$f_i(\lambda \mathbf{x} + (1-\lambda)\mathbf{x}^0) \geq \lambda f_i(\mathbf{x}) + (1-\lambda)f_i(\mathbf{x}^0)$. Since F is increasing, $F(f_1(\lambda \mathbf{x} + (1-\lambda)\mathbf{x}^0), \ldots, f_m(\lambda \mathbf{x} + (1-\lambda)\mathbf{x}^0))$
$\geq F(\lambda f_1(\mathbf{x}) + (1-\lambda)f_1(\mathbf{x}^0), \ldots, \lambda f_m(\mathbf{x}) + (1-\lambda)f_m(\mathbf{x}^0)) \geq F(f_1(\mathbf{x}^0), \ldots, f_m(\mathbf{x}^0))$, by quasiconcavity of F.

2.6

1. (a) $f(x, y) \approx -1 - x - y - \frac{1}{2}x^2 - \frac{1}{2}y^2$ (b) $f(x, y) \approx 1 + x + \frac{1}{2}x^2 + xy$ (c) $f(x, y) \approx x^2 + y^2$

2.7

1. The Jacobian is x_1. We find that $x_1 = y_1 + y_2$, $x_2 = y_2/(y_1 + y_2)$ (provided $y_1 + y_2 \neq 0$). The transformation maps the given rectangle onto a quadrilateral in the $y_1 y_2$-plane determined by the inequalities $1 \leq y_1 + y_2 \leq 2$ and $y_1 \leq y_2 \leq 2y_1$.

3. (a) $J = r$ (b) $T(r, 0) = T(r, 2\pi)$

5. (a) The partial derivatives obviously exist and are continuous for $(x, y) \neq (0, 0)$. Moreover, $f'_1(0, 0) = \lim_{h \to 0}[f(h, 0) - f(0, 0)]/h = \lim_{h \to 0} 0 = 0$, and similarly $f'_2(0, 0) = 0$. (b) Every directional derivative clearly exists for $(x, y) \neq (0, 0)$, because f is continuously differentiable at such points. If $\mathbf{a} = (a_1, a_2) \neq \mathbf{0}$, $f'_\mathbf{a}(0, 0) = \lim_{h \to 0}[f(ha_1, ha_2) - f(0, 0)]/h = \lim_{h \to 0}(a_1 a_2^2/(a_1^2 + h^2 a_2^2)) = a_2^2/a_1$ if $a_1 \neq 0$. If $a_1 = 0$, then $f'_\mathbf{a}(0, 0) = 0$. (c) $f(y^2, y) = 1/2$ for all $y \neq 0$ and $f(0, 0) = 0$, so f cannot be continuous at $(0, 0)$. Differentiability implies continuity, so f is not differentiable.

2.8

1. (a) $f'_y = 3y^2 + 1 \neq 0$, $y' = -f'_x/f'_y = -3x^2/(3y^2 + 1) = 0$ at $x = 0$. (b) $f'_y = 1 + x \cos(xy) = 1 \neq 0$ at $x_0 = 0$, $y' = 0$.

3. u'_x, v'_x, and w'_x must satisfy $u'_x - v'_x - 3w'_x = 0, -2 + u'_x - w'_x = 0, 2 - u'_x - v'_x + 3w'_x = 0$. The unique solution is $u'_x = 5/2$, $v'_x = 1$, $w'_x = 5/2$.

5. $\partial(F, G)/\partial(u, v) = -2u^2 + 4uv + 2v^2$, so around points where this expression is different from 0, one can express u and v as C^1 functions of x and y: $u = f(x, y)$ and $v = g(x, y)$. At $(x_0, y_0, u_0, v_0) = (2, 1, -1, 2)$ (which does satisfy the equations), $\partial(F, G)/\partial(u, v) = -2$ and $f'_x(2, 1) = 1/2$, $f'_y(2, 1) = 6$, $g'_x(2, 1) = 1$, and $g'_y(2, 1) = 2$.

2.9

1. (a) 3 degrees of freedom. (b) $f'(Y - T) \neq 1$ is sufficient.

3. $\partial v/\partial y = g'_1(\partial \varphi/\partial y) + g'_2 = g'_1(-f'_2/f'_1) + g'_2 = 0$, because $f'_1 g'_2 = f'_2 g'_1$.

5. (a) $u'_x = 3/2$, $v'_x = 5/(6 \ln 3)$ (b) $f(u) = u - ae^{u(b-1)}$ is strictly increasing because $b \leq 1$. Also $f(0) \leq 0$ and $f(1) \geq 0$. (c) Let $a = (1 + xy)/2$ and $b = x$, and use the result from (b). This gives a unique value of u. Because $u \in [0, 1]$, the first equation then gives a unique value of v.

2.10

1. The leading principal minors are 1 and 1, but $\mathbf{x}'\mathbf{Ax} = (x_1 + x_2)^2$, which is 0 when $x_2 = -x_1$.

Chapter 3

3.1

1. The Hessian matrix is $\mathbf{g}''(x, y) = \begin{pmatrix} g''_{11} & g''_{12} \\ g''_{21} & g''_{22} \end{pmatrix} = \begin{pmatrix} 6x & 0 \\ 0 & 6y \end{pmatrix}$. We see that g is (strictly) convex in its domain. Stationary point where $3x^2 - 3 = 0$ and $3y^2 - 2 = 0$, so $(1, \sqrt{6}/3)$ is the only stationary point. It is a (global) minimum point for g, and $g_{\min} = g(1, \sqrt{6}/3) = -2 - 4\sqrt{6}/9$.

3. (a) $v_1^* = \frac{1}{216} p^6 q_1^{-3} q_2^{-3}$, $v_2^* = \frac{1}{144} p^6 q_1^{-2} q_2^{-4}$ (b) $\pi^*(p, q_1, q_2) = \frac{1}{432} p^6 q_1^{-2} q_2^{-3}$. The equalities in (*) follow easily.

5. $x^*(r, s) = \frac{1}{2} r^2$ and $y^*(r, s) = \frac{3}{16} s^2$. Moreover, $f^*(r, s) = \frac{1}{4} r^4 + \frac{9}{32} s^4$, so $\partial f^*/\partial r = r^3$ and $\partial f/\partial r = 2rx$, so $\partial f(x^*, y^*, r, s)/\partial r = 2rx^* = r^3$. Also, $\partial f^*/\partial s = \partial f(x^*, y^*, r, s)/\partial s = \frac{9}{8} s^3$.

3.2

1. The only stationary point is $(0, 0, 0)$. The leading principal minors of the Hessian are $D_1 = 2$, $D_2 = 3$, and $D_3 = 4$, so $(0, 0, 0)$ is a local minimum point by Theorem 3.2.1(a).

3. (a) Stationary points where $x^2 = y$ and $y^2 = x$. Then $y^4 = y$, with the solutions $y = 0$ and $y = 1$. Hence the stationary points are $(x, y) = (0, 0)$ and $(1, 1)$. The quadratic form is $-6h_1 h_2$ at $(0, 0)$ and $6(h_1^2 - h_1 h_2 + h_2^2)$ at $(1, 1)$.   (b) $-6h_1 h_2$ is indefinite, so $(0, 0)$ is not a local extreme point. Completing the squares we see that $6(h_1^2 - h_1 h_2 + h_2^2) = 6[(h_1 - \frac{1}{2} h_2)^2 + \frac{3}{4} h_2^2] > 0$ for $(h_1, h_2) \neq (0, 0)$, so this form is positive definite and $(1, 1)$ is a local minimum point.   (c) (1)–(3) implies that $(0, 0)$ is a saddle point and that $(1, 1)$ a local minimum point.

5. It is easy to see that $(0, 0)$ is the only stationary point. The second derivatives are $f''_{11}(0, 0) = 2$, $f''_{12}(0, 0) = 0$, and $f''_{22}(0, 0) = 2$, so $(0, 0)$ is a local minimum point. It is not a global minimum point because $f(x, -2) = -x^2 + 4$ tends to $-\infty$ as $x \to \infty$.

3.3

1. (a) $x^* = a/6$, $y^* = a/3$, $z^* = a/6$, $\lambda = -a/3$. (The Lagrangian is concave as a sum of concave functions.)
(b) $f^*(a) = 100 - a^2/6$. We see that $df^*(a)/da = \lambda$.

3. (a) With $\mathcal{L} = e^x + y + z - \lambda_1(x + y + z) - \lambda_2(x^2 + y^2 + z^2)$, the first-order conditions are (i) $\partial\mathcal{L}/\partial x = e^x - \lambda_1 - 2\lambda_2 x = 0$, (ii) $\partial\mathcal{L}/\partial y = 1 - \lambda_1 - 2\lambda_2 y = 0$, (iii) $\partial\mathcal{L}/\partial z = 1 - \lambda_1 - 2\lambda_2 z = 0$. From (ii) and (iii), $\lambda_2 y = \lambda_2 z$, so (A) $\lambda_2 = 0$ or (B) $y = z$, etc. Four candidates: $(0, 0, 1)$ and $(0, 1, 0)$ with $\lambda_1 = 1$, $\lambda_2 = 0$; $(1, 0, 0)$ with $\lambda_1 = 1$, $\lambda_2 = \frac{1}{2}(e - 1)$; $(-\frac{1}{3}, \frac{2}{3}, \frac{2}{3})$ with $\lambda_1 = \frac{1}{3} + \frac{2}{3} e^{-1/3}$ and $\lambda_2 = \frac{1}{2} - \frac{1}{2} e^{-1/3}$. The value of the objective function is highest, and equal to e, at $(1, 0, 0)$. (The maximum exists by the extreme-value theorem.)
(b) $\Delta f^* \approx \lambda_1 \cdot (0.02) + \lambda_2 \cdot (-0.02) = 0.02 - 0.02 \cdot \frac{1}{2}(e - 1) = 0.01(3 - e)$.

5. (a) Maximum 1 at $(-3\sqrt{10}/10, \sqrt{10}/10, 0)$ and at $(3\sqrt{10}/10, -\sqrt{10}/10, 0)$ with $\lambda_1 = 1$, $\lambda_2 = 0$.
(b) $\Delta f^* \approx 1 \cdot 0.05 + 0 \cdot 0.05 = 0.05$.

7. (a) The constraints have the unique solution $(x, y) = (\frac{1}{2}\sqrt{2}, \frac{1}{2}\sqrt{2})$, and this pair with $z = 0$ must solve the problem.
(b) With $\mathcal{L} = x^2 + (y-1)^2 + z^2 - \lambda(x+y) - \mu(x^2 + y^2)$, $\mathcal{L}'_z = 0$ at $z = 0$, and the constraints give the same solution as before. But the equations $\mathcal{L}'_x = 0$ and $\mathcal{L}'_y = 0$ give a contradiction. (The matrix in (5) is here $\begin{pmatrix} 1 & 1 & 0 \\ 2x & 2y & 0 \end{pmatrix}$, which has rank 1 when $x = y$.)

3.4

1. (a) $(x, y) = (\pm 1, 0)$ with $\lambda = 1/4$ and $(0, \pm\sqrt{2})$ with $\lambda = 1/2$.   (b) $B_2(\pm 1, 0) = -64$, so $(\pm 1, 0)$ are local minimum points. $(-1)^2 B_2(0, \pm\sqrt{2}) = 64$, so $(0, \pm\sqrt{2})$ are local maximum points.
(c) The constraint curve is an ellipse, and the problem is to find those points on the curve that have the smallest and the largest (square) distance from $(0, 0)$.

3. At $(1, 0, 0)$ with $\lambda_1 = 1$, $\lambda_2 = -1$, we have $(-1)^3 B_3 = 16 > 0$, which gives a local maximum.
At $(-1/3, -2/3, -2/3)$ with $\lambda_1 = -1$, $\lambda_2 = 1/3$, we have $(-1)^2 B_3 = 16 > 0$, which gives a local minimum.

3.5

1. The solution is obvious: To maximize $1 - x^2 - y^2$ you must have x and y as small as they are allowed to be, i.e. $x = 2$ and $y = 3$. With $\mathcal{L} = 1 - x^2 - y^2 - \lambda(-x) - \mu(-y)$, the first-order conditions for (x^*, y^*) to solve the problem are: (i) $-2x^* + \lambda = 0$;   (ii) $-2y^* + \mu = 0$;   (iii) $\lambda \geq 0$ ($\lambda = 0$ if $x^* > 2$);   (iv) $\mu \geq 0$ ($\mu = 0$ if $y^* > 3$). Since $x^* \geq 2$, (i) implies $\lambda = 2x^* > 0$, and since $y^* \geq 3$, (ii) implies $\mu = 2y^* > 0$, so from (iii) and (iv) we conclude that $x^* = 2$, $y^* = 3$. This is an optimal solution since $\mathcal{L}$ is concave in (x, y).

3. (a) max $-4\ln(x^2 + 2) - y^2$ subject to $-x^2 - y \leq -2$, $-x \leq -1$. The necessary Kuhn–Tucker conditions are:
(i) $-\dfrac{8x}{x^2 + 2} + 2\lambda_1 x + \lambda_2 = 0$; (ii) $-2y + \lambda_1 = 0$; (iii) $\lambda_1 \geq 0$ ($\lambda_1 = 0$ if $x^2 + y > 2$); (iv) $\lambda_2 \geq 0$ ($\lambda_2 = 0$ if $x \geq 1$).
(b) $(x, y, \lambda_1, \lambda_2) = (\sqrt[4]{2}, 2 - \sqrt{2}, 4 - 2\sqrt{2}, 0)$

5. Kuhn–Tucker conditions: (i) $-2(x - 1) - 2\lambda x = 0$; (ii) $-2ye^{y^2} - 2\lambda y = 0$; (iii) $\lambda \geq 0$ ($\lambda = 0$ if $x^2 + y^2 < 1$). The solution is $x = 1$, $y = 0$, and $\lambda = 0$. Because the Lagrangian is concave, this is the optimal solution. Note that for the optimal solution $\lambda = 0$ *and* $x^2 + y^2 = 1$.

7. (a) For $a \geq 3b$, $(x, y, z) = (b, \frac{1}{2}(a - b), \frac{1}{2}(a - b))$ with $\lambda_1 = e^{-(a-b)/2}$ and $\lambda_2 = e^{-b} - e^{-(a-b)/2}$. For $a < 3b$, $x = y = z = \frac{1}{3}a$ with $\lambda_1 = e^{-a/3}$ and $\lambda_2 = 0$.   (b) For $a \geq 3b$, $f^*(a, b) = 100 - e^{-b} - 2e^{-(a-b)/2}$ and $\partial f^*/\partial a = \lambda_1$, $\partial f^*/\partial b = \lambda_2$. For $a < 3b$, $f^*(a, b) = 100 - 3e^{-a/3}$ and $\partial f^*/\partial a = \lambda_1$, $\partial f^*/\partial b = \lambda_2$.
(c) Let $g(a) = 100 - 3e^{-a/3}$, $h(a) = 99 - 2e^{-a/2}$. Then $F^*(a) = g(a)$ if $a < 0$, $F^*(a) = h(a)$ if $a \geq 0$. The functions g and h are both concave. Moreover, $g(0) = h(0)$ and $g'(0) = h'(0)$, so their graphs have a common tangent at the point corresponding to $a = 0$. It follows that F^* is concave.

3.6

1. Because $(x + y - 2)^2 \leq 0$, the constraint is equivalent to $x + y - 2 = 0$ and the solution is $(x, y) = (1, 1)$. The Kuhn–Tucker conditions are $y - 2\lambda(x + y - 2) = 0$ and $x - 2\lambda(x + y - 2) = 0$. Letting $(x, y) = (1, 1)$ yields the contradiction $1 = 0$. Note that $g_1'(x, y) = g_2'(x, y) = 2(x + y - 2) = 0$ for $x = y = 1$, so the gradient of g at $(1, 1)$ is $(0, 0)$, which is not a linearly independent set of vectors. Thus, the constraint qualification does not hold at $(1, 1)$.

3.7

1. (a) $1 - x^2 - y^2 \leq 1$ for all $x \geq 0$, $y \geq 0$, so the optimal solution must be $x = y = 0$.
(b) With $\mathcal{L} = 1 - x^2 - y^2$, the Kuhn–Tucker conditions are   (i) $\partial \mathcal{L}/\partial x = -2x \leq 0 (= 0$ if $x > 0$);
(ii) $\partial \mathcal{L}/\partial y = -2y (= 0$ if $y > 0$). The only solution is obviously $x = y = 0$. (The Lagrangian is concave.)

3. (a) With $\mathcal{L} = \ln(1 + x) + y - \lambda(px + y)$, the Kuhn–Tucker conditions are: (i) $1/(1 + x^*) - \lambda p \leq 0 (= 0$ if $x^* > 0$); (ii) $1 - \lambda \leq 0 (= 0$ if $y^* > 0$); (iii) $\lambda \geq 0$ ($\lambda = 0$ if $px^* + y^* < m$).
(b) $x = -1 + 1/p$, $y = m + p - 1$, with $\lambda = 1$ is the solution for all $p \in (0, 1]$ and $m > 1$. ($\mathcal{L}(x, y)$ *is concave in* (x, y).)

5. Using (A) with $\mathbf{x} = \hat{\mathbf{x}}$ implies that $f(\mathbf{x}^*) - \sum_{j=1}^{m} \lambda_j g_j(\mathbf{x}^*) \geq f(\hat{\mathbf{x}}) - \sum_{j=1}^{m} \lambda_j g_j(\hat{\mathbf{x}})$. But, because $\hat{\mathbf{x}}$ also solves (1), $f(\hat{\mathbf{x}}) = f(\mathbf{x}^*)$ and then $\sum_{j=1}^{m} \lambda_j g_j(\hat{\mathbf{x}}) \geq \sum_{j=1}^{m} \lambda_j g_j(\mathbf{x}^*)$. Thus, because $\lambda_j \geq 0$ and $g_j(\hat{\mathbf{x}}) \leq b_j$, $j = 1, \ldots, m$, and also because of (5), we have

$$\sum_{j=1}^{m} \lambda_j b_j \geq \sum_{j=1}^{m} \lambda_j g_j(\hat{\mathbf{x}}) \geq \sum_{j=1}^{m} \lambda_j g_j(\mathbf{x}^*) = \sum_{j=1}^{m} \lambda_j b_j \qquad (*)$$

Here the two middle terms, being squeezed between two equal numbers, must themselves be equal. Therefore $f(\hat{\mathbf{x}}) - \sum_{j=1}^{m} \lambda_j g_j(\hat{\mathbf{x}}) = f(\mathbf{x}^*) - \sum_{j=1}^{m} \lambda_j g_j(\mathbf{x}^*) \geq f(\mathbf{x}) - \sum_{j=1}^{m} \lambda_j g_j(\mathbf{x})$ for all $\mathbf{x} \geq \mathbf{0}$, proving (A). Also, if $g_k(\hat{\mathbf{x}}) < b_k$ and $\lambda_k > 0$ for any k, then $\sum_{j=1}^{m} \lambda_j(g_j(\hat{\mathbf{x}}) - b_j) < 0$, which contradicts $(*)$. Thus $\hat{\mathbf{x}}$ satisfies (A)–(C).

3.8

1. (a) With $\mathcal{L}(x, y, z, a) = x^2 + y^2 + z^2 - \lambda_1(2x^2 + y^2 + z^2 - a^2) - \lambda_2(x + y + z)$, the necessary conditions are:
(i) $\partial\mathcal{L}/\partial x = 2x - 4\lambda_1 x - \lambda_2 = 0$; (ii) $\partial\mathcal{L}/\partial y = 2y - 2\lambda_1 y - \lambda_2 = 0$; (iii) $\partial\mathcal{L}/\partial z = 2z - 2\lambda_1 z - \lambda_2 = 0$;
(iv) $\lambda_1 \geq 0$ ($\lambda_1 = 0$ if $2x^2 + y^2 + z^2 < a^2$). Solution: $(x^*, y^*, z^*) = (0, \pm\frac{1}{2}\sqrt{2}\,a, \mp\frac{1}{2}\sqrt{2}\,a)$, with $\lambda_1 = 1, \lambda_2 = 0$
both solve the problem. (b) $f^*(a) = a^2$ so $df^*(a)/da = 2a$, and $\partial\mathcal{L}(x^*, y^*, z^*, a)/\partial a = 2\lambda_1 a = 2a$.

3. (a) $x = \pm\frac{1}{2}a\sqrt{2}$, $y = 0$ (b) $x = 0$, $y = \pm\frac{1}{2}r$ (c) The admissible set is the area between two ellipses, and the problem is to find the largest and the smallest distance from the origin to a point in this admissible set.

Chapter 4

4.1

1. (a) $x - x^3 + C$ (b) $-\frac{1}{3}x^{-3} + C$ (c) $\int(1 - x^2)^2\,dx = \int(1 - 2x^2 + x^4)\,dx = x - \frac{2}{3}x^3 + \frac{1}{5}x^5 + C$

3. (a) $64/3 - 12\sqrt{3}$. (Substitute $u = \sqrt{4 - x^2}$.) (b) $2 - 6\ln\frac{7}{6}$. (Substitute $u = 3 + \sqrt{t + 8}$. Then $u - 3 = \sqrt{t + 8}$
and $(u - 3)^2 = t + 8$. Differentiation yields $2(u - 3)\,du = dt$, etc.) (c) $\frac{8}{9}e^3 + \frac{4}{9}$. (Integration by parts.)

5. (a) $1 + \ln\frac{9}{4}$ (b) $\frac{1}{2}$. (Substitute $u = 1 + \sqrt{x}$, then integration by parts.) (c) $45/2 - 3\ln 4$. (Substitute $u = 1 + x^{1/3}$.)

4.2

1. (a) $F'(x) = \int_1^2 e^{xt}\,dt = \frac{1}{x}(e^{2x} - e^x)$ (b) $F'(x) = \int_1^e \frac{1}{x}\,dt = \frac{1}{x}(e - 1)$ (c) $F'(x) = \int_0^1 \frac{-te^{-t}}{(1 + xt)^2}\,dt$
(d) $F'(x) = \int_3^8 \frac{2t^3}{(1 - xt)^3}\,dt$

3. (a) $F'(x) = 16x^3$ (b) $F'(x) = x^6 + 3x^5 + 5x^4$ (c) $F'(x) = 2x - \frac{1}{2}x^{-\frac{1}{2}}\cos(x - x^4) + 4x^3\int_{\sqrt{x}}^{x^2}\sin(t^2 - x^4)\,dt$
(d) $F'(x) = 2e^{2x}\sin(e^{2x} + x) - e^x\sin(e^x + x) + \int_{e^x}^{e^{2x}}\cos(t + x)\,dt = (2e^{2x} + 1)\sin(e^{2x} + x) - (e^x + 1)\sin(e^x + x)$

5. $M'(t) = \int_{-\infty}^{\infty} xe^{tx}f(x)\,dx$, and so $M'(0) = \int_{-\infty}^{\infty} xf(x)\,dx$. By induction, $M^{(n)}(t) = \int_{-\infty}^{\infty} x^n e^{tx}f(x)\,dx$ and
$M^{(n)}(0) = \int_{-\infty}^{\infty} x^n f(x)\,dx$.

7. $dF(\sigma_k)/d\sigma_k = \int_{-\infty}^{+\infty} U'(\mu_k + \sigma_k z)(d\mu_k/d\sigma_k + z)f(z, 0, 1)\,dz$

9. We have $z(t) = \int_t^{2t} F(\tau, t)\,d\tau$, where $F(\tau, t) = x(\tau)e^{-\int_t^\tau r(s)\,ds}$. Leibniz's formula gives $\dot{z}(t) = 2F(2t, t) -$
$F(t, t) + \int_t^{2t}(\partial F(\tau, t)/\partial t)\,d\tau = 2x(2t)e^{-\int_t^{2t} r(s)\,ds} - x(t) + \int_t^{2t} x(\tau)e^{-\int_t^\tau r(s)\,ds}r(t)\,d\tau = 2x(2t)p(t) - x(t) +$
$\int_t^{2t} F(\tau, t)r(t)\,d\tau = 2p(t)x(2t) - x(t) + r(t)z(t)$, and therefore $\dot{z}(t) - r(t)z(t) = 2p(t)x(2t) - x(t)$.

4.3

1. (a) $\frac{1}{2}\sqrt{\pi/a}$. (Substitute $t = \sqrt{a}x$ and use (3).) (b) 1. (Substitute $t = x/\sqrt{2}$ and use (3).)

3. $n! = \Gamma(n + 1) = \sqrt{2\pi}(n + 1)^{n+1/2}e^{-(n+1)}e^{\theta/12(n+1)} = s_n\sqrt{2\pi n}\,(n/e)^n$, where
$s_n = (n + 1)^{n+1/2}n^{-(n+1/2)}e^{-1}e^{\theta/12(n+1)} = \sqrt{1 + 1/n}\,(1 + 1/n)^n e^{-1}e^{\theta/12(n+1)} \to 1$ as $n \to \infty$.

5. (a) Introduce $u = \lambda x$ as a new variable. Then

$$\int_{-\infty}^{\infty} f(x)\,dx = \frac{\lambda^\alpha}{\Gamma(\alpha)}\int_0^\infty x^{\alpha-1}e^{-\lambda x}\,dx = \frac{\lambda^\alpha}{\Gamma(\alpha)}\int_0^\infty (u/\lambda)^{\alpha-1}e^{-u}\frac{1}{\lambda}\,du = \frac{1}{\Gamma(\alpha)}\int_0^\infty u^{\alpha-1}e^{-u}\,du = 1$$

(b) $M(t) = \lambda^\alpha(\Gamma(\alpha))^{-1}\int_0^\infty x^{\alpha-1}e^{-(\lambda-t)x}\,dx$. Introduce $u = \lambda - t$ as a new variable. Then $M(t) = (\lambda/(\lambda - t))^\alpha$.
$M'(0) = \alpha/\lambda$ (the expectation in the gamma distribution).

4.4

1. (a) $\int_0^2 (\int_0^1 (2x + 3y + 4)\,dx)\,dy = \int_0^2 (|_{x=0}^{x=1}(x^2 + 3xy + 4x))\,dy = \int_0^2 (5 + 3y)\,dy = |_0^2 (5y + \frac{3}{2}y^2) = 16$

(b) $\frac{1}{6}ab^2(3a - b)$ (c) $16\ln 2 - 3\ln 3 - 5\ln 5$ (d) $1/8 - 1/4\pi$

3. $k_a = 2 + \dfrac{4}{a^2 + 3a} > 2$ for all $a > 0$.

5. The innermost integral is $\displaystyle\int_0^1 (x_1^2 + x_2^2 + \cdots + x_n^2)\,dx_1 = \Big|_0^1 [\frac{1}{3}x_1^3 + x_1(x_2^2 + x_3^2 + \cdots + x_n^2)] = \frac{1}{3} + x_2^2 + x_3^2 + \cdots + x_n^2.$

Next, $\displaystyle\int_0^1 [\frac{1}{3} + x_2^2 + x_3^2 + \cdots + x_n^2]\,dx_2 = \Big|_0^1 [\frac{1}{3}x_2 + \frac{1}{3}x_2^3 + x_2(x_3^2 + x_4^2 + \cdots + x_n^2)] = \frac{2}{3} + x_3^2 + x_4^2 + \cdots + x_n^2$, etc.
By induction, $I = n/3$.

4.5

1. (a) 11/120. See Fig. 4.5.1(a). (Here $\int_{x^2}^x (x^2 + xy)\,dy = |_{y=x^2}^{y=x}(x^2 y + \frac{1}{2}xy^2) = \frac{3}{2}x^3 - x^4 - \frac{1}{2}x^5$. This gives
$\int_0^1 (\int_{x^2}^x (x^2 + xy)\,dy)\,dx = \int_0^1 (\frac{3}{2}x^3 - x^4 - \frac{1}{2}x^5)\,dx = |_0^1 (\frac{3}{8}x^4 - \frac{1}{5}x^5 - \frac{1}{12}x^6) = \frac{11}{120}.$)
(b) $\int_0^1 (\int_y^{\sqrt{y}} (x^2 + xy)\,dx)\,dy = \int_0^1 (\frac{1}{3}y\sqrt{y} + \frac{1}{2}y^2 - \frac{5}{6}y^3)\,dy = \frac{11}{120}.$ See Fig. 4.5.1(b).

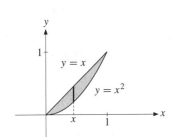

Figure 4.5.1(a)

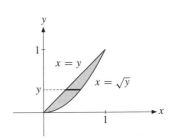

Figure 4.5.1(b)

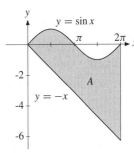

Figure 4.5.7

3. The double integral gives the area of A.

5. $\displaystyle\int_4^5 (\int_0^{\sqrt{25-y^2}} 2x\,dx)\,dy + \int_0^4 (\int_0^{3y/4} 2x\,dx)\,dy = 14/3 + 12 = 50/3.$

7. Figure 4.5.7 shows the set A. We get $\iint_A 2y\cos x\,dx\,dy = \int_0^{2\pi} (\int_{-x}^{\sin x} 2y\cos x\,dy)\,dx$. Here $\int_{-x}^{\sin x} 2y\cos x\,dy = |_{-x}^{\sin x} y^2\cos x = \sin^2 x\cos x - x^2\cos x$. So $\iint_A 2y\cos x\,dx\,dy = \int_0^{2\pi} (\sin^2 x\cos x - x^2\cos x)\,dx = |_0^{2\pi} (\frac{1}{3}\sin^3 x - x^2\sin x - 2x\cos x + 2\sin x) = -4\pi$. (You need integration by parts to get $\int x^2\cos x\,dx = x^2\sin x + 2x\cos x - 2\sin x + C$.)

9. (a) $\displaystyle\int_0^a (\int_0^b f(\xi_1, \xi_2)\,d\xi_2))\,d\xi_1$, where $a = \frac{1}{q_1}$, $b = \frac{1}{q_2} - \frac{q_1\xi_1}{q_2}$

(b) $\displaystyle\int_0^c (\int_0^d f(\xi_1, \xi_2)\,d\xi_1)\,d\xi_2$, where $c = \frac{1}{q_2}$, $d = \frac{1}{q_1} - \frac{q_2\xi_2}{q_1}$ (c) $\dfrac{\partial g}{\partial q_1} = -\frac{1}{q_2}\int_0^{\frac{1}{q_1}} \xi_1 f(\xi_1, \frac{1}{q_2} - \frac{q_1\xi_1}{q_2})\,d\xi_1$

4.6

1. (a) Use the same subdivision as in Example 1, except that $j = 0, \ldots, 2n - 1$. Then $(2x_i^* - y_j^* + 1)\Delta x_i\Delta y_j = (2\frac{i}{n} - \frac{j}{n} + 1)\frac{1}{n}\frac{1}{n} = 2\frac{i}{n^3} - \frac{j}{n^3} + \frac{1}{n^2}$, and $\sum_{j=0}^{2n-1} \sum_{i=0}^{n-1} (2\frac{i}{n^3} - \frac{j}{n^3} + \frac{1}{n^2}) = 2\frac{1}{n^3}\sum_{j=0}^{2n-1}(\sum_{i=0}^{n-1} i) - \frac{1}{n^3}\sum_{i=0}^{n-1}(\sum_{j=0}^{2n-1} j) + \frac{1}{n^2}\sum_{j=0}^{2n-1}(\sum_{i=0}^{n-1} 1) = 2\frac{1}{n^3}\sum_{j=0}^{2n-1}\frac{1}{2}n(n-1) - \frac{1}{n^3}\sum_{i=0}^{n-1}\frac{1}{2}(2n-1)2n + \frac{1}{n^2}\sum_{j=0}^{2n-1} n = 2\frac{1}{n^3}\frac{1}{2}n(n-1)2n - \frac{1}{n^3}\frac{1}{2}(2n-1)2nn + \frac{1}{n^2}n2n = 2 - \frac{1}{n} \to 2$ as $n \to \infty$.

(b) $\int_0^2 (\int_0^1 (2x - y + 1)\,dx)\,dy = \int_0^2 (|_0^1 (x^2 - xy + x))\,dy = \int_0^2 (2 - y)\,dy = 2.$

4.7

1. (a) See Fig. 4.7.1. $\iint_A (x + xy)\, dx\, dy = \int_0^2 \left(\int_{2-x}^{x+2} (x + xy)\, dy \right) dx + \int_2^4 \left(\int_{x-2}^{6-x} (x + xy)\, dy \right) dx = \int_0^2 6x^2\, dx +$
$\int_2^4 (-6x^2 + 24x)\, dx = 16 + 32 = 48$ (b) $\int_2^6 \left[\int_{-2}^2 (\frac{1}{2}u + \frac{1}{2}v + \frac{1}{4}v^2 - \frac{1}{4}u^2) \frac{1}{2}\, du \right] dv = \int_2^6 (\frac{1}{2}v^2 + v - \frac{2}{3})\, dv = 48$

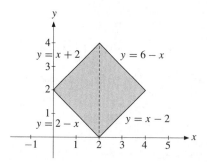

Figure 4.7.1

3. (a) $\pi/64$. ($\iint_A x^2\, dx\, dy = \int_0^{2\pi} \left(\int_0^{1/2} (r^2 \cos^2 \theta) r\, dr \right) d\theta = \int_0^{2\pi} \cos^2 \theta\, d\theta \int_0^{1/2} r^3\, dr = \pi/64$.)   (b) $\pi/64$

5. (a) $\pi/2$. (Using polar coordinates: $\iint_{A_1} (1 - x^2 - y^2)\, dx\, dy = \int_0^{2\pi} d\theta \int_0^1 (1 - r^2) r\, dr = \pi/2$.)
  (b) 144/25 (Introduce $u = -2x + y$, $v = 3x + y$, so $x = -\frac{1}{5}u + \frac{1}{5}v$, $y = \frac{3}{5}u + \frac{2}{5}v$. Then $J = -\frac{1}{5}$, and
  $\iint_{A_3} (x + y)\, dx\, dy = \int_4^8 \frac{1}{5} \left(\int_{-1}^1 (\frac{2}{5}u + \frac{3}{5}v)\, du \right) dv = 144/25$.)

4.8

1. (a) $\frac{1}{2}\pi$. (Introducing polar coordinates and letting $A_n = \{(x, y) : x^2 + y^2 \geq n^2\}$, we get $\iint_{A_n} (x^2 + y^2)^{-3}\, dx\, dy =$
$\int_0^{2\pi} \left(\int_1^n r^{-6} r\, dr \right) d\theta = \int_0^{2\pi} d\theta \int_1^n r^{-5}\, dr = \frac{1}{2}\pi(1 - 1/n^4) \to \frac{1}{2}\pi$ as $n \to \infty$.)
  (b) Convergence to $\pi/(p - 1)$ for $p > 1$. Divergence for $p \leq 1$. ($\iint_{A_n} (x^2 + y^2)^{-p}\, dx\, dy = \int_0^{2\pi} d\theta \int_1^n r^{1-2p}\, dr$.
  Then look at $p > 1$, $p = 1$, and $p < 1$ separately.)

3. (a) Introducing polar coordinates, $\iint_{x^2+y^2 \leq 1} k\sqrt{1 - x^2 - y^2}\, dx\, dy = k \int_0^{2\pi} d\theta \int_0^1 \sqrt{1 - r^2} \cdot r\, dr = 2\pi k/3$, so
  $k = 3/2\pi$.   (b) $f_X(x) = (3/2\pi) \int_{x^2+y^2 \leq 1} \sqrt{1 - x^2 - y^2}\, dy = (3/2\pi) \int_{-a \leq y \leq a} \sqrt{a^2 - y^2}\, dy = (3/2\pi)\frac{1}{2}\pi a^2 =$
  $\frac{3}{4}(1 - x^2)$, where $a = \sqrt{1 - x^2}$.

5. (a) Put $F(x, y) = \int_{-\infty}^x G(u, y)\, du$, with $G(u, y) = \int_{-\infty}^y f(u, v)\, dv$. Then $F_1'(x, y) = G(x, y)$ and $F_{12}''(x, y) =$
  $G_2'(x, y) = f(x, y)$.   (b) From $F(x, y) = \frac{1}{4}(2 - e^{-x})(2 - e^{-y})$ we easily find that $F_{12}''(x, y) = \frac{1}{4}e^{-x}e^{-y} = \frac{1}{4}e^{-x-y}$
  for $x \geq 0$, $y \geq 0$.

7. (a) π. (Introducing polar coordinates and defining A_n as in Example 3, we get $\iint_{A_n} x^2(x^2 + y^2)^{-3/2}\, dx\, dy =$
  $\int_0^{2\pi} \left(\int_{1/n}^1 (r^2 \cos^2 \theta) r^{-3} r\, dr \right) d\theta = \int_0^{2\pi} \cos^2 \theta\, d\theta \int_{1/n}^1 dr = \pi(1 - 1/n) \to \pi$ as $n \to \infty$.)
  (b) π. ($\iint_A \frac{-\ln(x^2 + y^2)}{\sqrt{x^2 + y^2}}\, dx\, dy = \lim_{n \to \infty} \int_0^{\pi/2} d\theta \int_{1/n}^1 (-\ln r^2/r) r\, dr = -\pi \lim_{n \to \infty} \int_{1/n}^1 \ln r\, dr$, etc.)

Chapter 5

5.1

1. If $x(t) = Ce^{-t} + \frac{1}{2}e^t$, then $\dot{x}(t) + x(t) = -Ce^{-t} + \frac{1}{2}e^t + Ce^{-t} + \frac{1}{2}e^t = e^t$.

3. Differentiate $xe^{tx} = C$ implicitly to obtain $\dot{x}e^{tx} + x[e^{tx}(x + t\dot{x})] = 0$. Cancelling e^{tx} and rearranging gives $(1 + tx)\dot{x} = -x^2$.

5. If $x = Ct - C^2$, then $\dot{x} = C$, so $\dot{x}^2 = C^2$ and $t\dot{x} - x = tC - Ct + C^2 = C^2$. If $x = \frac{1}{4}t^2$, then $\dot{x} = \frac{1}{2}t$, so $\dot{x}^2 = \frac{1}{4}t^2$, and $t\dot{x} - x = \frac{1}{4}t^2$. We conclude that $x = Ct - C^2$ is not the general solution.

5.2

1. See Fig. 5.2.1. (The solutions are $x = Ct$, for $t \neq 0$, with C an arbitrary constant.)

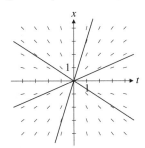

Figure 5.2.1

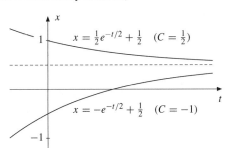

Figure 5.4.1

5.3

1. $\int x^2\, dx = \int(t + 1)\, dt$, so $\frac{1}{3}x^3 = \frac{1}{2}t^2 + t + C$, or $x = \sqrt[3]{\frac{3}{2}t^2 + 3t + 3C}$. We find $C = -7/6$.

3. (a) $x = Cte^{-t}$; $C = 1$. (Separate: $dx/x = [(1/t) - 1]\, dt$. Integrate: $\ln|x| = \ln|t| - t + C_1$. Hence, $|x| = e^{\ln|t| - t + C_1} = e^{\ln|t|}e^{-t}e^{C_1} = C_2|t|e^{-t} = Cte^{-t}$, where $C = \pm C_2 = \pm e^{C_1}$.) (b) $x = C\sqrt[3]{1 + t^3}$; $C = 2$.

(c) $x = \sqrt{t^2 - 1}$. (General solution: $x^2 - t^2 = C$.) (d) $x = \dfrac{1 - e^{-2t}}{1 + e^{-2t}}$. (*Hint*: : $e^{2t}\dot{x} = (x + 1)^2$.)

5. In both cases $\dot{N}$ depends on both N *and* t. (In Fig. A, for instance, $N(t_1) = N(t_2)$, but $\dot{N}(t_1) \neq \dot{N}(t_2)$.)

7. (a) $K = \left[\dfrac{An_0^\alpha a^b}{\alpha v + \varepsilon}(1 - b + c)e^{(\alpha v + \varepsilon)t} + C\right]^{1/(1-b+c)}$ (b) $|\alpha x - \beta|^{(\beta/\alpha)}|x - a|^{-a} = Ce^{(\alpha a - \beta)t}$

9. Using the given identity, (*) implies $\displaystyle\int \left(\frac{1}{y} + \frac{\alpha y^{\varrho-1}}{1 - \alpha y^\varrho}\right) dy = \int \frac{dx}{x}$. Integration yields $\ln y - (1/\varrho)\ln|1 - \alpha y^\varrho| = \ln x + C_1$. Multiplying both sides by ϱ leads to $\ln y^\varrho - \ln|1 - \alpha y^\varrho| = \ln x^\varrho + C_1\varrho$, or $\ln|y^\varrho/(1 - \alpha y^\varrho)| = \ln e^{C_1\varrho}x^\varrho$. Hence, $y^\varrho/(1 - \alpha y^\varrho) = Cx^\varrho$, with $C = \pm e^{C_1\varrho}$. Putting $\beta = 1/C$ and solving for y yields (**).

5.4

1. $x = Ce^{-t/2} + \frac{1}{2}$. The equilibrium state $x^* = 1/2$ is stable. See Fig. 5.4.1.

3. Applying (4) with $a = -1$ and $b(t) = t$ yields $x = Ce^t + e^t\int t\, e^{-t}\, dt$. Integrating by parts, $\int t e^{-t}\, dt = -te^{-t} + \int e^{-t}\, dt = -te^{-t} - e^{-t}$, and so the solution is $x = Ce^t - t - 1$.

5. (a) Because $C = aY + b$ and $I = k\dot{C} = ka\dot{Y}$, equation (i) implies $Y = C + I = aY + b + ka\dot{Y}$. Then solve for $\dot{Y}$.
(b) $Y(t) = [Y_0 - b/(1 - a)]e^{(1-a)t/ka} + b/(1 - a)$ and $I(t) = (1 - a)Y(t) - b$ (c) $1/(1 - a)$

7. (a) $\dot{x} + (2/t)x = -1$. Apply (6) with $a(t) = 2/t$ and $b = -1$. Then $\int a(t)\, dt = \int(2/t)\, dt = 2\ln|t| = \ln|t|^2 = \ln t^2$ and so $\exp(\int a(t)\, dt) = \exp(\ln t^2) = t^2$. Then $x = (1/t^2)[C + \int t^2(-1)\, dt] = Ct^{-2} - \frac{1}{3}t$.
(b) Here $\int a(t)\, dt = -\int(1/t)\, dt = -\ln t$, and (6) yields the solution $x = Ct + t^2$.
(c) In this case, $\int a(t)\, dt = -\frac{1}{2}\ln(t^2 - 1)$, and (6) yields the solution $x = C\sqrt{t^2 - 1} + t^2 - 1$ (d) $x = Ct^2 + 2a^2/3t$

9. Substituting T for t_0 and x_T for x_0, equation (7) yields $x = x_T e^{-\int_T^t a(\xi)\,d\xi} + \int_T^t b(\tau) e^{-\int_\tau^t a(\xi)\,d\xi}\,d\tau = x_T e^{\int_t^T a(\xi)\,d\xi} -$ $\int_t^T b(\tau) e^{-\int_\tau^t a(\xi)\,d\xi}\,d\tau$.

11. (a) $x(t) = X(t)/N(t)$ increases with t if $\alpha\sigma \geq \rho$. When $\sigma = 0.3$ and $\rho = 0.03$, this implies that $\alpha \geq 0.1\,(= 10\,\%)$.
(b) It suffices to note that $(1 - e^{-\xi t})/\xi > 0$ whenever $\xi \neq 0$ (look at $\xi > 0$ and $\xi < 0$ separately). Then apply this with $\xi = \alpha\sigma - \mu$. Faster growth per capita is to be expected because foreign aid contributes positively.

(c) Using equation (**), note that $x(t) = \left[x(0) + \left(\dfrac{\sigma}{\alpha\sigma - \mu}\right)\dfrac{H_0}{N_0}\right]e^{-(\rho - \alpha\sigma)t} + \left(\dfrac{\sigma}{\mu - \alpha\sigma}\right)\dfrac{H_0}{N_0}e^{(\mu-\rho)t}$. Even if $\alpha\sigma < \rho$, this is positive and increasing for large t as long as $\mu > \rho$. So foreign aid must grow faster than the population.

5.5

1. Separating the variables, $3x^2 dx = -2t\,dt$, so $\int 3x^2 dx = -2\int t\,dt$, which gives $x^3 + t^2 = C$. Alternatively, with $f(t, x) = 2t$ and $g(t, x) = 3x^2$, we have $f'_x = g'_t = 0$ so the equation is exact. From (8), $h(t, x) = \int_{t_0}^t 2\tau\,d\tau + \int_{x_0}^x 3\xi^2\,d\xi = t^2 + x^3 - t_0^2 - x_0^3$, so the solution is given implicitly by $t^2 + x^3 - t_0^2 - x_0^3 = C_1$, i.e. $t^2 + x^3 = C$, or $x = \sqrt[3]{C - t^2}$.

5.6

1. (a) Putting $z = x^{-1}$ leads to $\dot{z} = (2/t)z - 1$ whose solution is $z = Ct^2 + t$. Thus $x = (Ct^2 + t)^{-1}$.
(b) $x = (Ce^{2t} - e^t)^2$ (c) $x = (1 + \ln t + Ct)^{-1}$ and $x \equiv 0$.

3. $K = \{Ce^{-\alpha\delta(1-b)t} + \alpha A n_0^a (1 - b)e^{(av+\varepsilon)t}/(av + \varepsilon + \alpha\delta(1 - b))\}^{1/(1-b)}$

5. (a) $x = tz$ yields $\dot{x} = z + t\dot{z}$, which inserted into the given equation yields $\dot{z} = -f(t)z^2$.
(b) The general solution: $x = 4t/(\ln(2 + t^4) + C)$. $C = 4 - \ln 3$ gives the solution through $(1, 1)$.

7. $x = \dfrac{At^3 - t}{At^2 + 1}$

5.7

1. (a) $x = 1$ is unstable. See Fig. 5.7.1(a).   (b) $x = 12$ is stable. See Fig. 5.7.1(b).   (c) $x = -3$ is stable; $x = 3$ is unstable. See Fig. 5.7.1(c).

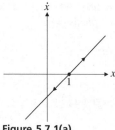

Figure 5.7.1(a)

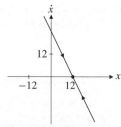

Figure 5.7.1(b)

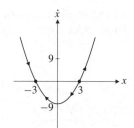

Figure 5.7.1(c)

3. (a) $x(t) = (1 + Ae^t)/(1 - Ae^t)$ where $A = (x_0 - 1)/(x_0 + 1)$ for $x_0 \neq -1$. For $x_0 = -1$, $x(t) \equiv -1$. For $x_0 \neq 1$, $x(t) \to -1$ as $t \to \infty$. If $x_0 > 1$, which occurs when $0 < A < 1$, $x(t) \to \infty$ as $t \to (-\ln A)^-$, and $x(t) \to -\infty$ as $t \to (-\ln A)^+$. For $x_0 = 1$, $x(t) \equiv 1$. See Fig. 5.7.3(a) for some integral curves.
(b) $x = -1$ is stable; $x = 1$ is unstable. See Fig. 5.7.3(b).

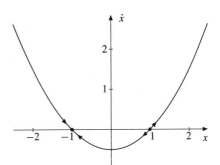

Figure 5.7.3(a)   **Figure 5.7.3(b)**

5.8

1. $F(t, x) = 2x/t$ is not continuous at $t = 0$, so the conditions in Theorem 5.8.1 are not satisfied at $(0, 0)$.

3. $x(t) = 1 + \frac{1}{1!}t + \frac{1}{2!}t^2 + \ldots = e^t$. $(x_0(t) \equiv 1, x_1(t) = 1 + \int_0^t ds = 1 + t, x_2(t) = 1 + \int_0^t (1 + s)\, ds = 1 + t + \frac{1}{2!}t^2,$
etc.)

5. See Fig. 5.8.5. For $t < a$, $\dot{\varphi}(t) = -2(t - a) = 2(a - t) = 2\sqrt{(a - t)^2} = 2\sqrt{|\varphi(t)|}$. The argument for $t > b$ is
similar. For t in (a, b) we have $\dot{\varphi}(t) = 0 = 2\sqrt{|\varphi(t)|}$. For $t < a$, $(\varphi(t) - \varphi(a))/(t - a) = -(t - a)^2/(t - a) = -(t - a) = a - t$, and for t slightly larger than a, $(\varphi(t) - \varphi(a))/(t - a) = 0$. It follows that when t is near a,
$|(\varphi(t) - \varphi(a))/(t - a)| \leq |t - a|$, so φ is differentiable at a, and $\dot{\varphi}(a) = \lim_{t \to a}(\varphi(t) - \varphi(a))/(t - a) = 0 = 2\sqrt{|\varphi(a)|}$. In the same way we show that the differential equation is satisfied at $t = b$.

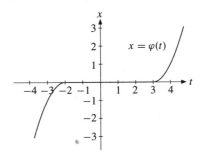

Figure 5.8.5

Chapter 6

6.1

1. (a) $\dot{x} = \int t\, dt = \frac{1}{2}t^2 + A$, so $x = \int (\frac{1}{2}t^2 + A)\, dt = \frac{1}{6}t^3 + At + B$ (b) $x = -\sin t + At + B$
(c) $x = e^t + \frac{1}{12}t^4 + At + B$

3. $x = Ae^t - \frac{1}{2}t^2 - t + B$ from Example 2. With $x(0) = 1$ and $x(1) = 2$ we get $A + B = 1$ and $Ae + B = 7/2$,
so that $A = 5/(2e - 2)$ and $B = 1 - A$.

5. (a) Let $w(y) = u'(y)$. Then $-w'(y)/w(y) = \lambda$, so that $w'(y) = -\lambda w(y)$, which has the solution $w(y) = Ae^{-\lambda y}$.
Integration gives $u(y) = \int w(y)\, dy = -(A/\lambda)e^{-\lambda y} + B$ if $\lambda \neq 0$. For $\lambda = 0$ we get $u(y) = Ay + B$.

(b) Let $w(y) = u'(y)$. Then $-yw'(y)/w(y) = k$, which is separable, with the solution $w(y) = Ay^{-k}$. Then for $k \neq 1$, $u(y) = \int Ay^{-k}\, dy = Ay^{1-k}/(1-k) + B$. For $k = 1$, $w(y) = A \ln y + B$.

7. (a) $u'_x = \alpha e^{t\alpha^2} e^{\alpha x}$, $u'_{xx} = \alpha^2 e^{t\alpha^2} e^{\alpha x}$, $u'_t = \alpha^2 e^{t\alpha^2} e^{\alpha x}$, so $u''_{xx} = u'_t$.
(b) $u'_x = g'(y)t^{-1/2}$, $u''_{xx} = g''(y)t^{-1}$, and $u'_t = -\frac{1}{2}g'(y)xt^{-3/2}$, so $g''(y)/g'(y) = -\frac{1}{2}y$. With $w(y) = g'(y)$ this gives $w'(y)/w(y) = -\frac{1}{2}y$, with the solution $\ln|w(y)| = -\frac{1}{4}y^2 + C$. Hence, $|w(y)| = e^{-\frac{1}{4}y^2 + C} = e^{-\frac{1}{4}y^2}e^C$, so $w(y) = Ae^{-\frac{1}{4}y^2}$, where $A = \pm e^C$. It follows that $u(y) = A\int e^{-\frac{1}{4}y^2}\, dy + B$.

6.2

1. (a) With $u_2 = te^t$ we get $\dot{u}_2 = e^t + te^t$ and $\ddot{u}_2 = e^t + e^t + te^t = 2e^t + te^t$, so $\ddot{u}_2 - 2\dot{u}_2 + u_2 = 0$. In the same way we prove that $u_1 = e^t$ satisfies the equation. If $u_2 = ku_1$ for all t, then $t = k$ for all t, which is absurd. Thus the general solution is $x(t) = Ae^t + Bte^t$, where A and B are arbitrary constants.
(b) One particular solution is $u^*(t) = 3$, so the general solution is $x(t) = Ae^t + Bte^t + 3$.

3. (a) $x = Ae^{2t} + Be^{-3t}$ (b) $x = Ae^{2t} + Be^{-3t} - t - \frac{1}{6}$

5. General solution: $x = A(t+a)^{-1} + B(t+b)^{-1}$. (Inserting $x = (t+k)^{-1}$ into the differential equation yields $k = a$ or $k = b$.)

6.3

1. (a) $x = Ae^{\sqrt{3}t} + Be^{-\sqrt{3}t}$ (b) $x = e^{-2t}(A\cos 2t + B\sin 2t)$ (c) $x = A + Be^{-8t/3}$
(d) $x = e^{-t/2}(A + Bt)$ (e) $x = Ae^{-3t} + Be^{2t} - 4/3$ (f) $x = Ae^{-t} + Be^{-2t} + (1/42)e^{5t}$

3. (a) $x = -(6+t)e^{-t} + t^2 - 4t + 6$ (b) $x = \frac{1}{2}\sin 2t + (\pi/2 + 1/4)\cos 2t + t + 1/4$

5. Using formula B.1.8, $C\cos(\beta t + D) = C\cos\beta t \cos D - C\sin\beta t \sin D = A\cos\beta t + B\sin\beta t$ provided that $A = C\cos D$ and $B = -C\sin D$. This requires $C = \sqrt{A^2 + B^2}$ and $D = \tan^{-1}(-B/A)$.

7. (a) $x = At^{-1} + Bt^{-3}$ (b) $x = At + Bt^3 - t^2$

9. $\ddot{p} + \lambda^2 p = a(d_0 - s_0)$ where $\lambda = [a(s_1 - d_1)]^{1/2}$. Solution: $p = A\cos\lambda t + B\sin\lambda t + (d_0 - s_0)/(s_1 - d_1)$.

6.4

1. (b), (d), and (f) are globally asymptotically stable, the others are not.

6.5

1. (a) $x = Ae^t + Be^{-t} - t$, $y = Ae^t - Be^{-t} - 1$. (Differentiating the first equation w.r.t. t gives $\ddot{x} = \dot{y}$, and substituting from the second equation we get $\ddot{x} = x + t$. The methods of Section 6.3 give the solution for x. Then from the first the equation we get $y = \dot{x}$.)   (b) $x = Ae^{\sqrt{2}t} + Be^{-\sqrt{2}t}$, $y = A(\sqrt{2} - 1)e^{\sqrt{2}t} - B(\sqrt{2} + 1)e^{-\sqrt{2}t}$
(c) $x = Ae^{-t} + Be^{3t} + t - \frac{2}{3}$, $y = Ae^{-t} - \frac{1}{3}Be^{3t} + \frac{2}{3}t - \frac{7}{9}$

3. (a) $x = Ae^{(1+\sqrt{2})t} + Be^{(1-\sqrt{2})t}$ (b) $x = Ae^{(1+\sqrt{2})t} + Be^{(1-\sqrt{2})t}$, $p = A\sqrt{2}e^{(\sqrt{2}-1)t} - B\sqrt{2}e^{(-\sqrt{2}-1)t}$.

5. $dy/dx = \dot{y}/\dot{x} = x/y$, a separable equation whose solution curve through $x = 1$, $y = \sqrt{2}$ is $y^2 = 1 + x^2$. Then $\dot{x} = t$, whose solution through $t = 1$, $x = 1$ is $x = \frac{1}{2}(1 + t^2)$, implying that $y = \sqrt{1 + \frac{1}{4}(1 + t^2)^2}$.

6.6

1. (a) $\mathbf{A} = \begin{pmatrix} 1 & -8 \\ 2 & -4 \end{pmatrix}$. Hence, $\text{tr}(\mathbf{A}) = -3$ and $\det(\mathbf{A}) = 12$, so the system is globally asymptotically stable.
(b) The trace is equal to 0, so the system is not globally asymptotically stable.
(c) The trace is equal to -3 and the determinant is 8, so the system is globally asymptotically stable.

3. (i) $x = Ae^t + Be^{-t} - 5$, $y = -Be^{-t} + 2$.   (ii) For the homogeneous system $\dot{x} = x + 2y$, $\dot{y} = -y$, the associated

matrix is $\begin{pmatrix} 1 & 2 \\ 0 & -1 \end{pmatrix}$. Since the trace is 0, the system is not globally asymptotically stable. The eigenvalues are

$\lambda_1 = 1$ and $\lambda_2 = -1$, with corresponding eigenvectors $\begin{pmatrix} 1 \\ 0 \end{pmatrix}$ and $\begin{pmatrix} 1 \\ -1 \end{pmatrix}$. According to (6.5.9), the solution

of the homogeneous system is $\begin{pmatrix} x \\ y \end{pmatrix} = Ae^t \begin{pmatrix} 1 \\ 0 \end{pmatrix} + Be^{-t} \begin{pmatrix} 1 \\ -1 \end{pmatrix} = \begin{pmatrix} Ae^t + Be^{-t} \\ -Be^{-t} \end{pmatrix}$. The equilibrium point is

$(-5, 2)$. Define (see Example 6.5.4) $z = x + 5$ and $w = y - 2$. Then $\dot{z} = \dot{x}$ and $\dot{w} = \dot{y}$, so the system reduces
to $\dot{z} = (z - 5) + 2(w + 2) + 1 = z + 2w$ and $\dot{w} = -(w + 2) + 2 = -w$. According to the solution of the
homogeneous system, the solution is $z = Ae^t + Be^{-t}$ and $w = -Be^{-t}$. The solution of the given system is
therefore $x = z - 5 = Ae^t + Be^{-t} - 5$ and $y = w + 2 = -Be^{-t} + 2$, the same solution as in (i).

6.7

1. (a) $x = Ae^t + Be^{-t}$, $y = Ae^t - Be^{-t}$. $(0, 0)$ is the only equilibrium point. See Fig. 6.7.1(a).
(b) See Problem 6.5.1(b). $(0, 0)$ is the only equilibrium point. See Fig. 6.7.1(b).
(c) $x = Ae^{-t} + Be^{-3t}$, $y = \frac{1}{2}Ae^{-t} + Be^{-3t}$. $(0, 0)$ is the only equilibrium point. See Fig 6.7.1(c).

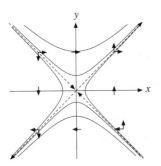

Figure 6.7.1(a)

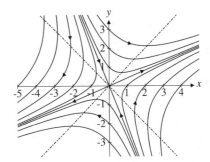

Figure 6.7.1(b)

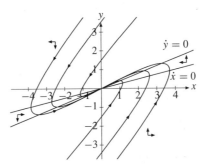

Figure 6.7.1(c)

3. See Fig. 6.7.3(a). (The nullclines are $C = AK^\alpha = 2\sqrt{K}$ and $K = (\alpha A/r)^{1/(1-\alpha)} = 400$.) A more detailed phase
diagram with some solution curves is given in Fig. 6.7.3(b).

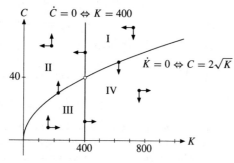

Figure 6.7.3(a)

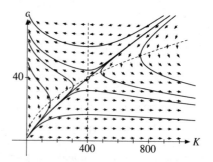

Figure 6.7.3(b)

5. $(x(t), y(t)) = (e^{-t}, e^{\frac{1}{2}(e^{-2t}-1)}) \to (0, e^{-\frac{1}{2}})$ as $t \to \infty$.

6.8

1. (a) $\mathbf{A}(0, 0) = \begin{pmatrix} -1 & 0 \\ 2 & -2 \end{pmatrix}$, $\mathrm{tr}(\mathbf{A}) = -3$, and $\det(\mathbf{A}) = 2$, so $(0, 0)$ is locally asymptotically stable.

(b) $\mathbf{A}(1, 1) = \begin{pmatrix} 4 & -2 \\ 1 & 0 \end{pmatrix}$, $\mathrm{tr}(\mathbf{A}) > 0$, so $(1, 1)$ is not locally asymptotically stable.

(c) $\mathbf{A}(0, 0) = \begin{pmatrix} 0 & -1 \\ 1 & 0 \end{pmatrix}$, so $\mathrm{tr}(\mathbf{A}) = 0$, and Theorem 6.8.1 does not apply.

(d) $\mathbf{A}(0, 0) = \begin{pmatrix} 2 & 8 \\ -1 & -3 \end{pmatrix}$, $\mathrm{tr}(\mathbf{A}) = -1$ and $\det(\mathbf{A}) = 2$, so $(0, 0)$ is locally asymptotically stable.

3. With $f(q, p) = a(p - c(q))$ and $g(q, p) = b(D(p) - q)$, the matrix $\mathbf{A}$ in Theorem 6.8.1, evaluated at (q^*, p^*), is
$\mathbf{A} = \begin{pmatrix} -ac'(q^*) & a \\ -b & bD'(p^*) \end{pmatrix}$. If $D'(p^*) < 0$ and $c'(q^*) > 0$, then $\mathrm{tr}(\mathbf{A}) < 0$ and $\det(\mathbf{A}) > 0$, so that (q^*, p^*) is locally asymptotically stable.

5. (a) $(K^*, P^*) = \left(\left(\frac{s}{\delta}\right)^{1/(1-\alpha)}, \frac{1}{\gamma}\left(\frac{s}{\delta}\right)^{\beta/(1-\alpha)} \right)$. The matrix $\mathbf{A}(K^*, P^*)$ is $\begin{pmatrix} -(1-\alpha)\delta & 0 \\ \beta(K^*)^{\beta-1} & -\gamma \end{pmatrix}$. Thus $\mathrm{tr}(\mathbf{A}) = -(1-\alpha)\delta - \gamma < 0$ and $\det(\mathbf{A}) = (1-\alpha)\delta\gamma > 0$, so (K^*, P^*) is locally asymptotically stable.

(b) $K(t) = \left[(K_0^{1-\alpha} - s/\delta)e^{-\delta(1-\alpha)t} + s/\delta \right]^{1/(1-\alpha)} \to (s/\delta)^{1/(1-\alpha)} = K^*$ as $t \to \infty$.

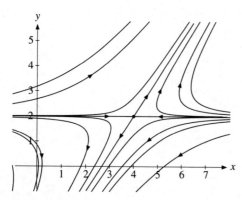

Figure 6.9.1

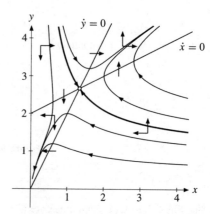

Figure 6.9.3

6.9

1. (a) $\mathbf{A} = \begin{pmatrix} -1/2 & 1 \\ 0 & 1 \end{pmatrix}$. Since $\det(\mathbf{A}) = -1/2 < 0$, the equilibrium point $(4, 2)$ is a local saddle point. The

eigenvalues of $\mathbf{A}$ are $\lambda_1 = -1/2$ and $\lambda_2 = 1$. An eigenvector associated with $\lambda_1 = -1/2$ is $\begin{pmatrix} 1 \\ 0 \end{pmatrix}$.

(b) See Fig. 6.9.1. The solution curves that converge to the equilibrium point are given by $x(t) = (x(0)-4)e^{-t/2}+4$, $y = 2$. (One for $x(0) < 4$, one for $x(0) > 4$.)

3. (a) $(x_0, y_0) = (4/3, 8/3)$. It is a (local) saddle point because the Jacobian at $(4/3, 8/3)$ is $\mathbf{A} = \begin{pmatrix} -2/3 & 4/3 \\ 2 & -1 \end{pmatrix}$, and $|\mathbf{A}| = -2$.   (b) See Fig. 6.9.3.

Chapter 7

7.1

1. $x = C_1 e^t + C_2 e^{-t} + C_3 e^{2t} + 5$

3. $x = A \sin t + B \cos t + \sin t \displaystyle\int \frac{\cos t}{t}\, dt - \cos t \displaystyle\int \frac{\sin t}{t}\, dt$. (The integrals cannot be evaluated.)

7.2

1. (a) $x = (C_1 + C_2 t + C_3 t^2)e^{-t} + 3$ (b) $x = C_1 e^{2t} + C_2 t e^{2t} + e^{-t/2}(C_3 \cos \frac{1}{2}\sqrt{3}\,t + C_4 \sin \frac{1}{2}\sqrt{3}\,t) + \frac{1}{2}t - \frac{1}{4}$

3. (a) $\dddot{K} - p\ddot{K} + q\dot{K} = 0$, where $p = \gamma_1 \kappa + \gamma_2 + \mu$ and $q = (\gamma_1 \kappa + \gamma_2)\mu - (\gamma_1 \sigma + \gamma_3)\mu_0$.
(b) The characteristic equation is $r(r^2 - pr + q) = 0$, and $r^2 - pr + q = 0$ has two different real roots not equal to 0 provided $p^2 > 4q$ and $q \neq 0$.

7.3

1. Using (3)(c), $a_1 = 3 > 0$, $a_3 = 1 > 0$, and $a_1 a_2 - a_3 = 8 > 0$. The equation is globally asymptotically stable.

7.4

1. $x_1 = Ae^{-t}+Be^{-2t}+Ce^{2t}$, $x_2 = Ae^{-t}-Be^{-2t}+Ce^{2t}$, $x_3 = -Ae^{-t}+2Ce^{2t}$. (We find that $\dddot{x}_1+\ddot{x}_1-4\dot{x}_1-4x_1 = 0$, with characteristic polynomial $r^3 + r^2 - 4r - 4 = (r + 1)(r^2 - 4)$.)

7.5

1. (a) $V(x, y) = x^2 + y^2$ is positive definite and $\dot{V} = 2x\dot{x} + 2y\dot{y} = 2x(-y-x^3)+2y(x-y^3) = -2x^4 - 2y^4 < 0$ for all $(x, y) \neq (0, 0)$. According to Theorem 7.5.2 the equilibrium point $(0, 0)$ is locally asymptotically stable. Since $V(x, y) = x^2 + y^2 \to \infty$ as $\|(x, y) - (0, 0)\| = \|(x, y)\| = \sqrt{x^2 + y^2} \to \infty$, the equilibrium point is globally asymptotically stable according to Theorem 7.5.3.

3. $V(\mathbf{x})$ is positive definite. Moreover, $\dot{V}(\mathbf{x}) = \sum_{i=1}^n -u_i'(\mathbf{x})u_i'(\mathbf{x}) = -(\nabla u(\mathbf{x}))^2 < 0$ for $\mathbf{x} \neq \mathbf{0}$, and we conclude that $\mathbf{0}$ is locally asymptotically stable.

5. (x_0, y_0) is locally asymptotically stable.

7.7

1. (a) By integration, $z = \frac{1}{4}x^4 + \frac{1}{2}x^2y^2 - e^xy + \varphi(y)$, where φ is an arbitrary differentiable function.
(b) $z = 3x + \varphi(y - 2x)$, where φ is an arbitrary differentiable function.
(c) $z = \dfrac{x}{1 + x\varphi(1/y - 1/x)}$ (The equations in (3) are both separable, $dy/dx = y^2/x^2$ and $dz/dx = z^2/x^2$. The solutions are $-1/y = -1/xy + C_1$, $-1/z = -1/x + C_2$. The general solution is therefore $\Phi(1/x - 1/y,\ 1/x - 1/z) = 0$, or $1/z = 1/x - \varphi(1/x - 1/y)$, and hence $z = \dfrac{x}{1 - x\varphi(1/x - 1/y)}$, where φ is an arbitrary differentiable function.)

3. (a) $z = x + \varphi(xy)$, where φ is an arbitrary differentiable function.   (b) The condition $f(x, 1) = x^2$ implies that $x + \varphi(x) = x^2$. Thus $\varphi(x) = -x + x^2$ for all x, and hence $f(x, y) = x + \varphi(xy) = x - xy + (xy)^2$.

5. The equations in (3) are $dx_2/dx_1 = -f(x_1)$ and $dU/dx_1 = 0$, with the solutions $x_2 = -F(x_1) + C_1$ and $U = C_2$, where F is an indefinite integral of f and C_1 and C_2 are constants. The solutions of the equation are therefore given by $\Phi(x_2 + F(x_1), U) = 0$, and thus $U = \varphi(x_2 + F(x_1)) = \varphi(x_2 + \int f(x_1)\,dx_1)$.

7. The equations in (3) are $dv_2/dv_1 = v_2/v_1$ and $dx/dv_1 = x\varepsilon(x)/v_1$, with the solutions $v_2/v_1 = C_1$, $f(x) - \ln v_1 = C_2$, where $f(x) = \int (1/x\varepsilon(x))\,dx$. Since $f'(x) = 1/x\varepsilon(x) > 0$, f strictly increasing, and has an inverse f^{-1} that is also strictly increasing. The general solution is $\Phi(v_2/v_1,\ f(x) - \ln v_1) = 0$, or $f(x) = \ln v_1 + \varphi(v_2/v_1)$. Hence, $x = f^{-1}(\ln v_1 + \varphi(v_2/v_1))$. Define $g(v_1, v_2) = e^{\ln v_1 + \varphi(v_2/v_1)} = v_1 e^{\varphi(v_2/v_1)}$. Then g is homogeneous of degree 1, and we see that $x = f^{-1}(\ln(g(v_1, v_2))$. The composition F of the two increasing functions f^{-1} and $\ln$ is increasing. It follows that $x = F(g(v_1, v_2))$ is homothetic.

Chapter 8

8.1

1. (i) $J(x) = \int_0^1 [(e^2 - 1)^2 t^2 + (e^2 - 1)^2]\,dt = (e^2 - 1)^2\ \big|_0^1\ (\frac{1}{3}t^3 + t) = (4/3)(e^2 - 1)^2$
(ii) $J(x) = \int_0^1 [(e^{1+t} - e^{1-t})^2 + (e^{1+t} + e^{1-t})^2]\,dt = e^4 - 1$. We find that $e^4 - 1 < (4/3)(e^2 - 1)^2$.

8.2

1. With $F(t, x, \dot{x}) = 4xt - \dot{x}^2$, $F'_x = 4t$ and $F'_{\dot{x}} = -2\dot{x}$, so the Euler equation is $4t - (d/dt)(-2\dot{x}) = 0$, or $\ddot{x} = -2t$. The general solution is $x = -\frac{1}{3}t^3 + At + B$. The boundary conditions yield $A = -1$ and $B = 2$. The function F is (for t fixed) concave in $(x, \dot{x})$, so we have found the solution.

3. (a) $\ddot{x} - x = e^t$ (b) $\ddot{x} - a\dot{x} + a = 0$ (c) $\ddot{x} - a\dot{x} + (a - 2)x = 0$ (d) $\ddot{x} + (1/t)\dot{x} = 1$

5. Euler equation: $\ddot{x} - \frac{1}{2}x = \frac{1}{2}t$. General solution: $x(t) = Ae^{\frac{1}{2}\sqrt{2}t} + Be^{-\frac{1}{2}\sqrt{2}t} - t$. With $x(0) = 0$ and $x(1) = 1$, $A = -B = 2/(e^{\frac{1}{2}\sqrt{2}} - e^{-\frac{1}{2}\sqrt{2}})$. With $F(t, x, \dot{x}) = x^2 + tx + tx\dot{x} + \dot{x}^2$, we have $F''_{xx} = 2 > 0$ and $F''_{xx}F''_{\dot{x}\dot{x}} - (F''_{x\dot{x}})^2 = 4 - t^2 > 0$ for $t \in [0, 1]$, F is (strictly) convex, so we have found the solution.

7. Euler equation: $t^2\ddot{x} + 2t\dot{x} - \frac{1}{2}x = 0$. General solution: $x(t) = At^{a_1} + Bt^{a_2}$, where $a_{1,2} = \frac{1}{2}(-1 \pm \sqrt{3})$. (See equation (6.3.8).) The boundary conditions yield: $A = -B = (2^{a_1} - 2^{a_2})^{-1}$. $F(t, x, \dot{x}) = x^2 + tx\dot{x} + t^2\dot{x}^2$ is convex, so we have found the solution.

8.3

1. The function $x(t) = a(t - t^2)$ is admissible and makes the integral equal to $11a^2/30$, which tends to ∞ as $a \to \infty$, so the conclusion follows.

3. The Euler equation is $(d/dt)(t\dot{x}) = 0$, so $x = A + B\ln t$ for $t > 0$. When $a \in (0, 1)$ the only solution satisfying the boundary conditions is $x(t) = 1 - \ln t / \ln a$. The integrand is convex in $(x, \dot{x})$, so this is the solution. For $a = 0$ there are no solutions to the necessary conditions, so there are no solution in this case.

8.4

1. $4\ddot{K} - 15\dot{K} + 14K = 0$. The solution is $K = Ae^{2t} + Be^{\frac{7}{4}t}$, where $A = P(K_T - K_0 e^{\frac{7}{4}T})$, $B = P(K_0 e^{2T} - K_T)$ with $P = (e^{2T} - e^{\frac{7}{4}T})^{-1}$

3. The Euler equation is $U_C'(f_K' - \delta) + (d/dt)U_C' = 0$, or $U_C'(f_K' - \delta) + U_{CC}''\dot{C} + U_{Ct}'' = 0$. We deduce that $\dot{C}/C = [(-U_{Ct}''/U_C') - (f_K' - \delta)]/\hat{\omega}$, where $\hat{\omega}$ is the elasticity w.r.t. consumption of the marginal utility of consumption.

8.5

1. $F(t, x, \dot{x}) = t\dot{x} + \dot{x}^2$ is convex in $(x, \dot{x})$. Euler equation: $-\frac{d}{dt}(t + 2\dot{x}) = 0$, and so $t + 2\dot{x} = A$ for some constant A. Integrating with $x(0) = 1$ yields $x(t) = -\frac{1}{4}t^2 + \frac{1}{2}At + 1$.
Case (i): Condition (2) is $(F_{\dot{x}}')_{t=1} = 1 + 2\dot{x}(1) = 0$, which reduces to $A = 0$, and the solution is $x = -\frac{1}{4}t^2 + 1$.
Case (ii): Condition (3) is here $(F_{\dot{x}}')_{t=1} = 1 + 2\dot{x}(1) \leq 0 \ (= 0 \text{ if } x(1) > 1)$, which reduces to $A \leq 0 \ (= 0 \text{ if } x(1) > 1)$. With $A = 0$, $x(1) = -\frac{1}{4} + 1 < 1$. Thus $A > 0$ and $x(1) = 1$, so the solution is $x = -\frac{1}{4}t^2 + \frac{1}{4}t + 1$.

3. Replace G in the integrand by $G = (r_1/r_2)\bar{Y} - (1/r_2)\dot{\bar{Y}}$. Euler equation: $\ddot{\bar{Y}} = m^2\bar{Y}$ with $m^2 = (\alpha_2 r_1^2 + \alpha_1 r_2^2)/\alpha_2$. Solution: $\bar{Y} = Ae^{mt} + Be^{-mt}$, where $A = (r_1 + m)Y_0 / (e^{2mT}(m - r_1) + (m + r_1))$, $B = Y_0 - A$.

5. (a) The conditions are $-(d/dt)[C_{\dot{x}}'(t, \dot{x})e^{-rt}] = 0$ and $C_{\dot{x}}'(5, \dot{x}(5)) \geq 0 \ (= 0 \text{ if } x(5) > 1500)$.
(b) $x(t) = 300t$, implying that planting takes place at the constant rate of 300 acres per year.

8.6

1. Equation (3) takes the form $-2x + \frac{d^2}{dt^2}(2\ddot{x}) = 0$, so $d^4x/dt^4 - x = 0$, whose general solution is $x = Ae^t + Be^{-t} + C\cos t + D\sin t$. (The characteristic equation is $(r^2 - 1)(r^2 + 1) = 0$.)   The only solution that satisfies the boundary conditions is $x = \cos t$.

Chapter 9

9.2

1. The Hamiltonian is $H = e^t x - u^2 + p(-u)$, so $H_x' = e^t$ and $H_u' = -2u - p$. Because $U = (-\infty, \infty)$, (7) implies that $u^*(t) = -\frac{1}{2}p(t)$. (5) reduces to $\dot{p} = -e^t$, $p(2) = 0$, from which it follows that $p(t) = -e^t + e^2$. Hence, $u^*(t) = \frac{1}{2}e^t - \frac{1}{2}e^2$. From $\dot{x}^* = -u^*(t) = -\frac{1}{2}e^t + \frac{1}{2}e^2$ and $x^*(0) = 0$, we find $x^*(t) = \frac{1}{2}(e^2 t - e^t + 1)$. The Hamiltonian is a sum of concave functions, so $u^*(t) = \frac{1}{2}e^t - \frac{1}{2}e^2$ is the optimal control.

3. $u^*(t) = -\frac{1}{2}t + \frac{1}{2}$, $x^*(t) = \frac{1}{4}t^2 - \frac{1}{2}t$, with $p(t) = t - 1$. (The Hamiltonian is $H = -(x + u^2) - pu$. Note that the first minus sign is inserted because we minimize the criterion.)

5. $u^*(t) = \frac{1}{2}(e^{T-t} - 1)$, $x^*(t) = \frac{1}{4}e^{T+t} - \frac{1}{4}e^{T-t} - \frac{1}{2}e^t + \frac{1}{2}$, $p(t) = e^{T-t} - 1$

9.4

1. $u^*(t) = 1$ with $x^*(t) = t$ is the obvious optimal solution.   We find that $V(T) = \int_0^T x^*(t)\,dt = \int_0^T t\,dt = \frac{1}{2}T^2$. The Hamiltonian is $H = x + pu$, so $\dot{p} = -H_x' = -1$, with $p(T) = 0$. Thus, $p = T - t$. The optimal control must maximize $p(t)u = (T - t)u$ for $u \in [0, 1]$, so $u^*(t) = 1$. As before, $x(t) = t$. The Hamiltonian is linear and hence concave in (x, u).

3. (a) $u^*(t) \equiv 0$, $x^*(t) \equiv x_0$ (b) $u^*(t) = -1$ and $x^*(t) = x_0 - t$ in $[0, \sqrt{T^2 - 4}]$; $u^*(t) = -\frac{1}{4}(T^2 - t^2)$ and $x^*(t) = \frac{1}{12}t^3 - \frac{1}{4}tT^2 + x_0 + (\frac{1}{6}T^2 - \frac{2}{3})\sqrt{T^2 - 4}$ in $(\sqrt{T^2 - 4}, T]$

5. (a) With $H = -(u^2 + x^2) + pau$, (6) gives $\dot{p} = 2x^*$, and (5) implies $u^* = 0$ if $-2u^* + ap < 0$, $u^* = 1$ if $-2u^* + ap > 0$. Condition (7)(c') yields $p(T) = 0$. If $a \geq 0$, $u^*(t) = 0$, $x^*(t) = 1$, and $p(t) = -2(T - t)$.

   (b) If $a < 0$, $u^*(t) = \dfrac{1}{1 + e^{2aT}}(e^{at} - e^{2aT}e^{-at})$, $p(t) = \dfrac{2u^*(t)}{a}$, $x^*(t) = \dfrac{e^{at} + e^{2aT}e^{-at}}{1 + e^{2aT}}$.

7. (a) With $H = -(ax + bu^2) + pu$ we have $\dot{p} = -H'_x = a$, and $u^*(t)$ maximizes $-bu^2 + p(t)u$ for $u \geq 0$.

   (b) For $B \geq aT^2/4b$: $u^*(t) = a(2t - T)/4b + B/T$.

   For $B < aT^2/4b$: $u^*(t) = 0$ in $[0, t^*]$, $u^*(t) = a(t - t^*)/2b$ in $(t^*, T]$, $t^* = T - 2\sqrt{bB/a}$.

9. (a) Show that $p_0 + p(t)$ must be 0. Hence, $p(t) \equiv -1$, and $H \equiv 0$.

   (b) $\max \int_0^2 u(t)\,dt = \max \int_0^2 \dot{x}(t)\,dt = \max x(2) = 1$.

9.5

1. The Euler equation is $\ddot{x} = -e^{-t}$. The solution is $x = -e^{-t} + e^{-1}t + 1$. To solve it as a control problem, put $\dot{x} = u$.

3. The Euler equation is $-\frac{d}{dt}[(-2 - 2\dot{x})e^{-t/10}] = 0$, which implies $\dot{x} = Ae^{t/10} - 1$, for some constant A. Integrate and use the boundary conditions to get the solution $x = 1 - t$. (Alternative form of the Euler equation: $\ddot{x} - \frac{1}{10}\dot{x} - \frac{1}{10} = 0$.)
   The control problem is: $\max \int_0^1 (-2u - u^2)e^{-t/10}\,dt$, $\dot{x} = u$, $x(0) = 1$, $x(1) = 0$. We find that $u^*(t) = -1$, $p(t) = 0$, and $x(t) = 1 - t$.

5. (a) With $H = U(x) - b(x) - gz + pax$, the conditions are: (i) x^* maximizes $U(x) - b(x) - gz^* + p(t)ax$ for $x \geq 0$; (ii) $\dot{p} = g$, $p(T) = 0$. From (ii) we immediately get $p(t) = g(t - T)$. Moreover, $\partial H^*/\partial x = 0$ yields (∗).

   (b) H is concave in (z, x), so Mangasarian's theorem applies. We find that $dx^*/dt = -ag/(U'' - b'') > 0$.

9.6

1. (a) $u^*(t) = T - t$, $x^*(t) = x_0 + Tt - \frac{1}{2}t^2$, with $p(t) = T - t$

   (b) $V(x_0, T) = x_0 T + \frac{1}{6}T^3$ and the relevant equalities in (5) are easily verified.

3. Using the results in the answers to Problem 9.4.4 (b), we find: $\partial V/\partial x_0 = x_1 - x_0 = p(0)$, $\partial V/\partial x_1 = T + x_0 - x_1 = -p(T)$, $\partial V/\partial T = x_1$, and $H^*(T) = x^*(T) + p(T)u^*(T) = x_1$.

5. (a) We get $x^*(t) = x_0$. For $x_0 < 0$, $u^* = 0$ maximizes $H = x_0 u$. For $x_0 > 0$, $u^* = 1$ maximizes $H = x_0 u$.

   (b) $V(x_0) = 0$ when $x_0 < 0$ and $V(x_0) = x_0$ when $x_0 \geq 0$, so V is not differentiable at 0.

9.7

1. (a) $u^*(t) = p(t) = t + x_1 - x_0 - \frac{1}{2}$, $x^*(t) = \frac{1}{2}t^2 + (x_1 - x_0 - \frac{1}{2})t + x_0$

   (b) Easily verified by differentiating under the integral sign.

3. (a) $u^*(t) = \dfrac{\alpha - 2\beta}{e^{(\alpha - 2\beta)T} - 1}e^{2(\alpha - \beta)t}$, $x^*(t) = \dfrac{e^{(\alpha - 2\beta)T}}{e^{(\alpha - 2\beta)T} - 1} - \dfrac{e^{2(\alpha - \beta)t}}{e^{(\alpha - 2\beta)T} - 1}$, $p(t) = \sqrt{\dfrac{e^{(\alpha - 2\beta)T} - 1}{4(\alpha - 2\beta)}}\,e^{-\alpha t}$

   (*Hint:* Argue why $u^*(t) > 0$.)   (b) The solution is still as in (a).

9.8

1. (a) $u^*(t) = \frac{1}{2} - t$, $x^*(t) = \frac{1}{2}t(1 - t)$, $p(t) = u^*(t)$, $T^* = \frac{1}{2}$ (b) $u^*(t) \equiv 6$, $T^* = 8/3$

3. (a) $u^*(t) = \frac{1}{2}ae^{(\alpha - \beta)t} - \frac{1}{2}\bar{p}e^{(r - \beta)t}$. For $\alpha = \beta = 0$, $x^*(t) = K - \frac{1}{2}at + \frac{\bar{p}}{2r}(e^{rt} - 1)$ with $\bar{p} = \frac{2r}{e^{rT} - 1}(\frac{1}{2}aT - K)$.

   (b) $u^*(T^*) = \frac{1}{2}(a - z)$, where $z = \bar{p}e^{rT^*}$. The condition $H^*(T^*) = 0$ reduces to $z^2 - 2az + a^2 - 4c = 0$, with (the only admissible) solution $z = a - 2\sqrt{c}$, which is positive because $a^2 > 4c$. The equation for determining T^* is $\varphi(T^*) = arT^* - (a - 2\sqrt{c}) + (a - 2\sqrt{c})e^{-rT^*} - 2rK = 0$. (Look at $\varphi(0)$, $\varphi(\infty)$, and the sign of $\varphi'(T^*)$.)

9.9

1. With $H^c = -x^2 - \frac{1}{2}u^2 + \lambda(x+u)$, $\partial H^c/\partial u = -u+\lambda$ and $\partial H^c/\partial x = -2x+\lambda$. Since the control region is $\mathbb{R}$ and H^c is concave in (x, u), the maximum condition (3) reduces to $\partial (H^c)^*/\partial u = 0$, so $u^*(t) = \lambda(t)$. Moreover, (4) and (5)(c') give $\dot\lambda - 2\lambda = -\partial (H^c)^*/\partial x = 2x^* - \lambda$ with $\lambda(T) = 0$. Thus x^* and λ must be solutions to the system $\dot x = x + \lambda$, $\dot\lambda = 2x + \lambda$. From this system we derive the following second-order differential equation in x, $\ddot x - 2\dot x - x = 0$. The general solution is $x = Ae^{(1+\sqrt2)t} + Be^{(1-\sqrt2)t}$. Then $u^* = \lambda = \dot x^* - x^* = A\sqrt2\, e^{(\sqrt2+1)t} - B\sqrt2\, e^{(1-\sqrt2)t}$. Because $x^*(0) = 1$ and $\lambda(T) = 0$, we find that $A = (1 + e^{2\sqrt2 T})^{-1}$ and $B = e^{2\sqrt2 T}(1 + e^{2\sqrt2 T})^{-1}$.

3. $H^c = -2u - u^2 + \lambda u$. $\partial (H^c)^*/\partial u = 0$ when $u^* = \frac{1}{2}\lambda - 1$, and $\dot\lambda - \frac{1}{10}\lambda = -\partial (H^c)^*/\partial x = 0$. We find $u^* = -1$, $x^* = 1 - t$, and $\lambda = 0$.

9.10

1. $u^*(t) = 1 - \frac{1}{2}t$, $x^*(t) = -\frac{1}{4}t^2 + t + 1$, $p(t) = 2$

3. In $[0, 9]$, $s^*(t) = 1$, $k^*(t) = (\frac{1}{2}t + 1)^2$, and $p(t) = 11/(t + 2)$. In $(9, 10]$, $s^*(t) = 0$, $k^*(t) = 30.25$, and $p(t) = \frac{20}{11} - \frac{1}{11}t$.

5. (a) $u^*(t) = -2ae^t$, $x^*(t) = a(3e^{2T-t} - e^t)$, $p(t) = 2u^*(t)$, where $a = \dfrac{x_0}{3e^{2T} - 1}$.   (b) $V(x_0, T) = \dfrac{-2(x_0)^2}{3e^{2T} - 1}$

7. The only problem is to prove that $p(t_1) = S'(x^*(t_1))$: From $p = q + S'(x^*)$ we get $\dot q = \dot p - S''(x^*)\dot x^* = \dot p - S''(x^*)g^*$. Moreover, $\partial H_1^*/\partial x = \partial f^*/\partial x + S''(x^*)g^* + S'(x^*)\partial g^*/\partial x + q\partial g^*/\partial x$. Hence $\dot q = -\partial H_1^*/\partial x$ implies that $\dot p = -\partial H^*/\partial x$.

9.11

1. $u^*(t) = 2e^{-0.1t}$, $x^*(t) = 10e^{-0.1t}$

3. $V = (1 - \delta)^{-1}[(\rho - r)/\delta + r]^{-\delta}(A_0 + w/r)^{1-\delta}$. As ρ increases, V decreases. As w increases, V increases. We see that $\partial V/\partial A_0 = \lambda(0) = \bar\lambda$.

9.12

1. (a) $H^c = ax - \frac{1}{2}u^2 + \lambda(-bx + u)$. System (2) is $\dot x = -bx + \lambda$, $\dot\lambda = -a + (b + r)\lambda$. The equilibrium point is $(\bar x, \bar\lambda) = (a/b(b + r), a/(b + r))$.   (b) The phase diagram is similar to Figure 9.12.1. (c) $x^*(t) = (x_0 - a/b(r + b))e^{-bt} + a/b(r + b)$, $u^*(t) = \lambda(t) = \bar\lambda$ solve the problem. (d) Easy verification. (Differentiate under the integral sign.)

3. (a) With $H^c = \ln c + \lambda(AK^\alpha - c)$, $\partial (H^c)^*/\partial c = 0$ implies $1/c^* - \lambda = 0$, or $c^*\lambda = 1$. Taking ln of each side and differentiating w.r.t. t yields $\dot c^*/c^* + \dot\lambda/\lambda = 0$. Also, $\dot\lambda - r\lambda = -\partial (H^c)^*/\partial K = -\lambda\alpha A(K^*)^{\alpha-1}$, or $\dot\lambda/\lambda = r - \alpha A(K^*)^{\alpha-1}$. It follows that if $K = K^*(t) > 0$ and $c = c^*(t) > 0$ solve the problem, then the second equation in $(*)$ holds. (The first equation is part of the problem.) (b) The Jacobian matrix evaluated at $(\bar K, \bar c) = (400, 40)$ is $J = \begin{pmatrix} 1/20 & -1 \\ -1/400 & 0 \end{pmatrix}$ and $|J| = -1/400 < 0$, so the equilibrium point is a saddle point. (c) If $K_0 = 100$ and $T = \infty$ the solution curve converges to the equilibrium point. For sufficient conditions, see Note 9.11.4.

Chapter 10

10.1

1. If $y(t) = \int_{t_0}^t G(\tau, x(\tau), \dot x(\tau))\, d\tau$, then $\dot y(t) = G(t, x(t), \dot x(t))$, so the control problem is:

$$\max \int_{t_0}^{t_1} F(t, x, u)\, dt, \quad \begin{cases} \dot x = u \\ \dot y = G(t, x, u) \end{cases} \quad \begin{array}{l} x(t_0) = x^0, \ x(t_1) = x^1 \\ y(t_0) = 0, \ y(t_1) = K \end{array}$$

3. $f(\lambda\mathbf{x}_1+(1-\lambda)\mathbf{x}_2) \geq F(\lambda\mathbf{x}_1+(1-\lambda)\mathbf{x}_2, \lambda\mathbf{u}_1+(1-\lambda)\mathbf{u}_2) \geq \lambda F(\mathbf{x}_1, \mathbf{u}_1)+(1-\lambda)F(\mathbf{x}_2, \mathbf{u}_2) = \lambda f(\mathbf{x}_1)+(1-\lambda)f(\mathbf{x}_2)$.
Concavity of g is proved in a similar manner.

10.2

1. $u^*(t) = -1$ in $[0, 4 - \sqrt{2}]$, $u^*(t) = 1$ in $(4 - \sqrt{2}, 4]$, $p_1(t) = t - 4$, $p_2(t) = -\frac{1}{2}(t - 4)^2$.
($H = 10 - x_1 + u + p_1 x_2 + p_2 u$, and $u^*(t) = 1$ if $p_2(t) > -1$, $u^*(t) = 0$ if $p_2(t) < -1$. $\dot{p}_1 = 1$ and $p_1(4) = 0$,
so $p_1(t) = t - 4$. Since $\dot{p}_2 = -p_1$ and $p_2(4) = 0$, we have $p_2(t) = -\frac{1}{2}(t - 4)^2$. Note that $p_2(t) > -1$ iff
$t > 4 - \sqrt{2}$.)

3. (a) $u_1^*(t) = \begin{cases} 1 & \text{if } t \in [0, T - 2] \\ 0 & \text{if } t \in (T - 2, T] \end{cases}$, $\quad u_2^*(t) = \begin{cases} 1 & \text{if } t \in [0, T - 5] \\ 0 & \text{if } t \in (T - 5, T] \end{cases}$, $\quad x_1^*(t) = \begin{cases} t & \text{if } t \in [0, T - 2] \\ T - 2 & \text{if } t \in (T - 2, T] \end{cases}$

$x_2^*(t) = \begin{cases} t & \text{if } t \in [0, T - 5] \\ T - 5 & \text{if } t \in (T - 5, T] \end{cases}$, $\quad p_1(t) = \frac{1}{2}(T - t)$, $\quad p_2(t) = \frac{1}{5}(T - t)$

(b) $u_1^*(t) = u_2^*(t) = 1$ and $x_1^*(t) = x_2^*(t) = t$ for all t, $p_1(t) = 3 + \frac{1}{2}(T - t)$, $p_2(t) = 2 + \frac{1}{5}(T - t)$.

5. $u^*(t) = 0$ in $[0, t_*]$, $u^*(t) = 1$ in $(t_*, t_{**}]$, and $u^*(t) = 0$ in $(t_{**}, T]$, where $t_* = T - \frac{1}{bc}(1 + \sqrt{1 - 2bc})$ and
$t_{**} = T - \frac{1}{bc}(1 - \sqrt{1 - 2bc})$.

7. $u^*(t) = \begin{cases} 1 & \text{if } t \leq 1 \\ 0 & \text{if } t > 1 \end{cases}$, $\quad x^*(t) = \begin{cases} t + 1 & \text{if } t \leq 1 \\ 2 & \text{if } t > 1 \end{cases}$, $\quad y^*(t) = \begin{cases} t & \text{if } t \leq 1 \\ 1 & \text{if } t > 1 \end{cases}$, $\quad p_1(t) = 2 - t$, $p_2(t) = -\frac{1}{2}$.

10.3

1. $u^*(t) = 1$ in $[0, -\ln r]$, $u^*(t) = 0$ in $(-\ln r, \infty)$

10.4

1. (i) $(x(t), u(t)) = (e^t - 1, 1)$ is admissible; (ii) $N(t, x)$ is the rectangle $\{(r, s) : r \leq x, x - 1 \leq s \leq x + 1\}$, which
surely is convex. (Draw a graph.) (iii) When $|u| \leq 1$, $|x + u| \leq |x| + 1$, so condition (2) in Note 2 is also satisfied.
We conclude from Theorem 10.4.1 that the problem has an optimal solution.

3. $u^*(t) = 0$, $x^*(t) = t + 4$ and $p(t) = -t^2 - 8t + 105/16$ for $t \in [0, \frac{3}{4}]$; $u^*(t) = 2$, $x^*(t) = -3t + 7$ and
$p(t) = 3t^2 - 14t + 141/16$ for $t \in (\frac{3}{4}, 1]$. (*Hint:* $u = u^*(t)$ maximizes $-p(t)u^2$ for $u \in [-1, 2]$. Then $u^*(t)$ must
be 2 if $p(t) < 0$ and 0 if $p(t) > 0$. When $u = -2$, $\dot{x} = -3$ and with $x(0) = 4$, $x = 4 - 3t$, which is ≥ 1 in $[0, 1]$.
Thus any admissible $x(t)$ is positive and $\dot{p}(t) = -2x^*(t) < 0$ so $p(t)$ is strictly decreasing, etc.)

10.6

1. (a) $H = -\frac{1}{2}u^2 - x - pu$ and $\mathcal{L} = H + q(x - u)$. H is concave in (x, u) and $h(t, x, u) = x - u$ is linear and
therefore quasiconcave. Here (i) $\partial\mathcal{L}^*/\partial u = -u^*(t) - p(t) - q(t) = 0$, (ii) $q(t) \geq 0$ ($= 0$ if $x^*(t) > u^*(t)$),
(iii) $\dot{p}(t) = 1 - q(t)$, with $p(2) = 0$. (b) $u^*(t) = x^*(t) = e^{-t}$, $p(t) = (t^* - \frac{1}{2}(t^*)^2)e^t - 1 - \frac{1}{2}e^{-t}$, $q(t) =$
$-e^{-t} - p(t)$ in $[0, t^*]$; $u^*(t) = 2 - t$, $x^*(t) = \frac{1}{2}t^2 - 2t + 2 + t^* - \frac{1}{2}(t^*)^2$, $p(t) = t - 2$, $q(t) = 0$ in $(t^*, 2]$,
with t^* determined by $e^{-t^*} = 2 - t^*$. ($t^* \approx 1.84$.) (Note that one has to check that $q(t) \geq 0$ in $[0, t^*]$, and that
$x^*(t) \geq u^*(t)$ in $(t^*, 2]$.

3. $u^*(t) = c$, $x^*(t) = (x_0 - c/a)e^{at} + c/a$, $p(t) = e^{a(t' - t)}$, $q_1(t) = e^{a(t' - t)} - 1$, $q_2(t) = 0$ in $[0, t']$. $u^*(t) =$
$ax_*(t)$, $x^*(t) = (x_0 - c/a)e^{at^*} + c/a$, $p(t) = a(t' - t) + 1$, $q_1(t) = 0$, $q_2(t) = a(t - t')$ in $[t', T]$, where
$t' = \max\{T - 1/a, t''\}$, $t'' = (1/a)\ln[(x_T - c/a)/(x_0 - c/a)]$.

10.7

1. In $[0, \sqrt{2}]$: $u^*(t) = 0$, $x^*(t) = 1 - \frac{1}{2}t^2$, $p(t) = t + 1 - \sqrt{2}$, and $q(t) = 0$. In $(\sqrt{2}, 5]$: $u^*(t) = t$, $x^*(t) = 0$,
$q(t) = 1$ with $p(t) = 1$ in $(\sqrt{2}, 5)$ and $p(5) = 0$, with $\beta = 1$.

3. $u^*(t) = \frac{1}{2}(t - 2)$, $x^*(t) = \frac{1}{4}(t - 2)^2$, $p(t) = t - 2$, and $q(t) = 0$ in $[0, 2]$;
$u^*(t) = 0$, $x^*(t) = 0$, $p(t) = 0$, $q(t) = 1$ in $(2, 10]$, with $\beta = 0$.

Chapter 11

11.1

1. (a) According to (4), $x_t = 5 \cdot 2^t - 4$ (b) $x_t = (1/3)^t + 1$ (c) $x_t = (-3/5)(-3/2)^t - 2/5$ (d) $x_t = -3t + 3$

3. (a) Because the parameters are positive, y_{k+1} is positive provided $y_k > 0$. Since y_0 is positive, so is y_1 a.s.o.
   (b) Substituting $y_t = 1/x_t$ gives $x_{t+1} = (a/c)x_t + b/c$. When $a = 2$, $b = 3$, and $c = 4$, the equation is $x_{t+1} = (1/2)x_t + 3/4$. When $x_0 = 1/y_0 = 2$, the solution is $x_t = (1/2)^{t+1} + 3/2$, and hence $y_t = \left[(1/2)^{t+1} + 3/2\right]^{-1}$. Then $y_t \to 2/3$ as $t \to \infty$.

5. $x_1 = \sqrt{x_0 - 1} = \sqrt{5 - 1} = 2$, $x_2 = \sqrt{x_1 - 1} = \sqrt{2 - 1} = 1$, and $x_3 = \sqrt{1 - 1} = \sqrt{0} = 0$. Then $x_4 = \sqrt{0 - 1} = \sqrt{-1}$, which is not a real number.

11.2

1. $a_t = (1.2)^t \cdot 1000 + 50 \sum_{k=1}^{t}(1.2)^{t-k} = (1.2)^t \cdot 1000 + 50 \frac{(1.2)^t - 1}{1.2 - 1} = 1250(1.2)^t - 250$

3. (a) Let the remaining debt on 1 January in year n be L_n. Then $L_0 = L$. Since the payment on the principal in year n is $L_{n-1} - L_n$ and interest is rL_{n-1}, we have $L_{n-1} - L_n = \frac{1}{2}rL_{n-1}$, $n = 1, 2, \ldots$. The solution is $L_n = (1 - \frac{1}{2}r)^n L$.
   (b) $(1 - r/2)^{10}L = (1/2)L$ implies that $r = 2 - 2 \cdot 2^{-1/10} \approx 0.133934$ (c) Remaining payment in the nth year will be $L_{n-1} - L_n + rL_{n-1} = (3/2)r(1 - \frac{1}{2}r)^{n-1}L$. The loan will never be complete paid since $L_n > 0$ for all n (but it does tend to 0 in the limit as $n \to \infty$.

11.3

1. (a) $x_{t+1} = A + B2^{t+1} = A + 2B2^t$ and $x_{t+2} = A + B2^{t+2} = A + 4B2^t$, so $x_{t+2} - 3x_{t+1} + 2x_t = A + 4B2^t - 3A - 6B2^t + 2A + 2B2^t = 0$ for all t.   (b) Direct verification as in (a).

3. $x_t = A\,3^t + B\,4^t$ is a solution. Substituting $t = 0$ and $t = 1$ yields $A + B = x_0$ and $3A + 4B = x_1$, with solution $A = 4x_0 - x_1$ and $B = -3x_0 + x_1$. So $x_t = A\,3^t + B\,4^t$ is the general solution of the given equation.

11.4

1. (a) $x_t = A2^t + B4^t$ (b) $x_t = A4^t + Bt4^t$ (c) $x_t = A\sqrt{3}^t \cos \theta t + B\sqrt{3}^t \sin \theta t$, where $\cos \theta = -\sqrt{3}/3$
   (d) $x_t = \left(\frac{\sqrt{6}}{3}\right)^t (A \cos \frac{\pi}{2}t + B \sin \frac{\pi}{2}t) + \frac{4}{5}$

3. (a) $Y_t^* = b/(1 - a)$ (b) $m^2 - a(1 + c)m + ac = 0$. Two different real roots, a double real root, two complex roots according as $a(1 + c)^2 - 4c > 0, = 0$, or < 0.

5. $D_n = Am_1^t + Bm_2^t$, where $m_{1,2} = 2(ab + 1 \pm \sqrt{1 + 2ab}\,)$

7. (a) Stable since $|a| = 0 < 1 - \frac{1}{3}$ and $b = -\frac{1}{3} < 1$.   (b) Not stable   (c) Stable

9. (a) $Y_t^* = \dfrac{a(1 + g)^t}{(1 + g)^2 - b(1 + g) - kg}$ (when the denominator is $\neq 0$).
   (b) $(b + k)^2 < 4k$ (c) $r = \sqrt{k}$. Damped oscillations if $k < 1$.

11. Claim: When $\frac{1}{4}a^2 \geq b$, $f(m) = m^2 + am + b = 0$ has both roots in the interval $(-1, 1)$ iff $|a| < 1 + b$ and $b < 1$. If both roots belong to $(-1, 1)$, it is necessary that $f(-1) > 0$, $f(1) > 0$, $f'(-1) < 0$, and $f'(1) > 0$. Hence, $1 - a + b > 0$, $1 + a + b > 0$, $-2 + a < 0$, and $a + 2 > 0$, These four inequalities are equivalent to $|a| < 1 + b$ and $|a| < 2$. But then $b \leq \frac{1}{4}a^2 < 1$ since the roots are real. On the other hand, if $|a| < 1 + b$ and $b < 1$, then $f(-1) > 0$, $f(1) > 0$, and $|a| < 2$. Hence $f'(-1) = -2 + a < 0$ and $f'(1) = 2 + a > 0$.

11.5

1. (a) $x_t = A + Bt + C(-2)^t$. (The characteristic polynomial is $(r - 1)^2(r + 2)$.)
   (b) $x_t = (A + Bt) \cos \frac{\pi}{2}t + (C + Dt) \sin \frac{\pi}{2}t + 2$. (The characteristic polynomial is $(r^2 + 1)^2$.)

3. A triangle with corners at $(-2, 1)$, $(2, 1)$, and $(0, -1)$.   **5.** (a) $\beta\sigma < 4(1 - \alpha)\alpha$ (b) $(1 + \alpha)\beta\sigma < 4\alpha$ and $\alpha < 1$

11.6

1. (a) $x_t = \frac{3}{2} - \frac{1}{2}(-1)^t$, $y_t = \frac{3}{4} + \frac{1}{4}(-1)^t$. (From the equations we deduce that $x_{t+2} = x_t$, etc.)
(b) $x_t = -\frac{1}{3} + \frac{1}{3}(-2)^t + \frac{1}{2}t(3 - t)$, $y_t = -\frac{1}{3} + \frac{1}{3}(-2)^t$, $z_t = \frac{2}{3} + \frac{1}{3}(-2)^t + \frac{1}{2}t(t - 1)$

3. (a) $y_{t+1} - 0.92y_t + 0.18894y_{t-1} = 0$ (b) Solutions of the characteristic equation: $m_1 \approx 0.61$, $m_2 \approx 0.31$. Thus $y_t \approx A(0.61)^t + B(0.31)^t$, $i_t \approx 1.47y_{t+1} - 0.72y_t$, etc.

11.7

1. Let $g(x) = f(x) - x$. Then $g(\xi_1) = \xi_2 - \xi_1$ and $g(\xi_2) = \xi_1 - \xi_2$ have opposite signs, and the intermediate value theorem implies that g has a zero x^* somewhere between ξ_1 and ξ_2. Then $f(x^*) = x^*$, so x^* is an equilibrium state.

3. The cycle points are $\xi_1 = (25 - 3\sqrt{5})/10 \approx 1.82918$, $\xi_2 = (25 + 3\sqrt{5})/10 \approx 3.17082$. Since $f'(\xi_1)f'(\xi_2) = -4/5$, the cycle is locally asymptotically stable. The equilibrium states are $x_1 = (15 - \sqrt{145})/10 \approx 0.29584$, $x_2 = (15 + \sqrt{145})/10 \approx 2.70416$, with $f'(x_1) = 1 + \sqrt{29/5}$, $f'(x_2) = 1 - \sqrt{29/5} \approx -1.40832$. It follows that both equilibria are locally unstable. It is also clear that x_2 lies between ξ_1 and ξ_2.

Chapter 12

12.1

1. (a) $J_2(x) = 1 - x^2$ for $u_2^*(x) = 0$, $J_1(x) = 2 - 5x^2/3$ for $u_1^*(x) = x/3$, $J_0(x) = 3 - 21x^2/11$ for $u_0^*(x) = 5x/11$. It follows that $u_0^*(5) = 25/11$. Hence $x_1^* = 5 - 25/11 = 30/11$, so $u_1^*(30/11) = 10/11$, and finally, $u_2^*(x) = 0$ and $x_2^* = 20/11$.   (b) $x_1 = 5 - u_0$, $x_2 = 5 - u_0 - u_1$. The sum in (∗) is $S(u_0, u_1, u_2) = -22 - 2u_0^2 - (5 - u_0)^2 - 2u_1^2 - (5 - u_0 - u_1)^2 - 2u_2^2$. This concave function has a maximum for $u_0 = 25/11$, $u_1 = 10/11$, $u_2 = 0$.

3. (a) With $\beta = (1 + r)^{-1}$, $J_T(x) = \beta^T x$ for $u_T^*(x) = 1$. For $\beta\rho < 1$, $J_{T-1}(x) = \beta^{T-1}x$ with $u_{T-1}^*(x) = 1$; for $\beta\rho \geq 1$, $J_{T-1}(x) = \rho\beta^T x$ with $u_{T-1}^*(x) = 0$.   (b) For $\beta\rho < 1$, $P_s = \beta^s$; for $\beta\rho \geq 1$, $P_s = \beta^T \rho^{T-s}$.
(c) For $\beta\rho < 1$, $J_0(x) = x$ and $u_1 = \cdots = u_T = 1$; for $\beta\rho \geq 1$, $J_0(x) = \beta^T \rho^T x$ and $u_1 = \cdots = u_T = 0$.

5. $J_T(x) = \ln x$, $u_T^*(x)$ is arbitrary, $J_{T-t}(x) = \ln x + C$ with $C = \ln(3/2) - 1/3$. The optimal controls are $u_0^*(x) = u^*(x) = \cdots = u_{T-1}^*(x) = 1/2$. The difference equation for x_t^* is $x_{t+1}^* = \frac{3}{2}x_t^*$, with $x_0^* = x_0$. The solution of this first-order difference equation is $x_t^* = (\frac{3}{2})^t x_0$.

7. (a) $J_T(x) = -\alpha e^{-\gamma x}$, $J_{T-1}(x) = -2\sqrt{\alpha}e^{-\gamma x}$, $J_{T-2}(x) = -2^{3/2}\alpha^{1/4}e^{-\gamma x}$.
(b) The difference equation for α_t is $\alpha_{t-1} = 2\sqrt{\alpha_t}$, $t = T, \ldots, 1$.

12.2

1. (a) $F(t, x_t, x_{t+1}) = 1 - x_t^2 - 2(x_t - x_{t+1})^2$ for $t = 0, 1$; $F(2, x_2, x_3) = 1 - x_2^2$. The Euler equation is $x_2 - (5/2)x_1 + x_0 = 0$ (for $t = 0$), $x_2 - (2/3)x_1 = 0$ (for $t = 1$). With $x_0 = 5$ we find $x_1 = 30/11$ and $x_2 = 20/11$, as in Problem 12.1.1.

12.3

1. (a) $(\alpha - \frac{2}{3})(1 + \alpha\beta)^2 = \alpha\beta(1 + \alpha\beta)$, and the only positive solution is $\alpha = \frac{1}{2\beta}\left(\frac{5\beta}{3} - 1 + \sqrt{(\frac{5\beta}{3} - 1)^2 + \frac{8\beta}{3}}\right)$. $u^*(t) = -\alpha\beta x/(1 + \alpha\beta)$.   (b) (2) applies for $x \in X(x_0) \subset [-x_0, x_0]$, $u \in [-x_0, x_0]$.

12.4

1. (a) $H = 1 - (x^2 + 2u^2) + p(x - u)$ for $t = 0, 1$ and $H = 1 - (x^2 + 2u^2)$ for $t = 2$. Condition (3) yields $p_0 = -4u_0^*$ and $p_1 = -4u_1^*$, and condition (3) gives $p_0 = -2x_1^* + p_1$ and $p_1 = -2x_2^*$.   (b) Of course, $x_1^* = x_0^* - u_0^* = 5 - u_0^*$ and $x_2^* = x_1^* - u_1^* = 5 - u_0^* - u_1^*$. From all these equation we get $u_0^* = 25/11$, $u_1^* = 10/11$, $u_2^* = 0$. (Start by eliminating p_0 and p_1.)   (c) The Hamiltonian is concave in (x, u), so we have found the solution.

12.5

1. (a) $I = 12 - 2u_0 - 2u_0^2 - u_1 - 2u_1^2 - 2u_2^2 - 2v_0 - v_0^2 - v_1 - v_1^2 - v_2^2$. Since I is concave as a sum of concave function, the unique stationary point $(u_0, v_0, u_1, v_1, u_2, v_2) = \left(-\frac{1}{2}, -1, -\frac{1}{4}, -\frac{1}{2}, 0, 0\right)$ solves the problem.

(b) $J_2(x, y) = \max_{u, v \in \mathbb{R}}(1 + x - y - 2u^2 - v^2) = 1 + x - y$ for $u_2^* = v_2^* = 0$. $J_1(x, y) = \frac{19}{8} + 2x - 2y$ for $u_1^* = -\frac{1}{4}$, $v_1^* = -\frac{1}{2}$, and $J_0(x, y) = \frac{39}{8} + 3x - 3y$ for $u_0^* = -\frac{1}{2}$, $v_0^*(x, y) = -1$.

(c) $H(t, x, u, p) = 1 + x - y - 2u^2 - v^2 + p^1(x - u) + p^2(y + v)$ for $t = 0, 1$, $H(t, x, u, p) = 1 + x - y - 2u^2 - v^2$ for $t = 2$. Condition (3) yields for $t = 0, 1$: $-4u_t - p_t^1 = 0$ and $-2v_t + p_t^2 = 0$. For $t = 2$ it yields $-4u_2 = 0$ and $-2v_2 = 0$ Hence, $u_0 = -\frac{1}{4}p_0^1$, $u_1 = -\frac{1}{4}p_1^1$, $u_2 = 0$, $v_0 = \frac{1}{2}p_0^2$, $v_1 = \frac{1}{2}p_1^2$, $v_2 = 0$. From (4) and (6)(c′), $p_0^1 = 1 + p_1^1$, $p_2^1 = 0$, $p_0^2 = -1 + p_1^2$, $p_2^2 = 0$. Moreover, from (5), $p_1^1 = 1 + p_2^1$, $p_1^1 = -1 + p_2^2$. Finally, $x_1 = x_0 - u_0 = 5 - u_0$, $x_2 = x_1 - u_1$, $y_1 = y_0 + v_0$, $y_2 = y_1 + v_1$. From these equations we find the same solution as before.

3. $x_t = \beta^t x_0$. (With $H = \beta^t \ln(x - u) + pu$, the relevant conditions are: (i) $\partial H^*/\partial u = p_t - \beta^t/(x_t^* - u_t^*) = 0$, (ii) $p_{t-1} = \partial H^*/\partial x = \beta^t/(x_t^* - u_t^*)$, (iii) $\underline{\lim}_{t \to \infty} p_t(x_t - x_t^*) \geq 0$, (iv) $x_{t+1}^* = u_t^*$, $x^*(0) = x_0$. From (i) and (ii) we get, $p_{t-1} = p_t$, so $p_t = \bar{p}$, a constant. From (i) and (iv), $x_{t+1}^* = x_t^* - \beta^t/\bar{p}$, with solution $x_t^* = (x_0 - 1/\bar{p}(1 - \beta) + \beta^t/\bar{p}(1 - \beta)/\bar{p}$.

12.6

1. $\alpha_{t-1} = 2(\alpha_t K)^{1/2}$, $u_{t-1} = x - (1/2\gamma)\ln(\alpha_t K)$; $\alpha_T = \delta$. (If $J(t, x) = -\alpha_t e^{-\gamma x}$, writing $x_{t-1} = x$, $u_{t-1} = u$, and $V_t = V$, the optimality equation is $J(t - 1, x) = -\alpha_{t-1}e^{-\gamma x} = \max_u\{-e^{-\gamma u} - \alpha_t E e^{-\gamma(2x - u + V)}\} = \max_u\{-e^{-\gamma u} - \alpha_t K e^{-\gamma(2x - u)}\}$. The first-order condition is $\gamma e^{-\gamma u} - \gamma \alpha_t K e^{-2\gamma x + \gamma u} = 0$, with solution $u = u_{t-1} = x - (1/2\gamma)\ln(\alpha_t K)$, so $-\alpha_{t-1}e^{-\gamma x} = -e^{\frac{1}{2}\ln(\alpha_t K)}e^{-\gamma x} - \alpha_t K e^{-\gamma x}e^{-\frac{1}{2}\ln(\alpha_t K)}$. Hence, $\alpha_{t-1} = 2(\alpha_t K)^{1/2}$, $\alpha_T = \delta$.)

3. $J(t, x_t) = k_t + a_t x_t$, $a_t = a2^{t-T}$, $k_{t-1} = k_t + 2/a_t$, $k_T = 0$

5. $J(T, x) = x$, $J(t, x) = 2^{T-t}x + b_t$ where $b_{t-1} = 2^{T-t}/\lambda + b_t$, $b_T = 0$; $u_T = 0$, u_{T-1} arbitrary, $u_t = 1, t < T - 1$.

7. (a) and (b): $J(t, x) = \max\{x^2, a_t + 2x^2\}$ where $a_{t-1} = -1 + \frac{1}{4}a_t$, $a_{T-1} = -1$, $u_t = 0$ if $a_t + x^2 \leq 0$, $u_t = 1$ if $a_t + x^2 > 0$.

9. $u_t = \bar{u} = (\hat{q} - \hat{p})/(\hat{q} + \hat{p})$, where $\hat{q} = q^{-1/\alpha}$, $\hat{p} = p^{-1/\alpha}$, $J(t, x) = A_t x^{1-\alpha}$, $A_{t-1} = A_t[p(1 + \bar{u})^{1-\alpha} + q(1 - \bar{u})^{1-\alpha}]$

11. $x_1 = x_0 - 1 - v_1$, $x_2 = x_1 - 1 - v_2$, $x_3 = x_2 + \frac{1}{2}$

12.7

1. (a) $J(x) = ax^2 + b$, $\hat{a} = [1 - 2\beta - \sqrt{1 + 4\beta^2}]/2\beta$, $\hat{b} = \hat{a}\beta d/(1 - \beta)$. (With $J(x) = ax^2 + b$, the Bellman equation is $ax^2 + b = \max_u\{-u^2 - x^2 + \beta E[a(x + u + V)^2 + b]\} = \max_u\{-u^2 - x^2 + \beta a(x + u)^2 + \beta ad + \beta b\}$. Maximizing this concave function yields $u = \beta ax/(1 - \beta a)$. Hence, $ax^2 + b = -x^2\beta^2 a^2/(1 - \beta a)^2 - x^2 + \beta ax^2/(1 - \beta a)^2 + \beta ad + \beta b$ for all x, or $[a + \beta^2 a^2/(1 - \beta a)^2 + 1 - \beta a/(1 - \beta a)^2]x^2 - (\beta ad + \beta b - b) = 0$ for all x. In particular, $a + 1 - \beta a/(1 - \beta a) = 0$. Solving this second-order equation gives $a = [1 - 2\beta - \sqrt{1 + 4\beta^2}]/2\beta$, and then $b = a\beta d/(1 - \beta)$.)

(b) $J(t, x) = \beta^t(a_t x^2 + b_t)$, $a_{t-1} = -1 + \beta^2 a_t^2/(1 - \beta a_t)^2 + \beta a_t/(1 - \beta a_t)^2 = -1 + \beta a_t/(1 - \beta a_t)$, $a_T =_1$, $b_{t-1} = \beta b_t \beta a_t d$, $b_T = 0$, $a_T = 1$. To find $\lim_{T \to \infty} J(0, x_0, T)$, we need to find $\lim_{T \to \infty} a_0$ and $\lim_{T \to \infty} b_0$, (for any t, a_t and b_t depends on T), write in particular $a_0 = a_0^T$, $b_0 = b_0^T$. To find these limits is the same as finding the limits $\lim_{t \to -\infty} a_t$, $\lim_{t \to -\infty} b_t$ when T is fixed. The function $\phi(x) = -1 + \beta x/(1 - \beta x)$, is increasing (calculate its derivative), and, since $a_{T-1} < a_T$ and this continuous backwards: $a_{t-1} < a_t$ for all t. Letting $t \to -\infty$ in the difference equation for a_t gives that the limit $a = \lim_{t \to}$, satisfies $a = -1 + \beta a/(1 - \beta a)$ (so a is $> -\infty$), in fact has the same value as in a). In a similar way, b_t decreases when t decreases, and its limit, denoted b, when taking limits in the equation for b_{t-21} gives $b = \beta b + \beta ad$, i.e. b is also as in a). Then, evidently, $J(0, x, T) = a_0^T x^2 + b_0^T \to ax^2 + b = J(x)$ when $T \to \infty$.

Chapter 13

13.1

1. $d(\mathbf{x}, \mathbf{y}) \geq |x_j - y_j|$ for all j, so if $d(\mathbf{x}, \mathbf{y}) < r$, then $|x_j - y_j| < r$, which means that $-r < x_j - y_j < r$.

3. $d(\mathbf{x}, \mathbf{y}) = \sqrt{\sum_{j=1}^{n}(x_j - y_j)^2} \leq \sum_{j=1}^{n} \sqrt{(x_j - y_j)^2} = \sum_{j=1}^{n} |x_j - y_j|$

5. See Figure 13.1.5. S is closed because it contains all its boundary points, which are the points on the curve.

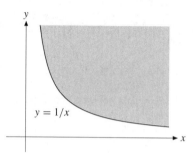

Figure 13.1.5

7. Closedness: The points $(2n, 1)$ are boundary points of A and B, but do not belong either of those sets, so A and B are not closed. C is closed because it contains all its boundary points. Openness: A and C are not open since no ball (two-dimensional disk) at all can be contained in A or C. B is obviously open, because it is the union of a family of open rectangles.

9. (a) If $\mathbf{x} \in$ int S, then there is an open ball B around $\mathbf{x}$ such that $B \subseteq S$. But then $B \subseteq T$ as well, so $\mathbf{x}$ is an interior point of T. If $\mathbf{y} \in \mathrm{cl}(S)$, then every open ball around $\mathbf{y}$ has a nonempty intersection with S. Obviously any such ball also meets T, and so $\mathbf{y}$ belongs to the closure of T.
(b) Let $\mathbf{y}$ be a point in the closure of $\mathrm{cl}(S)$. We want to show that $\mathbf{y} \in \mathrm{cl}(S)$. In order to show this, it is sufficient to show that every open ball around $\mathbf{y}$ intersects S. Thus, let B be an open ball around $\mathbf{y}$. Since $\mathbf{y}$ is in the closure of $\mathrm{cl}(S)$, the intersection $B \cap \mathrm{cl}(S)$ is nonempty. Let $\mathbf{z}$ be any point in this intersection. Since $\mathbf{z} \in B$ and B is open, there is an open ball B' around $\mathbf{z}$ such that $B' \subseteq B$. And since $\mathbf{z} \in \mathrm{cl}(S)$, there is at least one point $\mathbf{w}$ in $B' \cap S$. Then $\mathbf{w} \in B \cap S$, and so $B \cap S \neq \emptyset$. Hence, $\mathrm{cl}(S)$ is closed.

11. 0 belongs to the closure of $\bigcup_i A_i$, but not to $\bigcup_i A_i$ itself.

13. $\partial \mathbb{Q} = \mathbb{R}$, because arbitrarily close to any number in $\mathbb{R}$, we can find a rational number. Hence, $\overline{\mathbb{Q}} = \mathbb{Q} \cup \partial \mathbb{Q} = \mathbb{R}$. Since every open interval contains irrational numbers, $\mathrm{int}(\mathbb{Q}) = \emptyset$.

15. (a) and (c) are false, (b) and (d) are true.

13.2

1. (a) $\mathbf{x}_k \to (0, 1)$ (b) $\mathbf{x}_k \to (1, e)$. (Recall that $(1 + 1/k)^k \to e = 2.71828\ldots$ as $k \to \infty$).)
(c) $\mathbf{x}_k$ does not converge.   (d) $\mathbf{x}_k \to (\frac{1}{3}, 0)$.

3. Suppose $\{\mathbf{x}_k\}$ is a sequence in $\mathbb{R}^n$ converging to $\mathbf{x}$. Given $\varepsilon > 0$, choose a natural number N such that $\|\mathbf{x}_k - \mathbf{x}\| < \varepsilon/2$ for all $k > N$. Then for $k > N$ and $m > N$, $\|\mathbf{x}_k - \mathbf{x}_m\| = \|(\mathbf{x}_k - \mathbf{x}) + (\mathbf{x} - \mathbf{x}_m)\| \leq \|\mathbf{x}_k - \mathbf{x}\| + \|\mathbf{x} - \mathbf{x}_m\| < \varepsilon/2 + \varepsilon/2 = \varepsilon$. Therefore $\{\mathbf{x}_k\}$ is a Cauchy sequence.

13.3

1. Define the continuous functions f and g from $\mathbb{R}^2$ into $\mathbb{R}$ by $f(x, y) = 2x - y$ and $g(x, y) = x - 3y$. Both these functions are continuous, and so the sets $f^{-1}(-\infty, 2)$ and $g^{-1}(-\infty, 5)$ are both open. S is open as the intersection of these open sets.

3. (a) $S = \mathbb{R}$, $f(x) = e^x$, $f(S) = (0, \infty)$ (b) $S = \mathbb{R}$, $f(x) = e^{x^2}$, $f(S) = [1, \infty)$ (c) $S = (0, 1)$, $f(x) = 1/x$

5. The intersection of S and $\bar{B}(y; r)$ is closed and bounded, hence compact. Then $h(\mathbf{x})$ attains a minimum at some point $\mathbf{x}''$ in $S \cap \bar{B}(y; r)$, and $\mathbf{x}''$ is the required point.

13.4

1. (a) S is compact and f is continuous, so by Theorem 13.4.1, v is continuous.
(b) The set $\mathrm{cl}(T) = \{(y, z) : y \geq 0, z \geq 0, y^2 + z^2 \leq 4\}$ (the closure of T) is compact. Hence, for any x, $f(x, y, z)$ will attain a maximum value at some point (y_x, z_x) in $\mathrm{cl}(T)$. Obviously, $y_x > 0$ and $z_x > 0$, so $(y_x, z_x) \in T$. This implies that the supremum value of $f(x, y, z)$ over T is attained at (y_z, x_z). Hence, $w(x) = \max_{(y,z)\in\mathrm{cl}(T)} f(x, y, z)$, and by Theorem 13.4.1, w is continuous.

13.5

1. Let $\mathbf{z}$ and $\mathbf{w}$ belong to $Q = aS + bT$, and thus $\mathbf{z} = a\mathbf{x}_1 + b\mathbf{y}_1$ and $\mathbf{w} = a\mathbf{x}_2 + b\mathbf{y}_2$, where $\mathbf{x}_1$, $\mathbf{x}_2$ belongs to S and $\mathbf{y}_1$, $\mathbf{y}_2$ belongs to T. Let $\lambda \in [0, 1]$. We must prove that $\lambda\mathbf{z} + (1 - \lambda)\mathbf{w} \in Q$. Easy calculations yield $\lambda\mathbf{z} + (1 - \lambda)\mathbf{w} = \lambda(a\mathbf{x}_1 + b\mathbf{y}_1) + (1 - \lambda)(a\mathbf{x}_2 + b\mathbf{y}_2) = a(\lambda\mathbf{x}_1 + (1 - \lambda)\mathbf{x}_2) + b(\lambda\mathbf{y}_1 + (1 - \lambda)\mathbf{y}_2)$, which belongs to $Q = aS + bT$ because $\lambda\mathbf{x}_1 + (1 - \lambda)\mathbf{x}_2 \in S$ and $\lambda\mathbf{y}_1 + (1 - \lambda)\mathbf{y}_2 \in T$ due to the convexity of S and T.

3. (c) $\mathrm{co}(S) =$ the set of all points in the triangle with vertices at $(0, 0)$, $(a, 0)$, and $(0, a)$.
(d) $\mathrm{co}(S)$ is the closed square with the four points as extreme points.

5. $\lambda\mathbf{x} + (1 - \lambda)\mathbf{y} = \sum_{i=1}^{p} \lambda\lambda_i\mathbf{u}_i + \sum_{j=1}^{q}(1 - \lambda)\mu_j\mathbf{v}_j$, and $\sum_{i=1}^{p} \lambda\lambda_i + \sum_{j=1}^{q}(1 - \lambda)\mu_j = \lambda + (1 - \lambda) = 1$.

7. Mathematical induction.

13.6

1. Use Theorem 13.6.1 to find a hyperplane that strictly separates S from the origin.

3. *Hint:* If x is interior in $\bar{S}$, there exists an n-cube contained in $\bar{S}$, with x as its centre point. Arbitrarily close to each corner z_j of the cube there is a point y_j from S, and when the y_j are sufficiently close to z_j, then evidently x lies in the interior of the convex hull of the points y_j.

5. The statement is false. Consider two intersecting straight lines in $\mathbb{R}^2$.

13.7

1. $(\mathbf{I} - \mathbf{A})\mathbf{x} = \mathbf{1}$ reduces to $\frac{2}{3}x_1 - \frac{1}{2}x_2 = 1$ and $-\frac{1}{9}x_1 + \frac{2}{3}x_2 = 1$. This system has the solution $x_1 = 3$, $y_1 = 2$. Hence $\mathbf{A}$ is productive.

Chapter 14

14.1

1. The domain of F is closed, and the graph is closed. F is obviously not upper hemicontinuous at $x = 0$.

3. The domain of F is closed, and the graph is closed. To show l.h.c., for any $y^0 \in F(x^0)$, if $x_n \to x^0$, choose $y_n = \min\{y^0, 1/x_n\}$ (let $y_n = y^0$ if $x_n = 0$). Then $y_n \to y^0$, with $y^0 \in F(x^0)$.

5. For a sufficiently large number $\alpha > 0$, both $F(\mathbf{x}^0)$ and $G(\mathbf{x}^0)$ are contained in the ball $B(\mathbf{0}; \alpha)$. Then there exists a $\delta > 0$ such that $F(\mathbf{x}) \subseteq B(\mathbf{0}; \alpha + 1)$ and $G(\mathbf{x}) \subseteq B(\mathbf{0}; \alpha + 1)$ whenever $\|\mathbf{x} - \mathbf{x}^0\| < \delta$. Then $H(\mathbf{x}) \subseteq B(\mathbf{0}; 2\alpha + 2)$ for such $\mathbf{x}$. Hence, by Theorem 14.1.3 it suffices to prove that $H(\mathbf{x})$ has a closed graph at $\mathbf{x}^0$. Let $\mathbf{x}_n \to \mathbf{x}^0$, $\mathbf{h}_n \to \mathbf{h}$, $\mathbf{h}_n \in H(\mathbf{x}_n)$. Then $\mathbf{h}_n = \mathbf{f}_n + \mathbf{g}_n$ for some $\mathbf{f}_n$ in $F(\mathbf{x}_n)$ and $\mathbf{g}_n$ in $G(\mathbf{x}_n)$. A subsequence $(\mathbf{f}_{n_j}, \mathbf{g}_{n_j})$ converges to some point $(\mathbf{f}, \mathbf{g}) \in F(\mathbf{x}^0) \times G(\mathbf{x}^0)$. Then $\mathbf{h} = \mathbf{f} + \mathbf{g} \in H(\mathbf{x}^0)$.

7. The sequence property described in the problem implies that F has a closed graph at $\mathbf{x}^0$. Thus by Theorem 14.1.3, it suffices to show that $F(\mathbf{x})$ is locally bounded near $\mathbf{x}^0$. If it is not, then for every k there is a pair $\mathbf{x}^k$, $\mathbf{y}^k$ such that $\|\mathbf{x}^k - \mathbf{x}^0\| < 1/k$, $\|\mathbf{y}^k\| > k$, and $\mathbf{y}^k \in F(\mathbf{x}^k)$. But $\{\mathbf{y}^k\}$ contains no convergent subsequence. (It is also true that if F is compact-valued and upper hemicontinuous at $\mathbf{x}^0$, then the sequence property in the problem holds, but the proof of this fact is more difficult.)

9. For a point $(\mathbf{x}, \mathbf{y})$ with $\mathbf{x} \in X$ and $\mathbf{y} \in \mathcal{P}(\mathbf{x})$, let $\mathbf{A} = \{\partial g_i(\mathbf{x}, \mathbf{y})/\partial x_j\}_{i \in I}$, where $I = \{i : g_i(\mathbf{x}, \mathbf{y}) = b_i\}$. Then $\mathbf{Az} = \mathbf{1}$ has a solution $\mathbf{z}$. Hence, for all $\delta > 0$ that are small enough, $g_i(\mathbf{x} - \delta\mathbf{z}, \mathbf{y}) < 0$ for all i in I, and also for the other i's, so $\mathbf{y} \in \overline{\mathcal{P}^\circ(\mathbf{x})}$.

11. Let $\mathbf{z}^0 \in H(\mathbf{x}^0)$. Then $\mathbf{z}^0 \in G(\mathbf{y}^0)$ for some $\mathbf{y}^0 \in F(\mathbf{x}^0)$. Let V be a neighbourhood of $\mathbf{z}^0$. Then there exists a neighbourhood U of $\mathbf{y}^0$ such that $V \cap G(\mathbf{y}) \neq \emptyset$ for $\mathbf{y}$ in U. Moreover, there is a neighbourhood N of $\mathbf{x}^0$ such that $U \cap F(\mathbf{x}) \neq \emptyset$ when $\mathbf{x} \in N$. Let $\mathbf{x} \in N$ and $\mathbf{y} \in U \cap F(\mathbf{x})$. Then $V \cap G(\mathbf{y}) \neq \emptyset$, and if $\mathbf{z} \in V \cap G(\mathbf{y})$, then $\mathbf{z} \in G(\mathbf{y})$, $\mathbf{y} \in F(\mathbf{x})$, so $\mathbf{z} \in H(\mathbf{x})$.

14.2

1. $V(x) = \begin{cases} -x & \text{if } x \leq 0 \\ x^2/4 - x & \text{if } x \in (0, 2], \\ -1 & \text{if } x > 2 \end{cases}$ $\qquad Y^*(x) = \begin{cases} \{0\} & \text{if } x \leq 0 \\ \{-\sqrt{x/2}, \sqrt{x/2}\} & \text{if } x \in (0, 2] . \\ \{-1, 1\} & \text{if } x > 2 \end{cases}$

3. For $\mathbf{p} \gg \mathbf{0}, m > 0$, both the demand correspondence and the indirect utility function are continuous. Quasiconcavity entails convexity of each set $\xi(\mathbf{p}, m)$.

14.4

1. $\frac{1}{2}(x^* + 1) = x^*$ would imply $x^* = 1$. The interval $(0, 1)$ is not closed, so Brouwer's theorem does not apply.

3. Suppose $\mathbf{x} \in \Delta^{n-1}$. Then the ith component of the vector $\mathbf{Ax}$ is equal to $\sum_{j=1}^n a_{ij}x_j$, which is ≥ 0 because all the x_j and all the a_{ij} are nonnegative. Moreover, the sum of all the components of $\mathbf{Ax}$ is $\sum_{i=1}^n \left(\sum_{j=1}^n a_{ij}x_j\right) = \sum_{j=1}^n x_j \sum_{i=1}^n a_{ij} = \sum_{j=1}^n x_j = 1$. Thus the linear, and therefore continuous, transformation $\mathbf{x} \mapsto \mathbf{Ax}$ maps Δ^{n-1} into itself. By Brouwer's theorem there exists an $\mathbf{x}^*$ in S such that $\mathbf{Ax}^* = \mathbf{x}^*$. Thus $\lambda = 1$ is an eigenvalue for $\mathbf{A}$, and $\mathbf{x}^*$ is an eigenvector.

5. We shall show that x^* is a fixed point for f.
(1) If $x^* > 0$, then for every natural number n, we can find an x_n in A with $x^* - 1/n < x_n \leq x^*$. Since $f(x_n) \geq x_n$, we get $f(x^*) \geq \overline{\lim}_{s \to x^*-} f(s) \geq \overline{\lim}_n f(x_n) \geq \overline{\lim}_n x_n = x^*$.
(2) If $x^* < 1$, then $f(s) < s$ for every $s > x^*$, and so $f(x^*) \leq \overline{\lim}_{s \to x^*+} f(s) \leq \overline{\lim}_{s \to x^*+} s = x^*$.
(3) It follows from (1) and (2) that, if $0 < x^* < 1$, then $f(x^*) \leq x^* \leq f(x^*)$, so $f(x^*) = x^*$.
(4) It also follows that, if $x^* = 0$, then $0 \leq f(0) = f(x^*) \leq x^* = 0$, and if $x^* = 1$, then $1 \geq f(x^*) \geq x^* = 1$. Hence, in every case, we get $f(x^*) = x^*$.

14.5

1. The budget set does not change if $\mathbf{p}$ is replaced by $\lambda\mathbf{p}$, $\lambda > 0$.

Appendix A

A.1

1. Suppose that $\{\{a\}, \{a, b\}\} = \{\{c\}, \{c, d\}\}$. There are two cases to consider: $a = b$ and $a \neq b$. If $a = b$, then $\{a, b\} = \{a\}$, and so $\{\{c\}, \{c, d\}\} = \{\{a\}, \{a, b\}\} = \{\{a\}\}$. But then $\{c, d\} = \{c\} = \{a\}$, so $c = d = a = b$. If $a \neq b$, then $\{a, b\}$ is a two-element set, and we must have $\{c\} = \{a\}$ and $\{c, d\} = \{a, b\}$. This shows that $c = a$, and therefore $d = b$.

3. $D_f = \{0, 1\}$, $f(0) = 0$, $f(1) = 0$, $S_1 = \{0\}$, $S_2 = \{1\}$.

5. The inclusions $S \subseteq f^{-1}(f(S))$ and $f(f^{-1}(T)) \subseteq T$ follow immediately from the definitions of direct and inverse images. If $x \in f^{-1}(T)$, then $f(x) \in T$ and $x \in \text{range}(f)$, and it follows that $f^{-1}(T) \subseteq f^{-1}(T \cap \text{range}(f))$. The opposite inclusion is obvious, since $T \cap \text{range}(f) \subseteq T$. To show that the first two inclusions cannot always be replaced by equality signs, define $f : \mathbb{R} \to \mathbb{R}$ by $f(x) = x^2$, and let $S = [0, 2]$ and $T = [-1, 1]$. Then $f^{-1}(f(S)) = f^{-1}([0, 4]) = [-2, 2] \neq S$, and $f(f^{-1}(T)) = f([-1, 1]) = [0, 1] \neq T$.

A.2

1. $\sup A = 7$, $\inf A = -3$; $\sup B = 1$, $\inf B = 0$; $\sup C = \infty$, $\inf C = \sqrt{3}$.

3. It follows from $r^2 > 2$ that $s = (2 + r^2)/2r < (r^2 + r^2)/2r = r$. Moreover, $s^2 - 2 = (4 + 4r^2 + r^4)/4r^2 - 2 = (4 - 4r^2 + r^4)/4r^2 = (2 - r^2)^2/4r^2 > 0$.

A.3

1. $x_1 = 1 < 4$, and if $x_k < 4$, then $x_{k+1} = 2\sqrt{x_k} < 2\sqrt{4} = 4$. By induction $x_k < 4$ for all k. Moreover, $x_k > 0$ for all k and $x_{k+1} = 2\sqrt{x_k} = \sqrt{4x_k} > \sqrt{x_k^2} = x_k$. Hence $\{x_k\}$ is increasing. By Theorem A.3.1 the sequence is convergent. Let its limit be x. By taking the limit as $k \to \infty$ in $x_{k+1} = 2\sqrt{x_k}$, we obtain $x = 2\sqrt{x}$, or $x^2 = 4x$, and thus $x = 4$.

3. According to Theorem A.2.1 (b), for each natural number n, because $1/n > 0$, there exists a number in A, call it x_n, such that $x_n > b^* - 1/n$. Because $x_n \leq b^*$, we have $|x_n - b^*| < 1/n$. It follows that $x_n \to b^*$ as $n \to \infty$.

5. (a) Note that $x_k + y_k = 1$ and $x_k y_k = \frac{1}{4}(1 - (-1)^{2k}) = 0$ for all k. The required limits are: $\overline{\lim}_{k\to\infty} x_k = 1$, $\overline{\lim}_{k\to\infty} y_k = 1$, $\overline{\lim}_{k\to\infty}(x_k + y_k) = 1$, $\overline{\lim}_{k\to\infty}(x_k y_k) = 0$. $\underline{\lim}_{k\to\infty} x_k = 0$, $\underline{\lim}_{k\to\infty} y_k = 0$, $\underline{\lim}_{k\to\infty}(x_k + y_k) = 1$, $\underline{\lim}_{k\to\infty}(x_k y_k) = 0$.
(b) (i): For each natural number n, let $M_n = \sup\{x_k : k \geq n\}$ and $N_n = \sup\{y_k : k \geq n\}$. Then for all $k \geq n$, we have $x_k \leq M_n$ and $y_k \leq N_n$, and so $x_k + y_k \leq M_n + N_n$. Thus $\sup\{x_k + y_k : k \geq n\} \leq M_n + N_n \leq \lim_{n\to\infty}(M_n + N_n) = \lim_{n\to\infty} M_n + \lim_{n\to\infty} N_n$, or $\overline{\lim}_{k\to\infty}(x_k + y_k) \leq \overline{\lim}_{k\to\infty} x_k + \overline{\lim}_{k\to\infty} y_k$.
The proof of (ii) is similar and is left to the reader.

7. Suppose that $x \neq y$. Let $\varepsilon = |x - y|$. Since $\varepsilon/2 > 0$, there exist numbers N and M such that $|x_n - x| < \varepsilon/2$ for all $n > N$ and $|x_n - y| < \varepsilon/2$ for all $n > M$. Then for $n > \max\{N, M\}$, we get $|x - y| = |x - x_n + x_n - y| \leq |x_n - x| + |x_n - y| < \varepsilon/2 + \varepsilon/2 = \varepsilon$, a contradiction.

9. (a) $a_1 = 2$, $a_2 = 2.25$, $a_3 \approx 2.3704$, $a_4 \approx 2.4414$; $b_1 = 4$, $b_2 = 3.375$, $b_3 \approx 3.1605$, $b_4 \approx 3.0518$. (b) The inequality is valid for $n = 1$. Suppose $(1 + x)^n \geq 1 + nx$ for $x \geq -1$. Then $(1 + x)^{n+1} = (1 + x)^n(1 + x) \geq (1 + nx)(1 + x) = 1 + (n + 1)x + nx^2 \geq 1 + (n + 1)x$. The last inequality is strict if $x \neq 0$.
(c) With $x = -1/n^2 \neq 0$, the inequality yields $(1 - 1/n^2)^n > 1 - 1/n$. Multiplying by $(n/(n - 1))^n$ yields $(1 + 1/n)^n > (1 + 1/(n - 1))^{n-1}$. (d) Left to the reader. (e) The sequence $\{a_n\}$ is increasing and bounded above (by any b_n). The sequence $\{b_n\}$ is decreasing and bounded below (by any a_n). Thus both sequences converge.

Appendix B

B.1

1. See Fig. B.1.1. $OB = BP = \frac{1}{2}\sqrt{2}$ by Pythagoras's theorem. Hence, $\sin 45° = \sin \pi/4 = BP/OP = \frac{1}{2}\sqrt{2} = \cos \pi/4$, whereas $\tan 45° = \tan \pi/4 = \sin(\pi/4)/\cos(\pi/4) = 1$.

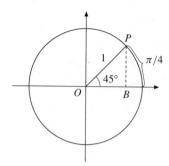

Figure B.1.1

3. $\cos(x - y) = \cos(x + (-y)) = \cos x \cos(-y) - \sin x \sin(-y) = \cos x \cos y + \sin x \sin y$

5. $\tan(x + \pi) = \dfrac{\sin(x + \pi)}{\cos(x + \pi)} = \dfrac{\sin x \cos \pi + \cos x \sin \pi}{\cos x \cos \pi - \sin x \sin \pi} = \dfrac{-\sin x}{-\cos x} = \tan x$

$\sin(x + \frac{1}{2}\pi) = \sin x \cos \frac{1}{2}\pi + \cos x \sin \frac{1}{2}\pi = (\sin x) \cdot 0 + (\cos x) \cdot 1 = \cos x$

$\cos(x + \frac{1}{2}\pi) = \cos x \cos \frac{1}{2}\pi - \sin x \sin \frac{1}{2}\pi = - \sin x$

7. (a) $\sqrt{2} \sin(x + \pi/4) - \cos x = \sqrt{2}(\sin x \cos \pi/4 + \cos x \sin \pi/4) - \cos x$
$= \sqrt{2}(\sin x \cdot 1/\sqrt{2} + \cos x \cdot 1/\sqrt{2}) - \cos x = \sin x$ (b) $\tan(\alpha + \beta)$ (c) $- \cos a / \sin a$

9. $\sin(x + y) \sin(x - y) = (\sin x \cos y + \cos x \sin y)(\sin x \cos y - \cos x \sin y) =$
$\sin^2 x \cos^2 y - \cos^2 x \sin^2 y = \sin^2 x (1 - \sin^2 y) - (1 - \sin^2 x) \sin^2 y = \sin^2 x - \sin^2 y$

11. (a) Because $|f(x)| = |(1/2)^x \sin x| \le (1/2)^x$ for all x, and $(1/2)^x \to 0$ as $x \to \infty$, the oscillations die out.
(b) Because $2^x \to \infty$ as $x \to \infty$, the oscillations explode.

13. $(AC)^2 = (BD)^2$ yields $(\cos x - \cos y)^2 + (\sin x - (- \sin y))^2 = (\cos(x + y) - 1)^2 + \sin^2(x + y)$. Expanding and using (2) three times eventually gives formula (8).

B.2

1. (a) $y' = \frac{1}{2} \cos \frac{1}{2}x$ (b) $y' = \cos x - x \sin x$ (c) $y' = \dfrac{2x}{\cos^2 x^2}$ (d) $y' = e^{2x}(2 \cos x - \sin x)$

3. (a) $\cos x - \sin x$ (b) $5x^4 \sin x + x^5 \cos x + (1/2\sqrt{x}) \cos x - \sqrt{x} \sin x$

(c) $\dfrac{1}{(x^2 + 1)^2} \left[\left(\dfrac{1}{2\sqrt{x}} - \dfrac{3x\sqrt{x}}{2} \right) \cos x - \sqrt{x}\,(1 + x^2) \sin x \right]$

5. (a) 2 (b) m/n (c) 1/2

7. $p'(t) = -\lambda C_1 \sin \lambda t + \lambda C_2 \cos \lambda t$ and $p''(t) = -\lambda^2 C_1 \cos \lambda t - \lambda^2 C_2 \sin \lambda t$, so
$p''(t) + \lambda^2 p(t) = C_0 \lambda^2$. Thus, $K = C_0 \lambda^2$.

9. (a) $\dfrac{2}{\sqrt{1 - 4x^2}}$ (b) $\dfrac{2x}{1 + (x^2 + 1)^2}$ (c) $- \dfrac{1}{2\sqrt{x}\sqrt{1 - x}}$

11. (a) $- \ln |\cos x| + C$ (b) $e^{\sin x} + C$ (c) $- \frac{1}{6} \cos^6 x + C$

B.3

1. (a) $z + w = 5 - 2i$ (b) $zw = 21 - 9i$ (c) $z/w = (-3 - 7i)/6$ (d) $|z| = \sqrt{2^2 + (-5)^2} = \sqrt{29}$

3. (a) $\frac{1}{2}(1 + 5i)$ (b) $-3 - 4i$ (c) $(31 + 27i)/26$ (d) i

REFERENCES

Arkin V. I. and L. V. Evstigneev (1987): *Stochastic Models of Control and Economic Dynamics*. Academic Press.

Arrow, K. J. (1951): "An extension of the basic theorems of classical welfare economics", in J. Neyman (ed.), *Proceedings of the Second Berkeley Symposium on Mathematical Statistics and Probability*. University of California Press.

Arrow, K. J. and M. Kurz (1970): *Public Investment, the Rate of Return, and Optimal Fiscal Policy*. The Johns Hopkins Press.

Atkinson, A. B. (1971): "Capital taxes, the redistribution of wealth and individual savings". *Review of Economic Studies*, 38.

Aubin, J.-P. and H. Frankowska (1990): *Set-Valued Analysis*. Birkhäuser.

Barro, R. J. and X. Sala-i-Martin (1995): *Economic Growth*. McGraw-Hill.

Bertsekas, D. P. (1976): *Dynamic Programming and Stochastic Control*. Academic Press.

Blanchard, O. and S. Fischer (1989): *Lectures on Macroeconomics*. MIT Press.

Cesari, L. (1983): *Optimization – Theory and Applications*. Springer-Verlag.

Chipman, J. S. (1950): "The multi-sector multiplier". *Econometrica*, 18.

Clarke, F. H. (1983): *Optimization and Nonsmooth Analysis*. John Wiley & Sons.

Coddington, E. A. and N. Levinson (1955): *Theory of Ordinary Differential Equations*. McGraw-Hill.

Dorfman, R. (1969): "An economic interpretation of optimal control theory". *American Economic Review*, Vol. LIX, 5.

Faddeeva, V. N. (1959): *Computational Methods of Linear Algebra*. Dover Publications, Inc.

Farebrother, R. W. (1977): "Necessary and sufficient conditions for a quadratic form to be positive whenever a set of homogeneous linear constraints is satisfied". *Linear Algebra and its Applications*, 16.

Fleming, W. H. and R. W. Rishel (1975): *Deterministic and Stochastic Control*. Springer-Verlag.

Fraleigh J. B. and R. A. Beauregard (1995): *Linear Algebra.* Addison-Wesley.

Frisch, R. (1970): "Econometrics in the world of today". In *Induction, Growth and Trade: Essays in Honour of Sir Roy Harrod*, ed. by W. A. Eltis, M. F. Scott, J. N. Wolfe. Clarendon Press.

Gandolfo, G. (1980): *Economic Dynamics: Methods and Models*, 2. rev. ed. North-Holland.

Gantmacher, F. R. (1959): *The Theory of Matrices*, Vol. 2. Chelsea Publishing Co.

Gelfand, I. M. and S. V. Fomin (1963): *Calculus of Variations.* Prentice-Hall.

Goldberg, S. (1958): *Introduction to Difference Equations.* John Wiley & Sons.

Haavelmo, T. (1954): *A Study in the Theory of Economic Evolution*, 3. ed. Contributions to Economic Analysis III. North-Holland.

Halkin, H. (1974): "Necessary conditions for optimal control problems with infinite horizons". *Econometrica*, 42.

Hartman, P. (1982): *Ordinary Differential Equations*, 2. ed. Birkhäuser.

Hernández-Lerma, O. and J. B. Lasserre (1996): *Discrete-Time Markov Control Processes.* Springer-Verlag.

Hestenes, M. R. (1966): *Calculus of Variations and Optimal Control Theory.* John Wiley & Sons.

Hildebrand, F. B. (1968): *Finite-Difference Equations and Simulations.* Prentice-Hall.

Hirsch, M. and S. Smale (1974): *Differential Equations, Dynamical Systems, and Linear Algebra.* Academic Press.

Hotelling, H. (1931): "The economics of exhaustible resources". *Journal of Political Economy*, 39.

Ichiishi, T. (1983): *Game Theory for Economic Analysis.* Academic Press.

Johansen, L. (1972): *Production Functions.* North-Holland.

Kamien, M. I. and N. I. Schwartz (1991): *Dynamic Optimization. The Calculus of Variations and Optimal Control in Economics and Management*, 2. ed. North-Holland.

LaSalle, J. and S. Lefschetz (1961): *Stability by Liapunov's Direct Method. With Applications.* Academic Press.

Lee, E. B. and L. Markus (1967): *Foundations of Optimal Control Theory.* John Wiley & Sons.

Léonard, D. and N. V. Long (1992): *Optimal Control Theory and Static Optimization in Economics.* Cambridge University Press.

Lewis, D. W. (1991): *Matrix Theory.* World Scientific, Singapore.

Marsden, J. E. and M. J. Hoffman (1993): *Elementary Classical Analysis*, 2. ed. W. H. Freeman and Co.

Mas-Colell, A. (1995): *The theory of general economic equilibrium. A differentiable approach.* Cambridge University Press.

Mas-Colell, A., M. D. Whinston, and J. R. Green (1995): *Microeconomic Theory.* Oxford University Press.

Munkres, J. R. (1991): *Analysis on Manifolds.* Addison-Wesley.

Nikaido, H. (1970): *Introduction to Sets and Mappings in Modern Economics.* North-Holland.

Olech, C. (1963): "On the global stability of an autonomous system on the plane". *Contributions to Differential Equations*, Vol. 1. Interscience.

Ortega, J. M and W. C. Rheinboldt (1970): *Iterative Solution of Nonlinear Equations in Several Variables.* Academic Press.

Parthasarathy, T. (1983): *On Global Univalence Theorems*. Lecture Notes in Mathematics, No. 977, Springer.

Pontryagin, L. S., V. G. Boltyanskii, R. V. Gamkrelidze and E. F. Mishchenko (1962): *The Mathematical Theory of Optimal Processes*. Interscience.

Protter, M. H. and C. B. Morrey, Jr. (1991): *A First Course in Real Analysis*. 2. ed. Springer.

Ramsey, F. P. (1928): "A mathematical theory of saving". *Economic Journal*. Vol. 38.

Rockafellar, R. T. (1970): *Convex Analysis*. Princeton University Press.

Scarf, H. (1973) (with the collaboration of T. Hansen): *The Computation of Economic Equilibria*. Cowles Foundation Monograph 24. Yale University Press.

Seierstad, A. and K. Sydsæter (1987): *Optimal Control Theory with Economic Applications*. North-Holland.

Shell, K. (1967): "Optimal program of capital accumulation for an economy in which there is exogenous technical change". In K. Shell (Ed.) *Essays on the Theory of Optimal Economic Growth*. M.I.T. Press.

Stokey, N. L. and R. E. Lucas with E. C. Prescott (1989): *Recursive Methods in Economic Dynamics*. Harvard University Press.

Zauderer, E. (1989): *Partial Differential Equations of Applied Mathematics*, 2. ed. John Wiley & Sons.

INDEX